Chemistry

ADDISON-WESLEY

ANTONY C. WILBRAHAM

DENNIS D. STALEY

MICHAEL S. MATTA

EDWARD L. WATERMAN

Prentice
Hall

Needham, Massachusetts
Upper Saddle River, New Jersey
Glenview, Illinois

Program Components

Student Edition

Teacher's Edition

Teaching Resources
- Chapter Review Modules
- Solutions Manual for Chapter Reviews
- Laboratory Practicals
- Laboratory Recordsheets
- Graphing Calculator Problems
- Overhead Transparency Preview
- Spanish Supplement
- Block Scheduling Guide
- How to Assess Student Work

Overhead Transparency Package

Laboratory Manual, ATE

Laboratory Manual

Small-Scale Chemistry Laboratory Manual, ATE

Small-Scale Chemistry Laboratory Manual

Probeware Lab Manual for Computers and Calculators

Guided Reading and Study Workbook, ATE

Guided Reading and Study Workbook

Prentice Hall Assessment System

Color Transparencies

Chem ASAP! CD-ROM

ActivChemistry CD-ROM

Resource Pro CD-ROM

Assessment Resources CD-ROM

Web site at www.phschool.com

SCIENCE NEWS at www.phschool.com

The Chemistry Place Internet Site

Chemistry Alive! Videodisc

Small-Scale Lab Video and Videodisc

CHEMedia™ Videodiscs

Problem Pro CD-ROM

Cover photographs: Clockwise from top left: Test tube with zinc in acid, Richard Megna, Fundamental Photographs; Molecular structure of buckyball, Ken Eward, Photo Researchers; Bunsen burner flame, and flask containing precipitate of lead iodide, Richard Megna, Fundamental Photographs; Scanning tunneling microscope image, Fran Heyl Associates.

About the cover: The collage of images on the cover illustrates the beauty and excitement of chemistry: the old and the new; the macro view and the micro view; the applied and the theoretical. Cover designed by Amanda Kavanagh/Ark Design, New York.

STAFF CREDITS

The people who made up the **Addison-Wesley Chemistry** team—representing design services, editorial, editorial services, electronic publishing technology, manufacturing & inventory planning, market research, marketing services, online services & multimedia development, planning & budgeting, product planning, production services, project office, and publishing processes—are listed below. Bold type denotes the core team members.

Barbara A. Bertell, **Peggy Bliss, Kristen Cetrulo Braghi, Kathy Dempsey, Frederick Fellows, Thomas Ferreira, Joel Gendler, Jerry Hooten, Ellen Levinger,** Diahanne Lucas, Marie Mathis, Paul Murphy, Jane Orner, **Matthew Raycroft,** Wendy Chadbourne Simpson, **Dori Steinhauff,** Chris Wawack, Helen Young

Prentice Hall

ISBN 0-13-054384-5

8 9 10   05 04

Brief Contents

Contents

Labs & Activities

DISCOVER IT!

MINI LAB

SMALL-SCALE LAB

Probe or sensor versions available in the Probeware Lab Manual.

Features

Chemistry Serving...

LiNK TO

CHEMISTRY IN CAREERS

CHEMath

CHEMISTRY FOR THE NEW CENTURY!

*A*ddison-Wesley Chemistry is a comprehensive and motivating program that builds problem-solving skills and stresses the relevance and application of chemistry to your present and future life.

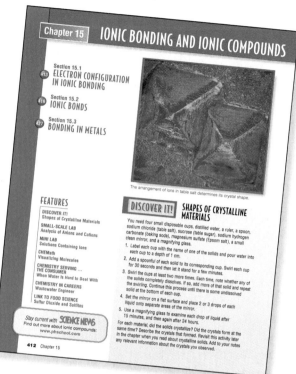

SCIENCE NEWS

Keep current with *Science News!* Find weekly science updates on the web, brought to you by *Science News* magazine.
www.phschool.com

Section Openers

Each section begins with an opportunity to learn about the applications and uses of chemistry in your everyday world. These short readings end with a question that you will be able to answer by reading the text in that section.

Discover It!

These activities provide opportunities to explore ideas and discover concepts of chemistry—before you read about them.

Objectives and Key Terms

The objectives describe what you should focus on as you read the section. The key terms, printed in bold type, are the vocabulary words you should be able to define.

Recognize the Relevance

Chemistry Serving...

This feature is designed to illustrate the important roles chemistry plays in serving the **Environment, Industry, Society,** and the **Consumer.**

Chemistry in Careers

Highlighted on each **Chemistry Serving...** page, and featured on pages 868–881, Chemistry in Careers discusses career opportunities that require an understanding of chemistry.

Link To...

This feature illustrates how concepts in chemistry relate to both science and non-science disciplines.

Appreciate the Process

Probeware Lab Manual

This supplementary lab manual provides exciting opportunities for high-tech lab work.

Small-Scale Labs

These labs require inexpensive, locally available equipment to carry out sophisticated and diverse chemical investigations on a small scale. You will use a variety of skills to hypothesize, experiment, observe, analyze, conclude, and apply your conclusions to other situations.

Mini Lab

Mini Lab activities are quick and effective hands-on opportunities to apply chemistry concepts and skills. Requiring minimal equipment, they enhance the concepts they are located near.

Reinforce Skills

(See sample page at left — section 4.3 "Converting Complex Units," Sample Problem 4-10, and Practice Problems.)

Sample Problems and Practice Problems

Problem solving is an essential skill in chemistry. Sample problems provide an opportunity to sharpen this skill as you **analyze** the problem, **calculate** the answer, **evaluate** the results, and **practice** similar problems.

CHEMath

These features review specific math skills and explain why each skill is essential to success in chemistry. CHEMath features are distributed throughout the textbook to provide a point-of-use math refresher. CHEMath provides step-by-step explanations and practice problems.

Section Review

Evaluate what you have learned in each section by answering the section review questions.

Understand the Concepts

Student Study Guide

The Student Study Guide checks your understanding of **Key Terms** and **Key Equations and Relationships.** You will also find a **Summary** of important concepts and **Concept Maps** to further test your understanding. The Guided Study Workbook provides active reading and guided practice—a great way to prepare for tests!

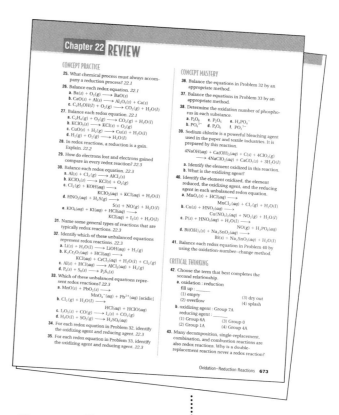

Chapter Review

The questions in **Concept Practice, Concept Mastery, Critical Thinking, Cumulative Review,** and **Concept Challenge** assess your comprehension of the chapter content. Selected questions identified by the calculator icon enhance proficiency in the use of this technology. Further instructions and practice problems are provided in the **Graphing Calculator** ancillary.

Standardized Test Prep

In each chapter, a practice test using a variety of formats prepares you for state and national exams. The Prentice Hall Assessment System has instruction in test-taking strategies and additional practice tests.

Incorporate Technology

Chem ASAP!

The Chem ASAP! CD-ROM is an easy-to-use learning and reference tool directly tied into the textbook. It is designed to help you understand chemistry concepts and master problem-solving skills through the use of **Animations, Simulations, Assessment** questions, and guided **Problem-Solving** tutorials.

Animations

Each narrated animation brings the textbook to life as it illustrates important chemistry concepts, chemical processes, and applications of technology.

Simulations

Each simulation reinforces your understanding of important concepts and allows you to manipulate variables, observe results, and draw conclusions.

Assessment

More than 500 interactive assessment questions allow you to check your understanding of key concepts and ideas from each section of the textbook.

Problem-Solving

Interactive tutorials guide you through detailed solutions of nearly 100 Practice Problems found in the textbook. Each tutorial follows the 3-step problem-solving approach and concludes with an additional related Practice Problem.

Additional Features

- ▶ **Periodic Table**—contains a wealth of easily accessed information
- ▶ **Glossary**—includes the complete textbook glossary along with audio pronunciations
- ▶ **Concept Mapping Tool**—easily creates custom concept maps relating key ideas
- ▶ **Take It to The Net**—directly connect to www.phschool.com from Chem ASAP!

... and More Technology

 ## Overhead Transparencies

The Overhead Transparency Package contains 80 color transparencies and a Teaching Guide. The transparencies, reproductions of art from the textbook, have been selected to help students visualize difficult-to-understand concepts. The Teaching Guide provides instructional strategies that include questions and answers for each transparency.

 ## Videodiscs and Videotapes

Chemistry Alive! Videodisc This informative series of 27 fascinating chemistry demonstrations performed by master teachers Lee Marek and Robert Lewis brings fast-paced fun and solid chemistry instruction into the classroom.

Small-Scale Lab Video and Videodisc Author Ed Waterman demonstrates small-scale techniques and discusses the advantages of small-scale labs.

CHEMedia™ Videodiscs Five videodiscs add real-world connections to chemistry topics through demos, field trips, animations, and explorations.

 ## Internet

SCIENCE NEWS Keep current with *Science News!* Weekly science updates keep you informed with the latest chemistry news and discoveries.
www.phschool.com

www.phschool.com
Enhance every chapter with Internet activities, self-tests, dynamic links, and career information.

The Chemistry Place This premier Internet chemistry site for students and teachers includes the latest chemistry research presented by prestigious resident faculty, extensive learning activities, members' forum, and more.

 ## CD-ROMs

Chem ASAP! CD-ROM An easy-to-use learning and reference tool provided on CD-ROM to every student, Chem ASAP! is designed to help students master chemistry concepts and problem-solving skills. Nearly 300 in-text references to Animations, Simulations, Assessment questions, and Problem-Solving tutorials contained in Chem ASAP! ensure that the CD-ROM is easily and effectively integrated into daily instruction.

Resource Pro CD-ROM The complete Teacher's Resource Package is available in a customizable CD-ROM format that also includes an integrated comprehensive lesson planner. Supplementary materials can be accessed by chapter or by title. Planning can be done for a day, week, term, or year for regular or block schedules.

ActivChemistry™ CD-ROM A virtual chemistry laboratory on CD-ROM, ActivChemistry lets students simulate laboratory experiments on the computer. The CD-ROM includes 17 lessons correlated to Addison-Wesley Chemistry and can be used as an authoring tool to create custom experiments and lessons.

Assessment Resources Traditional and alternative testing for every section in the textbook is provided by this easy-to-use-and-edit CD-ROM for Windows and Macintosh.

Problem Pro CD-ROM Includes options for customizing and generating a virtual endless number of practice–problem worksheets.

Probeware Lab Manual for Computers and Calculators Whether you are using Vernier, TI, or PASCO probes and sensors, you will find easy-to-use labs with step-by-step instructions. CD-ROM included for quick start-up and technical support.

The Authors...

Antony C. Wilbraham

Antony Wilbraham is an Emeritus Professor of Chemistry. He taught college-level chemistry for more than twenty-five years at Southern Illinois University at Edwardsville, Illinois, where he was also Director of Hazardous Waste Management. In 1978, he received the University Teaching Excellence Award. Dr. Wilbraham has been writing high school and college-level chemistry textbooks and related ancillaries for more than twenty years and has published extensively in science journals for over thirty years. He is a member of the American Chemical Society, a member of the National Science Teachers Association, and a Fellow of the Royal Society of Chemistry.

Dennis D. Staley

Dennis Staley is an Instructor in the Department of Chemistry and the Office of Science and Math Education at Southern Illinois University at Edwardsville, Illinois. He has been teaching high school and college-level chemistry for more than twenty years. In 1981 he received the University Teaching Excellence Award. Mr. Staley has been writing high school and college-level chemistry textbooks and related ancillaries for more than twenty years. He is a member of the American Chemical Society and a member of the National Science Teachers Association.

Michael S. Matta

Michael Matta is an Emeritus Professor of Chemistry. He was a professor of chemistry at Southern Illinois University at Edwardsville, Illinois, from 1969 to 1996, and served as Department Chair from 1980 to 1983. In 1973, Dr. Matta received the University Teaching Excellence Award. He has been developing and writing high school and college-level chemistry textbooks and related ancillaries for more than twenty years and has published extensively in scientific journals. He is a member of the American Chemical Society, the National Science Teachers Association, and the American Association for the Advancement of Science.

Edward L. Waterman

Ed Waterman has taught chemistry, advanced placement chemistry, and organic and biochemistry since 1976 at Rocky Mountain High School in Fort Collins, Colorado. Mr. Waterman conducts workshops for teachers on such topics as small-scale chemistry laboratory, advanced placement chemistry, block scheduling, Internet for the chemistry classroom, and virtual chemistry on CD-ROM. Mr. Waterman holds a Bachelor of Science degree in chemistry from Montana State University and a Master of Science degree in chemistry from Colorado State University.

Content Reviewers

Dr. John I. Gelder
Oklahoma State University
Stillwater, OK

Dr. Jameica Hill
Wofford College
Spartanburg, SC

Dr. Samuel Kounaves
Tufts University
Medford, MA

Dr. Doris Lewis
Suffolk University
Boston, MA

Dr. Lorraine Rellick
Capital University
Columbus, OH

Dr. David Taylor
Slippery Rock University
Slippery Rock, PA

Anita Dunn Thurwachter
Austin Community College
Austin, TX

Teacher Reviewers

Sidney Jay Abramowitz
Stamford High School
Stamford, CT

Christy Alexander
Permian High School
Odessa, TX

Max Ceballos
Edinburg High School
Edinburg, TX

Charles DiSapio
Stamford High School
Stamford, CT

Ron Dunaway
Monterey High School
Lubbock, TX

Lewis Hitzrot
Phillips Exeter Academy
Exeter, NH

Judy Mosher
Indian River High School
Chesapeake, VA

Terrie Reed
Permian High School
Odessa, TX

Mark Sandomir
Mountain View High School
Mesa, AZ

Victoria Sanftner
Montwood High School
El Paso, TX

Pamela Shlachtman
South Dade High School
Miami, FL

Sharron Story
Monterey High School
Lubbock, TX

Dorothy Thomas
Forth Worth ISD
Fort Worth, TX

David Tuskey
Clover Hill High School
Midlothian, VA

Kevin Williams
Edgewater High School
Orlando, FL

Senior Texas Consultant
Susan M. Cory
Cypress Fairbanks ISD
Houston, TX

Safety Reviewer

Sally Busboom
Austin ISD
Austin, TX

Chapter 1

INTRODUCTION TO CHEMISTRY

The Galileo spacecraft collects data about Jupiter and its moons.

FEATURES

DISCOVER IT!
Solid, Liquid, or What?

SMALL-SCALE LAB
Introduction to Small-Scale Chemistry

MINI LAB
Bubbles!

CHEMISTRY SERVING ... SOCIETY
Chemistry in the Information Age

CHEMISTRY IN CAREERS
Chemist

LINK TO FOOD SCIENCE
Chemistry in the Kitchen

LINK TO ATMOSPHERIC SCIENCE
Predicting the Formation of the Ozone Hole

Stay current with **SCIENCE NEWS**
Find out more about chemistry:
www.phschool.com

DISCOVER IT!   SOLID, LIQUID OR WHAT?

You need a measuring spoon, cornstarch, a small bowl (such as a cereal bowl), and water.

1. Add 3 heaping tablespoons of cornstarch to the bowl, and then add 3 tablespoons of water.

2. Stir the contents of the bowl thoroughly and let stand for 5 minutes.

3. Slowly push your finger into the mixture. Repeat with your fist.

4. Quickly jab your finger into the mixture. Repeat with your fist.

5. Take a handful of the mixture and form a ball. Squeeze and release the ball several times.

What happens when you slowly push into the mixture with your finger or fist? When you jab it? When you squeeze the ball? When you release the ball? What condition seems to determine whether the mixture behaves like a solid or a liquid? When you have completed the chapter, return to this activity. What hypotheses can you form? How can you test them?

CHEMISTRY

The Galileo spacecraft was placed in orbit around Jupiter to collect data about the planet and its moons. Instruments aboard Galileo analyzed the atmosphere of the moon Io and found large amounts of sulfur and sulfur dioxide. The presence of these chemicals verified that the volcanos on Io's surface are active. Chemistry allowed scientists to study the geology of a distant object in the solar system. **What is chemistry, and what are some of its different branches?**

objectives
▶ Define chemistry and differentiate among its traditional divisions
▶ List several reasons to study chemistry

key terms
▶ chemistry
▶ organic chemistry
▶ inorganic chemistry
▶ analytical chemistry
▶ physical chemistry
▶ biochemistry

What Is Chemistry?

Anyone who has ever watched a toddler explore a new environment knows that people are born with a natural curiosity about the world: a world of vivid colors and different textures, of simple and complex objects, of things that move and things that are permanently fixed. As the toddler grows, he or she learns to name observable things and, as much as possible, to figure out how they work. The desire to know more and more about the world grows as well. This desire, a lifelong attribute, is what compels humans to discover, build, and invent.

Chemistry is one branch of knowledge that grew from human curiosity about the world. **Chemistry** is the study of the composition of matter—the stuff things are made of—and the changes that matter undergoes. In fact, as you can see in **Figure 1.2** on page 4, the Japanese symbols that make up the word for chemistry mean "change study."

Much of chemistry is very practical and has obvious applications to everyday life. Perhaps you are wearing clothes made of synthetic fibers or natural fibers that have been dyed. The pan your dinner was cooked in may have a nonstick surface. Or perhaps you recently used nail-polish remover or hair spray. Other aspects of chemistry are theoretical, or without everyday application. But what is theoretical one day may become practical the next. For example, fifty years ago it would have been difficult to conceive of the impact of plastics or computers on our everyday lives.

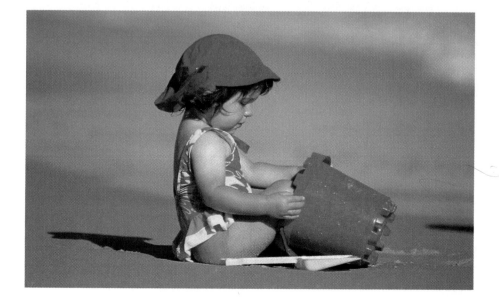

Figure 1.1
Children learn by watching and doing. This toddler is learning about sand and ocean water, as well as exploring the uses of a pail, as she experiences a day at the beach.

Figure 1.2

The Japanese characters for chemistry literally mean "change study." Chemistry concerns the changes that matter undergoes, such as the rusting of metal, the transformation of liquid water to steam, and the burning of a match.

Traditionally, chemistry has been divided into five major areas of study. Organic chemistry was originally the study of substances from living organisms. Today, with a few exceptions, **organic chemistry** is the study of essentially all substances containing carbon. **Inorganic chemistry** specializes primarily in substances that do not contain carbon. These are mainly substances from nonliving things. **Analytical chemistry** is concerned with the composition of substances. Finding minute quantities of a particular medication in blood requires the practice of analytical chemistry. **Physical chemistry** is concerned with theories and experiments that describe the behavior of chemicals. For example, the stretching of nylon can be explained using the concepts of physical chemistry. Finally, **biochemistry** is the study of the chemistry of living organisms. The processes of digestion, blood clotting, and respiration, to name just a few, are explained by biochemistry. These five subdivisions of chemistry often overlap; for example, one cannot learn the composition of an organic or inorganic substance without being skilled in analytical chemistry.

Chemistry is central to modern science and to almost all human endeavors, as you can see from **Figure 1.4.** Today, many chemists work in teams with other scientists—biologists, geologists, physicists, physiologists, physicians, and environmental scientists—as well as with engineers.

Figure 1.3

The flowering cactus and the surrounding vegetation in this scene contain many organic compounds; the rocks and the mountains in the background are made of inorganic compounds.

Why Study Chemistry?

All the wonderful people and things that fill the world around you involve chemistry in one way or another! You are made from chemicals, and you use chemicals every day—when you breathe, drink a glass of water, wash your hair, or eat a snack. These common activities—and many, many

Figure 1.4
Chemistry is everywhere in your everyday life. In what ways do these photographs "say" chemistry to you?

FOOD SCIENCE

Chemistry in the Kitchen

Chemical reactions underlie your most wonderful successes (or dismal disasters) in the kitchen. The cut surfaces of apples, pears, and bananas turn brown

upon exposure to oxygen in the air. Light, fluffy cakes result when baking powder reacts with acid in the batter to produce carbon dioxide. When sugar is heated, it forms dark-brown caramel. Heating the protein structure in eggs changes their texture from slimy to firm when they are boiled, scrambled, or fried. The tasty brown coating on the surface of roasted and grilled meats is formed by a complex series of chemical changes. Although tradition governs most of our behavior in the kitchen, food scientists are constantly searching for new and improved methods to prepare, present, and preserve food.

others—all involve chemicals and chemistry. Your natural desire to understand how these things work is perhaps the best reason to study chemistry. Chemistry, with its focus on the workings of the natural world, helps satisfy your need to know and understand.

Every day, you make choices: what to eat, what to wear, when and how much to study. As a citizen of this planet you will also be asked to act on questions of much greater importance. Is nuclear power acceptable or are there better alternative energy sources? What are appropriate responses to the problems of global warming and ozone depletion? Given limited resources, what deserves more support: the space program or finding a cure for cancer? Should experiments that involve manipulating heredity be regulated or forbidden? Knowledge of the basics of chemistry and other sciences can help you arrive at informed opinions and take appropriate actions on these questions.

Although relatively few people become professional chemists, a career in chemistry can be a satisfying one, indeed. This introductory course can help you decide whether chemistry is a career for you. As a chemist, you might develop new products such as textiles, paints, medicines, or cosmetics. Perhaps you would find methods to reduce pollution, clean up the environment, or prevent the destruction of the ozone layer. You could share your knowledge through teaching, analyzing pharmaceuticals, or checking the quality of manufactured goods.

Very often, chemistry is used to attain a specific goal. The goal might be to formulate a new paint or adhesive or to set up procedures for a new medical test. Such goals are examples of applied chemistry, or chemical technology. In applied chemistry, scientific knowledge is used in ways that can either benefit or harm people and/or the environment. Political and social debates about the uses of scientific knowledge are often really debates about the risks and benefits of technology. In addition to applied chemistry, there is pure chemistry. Like other pure sciences, pure chemistry accumulates knowledge for its own sake. As you read on in this textbook, you will recognize many ways in which chemistry affects your life. And perhaps you will consider a career in chemistry!

section review 1.1

1. Match the numbered terms in the right column with the lettered terms in the left column.

   a. technology   (1) life

   b. organic chemistry   (2) matter and its changes

   c. biochemistry   (3) carbon

   d. chemistry   (4) applications

   e. analytical chemistry   (5) composition

2. List three reasons to study chemistry.

3. Explain the difference between pure and applied chemistry.

 Chem ASAP! Assessment 1.1 Check your understanding of the important ideas and concepts in Section 1.1.

CHEMISTRY FAR AND WIDE

objectives
▶ Summarize ways in which chemistry affects your daily life
▶ Describe the impact of chemistry on various fields of science

*E*very autumn thousands of visitors travel to New England to view the breathtakingly beautiful colors of the foliage. These colors—vivid oranges, yellows, reds, and purples—appear as the trees approach the winter months when growth no longer takes place. The bright pigments are produced by a complex chemical process, which depends on changes in temperature and hours of sunlight. This process is only one of many that occur all around you—and even inside you! **What aspects of life involve chemistry?**

Materials

People have used chemistry to their advantage throughout history. Almost 3000 years ago, early chemists produced iron from iron ore by heating the ore with carbon. The invention of steel followed, in about 500 B.C. Steel and other mixtures of metals, such as brass and bronze, are important structural materials, as are the many recently developed ceramics. But today is primarily the age of plastics. Plastics, also called polymers, are gigantic molecules with many important properties. Chemists have learned to tailor these properties to meet specific needs. The most important property of structural plastics is their high strength-to-weight ratio. A piece of plastic with the same weight as a piece of steel may be as much as five or six times stronger than the steel! A high strength-to-weight ratio makes polymers perfect for the protective weaving in bullet-resistant vests and for structural automobile body panels. The resulting reduction in the weight of the vehicle increases fuel efficiency. An automobile contains more than 500 pounds of polymers, if one counts the rubber, paint, sealants, lubricants, and upholstery.

Figure 1.5
People have always used the materials of chemistry. Bronze is a mixture that has been used since ancient times. Ceramic tiles on a space shuttle help to protect it from overheating. Light passing through optical fibers is used to transmit telephone messages. Optical fibers are made mainly from silicon dioxide (SiO_2), which is found in sand.

Your home contains a dazzling array of plastic items. Do you refrigerate leftovers in plastic food wrap, use nonstick cooking utensils, or water the lawn with a plastic hose? Perhaps you walk on a polyester or nylon carpet. You may be wearing wrinkle-resistant clothing woven from polyester fibers mixed with natural fibers of cotton or wool. The plumbing in your home could be made from polyvinyl chloride (PVC) pipe, and your walls may contain polystyrene insulation covered with a polyethylene vapor barrier. You have probably seen lawn and patio furniture made from plastic, as well as kitchen counters covered with heat- and moisture-resistant polymers. To repair a piece of furniture, you might use an epoxy resin polymer to produce a bond stronger than the wood itself. Fabrics such as nylon and Dacron™ make up many of the clothes you wear everyday. Bowling balls, billiard balls, tennis rackets, and other sports equipment are made from polymers. None of these materials would exist if it were not for the efforts of chemists.

But plastics are not the only materials produced by chemists. Black-and-white and color photographs are produced by the interaction of light with chemicals. Personal computers rely on silicon memory chips. Telephone communications are transmitted over lines made from optical fibers. These are only a few examples, but surely you get the idea.

Energy

Population growth and increased standards of living around the globe create ever-greater demands for energy to power homes and factories. Where will this energy come from? There are only two ways to provide it: conserve energy and produce more energy. Chemistry plays an essential role in both of these options. Some methods of conserving energy are obvious, others less so. But from energy-efficient fuels to safe and effective insulation materials to roadways lighted with sodium lamps, chemistry is creating new and exciting energy conservation methods.

Figure 1.6

In a continuing effort to conserve energy, efficient outdoor lighting methods, such as high intensity discharge, have been a focus of chemists. Chemists are also helping to develop renewable energy resources, such as solar power and wind power, to replace the ever-shrinking supply of fossil fuels.

Energy from sunlight

Carbon + Water dioxide → Photosynthesis → Glucose + Oxygen (a sugar)

$6CO_2 + 6H_2O \longrightarrow C_6H_{12}O_6 + 6O_2$

Most of our energy needs are filled by burning fossil fuels. But the supply of fossil fuels is limited. Because they are a nonrenewable resource, someday they will run out. Much of the world's petroleum is difficult or impossible to extract from Earth. However, an enormous reserve of petroleum could become available if tar sands and oil shales were coaxed into giving up the oil they contain. In addition, coal, lignite, and peat are potential sources of petroleum products. Even garbage can be converted into natural gas. Chemists are currently working on these and other exciting possibilities.

Scientists are also working to provide new and perhaps inexhaustible sources of energy. Sunlight is the greatest source of energy available on Earth. Plants capture some of the sun's energy in the food-making process called photosynthesis. But only about 0.1% of the energy that strikes Earth is used by all the plant life in the world. Scientists are working to develop devices that efficiently convert the energy of sunlight into electrical energy. If they succeed, the electrical energy might be used to decompose ordinary water into hydrogen and oxygen. Hydrogen could then be burned as a renewable and nonpolluting fuel.

The development of batteries for the storage of energy is another goal of chemists. Early flashlight batteries, known as dry cells, did not last long in use. Dry cells were subsequently replaced by alkaline batteries, an improved design offering significantly longer life. The lithium–iodine battery is a recent advancement in the ongoing evolution of the battery. The lithium–iodine battery is an important improvement. Used in cardiac pacemakers, lithium–iodine batteries are small and efficient and can last as long as ten years. Electric automobiles will need powerful storage batteries to make them a practical alternative to vehicles with internal-combustion engines. Fuel cells under development are a promising source of pollution-free energy.

Figure 1.8
From entertainment devices to watches to medical appliances such as hearing aids, batteries have numerous applications. The development of practical electric automobiles is on the horizon. Just imagine what life would be like without batteries!

Figure 1.9

The sun's energy is produced by nuclear fusion. Nuclear power plants produce energy by nuclear fission.

Nuclear fission and nuclear fusion may also provide energy for the future. Nuclear fission, the process used in nuclear power plants, has been responsible for some serious nuclear accidents. However, if scientists learn enough about containing and controlling nuclear reactions and disposing of the waste, nuclear power may again achieve prominence as an energy source. Nuclear fusion, the process that produces the sun's energy, could be pollution-free. Research into producing energy from nuclear fusion on Earth is in its infancy. Scientists are currently concerned with methods for producing and containing the energy of nuclear fusion.

Medicine and Biotechnology

Every year, the chemical industry produces millions of pounds of such medically important substances as vitamin C, penicillin, and aspirin. However, the synthesis of vitamins and medicines is far from the only role that chemistry plays in the health and biological sciences. No endeavors have benefited more from advances in chemistry than medicine and biotechnology. Much of this benefit derives from the ability of scientists to determine the spatial arrangement of atoms in complex biological molecules such as proteins. Many medicines are effective because they interact in a very specific way with biological molecules. Knowledge of the molecular structure of the target biological molecule greatly assists the design of safe and effective drug molecules. Medicines to reduce high blood pressure, high blood cholesterol, and some cancers have been developed in this way.

Chemistry is also providing new materials for medical applications. Diseased or weakened arteries can be replaced surgically with tubes made of Dacron™ polymers. Hipbones are replaced by substitutes made from metal alloys, or mixtures, of tungsten and cobalt. Much progress has been made in the development of synthetic blood and skin.

Genes, the units of heredity in living organisms, are composed of deoxyribonucleic acid (DNA). The discovery of DNA's molecular structure and of many of the details of its role in heredity has resulted in major advances in biology and biotechnology. With the information gathered thus far and the continuing efforts of the Human Genome Project, scientists worldwide expect to be able to identify and determine the molecular structures of all human genes. Such knowledge will have significant applications in medicine, genetics, agriculture, and even economics!

Figure 1.10
You are who you are because of genes, which are segments of DNA. Molecular models, such as this intricate segment of DNA, help scientists unravel the mysteries of the world around us.

Among other things, biotechnology involves the transfer of genes from one organism to another. Using this technology, human genes have been inserted into bacteria that then become factories for the production of human substances such as insulin, which is used to treat diabetes. In a few cases, a human genetic disease has been cured or its symptoms alleviated by replacing a faulty gene with a normal gene. Through biotechnology, completely normal sheep and cattle have been produced from a single adult cell of these animals by a process called cloning. The offspring of cloning, called a clone, is an exact genetic copy of its parent. Cloned cattle can produce human proteins in their milk. If in the future, cloned animals can provide a continuous supply of proteins that can be used to treat human diseases, one of the goals of biotechnology will have been realized.

Figure 1.11
More than an identical twin? Dolly was cloned from a single cell from her mother.

Agriculture

Chemistry plays an important role in efforts to increase the world's food supply and to protect crops. Developing hardier and more productive plants is a key to these efforts. Studies of photosynthesis, the food-making process in plants, and nitrogen fixation, the process by which atmospheric nitrogen gas is converted into usable nitrogen compounds, may lead to the development of plants that use these processes more efficiently. Why do you think such plants would be valuable? Advances in the understanding of plant hormones, which regulate plant growth, represent another opportunity to increase the strength and viability of plants and, thus, increase the world's food supply.

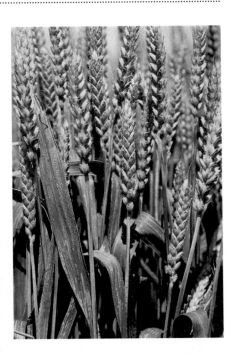

Figure 1.12

Insecticides, herbicides, and fungicides are used to protect crops from pests and disease. The effects of insect infestation, corn smut, and wheat rust are apparent in these ruined crops.

Figure 1.13

Do not take clean air for granted! As our roads grow more crowded, smog pollution becomes a problem chemists and others work hard to combat.

In addition to developing hardier and more productive plants, scientists are also focusing on safer and more effective ways to protect crops. In the past, insecticides, herbicides, and fungicides were quite nonspecific. Today, the trend is toward chemicals that are more specific for the condition they are designed to treat. For example, many newer insecticides are similar in molecular structure to natural protectants produced by the plants themselves. The discovery of more than 100 pheromones, which include insect sex attractants, is also being used in the battle against pests. These molecules have proved effective in attracting and trapping such pests as gypsy moths and boll weevils. Chemists are also working to create more pest-resistant and blight-resistant plants. Recombinant DNA technology is helping to breed plants with genetic resistance to their natural enemies.

The Environment

Progress has its price: Every new development has both risks and benefits. Society, often through the political process, must decide whether the benefits of a new development outweigh its risks. This is especially true for environmental protection.

Chemists work with environmental scientists to identify pollutants, prevent or minimize environmental pollution, and clean up toxic wastes. One example of this teamwork involves the battle against the irritating smog that envelops many of the world's cities. Nitrogen oxides emitted by the internal-combustion engines of automobiles are a major contributor to smog. To combat these pollutants, scientists designed catalytic converters that remove nitrogen oxides from automobile exhaust. Pollution caused by burning fossil fuels such as coal is another example of a problem chemists and environmental scientists are tackling together. Burning coal produces sulfur compounds. Gaseous sulfur compounds are components of acid rain, which as you probably know is harmful to forests and lakes. Electrostatic precipitators and scrubbers help remove sulfur compounds from the gas emitted by power plants and factories.

Figure 1.14
Acid rain changed the appearance of this marble statue of George Washington from what it was 60 years ago (left) to what it is today (right). What causes acid rain?

The most abundant pollutant generated by humans, carbon dioxide, is produced by the combustion of fossil fuels. Earth's surface is warmed naturally by the greenhouse effect, which is similar to the heating of an automobile's interior on a sunny day. The increasing amounts of carbon dioxide released into the atmosphere each year trap more of the sun's heat on Earth's surface than is natural, or even normal. The result of this increased amount of heat is global warming. Global warming could drastically alter weather patterns, sea levels, and agriculture around the world. In a worldwide effort, nations are working independently and collectively to reduce carbon dioxide emissions.

Scientists are also concerned about the thinning of the ozone layer. The ozone layer protects Earth from the sun's harmful ultraviolet rays. Why is that important? One reason for the depletion of the ozone layer is the presence of chlorofluorocarbons, most notably Freon, which are a family of fluorine-chlorine-containing hydrocarbons that were originally used in refrigeration and air-conditioning equipment. Methyl bromide, used in agriculture, may also contribute to the thinning of the ozone layer. When depletion of the ozone layer was discovered, chemists provided an explanation of the processes causing the deterioration. With this knowledge, they then began to design new compounds to replace the chlorofluorocarbons.

ATMOSPHERIC SCIENCE

Predicting the Formation of the Ozone Hole

In the 1970s, F. Sherwood Rowland and Mario Molina predicted that certain chlorine-containing compounds, such as chlorofluorocarbons (CFCs), might damage the ozone layer. The use of these compounds in aerosol sprays was banned in 1978. A decade later, British researchers showed that the ozone layer over the South Pole disappeared each year in the Antarctic spring. Since then, thinning of the ozone layer has been observed in other places around the globe. Work by atmospheric chemists has confirmed the idea of Rowland and Molina, and scientists now believe that a single chlorine atom can destroy millions of ozone molecules. In 1995, Rowland, Molina, and Paul Crutzen, a German atmospheric chemist who had also studied ozone depletion, received the Nobel Prize in chemistry for their work.

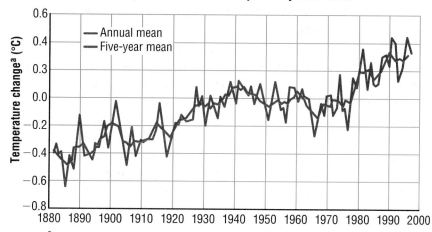

Global mean temperature has risen fairly steadily since 1880.

— Annual mean
— Five-year mean

Temperature change^a (°C)

[a]Difference in global surface-air temperature from the 1951–1980 average.
Source: National Aeronautics and Space Administration's Goddard Institute for Space Studies
C&E News Nov. 17, 1997

Figure 1.15
There has been a steady rise in the global mean temperature since 1880. How would you describe the overall trend?

Figure 1.16

This astronaut is walking on the moon to collect samples of the lunar surface, an example of which is shown in the inset photograph.

Figure 1.17

Samples of the surface of Mars were analyzed by remote control. This photograph, taken by the Mars Pathfinder, shows the Sojourner making observations of the rock named Yogi. Why is such information valuable?

Astronomy and Space Exploration

In the early nineteenth century, scientists first learned that by analyzing light transmitted to Earth by stars and other celestial objects, they could gain a "window" into the chemical composition of these objects. Obtaining similar information about the composition of the moon and planets is more difficult because these objects do not generate their own light. However, space exploration of Earth's moon and Mars is now providing some of this vital information. More than 850 pounds of moon rocks brought to Earth by various missions have been chemically analyzed. The moon rocks collected by Apollo astronauts were formed from volcanic material, suggesting that vast oceans of molten lava once covered the moon's surface. Chemical analysis of the atmosphere of Mars reveals the presence of primarily carbon dioxide, with smaller amounts of nitrogen, argon, oxygen, carbon monoxide, water vapor, and other gases. The Sojourner robotic vehicle, delivered to the surface of Mars by the Mars Pathfinder spacecraft, has analyzed and determined the chemical composition of Mars rocks. The composition of these rocks, particularly those known as conglomerates, indicates that a large amount of water once existed on the surface of Mars. Geologists are using this information to learn more about the formation of Earth and other planets, as well as to determine whether life as we know it could exist elsewhere in the solar system.

section review 1.2

4. Explain how chemistry affects your daily life.

5. Name at least three areas of science in which chemistry plays an important role.

6. How might plant crops improve as a result of agricultural research? Why would such improvement be important?

7. Name at least three items that are made completely or partially of plastic.

 Chem ASAP! Assessment 1.2 Check your understanding of the important ideas and concepts in Section 1.2.

THINKING LIKE A SCIENTIST

In March 1989, two chemists reported the discovery of an ordinary laboratory procedure for producing a nuclear fusion reaction. Their "cold fusion" reaction was relatively simple, using apparatus similar to that used for the electrolysis of water, yet it caused much excitement in the scientific community. Nuclear fusion, you see, is a thermonuclear reaction; that is, it involves the combination of two nuclei to produce one nucleus of heavier mass and the release of extraordinary amounts of energy. In fact, the energy released from the sun is the result of nuclear fusion. The prospect of producing huge quantities of energy to meet society's increasing demands by rather ordinary means ignited much interest and excitement. Many scientists rushed to duplicate the experiment. But after many failures, the dream of using cold fusion to obtain inexpensive, unlimited energy died. According to the scientific method, the results of an experiment must be reproducible if they are to be accepted. **What are the steps of the scientific method?**

objectives
- ▶ Describe the steps involved in the scientific method
- ▶ Distinguish between a theory and a scientific law

key terms
- ▶ scientific method
- ▶ observation
- ▶ hypothesis
- ▶ experiment
- ▶ theory
- ▶ scientific law

The Scientific Method

As you read the previous section, perhaps you found yourself thinking, "Who does these exciting and important things?" Scientists may seem to be special people because they obtain valuable—and sometimes spectacular—results. Nevertheless, as a Nobel Prize winner in science has said, science is about "ordinary people doing ordinary things."

An important discovery may involve some luck, but one must be prepared to recognize the lucky event. Alexander Fleming noticed that infectious bacteria failed to grow on portions of a bacterial culture where mold was growing. Fleming was very observant and scientifically prepared to realize the importance of this chance observation, which led to one of the greatest scientific achievements of all time. Do you know what Fleming's discovery was? Most scientific advances, however, involve little or no luck. A logical, systematic approach to the solution of a difficult problem is often the best method, as well as the most powerful tool that ordinary people—you and scientists included—have at their disposal.

The **scientific method** is one logical approach to the solution of scientific problems. The scientific method is useful for solving many kinds of problems because it is closely related to ordinary common sense. Suppose you want to use a flashlight, but when you turn it on it does not light. You have made an **observation**—that is, you have used your senses to obtain information directly. In this case, your observation is that the flashlight does not light. This raises a question: What is wrong with the flashlight? You guess that the flashlight batteries are probably dead. By guessing, you have proposed a reason for your observation. You have made a **hypothesis,** or a proposed explanation or reason for what is observed. In the scientific method, scientists typically first observe something of scientific interest and then propose a hypothesis.

Returning to your flashlight problem, you will probably want to test your hypothesis with an experiment. An **experiment** is a means to test a hypothesis. Most likely, you will put new batteries in the flashlight. If the

Figure 1.18
When you make observations, keep both eyes open.

If experiments prove your hypothesis false, then go back and propose a new hypothesis.

Observations → **Hypothesis** ? → **Experiments** → **Theory**

The theory is tested by further experiments and modified if necessary.

Figure 1.19
This outline of the scientific method shows how observations lead to the development of hypotheses and theories. Note that if experiments prove a hypothesis false, a new hypothesis must be proposed.

flashlight lights, you can be fairly certain from the one experiment that your hypothesis is true. Scientists also perform experiments to test their hypotheses. For the results of an experiment to be accepted, the experiment must produce the same result no matter how many times it is repeated, or by whom. The repeatability of scientific experiments distinguishes science from nonscientific fields.

Many different kinds of experiments may be needed to learn whether a hypothesis is valid. A scientific hypothesis is useful only if it accounts for what scientists observe in many situations. Suppose the flashlight does not work after you replace the batteries. What does this indicate about your hypothesis? When experimental data do not fit a hypothesis, the hypothesis must be rejected or changed. The new or refined hypothesis is then subjected to further experimental testing. Again, returning to the flashlight problem, you might now decide to replace the light bulb because replacing the batteries was not helpful. The original, false hypothesis (dead batteries) has led to a new hypothesis (burnt-out bulb) and a new experiment to test it. The scientific method of observing, hypothesizing, and experimenting is repeated until the hypothesis fits all the observed experimental facts. **Figure 1.19** outlines the major features of the scientific method.

Once a scientific hypothesis meets the test of repeated experimentation, it may be elevated to a higher level of ideas. It may become a theory. A **theory** is a broad and extensively tested explanation of why experiments give certain results. A theory can never be proved because it is always possible that a new experiment will disprove it. But theories are very useful because they help you form mental pictures of objects or processes that cannot be seen. Moreover, theories give you the power to predict the behavior of natural systems.

Figure 1.20
A scientific law summarizes the results of many observations and experiments.

Observations → **Experiments** → **Scientific law**

MINI LAB

Bubbles!

PURPOSE

To test the hypothesis that bubble making can be affected by adding chemicals to a bubble-blowing mixture.

MATERIALS

- 3 plastic cups
- 3 teaspoons liquid dish detergent
- measuring cup
- 150 mL water
- $\frac{1}{2}$ teaspoon sugar
- $\frac{1}{2}$ teaspoon salt
- drinking straw

PROCEDURE

1. Label three cups 1, 2, and 3. Measure 1 teaspoon liquid dish detergent into each cup. Use the measuring cup to add 50 mL water to each cup, then swirl the cups to make a clear mixture.

2. Add $\frac{1}{2}$ teaspoon table sugar to cup 2 and add $\frac{1}{2}$ teaspoon table salt to cup 3. Swirl each cup for 1 minute.

3. Dip the drinking straw into cup 1, withdraw it, and blow gently into the straw to make the largest bubble you can. Practice making bubbles until you feel you have reasonable control over your bubble production.

4. Repeat Step 3 with the mixtures in cups 2 and 3.

ANALYSIS AND CONCLUSIONS

1. Did you observe any differences in your bubble making using the mixtures in cup 1 and cup 2?

2. Did you observe any differences in your bubble making using the mixtures in cup 1 and cup 3?

3. What can you conclude about the effects of table sugar and table salt on your ability to produce bubbles?

4. Propose another hypothesis based on bubble making and design an experiment to test your hypothesis.

Scientific Laws

A **scientific law** is a concise statement that summarizes the results of many observations and experiments. A scientific law describes a natural phenomenon without attempting to explain it. Scientific laws can often be expressed by simple mathematical relationships. Gay-Lussac's law summarizes what happens when a sealed, gas-filled container is heated: The pressure of a gas is directly proportional to the Kelvin temperature at constant volume. Pressure can thus rise dangerously and lead to an explosion. Gay-Lussac's law states what happens; a theory explains why.

portfolio project

Antoine Lavoisier used the scientific method to disprove a popular explanation for burning called the phlogiston theory. Research the history of this theory. Describe the experiments Lavoisier used to demonstrate that phlogiston did not exist.

section review 1.3

8. Describe the steps involved in the scientific method. Give an example.

9. Distinguish among a theory, a hypothesis, and a scientific law.

10. Why should a hypothesis be developed before experiments take place?

11. In Chapter 2, you will learn that matter is neither created nor destroyed in any chemical change. Is this statement a theory or a law?

 Chem ASAP! Assessment 1.3 Check your understanding of the important ideas and concepts in Section 1.3.

SMALL-SCALE LAB

INTRODUCTION TO SMALL-SCALE CHEMISTRY

PURPOSE

The small-scale chemistry experiments in this textbook are designed to help you learn chemistry by doing chemistry. Each experiment provides the opportunity to interact with matter, make observations, and interpret what you see. As you solve problems, you will become more inventive. You will be encouraged to ask questions and find creative ways to answer them. You may even be able to contribute some original ideas and discoveries to chemistry. Most of all, you will have fun while learning chemistry.

The small-scale experiments in each chapter have been carefully designed to minimize the risk of injury. However, safety is also your responsibility. You are expected to behave in a way that is consistent with safe laboratory practices.

The following rules are essential for keeping you safe in the laboratory. You are responsible for knowing these rules and following them at all times. Some rules address pre-lab preparation; other rules address proper laboratory procedures.

1. Recognize that all laboratory procedures involve some degree of risk. Read the entire procedure before you begin. Listen to all your teacher's instructions. When in doubt about a procedure, ask your teacher.

2. Do only the assigned experiments. Do any experiment only when your teacher is present and has given you permission to work.

3. Know the location and operation of the following safety equipment: fire extinguisher, fire blanket, emergency shower, and eye wash station.

4. Know the location of emergency exits and escape routes. To make it easy to exit quickly, do not block walkways with furniture. Keep your work area orderly and free of personal belongings such as coats and backpacks.

5. Protect your clothing and hair from chemicals and sources of heat. Tie back long hair and roll up loose sleeves when working in the laboratory. Avoid wearing bulky or loose-fitting clothing.

Remove dangling jewelry. Wear closed-toe shoes at all times in the laboratory.

6. Report any accident, no matter how minor, to your teacher.

7. Wear safety glasses at all times when working in the laboratory. Safety glasses are designed to protect your eyes from injury. While working in the laboratory, do not rub your eyes, because chemicals are easily transferred from your hands to your eyes.

    If, despite these precautions, you get a chemical in your eye, remove any contact lenses and immediately wash your eye with a continuous stream of running water for at least 15 minutes.

8. To reduce danger, waste, and cleanup, always use minimal amounts of the chemicals specified for an experiment. This small-scale approach also saves time.

9. Use small-scale pipets for the controlled delivery of liquids, one drop at a time.

10. Never taste any chemical used in the laboratory, including food products that are the subject of an investigation. Treat all items as though they are contaminated with unknown chemicals that may be toxic. Keep all food and drink that is not part of an experiment out of the laboratory. Do not eat, drink, or chew gum in the laboratory.

    If you accidentally ingest a substance, notify your teacher immediately.

11. Do not use chipped or cracked glassware. Do not handle broken glass. If glassware does break, notify your teacher and nearby classmates. Discard broken glassware according to your teacher's instructions.

    If, despite these precautions, you receive a minor cut, allow it to bleed for a short time. Wash the injured area under cold running water and notify your teacher. More serious cuts or puncture wounds require immediate medical attention.

12. Do not handle hot glassware or equipment. You can prevent burns by being aware that hot and cold equipment can look exactly the same.

    If you are burned, immediately run cold water over the burned area for several minutes until the pain is reduced. Cooling also helps the burn to heal. Ask a classmate to notify your teacher.

13. Recognize that the danger of an electrical shock is greater in the presence of water. Keep electrical appliances away from sinks and faucets to minimize the risk of electrical shock. Be careful not to spill water or other liquids in the vicinity of an electrical appliance.

    If, despite these precautions, you spill water near an appliance, stand back, notify your teacher, and warn other students in the area.

14. Safety begins and continues with a clean laboratory. Report any chemical spills immediately to your teacher. Follow your teacher's instructions for cleaning up spills. Warn other students about the identity and location of spilled chemicals.

    If, despite these precautions, a corrosive chemical gets on your skin or clothing, wash the affected area with cold running water for several minutes.

15. Dispose of chemicals in a way that protects you, your classmates, and the environment. Always follow your teacher's directions for cleanup and disposal. Clean your small-scale reaction surface by draining the contents onto a paper towel. Then wipe the surface with a damp paper towel and dry the surface completely. Dispose of the paper towels in the waste bin. Wash your hands thoroughly with soap and water before leaving the laboratory.

16. Take appropriate precautions whenever any one of the following safety symbols appears in an experiment.

Eye Hazard
Wear safety goggles.

Clothing Hazard
Wear a lab coat or apron when using corrosive chemicals or chemicals that can stain clothing.

Fire Hazard
Tie back hair and loose clothing.
Do not use a burner near flammable materials.

Inhalation Hazard
Avoid inhaling this substance.

Corrosive Substance Hazard
Wear safety goggles and a laboratory apron.
Do not touch chemicals.

Poison Hazard
Do not chew gum, drink, or eat in the laboratory. Keep your hands away from your face.

Electrical Hazard
Use care when using electrical equipment.

Thermal Burn Hazard
Do not touch hot equipment.

Breakage Hazard
Do not use chipped or cracked glassware.
Do not heat the bottom of a test tube.

Disposal Hazard
Dispose of this chemical only as directed.

HOW TO STUDY CHEMISTRY

objectives

▶ Explain why learning chemistry requires daily effort

▶ Describe the importance of writing in the study of chemistry

*D*o you recognize any of the images in this photograph of your textbook cover? The images were chosen to capture the beauty and excitement of chemistry: the old and the new; the macro view and the micro view; the applied and the theoretical. We wrote this textbook to help you understand and appreciate chemistry—a subject that explains your daily observations and experiences. **How can you make your study of chemistry more effective and enjoyable?**

Understanding and Applying Concepts

Like anything worth doing, learning chemistry requires effort on your part. But the reward is worth the effort. You have to read carefully and take notes. You need to study often rather than waiting until you are facing a test. For your study to be effective, find a quiet, well-lit place away from distractions such as the television or loud music. Then pick up a pencil and begin.

Chemistry deals with scientific facts—facts that can be discovered by making observations and doing experiments. Your chemistry experience will include a great deal of observing and experimenting. Because discovering scientific facts usually takes a lot of time and effort, you often will need to rely on information that others have discovered.

You will need to understand the chemical concepts behind some new vocabulary and many familiar words. For example, the word *diamond* contains many layers of chemical meaning. When most people hear the word, they think of a glittering gem. Did you know that diamond is one of the hardest known substances? Or that it is a form of the element carbon? Or that it has a highly ordered molecular structure? Chemistry will help you make connections between the visible, macroscopic world and the microscopic world—a world that is too small to be seen with the unaided eye.

To reinforce what you are learning in your classroom and laboratory, connect the chemical concepts with your experiences outside the classroom. Try to visualize reactions you observe at the level of atoms and molecules. Use resources such as newspapers, television, and the Internet to keep up with developments in chemistry.

Figure 1.21

The images shown here reveal a lot about the subject of chemistry. Can you explain the concepts they illustrate? When you have completed your study of this exciting subject, return to these images and find out exactly what you have learned!

Water vapor: H₂O(*g*)

Ice: H₂O(*s*)

Water: H₂O(*l*)

Figure 1.22
Drawings can help you visualize those parts of matter that are too small to be seen, even with a powerful microscope. Here you see the submicroscopic world of water, ice, and water vapor.

Using Your Textbook

This textbook will be your companion throughout your chemistry course. As its authors, we think the textbook is a "good read." But you should not read a textbook as you do a novel. Before reading a section in detail, read once through quickly to get a content overview. Take notes during the second, detailed reading. Combining reading with writing helps you retain information. Use the objectives and key terms to focus your reading. The tables, illustrations, and figure captions are an important part of the content. Visual representations like the one in **Figure 1.22** help to make concepts clearer. Solve any Practice Problems as they appear and compare your answers with those given in Appendix C.

Throughout your textbook, you will see references to a Chem ASAP! CD, which is designed to help you learn chemistry *As Soon As Possible*. If you have access to this CD, use its animations and simulations to visualize the concepts presented in your textbook. CHEM ASAP! also provides a format that leads you through selected Practice Problems. After completing a chapter, use the section summaries in the Student Study Guide to review what you have learned. Test your knowledge by writing definitions for the key terms and answering chapter review problems assigned by your teacher. The answers to odd-numbered problems are in Appendix C. If you are unable to solve a problem or understand a concept after a reasonable amount of effort, move on to the next topic or problem. Ask your teacher or study group for help with the difficult problem or concept.

Figure 1.23
The Chem ASAP! CD-ROM has animations, simulations, assessment exercises, and problems that are designed to be used with your textbook.

Chem ASAP!

Animations

Simulations

Assessment

Problem-Solving

Figure 1.24
Working in a group often leads to the biggest discoveries!

On Your Own

You can be even more successful in your study of chemistry if you go beyond the textbook. For example, draw your own diagrams to illustrate important concepts and definitions. Or make flashcards for important formulas, equations, terms, and definitions. Quiz yourself and your classmates often to evaluate your understanding.

As you learned in Section 1.1, chemistry is often practiced as a group activity. Adopting this method might well enhance your study of chemistry. Many students form study groups with their classmates to work on difficult problems, talk through complex concepts, or gain a new perspective on what they are learning. Like writing, talking helps. If you cannot belong to a study group, explain chemistry to your friends, classmates, and family.

Tests and Quizzes

Learning chemistry can be a lot of fun! However, it is very likely that as part of your study, you will be required to take tests and quizzes. Cramming for a test at the last second is never a good idea. It is much more beneficial to set aside a certain amount of time to study every day. How much time you set aside depends on how long it takes you to do the work. When test time comes, reviewing the work that you have already completed should be part of your preparation. Remember, exhaustion is your mind's enemy. Get enough sleep the night before the test. When you get the test, read it over quickly. Determine which parts of the test you can answer immediately or work out rapidly. Complete those parts first. Reserve any difficult questions for last. Show all of your work when answering problem-solving questions. After you have solved a numerical problem, evaluate your answer to be certain that it makes sense. If you have time, go over the entire test to check for errors. Remember, the best way to avoid panic and unwelcome surprises is to be well prepared.

portfolio project

Design a study strategy or plan that you can use to learn chemistry. Discuss your plan with your teacher and share it with your classmates. Then use your plan throughout this course.

section review 1.4

12. Explain why it is important to study chemistry every day.

13. Why is chemistry best studied with a pencil in hand?

14. Explain the value of discussing chemistry with others.

15. Briefly describe what your strategy for studying chemistry will be throughout the upcoming year.

Chem ASAP! **Assessment 1.4** Check your understanding of the important ideas and concepts in Section 1.4.

CHEMISTRY IN THE INFORMATION AGE

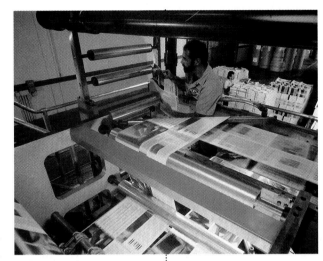

The general public needs to understand science. Citizens are often asked to make decisions about topics such as watershed protection, water quality, or waste disposal. These issues can affect the well-being of individuals and communities.

The way that scientists communicate with each other and with the general public has changed over the centuries. In earlier centuries, scientists exchanged ideas through letters. They also formed societies that met now and then to discuss the latest findings of their members. When societies began to publish journals, scientists could use the journals to keep up with experimental data. If results were published in an unfamiliar language or in an obscure journal, they might be lost for decades, as were Gregor Mendel's studies of heredity.

Nowadays, such a communication gap would be unlikely. Scientists exchange ideas with other scientists by phone, by e-mail, and at international conferences. Scientists still publish their results in scientific journals. These journals are the most reliable sources of information about new discoveries because articles are not published until they are reviewed by two or three experts in the author's field. The reviewers point out any errors in the author's hypothesis or experimental design. Reviewers may suggest that the author do more work to strengthen the argument before publishing. The review process can be painful for a scientist, but it is good for science as a whole because work that is not well founded is usually not published.

Because the review process can take from six months to a year, or even longer, some journals publish preliminary results on the Internet. Preliminary results should be treated with caution because such results are subject to change.

One advantage of the Internet is that anyone can get access to its information. One disadvantage is that anyone can post information on the Internet without first having that information reviewed. To judge the reliability of information you find on the Internet, you have to consider the source.

You also need to treat the scientific articles you read in newspapers and magazines or the news you listen to on television with similar caution. Sometimes scientific reports in the popular media are a poor reflection of the actual work done by scientists. If a media outlet has a reporter who specializes in science, the chances are better that the report will not have major distortions, gaps, or errors. But even the best reporter may have limited time to prepare an article and limited space in which to describe the topic. Also, the reporter may need to simplify a complex issue to reach the widest possible audience. Should you avoid reading about science in the popular press? Absolutely not! There are too many important advances worthy of your attention. But you should look for reliable sources and approach the news with a certain amount of healthy skepticism. Links provided through the Prentice Hall web site are good sources of current data.

> To judge the reliability of information you find on the Internet, you have to consider the source.

Take It to the NET
For interactive study and review, go to www.phschool.com

KEY TERMS

- analytical chemistry *p. 4*
- biochemistry *p. 4*
- chemistry *p. 3*
- experiment *p. 15*
- hypothesis *p. 15*
- inorganic chemistry *p. 4*
- observation *p. 15*
- organic chemistry *p. 4*
- physical chemistry *p. 4*
- scientific law *p. 17*
- scientific method *p. 15*
- theory *p. 16*

CONCEPT SUMMARY

1.1 Chemistry

- Chemistry is the study of the composition of matter and the changes that matter undergoes.
- Analytical chemistry, biochemistry, inorganic chemistry, organic chemistry, and physical chemistry are the traditional divisions of chemistry.
- Chemistry helps you to understand your world and to make informed decisions about scientific issues. Chemistry is an excellent career for some people.
- Applied chemistry, or chemical technology, is chemistry used to attain a specific goal. Pure chemistry accumulates knowledge for its own sake.

1.2 Chemistry Far and Wide

- Chemistry reaches into such diverse areas as materials science, energy, medicine and biotechnology, agriculture, environmental studies, and astronomy and space exploration.
- Progress has its price. Every new development has its risks and benefits. Society must decide in which direction the balance shifts.

1.3 Thinking Like a Scientist

- The scientific method provides a logical approach to the solution of scientific problems.
- The steps of the scientific method include observations, hypotheses, experiments, theories, and scientific laws.
- An observation is information gathered directly by using the senses. A hypothesis is a proposed explanation or reason for what is observed. An experiment is a means to test a hypothesis. A scientific experiment must be repeatable.
- A theory is a broad and extensively tested explanation of why experiments give certain results. A scientific law describes a natural phenomenon but does not explain it.

1.4 How to Study Chemistry

- You can study chemistry alone or in groups.
- It is important to learn the language and vocabulary of chemistry.
- Your textbook is an important aid in your studies.

CHAPTER CONCEPT MAP

Use these terms to construct a concept map that organizes the major ideas of this chapter.

 Chem ASAP! Concept Map 1
Create your Concept Map using the computer.

CONCEPT PRACTICE

16. Define chemistry. What is matter? *1.1*

17. Describe the difference between chemistry and chemical technology. *1.1*

18. Match each numbered term with a lettered term. *1.1*

a. physical chemistry	(1) composition
b. organic chemistry	(2) life
c. analytical chemistry	(3) carbon
d. inorganic chemistry	(4) behavior
e. biochemistry	(5) without carbon

19. Match each numbered photograph with the lettered field of chemistry it best represents. *1.2*

a. materials science
b. energy
c. medicine and biotechnology
d. agriculture
e. environment
f. astronomy and space

(1)

(2)

(3)

(4)

(5)

(6)

20. How might advances in energy research affect your life? *1.2*

21. Why is the ozone layer surrounding Earth important? *1.2*

22. Give at least two benefits of replacing some of the steel in automobiles with plastics. *1.2*

23. What is the purpose of an experiment as part of the scientific method? *1.3*

24. Describe two situations in which you used at least part of the scientific method. *1.3*

25. You perform an experiment and get unexpected results. According to the scientific method, what should you do next? *1.3*

26. Which of the following is not a part of the scientific method? *1.3*
   a. hypothesis **c.** guess
   b. experiment **d.** theory

27. Compare and contrast the study of chemistry with the study of a language. *1.4*

28. Which statement about the study of chemistry is false? *1.4*
   a. The chemistry textbook is an important study aid.
   b. Chemistry is mostly memorization.
   c. It is better to study on a regular basis than to cram before a test.
   d. A study group is beneficial.
   e. Discussing chemistry with family and friends is helpful.

CONCEPT MASTERY

29. You find a sealed box with strings protruding from three holes, as shown in the diagram. When you tug string **a**, it becomes longer and string **c** becomes shorter. When you tug string **b**, it becomes longer, but strings **a** and **c** are unaffected. Make a diagram showing the arrangement of the strings inside the box.

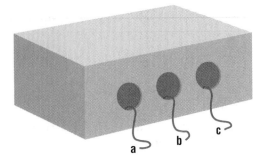

30. You have a sore throat, so you go to the doctor. The doctor examines your throat and says she thinks you have strep throat. She takes a sample to test for strep bacteria. What parts of the scientific method is the doctor applying?

31. You perform an experiment and find that the results do not agree with theory. Is something wrong with your experiment?

32. Explain why chemistry might be useful in any career.

CRITICAL THINKING

33. Choose the term that best completes the second relationship.
   a. seed:plant
      data:_____
      (1) theory   (3) experiment
      (2) techniques   (4) scientific method
   b. hub:wheel
      chemistry:_____
      (1) tire   (3) science
      (2) hypothesis   (4) theory
   c. part:whole
      theory:_____
      (1) scientific method   (3) observation
      (2) experiment   (4) law

34. Comment on the idea that science accepts what works and rejects what does not work.

35. Occasionally you may read about important discoveries being made accidentally. Louis Pasteur said, "Chance favors the prepared mind." Are these two statements contradictory? Explain.

36. Criticize the statement, "Theories are proven by experiments."

37. Refer back to question 28 and provide an explanation for each statement that is true. Correct the statement that is false.

Select the choice that best answers each question or completes each statement.

1. The branch of chemistry that studies most carbon-containing substances is ___ chemistry.
   a. physical
   b. inorganic
   c. analytical
   d. organic

2. An analytical chemist is most likely to
   a. explain why paint is stirred before it is used.
   b. explain what forces keep paint attached to the steel frame of an automobile.
   c. identify the type of paint chips found at the scene of a hit-and-run accident.
   d. investigate the effect of leaded paint on the development of a young child.

3. The greatest source of energy on Earth is
   a. petroleum.
   b. sunlight.
   c. electricity.
   d. nuclear power.

4. Chemists who work in the biotechnology field are most likely to work with
   a. x-ray technicians.
   b. geologists.
   c. physicians.
   d. physicists.

5. Increased levels of carbon dioxide in the atmosphere can cause
   a. smog.
   b. acid rain.
   c. global warming.
   d. ozone depletion.

Respond to each statement in questions 6–8.

6. Someone who wears contact lenses does not have to wear safety glasses.

7. Eating food that is left over from an experiment is an alternative to discarding the food.

8. For a student who has read the procedure, the teacher's pre-lab instructions are unnecessary.

Use the atomic windows to answer question 9.

9. The air you breathe is composed of about 20% oxygen and 80% nitrogen. Which atomic window best represents a sample of air?

a.
c.
b.
d.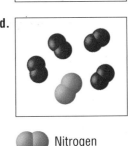

⬤⬤ Oxygen   ⬤⬤ Nitrogen

Use this paragraph to answer questions 10–12.

(1) On a cold morning, your car does not start. (2) You say, "Oh no! The battery is dead!". (3) Your friend who works on cars uses a battery tester and finds that the battery has a full charge. (4) Your friend notices a lot of corrosion on the battery terminals. (5) Your friend says "Maybe corrosion is causing a bad connection in the electrical circuit, preventing the car from starting." (6) Your friend cleans the terminals and the car starts.

10. Which statements are observations?

11. Which statements are hypotheses?

12. Which statement describes an experiment?

For each question there are two statements. Decide whether each statement is true or false. Then decide whether Statement II is a correct explanation for Statement I.

Statement I		**Statement II**
13. A hypothesis may be rejected after an experiment.	BECAUSE	Experiments are used to test hypotheses.
14. Fossil fuels are nonrenewable resources.	BECAUSE	Only about 1% of the energy in sunlight is captured by plant life on Earth.
15. Theories help you model objects or processes that cannot be seen.	BECAUSE	Theories summarize the results of many observations and experiments.
16. Ideally, insecticides, herbicides, and fungicides should be nonspecific.	BECAUSE	Scientists are looking for safer, more effective ways to protect crops.
17. All Internet sites that provide scientific information are equally reliable.	BECAUSE	All information on these sites is reviewed by qualified scientists.

Chapter 2

MATTER AND CHANGE

FEATURES

DISCOVER IT!
Classifying Matter

SMALL-SCALE LAB
1 + 2 + 3 = Black!

MINI LAB
Mixtures

CHEMISTRY SERVING ... INDUSTRY
Barriers to Heat Flow

CHEMISTRY IN CAREERS
Materials Scientist

LINK TO PHYSICS
Changing States of Matter

LINK TO LINGUISTICS
Origins of Element Names

LINK TO ENGINEERING
Chemical Engineers

Stay current with **SCIENCE NEWS**
Find out more about matter and change:
www.phschool.com

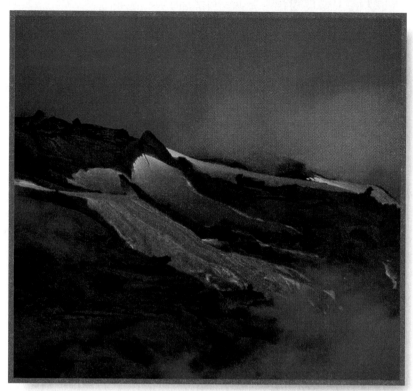

Hot lava from a volcano changes ocean water to steam.

DISCOVER IT! CLASSIFYING MATTER

You need four small clear containers, sugar, baking powder, flour, baking soda, water, a half-cup measure (about 120 mL), a half-teaspoon measure (about 2.5 mL), a spoon, tape or self-adhesive labels, and a pen.

1. Label the containers with the names of the four white solids (sugar, baking powder, flour, baking soda).
2. Pour a half-cup of water into each of the four containers.
3. Without stirring, add a half-teaspoon of each white solid to its corresponding container. Take note of any reaction between the solid and the water. Wipe the spoon between each addition.
4. Stir the contents of each container for at least 45 seconds, observing what happens to each of the white solids. Rinse the spoon with water between stirrings.

Which solid could you distinguish from the other three after the initial mixing with water? How? Can you distinguish completely among the remaining three solids based on the results of Step 4? Why or why not? Make a list of the distinguishing characteristics you have just explored, and add to it as you read this chapter.

MATTER

*A*s incredibly hot molten lava from a volcano reaches the ocean, the thick liquid lava cools to form solid rock. At the same time, some of the liquid water is heated to form a gas called steam. **What are the characteristics of solids, liquids, and gases, and how do their shapes and volumes differ?**

Properties of Matter

Look around you. All the things you see are examples of matter. But what exactly is matter? What forms does matter take? What can cause matter to change its form? **Matter** is defined as anything that has mass and takes up space. The **mass** of an object is the amount of matter the object contains. A golf ball has a greater mass than a table-tennis ball. The golf ball, therefore, contains more matter.

Everything is made up of matter. However, materials may differ in terms of the kind of matter they contain. For example, table sugar is one particular kind of matter, with the chemical name sucrose. Table sugar is always 100% sucrose. It always has the same makeup, or chemical composition. Matter that has a uniform and definite composition is called a **substance.** Substances, also referred to as pure substances, contain only one kind of matter. Lemonade is not a substance because not all samples of lemonade are identical. Lemonade contains more than one kind of matter and the relative amounts of each kind may differ. For example, different pitchers of lemonade may have varying amounts of sugar, lemon juice, or water, and may taste different. Thus they have different compositions.

All samples of a substance have identical physical properties. For example, all crystals of sucrose taste sweet and dissolve completely in water. A **physical property** is a quality or condition of a substance that can be observed or measured without changing the substance's composition. Physical properties include color, solubility, odor, hardness, density, melting point, and boiling point.

Scan the physical properties of the common substances listed in **Table 2.1.** Such physical properties help chemists identify the substances.

Table 2.1

Physical Properties of Some Common Substances						
Substance	Formula	State	Color	Melting point (°C)	Boiling point (°C)	Density (g/cm³)
Neon	Ne	gas	colorless	−249	−246	0.0009
Oxygen	O_2	gas	colorless	−218	−183	0.0014
Chlorine	Cl_2	gas	greenish-yellow	−101	−34	0.0032
Ethanol	C_2H_5OH	liquid	colorless	−117	78	0.789
Mercury	Hg	liquid	silvery-white	−39	357	13.5
Bromine	Br_2	liquid	red-brown	−7	59	3.12
Water	H_2O	liquid	colorless	0	100	1.00
Sulfur	S	solid	yellow	113	445	2.07
Sucrose	$C_{12}H_{22}O_{11}$	solid	white	185	d*	1.59
Sodium chloride	NaCl	solid	white	801	1413	2.17

d*, decomposes on heating

Table 2.2

Important Properties of the States of Matter			
Property	Solid	Liquid	Gas or vapor
Shape	definite	indefinite	indefinite
Volume	definite	definite	indefinite
Expansion on heating	very slight	moderate	great
Compressibility	almost incompressible	almost incompressible	readily compressible

For example, a colorless liquid that was found to boil at 100 °C and melt at 0 °C would likely be water. A colorless liquid that boiled at 78 °C and melted at −117 °C would most certainly not be water. Which substance in **Table 2.1** has these physical properties?

States of Matter

You are very familiar with the substance called water. Under certain circumstances, however, you use the words ice and steam to refer to what is really the same substance. You use these three names because water—like most other substances—can exist in three different physical states: solid, liquid, and gas. The physical state of a substance is a physical property of that substance. Certain characteristics, summarized in **Table 2.2,** distinguish the three states of matter.

Coal, sugar, ice, and iron are examples of materials that are solids. A **solid** is matter that has a definite shape and volume. The shape of a solid does not depend on the shape of its container. The particles in a solid are packed tightly together, as shown in **Figure 2.1a.** As a result, solids are almost incompressible—that is, they cannot be squashed into a smaller volume. In addition, they expand only slightly when heated.

Water, milk, and blood are examples of liquids. The particles in a liquid are in close contact with one another, but unlike solid particles, they are not rigidly packed. A liquid can flow; that is, it can take the shape of the container in which it is placed. The amount of space, or volume, occupied by a sample of a liquid is the same no matter what shape it takes. This

(a) Particles in a solid   (b) Particles in a liquid   (c) Particles in a gas

Chem ASAP!

Animation 1
Relate the states of matter to kinetic energy and temperature.

Figure 2.1

Compare the structured arrangement of the particles in a solid, a liquid, and a gas. (a) The particles in a solid are packed closely together in a rigid arrangement. A solid thus has a definite shape and volume. (b) The particles in a liquid contact one another yet have more freedom to move than the particles in a solid. A liquid can flow and takes on the shape of its container. (c) The particles in a gas are relatively far apart and are free to move anywhere inside their container. A gas thus has an indefinite shape and indefinite volume.

unchanging volume is said to be fixed or constant. A **liquid** is thus a form of matter that flows, has a fixed volume, and takes the shape of its container. Liquids are almost incompressible, but they tend to expand when heated.

Like liquids, gases flow to take the shape of the container that holds them. The particles in a gas are spaced far apart. Unlike liquids, gases expand without limit to fill any space. Thus a **gas** is a form of matter that takes both the shape and volume of its container. Gases are also easily compressed.

The words gas and vapor should not be used interchangeably; there is a difference. The term gas is limited to those substances that exist in the gaseous state at ordinary room temperature. For example, air is a mixture of gases including oxygen and nitrogen. The word **vapor** describes the gaseous state of a substance that is generally a liquid or solid at room temperature. Steam, the gaseous form of water, is referred to as a vapor because water is a liquid at room temperature. Moist air contains water vapor.

Physical Changes

Matter can be changed in many ways without altering the chemical composition of the material. Such a change, which alters a given material without changing its composition, is called a **physical change.** Cutting, grinding, and bending a material are examples of physical changes. A change in temperature may also bring about a physical change, such as the melting of the metal gallium, shown in **Figure 2.2.** The melting of ice, the freezing of water, the conversion of water to steam, and the condensation of steam to water are all examples of physical changes—changes that do not alter the chemical composition of the water.

Words such as boil, freeze, dissolve, melt, condense, break, split, crack, grind, cut, crush, and bend usually signify a physical change. Table salt (sodium chloride) is a white solid at room temperature. It can be made to undergo physical changes. For example, it can melt to form a liquid or boil to form a vapor. The temperatures at which these changes of state occur in sodium chloride are very different from the corresponding changes for water. Sodium chloride melts (becomes a liquid) at 801 °C and boils (becomes a vapor) at 1413 °C—high temperatures compared with water's melting and boiling points of 0 °C and 100 °C, respectively.

Figure 2.2
The melting point of gallium metal is 30 °C. What is the approximate Celsius temperature of the hand shown holding the gallium? How can you tell?

PHYSICS

Changing States of Matter
Changes of state are typically associated with changes in temperature. However, the state of matter can also be affected by other variables. Thixotropic materials are solidlike materials that liquefy when subjected to shearing forces. For example, many paints are thixotropic; they thin out when brushed on a surface and thicken when the brush strokes stop, thus keeping the paint from sliding off the wall! A shearing force has an opposite effect on quicksand. Quick movements "thicken" the quicksand and make it much more difficult for a person or animal trapped in it to move.

---

section review 2.1

1. Is every sample of matter a substance? Explain.

2. Contrast the characteristics of the three states of matter.

3. Which of the following are physical changes?

   a. making caramel from sugar   **c.** freezing mercury

   b. carving a wooden figurine   **d.** dissolving salt in water

4. Use **Table 2.1** to answer the following questions.

   a. Which of the liquids listed has the highest boiling point?

   b. What two properties of sucrose distinguish it from sodium chloride?

   c. What single property do neon, oxygen, and ethanol have in common?

 Chem ASAP! Assessment 2.1 Check your understanding of the important ideas and concepts in Section 2.1.

objectives

▶ Categorize a sample of matter as a substance or a mixture

▶ Distinguish between homogeneous and heterogeneous samples of matter

key terms

▶ mixture

▶ heterogeneous mixture

▶ homogeneous mixture

▶ solutions

▶ phase

▶ distillation

MIXTURES

In 1848, gold was discovered in the foothills near Placerville, California. This discovery led to a massive gold rush in the following year. Many people in the California foothills still pan for gold as a hobby. Panning separates gold out of a mixture of gold and sand. **What is a mixture, and how can it be separated?**

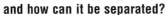

Classifying Mixtures

You might prepare a salad by tossing lettuce, tomatoes, cucumbers, and celery with some vinegar and oil. The result is not only nutritious; it is also a mixture. In this section, you will learn how to identify and classify mixtures.

Most samples of matter are obviously mixtures. For example, you can easily recognize chicken noodle soup as a mixture of chicken pieces, noodles, and broth. Recognizing other materials as mixtures may be much harder. Air is a mixture of gases, but its components cannot be distinguished by eye, even through a microscope.

A **mixture** is a physical blend of two or more substances. One important characteristic of mixtures is that their compositions may vary. A dinner salad can have varying amounts of tomatoes or celery in it. The composition of air in a forest may differ from that in an industrial city, particularly in the amounts of pollutants. Blood, a mixture of water, various chemicals, and cells, varies somewhat in composition from one individual to another and, from time to time, in a given individual.

Mixtures can be of two basic kinds: heterogeneous or homogeneous. **Figure 2.3** gives examples of each kind. A **heterogeneous mixture** is one that is not uniform in composition. If you were to sample one portion of such a mixture, its composition would be different from that of another portion. Why is the salad described above heterogeneous? A **homogeneous mixture** in contrast, is one that has a completely uniform composition. Its components are evenly distributed throughout the sample. A sample of salt water is the same throughout. Thus salt water is an example of a homogeneous mixture.

Figure 2.3

All of these items are mixtures. The bar of soap and the beverage are homogeneous mixtures; they have uniform compositions. The salad is a heterogeneous mixture; it consists of several phases containing components that are not evenly distributed. What other everyday items can you identify as either homogeneous or heterogeneous mixtures?

Table 2.3

Some Common Types of Solutions	
System	Examples
Gas–gas	Carbon dioxide and oxygen in nitrogen (air)
Liquid–gas	Water vapor in air (moist air)
Gas–liquid	Carbon dioxide in water (soda water)
Liquid–liquid	Acetic acid in water (vinegar)
Solid–liquid	Sodium chloride in water (brine)
Solid–solid	Copper in silver (sterling silver, an alloy)

Homogeneous mixtures are so important in chemistry that chemists give them the special name of **solutions.** As **Table 2.3** shows, solutions may be gases, liquids, or solids. If you were to take a sample from any portion of a solution of sugar in water, you would find that it has the same composition as any other portion. Any part of a system with uniform composition and properties is called a **phase.** Thus a homogeneous mixture consists of a single phase. A heterogeneous mixture consists of two or more phases. A mixture of vinegar and oil is an example of a heterogeneous mixture with two phases. When the mixture is left unshaken, the separate phases are visible; the oil phase floats on the water phase.

Separating Mixtures

Some mixtures can be separated into their components by simple physical methods. You might use a fork to separate taco filling into meat, lettuce, cheese, and tomatoes. But separating the grayish mixture of powdered yellow sulfur and black iron filings, shown in **Figure 2.4,** is not so simple. The individual particles of sulfur and iron can be readily distinguished from one another under a microscope, so the mixture is heterogeneous. What property of iron makes using a magnet an effective way to separate the mixture?

Tap water is a homogeneous mixture of water plus other substances that are dissolved in it. How would you separate the components in tap water? One method is called distillation. In **distillation,** a liquid is boiled to produce a vapor that is then condensed again to a liquid. **Figure 2.5** on page 34 shows an apparatus that can be used to perform a distillation. When water containing dissolved solids is distilled, it is first heated in a flask to form steam that enters a glass tube. The solid substances that originally dissolved in the water remain in the distillation flask because they do not change into a vapor. The steam cools and forms droplets of water inside the tube. The water drips into a receiver, where it is collected. The resulting distilled water is pure except for the dissolved gases it contains. Water from which even the dissolved gases are removed is a pure substance.

Figure 2.4

The mixture of iron filings and sulfur can be separated using a magnet.

Figure 2.5

A solution of impure water is being distilled. As the solution boils, the water turns into steam, leaving the impurities behind in the distillation flask. As the steam passes through the water-cooled condenser, it turns to liquid. The distilled water is collected in the receiver flask.

Practice Problems

5. What physical properties could be used to separate iron filings from salt?

6. Which of the following are homogeneous? Heterogeneous?
   a. spaghetti sauce
   b. glass
   c. muddy water
   d. cough syrup
   e. mixture of nitrogen gas and helium gas

Chem ASAP!

Problem-Solving 6
Solve Problem 6 with the help of an interactive guided tutorial.

Sample Problem 2-1

How can a mixture of iron filings and aluminum filings be separated?

1. **ANALYZE** *Plan a problem-solving strategy.*
List the properties of iron and aluminum and look for something that would be useful in separating the mixture.

2. **SOLVE** *Apply the problem-solving strategy.*

Iron:	Aluminum:
• metal	• metal
• grayish	• grayish
• not soluble in water	• not soluble in water
• attracted to a magnet	• not attracted to a magnet

Make use of a property that differentiates the metals; use a magnet to attract the iron filings.

3. **EVALUATE** *Does the result make sense?*
Because the magnet attracts iron but not aluminum filings, the iron would be removed while the aluminum would be left behind.

MINI LAB

MIXTURES

PURPOSE

To separate a mixture using paper chromatography.

MATERIALS

- green marking pens
- strips of filter paper
- metric ruler
- clear plastic tape
- pencil
- rubbing alcohol
- clear plastic drinking cups
- clear plastic wrap
- water

PROCEDURE

1. Use the marking pen to draw a horizontal line across the width of a strip of filter paper, 2 cm from one end of the strip.

2. Tape the unmarked end of the filter paper to the center of a pencil so that the strip hangs down when the pencil is held horizontally.

3. Working in a well-ventilated room, pour rubbing alcohol into a plastic cup to a depth of 1 cm.

4. Rest the pencil on the rim of the cup so that the end of the paper strip with the ink mark is just barely in contact with the rubbing alcohol. Carefully cover the top of the cup with plastic wrap.

5. Observe for 15 minutes.

6. If time permits, repeat this lab using different brands and different colors of pens. Also, try using water in place of rubbing alcohol.

ANALYSIS AND CONCLUSIONS

1. What appeared on the filter paper?

2. What did the results indicate about the nature of the green ink? Is the ink a mixture?

---

section review 2.2

7. What is the difference between a heterogeneous and a homogeneous mixture?

8. Describe a procedure that could be used to separate a mixture consisting of sand and salt.

9. Classify each of the following as a substance or a mixture.

    a. silver

    b. alphabet soup

    c. textbook

    d. table salt (sodium chloride)

10. Describe in your own words the difference between a pure substance and a mixture.

11. Describe ways in which the various components of a mixture can be separated.

12. Explain the term phase as it relates to homogeneous and heterogeneous mixtures.

Chem ASAP! Assessment 2.2 Check your understanding of the important ideas and concepts in Section 2.2.

objectives

► Explain the difference between an element and a compound
► Identify the chemical symbols of common elements, and name common elements, given their symbols

key terms

► elements
► compounds
► chemical symbol

ELEMENTS AND COMPOUNDS

Most people like sugar, a compound made of the elements carbon, hydrogen, and oxygen. Pure carbon is a black solid substance, pure hydrogen is a flammable gas, and pure oxygen is a gas that supports combustion. Yet these three elements combine in a particular way to form the white, sweet-tasting compound called sugar. **What is the difference between an element and a compound?**

Distinguishing Elements and Compounds

As you learned in the preceding section, a mixture can be physically separated into its components. Such a separation may yield pure substances, which have uniform and definite compositions. Substances themselves can be classified into two groups: elements and compounds. **Elements** are the simplest forms of matter that can exist under normal laboratory conditions. Elements cannot be separated into simpler substances by chemical means. They are the building blocks for all other substances. Oxygen, hydrogen, and carbon are examples of elements.

Two or more elements can combine chemically with one another to form compounds. For example, oxygen, hydrogen, and carbon can combine to produce the compound sucrose, or common table sugar. **Compounds** are substances that can be separated into simpler substances only by chemical means. There are a variety of chemical processes that can be used to separate compounds into simpler substances. Heating, as the photographs in **Figure 2.6** show, is one of these processes.

Heating a thin layer of sugar in a skillet demonstrates the difference between elements and compounds. With gentle heating, the sugar turns light brown. With continued heating, it turns black, breaking down completely into carbon and water vapor. This experiment shows that sugar is a compound, not an element. The chemical changes caused by strong heating break down the sugar into two different substances: carbon and water. But the question remains: Can the water and the carbon that are produced also be broken down, or are they elements? It turns out that water can be broken down into hydrogen and oxygen by another chemical change. Thus water, like sugar, is a compound. However, the carbon that is

Figure 2.6

*To be separated into their component elements, compounds must undergo a chemical change. Here sugar is heated in a process known as caramelization. The intermediate and final products in photos **(b)** and **(c)** look very different from the sugar in photo **(a)**. As water is completely removed, all that remains is charred, hardened carbon.*

(a)

(b)

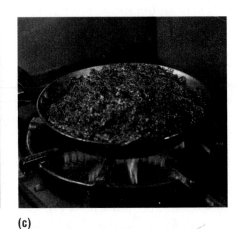

(c)

produced by the heating process cannot be broken down into simpler substances. This shows that carbon is an element, not a compound. The following diagram illustrates the overall process just described.

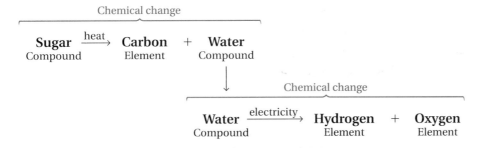

In general, the properties of compounds are quite different from those of their component elements. For example, the sugar placed in the skillet was a sweet, white solid, but the carbon that remained was a black, tasteless solid. Water is a colorless liquid, but oxygen and hydrogen are colorless gases. Table salt (sodium chloride) is a compound of the elements sodium and chlorine. Sodium is a soft metal that reacts explosively with water. Chlorine is a pale yellow-green poisonous gas. **Figure 2.7** shows how the physical appearances of sodium, chlorine, and sodium chloride differ.

Figure 2.7

The compound sodium chloride is common table salt. It is composed of the elements sodium (below: a solid, stored under oil) and chlorine (far left: a gas). The photos show each substance in use: the highly reactive chlorine used to disinfect water, the sodium chloride used to season food, and the sodium used in a street lamp. Why must sodium metal ordinarily be stored under oil?

Deciding whether a sample of matter is a substance or a mixture can sometimes be difficult. After all, a homogeneous mixture looks like a substance. In some cases, you can decide by considering whether the material in question is always a single kind of material. For example, how would you classify gasoline? Based on its physical appearance, you might conclude that gasoline is a pure substance. However, it must be a mixture, because it exists in many different grades. Gasoline can have many different octane ratings and it may or may not contain alcohol. **Figure 2.8** summarizes some information about elements, compounds, and mixtures.

Figure 2.8

Any sample of matter can be classified as an element, a compound, or a mixture. Note some of the characteristics of each. Can you name other examples of elements, compounds, and mixtures?

Sample Problem 2-2

When a blue solid is heated in the absence of air, two other substances—a colorless gas and a white solid—are formed. Which of these substances are elements and which are compounds? Is it possible to tell? Explain.

1. **ANALYZE** *Plan a problem-solving strategy.*
   List the known facts and determine if there is enough information to identify the substances by type (element or compound).
   • A blue solid is changed into two substances (a colorless gas and a white solid) when heated in the absence of air.
   • Compounds can be chemically broken down to simpler substances, but elements cannot be.
   • Heating can cause a chemical change.

2. **SOLVE** *Apply the problem-solving strategy.*
   The blue solid was separated into two different substances by heating. Therefore, it must be a compound. The two resulting substances may be either elements or compounds—it is impossible to tell based on the information given.

3. **EVALUATE** *Does the result make sense?*
   Given the limited amount of known information, the conclusions reached are reasonable.

Practice Problem

13. A clear liquid in an open container is allowed to evaporate. After three days, a solid residue is left. Was the original liquid an element, a compound, or a mixture? How do you know?

Chem ASAP!

Problem-Solving 13
Solve Problem 13 with the help of an interactive guided tutorial.

Symbols and Formulas

Carbon, hydrogen, oxygen, sodium, and chlorine are only a few of the more than 100 known elements. All matter in the universe is composed of these elements. Each element is represented by a one- or two-letter **chemical symbol.** The symbols for most elements consist of the first one or two letters of the element's name. **Table A.1** in the appendix gives the names and symbols for all of the elements. What is the symbol for the element ytterbium?

Note that the first letter of a chemical symbol is always capitalized. If a second letter is used, it is lowercase. Some chemical symbols are derived from Latin or Greek names for the element. In those cases, the symbol does not resemble the common name. **Table 2.4** lists such cases.

Figure 2.9
Many different symbols have been developed over time to represent chemicals, processes, and phenomena. This figure shows symbols used by the important eighteenth-century English chemist John Dalton, as well as some Chinese and alchemist symbols.

LINGUISTICS

Origins of Element Names

Many elements are named for the people who discovered them or the places where they were discovered. Some elements were given descriptive names taken from classical Latin or Greek. Others were named for figures in mythology. Polonium is named for Poland, the native land of Marie Curie, the discoverer of radium. Californium was discovered at the University of California. The word chlorine comes from the Greek *chloros*, meaning greenish-yellow; chlorine is a greenish-yellow gas. The name calcium is derived from the Latin *calx*, meaning lime. Calcium is a major component of limestone. You can find the origins of elements' names by consulting a dictionary or encyclopedia.

Table 2.4

Symbols and Name Origins for Some Elements		
Name	**Symbol**	**Latin or other name**
Sodium	Na	*natrium*
Potassium	K	*kalium*
Antimony	Sb	*stibium*
Copper	Cu	*cuprum*
Gold	Au	*aurum*
Silver	Ag	*argentum*
Iron	Fe	*ferrum*
Lead	Pb	*plumbum*
Mercury	Hg	*hydrargyrum* (from Greek)
Tin	Sn	*stannum*
Tungsten	W	*wolfram* (from German)

Chemical symbols provide a shorthand way to write the chemical formulas of compounds. The compound water is composed of the elements hydrogen (H) and oxygen (O). The formula for water is H_2O. The formula for sucrose, or table sugar, is $C_{12}H_{22}O_{11}$. Sucrose is composed of the elements carbon (C), hydrogen (H), and oxygen (O). The subscript numbers in chemical formulas represent the proportions of the various elements in the compound. The elements that make up a compound are always present in the same proportions. Thus, in the case of water, there are always two parts of hydrogen for each part of oxygen. A specific compound is always made up of the same elements in the same proportions. Thus, the formula for a specific chemical compound is always the same.

section review 2.3

14. How can you distinguish between an element and a compound?

15. Write the chemical symbols for each of the following elements.

    a. copper   **d.** silver

    b. oxygen   **e.** sodium

    c. phosphorus   **f.** helium

16. Name the chemical elements represented by the following symbols.

    a. Sn   **c.** S   **e.** P

    b. Ca   **d.** Cd   **f.** Cl

17. Classify each of these samples of matter as an element, a compound, or a mixture.

    a. spaghetti sauce   **d.** river water

    b. glass   **e.** cough syrup

    c. table sugar   **f.** nitrogen

18. What elements make up the pain reliever acetaminophen, chemical formula $C_8H_9O_2N$? Which element is present in the greatest proportion by number of atoms?

portfolio project

Choose an element whose symbol does not seem to match its name. Research the origin of the symbol.

 Chem ASAP! Assessment 2.3 Check your understanding of the important ideas and concepts in Section 2.3.

CHEMICAL REACTIONS

*O*ver a period of time, objects made out of iron will rust if they are left exposed to air. Rust is the product of a chemical reaction involving the reactants iron and oxygen. **What is a chemical reaction, and what are reactants and products?**

objectives
▶ Differentiate between physical and chemical changes in matter
▶ Apply the law of conservation of mass

key terms
▶ chemical reaction
▶ reactants
▶ products
▶ chemical property
▶ law of conservation of mass

Changing Reactants to Products

Just as every substance has physical properties, each also has properties that relate to the kinds of chemical changes it can undergo. For example, iron has the property of being able to combine with oxygen to form rust. Such a change is an example of a chemical reaction. In a **chemical reaction,** one or more substances change into new substances. The original substances iron and oxygen combine to form a new substance, iron oxide, or rust. In chemical reactions, the starting substances are called **reactants,** and the substances formed are called **products.** What are the reactants in the reaction just described? What is the product?

The ability of a substance to undergo a chemical reaction and to form new substances is called a **chemical property.** Rusting is a chemical property of iron. Chemical properties are observed only when a substance undergoes a chemical change. A chemical change always results in a change in chemical composition of the substances involved. Words such as burn, rot, rust, decompose, ferment, explode, and corrode usually signify a chemical change.

To help distinguish physical changes from chemical changes, recall the mixture of sulfur and iron filings discussed earlier. The separation of these substances by means of a magnet was an example of a physical change. If the same mixture is heated, however, a chemical reaction takes place. The sulfur and iron change into a new substance, iron sulfide. This change can be written in shorthand form as follows:

$$\text{iron} + \text{sulfur} \xrightarrow{\text{heat}} \text{iron sulfide}$$

Figure 2.10
The fizz of an antacid tablet dropped into a glass of water, the brilliance of fireworks exploding in the night sky, and the magnificent colors of autumn leaves are all examples of the chemical reactions you can see all around you.

(a)   (b)

Figure 2.11

*The formation of a gas or a solid from a liquid or the production of a color change are common indications that a chemical change may be taking place. **(a)** Zinc metal reacts with sulfuric acid solution to release hydrogen gas. **(b)** A red solid of silver chromate forms when a yellow solution of sodium chromate is added to a colorless solution of silver nitrate.*

ENGINEERING

Chemical Engineers

Chemical engineers are employed by many industries, including companies that produce fuels, metals, plastics, chemicals, cosmetics, drugs, rubber, paper, paints, and foods. Chemical engineers must determine whether a reaction can be done in large enough amounts for mass production. They plan the layout of an industrial plant, design or select the equipment, and supervise the plant's construction and operation. They may add safety or pollution control features to comply with federal and state regulations. Chemical engineers are responsible for ensuring that the plant operates efficiently. They must also be aware of production costs and stay within a budget. Many engineering and technical schools offer degrees in chemical engineering. The course of study emphasizes chemistry, physics, mathematics, economics, writing, and computers. Specialized engineering courses are also required.

The arrow in the formula stands for the words "change into" or "produce." The reactants are written to the left of the arrow, the products to the right. How would you represent, in shorthand form, the reaction in which hydrogen and oxygen produce water? Several common chemical reactions are illustrated in **Figure 2.10** on page 41. You are probably familiar with many other chemical reactions.

How can you tell whether a chemical reaction has taken place? In general, there are several clues that may serve as a guide. The first is that energy is always absorbed or given off in chemical reactions. When you cook food, chemical changes that involve an absorption of heat take place. When you burn natural gas on a stove (another chemical reaction), heat is given off. However, energy is also absorbed or given off when the physical state of matter changes. Therefore, an energy change in itself is not proof of a chemical change. Other clues include a change in color or odor or the production of a gas or a solid from a liquid. See **Figure 2.11** for examples of chemical reactions that produce such changes. Once again, however, such clues are not always proof of a chemical change. For example, gas or vapor formation can be the result of a change of physical state and not a chemical change. When water boils, it changes from a liquid to a vapor, but the change is physical only; its chemical composition remains the same. A final indicator of chemical change is irreversibility. Physical changes, especially those involving a change of state, are usually reversible. Water can be melted and then refrozen. In contrast, most chemical changes are not easily reversed. For example, once iron has reacted with oxygen to form rust (iron oxide), as happens on a car, you cannot easily reverse the process and turn the rust back into iron.

Conservation of Mass

Combustion, or burning, is an example of one of the most familiar chemical changes. When you burn a lump of coal, atmospheric oxygen combines with the coal. The reaction produces carbon dioxide gas, water vapor, and a small ash residue. This change seems to involve a reduction in the amount of matter. A sizable piece of matter seems to have produced only a trace of ash. However, careful measurements show that the total mass of the reactants (the coal and the oxygen consumed) equals the total mass of the products (the carbon dioxide, water vapor, and ash) when the gases involved are taken into account.

During any chemical reaction, the quantity of matter is unchanged. The mass of products is always equal to the mass of reactants. Constancy of mass also holds for physical changes. For example, when 10 grams of ice melt, 10 grams of liquid water are obtained. Again, in this physical process, mass remains the same. Similar observations have been recorded for all chemical and physical changes studied. The **law of conservation of mass** is reflected in these observations and states that in any physical change or chemical reaction, mass is neither created nor destroyed; it is conserved. In every case, the mass of the products equals the mass of the reactants. One example of the conservation of mass is shown in **Figure 2.12.**

(a)

(b)

Figure 2.12

Magnesium wire inside an old-fashioned flashbulb burns in oxygen gas to produce magnesium oxide. How do the mass readings for the unused bulb (a) and the used bulb (b) compare? What does this show about mass during the chemical reaction?

section review 2.4

19. **a.** State the difference between a physical change and a chemical change, and list three likely indications that a chemical change has occurred. Which indication is most suggestive of a chemical reaction?

   b. State the law of conservation of mass. How does the mass of reactants compare with the mass of products in a given reaction?

20. Classify the following changes as physical or chemical.

   a. Cookies are baked.   **d.** A firefly emits light.

   b. Water boils.   **e.** Milk spoils.

   c. Salt dissolves in water.   **f.** A metal chair rusts.

21. Consider the law of conservation of mass as you answer this problem. When ammonium nitrate (NH_4NO_3) breaks down explosively, it forms nitrogen gas (N_2), oxygen gas (O_2), and water (H_2O). When 40 grams of ammonium nitrate explode, 14 grams of nitrogen and 8 grams of oxygen are formed. How many grams of water are formed?

22. State several physical or chemical properties that could be used to distinguish between each of the following pairs of substances and mixtures.

   a. gasoline and water   **c.** water and a saltwater solution

   b. copper and silver   **d.** aluminum and steel

23. Hydrogen and oxygen react chemically to form water. How much water would be formed if 4.8 grams of hydrogen reacted with 38.4 grams of oxygen?

 Chem ASAP! Assessment 2.4 Check your understanding of the important ideas and concepts in Section 2.4.

SMALL-SCALE LAB

1 + 2 + 3 = BLACK!

SAFETY

Wear your safety glasses and follow standard safety procedures as outlined on page 18.

PURPOSE

To make macroscopic observations of chemical reactions and use them to solve problems.

MATERIALS

- pencil
- ruler
- chemicals shown in Figure A
- paper
- reaction surface
- pipette

PROCEDURE

Draw two grids similar to Figure A on separate sheets of paper. Make each square 2 cm on each side. Place a reaction surface over one of the grids and add one drop, one piece, or a few grains of each chemical, as shown in Figure A. Stir by blowing air through an empty pipette. Use the second grid as a data table to record your observations for each solution.

Figure A

ANALYSIS

Using your experimental data, record the answers to the following questions below your data table.

1. What color is a mixture of NaOCl and KI?

2. What happens when you mix NaOCl, KI, and starch?

3. NaOCl is a powerful bleaching agent as indicated by its reaction with KI and starch. Is hydrogen peroxide (H_2O_2) a bleaching agent? Explain.

4. What happens when you add NaOCl and KI to paper? What ingredient does this suggest the paper contains?

5. What ingredient is contained in cereal? How do you know?

YOU'RE THE CHEMIST!

The following small-scale activities allow you to develop your own procedures and analyze the results.

1. **Design It!** Design and carry out an experiment to see which foods contain starch.

2. **Design It!** Read the label on a package of iodized salt. How much KI does iodized salt contain? Design an experiment to prove the presence of KI in iodized salt and the absence of KI in regular salt.

3. **Design It!** Laundry detergents, automatic dish washing liquids, and cleansers sometimes contain a bleaching agent similar to NaOCl. The purpose of the bleach is to whiten clothes and remove stains. Design an experiment to decide which laundry detergents and cleansers contain bleach.

4. **Design It!** Antacid tablets and other pharmaceuticals often contain starch as a binder to hold the ingredients in the tablet together. Design and carry out an experiment to explore various antacid tablets to see if they contain starch.

5. **Analyze It!** Mix one drop of NaOCl on a piece of colored construction paper. What happens? Try inventing a technique that will create some original "bleach art."

6. **Analyze It!** Other bleaching agents include $FeCl_3$, KIO_3, $KMnO_4$, and $NaNO_2$. Try mixing these with KI and starch to see what happens. What is the best agent to detect the presence of KI in table salt?

BARRIERS TO HEAT FLOW

Will a hot drink stay hotter in a paper cup or in a foam cup? You probably know from experience that the foam cup will work better. In fact, the same foam cup will also do a good job of keeping a cold drink cold. The foam cup is effective at these jobs because polystyrene foam is a good thermal insulator.

A thermal insulator is a material that works as a barrier to the movement of thermal energy through matter. Thermal energy spreads from areas of higher temperature to areas of lower temperature, often very rapidly. This means that something hot, such as tea, will tend to lose its thermal energy to its surroundings. It also means that something cold, such as iced tea, will tend to be warmed by its surroundings. An insulator can slow the movement of thermal energy that causes the undesirable change in temperature.

Thermal insulators are everywhere in human society. They are used to keep houses warm and freezers cold. They keep you warm on a cold day and allow you to pick up a hot pan without getting burned. Because of the importance of insulators, chemists are always at work manipulating matter to make materials with good insulating properties.

> Chemists are always at work manipulating matter to make materials with good insulating properties.

Many of the best insulators are materials in which air is trapped. Air is a good barrier to the movement of thermal energy as long as the air is not moving, and trapped pockets of air satisfy this requirement well.

Using insulation that has a network of thin fibers is an effective way to trap air. Consider fiberglass insulation, which is often used to insulate the walls and ceilings of houses. Fiberglass is just what its name implies—thin fibers of glass (silicon dioxide) that have been woven together. A wool sweater or fleece jacket insulates your body in the same way as fiberglass.

Foams are another type of insulating material. Foams differ from fiber networks in that their air pockets are completely enveloped by the solid material that makes up the framework of the foam.

Traditional polystyrene foam and other similar foams are excellent insulators, but researchers knew they could take these foams a step further. Their goal was to make foams with as little mass as possible for a given volume. The researchers succeeded in developing several new high-tech foams, which are very effective insulators.

One of these new foams, SEAgel, is made of agar, a carbohydrate material that comes from seaweed. SEAgel begins as a gelatin-like mixture of agar and water. Then it is freeze-dried to remove the water. What is left is a honeycomb of dried agar filled with air. The sample in the photograph is light enough to float on soap bubbles. In fact, SEAgel is among the least dense solids known with a density approximately equal to that of air! SEAgel is a very lightweight and efficient insulator. Because it is made entirely of biological material, it is completely biodegradable.

Take It to the NET
For interactive study and
review, go to www.phschool.com

KEY TERMS

- chemical property *p. 41*
- chemical reaction *p. 41*
- chemical symbol *p. 39*
- compound *p. 36*
- distillation *p. 33*
- element *p. 36*
- gas *p. 31*
- heterogeneous mixture *p. 32*

- homogeneous mixture *p. 32*
- law of conservation of mass *p. 43*
- liquid *p. 31*
- mass *p. 29*
- matter *p. 29*
- mixture *p. 32*
- phase *p. 33*

- physical change *p. 31*
- physical property *p. 29*
- product *p. 41*
- reactant *p. 41*
- solid *p. 30*
- solution *p. 33*
- substance *p. 29*
- vapor *p. 31*

KEY RELATIONSHIP

- Law of conservation of mass:

  mass of reactants = mass of products

CONCEPT SUMMARY

2.1 Matter
- Matter has mass and occupies space.
- The three common states of matter are solid, liquid, and gas.
- A pure substance contains one kind of matter.

2.2 Mixtures
- A mixture is a physical combination of two or more substances that can be separated by physical means.
- Heterogeneous mixtures are not uniform in composition.
- Homogeneous mixtures, also called solutions, have uniform properties throughout and may be gases, liquids, or solids.

2.3 Elements and Compounds
- Elements are the simplest forms of matter that exist under normal conditions.
- Elements are always present in the same ratio in a given compound.

- Properties of a compound are usually different from those of the elements composing it.
- Chemical methods are required to separate compounds into their constituent elements.
- Each element is represented by a one- or two-letter chemical symbol. Chemical symbols of the elements are used as a shorthand method of writing chemical formulas of compounds.

2.4 Chemical Reactions
- A physical change is a change in the physical properties of a substance without a change in chemical composition.
- A chemical change is a change in the chemical composition of a substance.
- In a chemical change (chemical reaction), reactants are converted to products. Mass is conserved in any physical or chemical change.

CHAPTER CONCEPT MAP

Use these terms to construct a concept map that organizes the major ideas of this chapter.

 Chem ASAP! Concept Map 2
Create your Concept Map using the computer.

- chemical reaction
- matter
- substance
- element
- law of conservation of mass
- heterogeneous mixture
- homogeneous mixture
- physical property
- compound
- physical change
- chemical property

CONCEPT PRACTICE

24. List three physical properties of an iron nail. *2.1*

25. What is the physical state of each of the following items at room temperature? *2.1*
    a. gold   d. paraffin wax
    b. gasoline   e. rubbing alcohol
    c. helium   f. mercury

26. In which state of matter do the following exist at room temperature? *2.1*
    a. diamond   d. mercury
    b. oxygen   e. clay
    c. cooking oil   f. neon

27. Fingernail-polish remover (mostly acetone) is a liquid at room temperature. Would you describe acetone in the gaseous state as a vapor or a gas? Explain. *2.1*

28. List three substances that you have experienced in at least two physical states. *2.1*

29. Use **Table 2.1** to identify four substances that undergo a physical change if the temperature is decreased from 50 °C to −50 °C. Describe the nature of the physical change. *2.1*

30. Classify each of the following as homogeneous or heterogeneous mixtures. *2.2*
    a. blood
    b. chocolate-chip ice cream
    c. brass (a blend of copper and zinc)
    d. motor oil
    e. black coffee

31. How many phases does every solution have? Explain. *2.2*

32. Classify each of the following as an element or a mixture. *2.3*
    a. silver   d. oxygen
    b. pine tree   e. iced tea
    c. orange juice f. air

33. Name the elements found in each of the following compounds. *2.3*
    a. ammonium chloride (NH_4Cl)
    b. potassium permanganate ($KMnO_4$)
    c. isopropyl alcohol (C_3H_7OH)
    d. calcium iodide (CaI_2)

34. List four indications that a chemical change has probably taken place. *2.4*

35. Classify each of the following as a physical or chemical change. *2.4*
    a. bending a piece of wire
    b. burning coal
    c. cooking a steak
    d. cutting grass

36. When powdered iron is left exposed to the air, it rusts. Explain why the rust weighs more than the original powdered iron. *2.4*

37. A friend observes a burning candle and comments that the wax is lost as the candle burns. Having recently studied the law of conservation of mass, how would you correct your friend? *2.4*

CONCEPT MASTERY

38. Devise a way to separate sand from a mixture of charcoal, sand, sugar, and water.

39. Imagine first standing in the kitchen of your home and then in the middle of a park. When you view the surroundings in each location do you see mostly elements, compounds, or mixtures?

40. Use **Table 2.1** to answer each question.
    a. Which property most easily distinguishes sulfur from the other solid substances?
    b. How many of these substances are elements?
    c. Which compound has the highest boiling point?
    d. The solids are gradually heated. Which one will melt first?

41. Identify each of the following as a mixture or a compound. For the mixtures, classify each as homogeneous or heterogeneous.
    a. soda   e. egg
    b. candle wax   f. ice
    c. fog   g. gasoline
    d. ink   h. blood

42. Classify the following properties of the element silicon as chemical or physical properties.
    a. blue-gray color
    b. brittle
    c. insoluble in water
    d. melts at 1410 °C
    e. reacts vigorously with fluorine

43. How do you know that each of these is a chemical change?
   a. Food spoils.
   b. A foaming antacid tablet fizzes in water.
   c. A ring of scum forms around your bathtub.
   d. Iron rusts.
   e. A firecracker explodes.

CRITICAL THINKING

44. Choose the numbered term that best completes the second relationship.

   a. initial : final   reactant : _____
   (1) product   (3) matter
   (2) mixture   (4) compound

   b. words : sentence   elements : _____
   (1) reactant   (3) compound
   (2) theory   (4) substance

45. Compare the relationships among individual particles in the three states of matter.

46. Explain why this statement is false. "Because there is no change in composition during a physical change, the appearance of the substance will not change."

CONCEPT CHALLENGE

47. The mass of the elements iron and oxygen were measured in four samples of a rust-colored substance believed to be a compound. The amount of iron and oxygen found in each sample is shown on the graph.

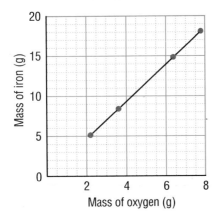

   a. Do you think each sample is of the same compound? Explain.
   b. Another sample of similar material was found to contain 9.9 g of iron and 3.4 g of oxygen. Is this the same substance as the other four? Explain.

48. Five elements make up 97.9% of the mass of the human body. These elements are oxygen (64.8%), carbon (18.1%), hydrogen (10.0%), nitrogen (3.1%), and calcium (1.9%). Compare these data with those in the pie graph below, which shows the five most abundant elements by mass in Earth's crust, oceans, and atmosphere.

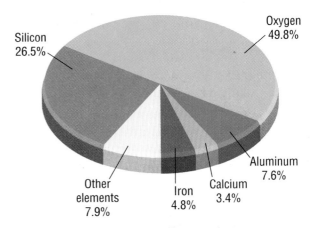

   a. Which elements are abundant in both Earth's surface and the human body?
   b. Which elements are abundant in Earth's surface but not in the human body?
   c. Would you expect the compounds making up the human body to be the same as or different from those found in rocks, water, and air? Explain your answer based on the evidence in the pie graph and the data above.

49. These questions refer to the substances in **Table 2.1**.
   a. How many of these substances are in the liquid state at 125 °C?
   b. Describe the physical properties of one of these substances that led you to the answer.
   c. The substances in the table are listed in order of increasing melting point. Propose another way that these data could be arranged.

50. Each day of your life you encounter some chemical changes that are helpful and some that are harmful. Cite three examples of each. For each example, list the indications that identified the change as chemical.

Select the choice that best answers each question or completes each statement.

1. Which of the following is *not* a chemical change?
   a. paper being shredded
   b. steel rusting
   c. charcoal burning
   d. a newspaper yellowing in the sun

2. Which phrase best describes an apple?
   a. heterogeneous mixture
   b. homogeneous compound
   c. heterogeneous substance
   d. homogeneous mixture

3. Which element is paired with the wrong symbol?
   a. sulfur, S   c. nitrogen, N
   b. potassium, P   d. silicon, Si

4. Which of these properties could *not* be used to distinguish between table salt and table sugar?
   a. boiling point   c. density
   b. melting point   d. color

5. The state of matter characterized by a definite volume and an indefinite shape is a
   a. solid.   c. liquid.
   b. mixture.   d. gas.

Use the atomic windows to answer question 6.

6. The species in window (a) react. Use the law of conservation of mass to determine which window best represents the reaction products.

a.

c.

b.

d.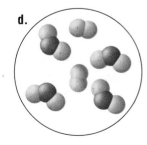

The lettered choices below refer to questions 7–10. A lettered choice may be used once, more than once, or not at all.

   (A) compound
   (B) heterogeneous mixture
   (C) element
   (D) homogeneous mixture

Which description correctly identifies each of the following materials?

7. air

8. carbon monoxide

9. zinc

10. mushroom pizza

Use the data table to answer questions 11–14.

Mass of magnesium (g)	Mass of oxygen (g)	Mass of magnesium oxide (g)
5.0	3.3	8.3
6.5	(a)	10.8
13.6	9.0	(b)
(c)	12.5	31.5

11. Magnesium metal burns vigorously in oxygen to produce the compound magnesium oxide. Use the law of conservation of mass to identify the masses labeled (a), (b), and (c) in the table.

12. Use the data in the completed table to construct a graph with mass of magnesium on the *x*-axis and mass of magnesium oxide on the *y*-axis.

13. How many grams of magnesium oxide form when 8.0 g of magnesium are burned?

14. How many grams of magnesium and oxygen react to form 20.0 g of magnesium oxide?

Use the data table to answer questions 15–17.

Substance	Color	Melting point (°C)	Boiling point (°C)
bromine	red-brown	−7	59
chlorine	green-yellow	−101	−34
ethanol	colorless	−117	78
mercury	silver-white	−39	357
neon	colorless	−249	−246
sulfur	yellow	113	445
water	colorless	0	100

15. Which colorless substance is a liquid at −30 °C?

16. Which colorless substance is a gas at 60 °C?

17. Which substance is a solid at 7 °C?

FEATURES

DISCOVER IT!
Exploring Density

SMALL-SCALE LAB
Measurement

MINI LAB
Accuracy and Precision

CHEMath
What Is an Equation?

CHEMISTRY SERVING … THE CONSUMER
These Standards Are Worth the Weight

CHEMISTRY IN CAREERS
Analytical Chemist

LINK TO ART
Measurement and Art

LINK TO ENGINEERING
Computer-Aided Design

Stay current with **SCIENCE NEWS**
Find out more about measurement:
www.phschool.com

Cranberries float on water in a cranberry bog.

DISCOVER IT! EXPLORING DENSITY

You need three beakers, a graduated cylinder, a colorless cylindrical glass or plastic container, shampoo, water, rubbing alcohol, red food coloring, a medicine dropper, a spoon or stirring rod, and small solid objects (such as a paper clip, plastic soda-bottle cap, chalk, ball of aluminum foil, aluminum nail, piece of uncooked pasta, dried bean, or piece of cork).

1. Pour about 250 mL each of shampoo, water, and rubbing alcohol into separate beakers.

2. Stir a drop of food coloring into the rubbing alcohol and the shampoo.

3. Carefully pour each liquid (in the following order: shampoo, water, rubbing alcohol) down the inside of the colorless cylindrical container to a depth of 2.5 cm (about 1 in.).

4. Record the positions of the three layers of liquids.

5. Gently add each small solid object to the layered liquids and record its resting location.

Propose an explanation for the order of layering of the liquids. Do you think it would make any difference if you added the liquids in a different order? Why or why not? After completing this chapter, reevaluate your explanation and revise it if necessary.

In horse racing, the finish is sometimes so close that the winner can only be determined by a photograph taken at the instant the horses cross the finish line. In the 130th Belmont Stakes, for example, the horse named Real Quiet, the winner of both the Kentucky Derby and the Preakness, was beaten by only the length of a nose in the final race for the Triple Crown. Chemistry also requires making accurate and often very small measurements. **What types of measurements are made in chemistry?**

objectives

▶ Distinguish between quantitative and qualitative measurements
▶ Convert measurements to scientific notation

key terms

▶ qualitative measurements
▶ quantitative measurements
▶ scientific notation

Qualitative and Quantitative Measurements

Everyone makes and uses measurements. For example, you decide how to dress in the morning based on the temperature outside. You measure the ingredients for your favorite cookie recipe. If you were building a cabinet for your stereo system, you would carefully measure the length of each piece of wood.

Measurements are fundamental to the experimental sciences as well. For that reason, it is important to be able to make measurements and to decide whether a measurement is correct. In chemistry, you will use the International System of Measurements (SI).

Not all measurements give the same amount of information. For example, how might you determine whether someone who is sick has a fever? You might simply touch the person's forehead and think, "Yes! This person feels feverish." This is an example of a qualitative measurement. **Qualitative measurements** give results in a descriptive, nonnumerical form. If several people touch the sick person's forehead, their qualitative measurements may not agree with yours. One reason for this is that a person's own temperature influences his or her perception of how warm another person feels. By using a thermometer, however, each person can eliminate this personal bias. The temperature takers will each report a numerical value, or quantitative measurement. **Quantitative measurements** give results in a definite form, usually as numbers and units. For example, the thermometer might reveal the person's temperature to be 39.2 °C (102.5 °F). This measurement has a definite value that can be compared with the person's temperature at a later time to check for changes. Yet this measurement, however definite, can be no more reliable than the instrument used to make the measurement and the care with which it is used and read.

Figure 3.1

Instruments are needed to make quantitative measurements. A meat thermometer, a radar gun, and a grocery scale are common instruments used to measure temperature, speed, and weight, respectively.

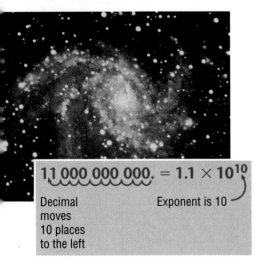

$$11\,000\,000\,000. = 1.1 \times 10^{10}$$

Decimal moves 10 places to the left

Exponent is 10

Figure 3.2

Expressing very large numbers, such as the estimated number of stars in a galaxy, is easier if scientific notation is used. The number of decimal places moved is equal to the exponent.

Scientific Notation

In chemistry, you will often encounter very small and very large numbers. The mass of an atom of gold, for example, is 0.000 000 000 000 000 000 000 327 gram. A gram of hydrogen contains 602 000 000 000 000 000 000 000 hydrogen atoms. Writing and using such small or large numbers is very cumbersome. You can work more easily with these numbers by writing them in scientific, or exponential, notation.

In **scientific notation,** a number is written as the product of two numbers: a coefficient and 10 raised to a power. For example, the number 36 000 is written in scientific notation as 3.6×10^4. The coefficient in this number is 3.6. In scientific notation, the coefficient is always a number greater than or equal to one and less than ten. The power of 10, or exponent, in this example is 4. The exponent indicates how many times the coefficient 3.6 must be multiplied by 10 to equal the number 36 000.

$$3.6 \times 10^4 = 3.6 \times 10 \times 10 \times 10 \times 10 = 36\,000$$

For numbers greater than ten, the exponent is positive and equals the number of places the original decimal point has been moved to the left to write the number in scientific notation. Numbers less than ten have a negative exponent. For example, the number 0.0081 written in scientific notation is 8.1×10^{-3}. The exponent -3 indicates that the coefficient 8.1 must be divided by 10 three times to equal 0.0081, as shown in **Figure 3.3.**

$$8.1 \times 10^{-3} = \frac{8.1}{10 \times 10 \times 10} = 0.0081$$

For numbers less than ten, the value of the exponent equals the number of places the original decimal point has been moved to the right to write the number in scientific notation. Can you express the mass of a single atom of gold, which is 0.000 000 000 000 000 000 000 327 gram, in scientific notation? Try it!

Multiplication and Division Using scientific notation makes calculating more straightforward. To multiply numbers written in scientific notation, multiply the coefficients and add the exponents. For example,

$$(3.0 \times 10^4) \times (2.0 \times 10^2) = (3.0 \times 2.0) \times 10^{4+2} = 6.0 \times 10^6$$

Figure 3.3

A tiny distance, such as that between the atoms in this electron micrograph, can be expressed conveniently in scientific notation. The direction in which the decimal point is moved determines the sign of the exponent. What is the sign of the exponent in this case?

$$0.0081 = 8.1 \times 10^{-3}$$

Decimal moves 3 places to the right.

Exponent is -3

To divide numbers written in scientific notation, first divide the coefficients. Then subtract the exponent in the denominator (bottom) from the exponent in the numerator (top). For example,

$$\frac{3.0 \times 10^4}{2.0 \times 10^2} = \frac{3.0}{2.0} \times 10^{4-2} = 1.5 \times 10^2$$

Addition and Subtraction Before you add or subtract numbers written in scientific notation, you must make the exponents the same because the exponents determine the locations of the decimal points in the original numbers. The decimal points must be aligned before you add two numbers. For numbers in scientific notation, making the exponents the same aligns the decimal points. For example, when adding 5.40×10^3 to 6.0×10^2, you must adjust the exponents to make them the same. You can choose to adjust 6.0×10^2 to 0.60×10^3.

$$
\begin{array}{r}
5.40 \times 10^3 \\
+\ 0.60 \times 10^3 \\
\hline
6.00 \times 10^3
\end{array}
$$

section review 3.1

1. **a.** What is the difference between a qualitative measurement and a quantitative measurement?

   b. How is a number converted to scientific notation?

2. Classify each statement as either qualitative or quantitative.

   a. The basketball is brown.

   b. The diameter of the basketball is 31 centimeters.

   c. The air pressure in the basketball is 12 pounds per square inch.

   d. The surface of the basketball has indented seams.

3. Write each measurement in scientific notation.

   a. the length of a football field, 91.4 meters

   b. the diameter of a carbon atom, 0.000 000 000 154 meter

   c. the radius of Earth, 6 378 000 meters

   d. the diameter of a human hair, 0.000 008 meter

   e. the average distance between the center of the sun and the center of Earth, 149 600 000 000 meters

4. Solve each problem, and express each answer in correct scientific notation.

   a. $(4 \times 10^7) \times (2 \times 10^{-3})$

   b. $\dfrac{(6.3 \times 10^{-2})}{(2.1 \times 10^4)}$

   c. $(4.6 \times 10^3) - (1.8 \times 10^3)$

   d. $(7.1 \times 10^{-2}) + (5 \times 10^{-3})$

 Chem ASAP! Assessment 3.1 Check your understanding of the important ideas and concepts in Section 3.1.

ART

Measurement and Art
Although some people believe that art and science are very different, artists and scientists share many of the same methods in their work. For example, artists and scientists are both concerned with measurements. A sculptor designing a realistic statue of a human figure must be certain that the head and its features, as well as the arms, legs, and body, are in proportion to each other. An artist may use a pantograph in making scale drawings. A pantograph is a device in which a pencil traced over an original drawing creates a new drawing that is larger or smaller in scale than the original drawing.

UNCERTAINTY IN MEASUREMENTS

objectives

▶ Distinguish among the accuracy, precision, and error of a measurement
▶ Identify the number of significant figures in a measurement and in the result of a calculation

key terms

▶ accuracy
▶ precision
▶ accepted value
▶ experimental value
▶ error
▶ percent error
▶ significant figures

*O*n July 4, 1997, the Mars Pathfinder spacecraft landed on Mars. Shortly after landing, the spacecraft released a small robotic rover called Sojourner to explore the Martian surface around the landing site in Ares Vallis. NASA scientists had to make thousands of precise calculations to ensure that Pathfinder reached its destination safely. All measurements have some uncertainty. **How do scientists ensure the accuracy and precision of their measurements?**

Accuracy, Precision, and Error

Your success in the chemistry lab and in many of your daily activities depends on your ability to make reliable measurements. Ideally, measurements are both correct and reproducible.

Correctness and reproducibility relate to the concepts of accuracy and precision, two words that mean the same thing to many people. In chemistry, however, their meanings are quite different. **Accuracy** is a measure of how close a measurement comes to the actual or true value of whatever is measured. **Precision** is a measure of how close a series of measurements are to one another. Note that the precision of a measurement depends on more than one measurement.

By contrast, an individual measurement may be accurate or inaccurate. Darts on a dartboard illustrate accuracy and precision in measurement. Let the bull's-eye of the dartboard represent the true, or correct, value of what you are measuring. The closeness of a dart to the bull's-eye corresponds to the degree of accuracy. The closer it comes to the bull's-eye, the more accurately the dart was thrown. The closeness of several darts to one another corresponds to the degree of precision. The closer together the darts are, the greater the precision and the reproducibility. Look at **Figure 3.4** as you consider the following outcomes.

(a) All of the darts land close to the bull's-eye and to one another. Closeness to the bull's-eye means that the degree of accuracy is great. Each dart in the bull's-eye corresponds to an accurate measurement of a value. Closeness of the darts to one another indicates high precision.

Figure 3.4

*The distribution of darts illustrates the difference between accuracy and precision. **(a)** Good accuracy and good precision: The darts are close to the bull's-eye and to one another. **(b)** Poor accuracy and good precision: The darts are far from the bull's-eye but close to one another. **(c)** Poor accuracy and poor precision: The darts are far from the bull's-eye and from one another.*

(a) Good accuracy
Good precision

(b) Poor accuracy
Good precision

(c) Poor accuracy
Poor precision

Figure 3.5
This scale has not been properly zeroed. So the reading obtained for the person's weight is inaccurate. There is a difference between the person's correct weight and the measured value.

(b) All of the darts land close to one another but far from the bull's-eye. The precision is high because of the closeness of grouping and thus the high level of reproducibility. The results are inaccurate, however, because of the distance of the darts from the bull's-eye.

(c) The darts land far from one another and from the bull's-eye. The results are both inaccurate and imprecise.

To evaluate the accuracy of a measurement, it must be compared with the correct value. Suppose you use a thermometer to measure the boiling point of pure water at standard atmospheric pressure. The thermometer reads 99.1 °C. You probably know that the true or accepted value of the boiling point of pure water under these conditions is actually 100.0 °C. There is a difference between the **accepted value,** which is the correct value based on reliable references, and the **experimental value,** the value measured in the lab. The difference between the accepted value and the experimental value is called the **error.**

$$\text{Error} = \text{experimental value} - \text{accepted value}$$

Error can be positive or negative depending on whether the experimental value is greater than or less than the accepted value.

For the boiling-point measurement, the error is 99.1 °C − 100.0 °C, or −0.9 °C. The magnitude of the error shows the amount by which the experimental value is too high or too low, compared with the accepted value. Often, it is useful to calculate the relative error, or percent error. The **percent error** is the absolute value of the error divided by the accepted value, multiplied by 100%.

$$\text{Percent error} = \frac{|\text{error}|}{\text{accepted value}} \times 100\%$$

Using the absolute value of the error means that the percent error will always be a positive value. For the boiling-point measurement, the percent error is calculated as follows.

$$\text{Percent error} = \frac{|99.1\ °\text{C} - 100.0\ °\text{C}|}{100.0\ °\text{C}} \times 100\%$$

$$= \frac{0.9\ °\cancel{C}}{100.0\ °\cancel{C}} \times 100\%$$

$$= 0.009 \times 100\%$$

$$= 0.9\%$$

ENGINEERING

Computer-Aided Design

Measurement is important, but making or specifying a large number of measurements can be very time consuming. An engineer designing a complex machine must specify hundreds of dimensions. Today, computer-aided design (CAD) programs have replaced many tedious aspects of technical design. A CAD program usually permits a designer to begin with a few important elements and measurements of the object being designed. As the design progresses, the program computes the dimensions of added elements and produces drawings of the object from any perspective the designer desires. When one dimension in a design is changed, CAD programs automatically adjust all of the other dimensions in proportion. The introduction of CAD programs has reduced the time needed to design complex items as well as the number of errors that plague big projects.

Chem ASAP!

Animation 2
See how the accuracy of a calculated result depends on the sensitivity of the measuring instruments.

Significant Figures in Measurements

If you use a liquid-filled thermometer that is calibrated in 1 °C intervals, you can easily read the temperature to the nearest degree. With such a thermometer, however, you can also estimate the temperature to about the nearest tenth of a degree by noting the closeness of the liquid inside to the calibrations. Suppose you estimate a temperature that lies between 23 °C and 24 °C to be 24.3 °C. This estimated number has three digits. The first two digits (2 and 4) are known with certainty. But the rightmost digit has been estimated and involves some uncertainty. These reported digits all convey useful information, however, and are called significant figures. The **significant figures** in a measurement include all of the digits that are known, plus a last digit that is estimated. Measurements must always be reported to the correct number of significant figures because, as you will soon learn, calculated answers depend upon the number of significant figures in the values used in the calculation.

Suppose you take someone's temperature with a thermometer that is calibrated in 0.1 °C intervals. You can read the temperature with virtual certainty to the nearest 0.1 °C, and you can estimate it to the nearest 0.01 °C. You might report the temperature as 35.82 °C. This measurement has four significant figures, the rightmost of which is uncertain. Instruments differ in the number of significant figures that can be obtained from them and thus in the precision of measurements. The three meter sticks in **Figure 3.6** can be used to make successively more precise measurements of the board.

To determine whether a digit in a measured value is significant, you need to apply the following rules.

1. Every nonzero digit in a reported measurement is assumed to be significant. The measurements 24.7 meters, 0.743 meter, and 714 meters each express a measure of length to three significant figures.

Figure 3.6
Three differently calibrated meter sticks can be used to measure the length of a board. What measurement is obtained in each case? Are there differences in the number of significant figures in the three measurements? Explain.

2. Zeros appearing between nonzero digits are significant. The measurements 7003 meters, 40.79 meters, and 1.503 meters each have four significant figures.

3. Leftmost zeros appearing in front of nonzero digits are not significant. They act as placeholders. The measurements 0.0071 meter, 0.42 meter, and 0.000 099 meter each have only two significant figures. The zeros to the left are not significant. By writing the measurements in scientific notation, you can get rid of such placeholding zeros: in this case, 7.1×10^{-3} meter, 4.2×10^{-1} meter, and 9.9×10^{-5} meter.

4. Zeros at the end of a number and to the right of a decimal point are always significant. The measurements 43.00 meters, 1.010 meters, and 9.000 meters each have four significant figures.

Figure 3.7
Two differently calibrated graduated cylinders are used to measure the volume of a liquid. Which cylinder would give more precise measurements?

5. Zeros at the rightmost end of a measurement that lie to the left of an understood decimal point are not significant if they serve as placeholders to show the magnitude of the number. The zeros in the measurements 300 meters, 7000 meters, and 27 210 meters are not significant. The numbers of significant figures in these values are one, one, and four, respectively. If such zeros were known measured values, however, then they would be significant. For example, if the value of 300 meters resulted from a careful measurement rather than a rough, rounded measurement, the zeros would be significant. Ambiguity is avoided if measurements are written in scientific notation. For example, if all of the zeros in the measurement 300 meters were significant, writing the value as 3.00×10^2 meters makes it clear that these zeros are significant.

6. There are two situations in which measurements have an unlimited number of significant figures. The first involves counting. If you carefully count that there are 23 people in your classroom, then there are exactly 23 people, not 22.9 or 23.1. This measurement can only be a whole number and has an unlimited number of significant figures, in the form of zeros understood to be to the right of the decimal point; thus, 23.000 000 … is understood. The second situation of unlimited significant figures involves exactly defined quantities, such as those usually used within a system of measurement. When, for example, you write 60 minutes = 1 hour, these quantities have an unlimited number of significant figures; there are exactly 60 minutes in an hour, by definition. It is important to recognize when quantities are exact and to round calculated answers correctly in problems involving such values.

Sample Problem 3-1

An engineer made the following measurements. How many significant figures are in each measurement?

  a. 123 meters   **e.** 30.0 meters
  b. 0.123 meter   **f.** 22 meter sticks
  c. 40 506 meters   **g.** 0.070 80 meter
  d. 9.8000×10^4 meters   **h.** 98 000 meters

1. **ANALYZE** *Plan a problem-solving strategy.*
   The location of each zero in the measurement and the location of the decimal point determine which of the rules apply for determining significant figures. These locations are known by examining each measurement value.

2. **SOLVE** *Apply the problem-solving strategy.*
   Examine each measurement and apply the rules for determining significant figures. All nonzero digits are significant (rule 1). Use rules 2–5 to determine if the zeros are significant.

   a. 3 (rule 1)   **e.** 3 (rule 4)
   b. 3 (rule 3)   **f.** unlimited (rule 6)
   c. 5 (rule 2)   **g.** 4 (rules 2, 3, 4)
   d. 5 (rule 4)   **h.** 2 (rule 5)

3. **EVALUATE** *Do the results make sense?*
   The rules for determining significant digits have been correctly applied in each case.

Practice Problems

5. Determine the number of significant figures in each measurement.
   a. 0.057 30 meter
   b. 8765 meters
   c. 0.000 73 meter
   d. 40.007 meters
6. How many significant figures are in each measurement?
   a. 143 grams
   b. 0.074 meter
   c. 8.750×10^{-2} gram
   d. 1.072 meters

Figure 3.8
The room shown in the blueprint measures 11 feet by 16 feet. What is the calculated area of the room to the correct number of significant figures?

Significant Figures in Calculations

Rounding Suppose you use a calculator to find the area of a floor that measures 7.7 meters by 5.4 meters. The calculator would give an answer of 41.58 square meters. The calculated area is expressed to four significant figures. However, each of the measurements used in the calculation is expressed to only two significant figures. It is important to know that the calculated area cannot be more precise than the measured values used to obtain it.

The calculated area must be rounded to make it consistent with the measurements from which it was calculated. In general, an answer cannot be more precise than the least precise measurement from which it was calculated.

To round a number, you must first decide how many significant figures the answer should have. This decision depends on the given measurements and on the mathematical process used to arrive at the answer. Once you know the number of significant figures your answer should have, round to that many digits, counting from the left. If the digit immediately to the right of the last significant digit is less than 5, it is simply dropped and the value of the last significant digit stays the same. If the digit in question is 5 or greater, the value of the digit in the last significant place is increased by 1. For example, rounding 56.312 meters to four significant figures produces the result 56.31 meters because 2, the digit to the right of the last significant digit, is less than 5. Rounding 56.316 meters gives the result 56.32 meters because 6, the digit to the right of the last significant figure, is greater than 5.

Sample Problem 3-2

Round each measurement to the number of significant figures shown in parentheses. Write the answers in scientific notation.
   a. 314.721 meters (4)
   b. 0.001 775 meter (2)
   c. 64.32×10^{-1} meters (1)
   d. 8792 meters (2)

1. **ANALYZE** *Plan a problem-solving strategy.*
   Using the rules for determining significant figures, round each number. Then, apply the rules for expressing numbers in scientific notation.

2. **SOLVE** *Apply the problem-solving strategy.*
   Count from the left and apply the rule to the digit immediately to the right of the digit to which you are rounding. The arrows point to the digit immediately following the last significant digit. (The number of significant figures for each is shown in parentheses.)

   a. 314.721 meters
      ↑
      2 is less than 5, so do not round up.
      314.7 meters (4) = 3.147×10^2 meters

   b. 0.001 775 meter
      ↑
      7 is greater than 5, so round up.
      0.0018 meter (2) = 1.8×10^{-3} meter

   c. 64.32×10^{-1} meters
      ↑
      4 is less than 5, so do not round up.
      60×10^{-1} meters (1) = 6 meters

      (Note that 6 meters can be expressed in scientific notation as 6×10^0 meters.)

   d. 8792 meters
      ↑
      9 is greater than 5, so round up.
      8800 meters (2) = 8.8×10^3 meters

3. **EVALUATE** *Do the results make sense?*
   The rules for rounding and for writing numbers in scientific notation have been correctly applied.

Practice Problems

7. Round each measurement to three significant figures. Write your answers in scientific notation.
   a. 87.073 meters
   b. 4.3621×10^8 meters
   c. 0.015 52 meter
   d. 9009 meters
   e. 1.7777×10^{-3} meter
   f. 629.55 meters
8. Round each measurement in Practice Problem 7 to one significant figure. Write your answers in scientific notation.

Chem ASAP!
Problem-Solving 7
Solve Problem 7 with the help of an interactive guided tutorial.

Addition and Subtraction The answer to an addition or subtraction calculation should be rounded to the same number of decimal places (not digits) as the measurement with the least number of decimal places. Work through Sample Problem 3-3 below which provides examples of rounding in addition and subtraction calculations.

Sample Problem 3-3

Perform the following addition and subtraction operations. Give each answer to the correct number of significant figures.
  a. 12.52 meters + 349.0 meters + 8.24 meters
  b. 74.626 meters − 28.34 meters

1. **ANALYZE** *Plan a problem-solving strategy.*
Perform the required math operation and then analyze each measurement to determine the number of decimal places required in the answer.

2. **SOLVE** *Apply the problem-solving strategy.*
Round the answers to match the measurement with the least number of decimal places.

  a. Align the decimal points and add the numbers.

$$
\begin{array}{r}
12.52 \text{ meters} \\
349.0 \text{ meters} \\
+\ \ 8.24 \text{ meters} \\
\hline
369.76 \text{ meters}
\end{array}
$$

The second measurement (349.0 meters) has the least number of digits (one) to the right of the decimal point. Thus the answer must be rounded to one digit after the decimal point. The answer is rounded to 369.8 meters, or 3.698×10^2 meters.

  b. Align the decimal points and subtract the numbers.

$$
\begin{array}{r}
74.626 \text{ meters} \\
-\ 28.34 \text{ meters} \\
\hline
46.286 \text{ meters}
\end{array}
$$

The answer must be rounded to two digits after the decimal point to match the second measurement. The answer is 46.29 meters, or 4.629×10^1 meters.

3. **EVALUATE** *Do the results make sense?*
The mathematical operations have been correctly carried out and the resulting answers are reported to the correct number of decimal places.

Practice Problems

9. Perform each operation. Give your answers to the correct number of significant figures.
  a. 61.2 meters + 9.35 meters + 8.6 meters
  b. 9.44 meters − 2.11 meters
  c. 1.36 meters + 10.17 meters
  d. 34.61 meters − 17.3 meters
10. Find the total mass of three diamonds that have masses of 14.2 grams, 8.73 grams, and 0.912 gram.

Chem ASAP!

Problem-Solving 10
Solve Problem 10 with the help of an interactive guided tutorial.

Multiplication and Division In calculations involving multiplication and division, you need to round the answer to the same number of significant figures as the measurement with the least number of significant figures.

You can see in **Figure 3.9** that the calculator answer (5.7672) must be rounded to three significant figures because each measurement used in the calculation has only three significant figures.

The position of the decimal point has nothing to do with the rounding process when multiplying and dividing measurements. The position of the decimal point is important only in rounding the answers of addition or subtraction problems.

Figure 3.9

This calculator was used to multiply the length and width measurements of a bolt of fabric, 3.24 meters by 1.78 meters, each of which has three significant figures. The area of the fabric is really not known with the precision suggested by the calculator. What is the product when correctly rounded?

Sample Problem 3-4

Perform the following operations. Give the answers to the correct number of significant figures.
  a. 7.55 meters × 0.34 meter
  b. 2.10 meters × 0.70 meter
  c. 2.4526 meters ÷ 8.4
  d. 0.365 meter ÷ 0.0200

1. **ANALYZE Plan a problem-solving strategy.**
   Perform the required math operation and then analyze each of the original numbers to determine the correct number of significant figures required in the answer.

2. **SOLVE Apply the problem-solving strategy.**

   Round the answers to match the measurement with the least number of significant figures.

   a. 7.55 meters × 0.34 meter = 2.567 square meters = 2.6 square meters
   (0.34 meter has two significant figures.)

   b. 2.10 meters × 0.70 meter = 1.47 square meters = 1.5 square meters
   (0.70 meter has two significant figures.)

   c. 2.4526 meters ÷ 8.4 = 0.291 976 meter = 0.29 meter
   (8.4 has two significant figures.)

   d. 0.365 meter ÷ 0.0200 = 18.25 meters = 18.3 meters
   (Both numbers have three significant figures.)

3. **EVALUATE Do the results make sense?**
   The mathematical operations have been performed correctly, and the resulting answers are reported to the correct number of places.

Practice Problems

11. Solve each problem. Give your answers to the correct number of significant figures and in scientific notation.
    a. 8.3 meters × 2.22 meters
    b. 8432 meters ÷ 12.5
    c. 35.2 seconds × 1 minute/ 60 seconds

12. Calculate the volume of a warehouse that has inside dimensions of 22.4 meters by 11.3 meters by 5.2 meters. (Volume = $l \times w \times h$)

Chem ASAP!

Problem-Solving 12
Solve Problem 12 with the help of an interactive guided tutorial.

MINI LAB

Accuracy and Precision

PURPOSE

To measure the dimensions of an object as accurately and precisely as possible and to apply rules for rounding answers calculated from the measurements.

MATERIALS

- index card (3″ × 5″)
- metric ruler

PROCEDURE

1. Use a metric ruler to measure in centimeters the length and width of an index card as accurately and precisely as you can. The hundredths place in your measurement should be estimated.

2. Calculate the perimeter [2 × (length + width)] and the area (length × width) of the index card. Write both your unrounded answers and your correctly rounded answers on the chalkboard.

ANALYSIS AND CONCLUSIONS

1. How many significant figures are in your measurements of length and of width?

$l = ?$ cm

perimeter = $2(\ell + w)$
area = $\ell \times w$

$w = ?$ cm

2. How do your measurements compare with those of your classmates?

3. How many significant figures are in your calculated value for the area? In your calculated value for the perimeter? Do your rounded answers have as many significant figures as your classmates' measurements?

4. Assume that the correct (accurate) length and width of the card are 12.70 cm and 7.62 cm, respectively. Calculate the percent error for each of your two measurements.

---

section review 3.2

13. Explain the differences between accuracy, precision, and error of a measurement.

14. Determine the number of significant figures in each of the following measurements and calculation results.

    a. 12 basketball players
    b. 0.010 square meter
    c. 507 thumbtacks
    d. 0.070 020 meter
    e. 10 800 meters
    f. 5.00 cubic meters

15. Solve the following and express each answer in scientific notation.

    a. $(5.3 \times 10^4) + (1.3 \times 10^4)$
    b. $(7.2 \times 10^{-4}) \div (1.8 \times 10^3)$
    c. $10^4 \times 10^{-3} \times 10^6$
    d. $(9.12 \times 10^{-1}) - (4.7 \times 10^{-2})$
    e. $(5.4 \times 10^4) \times (3.5 \times 10^9)$
    f. $(1.2 \times 10^2) \times (8.9 \times 10^2)$

16. A technician experimentally determined the boiling point of octane to be 124.1 °C. The actual boiling point of octane is 125.7 °C. Calculate the error and the percent error.

portfolio project

Interview workers who construct buildings or highways about the importance of accurate measurements.

 Chem ASAP! Assessment 3.2 Check your understanding of the important ideas and concepts in Section 3.2.

objectives
▸ List SI units of measurement and common SI prefixes
▸ Distinguish between the mass and weight of an object

key terms
▸ International System of Units (SI)
▸ meter (m)
▸ volume
▸ liter (L)
▸ weight
▸ kilogram (kg)
▸ gram (g)

*W*eights and measures were among the earliest human inventions. Length units were used for construction; units of weight were needed for trading goods. Body parts made convenient units of length. An inch was measured with a thumb, a foot was the length of a foot, and a yard was the distance from one's nose to the tip of an extended arm. Archeologists think that polished stones found in the ruins of ancient Babylonian cities were standards of weight. The carat measures the mass of gold, silver, and gems. Arabs based the carat on the seed of the carob plant. **What system do modern scientists use for measurement?**

Units of Length

When you make a measurement, you must assign the correct units to the numerical value. Without the units, it is impossible to communicate the measurement clearly to others. Imagine the confusion that would follow if someone told you to "walk five in that direction." Your immediate response would be "Five what? Feet, meters, yards, miles?"

All measurements depend on units that serve as reference standards. The standards of measurement used in science are those of the metric system. The metric system is important because of its simplicity and ease of use. All metric units are based on 10 or multiples of 10. As a result, you can convert between units easily. The metric system was originally established in France in 1790. The **International System of Units** (abbreviated **SI,** after the French name, *Le Systéme International d'Unités*) is a revised version of the metric system. The SI was adopted by international agreement in 1960. There are seven SI base units, which are listed in **Table 3.1.** From these base units, all other SI units of measurement can be derived. Derived units are used for measurements such as volume, density, and pressure.

Table 3.1

Units of Measurement				
Quantity	**SI base unit or SI derived unit**	**Symbol**	**Non-SI unit**	**Symbol**
Length	meter*	m		
Volume	cubic meter	m^3	liter	L
Mass	kilogram*	kg		
Density	grams per cubic centimeter	g/cm^3		
	grams per milliliter	g/mL		
Temperature	kelvin*	K	degree Celsius	°C
Time	second*	s		
Pressure	pascal	Pa	atmosphere	atm
			millimeter of mercury	mm Hg
Energy	joule	J	calorie	cal
Amount of substance	mole*	mol		
Luminous intensity	candela*	cd		
Electric current	ampere*	A		

*denotes SI base unit

Table 3.2

		Commonly Used Prefixes in the Metric System		
Prefix	Symbol	Meaning	Factor	Scientific notation
mega	M	1 million times larger than the unit it precedes	1 000 000	10^6
kilo	k	1000 times larger than the unit it precedes	1000	10^3
deci	d	10 times smaller than the unit it precedes	1/10	10^{-1}
centi	c	100 times smaller than the unit it precedes	1/100	10^{-2}
milli	m	1000 times smaller than the unit it precedes	1/1000	10^{-3}
micro	μ	1 million times smaller than the unit it precedes	1/1 000 000	10^{-6}
nano	n	1000 million times smaller than the unit it precedes	1/1 000 000 000	10^{-9}
pico	p	1 trillion times smaller than the unit it precedes	1/1 000 000 000 000	10^{-12}

Figure 3.10

A meter stick is divided into 100 centimeters (cm). Each centimeter is further divided into 10 millimeters (mm). How many millimeters are there in a meter?

All measured quantities can be reported in SI units. Sometimes, however, non-SI units are preferred for convenience or for practical reasons. **Table 3.1** also lists some derived SI units and non-SI units of measurement that are used in this textbook.

Size is an important property of matter. In SI, the basic unit of length, or linear measure, is the **meter (m)**. All measurements of length can be expressed in meters. (The length of a page in this book is about one-fourth of a meter.) For very large and very small lengths, however, it may be more convenient to use a unit of length that has a prefix. **Table 3.2** lists the prefixes in common use. For example, the prefix *milli-* means 1/1000, so a millimeter (mm) is 1/1000 of a meter, or 0.001 m. A hyphen (-) measures about 1 mm.

For large distances, it is usually most appropriate to express measurements in kilometers (km). The prefix *kilo-* means 1000, so 1 km equals 1000 m. A standard marathon distance race of about 42 000 m is more conveniently expressed as 42 km (42 × 1000 m). **Table 3.3** summarizes the relationships among units of length.

Table 3.3

		Metric Units of Length		
Unit	Symbol	Relationship	Example	
Kilometer	km	1 km = 10^3 m	length of about five city blocks	≈ 1 km
Meter	m	base unit	height of doorknob from the floor	≈ 1 m
Decimeter	dm	10^1 dm = 1 m	diameter of large orange	≈ 1 dm
Centimeter	cm	10^2 cm = 1 m	width of shirt button	≈ 1 cm
Millimeter	mm	10^3 mm = 1 m	thickness of dime	≈ 1 mm
Micrometer	μm	10^6 μm = 1 m	diameter of bacterial cell	≈ 1 μm
Nanometer	nm	10^9 nm = 1 m	thickness of RNA molecule	≈ 1 nm

Figure 3.11
These photographs should give you some idea of the relative sizes of some different units of volume. The volume of 20 drops of liquid from a medicine dropper is approximately 1 milliliter (mL). A sugar cube is 1 centimeter (cm) on each edge and has a volume of 1 cubic centimeter (cm³). These two volumes are equivalent; that is, a volume of 1 mL is the same as a volume of 1 cm³. A gallon of milk has about twice the volume of a two-liter bottle of soda. Note that a gallon is a non-SI unit and it is used here only for comparison purposes.

Units of Volume

The space occupied by any sample of matter is called its **volume.** You calculate the volume of any cubic or rectangular solid by multiplying its length by its width by its height. The unit for volume is thus derived from units of length. The SI unit of volume is the amount of space occupied by a cube that is 1 m along each edge. This volume is a cubic meter (m^3). An automatic dishwasher has a volume of about 1 m^3.

A more convenient unit of volume for everyday use is the liter, a non-SI unit. A **liter** (L) is the volume of a cube that is 10 centimeters (cm) along each edge (10 cm × 10 cm × 10 cm = 1000 cm^3 = 1 L). A decimeter (dm) is equal to 10 cm, so 1 L is also equal to 1 cubic decimeter (dm^3). A smaller non-SI unit of volume is the milliliter (mL); 1 mL is 1/1000 of a liter. Thus there are 1000 mL in 1 L. Because 1 L is defined as 1000 cm^3, 1 mL and 1 cm^3 are the same volume. The units milliliter and cubic centimeter are thus used interchangeably. **Table 3.4** summarizes the most commonly used relationships among units of volume.

Table 3.4

Metric Units of Volume				
Unit	**Symbol**	**Relationship**	**Example**	
Liter	L	base unit	quart of milk	≈ 1 L
Milliliter	mL	10^3 mL = 1 L	20 drops of water	≈ 1 mL
Cubic centimeter	cm^3	1 cm^3 = 1 mL	cube of sugar	≈ 1 cm^3
Microliter	μL	10^6 μL = 1 L	crystal of table salt	≈ 1 μL

Figure 3.12

Shown left to right are five types of glassware used to measure volume: Erlenmeyer flask, buret, graduated cylinder, beaker, and volumetric flask. Beakers, Erlenmeyer flasks, and graduated cylinders are used to measure approximate volumes. Volumetric flasks and burets allow more precise measurements. What would you use to measure a large volume, such as 1 L, accurately?

Figure 3.13

An astronaut's weight on the moon is one-sixth as much as it is on Earth. Earth exerts six times the force of gravity as the moon. The astronaut's lowered weight accounts for his ability to jump high on the moon. How does his mass on the moon compare with his mass on Earth?

There are many devices for measuring the volume of a liquid. Examples of volumetric glassware are shown in **Figure 3.12.** A graduated cylinder is useful for dispensing approximate volumes. A pipet or buret must be used, however, when accuracy is important. A volumetric flask contains a specified volume of liquid when it is filled to the calibration mark. Volumetric flasks are available in many sizes. A syringe is used to measure small volumes of liquids for injection.

The volume of any solid, liquid, or gas will change with temperature (although the change is much more dramatic for gases). Accurate volume-measuring devices are calibrated at a given temperature—usually 20 degrees Celsius (20 °C), which is about normal room temperature.

Units of Mass

The astronaut shown saluting on the surface of the moon in **Figure 3.13** weighs one-sixth of what he weighs on Earth. The reason for this difference is that the force of gravity on Earth is about six times what it is on the moon. **Weight** is a force that measures the pull on a given mass by gravity. Weight is different from mass, which is a measure of the quantity of matter. Although the weight of an object can change with its location, its mass remains constant regardless of its location—whether it is on Earth or on the moon. Objects can thus become weightless, but they can never become massless.

The mass of an object is measured in comparison to a standard mass of 1 **kilogram (kg)**, which is the basic SI unit of mass. A kilogram was originally defined as the mass of 1 L of liquid water at 4 °C. A cube of water

Table 3.5

Metric Units of Mass			
Unit	Symbol	Relationship	Example
Kilogram (base unit)	kg	$1 \text{ kg} = 10^3 \text{ g}$	small textbook $\approx$ 1 kg
Gram	g	$1 \text{ g} = 10^{-3} \text{ kg}$	dollar bill $\approx$ 1 g
Milligram	mg	$10^3 \text{ mg} = 1 \text{ g}$	ten grains of salt $\approx$ 1 mg
Microgram	μg	$10^6 \text{ } \mu\text{L} = 1 \text{ g}$	particle of baking powder $\approx$ 1 μg

at 4 °C measuring 10 cm on each edge would have a volume of 1 L and a mass of 1000 grams (g), or 1 kg. A **gram (g)** is 1/1000 of a kilogram and is a more commonly used unit of mass in chemistry. The mass of 1 cm³ of water at 4 °C is 1 g. The relationships among units of mass are shown in **Table 3.5.**

You can use a platform balance to measure the mass of an object. The object is placed on one side of the balance, and standard masses are added to the other side until the balance beam is level, as shown in **Figure 3.14.** The unknown mass is equal to the sum of the standard masses. Laboratory balances range from very sensitive instruments with a maximum capacity of only a few milligrams to devices for measuring quantities in kilograms. An analytical balance is used to measure objects of less than 100 g and can determine mass to the nearest 0.0001 g (0.1 mg).

Figure 3.14
A platform balance compares an unknown mass with a known mass. The mass of the water and the flask is the same as the sum of the standard masses.

section review 3.3

17. Name the quantity measured by each of the following SI units and give the SI symbol of the unit.

a. mole

d. pascal

b. kilogram/cubic meter

e. meter

c. second

f. kilogram

18. State the difference between mass and weight.

19. What is the symbol and meaning of each prefix?

a. *milli-*

c. *deci-*

b. *nano-*

d. *centi-*

20. As you climbed a mountain and the force of gravity decreased, would your weight increase, decrease, or remain constant? How would your mass change?

21. What is the volume of a paperback book 21 cm tall, 12 cm wide, and 3.5 cm thick?

22. List these units in order, from largest to smallest.

a. 1 dm³

d. 1 L

b. 1 μL

e. 1 cL

c. 1 mL

f. 1 dL

 Chem ASAP! Assessment 3.3 Check your understanding of the important ideas and concepts in Section 3.3.

DENSITY

objectives
▶ Calculate the density of an object from experimental data
▶ List some useful applications of the measurement of specific gravity

key terms
▶ density
▶ specific gravity
▶ hydrometer

Have you ever wondered why some objects float in water, while others sink? If you think that these cranberries float because they are lightweight, you are only partially correct.
What measurements would you need to make to determine whether an object would float in water?

Determining Density

Has anyone ever tried to trick you with this question: "Which is heavier, a pound of lead or a pound of feathers?" Most people would not give the question much thought and would incorrectly answer "lead." Of course, a pound of lead has the same mass as a pound of feathers. What concept, instead of mass, are people really thinking of when they answer this question?

Most people are incorrectly applying a perfectly correct idea: namely, that if a piece of lead and a feather of the same volume are weighed, the lead would have a greater mass than the feather. It would take a much larger volume of feathers to equal the mass of a given volume of lead.

Table 3.6

Substance	Cube of substance (face shown actual size)	Mass (g)	Volume (cm³)	Density (g/cm³)
Relationship Between Volume and Density for Identical Masses of Common Substances				
Lithium		10	19	0.53
Water		10	10	1.0
Aluminum		10	3.7	2.7
Lead		10	0.88	11.4

Table 3.7

Densities of Some Common Materials			
Solids and Liquids		Gases	
Material	Density at 20 °C (g/cm³)	Material	Density at 20 °C (g/L)
Gold	19.3	Chlorine	2.95
Mercury	13.6	Carbon dioxide	1.83
Lead	11.4	Oxygen	1.33
Aluminum	2.70	Air	1.20
Table sugar	1.59	Nitrogen	1.17
Water (4 °C)	1.000	Neon	0.84
Corn oil	0.922	Ammonia	0.718
Ice (0 °C)	0.917	Methane	0.665
Ethanol	0.789	Helium	0.166
Gasoline	0.66–0.69	Hydrogen	0.084

The important relationship in this case is between the object's mass and its volume. This relationship is called density. **Density** is the ratio of the mass of an object to its volume.

$$\text{Density} = \frac{\text{mass}}{\text{volume}}$$

A 10.0-cm³ piece of lead, for example, has a mass of 114 g. What, then, is the density of lead? If you substitute the mass and volume into the equation above, you can see that the density of lead is as follows.

$$\frac{114 \text{ g}}{10.0 \text{ cm}^3} = 11.4 \text{ g/cm}^3$$

Note that when mass is measured in grams, and volume in cubic centimeters, density has units of grams per cubic centimeter (g/cm³).

Table 3.6 compares the density of four substances. Why does each 10-g sample have a different volume? The volumes vary because the substances have different densities. Density is a characteristic property that depends only on the composition of a substance, not on the size of the sample. With a mixture, density can vary because the composition of a mixture can vary.

What do you think will happen if glycerine (glycerol) and corn oil are poured into a beaker of water? Using **Table 3.7,** you can see that the density of corn oil is less than the density of water. For that reason, the corn oil floats on top of the water. As you can see in **Figure 3.15,** the glycerol sinks below the water because its density is greater than the density of water. Other liquids with different densities are also shown.

You have probably seen a helium-filled balloon rapidly rise to the ceiling when it is released. Whether a gas-filled balloon will sink or rise when released depends on how the density of the gas compares with the density of air. The densities of various gases are given in **Table 3.7.** Would a carbon dioxide-filled balloon sink or rise in air?

What happens to the density of a substance as its temperature increases? Experiments show that the volume of most substances increases as the temperature increases. Meanwhile, the mass remains the same

— Corn oil

— Water

— Glycerol

Figure 3.15
Because of differences in density, the blue-colored glycerol sinks below the surface of the water, and the amber-colored corn oil floats on top of the water. Is the red-colored liquid more or less dense than glycerol? How do you know?

Simulation 1
Rank materials according to their densities.

CHEMath

WHAT IS AN EQUATION?

You will encounter numerous equations as you read through this textbook. You should consider every equation as a powerful and easy-to-use tool for simplifying and applying complex relationships. Furthermore, once you understand the basics of what equations are and how they are used, you will find they are usually solved using simple math.

The Equation An equation is a mathematical sentence that uses an equal sign ($=$) to represent two different expressions that have the same value. In addition to the equal sign, an equation may contain a combination of words, numbers, variables, or mathematical functions. An example of an equation that contains numbers is:

$$5 + 4 = 9$$

Each side of the equation is separated by the equal sign and is equivalent; $5 + 4$ is simply another way to write 9. An example of a word equation is:

The perimeter of a square is equal to the sum of the lengths of its four equal sides.

Although the above statement is correct, it can be stated much more concisely by the following mathematical equation:

$$\text{perimeter} = 4 \times \text{length of a side}$$

This can be further simplified by replacing the words with variables that represent the words. Letting p represent the perimeter, and L represent the length of each side yields,

$$p = 4 \times L$$
$$p = 4L$$

Units in Equations $5 + 4 = 9$ is an example of an equation that contains no units. Many equations do involve units, however, and you can use the units as a way to check that the equation is correct. Because both sides of an equation are equal, the units on each side of an equation must also be equal. Consider the following equation:

$$\text{mass}_{\text{total}} = \text{mass}_{\text{beaker}} + \text{mass}_{\text{chemical}}$$

Both sides of this equation must contain units of mass, such as grams or kilograms. If the units on both sides of the equation are not the same, the answer must be incorrect.

Solving Equations It is very important to realize that both sides of an equation are always equal to each other. This is important because you can use this fact to help solve for an unknown value.

You only need to remember a single rule when solving an equation for a specific quantity: whatever you do on one side of the equation must be done on the other side of the equation. For example, reconsider the perimeter equation.

$$p = 4L$$

If you need to calculate the length of a single side of the square (L), you must solve the equation for L. In other words the variable L must be isolated from everything else. To isolate L you can divide the right side of the equation by 4. However, remember you must also divide the left side by 4 as shown below.

$$p = 4L \qquad \frac{p}{4} = \frac{4L}{4} \qquad \frac{p}{4} = \frac{4L}{4} \qquad \frac{p}{4} = L$$
$$L = \frac{p}{4}$$

Practice Problems

A. Write a word equation for money earned each week from a part-time job.

B. Solve the equation $K = {}^{\circ}C + 273$ for ${}^{\circ}C$.

C. Using the equation $K = {}^{\circ}C + 273$, calculate K if ${}^{\circ}C = 200$.

D. Solve the equation $\text{density} = \dfrac{\text{mass}}{\text{volume}}$ for mass.

E. Using the equation $\text{density} = \dfrac{\text{mass}}{\text{volume}}$, calculate density if mass $= 228$ g and volume $= 102$ cm^3.

F. Repeat problem D, but solve for volume.

G. Solve the following equation for y.

$$\frac{2y}{x^2} + 3 = 4z$$

Figure 3.16
Solid paraffin sinks in melted paraffin (left), but ice floats in water (right). What does this tell you about the densities of each of these two substances in the solid and liquid states?

despite the temperature and volume changes. Because density is mass divided by volume, the density of a substance generally decreases as its temperature increases. As you will learn in Chapter 17, water is an important exception. Over a certain range of temperatures, the volume of water increases as its temperature decreases. Ice, or solid water, floats because it is less dense than liquid water. Compare the densities of the substances shown in **Figure 3.16.**

Sample Problem 3-5

A copper penny has a mass of 3.1 g and a volume of 0.35 cm³. What is the density of copper?

1. **ANALYZE List the knowns and the unknown.**

   Knowns:
   - mass = 3.1 g
   - volume = 0.35 cm³

   Unknown:
   - density = ? g/cm³

   Use the known values and the definition of density,

   $$\text{density} = \frac{\text{mass}}{\text{volume}},$$

   to calculate the density of copper.

2. **CALCULATE Solve for the unknown.**
   The equation is already set up to solve for the unknown. Substitute the known values for mass and volume, and calculate the density.

   $$\text{density} = \frac{\text{mass}}{\text{volume}} = \frac{3.1 \text{ g}}{0.35 \text{ cm}^3} = 8.8571 \text{ g/cm}^3$$

   $$= 8.9 \text{ g/cm}^3 \text{ (rounded to two significant figures)}$$

3. **EVALUATE Does the result make sense?**
   A piece of copper with a volume of about 0.3 cm³ has a mass of about 3 g. Thus, about three times that volume of copper, 1 cm³, should have a mass three times larger, about 9 g. This estimate agrees with the calculated result.

Practice Problems

23. A student finds a shiny piece of metal that she thinks is aluminum. In the lab, she determines that the metal has a volume of 245 cm³ and a mass of 612 g. Calculate the density. Is the metal aluminum?

24. The density of silver at 20 °C is 10.5 g/cm³. What is the volume of a 68-g bar of silver?

Chem ASAP!

Problem-Solving 24
Solve Problem 24 with the help of an interactive guided tutorial.

Specific Gravity

Specific gravity is a comparison of the density of a substance with the density of a reference substance, usually at the same temperature. Water at 4 °C, which has a density of 1 g/cm³, is commonly used as the reference substance. In that case,

$$\text{Specific gravity} = \frac{\text{density of substance (g/cm}^3)}{\text{density of water (g/cm}^3)}$$

Note that the units in the equation cancel — specific gravity has no units.

The specific gravity of a liquid can be measured with a device called a **hydrometer.** As is shown in **Figure 3.17a,** the depth to which the hydrometer sinks depends on the specific gravity of the liquid tested. The calibration mark on the hydrometer stem at the surface of the liquid indicates the specific gravity of the liquid.

Specific-gravity measurements are commonly used for various practical purposes. A physician uses the measured specific gravity of a patient's urine to help diagnose certain diseases, such as diabetes. You can check the condition of the antifreeze in your car by measuring the specific gravity of the solution in the radiator. The hydrometer in **Figure 3.17** is being used to measure the specific gravity of the acid in an automobile battery.

Figure 3.17

(a) A hydrometer is a sealed tube with a weight in the bottom. It is used to measure the specific gravity of a liquid. The higher the hydrometer floats, the higher the specific gravity of the liquid tested. (b) In the photograph, the concentration of acid in an automobile battery is checked with a hydrometer.

Hydrometer

Specific gravity read here

Liquid being measured

Weight

(a)   **(b)**

section review 3.4

25. How is density calculated from measured data?

26. A weather balloon is inflated to a volume of 2.2×10^3 L with 37.4 g of helium. What is the density of helium, in grams per liter?

27. List some applications of the measurement of specific gravity.

28. A plastic ball with a volume of 19.7 cm³ has a mass of 15.8 g. What is its density? Would this ball sink or float in a container of gasoline?

29. Given samples of gold, gasoline, ice, mercury, lead, and aluminum, which substances have the highest and lowest specific gravities?

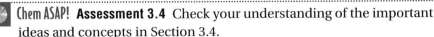

Chem ASAP! **Assessment 3.4** Check your understanding of the important ideas and concepts in Section 3.4.

MEASUREMENT

PURPOSE

To make precise and accurate measurements and to use fundamental data to calculate derived quantities.

MATERIALS

- pencil
- balance
- paper
- rectangular block
- ruler
- calculator

PROCEDURE

1. Use your ruler to measure the length, width, and height of a rectangular block in centimeters. Be sure to estimate between the lines of the ruler's smallest markings and report each measurement so that it includes the estimated number. Draw a diagram of the block and label its dimensions.

2. Measure and record the mass of the block. Estimate between the lines of the smallest markings of the balance and report your measurement in grams. (*Note:* If you are using a digital balance, the last number often blinks, or oscillates, between two or more numbers. Recording this last digit is similar to estimating between the markings on a balance.)

ANALYSIS

Using your experimental data, record the answers to the following questions.

1. How many significant figures do each of your measurements have?

2. Calculate the perimeter of each face of the rectangular block. Report the answer to the correct number of significant figures. (The perimeter of a face is the sum of the four edges of that face.)

3. Calculate the area of each face. Include the proper unit with your calculated value for area. Round your value to the correct number of significant figures.
(Area = length × width)

4. Calculate the volume of the block in units of cubic centimeters. Round your value to the correct number of significant figures.
(Volume = length × width × height)

5. Express the volume of your block in liters.
(1 L = 1000 cm^3)

6. Express the mass of your block in milligrams.
(1 g = 1000 mg)

YOU'RE THE CHEMIST

The following small-scale activities allow you to develop your own procedures and analyze the results.

1. **Analyze It!** Density is a measure of how tightly matter is packed together.

$$\text{Density} = \frac{\text{mass}}{\text{volume}}$$

   Calculate the density of the block in units of grams per cubic centimeter (g/cm^3). Convert your calculated density into units of grams per liter (g/L), milligrams per cubic centimeter (mg/cm^3), and kilograms per liter (kg/L).
(1 kg = 1000 g)

2. **Design It!** Make the necessary measurements to calculate the volume and density of a cylindrical block. The volume is determined from the following equation.

$$V = \pi r^2 h$$

$\pi \approx 3.1416$
r = radius
h = height

3. **Design It!** Make the necessary measurements to calculate the volume and density of a block that has had one or more holes drilled in it. Assume each hole is cylindrical and account for them in your calculations. What approximations must you make?

► Convert between the Celsius and Kelvin temperature scales

key terms
► temperature
► Celsius scale
► Kelvin scale
► absolute zero

TEMPERATURE

In 1911, a Dutch physicist named Heike Kamerlingh Onnes discovered that when mercury is cooled to near absolute zero (−460 °F), it loses all resistance to electrical current. This state is known as superconductivity. If a material could be found that would superconduct at room temperature (around 64 °F), it would revolutionize the computer industry and other electronics industries. **Which temperature scale has its zero point at absolute zero?**

Measuring Temperature

When you hold a glass of hot water, the glass feels hot because heat transfers from the glass to your hand. When you hold an ice cube, it feels cold because heat transfers from your hand to the ice cube. The **temperature** of an object determines the direction of heat transfer. When two objects at different temperatures are in contact, heat moves from the object at the higher temperature to the object at the lower temperature. In Chapter 10, you will learn how the temperature of an object is related to the energy and motion of particles.

Almost all substances expand with an increase in temperature and contract as the temperature decreases (a very important exception is water). These properties are the basis for the common mercury-in-glass thermometer, shown in **Figure 3.19.** The liquid mercury in the thermometer expands and contracts more than the volume of the glass bulb that holds it, producing changes in the column height of the mercury.

Temperature Scales

Several temperature scales have been devised. The Celsius scale of the metric system is named after the Swedish astronomer Anders Celsius (1701–1744). It uses two readily determined temperatures as reference temperature values: the freezing point and the boiling point of water. The **Celsius scale** sets the freezing point of water at 0 °C and the boiling point of water at 100 °C. The distance between these two fixed points is divided into 100 equal intervals, or degrees Celsius (°C).

Another temperature scale used in the physical sciences is the Kelvin, or absolute, scale. This scale is named for Lord Kelvin (1824–1907), a Scottish physicist and mathematician. On the Kelvin scale, the freezing point of water is 273.15 kelvins (K), and the boiling point is 373.15 K. Notice that with the Kelvin scale, the degree sign is not used. You can use **Figure 3.19** to compare the Celsius and Kelvin scales. The zero point on the Kelvin scale, 0 K, or **absolute zero,** is equal to −273.15 °C. For problems in this text, you can round −273.15 °C to −273 °C. Because one degree on the Celsius scale is equivalent to one kelvin on the Kelvin scale, converting from one temperature scale to the other is easy. You simply add or subtract 273, as shown in the following equations.

$$K = °C + 273$$
$$°C = K − 273$$

Figure 3.18

Temperatures on Earth range from the scorching heat of a desert, to the frigid cold of the Antarctic, to the normal human body temperature of 37 °C. What is the hottest temperature ever recorded? The coldest?

Celsius

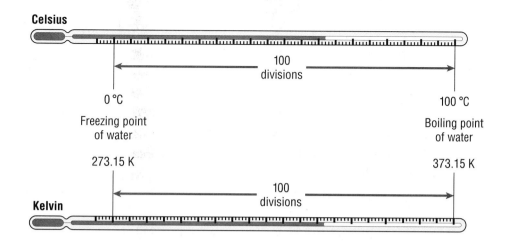

Figure 3.19
These thermometers show a comparison of the Celsius and Kelvin temperature scales. Note that a 1 °C change on the Celsius scale is equal to a 1 K change on the Kelvin scale. What is a change of 10 K equivalent to on the Celsius scale?

Sample Problem 3-6

Normal human body temperature is 37 °C. What is that temperature in kelvins?

1. **ANALYZE** *List the knowns and the unknown.*

   Known:
   • Temperature in °C = 37 °C

   Unknown:
   • Temperature in K = ? K

   Use the known value and the equation $K = °C + 273$ to calculate the temperature in kelvins.

2. **CALCULATE** *Solve for the unknown.*
   Substitute the known value for the Celsius temperature into the equation and solve.
   $$K = °C + 273$$
   $$= 37 + 273 = 310 \text{ K}$$

3. **EVALUATE** *Does the result make sense?*
   You should expect the Kelvin temperature to be in this range because the freezing point of water is 273.15 K and the boiling point of water is 373.15 K; normal body temperature is between these two values.

Practice Problems

30. Liquid nitrogen boils at 77.2 K. What is this temperature in degrees Celsius?

31. The element silver melts at 960.8 °C and boils at 2212 °C. Express these temperatures in kelvins.

Chem ASAP!

Problem-Solving 31
Solve Problem 31 with the help of an interactive guided tutorial.

section review 3.5

32. State the relationship between degrees Celsius and kelvins.

33. Chocolate cookies are baked at 190 °C. Express this temperature in kelvins.

34. Surgical instruments may be sterilized by heating at 170 °C for 1.5 hours. Convert 170 °C to kelvins.

35. The boiling point of the element argon is 87 K. What is the boiling point of argon in degrees Celsius?

Chem ASAP! Assessment 3.5 Check your understanding of the important ideas and concepts in Section 3.5.

THESE STANDARDS ARE WORTH THE WEIGHT

Imagine the confusion if every soft drink manufacturer defined a liter differently, or if the mass of a kilogram depended on where you live. As a consumer, you rely on units of mass, time, and length being unchanging and consistent, whether you buy a kilogram of ice cream, a half-hour of Internet access, or 10 000 square meters of land.

Luckily, you usually do not have to question the consistency of units of measurement because standards for each unit have been defined and agreed upon. But humans have not always had as good a system of standards as we have today. Throughout history, standards of measurement have become more precise and more consistent, and they continue in this direction today.

Using units that were based on body measurements was not a very reliable system of measurement. There could be great variation in the size of people's thumbs or the length of people's feet. In other words, thumbs and feet were not consistent units. People needed standards that did not change.

In 1790, with the establishment of the metric system, the French became the first to adopt measurement standards that were close to being precise. The meter was defined as one ten-millionth of the distance from the equator to the North Pole along the meridian that passes through Paris. The second was defined as $\frac{1}{86\,400}$ of the average day.

As scientific measurement techniques became more precise, the definitions of these and other base units also became more precise. For example, the meter is now defined as the distance traveled by light in a vacuum in $\frac{1}{299\,792\,458}$ of a second. The second itself is defined in terms of the number of cycles of radiation given off by a specific isotope of the element cesium.

As a consumer, you rely on units of mass, time, and length being unchanging and consistent.

The standard for one base unit—the kilogram—has not changed since it was originally established. A piece of metal (a platinum-iridium alloy shown here) that was cast more than 100 years ago is still used as the standard of mass. It resides in a triple bell jar in Sevres, France, and has been removed only three times since 1889. But this kilogram standard has a problem because contaminants can build up on its surface despite the layers of protection. It might seem like an easy task to find a more precise modern standard for the kilogram, but this goal has so far been a challenge to scientists.

How about defining a kilogram as a given number of atoms of a particular element? Scientists thought of that idea a few years ago, using ultra-pure spheres of silicon as the standard. However, the presence of lattice holes (empty spaces in the crystalline structure of silicon) led to different estimates of the number of atoms in a given mass. This problem has almost been solved, and the "atom counters" are getting close to the goal of defining a new kilogram standard. Another group of researchers, the "force measurers," have a competing idea. Their method uses a Watt balance (a type of balance that uses electromagnetic force) to express the mass of a kilogram in terms of the base units of voltage and current. Either way, the old kilogram may soon have a more modern definition.

CHEMISTRY IN CAREERS

☆ ☆

ANALYTICAL CHEMIST
Interested in a career with a focus on measurement and problem solving? See page 869.

CHEMIST NEEDED

TAKE IT TO THE NET
Find out more about career opportunities:
www.phschool.com

CHEMICAL SPECIALIST
Local food service distributor seeks responsible self-motivated individ-

Take It to the NET
For interactive study and review, go to www.phschool.com

KEY TERMS

- absolute zero *p. 74*
- accepted value *p. 55*
- accuracy *p. 54*
- Celsius scale *p. 74*
- density *p. 69*
- error *p. 55*
- experimental value *p. 55*
- gram (g) *p. 67*
- hydrometer *p. 72*

- International System of Units (SI) *p. 63*
- Kelvin scale *p. 74*
- kilogram (kg) *p. 66*
- liter (L) *p. 65*
- meter (m) *p. 64*
- percent error *p. 55*
- precision *p. 54*
- qualitative measurement *p. 51*

- quantitative measurement *p. 51*
- scientific notation *p. 52*
- significant figure *p. 56*
- specific gravity *p. 72*
- temperature *p. 74*
- volume *p. 65*
- weight *p. 66*

KEY EQUATIONS

- Error = experimental value − accepted value

- Percent error = $\dfrac{|\text{error}|}{\text{accepted value}} \times 100\%$

- Density = $\dfrac{\text{mass}}{\text{volume}}$

- Specific gravity = $\dfrac{\text{density of substance}}{\text{density of water}}$

- K = °C + 273

- °C = K − 273

CONCEPT SUMMARY

3.1 The Importance of Measurement
- Measurements can be qualitative or quantitative.
- Very large and very small numbers are best expressed in scientific notation.

3.2 Uncertainty in Measurements
- The accuracy of a measurement describes how close a measurement comes to the true value.
- The precision of a measurement depends on its reproducibility.
- Measurements and calculations must always be reported to the correct number of significant figures.

3.3 International System of Units
- The International System of Units (SI) is the measurement system used by scientists.

- The SI has seven base units from which all other SI units of measurement are derived.
- The quantity of matter an object contains is its mass. Weight is not the same as mass. Weight is the measure of the pull of gravity on an object of given mass.

3.4 Density
- The ratio of the mass of an object to its volume is its density. The unit of density is g/cm^3.
- Specific gravity is the ratio of the density of a substance to the density of water.

3.5 Temperature
- Temperature difference determines the direction of heat flow between two bodies.
- Temperature is measured on the Celsius and Kelvin scales.

CHAPTER CONCEPT MAP

Use these terms to construct a concept map that organizes the major ideas of this chapter.

 Chem ASAP! Concept Map 3
Create your Concept Map using the computer.

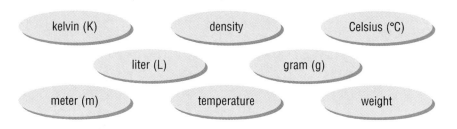

kelvin (K) density Celsius (°C)

liter (L) gram (g)

meter (m) temperature weight

CONCEPT PRACTICE

36. Identify the following as quantitative or qualitative measurements. *3.1*
   a. A flame is hot.
   b. A candle has a mass of 90 g.
   c. Wax is soft.
   d. A candle's height decreases 4.2 cm/hr.

37. Which of these synonyms or characteristics apply to the concept of accuracy? Which apply to the concept of precision? *3.2*
   a. multiple measurements
   b. correct
   c. repeatable
   d. reproducible
   e. single measurement
   f. true value

38. Under what circumstances could a series of measurements of the same quantity be precise but inaccurate? *3.2*

39. Three students made multiple weighings of a copper cylinder, each using a different balance. The correct mass of the cylinder had been previously determined to be 47.32 g. Describe the accuracy and precision of each student's measurements. *3.2*

Mass of Cylinder (g)			
	Lissa	Lamont	Leigh Anne
Weighing 1	47.13	47.45	47.95
Weighing 2	47.94	47.39	47.91
Weighing 3	46.83	47.42	47.89
Weighing 4	47.47	47.41	47.93

40. Comment on the accuracy and precision of these basketball free-throw shooters. *3.2*
   a. 99 of 100 shots are made.
   b. 99 of 100 shots hit the front of the rim and bounce off.
   c. 33 of 100 shots are made; the rest miss.

41. How many significant figures are in each underlined measurement? *3.2*
   a. 60 s = 1 min
   b. 9 innings in a baseball game
   c. 1 km = 1000 m
   d. 47.70 g of copper
   e. 25 computers
   f. 0.0950 m of gold chain

42. Round each of these measurements to three significant figures. *3.2*
   a. 98.473 L
   b. 0.000 763 21 cg
   c. 57.048 m
   d. 12.17 °C
   e. $0.007\ 498\ 3 \times 10^4$ mm
   f. 1764.9 mL

43. Write each of the rounded measurements in Problem 42 in scientific notation. *3.2*

44. Round each of the answers correctly. *3.2*
   a. 8.7 g + 15.43 g + 19 g = 43.13 g
   b. 4.32 cm × 1.7 cm = 7.344 cm^2
   c. 853.2 L − 627.443 L = 225.757 L
   d. 38.742 kg ÷ 0.421 = 92.023 75 kg
   e. 5.40 m × 3.21 m × 1.871 m = 32.431 914 m^3
   f. 5.47 m^3 + 11 m^3 + 87.300 m^3 = 103.770 m^3

45. Express each of the rounded answers in Problem 44 in scientific notation. *3.2*

46. How are the error and the percent error of a measurement calculated? *3.2*

47. Why is the percent error of a measurement always positive? *3.2*

48. A student estimated the volume of a liquid in a beaker as 200 mL. When she poured the liquid into a graduated cylinder, she measured the volume as 208 mL. What is the percent error of the estimated volume from the beaker, taking the measurement in the graduated cylinder as the accepted value? *3.2*

49. Water with a mass of 35.4 g is added to an empty flask with a mass of 87.432 g. The mass of the flask and the water is 146.72 g after a rubber stopper is added. Express the mass of the stopper to the correct number of significant figures. *3.2*

50. List at least two advantages of using SI units for measuring. *3.3*

51. List the SI base unit of measurement for each of these quantities. *3.3*
   a. time   **c.** temperature
   b. length   **d.** mass

52. Use the tables in this chapter to order these lengths from smallest to largest. Give each measurement in terms of meters. *3.3*
   a. centimeter   **e.** meter
   b. micrometer   **f.** nanometer
   c. kilometer   **g.** decimeter
   d. millimeter   **h.** picometer

53. Measure each dimension using a unit with the appropriate prefix. *3.3*
   a. the height of this letter: I
   b. the width of **Table 3.3**
   c. the height of this page

54. From what unit is a measure of volume derived? *3.3*

55. What is the volume of a glass cylinder with an inside diameter of 6.0 cm and a height of 28 cm? (The volume of a cylinder equals pi × radius squared × height, or $V = 3.14\ r^2h$.) *3.3*

56. Match the approximate volume with each item. *3.3*
   a. orange   (1) 30 m^3
   b. basketball   (2) 200 cm^3
   c. van   (3) 20 L
   d. aspirin tablet   (4) 200 mm^3

57. How many grams are in each of these quantities? *3.3*
   a. 1 cg   b. 1 μg   c. 1 kg   d. 1 mg

58. Astronauts in space are said to have apparent weightlessness. Explain why it is incorrect to say that they are massless. *3.3*

59. Match the approximate mass with each item. *3.3*
   a. peanut   (1) 400 cg
   b. pear   (2) 50 mg
   c. stamp   (3) 60 kg
   d. person   (4) 150 g

60. Would the density of a person be the same on the surface of Earth as it is on the surface of the moon? Explain. *3.4*

61. A shiny, gold-colored bar of metal weighing 57.3 g has a volume of 4.7 cm^3. Is the metal bar pure gold? *3.4*

62. Why doesn't a measure of specific gravity have a unit? *3.4*

63. Use the values in **Table 3.7** to calculate the specific gravity of the following substances at 20 °C. *3.4*
   a. aluminum
   b. mercury
   c. ice

64. Three balloons filled with neon, carbon dioxide, and hydrogen are released into the atmosphere. Using the data in **Table 3.7**, describe the movement of each balloon. *3.4*

65. Which would melt first, germanium with a melting point of 1210 K or gold with a melting point of 1064 °C? *3.5*

CONCEPT MASTERY

66. List two possible reasons for precise, but inaccurate, measurements.

67. Rank these numbers from smallest to largest.
   a. 5.3×10^4 d. 0.0057
   b. 57×10^3 e. 5.1×10^{-3}
   c. 4.9×10^{-2} f. 0.0072×10^2

68. Criticize this statement: "When two measurements are added together, the answer can have no more significant figures than the measurement with the least number of significant figures."

69. Fahrenheit is a third temperature scale. Use the data in the table or the graph to derive an equation for the relationship between the Fahrenheit and Celsius temperature scales.

	°C	°F
Melting point of selenium	221	430
Boiling point of water	100	212
Normal body temperature	37	98.6
Freezing point of water	0	32
Boiling point of chlorine	−34.6	−30.2

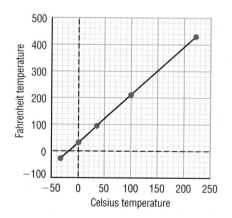

70. Which is larger?
   a. 1 centigram or 1 milligram
   b. 1 liter or 1 centiliter
   c. 1 calorie or 1 kilocalorie
   d. 1 millisecond or 1 centisecond
   e. 1 microliter or 1 milliliter
   f. 1 cubic millimeter or 1 cubic decimeter

71. Criticize this statement: "When a number is rounded, the last significant figure is dropped if it is less than 5."

72. A piece of wood sinks in gasoline but floats in ethanol. Give a range of possible densities for the wood.

73. Is it possible for an object to lose weight but at the same time not lose mass? Explain.

74. How has the egg been suspended in the clear liquid?

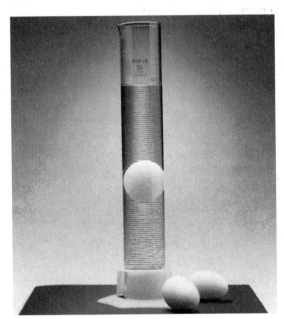

CRITICAL THINKING

75. Choose the term that best completes the second relationship.
   a. mass:kilograms   money: _____
      (1) hot   (3) coins
      (2) dollars   (4) spending
   b. foot:inch   meter: _____
      (1) millimeter   (3) kilometer
      (2) liter   (4) kilogram

76. Is it possible for experimental data to be accurate but imprecise?

77. You are hired to count the number of ducks on three northern lakes during the summer. In the first lake, you estimate 500 000 ducks; in the second, 250 000 ducks; and in the third, 100 000 ducks. You record that you have counted 850 000 ducks. As you drive away, you see 15 ducks fly in from the south and land on the third lake. Do you change the number of ducks that you report? Justify your answer.

78. Why is there a range of values given for the density of gasoline on **Table 3.8**?

CUMULATIVE REVIEW

79. What is a general goal of the scientific method?

80. What is the correct symbol for each element?
   a. sodium   d. copper
   b. aluminum   e. sulfur
   c. chlorine   f. strontium

81. Classify each of the following as a chemical or physical change.
   a. grass growing
   b. sugar dissolving in water
   c. crushing a rock
   d. cooking potatoes
   e. bleaching clothes
   f. boiling water

82. How would you separate a mixture of ground glass and salt?

83. How can you distinguish between a homogeneous mixture and a compound?

CONCEPT CHALLENGE

84. If ice were denser than water, it would certainly be easier to pour water from a pitcher of ice cubes and water. Can you imagine situations of more consequence?

85. The mass of a cube of iron is 355 g. Iron has a density of 7.87 g/cm^3. What is the mass of a cube of lead that has the same dimensions?

86. Equal amounts of mercury, water, and corn oil are added to a beaker.
   a. Describe the arrangement of the layers of liquids in the beaker.
   b. A small sugar cube is added to the beaker. Describe its location.
   c. What change will occur to the sugar cube over time?

87. Plot these data that show how the mass of sulfur increases with an increase in volume. Determine the density of sulfur from the slope of the line.

Mass of sulfur (g)	Volume of sulfur (cm^3)
23.5	11.4
60.8	29.2
115	55.5
168	81.1

Select the choice that best answers each question or completes each statement.

1. Which of these measurements have four significant figures?

    I. 3.045 g
    II. 0.0450 g
    III. 3.0×10^4 g
    IV. 4.050 g

    a. I and III only
    b. II and IV only
    c. I and IV only
    d. I, II, and IV only

2. A graduated cylinder contains 44.2 mL of water. A 48.6-g piece of metal is dropped into the cylinder. When the metal is completely covered with water, water rises to the 51.3 mL mark. What is the density of the metal?

    a. 0.95 g/mL   **c.** 7.1 g/mL
    b. 6.8 g/mL   **d.** 0.15 g/mL

3. Which of these series of units is ordered from smallest to largest?

    a. μg, cg, mg, kg   **c.** μs, ns, cs, s
    b. mm, dm, m, km   **d.** nL, mL, dL, cL

4. Which answer represents the measurement 0.00428 g rounded off to two significant figures?

    a. 4.28×10^3 g   **c.** 4.3×10^3 g
    b. 4.3×10^{-3} g   **d.** 4.0×10^{-3} g

Use these data to answer questions 5 and 6.

At 20 °C, the density of air is 1.20 g/L. Nitrogen's density is 1.17 g/L. Oxygen's density is 1.33 g/L.

5. Will balloons filled with oxygen and balloons filled with nitrogen rise or sink in air?

6. Air is mainly a mixture of nitrogen and oxygen. Which gas is the main component? Explain.

Use the data table to answer questions 7–10.

Body density (g/cm³)	Percent body fat (%)
1.01	38.3
1.03	29.5
1.05	21.0
1.07	12.9
1.09	5.07

7. What is the relationship between the density of a person's body and the percent of body fat?

8. Plot a graph with body density on the *x*-axis and percent body fat on the *y*-axis.

9. Are the variables directly or inversely related?

10. Use the graph to estimate the percent body fat of a person with a body density of 1.06 g/cm³.

Use the atomic windows below to answer questions 11 and 12.

The atomic windows represent particles of the same gas occupying the same volume at the same temperature. The systems differ only in the number of gas particles per unit volume.

11. List the windows in order of decreasing density.

12. Compare the density of the gas in window (a) to the density of the gas in window (b).

For each question there are two statements. Decide whether each statement is true or false. Then decide whether Statement II is a correct explanation for Statement I.

Statement I		Statement II
13. When a marshmallow is squashed, its mass and density do not change.	BECAUSE	Squashing an object does not change the amount of matter present.
14. There are five significant figures in the measurement 0.00450 m.	BECAUSE	All zeros to the right of a decimal point in a measurement are significant.
15. Precise measurements will always be accurate measurements.	BECAUSE	A value that is measured 10 times in a row must be accurate.
16. A temperature in kelvins is always numerically larger than the same temperature in degrees Celsius.	BECAUSE	A temperature in kelvins equals a temperature in degrees Celsius plus 273.

PROBLEM SOLVING IN CHEMISTRY

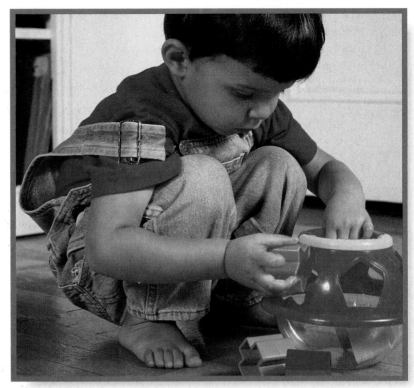

A child practices problem solving with shape-sorter toys.

FEATURES

Stay current with **SCIENCE NEWS**
Find out more about problem solving:
www.phschool.com

DISCOVER IT! TESTING PROBLEM-SOLVING SKILLS

You need five index cards, or five sheets of paper, and five pencils.

1. Copy the following problem onto each of the index cards: "The height of a graduated cylinder is 24 cm plus one-half of its height. How tall is the graduated cylinder?"

2. Work the problem yourself and then compare your answer with the solution provided by your teacher. How did you do?

3. Ask four family members or friends (not in your chemistry class) to work the problem.

4. How did they do?

Congratulate those who got the correct answer on their first try. Ask them how they got the answer. Point out to those who could not solve the problem that if they had checked their work they might have caught their initial error in reasoning. Show them that sketching the problem statement would have been useful in solving this problem. As you solve the problems in this chapter, make note of the problem-solving skills you use.

WHAT DO I DO NOW?

*S*hape-sorter toys fascinate young children. Typically, the children take one shape and try it in every hole over and over again until they find the right one. As adults, we can use information we have gathered about the distinction between shapes to evaluate the toy and place the star in the star-shaped hole. So although trial and error is one method of problem solving, it is usually not the best one. **What is the most effective way to solve problems?**

Skills Used in Solving Problems

Do you like word problems? You know the kind: "Sally is twice as old as Sara, who is three years younger than Suzy. What will Sally's age be one year from now if Suzy is one-third as old as twelve-year-old Sonja will be nine years from now?" (The answer is nine years old.) If problems such as this seem confusing, rest assured: None of the problems you will encounter in this textbook are that difficult. However, problem solving may be an area in which you feel less than proficient. This chapter will teach you how to become a good problem solver—and perhaps even to enjoy the process.

One way to become a better problem solver is to learn and use various problem-solving techniques. These techniques will turn out to apply to many situations, not just to your chemistry studies. You probably already use many problem-solving skills in everyday situations as well as in classes like algebra. Can you think of an instance in which you have used such skills today?

Problem solving involves developing a plan. Suppose one of your good friends moved to a distant state and then invited your family for a visit. You would face the problem of getting to the new location. You might fly to the airport closest to your friend's house and then rent a car to drive the rest of the way. But before you drove there, you would need to identify your destination on a road map like that in **Figure 4.1.** On the map, you see several alternate routes between the airport and your friend's town. You would have to select and plan a specific route to get from your starting point to your destination. Without the proper planning, your trip might be difficult.

Figure 4.1

Carefully planning your route helps ensure a successful trip. What are some possible routes for traveling from Meacham Field to Arlington?

A Three-Step Problem-Solving Approach

As you may have noted in Chapter 3, the techniques used in this book to solve problems are conveniently organized into a three-step problem-solving approach. While this approach is not the only strategy for solving problems, we believe it is the most helpful and effective. Thus we recommend that you follow it when working on the problems in this textbook. You will now examine the steps in detail.

Step 1. *ANALYZE* Solving a word problem is not too different from taking a trip to a new place. You must determine where you are starting from (identify the known), where you are going (identify the unknown), and how you are going to get there (plan a solution). What is known in a word problem may include a measurement and one or more relationships or equations that link measurements. You identify the unknown by reading the problem carefully to be sure that you understand what the problem is asking you to find. If the problem is long, you might need to read it several times. If the problem is to have a numerical answer, write down the units that the answer should have before you begin your solution.

Planning a solution—figuring out how to get from the known to the unknown—is obviously at the heart of problem solving. Sketching a picture that represents the problem may help you visualize a relationship between the known and the unknown. It might also suggest a way to break the problem down into two or more simpler problems. The solutions to the simpler problems can then be combined to solve the more complex problem. At this point, you might need to use resources such as tables or figures to find other facts or relationships. For example, you might need to look up a constant or an equation that relates a known measurement to an unknown measurement.

Step 2. *CALCULATE* If you have done a good job planning your solution, doing the calculation is usually straightforward. The calculation may involve substituting known quantities and doing the arithmetic needed to solve an equation for the unknown. Sometimes more than one equation may be needed in the solution. In some problems, you might need to convert a measurement to a different form.

Step 3. *EVALUATE* Once you have done the calculation, you must evaluate your answer. Does the answer make sense? Is it reasonable? Is it written in the correct unit? Solving the problem should give an answer with the correct unit. If it does not, you may have set up the equation incorrectly. The answer should also be expressed to the correct number of significant figures. Where appropriate, the answer should be written in scientific notation. Most importantly, you must check your work. Reread the problem to make sure that what the problem asked for is what you have found. Did you copy down the given facts correctly? Check your math. Often, you can estimate an appropriate answer as a quick check.

With slight modifications, this three-step approach can be used for both numeric and nonnumeric problems. With some practice, you will soon find yourself applying it without difficulty to all sorts of situations. Sample Problem 4-1 on page 86 illustrates how the approach is used.

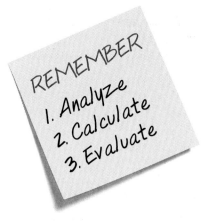

REMEMBER
1. Analyze
2. Calculate
3. Evaluate

Figure 4.2
The three-step approach to solving problems in chemistry is a useful and effective strategy that you should employ throughout this course—and in other problem-solving situations.

CHEMath

CALCULATOR SKILLS

Chemistry problems often involve calculations that are too complicated to do by hand. Thus the correct use of a calculator is essential to your success in this course. You will also find your calculator is very useful for solving a variety of problems in your everyday life.

The following instructions will help you use a typical scientific calculator. Be aware, however, that your calculator may vary slightly from the instructions that follow.

Addition, subtraction, multiplication, and division are entered much as they appear on paper. Use the change-sign key, +/−, to enter negative numbers, and use parentheses as appropriate. For example:

Enter 4×1.25 as 4 ⊗ 1 ⊡ 25 =.

Enter $10 \div (-0.4)$ as 10 ÷ 0 ⊡ 4 +/− =.

Enter $3 \times (2 + 3)$ as 3 × (2 + 3) =.

In chemistry, you will encounter many numbers written in scientific notation (see page 52). You can enter these numbers using the EXP key (labeled EE or E on some calculators). For example, the mass of an electron is 9.11×10^{-28} g, which you would enter as 9 ⊡ 11 EXP +/− 28. How would you calculate the mass of three electrons?

Different calculators may have different square root keys. Some calculators have a $\sqrt{x}$ or SQRT key, but others require a two-key process using INV x^2. To find the square root of 16, enter 16 $\sqrt{x}$, 16 SQRT, or 16 INV x^2, depending on your calculator.

To calculate powers, use the y^x key. For example, find 5^3 by pressing 5 y^x 3 =. When the exponent is 2, you can use the x^2 key. To calculate 8^2, enter 8 x^2 =.

Example 1

Use a calculator to evaluate $4^2 \times (10 + \sqrt{10\,609}\,)$.

Enter 4 x^2 × (10 + 10 609 $\sqrt{x}$) =.

The expression is equal to 1808.

Example 2

One atom of gold has a mass of 3.271×10^{-22} g. What is the mass of 158 atoms of gold?

The mass of 158 atoms of gold is given by $(158 \text{ atoms gold}) \times \dfrac{3.271 \times 10^{-22}\,\text{g}}{1 \text{ atom gold}}$.

158 × 3.271 EXP +/− 22 = 5.16818×10^{-20}

Rounding to four significant figures, the mass is 5.168×10^{-20} g.

Practice Problems

Prepare for upcoming problems in this chapter by using a calculator to solve each of the following problems.

A. Evaluate 7.823×15.76.

B. Evaluate $89^2 + 17^3 + 5^6$.

C. Evaluate $\dfrac{35 + \sqrt{529}}{2.9 \times 10^{17}}$.

D. The volume of a sphere with radius r is given by $\dfrac{4}{3}\pi r^3$. Find the volume of a sphere with a radius of 3.00 cm.

E. Find the number of atoms in 7.000 g of gold by evaluating $(7.000 \text{ g}) \times \dfrac{1 \text{ atom gold}}{3.271 \times 10^{-22}\,\text{g}}$.

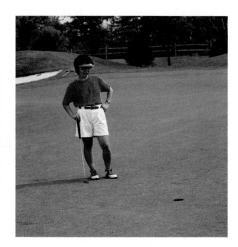

Figure 4.3
The three-step problem-solving approach is much like the approach used in many non-science situations. Here, the golfer analyzes the situation, assessing what is known about variables such as the ball's position and distance from the hole. Then she acts on her analysis by attempting her putt. Her evaluation reveals she has been successful! Careful analysis and execution have produced the desired outcome.

Sample Problem 4-1

What is the mass, in grams, of a piece of lead that has a volume of 19.84 cm³?

1. **ANALYZE** *List the knowns and the unknown.*

Knowns:
- volume of lead = 19.84 cm³
- density = relationship between the mass and volume of a substance = $\dfrac{\text{mass}}{\text{volume}}$

The density of lead is not given in the problem, so you must look it up. According to **Table 3.7** on page 69, the density of lead is 11.4 g/cm³.

- density of lead = 11.4 g/cm³

Unknown:
- mass = ? g

Using the known values for the volume and density of lead and the equation for density, density = $\dfrac{\text{mass}}{\text{volume}}$, the unknown mass can be determined.

2. **CALCULATE** *Solve for the unknown.*

The definition for density is an algebraic relationship that includes the unknown variable (mass) and two variables whose values are known in this problem (volume and density). Solve the equation for the unknown variable (mass) by rearranging the equation to isolate mass on one side of the equation. To do so, multiply both sides of the equation by the volume and cancel like terms.

$$\text{density} = \frac{\text{mass}}{\text{volume}}$$

$$\frac{\text{volume}}{1} \times \text{density} = \frac{\text{mass}}{\text{volume}} \times \frac{\text{volume}}{1}$$

Sample Problem 4-1 (cont.)

Canceling like terms yields:

$$\frac{\text{volume}}{1} \times \text{density} = \frac{\text{mass}}{\text{volume}} \times \frac{\text{volume}}{1}$$

$$\text{volume} \times \text{density} = \text{mass}$$
(or, mass = volume × density)

Substitute the known values for volume and density, and carry out the calculation.

$$\text{mass} = 19.84 \text{ cm}^3 \times 11.4 \text{ g/cm}^3 = 226.176 \text{ g}$$

Finally, round the answer to the correct number of significant figures (three) to match the number of figures in 11.4 g/cm³.

$$\text{mass} = 226 \text{ g}$$

3. **EVALUATE** *Does the result make sense?*
Evaluating the answer involves a number of checks. Has the unknown been found? Yes, the problem asked for the mass of lead. Do the units in the solution cancel so that the calculated answer has the correct units? Yes, the answer is given in grams, a unit of mass. Does the numerical value of the answer make sense? Yes, estimating an answer based on the approximate volume and the approximate density gives an estimated mass close to the calculated result. Is the number of significant figures correct? Yes, the answer to a multiplication calculation can have no more significant figures than the measurement with the smallest number of significant figures.

Here is another Sample Problem. Although it is somewhat different from Sample Problem 4-1, the problem-solving process is the same. Notice that this problem includes Practice Problems for you to solve on your own.

Sample Problem 4-2

What is the volume, in cubic centimeters, of a sample of cough syrup that has a mass of 50.0 g? The density of the cough syrup is 0.950 g/cm³.

1. **ANALYZE** *List the knowns and the unknown.*

Knowns:
- mass of cough syrup = 50.0 g
- density of cough syrup = 0.950 g/cm³
- $\text{density} = \dfrac{\text{mass}}{\text{volume}}$

Unknown:
- volume of cough syrup = ? cm³

Using the known values for the mass and density and the equation for density, the unknown volume can be determined.

Sample Problem 4-2 (cont.)

2. **CALCULATE** *Solve for the unknown.*

The equation for density must be solved for volume. Multiplying both sides of the equation by volume yields:

$$\text{volume} \times \text{density} = \frac{\text{mass}}{\cancel{\text{volume}}} \times \cancel{\text{volume}}$$

$$\text{volume} \times \text{density} = \text{mass}$$

Dividing both sides of the equation by density yields the desired result—the equation solved for volume.

$$\frac{\text{volume} \times \cancel{\text{density}}}{\cancel{\text{density}}} = \frac{\text{mass}}{\text{density}}$$

$$\text{volume} = \frac{\text{mass}}{\text{density}}$$

Substituting the known values and solving yields the volume.

$$\text{volume} = \frac{50.0 \cancel{g}}{0.950 \cancel{g}/\text{cm}^3} = 52.6316 \text{ cm}^3$$

Rounding to three significant figures gives 52.6 cm^3.

3. **EVALUATE** *Does the result make sense?*

Substituting the known mass and the calculated volume into the equation for density yields a result of 0.950 g/cm^3. This agrees with the known density. The unit obtained is the desired unit of volume. The answer has three significant figures as required.

Practice Problems

1. The density of silicon is 2.33 g/cm^3. What is the volume of a piece of silicon that has a mass of 62.9 g?
2. Helium has a boiling point of 4 K. This is the lowest boiling point of any liquid. Express this temperature in degrees Celsius.

section review 4.1

3. List three useful problem-solving skills.

4. State in your own words the three suggested steps for solving word problems.

5. Identify the statements that correctly complete the sentence: Good problem solvers

   a. read a problem only once.

   b. check their work.

   c. break complex problems down into one or more simpler problems.

   d. look for relationships among pieces of information.

6. A small piece of gold has a volume of 1.35 cm^3.

   a. What is the mass, given that the density of gold is 19.3 g/cm^3?

   b. What is the value of this piece if the market value of gold is $11/g?

7. What is normal body temperature (37 °C) on the Kelvin scale?

8. Match the steps taken in the trip described on page 83 with the three problem-solving steps used in chemistry problems.

 Chem ASAP! **Assessment 4.1** Check your understanding of the important ideas and concepts in Section 4.1.

SIMPLE CONVERSION PROBLEMS

Perhaps you have traveled abroad or are planning to do so. If so, you know—or will soon discover—that different countries have different currencies. As a tourist, exchanging money is essential to the enjoyment of your trip. After all, you must pay for your meals, hotel, transportation, gift purchases, and tickets to exhibits and events. Because each country's currency compares differently with the U.S. dollar, knowing how to convert currency units correctly is very important.
Is there a simple and effective method for making conversions?

objectives
▶ Construct conversion factors from equivalent measurements
▶ Apply the techniques of dimensional analysis to a variety of conversion problems
key terms
▶ conversion factor
▶ dimensional analysis

Conversion Factors

If you think about any number of everyday situations, you will realize that a quantity can usually be expressed in several different ways. For example, 1 dollar = 4 quarters = 10 dimes = 20 nickels = 100 pennies. These are all expressions, or measurements, of the same amount of money. The same thing is true of scientific quantities. For example, 1 meter = 10 decimeters = 100 centimeters = 1000 millimeters. These are different ways to express the same length.

Whenever two measurements are equivalent, a ratio of the two measurements will equal 1, or unity. For example, you can divide both sides of the equation 1 m = 100 cm by 1 m or by 100 cm.

$$\frac{1\ m}{1\ m} = \frac{100\ cm}{1\ m} = 1 \qquad \text{or} \qquad \frac{1\ m}{100\ cm} = \frac{100\ cm}{100\ cm} = 1$$

conversion factors

A ratio of equivalent measurements, such as $\frac{100\ cm}{1\ m}$ or $\frac{1\ m}{100\ cm}$, is called a **conversion factor.** In a conversion factor, the measurement in the numerator (on the top) is equivalent to the measurement in the denominator (on the bottom). The conversion factors above are read "one hundred centimeters per meter" and "one meter per hundred centimeters." **Figure 4.4** illustrates another way to look at the relationship in a conversion factor.

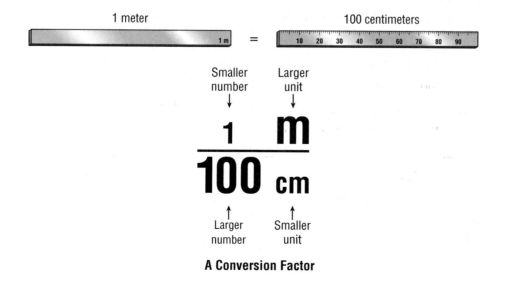

A Conversion Factor

Figure 4.4
The two parts of a conversion factor, the numerator and the denominator, are equal. The smaller number is part of the quantity with the larger unit; for example, a meter is physically larger than a centimeter. The larger number is part of the quantity with the smaller unit.

<u>Chem ASAP!</u>
Animation 3
Learn how to select the proper conversion factor and how to use it.

Conversion factors are useful in solving problems in which a given measurement must be expressed in some other unit of measure. When a measurement is multiplied by a conversion factor, the numerical value is generally changed, but the actual size of the quantity measured remains the same. For example, even though the numbers in the measurements 1 g and 10 dg (decigrams) differ, both measurements represent the same mass. In addition, conversion factors within a system of measurement are defined or exact quantities. Therefore, they have an unlimited number of significant figures. How would a conversion factor affect the rounding of a calculated answer?

Here are some additional examples of pairs of conversion factors written from equivalent measurements. The relationship between grams and kilograms is 1000 g = 1 kg. Possible conversion factors are:

$$\frac{1000 \text{ g}}{1 \text{ kg}} \quad \text{and} \quad \frac{1 \text{ kg}}{1000 \text{ g}}$$

The relationship between nanometers and meters is 10^9 nm = 1 m. The possible conversion factors are:

$$\frac{10^9 \text{ nm}}{1 \text{ m}} \quad \text{and} \quad \frac{1 \text{ m}}{10^9 \text{ nm}}$$

What conversion factors can you write based on the relationship 1 L = 1000 mL?

Dimensional Analysis

No one method is best for solving every type of problem. Several good approaches are available, and generally one of the best is dimensional analysis. **Dimensional analysis** is a way to analyze and solve problems using the units, or dimensions, of the measurements. The best way to explain this problem-solving technique is to use it to solve an everyday situation and then to apply the technique to a chemistry problem.

Sample Problem 4-3 uses dimensional analysis and the problem-solving techniques you learned in Section 4.1.

Sample Problem 4-3

Your school club has sold 600 tickets to a chili-supper fundraising event, and you have volunteered to make the chili. You have a chili recipe that serves ten. The recipe calls for two teaspoons of chili powder. How much chili powder do you need for 600 servings?

1. **ANALYZE** *List the knowns and the unknown.*

   Knowns:
   - servings = 600
   - 10 servings = 2 tsp chili powder

   Unknown:
   - amount of chili powder = ? tsp

   The correct conversion factor has the known unit in the denominator and the unknown unit in the numerator.

Sample Problem 4-3 (cont.)

2. *CALCULATE* Solve for the unknown.

The known measurement (600 servings) must be converted to teaspoons. Use the relationship between servings of chili and teaspoons of chili powder from the recipe to write a conversion factor that has the unit of the known in the denominator. The known unit will cancel, resulting in an answer that has the unit of the unknown.

The correct conversion factor is $\dfrac{2 \text{ tsp chili powder}}{10 \text{ servings}}$.

$$600 \; \text{servings} \times \frac{2 \text{ tsp chili powder}}{10 \; \text{servings}} = 120 \text{ tsp chili powder}$$

3. *EVALUATE* Does the result make sense?

The known measurement has been multiplied by a conversion factor (which equals unity). This gives another measurement: 120 teaspoons of chili powder. Because the size of the recipe was increased by a factor of 60, the amount of chili powder must also increase by a factor of 60. The unit of the known (servings) has canceled leaving the answer with the correct unit (tsp).

The answer to this problem has now generated a problem of a different sort. Do you really take the time to measure out 120 teaspoons of chili powder or do you just estimate and pour in several cans? Obviously, the first option would be tedious and the second could be dangerous! Why not measure out the chili powder by the cup? The question then becomes: How many cups are there in 120 teaspoons of chili powder? To solve this problem, you need to know the relationship between teaspoons and cups. This information and other volume relationships can be found in a cookbook. The given relationships do not include the one between teaspoons and cups, but they do include the following:

$$3 \text{ teaspoons} = 1 \text{ tablespoon}$$
$$16 \text{ tablespoons} = 1 \text{ cup}$$

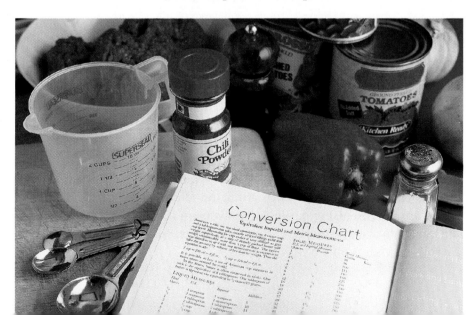

Figure 4.5
When you prepare chili, you need to know how to measure and convert units. Relationships among various measurements of volume used in cooking can be found in a conversion table in a cookbook.

Sample Problem 4-4

How many cups are in 120 teaspoons of chili powder?

1. **ANALYZE** *List the knowns and the unknown.*
   Knowns:
   - amount of chili powder = 120 teaspoons
   - 3 teaspoons = 1 tablespoon
   - 16 tablespoons = 1 cup

   Unknown:
   - amount of chili powder = ? cups

   The first conversion factor must be written with the unit teaspoons in the denominator. The second conversion factor must be written with the unit tablespoons in the denominator. This will provide the desired unit in the answer.

2. **CALCULATE** *Solve for the unknown.*
   Start with the known, 120 tsp chili powder. Use the first relationship to write a conversion factor that expresses 120 tsp as tablespoons. The unit teaspoons must be in the denominator so that the known unit will cancel. Then use the second conversion factor to change the unit tablespoons into the unit cups. This conversion factor must have the unit tablespoons in the denominator. The two conversion factors can be used together in a simple overall calculation.

$$120 \text{ teaspoons} \times \frac{1 \text{ tablespoon}}{3 \text{ teaspoons}} \times \frac{1 \text{ cup}}{16 \text{ tablespoons}} = 2.5 \text{ cups}$$

3. **EVALUATE** *Does the result make sense?*
   The numerical result makes sense because there are approximately 50 tsp in a cup, and 120 tsp should be between 2 and 3 cups. The unit in the solution is the desired unit (cups). Before you do the actual arithmetic, it is a good idea to make sure that the units cancel and that the numerator and denominator of each conversion factor are equal to each other.

Figure 4.6
How many pounds of apples can you buy with $4.00 if the price of apples is $1.39/lb? Solve this problem using dimensional analysis.

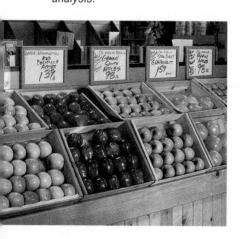

There is usually more than one way to solve a problem. When you first read the previous Sample Problems, you may have thought about different and equally correct ways to approach and solve some of the problems. Some problems are easily worked with simple algebra. Dimensional analysis provides you with a different approach. In each case, you should choose the problem-solving method that works best. What are some of the advantages of mastering more than one approach to problem solving?

In solving a problem, you should try to focus on the reasoning you are using at each step. In other words, think the solution through. Try to understand why you are using particular conversion factors in progressing from the known to the unknown. With perseverance, you can learn to apply and sharpen all your problem-solving skills.

Sample Problem 4-5

The directions for an experiment ask each student to measure out 1.84 g of copper (Cu) wire. The only copper wire available is a spool with a mass of 50.0 g. How many students can do the experiment before the copper runs out?

1. **ANALYZE** *List the knowns and the unknown.*

   Knowns:
   - mass of copper available = 50.0 g Cu
   - Each student needs 1.84 grams of copper, or $\dfrac{1.84 \text{ g Cu}}{\text{student}}$.

   Unknown:
   - number of students = ? students

   From the known mass of copper, calculate the number of students that can do the experiment. The desired conversion is mass of copper → number of students.

2. **CALCULATE** *Solve for the unknown.*

   Because students is the desired unit for the answer, the conversion factor should be written with students in the numerator.

   $$50.0 \text{ g Cu} \times \frac{1 \text{ student}}{1.84 \text{ g Cu}} = 27.174 \text{ students} = 27 \text{ students}$$

   Note that because students cannot be fractional, the result is shown rounded to a whole number.

3. **EVALUATE** *Does the result make sense?*

   The number of students (27) seems to be a reasonable answer. The approximate calculation using the ratio $\dfrac{1 \text{ student}}{2 \text{ g Cu}}$ gives an approximate answer of 25 students. The unit of the answer (students) is the one desired.

Practice Problems

9. An experiment requires that each student use an 8.5-cm length of magnesium ribbon. How many students can do the experiment if there is a 570-cm length of magnesium ribbon available?

10. A 1.00-degree increase on the Celsius scale is equivalent to a 1.80-degree increase on the Fahrenheit scale. If a temperature increases by 48.0 °C, what is the corresponding temperature increase on the Fahrenheit scale?

Converting Between Units

In chemistry, as in many other subjects, you often need to express a measurement in a unit different from the one given or measured initially. For example, suppose a laboratory experiment requires 7.5 dg of magnesium metal, and 100 students will do the experiment. How many grams of magnesium should your teacher have on hand? This is a typical conversion problem because you need to express a given measurement in a different unit. As you have seen, conversion problems are easily solved using dimensional analysis.

Figure 4.7

Architects use many conversion factors to draw buildings to scale accurately. If 10 mm on a scaled drawing equals 2 actual meters, what is the length of this room, front to back, as indicated by the red arrow?

As you work through the examples that follow, notice that the three-step problem-solving approach is applied to each.

Sample Problem 4-6

Express 750 dg in grams.

1. **ANALYZE** *List the knowns and the unknown.*

   Knowns:
   - mass = 750 dg
   - 1 g = 10 dg

   Unknown:
   - mass = ? g

   The desired conversion is decigrams → grams. Using the expression relating the units, 10 dg = 1 g, multiply the given mass by the proper conversion factor.

2. **CALCULATE** *Solve for the unknown.*

   The correct conversion factor is $\dfrac{1\,g}{10\,dg}$ because the known unit is in the denominator and the unknown unit is in the numerator.

   $$750\ \cancel{dg} \times \frac{1\,g}{10\,\cancel{dg}} = 75\ g$$

3. **EVALUATE** *Does the result make sense?*

   Because the unit gram represents a larger mass than the unit decigram, it makes sense that the number of grams is less than the given number of decigrams. The unit of the known (dg) cancels, and the answer has the correct unit (g). The answer also has the correct number of significant figures.

Practice Problems

11. Using tables from Chapter 3, convert the following.
    a. 0.044 km to meters
    b. 4.6 mg to grams
    c. 8.9 m to decimeters
    d. 0.107 g to centigrams
12. Convert the following.
    a. 15 cm³ to liters
    b. 7.38 g to kilograms
    c. 0.67 s to milliseconds
    d. 94.5 g to micrograms

Chem ASAP!

Problem-Solving 12
Solve Problem 12 with the help of an interactive guided tutorial.

Sample Problem 4-7

What is the volume of a pure silver coin that has a mass of 14 g? The density of silver (Ag) is 10.5 g/cm³.

1. **ANALYZE** *List the knowns and the unknown.*

   Knowns:
   - mass of coin = 14 g
   - density of silver = 10.5 g/cm³

   Unknown:
   - volume of coin = ? cm³

   This problem can be solved by using algebra, or it can be solved by using a conversion factor. Convert the given mass of the coin into a corresponding volume. The density of silver gives the needed relationship between mass and volume. Multiply the mass of the coin by the proper conversion factor to yield an answer in cm³.

Practice Problems

13. Use dimensional analysis and the given densities to make the following conversions.
    a. 14.8 g of boron to cubic centimeters of boron. The density of boron is 2.34 g/cm³.
    b. 2.8 L of argon to grams of argon. The density of argon is 1.78 g/L.
    c. 4.62 g of mercury to cubic centimeters of mercury. The density of mercury is 13.5 g/cm³.

Sample Problem 4-7 (cont.)

2. **CALCULATE** *Solve for the unknown.*

The correct conversion factor is $\dfrac{1 \text{ cm}^3 \text{ Ag}}{10.5 \text{ g Ag}}$ because the known unit is in the denominator and the unknown unit is in the numerator.

$$14 \text{ g Ag} \times \frac{1 \text{ cm}^3 \text{ Ag}}{10.5 \text{ g Ag}} = 1.3 \text{ cm}^3 \text{ Ag}$$

3. **EVALUATE** *Does the result make sense?*

Because a mass of 10.5 g of silver has a volume of 1 cm³, it makes sense that 14.0 g of silver should have a volume slightly larger than 1 cm³. The answer has two significant figures because the given mass has two significant figures.

Practice Problems (cont.)

14. Rework the preceding problems by applying the equation:

$$\text{density} = \frac{\text{mass}}{\text{volume}}.$$

Chem ASAP!

Problem-Solving 13
Solve Problem 13 with the help of an interactive guided tutorial.

section review 4.2

15. What conversion factor would you use to convert between these pairs of units?

   a. minutes to hours

   b. grams of water to cubic centimeters of water

   c. grams to milligrams

   d. cubic decimeters to milliliters

16. Make the following conversions. Express your answers in scientific notation.

   a. 36 cm to meters

   b. 14.8 g to micrograms

   c. 1.44 kL to liters

   d. 68.9 m to decimeters

   e. 3.72×10^{-3} kg to grams

   f. 66.3 L to cubic centimeters

   g. 0.0371 m to kilometers

17. A 2.00-kg sample of bituminous coal is composed of 1.30 kg of carbon, 0.20 kg of ash, 0.15 kg of water, and 0.35 kg of volatile (gas-forming) material. Using this information, determine how many kilograms of carbon are in 125 kg of this coal.

18. Which of the following linear measures is the longest?

   a. 6×10^4 cm

   b. 6×10^6 mm

   c. 0.06 km

   d. 6×10^9 nm

19. An atom of gold has a mass of 3.271×10^{-22} g. How many atoms of gold are in 5.00 g of gold?

 Chem ASAP! Assessment 4.2 Check your understanding of the important ideas and concepts in Section 4.2.

portfolio project

Develop four charts of conversion factors for units of length, volume, area, and mass. Include common non-SI units such as miles, gallons, acres, and tons. Provide both the names and the abbreviations of the units.

SMALL-SCALE LAB

NOW WHAT DO I DO?

PURPOSE
To solve problems by making accurate measurements and applying mathematics.

MATERIALS
- pencil
- paper
- meter stick
- balance
- pair of dice
- aluminum can
- calculator
- small-scale pipet
- water
- a pre- and a post-1982 penny
- 8-well strip
- plastic cup

PROCEDURE

1. Determine the mass, in grams, of one drop of water. To do this, measure the mass of an empty cup. Add 50 drops of water from a small-scale pipet to the cup and measure its mass again. Subtract the mass of the empty cup from the mass of the cup with water in it. To determine the average mass in grams of a single drop, divide the mass of the water by the number of drops (50). Repeat this experiment until your results are consistent.

2. Determine the mass of a pre-1982 penny and a post-1982 penny.

ANALYSIS
Using your experimental data, record the answers to the following questions.

1. What is the average mass of a single drop of water in milligrams? (1 g = 1000 mg)

2. The density of water is 1.00 g/cm^3. Calculate the volume of a single drop in cm^3 and mL. (1 mL = 1 cm^3) What is the volume of a drop in microliters (μL)? (1000 μL = 1 mL)

3. What is the density of water in units of mg/cm^3 and mg/mL? (1 g = 1000 mg)

4. Pennies made before 1982 consist of 95.0% copper and 5.0% zinc. Calculate the mass of copper and the mass of zinc in the pre-1982 penny.

5. Pennies made after 1982 are made of zinc with a thin copper coating. They are 97.6% zinc and 2.4% copper. Calculate the mass of copper and the mass of zinc in the newer penny.

6. Why does one penny have less mass than the other?

YOU'RE THE CHEMIST
The following small-scale activities allow you to develop your own procedures and analyze the results.

1. **Design It!** Design an experiment to determine if the size of drops varies with the angle at which they are delivered from the pipet. Try vertical (90°), horizontal (0°), and halfway between (45°). Repeat until your results are consistent.

2. **Analyze It!** What is the best angle to hold a pipet for ease of use and consistency of measurement? Explain. Why is it important to expel the air bubble before you begin the experiment?

3. **Design It!** Make the necessary measurements to determine the volume of aluminum used to make an aluminum soda can. *Hint:* Look up the density of aluminum in your textbook.

4. **Design It!** Design and carry out some experiments to determine the volume of liquid that an aluminum soda can will hold.

5. **Design It!** Measure a room and calculate the volume of air it contains. Estimate the percent error associated with not taking into account the furniture and people in the room.

6. **Design It!** Make the necessary measurements and do the necessary calculations to determine the volume of a pair of dice. First ignore the volume of the dots on each face, and then account for the volume of the dots. What is your error and percent error when you ignore the holes?

7. **Design It!** Design an experiment to determine the volume of your body. Write down what measurements you would need to make and what calculations you would do. What additional information might be helpful?

MORE-COMPLEX PROBLEMS

*A*rchitectural wonders like the Guggenheim Museum in Bilbao, Spain, are a testament to the vision, knowledge, and skills of all those associated with the construction. Solving the myriad problems that accompany the building of such structures is an essential first step that often involves converting complex units.

How can complex conversions be calculated?

objectives

▶ Solve problems by breaking the solution into steps
▶ Convert complex units, using dimensional analysis

Multistep Problems

Many complex tasks in your everyday life are best handled by breaking them down into manageable parts. For example, if you were cleaning a car, you might first vacuum the inside, then wash the exterior, then dry the exterior, and finally put on a fresh coat of wax. Similarly, many complex word problems are more easily solved by breaking the solution down into steps.

When converting between units, it is often necessary to use more than one conversion factor. Sample Problem 4-8 illustrates the use of multiple conversion factors.

Sample Problem 4-8

What is 0.073 cm in micrometers?

---

1. ANALYZE List the knowns and the unknown.

Knowns:
- length = 0.073 cm = 7.3×10^{-2} cm
- 10^2 cm = 1 m
- 1 m = 10^6 μm

Unknown:
- length = ? μm

The desired conversion is from centimeters to micrometers. The problem can be solved in a two-step conversion.

---

2. CALCULATE Solve for the unknown.

First, change centimeters to meters; then change meters to micrometers: centimeters → meters → micrometers. Each conversion factor must be written so that the unit in the denominator cancels the unit in the numerator of the previous factor.

$$7.3 \times 10^{-2} \, cm \times \frac{1 \, m}{10^2 \, cm} \times \frac{10^6 \, \mu m}{1 \, m} = 7.3 \times 10^2 \, \mu m$$

---

3. EVALUATE Does the result make sense?

Because a micrometer is a much smaller unit than a centimeter, the answer should be numerically larger than the given measurement. The units have canceled correctly, and the answer has the correct number of significant figures.

Practice Problems

20. The radius of a potassium atom is 0.227 nm. Express this radius in centimeters.

21. Earth's diameter is 1.3×10^4 km. What is the diameter expressed in decimeters?

Figure 4.8

A complex process, such as building a house, must be broken down into several simpler steps. Each of those steps is generally executed in logical order so that the product of the process is the desired one. Obviously one of the steps in this example involved the removal of a tree!

Here is another example of a multistep problem. You probably do not know how many seconds are in one day. However, you can easily calculate this quantity by using dimensional analysis and equivalent expressions of time that you do know.

Sample Problem 4-9

How many seconds are there in exactly one day?

1. **ANALYZE** *List the knowns and the unknown.*

   Knowns:
   - length of time = 1 day
   - 1 day = 24 hr
   - 1 hr = 60 min
   - 1 min = 60 s

   Unknown:
   - length of time = ? s

   The desired conversion is days $\longrightarrow$ seconds.

2. **CALCULATE** *Solve for the unknown.*

   As identified in the first step, the conversion required is from days to seconds. This conversion can be carried out by the following sequence of conversions: day $\longrightarrow$ hours $\longrightarrow$ minutes $\longrightarrow$ seconds. Each conversion factor in the series must be written so that the unit in the denominator cancels the unit in the numerator of the previous factor.

   $$1\ \text{day} \times \frac{24\ \text{hr}}{\text{day}} \times \frac{60\ \text{min}}{\text{hr}} \times \frac{60\ \text{s}}{\text{min}} = 8.6400 \times 10^4\ \text{s}$$

3. **EVALUATE** *Does the result make sense?*

   A large number is expected because a second is a much smaller unit than a day. The numerator and denominator of the conversion factors have canceled correctly to yield the desired unit.

Practice Problems

22. How many minutes are there in exactly one week?

23. How many seconds are in exactly a 40-hr work week?

Chem ASAP!

Problem-Solving 23

Solve Problem 23 with the help of an interactive guided tutorial.

Converting Complex Units

Many common measurements are expressed as a ratio of two units. For example, the results of international car races often give average lap speeds in kilometers per hour. You measure the densities of solids and liquids in grams per cubic centimeter. You measure the gas mileage in a car in miles per gallon of gasoline. If you use dimensional analysis, converting these complex units is just as easy as converting single units. It will just take multiple steps to arrive at an answer.

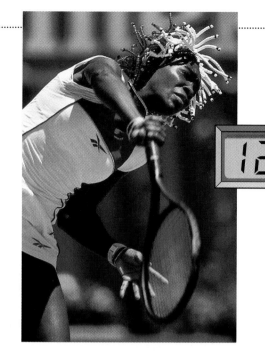

Figure 4.9
Different units are used in different settings. The speed of Venus Williams's record-setting serve was displayed in mi/h. What would this service speed be in km/s?

Sample Problem 4-10

The density of manganese is 7.21 g/cm³. What is the density of manganese expressed in units of kg/m³?

1. **ANALYZE List the knowns and the unknown.**

   Knowns:
   - density of manganese = 7.21 g/cm³
   - 10^3 g = 1 kg
   - 10^6 cm³ = 1 m³

   Unknown:
   - density of manganese = ? kg/m³

   The desired conversion is g/cm³ → kg/m³. The mass unit in the numerator must be changed from grams to kilograms: g → kg. In the denominator, the volume unit must be changed from cubic centimeters to cubic meters: cm³ → m³. Note that the relationship between cm³ and m³ was determined from the relationship between cm and m. Cubing the relationship 10^2 cm = 1 m yields $(10^2 \text{ cm})^3 = (1 \text{ m})^3$, or 10^6 cm³ = 1 m³.

2. **CALCULATE Solve for the unknown.**

$$\frac{7.21 \text{ g}}{1 \text{ cm}^3} \times \frac{1 \text{ kg}}{10^3 \text{ g}} \times \frac{10^6 \text{ cm}^3}{1 \text{ m}^3} = 7.21 \times 10^3 \text{ kg/m}^3$$

3. **EVALUATE Does the result make sense?**
   Because the physical size of the volume unit m³ is so much larger than cm³ (10^6 times), the calculated value of the density should be larger than the given value even though the mass unit is also larger (10^3 times). The units cancel, the conversion factors are correct, and the answer has the correct ratio of units.

Practice Problems

24. Gold has a density of 19.3 g/cm³. What is the density in kilograms per cubic meter?
25. There are 7.0×10^6 red blood cells (RBC) in 1.0 mm³ of blood. How many red blood cells are in 1.0 L of blood?

Chem ASAP!

Problem-Solving 25
Solve Problem 25 with the help of an interactive guided tutorial.

MINI LAB

DIMENSIONAL ANALYSIS

PURPOSE

To apply the problem-solving technique of dimensional analysis to conversion problems.

MATERIALS

- 3 inch × 5 inch index cards or paper cut to approximately the same size
- pen

PROCEDURE

A conversion factor is a ratio of equivalent measurements. For any relationship, you can write two ratios. On a conversion factor card you can write one ratio on each side of the card.

1. Make a conversion factor card for each metric relationship shown in **Tables 3.3, 3.4,** and **3.5.** Show the inverse of the conversion factor on the back of each card.

2. Make a conversion factor card showing the mass–volume relationship for water (1.00 g H_2O = 1.00 mL H_2O). Show the inverse of the conversion factor on the back of the card.

3. Use the appropriate conversion factor cards to set up solutions to Sample Problems 4-6 and 4-8. Notice that in each solution, the unit in the denominator of the conversion factor cancels the unit in the numerator of the previous conversion factor.

4. Use conversion factor cards to set up solutions to Problem 28, below.

ANALYSIS AND CONCLUSIONS

1. What is the effect of multiplying a given measurement by one or more conversion factors?

2. Use your conversion factor cards to set up solutions to these problems.

   a. 78.5 cm = ? m

   b. 0.056 L = ? cm^3

   c. 77 kg =? mg

   d. 4.54 mL H_2O = ? mg H_2O

   e. 0.087 nm = ? dm

   f. 78.5 g H_2O = ? L H_2O

   g. 0.96 cm = ? μm

   h. 0.0067 mm = ? nm

section review 4.3

26. How can you solve a complicated problem more easily?

27. How are complex units dealt with in calculations?

28. Convert the following. Express your answers in scientific notation.

    a. 7.5×10^4 nm to kilometers   **c.** 0.764 km to centimeters

    b. 3.9×10^5 mg to decigrams   **d.** 2.21×10^{-4} dL to microliters

29. Light travels at a speed of 3.00×10^{10} cm/s. What is the speed of light in kilometers per hour?

30. A bar of gold measures 4.5 cm by 6.5 cm by 1.6 dm. Calculate the mass of the gold bar in kilograms. The density of gold is 19.3 g/cm^3.

31. What is the mass, in kilograms, of 14.0 L of gasoline? (Assume that the density of gasoline is 0.680 g/cm^3.)

 Chem ASAP! **Assessment 4.3** Check your understanding of the important ideas and concepts in Section 4.3.

NATURE'S MEDICINE CABINET

You have probably taken drugs such as aspirin and decongestants several times in your life. Have you ever wondered whom you should thank for the welcome relief these drugs provide? In some cases, the "inventor" of the drug was not a white-coated chemist but a green-leafed plant!

In many ways, plants are the master chemists of the world. For millions of years, they have been busily evolving the ability to manufacture an array of chemical compounds. Many of these compounds have obvious uses for the plant — defense against plant-eating insects, for example. Others are by-products of growth processes of plants. A sizable number of plant compounds have some kind of property or chemical activity that makes them useful to humans as medicine.

Humans have known about the medicinal properties of plants for a long time. Before modern science, humans used plant extracts to treat illnesses and injuries, without understanding the chemical basis of the treatment. Today, chemists and medical researchers continue to look to plants as either the source or inspiration for new drugs.

The story of aspirin is a good example of the on-going link between plant compounds and drugs for humans. The first aspirin-like drug was an extract from the bark of willow trees, which was used by native North Americans to alleviate pain and fever.

> In many ways, plants are the master chemists of the world.

In the 1800s, chemists begin to search for the active ingredient in willow bark. They isolated a substance that had the fever-reducing effect and called it salicin, after *Salix*, the Latin name for the willow. Then chemists worked on synthesizing a compound in the laboratory with the same effects. They succeeded in making salicylic acid, which worked well to reduce fever but was very irritating to the stomach. Finally, in 1899, a German company began marketing a derivative of salicylic acid that did not upset the stomach but that still reduced fever and pain. They called it aspirin.

Many other common drugs have their roots in plant chemistry. The active ingredient in many decongestants, for example, is closely related to a compound in the ephedra plant called ephedrine. Plants are also a continuing source of new drugs. For example, a drug called taxol, extracted from the bark of the Pacific yew tree, has been shown to be effective in fighting both breast and ovarian cancer.

There are also some plant compounds that have been known for a long time to have medicinal properties but that are only now beginning to be recognized as effective drugs by scientists. One of these is contained in the plant called St. John's wort. Extracts of this plant have been shown to counteract depression, one of the most common mental disorders. The active ingredient in St. John's wort is related to a new class of drugs called selective serotonin re-uptake inhibitors (SSRIs), which are also used to treat depression. St. John's wort and the SSRI drugs both work by changing how the body uses serotonin, a hormone that plays a key part in mood regulation.

The next time you take a stroll in the woods, think about the wealth of chemical compounds contained in the flora around you. One of those compounds might someday offer a cure for what ails you.

CHEMISTRY IN CAREERS

☆☆☆☆☆☆☆☆☆☆☆☆☆☆☆☆☆☆☆☆☆

TAKE IT TO THE NET
Find out more about career opportunities:

www.phschool.com

CHEMICAL SPECIALIST
Local food service distributor seeks responsible self-motivated individ.

MEDICAL LABORATORY TECHNICIAN
Process sera for blood tests; determine cholesterol and enzyme levels.
See page 869.

CHEMIST NEEDED

STUDENT STUDY GUIDE

Take It to the NET
For interactive study and
review, go to www.phschool.com

KEY TERMS

▸ conversion factor *p. 89*
▸ dimensional analysis *p. 90*

CONCEPT SUMMARY

4.1 What Do I Do Now?

• Problem solving is a skill learned through practice. The more you practice, the more proficient you become.

• Problem solving involves developing a plan. In this textbook, a three-step approach is the plan used. The three steps are: analyze, calculate, and evaluate.

• To analyze a word problem, identify both the knowns and the unknown. Then plan a solution and do the calculations.

• In the final step, evaluate whether the answer to a word problem seems reasonable and whether the answer has the correct number of significant figures.

• No problem-solving method can replace the need for you to read carefully and to think through the steps needed to solve a given problem.

• A good problem-solving strategy can be applied to all sorts of situations—not just chemistry problems.

4.2 Simple Conversion Problems

• Any two measurements that are equal to one another but expressed in different units can be written as a ratio.

• A ratio of equivalent measurements is called a conversion factor and is equal to unity.

• Conversion factors are used in the problem-solving technique of dimensional analysis.

• A ratio of equivalent measurements has two forms. The correct conversion factor for solving a particular problem will have the known unit in the denominator and the unknown unit in the numerator.

• Conversion problems in which you are asked to express a measurement in some other unit are easily solved using dimensional analysis.

• In dimensional analysis, units are used to help write the solution to a problem.

4.3 More-Complex Problems

• Many complex problems, whether they be in chemistry or in your daily life, can be successfully solved by breaking the solution down into steps.

• More than one conversion factor may be required in some more-complex conversion problems.

• The given measurement in a rate problem has a ratio of units.

• Rate problems are solved by converting the unit in the numerator followed by converting the unit in the denominator.

CHAPTER CONCEPT MAP

Use these terms to construct a concept map that organizes the major ideas of this chapter.

| algebra | conversion factor | denominator |
| dimensional analysis | numerator | problem solving |

 Chem ASAP! **Concept Map 4**
Create your Concept Map
using the computer.

CONCEPT PRACTICE

32. In which step of the three-step problem-solving approach is a problem-solving strategy developed? *4.1*

33. A volume of 5.00 mL of mercury is added to a beaker that has a mass of 87.3 g. What is the mass of the beaker with the added mercury? *4.1*

34. What is the name given to a ratio of two equivalent measurements? *4.2*

35. One measure of area is the hectare, which is equal to 10 000 m². What does the ratio $\dfrac{10^4 \text{ m}^2}{\text{hectare}}$ equal? *4.2*

36. Write six conversion factors involving these units of measure: 1 g = 100 cg = 10^3 mg. *4.2*

37. What must be true for a ratio of two measurements to be a conversion factor? *4.2*

38. One of the first mixtures of metals used by dentists for tooth fillings consisted of 26.0 g of silver, 10.8 g of tin, 2.4 g of copper, and 0.8 g of zinc. How much silver is in a 25.0 g sample of this amalgam? *4.2*

39. How do you know which unit of a conversion factor must be in the denominator (on the bottom)? *4.2*

40. The density of dry air measured at 25 °C is 1.19×10^{-3} g/cm³. What is the volume of 50.0 g of air? *4.2*

41. List at least two things you should do after you have calculated the answer to a problem on your calculator. *4.2*

42. Have you ever found yourself sitting through a terrible movie, counting the minutes that remain? If a movie has 0.20 hour remaining, how many seconds of movie remain? *4.3*

43. Make the following conversions. *4.3*
   a. 157 cs to seconds
   b. 42.7 L to milliliters
   c. 261 nm to millimeters
   d. 0.065 km to decimeters
   e. 642 cg to kilograms
   f. 8.25×10^2 cg to nanograms

44. Make the following conversions. *4.3*
   a. 0.44 mL/min to microliters per second
   b. 7.86 g/cm² to milligrams per square millimeter
   c. 1.54 kg/L to grams per cubic centimeter

45. How many milliliters are contained in 1 m³? *4.3*

46. Complete this table so that the measurements in each row have the same value. *4.3*

mg	g	cg	kg
6.6×10^3		28.3	
	2.8×10^{-4}		

47. A cheetah can run 112 km/h over a 100-m distance. What is this speed in meters per second? *4.3*

CONCEPT MASTERY

48. A flask that can hold 158 g of water at 4 °C can hold only 127 g of ethanol. What is the density of ethanol?

49. A watch loses 0.15 s every minute. How many minutes will the watch lose in 1 day?

50. A tank measuring 28.6 cm by 73.0 mm by 0.72 m is filled with olive oil that has a mass of 1.38×10^4 g. What is the density of olive oil in kilograms per liter?

51. Alkanes are a class of molecules that have the general formula C_nH_{2n+2}, where n is an integer. The table below gives the boiling points for the first five alkanes with an odd number of carbon atoms. Using the table, construct a graph with number of carbon atoms on the x-axis.

Boiling point (°C)	Number of carbon atoms
−162.0	1
−42.0	3
36.0	5
98.0	7
151.0	9

   a. What are the approximate boiling points for the C_2, C_4, C_6, and C_8 alkanes?
   b. Which of these nine alkanes are gases at room temperature (20 °C)?
   c. How many of these nine alkanes are liquids at 350 K?
   d. What is the approximate increase in boiling point per additional carbon atom in this series of alkanes?

52. Earth is approximately 1.5×10^8 km from the sun. How many minutes does it take light to travel from the sun to Earth? The speed of light is 3.0×10^8 m/s.

53. What is the mass of a cube of aluminum that is 3.0 cm on each edge? The density of aluminum is 2.7 g/cm^3.

54. The average density of Earth is 5.52 g/cm^3. Express this density in units of kg/dm^3.

55. How many kilograms of water (at 4 °C) are needed to fill an aquarium that measures 40.0 cm by 20.0 cm by 30.0 cm?

CRITICAL THINKING

56. Choose the term that best completes the second relationship.
    a. journey : route   problem : _____
       (1) unknown   (3) known
       (2) plan   (4) calculate
    b. meter : 100 cm   gram : _____
       (1) 0.001 kL   (3) 1000 mg
       (2) 100 cm   (4) 100 kg

57. You have solved many word problems up to this point. Review the techniques for solving word problems. Which step is most difficult for you? What kind of problems do you find most difficult to solve?

58. Why are units so important in working word problems?

CUMULATIVE REVIEW

59. Describe how the law of conservation of mass applies to a burning campfire.

60. List three physical properties of each of the following objects in the accompanying photo.
    a. the glass
    b. the soda
    c. the ice cube
    d. the bubbles

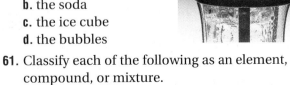

61. Classify each of the following as an element, compound, or mixture.
    a. an egg   c. dry ice (CO_2)
    b. a cake   d. iron powder

62. The melting point of silver is 962 °C. Express this temperature in kelvins.

63. Identify the larger quantity in each of these pairs of measurements.
    a. centigram, milligram
    b. deciliter, kiloliter
    c. millisecond, microsecond
    d. cubic decimeter, milliliter
    e. micrometer, nanometer

64. Name three physical and three chemical changes that you have seen today.

65. How many significant figures are in each of these measurements?
    a. 5.12 g   d. 0.045 04 mm
    b. 3.456×10^6 kg   e. 985.20 K
    c. 0.000 078 dm^3 f. 65.02 s

66. Round each of the measurements in Problem 65 to two significant figures.

CONCEPT CHALLENGE

67. Sea water contains 8.0×10^{-1} cg of the element strontium per kilogram of sea water. Assuming that all the strontium could be recovered, how many grams of strontium could be obtained from one cubic meter of sea water? Assume the density of sea water is 1.0 g/mL.

68. When 121 g of sulfuric acid is added to 400 mL of water, the resulting solution's volume is 437 mL. What is the specific gravity of the resulting solution?

69. How tall is a rectangular block of balsa wood measuring 4.4 cm wide and 3.5 cm deep that has a mass of 98.0 g? The specific gravity of balsa wood is 0.20.

70. The density of dry air at 20 °C is 1.20 g/L. What is the mass of air, in kilograms, of a room that measures 25.0 m by 15.0 m by 4.0 m?

71. Different volumes of the same liquid were added to a flask on a balance. After each addition of liquid, the mass of the flask with the liquid was measured. Graph the data using mass as the dependent variable. Use the graph to answer these questions.

Volume (mL)	14	27	41	55	82
Mass (g)	103.0	120.4	139.1	157.9	194.1

a. What is the mass of the flask?
b. What is the density of the liquid?

Select the choice that best answers each question or completes each statement.

1. Which of these conversion factors is *not* correct?
   a. $1 \text{ m}/10^2 \text{ mm}$
   b. $10^9 \text{ ns}/1 \text{ s}$
   c. $1 \text{ dm}^3/1 \text{ L}$
   d. $1 \text{ g}/10^6 \text{ μg}$

2. An over-the-counter medicine has 325 mg of its active ingredient per tablet. How many grams does this mass represent?
   a. 325 000 g
   b. 32.5 g
   c. 3.25 g
   d. 0.325 g

3. The density of zinc is 9.394 g/cm^3 at 20 °C. What is the volume of a sphere of zinc that has a mass of 15.6 g? ($V = 4/3\pi r^3$; $\pi = 3.14$)
   a. 1.66 cm^3
   b. 6.21 cm^3
   c. 0.602 cm^3
   d. 147 cm^3

4. If $10^4 \text{ μm} = 1 \text{ cm}$, how many $\text{μm}^3 = 1 \text{ cm}^3$?
   a. 10^4
   b. 10^6
   c. 10^8
   d. 10^{12}

5. How many meters does a car moving at 95 km/h travel in 1.0 s?
   a. 1.6 m
   b. 340 m
   c. 1600 m
   d. 26 m

6. If a substance contracts when it freezes, its
   a. density will remain the same.
   b. density will increase.
   c. density will decrease.
   d. change in density cannot be predicted.

For questions 7–10, identify the known and the unknown. Include units in your answers.

7. The density of water is 1.0 g/mL. How many deciliters of water will fill a 0.5-L bottle.

8. A 34.5-g gold nugget is dropped into a graduated cylinder containing water. By how many milliliters does the measured volume increase? The density of water is 1.0 g/mL. The density of gold is 19.3 g/cm^3.

9. A watch loses 0.2 s every minute. How many minutes will the watch lose in a day?

10. Eggs shipped to market are packed 12 eggs to a carton and 20 cartons to a box. A crate holds 4 boxes. Crates are stacked on a truck 5 crates wide, 6 crates deep, and 5 crates high. How many eggs are there in 5 truckloads?

11. Based on the prices displayed on the gas pumps, which station offers a lower price for gasoline? (1 gal = 3.79 L)

The lettered choices below refer to questions 12–15. A lettered choice may be used once, more than once, or not at all.

   (A) 60 min/h
   (B) 1 min/60 s
   (C) 1 h/60 min
   (D) 60 s/1 min

Which conversion factors are needed to do each of the following conversions?

12. number of seconds to cook a 3-minute egg

13. number of hours in 1000 s

14. number of minutes in "Wait just a second."

15. number of minutes in an 8-hour workday

Use the drawing to answer questions 16–18. The scale models show the relative sizes of a helium atom (left) and a xenon atom (right).

16. Use the metric ruler provided to determine the diameter of each model atom in millimeters.

17. Calculate the ratio of the diameter of the helium atom to the diameter of the xenon atom.

18. Calculate the ratio of the volume of the helium atom to the volume of the xenon atom. Assume that the atoms are perfect spheres. ($V = 4/3\pi r^3$; $\pi = 3.14$)

FEATURES

DISCOVER IT!
Electric Charge

SMALL-SCALE LAB
The Atomic Mass of Candium

MINI LAB
Using Inference: The Black Box

CHEMath
Using Positive and Negative Numbers

CHEMISTRY SERVING ... SOCIETY
Ask an Artifact for a Date!

CHEMISTRY IN CAREERS
Archaeologist

LINK TO HUMANITIES
Philosophy of Science

Stay current with **SCIENCE NEWS**
Find out more about atomic structure:
www.phschool.com

Each bright spot on this image represents one gold atom.

DISCOVER IT! ELECTRIC CHARGE

You need four 25-cm lengths of clear plastic tape and a metric ruler.

1. Firmly stick two of the 25-cm pieces of tape side-by-side, about 10 cm apart, on your desk top. Leave 2 to 3 cm of tape sticking over the edge of the desk. Grasp the free ends of the tapes and pull sharply upward to peel the tape pieces off of the desk. Slowly bring the pieces, which have similar charges, toward one another. What do you observe?

2. Pull the third and fourth pieces of tape between your thumb and forefinger several times, as if you were trying to clean each one. Slowly bring these two pieces of tape, which now have similar charges, toward one another. What do you observe?

3. Predict what might happen if you brought a piece of tape pulled from your desk top close to a piece of tape pulled between your fingers. Try it! What happens?

Do you think the pieces of tape used in Step 1 have the same charge as the pieces used in Step 2? Explain. After reading about charged particles in this chapter, return to this activity and re-evaluate your answer.

ATOMS

*I*n 1981, Swiss scientists Gerd Binnig and Heinrich Rohrer completed the construction of the scanning tunneling microscope. Their device, which they first tested using a specimen of gold, produces an image of individual atoms, often seen as rows of bright spots on a monitor as seen here. The scanning tunneling microscope is used today to study how atoms are arranged on the surface of many different materials. Binnig and Rohrer won the Nobel Prize for Physics in 1986 for their invention. **Why was an image of individual atoms considered such an important breakthrough?**

objectives
▶ Summarize Dalton's atomic theory
▶ Describe the size of an atom

key terms
▶ Dalton's atomic theory
▶ atom

Early Models of the Atom

Have you ever been asked to believe in something you could not see? Using your unaided eyes, you cannot see the tiny fundamental particles that make up matter. Yet all matter is composed of such particles. Democritus of Abdera, a teacher who lived in Greece during the fourth century B.C., first suggested the existence of these particles, which he called atoms. He believed that these atoms were indivisible and indestructible. Although Democritus's ideas agreed with later scientific theory, they were not useful in explaining chemical behavior. They also lacked experimental support because scientific testing was unknown at that time.

The real nature of atoms and the connection between observable changes and events at the atomic level were not established for more than 2000 years after Democritus. The modern process of discovery regarding atoms began with John Dalton (1766–1844), an English schoolteacher. Unlike Democritus, Dalton performed experiments to test and correct his atomic theory. Dalton studied the ratios in which elements combine in chemical reactions. Based on the results of his experiments, Dalton formulated hypotheses and theories to explain his observations. The result was **Dalton's atomic theory,** which includes the ideas illustrated in **Figure 5.1** and listed below.

1. All elements are composed of tiny indivisible particles called atoms.
2. Atoms of the same element are identical. The atoms of any one element are different from those of any other element.

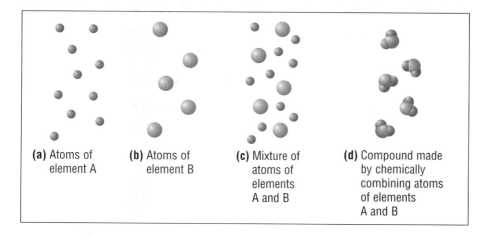

(a) Atoms of element A

(b) Atoms of element B

(c) Mixture of atoms of elements A and B

(d) Compound made by chemically combining atoms of elements A and B

Figure 5.1

According to Dalton's atomic theory, an element is composed of only one kind of atom, and a compound is composed of particles that are chemical combinations of different kinds of atoms.

Atomic Structure and the Periodic Table **107**

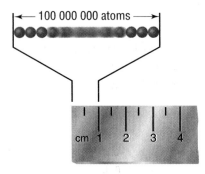

← 100 000 000 atoms →

cm 1 2 3 4

Figure 5.2

If 100 000 000 copper atoms were placed side by side, they would form a line 1 cm long. What is this number of atoms written in scientific notation?

3. Atoms of different elements can physically mix together or can chemically combine with one another in simple whole-number ratios to form compounds.
4. Chemical reactions occur when atoms are separated, joined, or rearranged. Atoms of one element, however, are never changed into atoms of another element as a result of a chemical reaction.

Just How Small Is an Atom?

A coin the size of a penny and composed of pure copper (Cu) illustrates Dalton's concept of the atom. Imagine grinding the copper coin into a fine dust. Each speck in the small pile of shiny red dust would still have the properties of copper. If by some means you could continue to make the copper dust particles smaller, you would eventually come upon a particle of copper that could no longer be divided and still have the properties of copper. This final particle is called an **atom,** defined in its modern sense as the smallest particle of an element that retains the properties of that element.

Copper atoms are very small. A pure copper coin the size of a penny contains about 2.4×10^{22} atoms. By comparison, Earth's population is only about 6×10^{9} people. There are about 4×10^{12} as many atoms in the coin as there are people on Earth. If you could line up 100 000 000 copper atoms side by side, they would produce a line only 1 cm long, as shown in **Figure 5.2.**

Does seeing individual atoms seem impossible? Despite their small size, individual atoms are observable with the proper instrument. As you read in the introduction to this section, and as **Figure 5.3** shows, a scanning tunneling microscope provides a visual image of individual atoms. Individual atoms can even be moved around and arranged in patterns. The ability to move individual atoms holds future promise for the creation of atomic-sized electronic devices, such as circuits and computer chips. This atomic-scale technology could someday be applied to communications and space exploration.

Figure 5.3

A scanning tunneling microscope can be used to view the surface of individual atoms, such as the gold atoms shown here.

section review 5.1

1. In your own words, state the main ideas of Dalton's atomic theory.

2. Characterize the size of an atom.

3. Democritus and Dalton both proposed that matter consists of atoms. How did their approaches to reaching that conclusion differ?

 Chem ASAP! Assessment 5.1 Check your understanding of the important ideas and concepts in Section 5.1.

*A*toms are so small they can only be visualized with a scanning tunneling microscope. How do scientists study the even smaller particles that make up atoms? Scientists study the makeup of atoms by breaking them apart! The atoms are accelerated to tremendous speeds—nearly the speed of light—in giant devices called particle accelerators. Then the atoms are smashed into one another, causing the particles within them to be released. Although scientists cannot actually see the particles, they can use the device shown here, called a bubble chamber, to see the tracks these particles make. **What are the component particles that scientists have discovered within atoms?**

objectives
▶ Distinguish among protons, electrons, and neutrons in terms of relative mass and charge
▶ Describe the structure of an atom, including the location of the protons, electrons, and neutrons with respect to the nucleus

key terms
▶ electrons
▶ cathode ray
▶ protons
▶ neutrons
▶ nucleus

Electrons

Much of Dalton's atomic theory is accepted today. One important change, however, is that atoms are now known to be divisible. They can be broken down into even smaller, more fundamental particles. Dozens of kinds of subatomic particles are unleashed when powerful devices known as atom smashers are used to fracture atoms. You will now learn about three kinds of subatomic particles.

Electrons are negatively charged subatomic particles. The English physicist J. J. Thomson (1856–1940) discovered electrons in 1897. Thomson performed experiments that involved passing electric current through gases at low pressure. He sealed the gases in glass tubes fitted at both ends with metal disks called electrodes. **Figure 5.4** shows the kind of apparatus he used. The electrodes were connected to a source of high-voltage electricity. One electrode, the anode, became positively charged. The other electrode, the cathode, became negatively charged. A glowing beam formed between the electrodes. This beam, which traveled from the cathode to the anode, is called a **cathode ray.**

Thomson found that cathode rays are attracted to metal plates that have a positive electrical charge. Plates that carry a negative electrical charge repel the rays. **Figure 5.5** on page 110 shows the deflection of cathode rays. Thomson knew that opposite charges attract and like charges repel, so he proposed that a cathode ray is a stream of tiny negatively charged

Figure 5.4

In a cathode-ray tube, electrons travel as a ray from the cathode (−) to the anode (+). A television tube is a specialized type of cathode-ray tube.

High voltage

Gas at very low pressure

Metal disk (cathode)

Vacuum pump

Cathode ray (electrons)

Metal disk (anode)

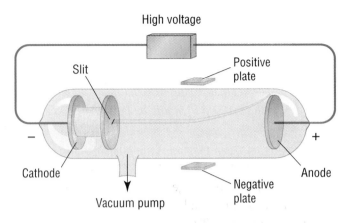

High voltage

Slit

Positive plate

Cathode

Vacuum pump

Negative plate

Anode

Figure 5.5

Cathode rays are deflected by a magnet and attracted by a positively charged plate. This shows that the particles that make up the rays are negatively charged.

particles moving at high speed. Thomson named these particles electrons. Thomson also showed that the production of cathode rays did not depend on the kind of gas in the cathode-ray tube or the type of metal used for the electrodes. He concluded that electrons must be parts of the atoms of all elements. By 1900, Thomson and others had determined that an electron's mass is about 1/2000 the mass of a hydrogen atom.

The American scientist Robert A. Millikan (1868–1953) carried out experiments that allowed him to find the quantity of charge carried by an electron. He also determined the ratio of the charge to the mass of an electron. Millikan used these two values to calculate an accurate value for the mass of the electron. Millikan's values for electron charge and mass, reported in 1916, are very similar to those accepted today. An electron carries exactly one unit of negative charge, and its mass is 1/1840 the mass of a hydrogen atom.

Protons and Neutrons

If cathode rays are electrons given off by atoms, what remains of the atoms that have lost the electrons? For example, after a hydrogen atom (the lightest kind of atom) loses an electron, what is left? You can think through this problem using four simple ideas about matter and electric charges. First, atoms have no net electric charge; they are electrically neutral. (One important piece of evidence for electrical neutrality is that you do not receive an electric shock every time you touch something!) Second, electric charges are carried by particles of matter. Third, electric charges always exist in whole-number multiples of a single basic unit; that is, there are no fractions of charges. Fourth, when a given number of negatively charged particles combines with an equal number of positively charged particles, an electrically neutral particle is formed.

Considering all of this information, it follows that a particle with one unit of positive charge should remain when a typical hydrogen atom loses an electron. Evidence for such a positively charged particle was found in 1886, when E. Goldstein observed a cathode-ray tube and found rays traveling in the direction opposite to that of the cathode rays. He called these rays canal rays and concluded that they were composed of positive particles. Such positively charged subatomic particles are called **protons.** Each proton has a mass about 1840 times that of an electron.

In 1932, the English physicist James Chadwick (1891–1974) confirmed the existence of yet another subatomic particle: the neutron. **Neutrons** are

Table 5.1

Properties of Subatomic Particles				
Particle	Symbol	Relative electrical charge	Relative mass (mass of proton = 1)	Actual mass (g)
Electron	e^-	1−	1/1840	9.11×10^{-28}
Proton	p^+	1+	1	1.67×10^{-24}
Neutron	n^0	0	1	1.67×10^{-24}

subatomic particles with no charge but with a mass nearly equal to that of a proton. Thus the fundamental building blocks of atoms are the electron, the proton, and the neutron. **Table 5.1** summarizes the properties of these subatomic particles.

The Atomic Nucleus

When subatomic particles were discovered, scientists wondered how these particles were put together in an atom. This was a difficult question to answer, given how tiny atoms are. Most scientists thought it likely that the electrons were evenly distributed throughout an atom filled uniformly with positively charged material. In 1911, Ernest Rutherford (1871–1937) and his coworkers at the University of Manchester, England, decided to test this theory of atomic structure. Their test used relatively massive alpha particles, which are helium atoms that have lost their two electrons and have a double positive charge because of the two remaining protons. In the experiment, illustrated in **Figure 5.6,** Rutherford directed a narrow beam of alpha particles at a very thin sheet of gold foil. According to the prevailing theory, the alpha particles should have passed easily through the gold, with only a slight deflection due to the positive charge thought to be spread out in the gold atoms.

Chem ASAP!

Animation 4
Take a look at Rutherford's gold-foil experiment, its results, and its conclusions.

Figure 5.6

(a) To learn more about the nature of the atom, Rutherford and his coworkers aimed a beam of alpha particles at a sheet of gold foil surrounded by a fluorescent screen. They found that most of the particles passed through the foil with no deflection at all. A few particles were greatly deflected. (b) Rutherford concluded that most of the alpha particles pass through the gold foil because the atom is mostly empty space. The mass and positive charge are concentrated in a small region of the atom. Rutherford called this region the nucleus. Particles that approach the nucleus closely are greatly deflected.

Atomic Structure and the Periodic Table **111**

Figure 5.7
If an atom were the size of this stadium, then its nucleus would be about the size of a marble!

To everyone's surprise, the great majority of alpha particles passed straight through the gold atoms, without deflection. Even more surprisingly, a small fraction of the alpha particles bounced off the gold foil at very large angles. Some even bounced straight back toward the source. Rutherford later recollected, "It was about as credible as if you had fired a 15-inch shell at a piece of tissue paper, and it came back and hit you."

Based on the experimental results, Rutherford suggested a new theory of the atom. He proposed that the atom is mostly empty space, thus explaining the lack of deflection of most of the alpha particles. He concluded that all the positive charge and almost all the mass are concentrated in a small region that has enough positive charge to account for the great deflection of some of the alpha particles. He called this region the nucleus. The **nucleus** is the central core of an atom and is composed of protons and neutrons. It is tiny compared with the atom as a whole. See **Figure 5.7.**

MINI LAB

Using Inference: The Black Box

PURPOSE

To determine the shape of a fixed object inside a sealed box without opening the box.

MATERIALS

- box containing a regularly shaped object fixed in place and a loose marble

PROCEDURE

1. Do not open the box.

2. Carefully manipulate the box so that the marble moves around the fixed object.

3. Gather data (clues) that describe the movement of the marble.

4. Sketch a picture of the object in the box, showing its shape, size, and location within the box.

5. Repeat this activity with a different box containing a different object.

ANALYSIS AND CONCLUSIONS

1. Find a classmate who had the same lettered box that you had. Compare your findings and try to come to agreement about the shape and location of the fixed object.

2. What experiment that contributed to a better understanding of the atom does this activity remind you of?

section review 5.2

4. What are the charges and relative masses of the three main subatomic particles?

5. Describe the basic structure of an atom.

6. Describe Thomson's, Millikan's, and Rutherford's contributions to atomic theory. Include their experiments if appropriate.

 ChemASAP! Assessment 5.2 Check your understanding of the important ideas and concepts in Section 5.2.

DISTINGUISHING BETWEEN ATOMS

"*R*ose is a rose is a rose is a rose," wrote the famous author Gertrude Stein. Of course, this is not true when it comes to the color of roses, which can range from the familiar red or white to yellow or even lavender. In all, there are more than 13 000 colorful varieties of roses. Just as roses come in different varieties, a given chemical element can come in different "varieties" called isotopes.

What is an isotope, and how does one isotope of an element differ from another?

Atomic Number

Atoms are composed of electrons, protons, and neutrons. Protons and neutrons make up the small, dense nucleus. Electrons surround the nucleus and occupy most of the volume of the atom. How, then, are atoms of hydrogen, for example, different from atoms of oxygen? Examine **Table 5.2.** Compare the entries for hydrogen and oxygen. You should notice that a hydrogen atom has one proton in its nucleus, but an oxygen atom has eight protons in its nucleus. Elements are different because they contain different numbers of protons.

The **atomic number** of an element is the number of protons in the nucleus of an atom of that element. Because all hydrogen atoms have one proton, the atomic number of hydrogen is 1. Similarly, because all oxygen atoms have eight protons, the atomic number of oxygen is 8. The atomic number identifies an element.

Look again at **Table 5.2.** For each element listed, the number of protons equals the number of electrons. Remember that atoms are electrically neutral. Thus the number of electrons (negatively charged particles) in an atom must equal the number of protons (positively charged particles) in the nucleus. A hydrogen atom has one electron, and an oxygen atom has eight electrons. How is the number of electrons for a neutral atom of a given element related to the atomic number of that element?

Table 5.2

Atoms of the First Ten Elements						
Name	Symbol	Atomic number	Composition of the nucleus		Mass number	Number of electrons
			Protons	Neutrons*		
Hydrogen	H	1	1	0	1	1
Helium	He	2	2	2	4	2
Lithium	Li	3	3	4	7	3
Beryllium	Be	4	4	5	9	4
Boron	B	5	5	6	11	5
Carbon	C	6	6	6	12	6
Nitrogen	N	7	7	7	14	7
Oxygen	O	8	8	8	16	8
Fluorine	F	9	9	10	19	9
Neon	Ne	10	10	10	20	10

* Number of neutrons in the most abundant isotope. Isotopes are introduced later in Section 5.3.

CHEMath

USING POSITIVE AND NEGATIVE NUMBERS

In this chapter you are introduced to protons and electrons, particles with charges of $1+$ and $1-$ respectively. In addition to these charges, you will encounter a variety of positive and negative numbers throughout this course. The table below offers a review of basic mathematical operations related to positive and negative numbers.

BASIC CONCEPTS	EXAMPLE
Positive and negative numbers are used in many applications, including temperature scales. On a number line, the positive numbers are to the right of the *origin* (zero), and the negative numbers are to the left of the origin.	Negative Numbers — Origin ↓ — Positive Numbers $-4 \ -3 \ -2 \ -1 \ 0 \ +1 \ +2 \ +3 \ +4$
The *absolute value* of any number is its distance from the origin. Absolute values are always positive (or zero).	$|3| = $ (absolute value of 3) $= 3$ $|-2| = $ (absolute value of -2) $= 2$
The *opposite* of any number is a number having the same absolute value but the opposite sign.	The opposite of 8 is -8. The opposite of -5 is $-(-5)$, or 5.
ADDITION	
If the two numbers are both positive, add them as usual.	$5 + 16 = 21$
If the two numbers are both negative, add their absolute values and take the opposite.	To find $-6 + (-5)$, note that $6 + 5 = 11$. Therefore, $-6 + (-5) = -11$.
It the two numbers have opposite signs, subtract the smaller absolute value from the larger absolute value. Use the sign of the number with the larger absolute value.	To find $6 + (-3)$: $6 - 3 = 3$, so $6 + (-3) = 3$. To find $6 + (-8)$: $8 - 6 = 2$, so $6 + (-8) = -2$. To find $(-6) + 3$: $6 - 3 = 3$, so $(-6) + 3 = -3$. To find $(-6) + 8$: $8 - 6 = 2$, so $(-6) + 8 = 2$.
SUBTRACTION	
Subtracting any number is the same as adding its opposite.	$12 - 23 = 12 + (-23) = -11$ $6 - (-4) = 6 + 4 = 10$
MULTIPLICATION AND DIVISION	
If the two numbers have the same sign (both positive or both negative), the product or quotient is positive.	$3 \times 5 = 15$ $-24 \div (-8) = 3$
If the two numbers have opposite signs, the product or quotient is negative.	$4 \times (-3) = -12$ $-20 \div 5 = -4$
CHEMISTRY CONNECTION	
An *ion* is a charged atom. The net charge of an ion is (number of protons) $-$ (number of electrons).	If an ion has 3 protons and 5 electrons, its net charge is $3 - 5 = -2$.

Practice Problems

Practice using positive and negative numbers by performing each calculation.

A. $12 + (-4)$

B. $-5 - (-10)$

C. $4 \times (-10)$

D. $-21 \div (-7)$

E. $-36 + 17$

F. $8.7 - 11.3$

G. -3.1×0.20

H. $22.5 \div (-3.60)$

I. $-24.8 - (-4.7)$

J. $-5.5 \times (-1.8)$

K. Find the net charge of an ion with 15 protons and 18 electrons.

L. Find the net charge of an ion with 9 protons and 8 electrons.

M. An ion with a charge of $3-$ loses 2 electrons. What is its charge?

N. An ion with a charge of $1+$ gains 3 electrons. What is its charge?

Sample Problem 5-1

The element nitrogen (N) has an atomic number of 7. How many protons and how many electrons are in a neutral nitrogen atom?

1. **ANALYZE** *List the known and the unknowns.*

   Known:
   • atomic number = 7

   Unknowns:
   • number of protons = ?
   • number of electrons = ?

   The atomic number gives the number of protons, which in a neutral atom equals the number of electrons.

   atomic number = number of protons = number of electrons

2. **CALCULATE** *Solve for the unknowns.*

   atomic number = 7 = number of protons
                       = number of electrons

3. **EVALUATE** *Do the results make sense?*

   The relationships have been applied correctly. The seven electrons are needed to balance the seven protons.

Practice Problems

7. How many protons and electrons are in each atom?
   a. fluorine   **c.** calcium
   b. aluminum
8. Complete the table.

Element	Atomic number	Protons	Electrons
K	19	____	19
____	____	____	5
____	16	____	____
____	____	23	____

Mass Number

You know that most of the mass of an atom is concentrated in its nucleus and depends on the number of protons and neutrons. Look again at **Table 5.2** and note the number of protons and neutrons in helium and in carbon. The total number of protons and neutrons in an atom is called the **mass number.** A helium atom has two protons and two neutrons, so its mass number is 4. A carbon atom, which has six protons and six neutrons, has a mass number of 12.

If you know the atomic number and mass number of an atom of any element, you can determine the atom's composition. **Table 5.2** shows that an oxygen atom has an atomic number of 8 and a mass number of 16. Because the atomic number equals the number of protons, which equals the number of electrons, an oxygen atom has eight protons and eight electrons. The mass number of oxygen is 16 and is equal to the number of protons plus the number of neutrons. The oxygen atom, then, has eight neutrons, which is the difference between the mass number and the atomic number $(16 - 8 = 8)$. For any atom, the number of neutrons can be determined from the following equation.

Number of neutrons = mass number − atomic number

The composition of any atom can be represented in shorthand notation using atomic number and mass number. **Figure 5.8** on page 116 shows how an atom of gold is represented using this notation. The chemical symbol Au appears with two numbers written to its left. The atomic number is the subscript (a number positioned lower). The mass number is the superscript (a number positioned higher). How many neutrons does this gold (Au) atom have?

197
79 Au

Figure 5.8
Au is the chemical symbol for gold. How many electrons does a gold atom have?

You can also use the mass number and the name of the element to designate atoms. For example, atoms of hydrogen with a mass number of 1 may be designated hydrogen-1. Atoms of gold with a mass number of 197 are designated gold-197.

Sample Problem 5-2

How many protons, electrons, and neutrons are in the following atoms?

	Atomic number	Mass number
a. Beryllium (Be)	4	9
b. Neon (Ne)	10	20
c. Sodium (Na)	11	23

1. **ANALYZE** *List the knowns and the unknowns.*

Knowns:
• For each atom, the atomic number and mass number are known.

Unknowns:
• number of protons = ?
• number of electrons = ?
• number of neutrons = ?

Use the definitions of atomic number and mass number to calculate the numbers of protons, electrons, and neutrons.

2. **CALCULATE** *Solve for the unknowns.*
number of electrons = atomic number
a. 4   **b.** 10   **c.** 11
number of protons = atomic number
a. 4   **b.** 10   **c.** 11
number of neutrons = mass number − atomic number
a. 9 − 4 = 5   **b.** 20 − 10 = 10   **c.** 23 − 11 = 12

3. **EVALUATE** *Do the results make sense?*
The relationships among atomic number, number of protons, number of neutrons, number of electrons, and mass number have been applied correctly.

Practice Problems

9. How many neutrons are in each atom?
   a. $^{16}_{8}$O   **c.** $^{108}_{47}$Ag   **e.** $^{207}_{82}$Pb
   b. $^{32}_{16}$S   **d.** $^{80}_{35}$Br

10. Use **Table 5.2** and **Figure 5.8** to express the composition of each atom in shorthand form.
    a. carbon-12
    b. fluorine-19
    c. beryllium-9

11. For each atom in Problem 9, identify the number of electrons.

Chem ASAP!

Problem-Solving 9
Solve Problem 9 with the help of an interactive guided tutorial.

Isotopes

Figure 5.9 shows that there are three different kinds of neon atoms. How do these atoms differ? All have the same number of protons (10) and electrons (10), but they each have different numbers of neutrons. Atoms that have the same number of protons but different numbers of neutrons are called **isotopes.** Because isotopes of an element have different numbers of neutrons, they also have different mass numbers. Despite these differences, isotopes are chemically alike because they have identical numbers of protons and electrons, which are the subatomic particles responsible for

Neon-20
10 protons
10 neutrons
10 electrons

Neon-21
10 protons
11 neutrons
10 electrons

Neon-22
10 protons
12 neutrons
10 electrons

10e⁻

10p⁺
10n⁰

10e⁻

10p⁺
11n⁰

10e⁻

10p⁺
12n⁰

chemical behavior. How does the discovery of isotopes contradict Dalton's atomic theory?

There are three known isotopes of hydrogen. Each isotope of hydrogen has one proton in its nucleus. The most common hydrogen isotope has no neutrons. It has a mass number of 1 and is called hydrogen-1 ($_{1}^{1}$H) or simply hydrogen. The second isotope has one neutron and a mass number of 2. It is called either hydrogen-2 ($_{1}^{2}$H) or deuterium. The third isotope has two neutrons and a mass number of 3. This isotope is called hydrogen-3 ($_{1}^{3}$H) or tritium.

Figure 5.9
Neon-20, neon-21, and neon-22 are three isotopes of neon, a gaseous element used in lighted signs. How are these isotopes different? How are they the same?

Sample Problem 5-3

Two isotopes of carbon are carbon-12 and carbon-13. Write the symbol for each isotope using superscripts and subscripts to represent the mass number and the atomic number.

1. ANALYZE *Plan a problem-solving strategy.*
Knowns:
- two isotopes of carbon:
  carbon-12 and carbon-13

Unknowns:
- each isotope's symbol

Write the symbol for carbon and place the mass number to the left of the symbol as a superscript. Place the atomic number to the left of the symbol as a subscript.

2. SOLVE *Apply the problem-solving strategy.*
Based on **Table 5.2,** the symbol for carbon is C and the atomic number is 6. The mass number for each isotope is given by its name. For carbon-12, the symbol is $_{6}^{12}$C. For carbon-13, the symbol is $_{6}^{13}$C.

3. EVALUATE *Do the results make sense?*
The concepts of atomic number and mass number have been applied correctly, and the information is positioned properly next to the chemical symbols.

Practice Problems

12. Three isotopes of oxygen are oxygen-16, oxygen-17, and oxygen-18. Write the complete symbol for each, including the atomic number and mass number.

13. The three isotopes of chromium are chromium-50, chromium-52, and chromium-53. How many neutrons are in each isotope, given that chromium always has an atomic number of 24?

Chem ASAP!
Problem-Solving 13
Solve Problem 13 with the help of an interactive guided tutorial.

Atomic Mass

A glance back at **Table 5.1** on page 111 shows that the actual mass of a proton or a neutron is very small (1.67×10^{-24} g). The mass of an electron is 9.11×10^{-28} g, which is negligible in comparison. Given these values, the mass of even the largest atom is incredibly small. Since the 1920s, it has been possible to determine these tiny masses by using a mass spectrometer. With this instrument, the mass of a fluorine atom was found to be 3.155×10^{-23} g, and the mass of an arsenic atom was found to be 1.244×10^{-22} g. Such data about the actual masses of individual atoms can provide useful information, but, in general, these values are inconveniently small and impractical to work with. Instead, it is more useful to compare the relative masses of atoms using a reference isotope as a standard. The isotope chosen is carbon-12. This isotope of carbon was assigned a mass of exactly 12 atomic mass units. An **atomic mass unit (amu)** is defined as one-twelfth the mass of a carbon-12 atom. Using these units, a helium-4 atom, with a mass of 4.0026 amu, has about one-third the mass of a carbon-12 atom. How many carbon-12 atoms would have about the same mass as a nickel-60 atom?

A carbon-12 atom has six protons and six neutrons in its nucleus, and its mass is set as 12 amu. The twelve protons and neutrons account for nearly all of this mass. Therefore the mass of a single proton or a single neutron is about one-twelfth of 12 amu, or about 1 amu. Because the mass of any single atom depends mainly on the number of protons and neutrons in the nucleus of the atom, you might predict that the atomic mass of an element should be a whole number. However, that is not usually the case. For example, the atomic mass of chlorine (Cl) is 35.453 amu. How can such an atomic mass be explained? The explanation involves the relative abundance of the naturally occurring isotopes of the element.

In nature, most elements occur as a mixture of two or more isotopes. Each isotope of an element has a fixed mass and a natural percent abundance. Consider the three isotopes of hydrogen discussed earlier in this section. According to **Table 5.3**, almost all naturally occurring hydrogen (99.985%) is hydrogen-1. The other two isotopes are present in trace amounts. Notice that

Figure 5.10

Chlorine is a reactive element used to disinfect swimming pools. It is made up of two isotopes: chlorine-35 and chlorine-37. Because there is more chlorine-35 than chlorine-37, the atomic mass of chlorine, 35.453 amu, is closer to 35 than to 37; it is a weighted average.

Ratio of chlorine atoms in natural abundance: three $_{17}^{35}Cl$ to one $_{17}^{37}Cl$

$_{17}^{35}Cl$ $_{17}^{35}Cl$ $_{17}^{35}Cl$ $_{17}^{37}Cl$

$17p^+$ $17p^+$ $17p^+$ $17p^+$
$18n^0$ $18n^0$ $18n^0$ $20n^0$

Total number of protons in three $_{17}^{35}Cl$ atoms and one $_{17}^{37}Cl$ atom

$(17 + 17 + 17 + 17)$

Total number of neutrons in three $_{17}^{35}Cl$ atoms and one $_{17}^{37}Cl$ atom

$(18 + 18 + 18 + 20)$

$$\frac{68 + 74}{4} = 35.5 \text{ amu}$$

Weighted Average Mass of a Chlorine Atom

Table 5.3

Natural Percent Abundance of Stable Isotopes of Some Elements				
Name	Symbol	Natural percent abundance	Mass (amu)	"Average" atomic mass
Hydrogen	$^{1}_{1}H$	99.985	1.0078	
	$^{2}_{1}H$	0.015	2.0141	1.0079
	$^{3}_{1}H$	negligible	3.0160	
Helium	$^{3}_{2}He$	0.0001	3.0160	4.0026
	$^{4}_{2}He$	99.9999	4.0026	
Carbon	$^{12}_{6}C$	98.89	12.000	12.011
	$^{13}_{6}C$	1.11	13.003	
Nitrogen	$^{14}_{7}N$	99.63	14.003	14.007
	$^{15}_{7}N$	0.37	15.000	
Oxygen	$^{16}_{8}O$	99.759	15.995	
	$^{17}_{8}O$	0.037	16.995	15.999
	$^{18}_{8}O$	0.204	17.999	
Sulfur	$^{32}_{16}S$	95.002	31.972	
	$^{33}_{16}S$	0.76	32.971	32.06
	$^{34}_{16}S$	4.22	33.967	
	$^{36}_{16}S$	0.014	35.967	
Chlorine	$^{35}_{17}Cl$	75.77	34.969	35.453
	$^{37}_{17}Cl$	24.23	36.966	
Zinc	$^{64}_{30}Zn$	48.89	63.929	
	$^{66}_{30}Zn$	27.81	65.926	
	$^{67}_{30}Zn$	4.11	66.927	65.38
	$^{68}_{30}Zn$	18.57	67.925	
	$^{70}_{30}Zn$	0.62	69.925	

HUMANITIES

Philosophy of Science

Modern philosophers search for wisdom in many areas of human life, such as medicine, the arts, and the sciences. Today's philosophers of science are primarily concerned with the critical analysis of scientific concepts and the ways in which these concepts are expressed. These philosophers analyze such concepts as number, space, force, and organism. The search for wisdom leads philosophers of science to debate questions that textbooks may lead you to believe are settled. For example, is the modern scientific method the only correct way to examine and explain the natural world? Or is there a better way, as yet unknown? In spite of the successes of the scientific method in explaining nature, philosophers of science are still studying such questions. These studies could greatly affect science if an improved scientific method were suggested. For this reason, philosophical questions and answers about the methods and concepts of science could be an important aid to scientific progress.

the atomic mass of hydrogen in **Table 5.3** (1.0079 amu) is very close to the mass of hydrogen-1 (1.0078 amu). The slight difference takes into account the larger masses, but smaller amounts, of the other two isotopes of hydrogen.

Now consider the two stable isotopes of chlorine listed in **Table 5.3**: chlorine-35 and chlorine-37. If you calculate the arithmetic mean of these two masses, you would get an average atomic mass of 35.968 amu ((34.969 amu + 36.966 amu)/2). A quick comparison with the value in **Table 5.3** indicates that 35.968 amu is higher than the actual value. To explain this, you need to know the natural percent abundance of the isotopes of chlorine. Chlorine-35 accounts for 75% of the naturally occurring chlorine atoms; chlorine-37 accounts for only 25%. See **Figure 5.10**.

The **atomic mass** of an element is a weighted average mass of the atoms in a naturally occurring sample of the element. A weighted average mass reflects both the mass and the relative abundance of the isotopes as they occur in nature.

Sample Problem 5-4

Which isotope of copper is more abundant: copper-63 or copper-65? (The atomic mass of copper is 63.546 amu.)

1. **ANALYZE Plan a problem-solving strategy.**
   Knowns:
   • isotopes of copper: copper-63 and copper-65
   • atomic mass of copper = 63.546 amu

   Unknown:
   • isotope that is more abundant

   This problem can be solved without any calculations by analyzing the atomic mass of copper relative to the masses of the two isotopes.

2. **SOLVE Apply the problem-solving strategy.**
   The atomic mass of 63.546 amu is closer to 63 than to 65. Thus, because the atomic mass is a weighted average of the isotopes, copper-63 must be more abundant than copper-65.

3. **EVALUATE Does the result make sense?**
   The relative abundance is reflected in the atomic mass, so it is reasonable that copper-63 must be more abundant.

Practice Problems

14. Boron has two isotopes: boron-10 and boron-11. Which is more abundant, given that the atomic mass of boron is 10.81?
15. There are three isotopes of silicon; they have mass numbers of 28, 29, and 30. The atomic mass of silicon is 28.086 amu. Comment on the relative abundance of these three isotopes.

Now that you know that the atomic mass of an element is a weighted average of the masses of its isotopes, you can calculate atomic mass based on relative abundance. To do this, you must know three values:

• the number of stable isotopes of the element,
• the mass of each isotope, and
• the natural percent abundance of each isotope.

Table 5.3 on the previous page shows these values for a few elements. For other elements, you can use standard chemistry reference books. Once you have these values for an element, multiply the atomic mass of each isotope by its abundance, expressed as a decimal, then add the results. Sample Problem 5-5 illustrates this method.

Sample Problem 5-5

Element X has two natural isotopes. The isotope with a mass of 10.012 amu (^{10}X) has a relative abundance of 19.91%. The isotope with a mass of 11.009 amu (^{11}X) has a relative abundance of 80.09%. Calculate the atomic mass of this element.

Sample Problem 5-5 (cont.)

1. ANALYZE *List the knowns and the unknown.*

Knowns: *Unknown:*
- isotope ^{10}X: • atomic mass of element X = ?
  mass = 10.012 amu
  relative abundance = 19.91% = 0.1991
- isotope ^{11}X:
  mass = 11.009 amu
  relative abundance = 80.09% = 0.8009

The mass each isotope contributes to the element's atomic mass can be calculated by multiplying the isotope's mass by its relative abundance. The atomic mass of the element is the sum of these contributions.

2. CALCULATE *Solve for the unknown.*

for ^{10}X:	10.012 amu × 0.1991 = 1.993 amu
for ^{11}X:	11.009 amu × 0.8009 = 8.817 amu
for element X:	atomic mass = 10.810 amu

3. EVALUATE *Does the result make sense?*

The calculated value is closer to the mass of the more abundant isotope, as would be expected.

Practice Problems

16. The element copper has naturally occurring isotopes with mass numbers of 63 and 65. The relative abundance and atomic masses are 69.2% for mass = 62.93 amu, and 30.8% for mass = 64.93 amu. Calculate the average atomic mass of copper.

17. Calculate the atomic mass of bromine. The two isotopes of bromine have atomic masses and relative abundance of 78.92 amu (50.69%) and 80.92 amu (49.31%).

Chem ASAP!

Problem-Solving 17
Solve Problem 17 with the help of an interactive guided tutorial.

section 5.3 review

18. Explain how the atomic number of an element identifies the element.

19. How can atomic number and mass number be used to find the numbers of protons, electrons, and neutrons?

20. An atom is identified as platinum-195.

    a. What does the number represent?

    b. Symbolize this atom using superscripts and subscripts.

21. How are isotopes of the same element alike? How are they different?

22. Determine the number of protons, electrons, and neutrons in each of the five isotopes of zinc.

23. List the number of protons, neutrons, and electrons in each pair of isotopes.

    a. $^{6}_{3}Li$, $^{7}_{3}Li$ **b.** $^{42}_{20}Ca$, $^{44}_{20}Ca$ **c.** $^{78}_{34}Se$, $^{80}_{34}Se$

24. The atomic masses of elements are generally not whole numbers. Explain why.

25. How is the atomic mass of an element calculated from isotope data?

26. Using the data for nitrogen listed in **Table 5.3,** calculate the average atomic mass of nitrogen. Show your work.

 Chem ASAP! Assessment 5.3 Check your understanding of the important ideas and concepts in Section 5.3.

portfolio project

An instrument called a mass spectrometer can be used to determine the masses and relative abundances of isotopes. Find out how this instrument works and make a poster to summarize your findings.

THE ATOMIC MASS OF CANDIUM

PURPOSE

To analyze the isotopes of candium and to calculate its atomic mass.

MATERIALS

- sample of candium
- balance
- pencil
- paper

PROCEDURE

Obtain a sample of candium. Separate the three isotopes (m&m's®, Skittles®, and Reese's Pieces®) and measure the mass of each isotope. Count the numbers of m&m's®, Skittles®, and Reese's Pieces®. Make a table similar to Figure A to record your measured and calculated data.

	m&m's®	Skittles®	Reese's Pieces®	Totals
Total mass (grams)				
Number				
Average mass (grams)				
Percent abundance				
Relative abundance				
Relative mass				

Figure A

ANALYSIS

Using the experimental data, record the answers to the following questions below your data table.

1. Calculate the average mass of each isotope by dividing its total mass by the number of particles of that isotope.

2. Calculate the percent abundance of each isotope by dividing its number of particles by the total number of particles and multiplying by 100.

3. Calculate the relative abundance of each isotope by dividing the percent abundance from Step 2 by 100.

4. Calculate the relative mass of each isotope by multiplying its relative abundance from Step 3 by its average mass.

5. Calculate the average mass of all candium particles by adding the relative masses. This average mass is the atomic mass of candium.

6. Explain the difference between percent abundance and relative abundance. What is the result when you total the individual percent abundances? The individual relative abundances?

7. The percent abundance of each kind of candy tells you how many of each kind of candy there are in every 100 particles. What does relative abundance tell you?

8. Compare the total values for rows 3 and 6 in the table. Explain why the totals differ and why the value in row 6 best represents atomic mass.

9. Explain any differences between the atomic mass of your candium sample and that of your neighbor. Explain why the difference would be smaller if larger samples were used.

YOU'RE THE CHEMIST

The following small-scale activities allow you to develop your own procedures and analyze the results.

1. **Analyze It!** Determine the atomic mass of a second sample of candium. How does it compare with the first? Suggest reasons for any differences between the samples.

2. **Design It!** Design and test methods to produce identical samples of candium. Try measuring mass or volume as a means of counting. Test these methods by counting each kind of candy in each sample you produce. Which method of sampling gives the most consistent results?

THE PERIODIC TABLE: ORGANIZING THE ELEMENTS

*H*ow do you know where to find products in the supermarket? From your experience, you probably know that different types of products are arranged according to similar characteristics in aisles or sections of aisles. Such a classification structure makes finding and comparing products easy. **Is there a way of arranging more than 100 known elements?**

objectives

▶ Describe the origin of the periodic table

▶ Identify the position of groups, periods, and the transition metals in the periodic table

key terms

▶ periodic table
▶ periods
▶ periodic law
▶ group
▶ representative elements
▶ metals
▶ alkali metals
▶ alkaline earth metals
▶ transition metals
▶ inner transition metals
▶ nonmetals
▶ halogens
▶ noble gases
▶ metalloids

Development of the Periodic Table

About 70 elements had been discovered by the mid-1800s, but until the work of the Russian chemist Dmitri Mendeleev (1834–1907), no one had found a way to relate the elements in a systematic, logical way. Mendeleev listed the elements in columns in order of increasing atomic mass. He then arranged the columns so that the elements with the most similar properties were side by side. He thus constructed the first **periodic table,** an arrangement of the elements according to similarities in their properties. As you can see in **Figure 5.11,** Mendeleev left blank spaces in the table because there were no known elements with the appropriate properties and masses.

Mendeleev and others were able to predict the physical and chemical properties of the missing elements. Eventually these elements were discovered and were found to have properties similar to those predicted.

In 1913, Henry Moseley (1887–1915), a British physicist, determined the atomic number of the atoms of the elements. Moseley arranged the elements in a table by order of atomic number instead of atomic mass. That is the way the periodic table is arranged today.

Figure 5.11
A version of Dmitri Mendeleev's periodic table is shown here.

				Ti = 50	Zr = 90	? = 180.
				V = 51	Nb = 94	Ta = 182.
				Cr = 52	Mo = 96	W = 186.
				Mn = 55	Rh = 104,4	Pt = 197,4
				Fe = 56	Ru = 104,4	Ir = 198.
			Ni = Co = 59	Pl = 106,6	Os = 199
H = 1				Cu = 63,4	Ag = 108	Hg = 200
	Be = 9,4	Mg = 24	Zn = 65,2	Cd = 112	
	B = 11	Al = 27,4	? = 68	Ur = 116	Au = 197?
	C = 12	Si = 28	? = 70	Sn = 118	
	N = 14	P = 31	As = 75	Sb = 122	Bi = 210
	O = 16	S = 32	Se = 79,4	Te = 128?	
	F = 19	Cl = 35,5	Br = 80	I = 127	
Li = 7	Na = 23	K = 39	Rb = 85,4	Cs = 133	Tl = 204
		Ca = 40	Sr = 87,6	Ba = 137	Pb = 207.
		? = 45	Ce = 92		
		?Er = 56	La = 94		
		?Yt = 60	Di = 95		
		?In =75,6	Th = 118?		

Figure 5.12

Elements are arranged in the modern periodic table in order of atomic number. The symbols are color coded according to the natural state of the elements: red for gases, black for solids, green for liquids (mercury and bromine), and white for elements that do not occur naturally.

The Modern Periodic Table

The most commonly used form of the modern periodic table, sometimes called the long form, is shown in **Figure 5.12.** Each element is identified by its symbol placed in a square. The atomic number of the element is shown centered above the symbol. The atomic mass and the name of the element are shown below the symbol. Notice that the elements are listed in order of increasing atomic number, from left to right and from top to bottom. Hydrogen (H), the lightest element, is in the top left corner. Helium (He), atomic number 2, is at the top right. Lithium (Li), atomic number 3, is at the left end of the second row.

The horizontal rows of the periodic table are called **periods.** There are seven periods. The number of elements per period ranges from 2 (hydrogen and helium) in period 1, to 32 in period 6. The properties of the elements within a period change as you move across it from element to element. The pattern of properties within a period repeats, however, when you move from one period to the next. This gives rise to the **periodic law:** When the elements are arranged in order of increasing atomic number, there is a periodic repetition of their physical and chemical properties. The arrangement of the elements into periods has an important consequence. Elements that have similar chemical and physical properties end up in the same column in the periodic table.

Each vertical column of elements in the periodic table is called a **group,** or family. The elements in any group of the periodic table have similar physical and chemical properties. Each group is identified by a number and the letter A or B. Look at the first column on the left. It includes the elements H, Li, Na, K, Rb, Cs, and Fr. This first column is designated Group 1A. Except for hydrogen, all of the Group 1A elements react vigorously, even explosively, with water. The next column to the right, Group 2A, starts with Be. Next comes Group 3A, toward the right of the table. The Group A elements are made up of Group 1A through Group 7A and Group 0 (the group at the far right). Group A elements are called the **representative elements** because they exhibit a wide range of both physical and chemical properties.

The representative elements can be divided into three broad classes. The first are **metals,** which have a high electrical conductivity and a high luster when clean. They are ductile (able to be drawn into wires) and malleable (able to be beaten into thin sheets). Except for hydrogen, the representative elements on the left side of the periodic table are metals. The Group 1A elements are called the **alkali metals,** and the Group 2A elements are called the **alkaline earth metals.** Most of the remaining elements that are not Group A elements are also metals. These include the **transition metals** and the **inner transition metals,** which together make up the Group B elements. Copper, silver, gold, and iron are familiar transition metals. The inner transition metals, which appear below the main body of the periodic table, are also called the rare-earth elements. Approximately 80% of all of the elements are metals. With one exception, all metals are solids at room temperature. **Figure 5.14** on page 126 shows the exception to this rule. What is the name, symbol, and physical state of this element?

Sodium emits bright yellow light during a flame test.

Potassium reacts violently with water.

Figure 5.13
The elements in the periodic table vary greatly in their properties.

Chromium, the principal element in chrome plating, resists corrosion.

Iodine exists as a solid and a vapor at 25°C.

Because of its malleability, silver is easily stamped into coins.

Figure 5.14

Mercury, a transition metal, is the only metallic element that is a liquid at room temperature. It is used in thermometers and barometers and as the electrical contact in a thermostat.

Figure 5.15

Sulfur is a low-melting point nonmetallic element that occurs as a crystalline solid or in the amorphous (formless) state. It is often mined through a process involving the pumping of hot water, which melts the sulfur. Sulfur is used primarily in the manufacture of sulfuric acid.

The nonmetals occupy the upper-right corner of the periodic table. **Nonmetals** are elements that are generally nonlustrous and that are generally poor conductors of electricity. Some of these elements, such as oxygen and chlorine, are gases at room temperature. Others, such as sulfur, shown in **Figure 5.15,** are brittle solids. One element, bromine, is a fuming dark-red liquid at room temperature. Two groups of nonmetals are given special names. The nonmetals of Group 7A are called the **halogens,** which include chlorine and bromine. The nonmetals of Group 0 are known as the **noble gases,** which are sometimes called the inert gases because they undergo few chemical reactions. The noble gas neon is used to fill the glass tubes of neon lights.

Notice the heavy stair-step line in **Figure 5.12.** This line divides the metals from the nonmetals. Most of the elements that border this line are **metalloids,** elements with properties that are intermediate between those of metals and nonmetals. Silicon and germanium are two important metalloids that are used in the manufacture of computer chips and solar cells.

Without the help of the periodic table, it would be quite difficult to learn and remember the chemical and physical properties of the more than 100 elements. Instead of memorizing their properties separately, you need only learn the general behavior and trends within the major groups. This gives you a useful working knowledge of the properties of most elements.

section 5.4 review

27. Describe how the periodic table was developed.

28. What criteria did Mendeleev use to construct his periodic table of the elements?

29. Relate group, period, and transition metals to the periodic table.

30. Identify each element as a metal, metalloid, or nonmetal.

   a. gold   **b.** silicon   **c.** manganese   **d.** sulfur   **e.** barium

31. Which of the elements listed in the preceding question are representative elements?

32. Name two elements that have properties similar to those of the element calcium.

 ChemASAP! Assessment 5.4 Check your understanding of the important ideas and concepts in Section 5.4.

ASK AN ARTIFACT FOR A DATE!

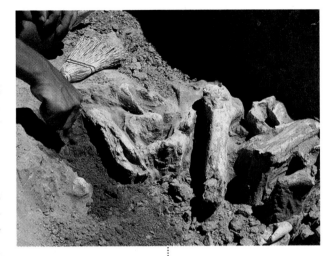

A human skeleton is discovered when construction begins on a new school. Is it the remains of someone who died within the past 200 years? Perhaps it is the remains of an early Native American who lived in the area 9000 years ago. An archaeologist is called to the site. She examines the skeleton and finds evidence that it may be very old. To determine its age, she uses a technique called radiometric dating.

Radiometric dating is based on two important facts: each element exists as more than one isotope, and some of these isotopes undergo radioactive decay. As you know, isotopes are atoms with the same number of protons and electrons but with different numbers of neutrons. Isotopes with an unstable ratio of protons and neutrons are radioactive. An atom of a radioactive isotope will emit radiation, changing into an atom of a different element. Although it is impossible to predict when a single atom of a radioactive isotope will decay, a large group of such atoms has a regular and predictable rate of decay. The amount of time it takes for half the atoms in a sample of a certain isotope to decay is called the half-life of that isotope.

When scientists want to date an artifact that was once part of a living organism, they often use a kind of radiometric dating called carbon-14 ($^{14}_{6}C$) dating. This method involves measuring the amount of the isotope carbon-14 in the artifact.

How is the amount of carbon-14 in an artifact related to its age? Carbon-14 is a radioactive isotope of carbon, with a half-life of 5730 years. It is present in small amounts in the environment, along with the two stable and more common isotopes of carbon, $^{12}_{6}C$ and $^{13}_{6}C$. The ratio of $^{14}_{6}C$ to the other carbon isotopes is relatively constant throughout the environment because $^{14}_{6}C$ is produced at a constant rate in the upper atmosphere by high-energy cosmic rays and is spread evenly throughout the biosphere. Living organisms all have the same ratio of $^{14}_{6}C$ to stable carbon in their bodies because they are constantly exchanging carbon with the environment.

When an organism dies, however, it stops exchanging carbon with the environment. The radioactive $^{14}_{6}C$ atoms in the remains of the organism decay at the rate characteristic of $^{14}_{6}C$ without being replaced by new ones. Therefore, the ratio of $^{14}_{6}C$ to stable carbon in an organism begins to change in a regular, predictable way at the moment the organism dies.

To determine the age of once-living remains, a scientist can find the ratio of $^{14}_{6}C$ to stable carbon in the remains and compare it with the ratio that should have been in the organism when it was alive. If a once-living artifact contains half the $^{14}_{6}C$ of a living organism, for example, it must be about 5730 years old—the amount of time equal to one half-life of carbon-14.

Carbon-14 dating can give accurate ages of artifacts that are up to about 40 000 years old. When objects are much older than that, the amount of $^{14}_{6}C$ they contain is so small that the use of carbon-14 dating is impractical.

> Carbon-14 dating can give accurate ages of artifacts that are up to about 40 000 years old.

CHEMISTRY IN CAREERS

☆☆☆☆☆☆☆☆☆☆☆☆☆☆☆☆☆☆☆☆☆☆

TAKE IT TO THE NET
Find out more about career opportunities:

www.phschool.com

CHEMICAL SPECIALIST
Local food service distributor seeks responsible self-motivated individ-

ARCHAEOLOGIST
Use carbon-14 dating and other chemical techniques to estimate the age and composition of artifacts.
See page 870.

CHEMIST FEDE

Take It to the NET
For interactive study and
review, go to www.phschool.com

KEY TERMS

- alkali metal *p. 125*
- alkaline earth metal *p. 125*
- atom *p. 108*
- atomic mass *p. 120*
- atomic mass unit (amu) *p. 118*
- atomic number *p. 113*
- cathode ray *p. 109*
- Dalton's atomic theory *p. 107*
- electron *p. 109*

- group *p. 124*
- halogen *p. 126*
- inner transition metal *p. 125*
- isotope *p. 116*
- mass number *p. 115*
- metal *p. 125*
- metalloid *p. 126*
- neutron *p. 110*
- noble gas *p. 126*

- nonmetal *p. 126*
- nucleus *p. 112*
- period *p. 124*
- periodic law *p. 124*
- periodic table *p. 123*
- proton *p. 110*
- representative element *p. 125*
- transition metal *p. 125*

KEY EQUATIONS AND RELATIONSHIPS

- atomic number = number of protons = number of electrons
- number of neutrons = mass number − atomic number

CONCEPT SUMMARY

5.1 Atoms
- Elements are composed of atoms, which are the basic building blocks of matter.
- The atoms of a given element are different from the atoms of all other elements.

5.2 Structure of the Nuclear Atom
- Atoms contain positively charged protons, negatively charged electrons, and electrically neutral neutrons.
- The nucleus of an atom is composed of protons and neutrons. The electrons surround the nucleus and occupy most of the volume of the atom.

5.3 Distinguishing Between Atoms
- The number of protons in an atom's nucleus is the atomic number of that element.
- Because atoms are electrically neutral, an atom has the same number of protons and electrons.

- The sum of the number of protons and number of neutrons is the mass number of an atom.
- Atoms with the same number of protons but different numbers of neutrons are called isotopes.
- The atomic mass of an element is expressed in atomic mass units (amu).
- The atomic mass of an element is a weighted average of all the naturally occurring isotopes of that element.

5.4 The Periodic Table: Organizing the Elements
- In the periodic table, the elements are organized into groups (vertical columns) and periods (horizontal rows) in order of increasing atomic number.
- Elements that have similar chemical properties are in the same group.
- Elements in the periodic table are classified as metals, nonmetals, or metalloids.

CHAPTER CONCEPT MAP

Use these terms to construct a concept map that organizes the main ideas of this chapter.

 Chem ASAP! Concept Map 5
Create your Concept Map using the computer.

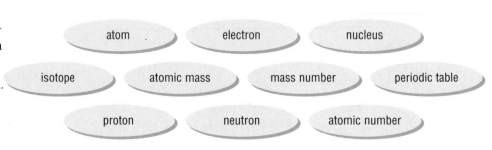

atom   electron   nucleus

isotope   atomic mass   mass number   periodic table

proton   neutron   atomic number

CONCEPT PRACTICE

33. With which of these statements would John Dalton have agreed in the early 1800s? For each, explain why or why not? *5.1*
   a. Atoms are the smallest particles of matter.
   b. The mass of an iron atom is different from the mass of a copper atom.
   c. Every atom of silver is identical to every other atom of silver.
   d. A compound is composed of atoms of two or more different elements.

34. What experimental evidence did Thomson have for each statement? *5.2*
   a. Electrons have a negative charge.
   b. Atoms of all elements contain electrons.

35. Would you expect two electrons to attract or repel each other? *5.2*

36. How did the results of Rutherford's gold foil experiment differ from his expectations? *5.2*

37. What is the charge, positive or negative, of the nucleus of every atom? *5.2*

38. Why is an atom electrically neutral? *5.3*

39. What does the atomic number of each atom represent? *5.3*

40. How many protons are in the nuclei of the following atoms? *5.3*
   a. phosphorus   **d.** cadmium
   b. molybdenum   **e.** chromium
   c. aluminum   **f.** lead

41. What is the difference between the mass number and the atomic number of an atom? *5.3*

42. Complete this table. *5.3*

Atomic number	Mass number	Number of protons	Number of neutrons	Number of electrons	Symbol of element
9			10		
		14	15		
		47	25		
	55	25			

43. Name two ways that isotopes of an element differ. *5.3*

44. How can there be more than 1000 different atoms when there are only about 100 different elements? *5.3*

45. What data must you know about the isotopes of an element to calculate the atomic mass of the element? *5.3*

46. What is the atomic mass of an element? *5.3*

47. Look up the word *periodic* in the dictionary. Propose a reason for the naming of the periodic table. *5.4*

48. How did Moseley's arrangement of the elements differ from that of Mendeleev? *5.4*

49. Give the symbol of each element. *5.4*
   a. the nonmetal in Group 4A
   b. the inner transition metal with the lowest atomic number
   c. all of the nonmetals for which the atomic number is a multiple of five
   d. the two elements that are liquid at room temperature
   e. the metal in Group 5A

CONCEPT MASTERY

50. Compare the relative size and relative density of an atom with its nucleus.

51. Imagine you are standing on the top of a boron-11 nucleus. Describe the numbers and kinds of subatomic particles you would see looking down into the nucleus, and those you would see looking out from the nucleus.

52. What parts of Dalton's atomic theory no longer agree with the current picture of the atom?

53. The four isotopes of lead are shown below, each with its percent by mass abundance and the composition of its nucleus. Using these data, calculate the approximate atomic mass of lead.

82p 122n	82p 124n	82p 125n	82p 126n
1.37%	26.26%	20.82%	51.55%

54. Dalton's atomic theory was not correct in every detail. Should this be taken as a criticism of Dalton as a scientist? Explain.

55. Why are atoms considered the basic building blocks of matter even though smaller particles, such as protons and electrons, exist?

56. The following table shows some of the data collected by Rutherford and his colleagues during their gold foil experiment.

Angle of deflection (degrees)	Number of deflections
5	8 289 000
10	502 570
15	120 570
30	7800
45	1435
60	477
75	211
>105	198

a. What percentage of the alpha particle deflections were 5° or less?

b. What percentage of the deflections were 15° or less?

c. What percentage of the deflections were 60° or greater?

CRITICAL THINKING

57. Choose the term that best completes the second relationship.

a. female:male   proton:_____
(1) atom   (3) electron
(2) neutron   (4) quark

b. cow:horse   neutron:_____
(1) proton   (3) atom
(2) nucleus   (4) quark

c. atom:proton   house:_____
(1) school   (3) planet
(2) nucleus   (4) brick

58. How could you modify Rutherford's experimental procedure to determine the relative sizes of different nuclei?

59. Rutherford's atomic theory proposed a dense nucleus surrounded by very small electrons. This implies that atoms are composed mainly of empty space. If all matter is mainly empty space, why is it impossible to walk through walls or pass your hand through your desk?

60. This chapter illustrates the scientific method in action. What happens when new experimental results cannot be explained by the existing theory?

61. Do you think there are more elements left to be discovered? Explain your answer.

CUMULATIVE REVIEW

62. Oxygen and hydrogen react explosively to form water. In one reaction, 6 g of hydrogen combines with oxygen to form 54 g of water. How much oxygen was used?

63. How many significant figures are in each measurement?
a. 4.607 mg   c. 0.001 50 mL
b. 4.35×10^4 km   d. 60.09 kg

64. The law of conservation of mass was introduced in Chapter 2. Use Dalton's atomic theory to explain this law.

65. An aquarium measures 55.0 cm × 1.10 m × 80.0 cm. How many cm^3 of water will this aquarium hold?

66. What is the mass of 5.42 cm^3 of platinum? The density of platinum is 22.5 g/cm^3.

67. Classify each as an element, a compound, or a mixture.
a. sulfur   d. orange
b. salad oil e. cardboard
c. newspaper f. apple juice

CONCEPT CHALLENGE

68. Diamond and graphite are both composed of carbon atoms. The density of diamond is 3.52 g/cm^3. The density of graphite is 2.25 g/cm^3. In 1955, scientists successfully made diamond from graphite. Using the relative densities, imagine what happens at the atomic level when this change occurs. Then suggest how this synthesis may have been accomplished.

69. Lithium has two naturally occurring isotopes. Lithium-6 has an atomic mass of 6.015 amu; lithium-7 has an atomic mass of 7.016 amu. The atomic mass of lithium is 6.941 amu. What is the percentage of naturally occurring lithium-7?

70. When the masses of the particles that make up an atom are added together, the sum is always larger than the actual mass of the atom. The missing mass, called the mass defect, represents the matter converted into energy when the nucleus was formed from its component protons and neutrons. Calculate the mass defect of a chlorine-35 atom by using the data in **Table 5.1.** The actual mass of a chlorine-35 atom is 5.81×10^{-23} g.

Select the choice that best answers each question or completes each statement.

1. An atom composed of 16 protons, 16 electrons, and 16 neutrons is
   a. $^{48}_{16}S$
   b. $^{16}_{32}Ge$
   c. $^{32}_{16}S$
   d. $^{16}_{32}S$.

2. Which element is *not* a transition metal?
   a. aluminum
   b. silver
   c. iron
   d. zirconium

3. Which of these subatomic particle descriptions is *incorrect*?
   a. proton: positive charge, in nucleus, mass of ≈ 1 amu
   b. electron: negative charge, mass of ≈ 0 amu, in nucleus
   c. neutron: mass of ≈ 1 amu, no charge

4. Which of these statements about the periodic table are correct?
   I. Elements are arranged in order of increasing atomic mass.
   II. A period is a horizontal row.
   III. Nonmetals are located on the right side of the table.
   a. I only
   b. I and II only
   c. I, II, and III
   d. I and III only
   e. II and III only

5. Thallium has two isotopes, thallium-203 and thallium-205. Thallium's atomic number is 81 and its atomic mass is 204.38 amu. Which statement about the thallium isotopes is true?
   a. There is more thallium-203 in nature.
   b. Atoms of both isotopes have 81 protons.
   c. Thallium-205 atoms have fewer neutrons.
   d. The most common atom of thallium has a mass of 204.38 amu.

Use the art to answer question 6.

6. How many nitrogen-14 atoms (^{14}N) would you need to place on the right pan to balance the three calcium-42 atoms (^{42}Ca) on the left pan of the "atomic balance" below? Describe the method you used to determine your answer, including any calculations.

Use the diagram below to answer questions 7–9. The diagram shows gold atoms being bombarded with fast-moving alpha particles.

7. The large yellow spheres represent gold atoms. What do the small gray spheres represent?

8. List at least two characteristics of the small gray spheres.

9. Which subatomic particle cannot be found in the area represented by the gray spheres?

For each question there are two statements. Decide whether each statement is true or false. Then decide whether Statement II is a correct explanation for Statement I.

Statement I		Statement II
10. Every aluminum-27 atom has 27 protons and 27 electrons.	BECAUSE	The mass number of aluminum-27 is 27.
11. Isotopes of an element have different atomic masses.	BECAUSE	The nuclei of an element's isotopes contain different numbers of protons.
12. An electron is repelled by a negatively charged particle.	BECAUSE	An electron has a negative charge.
13. The element hydrogen is a metal.	BECAUSE	Hydrogen is on the left in the periodic table.

Chapter 6

CHEMICAL NAMES AND FORMULAS

FEATURES

DISCOVER IT!
Element Name Search

SMALL-SCALE LAB
Names and Formulas of Ionic Compounds

MINI LAB
Making Ionic Compounds

CHEMath
Prefixes and Suffixes

CHEMISTRY SERVING ...
THE CONSUMER
What's in a Name?

CHEMISTRY IN CAREERS
Pharmacist

LINK TO ENVIRONMENTAL AWARENESS
A Toxic Environmental Gas

Stay current with **SCIENCE NEWS**
Find out more about chemical formulas:
www.phschool.com

The first cola formula was made and sold in Waco, Texas.

DISCOVER IT! ELEMENT NAME SEARCH

You need a variety of ingredient labels from items such as breads, cake mixes, baking soda, cereals, soap, shampoo, conditioner, toothpaste, and antacids.

1. Select a variety of ingredient labels from the suggested items or from similar ones.

2. List all the ingredients that you recognize. Do not be discouraged by the many unfamiliar names—there are thousands upon thousands of substances used in everyday products.

3. With the help of a periodic table, make another list of all the ingredient names that contain the name of an element.

Did you find the same element name in more than one product? What element names are on both lists? Did all the ingredients have complex chemical-sounding names? How do the names of element-containing compounds compare with the other names on your list? Return to your list after completing this chapter and identify which are common names and which are systemic names.

INTRODUCTION TO CHEMICAL BONDING

objectives
▶ Distinguish between ionic and molecular compounds
▶ Define cation and anion and relate them to metal and nonmetal

key terms
▶ molecule
▶ molecular compounds
▶ ions
▶ cation
▶ anions
▶ ionic compounds

Globally, there are about 5 million lightning strikes each day during thunderstorms, snowstorms, and dust storms. Lightning is often observed during volcanic eruptions. Lightning strikes have been responsible for loss of life, forest fires, house fires, power outages, and aircraft accidents. A lightning strike is an electrical discharge that usually occurs between the negatively charged bottom of a cloud and the oppositely charged Earth below. Positive and negative charges are important in chemistry. **What role do positive and negative charges play in the formation of ions?**

Molecules and Molecular Compounds

Elements are the building materials of the substances that make up all living and nonliving things. Although there are only about 100 different elements, there are millions of different compounds made from their atoms. When scientists communicate, they must know which compounds they are discussing. Thus, naming compounds is an essential skill in chemistry.

In nature, only the noble gas elements, such as helium and neon, tend to exist as isolated atoms. They are monatomic; that is, they consist of single atoms, as shown in **Figure 6.1.** Many elements found in nature are in the

Figure 6.1

The noble gases, including helium and neon, are monatomic. That means they exist as single atoms. Helium, which is less dense than air, is often used to inflate balloons. The colors produced in what we commonly call neon lights are a result of passing an electric current through one or more noble gases. Neon actually produces an orange-red color. Helium gives a yellowish light, argon shines lavender, krypton produces a whitish light, and xenon gives blue.

Helium (He)

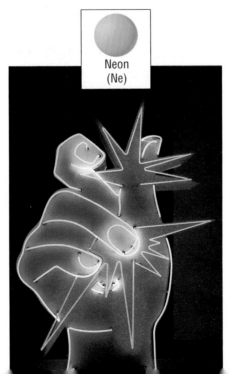

Neon (Ne)

Chemical Names and Formulas **133**

Figure 6.2

The diatomic molecule oxygen and the triatomic molecule ozone are both composed of atoms of oxygen. Ozone is produced during electrical discharges, such as lightning, and is found in a layer of Earth's stratosphere.

Water (H_2O)

Carbon monoxide (CO)

Figure 6.3

Water is a molecular compound with molecules composed of two hydrogen atoms and one oxygen atom. Carbon monoxide is a molecular compound with molecules composed of one carbon atom and one oxygen atom. Most molecular compounds are gases, liquids, or low-melting solids.

form of molecules. A **molecule** is the smallest electrically neutral unit of a substance that still has the properties of the substance. Molecules are made up of two or more atoms that act as a unit, as shown in **Figure 6.2.** For example, the oxygen gas in the air you breathe consists of oxygen molecules that contain two oxygen atoms each. Oxygen is an example of a diatomic molecule. Ozone is another molecular form of oxygen. In Earth's atmosphere, ozone absorbs harmful ultraviolet radiation from the sun. Each molecule of ozone is composed of three oxygen atoms. Therefore, ozone is a triatomic molecule.

Atoms of different elements may combine chemically to form compounds. In many compounds, the atoms combine to form molecules. Compounds composed of molecules are called **molecular compounds.**

Molecular compounds tend to have relatively low melting and boiling points. Many of these compounds thus exist as gases or liquids at room temperature. The molecules in most molecular compounds are composed of the atoms of two or more nonmetals. For example, one atom of carbon can combine with one atom of oxygen to produce one molecule of a compound known as carbon monoxide. Carbon monoxide is a poisonous gas produced by the burning of gasoline in internal-combustion engines. Two hydrogen atoms can combine with one oxygen atom to produce one molecule of the compound water. The molecules of a given molecular compound are all the same. However, they differ from the molecules of all other molecular compounds. As you can see in **Figure 6.3,** all carbon monoxide molecules are identical, but carbon monoxide molecules are different from water molecules. Do the compounds carbon monoxide and water consist of diatomic or triatomic molecules?

Ions and Ionic Compounds

Not all compounds are molecular. Many compounds are composed of particles called ions. **Ions** are atoms or groups of atoms that have a positive or negative charge. An ion forms when an atom or group of atoms loses or gains electrons. Recall that an atom is electrically neutral because it has equal numbers of protons and electrons. For example, an atom of sodium (Na) has 11 positively charged protons and 11 negatively charged electrons. The net charge on a sodium atom is zero $[11 + (-11) = 0]$. In forming a chemical compound, however, an atom of sodium tends to lose one of its electrons. The number of electrons in the atom is then no longer equal to the number of protons. The atom of sodium becomes an ion. Because there are more positive charges (protons) than negative charges (electrons), the sodium ion has a positive charge.

Atoms of the metallic elements, such as sodium, tend to form ions by losing one or more electrons. Such ions are called cations. A **cation** is any atom or group of atoms that has a positive charge. A cation has fewer electrons than the electrically neutral atom from which it formed. An ionic charge is written as a number followed by a sign. Look at **Figure 6.4.** Because a sodium cation has 11 protons but only 10 electrons, it must have a charge of 1+. The number 1 is usually omitted when writing the complete symbol for the ion; thus Na^{1+} and Na^+ are equivalent. Magnesium (Mg) is another example of an atom that tends to form cations. Magnesium does so by losing two electrons. Therefore, a magnesium cation has a charge of 2+ because it has 12 protons but only 10 electrons. Its symbol is Mg^{2+}.

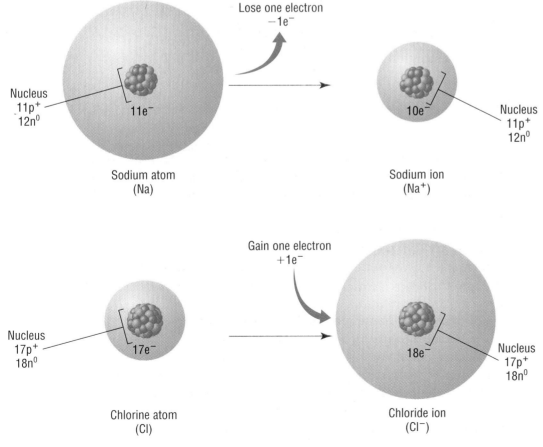

Nucleus
$11p^+$
$12n^0$

$11e^-$

Lose one electron
$-1e^-$

$10e^-$

Nucleus
$11p^+$
$12n^0$

Sodium atom
(Na)

Sodium ion
(Na^+)

Gain one electron
$+1e^-$

Nucleus
$17p^+$
$18n^0$

$17e^-$

$18e^-$

Nucleus
$17p^+$
$18n^0$

Chlorine atom
(Cl)

Chloride ion
(Cl^-)

Chem ASAP!

Animation 5
Discover the different ways that atoms of elements combine to form compounds.

Figure 6.4

A sodium atom loses an electron to become a positively charged sodium ion. A chlorine atom gains an electron to become a negatively charged chloride ion. What are the names for positively and negatively charged ions?

For metallic elements, the name of a cation is the same as the name of the element. As you have already seen, a sodium atom forms a sodium cation. Likewise, a lithium atom (Li) forms a lithium cation (Li^+), and an aluminum atom (Al) forms an aluminum cation (Al^{3+}). How many electrons does an aluminum atom lose to form an aluminum cation?

Although their names are the same, there are many important chemical differences between metals and their cations. Sodium metal, for example, reacts explosively with water. By contrast, sodium cations are quite unreactive. As you may know, they are a component of table salt, a compound that is very stable in water.

Atoms of nonmetallic elements tend to form ions by gaining one or more electrons. In this way they form **anions,** which are atoms or groups of atoms that have a negative charge. An anion has more electrons than the electrically neutral atom from which it formed. Look again at **Figure 6.4** on the preceding page to see what happens when a chlorine atom (Cl) gains one electron to form an anion. The chloride anion has 17 protons and 18 electrons. Therefore, it has an ionic charge of 1−. The chloride anion is written as Cl^-. Here again, the number 1 is usually omitted when writing the complete symbol for the ion. Another common anion is the oxide anion. An oxygen atom gains two electrons in forming this ion, so the oxide anion has an ionic charge of 2−. It is written O^{2-}. Notice that the name of an anion of a nonmetallic element is not the same as the element name. The name of the anion typically ends in -*ide*. Thus a sulfur atom (S) forms a sulfide anion (S^{2-}), and a bromine atom (Br) forms a bromide anion (Br^-).

Sample Problem 6-1

Write the symbol and name of the ion formed when
   a. a strontium atom loses two electrons.
   b. an iodine atom gains one electron.

1. **ANALYZE** *Plan a problem-solving strategy.*
   a. An atom that loses electrons forms a positively charged ion (cation). The name of a cation of a metallic element is the same as the name of the element.
   b. An atom that gains electrons forms a negatively charged ion (anion). The name of an anion of a nonmetallic element ends in -*ide*.

2. **SOLVE** *Apply the problem-solving strategy.*
   a. Sr^{2+}, strontium ion (a cation)
   b. I^-, iodide ion (an anion)

3. **EVALUATE** *Do the results make sense?*
   It makes sense that a metal atom that loses two negatively charged electrons should form a cation with a 2+ charge. It also makes sense that a nonmetal atom that gains one electron should form an anion with a 1− charge. The names conform to the naming convention.

Practice Problems

1. Give the name and symbol of the ion formed when
   a. a sulfur atom gains two electrons.
   b. an aluminum atom loses three electrons.
   c. a calcium atom loses two electrons.
2. How many electrons are lost or gained in forming each ion?
   a. Ba^{2+} **b.** As^{3-} **c.** Cu^{2+}

Chem ASAP!

Problem-Solving 1
Solve Problem 1 with the help of an interactive guided tutorial.

Compounds composed of cations and anions are called **ionic compounds.** Ionic compounds are usually composed of metal cations and nonmetal anions. One example of an ionic compound is sodium chloride, or table salt, which is composed of sodium cations and chloride anions. Another example is calcium oxide, commonly known as lime, which is composed of calcium cations and oxide anions. Although they are composed of ions, ionic compounds are electrically neutral. The total positive charge of the cations equals the total negative charge of the anions. Ionic compounds are usually solid crystals at room temperature, and they melt at high temperatures. **Table 6.1** summarizes some of the important differences between the properties of molecular compounds and ionic compounds. Knowing the differences in these properties can often be helpful in distinguishing between molecular and ionic compounds.

Table 6.1

Characteristics of Molecular and Ionic Compounds		
Characteristic	**Molecular compound**	**Ionic compound**
Representative unit	Molecule	Formula unit (balance of oppositely charged ions)
Type of elements	Nonmetallic	Metallic combined with nonmetallic
Physical state	Solid, liquid, or gas	Solid
Melting point	Low (usually below 300 °C)	High (usually above 300 °C)

section review 6.1

3. List three characteristics that distinguish ionic compounds from molecular compounds.

4. What is a cation? What is an anion? Relate the two to metals and to nonmetals.

5. What does the presence of an -*ide* ending on the name of an ion tell you about that ion?

6. What are the only elements that exist in nature as isolated atoms? What term is used to describe such elements?

7. What is a molecule? What is the difference between a diatomic molecule and a triatomic molecule? Give an example of each.

8. Write the symbol and name for the cation formed when

  a. a potassium atom loses one electron.

  b. a zinc atom loses two electrons.

9. Write the symbol and name for the anion formed when

  a. a fluorine atom gains one electron.

  b. a sulfur atom gains two electrons.

 Chem ASAP! Assessment 6.1 Check your understanding of the important ideas and concepts in Section 6.1.

objectives

▶ Distinguish among chemical formulas, molecular formulas, and formula units

▶ Use experimental data to show that a compound obeys the law of definite proportions

key terms

▶ chemical formula
▶ molecular formula
▶ formula unit
▶ law of definite proportions
▶ law of multiple proportions

REPRESENTING CHEMICAL COMPOUNDS

*O*n *the surface, identical twins may appear to be exactly the same. After all, they were formed from the same fertilized egg. On closer inspection, however, twins can be very different. Twins share some physical characteristics but are never completely alike. The same is true for chemical compounds made from the same elements. There are pairs of compounds that contain the same elements but have very different physical and chemical properties.* **How can two elements combine to form more than one chemical compound?**

Chemical Formulas

Chemists have identified more than ten million chemical compounds. Some of these are molecular compounds, such as the proteins and hormones in your body. Others, such as the salts in body fluids, are ionic compounds. No two of these compounds have identical properties. In this section, you will learn how a chemical formula represents the composition of each of these chemical substances.

A **chemical formula** shows the kinds and numbers of atoms in the smallest representative unit of the substance. You can represent the chemical formulas of monatomic elements by means of their atomic symbols. For example, helium and neon have the chemical formulas He and Ne, respectively. If the molecules of the element each have more than one atom, a number is used as a subscript. For example, the diatomic form of oxygen has the formula O_2 (read as "oh two"). The names and chemical formulas of the seven diatomic elements pictured in **Figure 6.5** are hydrogen (H_2), fluorine (F_2), oxygen (O_2), nitrogen (N_2), chlorine (Cl_2), bromine (Br_2), and iodine (I_2). Because of the importance of these elements, you should remember their names and formulas. The ozone molecule, which is composed of three atoms of oxygen, has the formula O_3.

Molecular Formulas

The chemical formula of a molecular compound is called a molecular formula. A **molecular formula** shows the kinds and numbers of atoms present in a molecule of a compound. A water molecule is a tightly bound unit of two hydrogen atoms and one oxygen atom. The molecular formula of water is H_2O. Notice that a subscript written after the symbol indicates the number of atoms of each element. If there is only one atom, the subscript 1 is omitted. The molecular formula of carbon dioxide is CO_2. This formula represents a molecule containing one carbon atom and two oxygen atoms. As shown in **Figure 6.6,** ethane, a component of natural gas, is also a molecular compound. The molecular formula for ethane is C_2H_6. According to this formula, one molecule of ethane contains two carbon atoms and six hydrogen atoms.

Although a molecular formula shows the composition of a molecule, it tells you nothing about the molecule's structure. In other words, it does not show the arrangement of the various atoms. As shown in **Figure 6.7,** a variety of diagrams and molecular models can be used to

Hydrogen (H_2)

Fluorine (F_2)

Oxygen (O_2)

Nitrogen (N_2)

Chlorine (Cl_2)

Bromine (Br_2)

Iodine (I_2)

Figure 6.5

These models represent seven nonmetallic elements that exist as diatomic molecules. What does the subscript 2 indicate in each case?

Figure 6.6
Ethane is a component of natural gas. What information is given in its molecular formula, C_2H_6?

show the arrangement of the atoms in a molecule of ammonia gas (NH_3). Diagrams and molecular models such as these will be used throughout the textbook to illustrate the arrangement of atoms in a molecule.

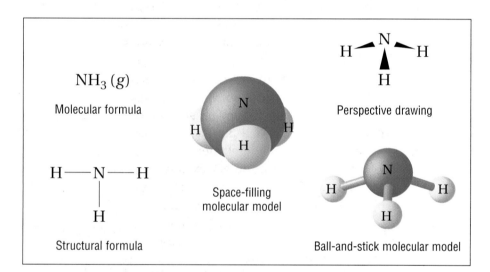

Figure 6.7
Ammonia (NH_3) is used in solution as a cleaning agent. Here are some ways the ammonia molecule can be represented and visualized.

Look at **Figure 6.8** to see the chemical formulas and structures of some other molecular compounds. On the basis of its molecular structure, what do you know about a molecule of ethanol?

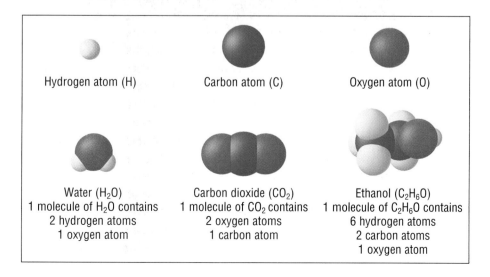

Figure 6.8
The formula of a molecular compound indicates the numbers and kinds of atoms in a molecule of the compound. The arrangement of the atoms within a molecule is called the molecular structure. Which of these molecules has the greatest number of oxygen atoms?

Formula Units

Chemical formulas can also be written for ionic compounds. In this case, however, the formula does not represent a molecule. Recall that sodium chloride (table salt) is an ionic compound. Sodium chloride is composed of equal numbers of sodium cations (Na^+) and chloride anions (Cl^-). As you can see in **Figure 6.9,** the ions in solid NaCl are arranged in an orderly pattern. There are no separate molecular units, only a continuous array of ions. To represent an ionic compound, chemists use a **formula unit,** which is the lowest whole-number ratio of ions in the compound. For sodium chloride, the lowest whole-number ratio of the ions is 1:1 (one Na^+ to each Cl^-). Thus the formula unit for sodium chloride is NaCl. Notice that although ionic charges are used to derive the correct formula, they are not shown when you write the formula unit of the compound.

The ionic compound magnesium chloride contains magnesium cations (Mg^{2+}) and chloride anions (Cl^-). In magnesium chloride, the ratio of magnesium cations to chloride anions is 1:2 (one Mg^{2+} to two Cl^-). So its formula unit is $MgCl_2$. Because there are twice as many chloride anions (each with a 1− charge) as magnesium cations (each with a 2+ charge), the compound is electrically neutral. What is the ratio of aluminum to chloride ions in $AlCl_3$?

Remember, there is no such thing as a molecule of sodium chloride or magnesium chloride. Instead, these compounds exist as collections of positively and negatively charged ions arranged in repeating three-dimensional patterns.

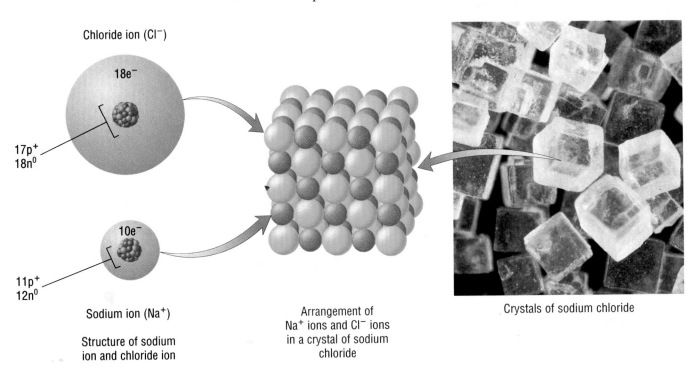

Chloride ion (Cl^-)

$18e^-$

$17p^+$
$18n^0$

$10e^-$

$11p^+$
$12n^0$

Sodium ion (Na^+)

Structure of sodium ion and chloride ion

Arrangement of Na^+ ions and Cl^- ions in a crystal of sodium chloride

Crystals of sodium chloride

Figure 6.9

Sodium cations and chloride anions form a repeating three-dimensional array in sodium chloride (NaCl). Chemists use a formula unit to represent ionic compounds such as sodium chloride. How many ions make up a single formula unit of this compound?

(a)

(b)

The Laws of Definite and Multiple Proportions

Consider the compound magnesium sulfide (MgS). It is produced by the combination of two kinds of ions, magnesium cations and sulfide anions. If you could take 100.00 g of magnesium sulfide and break it down into its elements, you would always obtain 43.13 g of magnesium and 56.87 g of sulfur. The ratio of these masses is 43.13/56.87 or 0.7584:1. The way the magnesium sulfide formed or the size of the sample does not change this mass ratio. Like all compounds, MgS obeys the **law of definite proportions,** which states that in samples of any chemical compound, the masses of the elements are always in the same proportions. This law is consistent with Dalton's atomic theory. If atoms combine in simple whole-number ratios, as Dalton postulated, it follows that their proportions by mass must always be the same.

In the early 1800s, Dalton and others studied pairs of compounds that contain the same elements but have different physical and chemical properties. For example, **Figure 6.10** shows two compounds—water (H_2O) and hydrogen peroxide (H_2O_2)—formed by the elements hydrogen and oxygen. The formulas of these compounds were not known in Dalton's time. Each compound obeys the law of definite proportions. In every sample of hydrogen peroxide, 16.0 g of oxygen are present for each 1.0 g of hydrogen. The mass ratio of oxygen to hydrogen is always 16 to 1. In every sample of water, the mass ratio of oxygen to hydrogen is always 8 to 1. If a sample of hydrogen peroxide has the same mass of hydrogen as a sample of water, the ratio of the masses of oxygen in the two compounds is exactly 2:1.

$$\frac{16 \text{ g O (in } H_2O_2 \text{ sample that has 1 g H)}}{8 \text{ g O (in } H_2O \text{ sample that has 1 g H)}} = \frac{16}{8} = \frac{2}{1} = 2{:}1$$

Using the results from these kinds of studies, Dalton stated the **law of multiple proportions:** Whenever two elements form more than one compound, the different masses of one element that combine with the same mass of the other element are in the ratio of small whole numbers. **Figure 6.11** illustrates the law of multiple proportions.

Figure 6.10
Water and hydrogen peroxide both contain only atoms of hydrogen and oxygen. Nevertheless, they have different chemical and physical properties. Water **(a)** *does not bleach dyes, whereas hydrogen peroxide* **(b)** *bleaches most dyes. What is the formula of hydrogen peroxide?*

Figure 6.11
This is an example of Dalton's law of multiple proportions. Two compounds, C and D, contain equal masses of B. The ratio of the masses of A in these compounds is 5:10 or 1:2 (a small whole-number ratio).

Chemical Names and Formulas **141**

Sample Problem 6-2

Carbon reacts with oxygen to form two compounds. Compound A contains 2.41 g of carbon for each 3.22 g of oxygen. Compound B contains 6.71 g of carbon for each 17.9 g of oxygen. What is the lowest whole-number mass ratio of carbon that combines with a given mass of oxygen?

1. **ANALYZE** *Plan a problem-solving strategy.*

   The law of multiple proportions applies to two different compounds composed of the same two elements. For each compound, find the grams of carbon that combine with each 1.00 g of oxygen by dividing the mass of carbon by the mass of oxygen. Then find the ratio of the masses of carbon in the two compounds by dividing one into the other. Confirm that the ratio is a low whole-number ratio.

2. **SOLVE** *Apply the problem-solving strategy.*

   Compound A $\quad \dfrac{2.41 \text{ g C}}{3.22 \text{ g O}} = \dfrac{0.748 \text{ g C}}{1.00 \text{ g O}}$

   Compound B $\quad \dfrac{6.71 \text{ g C}}{17.9 \text{ g O}} = \dfrac{0.375 \text{ g C}}{1.00 \text{ g O}}$

   Compare the masses of carbon per gram of oxygen.

   $$\frac{0.748 \text{ g C (in compound A)}}{0.375 \text{ g C (in compound B)}} = \frac{1.99}{1} = \text{roughly } \frac{2}{1} = 2:1$$

   The mass ratio of carbon per gram of oxygen in the compounds is 2:1.

3. **EVALUATE** *Does the result make sense?*

   The ratio is a low whole-number ratio, as expected. For a given mass of oxygen, there is twice the mass of carbon in compound A as in compound B.

Practice Problems

10. Lead forms two compounds with oxygen. One compound contains 2.98 g of lead combined with 0.461 g of oxygen. The other compound contains 9.89 g of lead combined with 0.763 g of oxygen. What is the lowest whole-number mass ratio of lead in the two compounds that combines with a given mass of oxygen?

11. In the compound nitrous oxide, also known as laughing gas and used as an anesthetic in dentistry, the mass ratio of nitrogen to oxygen is 7:4. A 68-g sample of a compound composed of nitrogen and oxygen contains 42 g of nitrogen. Is the sample nitrous oxide? Explain.

Chem ASAP!

Problem-Solving 11
Solve Problem 11 with the help of an interactive guided tutorial.

section review 6.2

12. Differentiate among a chemical formula, a molecular formula, and a formula unit.

13. How are experimental data used to show that a compound obeys the law of definite proportions?

14. Which law is illustrated by this statement: "In every sample of carbon monoxide, the mass ratio of carbon to oxygen is 3:4"?

15. Which law is illustrated by this statement: "When carbon and oxygen form the compounds carbon monoxide and carbon dioxide, the different masses of carbon that combine with the same mass of oxygen are in the ratio of 2:1"?

 Chem ASAP! **Assessment 6.2** Check your understanding of the important ideas and concepts in Section 6.2.

IONIC CHARGES

*I*n the play Romeo and Juliet, William Shakespeare wrote, "What's in a name? That which we call a rose/By any other name would smell as sweet." What we call a rose in English is rosa in Spanish, warda in Arabic, and julab in Hindi. To truly understand someone from another culture, you must first learn their language. Similarly, to understand chemistry, you must learn its language. Learning the language of chemistry involves learning the names of ionic compounds. **What are the rules for naming monatomic and polyatomic ions?**

objectives

▸ Use the periodic table to determine the charge on an ion
▸ Define a polyatomic ion and give the names and formulas of the most common polyatomic ions

key terms

▸ monatomic ions
▸ polyatomic ions

Monatomic Ions

To write chemical formulas for ionic compounds, you must know the types of ions that atoms tend to form. That means you must know the ionic charges typically obtained by the elements. For **monatomic ions,** or ions consisting of only one atom, the ionic charges can often be determined by using the periodic table.

Recall that metallic elements tend to lose electrons. Lithium, sodium, and potassium (in Group 1A) form cations. These ions have a 1+ charge (Li^+, Na^+, and K^+), as do all the other Group 1A ions. Magnesium and calcium are Group 2A metals. They form cations with a 2+ charge (Mg^{2+} and Ca^{2+}), as do all the other Group 2A metals. Aluminum is the only common Group 3A metal. As you might expect, it forms a 3+ cation (Al^{3+}). Thus the metals in Groups 1A, 2A, and 3A lose electrons when they form cations. The ionic charge is positive and is numerically equal to the group number.

The numerical charge of an ion of a Group A nonmetal is determined by subtracting the group number from 8. Because nonmetals tend to gain electrons and form anions, the sign of the charge is negative. For example, the elements in Group 7A form anions with a 1− charge (8 − 7 = 1). The anions for this group include fluoride (F^-) and chloride (Cl^-). Anions of nonmetals in Group 6A have a 2− charge (8 − 6 = 2); the oxide anion (O^{2-}) is an example. The three nonmetals in Group 5A can form anions with a 3− charge (8 − 5 = 3); one example is the nitride ion (N^{3-}). **Table 6.2** summarizes the ionic charges of representative elements that can be obtained from the periodic table. What is the charge of an iodide ion?

Table 6.2

Ionic Charges of Representative Elements							
1A	2A	3A	4A	5A	6A	7A	0
Li^+	Be^{2+}			N^{3-}	O^{2-}	F^-	
Na^+	Mg^{2+}	Al^{3+}		P^{3-}	S^{2-}	Cl^-	
K^+	Ca^{2+}			As^{3-}	Se^{2-}	Br^-	
Rb^+	Sr^{2+}					I^-	
Cs^+	Ba^{2+}						

Figure 6.12

Many compounds containing the Fe²⁺ ion are blue-green, whereas those compounds containing the Fe³⁺ ion tend to be yellow-brown. Note that the ions can be named by means of the Stock system as iron(II) and iron(III) or by means of the classical system as ferrous (the lower charge) and ferric (the higher charge).

The majority of the elements in the two remaining representative groups, 4A and 0, usually do not form ions. The elements in Group 0 rarely form compounds. Ordinarily, the two nonmetals in Group 4A, carbon and silicon, are found in molecular compounds.

Unlike the cations of the Group 1A, 2A, and 3A metals, many of the cations of transition metals have more than one common ionic charge. (This is also a characteristic of cations of tin and lead, the two metals in Group 4A.) For example, the transition metal iron forms two common cations, Fe^{2+} and Fe^{3+}. There are two methods of naming such cations. The preferred method is called the Stock system. As part of the name of the element, a Roman numeral in parentheses indicates the numerical value of the charge. As you will discover if you look at **Table 6.3,** when using the Stock system, the cation Fe^{2+} is named the iron(II) ion. This is read as the "iron two ion." Note that there is no space between the element name and the first parenthesis.

An older, less preferred method of naming these cations uses a root word with different suffixes at the end of the word. The older, or classical, name of the element is used to form the root word—for example *ferr-*, from *ferrum,* which is Latin for iron. The suffix *-ous* is used to name the cation with the lower of the two ionic charges. The suffix *-ic* is used with the higher of the two ionic charges. Using this system, Fe^{2+} is the ferr*ous* cation, and Fe^{3+} is the ferr*ic* cation, as shown in **Table 6.3.** Notice that you can usually identify an element from what may be an unfamiliar classical name by looking for the symbol of the element in the name. Thus *fe*rrous (Fe) is iron; *cu*prous (Cu) is copper; and *sta*nnous (Sn) is tin. A major disadvantage of using the classical name for ions is that they do not tell you the actual charge of the ion. The name tells you only that the cation has either the smaller (*-ous*) or the larger (*-ic*) charge of the pair.

Table 6.3

Formulas and Names of Common Metal Ions with More than One Ionic Charge		
Formula	**Stock name**	**Classical name**
Cu^+	Copper(I) ion	Cuprous ion
Cu^{2+}	Copper(II) ion	Cupric ion
Fe^{2+}	Iron(II) ion	Ferrous ion
Fe^{3+}	Iron(III) ion	Ferric ion
*Hg_2^{2+}	Mercury(I) ion	Mercurous ion
Hg^{2+}	Mercury(II) ion	Mercuric ion
Pb^{2+}	Lead(II) ion	Plumbous ion
Pb^{4+}	Lead(IV) ion	Plumbic ion
Sn^{2+}	Tin(II) ion	Stannous ion
Sn^{4+}	Tin(IV) ion	Stannic ion
Cr^{2+}	Chromium(II) ion	Chromous ion
Cr^{3+}	Chromium(III) ion	Chromic ion
Mn^{2+}	Manganese(II) ion	Manganous ion
Mn^{3+}	Manganese(III) ion	Manganic ion
Co^{2+}	Cobalt(II) ion	Cobaltous ion
Co^{3+}	Cobalt(III) ion	Cobaltic ion

*A diatomic elemental ion.

A few transition metals have only one ionic charge. The names of these cations do not have a Roman numeral. These exceptions include silver, with cations that nearly always have a 1+ charge (Ag^+), and cadmium and zinc, with cations that nearly always have a 2+ charge (Cd^{2+} and Zn^{2+}). As **Figure 6.13** shows, many transition metal compounds are used as pigments.

Figure 6.13
Many transition metals form brightly colored compounds that are used in making artists' paints.

Sample Problem 6-3

What is the charge of the ion typically formed by each element? (For transition metals with more than one common ionic charge, the number of electrons lost is indicated.)

  a. sulfur   **d.** argon
  b. lead, 4 electrons lost   **e.** bromine
  c. strontium   **f.** copper, 1 electron lost

1. ANALYZE *Plan a problem-solving strategy.*

a.–f. The charge of the ion of a representative (Group A) element is determined by that element's location in the periodic table. Group A metals have a positive charge equal to the group number. The charge of a Group A nonmetal is negative and numerically equal to 8 minus the group number. Ionic charges of transition metals cannot usually be read from the periodic table but can be determined from the number of electrons lost in forming the ion.

2. SOLVE *Apply the problem-solving strategy.*

  a. 2− (nonmetal in Group 6A; 8 − 6 = 2)
  b. 4+ (4 electrons lost)
  c. 2+ (metal in Group 2A)
  d. no ion formed (in Group 0)
  e. 1− (nonmetal in Group 7A; 8 − 7 = 1)
  f. 1+ (1 electron lost)

3. EVALUATE *Do the results make sense?*

As expected, the metals formed positively charged ions (cations) by losing one or more electrons. The nonmetals formed negatively charged ions (anions) by gaining one or more electrons.

Practice Problems

16. What is the charge of the typical ion of each element?
  a. selenium   **c.** cesium
  b. barium   **d.** phosphorus

17. How many electrons does the neutral atom gain or lose when each ion forms?
  a. Fe^{3+} **c.** Cu^+
  b. O^{2-} **d.** Cd^{2+}

Chem ASAP!

Problem-Solving 16
Solve Problem 16 with the help of an interactive guided tutorial.

Sample Problem 6-4

Name the ions in Sample Problem 6-3. Classify each as a cation or an anion.

1. **ANALYZE** *Plan a problem-solving strategy.*
   a.–f. Apply the different rules for naming cations and anions. The names of nonmetallic anions end in *-ide.* Metallic cations take the name of the metal. If the metal has more than one common ionic charge, a Roman numeral or classical name with a suffix is used.

2. **SOLVE** *Apply the problem-solving strategy.*
   a. sulfide ion, anion
   b. lead(IV) or plumbic ion, cation
   c. strontium ion, cation
   d. a noble gas, no ion formed
   e. bromide ion, anion
   f. copper(I) or cuprous ion, cation

3. **EVALUATE** *Do the results make sense?*
   The rules have been applied correctly. Each name uniquely identifies an ion and provides sufficient information for the formula of the ion to be written.

Practice Problems

18. Name each ion in Practice Problem 16. Identify each as an anion or a cation.
19. Name each ion in Practice Problem 17.

Polyatomic Ions

All the ions mentioned to this point are monatomic ions; that is, they are composed of only one atom. Unlike monatomic ions, the sulfate anion is composed of one sulfur atom and four oxygen atoms. These five atoms together form a sulfate anion. It has a 2− charge and is written SO_4^{2-}. **Polyatomic ions,** such as sulfate, are tightly bound groups of atoms that behave as a unit and carry a charge. You can see the structures of some polyatomic ions in **Figure 6.14.**

Figure 6.14
These models show the arrangement of atoms in four common polyatomic ions.

Nitrate ion
(NO_3^-)

Phosphate ion
(PO_4^{3-})

Sulfate ion
(SO_4^{2-})

Ammonium ion
(NH_4^+)

Table 6.4 lists the names and formulas of some common polyatomic ions. The ions are grouped by charge. Observe that the names of most of the polyatomic anions end in -*ite* or -*ate*. However, there are three important exceptions: the positively charged ammon*ium* cation (NH_4^+) and two polyatomic anions that end in -*ide,* the cyan*ide* ion (CN^-) and the hydrox*ide* ion (OH^-).

Examine the relationships among the polyatomic ions below for which there is an -*ite*/-*ate* pair. Look at the charge on each ion in the pair, the number of oxygen atoms, and the endings on each name. You should be able to discern a pattern in the naming convention.

-*ite*	-*ate*
SO_3^{2-}, sulfite	SO_4^{2-}, sulfate
NO_2^-, nitrite	NO_3^-, nitrate
ClO_2^-, chlorite	ClO_3^-, chlorate

The charge on each polyatomic ion in a given pair is the same. The -*ite* ending indicates one less oxygen atom than the -*ate* ending. However, the ending does not tell you the actual number of oxygen atoms in the ion. For example, the nit*rite* ion has two oxygen atoms and the sulf*ite* ion has three oxygen atoms.

When the formula for a polyatomic ion begins with H (hydrogen), you can imagine the H to represent a hydrogen ion (H^+) combined with another polyatomic ion. For example, HCO_3^- is a combination of H^+ and CO_3^{2-}.

Table 6.4

Common Polyatomic Ions					
1− charge		**2− charge**		**3− charge**	
Formula	Name	Formula	Name	Formula	Name
$H_2PO_4^-$	Dihydrogen phosphate	HPO_4^{2-}	Hydrogen phosphate	PO_3^{3-}	Phosphite
$C_2H_3O_2^-$	Acetate	$C_2O_4^{2-}$	Oxalate	PO_4^{3-}	Phosphate
HSO_3^-	Hydrogen sulfite	SO_3^{2-}	Sulfite		
HSO_4^-	Hydrogen sulfate	SO_4^{2-}	Sulfate	**1+ charge**	
HCO_3^-	Hydrogen carbonate	CO_3^{2-}	Carbonate	Formula	Name
NO_2^-	Nitrite	CrO_4^{2-}	Chromate	NH_4^+	Ammonium
NO_3^-	Nitrate	$Cr_2O_7^{2-}$	Dichromate		
CN^-	Cyanide	SiO_3^{2-}	Silicate		
OH^-	Hydroxide				
MnO_4^-	Permanganate				
ClO^-	Hypochlorite				
ClO_2^-	Chlorite				
ClO_3^-	Chlorate				
ClO_4^-	Perchlorate				

(a)

(b)

(c)

Figure 6.15

(a) This cloth shows the effect of sodium hypochlorite (NaClO) when it is used as a laundry bleach. (b) Ammonium phosphate ((NH₄)₃PO₄) is used as a fertilizer. (c) Some antacids contain the hydrogen carbonate anion.

Note that the charge on the new ion is the algebraic sum of the ionic charges.

$$H^+ + CO_3^{2-} \longrightarrow HCO_3^-$$
carbonate   hydrogen carbonate

$$H^+ + PO_4^{3-} \longrightarrow HPO_4^{2-}$$
phosphate   hydrogen phosphate

$$H^+ + HPO_4^{2-} \longrightarrow H_2PO_4^-$$
hydrogen phosphate   dihydrogen phosphate

The hydrogen carbonate anion (HCO_3^-), the hydrogen phosphate anion (HPO_4^{2-}), and the dihydrogen phosphate ($H_2PO_4^-$) anion are all essential components of living systems. In contrast, the cyanide ion (CN^-) is extremely poisonous to living systems because it blocks a cell's means of producing energy. Most laundry and household bleaches contain the hypochlorite anion (ClO^-). According to **Table 6.4,** what is the formula for the hydrogen sulfite polyatomic ion?

section review 6.3

20. How can the periodic table be used to determine the charge of an ion? Use a specific example to explain.

21. Explain what is meant by a polyatomic ion.

22. Using only the periodic table, name and write the formula for the typical ion of each representative element.

   a. potassium   **c.** argon   **e.** beryllium

   b. sulfur   **d.** bromine   **f.** sodium

23. Write the formula (including charge) for each ion.

   a. ammonium ion   **d.** nitrate ion   **g.** permanganate ion

   b. tin(II) ion   **e.** cyanide ion   **h.** manganese(II) ion

   c. chromate   **f.** iron(III) ion

portfolio project

Sodium ions (Na^+) and potassium ions (K^+) are needed for the human body to function. Research where these ions are most likely to be found in the body and the roles they play.

 Chem ASAP! **Assessment 6.3** Check your understanding of the important ideas and concepts in Section 6.3.

IONIC COMPOUNDS

*D*r Pepper®, the oldest of the major brand soft drinks in the United States, was first made and sold in Waco, Texas, in 1885. How does Dr Pepper continue to maintain the unique flavor associated with it? A specific formula, listing exact amounts of each ingredient, must be followed. Understandably, the formula for Dr Pepper is a closely guarded secret. In chemistry, however, there are no secret ingredients! Once you know the rules, you can write the formula for any chemical compound. **How do you write the formulas for ionic compounds?**

objectives
▶ Apply the rules for naming and writing formulas for binary ionic compounds
▶ Apply the rules for naming and writing formulas for ternary ionic compounds

key terms
▶ binary compounds
▶ ternary compound

Writing Formulas for Binary Ionic Compounds

In the days before the science of chemistry developed, the person who discovered a new compound often got to name it anything he or she wished. It was not uncommon for the name to describe some property of the substance or its source. For example, a common name for potassium carbonate (K_2CO_3) is potash. The name evolved because the compound was obtained by boiling wood ashes in iron pots. Laughing gas is the common name for the gaseous compound dinitrogen monoxide (N_2O) because people may laugh when they inhale it. Baking soda is added to batter to make cakes rise as they bake. Plaster of paris, gypsum, and lye are other common names of chemical compounds. Unfortunately, however, such names do not tell you anything about the chemical composition of the compound.

As the science of chemistry developed, it became obvious that some systematic method of naming chemical compounds was needed for consistency and clarity. A chemical compound's name should indicate its composition, behavior, and how it is related to other compounds. The rest of this chapter is devoted to examining the system of naming inorganic compounds, which are generally compounds that do not contain the element carbon.

The ionic compound potassium chloride (KCl) is composed of potassium cations (K^+) and chloride anions (Cl^-). Compounds composed of two elements are called **binary compounds.** Potassium chloride is a binary compound. In writing the formula for potassium chloride (or any other ionic compound), the positive charge of the cation must balance the negative charge of the anion. In other words, the net ionic charge of the formula must be zero. In potassium chloride, the charge of each K^+ cation is balanced by the charge of each Cl^- anion. The potassium and chloride ions combine in a 1:1 ratio. For each K^+ there is one Cl^-. Thus the formula for potassium chloride is KCl. The net ionic charge of the formula unit is zero. Notice that in this formula, and in the formulas for essentially all ionic compounds, the cation is written first: K before Cl.

The binary ionic compound calcium bromide is composed of calcium cations (Ca^{2+}) and bromide anions (Br^-). Each calcium ion with its 2+ charge must combine with (or be balanced by) two bromide ions, each with a 1− charge. The ions must combine in a 1:2 ratio. For each Ca^{2+} there are two Br^-. The formula for calcium bromide is $CaBr_2$, with a net ionic charge of zero.

Chem ASAP!
Simulation 2
Combine ions and derive the chemical formulas for several ionic compounds.

Figure 6.16
The rusting of a tractor produces iron(III) oxide, or rust, which is a binary ionic compound.

Figure 6.16 shows an example of the formation of rust, or iron(III) oxide. What is the formula for rust? Recall that a Roman numeral shows the charge of the metal ion. Thus this compound consists of Fe^{3+} cations combined with oxide anions (O^{2-}). Writing a balanced formula for this compound involves finding the least common multiple of the charges. Because $3 \times 2 = 6$, two Fe^{3+} cations (a 6+ charge) will balance three O^{2-} anions (a 6− charge). The balanced formula, then, is Fe_2O_3.

Another approach to writing a balanced formula for a compound is to use the crisscross method. In this method, the numerical charge of each ion is crossed over and used as a subscript for the other ion. The signs of the numbers are dropped.

$$Fe^{3+} \quad O^{2-}$$

$$Fe_2O_3$$
$$2(3+) + 3(2-) = 0$$

If you use the crisscross method to write the formula for a compound such as calcium sulfide (which contains Ca^{2+} and S^{2-}), however, you would obtain the result Ca_2S_2. Remember that formulas for ionic compounds show the lowest whole-number ratio of ions. The formula for calcium sulfide, written correctly, is thus reduced to CaS.

$$Ca^{2+} \quad S^{2-}$$

$$Ca_2S_2 \text{ reduces to CaS}$$
$$1(2+) + 1(2-) = 0$$

Of course, if the magnitudes of the charges of the cation and anion are the same, as they are in this case, the charges will balance. There is no reason even to use the crisscross method. The ions will simply combine in a 1:1 ratio.

Sample Problem 6-5

Write formulas for these binary ionic compounds.
  a. copper(II) sulfide
  b. potassium nitride

1. **ANALYZE** *Plan a problem-solving strategy.*
   a.–b. Binary ionic compounds are composed of a monatomic cation and a monatomic anion. The ionic charges in an ionic compound must balance (add up to zero), and there must be a lowest whole-number ratio of ions. The formula for the cation appears first in the formula for the compound.

2. **SOLVE** *Apply the problem-solving strategy.*
   Write the formula (symbol and charge) for each ion in each compound.
   a. Cu^{2+} and S^{2-} **b.** K^{+} and N^{3-}
   Balance the formula using appropriate subscripts.

   a. Cu^{2+} S^{2-} **b.** K^{+} N^{3-}
   CuS   K₃N

   $$ \text{CuS} \qquad\qquad \text{K}_3\text{N} $$

3. **EVALUATE** *Do the results make sense?*
   The ions are in the lowest whole-number ratio and the net ionic charge is zero: $1(2+) + 1(2-) = 0$ and $3(1+) + 1(3-) = 0$.

Practice Problems

24. Write formulas for compounds formed from these pairs of ions.
    a. Ba^{2+}, S^{2-} **c.** Ca^{2+}, N^{3-}
    b. Li^{+}, O^{2-} **d.** Cu^{2+}, I^{-}
25. Write formulas for these compounds.
    a. sodium iodide
    b. stannous chloride
    c. potassium sulfide
    d. calcium iodide

Chem ASAP!
Problem-Solving 25
Solve Problem 25 with the help of an interactive guided tutorial.

Naming Binary Ionic Compounds

So far, you have written the formulas for ionic compounds when given their names. What if you wanted to do the reverse? Suppose, for example, you wanted to write the name of the binary ionic compound that has the formula of CuO. Your first guess might be to write the name of the metallic cation (copper) followed by the name of the nonmetallic anion (oxide). However, the name copper oxide is incomplete. Recall that copper commonly forms two cations: Cu^{+} and Cu^{2+}, called copper(I) and copper(II), respectively. How can you tell which of these cations forms the compound CuO? Working backward will help. The formula indicates that the copper cation and the oxide anion combine in a 1:1 ratio. You know that the oxide anion always has a 2– charge. The charge of the copper cation must therefore be 2+ (to balance the 2– charge). The compound CuO must be copper(II) oxide. Recall that iron is another element that forms two cations: Fe^{2+} and Fe^{3+}.

It is helpful to know the common ionic charges of transition metals: for example, tin forms cations with 2+ and 4+ charges. However, you must still determine which of the cations is in a particular compound. Thus the compound SnO_2 must be tin(IV) oxide, because only the tin(IV) cation (Sn^{4+}) can balance the two oxide anions, each of which has a 2– charge. **Figure 16.17,** on page 153, shows examples of compounds consisting of these ions. What is the name of the compound that has the formula SnO?

CHEMath

PREFIXES AND SUFFIXES

Throughout this textbook you will encounter many new words. Some of them may seem intimidating at first, but don't be discouraged. You can get an idea of what a word means by analyzing its prefix or suffix. Prefixes and suffixes are one or more letters added to the beginning or end of a root word to modify the root word's meaning. Prefixes are added to the beginning of a root word and suffixes are added to the end. You can use what you learn about prefixes and suffixes to interpret and write the names of chemical compounds.

Measurements You already use prefixes to modify the magnitude of SI units. By adding prefixes to such root words as meter, liter, and gram, you can increase or decrease the magnitude of the unit. For example, if you write the prefix *kilo-* before the root word meter, you get kilometer. There are one thousand meters in a kilometer. If instead you write the prefix *centi-* before the root word meter, you get the word centimeter. There are one hundred centimeters in a meter. **Table 3.2** lists common prefixes used with SI units.

Chemical Compounds Prefixes and suffixes are also found in the names of chemical compounds. All binary compounds, for example, end in the suffix *-ide*. So whenever you see the name of a compound with the suffix *-ide*, such as carbon monoxide, you know that the compound is generally a binary compound. What is a binary compound? The prefix *bi-* means two, so a binary compound is one that contains only two elements.

In one type of binary compound, known as a molecular compound, prefixes are used to indicate the number of atoms in the chemical formula. In the compound carbon monoxide (CO), the prefix *mono-* indicates that there is one oxygen atom. In the compound carbon dioxide (CO_2), the prefix *di-* indicates that there are two oxygen atoms. **Table 6.5** lists the prefixes used to count up to ten atoms.

As you read this chapter, you will also encounter compounds whose names have the suffixes *-ite* or *-ate.* Compounds such as these contain polyatomic ions. The prefix *poly-* means many. Most polyatomic ions consist of three or more atoms.

The suffixes *-ite* or *-ate* relate to the number of oxygen atoms in the ion. An ion whose name ends in *-ite* has one less oxygen atom than the ion that ends in *-ate.* For example, the nitrite ion, NO_2^-, has two oxygen atoms and the nitrate ion, NO_3^-, has three. Neither suffix, however, indicates the specific number of oxygen atoms in the ion. **Table 6.4** lists several examples of common polyatomic ions.

Example 1

Give the name for BCl_3.

This is a binary compound so its name ends with the suffix *-ide.* Attach the suffix to the second element, giving the name chloride. Then use prefixes to indicate the relative number of atoms in the formula. There are three atoms of chlorine (*tri-*) and one atom of boron (*mono-*). The *mono-* prefix is omitted at the beginning of a name, so the name of the compound is boron trichloride.

Example 2

Write the formula for dinitrogen pentoxide.

First, use the prefixes to determine the subscript of each element in the formula. The prefix *di-* indicates two nitrogen atoms and the prefix *penta-* indicates five oxygen atoms. Next, write the correct symbols for the elements with the appropriate subscripts. The symbol for nitrogen is N and the symbol for oxygen is O. So the formula is N_2O_5.

Practice Problems

Prepare for upcoming problems in this chapter by solving each of the following.

A. According to **Table 3.2**, what prefix would you use to write 0.001 gram?

B. Use **Table 6.5** to determine the number of chlorine atoms that are in a molecule of carbon tetrachloride.

C. Which of the following is a binary compound: dinitrogen monoxide or calcium carbonate?

D. Give the name for NO_2.

E. Which ion is chlorite and which is chlorate: ClO_2^-, ClO_3^-.

Figure 6.17

Tin forms two ions: Sn^{2+} (tin(II) or stannous) and Sn^{4+} (tin(IV) or stannic). Stannous fluoride is used in some toothpastes to toughen enamel. Stannic sulfide is used to mimic the appearance of gold. What are the formulas of these two tin compounds?

Sample Problem 6-6

Name these binary ionic compounds.
  a. CoI_2
  b. Cs_2O

1. *ANALYZE Plan a problem-solving strategy.*

a.–b. Confirm that the compound is a binary ionic compound; that is, it is composed of a one-element metallic cation and a one-element nonmetallic anion. Name the compound by naming the ions in the order written in the formula: cation name followed by anion name. The name of a transition metal ion that has more than one common ionic charge must include a Roman numeral indicating the charge.

2. *SOLVE Apply the problem-solving strategy.*

Name the cation, followed by the name of the anion, using the crisscross method as needed. Use Roman numerals where appropriate.
  a. cobalt(II) iodide or cobaltous iodide

  b. cesium oxide

3. *EVALUATE Do the results make sense?*

As a check, try to write the formula for the original compound using the ions from the name you have written. The check leads to the correct formulas: Co^{2+} and I^- make CoI_2, and Cs^+ and O^{2-} make Cs_2O.

Practice Problems

26. Write names for these binary ionic compounds.
  a. ZnS   **c.** BaO
  b. KCl   **d.** $CuBr_2$
27. Write names for these binary ionic compounds.
  a. CaO   **c.** FeS
  b. Cu_2Se **d.** AlF_3

Ternary Ionic Compounds

The pearl and the oyster shell shown in **Figure 6.18** are both made of calcium carbonate ($CaCO_3$), an ionic compound. Calcium carbonate is an example of a **ternary compound,** or a compound that contains atoms of three different elements. Usually, ternary ionic compounds contain a polyatomic ion. How would you write the formula for calcium nitrate? The procedure is the same as that for binary ionic compounds. First, write the formula (symbol and charge) for each ion. Then balance the charges. Remember that an -*ate* or -*ite* ending on the name of a compound indicates that the compound contains a polyatomic anion that includes oxygen. The only two common polyatomic ions that end in -*ide* are the hydroxide and cyanide ions.

Calcium nitrate is composed of calcium cations (Ca^{2+}) and polyatomic nitrate anions (NO_3^-). In calcium nitrate, two nitrate anions, each with a 1− charge, are needed to balance the 2+ charge of each calcium cation, as shown below.

$$Ca(NO_3)_2$$

Notice that parentheses are used around the nitrate ion in the formula because more than one nitrate anion is needed. The 2 that follows the parentheses shows that two nitrate anions are needed.

When more than a single polyatomic ion are needed to balance a formula, parentheses in the formula set off the polyatomic ion. This is the only time parentheses are used. For example, the formula for strontium sulfate is simply $SrSO_4$ because only a single polyatomic sulfate anion is needed to balance the strontium cation.

Figure 6.18

Some examples of ternary ionic compounds are shown here. Oysters produce calcium carbonate as they form their shells and produce pearls, which develop around irritant particles, such as grains of sand. The mineral celestite is composed of strontium sulfate, which usually occurs as white crystals but is sometimes blue. Most strontium compounds are produced from celestite. Ammonium dichromate is often used to sensitize silkscreens to light, creating a negative image that can be used to make the positive print. Here you can see the varied results of the silkscreening process.

Lithium carbonate is a ternary compound composed of lithium cations (Li^+) and polyatomic carbonate anions (CO_3^{2-}).

$$Li \quad \overset{①+}{\underset{}{}} \quad \times \quad (CO_3) \overset{②-}{\underset{}{}}$$

$$Li_2CO_3$$

In lithium carbonate, two lithium cations, each with a 1+ charge, are needed to balance the 2− charge of one carbonate anion. Parentheses are not needed to set off the polyatomic carbonate anion. Lithium carbonate can be prescribed to patients who have mood disorders, such as manic-depressive, or bipolar, disorder. A person with bipolar disorder experiences distressing mood swings, from elation to depression and back again. Lithium ions probably exert their mood-stabilizing effects on neurotransmission, which is how messages are sent between nerve cells, including those in the brain.

Sample Problem 6-7

Write formulas for these ternary ionic compounds.
a. potassium sulfate   **b.** magnesium hydroxide

1. ANALYZE *Plan a problem-solving strategy.*
a.–b. The general rules for writing a formula for an ionic compound apply. Write the formula for each ion in the order listed in the name (cation followed by anion), then use subscripts to balance the charges (net charge = 0). If more than one polyatomic ion is needed to balance a formula, place the polyatomic ion formula in parentheses, followed by a subscript showing the number needed.

2. SOLVE *Apply the problem-solving strategy.*

a. $K \overset{①+}{\underset{}{}} \quad \times \quad (SO_4) \overset{②-}{\underset{}{}}$

$$K_2SO_4$$

Two potassium cations with 1+ charges are needed to balance the 2− charge on one sulfate anion. The formula for potassium sulfate is thus K_2SO_4.

b. $Mg \overset{②+}{\underset{}{}} \quad \times \quad (OH) \overset{①-}{\underset{}{}}$

$$Mg(OH)_2$$

Two hydroxide anions with 1− charges are needed to balance the 2+ charge on one magnesium cation. The formula for magnesium hydroxide must make use of parentheses.

3. EVALUATE *Do the results make sense?*
The ionic charges correctly add up to zero: $2(1+) + 1(2-) = 0$ and $1(2+) + 2(1-) = 0$.

Practice Problems

28. Write formulas for compounds formed from these pairs of ions.
    a. NH_4^+, SO_3^{2-}
    b. calcium ion, phosphate ion
    c. Al^{3+}, NO_3^-
    d. potassium ion, chromate ion
29. Write formulas for these compounds.
    a. lithium hydrogen sulfate
    b. chromium(III) nitrite
    c. mercury(II) bromide
    d. ammonium dichromate

Chem ASAP!
Problem-Solving 28
Solve Problem 28 with the help of an interactive guided tutorial.

When naming ternary ionic compounds from their formulas, you must first recognize the polyatomic ions. Like binary ionic compounds, ternary ionic compounds are named by naming the ions, cation first. For example, the compound $K_2Cr_2O_7$ consists of two K^+ ions combined with one $Cr_2O_7^{2-}$ polyatomic ion. Its name is potassium dichromate.

Sample Problem 6-8

Name these compounds.
- **a.** LiCN
- **b.** $Sr(H_2PO_4)_2$
- **c.** $(NH_4)_2C_2O_4$
- **d.** $Fe(ClO_3)_3$

1. **ANALYZE** *Plan a problem-solving strategy.*
   a.–d. If a formula has three or more different elements, the first thing to do is see whether you can recognize a polyatomic ion in the formula for the compound. Name a compound that has one or more polyatomic ions by naming the ions in the order listed in the formula, cation followed by anion.

2. **SOLVE** *Apply the problem-solving strategy.*
   a. lithium cyanide
   b. strontium dihydrogen phosphate
   c. ammonium oxalate
   d. iron(III) chlorate (Iron is a transition metal that can form more than one ion; its name must include a Roman numeral.)

3. **EVALUATE** *Do the results make sense?*
   Reversing the process as a check and using the names written to write formulas lead correctly back to the given formulas.

Practice Problems

30. Name each ternary ionic compound.
    a. CaC_2O_4
    b. KClO
    c. $KMnO_4$
    d. Li_2SO_3
31. Write names for these compounds.
    a. $Al(OH)_3$
    b. $NaClO_3$
    c. $Sn_3(PO_4)_2$
    d. Na_2CrO_4

section review 6.4

32. How are formulas written for binary ionic compounds, given their names? How is the reverse done?

33. How are formulas written for ternary ionic compounds, given their names? How is the reverse done?

34. Write the name or formula, as appropriate.

    a. chromium(III) nitrite
    b. $Mg_3(PO_4)_2$
    c. LiF
    d. sodium perchlorate
    e. $Pb(C_2H_3O_2)_2$
    f. magnesium hydrogen carbonate

35. When are parentheses used in writing a chemical formula?

36. What condition must be met in writing a balanced formula for an ionic compound?

 Chem ASAP! **Assessment 6.4** Check your understanding of the important ideas and concepts in Section 6.4.

NAMES AND FORMULAS OF IONIC COMPOUNDS

SAFETY

Wear safety glasses and follow the standard safety procedures, as outlined on page 18.

PURPOSE

To observe the formation of compounds, and to write their names and formulas.

MATERIALS

- pencil
- chemicals shown in Figure A
- paper
- ruler
- reaction surface

PROCEDURE

On separate sheets of paper, draw two grids similar to Figure A. Make each square 2 cm on each side. Draw black Xs on only one of the grids. Place a reaction surface over the grid with black Xs and add the chemicals as shown in Figure A. Use the other grid as a data table to record your observations for each solution.

Figure A

ANALYSIS

Using the experimental data, record the answers to the following questions below your data table.

1. Describe each precipitate that forms as milky, grainy, cloudy, or gelatinous. Which mixture(s) did not form a precipitate?

2. Write the formulas and names of the chemical compounds produced in the mixings.

YOU'RE THE CHEMIST

The following small-scale activities allow you to develop your own procedures and analyze the results.

1. **Analyze It!** Repeat the above experiment, using the chemicals in Figure B. Identify the precipitates, write their formulas, and name them.

Figure B

2. **Analyze It!** In ionic equations, the precipitate is written to the right of the arrow, and the ions that produced it are to the left.

   Write ionic equations for the precipitates formed from the reactions related to Figure B.

MOLECULAR COMPOUNDS AND ACIDS

objectives
▶ Apply the rules for naming and writing formulas for binary molecular compounds
▶ Name and write formulas for common acids

*G*old was one of the first metals to attract human attention. When gold was discovered in California in the late 1840s, people from all over the world came to make their fortune. Today, gold is still greatly prized and valued. But whereas one milligram of gold is worth only about one cent, one kilogram of gold is worth approximately $10,000. In this case, using the correct prefix makes quite a difference! Prefixes are important in chemistry too. **What do prefixes tell you about the composition of binary molecular compounds?**

Binary Molecular Compounds

Unlike binary ionic compounds, binary molecular compounds are composed of two nonmetallic elements. This difference affects the naming of these compounds, as well as the writing of their formulas. Because binary molecular compounds are composed of molecules, ionic charges are not used to assign formulas or names to them. In addition, when two nonmetallic elements combine, they often can do so in more than one way. For example, the elements carbon and oxygen combine to form two different gaseous compounds, CO and CO_2. (They also form two different polyatomic ions, CO_3^{2-} and $C_2O_4^{2-}$.) How would you name a binary compound formed by the combination of carbon and oxygen atoms? It might seem satisfactory to call it carbon oxide. However, the two carbon oxides, CO and CO_2, are very different compounds. Sitting in a room with small amounts of the carbon oxide CO_2 in the air would not present any problems. You exhale CO_2 as a product of your body chemistry. Thus it is normally present in the air you breathe. On the other hand, if the same amount of the other carbon oxide, CO, were in the room, you could very well die of asphyxiation as a result. The binary compound CO is a poisonous gas that interferes with the blood's

Figure 6.19

Carbon dioxide (CO_2) and carbon monoxide (CO) are both binary molecular compounds of carbon and oxygen, but they differ considerably in properties. Carbon dioxide is a nonpoisonous product of respiration, but carbon monoxide is an extremely toxic product of incomplete burning, such as occurs in automobile gasoline engines.

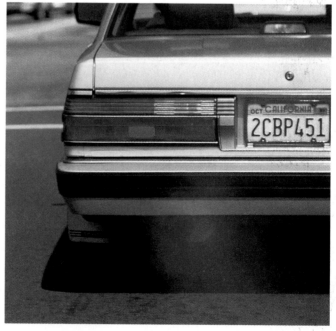

ability to carry oxygen to body cells. Obviously, a naming system that distinguishes between these two compounds is needed.

Prefixes help distinguish between different compounds. **Table 6.5** lists the prefixes used to name binary molecular compounds. These prefixes tell how many atoms of each element are present in each molecule (and in the formula) of the compound. According to the table, the prefix *mono*-indicates the presence of the single oxygen atom in CO. The prefix *di*-indicates the presence of the two oxygen atoms in CO_2. The two compounds of carbon and oxygen, CO and CO_2, are thus named carbon monoxide and carbon dioxide, respectively. Notice that the second element in the name ends with -*ide*. The names of all binary molecular compounds end in -*ide*, just as was the case for binary ionic compounds. Also note that the vowel at the end of a prefix often is dropped when the name of the element begins with a vowel. For CO, you would write monoxide, not monooxide. If there is just a single atom of the first element in the name, omit the prefix *mono*- for that element. How many chlorine atoms are there in carbon tetrachloride, a toxic substance once used in the dry cleaning of clothes?

Writing formulas for binary molecular compounds, given their names, is quite easy. Use the prefixes to tell you the subscript of each element in the formula. Then write the correct symbols for the two elements, with the appropriate subscripts. For example, the formula for tetraiodine nonoxide is I_4O_9. The prefix *tetra*- indicates four iodine atoms, and the prefix *nona*- indicates nine oxygen atoms in the molecule. How would you write formulas for sulfur trioxide and phosphorus pentafluoride?

Table 6.5

Prefixes Used in Naming Binary Molecular Compounds	
Prefix	Number
mono-	1
di-	2
tri-	3
tetra-	4
penta-	5
hexa-	6
hepta-	7
octa-	8
nona-	9
deca-	10

Sample Problem 6-9

Name these binary molecular compounds.
a. N_2O **b.** PCl_3 **c.** SF_6

1. *ANALYZE Plan a problem-solving strategy.*
a.–c. Confirm that the compound is a binary molecular compound—that is, the compound is composed of two non-metals. The name must reflect the composition of the compound's molecule. Name the elements in the order listed in the formulas. Prefixes indicate the number of each kind of atom. The suffix of the name of the second element is -*ide*.

2. *SOLVE Apply the problem-solving strategy.*
a. The formula N_2O contains two nitrogen atoms (prefix *di*-) and one oxygen atom (prefix *mono*-). The name of the compound is dinitrogen monoxide.
b. phosphorus trichloride
c. sulfur hexafluoride

3. *EVALUATE Do the results make sense?*
Each name provides sufficient information to regenerate the correct formula.

Practice Problems

37. Name these binary molecular compounds.
a. OF_2 **b.** Cl_2O_8 **c.** SO_3
38. Write formulas for the following binary molecular compounds.
a. nitrogen trifluoride
b. disulfur dichloride
c. dinitrogen tetroxide

Chem ASAP!

Problem-Solving 37
Solve Problem 37 with the help of an interactive guided tutorial.

Figure 6.20
Acids are used for many purposes. The nitric acid shown here is being used to etch a metal plate that will be used to create an artist's print.

ENVIRONMENTAL AWARENESS

A Toxic Environmental Gas

The binary molecular compound carbon monoxide is a colorless, odorless, flammable gas used to manufacture numerous organic and inorganic chemicals. This gas is also highly toxic to humans. Upon inhalation, carbon monoxide binds to the hemoglobin molecules in red blood cells, where it replaces oxygen. Carbon monoxide binds to hemoglobin about 200 times more effectively than oxygen does. This keeps the red blood cells from carrying oxygen to body tissues. Therefore, at very low levels carbon monoxide is a fast-acting poison that may cause serious illness or death. At peak traffic times, the level of carbon monoxide around streets and highways may reach as high as 100 parts per million (ppm) of air. In the United States, automobiles must have catalytic converters, which change toxic carbon monoxide to less toxic carbon dioxide. Carbon monoxide is also present in cigarette smoke. It takes several hours to replace the carbon monoxide in a smoker's blood after only one cigarette.

Naming Common Acids

Acids are a special group of compounds. As you will see in Chapter 20, there are several definitions of acids. For now, it is sufficient to know that under the more common definition, acids are compounds that produce hydrogen ions when dissolved in water. When naming acids and writing their formulas, you can consider them to be combinations of anions connected to as many hydrogen ions (H^+) as are needed to make the molecule electrically neutral.

Many industrial processes, including steel and fertilizer manufacturing, use acids. There are a few acids that you will regularly use in the laboratory. You should know the names and formulas of these acids:

Hydrochloric acid	HCl
Sulfuric acid	H_2SO_4
Nitric acid	HNO_3
Acetic acid	$HC_2H_3O_2$
Phosphoric acid	H_3PO_4
Carbonic acid	H_2CO_3

section review 6.5

39. How are formulas written for binary molecular compounds, given their names? How is the reverse done?

40. Give the name or formula for these common acids.

    a. H_2SO_4 **b.** H_2CO_3 **c.** nitric acid   **d.** phosphoric acid

41. Write the formula or name for these compounds.

    a. CS_2 **c.** carbon tetrabromide

    b. Cl_2O_7 **d.** diphosphorus trioxide

42. What element typically appears in the formula of a common acid?

 ChemASAP! Assessment 6.5 Check your understanding of the important ideas and concepts in Section 6.5.

SUMMARY OF NAMING AND FORMULA WRITING

objectives

▶ Use the flowchart in **Figure 6.21** to write the name of a compound when given its chemical formula

▶ Use the flowchart in **Figure 6.23** to write a chemical formula when given the name of a compound

*I*n the average home, there are probably hundreds of chemicals, including cleaning products, drugs, and pesticides. Most people would not know what to do if some of these chemicals accidentally mixed together and began to react, or, even worse, if a small child ingested one of these chemicals. A phone call to a poison-control center can provide life-saving information to victims of such poisonings. On the inside front cover of most phone books is a list of phone numbers for regional centers and other emergency numbers. **Why would knowing the correct name of a chemical be important to a poison-control center worker?**

Practicing Skills: Follow the Arrows

In this chapter, you have learned two basic skills: writing chemical formulas and naming chemical compounds. If this is the first time you have tried to master these skills, you may feel a little overwhelmed at this point. For example, you may find it difficult to know when to use prefixes and Roman numerals in a name, and when not to do so. Or you may have trouble determining if a compound's name should end in *-ate, -ide,* or *-ite.* The flowchart in **Figure 6.21** is designed to help you name compounds correctly. Follow the arrows on the flowchart to find directions for naming a particular compound. By using the flowchart while working exercises, you will increase your skill at naming compounds.

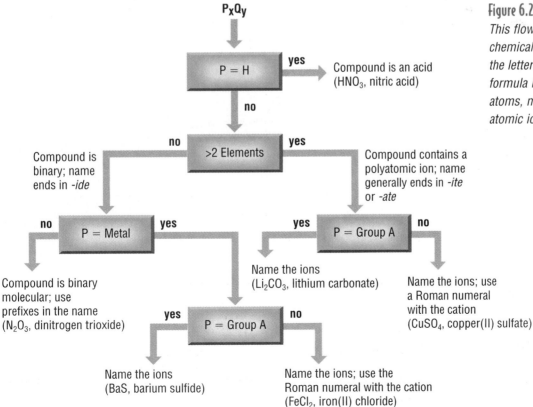

Figure 6.21

This flowchart will help you name chemical compounds. Begin with the letters P and Q in the general formula P_xQ_y. P and Q can be atoms, monatomic ions, or polyatomic ions.

Figure 6.22

Artists Palette at Death Valley, in California, boasts many colorful rock formations. The colors indicate the presence of salts of iron, potassium, aluminum, magnesium, and manganese. These salts, some of which are complex compounds, are named and their formulas are written according to the rules you have learned here.

In writing a chemical formula from a chemical name, it is helpful to remember the following rules.

1. In an ionic compound, the net ionic charge is zero.
2. An *-ide* ending generally indicates a binary compound.
3. An *-ite* or *-ate* ending means there is a polyatomic ion that includes oxygen in the formula.
4. Prefixes in a name generally indicate that the compound is molecular. They show the number of each kind of atom in the molecule.
5. A Roman numeral after the name of a cation shows the ionic charge of the cation.

Figure 6.23 ▶

This flowchart will help you write a chemical formula when given a chemical name.

MINI LAB

Making Ionic Compounds

PURPOSE

Mix cations and anions to make ionic compounds.

MATERIALS

- 9 small test tubes
- test tube rack
- 6 solutions in plastic dropper bottles containing the following ions:
  Solution A
  (Fe^{3+} ion)
  Solution B
  (Ag^+ ion)
  Solution C
  (Pb^{2+} ion)
  Solution X
  (CO_3^{2-} ion)
  Solution Y
  (OH^- ion)
  Solution Z
  (PO_4^{3-} ion)

PROCEDURE

1. Label three test tubes A, three test tubes B, and three test tubes C.

2. Add 10 drops (0.5 mL) of solutions A, B, and C to each of their respective labeled test tubes.

3. Add 10 drops of solution X to one test tube of A, 10 drops to one test tube of B, and 10 drops to one test tube of C. Observe each for the formation of a solid material.

4. Make a 3-by-3 grid in which to record your observations. Label the rows A, B, and C. Label the columns X, Y, and Z. Write a short description of the solid material you observed forming in each test tube.

5. Repeat Steps 3 and 4, adding 10 drops of solution Y to test tubes A, B, and C.

6. Repeat Steps 3 and 4, adding 10 drops of solution Z to test tubes A, B, and C.

ANALYSIS AND CONCLUSIONS

1. Can mixing a cation and an anion lead to the formation of an insoluble (does not dissolve in water) ionic compound?

2. Write the correct formula for each ionic compound formed.

3. Name each ionic compound formed.

4. Do you think mixing together a solution of any cation with a solution of any anion will always lead to the formation of an insoluble ionic compound?

---

section review 6.6

43. Name these compounds, using **Figure 6.21** as an aid if necessary.

    a. $CaCO_3$ **c.** $PbCrO_4$ **e.** $SnCr_2O_7$

    b. $KMnO_4$ **d.** $CaHPO_4$ **f.** Mg_3P_2

44. Write formulas for these compounds, using **Figure 6.23** as an aid if necessary.

    a. tin(II) hydroxide

    b. barium fluoride

    c. tetraiodine nonoxide

    d. iron(III) oxalate

    e. calcium sulfide

    f. aluminum hydrogen carbonate

 Chem ASAP! Assessment 6.6 Check your understanding of the important ideas and concepts in Section 6.6.

Chemistry Serving...the Consumer

WHAT'S IN A NAME?

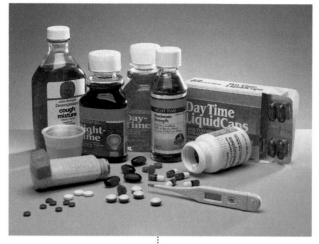

When it comes to drugs and medicines, chemical naming can get very complex and even confusing. Consider the example of a drug commonly prescribed for lowering blood pressure. Its chemical name is 4-[2'-hydroxy-3'-[(1-methylethyl) amino] propoxy]-benzeneacetamide, but a pharmacist is not likely to know the drug by this name. So a doctor would write Tenormin® on a prescription. Alternatively, the doctor could write Atenolol, Alinor, Altol, Antipressan, Atcardil, AteHexal, Atenil, Betablok, Betacard, Felo-Bits, or Myocord. Or if the doctor did not like any of those names, he or she could put down Normiten, Oraday, Premorine, Prenolol, Seles, Tenolol, or Vericordin. Any of these names would get the patient the same chemical compound— 4-[2'-hydroxy-3'-[(1-methylethyl) amino] propoxy]-benzeneacetamide.

Why are there so many names for the same drug? A drug is assigned a single generic name, such as Atenolol, by an international council that includes the World Health Organization. There are many brand names, such as Ternormin®, which are assigned by the companies that develop and produce the drug.

When a manufacturer develops a drug, it puts to work teams of chemists and pharmacists who spend many years doing expensive research. Then the company must test the drug and prove it safe and effective, another lengthy and costly process. Eventually, the company submits the drug to the Food and Drug Administration (FDA) for review. If the FDA approves the drug, the company can finally market it. At this point, the marketing department of the manufacturer names the drug. The name, which then becomes a brand name, is often descriptive of what the drug does but usually has nothing to do with the actual chemical name of the drug.

> A drug is assigned a single generic name by an international council that includes the World Health Organization.

Because manufacturers invest so much time and money in developing a new drug, they must protect their investment. They do this by patenting the drug. The patent gives the company the exclusive right to produce and market the drug for 17 years.

After the patent expires, other companies can manufacture the drug. Because these companies do not have to do all the development and testing, they can sell the drug at a lower cost than the original manufacturer can. Although other companies can manufacture the drug after the patent expires, they cannot market their versions under the same brand name. Each company gives its version of the drug a different brand name. If the market for the drug is large, many different companies may be motivated to produce and sell the drug. Thus, there can be many brand names for a single drug. Doctors often write prescriptions using only the generic name. The pharmacist fills the prescription with whatever brand is in stock. The FDA assures that all available drugs are safe and effective.

To fill prescriptions correctly, pharmacists must keep track of all the different brand names and generic names. To do this, pharmacists use a variety of resources, such as the *Physicians Desk Reference*. Most larger pharmacies have computer programs that suggest substitutions automatically.

CHEMISTRY IN CAREERS

☆☆☆☆☆☆☆☆☆☆☆☆☆☆☆☆☆☆☆☆☆☆

PHARMACIST
Fill prescriptions, determining generic-drug substitutions and advising customers on recommended dosage and usage. See page 870.

TAKE IT TO THE NET

Find out more about career opportunities:
www.phschool.com

CHEMICAL SPECIALIST
Local food service distributor seeks responsible self-motivated individ-

Take It to the NET
For interactive study and review, go to www.phschool.com

KEY TERMS

- anion *p. 136*
- binary compound *p. 149*
- cation *p. 135*
- chemical formula *p. 138*
- formula unit *p. 140*

- ion *p. 135*
- ionic compound *p. 137*
- law of definite proportions *p. 141*
- law of multiple proportions *p. 141*
- molecular compound *p. 134*

- molecular formula *p. 138*
- molecule *p. 134*
- monatomic ion *p. 143*
- polyatomic ion *p. 146*
- ternary compound *p. 154*

KEY RELATIONSHIP

- For ionic compounds, net ionic charge = 0.

CONCEPT SUMMARY

6.1 Introduction to Chemical Bonding
- Every substance is either an element or a compound.
- A compound consists of more than one kind of atom.
- A compound is either molecular or ionic in nature.

6.2 Representing Chemical Compounds
- Molecular compounds are composed of two or more nonmetals.
- A molecular formula shows the number and kinds of atoms present in a molecule of a compound.
- Ionic compounds are composed of oppositely charged ions (cations and anions) combined in electrically neutral groupings.
- A formula unit gives the lowest whole-number ratio of ions in the compound.

6.3 Ionic Charges
- The charges of the ions of the representative elements can be determined by the position of these elements in the periodic table.
- Most transition metals have more than one common ionic charge.

- A polyatomic ion is a group of atoms that behaves as a unit and has a charge.

6.4 Ionic Compounds
- Binary (two-element) ionic compounds are named by writing the name of the cation followed by the name of the anion. Binary compounds end in *-ide*.
- When a cation can have more than one ionic charge, a Roman numeral is used in the name.
- Ternary ionic compounds contain at least one polyatomic ion. The names of these compounds generally end in *-ite* or *-ate*.

6.5 Molecular Compounds and Acids
- Binary molecular compounds are composed of two nonmetallic elements.
- The name of a binary molecular compound always ends in *-ide*.
- Prefixes are used to show how many atoms of each element are present in a molecule of the compound.

6.6 Summary of Naming and Formula Writing
- The use of a flowchart is helpful in naming compounds.

CHAPTER CONCEPT MAP

Use these terms to construct a concept map that organizes the major ideas of this chapter.

 Chem ASAP! **Concept Map 6**
Create your Concept Map using the computer.

anion · binary compound · cation · ionic compound · law of definite proportions · metal · molecular compound · nonmetal · ternary compound

CONCEPT PRACTICE

45. Describe two ways that an ion forms from an atom. *6.1*

46. State the number of electrons either lost or gained in forming each ion. *6.1*
 a. Br^- **d.** Ca^{2+}
 b. Na^+ **e.** Cu^+
 c. As^{3-} **f.** H^-

47. Name each ion in Problem 46. Identify each as an anion or a cation. *6.1*

48. If ionic compounds are composed of charged particles (ions), why isn't every ionic compound either positively or negatively charged? *6.2*

49. Would you expect the following pairs of atoms to combine chemically to give an ionic or a molecular compound? *6.2*
 a. Li and S   **d.** F and Cl
 b. O and S   **e.** I and K
 c. Al and O   **f.** H and N

50. Four students heat different masses of a blue substance. The blue substance decomposes into a white powder and a colorless gas. The mass of the white powder and the mass of the colorless gas for each sample is plotted on the graph below. *6.2*

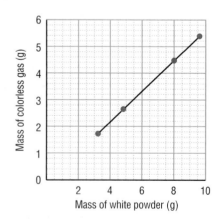

 a. Does the graph support the idea that all four samples of blue substance are the same material? Explain.
 b. Assuming the blue powder is a compound, what law do the data presented here demonstrate?
 c. On heating, a fifth sample of the same blue substance gives 6.2 g of white powder. How many grams of colorless gas are also produced?

51. Identify the number and kinds of atoms present in a molecule of each compound. *6.2*
 a. ascorbic acid (vitamin C), $C_6H_8O_6$
 b. monosodium glutamate (MSG), $C_5H_8O_4Na$
 c. sucrose (table sugar), $C_{12}H_{22}O_{11}$
 d. trinitrotoluene (TNT), $C_7H_5N_3O_6$
 e. ammonium nitrate (fertilizer), NH_4NO_3

52. The melting point of a compound is 1240 °C. Is this compound an ionic or a molecular compound? *6.2*

53. Write the symbol for each ion. Be sure to include the charge. *6.3*
 a. oxide ion   **d.** nitride ion
 b. lead(II) ion   **e.** cupric ion
 c. lithium ion   **f.** fluoride ion

54. Name the following ions. Use Table 6.3 if necessary. *6.3*
 a. Ba^{2+} **c.** Ag^+ **e.** P^{3-}
 b. I^- **d.** Hg^{2+} **f.** Sn^{4+}

55. Write the names and formulas of the two polyatomic anions in **Table 6.4** with names that do not end in *-ite* or *-ate*. *6.3*

56. Without consulting **Table 6.4,** name the following ions. *6.3*
 a. OH^- **e.** HPO_4^{2-}
 b. Pb^{4+} **f.** $Cr_2O_7^{2-}$
 c. SO_4^{2-} **g.** Al^{3+}
 d. O^{2-} **h.** ClO_2^-

57. What is the net ionic charge of every ionic compound? Explain. *6.4*

58. Write formulas for compounds composed of these pairs of ions. *6.4*
 a. Na^+, O^{2-} **c.** K^+, Cl^-
 b. Sn^{4+}, S^{2-} **d.** Mg^{2+}, N^{3-}

59. How do you determine the charge of a transition metal cation from the formula of an ionic compound? *6.4*

60. When must parentheses be used in a formula? *6.4*

61. Write the formulas for these compounds. *6.4*
 a. calcium carbonate
 b. barium hydrogen carbonate
 c. lithium hypochlorite
 d. tin(IV) dichromate

62. Complete the table on the following page by writing correct formulas for the compounds formed by combining positive and negative ions. Then name each compound. *6.4*

	NO_3^-	CO_3^{2-}	CN^-	PO_4^{3-}
NH_4^+				
Sn^{4+}				
Fe^{3+}				
Mg^{2+}				

63. What are the components of a binary molecular compound? *6.5*

64. Write the formula or name for these compounds. *6.5*
   a. boron trichloride
   b. dinitrogen tetrahydride
   c. N_2O_5
   d. CCl_4

65. Give the name or the formula for these acids. *6.5*
   a. HCl
   b. HNO_3
   c. sulfuric acid
   d. acetic acid

66. Which prefix indicates each of the following numbers of atoms in a molecular compound formula? *6.5*
   a. 3   **b.** 1   **c.** 2   **d.** 6   **e.** 5   **f.** 4

CONCEPT MASTERY

67. Name these compounds.
   a. $NaClO_3$
   b. Hg_2Br_2
   c. K_2CrO_4
   d. AlI_3
   e. SnO_2
   f. $Fe(C_2H_3O_2)_3$
   g. $KHSO_4$
   h. CaH_2

68. Write formulas for these compounds.
   a. potassium permanganate
   b. calcium hydrogen carbonate
   c. dichlorine heptoxide
   d. trisilicon tetranitride
   e. sodium dihydrogen phosphate
   f. phosphorus pentabromide
   g. carbon tetrachloride

69. Name each substance. Use **Figure 6.21** if necessary.
   a. $LiClO_4$
   b. Cl_2O
   c. HgF_2
   d. CaO
   e. $Ba_3(PO_4)_2$
   f. I_2
   g. $SrSO_4$
   h. $CuC_2H_3O_2$

70. Write formulas for these compounds.
   a. magnesium sulfide
   b. nitrogen gas
   c. barium hydroxide
   d. copper(II) nitrite
   e. sulfite ion
   f. calcium carbonate
   g. sodium bromide
   h. ferric sulfate

71. Name each compound.
   a. $Mg(MnO_4)_2$
   b. $Be(NO_3)_2$
   c. K_2CO_3
   d. N_2H_4
   e. $LiOH$
   f. BaF_2
   g. PI_3
   h. ZnO

72. The United States produces thousands of different kinds of inorganic chemicals. The following data table shows the amounts (in billions of kg) of the top ten inorganic chemicals produced in a recent year.

Chemical	Amount produced (billions of kg)
Sulfuric acid	39.4
Nitrogen	26.9
Oxygen	17.7
Ammonia	16.5
Lime	16.3
Phosphoric acid	11.2
Sodium hydroxide	11.0
Chlorine	10.3
Sodium carbonate	9.3
Nitric acid	6.8

   a. For what percentage of the total production of the top ten did lime (calcium oxide) account?
   b. Three diatomic gases are on the list. What are their names and what was their total production?
   c. For what percentage of the total production of the top ten did the three acids account?
   d. Write formulas for the top ten inorganic chemicals.

73. Write formulas for these compounds.
   a. calcium bromide
   b. silver chloride
   c. aluminum carbide
   d. nitrogen dioxide
   e. tin(IV) cyanide
   f. lithium hydride
   g. strontium acetate
   h. sodium silicate

CRITICAL THINKING

74. Choose the term that best completes the second relationship.
   a. black : white
      cation : _____
      (1) anion
      (2) metal
      (3) sodium ion
      (4) iron ion
   b. plant : oak tree
      anion : _____
      (1) sodium ion
      (2) magnesium ion
      (3) cation
      (4) chloride ion
   c. molecular compound : molecule
      ionic compound : _____
      (1) cation
      (2) formula unit
      (3) anion
      (4) metalloid

75. Compare and contrast the information conveyed by a molecular formula with that given by a formula unit of a compound.

76. Where on the periodic table will you find the two elements in a binary molecular compound?

77. Why is it important for chemists to have a scientific system of writing chemical names and formulas?

78. Criticize this statement: "The ionic charge of any metal can be determined from the position of the element in the periodic table."

79. Summarize the rules that chemists use for naming ionic compounds. What is the purpose for each rule?

CUMULATIVE REVIEW

80. Make the following conversions.
    a. 775 mL to microliters (μL)
    b. $-65\,°C$ to K
    c. 8.32 mg Ag to centigrams of silver (cg Ag)

81. How many protons and electrons are in each ion?
    a. magnesium ion   c. strontium ion
    b. bromide ion   d. sulfide ion

82. List five properties of the chair you are sitting on. Classify each as physical or chemical.

83. A student finds that 6.62 g of a substance occupies a volume of 12.3 cm³. What is the density of the substance?

CONCEPT CHALLENGE

84. The *Handbook of Chemistry and Physics* is a reference work that contains a wealth of information about elements and compounds. Two sections of this book you might use are "Physical Constants of Inorganic Compounds" and "Physical Constants of Organic Compounds." To familiarize yourself with this work, make a table with these headings: Name, Formula, Crystalline form or color, Density, Melting point (°C), Boiling point (°C), and Solubility in water. Enter these substances in the body of the table: ammonium chloride, barium, barium sulfate, bromine, calcium carbonate, chlorine, copper(II) sulfate pentahydrate, iodine, iron(II) sulfate pentahydrate, mercury, potassium carbonate, and sulfur. Use the *Handbook* to complete the table.

85. Use the table you prepared for Problem 84 to answer the following questions.
    a. You have two unlabeled bottles, each containing a white powder. One of the substances is calcium carbonate, and the other is potassium carbonate. Describe a simple physical test you could carry out to distinguish between these two compounds.
    b. How would you distinguish between samples of copper(II) sulfate pentahydrate and iron(II) sulfate pentahydrate?
    c. A bottle contains a mixture of ammonium chloride and barium sulfate. What method could you use to separate these two compounds?
    d. List the elements in the table in order of increasing density. Identify the elements as metals or nonmetals.
    e. List the compounds in the table in order of decreasing density.
    f. Calculate the mass of 47.0 cm³ of mercury.
    g. Calculate the volume of 16.6 g of sulfur.
    h. How would you distinguish among the Group 7A elements (halogens) listed in the table?

Select the choice that best answers each question or completes each statement.

1. Identify the pair in which the formula does *not* match the name.
   a. sulfite, SO_3^{2-}
   b. dichromate, $Cr_2O_7^{2-}$
   c. hydroxide, OH^-
   d. nitrite, NO_3^-
   e. perchlorate, ClO_4^-

2. Which of these compounds are ionic?
   I. $CaSO_4$
   II. N_2O_4
   III. NH_4NO_3
   IV. CaS
   a. I and II only
   b. II and III only
   c. III and IV only
   d. I, III, and IV only
   e. I, II, III, and IV

3. A sample of aspirin contains 6.00 g of carbon and 3.56 g of oxygen. A second sample of aspirin contains 4.20 g of carbon. How many grams of oxygen are in the second sample?
   a. 2.49 g   c. 3.08 g
   b. 5.09 g   d. 2.44 g

4. The Roman numeral in manganese(IV) sulfide indicates the
   a. group number on the periodic table.
   b. positive charge on the manganese ion.
   c. number of manganese ions in the formula.
   d. the number of sulfide ions needed in the formula.

5. Which of these statements does *not* describe every binary molecular compound?
   a. Molecules of binary molecular compounds are composed of two atoms.
   b. The names of binary molecular compounds contain prefixes.
   c. The names of binary molecular compounds end in the suffix *–ide.*
   d. Binary molecular compounds are composed of two nonmetals.

6. What is the formula of ammonium carbonate?
   a. NH_4CO_3
   b. NH_4C
   c. $(NH_4)_2CO_3$
   d. NH_3CO_4
   e. $(NH_3)_2CO_4$

The lettered choices below refer to questions 7–11. A lettered choice may be used once, more than once, or not at all.
   (A) PQ
   (B) PQ_2
   (C) P_2Q
   (D) P_2Q_3

Which formula shows the correct ratio of ions in the compound formed by each pair of elements?

	Element P	Element Q
7.	aluminum	sulfur
8.	potassium	oxygen
9.	lithium	chlorine
10.	strontium	bromine
11.	sodium	sulfur

Use the data table to answer questions 12–13.

Cation	Anion			
	A	B	C	D
M	MA_2	(1)	(2)	MD
N	(3)	N_2B	(4)	(5)
P	PA_3	(6)	PC	$P_2(D)_3$

The table gives formulas for some of the ionic compounds formed when cations (M, N, P) combine with anions (A, B, C, D).

12. Use the given formulas to determine the ionic charge of each cation and anion.

13. Write formulas for compounds (1) through (6).

Use the atomic windows to answer questions 14–15.

a.
c.
b.
d.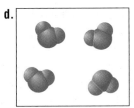

14. Identify the contents of each atomic window as a substance or a mixture.

15. Classify the contents as elements only, compounds only, or elements and compounds.

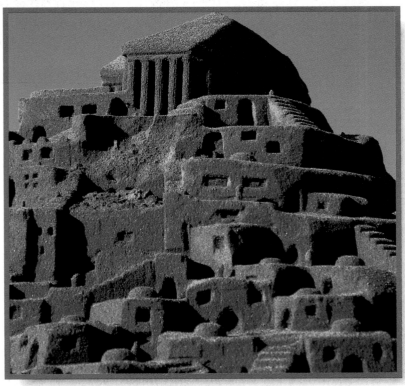

This sand sculpture contains millions of grains of sand.

FEATURES

DISCOVER IT!
Counting by Measuring Mass

SMALL-SCALE LAB
Measuring Mass as a Means of Counting

MINI LAB
Percent Composition

CHEMath
Fractions, Ratios, and Percent

CHEMISTRY SERVING ... THE ENVIRONMENT
Water Worth Drinking

CHEMISTRY IN CAREERS
Ecologist

Stay current with **SCIENCE NEWS**
Find out more about chemical quantities:
www.phschool.com

DISCOVER IT!

COUNTING BY MEASURING MASS

You need 100 paper clips of the same size and a centigram balance.

1. Find the mass of 25 paper clips. Divide the total mass by 25 to find the average mass of a paper clip. Repeat this step using 25 different paper clips until your average masses agree.

2. Select about 75% of your paper clips and find their mass. Without counting, calculate the number of paper clips in your sample.

3. Count the number of paper clips in your sample.

4. Repeat Steps 2 and 3 with a different sample size.

Did the number of paper clips you counted in the sample (Step 3) equal the number you calculated by mass (Step 2)? Explain how you would use the balance to count out 185 paper clips. What is the advantage of using a larger sample size in Step 1? What is a disadvantage? After completing this chapter, revisit this activity and suggest other ways you might count your paper clips.

THE MOLE: A MEASUREMENT OF MATTER

Every year, contestants from all over the world travel to Harrison Hot Springs in British Columbia, Canada to compete in the world championship sand sculpture contest. Each contestant creates a beautiful work of art out of millions of tiny grains of sand. **If you assume that sand is pure silicon dioxide (SiO$_2$), what chemical unit could you use to measure the amount of sand in a sand sculpture?**

What Is a Mole?

You live in a quantitative world. The grade you got on your last exam, the number of times you heard your favorite song on the radio yesterday, and the cost of a bicycle you would like to own are all important quantities to you. These are quantities that answer such questions as "how much?" or "how many?" Scientists spend time answering similar questions. How many kilograms of iron can be obtained from one kilogram of iron ore? How many grams of the elements hydrogen and nitrogen must be combined to make 200 grams of the fertilizer ammonia (NH$_3$)? These two questions illustrate that chemistry is a quantitative science. In your study of chemistry, you will analyze the composition of samples of matter. You will also perform chemical calculations relating quantities of reactants and products to chemical equations. To solve these and other problems, you will have to be able to measure the amount of matter you have.

How do you measure matter? One way is to count how many of something you have. For example, you can count the CDs in your collection or the number of pins you knock down when bowling. Another way to measure matter is to determine its mass or weight. You can buy potatoes by the kilogram or pound and gold by the gram or ounce. You can also measure matter by volume. For instance, people buy gasoline by the liter or gallon and take cough medicine by the milliliter or teaspoon. Often, more than one method of measurement—a count, a mass, a volume—can be used. For example, you can buy soda by the six-pack or by the liter. **Figure 7.2** on the following page shows how some everyday items are measured.

Figure 7.1
Jellybeans are often sold by either weight or mass.

Some of the units used when measuring always indicate a specific number of items. For example, a pair always means two. A pair of shoes is two shoes, and a pair of aces is two aces. Similarly, a dozen always means 12 (except for a baker's dozen which is 13). A dozen eggs is 12 eggs, a dozen pens is 12 pens, and a dozen donuts is 12 donuts.

Apples are commonly measured in three different ways. At a fruit stand, apples are often sold by the *count* (5 for $2.00). In a supermarket, you usually buy apples by weight ($0.89/pound) or *mass* ($1.95/kg). At an orchard, you can buy apples by *volume* ($9.00/bushel). Each of these different ways to measure apples—by count, by mass, and by volume—can be equated to a dozen apples.

By count:
1 dozen apples = 12 apples

For average-sized apples the following approximations can be used.

By mass:
1 dozen apples = 2.0 kg apples

By volume:
1 dozen apples = 0.20 bushel apples

Knowing how the count, mass, and volume of apples relate to a dozen apples allows you to convert between these units. For example, you could calculate the mass of a bushel of apples or the mass of 90 average-sized apples using conversion factors based on the unit relationships given above.

In chemistry, you will do calculations using a measuring unit called a mole. The mole, the SI unit that measures the amount of substance, is a unit just like the dozen. The mole can be related to the number of particles (a count), the mass, and the volume of an element or a compound just as a dozen was related to these three units for apples.

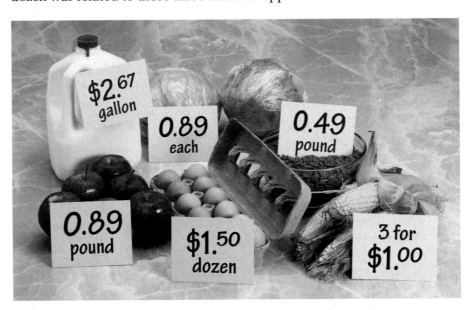

Figure 7.2
Items are often sold by different types of measurements, such as a count, a weight or mass, or a volume. Which of these common supermarket items are being sold by weight? By volume? By count?

Sample Problem 7-1

What is the mass of 90 average-sized apples?

1. **ANALYZE List the knowns and the unknown.**

   Knowns:
   - number of apples = 90 apples
   - 12 apples = 1 dozen apples
   - 1 dozen apples = 2.0 kg apples

   Unknown:
   - mass of 90 apples = ? kg

   The desired conversion is:

   number of apples $\longrightarrow$ mass of apples

   This conversion can be carried out by performing the following sequence of conversions:

   number $\longrightarrow$ dozens $\longrightarrow$ mass of apples

2. **CALCULATE Solve for the unknown.**

   The first conversion factor is $\dfrac{1 \text{ dozen apples}}{12 \text{ apples}}$.

   The second conversion factor is $\dfrac{2.0 \text{ kg apples}}{1 \text{ dozen apples}}$.

   Multiplying the original number of apples by these two conversion factors yields the answer in kilograms,

   $$90 \text{ apples} \times \frac{1 \text{ dozen apples}}{12 \text{ apples}} \times \frac{2.0 \text{ kg apples}}{1 \text{ dozen apples}}$$

   $$= 15 \text{ kg apples}$$

3. **EVALUATE Does the result make sense?**

   Because a dozen apples has a mass of 2.0 kg and 90 apples is less than 10 dozen apples, the mass should be less than 20 kg of apples (10 dozen × 2.0 kg/dozen).

Practice Problems

1. What is the mass of 0.50 bushel of apples?
2. Assume that a variety of apples has 8 seeds in each apple. How many apple seeds are in 14 kg of apples?

Chem ASAP!

Problem-Solving 1
Solve Problem 1 with the help of an interactive guided tutorial.

The Number of Particles in a Mole

In Chapter 2, you learned that matter is composed of different kinds of particles. One way to measure the amount of a substance is to count the number of particles in that substance. Because atoms, molecules, and ions are exceedingly small, the number of individual particles in a sample (even a very small sample) of any substance is very large. Counting the particles is not practical. However, you can count particles if you introduce a term that represents a specified number of particles. Just as a dozen eggs represents 12 eggs, a **mole (mol)** of a substance represents 6.02×10^{23} representative particles of that substance. The experimentally determined number 6.02×10^{23} is called **Avogadro's number,** in honor of Amedeo Avogadro di Quaregna (1776–1856).

The term **representative particle** refers to the species present in a substance: usually atoms, molecules, or formula units (ions). The representative particle of most elements is the atom. Iron is composed of iron atoms. Helium is composed of helium atoms. Seven elements, however, normally exist as diatomic molecules (H_2, N_2, O_2, F_2, Cl_2, Br_2, and I_2). The

Figure 7.3

Although Amedeo Avogadro clarified the difference between atoms and molecules, he did not calculate the value that is named after him. Avogadro's number was given his name to honor his contributions to science.

Figure 7.4
There are words other than mole used to describe a number of something— for example, a dozen (12) eggs, a gross (144) of pencils, and a ream (500 sheets) of paper.

representative particle of these elements and of all molecular compounds is the molecule. The molecular compounds water (H_2O) and sulfur dioxide (SO_2) are composed of H_2O and SO_2 molecules, respectively. For ionic compounds, the formula unit is the representative particle. The ionic compound calcium chloride is composed of $CaCl_2$ formula units. Calcium ions and chloride ions are present in a one to two ratio in this formula unit. **Table 7.1** summarizes the relationship between representative particles and moles of substances. Remember that a mole of any substance always contains 6.02×10^{23} representative particles.

Table 7.1

Representative Particles and Moles			
Substance	Representative particle	Chemical formula	Representative particles in 1.00 mol
Atomic nitrogen	Atom	N	6.02×10^{23}
Nitrogen gas	Molecule	N_2	6.02×10^{23}
Water	Molecule	H_2O	6.02×10^{23}
Calcium ion	Ion	Ca^{2+}	6.02×10^{23}
Calcium fluoride	Formula unit	CaF_2	6.02×10^{23}
Sucrose	Molecule	$C_{12}H_{22}O_{11}$	6.02×10^{23}

Sample Problem 7-2

How many moles of magnesium is 1.25×10^{23} atoms of magnesium?

1. **ANALYZE List the knowns and the unknown.**

Knowns:
- number of atoms = 1.25×10^{23} atoms Mg
- 1 mol Mg = 6.02×10^{23} atoms Mg

The desired conversion is:

$$\text{atoms} \longrightarrow \text{moles}$$

Unknown:
- moles = ? mol Mg

2. **CALCULATE Solve for the unknown.**

The conversion factor is $\dfrac{1 \text{ mol Mg}}{6.02 \times 10^{23} \text{ atoms Mg}}$.

Multiplying atoms of Mg by the conversion factor yields the answer.

$$1.25 \times 10^{23} \text{ atoms Mg} \times \frac{1 \text{ mol Mg}}{6.02 \times 10^{23} \text{ atoms Mg}}$$

$$= 2.08 \times 10^{-1} \text{ mol Mg}$$

3. **EVALUATE Does the result make sense?**
Because the given number of atoms is less than one-fourth of Avogadro's number, the answer should be less than one-fourth mole of atoms. The answer should have three significant figures.

Practice Problems

3. How many moles is 2.80×10^{24} atoms of silicon?
4. How many molecules is 0.360 mol of water?

Chem ASAP!

Problem-Solving 4
Solve Problem 4 with the help of an interactive guided tutorial.

Now suppose you want to determine how many atoms are in a mole of a compound. To do this, you must know how many atoms are in a representative particle of the compound. This number is determined from the chemical formula. For example, each molecule of carbon dioxide (CO_2) is composed of three atoms: one carbon atom and two oxygen atoms. A mole of carbon dioxide contains Avogadro's number of CO_2 molecules. Thus a mole of carbon dioxide contains three times Avogadro's number of atoms. A molecule of carbon monoxide (CO) consists of two atoms, so a mole of carbon monoxide contains two times Avogadro's number of atoms. To find the number of atoms in a mole of a compound, you must first determine the number of atoms in a representative particle of that compound and then multiply that number by Avogadro's number. **Figure 7.5** illustrates this idea with marbles (atoms) in cups (molecules).

Figure 7.5
A dozen cups of marbles contain more than a dozen marbles. Similarly, a mole of molecules contains more than a mole of atoms. How many atoms are in one mole of molecules if each molecule consists of six atoms?

Sample Problem 7-3

How many atoms are in 2.12 mol of propane (C_3H_8)?

1. **ANALYZE List the knowns and the unknown.**

   Knowns:
   - number of moles = 2.12 mol C_3H_8
   - 1 mol C_3H_8 = 6.02×10^{23} molecules C_3H_8
   - 1 molecule C_3H_8 = 11 atoms
     (3 carbon atoms and 8 hydrogen atoms)

   Unknown:
   - number of atoms = ? atoms

   The desired conversion is:

   $$moles \longrightarrow molecules \longrightarrow atoms$$

   Using the relationships among units given above, the desired conversion factors can be written.

2. **CALCULATE Solve for the unknown.**

   The first conversion factor is $\dfrac{6.02 \times 10^{23} \text{ molecules } C_3H_8}{1 \text{ mol } C_3H_8}$.

   The second conversion factor is $\dfrac{11 \text{ atoms}}{1 \text{ molecule } C_3H_8}$.

   Multiplying the moles of C_3H_8 by the proper conversion factors yields the answer.

   $$2.12 \text{ mol } C_3H_8 \times \frac{6.02 \times 10^{23} \text{ molecules } C_3H_8}{1 \text{ mol } C_3H_8} \times \frac{11 \text{ atoms}}{1 \text{ molecule } C_3H_8}$$

   $$= 1.4039 \times 10^{25} \text{ atoms} = 1.40 \times 10^{25} \text{ atoms}$$

3. **EVALUATE Does the result make sense?**
   Because there are 11 atoms in each molecule of propane and more than 2 mol of propane, the answer should be more than 20 times Avogadro's number of propane molecules. The answer has three significant figures based on the three significant figures in the given measurement.

Practice Problems

5. How many atoms are there in 1.14 mol SO_3?
6. How many moles are there in 4.65×10^{24} molecules of NO_2?

Figure 7.6
How big is a mole?

Chem ASAP!
Animation 6
Find out how Avogadro's
number is based on the relationship
between the amu and the gram.

Perhaps you are wondering just how large Avogadro's number is. The SI unit, the mole, is not related to the small burrowing animal of the same name shown in **Figure 7.6.** However, you can use this animal to help develop an appreciation for the size of the number 6.02×10^{23}. Assume that an average animal-mole is 15 cm long, 5 cm tall, and has a mass of 150 g. Based on this information, what is the mass of 6.02×10^{23} animal-moles?

$$6.02 \times 10^{23} \ \cancel{\text{animal-mole}} \times \frac{150 \text{ g}}{1 \ \cancel{\text{animal mole}}} = 9.03 \times 10^{25} \text{g}$$
$$= 9.03 \times 10^{22} \text{ kg}$$

The mass of animal-moles is equivalent to
- more than 1% of Earth's mass.
- more than 1.3 times the mass of the moon.
- more than 60 times the combined mass of Earth's oceans.

If spread over the entire surface of Earth, Avogadro's number of animal-moles would form a layer more than 8 million animal-moles thick.

What about the length of 6.02×10^{23} animal-moles?

$$6.02 \times 10^{23} \ \cancel{\text{animal-mole}} \times \frac{15 \text{ cm}}{1 \ \cancel{\text{animal mole}}} = 9.03 \times 10^{24} \text{cm}$$
$$= 9.03 \times 10^{19} \text{ km}$$

If lined up end-to-end, 6.02×10^{23} animal-moles would stretch from Earth to the nearest star, Alpha Centauri, more than two million times.

Suppose you could convince Avogadro's number of animal-moles to line up in 6 billion equal columns. Further suppose that each of the approximately 6 billion people on Earth counted the animal-moles in one column at the rate of 1000 animal-moles per second. Even with that many people counting that fast, it would still take more than 3000 years to count 6.02×10^{23} animal-moles! Are you beginning to understand how enormous Avogadro's number is?

The Mass of a Mole of an Element

You are always working with large numbers of atoms even if you are using microgram quantities. Even one billion atoms would be a very small amount of a substance. Working with grams of atoms is much easier. The **gram atomic mass (gam)** is the atomic mass of an element expressed in grams. For carbon, the gram atomic mass is 12.0 g. For atomic hydrogen, the gram atomic mass is 1.0 g. **Figure 7.7** shows one gram atomic mass of carbon, sulfur, mercury, and iron. Compare the gram atomic masses in the figure to the atomic masses in your periodic table. Notice that the gram atomic masses were rounded off to one place after the decimal point. All the examples and problems in this text use gram atomic masses that are rounded off in the same way. If your teacher uses a different rounding rule for gram atomic masses, your answers to problems may differ slightly from the answers given in the text.

You learned previously that the atomic mass of an element (the mass of a single atom) is expressed in atomic mass units (amu). Remember that atomic masses of atoms are relative values. The atomic masses of elements found in the periodic table are weighted average masses of the isotopes of

Figure 7.7

One gram atomic mass (gam) is shown for carbon, sulfur, mercury, and iron. Each of these quantities contains one mole, or 6.02 ×10²³ atoms, of that substance.

that element. As you can see in **Figure 7.8,** an average carbon atom (C) with an atomic mass of 12.0 amu is 12 times heavier than an average hydrogen atom (H) with an atomic mass of 1.0 amu. Therefore 100 carbon atoms are 12 times heavier than 100 hydrogen atoms. In fact, any number of carbon atoms is 12 times heavier than the same number of hydrogen atoms, as **Figure 7.8** demonstrates. Therefore 12.0 g of carbon atoms and 1.0 g of hydrogen atoms contain the same number of atoms.

The gram atomic masses of any two elements must contain the same number of atoms. If you were to compare 12.0 g of carbon atoms with 16.0 g of oxygen atoms, you would find they contain the same number of atoms. How many atoms are contained in the gram atomic mass of an element? You are now familiar with this quantity—the gram atomic mass of any element contains 1 mol of atoms (6.02×10^{23} atoms) of that element.

Figure 7.8

The mass ratio of equal numbers of carbon atoms to hydrogen atoms is always 12 to 1.

CARBON ATOMS		HYDROGEN ATOMS		MASS RATIO
Number	Mass (amu)	Number	Mass (amu)	$\dfrac{\text{Mass carbon}}{\text{Mass hydrogen}}$
●	12	○	1	$\dfrac{12\ \text{amu}}{1\ \text{amu}} = \dfrac{12}{1}$
●●	24 [2 × 12]	○○	2 [2 × 1]	$\dfrac{24\ \text{amu}}{2\ \text{amu}} = \dfrac{12}{1}$
●●●●● ●●●●●	120 [10 × 12]	○○○○○ ○○○○○	10 [10 × 1]	$\dfrac{120\ \text{amu}}{10\ \text{amu}} = \dfrac{12}{1}$
●●●●●●●●●● ●●●●●●●●●● ●●●●●●●●●● ●●●●●●●●●● ●●●●●●●●●●	600 [50 × 12]	○○○○○○○○○○ ○○○○○○○○○○ ○○○○○○○○○○ ○○○○○○○○○○ ○○○○○○○○○○	50 [50 × 1]	$\dfrac{600\ \text{amu}}{50\ \text{amu}} = \dfrac{12}{1}$
Avogadro's number	$(6.02 \times 10^{23}) \times (12)$	Avogadro's number	$(6.02 \times 10^{23}) \times (1)$	$\dfrac{(6.02 \times 10^{23}) \times (12)}{(6.02 \times 10^{23}) \times (1)} = \dfrac{12}{1}$

The mole can now be defined as the amount of substance that contains as many representative particles as the number of atoms in 12.0 g of carbon-12. You know that 12.0 g is the gram atomic mass of carbon-12. Because 12.0 g of carbon is the gram atomic mass of carbon, 12.0 g is 1 mol of carbon. The same relationship applies to hydrogen as well; that is, 1.0 g of hydrogen is 1 mol of hydrogen. Similarly, because 24.3 g is the gram atomic mass of magnesium, 24.3 g is 1 mol of magnesium (or 6.02×10^{23} atoms of magnesium). Thus the gram atomic mass is the mass of 1 mol of atoms of any element.

The Mass of a Mole of a Compound

What is the mass of a mole of a compound? To answer this question, you must first know the formula of the compound. The formula of a compound tells you the number of atoms of each element in a representative particle of that compound. For example, the formula of the molecular compound sulfur trioxide is SO_3. A molecule of SO_3 is composed of one atom of sulfur and three atoms of oxygen.

SO_3 =   1 S atom   +   3 O atoms

You can calculate the mass of a molecule of SO_3 by adding the atomic masses of the atoms making up the molecule. From the periodic table, the atomic mass of sulfur (S) is 32.1 amu. The mass of three atoms of oxygen is three times the atomic mass of a single oxygen atom (O): 3×16.0 amu = 48.0 amu. Thus the molecular mass of SO_3 is 32.1 amu + 48.0 amu = 80.1 amu.

1 S atom   3 O atoms

32.1 amu   +   16.0 amu + 16.0 amu + 16.0 amu = 80.1 amu

If you now substitute the unit grams for atomic mass units, you will have the gram molecular mass of SO_3. The **gram molecular mass (gmm)** of any molecular compound is the mass of 1 mol of that compound. The gmm equals the molecular mass expressed in grams. Thus 1 mol of SO_3 has a mass of 80.1 g.

Gram molecular masses may be calculated directly from gram atomic masses. For each element in a compound, find the number of grams of that element per mole of the compound. Then sum the masses of the elements in the compound. The gram molecular masses of the molecular compounds in **Figure 7.9** were obtained in this way. Try calculating the gram molecular mass values shown in **Figure 7.9** yourself. Do you get the same values? If not, review the calculation for sulfur trioxide shown above, then try again. Calculating gram molecular mass values is an important skill that you will use often in your study of chemistry.

Key

Glucose

Water

Paradichlorobenzene

1 mol of glucose molecules
(blood sugar)
180.0 g $C_6H_{12}O_6$ = 1 gmm $C_6H_{12}O_6$

1 mol of paradichlorobenzene
molecules (moth crystals)
147.0 g $C_6H_4Cl_2$ = 1 gmm $C_6H_4Cl_2$

1 mol of water molecules
18.0 g H_2O = 1 gmm H_2O

Figure 7.9
*One gram molecular mass (gmm)
is shown for each of three molecular compounds. Each of these
quantities contains 6.02×10^{23}
molecules. Do they each contain
the same number of atoms?*

Sample Problem 7-4

The molecular formula of hydrogen peroxide is H_2O_2. What is its gram molecular mass?

1. **ANALYZE** *List the knowns and the unknown.*

   Knowns:
   - molecular formula = H_2O_2
   - 1 gam H = 1 mol H = 1.0 g H
   - 1 gam O = 1 mol O = 16.0 g O

   Unknown:
   - gmm = ? g

   The molecular formula gives the number of moles of each element in 1 mol of hydrogen peroxide: 2 mol of hydrogen atoms and 2 mol of oxygen atoms. Moles of atoms are converted to grams by using conversion factors (g/mol) based on the gram atomic mass of each element. The sum of the masses of the elements gives the gram molecular mass.

2. **CALCULATE** *Solve for the unknown.*
   Use the proper conversion factors to convert moles of hydrogen and oxygen to grams of hydrogen and oxygen. Adding the results gives the answer.

   $$2 \text{ mol H} \times \frac{1.0 \text{ g H}}{1 \text{ mol H}} = 2.0 \text{ g H}$$

   $$2 \text{ mol O} \times \frac{16.0 \text{ g O}}{1 \text{ mol O}} = 32.0 \text{ g O}$$

   gram molecular mass of H_2O_2 = 34.0 g

3. **EVALUATE** *Does the result make sense?*
   The answer reflects the number of moles of atoms of each element and the gram atomic mass of each element. The answer is expressed to the tenth's place because the numbers being added are expressed to the tenth's place.

Practice Problems

7. Find the gram molecular mass of each compound.
   a. C_2H_6
   b. PCl_3
   c. C_3H_7OH
   d. N_2O_5
8. What is the mass of 1.00 mol of each substance?
   a. chlorine
   b. nitrogen dioxide
   c. carbon tetrabromide
   d. silicon dioxide

Figure 7.10

One gram formula mass (gfm) is shown for each of three ionic compounds. Each of these quantities contains 6.02×10^{23} formula units. Which of these compounds contains the greatest number of atoms?

1 mol of cobalt(II) chloride formula units
129.9 g CoCl$_2$ =1 gfm CoCl$_2$

1 mol of potassium dichromate formula units
294.2 g K$_2$Cr$_2$O$_7$ =1 gfm K$_2$Cr$_2$O$_7$

1 mol of potassium hydroxide formula units
56.1 g KOH = 1 gfm KOH

It is inappropriate to calculate the gram molecular mass of calcium iodide (CaI_2) because it is an ionic compound. The representative particle of an ionic compound is a formula unit, not a molecule. The mass of one mole of an ionic compound is the **gram formula mass (gfm)**. The gfm equals the formula mass expressed in grams. A gram formula mass is calculated the same way as a gram molecular mass: Simply sum the atomic masses of the ions in the formula of the compound. For example, the gram formula mass of calcium iodide is the gram atomic mass of calcium plus two times the gram atomic mass of iodine.

$$40.1 \text{ g Ca} + (2 \times 126.9 \text{ g I}) = 293.9 \text{ g CaI}_2$$

There are 293.9 g CaI_2 in 1 gfm or 1 mol CaI_2.

Figure 7.10 shows one gram formula mass of three ionic compounds. How many formula units are in each sample in the figure?

Sample Problem 7-5

What is the gram formula mass of ammonium carbonate $((NH_4)_2CO_3)$?

1. **ANALYZE** *List the knowns and the unknown.*

Knowns:
- formula unit = $(NH_4)_2CO_3$
- 1 gam N = 1 mol N = 14.0 g N
- 1 gam H = 1 mol H = 1.0 g H
- 1 gam C = 1 mol C − 12.0 g C
- 1 gam O = 1 mol O = 16.0 g O

Unknown:
- gfm = ? g

The formula shows that a mole of this ionic compound is composed of 2 mol of nitrogen atoms, 8 mol of hydrogen atoms, 1 mol of carbon atoms, and 3 mol of oxygen atoms. Moles of atoms are converted to grams by using conversion factors based on the gram atomic masses. The sum of the masses of the elements gives the gram formula mass.

Sample Problem 7-5 (cont.)

2. **CALCULATE** *Solve for the unknown.*

Using the proper conversion factors and adding the results gives the answer.

$$2 \text{ mol N} \times \frac{14.0 \text{ g N}}{1 \text{ mol N}} = 28.0 \text{ g N}$$

$$8 \text{ mol H} \times \frac{1.0 \text{ g H}}{1 \text{ mol H}} = 8.0 \text{ g H}$$

$$1 \text{ mol C} \times \frac{12.0 \text{ g C}}{1 \text{ mol C}} = 12.0 \text{ g C}$$

$$3 \text{ mol O} \times \frac{16.0 \text{ g O}}{1 \text{ mol O}} = 48.0 \text{ g O}$$

gram formula mass of $(NH_4)_2CO_3 = 96.0$ g

3. **EVALUATE** *Does the result make sense?*

The answer reflects the number of moles of atoms of each element and the gram atomic mass of each element. The answer is expressed to the tenth's place because the numbers being added are expressed to the tenth's place.

Practice Problems

9. Calculate the gram formula mass of each ionic compound.
   a. K_2O
   b. $CaSO_4$
   c. CuI_2
10. Find the gram formula mass of each compound.
    a. barium fluoride
    b. strontium cyanide
    c. sodium hydrogen carbonate
    d. aluminum sulfite

section review 7.1

11. Describe the relationship between Avogadro's number and one mole of any substance.

12. Find the gram formula mass of each compound.
    a. Li_2S
    b. $FeCl_3$
    c. $Ca(OH)_2$

13. How many oxygen atoms are in a representative particle of each substance?
    a. ammonium nitrate (NH_4NO_3), a fertilizer
    b. acetylsalicylic acid ($C_8H_8O_4$), the fever-reducing compound aspirin
    c. ozone (O_3), a disinfectant
    d. nitroglycerine ($C_3H_5(NO_3)_3$), an explosive

14. How many moles is each of the following?
    a. 1.50×10^{23} molecules NH_3
    b. 1 billion (1×10^9) molecules O_2
    c. 6.02×10^{22} molecules Br_2
    d. 4.81×10^{24} atoms Li

15. Distinguish among gram atomic mass, gram molecular mass, and gram formula mass.

portfolio project

Research the history of Avogadro's number. What elements other than carbon have been used to define a mole? Write a report that summarizes your findings.

 ChemASAP! Assessment 7.1 Check your understanding of the important ideas and concepts in Section 7.1.

objectives

▶ Use the molar mass to convert between mass and moles of a substance

▶ Use the mole to convert among measurements of mass, volume, and number of particles

key terms

▶ molar mass

▶ standard temperature and pressure (STP)

▶ molar volume

MOLE-MASS AND MOLE-VOLUME RELATIONSHIPS

If *you have ever been to a circus or a carnival, you may have seen a "Guess Your Weight" booth. The person in the booth will offer to guess your weight within a certain range or you win a prize. Is the person just guessing? Probably not. Based on tables that relate average weight to height, the person can probably come fairly close to estimating your weight by estimating your height. In a similar way, chemists use relationships between quantities of matter to solve problems.* **What molar relationship do chemists use to solve problems?**

The Molar Mass of a Substance

In the previous section, you learned three new terms: gram atomic mass (gam), gram molecular mass (gmm), and gram formula mass (gfm). Each is used to represent a mole of a particular kind of substance. The gram atomic mass of an element contains a mole of atoms. The gram molecular mass of a molecular compound contains a mole of molecules. The gram formula mass of an ionic compound contains a mole of formula units. Although these three terms have different specific meanings, we can use the broader term molar mass to refer to a mole of an element, a molecular compound, or an ionic compound. The **molar mass** of any substance is the mass (in grams) of one mole of the substance.

There are situations in which the term molar mass is unclear. Consider this example: What is the molar mass of oxygen? How you answer this question depends on your interpretation of it. If you assume the oxygen in the question is molecular oxygen (O_2), then the molar mass is 32.0 g (2×16.0 g)—its gram molecular mass. If you assume that the question is asking for the mass of a mole of oxygen atoms (O), then the answer is 16.0 g—its gram atomic mass. Throughout this textbook, the term molar mass is used unless there is the potential for confusion. In that case, a more specific term will be used or the formula of the substance will be given.

In the following Sample Problems, the molar mass of an element or compound is used to convert between grams and moles of a substance.

Sample Problem 7-6

How many grams are in 9.45 mol of dinitrogen trioxide (N_2O_3)?

··

1. **ANALYZE** *List the knowns and the unknown.*

Knowns:
- number of moles = 9.45 mol N_2O_3
- 1 mol N_2O_3 = 76.0 g N_2O_3

Unknown:
- mass = ? g N_2O_3

The number of grams of the compound must be calculated from the known number of moles of the compound. The desired conversion is moles $\longrightarrow$ grams.

Sample Problem 7-6 (cont.)

2. CALCULATE *Solve for the unknown.*

Multiply the given number of moles by the proper conversion factor relating moles of N_2O_3 to grams of N_2O_3.

$$9.45 \text{ mol } N_2O_3 \times \frac{76.0 \text{ g } N_2O_3}{1.00 \text{ mol } N_2O_3} = 718.2 \text{ g } N_2O_3$$

$$= 718 \text{ g } N_2O_3$$

3. EVALUATE *Does the result make sense?*

Because 1 mol N_2O_3 has a mass of 76.0 g, and there are almost ten moles of the compound, the answer should be about 700. The answer has been rounded to the correct number of significant figures.

Practice Problems

16. Find the mass, in grams, of each.
   a. 3.32 mol K
   b. 4.52×10^{-3} mol $C_{20}H_{42}$
   c. 0.0112 mol K_2CO_3
17. Calculate the mass, in grams, of 2.50 mol of each substance.
   a. sodium sulfate
   b. iron(II) hydroxide

Problem-Solving 16
Solve Problem 16 with the help of an interactive guided tutorial.

Whereas Sample Problem 7-6 used a conversion factor based on the molar mass to convert moles to grams, the following Sample Problem does the reverse, using a conversion factor based upon the molar mass to convert grams to moles.

Sample Problem 7-7

Find the number of moles in 92.2 g of iron(III) oxide (Fe_2O_3).

1. ANALYZE *List the knowns and the unknown.*

Knowns:
- mass = 92.2 g Fe_2O_3
- 1 mol Fe_2O_3 = 159.6 g Fe_2O_3

Unknown:
- number of moles = ? mol Fe_2O_3

From a known number of grams of a compound, the unknown number of moles of the compound must be calculated. The desired conversion is grams $\longrightarrow$ moles.

2. CALCULATE *Solve for the unknown.*

Multiply the given mass by the proper conversion factor relating mass of Fe_2O_3 to moles of Fe_2O_3.

$$92.2 \text{ g } Fe_2O_3 \times \frac{1.00 \text{ mol } Fe_2O_3}{159.6 \text{ g } Fe_2O_3} = 0.5776 \text{ mol } Fe_2O_3$$

$$= 0.578 \text{ mol } Fe_2O_3$$

3. EVALUATE *Does the result make sense?*

Because the given mass (about 90 g) is slightly larger than the mass of one-half mole of Fe_2O_3 (about 160 g), the answer should be slightly larger than one-half (0.5) of a mole.

Practice Problems

18. Find the number of moles in each quantity.
   a. 3.70×10^{-1} g B
   b. 27.4 g TiO_2
   c. 847 g $(NH_4)_2CO_3$
19. Calculate the number of moles in 75.0 g of each substance.
   a. dinitrogen trioxide
   b. nitrogen gas
   c. sodium oxide

Figure 7.11
The volume of eleven 2-liter soda bottles is 22 L. The volume of 1 mole of any gas at STP is a little more, 22.4 L.

The Volume of a Mole of Gas

If you look back at **Figure 7.9** on page 179, you will see that the volumes of one mole of different solid and liquid substances are not the same. For example, the volume of a mole of glucose (blood sugar) and one mole of paradichlorobenzene (moth crystals) are much larger than that of a mole of water. Unlike liquids and solids, the volumes of moles of gases are much more predictable under the same physical conditions.

The volume of a gas varies with a change in temperature or a change in pressure. Because of this variation, the volume of a gas is usually measured at a **standard temperature and pressure (STP).** Standard temperature is 0 °C. Standard pressure is 101.3 kPa, or 1 atmosphere (atm). At STP, 1 mol of any gas occupies a volume of 22.4 L. **Figure 7.11** should give you an idea of the volume occupied by 22.4 L. This quantity, 22.4 L, is known as the **molar volume** of a gas and is measured at STP. Because 1 mol of any substance contains Avogadro's number of particles, 22.4 L of any gas at STP contains 6.02×10^{23} representative particles of that gas. Would these values differ for gaseous elements compared with gaseous compounds?

Would 22.4 L of one gas also have the same mass as 22.4 L of another gas at STP? Probably not. A mole of a gas (22.4 L at STP) has a mass equal to its molar mass. Only gases with the same molar masses would have equal masses for equal volumes at STP.

Practice Problems

20. What is the volume at STP of these gases?
    a. 3.20×10^{-3} mol CO_2
    b. 0.960 mol CH_4
    c. 3.70 mol N_2
21. Assuming STP, how many moles are in these volumes?
    a. 67.2 L SO_2
    b. 0.880 L He
    c. 1.00×10^3 L C_2H_6

Chem ASAP!

Problem-Solving 20

Solve Problem 20 with the help of an interactive guided tutorial.

Sample Problem 7-8

Determine the volume, in liters, of 0.60 mol SO_2 gas at STP.

1. **ANALYZE** *List the knowns and the unknown.*

   Knowns:
   - moles = 0.60 mol SO_2
   - 1 mol SO_2 = 22.4 L SO_2

   Unknown:
   - volume = ? L SO_2

   The known is the number of moles and the unknown is the number of liters of SO_2. Use the relationship 1.00 mol SO_2 = 22.4 L SO_2 (at STP) to write the conversion factor needed to perform the conversion of moles $\longrightarrow$ liters.

2. **CALCULATE** *Solve for the unknown.*

$$0.60 \; \text{mol } SO_2 \times \frac{22.4 \text{ L } SO_2}{1 \text{ mol } SO_2} = 13.44 = 13 \text{ L } SO_2$$

3. **EVALUATE** *Does the result make sense?*

   Because 1 mol of any gas at STP has a volume of 22.4 L, 0.60 mol should have a volume slightly larger than 22.4/2 = 11.2 L. The answer should have two significant figures.

The density of a gas is usually measured in the units grams per liter (g/L). The experimentally determined density of a gas at STP is used to calculate the molar mass of that gas. The gas can be an element or a compound. As you can see in **Figure 7.12,** whether a gas-filled balloon sinks or floats is determined by the density of the gas in the balloon compared with the density of the surrounding air.

Sample Problem 7-9

The density of a gaseous compound containing carbon and oxygen is 1.964 g/L at STP. Determine the molar mass of the compound.

1. **ANALYZE List the knowns and the unknown.**

Knowns:
- density = 1.964 g/L
- 1 mol (gas at STP) = 22.4 L

Unknown:
- molar mass = ? g/mol

Use the relationship 1 mol (gas at STP) = 22.4 L to write the conversion factor needed to perform the required conversion.

$$\frac{g}{L} \longrightarrow \frac{g}{mol}$$

2. **CALCULATE Solve for the unknown.**

$$\frac{1.964 \text{ g}}{1 \text{ L}} \times \frac{22.4 \text{ L}}{1 \text{ mol}} = 43.9936 = 44.0 \text{ g/mol}$$

3. **EVALUATE Does the result make sense?**
The ratio of the calculated mass (44.0 g) to the volume (22.4 L) is about two, which is close to the known density. The answer should have three significant figures.

Practice Problems

22. A gaseous compound composed of sulfur and oxygen that is linked to the formation of acid rain has a density of 3.58 g/L at STP. What is the molar mass of this gas?
23. What is the density of krypton gas at STP?

Chem ASAP!

Problem-Solving 22
Solve Problem 22 with the help of an interactive guided tutorial.

The Mole Road Map

You have now examined a mole in terms of particles, mass, and volume of gases at STP. **Figure 7.13** on page 186 summarizes these relationships and illustrates the importance of the mole. To convert from one unit to another, you use the mole as an intermediate step. The form of the conversion factor depends on whether you are going from moles or to moles. You use the mole conversion factor in the same way you used the unit dozen to convert among mass, volume, and number of apples in Section 7.1. According to **Figure 7.13** on the following page, how many conversion factors are needed to convert from the mass of a gas to the volume of a gas (at STP)?

Figure 7.12

Helium is less dense than air. Balloons filled with helium must be tied to a heavy object to prevent them from floating away. The balloons sitting on the table are not tied down. How does the density of the gas in these balloons compare with the density of helium?

Figure 7.13
All paths lead to or from the mole on this mole conversion road map. The map shows the general form of the conversion factors needed to convert among volume, mass, and number of particles.

Chem ASAP!

Simulation 3
Practice using the mole road map to convert among mass, volume, and number of representative particles.

section review 7.2

24. Find the mass in grams of each quantity.

    a. 0.720 mol Be   **c.** 0.160 mol H_2O_2

    b. 2.40 mol N_2 **d.** 5.08 mol $Ca(NO_3)_2$

25. **a.** Calculate the number of molecules in 60.0 g NO_2.

    b. Calculate the volume, in liters, of 3.24×10^{22} molecules Cl_2 (STP).

    c. Calculate the mass, in grams, of 18.0 L CH_4 (STP).

26. Would three balloons, each containing the same number of molecules of a different gas at STP, have the same mass or the same volume? Explain.

27. Find the number of moles in each quantity.

    a. 5.00 g hydrogen molecules   **c.** 187 g Al

    b. 0.000264 g Li_2HPO_4 **d.** 333 g SnF_2

28. The densities of gases A, B, and C are 1.25 g/L, 2.86 g/L, and 0.714 g/L, respectively. Calculate the molar mass of each substance. Identify each substance as ammonia (NH_3), sulfur dioxide (SO_2), chlorine (Cl_2), nitrogen (N_2), or methane (CH_4).

Chem ASAP! Assessment 7.2 Check your understanding of the important ideas and concepts in Section 7.2.

MEASURING MASS AS A MEANS OF COUNTING

SAFETY

Wear your safety glasses and follow standard safety procedures as outlined on page 18.

PURPOSE

To determine the mass of several chemical compound samples and use the data to count atoms.

MATERIALS

- pencil
- paper
- plastic spoon
- chemicals shown in Figure A
- balance
- ruler

PROCEDURE

Measure the mass of one level teaspoon of sodium chloride (NaCl), water (H_2O), and calcium carbonate ($CaCO_3$). Make a table similar to Figure A to record your measured and calculated data.

	$H_2O(l)$	$NaCl(s)$	$CaCO_3(s)$
Mass (grams)			
Molar Mass (g/mol)			
Moles of each compound			
Moles of each element			
Atoms of each element			

Figure A

ANALYSIS

Using your data, record the answers to the following questions in or below your data table.

1. Calculate the moles of NaCl contained in one level teaspoon and record the result in your table.

$$\text{moles of NaCl} = ? \text{ g NaCl} \times \frac{1 \text{ mol NaCl}}{58.5 \text{ g}}$$

2. Repeat Step 1 for the other compounds in Figure A. Use the periodic table if necessary to calculate the molar mass of water and calcium carbonate.

3. Calculate the moles of each element present in the teaspoon-sized sample of H_2O.

$$\text{moles of H} = ? \text{ mol } H_2O \times \frac{2 \text{ mol H}}{1 \text{ mol } H_2O}$$

Repeat for all the other compounds in your table.

4. Calculate the number of atoms of each element present in the teaspoon-sized sample of H_2O.

$$\text{atoms of H} = ? \text{ mol H} \times \frac{6.02 \times 10^{23} \text{ atoms H}}{1 \text{ mol } H_2O}$$

Repeat for all the other compounds in your table.

5. Which of the three teaspoon-sized samples contains the greatest number of moles?

6. Which of the three compounds contains the most atoms?

YOU'RE THE CHEMIST!

The following small-scale activities allow you to develop your own procedures and analyze the results.

1. **Design It!** Can you use the technique of measuring volume as a means of counting? Design and carry out an experiment to do it!

2. **Design It!** Design an experiment that will determine the number of atoms of calcium, carbon, and oxygen it takes to write your name on the chalkboard with a piece of chalk. Assume chalk is 100 percent calcium carbonate, $CaCO_3$.

▶ Calculate the percent composition of a substance from its chemical formula or experimental data
▶ Derive the empirical formula and the molecular formula of a compound from experimental data

key terms
▶ percent composition
▶ empirical formula

Figure 7.14

Percent compositions, such as those found on this label, are frequently used in everyday life.

PERCENT COMPOSITION AND CHEMICAL FORMULAS

*G*rowing healthy plants requires more than just a green thumb. Lawn-care professionals, as well as most home gardeners, know the importance of fertilizers in maintaining healthy lawns and gardens. Lawn and garden fertilizers are labeled with three numbers, such as 15-10-15, which represent the relative amounts of nitrogen, phosphorus, and potassium, respectively. Relative quantities are similar to percentages and can be used to calculate percent composition.
What is the percent composition of a substance, and how is it calculated?

Calculating the Percent Composition of a Compound

If you have had any experience with lawn care, then you know that the amount of fertilizer you put on a lawn is important. The relative amount, or the percent, of each nutrient in the fertilizer is also important. In the spring, you may use a fertilizer that has a relatively high percent of nitrogen to "green" the grass. In the fall, you may want to use a fertilizer with a higher percent of potassium to strengthen the root system of the grass. Knowing the relative amounts of the components of a mixture or compound is often useful or important.

The relative amounts of each element in a compound are expressed as the **percent composition,** or the percent by mass of each element in a compound. The percent composition of a compound has as many percent values as there are different elements in the compound. As you can see in **Figure 7.15,** the percent composition of K_2CrO_4 is K = 40.3%, Cr = 26.8%, and O = 32.9%. These percents must total 100% (40.3% + 26.8% + 32.9% = 100%).

The percent by mass of an element in a compound is the number of grams of the element divided by the number of grams of the compound, multiplied by 100%.

$$\% \text{ mass of element E} = \frac{\text{grams of element E}}{\text{grams of compound}} \times 100\%$$

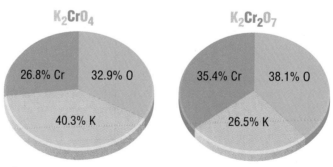

Potassium chromate, K_2CrO_4 Potassium dichromate, $K_2Cr_2O_7$

Figure 7.15

Potassium chromate (K_2CrO_4) is composed of 40.3% potassium, 26.8% chromium, and 32.9% oxygen. How does this differ from the percent composition of potassium dichromate ($K_2Cr_2O_7$), a compound composed of the same three elements?

Sample Problem 7-10

An 8.20-g piece of magnesium combines completely with 5.40 g of oxygen to form a compound. What is the percent composition of this compound?

1. **ANALYZE** *List the knowns and the unknown.*

   Knowns:
   - mass of magnesium = 8.20 g Mg
   - mass of oxygen = 5.40 g O
   - mass of compound = 8.20 g + 5.40 g = 13.60 g

   Unknowns:
   - percent Mg = ? % Mg
   - percent O = ? % O

   The percent by mass of an element in a compound is the mass of that element divided by the mass of the compound multiplied by 100%.

2. **CALCULATE** *Solve for the unknown.*

$$\% \text{ Mg} = \frac{\text{mass of Mg}}{\text{grams of compound}} \times 100\%$$

$$= \frac{8.2 \text{ g}}{13.6 \text{ g}} \times 100\% = 60.29412 = 60.3\%$$

$$\% \text{ O} = \frac{\text{mass of O}}{\text{grams of compound}} \times 100\%$$

$$= \frac{5.4 \text{ g}}{13.6 \text{ g}} \times 100\% = 39.70588 = 39.7\%$$

3. **EVALUATE** *Does the result make sense?*
   The percents of the elements add up to 100%: 60.3% + 39.7% = 100%.

Practice Problems

29. **a.** 9.03 g Mg combine completely with 3.48 g N to form a compound. What is the percent composition of this compound?

    b. 29.0 g Ag combine completely with 4.30 g S to form a compound. What is the percent composition of this compound?

30. When a 14.2-g sample of mercury(II) oxide is decomposed into its elements by heating, 13.2 g Hg is obtained. What is the percent composition of this compound?

Chem ASAP!

Problem-Solving 30
Solve Problem 30 with the help of an interactive guided tutorial.

To calculate the percent composition of a known compound, use the chemical formula to calculate the molar mass. This gives the mass of one mole of the compound. Then for each element, calculate the percent by mass in one mole of the compound. This is done by dividing the mass of each element in one mole of the compound by the molar mass and multiplying the result by 100%. Remember that the subscripts in the formula of the compound are used to calculate the grams of each particular element in a mole of that compound.

$$\% \text{ mass} = \frac{\text{grams of element in 1 mol compound}}{\text{molar mass of compound}} \times 100\%$$

Figure 7.16
The percent composition of water is always the same, regardless of the volume of the water sample. A sample of water is always 11.1% H and 88.9% O by mass.

CHEMath

FRACTIONS, RATIOS, AND PERCENT

In this chapter, you will use percents and ratios when calculating the composition of a substance or determining empirical and molecular formulas. Percents are also used in routine activities such as shopping—stores often have "percent-off" sales. To understand percents and ratios, you must first understand fractions.

A fraction is a special quotient that defines a quantity in terms of equal parts of a whole. The quotient $3 \div 4$ can be written as the fraction $\frac{3}{4}$, or three-fourths, which means three of the four equal parts that make up a whole. The top number of a fraction is the *numerator* and the bottom number is the *denominator.*

Fractions that represent the same quantity are *equivalent.* A fraction is in *lowest terms* if the numerator and denominator have no common factors. So, $\frac{4}{5}$ and $\frac{16}{20}$ are equivalent, but only $\frac{4}{5}$ is in lowest terms. To express a fraction in lowest terms, divide the numerator and denominator by their greatest common factor (GCF).

A *ratio* is a comparison of two quantities. Ratios are often written as fractions. If there are 10 dogs and 15 cats, the ratio of dogs to cats is 10 to 15, or $\frac{10}{15}$, or $\frac{2}{3}$. You can multiply or divide both quantities in a ratio by the same nonzero quantity without changing the value of the ratio. For example, multiplying quantities in the ratio $\frac{2}{3}$ by 5 yields $\frac{10}{15}$ (the original ratio).

A *percent* compares a number to 100. Thus, a ratio of $\frac{73}{100}$ can be written as 73%. 100% represents a whole, so 100% = 1.

You can think of 100% as a *conversion factor* that converts to percent. To convert a fraction or decimal to a percent, multiply by 100%. So, $\frac{3}{5}$ as a percentage is $\frac{3}{5} \times 100\% = 60\%$. This is the idea behind the formula for % mass on page 189.

Example 1

Sulfur makes up 26.7% of the mass of $NaHSO_4$. Find the mass of the sulfur in 16.8 g of $NaHSO_4$.

Since $NaHSO_4$ is 26.7% sulfur, 100 g of the compound would contain 26.7 g sulfur. So, you can use

$$\frac{26.7 \text{ g S}}{100 \text{ g NaHSO}_4}$$

as a conversion factor.

Conversion: grams $NaHSO_4 \longrightarrow$ grams S

$$16.8 \text{ g NaHSO}_4 \times \frac{26.7 \text{ g S}}{100 \text{ g NaHSO}_4} = 4.49 \text{ g S}$$

The mass of the sulfur is 4.49 g.

Example 2

100 g of a compound contains 1.88 mol O and 1.25 mol Fe. Write the mole ratio of oxygen to iron. Use whole numbers in lowest terms. (*Hint:* Each whole number is less than 10.)

Notice that the quantities are approximate, with three significant figures. The ratio is:

$$\frac{1.88}{1.25} = \frac{1.88 \div 1.25}{1.25 \div 1.25} = \frac{1.50}{1.00} = \frac{1.50 \times 2}{1.00 \times 2} = \frac{3.00}{2.00}$$

The mole ratio of oxygen to iron is 3 to 2.

Practice Problems

Prepare for upcoming problems in this chapter by solving each of the following.

A. Express the fractions $\frac{35}{42}$, $\frac{16}{78}$, and $\frac{36}{100}$ in lowest terms.

B. Aluminum makes up 52.9% of the mass of Al_2O_3. Find the mass of the aluminum in 24.3 g of Al_2O_3.

C. Hydrogen makes up 2.06% of the mass of H_2SO_4. Find the mass of the hydrogen in 185 g H_2SO_4.

D. 100 g of a compound contains 1.85 mol N and 4.63 mol O.

Write the mole ratio of nitrogen to oxygen.

Use whole numbers in lowest terms. (*Hint:* Each whole number is less than 10.)

Sample Problem 7-11

Calculate the percent composition of propane (C_3H_8).

1. ANALYZE List the knowns and the unknowns.

Knowns:
- molar mass C_3H_8 = 44.0 g/mol
- mass of C in 1 mol C_3H_8 = 36.0 g
- mass of H in 1 mol C_3H_8 = 8.0 g

Unknowns:
- percent C = ? % C
- percent H = ? % H

The percent mass of each element can be calculated by dividing the mass of that element in one mole of the compound by the molar mass of the compound and multiplying by 100%.

2. CALCULATE Solve for the unknowns.

$$\% \text{ C} = \frac{\text{mass of C}}{\text{grams of compound}} \times 100\%$$

$$= \frac{36.0 \text{ g}}{44.0 \text{ g}} \times 100\% = 0.818181 = 81.8\%$$

$$\% \text{ H} = \frac{\text{mass of H}}{\text{grams of compound}} \times 100\%$$

$$= \frac{8.0 \text{ g}}{44.0 \text{ g}} \times 100\% = 0.181818 = 18\%$$

3. EVALUATE Does the result make sense?

The percents of the elements add up to 100% after the answers are expressed to two significant figures.

Practice Problems

31. Calculate the percent composition of these compounds.
  a. ethane (C_2H_6)
  b. sodium bisulfate ($NaHSO_4$)
  c. ammonium chloride (NH_4Cl)
32. Calculate the percent nitrogen in these common fertilizers.
  a. $CO(NH_2)_2$
  b. NH_3
  c. NH_4NO_3

Using Percent as a Conversion Factor

You can use percent composition to calculate the number of grams of an element contained in a specific amount of a compound. To do this, you multiply the mass of the compound by a conversion factor that is based on the percent composition. In Sample Problem 7-11, you found that propane is 81.8% C. Thus in a 100-g sample, you would have 81.8 g C. Sample Problem 7-12 shows how the ratio 81.8 g C/100 g C_3H_8 can be used to solve for the mass of carbon contained in a specific amount of propane (C_3H_8).

Sample Problem 7-12

Calculate the mass of carbon in 82.0 g of propane (C_3H_8).

1. ANALYZE List the knowns and the unknown.

Knowns:
- mass C_3H_8 = 82.0 g
- percent by mass of C in C_3H_8 = 81.8% (from Sample Problem 7-11)

Unknown:
- mass of carbon = ? g C

The conversion is grams $C_3H_8 \longrightarrow$ grams C.

Practice Problems

33. Using Problem 31, calculate the mass of hydrogen in each of the following.
  a. 350 g C_2H_6
  b. 20.2 g $NaHSO_4$
  c. 2.14 g NH_4Cl

Practice Problems (cont.)

34. Calculate the grams of nitrogen in 125 g of each fertilizer.
   a. $CO(NH_2)_2$
   b. NH_3
   c. NH_4NO_3

Chem ASAP!

Problem-Solving 34
Solve Problem 34 with the help of an interactive guided tutorial.

2. CALCULATE *Solve for the unknown.*
A conversion factor based on the percent mass of carbon in propane is used. Sample Problem 7-11 showed that the percent composition of propane is 81.8% C and 18.2% H. Remember that 81.8% C means 81.8 g C per 100 g C_3H_8. This is the desired conversion factor.

$$82.0 \text{ g } C_3H_8 \times \frac{81.8 \text{ g C}}{100 \text{ g } C_3H_8} = 67.1 \text{ g C}$$

3. EVALUATE *Does the result make sense?*
Because carbon constitutes about 82% by mass of propane, it is logical that in this sample, carbon has a mass of about 82% of 82.0 g, or 67.1 g.

Calculating Empirical Formulas

Determining the percent composition of a compound has an important application. Percent composition data can be used to calculate the empirical formula of a compound. The **empirical formula** gives the lowest whole-number ratio of the atoms of the elements in a compound. For example, a compound may have the empirical formula CO. The empirical formula provides valuable information about the kinds and relative count of atoms or moles of atoms in molecules or formula units of a compound. As you can see in **Figure 7.17,** empirical formulas may be interpreted at the microscopic (atoms) or macroscopic (moles of atoms) level.

If you use the mole interpretation, an empirical formula is the lowest whole-number ratio of moles of atoms that combine to form a compound. An empirical formula may or may not be the same as a molecular formula. If the formulas are different, the molecular formula is a simple multiple of the empirical formula. The empirical formula of hydrogen peroxide (H_2O_2) for example, is HO.

For carbon dioxide, the empirical and molecular formulas are the same—CO_2. Dinitrogen tetrahydride, whose molecular formula is N_2H_4, has an empirical formula of NH_2 because this is the simplest ratio of nitrogen to hydrogen in the compound. **Figure 7.18** shows two compounds of carbon that have the same empirical formula but different molecular formulas.

Figure 7.17

A formula can be interpreted on a microscopic level in terms of atoms or on a macroscopic level in terms of moles of atoms.

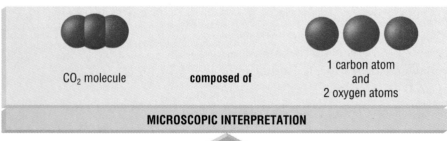

| CO_2 molecule | **composed of** | 1 carbon atom and 2 oxygen atoms |

MICROSCOPIC INTERPRETATION

CO₂

MACROSCOPIC INTERPRETATION

| 1 mol CO_2 | **composed of** | 6.02×10^{23} carbon atoms (1 mol C atoms) and $2 \times (6.02 \times 10^{23})$ oxygen atoms (2 mol O atoms) |

Sample Problem 7-13

What is the empirical formula of a compound that is 25.9% nitrogen and 74.1% oxygen?

1. **ANALYZE** *List the knowns and the unknown.*

   Knowns:
   - percent of nitrogen = 25.9% N
   - percent of oxygen = 74.1% O

   Unknown:
   - empirical formula = $N_?O_?$

   The lowest whole-number ratio of moles of nitrogen atoms to oxygen atoms, or the empirical formula, is to be calculated. The percent composition tells the ratio of masses of nitrogen atoms to oxygen atoms in the compound. The ratio of masses is changed to a ratio of moles by using conversion factors based on the molar mass of each element. This mole ratio is then reduced to the lowest whole-number ratio.

2. **CALCULATE** *Solve for the unknown.*

   In 100.0 g of the compound, there are 25.9 g N and 74.1 g O. These values are used to convert to moles.

   $$25.9 \text{ g N} \times \frac{1 \text{ mol N}}{14.0 \text{ g N}} = 1.85 \text{ mol N}$$

   $$74.1 \text{ g O} \times \frac{1 \text{ mol O}}{16.0 \text{ g O}} = 4.63 \text{ mol O}$$

   The mole ratio of nitrogen to oxygen is $N_{1.85}O_{4.63}$. This is not the correct empirical formula because it is not the lowest whole-number ratio. The correct values can be obtained by dividing both molar quantities by the smaller number of moles. This will give a 1 for the element with the smaller number of moles. However, this step may not give whole numbers for the other elements.

   $$\frac{1.85 \text{ mol N}}{1.85} = 1 \text{ mol N}$$

   $$\frac{4.63 \text{ mol O}}{1.85} = 2.50 \text{ mol O}$$

   Is the final answer $N_1O_{2.5}$? Obviously not. This formula still does not represent the lowest whole-number ratio. To obtain such a ratio, each part of the ratio is multiplied by a number (in this case 2) that converts the fraction to a whole number.

   $$1 \text{ mol N} \times 2 = 2 \text{ mol N}$$
   $$2.5 \text{ mol O} \times 2 = 5 \text{ mol O}$$

   The empirical formula is N_2O_5.

3. **EVALUATE** *Does the result make sense?*

   This is an empirical formula. The subscripts are whole numbers. As a further check, the percent composition of this empirical formula can be calculated. The percents of each element should equal the percents given in the original problem.

Figure 7.18
Ethyne (C_2H_2), also called acetylene, is a gas used in welder's torches. Styrene (C_8H_8) is used in making polystyrene. These two compounds have the same empirical formula. What is the empirical formula?

Practice Problems

35. Calculate the empirical formula of each compound.
   a. 94.1% O, 5.9% H
   b. 79.8% C, 20.2% H
   c. 67.6% Hg, 10.8% S, 21.6% O
   d. 27.59% C, 1.15% H, 16.09% N, 55.17% O

36. 1,6-diaminohexane is used to make nylon. What is the empirical formula of this compound if it is 62.1% C, 13.8% H, and 24.1% N?

Chem ASAP!

Problem-Solving 36
Solve Problem 36 with the help of an interactive guided tutorial.

Table 7.2

Comparison of Empirical and Molecular Formulas		
Formula (name)	Classification of formula	Molar mass
CH	Empirical	13
C_2H_2 (ethyne)	Molecular	26 (2 × 13)
C_6H_6 (benzene)	Molecular	78 (6 × 13)
CH_2O (methanal)	Empirical and Molecular	30
$C_2H_4O_2$ (ethanoic acid)	Molecular	60 (2 × 30)
$C_6H_{12}O_6$ (glucose)	Molecular	180 (6 × 30)

Calculating Molecular Formulas

Look at the two series of compounds in **Table 7.2.** Ethyne and benzene have the same empirical formula—CH. Glucose, ethanoic acid, and methanal have the same empirical formula—CH_2O. But as you can see, the compounds in each series have different molar masses. These molar masses are simple whole-number multiples of the molar mass of the empirical formulas, CH and CH_2O. The molecular formula of a compound is either the same as its experimentally determined empirical formula, or it is a simple whole-number multiple of it.

You can determine the molecular formula of a compound if you know its empirical formula and its molar mass. From the empirical formula, you can calculate the empirical formula mass (efm). This is simply the molar mass of the empirical formula. The known molar mass is then divided by the empirical formula mass. This gives the number of empirical formula units in a molecule of the compound and is the multiplier to convert the empirical formula to the molecular formula.

Practice Problems

37. Find the molecular formula of each compound given its empirical formula and molar mass.
   a. ethylene glycol (CH_3O), used in antifreeze, molar mass = 62 g/mol
   b. *p*-dichlorobenzene (C_3H_2Cl), mothballs, molar mass = 147 g/mol

38. Which pair of molecules has the same empirical formula?
   a. $C_2H_4O_2$, $C_6H_{12}O_6$
   b. $NaCrO_4$, $Na_2Cr_2O_7$

Chem ASAP!

Problem-Solving 37
Solve Problem 37 with the help of an interactive guided tutorial.

Sample Problem 7-14

Calculate the molecular formula of the compound whose molar mass is 60.0 g and empirical formula is CH_4N.

1. **ANALYZE** *List the knowns and the unknown.*

   Knowns:
   • empirical formula = CH_4N
   • molar mass = 60.0 g

   Unknown:
   • molecular formula = ?

2. **CALCULATE** *Solve for the unknown.*

   First calculate the empirical formula mass. Then divide the empirical formula mass into the molar mass. Multiply formula subscripts by this value to get the molecular formula.

Empirical formula	efm	Molar mass/efm	Molecular formula
CH_4N	30.0	60.0/30.0 = 2	$C_2H_8N_2$

3. **EVALUATE** *Does the result make sense?*

   The molecular formula has the molar mass of the compound and can be reduced to the empirical formula.

MINI LAB

Percent Composition

PURPOSE

To measure the percent of water in a series of crystalline compounds called hydrates.

MATERIALS

- centigram balance
- burner
- 3 medium-sized test tubes
- test tube holder
- test tube rack
- spatula
- hydrated salts of copper(II) sulfate, calcium chloride, and sodium sulfate

PROCEDURE

1. Label each test tube with the name of a salt. Weigh and record its mass.

2. Add 2–3 g of salt (a good-sized spatula full) to the appropriately labeled test tube. Weigh and record the mass of each test tube plus the salt.

3. Hold one of the tubes at a 45° angle and gently heat its contents over the burner, slowly passing it in and out of the flame. Note any change in the appearance of the solid salt.

4. As moisture begins to condense in the upper part of the test tube, gently heat the entire length of the tube. Continue heating until all of the moisture is driven from the tube. This may take 2–3 minutes. Repeat Steps 3 and 4 for the other two tubes.

5. Allow each tube to cool. Then weigh and record the mass of each test tube and the heated salt.

ANALYSIS AND CONCLUSIONS

1. Set up a data table so you can subtract the mass of the empty tube from the mass of the salt and the test tube, both before and after heating.

2. Calculate the difference between the mass of each salt before and after heating. This difference represents the amount of water lost by the hydrate on heating.

3. Calculate the percent by mass of water lost by each compound.

4. Which compound lost the greatest percent by mass of water? The least?

---

section review 7.3

39. Calculate the percent composition of the compounds that are formed from these reactions.

   a. 222.6 g N combines completely with 77.4 g O.

   b. 2.62 g Na and 4.04 g Cl are formed by the decomposition of table salt.

40. The compound methyl butanoate smells like apples. Its percent composition is 58.8% C, 9.8% H, and 31.4% O. Methyl butanoate's molar mass is 102 g/mol. What is its molecular formula?

41. Calculate the percent composition of each compound.

   a. calcium acetate ($Ca(C_2H_3O_2)_2$)   **b.** hydrogen cyanide (HCN)

42. Using the results of Problem 41, calculate the amount of hydrogen in the following amounts of these compounds.

   a. 124 g $Ca(C_2H_3O_2)_2$ **b.** 378 g HCN

43. Which of the following molecular formulas are also empirical formulas?

   a. ribose ($C_5H_{10}O_5$)   **c.** chlorophyll ($C_{55}H_{72}MgN_4O_5$)

   b. ethyl butyrate ($C_6H_{12}O_2$)   **d.** DEET ($C_{12}H_{17}ON$)

portfolio project

Find out whether your state sets standards for the composition of bottled water. If so, is all the bottled water sold tested or just water bottled in your state?

Chem ASAP! Assessment 7.3 Check your understanding of the important ideas and concepts in Section 7.3.

WATER WORTH DRINKING

When you turn on your faucet to get a glass of water, you might assume that the water coming out is safe to drink. You probably do not think about the many substances other than water that may be in your glass or how much of each of these substances the water contains.

Worrying about the quality of drinking water is the job of your local water supplier and the federal government's Environmental Protection Agency (EPA). The EPA has established drinking water standards that state and local governments must follow to ensure that water is safe. A drinking water standard sets an upper limit on a potentially harmful substance if that substance is present in the water. In addition to setting these standards, the EPA also requires that local water providers test their public water supplies regularly. Levels of minerals, chlorine and microorganisms such as bacteria are monitored.

Water standards are established by scientific study. Any naturally occurring or synthetic compounds that may be harmful when present in drinking water are examined by the EPA and by state and local water labs. Compounds found to have negative effects on human health and the environment are studied to determine at what level they begin to produce their harmful effects. Based on this research, standards are set for each contaminant. These regulations help ensure that good quality drinking water reaches your faucet.

The regulation and control of water quality requires measuring the concentration of each contaminant that may be contained in the water. Some contaminants are measured in exceedingly small units called parts per billion (ppb). Trace metals, such as mercury, and organic compounds, such as trihalomethane, are both measured in ppb. Such small units are used because very

You probably do not think about the many substances other than water that may be in your glass.

small amounts of these compounds can make humans ill or can have an adverse effect on the environment. Another unit commonly used is parts per million (ppm). Dissolved minerals such as sodium and calcium, chlorine, and levels of microorganisms, such as coliform bacteria, are measured in ppm.

The number of microorganisms in water is one of the most important aspects of water quality. If left unchecked, microorganisms could cause outbreaks of bacterial infections and other water-borne diseases. Local and state officials use an indicator species, coliform bacteria, to monitor microbiological water quality. If periodic water samples indicate too high a level of coliform bacteria, disinfectants such as chlorine must be added to the water distribution system to destroy potentially dangerous microorganisms.

Where water is treated with chlorine, tests are done frequently to ensure that levels of this disinfectant do not fall below 0.5 ppm. By contrast, the amount of sodium in drinking water may vary depending on the source of the water.

The mineral content of drinking water can vary widely by location. To find out the percent composition of your drinking water, check with your local government office or agriculture bureau. You may be surprised to find out what you are drinking!

Take It to the NET
For interactive study and review, go to www.phschool.com

KEY TERMS

- Avogadro's number *p. 173*
- empirical formula *p. 192*
- gram atomic mass (gam) *p. 176*
- gram formula mass (gfm) *p. 180*
- gram molecular mass (gmm) *p. 178*
- molar mass *p. 182*
- molar volume *p. 184*
- mole (mol) *p. 173*
- percent composition *p. 188*
- representative particle *p. 173*
- standard temperature and pressure (STP) *p. 184*

CONCEPT SUMMARY

7.1 The Mole: A Measurement of Matter

- The SI unit that measures the amount of substance is the mole.
- A mole of any substance is composed of Avogadro's number (6.02×10^{23}) of representative particles.
- The representative particle of most elements is the atom.
- A molecule is the representative particle of diatomic elements and molecular compounds.
- The representative particle of ionic compounds is a formula unit.
- The gram atomic mass (gam), gram molecular mass (gmm), and gram formula mass (gfm) are the mass of one mole of an element, a molecular compound, and an ionic compound, respectively.
- The molar mass of a substance is the mass in grams of one mole of that substance.
- One mole of any substance contains the same number of representative particles as one mole of any other substance.

7.2 Mole–Mass and Mole–Volume Relationships

- Multiplying the number of moles of a substance by its molar mass gives the mass of the substance.
- Dividing the mass of a substance by its molar mass gives the number of moles of that substance.
- One mole of any gas at STP (1 atm pressure and 0 °C) occupies a volume of 22.4 L.
- The density of any gas at STP is its molar mass divided by 22.4 L.

7.3 Percent Composition and Chemical Formulas

- The percent composition is the percent by mass of each element in a compound.
- The percent by mass of any element in a given compound is calculated by dividing the element's mass by the mass of the compound and multiplying by 100%.
- An empirical formula is the simplest whole-number ratio of atoms of the elements in a compound.

CHAPTER CONCEPT MAP

Use these terms to construct a concept map that organizes the major ideas of this chapter.

 Chem ASAP! **Concept Map 7** Create your Concept Map using the computer.

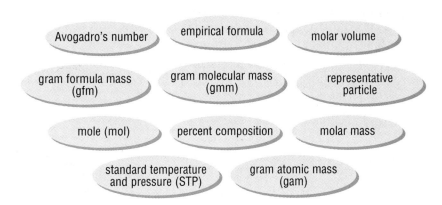

- Avogadro's number
- empirical formula
- molar volume
- gram formula mass (gfm)
- gram molecular mass (gmm)
- representative particle
- mole (mol)
- percent composition
- molar mass
- standard temperature and pressure (STP)
- gram atomic mass (gam)

CONCEPT PRACTICE

44. List three common ways that matter is measured. Give examples of each. *7.1*

45. Name the representative particle (atom, molecule, or formula unit) of each substance. *7.1*
a. oxygen   **c.** sulfur dioxide
b. sodium sulfide   **d.** potassium

46. How many hydrogen atoms are in a representative particle of each substance? *7.1*
a. $Al(OH)_3$ **c.** $(NH_4)_2HPO_4$
b. $H_2C_2O_4$ **d.** $C_4H_{10}O$

47. Which contains more molecules: 1.00 mol H_2O_2, 1.00 mol C_2H_6, or 1.00 mol CO? *7.1*

48. Which contains more atoms: 1.00 mol H_2O_2, 1.00 mol C_2H_6, or 1.00 mol CO? *7.1*

49. Find the number of representative particles in each substance. *7.1*
a. 3.00 mol Sn   **c.** 7.50 mol SO_2
b. 0.400 mol KCl   **d.** 4.80×10^{-3} mol NaI

50. Calculate the molar mass of each substance. *7.1*
a. H_3PO_4 **c.** $CaCO_3$ **e.** $C_4H_9O_2$
b. N_2O_3 **d.** $(NH_4)_2SO_4$ **f.** Br_2

51. Calculate the mass of 1.00 mol of each of these substances. *7.1*
a. silicon dioxide (SiO_2)
b. diatomic nitrogen (N_2)
c. iron(III) hydroxide ($Fe(OH)_3$)
d. copper (Cu)

52. List the steps you would take to calculate the molar mass of any compound. *7.1*

53. What is the gram molecular mass (gmm) of chlorine? *7.1*

54. Construct a numerical problem to illustrate the size of Avogadro's number. Exchange problems with a classmate and then compare your answers. *7.1*

55. How many moles is each of the following? *7.2*
a. 15.5 g SiO_2 **d.** 5.96 g KOH
b. 0.0688 g AgCl   **e.** 937 g $Ca(C_2H_3O_2)_2$
c. 79.3 g Cl_2 **f.** 0.800 g Ca

56. Find the mass of each substance. *7.2*
a. 1.50 mol C_5H_{12}
b. 14.4 mol F_2
c. 0.780 mol $Ca(CN)_2$
d. 7.00 mol H_2O_2
e. 5.60 mol NaOH
f. 3.21×10^{-2} mol Ni

57. Calculate the volume of each of the following gases at STP. *7.2*
a. 7.6 mol Ar
b. 0.44 mol C_2H_6
c. 1.20 mol O_2

58. What is the density of each of the following gases at STP? *7.2*
a. C_3H_8 **b.** Ne   **c.** NO_2

59. Find each of the following quantities. *7.2*
a. the volume, in liters, of 835 g SO_3 at STP
b. the mass, in grams, of a molecule of aspirin ($C_9H_8O_4$)
c. the number of atoms in 5.78 mol NH_4NO_3

60. Calculate the percent composition of each compound. *7.3*
a. H_2S **c.** $Mg(OH)_2$
b. $(NH_4)_2C_2O_4$ **d.** Na_3PO_4

61. Using your answers from Problem 60, calculate the number of grams of these elements. *7.3*
a. sulfur in 3.54 g H_2S
b. nitrogen in 25.0 g $(NH_4)_2C_2O_4$
c. magnesium in 97.4 g $Mg(OH)_2$
d. phosphorus in 804 g Na_3PO_4

62. Which of the following compounds has the highest iron content? *7.3*
a. $FeCl_2$ **c.** $Fe(OH)_2$
b. $Fe(C_2H_3O_2)_3$ **d.** FeO

63. You find that 7.36 g of a compound has decomposed to give 6.93 g of oxygen. The only other element in the compound is hydrogen. If the molar mass of the compound is 34.0 g/mol, what is its molecular formula? *7.3*

64. Classify each formula as an empirical or a molecular formula. *7.3*
a. S_2Cl_2 **c.** Na_2SO_3 **e.** $C_{17}H_{19}NO_3$
b. $C_6H_{10}O_4$ **d.** $C_5H_{10}O_5$ **f.** $(NH_4)_2CO_3$

65. What is the molecular formula for each compound? Each compound's empirical formula and molar mass is given. *7.3*
a. CH_2O, 90 g/mol
b. HgCl, 472.2 g/mol
c. $C_3H_5O_2$, 146 g/mol

66. Determine the molecular formula for each compound. *7.3*
a. 94.1% O and 5.9% H; molar mass = 34 g
b. 40.0% C, 6.6% H, and 53.4% O; molar mass = 120 g

67. How can you determine the molar mass of a gaseous compound if you do not know its molecular formula?

68. A series of compounds has the empirical formula CH_2O. The graph shows the relationship between the molar mass of the compounds and the mass of carbon in each compound.

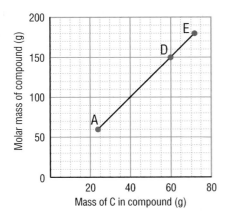

a. What are the molecular formulas for the compounds represented by data points A, D, and E?

b. Find the slope of the line. Is this value consistent with the empirical formula?

c. There are two other valid data points that fall on the line between points A and D. What are the *x, y* values for these data points?

69. Explain what is wrong with each statement.
   a. One mole of any substance contains the same number of atoms.
   b. The gram atomic mass of a compound is the atomic mass expressed in grams.
   c. One gram molecular mass of CO_2 contains Avogadro's number of atoms.

70. Which of the following contains the largest number of atoms?
   a. 82.0 g Kr
   b. 0.842 mol C_2H_4
   c. 36.0 g N_2

71. What is the total mass of a mixture of 3.50×10^{22} formula units Na_2SO_4, 0.500 mol H_2O, and 7.23 g AgCl?

72. Determine the empirical formula of each.
   a. 42.9% C and 57.1% O
   b. 32.00% C, 42.66% O, 18.67% N, and 6.67% H
   c. 71.72% Cl, 16.16% O, and 12.12% C

73. An imaginary "atomic balance" is shown below. Fifteen atoms of boron on the left side of the balance are balanced by six atoms of an unknown element E on the right side.

   a. What is the atomic mass of element E?
   b. What is the identity of element E?

74. A typical virus is 5×10^{-6} cm in diameter. If Avogadro's number of these virus particles were laid in a row, how many kilometers long would the line be?

75. Calculate the empirical formula for each compound.
   a. compound consisting of 0.40 mol Cu per 0.80 mol Br
   b. compound with 4 atoms of carbon for every 12 atoms of hydrogen

76. Choose the term that best completes the second relationship.
   a. dozen : eggs
   mole : _____
   (1) atoms
   (2) 6.02×10^{23}
   (3) size
   (4) grams
   b. gam : element
   gmm : _____
   (1) formula unit
   (2) molecule
   (3) ionic compound
   (4) molecular compound
   c. mole : Avogadro's number
   molar volume : _____
   (1) mole
   (2) water
   (3) STP
   (4) 22.4 L

77. How are the empirical and molecular formulas of a compound related?

78. Why does one mole of carbon have a smaller mass than one mole of sulfur? How are the atomic structures of these elements different?

79. One mole of any gas at STP equals 22.4 L of that gas. It is also true that different elements have different atomic volumes, or diameters. How can you reconcile these two statements?

CUMULATIVE REVIEW

80. How many protons, electrons, and neutrons are in each isotope?
    a. zirconium-90
    b. palladium-108
    c. bromine-81
    d. antimony-123

81. How many moles is 14.5 cm^3 of platinum? The density of platinum is 21.45 g/cm^3.

82. How does a molecule differ from an atom?

83. Convert each of the following.
    a. 4.72 g to mg
    b. 2.7 × 10^3 cm/s to km/h
    c. 4.4 mm to dm

84. Name these compounds
    a. Fe(OH)$_3$ c. Na$_2$CO$_3$
    b. NH$_4$I   d. CCl$_4$

85. Write formulas for these compounds.
    a. potassium nitrate
    b. copper(II) oxide
    c. magnesium nitride
    d. silver fluoride

CONCEPT CHALLENGE

86. Nitroglycerine contains 60% as many carbon atoms as hydrogen atoms; three times as many oxygen atoms as nitrogen atoms; and the same number of carbon and nitrogen atoms. The number of moles of nitroglycerine in 1 g is 0.00441. What is the molecular formula of nitroglycerine?

87. The density of nickel is 8.91 g/cm^3. How large a cube, in cm^3, would contain 2.00 × 10^{24} atoms of nickel?

88. Dry air is about 20.95% oxygen by volume. Assuming STP, how many oxygen molecules are in a 75.0-g sample of air? The density of air is 1.19 g/L.

89. The table below gives the molar mass and density of seven gases at STP.

Substance	Molar mass (g)	Density (g/L)
Oxygen	32.0	1.43
Carbon dioxide	44.0	1.96
Ethane	30.0	1.34
Hydrogen	2.0	0.089
Sulfur dioxide	64.1	2.86
Ammonia	17.0	0.759
Fluorine	38.0	1.70

a. Plot these data, with density on the x-axis.
b. What is the slope of the straight-line plot?
c. What is the molar mass of a gas at STP that has a density of 1.10 g/L?
d. A mole of a gas at STP has a mass of 56.0 g. Use the graph to determine its density.

90. The element gold has properties that have made it much sought after through the ages. A cubic meter of ocean water has 6 × 10^{-6} g gold. If the total mass of the water in Earth's oceans is 4 × 10^{20} kg, how many kilograms of gold are distributed throughout the oceans? (Assume that the density of seawater is 1 g/cm^3.) How many liters of seawater would have to be processed to recover 1 kg of gold (which has a value of about $8850 at 2001 prices)? Do you think this recovery operation is feasible?

91. Have you ever wondered how Avogadro's number was determined? Actually, Avogadro's number has been independently determined by about 20 different methods. In one approach, Avogadro's number is calculated from the volume of a film of a fatty acid floating on water. In another method, it is determined by comparing the electric charge of one electron with the electric charge of a mole of electrons. In a third method, the spacing between ions in an ionic substance can be determined by using a technique called x-ray diffraction. In the x-ray diffraction of sodium chloride, it has been determined that the distance between adjacent Na$^+$ and Cl$^-$ ions is 2.819 × 10^{-8} cm. The density of solid sodium chloride is 2.165 g/cm^3. By calculating the molar mass to four significant figures, you can determine Avogadro's number. What value do you obtain?

Select the choice that best answers each question or completes each statement.

1. Calculate the molar mass of ammonium phosphate, $(NH_4)_3PO_4$.
   a. 149.0   c. 242.0
   b. 113.0   d. 121.0

2. Based on the structural formula below, what is the empirical formula for tartaric acid, a compound found in grape juice?

$$HO—CH—COOH$$
$$|$$
$$HO—CH—COOH$$

   a. $C_2H_3O_3$
   b. $C_4H_6O_6$
   c. CHO
   d. $C_1H_{1.5}O_{1.5}$

3. How many hydrogen atoms are in six molecules of ethylene glycol, $HOCH_2CH_2OH$?
   a. 6
   b. 36
   c. $6 \times 6.02 \times 10^{23}$
   d. $36 \times 6.02 \times 10^{23}$

4. Which of these statements is true of a balloon filled with 1.00 mol $N_2(g)$ at STP?
   I. The balloon has a volume of 22.4 L.
   II. The contents of the balloon have a mass of 14.0 g.
   III. The balloon contains 6.02×10^{23} molecules.
   a. I only
   b. I and II only
   c. I and III only
   d. II and III only
   e. I, II, and III

5. Which of these compounds has the largest percent by mass of nitrogen?
   a. N_2O
   b. NO
   c. NO_2
   d. N_2O_3
   e. N_2O_4

6. Allicin, $C_6H_{10}S_2O$, is the compound that gives garlic its odor. A sample of allicin contains 3.0×10^{21} atoms of carbon. How many atoms of hydrogen does this sample contain?
   a. 1.8×10^{21} atoms
   b. 10 atoms
   c. 5.0×10^{21} atoms
   d. 1.0×10^{21} atoms

The lettered choices below refer to questions 7–11. A lettered choice may be used once, more than once, or not at all.
   (A) CH
   (B) CH_2
   (C) C_2H_5
   (D) CH_3
   (E) C_2H_3

Which of the formulas is the empirical formula for each of the following compounds?
   7. C_8H_{12}
   8. C_6H_6
   9. $C_{12}H_{24}$
   10. C_2H_6
   11. C_4H_{10}

Use the ball-and-stick models to answer questions 12–14. In the models, carbon is black, hydrogen is light blue, oxygen is red, and nitrogen is dark blue. Write the molecular formula for each compound. Then calculate its molar mass.

12.

Isopropanol

13.

Glycine

14.

Ethyl formate

CHEMICAL REACTIONS

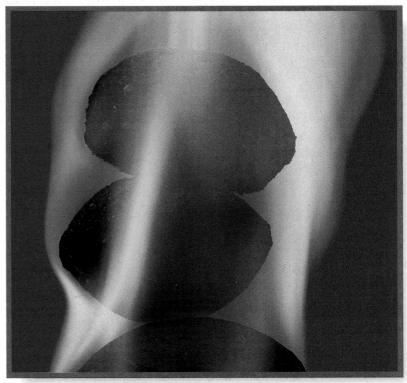

Combustion of carbon in charcoal briquettes produces heat and light.

FEATURES

DISCOVER IT!
Modeling Chemical Reactions

SMALL-SCALE LAB
Precipitation Reactions:
Formation of Solids

MINI LAB
Activity Series of Metals

CHEMISTRY SERVING ... SOCIETY
Combating Combustion

CHEMISTRY IN CAREERS
Firefighter

LINK TO PHYSIOLOGY
Hydrogen Peroxide

Stay current with **SCIENCE NEWS**
Find out more about chemical reactions:
www.phschool.com

DISCOVER IT!
MODELING CHEMICAL REACTIONS

You need 36 paper clips (12 each of 3 different colors).

1. Each paper clip represents a single atom. Designate a different color of paper clip to represent atoms of oxygen (O), hydrogen (H), or carbon (C). Make two molecules each of hydrogen (H_2) and methane (CH_4) and six molecules of oxygen (O_2).

2. "React" one H_2 with one O_2 by splitting the molecules and joining one oxygen atom to two hydrogen atoms. Because there is an unreacted oxygen atom, you must react it with another hydrogen molecule to form a second water molecule.

3. Summarize what happened in this reaction by placing the number of each molecule reacted or formed in front of its formula.

$$\_\_H_2 + \_\_O_2 \longrightarrow \_\_H_2O$$

4. Now "react" methane (CH_4) with oxygen (O_2) to produce carbon dioxide (CO_2) and water (H_2O). Start with one molecule of methane and one molecule of oxygen. Continue reacting molecules of CH_4 and O_2 until all the reactant atoms have been used to form products.

5. Summarize what happened in this reaction.

$$\_\_CH_4 + \_\_O_2 \longrightarrow \_\_CO_2 + \_\_H_2O$$

Summarize Dalton's atomic theory. How might the numbers and kinds of atoms to the left and right of the arrow ($\longrightarrow$) in the model reactions you performed support this theory?

DESCRIBING CHEMICAL CHANGE

*O*n May 6, 1937, the huge airship Hindenburg was heading for its landing site in Lakehurst, New Jersey, after an uneventful trans-Atlantic crossing. Suddenly, to the horror of observers on the ground, the airship erupted into a fireball as 210 000 cubic meters of hydrogen burst into flame. The chemical reaction that caused the disaster can be described simply as "hydrogen combines explosively with oxygen to produce water." **How do chemists describe chemical reactions?**

Word Equations

Every minute of the day chemical reactions take place—both inside you and around you. After a meal, a series of complex chemical reactions take place as your body digests food. Likewise, plants use sunlight to drive the photosynthetic processes needed to produce plant growth. Although the chemical reactions involved in photosynthesis and digestion are quite different, both of these chemical reactions are necessary to sustain life. What are some other reactions necessary for life?

Not every chemical reaction involves living things directly. The useful chemical reaction that produces electrical energy in a car battery is one example. The energy produced is used to start the car. At the same time, an undesirable chemical reaction might be occurring between the iron in the car fender and the oxygen in the air. This reaction produces rust. Many common reactions occur when food is grown or cooked. All chemical reactions, whether simple or complex, desirable or undesirable, involve changing substances.

It will be important for you to be able to describe a chemical reaction in writing. In a reaction, one or more substances (the reactants) change into one or more new substances (the products). Recall from Chapter 2 the shorthand method for writing a brief description of what happens in a chemical reaction. In writing reactions, separate the reactants from the products by writing an arrow (→), which means yields, gives, or reacts to produce.

$$\text{Reactants} \longrightarrow \text{products}$$

You may remember that John Dalton proposed an explanation for the way in which substances change in a chemical reaction. His atomic theory holds true today. As reactants are converted to products, the bonds holding the atoms together are broken and new bonds are formed. It is

Figure 8.1

Flour, sugar, salt, yeast, and water are the main ingredients for making leavened bread. The reactants (ingredients) undergo physical and chemical changes to form the product (baked bread). What are some indications in the pictures below that chemical reactions are taking place?

important to note that the atoms themselves are neither created nor destroyed; they are merely rearranged. This part of Dalton's theory explains the law of conservation of mass. Recall that this law states that in any physical or chemical change, mass is neither created nor destroyed. The atoms in the products are the same atoms that were in the reactants—they are just arranged differently.

Chemical reactions can be described in many different ways. For the example of rusting iron, you could say: "Iron reacts with oxygen to produce iron(III) oxide (rust)." Alternatively, you could identify the reactants and product in this reaction by writing a word equation.

$$\text{Iron} + \text{oxygen} \longrightarrow \text{iron(III) oxide}$$

In a word equation, the reactants are written to the left of the arrow, and the products are written to the right. Notice that the reactants are separated by a plus sign. Had there been two or more products, they also would have been separated by a plus sign.

Consider another example of a simple chemical reaction, one involving hydrogen peroxide, a common antiseptic. When you pour hydrogen peroxide on an open cut, bubbles of oxygen gas rapidly form. The production of a new substance, a gas, is visible evidence of a chemical change. Actually, two new substances are produced in this reaction, oxygen gas and liquid water. The statement "hydrogen peroxide reacts to form water and oxygen gas" describes this reaction. You can write this chemical reaction as a word equation.

$$\text{Hydrogen peroxide} \longrightarrow \text{water} + \text{oxygen}$$

A third common reaction is the burning of methane. Methane is the major component of natural gas, a common fuel for residential heating. When methane is burned to produce energy, a chemical reaction occurs. The word equation for this reaction must include all of the reactants and products. Burning a substance typically requires oxygen. The products of this chemical reaction are water and carbon dioxide. Thus the word equation is as follows.

$$\text{Methane} + \text{oxygen} \longrightarrow \text{carbon dioxide} + \text{water}$$

Figure 8.2

Some common chemical reactions. (a) Copper exposed to moist air forms a pale green coating of basic copper(II) carbonate. This type of coating is called a patina. (b) Glucose is fermented by yeast (shown) to form ethanol and carbon dioxide. (c) Plants carry out photosynthesis—the creation of glucose and oxygen from carbon dioxide, water, and sunlight.

(a) Copper + carbon dioxide + water ⟶ basic copper(II) carbonate

(b) Glucose $\xrightarrow{\text{yeast}}$ ethanol + carbon dioxide

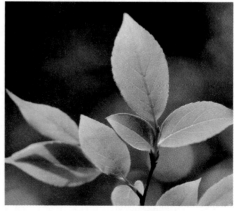

(c) Carbon dioxide + water $\xrightarrow{\text{light}}$ glucose + oxygen

Chemical Equations

Although word equations adequately describe chemical reactions, they are cumbersome. To communicate more effectively, you can use chemical formulas to write equations. In a **chemical equation,** the arrow separates the formulas of the reactants (on the left) from the formulas of the products (on the right). For instance, here is the chemical equation for rusting.

$$Fe + O_2 \longrightarrow Fe_2O_3$$

Such equations, which show just the formulas of the reactants and products, are skeleton equations. A **skeleton equation** is a chemical equation that does not indicate the relative amounts of the reactants and products involved in the reaction. Writing a skeleton equation with the correct formulas for the reactants and products is an important first step in obtaining a correct chemical equation.

You can indicate the physical state of a substance in the equation by putting a symbol after each formula. Use (s) for a solid, (l) for a liquid, (g) for a gas, and (aq) for an aqueous solution (a substance dissolved in water). Indicating the states in the chemical equation for rusting yields

$$Fe(s) + O_2(g) \longrightarrow Fe_2O_3(s)$$

In many chemical reactions, a catalyst is employed. A **catalyst** is a substance that speeds up the rate of a reaction but that is not used up in the reaction. Because a catalyst is neither a reactant nor a product, its formula is written above the arrow in a chemical equation. For example, **Figure 8.3** shows that the compound manganese(IV) oxide (MnO_2)(s) catalyzes the decomposition of an aqueous solution of hydrogen peroxide (H_2O_2)(aq) into water and oxygen. The skeleton equation is

$$H_2O_2(aq) \xrightarrow{\text{MnO}_2} H_2O(l) + O_2(g)$$

Many of the symbols commonly used in writing chemical equations are listed in **Table 8.1** on the following page.

Figure 8.3
Hydrogen peroxide slowly decomposes to form water and oxygen gas (left). The addition of manganese(IV) oxide (MnO_2) greatly speeds up the reaction, causing the rapid evolution of oxygen gas (right). Because it is not used up in the reaction, MnO_2 is a catalyst. The reaction produces enough heat to cause the water to boil; the white "smoke" in the photo is condensed water vapor.

Table 8.1

Symbols Used in Chemical Equations	
Symbol	**Explanation**
$+$	Used to separate two reactants or two products
$\longrightarrow$	"Yields," separates reactants from products
$\rightleftharpoons$	Used in place of $\longrightarrow$ for reversible reactions
(s)	Designates a reactant or product in the solid state; placed after the formula
(l)	Designates a reactant or product in the liquid state; placed after the formula
(g)	Designates a reactant or product in the gaseous state; placed after the formula
(aq)	Designates an aqueous solution; the substance is dissolved in water; placed after the formula
$\xrightarrow{\Delta}$ $\xrightarrow{\text{heat}}$	Indicates that heat is supplied to the reaction
$\xrightarrow{\text{Pt}}$	A formula written above or below the yield sign indicates its use as a catalyst (in this example, platinum)

Sample Problem 8-1

Write a skeleton equation for this chemical reaction: Solid sodium hydrogen carbonate reacts with hydrochloric acid to produce aqueous sodium chloride, water, and carbon dioxide gas. Include appropriate symbols.

1. *ANALYZE Plan a problem-solving strategy.*
Write the correct formula for each substance in the reaction, separate the reactants from the products, and indicate the state of each substance.

2. *SOLVE Apply the problem-solving strategy.*
First, write the formulas and states of the reactants.
• solid sodium hydrogen carbonate: $NaHCO_3(s)$
• hydrochloric acid: $HCl(aq)$
Then do the same for the products.
• aqueous sodium chloride: $NaCl(aq)$
• water: $H_2O(l)$
• carbon dioxide gas: $CO_2(g)$
Finally, write the equation.
$$NaHCO_3(s) + HCl(aq) \longrightarrow NaCl(aq) + H_2O(l) + CO_2(g)$$

3. *EVALUATE Does the result make sense?*
The rules for writing a skeleton equation have been properly applied. Formulas for the reactants are written first, followed by an arrow, followed by the formulas of the products.

Practice Problems

1. Write a skeleton equation for each chemical reaction. Include appropriate symbols from **Table 8.1**.
   a. Sulfur burns in oxygen to form sulfur dioxide.
   b. Heating potassium chlorate in the presence of the catalyst manganese dioxide produces oxygen gas. Potassium chloride is left as a solid.

2. Write a sentence that describes each chemical reaction.
   a. $KOH(aq) + H_2SO_4(aq) \longrightarrow$
      $H_2O(l) + K_2SO_4(aq)$
   b. $Na(s) + H_2O(l) \longrightarrow$
      $NaOH(aq) + H_2(g)$

Balancing Chemical Equations

You can write word equations similar to chemical equations for many everyday processes. For instance, you could write a word equation for the manufacture of bicycles. What do you need to make a bicycle? To simplify your task, limit yourself to four major components: frames, wheels, handlebars, and pedals. Your word equation for making a bicycle probably reads like this.

$$\text{Frame + wheel + handlebar + pedal} \longrightarrow \text{bicycle}$$
(reactants)   (product)

Your word equation is qualitatively correct. It shows the reactants (the kinds of parts) you need to make a product (a bicycle). If you were responsible for ordering parts to make a bicycle, however, this word equation would be inadequate. Why? It does not show a quantitative relationship; that is, it does not indicate the quantity of each part needed to make one bicycle.

A standard bicycle is composed of one frame (F), two wheels (W), one handlebar (H), and two pedals (P). Using these symbols, the formula for a bicycle is FW_2HP_2. The unbalanced skeleton equation for bicycle assembly is written as follows.

$$F + W + H + P \longrightarrow FW_2HP_2$$

An equation that does not indicate the quantity of the reactants needed to make the product is called an unbalanced equation. A complete description of the reaction would include both the kinds and the quantities of parts required. An equation that gives the correct quantity of each reactant and product is called a balanced equation. Numbers called **coefficients** are placed in front of the symbols for the respective parts. When no coefficient is written, it is assumed to be 1. The balanced equation for making a bicycle is shown below. If you had ten of each of the parts, how many bicycles could you make? Would you have any parts left over? If so, list them.

$$F \quad + \quad 2W \quad + \quad H \quad + \quad 2P \quad \longrightarrow \quad FW_2HP_2$$

For chemical equations to represent a chemical reaction correctly, you must first write the correct formulas for the reactants and the products using what you know about formulas for elements and compounds. This is always the first step in writing a chemical equation. The next step is to balance the chemical equation so that it is quantitatively correct, indicating the amounts of the reactants and products.

Balancing the chemical equation is necessary so that it obeys the law of conservation of mass. Remember, in a chemical reaction, atoms are not created or destroyed; they are simply rearranged. In every **balanced equation,** each side of the equation has the same number of atoms of each element.

LINK TO PHYSIOLOGY

Hydrogen Peroxide

Why does hydrogen peroxide decompose to water and oxygen when it comes into contact with blood? This rapid, foaming reaction is an example of chemical catalysis by a biological molecule. The enzyme catalase, found in living cells, catalyzes the breakdown of hydrogen peroxide. Catalase is a protein that contains an iron(II) ion at its center. The iron(II) ion is the actual site on the catalase molecule where the reaction takes place. When hydrogen peroxide is poured on a cut, it reacts with the iron(II) ions of catalase. This triggers the rapid release of atomic oxygen from the hydrogen peroxide. These energetic oxygen atoms produce the antiseptic effect of hydrogen peroxide.

Sometimes when you write the formulas for the reactants and products in an equation, the equation may already be balanced. One example of this is the equation for the burning of carbon in the presence of oxygen to produce carbon dioxide.

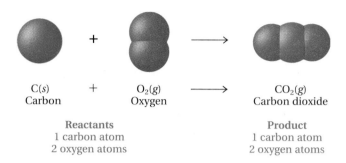

C(s)	+	$O_2(g)$	$CO_2(g)$
Carbon		Oxygen	Carbon dioxide

Reactants
1 carbon atom
2 oxygen atoms

Product
1 carbon atom
2 oxygen atoms

This equation is balanced. One carbon atom is on each side of the equation, and two oxygen atoms are on each side. You do not need to change the coefficients; they are all understood to be 1.

Another equation you have seen is the reaction of hydrogen with oxygen to form water.

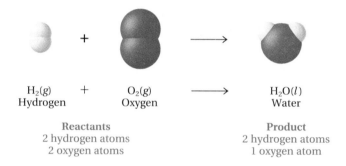

$H_2(g)$	+	$O_2(g)$	$H_2O(l)$
Hydrogen		Oxygen	Water

Reactants
2 hydrogen atoms
2 oxygen atoms

Product
2 hydrogen atoms
1 oxygen atom

This equation is not balanced even though the formulas for all of the reactants and products are correct. Count the atoms on both sides of the equation. There are two oxygen atoms on the reactant (left) side of the equation and only one oxygen atom on the product (right) side. As written, the equation does not obey the law of conservation of mass. What can you do to balance it? Many chemical equations can be balanced by trial and error. A few guidelines, however, will speed up the process.

Rules for Balancing Equations

1. Determine the correct formulas for all the reactants and products in the reaction, using what you know about elements and compounds. In some cases, you may also indicate in parentheses the state in which the reactants and products exist.

2. Write the formulas for the reactants on the left and the formulas for the products on the right with a yields sign ($\rightarrow$) in between. If two or more reactants or products are involved, separate their formulas with plus signs. When finished, you will have a skeleton equation.

3. Count the number of atoms of each element in the reactants and products. For simplicity, a polyatomic ion appearing unchanged on both sides of the equation is counted as a single unit.

4. Balance the elements one at a time by using coefficients. When no coefficient is written, it is assumed to be 1. It is best to begin the balancing operation with elements that appear only once on each side of the equation. You must not attempt to balance an equation by changing the subscripts in the chemical formula of a substance.

5. Check each atom or polyatomic ion to be sure that the equation is balanced.

6. Finally, make sure all the coefficients are in the lowest possible ratio that balances.

Now use these rules to balance the equation in Sample Problem 8-2 for the formation of water from hydrogen and oxygen.

Chem ASAP!

Simulation 4

Sharpen your skills by balancing chemical equations.

Sample Problem 8-2

Hydrogen and oxygen react to form water. Write a balanced equation for this reaction.

1. **ANALYZE** *Plan a problem-solving strategy.*
   Apply the rules for balancing equations to the word equation describing the reaction.

2. **SOLVE** *Apply the problem-solving strategy.*
   Write correct formulas to give the skeleton equation.

   $$H_2(g) + O_2(g) \longrightarrow H_2O(l)$$

   Counting the number of each atom shows that hydrogen is balanced but oxygen is not. If you put a coefficient of 2 in front of H_2O, the oxygen becomes balanced.

   $$H_2(g) + O_2(g) \longrightarrow 2H_2O(l)$$

   Now there are twice as many hydrogen atoms in the product as there are in the reactants. To correct this, put a coefficient of 2 in front of H_2. The equation is now balanced.

   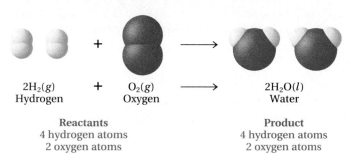

   | $2H_2(g)$ | + | $O_2(g)$ | $\longrightarrow$ | $2H_2O(l)$ |
   | Hydrogen | | Oxygen | | Water |

Reactants	Product
4 hydrogen atoms	4 hydrogen atoms
2 oxygen atoms	2 oxygen atoms

3. **EVALUATE** *Does the result make sense?*
   There are four hydrogen atoms and two oxygen atoms on each side of the chemical equation. The chemical formulas for the elements and compounds involved are correct, and the coefficients are in their lowest possible ratio: $2(H_2)$, $1(O_2)$, and $2(H_2O)$.

Practice Problems

3. Balance each equation.
   a. $AgNO_3 + H_2S \longrightarrow$
      $Ag_2S + HNO_3$
   b. $MnO_2 + HCl \longrightarrow$
      $MnCl_2 + H_2O + Cl_2$
   c. $Zn(OH)_2 + H_3PO_4 \longrightarrow$
      $Zn_3(PO_4)_2 + H_2O$

4. Rewrite these word equations as balanced chemical equations.
   a. hydrogen + sulfur $\longrightarrow$
      hydrogen sulfide
   b. iron(III) chloride + calcium hydroxide $\longrightarrow$ iron(III) hydroxide + calcium chloride

Chem ASAP!

Problem-Solving 4

Solve Problem 4 with the help of an interactive guided tutorial.

Figure 8.4

Notice the deposit of silver crystals on the copper wire when copper reacts with silver nitrate in aqueous solution.

Practice Problems

5. Balance the equation.
   $CO + Fe_2O_3 \longrightarrow Fe + CO_2$
6. Write the balanced chemical equation for the reaction of carbon with oxygen to form carbon monoxide.

Sample Problem 8-3

Figure 8.4 shows the reaction of copper metal and an aqueous solution of silver nitrate. Balance the equation for this reaction.

$$AgNO_3(aq) + Cu(s) \longrightarrow Cu(NO_3)_2(aq) + Ag(s)$$

1. **ANALYZE** *Plan a problem-solving strategy.*
   Apply the rules for balancing equations. Because the nitrate polyatomic ion appears as a reactant and a product, this ion can be balanced as a unit.

2. **SOLVE** *Apply the problem-solving strategy.*
   Put a coefficient of 2 in front of $AgNO_3(aq)$ to balance the nitrate ion.

   $$2AgNO_3(aq) + Cu(s) \longrightarrow$$
   $$Cu(NO_3)_2(aq) + Ag(s)$$

   By inspection, the silver is not balanced. Put a coefficient of 2 in front of $Ag(s)$.

   $$2AgNO_3(aq) + Cu(s) \longrightarrow$$
   $$Cu(NO_3)_2(aq) + 2Ag(s)$$

3. **EVALUATE** *Does the result make sense?*
   The equation is balanced, and the coefficients are in the lowest whole-number ratio.

Sample Problem 8-4

Aluminum reacts with oxygen in the air to form a thin protective coat of aluminum oxide. Balance the equation for this reaction.

$$Al(s) + O_2(g) \longrightarrow Al_2O_3(s)$$

1. **ANALYZE** *Plan a problem-solving strategy.*
   Apply the rules for balancing equations.

2. **SOLVE** *Apply the problem-solving strategy.*
   First balance the aluminum by placing a coefficient of 2 in front of $Al(s)$.

   $$2Al(s) + O_2(g) \longrightarrow Al_2O_3(s)$$

   There is now a situation that occurs quite frequently in balancing equations. It can be called the even-odd problem. Any whole-number coefficient placed in front of the O_2 will give an even number of oxygen atoms on the left. This is because the coefficient is always being multiplied by the subscript 2. How can the odd number of oxygen atoms in the product (right side) be made even to balance with the even number on the left? The simplest way to do this is to begin by multiplying the formula with the odd number of oxygen atoms by 2.

   $$2Al(s) + O_2(g) \longrightarrow 2Al_2O_3(s)$$

Practice Problems

7. Balance each equation.
   a. $FeCl_3 + NaOH \longrightarrow$
   $$Fe(OH)_3 + NaCl$$
   b. $CS_2 + Cl_2 \longrightarrow CCl_4 + S_2Cl_2$
   c. $CH_4 + Br_2 \longrightarrow CH_3Br + HBr$

Sample Problem 8-4 (cont.)

Now there are six oxygen atoms on the right. Balance the oxygens on the left with a 3 and rebalance the aluminum on the left with a 4.

$$4Al(s) + 3O_2(g) \longrightarrow 2Al_2O_3(s)$$

3. EVALUATE *Does the result make sense?*

There are equal numbers of each kind of atom in the reactants and product (4 aluminum and 6 oxygen). Also, the coefficients are in the lowest possible ratio. Suppose the equation for the formation of aluminum oxide was written

$$8Al(s) + 6O_2(g) \longrightarrow 4Al_2O_3(s)$$

Because this equation obeys the law of conservation of mass, it appears to be correct. It is incorrect, however, because the coefficients are not in their lowest possible ratio. Each of the coefficients can be divided by 2 to give the previous equation, which has the lowest whole-number ratio of coefficients.

Practice Problems (cont.)

8. Write the balanced chemical equations.

 a. sodium + water $\longrightarrow$ sodium hydroxide + hydrogen

 b. calcium hydroxide + sulfuric acid $\longrightarrow$ calcium sulfate + water

Chem ASAP!

Problem-Solving 8
Solve Problem 8 with the help of an interactive guided tutorial.

---

section review 8.1

9. Write word equations for the following chemical reactions.

 a. Pure copper can be produced by heating copper(II) sulfide in the presence of diatomic oxygen from the air. Sulfur dioxide gas is also produced in this reaction.

 b. Water is formed by the explosive reaction between hydrogen gas and oxygen gas.

 c. When baking soda (sodium hydrogen carbonate) is heated, it decomposes, forming the products sodium carbonate, carbon dioxide, and water.

10. Balance the following equations.

 a. $SO_2 + O_2 \longrightarrow SO_3$ **c.** $P + O_2 \longrightarrow P_4O_{10}$

 b. $Fe_2O_3 + H_2 \longrightarrow Fe + H_2O$ **d.** $Al + N_2 \longrightarrow AlN$

11. Write formulas and other symbols for these substances.

 a. sulfur trioxide gas

 b. potassium nitrate dissolved in water

 c. heat supplied to a chemical reaction

 d. metallic copper

 e. liquid mercury

 f. zinc chloride as a catalyst

12. How is the law of conservation of mass related to the balancing of a chemical equation?

portfolio project

Some products are marketed as biodegradable. What does *biodegradable* mean? Identify some biodegradable products. How do these products benefit the environment?

 Chem ASAP! Assessment 8.1 Check your understanding of the important ideas and concepts in Section 8.1.

TYPES OF CHEMICAL REACTIONS

The largest barbeque on record served more than 50 000 people! Charcoal briquettes fuel barbeque grills through the combustion of carbon. Have you ever felt the heat and smelled the smoke coming from a burning barbeque grill? The heat and smoke are actually the products of a combustion reaction. Combustion is one of many types of chemical reactions. **How can you identify the different types of chemical reactions?**

Classifying Reactions

Consider for a moment the number of possible chemical reactions. Because there are millions of known chemical compounds, it is logical to expect that millions of different chemical reactions can occur in nature or be carried out in the laboratory. Just as you learned to name many compounds in Chapter 6 by following a system of nomenclature rather than memorizing common names for thousands of different compounds, you can learn to recognize patterns of chemical behavior that allow you to predict the products in many chemical reactions.

There are several ways to categorize chemical reactions. One classification scheme identifies five general types of reactions: combination, decomposition, single-replacement, double-replacement, and combustion. Not all chemical reactions, however, fit uniquely into only one of these classes. Occasionally, a reaction may fit equally well into two of these categories. In spite of these exceptions, recognizing a reaction as a particular type is useful. Patterns of behavior in reactions will become apparent and allow you to predict the products of these reactions.

Combination Reactions

The first reaction type you will look at is the combination, or synthesis, reaction. As shown in **Figure 8.5,** magnesium metal and oxygen gas combine to form a new compound, magnesium oxide. In a **combination reaction,** two or more substances combine to form a single substance. The reactants of most common combination reactions are either two elements or two compounds. The product of a combination reaction is always a compound. What determines whether the compound formed is ionic or molecular? Several examples of the general types of combination reactions are explained in the following paragraphs.

When a Group A metal and a nonmetal react, the product is a compound that is a combination of the metal cation and the nonmetal anion. You should be able to write the correct formula of the product by considering the charges of the anions and cations. For example,

$$2K(s) + Cl_2(g) \longrightarrow 2KCl(s)$$

As shown in the two examples below, when two nonmetals react by combination, more than one product is often possible.

$$S(s) + O_2(g) \longrightarrow SO_2(g) \text{ sulfur dioxide}$$
$$2S(s) + 3O_2(g) \longrightarrow 2SO_3(g) \text{ sulfur trioxide}$$

Figure 8.5
When ignited, magnesium ribbon reacts with oxygen in the surrounding air to form magnesium oxide, a white solid. This is a combination reaction. Magnesium burns so brightly that it was once used to provide the light needed for flash photography. Flashbulbs have since been replaced by electronic flash units.

$$2Mg(s) + O_2(g) \longrightarrow 2MgO(s)$$
Magnesium   Oxygen   Magnesium oxide

More than one product may also result from the combination reaction of a transition metal and a nonmetal. (Remember Dalton's law of multiple proportions from Chapter 6.)

$$Fe(s) + S(s) \longrightarrow FeS(s) \text{ iron(II) sulfide}$$
$$2Fe(s) + 3S(s) \longrightarrow Fe_2S_3(s) \text{ iron(III) sulfide}$$

Some nonmetal oxides react with water to produce an acid, a compound that produces hydrogen ions in aqueous solution. You will learn about acids in chapter 20.

$$SO_2(g) + H_2O(l) \longrightarrow H_2SO_3(aq) \text{ sulfurous acid}$$

Some metallic oxides react with water to give a base, or a compound containing hydroxide ions. Again in this case, you can use the ionic charges to derive the formula for the product.

$$CaO(s) + H_2O(l) \longrightarrow Ca(OH)_2(aq) \text{ calcium hydroxide}$$

Sample Problem 8-5

Using the previous examples as guidelines, complete the following combination reactions.

a. $Al(s) + O_2(g) \longrightarrow$

b. $Cu(s) + S(s) \longrightarrow$ (two reactions possible)

c. $SO_3(g) + H_2O(l) \longrightarrow$

1. **ANALYZE** *Plan a problem-solving strategy.*

   a. Because aluminum is a Group A metal combining with a nonmetal, write the correct formula for the compound aluminum oxide by using ionic charges. Then balance the equation.

   b. Two reactions are possible because copper is a transition metal and has more than one common ionic charge (Cu^+ and Cu^{2+}). Balance the two possible equations.

   c. Reactions between water and nonmetal oxides usually yield an acid in solution when the two molecules combine.

2. **SOLVE** *Apply the problem-solving strategy.*

   For each reaction, write the skeleton equation first, then apply the rules for balancing equations.

   a. $Al(s) + O_2(g) \longrightarrow Al_2O_3(s)$
   $4Al(s) + 3O_2(g) \longrightarrow 2Al_2O_3(s)$ (balanced)

   b. For copper(II):
   $Cu(s) + S(s) \longrightarrow CuS(s)$ (balanced)
   For copper(I):
   $Cu(s) + S(s) \longrightarrow Cu_2S(s)$
   $2Cu(s) + S(s) \longrightarrow Cu_2S(s)$ (balanced)

   c. $SO_3(g) + H_2O(l) \longrightarrow H_2SO_4(aq)$ (balanced)

3. **EVALUATE** *Do the results make sense?*

   In **a.** and **b.** a metal reacts with a nonmetal and the formula of the product is written using ionic charges. In **c.** a nonmetal oxide combines with water to form an acid by "adding" the molecules together.

Practice Problems

13. Complete and balance these combination reactions.

   a. $Be + O_2 \longrightarrow$

   b. $SO_2 + H_2O \longrightarrow$

14. Write and balance an equation for the formation of each compound from its elements.

   a. strontium iodide (SrI_2)

   b. magnesium nitride (Mg_3N_2)

Chem ASAP!

Problem-Solving 14

Solve Problem 14 with the help of an interactive guided tutorial.

Decomposition Reactions

When calcium carbonate is heated, it decomposes or breaks down into two simpler compounds. This reaction is used to make lime (calcium oxide) from limestone (primarily calcium carbonate).

$$CaCO_3(s) \xrightarrow{\text{heat}} CaO(s) + CO_2(g)$$

Many other compounds also decompose with the addition of energy. The decomposition of mercury(II) oxide to yield mercury and oxygen is shown in **Figure 8.6**.

In a **decomposition reaction,** a single compound is broken down into two or more products. These products can be any combination of elements and compounds. It is usually very difficult to predict the products of decomposition reactions. However, as shown in **Figure 8.6,** when a simple binary compound breaks down you know the products will be the constituent elements. Extremely rapid decomposition reactions that produce gaseous products and heat are often the cause of explosions. As seen in the two reactions shown in **Figure 8.6** and **Figure 8.7,** most decomposition reactions require energy in the form of heat, light, or electricity.

Figure 8.6

When it is heated, orange-colored mercury(II) oxide decomposes into its constituent elements: liquid mercury and gaseous oxygen.

Figure 8.7

Decomposition in action! The powerful explosive force of dynamite comes from a decomposition reaction. What is usually added to the reactants of a decomposition reaction to start the reaction?

Chemical Reactions **215**

Sample Problem 8-6

Write a balanced equation for each decomposition reaction.

a. $H_2O(l) \xrightarrow{\text{electricity}}$ **b.** lead(IV) oxide $\xrightarrow{\text{heat}}$

1. *ANALYZE* **Plan a problem-solving strategy.**
   a. Water, a binary compound, breaks down into its elements. Balance the equation, remembering that hydrogen and oxygen are both diatomic molecules.
   b. Lead(IV) oxide decomposes into its constituent elements. Balance the equation.

2. *SOLVE* **Apply the problem-solving strategy.**
   For each reaction, write the skeleton equation first, then apply the rules for balancing equations.
   a. $H_2O(l) \xrightarrow{\text{electricity}} H_2(g) + O_2(g)$
        $2H_2O(l) \xrightarrow{\text{electricity}} 2H_2(g) + O_2(g)$ (balanced)
   b. $PbO_2(s) \xrightarrow{\text{heat}} Pb(l) + O_2(g)$ (balanced)

3. *EVALUATE* **Do the results make sense?**
   The formulas for the reactants and products are correct. The balanced equations have the same number and kinds of atoms on each side of the yields sign.

Practice Problems

15. Complete and balance these decomposition reactions.
    a. $HI \longrightarrow$
    b. $Mg(ClO_3)_2 \longrightarrow MgCl_2 +$
16. Write the formula for the binary compound that decomposes to each set of products.
    a. $H_2 + Br_2$
    b. $Na + Cl_2$

Single-Replacement Reactions

Dropping a small piece of potassium into a beaker of water creates a violent reaction, as shown in **Figure 8.8.** The reaction produces hydrogen gas and a large quantity of heat. The hydrogen gas released can ignite explosively.

Figure 8.8

The alkali metal potassium displaces hydrogen from water and forms a solution of potassium hydroxide in a single-replacement reaction. The heat of the reaction is often sufficient to ignite the hydrogen. Why are alkali metals stored under mineral oil or kerosene?

| $2K(s)$ | + | $2H_2O(l)$ | $\longrightarrow$ | $2KOH(aq)$ | + | $H_2(g)$ |
| Potassium | | Water | | Potassium hydroxide | | Hydrogen |

The reaction of potassium with water is a single-replacement reaction. Similar but much less spectacular reactions can occur when certain elements are put into an aqueous solution of a compound. In a **single-replacement reaction,** one element replaces a second element in a compound. Single-replacement reactions are also called single-displacement reactions. In the reaction shown in **Figure 8.8,** potassium replaces hydrogen, which is released as a flammable gas.

Whether one metal will displace another metal from a compound can be determined by the relative reactivities of the two metals. The **activity series of metals,** given in **Table 8.2,** lists metals in order of decreasing reactivity. A reactive metal will replace any metal listed below it in the activity series. Thus, as shown in **Figure 8.9,** iron will displace copper from a copper compound in solution. Magnesium displaces zinc from a zinc compound in solution, as well as silver from a silver compound in solution. By contrast, magnesium does not displace lithium or calcium from aqueous solutions of their compounds.

$$Mg(s) + Zn(NO_3)_2(aq) \longrightarrow Mg(NO_3)_2(aq) + Zn(s)$$

$$Mg(s) + 2AgNO_3(aq) \longrightarrow Mg(NO_3)_2(aq) + 2Ag(s)$$

$$Mg(s) + LiNO_3(aq) \longrightarrow \text{no reaction}$$

A nonmetal can also replace another nonmetal from a compound. This replacement is usually limited to the halogens (F_2, Cl_2, Br_2, and I_2). The activity of the halogens decreases as you go down Group 7A of the periodic table.

Table 8.2

Activity Series of Metals	
Name	**Symbol**
Lithium	Li
Potassium	K
Calcium	Ca
Sodium	Na
Magnesium	Mg
Aluminum	Al
Zinc	Zn
Iron	Fe
Lead	Pb
(Hydrogen)	(H)*
Copper	Cu
Mercury	Hg
Silver	Ag

(Decreasing reactivity — indicated by downward arrow at left)

*Metals from Li to Na will replace H from acids and water; from Mg to Pb they will replace H from acids only.

Figure 8.9

Some single-replacement reactions take place quietly, as when iron displaces copper from a compound in solution (left); the copper is deposited on the iron bolt. Other single-replacement reactions are violent, as when water is dropped onto sodium (right).

Chemical Reactions **217**

Sample Problem 8-7

Write a balanced chemical equation for each single-replacement reaction.

    a. $Zn(s) + H_2SO_4(aq) \longrightarrow$
    b. $Na(s) + H_2O(l) \longrightarrow$
    c. $Sn(s) + NaNO_3(aq) \longrightarrow$
    d. $Cl_2(g) + NaBr(aq) \longrightarrow$

1. **ANALYZE** *Plan a problem-solving strategy.*
       a. According to the activity series of metals, zinc displaces hydrogen from an acid and takes its place. Balance the equation, remembering that elemental hydrogen is diatomic.

       b. Sodium displaces hydrogen from water. As you balance the equation, you might find it helpful to write water as HOH and visualize it as being made of H^+ and OH^- ions.

       c. No displacement reaction occurs because tin is less reactive than sodium.

       d. Chlorine is more reactive than bromine and displaces bromine from its compounds. Balance the equation, remembering that bromine is diatomic and a liquid.

2. **SOLVE** *Apply the problem-solving strategy.*
   For each reaction, write the skeleton equation first, then apply the rules for balancing equations.

       a. $Zn(s) + H_2SO_4(aq) \longrightarrow ZnSO_4(aq) + H_2(g)$ (balanced)

       b. $Na(s) + HOH(l) \longrightarrow NaOH(aq) + H_2(g)$
           $2Na(s) + 2HOH(l) \longrightarrow 2NaOH(aq) + H_2(g)$ (balanced)

       c. no reaction

       d. $Cl_2(g) + NaBr(aq) \longrightarrow NaCl(aq) + Br_2(l)$
           $Cl_2(g) + 2NaBr(aq) \longrightarrow 2NaCl(aq) + Br_2(l)$ (balanced)

3. **EVALUATE** *Do the results make sense?*
   A single-replacement reaction occurs only when a more active metal (or nonmetal) displaces a less active metal (or nonmetal) from a compound. After ionic charges were used to write correct formulas for ionic products, the equations were balanced.

Practice Problem

17. Complete the equations for these single-replacement reactions that take place in aqueous solution. Balance each equation. If a reaction does not occur (use the activity series), write "no reaction."
        a. $Fe(s) + Pb(NO_3)_2(aq) \longrightarrow$
        b. $Cl_2(g) + NaI(aq) \longrightarrow$
        c. $Ca(s) + H_2O(l) \longrightarrow$

Chem ASAP!

Problem-Solving 17
Solve Problem 17 with the help of an interactive guided tutorial.

Double-Replacement Reactions

Many ionic compounds can dissolve in water to form solutions. When two solutions of ionic compounds are mixed, the result still may be a solution. This is what happens when solutions of sodium chloride and calcium nitrate are mixed. A second possible outcome is that ions in the solutions

$$K_2CO_3(aq) \quad + \quad BaCl_2(aq) \quad \longrightarrow \quad 2KCl(aq) \quad + \quad BaCO_3(s)$$

Potassium carbonate   +   Barium chloride   ⟶   Potassium chloride   +   Barium carbonate

react. **Figure 8.10** shows that mixing aqueous solutions of barium chloride and potassium carbonate results in a chemical reaction. Barium carbonate is the white precipitate formed. Potassium chloride, the other product of the reaction, remains in solution. **Double-replacement reactions** involve an exchange of positive ions between two reacting compounds. Such reactions generally take place between two ionic compounds in aqueous solution and are often characterized by the production of a precipitate. For a double-replacement reaction to occur, one of the following is usually true.

Figure 8.10

Aqueous solutions of barium chloride and potassium carbonate react in a double-replacement reaction to form barium carbonate, the white precipitate. Potassium chloride, the other product of the reaction, remains in solution. (In this figure, the polyatomic ion CO_3^{2-} is represented as a single sphere.)

1. One product is only slightly soluble and precipitates from solution. For example, the reaction of aqueous solutions of sodium sulfide and cadmium nitrate produces a yellow precipitate of cadmium sulfide.

$$Na_2S(aq) + Cd(NO_3)_2(aq) \longrightarrow CdS(s) + 2NaNO_3(aq)$$

2. One product is a gas that bubbles out of the mixture. For example, hydrogen cyanide gas is produced when aqueous sodium cyanide is mixed with sulfuric acid.

$$2NaCN(aq) + H_2SO_4(aq) \longrightarrow 2HCN(g) + Na_2SO_4(aq)$$

3. One product is a molecular compound such as water. Combining solutions of calcium hydroxide and hydrochloric acid produces water as one of the products.

$$Ca(OH)_2(aq) + 2HCl(aq) \longrightarrow CaCl_2(aq) + 2H_2O(l)$$

Practice Problems

18. Write the products for these double-replacement reactions. Then balance each equation.
   a. $NaOH + Fe(NO_3)_3 \longrightarrow$
      (Iron hydroxide is a precipitate.)
   b. $Ba(NO_3)_2 + H_3PO_4 \longrightarrow$
      (Barium phosphate is a precipitate.)
19. Write a balanced equation for each reaction.
   a. $KOH(aq) + H_3PO_4(aq) \longrightarrow$
   b. $H_2SO_4 + Al(OH)_3 \longrightarrow$

Chem ASAP!

Problem-Solving 18

Solve Problem 18 with the help of an interactive guided tutorial.

Sample Problem 8-8

Write a balanced chemical equation for each double-replacement reaction.
   a. $BaCl_2(aq) + K_2CO_3(aq) \longrightarrow$ (A precipitate of barium carbonate is formed.)
   b. $FeS(s) + HCl(aq) \longrightarrow$ (Hydrogen sulfide gas (H_2S) is formed.)

1. *ANALYZE Plan a problem-solving strategy.*
   a. The driving force behind the reaction is the formation of a precipitate. Write correct formulas of the products using ionic charges. Then balance the equation.
   b. A gas is formed in this double-replacement reaction. Use ionic charges to write the correct formula of the other product. Then balance the equation.

2. *SOLVE Apply the problem-solving strategy.*
   For each reaction, write the skeleton equation first, then apply the rules for balancing equations.
   a. $BaCl_2(aq) + K_2CO_3(aq) \longrightarrow BaCO_3(s) + KCl(aq)$
      $BaCl_2(aq) + K_2CO_3(aq) \longrightarrow BaCO_3(s) + 2KCl(aq)$
      (balanced)
   b. $FeS(s) + HCl(aq) \longrightarrow H_2S(g) + FeCl_2(aq)$
      $FeS(s) + 2HCl(aq) \longrightarrow H_2S(g) + FeCl_2(aq)$ (balanced)

3. *EVALUATE Do the results make sense?*
   After correct formulas of the ionic products were written using ionic charges, the equations were balanced. Also, each reaction follows one of the rules for double-replacement reactions.

Combustion Reactions

In a **combustion reaction,** an element or a compound reacts with oxygen, often producing energy as heat and light. Combustion reactions commonly involve hydrocarbons, compounds of hydrogen and carbon. The complete combustion of a hydrocarbon produces the compounds carbon dioxide and water. If the supply of oxygen is insufficient during a reaction, combustion will be incomplete. Elemental carbon and toxic carbon monoxide may be additional products. The complete combustion of a hydrocarbon releases a large amount of energy as heat. Thus hydrocarbons such as methane (CH_4), propane (C_3H_8), and butane (C_4H_{10}) are important fuels. The combustion reaction for methane is shown in **Figure 8.11.**

The reaction between some elements and oxygen is also an example of a combustion reaction. For example, both magnesium and sulfur will burn by reaction with oxygen. As what other type can these two reactions be classified?

$$2Mg(s) + O_2(g) \longrightarrow 2MgO(s)$$

$$S(s) + O_2(g) \longrightarrow SO_2(g)$$

Figure 8.11
Methane gas reacts with oxygen from the surrounding air in a combustion reaction to produce carbon dioxide and water. What else is produced in this reaction?

$CH_4(g)$ + $2O_2(g)$ ⟶ $CO_2(g)$ + $2H_2O(g)$
Methane   Oxygen   Carbon dioxide   Water

Sample Problem 8-9

Write balanced equations for the complete combustion of these compounds.
  a. benzene (C_6H_6)(l)
  b. methanol (CH_3OH)(l)

1. **ANALYZE** *Plan a problem-solving strategy.*
   Remember that oxygen is the other reactant in these combustion reactions. Also, because the reactions are complete, the only products are CO_2 and H_2O. Write the skeleton equation for each reaction, then balance the equation.

2. **SOLVE** *Apply the problem-solving strategy.*
   For each reaction, write the skeleton equation first, then apply the rules for balancing equations.
   a. $C_6H_6(l) + O_2(g) \longrightarrow CO_2(g) + H_2O(g)$
      $2C_6H_6(l) + 15O_2(g) \longrightarrow 12CO_2(g) + 6H_2O(g)$ (balanced)
   b. $CH_3OH(l) + O_2(g) \longrightarrow CO_2(g) + H_2O(g)$
      $2CH_3OH(l) + 3O_2(g) \longrightarrow 2CO_2(g) + 4H_2O(g)$ (balanced)

3. **EVALUATE** *Do the results make sense?*
   Each balanced equation has the lowest whole-number set of coefficients. Each side of the balanced equation has the same number and kinds of atoms.

Practice Problems

20. Write a balanced equation for the complete combustion of each compound.
   a. formic acid (HCOOH)
   b. heptane (C_7H_{16})
21. Write a balanced equation for the complete combustion of glucose ($C_6H_{12}O_6$).

Chem ASAP!

Problem-Solving 21
Solve Problem 21 with the help of an interactive guided tutorial.

Predicting Products of a Chemical Reaction

Now that you have an understanding of some of the basic reaction types, you can predict the products of many reactions. To predict the products of a chemical reaction successfully, you must recognize the possible type of reaction that the reactants can undergo. Keys to recognizing reaction types and predicting products are shown in **Figure 8.12.**

Some reactions do not fit any one of the five general types discussed so far. Another very important type of chemical reaction is an oxidation–reduction, or redox, reaction. This type of reaction is discussed in Chapters 22 and 23. Recognizing types of reactions is important, but the only way to determine the products of any reaction with certainty is to carry out the reaction in the laboratory.

Figure 8.12
The five types of chemical reactions discussed in this chapter are summarized here.

Combination Reaction

General Equation: R + S $\longrightarrow$ RS
Reactants: Generally two elements, or two compounds (where at least one compound is a molecular compound)
Probable Products: A single compound
Example: Burning magnesium in air

$$2Mg(s) + O_2(g) \longrightarrow 2MgO(s)$$

Decomposition Reaction

General Equation: RS $\longrightarrow$ R + S
Reactants: Generally a single binary or ternary compound
Probable Products: Two elements (for a binary compound), or two or more elements and/or compounds (for a ternary compound)
Example: Heating mercury(II) oxide

$$2HgO(s) \longrightarrow 2Hg(l) + O_2(g)$$

Single-Replacement Reaction

General Equation:

$$T + RS \longrightarrow TS + R$$

Reactants: An element and a compound. In a single-replacement reaction, an element replaces another element from a compound in aqueous solution. For a single-replacement reaction to occur, the element that is displaced must be less active than the element that is doing the displacing.

Probable Products: A different element and a new compound

Example: Potassium in water

$$2K(s) + 2H_2O(l) \longrightarrow 2KOH(aq) + H_2(g)$$

Double-Replacement Reaction

General Equation:

$$R^+S^- + T^+U^- \longrightarrow R^+U^- + T^+S^-$$

Reactants: Two ionic compounds. In a double-replacement reaction, two ionic compounds react by exchanging cations to form two different compounds.

Probable Products: Two new compounds. Double-replacement reactions are driven by the formation of a precipitate, a gaseous product, or water.

Example: Reaction of aqueous solutions of barium chloride and potassium carbonate.

$$K_2CO_3(aq) + BaCl_2(aq) \longrightarrow 2KCl(aq) + BaCO_3(s)$$

Combustion Reaction

General Equation:

$$C_xH_y + (x + y/4)\, O_2 \longrightarrow xCO_2 + (y/2)H_2O$$

Reactants: Oxygen and a compound of C, H, (O).
When oxygen reacts with an element or compound, combustion may occur.

Probable Products: CO_2 and H_2O
With incomplete combustion, C and CO may also be products.

Example: The combustion of methane gas in air

$$CH_4(g) + 2O_2(g) \longrightarrow CO_2(g) + 2H_2O(g)$$

MINI LAB

Activity Series of Metals

PURPOSE

To develop an activity series of metals.

MATERIALS

- 15 100-mL beakers
- 5 small strips each of copper, magnesium, and zinc metal
- steel wool or fine sandpaper
- aqueous solutions of the following:
  $CuSO_4$ (0.05M)
  $MgSO_4$ (0.05M)
  $NaCl$ (0.05M)
  $AgNO_3$ (0.05M)
  $ZnSO_4$ (0.05M)

PROCEDURE

1. Clean each strip of metal with the steel wool or sandpaper.

2. Label each beaker with the name of one of the solutions. There should be three beakers for each solution.

3. Pour 20.0 mL of each solution into each of its labeled beakers.

4. Divide the beakers into three groups, each with one beaker of each solution. Label one group of beakers copper, one magnesium, and one zinc. Place a strip of the corresponding metal into each beaker.

5. After 1, 5, and 15 minutes make observations of the metal strips and the solutions.

ANALYSIS AND CONCLUSIONS

1. In which solutions did the appearance of the metal change? (Ignore the formation of bubbles.)

2. Write a balanced equation for each reaction between a metal and a solution.

3. Based on the results of your experiment, construct an activity series for these five metals. Put the most active metal first.

section review 8.2

22. Balance each equation. Identify each as to type.

   a. $Pb(NO_3)_2 + K_2CrO_4 \longrightarrow PbCrO_4 + KNO_3$

   b. $Cl_2 + KI \longrightarrow KCl + I_2$

   c. $C_3H_6 + O_2 \longrightarrow CO_2 + H_2O$

   d. $Al(OH)_3 \longrightarrow Al_2O_3 + H_2O$

   e. $Li + O_2 \longrightarrow Li_2O$

   f. $HCl + Fe_2O_3 \longrightarrow FeCl_3 + H_2O$

   g. $MgCO_3 \longrightarrow MgO + CO_2$

   h. $Ba(CN)_2 + H_2SO_4 \longrightarrow BaSO_4 + HCN$

23. Complete and balance an equation for each reaction.

   a. $CaI_2 + Hg(NO_3)_2 \longrightarrow$ d. $C_2H_2 + O_2 \longrightarrow$

   b. $Al + Cl_2 \longrightarrow$ e. $MgCl_2 \longrightarrow$

   c. $Ag + HCl \longrightarrow$ f. $H_2O_2 \longrightarrow$

24. What three types of products drive double-replacement reactions?

 Chem ASAP! Assessment 8.2 Check your understanding of the important ideas and concepts in Section 8.2.

REACTIONS IN AQUEOUS SOLUTION

*The beauty of a limestone cavern is the direct result of chemical reactions involving water. Limestone caverns form as calcium carbonate reacts with carbon dioxide dissolved in water to form soluble calcium hydrogen carbonate. Addi-*tional carbon dioxide then converts the calcium hydrogen carbonate back into calcium carbonate, which precipitates out, leaving behind dramatic stalactites and stalagmites. **What causes the formation of a precipitate?**

objectives
▶ Write and balance net ionic equations
▶ Use solubility rules to predict the precipitate formed in double-replacement reactions

key terms
▶ complete ionic equation
▶ spectator ions
▶ net ionic equation

Net Ionic Equations

Our world is water-based. More than 70% of Earth's surface is covered by water, and about 66% of the adult human body is water. It is not surprising, therefore, that many important chemical reactions take place in water—that is, in aqueous solution.

The reaction of aqueous solutions of silver nitrate with sodium chloride to form solid silver chloride and aqueous sodium nitrate is a double-replacement reaction.

$$\text{AgNO}_3(aq) + \text{NaCl}(aq) \longrightarrow \text{AgCl}(s) + \text{NaNO}_3(aq)$$

As written, this equation continues the practice of representing ionic compounds by their formula units. This equation is more realistically written, however, if you recognize that most ionic compounds dissociate, or separate, into cations and anions when they dissolve in water. For example, when sodium chloride dissolves in water it separates into sodium ions (Na^+)(aq) and chloride ions (Cl^-)(aq). Similarly, silver nitrate dissociates into silver ions (Ag^+)(aq) and nitrate ions (NO_3^-)(aq).

You can now write a **complete ionic equation,** an equation that shows dissolved ionic compounds as their free ions.

$$\text{Ag}^+(aq) + \text{NO}_3^-(aq) + \text{Na}^+(aq) + \text{Cl}^-(aq) \longrightarrow$$
$$\text{AgCl}(s) + \text{Na}^+(aq) + \text{NO}_3^-(aq)$$

The equation can be simplified and made more useful by eliminating the ions that do not participate in the reaction. You do this by canceling the ions that appear on both sides of the equation.

$$\text{Ag}^+(aq) + \cancel{\text{NO}_3^-(aq)} + \cancel{\text{Na}^+(aq)} + \text{Cl}^-(aq) \longrightarrow$$
$$\text{AgCl}(s) + \cancel{\text{Na}^+(aq)} + \cancel{\text{NO}_3^-(aq)}$$

Ions that are not directly involved in a reaction are called **spectator ions.** Notice that the spectator ions appear on both sides of the equation. You can rewrite this equation leaving out the spectator ions. This gives you the **net ionic equation,** the equation that indicates only those particles that actually take part in the reaction.

$$\text{Ag}^+(aq) + \text{Cl}^-(aq) \longrightarrow \text{AgCl}(s)$$

In writing balanced net ionic equations, you must also balance the ionic charge. For the previous reaction, the net ionic charge on each side of the equation is zero and is therefore balanced. In other reactions, this may not be the case. Consider the following reaction.

$$\text{Pb}(s) + \text{AgNO}_3(aq) \longrightarrow \text{Ag}(s) + \text{Pb(NO}_3)_2(aq)$$

The nitrate ion is the spectator ion in this reaction. The net ionic equation is

$$Pb(s) + Ag^+(aq) \longrightarrow Ag(s) + Pb^{2+}(aq) \text{ (unbalanced)}$$

Although this equation is balanced with respect to atoms, the ionic charges do not balance. On the reactant side of the equation there is a single unit of positive charge. On the product side there are two units of positive charge. Placing the coefficient 2 in front of $Ag^+(aq)$ balances the charge. A coefficient of 2 in front of $Ag(s)$ rebalances the atoms.

$$Pb(s) + 2Ag^+(aq) \longrightarrow 2Ag(s) + Pb^{2+}(aq) \text{ (balanced)}$$

Of the five types of reactions identified in this chapter, both single- and double-replacement reactions generally can be written as net ionic equations.

Sample Problem 8-10

Identify the spectator ions and write balanced net ionic equations for these reactions.

    a. $HCl(aq) + ZnS(aq) \longrightarrow H_2S(g) + ZnCl_2(aq)$
    b. $Cl_2(g) + NaBr(aq) \longrightarrow Br_2(l) + NaCl(aq)$
    c. Aqueous solutions of iron(III) chloride and potassium hydroxide are mixed, forming a precipitate of iron(III) hydroxide.

---

1. *ANALYZE Plan a problem-solving strategy.*
Write the complete ionic equation for each reaction, showing any soluble ionic compounds as individual ions. Any aqueous ions that appear as both reactants and products are spectator ions and are eliminated to give the net ionic equation. Finally, balance the net ionic equation.

---

2. *SOLVE Apply the problem-solving strategy.*
    a. Write the complete ionic equation.

$$H^+(aq) + Cl^-(aq) + Zn^{2+}(aq) + S^{2-}(aq) \longrightarrow$$
$$H_2S(g) + Zn^{2+}(aq) + Cl^-(aq)$$

The spectator ions are Zn^{2+} and Cl^-. The balanced net ionic equation is

$$2H^+(aq) + S^{2-}(aq) \longrightarrow H_2S(g)$$

    b. Write the complete ionic equation.

$$Cl_2(g) + Na^+(aq) + Br^-(aq) \longrightarrow$$
$$Br_2(l) + Na^+(aq) + Cl^-(aq)$$

The spectator ion is Na^+. The balanced net ionic equation is

$$Cl_2(g) + 2Br^-(aq) \longrightarrow Br_2(l) + 2Cl^-(aq)$$

    c. Write the complete ionic equation.

$$Fe^{3+}(aq) + 3Cl^-(aq) + 3K^+(aq) + 3OH^-(aq) \longrightarrow$$
$$Fe(OH)_3(s) + 3K^+(aq) + 3Cl^-(aq)$$

The spectator ions are K^+ and Cl^-. The balanced net ionic equation is

$$Fe^{3+}(aq) + 3OH^-(aq) \longrightarrow Fe(OH)_3(s)$$

Practice Problems

25. Write balanced net ionic equations for each reaction.
    a. $Pb(ClO_4)_2(aq) + NaI(aq)$
        $\longrightarrow PbI_2(s) + NaClO_4(aq)$
    b. $Zn(s) + HCl(aq) \longrightarrow$
        $ZnCl_2(aq) + H_2(g)$
    c. $Ca(OH)_2(aq) + H_3PO_4(aq)$
        $\longrightarrow Ca_3(PO_4)_2(aq) + H_2O(l)$

Problem-Solving 25
Solve Problem 25 with the help of an interactive guided tutorial.

Sample Problem 8-10 (cont.)

3. **EVALUATE** *Do the results make sense?*
In each balanced net ionic equation, the number and kinds of atoms in the reactants equal the number and kinds of atoms in the product. The net charge of all the reactants equals the net charge of all the products.

Predicting the Formation of a Precipitate

You have seen that mixing solutions of two ionic compounds can sometimes result in the formation of an insoluble salt called a precipitate. The formation of a precipitate is predicted by using the general rules for solubility of ionic compounds, shown in **Table 8.3.** Should a precipitate form when aqueous solutions of $Na_2SO_4(aq)$ and $Ba(NO_3)_2(aq)$ are mixed? When these four ions are mixed, the two new compounds that might form are $NaNO_3$ and $BaSO_4$. These are the only two new combinations of cation and anion possible.

$$2Na^+(aq) + SO_4^{2-}(aq) + Ba^{2+}(aq) + 2NO_3^-(aq) \longrightarrow ?$$

Sodium nitrate will not form a precipitate because alkali metal salts and nitrate salts are soluble (Rules 1 and 2). Rule 4 indicates that barium sulfate is insoluble and therefore will precipitate. In this reaction Na^+ and NO_3^- are spectator ions. The net ionic equation for this reaction is as follows.

$$Ba^{2+}(aq) + SO_4^{2-}(aq) \longrightarrow BaSO_4(s)$$

The mixing of solutions of sodium sulfate and barium nitrate is shown in **Figure 8.13.** In this example, why is the formation of a precipitate from Na^+ and SO_4^{2-} or Ba^{2+} and NO_3^- not a concern?

Table 8.3

Solubility Rules for Ionic Compounds		
Compounds	**Solubility**	**Exceptions**
1. Salts of alkali metals and ammonia	Soluble	Some lithium compounds
2. Nitrate salts and chlorate salts	Soluble	Few exceptions
3. Sulfate salts	Soluble	Compounds of Pb, Ag, Hg, Ba, Sr, and Ca
4. Chloride salts	Soluble	Compounds of Ag and some compounds of Hg and Pb
5. Carbonates, phosphates, chromates, sulfides, and hydroxides	Most are insoluble	Compounds of the alkali metals and of ammonia

Figure 8.13
A precipitate forms when aqueous solutions of sodium sulfate and barium nitrate are mixed.

Sample Problem 8-11

Use the solubility rules in **Table 8.3** to identify the precipitate formed and write the net ionic equation for the reaction of aqueous potassium carbonate with aqueous strontium chloride.

1. ANALYZE *Plan a problem-solving strategy.*

Write the reactants showing each as dissociated free ions. Then look at possible new pairings of cation and anion that give an insoluble substance. Finally, eliminate the spectator ions and write the net ionic equation.

2. SOLVE *Apply the problem-solving strategy.*

$$2K^+(aq) + CO_3^{2-}(aq) + Sr^{2+}(aq) + 2NO_3^-(aq) \longrightarrow ?$$

Of the two possible combinations, KNO_3 is soluble (Rules 1 and 2) and $SrCO_3$ is insoluble (Rule 5). Thus the net ionic equation is

$$Sr^{2+}(aq) + CO_3^{2-}(aq) \longrightarrow SrCO_3(s)$$

3. EVALUATE *Does the result make sense?*

$SrCO_3$ is the only combination of cation and anion that gives a precipitate. The equation is balanced in terms of atoms and charge.

Practice Problems

26. Identify the precipitate formed when solutions of these ionic compounds are mixed. Write a net ionic equation.

$$NH_4Cl(aq) + Pb(NO_3)_2(aq) \longrightarrow$$

27. Write a complete ionic equation and a net ionic equation for the reaction of aqueous solutions of iron(III) nitrate and sodium hydroxide.

Chem ASAP!

Problem-Solving 26
Solve Problem 26 with the help of an interactive guided tutorial.

section review 8.3

28. Write a balanced net ionic equation for each reaction.

   a. $Pb(NO_3)_2(aq) + H_2SO_4(aq) \longrightarrow PbSO_4(s) + HNO_3(aq)$

   b. $Pb(C_2H_3O_2)_2(aq) + HCl(aq) \longrightarrow PbCl_2(s) + HC_2H_3O_2(aq)$

   c. $Na_3PO_4(aq) + FeCl_3(aq) \longrightarrow NaCl(aq) + FePO_4(s)$

   d. $(NH_4)_2S(aq) + Co(NO_3)_2(aq) \longrightarrow CoS(s) + NH_4NO_3(aq)$

29. Write a net ionic equation for each reaction.

   a. $HCl(aq) + AgNO_3(aq) \longrightarrow$

   b. $Pb(C_2H_3O_2)_2(aq) + LiCl(aq) \longrightarrow$

   c. $Na_3PO_4(aq) + CrCl_3(aq) \longrightarrow$

30. Identify the spectator ions in each reaction in Problem 29.

31. Identify the precipitate formed when solutions of these ionic compounds are mixed.

   a. $H_2SO_4 + BaCl_2 \longrightarrow$

   b. $Al_2(SO_4)_3 + NH_4OH \longrightarrow$

   c. $AgNO_3 + H_2S \longrightarrow$

   d. $CaCl_2 + Pb(NO_3)_2 \longrightarrow$

   e. $Ca(NO_3)_2 + Na_2CO_3 \longrightarrow$

 Chem ASAP! Assessment 8.3 Check your understanding of the important ideas and concepts in Section 8.3.

SMALL-SCALE LAB

PRECIPITATION REACTIONS: FORMATION OF SOLIDS

SAFETY

Wear safety glasses and follow standard safety procedures outlined on page 18.

PURPOSE

To observe, identify, and write balanced equations for precipitation reactions.

MATERIALS

- pencil
- paper
- ruler
- reaction surface
- chemicals shown in Figure A

	$AgNO_3$ (Ag^+)	$Pb(NO_3)_2$ (Pb^{2+})	$CaCl_2$ (Ca^{2+})
Na_2CO_3 (CO_3^{2-})	a	f	k
Na_3PO_4 (PO_4^{3-})	b	g	l
$NaOH$ (OH^-)	c	h	m
Na_2SO_4 (SO_4^{2-})	d	i	n
$NaCl$ (Cl^-)	e	j	o

Figure A

PROCEDURE

Draw two grids similar to Figure A on separate sheets of paper. Make each square 2 cm on each side. Draw large black Xs on only one of the grids. Place a reaction surface over the grid with black Xs and add the chemicals as shown in Figure A. Use the other grid as a data table to record your observations for each solution.

ANALYSIS

Using the experimental data, record the answers to the following questions below your data table.

1. Translate the following word equations into balanced chemical equations and explain how the equations represent what happens in grid spaces a and g.

   a. In grid space a, sodium carbonate reacts with silver nitrate to produce sodium nitrate and solid silver carbonate.

   b. In grid space g, sodium phosphate reacts with lead(II) nitrate to produce sodium nitrate and solid lead(II) phosphate.

2. Write a word equation to represent what happens in grid space m.

3. What happens in grid space d? Which other mixings gave similar results? Is it necessary to write an equation when no reaction occurs? Explain.

4. Write balanced equations for the other precipitation reactions you observed.

5. Write balanced net ionic equations for the other precipitation reactions you observed.

YOU'RE THE CHEMIST

The following small-scale activities allow you to develop your own procedures and analyze the results.

1. **Analyze It!** Mix a solution of potassium iodide (KI) with silver nitrate and then separately with lead(II) nitrate to discover two distinctively colored precipitates. Write balanced equations and net ionic equations for each reaction.

2. **Design It!** Table salt is mostly sodium chloride. Design and carry out an experiment to find out if table salt will form a precipitate with either lead(II) or silver nitrate.

3. **Design It!** Design and carry out an experiment to show that iodized table salt contains potassium iodide (KI).

COMBATING COMBUSTION

Many of the materials in the world around you—such as wooden structures, paper, trees, gasoline—are combustible. All it takes is a source of ignition to start a serious fire. In North America alone, fires kill more than 20 000 people and cause millions of dollars in property damage each year. Fighting fires is an important application of chemistry.

Fire, or combustion, is the rapid reaction of a fuel with oxygen. The fuel is heated to start the fire. Once started, a fire can be put out in three ways: (1) by cooling the fuel, (2) by cutting off the supply of oxygen, or (3) by trapping the combustion intermediates so they cannot react with oxygen.

Firefighters are called upon most often to fight fires involving solid fuel, such as the wooden frame of a house. This kind of fire is known as a Class A fire. In a Class A fire the burning materials produce flammable gases that sustain and spread the fire. Water can be used to extinguish Class A fires because (1) water cools the fuel to below its combustion temperature and (2) when liquid water vaporizes, the vapor dilutes the oxygen content of the surrounding air.

Wood, of course, is not the only material that can catch fire and burn. Cooking oil, greases, and flammable liquids are all extremely combustible, and when they burn the fire cannot easily be extinguished with water. A stream of water, in fact, might actually spread the burning liquid. These kinds of fires, called Class B, are often fought with carbon dioxide fire extinguishers. Because it is more dense than air, the carbon dioxide blankets the burning fire and extinguishes the fire by cutting off the oxygen supply. Class B fires can also be fought with chemical powders. Portable dry powder extinguishers found in homes contain monoammonium phosphate

> **In North America alone, fires kill more than 20 000 people and cause millions of dollars in property damage each year.**

(MAP). MAP is useful for Class A, B, and C fires. MAP coats hot surfaces with a sticky residue that excludes oxygen and stops combustion.

Another type of fire is one involving an energized electrical circuit. Known as Class C fires, these fires cannot be fought with water because water almost always contains enough dissolved salts to conduct electricity. Instead, Class C fires are fought with the same types of extinguishing agents as Class B fires.

As you may remember, certain metals, such as magnesium, can also burn. Fires involving metals are called Class D fires and must be extinguished with special dry chemical powder fire extinguishers. Applying water or carbon dioxide to a Class D fire is not wise because both compounds can actually react with the burning material.

When a whole forest of trees is burning, techniques somewhat different from those used for fires involving buildings are called for. Water can be used to extinguish a forest fire, but getting the water to the fire can be a problem. Airplanes or helicopters are used to dump fire retardant chemicals on brush or forest fires. The dry chemicals are usually a mixture of MAP, ammonium sulfate, and iron oxide. These chemicals form a sticky residue on hot surfaces. The residue acts as a barrier to oxygen. The chemicals also act as nutrients that encourage new growth of trees after the fire.

CHEMISTRY IN CAREERS

☆☆☆☆☆☆☆☆☆☆☆☆☆☆☆☆☆☆☆

FIREFIGHTER
Are you ready for action? Do you want to control combustion reactions? Firefighting may be just the career for you. See page 871.

TAKE IT TO THE NET
Find out more about career opportunities:
www.phschool.com

CHEMICAL SPECIALIST
Local food service distributor seek responsible, self-motivated indivic

CHEMIST NEEDED

KEY TERMS

- activity series of metals *p. 217*
- balanced equation *p. 207*
- catalyst *p. 205*
- chemical equation *p. 205*
- coefficient *p. 207*
- combination reaction *p. 212*

- combustion reaction *p. 220*
- complete ionic equation *p. 225*
- decomposition reaction *p. 215*
- double-replacement reaction *p. 219*

- net ionic equation *p. 225*
- single-replacement reaction *p. 217*
- skeleton equation *p. 205*
- spectator ion *p. 225*

CONCEPT SUMMARY

8.1 Describing Chemical Change

- A chemical reaction can be concisely represented by a chemical equation.
- The substances that undergo a chemical change are the reactants. The new substances formed are the products.
- Special symbols are written after formulas in equations to show a substance's state. The designations for a solid, liquid, or gas are (*s*), (*l*), and (*g*) respectively. A substance dissolved in water is designated (*aq*).
- A catalyst is a substance that increases reaction rate without being used up by the reaction. If a catalyst is used, its formula is written above the arrow.
- In accordance with the law of conservation of mass, a chemical equation must be balanced. In balancing an equation, coefficients are used so the same number of atoms of each element are on each side of the equation.

8.2 Types of Chemical Reactions

- In a combination reaction, there is always a single product. The reactants are two or more elements and/or compounds that combine.
- A decomposition reaction involves the breakdown of a single compound into two or more simpler substances.

- In a single-replacement reaction, the reactants and products are an element and a compound. The activity series of metals can be used to predict whether single-replacement reactions will take place.
- A double-replacement reaction involves the exchange of cations (or anions) between two compounds. This reaction generally takes place between two ionic compounds in aqueous solution.
- A combustion reaction always involves oxygen. The products of the complete combustion of a hydrocarbon are carbon dioxide and water.

8.3 Reactions in Aqueous Solution

- A complete ionic equation shows all dissolved ionic compounds as their free ions. It includes spectator ions as well as ions involved in the reaction.
- Both single- and double-replacement reactions can be written as net ionic equations in which spectator ions are deleted from both sides of the equation.
- The precipitate formed in a double-replacement reaction can be identified using a table of solubilities.

CHAPTER CONCEPT MAP

Use these terms to construct a concept map that organizes the major ideas of this chapter.

 ChemASAP! Concept Map 8
Create your Concept Map using the computer.

CONCEPT PRACTICE

32. Identify the reactants and products in each chemical reaction. *8.1*
    a. Hydrogen gas and sodium hydroxide are formed when sodium is dropped into water.
    b. In photosynthesis, carbon dioxide and water react to form oxygen gas and glucose.

33. How did John Dalton explain a chemical reaction using his atomic theory? *8.1*

34. What is the function of an arrow ($\longrightarrow$) and a plus sign (+) in a chemical equation? *8.1*

35. Write sentences that completely describe each of the chemical reactions shown in these skeleton equations. *8.1*
    a. $NH_3(g) + O_2(g) \xrightarrow{Pt} NO(g) + H_2O(g)$
    b. $H_2SO_4(aq) + BaCl_2(aq) \longrightarrow$
    $$BaSO_4(s) + HCl(aq)$$
    c. $N_2O_3(g) + H_2O(l) \longrightarrow HNO_2(aq)$

36. What is the purpose of a catalyst? *8.1*

37. Balance equations for each item. The formula for each product (object) is given. *8.1*
    a. a basketball team
    $$center + forward + guard \longrightarrow team$$
    $$C + F + G \longrightarrow CF_2G_2$$
    b. a tricycle
    $$frame + wheel + seat + pedal \longrightarrow tricycle$$
    $$F + W + S + P \longrightarrow FW_3SP_2$$

38. The equation for the formation of water from its elements, $H_2(g) + O_2(g) \longrightarrow H_2O(l)$, can easily be "balanced" by changing the formula of the product to H_2O_2. Explain why this is incorrect. *8.1*

39. Balance the following equations. *8.1*
    a. $PbO_2 \longrightarrow PbO + O_2$
    b. $Fe(OH)_3 \longrightarrow Fe_2O_3 + H_2O$
    c. $(NH_4)_2CO_3 \longrightarrow NH_3 + H_2O + CO_2$
    d. $NaCl + H_2SO_4 \longrightarrow Na_2SO_4 + HCl$
    e. $H_2 + Fe_3O_4 \longrightarrow Fe + H_2O$
    f. $Al + CuSO_4 \longrightarrow Al_2(SO_4)_3 + Cu$

40. Explain why it is useful to classify reactions by their type. *8.2*

41. How do you predict the correct formula for the combination reaction between a nonmetal and a Group A metal? *8.2*

42. What is a characteristic of every combination reaction? *8.2*

43. Write balanced chemical equations for the following combination reactions. *8.2*
    a. $Mg + O_2 \longrightarrow$
    b. $P + O_2 \longrightarrow$ diphosphorus pentoxide
    c. $Ca + S \longrightarrow$
    d. $Fe + O_2 \longrightarrow$ iron(II) oxide
    e. $N_2O_5 + H_2O \longrightarrow$

44. Write a balanced chemical equation for each decomposition reaction. *8.2*
    a. $Ag_2O(s) \xrightarrow{\Delta} ?$
    b. nickel(II) carbonate $\xrightarrow{\Delta}$
    $$nickel(II)\ oxide + ?$$
    c. ammonium nitrate $\xrightarrow{\Delta}$
    $$dinitrogen\ monoxide + water$$

45. What is a distinguishing feature of every decomposition reaction? *8.2*

46. For each of the following pairs, predict which element as an atom would displace the other element as an ion from a compound in aqueous solution. *8.2*
    a. iron and sodium
    b. silver and copper
    c. zinc and hydrogen (in HCl)

47. Use the activity series of metals to write a balanced chemical equation for each single-replacement reaction. *8.2*
    a. $Au(s) + KNO_3(aq) \longrightarrow$
    b. $Zn(s) + AgNO_3(aq) \longrightarrow$
    c. $Al(s) + H_2SO_4(aq) \longrightarrow$
    d. $Cu(s) + H_2O(l) \longrightarrow$
    e. $Al(s) + CuSO_4(aq) \longrightarrow$

48. Write a balanced equation for each of the following reactions. *8.2*
    a. $HCl(aq) + Ca(OH)_2(aq) \longrightarrow$
    b. $Ag_2SO_4(aq) + AlCl_3(aq) \longrightarrow$
    (Silver chloride is a precipitate.)
    c. $H_2C_2O_4(aq) + KOH(aq) \longrightarrow$
    d. $CdBr_2(aq) + Na_2S(aq) \longrightarrow$
    (Cadmium sulfide is a precipitate.)

49. What substance is common to all combustion reactions? *8.2*

50. Write a balanced equation for the complete combustion of each compound. *8.2*
    a. butene (C_4H_8)
    b. octane (C_8H_{18})
    c. glycerol ($C_3H_8O_3$)
    d. acetone (C_3H_6O)

51. Balance each equation and identify its type. *8.2*
    a. $Hf + N_2 \longrightarrow Hf_3N_4$
    b. $Mg + H_2SO_4 \longrightarrow MgSO_4 + H_2$
    c. $C_2H_6 + O_2 \longrightarrow CO_2 + H_2O$
    d. $Pb(NO_3)_2 + NaI \longrightarrow PbI_2 + NaNO_3$
    e. $Fe + O_2 \longrightarrow Fe_3O_4$
    f. $Pb(NO_3)_2 \longrightarrow PbO + NO_2 + O_2$
    g. $Hg(NO_3)_2 + NH_4SCN \longrightarrow$
    $$Hg(SCN)_2 + NH_4NO_3$$
    h. $(NH_4)_2SO_4 + NaOH \longrightarrow$
    $$NH_3 + H_2O + Na_2SO_4$$
    (*Hint:* There are two stepwise reactions in this equation.)

52. Complete each equation and then write a net ionic equation. *8.3*
    a. $Al(s) + H_2SO_4(aq) \longrightarrow$
    b. $HCl(aq) + Ba(OH)_2(aq) \longrightarrow$
    c. $Au(s) + HCl(aq) \longrightarrow$

53. What is a spectator ion? *8.3*

CONCEPT MASTERY

54. Each of these equations is "balanced" but incorrect. Find the errors and correctly balance each equation.
    a. $Cl_2 + NaI \longrightarrow NaCl_2 + I$
    b. $NH_3 \longrightarrow N + H_3$
    c. $Na + O_2 \longrightarrow NaO_2$
    d. $2Mg + H_2SO_4 \longrightarrow Mg_2SO_4 + H_2$
    e. $MgCl + CaOH \longrightarrow MgOH + CaCl$
    f. $H_2 + Cl_2 \longrightarrow H_2Cl_2$

55. Write a balanced chemical equation for each reaction. Use the necessary symbols from **Table 8.1** to describe the reaction completely.
    a. Bubbling chlorine gas through a solution of potassium iodide gives elemental iodine and a solution of potassium chloride.
    b. Bubbles of hydrogen gas and aqueous iron(III) chloride are produced when metallic iron is dropped into hydrochloric acid.
    c. Solid tetraphosphorus decoxide reacts with water to produce phosphoric acid.
    d. Solid silver oxide can be heated to give silver and oxygen gas.
    e. Iodine crystals react with chlorine gas to form solid iodine trichloride.
    f. Mercury metal is produced by heating a mixture of mercury(II) sulfide and calcium oxide. Additional products are calcium sulfide and calcium sulfate.

56. Write balanced chemical equations for these double-replacement reactions that occur in aqueous solution.
    a. Zinc sulfide is added to sulfuric acid.
    b. Sodium hydroxide reacts with nitric acid.
    c. Solutions of potassium fluoride and calcium nitrate are mixed.

57. Write a balanced chemical equation for each combination reaction.
    a. sodium oxide + water $\longrightarrow$
    b. hydrogen + bromine $\longrightarrow$
    c. dichlorine heptoxide + water $\longrightarrow$

58. Write a balanced chemical equation for each single-replacement reaction that takes place in aqueous solution. Write "no reaction" if a reaction does not occur.
    a. A piece of steel wool (iron) is placed in sulfuric acid.
    b. Mercury is poured into an aqueous solution of zinc nitrate.
    c. Bromine reacts with aqueous barium iodide.

59. Pieces of sodium and magnesium are dropped into separate water-filled test tubes (A and B). Tube A bubbles vigorously; Tube B does not.
    a. Which tube contains the sodium metal?
    b. Write an equation for the reaction in the tube containing the sodium metal. What type of reaction is occurring in this tube?

60. Write a balanced equation for the complete combustion of each compound. Assume that the products are carbon dioxide and water.
    a. octane (C_8H_{18})
    b. glucose ($C_6H_{12}O_6$)
    c. acetic acid ($HC_2H_3O_2$)

61. Write balanced chemical equations for these decomposition reactions.
    a. Aluminum can be obtained from aluminum oxide with the addition of a large amount of electrical energy.
    b. Heating tin(IV) hydroxide gives tin(IV) oxide and water.
    c. Silver carbonate decomposes into silver oxide and carbon dioxide when it is heated.

62. Write a balanced net ionic equation for each reaction. The product that is not in solution is given.
    a. $H_2C_2O_4 + KOH \longrightarrow$ [H_2O]
    b. $CdBr_2 + Na_2S \longrightarrow$ [CdS]
    c. $NaOH + Fe(NO_3)_3 \longrightarrow$ [$Fe(OH)_3$]

CRITICAL THINKING

63. Choose the term that best completes the second relationship.
  a. charcoal : ashes reactant : _____
  (1) equation   (3) heat
  (2) reaction   (4) product
  b. tool : hammer catalyst : _____
  (1) reaction   (3) sulfur
  (2) MnO_2 (4) combustion
  c. east : west combination : _____
  (1) decomposition (3) coefficient
  (2) reaction   (4) replacement

64. Why is smoking not permitted near an oxygen source? What would happen if a match were struck in a room filled with oxygen?

65. Alkanes are hydrocarbon molecules that have the general formula C_nH_{2n+2}. The graph shows the number of oxygen, carbon dioxide, and water molecules needed to balance the equations for the complete combustion of every alkane having from one to ten carbon atoms.

$$C_nH_{2n+2} + \underline{\quad} O_2 \longrightarrow \underline{\quad} CO_2 + \underline{\quad} H_2O$$

● ● ● Carbon dioxide
▲ ▲ ▲ Oxygen
■ ■ ■ Water

  a. Use the graph to write balanced equations for the combustion of C_5H_{12} and C_9H_{20}.
  b. Extrapolate the graph and write balanced equations for the combustion of $C_{12}H_{26}$ and $C_{17}H_{36}$.
  c. The coefficient for O_2 in the general equation is $n + \sqrt{\dfrac{n+1}{2}}$. What are the coefficients for CO_2 and H_2O?

CUMULATIVE REVIEW

66. Calculate the number of moles in each substance.
  a. 54.0 L of nitrogen dioxide (at STP)
  b. 1.68 g of magnesium ions
  c. 69.6 g of sodium hypochlorite
  d. 4.27×10^{24} molecules of carbon monoxide

67. What mass of gold (density = 19.3 g/cm³) occupies the same volume as 2.20 mol of aluminum (density = 2.70 g/cm³)?

68. Many coffees and colas contain the stimulant caffeine. The percent composition of caffeine is 49.5% C, 5.20% H, 16.5% O, and 28.9% N. What is the molecular formula of caffeine if its molar mass is 194.1 g/mol?

69. The white solid calcium chloride ($CaCl_2$) is used as a drying agent. The maximum amount of water absorbed by different quantities of $CaCl_2$ is given in the table below.

$CaCl_2$ (g)	$CaCl_2$ (mol)	H_2O (g)	H_2O (mol)
17.3		5.62	
48.8		15.8	
124		40.3	
337		109	

  a. Complete the table.
  b. Plot the moles of water absorbed (*y*-axis) versus the moles of $CaCl_2$.
  c. Based on your graph, how many molecules of water does each formula unit of $CaCl_2$ absorb?

CONCEPT CHALLENGE

70. Write a balanced chemical equation for each reaction. Classify each as to type.
  a. Sodium iodide reacts with phosphoric acid.
  b. Potassium oxide reacts with water.
  c. Heating sulfuric acid produces water, oxygen, and sulfur dioxide.
  d. Aluminum reacts with sulfuric acid.
  e. Pentane (C_5H_{12}) reacts with oxygen.

71. The mass of a proton and an electron are 1.67×10^{-24} g and 9.11×10^{-28} g, respectively.
  a. What is the mass of a mole of protons and a mole of electrons?
  b. How many electrons are equal in mass to one proton?

Select the choice that best answers each question or completes each statement.

1. When the equation $Fe_2O_3 + H_2 \longrightarrow Fe + H_2O$ is balanced using whole-number coefficients, H_2 has a coefficient of
   a. 6.   **b.** 3.   **c.** 2.   **d.** 1.

2. Identify the spectator ion is this reaction.
   $Ba(OH)_2(aq) + H_2SO_4(aq) \longrightarrow$
   $$BaSO_4(s) + H_2O(l)$$
   a. Ba^{2+}
   b. SO_4^{2-}
   c. OH^-
   d. H^+
   e. There is no spectator ion.

3. Magnesium ribbon reacts with an aqueous solution of copper(II) chloride in a single replacement reaction. The products of the balanced net ionic equation for the reaction are
   a. $Mg^{2+}(aq) + 2Cl^-(aq) + Cu(s)$.
   b. $Mg^+(aq) + Cl^-(aq) + Cu^+(aq)$.
   c. $Mg^{2+}(aq) + Cu(s)$.
   d. $Cu(s) + 2Cl^-(aq)$.

4. The expected products of the decomposition reaction of potassium oxide, K_2O, are
   a. $K^+(s)$ and $O^{2-}(g)$.
   b. $K^+(s)$ and $O_2(g)$.
   c. $K(s)$ and $O_2^{2-}(g)$.
   d. $K(s)$ and $O_2(g)$.

5. In an equation, the symbol Δ above the yields arrow means that
   a. a change is about to occur.
   b. heat is added to the reactants.
   c. a catalyst is needed for the reaction to occur.
   d. all of the above are correct.

Use the following description and data table to answer questions 6–8.

Dropper bottles labeled P, Q, and R contain one of three aqueous solutions: potassium carbonate, K_2CO_3; hydrochloric acid, HCl; and calcium nitrate, $Ca(NO_3)_2$. The table shows what happens when pairs of solutions are mixed.

Solution	P	Q	R
P	—	precipitate	no reaction
Q	precipitate	—	gas forms
R	no reaction	gas forms	—

6. Identify the contents of each dropper bottle.

7. Write the net ionic equation for the formation of the precipitate.

8. Write the complete ionic equation for the formation of the gas.

Use the atomic windows to answer question 9. Oxygen atoms are red; nitrogen atoms are blue.

a.

c.

b.

d.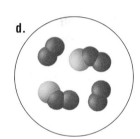

9. Which windows represents the reactants and the products for the following reaction?
   $2NO(g) + O_2(g) \longrightarrow 2NO_2(g)$

Use the diagram to answer questions 10–13.

10. When ammonium carbonate is heated, water, ammonia, and carbon dioxide are produced. What type of chemical reaction is occurring?

11. Write formulas for the reaction products.

12. Write a balanced equation for the reaction. Include states for reactants and products.

13. What purpose might the limewater serve?

Chapter 9 | STOICHIOMETRY

FEATURES

DISCOVER IT!
How Much Can You Make?

SMALL-SCALE LAB
Analysis of Baking Soda

MINI LAB
Limiting Reagents

CHEMath
Dimensional Analysis

CHEMISTRY SERVING … SOCIETY
Just the Right Volume of Gas

CHEMISTRY IN CAREERS
Quality Control Chemist

LINK TO AGRICULTURE
Ammonia in the Nitrogen Cycle

Stay current with **SCIENCE NEWS**
Find out more about stoichiometry:
www.phschool.com

A chemical reaction produces just enough gas to inflate an air bag.

DISCOVER IT! HOW MUCH CAN YOU MAKE?

You need twenty metal paper clips (symbol M), twenty identically colored vinyl-coated paper clips (symbol C), and one plastic sandwich bag.

1. Join together pairs of paper clips of the same color to form models representing 10 diatomic molecules of each reactant. Place these molecules in the plastic bag.

2. Without looking, choose 15 molecules from the plastic bag.

3. Line up the M_2 and C_2 molecules in two adjacent vertical rows.

4. Pair up reactant molecules in the $1:3$ M_2-to-C_2 ratio as shown in the equation $M_2 + 3C_2 \longrightarrow 2MC_3$.

5. Make the molecules "react" by taking them apart and forming two molecules of the product.

6. Continue making M_2 and C_2 react in a 1:3 ratio until you run out of one of the reactants.

List the number of each type of reactant molecule that was drawn from the bag. How many molecules of the product could you form? Which reactant molecule did you run out of first? How many molecules of each reactant remained at the completion of the reaction? Repeat the experiment and compare the results. Use what you learn in this chapter to provide an explanation for your observations.

THE ARITHMETIC OF EQUATIONS

*S*ilk, one of the most beautiful and luxurious of all fabrics, is spun from the cocoons of tiny silkworms. Silkworms have the unique ability to transform the leaves of mulberry trees into silk thread, which they use to weave their cocoons. More than 3000 cocoons are needed to produce enough silk to make just one elegant Japanese kimono. **How do chemists calculate the amount of reactants and products in chemical reactions?**

objectives
▶ Calculate the amount of reactants required or product formed in a nonchemical process
▶ Interpret balanced chemical equations in terms of interacting moles, representative particles, masses, and gas volume at STP

key term
▶ stoichiometry

Using Everyday Equations

Nearly everything you use is manufactured from chemicals—soaps, shampoos and conditioners, cassette tapes, cosmetics, medicines, and clothes. Obviously, for the manufacturer to make a profit, the cost of making any of these items cannot exceed the money paid for them. Therefore, the chemical processes used in manufacturing must be carried out economically. This is where balanced chemical equations help.

Equations are the recipes that tell chemists what amounts of reactants to mix and what amounts of products to expect. You can determine the quantities of reactants and products in a reaction from the balanced equation. When you know the quantity of one substance in a reaction, you can calculate the quantity of any other substance consumed or created in the reaction. Quantity usually means the amount of a substance expressed in grams or moles. But quantity could just as well be in liters, tons, or molecules. Can you name some other units you might use to measure the amount of matter?

The calculation of quantities in chemical reactions is a subject of chemistry called **stoichiometry.** Calculations using balanced equations are called stoichiometric calculations. For chemists, stoichiometry is a form of bookkeeping.

When you bake cookies, you probably use a recipe. A cookie recipe tells you the amounts of ingredients to mix together to make a certain number of cookies. If you need a larger number of cookies than the recipe provides, the amounts of ingredients can be doubled or tripled. In a way, a cookie recipe provides the same kind of information that a balanced chemical equation does. The ingredients are the reactants; the cookies are the products.

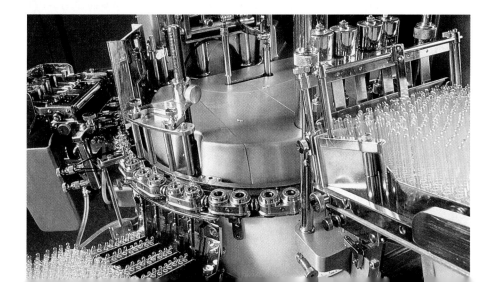

Figure 9.1
Just like cooking, manufacturing requires specific amounts of ingredients to get a certain number of products.

Here is another example, this time from the business world rather than from the world of cooking. Imagine you are in charge of manufacturing for the Tiny Tyke Tricycle Company. The business plan for Tiny Tyke requires the production of 128 custom-made tricycles each day. One of your responsibilities is to be sure that there are enough parts available at the start of each day to make these tricycles. To simplify this discussion, assume that the major components of the tricycle are the frame (F), the seat (S), the wheels (W), the handlebars (H), and the pedals (P). The finished tricycle has a "formula" of FSW_3HP_2. The balanced equation for the production of a tricycle is

$$F + S + 3W + H + 2P \longrightarrow FSW_3HP_2$$

This equation gives you the "recipe" to make a single tricycle: Making a tricycle requires one frame, one seat, three wheels, one handlebar, and two pedals.

Figure 9.2

A balanced equation can be thought of as a recipe. In the equation shown here, the tricycle parts are the reactants and the assembled tricycle is the product. How many pedals are needed to make four tricycles?

F + S + 3W + H + 2P ⟶ FSW_3HP_2

Sample Problem 9-1

In a five-day workweek, Tiny Tyke is scheduled to make 640 tricycles. How many wheels should be in the plant on Monday morning to make these tricycles?

1. **ANALYZE** *List the knowns and the unknown.*

   Knowns:
   • number of tricycles = 640 tricycles
   • 1 FSW_3HP_2 = 3 W (from balanced equation)

   Unknown:
   • number of wheels = ? wheels

   Use the conversion factor $\dfrac{3\text{ W}}{1\text{ FSW}_3\text{HP}_2}$ to calculate the unknown.

2. **CALCULATE** *Solve for the unknown.*

   $$640\ \cancel{FSW_3HP_2} \times \frac{3\text{ W}}{1\ \cancel{FSW_3HP_2}} = 1920\text{ W}$$

3. **EVALUATE** *Does the result make sense?*
   If 3 wheels are required for each tricycle, and a total of more than 600 tricycles are being made, then a number of wheels in excess of 1800 is a logical answer. The unit of the known cancels with the unit in the denominator of the conversion factor, and the answer is in the unit of the unknown. The conversion factor is exact and does not affect the rounding of the answer.

Practice Problems

1. How many tricycle seats, wheels, and pedals are needed to make 288 tricycles?
2. Write an equation that gives your own "recipe" for making a puppet or a piece of furniture.

Interpreting Chemical Equations

As you may recall from Chapter 7, ammonia is widely used as a fertilizer. Ammonia is produced industrially by the reaction of nitrogen with hydrogen.

$$N_2(g) + 3H_2(g) \longrightarrow 2NH_3(g)$$

What kinds of information can be derived from this equation?

1. **Particles** One molecule of nitrogen reacts with three molecules of hydrogen to produce two molecules of ammonia. Nitrogen and hydrogen will always react to form ammonia in this 1:3:2 ratio of molecules. So if you could make 10 molecules of nitrogen react with 30 molecules of hydrogen, you would expect to get 20 molecules of ammonia. Of course, it is not possible to count such small numbers of molecules and allow them to react. You could, however, take Avogadro's number of nitrogen molecules and make them react with three times Avogadro's number of hydrogen molecules. This would be the same 1:3 ratio of molecules of reactants. The reaction would form two times Avogadro's number of ammonia molecules.

2. **Moles** You know that Avogadro's number of representative particles is one mole of a substance. On the basis of the particle interpretation you just read, the equation tells you the number of moles of reactants and products. One mole of nitrogen molecules reacts with three moles of hydrogen molecules to form two moles of ammonia molecules. The coefficients of a balanced chemical equation indicate the relative numbers of moles of reactants and products in a chemical reaction. This is the most important information that a balanced chemical equation provides. Using this information, you can calculate the amounts of reactants and products. Does the number of moles of reactants equal the number of moles of product in this reaction?

Figure 9.3
Gardeners use ammonium salts as fertilizer. The nitrogen in these salts is essential to plant growth.

N₂(g)	+	3H₂(g)	→	2NH₃(g)
2 atoms N	+	6 atoms H	→	2 atoms N and 6 atoms H
1 molecule N₂	+	3 molecules H₂	→	2 molecules NH₃
10 molecules N₂	+	30 molecules H₂	→	20 molecules NH₃
$1 \times \left(\dfrac{6.02 \times 10^{23}}{\text{molecules N}_2} \right)$	+	$3 \times \left(\dfrac{6.02 \times 10^{23}}{\text{molecules H}_2} \right)$	→	$2 \times \left(\dfrac{6.02 \times 10^{23}}{\text{molecules NH}_3} \right)$
1 mol N₂	+	3 mol H₂	→	2 mol NH₃
28 g N₂	+	3 × 2 g H₂	→	2 × 17 g NH₃
		34 g reactants	→	34 g products
Assume STP 22.4 L	+	22.4 L 22.4 L 22.4 L	→	22.4 L 22.4 L
22.4 L N₂		67.2 L H₂		44.8 L NH₃

Figure 9.4
The balanced chemical equation for the formation of ammonia can be interpreted in several ways. How many molecules of NH₃ could be made from 5 molecules N₂ and 15 molecules H₂?

3. **Mass** A balanced chemical equation must obey the law of conservation of mass. This law states that mass can be neither created nor destroyed in an ordinary chemical or physical process. The mole interpretation supports this requirement. Remember that mass is related to the number of atoms in the chemical equation through moles. The mass of 1 mol of nitrogen (28.0 g) plus the mass of 3 mol of hydrogen (6.0 g) does equal the mass of 2 mol of ammonia (34.0 g). So although the number of moles of reactants does not equal the number of moles of product(s), the total number of grams of reactants does equal the total number of grams of product(s). Mass is conserved.

4. **Volume** If you assume standard temperature and pressure, the equation also tells you about the volumes of gases. Recall that 1 mol of any gas at STP occupies a volume of 22.4 L. It follows that 22.4 L of nitrogen reacts with 67.2 L (3×22.4 L) of hydrogen to form 44.8 L (2×22.4 L) of ammonia.

Look at **Figure 9.4** on the previous page. Do you see that mass and atoms are conserved in this chemical reaction? Mass and atoms are conserved in every chemical reaction. The mass of the reactants equals the mass of the products. The number of atoms of each reactant equals the number of atoms of that reactant in the product(s). Unlike mass and atoms, however, molecules, formula units, moles, and volumes of gases will not necessarily be conserved—although they may. Consider, for example, the formation of hydrogen iodide.

$$H_2(g) + I_2(g) \longrightarrow 2HI(g)$$

In this reaction, molecules, moles, and volume are all conserved. But in the majority of chemical reactions (including the reaction for the formation of ammonia), they are not. Only mass and atoms are conserved in every chemical reaction.

Figure 9.5
Hydrogen sulfide (H_2S) smells like rotten eggs. It escapes from the ground in volcanic areas.

Sample Problem 9-2

Hydrogen sulfide, a foul-smelling gas, is found in nature in volcanic areas. The balanced chemical equation for the burning of hydrogen sulfide is given below. Interpret this equation in terms of the interaction of the following three relative quantities.

   a. number of representative particles
   b. number of moles
   c. masses of reactants and products

$$2H_2S(g) + 3O_2(g) \longrightarrow 2SO_2(g) + 2H_2O(g)$$

1. **ANALYZE** *Plan a problem-solving strategy.*
   a. The coefficients in the balanced equation give the relative number of molecules of reactants and products.
   b. The coefficients in the balanced equation give the relative number of moles of reactants and products.
   c. A balanced chemical equation obeys the law of conservation of mass. The sum of the masses of the reactants must equal the sum of the masses of the products.

Practice Problems

3. Interpret the equation for the formation of water from its elements in terms of numbers of molecules and moles and volumes of gases at STP.

$$2H_2(g) + O_2(g) \longrightarrow 2H_2O(g)$$

Sample Problem 9-2 (cont.)

2. SOLVE *Apply the problem-solving strategy.*

a. 2 molecules H_2S react with 3 molecules O_2 to form 2 molecules SO_2 and 2 molecules H_2O.

b. 2 mol H_2S react with 3 mol O_2 to produce 2 mol SO_2 and 2 mol H_2O.

c. Multiply the number of moles of each reactant and product by its molar mass: 2 mol H_2S + 3 mol $O_2 \longrightarrow$ 2 mol SO_2 + 2 mol H_2O.

$$\left(2 \text{ mol} \times 34.1 \frac{g}{mol}\right) + \left(3 \text{ mol} \times 32.0 \frac{g}{mol}\right) \longrightarrow$$
$$\left(2 \text{ mol} \times 64.1 \frac{g}{mol}\right) + \left(2 \text{ mol} \times 18.0 \frac{g}{mol}\right)$$

$$68.2 \text{ g } H_2S + 96.0 \text{ g } O_2 \longrightarrow 128.2 \text{ g } SO_2 + 36.0 \text{ g } H_2O$$
$$164.2 \text{ g} = 164.2 \text{ g}$$

3. EVALUATE *Do the results make sense?*

Because all the substances in this reaction are molecular, the mole ratio of reactants and products equals the molecular ratio of reactants and products (2:3:2:2). The sum of the masses of the reactants equals the sum of the masses of the products.

Practice Problems (cont.)

4. Balance the equation for the combustion of acetylene:
$$C_2H_2(g) + O_2(g) \longrightarrow$$
$$CO_2(g) + H_2O(g)$$
Interpret the equation in terms of relative numbers of moles, volumes of gas at STP, and masses of reactants and products.

Chem ASAP!

Problem-Solving 4

Solve Problem 4 with the help of an interactive guided tutorial.

section review 9.1

5. Your school club has "adopted" a local nursing home and provides welcoming packages to new residents. Each welcoming package contains a toothbrush (B), three washcloths (W), a hand mirror (M), two decks of cards (C), and four small bottles of skin lotion (L).

a. Write a balanced equation for preparing a welcoming package ($BW_3MC_2L_4$).

b. Calculate the number of each item needed for 45 packages.

6. Balance this equation: $C_2H_5OH(l) + O_2(g) \longrightarrow CO_2(g) + H_2O(g)$.

a. Interpret the equation in terms of numbers of molecules and moles.

b. Show that the balanced equation obeys the law of conservation of mass.

7. Explain this statement: "Mass and atoms are conserved in every chemical reaction, but moles will not necessarily be conserved."

8. Interpret the following equation in terms of relative numbers of representative particles, numbers of moles, and masses of reactants and products.

$$2K(s) + 2H_2O(l) \longrightarrow 2KOH(aq) + H_2(g)$$

 Chem ASAP! Assessment 9.1 Check your understanding of the important ideas and concepts in Section 9.1.

objectives

▶ Construct mole ratios from balanced chemical equations and apply these ratios in mole-mole stoichiometric calculations

▶ Calculate stoichiometric quantities from balanced chemical equations using units of moles, mass, representative particles, and volumes of gases at STP

Chem ASAP!

Simulation 6
Strengthen your analytical skills by solving stoichiometric problems.

CHEMICAL CALCULATIONS

*A*ir bags inflate almost instantaneously upon impact. The effectiveness of air bags is based on the rapid conversion of a small mass of sodium azide into a large volume of gas. **How can stoichiometry be used to calculate the volume of gas produced in this reaction?**

Mole-Mole Calculations

As you just learned, a balanced chemical equation provides a wealth of quantitative information relating representative particles (atoms, molecules, formula units), moles of substances, and masses. Most important, a balanced chemical equation is essential for all calculations involving amounts of reactants and products: If you know the number of moles of one substance, the balanced chemical equation allows you to determine the number of moles of all other substances in the reaction.

Figure 9.6

Manufacturing plants produce ammonia by combining nitrogen with hydrogen. Ammonia is used in cleaning products, fertilizers, and in the manufacture of other chemicals.

Look again at the production of ammonia from nitrogen and hydrogen. The balanced equation for the reaction is

$$N_2(g) + 3H_2(g) \longrightarrow 2NH_3(g)$$

The most important interpretation of this equation is that 1 mol of nitrogen reacts with 3 mol of hydrogen to form 2 mol of ammonia. With this interpretation, you can relate moles of reactants to moles of product. The coefficients from the balanced equation are used to write conversion factors called mole ratios. The mole ratios are used to calculate the number of moles of product from a given number of moles of reactant or to calculate the number of moles of reactant from a given number of moles of product. Three of the mole ratios for this equation are

$$\frac{1 \text{ mol } N_2}{3 \text{ mol } H_2} \qquad \frac{2 \text{ mol } NH_3}{1 \text{ mol } N_2} \qquad \frac{3 \text{ mol } H_2}{2 \text{ mol } NH_3}$$

What are the other three mole ratios?

CHEMath

DIMENSIONAL ANALYSIS

Converting units is an essential skill for solving problems in chemistry and other sciences. In Section 4.2, you learned how to convert units using *dimensional analysis*. This page provides a chance for you to recall and brush up your skills prior to plunging into Chapter 9—a chapter requiring extensive use of dimensional analysis.

A *conversion factor* is a ratio of equivalent measurements. (Mole ratios, which are used frequently in Chapter 9, are a special type of conversion factor.) By definition, any conversion factor is equal to 1, so you can always multiply by a conversion factor without changing the value of an expression. By carefully choosing conversion factors and canceling units, you can convert any measurement into one expressed in the desired units.

For example, to convert 17 minutes into seconds, you would multiply by a conversion factor that relates the two units. From the relationship 1 minute = 60 seconds, the correct conversion factor can be written and applied.

$$17 \text{ min} \times \frac{60 \text{ s}}{1 \text{ min}} = 1020 \text{ s}$$

Dimensional analysis is also a powerful tool for preventing mistakes. The variables and constants in scientific formulas usually include units, and dimensional analysis can be used to ensure that the units on each side of an equation are the same. For example, consider the formula

$$\text{distance} = \text{velocity} \times \text{time}$$

$$\text{or } d = vt.$$

Notice the typical units in this equation:

$$\text{meters} = \frac{\text{meter}}{\text{second}} \times \text{seconds}$$

After canceling, both sides of the equation have the same units, meters. But if you were to write an incorrect equation using d, v, and t, the units would *not* balance and you would know, immediately, that your formula was incorrect!

Everyone makes mistakes. But if you pay attention to the units in all of your calculations, you will be able to identify and correct many of your mistakes before they cost you a few points and a lower grade.

Example 1

Ingrid drove 18 minutes at 40 km/h. Use $d = vt$ to find out how far she traveled.

Apply the formula: $d = vt = \dfrac{40 \text{ km}}{1 \text{ h}} \times 18 \text{ min}$

Notice that the time units do not cancel. (Minutes must be converted to hours.) Inserting the proper conversion factor and using dimensional analysis yields,

$$d = vt = \frac{40 \text{ km}}{1 \text{ h}} \times \frac{1 \text{ h}}{60 \text{ min}} \times 18 \text{ min} = 12 \text{ km}$$

She traveled a distance of 12 km.

Example 2

One mole of copper has a mass of 63.5 g. Find the number of moles in 6.00 kg of copper.

This problem requires two conversion factors. First, kilograms are converted to grams, and then grams are converted to moles.

$$6.00 \text{ kg Cu} \times \frac{1000 \text{ g Cu}}{1 \text{ kg Cu}} \times \frac{1 \text{ mol Cu}}{63.5 \text{ g Cu}} = 94.5 \text{ mol Cu}$$

There are 94.5 moles in 6.00 kg of copper.

Practice Problems

A. Convert a volume of 38.5 L to milliliters.

B. Boris rode a bicycle for 35 minutes at a 24 km/h. How far did he travel?

C. Convert a speed of 90 km/h to meters per second.

D. Convert a speed of 66 ft/s to mi/h. (1 mi = 5280 ft)

E. Convert a density of 158.7 kg/m^3 to g/cm^3.

F. One mole of sulfur has a mass of 32.1 g. Find the mass, in kilograms, of 64.8 moles of sulfur.

G. One mole of 2,2-dichlorohexane ($C_6H_{12}Cl_2$) has a mass of 155.1 g. Find the number of moles in 18.74 kg of 2,2-dichlorohexane.

Sample Problem 9-3

How many moles of ammonia are produced when 0.60 mol of nitrogen reacts with hydrogen?

1. ANALYZE List the known and the unknown.

Known:
- moles of nitrogen = 0.60 mol N_2

Unknown:
- moles of ammonia = ? mol NH_3

The conversion is mol $N_2 \rightarrow$ mol NH_3. According to the balanced equation, 1 mol N_2 combines with 3 mol H_2 to produce 2 mol NH_3. To determine the number of moles of NH_3, the given quantity of N_2 is multiplied by the form of the mole ratio from the balanced equation that allows the given unit to cancel.

2. CALCULATE Solve for the unknown.

$$0.60 \; \cancel{mol \; N_2} \times \frac{2 \; mol \; NH_3}{1 \; \cancel{mol \; N_2}} = 1.2 \; mol \; NH_3$$

3. EVALUATE Does the result make sense?

The balanced chemical equation shows that two moles of ammonia are produced for each mole of nitrogen reacted. Note that mole ratios from balanced equations are considered to be exact (defined numbers). They do not enter into the determination of significant figures in the answer.

Practice Problems

9. This equation shows the formation of aluminum oxide.

$$4Al(s) + 3O_2(g) \longrightarrow 2Al_2O_3(s)$$

  a. Write the six mole ratios that can be derived from this equation.

  b. How many moles of aluminum are needed to form 3.7 mol Al_2O_3?

10. According to the equation in Problem 9:

  a. How many moles of oxygen are required to react completely with 14.8 mol Al?

  b. How many moles of Al_2O_3 are formed when 0.78 mol O_2 reacts with aluminum?

In the mole ratio below, *W* is the unknown quantity. The values of *a* and *b* are the coefficients from the balanced equation. Thus a general solution for a mole-mole problem, such as Sample Problem 9-3, is given by

$$x \; \cancel{mol \; G} \times \frac{b \; mol \; W}{a \; \cancel{mol \; G}} = \frac{xb}{a} \; mol \; W$$

Given   Mole ratio   Calculated

Mass-Mass Calculations

No laboratory balance can measure substances directly in moles. Instead, as is shown in **Figure 9.7**, the amount of a substance is usually determined by measuring its mass in grams. From the mass of a reactant or product, the mass of any other reactant or product in a given chemical equation can be calculated. The mole interpretation of a balanced equation is the basis for this conversion. If the given sample is measured in grams, the mass can be converted to moles by using the molar mass. Then the mole ratio from the balanced equation can be used to calculate the number of moles of the unknown. If it is the mass of the unknown that needs to be determined, the number of moles of the unknown can be multiplied by the molar mass. As in mole-mole calculations, the unknown can be either a reactant or a product.

Figure 9.7

To determine the number of moles in a sample of a compound, first measure the mass of the sample. Then use the molar mass to calculate the number of moles in that mass.

Sample Problem 9-4

Calculate the number of grams of NH_3 produced by the reaction of 5.40 g of hydrogen with an excess of nitrogen. The balanced equation is

$$N_2(g) + 3H_2(g) \longrightarrow 2NH_3(g)$$

1. **ANALYZE** *List the knowns and the unknown.*

   Knowns:
   - mass of hydrogen = 5.40 g H_2
   - 3 mol H_2 = 2 mol NH_3 (from balanced equation)
   - 1 mol H_2 = 2.0 g H_2 (molar mass)
   - 1 mol NH_3 = 17.0 g NH_3 (molar mass)

   Unknown:
   - mass of ammonia = ? g NH_3

   The mass in grams of hydrogen will be used to find the mass in grams of ammonia: g $H_2 \longrightarrow$ g NH_3.

   The coefficients in the balanced equation show that 3 mol H_2 reacts with 1 mol N_2 to produce 2 mol NH_3. The following calculations need to be done:

   $$g\ H_2 \longrightarrow mol\ H_2 \longrightarrow mol\ NH_3 \longrightarrow g\ NH_3$$

2. **CALCULATE** *Solve for the unknown.*

   Convert the given (5.40 g H_2) to moles by using the molar mass of hydrogen.

   $$5.40\ \cancel{g\ H_2} \times \frac{1\ mol\ H_2}{2.0\ \cancel{g\ H_2}} = 2.7\ mol\ H_2$$

   Use the mole ratio from the balanced equation to calculate the number of moles of NH_3.

   $$2.7\ \cancel{mol\ H_2} \times \frac{2\ mol\ NH_3}{3\ \cancel{mol\ H_2}} = 1.8\ mol\ NH_3$$

   Convert the moles of NH_3 to grams of NH_3 by using the molar mass of ammonia.

   $$1.8\ \cancel{mol\ NH_3} \times \frac{17.0\ g\ NH_3}{1\ \cancel{mol\ NH_3}} = 31\ g\ NH_3$$

   This series of calculations can be combined:

   $$g\ H_2 \longrightarrow mol\ H_2 \longrightarrow mol\ NH_3 \longrightarrow g\ NH_3$$

   $$5.40\ \underset{\substack{\text{Given}\\\text{quantity}}}{\cancel{g\ H_2}} \times \underset{\substack{\text{Change given}\\\text{unit to moles}}}{\frac{1\ \cancel{mol\ H_2}}{2.0\ \cancel{g\ H_2}}} \times \underset{\substack{\text{Mole ratio}}}{\frac{2\ \cancel{mol\ NH_3}}{3\ \cancel{mol\ H_2}}} \times \underset{\substack{\text{Change moles}\\\text{to grams}}}{\frac{17.0\ g\ NH_3}{1\ \cancel{mol\ NH_3}}} = 31\ g\ NH_3$$

3. **EVALUATE** *Does the result make sense?*

   Because there are three conversion factors involved in this solution, it is more difficult to estimate an answer. However, because the molar mass of NH_3 is substantially greater than the molar mass of H_2, the answer should have a larger mass than the given mass. The answer should have two significant figures.

Practice Problems

11. Acetylene gas (C_2H_2) is produced by adding water to calcium carbide (CaC_2).

$$CaC_2(s) + 2H_2O(l) \longrightarrow$$
$$C_2H_2(g) + Ca(OH)_2(aq)$$

How many grams of acetylene are produced by adding water to 5.00 g CaC_2?

12. Using the same equation, determine how many moles of CaC_2 are needed to react completely with 49.0 g H_2O.

Chem ASAP!

Problem-Solving 11
Solve Problem 11 with the help of an interactive guided tutorial.

AGRICULTURE

Ammonia in the Nitrogen Cycle

Ammonia is part of the nitrogen cycle in nature. Earth's atmosphere contains 0.01 parts per million of ammonia, and small

amounts of ammonia occur in volcanic gases. Most ammonia cycles through the living world without returning to the atmosphere. Ammonia plays a role in several stages of the nitrogen cycle. Nitrogen-fixing bacteria form nodules, or swellings, on the roots of plants in the legume family, such as beans and clover plants. Here the bacteria change atmospheric nitrogen into ammonia molecules or ammonium ions. Other bacteria break down the nitrogenous material in dead plants and animals into ammonia molecules. Certain soil bacteria oxidize these molecules into nitrate ions, the form readily absorbed by plant roots. When a plant dies, this cycle begins again.

Figure 9.8
In this Hubble Space Telescope image, clouds of condensed ammonia are visible covering the surface of Saturn.

If the law of conservation of mass is true, how is it possible to make 31 g NH_3 from only 5.40 g H_2? Looking back at the equation for the reaction, you will see that hydrogen is not the only reactant. Another reactant, nitrogen, is also involved. If you were to calculate the number of grams of nitrogen needed to produce 31 g NH_3 and then compare the total masses of reactants and products, you would have an answer to this question. Go ahead and try it!

You can see from Sample Problem 9-4 that mass-mass problems can be solved in basically the same way as mole-mole problems. **Figure 9.9** reviews the steps for the mass-mass conversion of any given mass *(G)* and any wanted mass *(W)*.

1. The mass G is changed to moles of G (mass G $\longrightarrow$ mol G) by using the molar mass of G.

$$\text{mass } G \times \frac{1 \text{ mol } G}{\text{molar mass } G} = \text{mol } G$$

2. The moles of *G* are changed to moles of *W* (mol *G* $\rightarrow$ mol *W*) by using the mole ratio from the balanced equation.

$$\text{mol } G \times \frac{b \text{ mol } W}{a \text{ mol } G} = \text{mol } W$$

3. The moles of W are changed to grams of W (mol W $\rightarrow$ mass W) by using the molar mass of W.

$$\text{mol } W \times \frac{\text{molar mass } W}{1 \text{ mol } W} = \text{mass } W$$

Figure 9.9 also shows the steps for doing mole-mass and mass-mole stoichiometric calculations. For a mole-mass problem, the first conversion (from mass to moles) is skipped. For a mass-mole problem, the last conversion (from moles to mass) is skipped. You can use parts of the three-step process shown in **Figure 9.9** as they are appropriate to the problem you are solving.

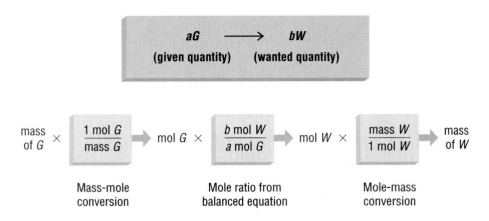

Figure 9.9

This general solution diagram indicates the steps necessary to solve a mass-mass stoichiometry problem: convert mass to moles, use the mole ratio, and then convert moles to mass. Is the given always a reactant?

Other Stoichiometric Calculations

As you already know, a balanced chemical equation indicates the relative number of moles of reactants and products. From this foundation, stoichiometric calculations can be expanded to include any unit of measurement that is related to the mole. The given quantity can be expressed in numbers of representative particles, units of mass, or volumes of gases at STP. The problems can include mass-volume, volume-volume, and particle-mass calculations. In any of these problems, the given quantity is first converted to moles. Then the mole ratio from the balanced equation is used to calculate the number of moles of the wanted substance. Once this has been determined, the moles are converted to any other unit of measurement related to the unit mole, as the problem requires. **Figure 9.10** summarizes these steps for a typical stoichiometric problem.

Figure 9.10

With your knowledge of conversion factors and this problem-solving approach you can solve a variety of stoichiometric problems. What conversion factor is used to convert moles to representative particles?

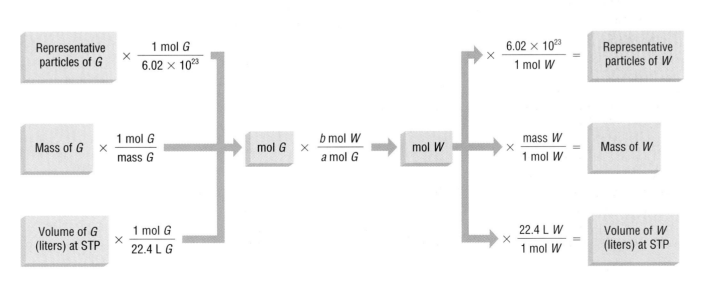

Figure 9.11
The electrolysis of water causes it to decompose into hydrogen and oxygen.

Sample Problem 9-5

How many molecules of oxygen are produced when a sample of 29.2 g of water is decomposed by electrolysis according to this balanced equation?

$$2H_2O(l) \xrightarrow{\text{electricity}} 2H_2(g) + O_2(g)$$

1. ANALYZE List the knowns and the unknown.

Knowns:
- mass of water = 29.2 g H_2O
- 2 mol H_2O = 1 mol O_2 (from balanced equation)
- 1 mol H_2O = 18.0 g H_2O (molar mass)
- 1 mol O_2 = 6.02×10^{23} molecules O_2

Unknown:
- molecules of oxygen = ? molecules O_2

Use appropriate conversion factors to convert the given quantity in grams to number of molecules.

2. CALCULATE Solve for the unknown.

$$29.2 \text{ g } H_2O \times \frac{1 \text{ mol } H_2O}{18.0 \text{ g } H_2O} \times \frac{1 \text{ mol } O_2}{2 \text{ mol } H_2O} \times \frac{6.02 \times 10^{23} \text{ molecules } O_2}{1 \text{ mol } O_2}$$

Given quantity   Change to moles   Mole ratio   Change to molecules

$$= 4.88 \times 10^{23} \text{ molecules } O_2$$

3. EVALUATE Does the result make sense?

The given mass of water should produce a little less than 1 mol of oxygen, or a little less than Avogadro's number of molecules. The answer should have three significant figures.

Practice Problems

13. How many molecules of oxygen are produced by the decomposition of 6.54 g of potassium chlorate ($KClO_3$)?

$$2KClO_3(s) \longrightarrow 2KCl(s) + 3O_2(g)$$

14. The last step in the production of nitric acid is the reaction of nitrogen dioxide with water.

$$3NO_2(g) + H_2O(l) \longrightarrow 2HNO_3(aq) + NO(g)$$

How many grams of nitrogen dioxide must react with water to produce 5.00×10^{22} molecules of nitrogen monoxide?

Sample Problem 9-6

Assuming STP, how many liters of oxygen are needed to produce 19.8 L SO_3 according to this balanced equation?

$$2SO_2(g) + O_2(g) \longrightarrow 2SO_3(g)$$

1. ANALYZE List the knowns and the unknown.

Knowns:
- volume of sulfur trioxide = 19.8 L
- 2 mol SO_3 = 1 mol O_2 (from balanced equation)
- 1 mol SO_3 = 22.4 L SO_3 (at STP)
- 1 mol O_2 = 22.4 L O_2 (at STP)

Unknown:
- volume of oxygen = ? L O_2

2. CALCULATE Solve for the unknown.

$$19.8 \text{ L } SO_3 \times \underbrace{\frac{1 \text{ mol } SO_3}{22.4 \text{ L } SO_3}}_{\substack{\text{Given} \\ \text{quantity}}} \times \underbrace{\frac{1 \text{ mol } O_2}{2 \text{ mol } SO_3}}_{\substack{\text{Change} \\ \text{to moles}}} \times \underbrace{\frac{22.4 \text{ L } O_2}{1 \text{ mol } O_2}}_{\substack{\text{Change} \\ \text{to liters}}} = 9.90 \text{ L } O_2$$

Given quantity — Change to moles — Mole ratio — Change to liters

3. EVALUATE Does the result make sense?

Because 2 mol SO_3 is produced for each 1 mol O_2 that reacts, the volume of O_2 should be half the volume of SO_3. The answer should have three significant figures.

Practice Problems

15. The equation for the combustion of carbon monoxide is

$$2CO(g) + O_2(g) \longrightarrow 2CO_2(g)$$

How many liters of oxygen are required to burn 3.86 L of carbon monoxide?

16. Phosphorus and hydrogen can be combined to form phosphine (PH_3).

$$P_4(s) + 6H_2(g) \longrightarrow 4PH_3(g)$$

How many liters of phosphine are formed when 0.42 L of hydrogen reacts with phosphorus?

Chem ASAP!

Problem-Solving 16

Solve Problem 16 with the help of an interactive guided tutorial.

In Sample Problem 9-6, did you notice that the 22.4 L/mol factors canceled out? This will always be true in a volume-volume problem. The coefficients in a balanced chemical equation indicate the relative numbers of moles. The coefficients also indicate the relative volumes of interacting gases. The volume can be expressed in any unit. What are some other units of volume?

Sample Problem 9-7

Nitrogen monoxide and oxygen gas combine to form the brown gas nitrogen dioxide. How many milliliters of nitrogen dioxide are produced when 3.4 mL of oxygen reacts with an excess of nitrogen monoxide? Assume conditions of STP.

$$2NO(g) + O_2(g) \longrightarrow 2NO_2(g)$$

1. ANALYZE List the knowns and the unknown.

Knowns:
- volume of oxygen = 3.4 mL O_2
- 1 mL O_2 = 2 mL NO_2
  (from balanced equation)

Unknown:
- volume of nitrogen dioxide = ? mL NO_2

Figure 9.12
The brown gas nitrogen dioxide is a component of photochemical smog, which builds up when still air hangs over a city or other pollution source. Persistent smog can pose a health danger.

Practice Problems

Consider this equation.

$$CS_2(l) + 3O_2(g) \longrightarrow$$
$$CO_2(g) + 2SO_2(g)$$

17. Calculate the volume of sulfur dioxide produced when 27.9 mL O_2 reacts with carbon disulfide.

18. How many deciliters of carbon dioxide are produced when 0.38 L SO_2 is formed?

Sample Problem 9-7 (cont.)

2. *CALCULATE* **Solve for the unknown.**

$$3.4 \text{ mL } O_2 \times \frac{2 \text{ mL } NO_2}{1 \text{ mL } O_2} = 6.8 \text{ mL } NO_2$$

Given quantity   Volume ratio

3. *EVALUATE* **Does the result make sense?**

The conversion is mL $O_2 \longrightarrow$ mL NO_2. The given quantity of O_2 is multiplied by the volume ratio from the balanced equation that allows the given unit to cancel. Because the volume ratio is 2 volumes NO_2 to 1 volume O_2, the calculated volume of NO_2 should be twice the given volume of O_2. The answer should have two significant figures.

section review 9.2

19. Isopropyl alcohol (C_3H_7OH) burns in air according to this equation:

$$2C_3H_7OH(l) + 9O_2(g) \longrightarrow 6CO_2(g) + 8H_2O(g)$$

   a. Calculate the moles of oxygen needed to react with 3.40 mol C_3H_7OH.

   b. Find the moles of each product formed when 3.40 mol C_3H_7OH reacts with oxygen.

20. What ratio is used to carry out each conversion?

   a. mol CH_4 to g CH_4

   b. L $CH_4(g)$ to mol $CH_4(g)$ (at STP)

   c. molecules CH_4 to mol CH_4

21. The combustion of acetylene gas is represented by this equation:

$$2C_2H_2(g) + 5O_2(g) \longrightarrow 4CO_2(g) + 2H_2O(g)$$

   a. How many grams of CO_2 and grams of H_2O are produced when 52.0 g C_2H_2 burns?

   b. How many grams of oxygen are required to burn 52.0 g C_2H_2?

   c. Use the answers from **a** and **b** to show that this equation obeys the law of conservation of mass.

portfolio project

Using the Internet or the library, research analytical balances. How small a mass or large a mass can these types of balances measure? Compare different balances to find out whether there is a relationship between precision and cost.

22. Tin(II) fluoride, formerly found in many kinds of toothpaste, is formed in this reaction:

$$Sn(s) + 2HF(g) \longrightarrow SnF_2(s) + H_2(g)$$

   a. How many liters of HF are needed to produce 9.40 L H_2 at STP?

   b. How many molecules of H_2 are produced by the reaction of tin with 20.0 L HF at STP?

   c. How many grams of SnF_2 can be made by reacting 7.42×10^{24} molecules of HF with tin?

 Chem ASAP! **Assessment 9.2** Check your understanding of the important ideas and concepts in Section 9.2.

SMALL-SCALE LAB

ANALYSIS OF BAKING SODA

SAFETY

Wear safety glasses and follow the standard safety procedure as outlined on page 18.

PURPOSE

To determine the mass of sodium hydrogen carbonate in a sample of baking soda using stoichiometry.

MATERIALS

- baking soda
- 3 plastic cups
- pipets of HCl, NaOH, and thymol blue
- soda straw
- balance
- pH sensor (optional)

PROCEDURE

 Sensor version available in the Probeware Lab Manual.

Prepare and analyze a sample of baking soda. Take care to write down the results of each step.

A. Measure the mass of a clean, dry plastic cup.

B. Using the straw as a scoop, fill one end with baking soda to a depth of about 1 cm. Add the sample to the cup and measure its mass again.

C. Place two HCl pipets that are about ¾ full into a clean cup and measure the mass of the system.

D. Transfer the contents of both HCl pipets to the cup containing baking soda. Swirl until the fizzing stops. Wait 5–10 minutes to be sure the reaction is complete. Measure the mass of the two empty HCl pipets in their cup again.

E. Add 5 drops of thymol blue to the plastic cup.

F. Place two full NaOH pipets in a clean cup and measure the mass of the system.

G. Add NaOH slowly to the baking soda/HCl mixture until the pink color just disappears. Measure the mass of the NaOH pipets in their cup again.

ANALYSIS

Using your experimental data, record the answers to the following questions below your data table.

1. Write a balanced equation for the reaction between baking soda ($NaHCO_3$) and HCl.

2. Calculate the mass in grams of the baking soda.

$$(\text{Step B} - \text{Step A})$$

3. Calculate the total mmol of $1M$ HCl.
   Note: Every gram of HCl contains 1 mmol.

$$(\text{Step C} - \text{Step D}) \times 1.00 \text{ mmol/g}$$

4. Calculate the total mmol of $0.5M$ NaOH.
   Note: Every gram of NaOH contains 0.5 mmol.

$$(\text{Step F} - \text{Step G}) \times 0.500 \text{ mmol/g}$$

5. Calculate the mmol of HCl that reacted with the baking soda. *Note:* The NaOH measures the amount of HCl that did not react.

$$(\text{Step 3} - \text{Step 4})$$

6. Calculate the mass of the baking soda from the reaction data.

$$(0.084 \text{ g/mmol} \times \text{Step 5})$$

7. Calculate the percent error of the experiment.

$$\frac{(\text{Step 2} - \text{Step 6})}{\text{Step 2}} \times 100\%$$

YOU'RE THE CHEMIST

The following small-scale activities allow you to develop your own procedures and analyze the results.

1. **Analyze It!** For each calculation you did, substitute each quantity (number and unit) into the equation and cancel the units to explain why each step gives the quantity desired.

2. **Design It!** Baking powder consists of a mixture of baking soda, sodium hydrogen carbonate, and a solid acid, usually calcium dihydrogen phosphate ($Ca(H_2PO_4)_2$). Design and carry out an experiment to determine the percentage of baking soda in baking powder.

LIMITING REAGENT AND PERCENT YIELD

objectives
- ▶ Identify and use the limiting reagent in a reaction to calculate the maximum amount of product(s) produced and the amount of excess reagent
- ▶ Calculate theoretical yield, actual yield, or percent yield given appropriate information

key terms
- ▶ limiting reagent
- ▶ excess reagent
- ▶ theoretical yield
- ▶ actual yield
- ▶ percent yield

If a carpenter had two table tops and seven table legs, he would have difficulty building more than one functional four-legged table. The first table would require four of the legs, leaving just three legs for the second table. In this case, the number of table legs is the limiting factor in the construction of four-legged tables. A similar concept applies in chemistry when knowing the exact amounts of reactants and products in a chemical reaction is crucial. **How does a limiting reagent affect a chemical reaction?**

What Is a Limiting Reagent?

Perhaps you know from your own experience that many cooks follow a recipe when making a new dish. They know that sufficient quantities of all the ingredients must be available. Suppose, for example, that you are preparing to make lasagna and you have more than enough meat, tomato sauce, ricotta cheese, eggs, mozzarella cheese, spinach, and seasoning on hand. However, you have only half a box of lasagna noodles. The amount of lasagna you can make will be limited by the amount of noodles you have. Thus the noodles are the limiting reagent in this baking venture. **Figure 9.13** illustrates another example of a limiting reagent in the kitchen. A chemist often faces a similar situation. It is impossible for a chemist to make a certain amount of a desired compound if there is an insufficient quantity of any of the required reactants.

As you know, a balanced chemical equation is a chemist's recipe—a recipe that can be interpreted on a microscopic scale (interacting particles) or on a macroscopic scale (interacting moles). The coefficients used to write

Figure 9.13
The amount of product is determined by the quantity of the limiting reagent. In this example, the rolls are the limiting reagent. No matter how much of the other ingredients you have, with two rolls you can make only two sandwiches.

the balanced equation give both the ratio of representative particles and the mole ratio. Recall the equation for the preparation of ammonia.

$$N_2(g) + 3H_2(g) \longrightarrow 2NH_3(g)$$

When one molecule (mole) of N_2 reacts with three molecules (moles) of H_2, two molecules (moles) of NH_3 are produced. What would happen if two molecules (moles) of N_2 reacted with three molecules (moles) of H_2? Would more than two molecules (moles) of NH_3 be formed? **Figure 9.14** shows both the particle and the mole interpretations of this problem.

Before the reaction takes place, nitrogen and hydrogen are present in a 2:3 molecule (mole) ratio. The reaction takes place according to the balanced equation. One molecule (mole) of N_2 reacts with three molecules (moles) of H_2 to produce two molecules (moles) of NH_3. At this point, all the hydrogen has been used up, and the reaction stops. One molecule (mole) of unreacted nitrogen is left in addition to the two molecules (moles) of NH_3 that have been produced by the reaction.

In this reaction, only the hydrogen is completely used up. It is called the limiting reagent. As the name implies, the **limiting reagent** limits or determines the amount of product that can be formed in a reaction. The reaction occurs only until the limiting reagent is used up. By contrast, the reactant that is not completely used up in a reaction is called the **excess reagent.** In this example, nitrogen is the excess reagent because some nitrogen will remain unreacted. You probably know that if you put a glass over a burning candle, the candle goes out. In this example of the combustion of candle wax, what is the limiting reagent?

Sometimes in problems, the given quantities of reactants are expressed in units other than moles. In such cases, the first step in the solution is to convert each reactant to moles. Then the limiting reagent can be identified, as in Sample Problem 9-8. Finally, the amount of product can be determined from the given amount of limiting reagent.

Chem ASAP!

Animation 8
Apply the limiting reagent concept to the production of iron from iron ore.

Figure 9.14
The "recipe" calls for 3 molecules of H_2 for every 1 molecule of N_2. In this particular experiment, H_2 is the limiting reagent and N_2 is in excess. Would the amount of products formed change if you started with 4 molecules of N_2 and 3 molecules of H_2?

Chemical Equations				
	$N_2(g)$	+	$3H_2(g)$	→	$2NH_3(g)$
"Microscopic recipe"	1 molecule N_2	+	3 molecules H_2	→	2 molecules NH_3
"Macroscopic recipe"	1 mol N_2	+	3 mol H_2	→	2 mol NH_3

Experimental Conditions			
	Reactants		Products
Before reaction	2 molecules N_2	3 molecules H_2	0 molecules NH_3
After reaction	1 molecule N_2	0 molecules H_2	2 molecules NH_3

Figure 9.15
Igniting sodium metal in chlorine gas produces a white smoke of NaCl and bright yellow light.

Practice Problems

23. The equation for the complete combustion of ethene (C_2H_4) is

    $$C_2H_4(g) + 3O_2(g) \longrightarrow 2CO_2(g) + 2H_2O(g)$$

    If 2.70 mol C_2H_4 is reacted with 6.30 mol O_2,
    a. identify the limiting reagent.
    b. calculate the moles of water produced.

24. The equation for the incomplete combustion of ethene (C_2H_4) is

    $$C_2H_4(g) + 2O_2(g) \longrightarrow 2CO(g) + 2H_2O(g)$$

    If 2.70 mol C_2H_4 is reacted with 6.30 mol O_2,
    a. identify the limiting reagent.
    b. calculate the moles of water produced.

Chem ASAP!

Problem-Solving 24
Solve Problem 24 with the help of an interactive guided tutorial.

Sample Problem 9-8

Sodium chloride can be prepared by the reaction of sodium metal with chlorine gas.

$$2Na(s) + Cl_2(g) \longrightarrow 2NaCl(s)$$

Suppose that 6.70 mol Na reacts with 3.20 mol Cl_2.
 a. What is the limiting reagent?
 b. How many moles of NaCl are produced?

1. *ANALYZE List the knowns and the unknown for a.*
Knowns:
 • moles sodium = 6.70 mol Na
 • moles chlorine = 3.20 mol Cl_2
 • 2 mol Na = 1 mol Cl_2 (from balanced equation)
Unknown:
 • limiting reagent = ?

The known amount of one of the reactants is multiplied by the mole ratio from the balanced equation to calculate the required amount of the other reactant. Sodium is chosen arbitrarily here: mol Na → mol Cl_2.

2. *CALCULATE Solve for the unknown.*

$$6.70 \; \cancel{\text{mol Na}} \times \frac{1 \text{ mol } Cl_2}{2 \; \cancel{\text{mol Na}}} = 3.35 \text{ mol } Cl_2$$

Given amount	Mole ratio	Required amount

This calculation indicates that 3.35 mol Cl_2 is needed to react with 6.70 mol Na. Because only 3.20 mol Cl_2 is available, however, chlorine becomes the limiting reagent. Sodium, then, must be in excess.

1. *ANALYZE List the knowns and the unknown for b.*
Knowns:
 • amount of limiting reagent = 3.20 mol Cl_2
 • 1 mol Cl_2 = 2 mol NaCl (from balanced equation)

Unknown:
 • moles of sodium chloride = ? mol NaCl

2. *CALCULATE Solve for the unknown.*

$$3.20 \; \cancel{\text{mol } Cl_2} \times \frac{2 \text{ mol NaCl}}{1 \; \cancel{\text{mol } Cl_2}} = 6.40 \text{ mol NaCl}$$

3. *EVALUATE Do the results make sense?*
Because the ratio of the given moles of sodium to chlorine was greater than 2:1, which is the ratio from the balanced equation, sodium should be in excess and chlorine should be the limiting reagent.

Sample Problem 9-9

As illustrated in **Figure 9.16,** the properties of copper(I) sulfide are very different from the properties of the elements copper and sulfur.

$$2Cu(s) + S(s) \longrightarrow Cu_2S(s)$$

a. What is the limiting reagent when 80.0 g Cu reacts with 25.0 g S?

b. What is the maximum number of grams of Cu_2S that can be formed?

....

1. ANALYZE *List the knowns and the unknown for* **a.**

Knowns:
- mass of copper = 80.0 g Cu
- mass of sulfur = 25.0 g S
- 2 mol Cu = 1 mol S (from balanced equation)

Unknown:
- limiting reagent = ?

The number of moles of each reactant must first be found:

$$g\,Cu \longrightarrow mol\,Cu$$
$$g\,S \longrightarrow mol\,S$$

The balanced equation is used to calculate the number of moles of one reactant needed to react with the given amount of the other reactant:

$$mol\,Cu \longrightarrow mol\,S$$

....

2. CALCULATE *Solve for the unknown.*

$$80.0\;\cancel{g\,Cu} \times \frac{1\;mol\,Cu}{63.5\;\cancel{g\,Cu}} = 1.26\;mol\,Cu$$

$$25.0\;\cancel{g\,S} \times \frac{1\;mol\,S}{32.1\;\cancel{g\,S}} = 0.779\;mol\,S$$

$$1.26\;\cancel{mol\,Cu} \times \frac{1\;mol\,S}{2\;\cancel{mol\,Cu}} = 0.630\;mol\,S$$

| Given quantity | Mole ratio | Needed amount |

Comparing the amount of sulfur needed (0.630 mol S) with the given amount (0.779 mol S) indicates that sulfur is in excess. Thus copper is the limiting reagent.

....

1. ANALYZE *List the knowns and the unknown for* **b.**

Knowns:
- limiting reagent = 1.26 mol Cu
- 2 mol Cu = 1 mol Cu_2S (from balanced equation)
- 1 mol Cu_2S = 159.1 g Cu_2S (molar mass)

Unknown:
- mass copper(I) sulfide = ? g Cu_2S

The limiting reagent, which was determined in the last step, is used to calculate the maximum amount of Cu_2S formed:

$$mol\,Cu \longrightarrow mol\,Cu_2S \longrightarrow g\,Cu_2S$$

Figure 9.16
Black crystalline copper(I) sulfide (bottom) is formed as a product when the reactants, sulfur (top left) and copper (top right), are heated together.

Practice Problems

25. Hydrogen gas can be produced in the laboratory by the reaction of magnesium metal with hydrochloric acid.

$$Mg(s) + 2HCl(aq) \longrightarrow MgCl_2(aq) + H_2(g)$$

a. Identify the limiting reagent when 6.00 g HCl reacts with 5.00 g Mg.

b. How many grams of hydrogen can be produced when 6.00 g HCl is added to 5.00 g Mg?

Sample Problem 9-9 (cont.)

2. **CALCULATE** *Solve for the unknown.*

$$1.26 \text{ mol Cu} \times \frac{1 \text{ mol Cu}_2\text{S}}{2 \text{ mol Cu}} \times \frac{159.1 \text{ g Cu}_2\text{S}}{1 \text{ mol Cu}_2\text{S}} = 1.00 \times 10^2 \text{ g Cu}_2\text{S}$$

The given quantity of copper, 80.0 g, could have been used for this step instead of the moles of copper, which were calculated in the very first step of the solution.

3. **EVALUATE** *Do the results make sense?*

Copper is the limiting reagent in this reaction. The maximum number of grams of Cu_2S produced should be more than the amount of copper that initially reacted because copper is combining with sulfur. The amount of Cu_2S produced should be less than the sum of copper and sulfur (80.0 g Cu + 25.0 g S = 105.0 g) because sulfur was in excess.

Practice Problems (cont.)

26. Acetylene (C_2H_2) will burn in the presence of oxygen.

$$2C_2H_2(g) + 5O_2(g) \longrightarrow$$
$$4CO_2(g) + 2H_2O(g)$$

How many grams of water can be produced by the reaction of 2.40 mol C_2H_2 with 7.4 mol O_2?

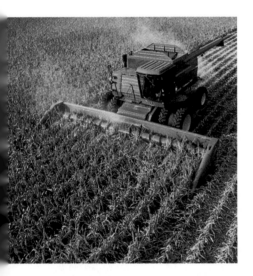

Figure 9.17

The productivity of a farm is measured in yield. Because growing conditions may vary from year to year, the actual yield often differs from the theoretical yield.

Calculating the Percent Yield

In theory, when a teacher gives an exam to the class, every student should get a grade of 100%. For a variety of reasons, this generally does not occur. Instead, the performance of the class is usually spread over a range of grades. Your exam grade, expressed as a percentage, is a quantity that shows how well you did on the exam (questions answered correctly) compared with how well you could have done if you had answered all the questions correctly (100%). This calculation is analogous to the percent yield calculation that you do in the laboratory when the product from a chemical reaction is less than you expected based on the balanced chemical equation.

So far in this chapter, you have probably assumed that when doing stoichiometric problems things do not go wrong in chemical reactions. This assumption is as faulty as assuming that all students will score 100% on an exam. When an equation is used to calculate the amount of product that will form during a reaction, a value representing the theoretical yield is obtained. The **theoretical yield** is the maximum amount of product that could be formed from given amounts of reactants. In contrast, the amount of product that actually forms when the reaction is carried out in the laboratory is called the **actual yield**. The actual yield is often less than the theoretical yield. The **percent yield** is the ratio of the actual yield to the theoretical yield expressed as a percent. The percent yield measures the efficiency of the reaction.

$$\text{Percent yield} = \frac{\text{actual yield}}{\text{theoretical yield}} \times 100\%$$

A percent yield should not normally be larger than 100%. Many factors cause percent yields to be less than 100%. Reactions do not always go to completion; when this occurs, less than the calculated amount of product is formed. Impure reactants and competing side reactions may cause unwanted products to form. Actual yield can also be lower than the theoretical yield due to a loss of product during filtration or in transferring

Figure 9.18
A batting average is actually a percent yield.

between containers. Moreover, if reactants or products have not been carefully measured, a percent yield of 100% is unlikely.

An actual yield is an experimental value. **Figure 9.19** shows a typical laboratory procedure for determining the actual yield of a product of a decomposition reaction. If you do not do an experiment, you cannot calculate a percent yield unless you are given the value of an actual yield. For reactions in which percent yields have been determined, you can calculate and therefore predict an actual yield if the reaction conditions remain the same. A farmer's crop yield could also be expressed as a percent yield. What factors would a farmer use to predict a theoretical yield?

Figure 9.19

(a) *The mass of sodium hydrogen carbonate ($NaHCO_3$), the reactant, is measured.*
(b) *The reactant is heated.* **(c)** *The mass of one of the products, sodium carbonate (Na_2CO_3), the actual yield, is measured after the reaction is completed. The percent yield can be calculated once the actual yield has been determined. What are the other products of this reaction?*

(a)   (b)   (c)

Sample Problem 9-10

Calcium carbonate is decomposed by heating, as shown in the following equation.

$$CaCO_3(s) \xrightarrow{\Delta} CaO(s) + CO_2(g)$$

a. What is the theoretical yield of CaO if 24.8 g CaCO$_3$ is heated?

b. What is the percent yield if 13.1 g CaO is produced?

1. *ANALYZE* **List the knowns and the unknown for a.**

Knowns:
- mass of calcium carbonate = 24.8 g CaCO$_3$
- 1 mol CaCO$_3$ = 1 mol CaO (from balanced equation)
- 1 mol CaCO$_3$ = 100.1 g CaCO$_3$ (molar mass)
- 1 mol CaO = 56.1 g CaO (molar mass)

Unknown:
- theoretical yield of calcium oxide = ? g CaO

The theoretical yield can be calculated using the mass of the reactant:

$$g\ CaCO_3 \longrightarrow mol\ CaCO_3 \longrightarrow mol\ CaO \longrightarrow g\ CaO$$

2. *CALCULATE* **Solve for the unknown.**

First, the theoretical yield of the reaction is calculated.

$$24.8\ g\ CaCO_3 \times \frac{1\ mol\ CaCO_3}{100.1\ g\ CaCO_3} \times \frac{1\ mol\ CaO}{1\ mol\ CaCO_3} \times \frac{56.1\ g\ CaO}{1\ mol\ CaO}$$

$$= 13.9\ g\ CaO$$

1. *ANALYZE* **List the knowns and the unknown for b.**

Knowns:
- actual yield = 13.1 g CaO
- theoretical yield = 13.9 g CaO (from **a**)

- percent yield = $\dfrac{\text{actual yield}}{\text{theoretical yield}} \times 100\%$

Unknown:
- percent yield = ? %

2. *CALCULATE* **Solve for the unknown.**

$$\text{percent yield} = \frac{\text{actual yield}}{\text{theoretical yield}} \times 100\%$$

$$\text{percent yield} = \frac{13.1\ g\ CaO}{13.9\ g\ CaO} \times 100\% = 94.2\%$$

3. *EVALUATE* **Does the result make sense?**

In this example, the actual yield is slightly less than the theoretical yield. Therefore, the percent yield should be slightly less than 100%. The answer should have three significant figures.

Practice Problems

27. When 84.8 g of iron(III) oxide reacts with an excess of carbon monoxide, 54.3 g of iron is produced.

$$Fe_2O_3(s) + 3CO(g) \longrightarrow$$
$$2Fe(s) + 3CO_2(g)$$

What is the percent yield of this reaction?

28. If 50.0 g of silicon dioxide is heated with an excess of carbon, 27.9 g of silicon carbide is produced.

$$SiO_2(s) + 3C(s) \longrightarrow$$
$$SiC(s) + 2CO(g)$$

What is the percent yield of this reaction?

Problem-Solving 28
Solve Problem 28 with the help of an interactive guided tutorial.

MINI LAB

Limiting Reagents

0.6 g Mg   1.2 g Mg   2.4 g Mg

PURPOSE

To illustrate the concept of a limiting reagent in a chemical reaction.

MATERIALS

- graduated cylinder
- balance
- 3 250-mL Erlenmeyer flasks
- 3 rubber balloons
- 4.2 g magnesium ribbon
- 300 mL 1.0M hydrochloric acid

PROCEDURE

1. Add 100 mL of the hydrochloric acid solution to each flask.

2. Weigh out 0.6 g, 1.2 g, and 2.4 g of magnesium ribbon, and place each sample into its own balloon.

3. Stretch the end of each balloon over the mouth of each flask. Do not allow the magnesium ribbon in the balloon to fall into the flask.

4. Magnesium reacts with hydrochloric acid to form hydrogen gas. When you mix the magnesium with the hydrochloric acid in the next step, you will generate a certain volume of hydrogen gas. How do you think the volume of hydrogen produced in each flask will compare?

5. Lift up on each balloon and shake the magnesium metal down into each flask. Observe the volume of gas produced until the reaction in each flask is completed.

ANALYSIS AND CONCLUSIONS

1. How did the volumes of hydrogen gas produced, as measured by the size of the balloons, compare? Did the results agree with your prediction?

2. Write a balanced equation for the reaction between magnesium metal and hydrochloric acid.

3. The 100 mL of hydrochloric acid contained 0.10 mol HCl. Show by calculation why the balloon with 1.2 g Mg inflated to about twice the size of the balloon with 0.60 g Mg.

4. Show by calculation why the balloons with 1.2 g and 2.4 g Mg inflated to approximately the same volume. What was the limiting reagent when 2.4 g Mg was added to the acid?

---

section review 9.3

29. What is a limiting reagent? An excess reagent?

30. What is the percent yield if 4.65 g of copper is produced when 1.87 g of aluminum reacts with an excess of copper(II) sulfate?

$$2Al(s) + 3CuSO_4(aq) \longrightarrow Al_2(SO_4)_3(aq) + 3Cu(s)$$

31. What is the difference between an actual yield and a theoretical yield? Which yield is larger for a given reaction? How are these values used to determine percent yield?

32. How many grams of SO_3 are produced when 20.0 g FeS_2 reacts with 16.0 g O_2 according to this balanced equation?

$$4FeS_2(s) + 15O_2(g) \longrightarrow 2Fe_2O_3(s) + 8SO_3(g)$$

 Chem ASAP! Assessment 9.3 Check your understanding of the important ideas and concepts in Section 9.3.

JUST THE RIGHT VOLUME OF GAS

The steering wheel shown here displays the letters SRS, which stand for Supplemental Restraint System and indicate that the steering wheel is equipped with an air bag. If you are lucky, you will never have to experience an air bag. But if you do have a front-end collision while driving, an air bag may save your life. A sensor in the front of the car detects the sudden deceleration and sends a signal to a cylinder containing a mixture of chemicals. In the cylinder, an igniter goes off, starting a series of chemical reactions that release a large volume of nitrogen gas. The gas fills the air bag, and you hit the soft bag instead of the steering wheel or dashboard. All this happens in less than a second.

The design of the air bag may sound fairly simple, but it was actually quite a challenge. Engineers had to come up with a system that was safe and effective and that would still work after many years of not being used. Perhaps most importantly, the bag had to inflate in less than a tenth of a second, and it had to inflate with exactly the right amount of gas. If it under-inflated it would not provide enough protection; if it overinflated it would cause injury or it might even rupture. To design an air bag inflation system that met these requirements, engineers had to choose the right chemical reactants and pay close attention to the stoichiometry of the reactions.

The inflation system that engineers settled on uses a series of chemical reactions that take place very quickly. The first reaction—set off by the igniter—is the decomposition of sodium azide into sodium metal and nitrogen gas

$$2NaN_3(s) \longrightarrow 2Na(s) + 3N_2(g).$$

By itself, this reaction cannot fill the air bag fast enough, and the sodium metal that is produced is

The engineers had to determine the exact quantity of each reactant to include in the reaction mixture and to allow for the change in gas density caused by the heat released in the reaction.

dangerously reactive. To solve these problems, the engineers included potassium nitrate in the mixture of reactants. The potassium nitrate reacts with the sodium produced in the first reaction, releasing even more nitrogen gas

$$10Na + 2KNO_3 \longrightarrow K_2O + 5Na_2O + N_2$$

The heat released by this reaction raises the temperature of the gaseous product, helping the bag inflate even faster. The heat causes all the solid reaction products to fuse together with SiO_2, powdered sand, which is also part of the reaction mixture. This forms a safe, unreactive glass.

The volume of gas produced by these reactions is the key factor in getting the proper bag inflation. The volume depends on both the quantity of reactants and the temperature of the gas. Thus, the engineers had to determine the exact quantity of each reactant to include in the reaction mixture and to allow for the change in gas pressure caused by the heat released in the reaction. Even the quantity of potassium nitrate included in the mixture had to be precisely determined to make sure no sodium metal was left over from the first reaction. So if an air bag ever saves you from injury in a front-end collision, be thankful that the chemical engineers who designed the air bag's inflation system knew their stoichiometry!

CHEMISTRY IN CAREERS

QUALITY CONTROL CHEMIST
Interested in a career maintaining high-quality standards?
See page 872.

TAKE IT TO THE NET
Find out more about career opportunities:
www.phschool.com

CHEMICAL SPECIALIST
Local food service distributor seeks responsible self-motivated individ-

CHEMIST NEEDED

Take It to the NET
For interactive study and review, go to www.phschool.com

KEY TERMS

- actual yield *p. 256*
- excess reagent *p. 253*
- limiting reagent *p. 253*
- percent yield *p. 256*
- stoichiometry *p. 237*
- theoretical yield *p. 256*

KEY EQUATIONS AND RELATIONSHIPS

- mole-mole relationship for $aG \longrightarrow bW$:

$$\underset{\text{Given}}{x \text{ mol } G} \times \underset{\text{Mole ratio}}{\frac{b \text{ mol } W}{a \text{ mol } G}} = \underset{\text{Calculated}}{\frac{xb}{a} \text{ mol } W}$$

- $\text{percent yield} = \dfrac{\text{actual yield}}{\text{theoretical yield}} \times 100\%$

CONCEPT SUMMARY

9.1 The Arithmetic of Equations

- The coefficients in a balanced chemical equation tell the relative number of moles of reactants and products.
- Chemists use moles to do chemical arithmetic, or stoichiometry.
- All stoichiometric calculations involving chemical reactions begin with a balanced equation because mass is conserved in every chemical reaction.
- The number and kinds of atoms in the reactants equal the number and kinds of atoms in the products.

9.2 Chemical Calculations

- Stoichiometric problems are solved using conversion factors derived from a balanced chemical equation.
- A conversion factor called a mole ratio relates the moles of a given substance to the moles of the desired substance.
- Units such as mass, volume of gases (at STP), and particles are converted to moles when working stoichiometry problems.

9.3 Limiting Reagent and Percent Yield

- Whenever quantities of two or more reactants are given in a stoichiometry problem, the limiting reagent must be identified.
- A limiting reagent is completely used up in a chemical reaction.
- The amount of limiting reagent determines the amount of product formed in a chemical reaction.
- If there is a single limiting reagent in a reaction, all the other reactants are in excess.
- A theoretical yield is the maximum amount of product that can be obtained from a given amount of reactants in a chemical reaction.
- An actual yield is the amount of product obtained when the reaction is carried out in the laboratory.
- A ratio of the actual yield to the theoretical yield, expressed as a percentage, is the percent yield of a reaction.

CHAPTER CONCEPT MAP

Use these terms to construct a concept map that organizes the major ideas of this chapter.

 Chem ASAP! **Concept Map 9**
Create your Concept Map using the computer.

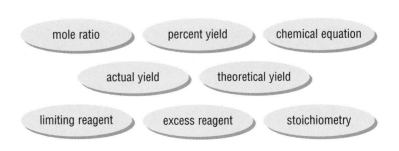

CONCEPT PRACTICE

33. Interpret each chemical equation in terms of interacting particles. *9.1*

a. $2KClO_3(s) \longrightarrow 2KCl(s) + 3O_2(g)$

b. $4NH_3(g) + 6NO(g) \longrightarrow 5N_2(g) + 6H_2O(g)$

c. $4K(s) + O_2(g) \longrightarrow 2K_2O(s)$

34. Interpret each equation in Problem 33 in terms of interacting numbers of moles of reactants and products. *9.1*

35. Calculate and compare the mass of the reactants with the mass of the products for each equation in Problem 33. Show that each balanced equation obeys the law of conservation of mass. *9.1*

36. Explain the term mole ratio in your own words. When would you use this term? *9.2*

37. Carbon disulfide is an important industrial solvent. It is prepared by the reaction of coke with sulfur dioxide. *9.2*

$$5C(s) + 2SO_2(g) \longrightarrow CS_2(l) + 4CO(g)$$

a. How many moles of CS_2 form when 2.7 mol C reacts?

b. How many moles of carbon are needed to react with 5.44 mol SO_2?

c. How many moles of carbon monoxide form at the same time that 0.246 mol CS_2 forms?

d. How many mol SO_2 are required to make 118 mol CS_2?

38. Methanol (CH_3OH) is used in the production of many chemicals. Methanol is made by reacting carbon monoxide and hydrogen at high temperature and pressure. *9.2*

$$CO(g) + 2H_2(g) \longrightarrow CH_3OH(g)$$

a. How many moles of each reactant are needed to produce 3.60×10^2 g CH_3OH?

b. Calculate the number of grams of each reactant needed to produce 4.00 mol CH_3OH.

c. How many grams of hydrogen are necessary to react with 2.85 mol CO?

39. The reaction of fluorine with ammonia produces dinitrogen tetrafluoride and hydrogen fluoride. *9.2*

$$5F_2(g) + 2NH_3(g) \longrightarrow N_2F_4(g) + 6HF(g)$$

a. If you have 66.6 g NH_3, how many grams of F_2 are required for complete reaction?

b. How many grams of NH_3 are required to produce 4.65 g HF?

c. How many grams of N_2F_4 can be produced from 225 g F_2?

40. What information about a chemical reaction is derived from the coefficients in a balanced equation? *9.2*

41. Lithium nitride reacts with water to form ammonia and aqueous lithium hydroxide. *9.2*

$$Li_3N(s) + 3H_2O(l) \longrightarrow NH_3(g) + 3LiOH(aq)$$

a. What mass of water is needed to react with 32.9 g Li_3N?

b. When the above reaction takes place, how many molecules of NH_3 are produced?

c. Calculate the number of grams of Li_3N that must be added to an excess of water to produce 15.0 L NH_3 (at STP).

42. What is the significance of the limiting reagent in a chemical process? What happens to the amount of any reagent that is present in an excess? *9.3*

43. How would you identify a limiting reagent in a chemical reaction? *9.3*

44. For each balanced equation, identify the limiting reagent for the given combination of reactants. *9.3*

a. $\underset{3.6 \text{ mol}}{2Al} + \underset{5.3 \text{ mol}}{3Cl_2} \longrightarrow 2AlCl_3$

b. $\underset{6.4 \text{ mol}}{2H_2} + \underset{3.4 \text{ mol}}{O_2} \longrightarrow 2H_2O$

c. $\underset{0.48 \text{ mol}}{2P_2O_5} + \underset{1.52 \text{ mol}}{6H_2O} \longrightarrow 4H_3PO_4$

d. $\underset{14.5 \text{ mol}}{4P} + \underset{18.0 \text{ mol}}{5O_2} \longrightarrow 2P_2O_5$

45. For each reaction in Problem 44, calculate the number of moles of product formed. *9.3*

46. For each reaction in Problem 44, calculate the number of moles of excess reagent remaining after the reaction. *9.3*

47. Heating an ore of antimony (Sb_2S_3) in the presence of iron gives the element antimony and iron(II) sulfide.

$$Sb_2S_3(s) + 3Fe(s) \longrightarrow 2Sb(s) + 3FeS(s)$$

When 15.0 g Sb_2S_3 reacts with an excess of Fe, 9.84 g Sb is produced. What is the percent yield of this reaction? *9.3*

48. In an experiment, varying masses of sodium metal are reacted with a fixed initial mass of chlorine gas. The amounts of sodium used and the amounts of sodium chloride formed are shown on the following graph. *9.3*

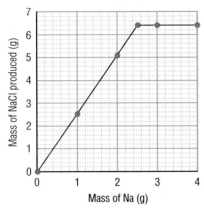

a. Explain the general shape of the graph.

b. Estimate the amount of chlorine gas used in this experiment at the point where the curve becomes horizontal.

49. What does the percent yield of a chemical reaction measure? *9.3*

50. The manufacture of compound F requires five separate chemical reactions. The initial reactant, compound A, is converted to compound B, compound B is converted to compound C, and so forth. The diagram below summarizes the stepwise manufacture of compound F, including the percent yield for each step. Provide the missing quantities or missing percent yields. Assume that the reactant and product in each step react in a one-to-one mole ratio. *9.3*

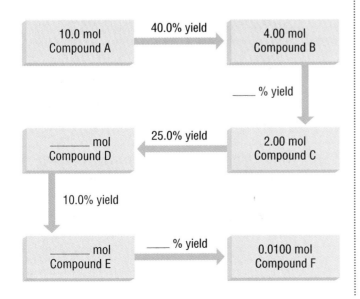

CONCEPT MASTERY

51. Calcium carbonate reacts with phosphoric acid to produce calcium phosphate, carbon dioxide, and water.

$$3CaCO_3(s) + 2H_3PO_4(aq) \longrightarrow$$
$$Ca_3(PO_4)_2(aq) + 3CO_2(g) + 3H_2O(l)$$

a. How many grams of phosphoric acid react with excess calcium carbonate to produce 3.74 g $Ca_3(PO_4)_2$?

b. Calculate the number of grams of CO_2 formed when 0.773 g H_2O is produced.

52. Nitric acid and zinc react to form zinc nitrate, ammonium nitrate, and water.

$$4Zn(s) + 10HNO_3(aq) \longrightarrow$$
$$4Zn(NO_3)_2(aq) + NH_4NO_3(aq) + 3H_2O(l)$$

a. How many atoms of zinc react with 1.49 g HNO_3?

b. Calculate the number of grams of zinc that must react with an excess of HNO_3 to form 29.1 g NH_4NO_3.

53. Hydrazine (N_2H_4) is used as rocket fuel. It reacts with oxygen to form nitrogen and water.

$$N_2H_4(l) + O_2(g) \longrightarrow N_2(g) + 2H_2O(g)$$

a. How many liters of N_2 (at STP) form when 1.0 kg N_2H_4 reacts with 1.0 kg O_2?

b. How many grams of the excess reagent remain after the reaction?

54. When 50.0 g of silicon dioxide is heated with an excess of carbon, 32.2 g of silicon carbide is produced.

$$SiO_2(s) + 3C(s) \longrightarrow SiC(s) + 2CO(g)$$

a. What is the percent yield of this reaction?

b. How many grams of CO gas are made?

55. If the reaction below proceeds with a 96.8% yield, how many kilograms of $CaSO_4$ are formed when 5.24 kg SO_2 reacts with an excess of $CaCO_3$ and O_2?

$$2CaCO_3(s) + 2SO_2(g) + O_2(g) \longrightarrow$$
$$2CaSO_4(s) + 2CO_2(g)$$

56. Ammonium nitrate will decompose explosively at high temperatures to form nitrogen, oxygen, and water vapor.

$$2NH_4NO_3(s) \longrightarrow 2N_2(g) + 4H_2O(g) + O_2(g)$$

What is the total number of liters of gas formed when 228 g NH_4NO_3 is decomposed? (Assume STP.)

57. Choose the term that completes the second relationship.

    a. equation:coefficients   balance:_____

      (1) moles   (3) weight

      (2) standard masses   (4) atoms

    b. actual:theoretical   experimental:_____

      (1) excess   (3) real

      (2) limiting   (4) calculated

58. Given a certain quantity of reactant, you calculate that a particular reaction should produce 55 g of a product. When you perform the reaction, you find that you have produced 63 g of product. What is your percent yield? What could have caused a percent yield greater than 100%?

59. Would the law of conservation of mass hold in a net ionic equation? Explain.

60. A bicycle-built-for-three has a frame, two wheels, six pedals, and three seats. The balanced equation for this bicycle is

$$F + 2W + 6P + 3S \longrightarrow FW_2P_6S_3$$

How many of each part are needed to make 29 bicycles-built-for-three?

    a. frames   **b.** wheels   **c.** pedals   **d.** seats

CUMULATIVE REVIEW

61. Write a balanced chemical equation for each reaction.

    a. When heated, lead(II) nitrate decomposes to form lead(II) oxide, nitrogen dioxide, and molecular oxygen.

    b. The complete combustion of isopropyl alcohol (C_3H_7OH) produces carbon dioxide and water vapor.

    c. When a mixture of aluminum and iron(II) oxide is heated, metallic iron and aluminum oxide are produced.

62. How many grams of beryllium are in 147 g of the mineral beryl ($Be_3Al_2Si_6O_{18}$)?

63. Balance each equation.

    a. $Ba(NO_3)_2(aq) + Na_2SO_4(aq) \longrightarrow$
                             $BaSO_4(s) + NaNO_3(aq)$

    b. $AlCl_3(aq) + AgNO_3(aq) \longrightarrow$
                             $AgCl(s) + Al(NO_3)_3(aq)$

    c. $H_2SO_4(aq) + Mg(OH)_2(aq) \longrightarrow$
                             $MgSO_4(aq) + H_2O(l)$

64. Write a net ionic equation for each reaction in Problem 63.

65. Identify the spectator ions in each reaction in Problem 63.

66. How many electrons, protons, and neutrons are in an atom of each isotope?

    a. titanium-47   **c.** oxygen-18

    b. tin-120   **d.** magnesium-26

67. What is the mass, in grams, of a molecule of benzene (C_6H_6)?

68. Write the formula for each compound.

    a. aluminum carbonate

    b. silicon dioxide

    c. potassium sulfide

    d. manganese(II) chromate

    e. sodium bromide

69. What is the molecular formula of oxalic acid, molar mass 90 g/mol? Its percent composition is 26.7% C, 2.2% H, and 71.1% O.

CONCEPT CHALLENGE

70. A car gets 9.2 kilometers to a liter of gasoline. Assuming that gasoline is 100% octane (C_8H_{18}), which has a specific gravity of 0.69, how many liters of air (21% oxygen by volume at STP) will be required to burn the gasoline for a 1250-km trip? Assume complete combustion.

71. Ethyl alcohol (C_2H_5OH) can be produced by the fermentation of glucose ($C_6H_{12}O_6$). If it takes 5.0 h to produce 8.0 kg of alcohol, how many days will it take to consume 1.0×10^3 kg of glucose? (An enzyme is used.)

$$C_6H_{12}O_6 \xrightarrow{enzyme} 2C_2H_5OH + 2CO_2$$

72. A 1004.0-g sample of $CaCO_3$ that is 95.0% pure gives 225 L CO_2 at STP when reacted with an excess of hydrochloric acid.

$$CaCO_3 + 2HCl \longrightarrow CaCl_2 + CO_2 + H_2O$$

What is the density (in g/L) of the CO_2?

73. The white limestone cliffs of Dover, England, contain a large percentage of calcium carbonate ($CaCO_3$). A sample of limestone weighing 84.4 g reacts with an excess of hydrochloric acid to form calcium chloride.

$$CaCO_3 + 2HCl \longrightarrow CaCl_2 + H_2O + CO_2$$

The mass of calcium chloride formed is 81.8 g. What is the percentage of calcium carbonate in the limestone?

Select the choice that best answers each question or completes each statement.

1. Nitric acid is formed by the reaction of nitrogen dioxide with water.

   $$3NO_2(g) + H_2O(l) \longrightarrow NO(g) + 2HNO_3(aq)$$

   How many mol of water are needed to react with 8.4 mol NO_2?
   a. 2.8 mol   c. 8.4 mol
   b. 3.0 mol   d. 25 mol

2. Phosphorus trifluoride is formed from its elements.

   $$P_4(s) + 6F_2(g) \longrightarrow 4PF_3(g)$$

   How many grams of fluorine are needed to react with 6.20 g of phosphorus?
   a. 2.85 g   c. 11.4 g
   b. 5.70 g   d. 37.2 g

3. Which of the following are needed to calculate the percent yield of a reaction?
   I. theoretical yield
   II. excess yield
   III. actual yield
   a. I only
   b. I and II only
   c. I and III only
   d. II and III only
   e. I, II, and III

4. According to the balanced equation for the combustion of ethane, C_2H_6,
   $$2C_2H_6(g) + 7O_2(g) \longrightarrow 4CO_2(g) + 6H_2O(l),$$
   for every molecule of ethane that reacts,
   a. 2 molecules of carbon dioxide are produced.
   b. 3 molecules of water are produced.
   c. Both (a) and (b) are correct.
   d. Neither (a) nor (b) is correct.

5. Magnesium nitride is formed in the reaction of magnesium metal with nitrogen gas.
   $$3Mg(s) + N_2(g) \longrightarrow Mg_3N_2(s)$$
   The reaction of 4.0 mol of nitrogen with 6.0 mol of magnesium produces
   a. 2.0 mol of Mg_3N_2 and 2.0 mol of excess N_2.
   b. 4.0 mol of Mg_3N_2 and 1.0 mol of excess Mg.
   c. 6.0 mol of Mg_3N_2 and 3.0 mol of excess N_2.
   d. no product because the reactants are not in the correct mole ratio.

Questions 6 and 7 involve the reaction between diatomic element P and diatomic element Q to form the compound P_3Q.

6. Write a balanced equation for the reaction between element P and element Q.

7. Based on the atomic windows below, identify the limiting reagent.

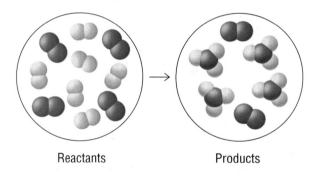

Reactants   Products

For each question there are two statements. Decide whether each statement is true or false. Then decide whether Statement II is a correct explanation for Statement I.

Statement I		Statement II
8. Every stoichiometry calculation uses a balanced equation.	BECAUSE	Every chemical reaction obeys the law of conservation of mass.
9. A percent yield is always greater than 0% and less than 100%.	BECAUSE	The actual yield in a reaction is never more than the theoretical yield.
10. The amount of the limiting reagent left after a reaction is zero.	BECAUSE	The limiting reagent is completely used up in a reaction.
11. The coefficients in a balanced equation represent the relative masses of the reactants and products.	BECAUSE	The mass of the reactants must equal the mass of the products in a chemical reaction.
12. A mole ratio is always written with the larger number in the numerator.	BECAUSE	A mole ratio will always be greater than one.

Stoichiometry **265**

Elk experience three states of water at Yellowstone National Park.

FEATURES

DISCOVER IT!
Observing Gas Pressure

SMALL-SCALE LAB
Kinetic Theory in Action

MINI LAB
Sublimation

CHEMath
Making and Interpreting Graphs

CHEMISTRY SERVING ...
THE ENVIRONMENT
Gases Can Alter Global Temperature

CHEMISTRY IN CAREERS
Climatologist

LINK TO MEDICINE
Cryogenics

LINK TO FOOD SCIENCE
Freeze-Drying

Stay current with **SCIENCE NEWS**
Find out more about states of matter:
www.phschool.com

DISCOVER IT! OBSERVING GAS PRESSURE

You need an index card, a graduated cylinder, water, and a small glass with a smooth, even rim.

1. Fill the glass to its rim with water.

2. Place the index card on top of the glass.

3. Working over a sink, use one hand to press the index card firmly to the top of the glass. Then quickly invert the glass, keeping your hand in place.

4. Remove your hand from the index card.

What did you observe when you removed your hand? Measure the volume of water in the glass. How many grams of water are in the glass? (Remember that 1 mL H_2O = 1 g H_2O.) What keeps the water inside the glass? As you read about the properties of gases in this chapter, re-examine this activity and see if you can improve your explanation of what occurred.

THE NATURE OF GASES

You are walking your dog in the woods, enjoying the great outdoors. Suddenly your dog begins to bark at what you believe is a black cat. But before you realize what it actually is, the damage is done. It's too late; the skunk has released its spray! Within seconds you smell that all-too recognizable smell. **How do the gaseous odor molecules travel from one place to another?**

objectives
▶ Describe the motion of gas particles according to the kinetic theory
▶ Interpret gas pressure in terms of kinetic theory

key terms
▶ kinetic energy
▶ kinetic theory
▶ gas pressure
▶ vacuum
▶ atmospheric pressure
▶ barometers
▶ pascal (Pa)
▶ standard atmosphere (atm)

Kinetic Theory

An ice cube is solid water; tap water is liquid water; and steam is gaseous water. Most substances commonly exist in only one of the three states of matter: solid, liquid, or gas. However, a substance in one state may change to another state with a change in temperature. You know that when cooled, water freezes to become ice, and steam condenses to form water. You also know that soon after you put on perfume, anyone nearby will be able to smell it. Obviously, the molecules of the perfume have moved through the air. How do you account for these behaviors? A model called the kinetic theory will help you find the answer.

The word kinetic refers to motion. The energy an object has because of its motion is called **kinetic energy.** The **kinetic theory** states that the tiny particles in all forms of matter are in constant motion. The following are the basic assumptions of the kinetic theory as it applies to gases.

1. A gas is composed of particles, usually molecules or atoms. These particles are considered to be small, hard spheres that have insignificant volume and are relatively far apart from one another. Between the particles there is empty space. No attractive or repulsive forces exist between the particles.

2. The particles in a gas move rapidly in constant random motion. They travel in straight paths and move independently of each other. As a result, gases fill their containers regardless of the shape and volume of the containers; uncontained gases diffuse into space without limit. The gas particles change direction only when they rebound from collisions with one another or with other objects. Measurements indicate that the average speed of oxygen molecules in air at 20 °C is an amazing 1700 km/h! At these high speeds, the odor molecules from a hot cheese pizza in Washington, D.C., should reach Mexico City in about 106 minutes. That does not happen, however, because the odor molecules are constantly striking molecules of air and rebounding in other directions. Their path of uninterrupted travel in a straight line is very short. The aimless path the gas molecules take is called a random walk. **Figure 10.1** on the following page illustrates a typical random walk.

3. All collisions are perfectly elastic. This means that during collisions kinetic energy is transferred without loss from one particle to another, and the total kinetic energy remains constant.

As you will learn next, the kinetic theory of gases is very helpful in explaining gas pressure.

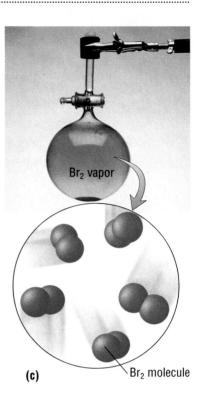

Figure 10.1

(a) Gas particles move randomly. They are constantly colliding with one another and with the walls of their containers. The collisions cause the particles to change direction frequently. (b) Every gas particle travels in a straight-line path until it collides with another particle, object, or wall. (c) A molecular view of a gas shows that the particles are relatively far apart and fill all available space. In this example, the gas is bromine vapor (Br_2).

Gas Pressure

Moving bodies exert forces when they collide with other bodies. Although a single gas particle is a moving body, the force it exerts is extremely small. Yet it is not hard to imagine that simultaneous collisions involving many such particles would produce a measurable force on an object. Gas pressure is the result of simultaneous collisions of billions of gas particles with an object. **Gas pressure** is defined as the force exerted by a gas per unit surface area of an object. If there are no gas particles present, there cannot be collisions, and there is consequently no pressure. Such an empty space, with no particles and no pressure, is called a **vacuum.**

Air exerts pressure on Earth because gravity holds air molecules in Earth's atmosphere. **Atmospheric pressure** results from the collisions of air molecules with objects. Atmospheric pressure decreases as you climb a mountain because the air layer around Earth thins out as elevation increases. **Barometers** are devices commonly used to measure atmospheric pressure. This pressure is dependent on weather.

The SI unit of pressure is the **pascal (Pa).** Atmospheric pressure at sea level is about 101.3 kilopascals (kPa). Two older units of pressure are millimeters of mercury (mm Hg) and atmospheres (atm). The origin of these units is the early use of mercury barometers similar to the one shown in **Figure 10.2.** Such a barometer was a straight glass tube filled with mercury and closed at one end. The tube was placed in a dish of mercury so that the open end was below the surface of mercury in the dish. The height of mercury in the tube depended on the pressure created by collisions of air molecules with the surface of the mercury in the dish. At sea level, this pressure is sufficient to support a mercury column about 760 mm high. One **standard atmosphere (atm)** is the pressure required to support 760 mm of mercury in a mercury barometer at 25 °C. That is, 1 atm = 760 mm Hg = 101.3 kPa.

Sea level   **On top of Mount Everest**

Figure 10.2

Typical atmospheric pressure at sea level in fair weather is 1 atm, which equals 760 mm Hg, or 101.3 kPa. Such atmospheric pressure supports a 760-mm column of mercury (101.3 kPa). On top of Mount Everest (at an altitude of 9000 m), the air exerts only enough pressure to support a 253-mm column of mercury. Express this pressure in kilopascals.

Many modern barometers do not contain mercury and are called aneroid barometers. In these devices, atmospheric pressure is related to the number of collisions of air molecules with a sensitive metal diaphragm. The diaphragm controls the movement of a pointer, which in turn indicates the pressure reading.

In the case of gases, it is important to be able to relate measured values to standards. Standard conditions are defined as a temperature of 0 °C and a pressure of 101.3 kPa, or 1 atm. This set of conditions is called standard temperature and pressure, or STP. What is standard temperature expressed on the Kelvin temperature scale?

Kinetic Energy and Kelvin Temperature

What happens when a substance is heated? The particles of the substance absorb energy, some of which is stored within the particles. This stored portion of the energy, or potential energy, does not raise the temperature of the

Figure 10.3

The standard lab barometer is still commonly used (left). An aneroid barometer (right) does not contain mercury.

CHEMath

MAKING AND INTERPRETING GRAPHS

A graph is used to display relationships or data visually. You will encounter many graphs in your study of chemistry. Graphs are also used in economics, physics, social studies, and other fields. Your local newspaper probably includes several graphs each week.

In a graph, the horizontal axis (or x-axis) represents the *independent variable* and the vertical axis (or y-axis) represents the *dependent variable*. For example, in the graph shown below, the independent variable is temperature, and the dependent variable is vapor pressure. So, this graph shows vapor pressure vs. temperature. When stating a relationship, you should always give the dependent variable first.

Vapor Pressure of Ethanol vs. Temperature

The *range* and *interval* for each axis determine the appearance of the graph. The range is given by the minimum and maximum values represented in the graph, and the interval is the distance between grid lines or tick marks. In the graph shown, the temperature range is 0 °C to 100 °C, and the temperature interval is 5 °C.

To make a graph, first choose appropriate ranges and scales. Choose the range for each axis so that all important data is included. The intervals should be convenient numbers (such as 1, 5, or 20) that result in an easy-to-read graph. After you draw and label the axes, plot the data. Each data point should be aligned with the correct values on the axes. When appropriate, connect the data with a smooth curve.

In Section 10.4, you will learn about the *phase diagram* for a substance (see Figure 10.18). A phase diagram is a pressure vs. temperature graph that has been divided into regions for each of the solid, liquid, and vapor phases. For a given pressure and temperature, you can determine from the graph if the substance is a solid, a liquid, or a gas.

Example 1

Refer to the graph above. Give the range and interval for vapor pressure. Then find the boiling point of ethanol when the atmospheric pressure is 60 kPa.

The vertical axis includes values from 0 kPa to 225 kPa with the grid lines 25 kPa apart. So, the vapor pressure range is 0 kPa to 225 kPa and the vapor pressure interval is 25 kPa.

To find the boiling point of ethanol when the atmospheric pressure is 60 kPa, notice that the curve appears to include the point (65 °C, 60 kPa). Therefore, the boiling point is about 65 °C at 60 kPa.

Practice Problems

Prepare for upcoming problems in this chapter by solving the following problems.

A. For the graph in Figure 10.11, what are the range and interval for temperature?

B. Refer to the graph above. Find the boiling point of ethanol when the atmospheric pressure is 90 kPa.

C. Refer to the graph above. What is the vapor pressure of ethanol when its temperature is 50 °C?

D. The table gives the vapor pressure of isopropyl alcohol (rubbing alcohol) at various temperatures. Graph the data. Connect the data points using a smooth curve.

Temperature (°C)	0	25	50	75	100	125
Vapor pressure (kPa)	1.11	6.02	23.9	75.3	198	452

Sample Problem 10-1

A gas is at a pressure of 1.50 atm. Convert this pressure to
   a. kilopascals.   **b.** millimeters of mercury.

1. **ANALYZE** *List the knowns and the unknowns.*

   Knowns:
   - pressure = 1.50 atm
   - 1 atm = 101.3 kPa
   - 1 atm = 760 mm Hg

   Unknowns:
   a. pressure = ? kPa
   b. pressure = ? mm Hg

   The given pressure is converted into the desired unit by multiplying by the proper conversion factor.

2. **CALCULATE** *Solve for the unknowns.*

   a. For the conversion atm $\longrightarrow$ kPa, the conversion factor is $\dfrac{101.3 \text{ kPa}}{1 \text{ atm}}$.

   $$1.50 \text{ atm} \times \frac{101.3 \text{ kPa}}{1 \text{ atm}} = 151.95 \text{ kPa} = 1.52 \times 10^2 \text{ kPa}$$

   b. For the conversion atm $\longrightarrow$ mm Hg, the conversion factor is $\dfrac{760 \text{ mm Hg}}{1 \text{ atm}}$.

   $$1.50 \text{ atm} \times \frac{760 \text{ mm Hg}}{1 \text{ atm}} = 1140 \text{ mm Hg} = 1.14 \times 10^3 \text{ mm Hg}$$

3. **EVALUATE** *Do the results make sense?*

   Because the conversion factor for calculating mm Hg is larger than the one for kPa, it makes sense that the value expressed in mm Hg is larger than the value in kPa. In each case the given unit cancels, and the answer has the desired unit. Each answer has the three significant figures required.

Practice Problems

1. What pressure, in kilopascals and in atmospheres, does a gas exert at 385 mm Hg?
2. The pressure at the top of Mount Everest is 33.7 kPa. Is that pressure greater or less than 0.25 atm?

Chem ASAP!

Problem-Solving 1
Solve Problem 1 with the help of an interactive guided tutorial.

substance. The remaining absorbed energy speeds up the particles—that is, increases their average kinetic energy—which results in an increase in temperature. The particles in any collection of atoms or molecules at a given temperature have a wide range of kinetic energies, from very low to very high. Most of the particles have kinetic energies somewhere in the middle of this range. Therefore average kinetic energy is used when discussing the kinetic energy of a collection of particles in a substance. **Figure 10.4** on the following page shows the distribution of kinetic energies of gas particles at two different temperatures. Notice that at the higher temperature there is a wider range of kinetic energies.

An increase in the average kinetic energy of particles causes the temperature of a substance to rise. As a substance cools, the particles tend to move more slowly, and their average kinetic energy declines. You could reasonably expect the particles of all substances to stop moving at some very low temperature. The particles would have no kinetic energy at that temperature because they would have no motion. Absolute zero (0 K, or

Figure 10.4

The blue curve shows the kinetic energy distribution of a typical collection of molecules at a fairly low temperature, such as the water molecules in iced tea. Notice that most molecules have intermediate energies. The red curve shows the energy distribution of molecules at a higher temperature, such as the water molecules in hot tea. How do the average kinetic energies of the two liquids compare?

Chem ASAP!

Animation 9
Observe particles in motion and discover the connection between temperature and kinetic energy.

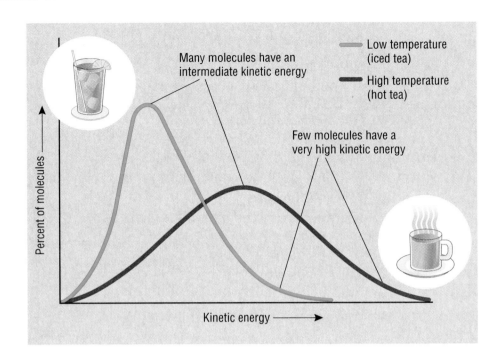

Low temperature (iced tea)

High temperature (hot tea)

Many molecules have an intermediate kinetic energy

Few molecules have a very high kinetic energy

Percent of molecules

Kinetic energy

LINK TO MEDICINE

Cryogenics

Cryogenics is the science of producing very low temperatures and studying the behavior of matter at such temperatures. Biological reactions slow down or even stop at very low temperatures. Biologists use this fact to study reactions more easily. In medicine, some tissues can be removed from the body and preserved by rapid freezing. They can later be used when thawed. Blood and cartilage are examples of such materials. Doctors also perform cryosurgery by freezing tissue instead of cutting it. Cryosurgery minimizes bleeding during operations, and healing is rapid with minimal scarring.

−273.15 °C) is the temperature at which the motion of particles theoretically ceases. Absolute zero has never been produced in the laboratory, although temperatures of about 0.000 001 K have been achieved. Would you expect to find negative temperatures on the Kelvin temperature scale?

The Kelvin temperature scale reflects the relationship between temperature and average kinetic energy. The Kelvin temperature of a substance is directly proportional to the average kinetic energy of the particles of the substance. For example, the particles in helium gas at 200 K have twice the average kinetic energy as the particles in helium gas at 100 K. As you will see later in this chapter, the effects of temperature on particle motion in liquids and solids are more complex than in gases. Nevertheless, at any given temperature the particles of all substances, regardless of physical state, have the same average kinetic energy.

section review 10.1

3. According to the assumptions of kinetic theory, how do the particles in a gas move?

4. Use kinetic theory to explain what causes gas pressure.

5. Express the pressure 545 mm Hg in kilopascals.

6. How can you raise the average kinetic energy of the water molecules in a glass of water?

7. A cylinder of oxygen gas is cooled from 300 K (27 °C) to 150 K (−123 °C). By what factor does the average kinetic energy of the oxygen molecules in the cylinder decrease?

 Chem ASAP! Assessment 10.1 Check your understanding of the important ideas and concepts in Section 10.1.

KINETIC THEORY IN ACTION

SAFETY

Wear safety glasses and follow the standard safety procedures as outlined on page 18.

PURPOSE

To observe color changes in the chemical reactions of gases and to interpret these changes in terms of kinetic theory.

MATERIALS

- clear plastic cup or Petri dish
- pencil
- paper
- ruler
- cotton swab
- medicine dropper
- reaction surface
- chemicals shown in Figure A and KI, $NaNO_2$, NH_4Cl, and NaOH

PROCEDURE

Use a clear plastic cup or Petri dish as a template to draw a large circle, as shown in Figure A. Place a reaction surface over the grid and add small drops of BTB (bromthymol blue) in the pattern shown by the small circles. Be sure the drops do not touch one another. Mix one drop each of HCl and $NaHSO_3$ in the center of the pattern. Place a clear plastic cup or Petri dish over the grid and observe what happens. Do not clean up until after you complete any assigned YOU'RE THE CHEMIST activities.

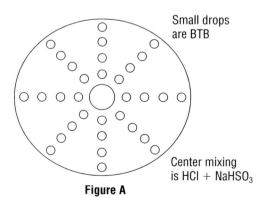

Small drops are BTB

Center mixing is HCl + $NaHSO_3$

Figure A

ANALYSIS

Using your experimental data, record the answers to the following questions below your data table.

1. Describe in detail the changes you observed in the drops of BTB over time. Draw pictures to illustrate the changes.

2. Draw a series of pictures showing how one of the BTB drops might look over time if you could view the drop from the side.

3. The BTB changed even though you added nothing to it. If the mixture in the center circle produced a gas, would this explain the change in the drops of BTB? Use kinetic theory to explain your answer.

4. Translate the following word equation into a balanced chemical equation: Sodium hydrogen sulfite reacts with hydrochloric acid to produce sulfur dioxide gas, water, and sodium chloride.

YOU'RE THE CHEMIST

The following small-scale activities allow you to develop your own procedures and analyze the results.

1. **Analyze It!** Carefully absorb the center mixture of the original experiment onto a cotton swab and replace it with one drop of NaOH and one drop of NH_4Cl. What happens? Explain in terms of kinetic theory. Ammonium chloride reacts with sodium hydroxide to produce ammonia gas, water, and sodium chloride. Write and balance a chemical equation to describe this reaction.

2. **Design It!** Design an experiment to observe the effect of the size of the BTB drops on the rate at which they change. Explain your results in terms of kinetic theory.

3. **Analyze It!** Repeat the original experiment, except use KI in place of BTB and mix sodium nitrite ($NaNO_2$) with hydrochloric acid (HCl) at the center. Record your results. Write and balance an equation: Sodium nitrite reacts with hydrochloric acid to produce nitrogen monoxide gas, water, sodium nitrate, and sodium chloride.

THE NATURE OF LIQUIDS

objectives
▶ Describe the nature of a liquid in terms of the attractive forces between the particles
▶ Differentiate between evaporation and boiling of a liquid, using kinetic theory

key terms
▶ vaporization
▶ evaporation
▶ vapor pressure
▶ boiling point
▶ normal boiling point

*T*he Kilauea volcano in Hawaii is the most active volcano in the world—it has been erupting for centuries. The hot lava oozes and flows, scorching everything in its path, occasionally including nearby houses. When the lava cools, it solidifies into rock. **What makes a liquid different from a solid?**

A Model for Liquids

You have just learned from the kinetic theory that gas pressure can be explained by assuming that gas particles have motion and that there is no attraction between the particles. The particles that make up liquids are also in motion, as **Figure 10.5** shows. Liquid particles are free to slide past one another. For that reason, both liquids and gases can flow, as you can see in **Figure 10.6.** However, the particles in a liquid are attracted to each other, while according to kinetic theory, those in a gas are not. The attractive forces between the molecules are called intermolecular forces.

The particles that make up liquids vibrate and spin while they move from place to place. All of these motions contribute to the average kinetic energy of the particles. Even so, most of the particles do not have enough kinetic energy to escape into the gaseous state. To do so, a particle must have sufficient kinetic energy to overcome the intermolecular forces that hold it together with the other particles. The intermolecular forces also reduce the amount of space between the particles in a liquid. Thus liquids are much more dense than gases. Increasing the pressure on a liquid has hardly any effect on its volume. The same is true of solids. For that reason, liquids and solids are known as condensed states of matter.

The interplay between the disruptive motions of particles and the attractive forces between them determines many of the physical properties of liquids. You will now explore two of these properties: vapor pressure and boiling point.

Figure 10.5

The particles in a liquid, such as the water in this lake, are close together but can move and slide around one another. The attractive forces between the particles generally prevent most of the particles from escaping the liquid and entering into the vapor state.

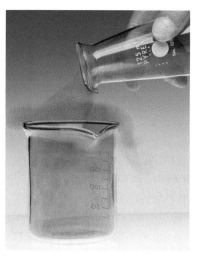

Figure 10.6
Both liquids and gases can flow. The liquid on the left is colored water. The gas on the right is bromine vapor. If a gas is denser than air, it can be poured from one container into another. These pictures were taken in a fume hood because bromine is toxic and corrosive. What will eventually happen to the gas in the uncovered beaker?

Evaporation

As you probably know from experience, water in an open vessel or a puddle eventually goes into the air. **See Figure 10.7a.** The conversion of a liquid to a gas or vapor is called **vaporization.** When such a conversion occurs at the surface of a liquid that is not boiling, the process is called **evaporation.** In evaporation, some molecules in the liquid break away and enter the gas or vapor state. Only those molecules of the liquid with a certain minimum kinetic energy can break away from the surface. Even some of the particles that do escape collide with air molecules and rebound into the liquid.

You may have noticed that a liquid evaporates faster when heated. This occurs because the added heat increases the average kinetic energy of the liquid's particles, enabling more of the particles to overcome the attractive forces keeping them in the liquid state. However, evaporation itself is a cooling process. The cooling occurs because the particles with the highest kinetic energy tend to escape first. The particles left in the liquid have a lower average kinetic energy than the particles that have escaped. Thus the liquid's temperature decreases. The process is similar to removing the fastest runner from a race. The remaining runners have a lower average speed.

Figure 10.7
(a) In an open container, water molecules evaporate from the liquid state and escape from the container. Equilibrium cannot be established in this system. (b) In a closed container, water molecules go into the vapor state, but they cannot escape from the system. They collect as a vapor above the liquid. A dynamic equilibrium between the water molecules in the vapor state and in the liquid state can be established.

<u>Chem ASAP!</u>
Animation 10
Observe the phenomenon of evaporation from a molecular perspective.

(a)   (b)

Figure 10.8

This sealed terrarium is in liquid–vapor equilibrium. The rate of vaporization of the liquid water equals the rate of condensation of the water vapor. Condensation appears on the inner surface of the glass.

You have observed the effects of evaporative cooling on hot days. When you perspire, water molecules in your perspiration absorb heat from your body and evaporate from your skin's surface. This evaporation leaves the remaining perspiration cooler. The perspiration that remains cools you further by absorbing more body heat. Can you relate this feeling to the chill you may possibly feel when getting out of a swimming pool on a warm, windy day?

The evaporation of a liquid in a closed container is somewhat different. **Figure 10.7b** on the previous page shows that no particles can escape into the outside air. When a partially filled container of liquid is sealed, some of the particles in the liquid vaporize. These particles collide with the walls of the sealed container and produce a **vapor pressure,** or a force due to the gas above the liquid. As time passes, the number of particles entering the vapor increases. Eventually, some of the particles will return to the liquid, or condense. The following equation illustrates the two opposing processes.

$$\text{Liquid} \underset{\text{condensation}}{\overset{\text{evaporation}}{\rightleftharpoons}} \text{Vapor (gas)}$$

After a time, the number of vapor particles condensing will equal the number of liquid particles vaporizing. The space in the container above the liquid is now saturated with vapor, and a dynamic equilibrium exists between the gas and the liquid. At the point of equilibrium,

Rate of evaporation of liquid = Rate of condensation of vapor

At equilibrium, the particles in the system continue to evaporate and condense, but there is no net change in the number of either liquid or vapor particles. The sealed terrarium in **Figure 10.8** is an example of a closed container at equilibrium. The moisture on the inner walls of the terrarium is a sign that equilibrium has been established. Particles that once evaporated are condensing, but other particles are evaporating to take their place. What would happen if the cover of the terrarium were punctured?

An increase in the temperature of a contained liquid increases the vapor pressure. This happens because the particles in the warmed liquid have increased kinetic energy. As a result, more of the particles will have the minimum kinetic energy necessary to escape the surface of the liquid. The particles escape the liquid and collide with the walls of the container at a greater frequency. **Table 10.1** gives the vapor pressures of some common liquids at various temperatures. The vapor pressure of a liquid can be determined by means of a device called a manometer.

Table 10.1

Vapor Pressures (kPa) of Several Substances at Various Temperatures						
	0 °C	20 °C	40 °C	60 °C	80 °C	100 °C
Water	0.61	2.33	7.37	19.92	47.34	101.33
Ethanol	1.63	5.85	18.04	47.02	108.34	225.75
Diethyl ether	24.70	58.96	122.80	230.65	399.11	647.87

12.2 mm Hg
= 1.63 kPa

Ethanol

Mercury

Ethanol at 0 °C

43.9 mm Hg
= 5.85 kPa

Ethanol

Mercury

Ethanol at room
temperature (20 °C)

Figure 10.9
*The height difference of
the mercury in the two arms
of the U-tube equals the vapor
pressure of the contained liquid
at that temperature. What
happens to the vapor pressure
as temperature increases?*

In a simple manometer, one end of a U-shaped glass tube containing mercury is attached to a container. The other end of the tube is open to the surrounding atmosphere. When the container is empty, the mercury levels on both sides of the U-tube are the same because both sides of the tube are at the same pressure. When a liquid is added to the container, the pressure in the container increases. The increase in pressure is due to the vapor pressure of the liquid. The vapor pressure of the liquid pushes the mercury on the container side of the U-tube; the levels of mercury in the U-tube are no longer the same. The vapor pressure of the liquid is thus equal to the difference in the levels of mercury. **Figure 10.9** illustrates the use of a manometer to determine the effect of temperature on the vapor pressure of a liquid.

Boiling Point

You know that the rate of evaporation of a liquid from an open container increases as heat is added. Heating allows larger numbers of particles at the liquid's surface to overcome the attractive forces keeping them in the liquid state. The remaining particles in the liquid move faster and faster as they absorb the heat that is being added. Consequently, their average kinetic energy increases. Therefore the temperature of the liquid increases. When the liquid is heated to a high enough temperature, many of the particles throughout the liquid have enough kinetic energy to vaporize. At that point, boiling (or vaporization throughout the liquid) occurs. The **boiling point** (bp) is the temperature at which the vapor pressure of the liquid is just equal to the external pressure. Bubbles of vapor form through-out the liquid, rise to the surface, and escape into the air as the liquid boils.

Sea Level

At 70 °C and 101.3 kPa, the atmospheric pressure at the surface of the liquid water is greater than the vapor pressure of the liquid. Bubbles of vapor cannot form in the liquid, and the liquid does not boil.

Sea Level

At the boiling point, the vapor pressure is equal to atmospheric pressure. Bubbles of vapor form in the liquid, and the liquid boils.

Atop Mount Everest

At high altitudes, the atmospheric pressure is lower than it is at sea level. Thus the liquid boils at a lower temperature.

Figure 10.10

A liquid boils when the vapor pressure of particles within the liquid equals the atmospheric pressure. What would happen to the boiling point of water at pressures above 101.3 kPa?

As you just learned, the boiling point is the temperature at which the vapor pressure of the liquid is just equal to the external pressure. Thus the boiling point of a liquid changes if the external pressure changes. **Figure 10.10** illustrates this point, using water as the example. Therefore the **normal boiling point** is defined as the boiling point of a liquid at a pressure of 101.3 kPa. **Table 10.2** shows the normal boiling points of various substances. It follows then that the normal boiling point decreases at lower pressures and increases at higher pressures. The vapor-pressure diagram of **Figure 10.11** illustrates this fact. At lower pressures, the boiling point decreases because the particles need less kinetic energy to escape the liquids. Similarly, at higher external pressures, a liquid's boiling point increases because the particles in the liquid need more kinetic energy to escape.

The normal boiling point of water is 100 °C. In Denver, however, water boils at about 95 °C. This is because Denver is 1600 m above sea level and has an average atmospheric pressure of only 85.3 kPa (or 640 mm Hg, or 0.84 atm). You may know about pressure cookers, which reduce cooking time. At the high pressure in the cooker, water boils well above 100 °C, so food cooks faster. Autoclaves, devices often used to sterilize medical instruments, operate in a similar way.

Table 10.2

The Normal Boiling Points of Several Common Substances	
Name and formula	Boiling point (°C)
Carbon disulfide (CS_2)	46.0
Chloroform ($CHCl_3$)	61.7
Ethanol (C_2H_6O)	78.5
Water (H_2O)	100.0

Figure 10.11
The intersection of a curve with the 101.3-kPa line indicates the normal boiling point of that substance. At about what temperature would ethanol boil in Denver, where the atmospheric pressure is 85.3 kPa?

Chem ASAP!

Animation 11
Relate vapor pressure and boiling point to intermolecular attractive forces.

Boiling is a cooling process similar to evaporation. In boiling, as in evaporation, the particles with the highest kinetic energy escape first when the liquid is at the boiling point. Turning off the source of external heat drops the liquid's temperature below its boiling point. Supplying more heat allows more particles to acquire enough kinetic energy to escape. However, the temperature of the boiling liquid never rises above its boiling point. If heat is supplied at a greater rate, the liquid only boils faster. The vapor produced is at the same temperature as that of the boiling liquid. It is important to note that although the vapor has the same kinetic energy, its potential (or stored energy) is much higher. Using this fact, which type of burn do you think is more severe: one from boiling water or one from an equal mass of steam at the same temperature?

section review 10.2

8. Describe the nature of liquids. Refer to the role of attractive forces in your answer.

9. Use kinetic theory to explain the differences between the particles in a gas and those in a liquid.

10. Use kinetic theory to explain the difference between evaporation and boiling of a liquid.

11. Use **Figure 10.11** to determine the boiling point of each liquid.

  a. ethanoic acid at 200 mm Hg

  b. chloroform at 600 mm Hg

  c. ethanol at 400 mm Hg

12. Explain why the boiling point of a liquid varies with atmospheric pressure.

13. Why does evaporation lower the temperature of a liquid?

portfolio project

Look for high-altitude cooking directions on packages of cake, brownie, or muffin mixes. Check the Internet for additional tips on high-altitude cooking.

 Chem ASAP! Assessment 10.2 Check your understanding of the important ideas and concepts in Section 10.2.

THE NATURE OF SOLIDS

▶ Describe how the degree of organization of particles distinguishes solids from gases and liquids

▶ Distinguish between a crystal lattice and a unit cell

▶ Explain how allotropes of an element differ

key terms

▶ melting point
▶ crystal
▶ unit cell
▶ allotropes
▶ amorphous solids
▶ glasses

*I*magine carbon atoms arranged in the shape of a soccer ball. Just such a structure, the buckminsterfullerene or buckyball, was discovered in 1985. Scientists are currently researching ways to make use of the buckyball's unique properties. Diamonds are also made of carbon atoms, and they too have unique properties that make them valuable for a variety of applications. **How many different molecular forms of carbon are there, and what are these forms called?**

A Model for Solids

The particles in liquids are relatively free to move. The particles in solids, however, are not, as **Figure 10.12** shows. Particles in a solid tend to vibrate about fixed points, rather than sliding from place to place. In most solids the particles are packed against one another in a highly organized pattern. Solids tend to be dense and incompressible. Because of the fixed positions about which their particles vibrate, solids do not flow to take the shape of their containers.

When you heat a solid, its particles vibrate more rapidly as their kinetic energy increases. The organization of particles within the solid breaks down and eventually the solid melts. The **melting point** (mp) is the temperature at which a solid turns into a liquid. At this temperature, the disruptive vibrations of the particles are strong enough to overcome the interactions that hold them in fixed positions. The melting process can be reversed by cooling the liquid so it freezes. The freezing of a liquid is thus the reverse of melting the corresponding solid. The melting and freezing points of a substance are at the same temperature. At that temperature, the liquid and solid substance are in equilibrium with each other.

$$\text{Solid} \underset{\text{freezing}}{\overset{\text{melting}}{\rightleftharpoons}} \text{Liquid}$$

In general, ionic solids have high melting points. This is because relatively strong forces hold them together. Sodium chloride, an ionic compound, has a rather high melting point of 801 °C. By contrast, molecular solids have relatively low melting points. For example, hydrogen chloride, a molecular compound, melts at −112 °C. What is the freezing point of hydrogen chloride? Not all solids melt, however. Wood and cane sugar, for example, decompose when heated.

Figure 10.12

The particles in a solid vibrate about fixed points. A solid melts when its temperature is raised to a level at which the vibrations of the particles become so intense that they disrupt the ordered structure.

Crystal Structure and Unit Cells

Most solid substances are crystalline. In a **crystal,** such as the one shown in **Figure 10.13,** the atoms, ions, or molecules that make up the solid substance are arranged in an orderly, repeating, three-dimensional pattern called the crystal lattice. All crystals have a regular shape. The shape of a crystal reflects the arrangement of the particles within the solid. The type of bonding that exists between the atoms determines the melting points of crystals.

Figure 10.13
The regular shape of a sodium chloride crystal (left) can be explained by the arrangement of sodium ions and chloride ions within the crystal (right). The ions are close together, packed in a regular array, and move very little relative to each other. What happens to the arrangement of the particles if the solid is heated sufficiently?

A crystal has sides, or faces. The angles at which the faces of a crystal intersect are always the same for a given substance and are characteristic of that substance. Crystals are classified into seven groups, or crystal systems that have the characteristic shapes shown in **Figure 10.14.** The seven crystal systems differ in terms of the angles between the faces and in the number of edges of equal length on each face.

Figure 10.14
Crystals are classified into the seven crystal systems shown here.

galena
$a = b = c$
$\alpha = \beta = \gamma = 90°$
Cubic

zircon
$a = b \neq c$
$\alpha = \beta = \gamma = 90°$
Tetragonal

topaz
$a \neq b \neq c$
$\alpha = \beta = \gamma = 90°$
Orthorhombic

gypsum
$a \neq b \neq c$
$\beta = \gamma = 90° \neq \alpha$
Monoclinic

amazonite
$a \neq b \neq c$
$\alpha \neq \beta \neq \gamma \neq 90°$
Triclinic

tourmaline
$a = b \neq c$
$\alpha = \beta = 90°, \gamma = 120°$
Hexagonal

calcite
$a = b = c$
$\alpha = \beta = \gamma \neq 90°$
Rhombohedral

The shape of a crystal depends on the arrangement of the particles within it. The smallest group of particles within a crystal that retains the geometric shape of the crystal is known as a **unit cell**. A crystal lattice is a repeating array of any one of fourteen kinds of unit cells. Each crystal system has from one to four types of unit cells that can be associated with that crystal system. **Figure 10.15** shows the three kinds of unit cells that can make up a cubic crystal system.

In a **simple cubic** unit cell, the atoms or ions are arranged at the corners of an imaginary cube.

In a **body-centered cubic** unit cell, the atoms or ions are at the corners and in the center of an imaginary cube.

In a **face-centered cubic** unit cell, the atoms or ions are in the center of each face of the imaginary cube (but there is no atom or ion at the center).

Figure 10.15

The top row shows spheres representing the atoms or ions of three different cubic lattices. The bottom row illustrates the cubic unit cells for these lattices.

Some solid substances can exist in more than one form. A good example is the element carbon. Diamond is one crystalline form of carbon. It forms when carbon crystallizes under tremendous pressure (thousands of atmospheres). A different crystalline form of carbon is graphite. The lead in a pencil is not really lead; it is graphite. In graphite, the carbon atoms are packed in sheets rather than in the extended three-dimensional array characteristic of diamond.

In 1985, a third form of carbon—buckminsterfullerene, or the buckyball—was discovered. The buckyball is a molecule with 60 or more carbon atoms arranged in a pattern that looks like a soccer ball. It is found in ordinary soot. **Figure 10.16** shows the arrangement of carbon atoms in diamond, graphite, and a buckyball. The physical properties of diamond, graphite, and buckyballs are quite different. Diamond has a high density and is very hard; graphite has a relatively low density and is soft. Buckyballs are hollow cages with great strength and rigidity. Diamond, graphite, and buckyballs are called allotropes of carbon because all are made of carbon atoms and all are solids. **Allotropes** are two or more different molecular forms of the same element in the same physical state.

Not all solids are crystalline in form; some solids are amorphous. **Amorphous solids** lack an ordered internal structure. Rubber, plastic, and asphalt are amorphous solids. Their atoms are randomly arranged.

In **diamond,** each carbon atom in the interior of the diamond is strongly bonded to four others, creating a rigid compact array. Diamond is the hardest known material.

In **graphite,** the carbon atoms are linked in widely spaced layers of hexagonal (six-sided) arrays. Weak bonds between these layers allow them to slide over one another, making graphite very soft.

In **buckminsterfullerene,** the so-called buckyball, 60 carbon atoms form a hollow sphere; the carbons are arranged in pentagons and hexagons as on a soccer ball.

Other examples of amorphous solids are **glasses**—transparent fusion products of inorganic substances that have cooled to a rigid state without crystallizing. Glasses are sometimes called supercooled liquids. The irregular internal structures of glasses are intermediate between those of a crystalline solid and a free-flowing liquid. Glasses do not melt at a definite temperature but gradually soften when heated. This softening with temperature is critical to the glassblower's art, as shown in **Figure 10.17.** When a crystalline solid is shattered, the fragments tend to have the same surface angles as the original solid. By contrast, when an amorphous solid, such as glass, is shattered, the fragments have irregular angles and jagged edges.

Figure 10.16

The differing arrangements of carbon atoms dramatically affect the properties of diamond, graphite, and buckminsterfullerene—the three forms of carbon. What are such different forms of an element called?

Figure 10.17

Because it is an amorphous solid, glass does not have a definite melting point. This glassblower is heating glass to make a beautiful vase.

section review 10.3

14. Explain the nature of solids and tell why they differ from liquids. Refer to the organization of particles in your answer.

15. How does the crystal lattice of a solid differ from its unit cell?

16. How do allotropes of an element differ?

 Chem ASAP! Assessment 10.3 Check your understanding of the important ideas and concepts in Section 10.3.

CHANGES OF STATE

objectives

▶ Interpret the phase diagram of water at any given temperature and pressure

▶ Describe the behavior of solids that change directly to the vapor state and recondense to solids without passing through the liquid state

key terms

▶ phase diagram

▶ triple point

▶ sublimation

All life on Earth requires water, which cycles through our ecosystem in three forms—solid ice, liquid water, and water vapor. You are familiar with these states in a variety of ways: raindrops in a spring shower, snowflakes from a winter blizzard, and water vapor making a summer day humid. **How are the solid, liquid, and vapor states related?**

Phase Diagrams

The relationships among the solid, liquid, and vapor states (or phases) of a substance in a sealed container are best represented in a single graph called a phase diagram. A **phase diagram** gives the conditions of temperature and pressure at which a substance exists as solid, liquid, and gas (vapor). **Figure 10.18** shows the phase diagram for water. Each of the three regions represents a pure phase of water. A line that separates any two regions gives the conditions at which those two phases exist in equilibrium. The curving line that separates water's vapor phase from its liquid phase reveals the equilibrium conditions for liquid and vapor; it also illustrates how the vapor pressure of water varies with temperature. Similarly, the other two curving lines give the conditions for equilibrium between liquid water and ice and between water vapor and ice. A unique feature of the diagram is the point at which all three curves meet. This meeting point, called the **triple point,** describes the only set of conditions at which all three phases can exist in equilibrium with one another. For water, the triple

Figure 10.18

The phase diagram for water shows the relationship among pressure, temperature, and physical state. At the triple point, ice, liquid water, and water vapor can exist at equilibrium. Freezing, melting, boiling, and condensation can all occur at the same time, as shown in the photograph.

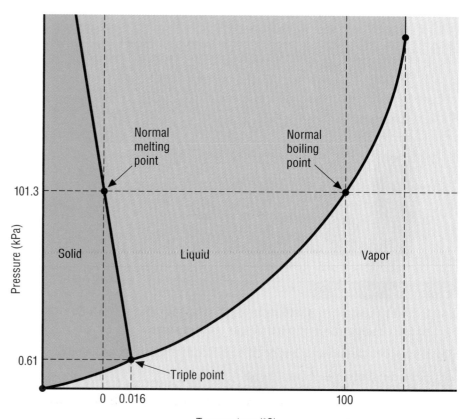

point is a temperature of 0.016 °C and a pressure of 0.61 kPa (0.0060 atm). The photograph in **Figure 10.18** shows that the triple point for water can be achieved in the laboratory.

Using a phase diagram, you can determine the changes in the melting point and boiling point of a substance with changes in external pressure. As shown in **Figure 10.18,** at a pressure of 101.3 kPa (1 atm), the normal boiling point and melting point of water are 100 °C and 0 °C, respectively. What happens if boiling and melting are carried out at pressures less than 101.3 kPa? A decrease in pressure lowers the boiling point and raises the melting point. What happens to the boiling point of water if the pressure is raised above atmospheric pressure?

When ice skaters move along the ice, the blades of their skates exert pressure which lowers the melting point of the ice. Consequently, the ice melts and a film of water forms under the blades of the skates. This film acts as a lubricant, enabling the skaters to glide gracefully over the ice.

Sublimation

If you hang wet laundry on a clothesline on a very cold day, the water in the clothes quickly freezes to ice. Eventually, however, the clothes become dry although the ice never thaws. The ice changes directly to water vapor without melting and passing through the liquid state. This is because solids, like liquids, have a vapor pressure. The vapor pressure of some solids can be high enough that they pass to a gas or vapor without becoming liquid. The change of a substance from a solid to a vapor without passing through the liquid state is called **sublimation.** Have you ever noticed that ice cubes left in the freezer for a long time get smaller? Can you propose an explanation?

Iodine is another example of a substance that undergoes sublimation. This violet-black solid ordinarily changes into a purple vapor without passing through a liquid state. Notice in **Figure 10.19** how dark crystals of iodine deposit on the underside of a watch glass placed on top of a beaker containing solid iodine that is being heated. The iodine vapor sublimes from iodine crystals in the bottom of the beaker and condenses to form crystals on the watch glass.

Chem ASAP!

Simulation 7
Predict the physical states present at different points on a phase diagram.

LiNK
TO

FOOD SCIENCE

Freeze-Drying
Astronauts and backpackers alike enjoy the benefits of foods preserved by freeze-drying. Freeze-dried foods are light-weight and conveniently re-constituted by adding water. They need no refrigeration because bacteria cannot multiply in the absence of moisture. The ready sublimation of ice at low pressure makes the process of freeze-drying possible. Food is frozen and then placed in a chamber attached to a vacuum pump. By lowering the pressure in the chamber below the vapor pressure of ice, the ice crystals sublime and the food is dried without the loss of its flavor.

Gaseous I_2 molecules

Solid I_2 molecules

Figure 10.19
When solid iodine is heated, the crystals sublime, going directly from the solid to the vapor state. When the purple vapor cools, solid crystals re-form without passing through the liquid state.

Sublimation is useful in many situations and processes. Freezing freshly brewed coffee and removing the water vapor with a vacuum pump makes freeze-dried coffee. Solid carbon dioxide (dry ice) is an important cooling material that also sublimes. Given its low temperature of $-78\,°C$ and the fact that it does not produce a liquid when it melts, dry ice is very useful for keeping frozen foods, such as ice cream, solid during shipping. Solid air fresheners contain a variety of substances that sublime at room temperature. Mothballs contain naphthalene. It is the naphthalene vapor that keeps away moths. Sublimation is also useful for separating substances. Organic chemists use this process to separate mixtures and to purify compounds.

MINI LAB

Sublimation

PURPOSE

To observe the sublimation of air freshener.

MATERIALS

- small pieces of solid air freshener
- small shallow container
- 2 clear plastic cups (8 oz each)
- hot tap water
- ice
- 3 thick cardboard strips

PROCEDURE

1. Place a few pieces of air freshener in one of the cups.

2. Bend the cardboard strips and place them over the rim of the cup that has the air freshener pieces.

3. Place the second cup inside the first. The base of the second cup should not touch the air freshener. Adjust the cardboard as necessary. This assembly is your sublimator.

4. Fill the top cup with ice. Do not get any ice or water in the bottom cup.

5. Fill the shallow container about one-third full with hot tap water.

6. Carefully place your sublimator in the hot water. Observe what happens.

Ice

Shallow container with hot water

Small pieces of air freshener

ANALYSIS AND CONCLUSIONS

1. Define sublimation.

2. What do you think would happen if the water in the shallow container was at room temperature? If it was boiling?

3. Why is it possible to separate the substances in some mixtures by sublimation?

---

section review 10.4

17. What general information can you get from a phase diagram for water at various temperatures and pressures?

18. Describe the process of sublimation. What is a practical use of this process?

19. Explain triple point.

 Chem ASAP! **Assessment 10.4** Check your understanding of the important ideas and concepts in Section 10.4.

GASES CAN ALTER GLOBAL TEMPERATURE

Gases in Earth's atmosphere called greenhouse gases act much like the glass ceiling of a greenhouse. Earth's heat radiates skyward where it is absorbed and re-emitted by the greenhouse gases in the atmosphere back toward the surface of Earth. This process is very similar to how glass traps heat inside a greenhouse. If greenhouse gases were not present in the atmosphere, Earth's heat would escape into space—Earth would be a lifeless planet! Without greenhouse gases, Earth would have an average surface temperature of only −18 °C. With these gases in place, however, Earth's average surface temperature is 15 °C.

The main greenhouse gases are water vapor, carbon dioxide, ozone, methane, nitrous oxide, and halogenated substances including chlorofluorocarbons (CFCs). Many activities release greenhouse gases. Some of these are natural processes while others are directly related to human actions. Human activities are adding larger and larger amounts of greenhouse gases into the atmosphere, resulting in an excess of trapped heat. This unnatural trapping of heat in the atmosphere is called global warming.

> **Without greenhouse gases, Earth would have an average surface temperature of only −18°C.**

Carbon dioxide is the largest contributor to global warming. Processes such as cellular respiration produce this gas naturally. In addition, the burning of fossil fuels and forests contributes heavily to the concentration of this gas.

CFCs are also contributors to global warming. These compounds are produced almost entirely from human actions. The manufacture of plastic foams and the evaporation of industrial solvents release CFCs. Some aerosol propellants give off CFCs, and CFC-based air conditioners and refrigerators can leak CFCs into the atmosphere. CFC molecules have a much greater effect on global warming than do carbon dioxide molecules.

Methane is another greenhouse gas capable of trapping more heat than carbon dioxide. The natural process of decomposition releases methane into the atmosphere. Landfills further contribute to methane's atmospheric concentration. In addition, methane is released as underground deposits of fossil fuels and natural gas are brought to the surface.

If the release of greenhouse gases by human activities continues unchecked, the potential for overall global climate changes increases, as does the threat to the survival of many species. The predicted changes in climate could cause droughts in some regions, floods in others, loss of biodiversity, and rising sea levels. These gases have the power to affect Earth's climate and its animal and plant life.

CHEMISTRY IN CAREERS

☆☆☆☆☆☆☆☆☆☆☆☆☆☆☆☆☆☆☆

TAKE IT TO THE NET
Find out more about career opportunities:

www.phschool.com

CHEMICAL SPECIALIST
Local food service distributor seeks responsible self-motivated individ-

CLIMATOLOGIST
Study the weather of the future and the past using supercomputers and ice core sampling.
See page 872.

CHEMIST NEEDED
Enviro Lab CO h

Take It to the NET
For interactive study and
review, go to www.phschool.com

KEY TERMS

- allotrope *p. 282*
- amorphous solid *p. 282*
- atmospheric pressure *p. 268*
- barometer *p. 268*
- boiling point *p. 277*
- crystal *p. 280*
- evaporation *p. 275*
- gas pressure *p. 268*

- glass *p. 283*
- kinetic energy *p. 267*
- kinetic theory *p. 267*
- melting point *p. 280*
- normal boiling point *p. 278*
- pascal (Pa) *p. 268*
- phase diagram *p. 284*

- standard atmosphere (atm) *p. 268*
- sublimation *p. 285*
- triple point *p. 284*
- unit cell *p. 282*
- vacuum *p. 268*
- vaporization *p. 275*
- vapor pressure *p. 276*

CONCEPT SUMMARY

10.1 The Nature of Gases

- The kinetic theory describes the motion of particles (atoms, ions, or molecules) in matter and the forces of attraction between them.
- The kinetic theory assumes that the volume occupied by a gas is mostly empty space and that the particles of a gas are far apart, move rapidly, and have random motion.
- The pressure of a gas results from the collisions of the gas particles with an object.
- Standard conditions are 0 °C and 1 atm.
- The temperature of a gas is directly proportional to the average kinetic energy of the particles.

10.2 The Nature of Liquids

- When the temperature of a gas is lowered enough, the gas condenses to a liquid.
- A liquid boils when its vapor pressure equals the external pressure.
- When a liquid that is not boiling changes to a vapor or gas, the process is called evaporation.
- The normal boiling point of a liquid is the temperature at which the vapor pressure is equal to 1 atm.

10.3 The Nature of Solids

- The movement of particles in a solid is restricted to vibrations about fixed points.
- Solids melt when the vibrations become greater than the forces holding the particles together.
- Most solids are crystalline. The particles are arranged in a repeating three-dimensional pattern known as a crystal lattice.
- The smallest subunit of a crystal lattice is the unit cell.
- An element may have two or more different molecular forms, called allotropes, in the same physical state.

10.4 Changes of State

- Most substances change their physical state and melt or vaporize as the temperature increases. Substances condense or freeze as the temperature decreases.
- While the physical state of a substance changes during a phase change, the temperature of the system remains constant.
- In sublimation, a solid can change directly to a gas or vapor without first becoming a liquid.

CHAPTER CONCEPT MAP

Use these terms to construct a concept map that organizes the major ideas of this chapter.

 Chem ASAP! Concept Map 10
Create your Concept Map using the computer.

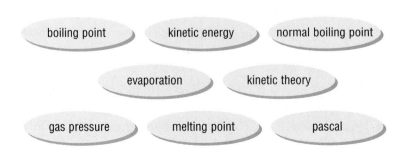

CONCEPT PRACTICE

20. What is meant by elastic collision? *10.1*

21. List the various units used to measure pressure, and identify the SI unit. *10.1*

22. Change 1656 kPa to atm. *10.1*

23. Convert 190 mm Hg to the following. *10.1*
  a. kilopascals
  b. atmospheres of pressure

24. How much pressure (in mm Hg) does a gas exert at 3.1 atm? *10.1*

25. Explain the relationship between the absolute temperature of a substance and the kinetic energy of its particles. *10.1*

26. How is the average kinetic energy of water molecules affected when you pour hot water from a kettle into cups at the same temperature as the water? *10.1*

27. What does the abbreviation STP represent? *10.1*

28. Express standard temperature in kelvins and standard pressure in kilopascals and in millimeters of mercury. *10.1*

29. What is significant about the temperature absolute zero? *10.1*

30. By what factor does the average kinetic energy of gas molecules in an aerosol container increase when the temperature is raised from 27 °C (300 K) to 627 °C (900 K)? *10.1*

31. A liquid is a condensed state of matter. Explain. *10.2*

32. Explain why liquids and gases differ *10.2*
  a. in physical state.
  b. in compressibility.

33. Compare the evaporation of a contained liquid with that of an uncontained liquid. *10.2*

34. Explain vapor pressure and dynamic equilibrium. *10.2*

35. Explain why increasing the temperature of a liquid increases its rate of evaporation. *10.2*

36. Would you expect an equilibrium vapor pressure to be reached above a liquid in an open container? Why? *10.2*

37. Describe the effect that increasing temperature has on the vapor pressure of a liquid. *10.2*

38. Distinguish between the boiling point and the normal boiling point of a liquid. *10.2*

39. Use the graph to answer each question. *10.2*

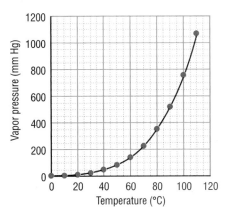

  a. What is the vapor pressure of water at 40 °C?
  b. At what temperature is the vapor pressure of water 600 mm Hg?
  c. What is the significance of the vapor pressure of water at 100 °C?

40. Use **Figure 10.11** to determine the temperature at which water will boil in an open vessel when the atmospheric pressure is 400 mm Hg. *10.2*

41. At the top of Mount Everest, water boils at only 69 °C. Use **Figure 10.11** to estimate the atmospheric pressure at the top of this mountain. *10.2*

42. Explain how boiling is a cooling process. *10.2*

43. Name at least one physical property that would permit you to distinguish a molecular solid from an ionic solid. *10.3*

44. Describe what happens when a solid is heated to its melting point. *10.3*

45. Molecular solids usually have lower melting points than ionic solids. Why? *10.3*

46. When you remove the lid from a food container that has been left in a freezer for several months, you discover a large collection of ice crystals on the underside of the lid. Explain what has happened. *10.4*

47. Any liquid stays at a constant temperature while it is boiling. Why? *10.4*

CONCEPT MASTERY

48. Describe evaporation, vapor pressure, and boiling point.

49. Mount McKinley (6194 m) in Alaska is the tallest peak in North America. The atmospheric pressure at its peak is 330 mm Hg. Find the boiling point of water there. Use **Figure 10.11**.

50. What causes atmospheric pressure, and why is it much lower on the top of a mountain than it is at sea level?

51. Why is the equilibrium that exists between a liquid and its vapor in a closed container called a dynamic equilibrium?

52. Pouring liquid nitrogen onto a balloon decreases the volume of the balloon dramatically, as shown in the photograph. Afterward, the balloon reinflates. Use kinetic theory to explain this sequence of events. The temperature of liquid nitrogen is −196 °C.

53. What happens to the average kinetic energy of the water molecules in your body when you get a fever?

54. The temperature of the gas in an aerosol container is 0 °C (273 K). To what temperature must this gas be raised to increase the average kinetic energy of the gas molecules by a factor of three?

55. Explain what happens at the melting point of a substance.

CRITICAL THINKING

56. Choose the term that best completes the second relationship.
    a. temperature : thermometer
       atmospheric pressure : _____
       (1) valve   (3) volume
       (2) barometer   (4) gauge
    b. evolution : organisms
       kinetic theory : _____
       (1) particles   (3) heat
       (2) temperature   (4) pressure

57. What everyday evidence suggests that all matter is in constant motion?

58. Is the average kinetic energy of the particles in a block of ice at 0 °C the same as or different from the average kinetic energy of the particles in a gas-filled weather balloon at 0 °C? Explain.

59. Are perfectly elastic collisions possible between objects that you can see?

60. How does perspiration help cool your body on a hot day?

61. Why do different liquids have different boiling points?

CUMULATIVE REVIEW

62. Balance these equations.
    a. $V_2O_5 + H_2 \rightarrow V_2O_3 + H_2O$
    b. $(NH_4)_2Cr_2O_7 \rightarrow Cr_2O_3 + N_2 + H_2O$
    c. $NH_3 + O_2 \rightarrow NO + H_2O$
    d. $C_6H_{14} + O_2 \rightarrow CO + H_2O$

63. What is the density of krypton gas at STP?

64. Hydrogen reacts with ethene (C_2H_4) to form ethane (C_2H_6).

$$C_2H_4 + H_2 \longrightarrow C_2H_6$$

What is the limiting reagent when 40.0 g C_2H_4 reacts with 3.0 g H_2?

65. How many moles is each substance?
    a. 888 g of sulfur dioxide
    b. 2.84×10^{22} molecules of ammonia
    c. 0.47 L of carbon dioxide (at STP)

66. Perchloric acid forms by the reaction of water with dichlorine heptoxide.

$$Cl_2O_7 + H_2O \longrightarrow 2HClO_4$$

    a. How many grams of Cl_2O_7 must react with an excess of H_2O to form 56.2 g $HClO_4$?
    b. How many mL of water are needed to form 3.40 mol $HClO_4$?

CONCEPT CHALLENGE

67. If the volume of the container in which there is a liquid–vapor equilibrium is changed, the vapor pressure is not affected. Why?

68. The ions in sodium chloride are arranged in a face-centered cubic pattern. Sketch a layer of the ions in a crystal of sodium chloride.

69. Using **Figure 10.14,** identify the crystal system described by these characteristics.
    a. three unequal axes mutually perpendicular
    b. three equal axes making equal angles with each other
    c. two equal axes and one unequal axis mutually perpendicular
    d. three unequal axes intersecting obliquely
    e. three axes equal and mutually perpendicular

Select the choice that best answers each question or completes each statement.

1. To double the average kinetic energy of helium atoms in a balloon at 27 °C, the temperature of the gas must be
   a. decreased to 150 K.
   b. increased to 600 K.
   c. increased to 450 K.
   d. increased to 54 °C.

2. Which sequence has the states of CH_3OH correctly ordered in terms of increasing average kinetic energy?
   a. $CH_3OH(s)$, $CH_3OH(g)$, $CH_3OH(l)$
   b. $CH_3OH(g)$, $CH_3OH(l)$, $CH_3OH(s)$
   c. $CH_3OH(l)$, $CH_3OH(g)$, $CH_3OH(s)$
   d. $CH_3OH(s)$, $CH_3OH(l)$, $CH_3OH(g)$

3. Which statement is *not* part of kinetic theory?
   a. Collisions between gas particles are elastic.
   b. All gas particles are in constant motion.
   c. All particles have identical kinetic energies.
   d. The motion of gas particles is random.

Use the drawing to answer questions 4–6. The same liquid is in each flask.

(a)   (b)

4. In which flask is the vapor pressure lower? Give a reason for your answer.

5. In which flask is the liquid at the higher temperature? Explain your answer.

6. How can the vapor pressure in each flask be determined?

Use the graph to answer questions 7–9.

7. What is the normal boiling point of ethanol?

8. Can chloroform be heated to 90 °C in an open container?

9. To what temperature must water be heated so that its vapor pressure equals the vapor pressure of ethanol at 60 °C?

For each question there are two statements. Decide whether each statement is true or false. Then decide whether Statement II is a correct explanation for Statement I.

Statement I		Statement II
10. In an open container, the rate of evaporation of a liquid always equals the rate of condensation.	BECAUSE	A dynamic equilibrium exists between a liquid and its vapor in an open container.
11. Water boils at a temperature below 100 °C on top of a mountain.	BECAUSE	Atmospheric pressure decreases with an increase in altitude.
12. The temperature of a substance always increases as heat is added to the substance.	BECAUSE	The average kinetic energy of the particles in a substance increase with an increase in temperature.
13. Solids have a fixed volume.	BECAUSE	Particles in a solid cannot move.
14. Gases are more compressible than liquids.	BECAUSE	There is more space between particles in a gas than between particles in a liquid.

Chapter 11

THERMOCHEMISTRY—HEAT AND CHEMICAL CHANGE

FEATURES

Stay current with **SCIENCE NEWS**
Find out more about thermochemistry:
www.phschool.com

Heat released by a burning match is absorbed by air.

DISCOVER IT! OBSERVING HEAT FLOW

You need a clean, medium-sized rubber band.

1. Hook your index fingers through each end of the rubber band. Without stretching the rubber band, place it against your upper lip or forehead. Note the temperature of the rubber band.

2. Move the rubber band away from your skin, quickly stretch and hold it, and then place it back against your skin. Note any temperature change.

3. Fully stretch the rubber band, and then allow it to return to its original shape. Place it against your skin and note any temperature change.

4. Repeat Steps 2 and 3 until you are certain of the temperature change in each step.

Did the rubber band feel cool or warm after it was stretched in Step 2? Did the rubber band feel cool or warm after it returned to its original shape in Step 3? Think about the temperature changes you observed and form some initial answers to the following questions. What is heat? In what direction does heat flow? As you work through this chapter, return to these questions.

*L*ava flowing out of an erupting volcano is very hot. Its temperature ranges from 550 °C to 1400 °C. As lava flows down the side of a volcano, it loses heat and begins to cool slowly. In some instances, the lava may flow into the ocean where it cools rapidly. **Why does lava cool more quickly in water than on land?**

Energy Transformations

Glowing campfires, the sun's rays, and rubbing your hands together all produce heat. However, other activities, such as melting ice and boiling water, absorb heat. **Thermochemistry** is concerned with the heat changes that occur during chemical reactions. In this chapter, you will examine heat and its effects on a number of chemical and physical processes. First, however, it is important to understand energy transformations.

When you buy gasoline, you are buying the stored potential energy it contains. This energy is used to do work, most often to propel a car. The controlled explosions of the gasoline in the car's engine transform the potential energy into useful work. Work is done when a force is used to move an object. **Energy** is the capacity for doing work or supplying heat. Unlike matter, energy is weightless, odorless, and tasteless. Energy is detected only because of its effects. Energy stored within the structural units of chemical substances is called **chemical potential energy.** Gasoline contains a significant amount of chemical potential energy. Different substances store different amounts of energy. The kinds of atoms and their arrangement in the substance determine the amount of energy stored in the substance.

Heat, represented by q, is energy that transfers from one object to another because of a temperature difference between them. Heat, itself, cannot be detected by the senses or by instruments. Only changes caused by heat can be detected. One of the effects of adding heat is a rise in the temperature of objects. It is the radiant heat of the sun's rays that makes a summer day hot. In this example, air is the object that absorbs heat and

objectives
▶ Explain the relationship between energy and heat
▶ Distinguish between heat capacity and specific heat

key terms
▶ thermochemistry
▶ energy
▶ chemical potential energy
▶ heat
▶ system
▶ surroundings
▶ universe
▶ law of conservation of energy
▶ endothermic process
▶ exothermic process
▶ calorie
▶ joule
▶ heat capacity
▶ specific heat capacity
▶ specific heat

Figure 11.1

Chemical potential energy is stored within the bonds of gasoline molecules (a). As the gasoline burns, the energy is released and is used to do work. In this example, the work is to propel race cars around the track (b).

(a)

(b)

Figure 11.2

The part of the universe being studied is the system. What constitutes the surroundings?

Figure 11.3

There are two directions in which the heat of a system can flow. (a) In an endothermic process, heat flows into the system from the surroundings. The system absorbs heat. (b) In an exothermic process, heat flows from the system to the surroundings. The system loses heat.

increases in temperature. Heat always flows from a warmer object to a cooler object. If two objects remain in contact, heat will flow from the warmer object to the cooler object until the temperature of both objects is the same.

Exothermic and Endothermic Processes

Essentially all chemical reactions and changes in physical state involve either the release or the absorption of heat. In studying heat changes, it is useful to define a **system** as the part of the universe on which you focus your attention. The **surroundings** include everything else in the universe. In thermochemical experiments, it is a good approximation to consider the region in the immediate vicinity of the system as the surroundings. In **Figure 11.2,** for example, the mixture of chemicals undergoing a reaction is the system, and everything else is the surroundings. Together, the system and its surroundings constitute the **universe.** A major goal of studying thermochemistry is to examine the flow of heat from the system to its surroundings, or the flow of heat from the surroundings to the system. The **law of conservation of energy** states that in any chemical or physical process, energy is neither created nor destroyed. All of the energy involved in a process can be accounted for as work, stored energy, or heat.

(a)

(b)

In thermochemical calculations the direction of the heat flow is given from the point of view of the system. Look at **Figure 11.3a.** Heat flowing into a system from its surroundings is defined as positive; q has a positive value. A process that absorbs heat from the surroundings is called an **endothermic process.** In an endothermic process, the system gains heat as the surroundings cool down. In **Figure 11.3b,** heat flows out of the system into its surroundings. This type of heat flow is given a negative value; q is negative because the system is losing heat. A process that releases heat to its surroundings is called an **exothermic process.** In an exothermic process, the system loses heat as the surroundings heat up. **Table 11.1** explains the sign convention for heat changes.

Table 11.1

Heat Change Sign Convention		
Direction of heat flow	**Sign** **Reaction type**	
Heat flows out of the system	Heat change < 0 (negative)	Exothermic
Heat flows into the system	Heat change > 0 (positive)	Endothermic

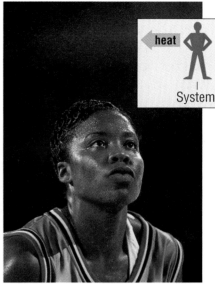

Figure 11.4

A fire helps keep you warm when you are out in the cold. If your body is the system, what is the fire? The human body cools itself by giving off heat when perspiration evaporates. What is the system here? Which of these processes is exothermic and which is endothermic?

In the photograph on the left in **Figure 11.4,** the system (the people) gains heat from its **surroundings** (the fire). As shown in the inset illustration, heat flows into the system from its surroundings. What kind of process is this? In the photograph on the right, the system (the body) cools as perspiration evaporates from the skin and heat flows to the surroundings. What kind of process is shown in this illustration?

Heat Capacity and Specific Heat

You have probably heard of someone exercising to burn off fat and calories. What does it mean to "burn calories"? During exercise your body generates heat, and this heat is measured in units called calories. The heat is generated as your body breaks down sugars and fats into carbon dioxide and water. Although there is not an actual fire burning the sugars and fats within your body, chemical reactions accomplish the same result. In breaking down 10 g of sugar, for example, your body generates a certain amount of heat. The same amount of heat would be produced if 10 g of sugar were completely burned in a fire, producing carbon dioxide and water.

A **calorie** is defined as the quantity of heat needed to raise the temperature of 1 g of pure water 1 °C. There is an important difference, however, between a calorie and a Calorie. The calorie, written with a small c, is defined above and is used except when referring to the energy contained in food. The dietary Calorie, written with a capital C, always refers to the energy in food. One dietary Calorie is actually equal to one kilocalorie, or 1000 calories.

$$1 \text{ Calorie} = 1 \text{ kilocalorie} = 1000 \text{ calories}$$

The statement "10 g of sugar has 41 Calories" means that 10 g of sugar releases 41 kilocalories of heat when completely burned to produce carbon dioxide and water.

Figure 11.5

Which food will warm you up more when you are cold: a bowl of hot soup, or two slices of hot buttered toast? Why?

PHYSIOLOGY

Dietary Calories

Your proper caloric intake depends on your level of physical activity. In an eight-hour day at a desk, you burn about 800 Calories. This is about the number of Calories in two helpings of spaghetti. When exercising, however, you become a relative biochemical blast furnace. In vigorous activities such as running and jumping, you expend 7–10 Calories per minute, or 420–600 Calories per hour. At these rates, a runner who covers a 26-mile marathon course in 3 hours might expend 1800 Calories, or the equivalent of 4.5 helpings of spaghetti.

The calorie is also related to the **joule,** the SI unit of heat and energy named after the English physicist James Prescott Joule (1818–1889). A joule is slightly less than one-fourth of a calorie. One joule of heat raises the temperature of 1 g of pure water 0.2390 °C. You can convert between calories and joules using the following relationships.

$$1 \text{ J} = 0.2390 \text{ cal} \qquad 4.184 \text{ J} = 1 \text{ cal}$$

The amount of heat needed to increase the temperature of an object exactly 1 °C is the **heat capacity** of that object. The heat capacity of an object depends on its mass as well as its chemical composition. The greater the mass of the object, the greater its heat capacity. A massive steel girder, for example, requires much more heat to raise its temperature 1 °C than a small steel nail does. Similarly, a cup of water has a much greater heat capacity than a drop of water. Besides varying with mass, the heat capacity of an object also depends on its chemical composition. It follows that different substances with the same mass may have different heat capacities.

On a sunny day, a 20 kg puddle of water may be cool, while a nearby 20 kg iron sewer cover may be too hot to touch. This situation illustrates how different heat capacities affect the temperature of objects. Assuming that both the water and the iron absorb the same amount of radiant energy from the sun, the temperature of the water changes less than the temperature of the iron because the specific heat capacity of water is larger.

Table 11.2

Specific Heat Capacities of Some Common Substances		
	Specific heat capacity	
Substance	**J/(g × °C)**	**cal/(g × °C)**
Water	4.18	1.00
Grain alcohol	2.4	0.58
Ice	2.1	0.50
Steam	1.7	0.40
Chloroform	0.96	0.23
Aluminum	0.90	0.21
Glass	0.50	0.12
Iron	0.46	0.11
Silver	0.24	0.057
Mercury	0.14	0.033

The **specific heat capacity,** or simply the **specific heat,** of a substance is the amount of heat it takes to raise the temperature of 1 g of the substance 1 °C. What is the relationship between specific heat and heat capacity? **Table 11.2** gives specific heats for some common substances. Water has a very high specific heat compared with the other substances in the table. You can see from the table that one calorie of heat raises the temperature of 1 g of water 1 °C. Metals, however, have low specific heats. One calorie of heat raises the temperature of 1 g of iron 9 °C. Thus water has a specific heat nine times that of iron. Heat affects the temperature of objects with a high specific heat much less than the temperature of those with a low specific heat. Just as it takes a lot of heat to raise the temperature of water, water also releases a lot of heat as it cools. Water in lakes and oceans absorbs heat from the air on hot days and releases it back into the air on cool days. As illustrated in **Figure 11.6,** this property of water is responsible for moderate climates in coastal areas. The specific heat of water is often used by farmers to protect their crops. In freezing weather, citrus crops are often sprayed with water to protect the fruit from damage. As the water freezes, it releases heat, which helps to prevent the fruit from freezing. The results of this procedure are shown in **Figure 11.7.**

To calculate the specific heat of a substance, you divide the heat input by the temperature change times the mass of the substance. The equation for specific heat (C) follows, where q is heat and m is mass. The symbol ΔT (read "delta T") in the equation represents the change in temperature. ΔT is calculated from the equation $\Delta T = T_f - T_i$, where T_f is the final temperature and T_i is the initial temperature.

$$C = \frac{q}{m \times \Delta T} = \frac{\text{heat (joules or calories)}}{\text{mass (g)} \times \text{change in temperature (°C)}}$$

As you can see from this equation, specific heat may be expressed in terms of joules or calories. Therefore, the units of specific heat are either $\text{J/(g} \times \text{°C)}$ or $\text{cal/(g} \times \text{°C)}$.

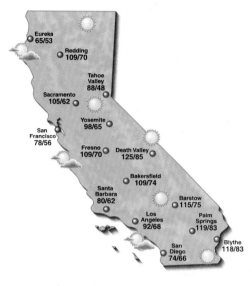

Figure 11.6

San Francisco is located on the Pacific coast. The high specific heat of the ocean helps keep the temperature in San Francisco much more moderate than that of towns and cities farther inland.

Figure 11.7

Water must give off a lot of heat in order to freeze. Sometimes farmers use water's high specific heat capacity to their advantage. In freezing weather, orange groves are often sprayed with water to protect the fruit from frost damage.

Thermochemistry **297**

CHEMath

REVIEW OF SIGNIFICANT FIGURES

This page offers you a chance to refresh your knowledge of significant figures before beginning this chapter—a chapter which involves solving problems containing numerous numerical values. As you learned in Section 3.2, a value in science must be reported using the correct number of *significant figures* (or digits). Answers cannot be more precise than the given data, as they would be misleading.

The rules for determining significant figures are summarized below. (Note that this list is a condensed version of the rules listed in Chapter 3.)

1. Nonzero digits are always significant.
2. A zero is significant only if it is
   a. at the right end of a number and after a decimal point, or
   b. between digits that are significant according to rule **1** or **2a.**

   Zeros to the left of nonzero digits or at the end of a quantity written as a whole number are "placeholders" and are *not* significant.
3. If a quantity is known to be exact, it has an unlimited number of significant figures.

4. If a quantity is written in scientific notation, all digits of the coefficient are significant.

For example, the significant digits in each number below are shown in blue.

30 400	3 significant figures
150.0	4 significant figures
2401	4 significant figures
168.030	6 significant figures
0.0058	2 significant figures
3.010×10^8	4 significant figures

When working with significant digits, *round up* the final significant digit *only if* the next digit is 5 or greater. When you do a calculation, round your final answer (not the intermediate steps) according to these rules:

Addition and Subtraction Round the result to the same number of decimal places as the measurement with the fewest decimal places.

Multiplication and Division Round the result to the same number of significant figures as the measurement with the fewest significant figures.

Example 1

Evaluate $2.34 + 1.2$ and express the answer with the correct number of significant figures.

2.34 has 2 decimal places and 1.2 has 1 decimal place. So, the answer should be rounded to 1 decimal place.

Without rounding, $2.34 + 1.2 = 3.54$.

After rounding 3.54 to 1 decimal place, the final answer is 3.5.

Example 2

Use the formula $C = \dfrac{q}{m \times \Delta T}$ to calculate C, the specific heat capacity, if $q = 516$ J, $m = 6.4$ g, and $\Delta T = 25.80$ °C.

Because 6.4 g has only 2 significant figures, the answer should be rounded to 2 significant figures.

$$C = \frac{516 \text{ J}}{6.4 \text{ g} \times 25.80 \text{ °C}} = 3.125 \frac{\text{J}}{\text{g} \times \text{°C}} = 3.1 \frac{\text{J}}{\text{g} \times \text{°C}}$$

Practice Problems

Find the number of significant figures in each quantity.

A. 1340   **B.** 0.06   **C.** 3.400×10^4 **D.** 0.00350   **E.** 16.0

Round each answer to the appropriate number of significant figures.

F. $16.382 + 17.5$ **I.** $317.04 \div 18.7$ **L.** Use the formula $C = \dfrac{q}{m \times \Delta T}$ to calculate C if

G. 1.4×6.03 **J.** $(6.030 \times 10^7) + (1.64 \times 10^5)$ $q = 14.80$ J, $m = 3.056$ g, and $\Delta T = 10.01$ °C.

H. $128.0 - 64.37$ **K.** $(3.0 \times 10^{15}) \div (2.19 \times 10^4)$

Sample Problem 11-1

The temperature of a piece of copper with a mass of 95.4 g increases from 25.0 °C to 48.0 °C when the metal absorbs 849 J of heat. What is the specific heat of copper?

1. **ANALYZE** *List the knowns and the unknown.*

Knowns:
- $m_{Cu} = 95.4$ g
- $\Delta T = (48.0\ °C - 25.0\ °C) = 23.0\ °C$
- $q = 849$ J

Unknown:
- $C_{Cu} = ?\ \dfrac{J}{g \times °C}$

Use the known values and the definition of specific heat, $C = \dfrac{q}{m \times \Delta T}$, to calculate the unknown value C_{Cu}.

2. **CALCULATE** *Solve for the unknown.*

Substitute the known values into the equation for the specific heat and solve.

$$C_{Cu} = \frac{q}{m \times \Delta T}$$

$$C_{Cu} = \frac{849\ J}{95.4\ g \times 23.0\ °C} = 0.387\ \frac{J}{g \times °C}$$

3. **EVALUATE** *Does the result make sense?*

Remember that water has a very high specific heat $(4.18\ J/(g \times °C))$. Metals, however, have low specific heats—values less than $4.18\ J/(g \times °C)$. Thus the calculated value of $0.387\ J/(g \times °C)$ seems reasonable.

Practice Problems

1. When 435 J of heat is added to 3.4 g of olive oil at 21 °C, the temperature increases to 85 °C. What is the specific heat of olive oil?
2. A 1.55-g piece of stainless steel absorbs 141 J of heat when its temperature increases by 178 °C. What is the specific heat of the stainless steel?
3. How much heat is required to raise the temperature of 250.0 g of mercury 52 °C?

Chem ASAP!

Problem-Solving 3
Solve Problem 3 with the help of an interactive guided tutorial.

section review 11.1

4. Define energy and explain how energy and heat are related.
5. Explain the difference between heat capacity and specific heat.
6. Will the specific heat of 50 g of a substance be the same as, or greater than, the specific heat of 10 g of the same substance?
7. On a sunny day, why does the concrete deck around an outdoor swimming pool become hot, while the water stays cool?
8. Using calories, calculate how much heat 32.0 g of water absorbs when it is heated from 25.0 °C to 80.0 °C. How many joules is this?
9. A chunk of silver has a heat capacity of 42.8 J/°C. If the silver has a mass of 181 g, calculate the specific heat of silver.
10. How many kilojoules of heat are absorbed when 1.00 L of water is heated from 18 °C to 85 °C?

 Chem ASAP! Assessment 11.1 Check your understanding of the important ideas and concepts in Section 11.1.

MEASURING AND EXPRESSING HEAT CHANGES

objectives

▶ Construct equations that show the heat changes for chemical and physical processes
▶ Calculate heat changes in chemical and physical processes

key terms

▶ calorimetry
▶ calorimeter
▶ enthalpy (*H*)
▶ thermochemical equation
▶ heat of reaction
▶ heat of combustion

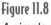

*A*s you know, a burning match gives off heat. When you strike a match, heat is released to the surroundings in all directions. As you have learned, heat cannot be detected by the senses or by instruments. **Is there a way to measure exactly how much heat is released from a burning match?**

Calorimetry

Energy changes occur in many systems, from the inner workings of a clock, to the eruption of volcanoes, to the formation of the solar system. Most chemical and physical changes you will encounter occur at constant atmospheric pressure. For example, a reaction in an open beaker, the formation of ice in a lake, and the reactions in many living organisms all occur at constant atmospheric pressure. By defining a thermodynamic variable called enthalpy—a variable that takes constant pressure into account—you can measure the energy changes that accompany chemical and physical processes.

Heat that is released or absorbed during many chemical reactions can be measured by calorimetry. **Calorimetry** is the accurate and precise measurement of heat change for chemical and physical processes. In calorimetry, the heat released by the system is equal to the heat absorbed by its surroundings. What law describes this relationship? To measure heat changes accurately and precisely, the processes must be carried out in an insulated container. The insulated device used to measure the absorption or release of heat in chemical or physical processes is called a **calorimeter.**

Foam cups, which keep hot drinks hot and cold drinks cold, are excellent heat insulators. Because they do not let much heat in or out, they can be used as simple calorimeters. In fact, the heat change for many chemical reactions can be measured in a constant-pressure calorimeter similar to the one shown in **Figure 11.8.** Because most chemical reactions and physical

Figure 11.8

A simple constant-pressure calorimeter is shown here. In a calorimeter, the thermometer measures the temperature change of the chemicals as they react in water. The stirrer is used to keep the solution at a uniform temperature. The chemical substances that react in solution constitute the system. Is the water, in which the chemicals dissolved, part of the system or part of the surroundings?

Thermometer

Stirrer

Foam lid
(loose fitting)

Water
(where reaction
takes place)

Nested foam cups
(insulation)

Table 11.3

Enthalpy Sign Convention	
Exothermic reaction	ΔH is negative $(\Delta H < 0)$
Endothermic reaction	ΔH is positive $(\Delta H > 0)$

changes carried out in the laboratory are open to the atmosphere, these changes occur at constant pressure. For systems at constant pressure, the heat content is the same as a property called the **enthalpy** *(H)* of the system. Heat changes for reactions carried out at constant pressure are the same as changes in enthalpy, symbolized as ΔH (read "delta H"). Because the reactions presented in this textbook occur at constant pressure, the terms heat and enthalpy are used interchangeably. In other words, $q = \Delta H$. Recalling the equation for specific heat, we can write the following relationship for the heat change in a chemical reaction carried out in aqueous solution.

$$q = \Delta H = m \times C \times \Delta T$$

ΔH is the heat change; m is the mass of the water; C is the specific heat capacity of water; and $\Delta T = T_f - T_i$. The sign of ΔH is negative for an exothermic reaction and positive for an endothermic reaction. **Table 11.3** summarizes the sign convention for enthalpy.

To measure the heat change for a reaction in aqueous solution in a foam cup calorimeter, you dissolve the reacting chemicals (the system) in known volumes of water (the surroundings). Then measure the initial temperature of each solution and mix the solutions in the foam cup. After the reaction is complete, measure the final temperature of the mixed solutions. Because you know the initial and final temperatures and the heat capacity of water, you can calculate the heat released or absorbed in the reaction using the equation for specific heat.

Calorimetry experiments can also be performed at constant volume using a device called a bomb calorimeter. A bomb calorimeter, similar to the one shown in **Figure 11.9,** measures the heat released from burning a compound. The calorimeter is a closed system; that is, the mass of the system is constant.

Chem ASAP!

Simulation 8
Simulate a combustion reaction and compare the ΔH results for several compounds.

Electrical leads
Oxygen intake valve
Thermometer
Insulated outer container
Firing element
Oxygen at high pressure
Sample to be burned
Steel bomb
Stirrer
Water

Figure 11.9

In a bomb calorimeter, a sample is burned in a constant-volume chamber in the presence of oxygen at high pressure. The heat that is released warms the water surrounding the chamber. By measuring the temperature increase of the water, it is possible to calculate the quantity of heat released during the combustion reaction.

Thermochemistry **301**

Sample Problem 11-2

To study the amount of heat released during a neutralization reaction (you will learn about neutralization in Chapter 21), 25.0 mL of water containing 0.025 mol HCl is added to 25.0 mL of water containing 0.025 mol NaOH in a foam cup calorimeter. At the start, the solutions and the calorimeter are all at 25.0 °C. During the reaction, the highest temperature observed is 32.0 °C. Calculate the heat (in kJ) released during this reaction. Assume the densities of the solutions are 1.00 g/mL.

1. **ANALYZE** *List the knowns and the unknown.*

Knowns:

HCl solution:
- V_{HCl} = 25.0 mL
- solution contains 0.025 mol HCl

NaOH solution:
- V_{NaOH} = 25.0 mL
- solution contains 0.025 mol NaOH

- $V_{final} = V_{HCl} + V_{NaOH}$
    = 25.0 mL + 25.0 mL = 50.0 mL
- T_i = 25.0 °C
- T_f = 32.0 °C
- C_{water} = 4.18 J/(g × °C)
- $Density_{solution}$ = 1.00 g/mL

Unknown:
- ΔH = ? kJ

The equation requires the mass of the water used in the experiment, but the mass is not known. Use dimensional analysis to determine the mass of the water. ΔT must also be calculated. Once m, C, and ΔT are known, use $\Delta H = m \times C \times \Delta T$ to solve for ΔH of the water.

2. **CALCULATE** *Solve for the unknown.*

First, calculate the total mass of the water. Only the final volume of the solution (V_f) is needed to make the calculation.

$$m = (50.0 \text{ mL}) \times \left(\frac{1.00 \text{ g}}{\text{mL}}\right) = 50.0 \text{ g}$$

Now calculate ΔT.

$$\Delta T = T_f - T_i \qquad \Delta T = 32.0 \text{ °C} - 25.0 \text{ °C} = 7.0 \text{ °C}$$

Substitute the values for m, C_{water}, and ΔT into the equation and solve for the unknown (ΔH).

$$\Delta H = m \times C \times \Delta T$$
$$= (50.0 \text{ g})(4.18 \text{ J/(g} \times \text{°C}))(7.0 \text{ °C})$$
$$= 1463 \text{ J} = 1.5 \times 10^3 \text{ J}$$

Convert joules to kilojoules.

$$\Delta H = (1.5 \times 10^3 \text{ J})\left(\frac{1 \text{ kJ}}{1000 \text{ J}}\right) = 1.5 \text{ kJ}$$

Practice Problems

11. A student mixed 50.0 mL of water containing 0.50 mol HCl at 22.5 °C with 50.0 mL of water containing 0.50 mol NaOH at 22.5 °C in a foam cup calorimeter. The temperature of the resulting solution increased to 26.0 °C. How much heat in kilojoules (kJ) was released by this reaction?

12. A small pebble is heated and placed in a foam cup calorimeter containing 25.0 mL of water at 25.0 °C. The water reaches a maximum temperature of 26.4 °C. How many joules of heat were released by the pebble?

Chem ASAP!

Problem-Solving 12

Solve Problem 12 with the help of an interactive guided tutorial.

Sample Problem 11-2 (cont.)

3. **EVALUATE** *Does the result make sense?*
The sign of ΔH for the water is positive; the water absorbs 1.5 kJ of heat. Therefore, this neutralization reaction releases 1.5 kJ of heat into the water in the calorimeter, so the sign of ΔH for the reaction is negative. About 4 J of heat is required to raise the temperature of 1 g of water 1 °C. Thus it would take about 200 J to raise the temperature of 50 g of water 1 °C. Further, about 1400 J, or 1.4 kJ, is needed to raise the temperature of 50 g of water 7 °C. This estimated answer is very close to the calculated value of ΔH for the neutralization reaction.

Thermochemical Equations

If you mix calcium oxide with water, an exothermic reaction takes place. The water in the mixture becomes warm. This reaction occurs when cement, which contains calcium oxide, is mixed to make concrete. When 1 mol of calcium oxide reacts with 1 mol of water, 1 mol of calcium hydroxide forms and 65.2 kJ of heat is released. You can show this in the chemical equation by including heat change as a product of the reaction. The diagram in **Figure 11.11a** shows the heat change that occurs in this exothermic reaction.

$$CaO(s) + H_2O(l) \longrightarrow Ca(OH)_2(s) + 65.2 \text{ kJ}$$

You can treat heat change in a chemical reaction like any other reactant or product in a chemical equation. An equation that includes the heat change is called a **thermochemical equation**. A **heat of reaction** is the heat change for the equation exactly as it is written. You will usually see heats of reaction reported as ΔH, which is the heat change at constant pressure. The physical state of the reactants and products must also be given. The standard conditions are that the reaction is carried out at 101.3 kPa (1 atmosphere) and that the reactants and products are in their usual physical states at 25 °C.

Figure 11.10
The reaction between iron(III) oxide and aluminum, called the thermite reaction, releases so much heat that the iron produced is in the molten state.
$$Fe_2O_3(s) + 2Al(s) \longrightarrow Al_2O_3(s) + 2Fe(l)$$

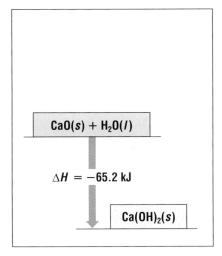

(a) Exothermic Reaction

CaO(s) + H₂O(l)

$\Delta H = -65.2$ kJ

Ca(OH)₂(s)

Na₂CO₃(s) + H₂O(g) + CO₂(g)

$\Delta H = 129$ kJ

2NaHCO₃(s)

(b) Endothermic Reaction

Figure 11.11
*These enthalpy diagrams show exothermic and endothermic processes: **(a)** the reaction of calcium oxide and water and **(b)** the decomposition of sodium hydrogen carbonate. In which case is the enthalpy of the reactant(s) higher than that of the product(s)?*

Thermochemistry **303**

The heat of reaction, or ΔH, in the above example is -65.2 kJ. Each mole of calcium oxide and water that react to form calcium hydroxide produces 65.2 kJ of heat.

$$CaO(s) + H_2O(l) \longrightarrow Ca(OH)_2(s) \qquad \Delta H = -65.2 \text{ kJ}$$

Other reactions absorb heat from the surroundings. For example, baking soda (sodium hydrogen carbonate) decomposes when it is heated, making it useful in baking. The carbon dioxide released in the reaction causes a cake to rise while baking. This process is endothermic, and the heat of reaction is 129 kJ.

$$2NaHCO_3(s) + 129 \text{ kJ} \longrightarrow Na_2CO_3(s) + H_2O(g) + CO_2(g)$$

Remember that ΔH is positive for endothermic reactions. Therefore, you can write the reaction as follows.

$$2NaHCO_3(s) \longrightarrow Na_2CO_3(s) + H_2O(g) + CO_2(g) \qquad \Delta H = 129 \text{ kJ}$$

Sample Problem 11-3

Using the equation for the reaction above, calculate the kilojoules of heat required to decompose 2.24 mol $NaHCO_3(s)$.

1. ANALYZE *List the knowns and the unknown.*

Knowns:
- 2.24 mol $NaHCO_3(s)$ decomposes   • $\Delta H = 129$ kJ

Unknown:
- $\Delta H = ?$ kJ

Use the thermochemical equation,

$$2NaHCO_3(s) + 129 \text{ kJ} \longrightarrow$$
$$Na_2CO_3(s) + H_2O(g) + CO_2(g),$$

to write a conversion factor relating kilojoules of heat and moles of $NaHCO_3$. Then use the conversion factor to determine ΔH for 2.24 mol $NaHCO_3$.

2. CALCULATE *Solve for the unknown.*

The thermochemical equation indicates that 129 kJ are needed to decompose 2 mol $NaHCO_3(s)$. Using this relationship, the conversion factor is

$$\frac{129 \text{ kJ}}{2 \text{ mol } NaHCO_3(s)}$$

Using dimensional analysis, solve for ΔH.

$$\Delta H = 2.24 \text{ mol } NaHCO_3(s) \times \frac{129 \text{ kJ}}{2 \text{ mol } NaHCO_3(s)}$$
$$= 144 \text{ kJ}$$

3. EVALUATE *Does the result make sense?*

Because the ΔH of 129 kJ refers to the decomposition of 2 mol $NaHCO_3(s)$, the decomposition of 2.24 mol should absorb about 10% more heat than 129 kJ, or slightly more than 142 kJ. The answer of 144 kJ is consistent with this estimate.

Practice Problems

13. When carbon disulfide is formed from its elements, heat is absorbed. Calculate the amount of heat (in kJ) absorbed when 5.66 g of carbon disulfide is formed.

$$C(s) + 2S(s) \longrightarrow CS_2(l)$$
$$\Delta H = 89.3 \text{ kJ}$$

14. The production of iron and carbon dioxide from iron(III) oxide and carbon monoxide is an exothermic reaction. How many kilojoules of heat are produced when 3.40 mol Fe_2O_3 reacts with an excess of CO?

$$Fe_2O_3(s) + 3CO(g) \longrightarrow$$
$$2Fe(s) + 3CO_2(g) + 26.3 \text{ kJ}$$

 Chem ASAP!

Problem-Solving 14
Solve Problem 14 with the help of an interactive guided tutorial.

Chemistry problems involving enthalpy changes are similar to stoichiometry problems. The amount of heat released or absorbed during a reaction depends on the number of moles of the reactants involved. The decomposition of 2 mol of sodium hydrogen carbonate, for example, requires 129 kJ of heat. Therefore, the decomposition of 4 mol of the same substance would require twice as much heat, or 258 kJ. **Figure 11.11b** on page 303 shows the heat changes for this reaction. In this and other endothermic processes, the potential energy of the product(s) is higher than the potential energy of the reactant(s).

The physical state of the reactants and products in a thermochemical reaction must also be stated. To see why, compare the following two equations for the decomposition of 1 mol of water.

$$H_2O(l) \longrightarrow H_2(g) + \tfrac{1}{2}O_2(g) \qquad \Delta H = 285.8 \text{ kJ}$$
$$H_2O(g) \longrightarrow H_2(g) + \tfrac{1}{2}O_2(g) \qquad \Delta H = 241.8 \text{ kJ}$$

$$\text{difference} = 44.0 \text{ kJ}$$

Although the two equations are very similar, the different physical states of the H_2O result in different ΔH values. In one case, the reactant is a liquid; in the other case, the reactant is a gas. The vaporization of 1 mole of liquid water to water vapor at 25 °C requires an extra 44.0 kJ of heat. Notice also that fractional coefficients are used here for O_2 because 1 mol H_2O is being decomposed.

$$H_2O(l) \longrightarrow H_2O(g) \qquad \Delta H = 44.0 \text{ kJ}$$

Table 11.4 lists heats of combustion for some common substances. The **heat of combustion** is the heat of reaction for the complete burning of one mole of a substance.

Table 11.4

Heats of Combustion at 25 °C		
Substance	Formula	ΔH (kJ/mol)
Hydrogen	$H_2(g)$	−286
Carbon	$C(s)$, graphite	−394
Carbon monoxide	$CO(g)$	−283
Methane	$CH_4(g)$	−890
Methanol	$CH_3OH(l)$	−726
Acetylene	$C_2H_2(g)$	−1300
Ethanol	$C_2H_5OH(l)$	−1368
Propane	$C_3H_8(g)$	−2220
Benzene	$C_6H_6(l)$	−3268
Glucose	$C_6H_{12}O_6(s)$	−2808
Octane	$C_8H_{18}(l)$	−5471
Sucrose	$C_{12}H_{22}O_{11}(s)$	−5645

BIOLOGY

Warmth from Fat

How do animals such as polar bears and seals survive the cold land and water temperatures where they live? A good coat of fur helps, but it is not enough to

keep them warm. These animals also have special fat cells that help generate heat. These special cells are in tissue called brown fat. The cells of brown fat are unlike other fat cells in the animal's body. Most other cells store chemical energy from the breakdown of carbohydrates and fatty acids in adenosine triphosphate (ATP). ATP acts as the central source of energy for the activities and growth of all animals. Heat is mostly a waste product in ATP-producing cells. The heat generated by the brown fat tissue, however, helps the animal keep relatively comfortable even at subzero temperatures.

Figure 11.12

The combustion of natural gas is an exothermic reaction. As bonds in methane, the main component of natural gas, and oxygen are broken and bonds in carbon dioxide and water are formed, large amounts of energy are released. This energy powers the engine of automobiles. Natural gas is an alternative to gasoline because it substantially reduces air pollution while increasing engine life.

The combustion of natural gas, which is mostly methane, is an exothermic reaction used to heat many homes around the country.

$$CH_4(g) + 2O_2(g) \longrightarrow CO_2(g) + 2H_2O(l) + 890 \text{ kJ}$$

This can also be written as follows.

$$CH_4(g) + 2O_2(g) \longrightarrow CO_2(g) + 2H_2O(l) \qquad \Delta H = -890 \text{ kJ}$$

Burning 1 mol of methane releases 890 kJ of heat. The heat of combustion (ΔH) for this reaction is -890 kJ per mole of carbon burned.

Like other heats of reaction, heats of combustion are reported as the enthalpy changes when the reactions are carried out at 101.3 kPa of pressure and the reactants and products are in their physical states at 25 °C.

section review 11.2

15. When 2 mol of solid magnesium (Mg) combines with 1 mole of oxygen gas (O_2), 2 mol of solid magnesium oxide (MgO) is formed and 1204 kJ of heat is released. Write the thermochemical equation for this combustion reaction.

16. Gasohol contains ethanol (C_2H_5OH)(l), which when burned reacts with oxygen to produce $CO_2(g)$ and $H_2O(g)$. How much heat is released when 12.5 g of ethanol burns?

$$C_2H_5OH(l) + 3O_2(g) \longrightarrow 2CO_2(g) + 3H_2O(g) \qquad \Delta H = -1235 \text{ kJ}$$

17. Explain the term heat of reaction.

18. Hydrogen gas and fluorine gas react to produce hydrogen fluoride. Calculate the heat change (in kJ) for the conversion of 15.0 g of hydrogen gas to hydrogen fluoride gas at constant pressure.

$$H_2(g) + F_2(g) \longrightarrow 2HF(g) \qquad \Delta H = -536 \text{ kJ}$$

19. Why is it important to give the physical state of a substance in a thermochemical reaction?

 Chem ASAP! **Assessment 11.2** Check your understanding of the important ideas and concepts in Section 11.2.

HEAT IN CHANGES OF STATE

When your body heats up, you start to sweat. The evaporation of sweat is your body's way of cooling itself to a normal temperature. **Why does the evaporation of sweat from your skin help to rid your body of excess heat?**

objectives

▶ Classify, by type, the heat changes that occur during melting, freezing, boiling, and condensing

▶ Calculate heat changes that occur during melting, freezing, boiling, and condensing

key terms

▶ molar heat of fusion
▶ molar heat of solidification
▶ molar heat of vaporization
▶ molar heat of condensation
▶ molar heat of solution

Heats of Fusion and Solidification

What happens if you place an ice cube on a table in a warm room? The ice cube is the system, and the table and air around it are the surroundings. The ice absorbs heat from its surroundings and begins to melt. The temperature of the ice and the water produced remains at 0 °C until all of the ice has melted. The temperature of the water begins to increase only after all of the ice has melted. In this section you will learn about heat changes that occur during changes of state.

Like ice cubes, all solids absorb heat as they melt to become liquids. The heat absorbed by one mole of a substance in melting from a solid to a liquid at a constant temperature is the **molar heat of fusion** (ΔH_{fus}). The heat lost when one mole of a liquid solidifies at a constant temperature is the **molar heat of solidification** (ΔH_{solid}). The quantity of heat absorbed by a melting solid is exactly the same as the quantity of heat lost when the liquid solidifies; that is, $\Delta H_{fus} = -\Delta H_{solid}$, as shown in **Figure 11.13**. Why is this true? **Table 11.5** on the following page gives heats of fusion of some substances.

The melting of 1 mol of ice at 0 °C to 1 mol of water at 0 °C requires the absorption of 6.01 kJ of heat. This quantity of heat is the molar heat of fusion. Likewise, the conversion of 1 mol of water at 0 °C to 1 mol of ice at 0 °C releases 6.01 kJ. This quantity of heat is the molar heat of solidification.

$$H_2O(s) \longrightarrow H_2O(l) \qquad \Delta H_{fus} = 6.01 \text{ kJ/mol}$$

$$H_2O(l) \longrightarrow H_2O(s) \qquad \Delta H_{solid} = -6.01 \text{ kJ/mol}$$

Chem ASAP!

Animation 12

Observe the phase changes as ice is converted to steam when heat is added.

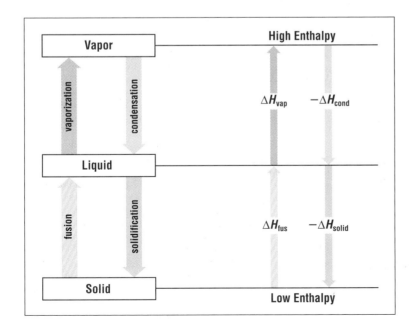

Figure 11.13

Enthalpy changes accompany changes in state. Fusion and vaporization are endothermic processes. Solidification and condensation are exothermic processes.

Table 11.5

		Heats of Physical Change			
Substance	Formula	Freezing point (K)	ΔH_{fus} (kJ/mol)	Boiling point (K)	ΔH_{vap} (kJ/mol)
Acetone	CH_3COCH_3	177.8	5.72	329.4	29.1
Ammonia	NH_3	195.3	5.65	239.7	23.4
Argon	Ar	83.8	1.2	87.3	6.5
Benzene	C_6H_6	278.7	9.87	353.3	30.8
Ethanol	C_2H_5OH	158.7	4.60	351.5	43.5
Helium	He	3.5	0.02	4.22	0.08
Hydrogen	H_2	14.0	0.12	20.3	0.90
Methane	CH_4	90.7	0.94	111.7	8.2
Methanol	CH_3OH	175.5	3.16	337.2	35.3
Neon	Ne	24.5	0.33	27.1	1.76
Nitrogen	N_2	63.3	0.72	77.4	5.58
Oxygen	O_2	54.8	0.44	90.2	6.82
Water	H_2O	273.2	6.01	373.2	40.7

MINI LAB

Heat of Fusion of Ice

PURPOSE

To estimate the heat of fusion of ice.

MATERIALS

- ice
- foam cup
- graduated cylinder
- thermometer
- hot water
- temperature probe (optional)

PROCEDURE

 Probe version available in the Probeware Lab Manual.

1. Fill a 100-mL graduated cylinder with hot tap water. Allow the filled cylinder to stand for 1 minute. Pour the water into the sink.

2. Use the graduated cylinder to measure 70 mL of hot water. Pour the water into the foam cup. Measure the temperature of the water.

3. Add a small ice cube to the cup of water and gently swirl the cup. Measure the temperature of the water immediately after the ice cube has completely melted.

4. Pour the water into the graduated cylinder and measure the volume.

5. Calculate the heat of fusion of ice (kJ/mol) by dividing the heat given up from the water by the moles of ice melted. *Hint:* The mass of ice melted is the same as the increase in the volume of the water: 1 g H_2O = 1 mL H_2O.

ANALYSIS AND CONCLUSIONS

1. Compare your experimental value for the heat of fusion of ice with the accepted value of 6.01 kJ/mol. Account for any error in your value.

2. Suggest some changes in this procedure that would improve the accuracy of the results.

Figure 11.14
Ice is commonly used to refrigerate perishable foods. What happens to the temperature of the ice as it begins to melt?

Sample Problem 11-4

How many grams of ice at 0 °C and 101.3 kPa could be melted by the addition of 2.25 kJ of heat?

1. ANALYZE List the knowns and the unknown.

Knowns:
- Initial conditions are 0 °C and 101.3 kPa.
- $\Delta H_{fus} = 6.01$ kJ/mol
- $\Delta H = 2.25$ kJ

Unknown:
- $m_{ice} = ?$ g

The conditions 0 °C and 101.3 kPa indicate that the standard conditions for the fusion of ice have been met. Use the chemical equation $H_2O(s) + 6.01$ kJ $\rightarrow H_2O(l)$ to find the number of moles of ice that can be melted by the addition of 2.25 kJ of heat. Convert moles of ice to grams of ice.

2. CALCULATE Solve for the unknown.

The required conversion factors come from ΔH_{fus} and the molar mass of ice. The conversion factors are

$$\frac{1 \text{ mol ice}}{6.01 \text{ kJ}} \quad \text{and} \quad \frac{18.0 \text{ g ice}}{1 \text{ mol ice}}$$

Multiply the known heat change (2.25 kJ) by the conversion factors

$$m_{ice} = 2.25 \text{ kJ} \times \frac{1 \text{ mol ice}}{6.01 \text{ kJ}} \times \frac{18.0 \text{ g ice}}{1 \text{ mol ice}}$$

$$= 6.74 \text{ g ice}$$

3. EVALUATE Does the result make sense?

6.01 kJ is required to melt 1 mol of ice. Because only about one-third of this amount of heat (roughly 2 kJ) is available, only about one-third mol of ice, or $\frac{18.0 \text{ g}}{3} = 6$ g, should melt. This estimate and the calculated answer are similar.

Practice Problems

20. How many grams of ice at 0 °C and 101.3 kPa could be melted by the addition of 0.400 kJ of heat?

21. How many kilojoules of heat are required to melt a 10.0 g popsicle at 0 °C and 101.3 kPa? Assume the popsicle has the same molar mass and heat capacity as water.

Chem ASAP!

Problem-Solving 21
Solve Problem 21 with the help of an interactive guided tutorial.

Heats of Vaporization and Condensation

When liquids absorb heat at their boiling points, they become vapors. Vaporization of a liquid, through boiling or evaporation, cools the environment around the liquid as heat flows from the surroundings to the liquid. The amount of heat necessary to vaporize one mole of a given liquid is called its **molar heat of vaporization. Table 11.5** on page 308 gives some values of molar heats of vaporization for various compounds. The values are derived at standard conditions: the reactions are carried out at one atmosphere pressure and the reactants and products are in their usual physical states at the same temperature.

The molar heat of vaporization of water is 40.7 kJ/mol. This means that in order to vaporize 1 mol of water, 40.7 kJ of energy must be supplied. This energy converts 1 mol of water molecules in the liquid state to 1 mol of water molecules in the vapor state, given the same temperature and 1 atm pressure. This process is described in the thermochemical equation below.

$$H_2O(l) \longrightarrow H_2O(g) \qquad \Delta H_{vap} = 40.7 \text{ kJ/mol}$$

Diethyl ether ($C_4H_{10}O$) is a low-boiling-point liquid (bp = 34.6 °C) that is a good solvent and was formerly used as an anesthetic. If diethyl ether is poured into a beaker on a warm, humid day, the ether will absorb heat from the beaker walls and evaporate very rapidly. If the beaker loses enough heat, the water vapor in the air may condense and freeze on the beaker walls. If so, a coating of frost will form on the outside of the beaker. Diethyl ether has a molar heat of vaporization (ΔH_{vap}) of 15.7 kJ/mol. Is this an endothermic or an exothermic process?

$$C_4H_{10}O(l) \longrightarrow C_4H_{10}O(g) \qquad \Delta H_{vap} = 15.7 \text{ kJ/mol}$$

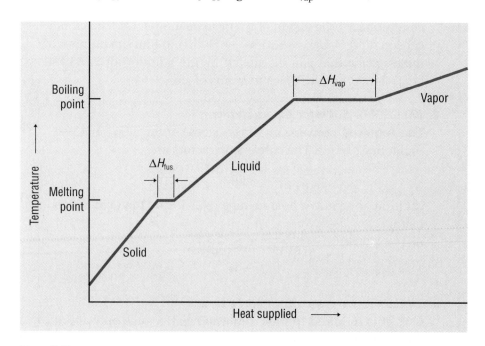

Figure 11.15

This graph shows the heating curve for water. Notice that the temperature remains constant during melting and vaporization. Notice also that it requires much more energy to vaporize liquid water than it does to melt the same mass of ice.

Condensation is the exact opposite of vaporization. Therefore, the amount of heat released when 1 mol of vapor condenses is called its **molar heat of condensation** (ΔH_{cond}). This value is numerically the same as the corresponding molar heat of vaporization, however the value has the opposite sign. Because energy is conserved in a physical change, $\Delta H_{vap} = -\Delta H_{cond}$. **Figure 11.15** summarizes the heat changes that occur as a solid is heated to a liquid and then to a gas. You should be able to identify certain trends regarding the temperature during changes of state and the energy requirements that accompany these changes from the graph. The large values for ΔH_{vap} and ΔH_{cond} are the reason hot vapors such as steam can be very dangerous. You can receive a scalding burn from steam when the heat of condensation is released as it touches your skin.

$$H_2O(g) \longrightarrow H_2O(l) \qquad \Delta H_{cond} = -40.7 \text{ kJ/mol}$$

Sample Problem 11-5

How much heat (in kJ) is absorbed when 24.8 g $H_2O(l)$ at 100 °C is converted to steam at 100 °C?

1. **ANALYZE List the knowns and the unknown.**

Knowns:
- mass of water converted to steam = 24.8 g
- ΔH_{vap} = 40.7 kJ/mol

Unknown:
- ΔH = ? kJ

The ΔH_{vap} in the following equation is given in kJ/mol, but the quantity of water is given in grams. Thus the first steps in the problem solution are to convert grams of water to moles of water and then multiply by ΔH_{vap}.

$$H_2O(l) + 40.7 \text{ kJ/mol} \longrightarrow H_2O(g)$$

2. **CALCULATE Solve for the unknown.**

The required conversion factors come from ΔH_{vap} and the molar mass of water.

$$\frac{1 \text{ mol } H_2O(l)}{18.0 \text{ g } H_2O(l)} \quad \text{and} \quad \frac{40.7 \text{ kJ}}{1 \text{ mol } H_2O(l)}$$

Multiply the known mass of water in grams by the conversion factors.

$$\Delta H = 24.8 \text{ g } H_2O(l) \times \frac{1 \text{ mol } H_2O(l)}{18.0 \text{ g } H_2O(l)} \times \frac{40.7 \text{ kJ}}{1 \text{ mol } H_2O(l)}$$
$$= 56.1 \text{ kJ}$$

3. **EVALUATE Does the result make sense?**

Knowing the molar mass of water is 18.0 g/mol, 24.8 g $H_2O(l)$ can be estimated to be somewhat less than 1.5 mol H_2O. Thus the calculated heat change should be somewhat less than 1.5 mol × 40 kJ/mol = 60 kJ, and it is.

Practice Problems

22. How much heat (in kJ) is absorbed when 63.7 g $H_2O(l)$ at 100 °C is converted to steam at 100 °C?

23. How many kilojoules of heat are absorbed when 0.46 g of chloroethane (C_2H_5Cl, bp 12.3 °C) vaporizes at its boiling point? The molar heat of vaporization of chloroethane is 26.4 kJ/mol.

Chem ASAP!

Problem-Solving 23
Solve Problem 23 with the help of an interactive guided tutorial.

Heat of Solution

Heat changes can also occur when a solute dissolves in a solvent. The heat change caused by dissolution of one mole of substance is the **molar heat of solution** (ΔH_{soln}). Sodium hydroxide provides a good example of an exothermic molar heat of solution. When 1 mol of sodium hydroxide (NaOH)(s) is dissolved in water, the solution can become so hot that it steams. The heat from this process is released as the sodium ions and the hydroxide ions separate and interact with the water. The temperature of the solution increases, releasing 445.1 kJ of heat as the molar heat of solution.

$$\text{NaOH}(s) \xrightarrow{\text{H}_2\text{O}(l)} \text{Na}^+(aq) + \text{OH}^-(aq)$$

$$\Delta H_{\text{soln}} = -445.1 \text{ kJ/mol}$$

A practical application of an exothermic reaction is how a hot pack works. A hot pack mixes calcium chloride ($CaCl_2$) and water, which produces the heat characteristic of an exothermic reaction.

$$\text{CaCl}_2(s) \xrightarrow{\text{H}_2\text{O}(l)} \text{Ca}^{2+}(aq) + 2\text{Cl}^-(aq)$$

$$\Delta H_{\text{soln}} = -82.8 \text{ kJ/mol}$$

The dissolution of ammonium nitrate (NH_4NO_3)(s) is an example of an endothermic process. When ammonium nitrate dissolves in water, the solution becomes so cold that frost may form on the outside of the container. Is heat absorbed or released as the ammonium and nitrate ions separate and interact with the water? Heat is released from the water and the temperature of the solution decreases. The cold pack allows water and ammonium nitrate (NH_4NO_3) to mix, producing an endothermic reaction.

$$\text{NH}_4\text{NO}_3(s) \xrightarrow{\text{H}_2\text{O}(l)} \text{NH}_4^+(aq) + \text{NO}_3^-(aq)$$

$$\Delta H_{\text{soln}} = 25.7 \text{ kJ/mol}$$

Figure 11.16 illustrates a practical application of heats of solution.

Figure 11.16
Cold packs and hot packs are available for a variety of medical uses.

Sample Problem 11-6

How much heat (in kJ) is released when 2.500 mol NaOH(s) is dissolved in water?

1. ANALYZE List the knowns and the unknown.

Knowns:

- $\Delta H_{soln} = -445.1$ kJ/mol
- amount of NaOH(s) dissolved: 2.500 mol

Unknown:

- $\Delta H = ?$ kJ

Use the heat of solution from the following chemical equation to solve for the amount of heat released (ΔH).

$$NaOH(s) + H_2O(l) \longrightarrow Na^+(aq) + OH^-(aq)$$
$$+ 445.1 \text{ kJ/mol}$$

2. CALCULATE Solve for the unknown.

Multiplying the number of mol NaOH and ΔH_{soln} will yield the value of the unknown (ΔH).

$$\Delta H = 2.500 \text{ mol NaOH}(s) \times \frac{-445.1 \text{ kJ}}{1 \text{ mol NaOH}(aq)} = -1113 \text{ kJ}$$

3. EVALUATE Does the result make sense?

By inspection, ΔH is 2.5 times greater than ΔH_{soln}, as it should be. Also, the heat of solution in the answer is negative, indicating an exothermic reaction. This is consistent with the heat of solution of sodium hydroxide discussed earlier in the text.

Practice Problems

24. How much heat (in kJ) is released when 0.677 mol NaOH(s) is dissolved in water?

25. How many moles of $NH_4NO_3(s)$ must be dissolved in water so that 88.0 kJ of heat is released from the water?

Chem ASAP!

Problem-Solving 25
Solve Problem 25 with the help of an interactive guided tutorial.

---

section review 11.3

26. Identify each heat change by name and classify each change as exothermic or endothermic.

   a. 1 mol $C_3H_8(l) \longrightarrow$ 1 mol $C_3H_8(g)$

   b. 1 mol NaCl(s) + 3.88 kJ/mol $\longrightarrow$ 1 mol NaCl(aq)

   c. 1 mol NaCl(s) $\longrightarrow$ 1 mol NaCl(l)

   d. 1 mol $NH_3(g) \longrightarrow$ 1 mol $NH_3(l)$

   e. 1 mol Hg(l) $\longrightarrow$ 1 mol Hg(s)

27. Heavy water, in which the hydrogens are hydrogen-2 instead of the more common hydrogen-1, is called deuterium oxide (D_2O). Solid D_2O melts at 3.78 °C. The molar heat of fusion of $D_2O(s)$ is 6.34 kJ/mol. How much heat is released when 8.46 g $D_2O(l)$ solidifies at its melting point?

28. Why is a burn from steam potentially far more serious than a burn from very hot water?

29. Why does an ice cube melt at room temperature?

 Chem ASAP! Assessment 11.3 Check your understanding of the important ideas and concepts in Section 11.3.

CALCULATING HEAT CHANGES

objectives
▶ Apply Hess's law of heat summation to find heat changes for chemical and physical processes
▶ Calculate heat changes using standard heats of formation

key terms
▶ Hess's law of heat summation
▶ standard heat of formation

*E*meralds are beautiful gemstones composed of the elements chromium, aluminum, silicon, oxygen, and beryllium. If you were interested in the heat changes that occur when an emerald is converted to its elements, it is more than likely that you would not want to destroy the emerald by measuring the heat changes directly. **Is there a way to determine the heat of reaction without actually performing the reaction?**

Hess's Law

It is possible to talk in general terms about the heat changes that take place in chemical reactions. However, most reactions occur in a series of steps. Suppose, for example, you need to know the heat of reaction for an intermediate step, but it is impossible for you to obtain the value directly. Fortunately, Hess's law makes it possible to measure a heat of reaction indirectly. Thus even when a direct measurement cannot be made, the heat of reaction can still be determined.

Elemental carbon exists as both graphite and diamond at 25 °C. Because graphite is more stable than diamond, you would expect the following process to take place.

$$C(\text{diamond}) \longrightarrow C(\text{graphite})$$

Fortunately for people who own diamonds, the conversion of diamond to graphite takes millions and millions of years. This enthalpy change cannot be measured directly because the reaction is far too slow. Hess's law, however, provides a way to calculate the heat of reaction. Hess's law is expressed by a simple rule: If you add two or more thermochemical equations to give a final equation, then you can also add the heats of reaction to give the final heat of reaction. This rule is **Hess's law of heat summation.**

You can use Hess's law to find the enthalpy changes for the conversion of diamond to graphite by using the following combustion reactions and **Figure 11.17.**

a. $C(s, \text{graphite}) + O_2(g) \longrightarrow CO_2(g)$ $\Delta H = -393.5$ kJ
b. $C(s, \text{diamond}) + O_2(g) \longrightarrow CO_2(g)$ $\Delta H = -395.4$ kJ

Write equation **a** in reverse to give:

c. $CO_2(g) \longrightarrow C(s, \text{graphite}) + O_2(g)$ $\Delta H = 393.5$ kJ

When you write a reverse reaction, you must also change the sign of ΔH. If you now add equations **b** and **c**, you get the equation for the conversion of diamond to graphite. The $CO_2(g)$ and $O_2(g)$ terms on both sides of the summed equations cancel, just as they do in algebra. Now if you also add the values of ΔH for equations **b** and **c**, you get the heat of reaction for this conversion.

$C(s, \text{diamond}) + \cancel{O_2(g)} \longrightarrow \cancel{CO_2(g)}$	$\Delta H = -395.4$ kJ
$\cancel{CO_2(g)} \longrightarrow C(s, \text{graphite}) + \cancel{O_2(g)}$	$\Delta H = 393.5$ kJ
$C(s, \text{diamond}) \longrightarrow C(s, \text{graphite})$	$\Delta H = -1.9$ kJ

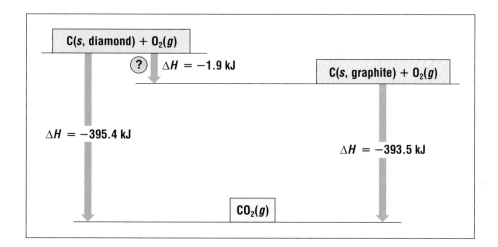

Figure 11.17

Hess's law is used to determine the enthalpy change of a very slow chemical process.

$C(s, diamond) \longrightarrow C(s, graphite)$

Thus the conversion of diamond to graphite is an exothermic process; its heat of reaction has a negative sign. Conversely, the change of graphite to diamond is an endothermic process. Some reactions give other products in addition to the product of interest. Suppose you want to determine the enthalpy change for the formation of carbon monoxide from its elements. The reaction is:

$$C(s, \text{graphite}) + \tfrac{1}{2}O_2(g) \longrightarrow CO(g) \qquad \Delta H = ?$$

Although it is easy to write the equation, carrying out the reaction in the laboratory as written is virtually impossible. Carbon dioxide (a "side product") is produced along with carbon monoxide (the "desired product"). Therefore, any measured heat of reaction is related to the formation of both $CO(g)$ and $CO_2(g)$, and not $CO(g)$ alone. You can solve the problem, however, using Hess's law and two reactions that can be carried out in the laboratory. The reactions are:

a. $C(s, \text{graphite}) + O_2(g) \longrightarrow CO_2(g) \qquad \Delta H = -393.5 \text{ kJ}$
b. $CO(g) + \tfrac{1}{2}O_2(g) \longrightarrow CO_2(g) \qquad\qquad \Delta H = -283.0 \text{ kJ}$

Writing the reverse of equation **b** and changing the sign of ΔH yields equation **c.**

c. $CO_2(g) \longrightarrow CO(g) + \tfrac{1}{2}O_2(g) \qquad \Delta H = 283.0 \text{ kJ}$

As shown on the following page, adding equations **a** and **c** gives the expression for the formation of $CO(g)$ from its elements. Notice that only $\tfrac{1}{2}O_2(g)$ cancels in the final equation. See **Figure 11.18.**

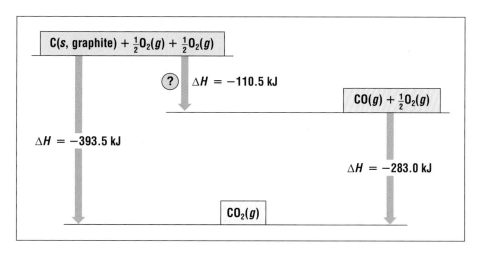

Figure 11.18

Hess's law is used to determine the enthalpy change for the reaction:

$C(s, graphite) + \tfrac{1}{2}O_2(g) \longrightarrow CO(g)$

Thermochemistry **315**

$$C(s, \text{graphite}) + O_2(g) \longrightarrow \cancel{CO_2(g)} \qquad \Delta H = -393.5 \text{ kJ}$$
$$\cancel{CO_2(g)} \longrightarrow CO(g) + \tfrac{1}{2}O_2(g) \qquad \Delta H = 283.0 \text{ kJ}$$

$$C(s, \text{graphite}) + \tfrac{1}{2}O_2(g) \longrightarrow CO(g) \qquad \Delta H = -110.5 \text{ kJ}$$

The formation of $CO(g)$ is exothermic; 110.5 kJ of heat is given off when 1 mol $CO(g)$ is formed from its elements.

Standard Heats of Formation

Sometimes it is hard to measure the heat change for a reaction. What are some examples where this might be the case? In such cases you can calculate the heat of reaction from standard heats of formation. The **standard heat of formation** (ΔH_f^0) of a compound is the change in enthalpy that accompanies the formation of one mole of a compound from its elements with all substances in their standard states at 25 °C.

The ΔH_f^0 of a free element in its standard state is arbitrarily set at zero. For example, $\Delta H_f^0 = 0$ for the diatomic molecules $H_2(g)$, $N_2(g)$, $O_2(g)$, $F_2(g)$, $Cl_2(g)$, $Br_2(l)$, and $I_2(s)$. Similarly, $\Delta H_f^0 = 0$ for the graphite form of carbon, $C(s, \text{graphite})$.

Many values of ΔH_f^0 have been measured. **Table 11.6** lists ΔH_f^0 values for some common substances. Standard heats of formation of compounds are handy for calculating heats of reaction at standard conditions. The standard heat of reaction (ΔH^0) is the difference between the standard heats of formation of all the reactants and products. This relationship can be expressed by the following equation.

$$\Delta H^0 = \Delta H_f^0(\text{products}) - \Delta H_f^0(\text{reactants})$$

Table 11.6

Standard Heats of Formation (ΔH_f^0) at 25 °C and 101.3 kPa					
Substance	ΔH_f^0 (kJ/mol)	Substance	ΔH_f^0 (kJ/mol)	Substance	ΔH_f^0 (kJ/mol)
$Al_2O_3(s)$	−1676.0	$Fe(s)$	0.0	$NO(g)$	90.37
$Br_2(g)$	30.91	$Fe_2O_3(s)$	−822.1	$NO_2(g)$	33.85
$Br_2(l)$	0.0	$H_2(g)$	0.0	$Na_2CO_3(s)$	−1131.1
$C(s, \text{diamond})$	1.9	$H_2O(g)$	−241.8	$NaCl(s)$	−411.2
$C(s, \text{graphite})$	0.0	$H_2O(l)$	−285.8	$O_2(g)$	0.0
$CH_4(g)$	−74.86	$H_2O_2(l)$	−187.8	$O_3(g)$	142.0
$CO(g)$	−110.5	$HCl(g)$	−92.31	$P(s, \text{white})$	0.0
$CO_2(g)$	−393.5	$H_2S(g)$	−20.1	$P(s, \text{red})$	−18.4
$CaCO_3(s)$	−1207.0	$I_2(g)$	62.4	$S(s, \text{rhombic})$	0.0
$CaO(s)$	−635.1	$I_2(s)$	0.0	$S(s, \text{monoclinic})$	0.30
$Cl_2(g)$	0.0	$N_2(g)$	0.0	$SO_2(g)$	−296.8
$F_2(g)$	0.0	$NH_3(g)$	−46.19	$SO_3(g)$	−395.7

Figure 11.19 is a diagram similar to others you have seen, except that it displays the standard heats of formation of the reactants hydrogen and oxygen and the product water. The heat difference between the reactants and products, −285.8 kJ/mol, is the standard heat of formation of liquid water from the gases hydrogen and oxygen. Does water have a lower or higher enthalpy than the elements from which it is formed? On what other basis can you account for your answer?

Figure 11.19
This enthalpy diagram shows the standard heat of formation of water.

Sample Problem 11-7

What is the standard heat of reaction (ΔH^0) for the reaction of gaseous carbon monoxide with oxygen to form gaseous carbon dioxide?

1. ANALYZE *List the knowns and the unknown.*

Knowns (from **Table 11.6**):
- $\Delta H_f^0 O_2(g) = 0$ kJ/mol (free element)
- $\Delta H_f^0 CO(g) = -110.5$ kJ/mol
- $\Delta H_f^0 CO_2(g) = -393.5$ kJ/mol

Unknown:
- $\Delta H^0 = ?$ kJ

Balance the equation of the reaction of $CO(g)$ with $O_2(g)$ to form $CO_2(g)$. Then determine ΔH^0 using the standard heats of formation of the reactants and products.

2. CALCULATE *Solve for the unknown.*

First, write the balanced equation.

$$2CO(g) + O_2(g) \longrightarrow 2CO_2(g)$$

Next, find and sum the ΔH_f^0 of all of the reactants, taking into account the number of moles of each.

$$\Delta H_f^0(\text{reactants}) = 2 \text{ mol } CO(g) \times \frac{-110.5 \text{ kJ}}{1 \text{ mol } CO(g)}$$

$$+ 1 \text{ mol } O_2(g) \times \frac{0 \text{ kJ}}{1 \text{ mol } O_2(g)}$$

$$= -221.0 \text{ kJ}$$

Then, find the ΔH_f^0 of the product in a similar way.

$$\Delta H_f^0(\text{product}) = 2 \text{ mol } CO_2(g) \times \frac{-393.5 \text{ kJ}}{1 \text{ mol } CO_2(g)}$$

$$= -787.0 \text{ kJ}$$

Finally, find the difference between $\Delta H_f^0(\text{products})$ and $\Delta H_f^0(\text{reactants})$.

$$\Delta H^0 = \Delta H_f^0(\text{products}) - \Delta H_f^0(\text{reactants})$$

$$\Delta H^0 = (-787.0 \text{ kJ}) - (-221.0 \text{ kJ})$$

$$\Delta H^0 = -566.0 \text{ kJ}$$

Practice Problems

30. Use the standard heats of formation to calculate the standard heats of reaction (ΔH^0) for these reactions.
   a. $Br_2(g) \longrightarrow Br_2(l)$
   b. $CaCO_3(s) \longrightarrow CaO(s) + CO_2(g)$
   c. $2NO(g) + O_2(g) \longrightarrow 2NO_2(g)$

31. With one exception, the standard heats of formation of $Na(s)$, $O_2(g)$, $Br_2(l)$, $CO(g)$, $Fe(s)$, and $He(g)$ are identical. What is the exception? Explain.

Chem ASAP!

Problem-Solving 30
Solve Problem 30 with the help of an interactive guided tutorial.

Sample Problem 11-7 (cont.)

3. **EVALUATE** *Does the result make sense?*

The ΔH^0 is negative. Therefore, the reaction is exothermic, as illustrated in **Figure 11.20**. This makes sense because the oxidation of carbon monoxide is a combustion reaction. Combustion reactions always release heat.

Figure 11.20

Hess's law is used to determine the enthalpy change for the reaction of carbon monoxide and oxygen.

$2CO(g) + O_2(g) \longrightarrow 2CO_2(g)$

---

section review 11.4

32. Calculate the enthalpy change (ΔH) in kJ for the following reaction.

$$2Al(s) + Fe_2O_3(s) \longrightarrow 2Fe(s) + Al_2O_3(s)$$

Use the enthalpy changes for the combustion of aluminum and iron:

$$2Al(s) + 1\tfrac{1}{2}O_2(g) \longrightarrow Al_2O_3(s) \qquad \Delta H = -1669.8 \text{ kJ}$$

$$2Fe(s) + 1\tfrac{1}{2}O_2(g) \longrightarrow Fe_2O_3(s) \qquad \Delta H = -824.2 \text{ kJ}$$

33. What is the standard heat of reaction (ΔH^0) for the decomposition of hydrogen peroxide?

$$2H_2O_2(l) \longrightarrow 2H_2O(l) + O_2(g)$$

34. State Hess's law of heat summation in your own words. Explain its usefulness.

35. What happens to the sign of ΔH when the reverse of a chemical reaction is written? Why?

 Chem ASAP! Assessment 11.4 Check your understanding of the important ideas and concepts in Section 11.4.

portfolio project

Some chefs use heavy cast iron skillets; others use lightweight stainless steel. Use what you have learned about heat capacity to list the advantages and drawbacks of these skillets. Write an advertisement for each skillet stressing only its positive features.

SMALL-SCALE LAB

HEAT OF COMBUSTION OF A CANDLE

SAFETY

Wear safety glasses and follow the standard safety procedures outlined on page 18. Keep the burning candle away from combustible materials.

PURPOSE

To observe a burning candle and calculate the heat associated with the combustion reaction.

MATERIALS

- candle
- aluminum foil
- safety matches
- ruler
- balance
- temperature probe (optional)

PROCEDURE

Probe version available in the Probeware Lab Manual.

Measure and record the length of a candle in centimeters. Place the candle on a small piece of aluminum foil and measure the mass of the foil–candle system. Note the time as you light the candle. Let the candle burn for about five minutes. While you wait, begin answering the ANALYSIS questions. After about 5 minutes, extinguish the candle and record the time. Measure the mass of the foil–candle system again. Do not try to measure the mass while the candle is burning.

ANALYSIS

Using your experimental data, answer the following questions.

1. Observe the candle burn and draw a picture of what you see.

2. Examine the flame closely. Is it the wax or the wick that burns?

3. If you said the wax, how does the wax burn without touching the flame? If you said the wick, what is the function of the wax?

4. If you could measure the temperature near the flame, you would find that the air is much hotter above the flame than it is beside it. Why? Explain.

5. Scientists have often wondered if a candle would burn well in zero gravity. How would zero gravity change the shape of the flame?

6. How much length and mass did the candle lose? Are these data more consistent with the wax or the wick burning?

7. Keeping in mind that 'wick' is also a verb, explain how a candle works.

8. The formula for candle wax can be approximated as $C_{20}H_{42}$. Write and balance an equation for the complete combustion of the candle wax.

9. Calculate the moles of candle wax burned in the experiment.

10. Calculate the heat of combustion of candle wax in kJ/mol. The standard heat of formation of candle wax ($C_{20}H_{42}$) is -2230 kJ/mol. The standard heats of formation of carbon dioxide and water are -394 kJ/mol and -242 kJ/mol, respectively. The heat of combustion of candle wax equals the sum of the heats of formation of the products minus the sum of the heats of formation of the reactants.

11. Calculate the kilojoules of heat released in your reaction. *Hint:* Multiply the number of moles of candle wax burned in the experiment by the heat of combustion of candle wax.

YOU'RE THE CHEMIST!

The following small-scale activities allow you to develop your own procedures and analyze the results.

1. **Design It!** Design an experiment to show that the candle wax does not burn with complete combustion.

2. **Design It!** Design an experiment to show that water is a product of the combustion of a candle.

HARNESSING SOLAR ENERGY

When you consider energy sources other than oil or coal, you may think of solar power. Solar power is energy from the sun, and it is free, clean, and readily available.

In theory, solar power is surely the most plentiful energy source available. The enormous power of the sun's rays can be harnessed by solar, or photovoltaic, cells. In reality, this process has been faced with problems that have prevented solar power from becoming a more prevalent part of your life. First, the sun does not always shine on a desired location with maximum power. The tilt of Earth on its axis, as well as weather conditions, can alter the amount of sunlight falling upon different locations. Second, solar cells are not very efficient at converting a "packet" of light energy, called a photon, into electricity. Finally, storing the electricity is not very practical because small batteries that can hold a lot of charge for extended periods of time have not yet been developed.

Instead of using the sun's energy to generate electricity, what about using it to heat an object directly? The sun's rays can be concentrated onto very small areas. Anyone who has used a magnifying glass to burn a hole in a sheet of paper knows this! The heat collected can be transferred to water, or oil, or even molten NaCl to be stored, or piped, to a remote area. This stored heat energy can then be converted to electricity. One of the drawbacks of this scheme is that some heat will always be lost because the heat-storing system is not at thermal equilibrium with its surroundings.

Scientists have also begun to take advantage of storing solar energy in the form of chemical energy. Think of it this way: It "costs" a certain amount of

In theory, solar power is the most plentiful energy source available. The enormous power of the sun's rays can be harnessed by solar, or photovoltaic, cells.

energy to break a chemical bond in a molecule; when the process is reversed, the energy "cost" is refunded in the form of heat energy. The first process is an example of an endothermic reaction, which requires heat to be supplied to the system for the reaction to occur. The second (reverse) reaction is exothermic, during which heat is released as a reaction product.

One system that uses endothermic and exothermic reactions has been successfully tested. In this system, the sun's rays are concentrated to heat a "solar reactor" to about 800 °C, where methane (CH_4) and carbon dioxide (CO_2) absorb the heat to form carbon monoxide (CO) and hydrogen gas (H_2). The product gases (CO and H_2) are cooled to room temperature and piped to a destination where they are recombined to release the energy that is stored in chemical bonds. This approach is significant because the product gases are not hot, so they do not lose heat to the surroundings. After the CO and H_2 react, heat, CH_4, and CO_2 are produced. The gases are used to start the process over again, and the heat is used to generate electricity.

Solar energy is a very dynamic field. Many researchers are actively seeking new and better ways to harness the world's most plentiful energy resource.

Chapter 11 STUDENT STUDY GUIDE

Take It to the NET
For interactive study and
review, go to www.phschool.com

KEY TERMS

- calorie *p. 295*
- calorimeter *p. 300*
- calorimetry *p. 300*
- chemical potential energy *p. 293*
- endothermic process *p. 294*
- energy *p. 293*
- enthalpy (*H*) *p. 301*
- exothermic process *p. 294*
- heat *p. 293*
- heat capacity *p. 296*
- heat of combustion *p. 305*

- heat of reaction *p. 303*
- Hess's law of heat summation *p. 314*
- joule *p. 296*
- law of conservation of energy *p. 294*
- molar heat of condensation *p. 311*
- molar heat of fusion *p. 307*
- molar heat of solidification *p. 307*

- molar heat of solution *p. 312*
- molar heat of vaporization *p. 310*
- specific heat *p. 297*
- specific heat capacity *p. 297*
- standard heat of formation *p. 316*
- surroundings *p. 294*
- system *p. 294*
- thermochemical equation *p. 303*
- thermochemistry *p. 293*
- universe *p. 294*

KEY EQUATIONS AND RELATIONSHIPS

- 1 Calorie = 1 kilocalorie = 1000 calories
- 1 J = 0.239 cal and 4.184 J = 1 cal
- $C = \dfrac{q}{m \times \Delta T} = \dfrac{\text{heat (joules or calories)}}{\text{mass (g)} \times \text{change in temperature (°C)}}$

- $\Delta H = m \times C \times \Delta T$, where $\Delta T = T_f - T_i$
- $\Delta H^0 = \Delta H_f^0(\text{products}) - \Delta H_f^0(\text{reactants})$

CONCEPT SUMMARY

11.1 The Flow of Energy—Heat

- Energy is the capacity to do work or to supply heat. The law of conservation of energy states that energy cannot be created or destroyed.
- A process is exothermic if heat flows from the system to the surroundings and endothermic if heat flows from the surroundings to the system.
- An object's heat capacity is the amount of heat it takes to change the object's temperature by exactly 1 °C. The specific heat capacity of a substance is the amount of heat it takes to raise the temperature of 1 g of the substance 1 °C.

11.2 Measuring and Expressing Heat Changes

- Thermochemical equations show the accompanying heat of reaction at constant pressure.
- Calorimetry measures heat changes associated with chemical reactions and phase changes.

11.3 Heat in Changes of State

- The molar heats of fusion, solidification, vaporization, and condensation describe the quantity of heat transferred to or from a system when one mole of substance undergoes a change of state at constant temperature.

11.4 Calculating Heat Changes

- Hess's law states that in a reaction that is the sum of two or more other reactions, ΔH for the overall process is the sum of the ΔH values for all of the constituent reactions.
- The enthalpy for the formation of one mole of a compound from its elements in standard states is the enthalpy of formation (H_f^0).
- The standard enthalpy change for a reaction (ΔH^0) can be calculated from the H_f^0 of the reactants and products.

CHAPTER CONCEPT MAP

Use these terms to construct a concept map that organizes the major ideas of this chapter.

 Chem ASAP! Concept Map 11
Create your Concept Map using the computer.

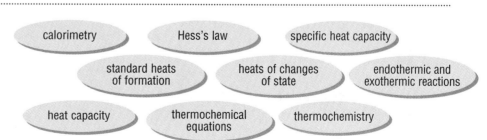

calorimetry   Hess's law   specific heat capacity

standard heats of formation   heats of changes of state   endothermic and exothermic reactions

heat capacity   thermochemical equations   thermochemistry

CONCEPT PRACTICE

36. Explain in your own words the law of conservation of energy. *11.1*

37. What always happens when two objects of different temperatures come in contact? Give an example from your own experience. *11.1*

38. Define potential energy in terms of chemistry. *11.1*

39. What factors determine the heat capacity of an object? *11.1*

40. What is the relationship between a calorie and a Calorie? *11.1*

41. Make the following conversions. *11.1*
a. 8.50×10^2 cal to Calories
b. 444 cal to joules
c. 1.8 kJ to joules
d. 4.5×10^{-1} kJ to calories

42. Why do you think it is important to define the system and the surroundings? *11.1*

43. Describe the sign convention that is used in thermochemical calculations. *11.1*

44. Two substances in a glass beaker chemically react, and the glass beaker becomes too hot to touch. *11.1*
a. Is this an exothermic or endothermic reaction?
b. If the two substances are defined as the system, what constitutes the surroundings?

45. Classify these processes as exothermic or endothermic. *11.1*
a. condensing steam
b. evaporating alcohol
c. burning alcohol
d. baking a potato

46. What special name is given to a heat change at constant pressure? *11.2*

47. What is the function of a calorimeter? *11.2*

48. There are some obvious sources of error in experiments that use foam cups as calorimeters. Name at least three. *11.2*

49. What special device would you use to measure the heat released at constant volume? *11.2*

50. Give the standard conditions for heat of combustion. *11.2*

51. What information is given in a thermochemical equation? *11.2*

52. Explain why ice melts at 0 °C without an increase of temperature, even though heat is flowing from the surroundings into the system (the ice). *11.3*

53. Calculate the quantity of heat gained or lost in the following changes. *11.3*
a. 3.50 mol of water freezes at 0 °C.
b. 0.44 mol of steam condenses at 100 °C.
c. 1.25 mol NaOH(s) dissolves in water.
d. 0.15 mol $C_2H_5OH(l)$ vaporizes at 78.3 °C.

54. Sodium acetate dissolves readily in water according to the following equation. *11.3*

$$NaC_2H_3O_2(s) \longrightarrow NaC_2H_3O_2(aq)$$
$$\Delta H = -17.3 \text{ kJ/mol}$$

Would this process increase or decrease the temperature of the water?

55. Explain the usefulness of Hess's law of heat summation in thermochemistry. *11.4*

56. A considerable amount of heat is required for the decomposition of aluminum oxide. *11.4*

$$2Al_2O_3(s) \longrightarrow 4Al(s) + 3O_2(g)$$
$$\Delta H = 3352 \text{ kJ}$$

a. What is the heat change for the formation of 1 mol of aluminum oxide from its elements?
b. Is the reaction exothermic or endothermic?

57. Calculate the heat change for the formation of lead(IV) chloride by the reaction of lead(II) chloride with chlorine. *11.4*

$$PbCl_2(s) + Cl_2(g) \longrightarrow PbCl_4(l)$$
$$\Delta H = ?$$

Use the following thermochemical equations.

$$Pb(s) + 2Cl_2(g) \longrightarrow PbCl_4(l)$$
$$\Delta H = -329.2 \text{ kJ}$$
$$Pb(s) + Cl_2(g) \longrightarrow PbCl_2(s)$$
$$\Delta H = -359.4 \text{ kJ}$$

58. From the following reactions: *11.4*

$$\tfrac{1}{2}N_2(g) + \tfrac{1}{2}O_2(g) \longrightarrow NO(g)$$
$$\Delta H = 90.4 \text{ kJ/mol}$$
$$\tfrac{1}{2}N_2(g) + O_2(g) \longrightarrow NO_2(g)$$
$$\Delta H = 33.6 \text{ kJ/mol}$$

determine the heat of reaction for:

$$NO(g) + \tfrac{1}{2}O_2(g) \longrightarrow NO_2(g)$$
$$\Delta H = ?$$

59. Calculate the heat change for the formation of copper(I) oxide from its elements. *11.4*

$$Cu(s) + \tfrac{1}{2}O_2(g) \longrightarrow CuO(s)$$

Use the following thermochemical equations to make the calculation.

$$CuO(s) + Cu(s) \longrightarrow Cu_2O(s)$$
$$\Delta H = -11.3 \text{ kJ}$$
$$Cu_2O(s) + \tfrac{1}{2}O_2(g) \longrightarrow 2CuO(s)$$
$$\Delta H = -114.6 \text{ kJ}$$

60. What is the standard heat of formation of a free element in its standard state? *11.4*

61. Consider the statement, "the more negative the value of ΔH_f^0, the more stable the compound." Is this statement true or false? Explain. *11.4*

62. Calculate the change in enthalpy (in kJ) for the following reactions. *11.4*
a. $CH_4(g) + 2O_2(g) \longrightarrow CO_2(g) + 2H_2O(l)$
b. $2CO(g) + O_2(g) \longrightarrow 2CO_2(g)$

63. What is the standard heat of formation of a compound? *11.4*

CONCEPT MASTERY

64. Equal masses of two substances absorb the same amount of heat. The temperature of substance A increases twice as much as the temperature of substance B. Which substance has the higher specific heat? Explain.

65. If 3.20 kcal of heat is added to 1.00 kg of ice at 0 °C, how much water at 0 °C is produced, and how much ice remains?

66. The amounts of heat required to change different quantities of carbon tetrachloride (CCl_4)(l) into vapor are given in the table.

Mass of CCl₄	Heat	
(g)	(J)	(cal)
2.90	652	156
7.50	1689	404
17.0	3825	915
26.2	5894	1410
39.8	8945	2140
51.0	11453	2740

a. Graph the data, using heat as the dependent variable.
b. What is the slope of the line?
c. The heat of vaporization of CCl_4(l) is 53.8 cal/g. How does this value compare with the slope of the line?

67. Calculate the heat change in calories when 45.2 g of steam at 100 °C condenses to water at the same temperature. What is the heat change in joules?

68. Find the enthalpy change for the formation of phosphorus pentachloride from its elements.

$$2P(s) + 5Cl_2(g) \longrightarrow 2PCl_5(s)$$

Use the following thermochemical equations.

$$PCl_5(s) \longrightarrow PCl_3(g) + Cl_2(g)$$
$$\Delta H = 87.9 \text{ kJ}$$
$$2P(s) + 3Cl_2(g) \longrightarrow 2PCl_3(g)$$
$$\Delta H = -574 \text{ kJ}$$

69. Use standard heats of formation (ΔH_f^0) to calculate the change in enthalpy for these reactions.
a. $2C(s, \text{graphite}) + O_2(g) \longrightarrow 2CO(g)$
b. $2H_2O_2(l) \longrightarrow 2H_2O(l) + O_2(g)$
c. $4NH_3(g) + 5O_2(g) \longrightarrow 4NO(g) + 6H_2O(g)$

70. An ice cube with a mass of 40.0 g melts in water originally at 25.0 °C.
a. How much heat does the ice cube absorb from the water when it melts? Report your answer in calories, kilocalories, and joules.
b. Calculate the number of grams of water that can be cooled to 0 °C by the melting ice cube.

71. The molar heat of vaporization of ethanol ($C_2H_5OH(l)$) is 43.5 kJ/mol. Calculate the heat required to vaporize 25.0 g of ethanol at its boiling point.

72. An orange contains 445 kJ of energy. What mass of water could this same amount of energy raise from 25.0 °C to the boiling point?

73. The combustion of ethane (C_2H_4) is an exothermic reaction.

$$C_2H_4(g) + 3O_2(g) \longrightarrow 2CO_2(g) + 2H_2O(l)$$
$$\Delta H = -1.39 \times 10^3 \text{ kJ}$$

Calculate the amount of heat liberated when 4.79 g C_2H_4 reacts with excess oxygen.

74. Calculate the heat change (ΔH) for the formation of nitrogen monoxide from its elements.

$$N_2(g) + O_2(g) \longrightarrow 2NO(g)$$

Use these thermochemical equations.

$$4NH_3(g) + 3O_2(g) \longrightarrow 2N_2(g) + 6H_2O(l)$$
$$\Delta H = -1.53 \times 10^3 \text{ kJ}$$
$$4NH_3(g) + 5O_2(g) \longrightarrow 4NO(g) + 6H_2O(l)$$
$$\Delta H = -1.17 \times 10^3 \text{ kJ}$$

75. How much heat must be removed from a 45.0-g sample of naphthalene ($C_{10}H_8$) at its freezing point to bring about solidification? The heat of fusion of naphthalene is 191.2 kJ/mol.

CRITICAL THINKING

76. Choose the term that best completes the second relationship.

a. kilojoules:heat

cm^3: _____

(1) mass   (3) energy

(2) volume   (4) weight

b. right:left

exothermic: _____

(1) combustion   (3) endothermic

(2) heat   (4) joule

c. thermometer:temperature

calorimeter: _____

(1) constant pressure   (3) endothermic

(2) reactants   (4) heat

77. Refer to **Figure 11.15.** Which region of the graph represents the coexistence of solid and liquid? Liquid and vapor?

CUMULATIVE REVIEW

78. What fraction of the average kinetic energy of hydrogen gas at 100 K does hydrogen gas have at 40 K?

79. How many hydrogen molecules are in 44.8 L $H_2(g)$ at STP?

80. Write the net ionic equation for the reaction of aqueous solutions of sodium chloride and silver acetate.

81. How many grams of oxygen are formed by the decomposition of 25.0 g of hydrogen peroxide?

$$2H_2O_2(l) \longrightarrow 2H_2O(l) + O_2(g)$$

CONCEPT CHALLENGE

82. The temperature of a person with an extremely high fever can be lowered with a sponge bath of isopropyl alcohol (C_3H_7OH). The heat of vaporization of this alcohol is 11.1 kcal/mol.

a. How many kilocalories of heat are removed from a person's skin when 175 g of isopropyl alcohol evaporates? How many kilojoules?

b. How many kilograms of water would this energy loss cool in lowering the temperature from 40.0 °C to 36.0 °C?

83. Ethane ($C_2H_6(g)$) can be formed by the reaction of ethene ($C_2H_4(g)$) with hydrogen gas.

$$C_2H_4(g) + H_2(g) \longrightarrow C_2H_6(g)$$

Use the heats of combustion for the following reactions to calculate the heat change for the formation of ethane from ethene and hydrogen.

$$2H_2(g) + O_2(g) \longrightarrow 2H_2O(l)$$
$$\Delta H = -5.72 \times 10^2 \text{ kJ}$$

$$C_2H_4(g) + 3O_2(g) \longrightarrow 2H_2O(l) + 2CO_2(g)$$
$$\Delta H = -1.401 \times 10^3 \text{ kJ}$$

$$2C_2H_6(g) + 7O_2(g) \longrightarrow 6H_2O(l) + 4CO_2(g)$$
$$\Delta H = -3.100 \times 10^3 \text{ kJ}$$

84. An ice cube at 0 °C was dropped into 30.0 g of water in a cup at 45.0 °C. At the instant that all of the ice was melted, the temperature of the water in the cup was 19.5 °C. What was the mass of the ice cube?

85. 41.0 g of glass at 95 °C is placed in 175 g of water at 21 °C in an insulated container. They are allowed to come to the same temperature. What is the final temperature of the glass-water mixture? The specific heat of glass is 2.1 cal/(g × °C).

86. The enthalpy of vaporization of water at various temperatures is given in the graph. From this graph, estimate the amount of heat required to convert 1 L of water to steam on the summit of Mount Everest (29 002 ft), where the boiling temperature of water is 70 °C.

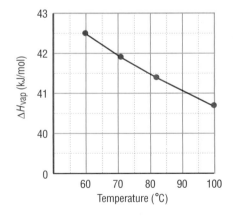

Select the choice that best answers each question or completes each statement.

1. The ΔH_{fus} of ethanol (C_2H_5OH) is 4.60 kJ/mol. How many kilojoules are required to melt 24.5 g of ethanol at its freezing point?
   a. 2.45 kJ   **c.** 245 kJ
   b. 5.33 kJ   **d.** 18.8 kJ

2. How much heat, in kilojoules, must be added to 178 g of water to increase the temperature of the water by 5.0 °C ?
   a. 890 kJ   **c.** 3.7 kJ
   b. 36 kJ   **d.** 0.093 kJ

3. The standard heat of formation of a free element in its standard state is always
   a. zero.
   b. positive.
   c. negative.
   d. higher for solids than gases.

4. If ΔH for the reaction $2HgO(s) \longrightarrow 2Hg(l) + O_2(g)$ is +181.66 kJ, then ΔH for the reaction $Hg(l) + 1/2 O_2(g) \longrightarrow HgO(s)$ is
   a. 90.83 kJ.   **c.** 181.66 kJ.
   b. −90.83 kJ.   **d.** −181.66 kJ.

5. The specific heat capacity of grain alcohol is ten times larger than the specific heat capacity of silver. A hot bar of silver with a mass of 55 g is dropped into an equal mass of cool alcohol. If the temperature of the silver bar drops 45 °C, the temperature of the alcohol
   a. increases 45 °C.
   b. decreases 4.5 °C.
   c. increases 4.5 °C.
   d. decreases 45 °C.

The lettered choices below refer to questions 6–9. A lettered choice may be used once, more than once, or not at all.

  (A) kJ/mol
  (B) (J × °C)/g
  (C) J/(g × °C)
  (D) kJ
  (E) kJ/°C

Which unit is appropriate for each of the following measurements?

6. heat of reaction

7. heat capacity

8. molar heat of fusion

9. specific heat capacity

Use the data table to answer questions 10–12. Alkanes are a class of compounds containing carbon and hydrogen that are often used as fuels.

Alkane	Heat of combustion (kJ/mol)
Methane, CH_4	−890
Ethane, C_2H_6	−1560
Propane, C_3H_8	−2220
Butane, C_4H_{10}	
Pentane, C_5H_{12}	−3540
Hexane, C_6H_{14}	−4160
Heptane, C_7H_{16}	−4810

10. Graph the data. Make the number of carbon atoms per molecule the independent variable.

11. Estimate the heat of combustion for butane.

12. Estimate the heat of combustion for the next alkane in the series, octane, C_8H_{18}.

Use the graph and table to answer questions 13–16. Assume 1.00 mol of substance in each container.

Substance	Freezing point (K)	ΔH_{fus} (kJ/mol)	Boiling point (K)	ΔH_{vap} (kJ/mol)
Ammonia	195.3	5.65	239.7	23.4
Benzene	278.7	9.87	353.3	30.8
Methanol	175.5	3.16	337.2	35.3
Neon	24.5	0.33	27.1	1.76

13. Calculate heat absorbed in region A for neon.

14. Calculate heat absorbed in region C for benzene.

15. Calculate heat absorbed in regions B and C for methanol. [specific heat = 81.6 J/(g × °C)]

16. Calculate heat absorbed in regions A, B, and C for ammonia. [specific heat = 35.1 J/(g × °C)]

Thermochemistry   **325**

A hot-air balloon rises when air inside the balloon is heated.

FEATURES

DISCOVER IT!
Observing Volume Changes

SMALL-SCALE LAB
Reactions of Acids with Carbonates

MINI LAB
Carbon Dioxide from Antacid Tablets

CHEMath
Solving Equations

CHEMISTRY SERVING … INDUSTRY
Diving Can Be a Gas

CHEMISTRY IN CAREERS
Commercial Diver

LINK TO PHYSICS
Cryostats

Stay current with **SCIENCE NEWS**
Find out more about gas behavior:
www.phschool.com

DISCOVER IT! OBSERVING VOLUME CHANGES

You need a spherical balloon, a marking pen, a tape measure, a freezer, and a sunny window.

1. Inflate the balloon and tie it closed. Use the marking pen to draw a line around the middle of the balloon. This is the circumference of the balloon.

2. Place the balloon in the freezer for half an hour. Remove it and quickly measure and record the circumference of the balloon in centimeters.

3. Place the balloon in a sunny window for half an hour. Measure and record the circumference of the balloon in centimeters.

4. Assume the balloon is a perfect sphere and calculate the volume for each circumference recorded. Use the following formula:

$$\text{Volume} = \frac{4\pi r^3}{3}$$

Note that $r = \dfrac{\text{circumference}}{2\pi}$

What do you observe about the volume of the balloon at the two temperatures? Use your results to suggest a relationship between temperature and volume when pressure remains constant. Refer back to your suggested relationship when you read about Charles's law later in this chapter.

THE PROPERTIES OF GASES

*Y*ou have probably seen huge, colorful, helium-filled balloons like this one in holiday parades. But what's wrong with Bullwinkle? As you can see, Bullwinkle isn't looking too good—he is deflating. The balloon is leaking helium and is beginning to sag and list. Soon Bullwinkle may collapse altogether. **How does kinetic theory explain why losing helium causes the balloon to sag and collapse?**

objectives
▶ Describe the properties of gas particles
▶ Explain how the kinetic energy of gas particles relates to Kelvin temperature

key terms
▶ compressibility

Kinetic Theory Revisited

This chapter discusses the ways in which simple kinetic molecular theory is used to explain gas behavior. You may have already observed some everyday examples of gas behavior. For example, you may have noticed that a sealed bag of potato chips bulges at its seams when placed in a sunny window. The air inside the bag exerts greater pressure as its temperature increases. Why does this happen? Kinetic theory can explain this and other gas behavior.

Recall from Chapter 10 that the kinetic theory of gases makes several basic assumptions. It assumes that gases consist of hard, spherical particles that have the following properties. First, the gas particles are so small in relation to the distances between them that their individual volumes can be assumed to be insignificant. The large relative distances between the gas particles means that there is considerable empty space between the particles. This assumption that gas particles are far apart explains the important property of gas compressibility. **Compressibility** is a measure of how much the volume of matter decreases under pressure. Gases, unlike solids or liquids, are easily compressed because of the space between the particles. Because gases are compressible, they are used in automobile airbags and other safety devices designed to absorb the energy of an impact. The energy of a collision is absorbed when the gas particles are forced closer together. As seen in **Figure 12.1,** gases can be used to absorb a considerable amount of energy.

Figure 12.1
An air bag cushions the impact of this crash dummy. How will the compressibility of gases protect the dummy from being broken?

Figure 12.2

According to kinetic theory, the particles of air in this balloon are not affected by attractive or repulsive forces. As a result, the air expands to fill the interior of the balloon evenly.

The second property of gas particles assumed by the kinetic theory is that no attractive or repulsive forces exist between the particles. As a result, gases are free to move inside their containers. In fact, a gas expands until it takes the shape and volume of its container.

The third assumption is that gas particles move rapidly in constant random motion. The particles travel in straight paths and move independently of each other. As you can see in **Figure 12.3,** only when a particle collides with another particle or object does it deviate from its straight-line path. Kinetic theory assumes further that these collisions between gas particles are perfectly elastic, which means that during a collision the total amount of kinetic energy remains constant and that the kinetic energy is transferred without loss from one particle to another. You should also recall that the average kinetic energy of a collection of gas particles is directly proportional to the Kelvin temperature of the gas.

Figure 12.3

Notice the random motion of the gas particles. Changes in direction occur only when particles collide with each other or with another object.

Gas particles in constant random motion

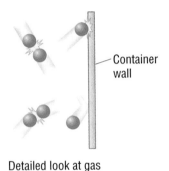

Container wall

Detailed look at gas particles colliding

Variables That Describe a Gas

Four variables are generally used to describe a gas. The variables and their common units are pressure (P) in kilopascals, volume (V) in liters, temperature (T) in kelvins, and number of moles (n). The gas laws that you will learn about in this chapter will enable you to predict gas behavior at specific conditions. Understanding the gas laws will help you understand everyday applications of gases such as in automobile airbags, scuba-diving equipment, and hot-air balloons, among many others.

section review 12.1

1. State the main assumptions of kinetic theory regarding gas particles.

2. Describe what happens to kinetic energy during gas particle collisions and as Kelvin temperature increases.

3. How does kinetic theory explain the compressibility of gases?

4. What variables and units are used to describe a gas?

Chem ASAP! Assessment 12.1 Check your understanding of the important ideas and concepts in Section 12.1.

SMALL-SCALE LAB

REACTIONS OF ACIDS WITH CARBONATES

SAFETY

Wear safety glasses and follow the standard safety procedures outlined on page 18.

PURPOSE

To observe and identify the reactions of carbonates that produce carbon dioxide gas.

MATERIALS

- pencil
- paper
- ruler
- reaction surface
- chemicals shown in Figure A

PROCEDURE

On separate sheets of paper, draw two grids similar to Figure A. Make each square 2 cm on each side. Place a reaction surface over one of the grids and add the chemicals as shown in Figure A. Use the second grid as a data table to record your observations for each reaction.

Figure A

ANALYSIS

Using your experimental data, record the answers to the following questions below your data table.

1. What common observation can you make for each of the mixings?

2. Write the name and formula of the gas produced in each reaction. Identify one other product formed in all of the reactions.

3. Hydrochloric acid reacts with sodium hydrogen carbonate to yield carbon dioxide, water, and sodium chloride. Convert this word equation into a chemical equation.

4. Write complete chemical equations for the reactions you observed in this experiment.

YOU'RE THE CHEMIST

The following small-scale activities allow you to develop your own procedures and analyze the results.

1. **Analyze It!** Add some HCl to $NaHCO_3$ and then add some HCl to Na_2CO_3. What do you observe? Is it possible to use HCl to distinguish between $NaHCO_3$ and Na_2CO_3? Explain.

2. **Analyze It!** Add some $FeCl_3$ to $NaHCO_3$ and then add some $FeCl_3$ to Na_2CO_3. Look carefully. What do you observe? Is it possible to use $FeCl_3$ to distinguish between $NaHCO_3$ and Na_2CO_3? Explain.

3. **Design It!** Most laundry detergents contain carbonates such as $NaHCO_3$ and Na_2CO_3. Design and carry out an experiment to determine which laundry detergents contain carbonate in some form. Using your method, is it possible to tell exactly which carbonate a detergent contains? Explain.

4. **Design It!** Experiment with chalk, antacid tablets, seashells, limestone, and marble to determine if they contain carbonates. How can you tell?

5. **Design It!** Experiment with powdered soft drink mixes to see if they contain citric acid. Record your results.

FACTORS AFFECTING GAS PRESSURE

objectives

▶ Explain how the amount of gas and the volume of the container affect gas pressure

▶ Infer the effect of temperature changes on the pressure exerted by a contained gas

Your raft blasts through a narrow opening between rocks and plummets over a short fall into the churning whitewater below. The raft bends and twists, absorbing some of the pounding energy of the river. The strength and flexibility of the raft are impressive. **What factors affect the gas pressure inside the raft and its resulting rigidity?**

Amount of Gas

Using the kinetic theory, you can predict and explain how gases will respond to a change of conditions. When you pump up a tire, for example, you should expect the pressure inside it to increase. See **Figure 12.4.** Collisions of gas particles with the inside walls of the tire result in the pressure that is exerted by the enclosed gas. By adding gas, you increase the number of gas particles, thus increasing the number of collisions, which explains why the gas pressure increases.

Figure 12.4

Using a pump to force more air particles into a partially deflated bicycle tire increases the pressure inside the tire.

Low pressure: Fewer gas particles inside tire

High pressure: More gas particles inside the tire

Figure 12.5

When a gas is pumped into a closed rigid container, the pressure increases in proportion to the number of gas particles added. If the number of gas particles doubles, the pressure doubles.

Now look at **Figure 12.5.** As long as gas temperature does not change, doubling the number of gas particles doubles the pressure. Tripling the number of gas particles triples the pressure, and so forth. With a powerful pump and a strong container, you can generate very high pressures by adding more and more gas. Once the pressure exceeds the strength of the container, however, the container will rupture.

100 kPa

200 kPa

200 kPa | Decreasing Pressure | 100 kPa

Figure 12.6
Gas pressure inside this constant-volume container decreases as gas particles escape. The gas at 100 kPa has exactly half the number of particles as the gas at 200 kPa.

In a similar way, letting the air out of a tire decreases the pressure inside the tire. The fewer particles inside exert less pressure. As you can see by looking at **Figure 12.6,** halving the number of gas particles in a given volume decreases the pressure by half.

When a sealed container of gas under pressure is opened, gas inside moves from the region of higher pressure to the region of lower pressure outside. This is the principle used in aerosol cans. You have probably used many aerosol products, from whipped cream, to hair spray and mousse, to the spray paint shown in **Figure 12.7.** The can of spray paint contains a gas at high pressure that acts as the propellant. The air outside the can is at a lower pressure. Pushing the spray button creates an opening between the inside of the can and the air outside. The high-pressure propellant gas flows to the lower pressure region outside, forcing paint out with it. As the propellant gas is depleted, the pressure inside the aerosol can decreases.

Volume

There are other ways to increase gas pressure. For example, you can raise the pressure exerted by a contained gas by reducing its volume. The more the gas is compressed, the greater is the pressure it exerts inside the container. Reducing the volume of a contained gas by half doubles the pressure, as **Figure 12.8** demonstrates. Increasing the volume of the contained gas has just the opposite effect. By doubling the volume, you halve the gas pressure because the same number of gas particles occupy a volume twice the original size.

Push button

Gas propellant (High pressure)

Outside air (Low pressure)

Product

Pressure-resistant curved bottom

Figure 12.7
The difference in pressure between the inside of the spray can and the air outside allows aerosol sprays to work. What is the pressure inside the can when the aerosol will no longer spray?

100 kPa

100 kPa

Volume = 1.0 L

200 kPa

200 kPa

Volume = 0.5 L

Figure 12.8
A piston, such as those used in engines, forces a gas in a cylinder to reduce in volume. A decrease in volume by half doubles the pressure the gas exerts.

Figure 12.9

When a gas in a container is heated from 300 K (27 °C) to 600 K (327 °C), the kinetic energy of the gas particles doubles. The doubling of the kinetic energy results in a doubling of the pressure exerted by the gas. Pressure buildup due to high temperatures may cause the container to explode.

Temperature

Raising the temperature of an enclosed gas provides yet another way to increase gas pressure. (Remember the potato chip bag mentioned in Section 12.1.) The speed and kinetic energy of gas particles increase as the particles absorb thermal energy. The faster-moving particles impact the walls of their container with more energy, exerting greater pressure, as shown in **Figure 12.9.** If the average kinetic energy of a gas doubles, the Kelvin temperature doubles and the pressure of the enclosed gas also doubles. A gas in a sealed container may thus generate enormous pressure when heated. For that reason, an aerosol can, even an empty one, carelessly thrown onto a fire is an explosion hazard.

By contrast, as the temperature of an enclosed gas decreases, the particles move more slowly and have less kinetic energy. They strike the container walls with less force. Halving the Kelvin temperature of a gas in a rigid container decreases the gas pressure by half.

section review 12.2

5. What effects do changes in the amount of gas and in the volume of the container have on gas pressure?

6. What is the effect of temperature change on the pressure of a contained gas?

7. What would you have to do to the volume of a gas to reduce its pressure to one-quarter of the original value, assuming that the gas is at a constant temperature?

8. Keeping temperature constant, how could you increase the pressure in a container by one hundredfold?

9. The manufacturer of an aerosol deodorant packaged in a 150-mL container wishes to produce a container of the same size that will hold twice as much gas. How will the pressure of the gas in the new product compare with that of the gas in the original container?

 Chem ASAP! Assessment 12.2 Check your understanding of the important ideas and concepts in Section 12.2.

portfolio project

Contact local tire stores or car dealers to find out what factors determine recommended tire pressure. Find out how and under what conditions to use a tire gauge. What are the typical units of pressure for a tire gauge? What can happen if tires are not properly inflated?

THE GAS LAWS

*B*ecause warm air is less dense than cooler air, the pilot of a hot-air balloon heats the air inside the balloon to make it rise. To make it fall, the pilot releases the heated air from the top of the balloon. **What is the effect of adding heat to a gas at constant pressure? What law describes this relationship?**

objectives
▶ State Boyle's law, Charles's law, Gay-Lussac's law, and the combined gas law
▶ Apply the gas laws to problems involving the temperature, volume, and pressure of a contained gas

key terms
▶ Boyle's law
▶ Charles's law
▶ Gay-Lussac's law
▶ combined gas law

The Pressure–Volume Relationship: Boyle's Law

Consider the effect of pressure on the volume of a contained gas while the temperature remains constant. When the pressure goes up, the volume goes down. Similarly, when the pressure goes down, the volume goes up. The first person to do a systematic quantitative study of this pressure–volume relationship was the Anglo-Irish chemist Robert Boyle (1627–1691). In 1662, Boyle proposed a law to describe this behavior of gases. **Boyle's law** states that for a given mass of gas at constant temperature, the volume of the gas varies inversely with pressure. In an inverse relationship, the product of the two variable quantities is constant.

Look at **Figure 12.10.** In the figure, a volume of 1.0 L (V_1) is at a pressure of 100 kPa (P_1). If you increase the volume to 2.0 L (V_2), the pressure decreases to 50 kPa (P_2). Observe that the product $P_1 \times V_1$ (100 kPa × 1.0 L = 100 kPa × L) is the same as the product $P_2 \times V_2$ (50 kPa × 2.0 L = 100 kPa × L). If you decrease the volume to 0.5 L, the gas pressure increases to 200 kPa. Again, the product of pressure times volume equals 100 kPa × L.

The product of pressure and volume at any two sets of conditions is always constant at a given temperature. The mathematical expression of Boyle's law is as follows:

$$P_1 \times V_1 = P_2 \times V_2$$

When you graph an inverse relationship, such as this one, the result is a curve, as shown in **Figure 12.10.**

Chem ASAP!

Simulation 9
Examine the relationship between gas volume and pressure.

$P_1 = 100$ kPa $P_2 = 50$ kPa $P_3 = 200$ kPa
$V_1 = 1.0$ L $V_2 = 2.0$ L $V_3 = 0.5$ L

$P_1 \times V_1 = P_2 \times V_2 = P_3 \times V_3 = 100$ L × kPa

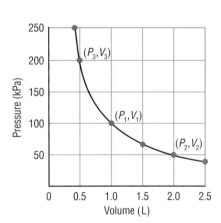

Figure 12.10
Boyle's law is studied by using a cylindrical container fitted with a frictionless, weightless piston. When the volume of a gas at constant temperature increases from V_1 to V_2, the pressure decreases from P_1 to P_2. When the volume decreases (to V_3), the pressure increases (to P_3). The graph illustrates Boyle's law. At any point on this curve, the product $P \times V$ of pressure (P) and volume (V) is a constant.

CHEMath

SOLVING EQUATIONS

Knowing which equation to use is the key first step in solving many problems. However, you must also master the skill of solving the equation for the unknown variable.

To solve an equation for one of its variables, isolate that variable on one side of the equal sign. In other words, the other variables and numbers in the equation must be on the other side of the equal sign.

For example, you are probably familiar with the equation for the area of a rectangle:

Area = base × height, or $A = bh$

As written, the equation solves for area (A). Notice that the variable A is on one side of the equal sign, while all of the other variables are on the other side of the equal sign. Variable A is therefore isolated.

If the variable you need to solve for is not already isolated, you will use addition, subtraction, multiplication, and division to isolate it. The key to the process is remembering that whatever you do on one side of the equation to isolate the variable, you must also do on the other side.

Example 1

Solve the equation $A = bh$ for the variable b.

You must isolate the variable b. Because b is multiplied by h, divide both sides of the equation by h.

$$\frac{A}{h} = \frac{bh}{h}$$

Canceling terms, $\dfrac{A}{h} = \dfrac{b\cancel{h}}{\cancel{h}}$ yields $\dfrac{A}{h} = b$. Thus $b = \dfrac{A}{h}$.

Example 2

This example involves one of the equations you will learn and use in this chapter.

Solve the equation $P_1 \times V_1 = P_2 \times V_2$ for the variable P_1.

$$P_1 \times V_1 = P_2 \times V_2$$

You must isolate the variable P_1. Because P_1 is multiplied by V_1, divide both sides by V_1.

$$\frac{P_1 \times V_1}{V_1} = \frac{P_2 \times V_2}{V_1}$$

Canceling terms, $\dfrac{P_1 \times \cancel{V_1}}{\cancel{V_1}} = \dfrac{P_2 \times V_2}{V_1}$ yields $P_1 = \dfrac{P_2 \times V_2}{V_1}$.

Practice Problems

Prepare for upcoming problems in this chapter by solving the following equations for the variable indicated.

A. Solve $P_1 \times V_1 = P_2 \times V_2$ for V_2.

B. Solve $\dfrac{V_1}{T_1} = \dfrac{V_2}{T_2}$ for T_2.

C. Solve $P_{total} = P_1 + P_2 + P_3$ for P_2.

D. Solve $\dfrac{P_1 \times V_1}{T_1} = \dfrac{P_2 \times V_2}{T_2}$ for T_1.

E. Solve $P \times V = n \times R \times T$ for T.

F. Solve $\dfrac{Rate_A}{Rate_B} = \dfrac{\sqrt{molar\ mass_B}}{\sqrt{molar\ mass_A}}$ for molar mass$_B$.

Sample Problem 12-1

A high-altitude balloon contains 30.0 L of helium gas at 103 kPa. What is the volume when the balloon rises to an altitude where the pressure is only 25.0 kPa? (Assume that the temperature remains constant.)

1. ANALYZE List the knowns and the unknown.

Knowns:
- $P_1 = 103$ kPa
- $V_1 = 30.0$ L
- $P_2 = 25.0$ kPa

Unknown:
- $V_2 = ?$ L

Use the known values and Boyle's law ($P_1 \times V_1 = P_2 \times V_2$) to calculate the unknown value (V_2).

2. CALCULATE Solve for the unknown.

Rearrange the expression for Boyle's law to isolate V_2.

$$V_2 = \frac{V_1 \times P_1}{P_2}$$

Substitute the known values for P_1, V_1, and P_2 into the equation and solve.

$$V_2 = \frac{30.0 \text{ L} \times 103 \text{ kPa}}{25.0 \text{ kPa}}$$

$$= 1.24 \times 10^2 \text{ L}$$

3. EVALUATE Does the result make sense?

Using kinetic theory, a decrease in pressure at constant temperature must correspond to a proportional increase in volume. The calculated result agrees with both the kinetic theory and the pressure–temperature relationship. Also, the units have canceled correctly and the answer is expressed to the proper number of significant figures.

Practice Problems

10. The pressure on 2.50 L of anesthetic gas changes from 105 kPa to 40.5 kPa. What will be the new volume if the temperature remains constant?

11. A gas with a volume of 4.00 L at a pressure of 205 kPa is allowed to expand to a volume of 12.0 L. What is the pressure in the container if the temperature remains constant?

Chem ASAP!

Problem-Solving 11
Solve Problem 11 with the help of an interactive guided tutorial.

The Temperature–Volume Relationship: Charles's Law

In 1787, the French physicist and balloonist Jacques Charles (1746–1823) investigated the quantitative effect of temperature on the volume of a gas at constant pressure. In every experiment, he observed an increase in the volume of a gas with an increase in temperature, and a decrease in volume with a decrease in temperature. In practice, the temperature–volume relationship for any gas can be measured only over a limited range because at low temperatures gases condense to form liquids.

From his quantitative studies, Charles observed that at constant pressure the graph of gas volume versus temperature yields a straight line. **Figure 12.11** shows such a graph for three different gas samples in balloons. In addition to the straight lines, another important feature emerged. The lines extended (extrapolated) to zero volume ($V = 0$) all intersect the temperature axis at the same point, −273.15 °C.

Figure 12.11

This graph shows the direct relationship between volume and temperature for three different gas samples in balloons at constant pressure. What is the significance of the temperature −273.15 °C?

Figure 12.12

This apparatus illustrates Charles's law. When a gas is heated at constant pressure, the volume increases. When a gas is cooled at constant pressure, the volume decreases.

100 kPa

100 kPa

V_1

V_2

$V_1 = 1\ L$
$T_1 = 300\ K$

$V_2 = 2\ L$
$T_2 = 600\ K$

$$\frac{V_1}{T_1} = \frac{V_2}{T_2} = 0.00333\ L/K$$

William Thomson (Lord Kelvin) realized the significance of this temperature value. He identified this value as absolute zero, the lowest possible temperature. It is the temperature at which the average kinetic energy of gas particles would theoretically be zero. This was the basis for the absolute temperature scale established by Kelvin in 1848. This scale is now called the Kelvin temperature scale. On the Kelvin temperature scale, 0 K corresponds to $-273.15\ °C$. Throughout this textbook, absolute zero expressed in degrees Celsius is rounded to -273. What is 0 °C in kelvins?

Charles's law summarizes Charles's observations and the findings of Kelvin. **Charles's law** states that the volume of a fixed mass of gas is directly proportional to its Kelvin temperature if the pressure is kept constant. In a direct relationship, such as this one, the ratio of the two quantities that change is a constant. In **Figure 12.12**, for example, a 1-L sample of gas (V_1) is at a temperature of 300 K (T_1). (Note that when solving gas-law problems, the temperature must always be expressed in kelvins.) When the temperature is increased to 600 K (T_2), the volume increases to 2 L (V_2). The ratio V_1/T_1 is equal to the ratio V_2/T_2. Moreover, at constant pressure, the ratio of volume to Kelvin temperature for a gas sample at any two sets of conditions is constant. Thus you can write Charles's law as follows:

$$\frac{V_1}{T_1} = \frac{V_2}{T_2}$$

The graph of a relationship such as Charles's law that is a direct proportion is a straight line. **Figure 12.13** provides a detailed look at the Charles's law relationship.

Chem ASAP!

Simulation 10

Examine the relationship between gas volume and temperature.

Figure 12.13

This graph illustrates Charles's law. At any point on this line, the ratio of volume (V) to temperature (T) is constant; in this case, V/T = 0.00333 L/K.

Volume increases (or decreases) by *this* amount when temperature increases (or decreases) by *this* amount.

Figure 12.14
The volume of a balloon in a beaker of ice water is less than it is in a beaker of hot water. Why?

Sample Problem 12-2

A balloon inflated in a room at 24 °C has a volume of 4.00 L. The balloon is then heated to a temperature of 58 °C. What is the new volume if the pressure remains constant?

1. ANALYZE List the knowns and the unknown.

Knowns:
- $V_1 = 4.00$ L
- $T_1 = 24$ °C
- $T_2 = 58$ °C

Unknown:
- $V_2 = ?$ L

Use the known values and Charles's law ($V_1/T_1 = V_2/T_2$) to calculate the unknown value (V_2).

2. CALCULATE Solve for the unknown.

Because the gas laws will be applied, express the temperatures in kelvins.

$$T_1 = 24\ °C + 273 = 297\ K$$

$$T_2 = 58\ °C + 273 = 331\ K$$

Rearrange the expression for Charles's law to isolate V_2.

$$V_2 = \frac{V_1 \times T_2}{T_1}$$

Substitute the known values for T_1, V_1, and T_2 into the equation and solve.

$$V_2 = \frac{4.00\ L \times 331\ \cancel{K}}{297\ \cancel{K}} = 4.46\ L$$

3. EVALUATE Does the result make sense?

From kinetic theory, the volume should increase with an increase in temperature (at constant pressure). This result agrees with the kinetic theory and Charles's law. The volume does increase with increasing temperature.

Practice Problems

12. If a sample of gas occupies 6.80 L at 325 °C, what will be its volume at 25 °C if the pressure does not change?

13. Exactly 5.00 L of air at −50.0 °C is warmed to 100.0 °C. What is the new volume if the pressure remains constant?

Chem ASAP!

Problem-Solving 13
Solve Problem 13 with the help of an interactive guided tutorial.

The Temperature–Pressure Relationship: Gay-Lussac's Law

On a hot summer day, the pressure in a car tire increases. This increase illustrates a relationship that was discovered in 1802 by Joseph Gay-Lussac (1778–1850), a French chemist. **Gay-Lussac's law** states that the pressure of a gas is directly proportional to the Kelvin temperature if the volume remains constant. See **Figure 12.15.** Because Gay-Lussac's law involves direct proportions, the ratios P_1/T_1 and P_2/T_2 are equal at constant volume. Therefore, assuming that the volume remains constant, you can write Gay-Lussac's law as follows:

$$\frac{P_1}{T_1} = \frac{P_2}{T_2}$$

Figure 12.15

When a gas is heated at constant volume, the pressure increases. When a gas is cooled at constant volume, the pressure decreases.

Chem ASAP!

Simulation 11

Explore the relationship between gas temperature and pressure.

$P_1 = 100$ kPa
$T_1 = 300$ K

$P_2 = 200$ kPa
$T_2 = 600$ K

Sample Problem 12-3

The gas left in a used aerosol can is at a pressure of 103 kPa at 25 °C. If this can is thrown onto a fire, what is the pressure of the gas when its temperature reaches 928 °C? (Calculating the answer to this problem will show you why it is dangerous to dispose of aerosol cans in a fire. Most aerosol cans carry warnings on their labels that clearly say not to incinerate (burn) or to store above a certain temperature.)

1. **ANALYZE List the knowns and the unknown.**

   Knowns:
   - $P_1 = 103$ kPa
   - $T_1 = 25$ °C
   - $T_2 = 928$ °C

   Unknown:
   - $P_2 = ?$ kPa

   Use the known values and Gay-Lussac's law ($P_1/T_1 = P_2/T_2$) to calculate the unknown (P_2). Remember, because this problem involves temperatures and a gas law, the temperatures must be expressed in kelvins.

Practice Problems

14. A gas has a pressure of 6.58 kPa at 539 K. What will be the pressure at 211 K if the volume does not change?

Sample Problem 12-3 (cont.)

2. **CALCULATE** *Solve for the unknown.*

First convert degrees Celsius to kelvins.

$$T_1 = 25 \,°C + 273 = 298 \text{ K}$$

$$T_2 = 928 \,°C + 273 = 1201 \text{ K}$$

Rearrange Gay-Lussac's law to isolate P_2.

$$P_2 = \frac{P_1 \times T_2}{T_1}$$

Substitute the known values for P_1, T_2, and T_1 into the equation and solve.

$$P_2 = \frac{103 \text{ kPa} \times 1201 \,\cancel{K}}{298 \,\cancel{K}} = 415 \text{ kPa}$$

$$= 4.15 \times 10^2 \text{ kPa}$$

3. **EVALUATE** *Does the result make sense?*

From the kinetic theory, one would expect the increase in temperature of a gas to produce an increase in pressure if the volume remains constant. The calculated value does show such an increase.

Practice Problems (cont.)

15. The pressure in an automobile tire is 198 kPa at 27 °C. At the end of a trip on a hot sunny day, the pressure has risen to 225 kPa. What is the temperature of the air in the tire? (Assume that the volume has not changed.)

Chem ASAP!

Problem-Solving 15
Solve Problem 15 with the help of an interactive guided tutorial.

The Combined Gas Law

If you have been wondering how to remember the individual expressions for the gas laws, there is really no need. A single expression, called the **combined gas law,** combines the three gas laws, as follows:

$$\frac{P_1 \times V_1}{T_1} = \frac{P_2 \times V_2}{T_2}$$

The other laws can be obtained from this law by holding one quantity (pressure, volume, or temperature) constant.

To illustrate, suppose you hold temperature constant ($T_1 = T_2$). Rearrange the combined gas law to get the two temperature terms on the same side of the equation and then cancel.

$$P_1 \times V_1 = \frac{P_2 \times V_2 \times \cancel{T_1}}{\cancel{T_2}}$$

$$P_1 \times V_1 = P_2 \times V_2$$

As you can see, you are left with Boyle's law. The same kind of process yields Charles's law when pressure remains constant and Gay-Lussac's law when volume remains constant.

In addition to providing a useful way of recalling the three previous gas laws, the combined gas law also enables you to do calculations for situations in which none of the variables are constant. In Sample Problem 12-4, on the following page, you will see how to use the combined gas law to calculate the new volume of a gas that results from changing both the pressure and the temperature.

Sample Problem 12-4

The volume of a gas-filled balloon is 30.0 L at 40 °C and 153 kPa pressure. What volume will the balloon have at standard temperature and pressure (STP)?

1. **ANALYZE** *List the knowns and the unknown.*

   Knowns:
   - $V_1 = 30.0$ L
   - $T_1 = 40$ °C
   - $T_2 = 273$ K (standard temperature)
   - $P_1 = 153$ kPa
   - $P_2 = 101.3$ kPa (standard pressure)

   Unknown:
   - $V_2 = ?$ L

   Use the known values and the combined gas law to calculate the unknown (V_2).

2. **CALCULATE** *Solve for the unknown.*

   Convert degrees Celsius to kelvins.

   $$T_1 = 40\,°C + 273 = 313\,K$$

   Rearrange the combined gas law to isolate V_2.

   $$V_2 = \frac{V_1 \times P_1 \times T_2}{P_2 \times T_1}$$

   Substitute the known quantities into the equation and solve.

   $$V_2 = \frac{30.0\,L \times 153\,kPa \times 273\,K}{101.3\,kPa \times 313\,K} = 39.5\,L$$

3. **EVALUATE** *Does the result make sense?*

   The temperature decreases; therefore, the temperature ratio is less than 1 (273 K/313 K). The pressure decreases, so the pressure ratio is greater than 1 (153 kPa/101.3 kPa). Recalculate by multiplying the initial volume of gas by these two ratios.

   $$V_2 = 30.0\,L \times \frac{153\,kPa}{101.3\,kPa} \times \frac{273\,K}{313\,K} = 39.5\,L$$

   The result is the same.

Practice Problems

16. A gas at 155 kPa and 25 °C occupies a container with an initial volume of 1.00 L. By changing the volume, the pressure of the gas increases to 605 kPa as the temperature is raised to 125 °C. What is the new volume?

17. A 5.00-L air sample at a temperature of −50 °C has a pressure of 107 kPa. What will be the new pressure if the temperature is raised to 102 °C and the volume expands to 7.00 L?

Chem ASAP!

Problem-Solving 17
Solve Problem 17 with the help of an interactive guided tutorial.

section review 12.3

18. State Boyle's law, Charles's law, and Gay-Lussac's law.

19. Briefly explain how the combined gas law can be reduced to the other three gas laws.

20. Write the mathematical equation for Boyle's law and explain the symbols. What must be true about the temperature?

21. A given mass of air has a volume of 6.00 L at 101 kPa. What volume will it occupy at 25.0 kPa if the temperature does not change?

 Chem ASAP! **Assessment 12.3** Check your understanding of the important ideas and concepts in Section 12.3.

IDEAL GASES

What if someone told you that all of the gas laws you just learned were wrong! In some ways, the person would be correct. The gas laws assume that gases behave in an ideal way, obeying the assumptions of kinetic theory. As it turns out, gases do not behave exactly this way. **What then is an ideal gas, and under what conditions do the gas laws apply?**

objectives
▶ Calculate the amount of gas at any specified conditions of pressure, volume, and temperature
▶ Distinguish between ideal and real gases

key terms
▶ ideal gas constant (R)
▶ ideal gas law

Ideal Gas Law

Up to this point in this textbook, you have worked with three variables regarding gas behavior: pressure, volume, and temperature. There is a fourth variable still to be considered: the amount of gas in the system, expressed in terms of the number of moles. Suppose you want to calculate the number of moles (n) of a gas in a fixed volume at a known temperature and pressure, as illustrated in **Figure 12.16.** The calculation of moles is possible by modifying the combined gas law. You can understand the modification by recognizing that the volume occupied by a gas at a specified temperature and pressure must depend on the number of gas particles. The number of moles of gas is directly proportional to the number of particles. Hence, moles must be directly proportional to volume as well. Therefore you can introduce moles into the combined gas law by dividing each side of the equation by n.

$$\frac{P_1 \times V_1}{T_1 \times n_1} = \frac{P_2 \times V_2}{T_2 \times n_2}$$

This equation shows that $(P \times V)/(T \times n)$ is a constant. This constancy holds for what are called ideal gases. A gas behaves ideally if it conforms to the gas laws. Ideal behavior depends upon certain conditions, as you will see later in this section.

If you could evaluate the constant $(P \times V)/(T \times n)$, you could then calculate the number of moles of gas at any specified values of P, V, and T. This constant is symbolized as R.

You can find the actual value of R, given an important fact about gases: 1 mol of every gas occupies 22.4 L at STP (101.3 kPa and 273 K). Inserting the values of P, V, T, and n into the equation:

$$R = \frac{P \times V}{T \times n} = \frac{101.3 \text{ kPa} \times 22.4 \text{ L}}{273 \text{ K} \times 1 \text{ mol}} = 8.31 \text{ (L} \times \text{kPa)}/(\text{K} \times \text{mol})$$

The **ideal gas constant** *(R)* has the value 8.31 (L $\times$ kPa)/(K $\times$ mol). Rearranging the equation for R, you obtain the usual form of the **ideal gas law:**

$$R = \frac{P \times V}{T \times n}$$

$$\text{or } P \times V = n \times R \times T$$

An advantage of the ideal gas law over the combined gas law is that it permits you to solve for the number of moles of a contained gas when P, V, and T are known.

Figure 12.16
When the temperature, pressure, and volume of a gas are known, you can use the ideal gas law to calculate the number of moles of the gas.

Sample Problem 12-5

You fill a rigid steel cylinder that has a volume of 20.0 L with nitrogen gas (N_2)(g) to a final pressure of 2.00×10^4 kPa at 28 °C. How many moles of N_2(g) does the cylinder contain?

1. **ANALYZE** *List the knowns and the unknown.*

   Knowns: *Unknown:*
   - $P = 2.00 \times 10^4$ kPa   - $n = ?$ mol N_2(g)
   - $V = 20.0$ L
   - $T = 28$ °C

   Use the known values and the ideal gas law to calculate the unknown (n).

2. **CALCULATE** *Solve for the unknown.*

   Convert degrees Celsius to kelvins.

   $$28\ °C + 273 = 301\ K$$

   Rearrange the ideal gas law to isolate n.

   $$n = \frac{P \times V}{R \times T}$$

   Substitute the known quantities P, V, R, and T into the equation and solve.

   $$n = \frac{2.00 \times 10^4\ \cancel{kPa} \times 20.0\ \cancel{L}}{8.31 \dfrac{\cancel{L} \times \cancel{kPa}}{\cancel{K} \times mol} \times 301\ \cancel{K}} = 160\ mol\ N_2(g)$$

   $$= 1.60 \times 10^2\ mol\ N_2(g)$$

3. **EVALUATE** *Does the result make sense?*

   The gas is at a high pressure, but the volume is not large. This means that a large number of moles of gas must be compressed into the volume. The large answer is thus reasonable, and the units have canceled correctly.

Practice Problems

22. When the temperature of a rigid hollow sphere containing 685 L of helium gas is held at 621 K, the pressure of the gas is 1.89×10^3 kPa. How many moles of helium does the sphere contain?

23. What pressure will be exerted by 0.450 mol of a gas at 25 °C if it is contained in a 0.650-L vessel?

Figure 12.17
Natural gas (mainly methane) is often found in underground pockets near petroleum reserves. In the past, excess gas was simply burned off, as shown here, involving a great waste of this energy resource.

Sample Problem 12-6

A deep underground cavern contains 2.24×10^6 L of methane gas $(CH_4)(g)$ at a pressure of 1.50×10^3 kPa and a temperature of 42 °C. How many kilograms of CH_4 does this natural-gas deposit contain?

1. **ANALYZE** *List the knowns and the unknown.*

   Knowns:
   - $P = 1.50 \times 10^3$ kPa
   - $V = 2.24 \times 10^6$ L
   - $T = 42$ °C

   Unknown:
   - $m = ?$ kg CH_4

   Calculate the number of moles (n) using the ideal gas law. Convert moles to grams, using the molar mass of methane, and then convert grams to kilograms.

2. **CALCULATE** *Solve for the unknown.*

   Convert degrees Celsius to kelvins.

   $$42 \,°C + 273 = 315 \text{ K}$$

   Rearrange the equation for the ideal gas law to isolate n, the number of moles of methane.

   $$n = \frac{P \times V}{R \times T}$$

   Substitute the known quantities into the equation to find the number of moles of methane.

   $$n = \frac{1.50 \times 10^3 \text{ kPa} \times (2.24 \times 10^6 \text{ L})}{8.31 \frac{\text{L} \times \text{kPa}}{\text{K} \times \text{mol}} \times 315 \text{ K}} = 1.28 \times 10^6 \text{ mol } CH_4$$

   Convert moles of methane to grams.

   $$\text{molar mass } CH_4 = \left(4 \text{ mol H} \times \frac{1.0 \text{ g H}}{1 \text{ mol H}}\right) + \frac{12.0 \text{ g C}}{1 \text{ mol C}}$$
   $$= 16.0 \text{ g } CH_4/\text{mol } CH_4$$

   A mole–mass conversion gives the number of grams of methane.

   $$1.28 \times 10^6 \text{ mol } CH_4 \times \frac{16.0 \text{ g } CH_4}{1 \text{ mol } CH_4} = 20.5 \times 10^6 \text{ g } CH_4$$
   $$= 2.05 \times 10^7 \text{ g } CH_4$$

   Convert this answer to kilograms.

   $$2.05 \times 10^7 \text{ g } CH_4 \times \frac{1 \text{ kg}}{1000 \text{ g}} = 2.05 \times 10^4 \text{ kg } CH_4$$

3. **EVALUATE** *Does the result make sense?*

   The volume and pressure of the methane are very large. It is reasonable that the cavern contains the large mass of methane gas found as the solution to the problem. Also, the units canceled correctly, and the answer is expressed to the proper number of significant figures.

Practice Problems

24. A child has a lung capacity of 2.20 L. How many grams of air do her lungs hold at a pressure of 102 kPa and a normal body temperature of 37 °C? Air is a mixture, but you may assume an average molar mass of 29 g/mol for air because air is about 20% O_2 (molar mass 32) and 80% N_2 (molar mass 28).

25. What volume will 12.0 g of oxygen gas $(O_2)(g)$ occupy at 25 °C and a pressure of 52.7 kPa?

Chem ASAP!

Problem-Solving 24
Solve Problem 24 with the help of an interactive guided tutorial.

Figure 12.18
Carbon dioxide freezes at −78.5 °C. The solid that forms (dry ice) can damage skin if touched. The dry ice in the photo is under water. As it sublimes, carbon dioxide gas bubbles up through the water and into the air. The cold gas causes water vapor in air to condense and form a white fog. Why is dry ice not as messy to use as ice?

The Ideal Gas Law and Kinetic Theory

The previous discussions of kinetic theory and the gas laws assumed that the gases were ideal gases. A truly ideal gas is one that follows the gas laws at all conditions of pressure and temperature. Such a gas would have to conform precisely to the assumptions of kinetic theory. Its particles could thus have no volume and could not be attracted to each other at all. As you probably suspect, there is no gas for which this is true. An ideal gas does not exist. Nevertheless, at many conditions of temperature and pressure, real gases behave very much like an ideal gas.

An important behavior of real gases that differs from that of a hypothetical ideal gas is that real gases can be liquefied and sometimes solidified by cooling and by applying pressure. Ideal gases cannot be. For example, when water vapor is cooled below 100 °C at standard atmospheric pressure, it condenses to a liquid. The behavior of other real gases is similar, although lower temperatures and greater pressures may be required. In some cases, such as carbon dioxide (as you learned in Chapter 10), the gas may be converted directly to a solid. Solid carbon dioxide sublimes readily back to the gas state, as shown in **Figure 12.18.**

Departures from the Ideal Gas Law

A gas that adheres very closely to the gas laws at some conditions of temperature and pressure is said to exhibit ideal behavior under those conditions. No gas behaves ideally at all temperatures and pressures.

You can analyze how much a gas departs from ideal behavior by considering the ratio $(P \times V)/(n \times R \times T)$. According to the ideal gas law, this ratio for an ideal gas equals 1 (to see that, just divide both sides of the ideal gas law by $n \times R \times T$). This ratio plotted against pressure gives a horizontal line for an ideal gas because the ratio is constant. See **Figure 12.19.** For real gases at high pressures, the ratio $(P \times V)/(n \times R \times T)$ may depart widely from the ideal constant value of 1. The ratio may be greater or less than 1; the deviation may be positive (above the line) or negative (below the line). The explanation for these departures, or deviations, from the ideal is based on two factors: the attractions between molecules and the volume of gas molecules.

Figure 12.19
For an ideal gas, the ratio $(P \times V)/(n \times R \times T)$ always equals 1. By contrast, real gases deviate from the ideal. What is the value of $(P \times V)/(n \times R \times T)$ for CO_2 at 40 °C and 10 000 kPa?

Ideal gas

Ideal gas
(Particles are
assumed to be
dimensionless
points.)

P_1 P_2

Real gas

Real gas
(Particles have
volume.)

P_1 P_2

Figure 12.20
As pressure increases, the actual volumes of individual gas molecules in a real gas are no longer insignificant. It becomes increasingly difficult to compress the gas beyond a certain point, no matter what pressure is applied.

PHYSICS

Cryostats
The containers that store and transport liquefied gases are called cryostats. Their design prevents heat from being transferred from the environment to the very cold liquid inside. The most widely used cryostats are called Dewar flasks, named after the Scottish scientist Sir James Dewar, who invented the containers in 1892. Dewar flasks are double-walled vessels with a vacuum between the walls, similar to the familiar Thermos™ bottle used to carry hot or cold drinks. Cryostats are very lightweight in comparison with compressed-gas cylinders. A given amount of a substance has a much smaller volume as a liquid than as a gas, even if the gas is under pressure. For these reasons, many gases are stored and transported in their liquefied form rather than as gases.

As you have read, simple kinetic theory assumes that gas particles are not attracted to each other and that the particles have no volume. These assumptions are incorrect. Gases and vapors could not be liquefied if there were no attractions between molecules. Also real gases are made up of actual physical particles, which do have a volume, as **Figure 12.20** illustrates.

The intermolecular forces that tend to hold the particles in a gas together effectively reduce the distance between particles. The gas therefore occupies less volume than is expected by the no-attractions assumption of the kinetic theory. This fact, considered alone, causes the $(P \times V)/(n \times R \times T)$ ratio to tend to be less than 1. At the same time, the molecules themselves occupy some volume, thus contradicting the zero-volume assumption of kinetic theory. This fact, on its own, causes the $(P \times V)/(n \times R \times T)$ ratio to tend to be greater than 1. One or the other of these two effects will usually dominate. In portions of the curves below the line, the intermolecular attractions dominate, causing the total volume to be less than ideal. In portions of the curves above the line, the effect of volume of the molecules dominates, causing the total volume to be greater than ideal. The temperature of the gas determines which of these two effects is the dominant one.

Compare the curves for $CH_4(g)$ at 0 °C and at 200 °C. At 0 °C, the methane molecules are moving relatively slowly. The attractions between the molecules are sufficiently strong so that, at low pressures, the curve is below the $(P \times V)/(n \times R \times T) = 1$ line. At higher pressures, the space between the molecules is reduced. The actual physical volume of the methane molecules now becomes important, and the curve is above the $(P \times V)/(n \times R \times T) = 1$ line. Raising the temperature to 200 °C increases the average kinetic energy of the methane molecules sufficiently to overcome the weak intermolecular attractive effects. Thus $(P \times V)/(n \times R \times T)$ is nearly equal to 1 at lower pressure at the elevated temperature. The ratio increases to greater than 1 only when the volume of the individual gas particles becomes important, as it does at high pressure.

The Behavior of Gases **345**

MINI LAB

Carbon Dioxide from Antacid Tablets

PURPOSE

To measure the amount of carbon dioxide gas given off when antacid tablets dissolve in water.

MATERIALS

- pencil
- graph paper
- tape measure
- clock or watch
- 3 rubber balloons (round)
- plastic medicine dropper
- water
- 6 antacid tablets
- pressure sensor (optional)

PROCEDURE

Sensor version available in the Probeware Lab Manual.

1. Break six antacid tablets into small pieces. Keep the pieces from each tablet in a separate pile. Put the pieces from one tablet into the first balloon. Put the pieces from two tablets into a second balloon. Put the pieces from three tablets into a third balloon.

2. After you use the medicine dropper to squirt about 5 mL of cold water into each balloon, immediately tie off each balloon.

3. Shake the balloons to mix the contents. Allow the contents to warm to room temperature.

4. Carefully measure and record the circumference of each balloon several times during the next 20 minutes.

5. Use the maximum circumference of each balloon to calculate the volume of each balloon. Assume that the balloons are spherical. (*Hint:* Volume of a sphere $= \dfrac{4\pi r^3}{3}$)

ANALYSIS AND CONCLUSIONS

1. Make a graph of balloon volume versus number of tablets. According to your graph, describe the relationship between the number of tablets used and the volume of the balloon.

2. Assume that the balloon is filled with carbon dioxide gas at 20 °C and standard pressure. Calculate the mass and the number of moles of CO_2 in each balloon at maximum inflation.

3. If a typical antacid tablet contains 2.0 g of sodium hydrogen carbonate, show how your carbon dioxide results compare with the theoretical values.

---

section review 12.4

26. How is it possible to calculate the amount of gas in a sample at given conditions of temperature, pressure, and volume?

27. What is the difference between an ideal gas and a real gas?

28. Explain the meaning of this statement: "No gas exhibits ideal behavior at all temperatures and pressures." At what conditions do real gases behave like ideal gases? Why?

29. Determine the volume occupied by 0.582 mol of a gas at 15 °C if the pressure is 81.8 kPa.

30. If 28.0 g of methane gas (CH_4) are introduced into an evacuated 2.00-L gas cylinder at a temperature of 35 °C, what is the pressure inside the cylinder? Note that the volume of the gas cylinder is constant.

 Chem ASAP! **Assessment 12.4** Check your understanding of the important ideas and concepts in Section 12.4.

GAS MOLECULES: MIXTURES AND MOVEMENTS

objectives
▶ State Avogadro's hypothesis, Dalton's law, and Graham's law
▶ Calculate moles, masses, and volumes of gases at STP
▶ Calculate partial pressures and rates of effusion

key terms
▶ Avogadro's hypothesis
▶ partial pressure
▶ Dalton's law of partial pressures
▶ diffusion
▶ effusion
▶ Graham's law of effusion

The top of Mount Everest is more than 29 000 feet above sea level. In addition to tents, food, warm clothes, and ropes, an expedition to climb Mount Everest requires cylinders of oxygen. Humans need a partial pressure of oxygen of at least 10.67 kPa to survive—continual exposure to less oxygen will result in death! **What is meant by the partial pressure of oxygen, and why does it decrease as altitude increases?**

Avogadro's Hypothesis

The particles that make up different gases are not the same size. For example, chlorine molecules have large numbers of electrons, protons, and neutrons. They are bigger and occupy more volume than hydrogen molecules, which have only two protons and two electrons. Early scientists recognized that there must be such size differences and assumed that collections of larger molecules must have larger volumes than collections of an equal number of small molecules. Thus many scientists reacted in disbelief in 1811 when they heard of **Avogadro's hypothesis:** Equal volumes of gases at the same temperature and pressure contain equal numbers of particles. It was as if Avogadro were suggesting that two rooms of the same size could be filled by the same number of objects, regardless of whether the objects were marbles or basketballs.

What Avogadro had in mind is not really so mysterious if you consider that the particles in a gas are very far apart, with nothing but space in between. Thus a collection of relatively large particles does not require much more space than the same number of relatively small particles. On average, there would be large expanses of space between the particles in either case, as shown in **Figure 12.21.** This was Avogadro's great insight, today easily demonstrated by experiment. At STP, 1 mol (6.02×10^{23}) of particles of any gas, regardless of the size of the particles, occupies a volume of 22.4 L.

Figure 12.21
The volume of a container easily accommodates the same number of relatively large or small particles, as long as the particles are not tightly packed. There is a great deal of empty space compared with the volume occupied by the particles. When the particles are tightly packed, large particles take up more space than small particles.

You can also understand Avogadro's hypothesis by thinking about the modern explanation for gas pressure. Equal numbers of particles of different gases in equal volumes at the same temperature should exert the same pressure because the particles have the same average kinetic energy and are contained within equal volumes. Thus whenever you have equal volumes of gases at the same temperature and pressure, the volumes should contain equal numbers of particles.

Sample Problem 12-7

Determine the volume (in L) occupied by 0.202 mol of a gas at standard temperature and pressure (STP).

1. **ANALYZE** *List the known and the unknown.*

   Known: *Unknown:*
   - $n = 0.202$ mol   - $V = ?$ L

   The number of moles of gas at STP is given. Convert from moles to the volume (V).

   $$\text{moles} \rightarrow \text{volume}$$

   The conversion factor for moles $\rightarrow$ volume at STP is 22.4 L/1 mol.

2. **CALCULATE** *Solve for the unknown.*

   Multiplying the known value by the conversion factor yields:

   $$V = 0.202 \text{ mol} \times \frac{22.4 \text{ L}}{1 \text{ mol}} = 4.52 \text{ L}$$

3. **EVALUATE** *Does the result make sense?*

   Because 1 mol of the gas occupies 22.4 L at STP, 0.202 mol of the gas should occupy about one-fifth of that volume, or about 4.5 L.

Practice Problems

31. What is the volume occupied by 0.250 mol of a gas at STP?
32. What volume does 0.742 mol of argon gas occupy at STP?

Sample Problem 12-8

How many oxygen molecules are in 3.36 L of oxygen gas at standard temperature and pressure (STP)?

1. **ANALYZE** *List the known and the unknown.*

   Known: *Unknown:*
   - $V = 3.36$ L   - ? molecules O_2

   The volume of O_2 at STP is known. To find the number of oxygen molecules, make the following conversion.

   $$\text{volume} \rightarrow \text{moles} \rightarrow \text{molecules}$$

   The conversion factors are 1 mol O_2/22.4 L O_2 and

   6.02×10^{23} molecules O_2/1 mol O_2, respectively.

Practice Problems

33. How many nitrogen molecules are in 5.12 L of the gas at STP?

Sample Problem 12-8 (cont.)

2. CALCULATE *Solve for the unknown.*

Multiplying the known value by the conversion factors yields:

$$3.36 \text{ L O}_2 \times \frac{1 \text{ mol O}_2}{22.4 \text{ L O}_2} \times \frac{6.02 \times 10^{23} \text{ molecules O}_2}{1 \text{ mol O}_2}$$

$$= 9.03 \times 10^{22} \text{ molecules O}_2$$

3. EVALUATE *Does the result make sense?*

The answer is reasonable: 3.36 L O_2 should contain about one-seventh mole of O_2 molecules. One-seventh of approximately 6×10^{23} molecules is about 9×10^{22} molecules.

Practice Problems (cont.)

34. What volume is occupied by 4.02×10^{22} molecules of helium gas at STP?

 Chem ASAP!

Problem-Solving 34
Solve Problem 34 with the help of an interactive guided tutorial.

Sample Problem 12-9

Determine the volume (in L) occupied by 14.0 g of nitrogen gas at STP.

1. ANALYZE *List the known and the unknown.*

Known:
- mass = 14.0 g $N_2(g)$

Unknown:
- $V = ? \text{ L}$

The mass of nitrogen is known. Convert the known mass to volume.

$$\text{mass} \rightarrow \text{moles} \rightarrow \text{volume}$$

The conversion factors are 1 mol N_2/molar mass N_2 and 22.4 L N_2/1 mol N_2, respectively. The conversion factors require the value of the molar mass of N_2.

2. CALCULATE *Solve for the unknown.*

First find the molar mass of N_2.

$$\text{molar mass N}_2 = 2 \text{ mol N} \times \frac{14.0 \text{ g N}}{1 \text{ mol N}}$$

$$= 28.0 \text{ g N}_2$$

Substitute the molar mass into the conversion factor, then solve for the volume of nitrogen gas.

$$14.0 \text{ g N}_2 \times \frac{1 \text{ mol N}_2}{28.0 \text{ g N}_2} \times \frac{22.4 \text{ L N}_2}{1 \text{ mol N}_2}$$

$$= 11.2 \text{ L N}_2$$

3. EVALUATE *Does the result make sense?*

The mass of nitrogen corresponds to one-half mole of N_2. One-half mole of gas at STP should occupy half of 22.4 L, or 11.2 L.

Practice Problems

35. What is the volume of a container that holds 8.80 g of carbon dioxide at STP?

36. A container holds 6.92 g of hydrogen gas at STP. What is the volume of the container?

Dalton's Law

The gases listed in **Table 12.1** make up a mixture called air. The particles in a gas mixture at the same temperature have the same average kinetic energy. Gas pressure depends only on the number of gas particles in a given volume and on their average kinetic energy—the kind of particle is unimportant. Each particle makes the same contribution to the pressure. Thus if you know the pressure exerted by each gas in a mixture, you can add the individual pressures to get the total gas pressure.

Table 12.1

Composition of Dry Air		
Component	**Volume (%)**	**Partial pressure (kPa)**
Nitrogen	78.08	79.11
Oxygen	20.95	21.22
Carbon dioxide	0.04	0.04
Argon and others	0.93	0.95
	100.00	101.32

Chem ASAP!

Animation 13

Observe the behavior of a mixture of nonreacting gases.

The contribution each gas in a mixture makes to the total pressure is called the **partial pressure** exerted by that gas. In a mixture of gases, the total pressure is the sum of the partial pressures of the gases.

$$P_{total} = P_1 + P_2 + P_3 + \ldots$$

This equation is one mathematical form of **Dalton's law of partial pressures:** At constant volume and temperature, the total pressure exerted by a mixture of gases is equal to the sum of the partial pressures of the component gases. The individual gases in containers a, b, and c of **Figure 12.22** are combined in container T. What partial pressure does each individual gas contribute to the total pressure of the mixture?

The fractional contribution to pressure exerted by each gas in a mixture does not change as the temperature, pressure, or volume changes. This fact has important implications for aviators and mountain climbers. For example, on top of Mount Everest, the total atmospheric pressure is reduced to 33.73 kPa (about one-third of its value at sea level). The partial pressure of oxygen is reduced by the same factor, to only 7.06 kPa (one-third the partial pressure of oxygen at sea level). This reduced oxygen

Figure 12.22

The sum of the pressures exerted by the gas in each of the three containers on the left is the same as the total pressure exerted by a mixture of the gases in the same volume, assuming the temperature stays the same. Dalton's law of partial pressures holds true because each gas exerts its own pressure independent of the pressure exerted by the other gases.

200 kPa (a) 500 kPa (b) 400 kPa (c) 1100 kPa (T)

pressure is insufficient for respiration because humans need an oxygen partial pressure of at least 10.67 kPa; some individuals need a higher partial pressure. **Figure 12.23** shows some of the steps jet pilots and mountaineers take to counteract high-altitude conditions.

Figure 12.23
High-altitude pilots and mountaineers must have supplemental oxygen supplies available when at high altitudes.

Sample Problem 12-10

Air contains oxygen, nitrogen, carbon dioxide, and trace amounts of other gases. What is the partial pressure of oxygen (P_{O_2}) at 101.30 kPa of total pressure if the partial pressures of nitrogen, carbon dioxide, and other gases are 79.10 kPa, 0.040 kPa, and 0.94 kPa, respectively.

1. ANALYZE *List the knowns and the unknown.*

Knowns:
- P_{N_2} = 79.10 kPa
- P_{CO_2} = 0.040 kPa
- P_{others} = 0.94 kPa
- P_{total} = 101.30 kPa

Unknown:
- P_{O_2} = ? kPa

Use the known values and Dalton's law of partial pressures ($P_{total} = P_{O_2} + P_{N_2} + P_{CO_2} + P_{others}$) to calculate the unknown value (P_{O_2}).

2. CALCULATE *Solve for the unknown.*

Rearrange the expression for Dalton's law to isolate P_{O_2}. Substitute the values for the partial pressures and solve the equation.

$$P_{O_2} = P_{total} - (P_{N_2} + P_{CO_2} + P_{others})$$
$$= 101.30 \text{ kPa} - (79.10 \text{ kPa} + 0.040 \text{ kPa} + 0.94 \text{ kPa})$$
$$= 21.22 \text{ kPa}$$

3. EVALUATE *Does the result make sense?*

The partial pressure of oxygen must be smaller than that of nitrogen because P_{total} is only 101.30 kPa. The other partial pressures are small, so an answer of 21.22 kPa seems reasonable.

Practice Problems

37. Determine the total pressure of a gas mixture that contains oxygen, nitrogen, and helium if the partial pressures of the gases are as follows: P_{O_2} = 20.0 kPa, P_{N_2} = 46.7 kPa, and P_{He} = 26.7 kPa.

38. A gas mixture containing oxygen, nitrogen, and carbon dioxide has a total pressure of 32.9 kPa. If P_{O_2} = 6.6 kPa and P_{N_2} = 23.0 kPa, what is P_{CO_2}?

Chem ASAP!

Problem-Solving 38
Solve Problem 38 with the help of an interactive guided tutorial.

Graham's Law

When you open a perfume bottle inside a room, the perfume molecules eventually spread throughout the room, and you can smell them everywhere. **Diffusion** is the tendency of molecules to move toward areas of lower concentration until the concentration is uniform throughout. **Figure 12.25** illustrates the diffusion process for bromine vapor. The concentrated bromine vapor tends to move outside the graduated cylinder toward an area where the bromine vapor concentration is less.

Much of the early work on diffusion was done in the 1840s by the Scottish chemist Thomas Graham (1805–1869). Graham measured the rates of **effusion,** the process in which a gas escapes through a tiny hole in its container. Graham noticed that gases of lower molar mass effuse faster than gases of higher molar mass. From his observations, he proposed **Graham's law of effusion:** The rate of effusion of a gas is inversely proportional to the square root of the gas's molar mass. Subsequently, this relationship was also shown to be true for the diffusion of gases. Thus the rate of diffusion of a gas is also inversely proportional to the square root of its molar mass.

To understand Graham's law, examine the relationship of the mass and speed of a moving body to the kinetic energy the body transfers when it strikes a stationary object (assuming perfectly elastic collisions). The mathematical expression that relates the mass (m) and the speed or velocity (v) of a body to its kinetic energy (KE) is $KE = \frac{1}{2}mv^2$. Suppose a small ball with a mass of 2 g traveling at 5 m/s has just enough kinetic energy to shatter a pane of glass. A ball bearing with a mass of only 1 g would need to travel faster (slightly more than 7 m/s) to have the same kinetic energy as the ball and to be able to shatter the same pane of glass.

Figure 12.24

White vapors of ammonium chloride form as the vapors from aqueous ammonia (NH_3)(aq) and hydrochloric acid (HCl)(aq) diffuse into the air. Aqueous ammonia used to be called ammonium hydroxide, a name seldom used today. What are the names and formulas of the molecules in the vapors? Which molecule diffuses faster? Why?

Chem ASAP!

Animation 14

Examine the processes of gas effusion and diffusion.

Figure 12.25

The diffusion of one substance through another is a relatively slow process. Here, bromine vapor is diffusing upward through the air in a graduated cylinder. After several hours, bromine vapors will mingle with air outside the cylinder.

There is an important principle here. If two bodies of different masses have the same kinetic energy, the lighter body must move faster. You already know that the particles of two different gases at the same temperature have the same average kinetic energy. Thus a gas particle of low mass should move faster than a gas particle of high mass if the gases are at the same temperature. The gas of lower molar mass should therefore diffuse and effuse faster.

It is easy to show that the above phenomenon is true by comparing two balloons: one filled with helium and the other filled with air. There are pores in a balloon that, although tiny, are still large enough for both helium atoms and molecules in air to pass through freely. Balloons filled with air stay inflated longer, because the main components of air—oxygen molecules and nitrogen molecules—are more massive than helium atoms. The air particles move more slowly; therefore, they diffuse and effuse more slowly than helium atoms. The fast-moving helium atoms, with molar masses of only 4 g, rapidly effuse through the pores in the balloon. The rate of effusion or diffusion is related only to the particle's speed. In a mathematical form, Graham's law can be written as follows for two gases, A and B.

$$\frac{Rate_A}{Rate_B} = \frac{\sqrt{molar\ mass_B}}{\sqrt{molar\ mass_A}}$$

In other words, the rates of effusion of two gases are inversely proportional to the square roots of their molar masses. Now compare the rates of effusion of the air component nitrogen (molar mass = 28.0 g) and helium (molar mass = 4.0 g):

$$\frac{Rate_{He}}{Rate_{N_2}} = \frac{\sqrt{28.0\ g}}{\sqrt{4.0\ g}} = \frac{5.3\ g}{2.0\ g} = 2.7$$

You can see that helium effuses and diffuses nearly three times faster than nitrogen at the same temperature.

section review 12.5

39. In your own words, briefly state Avogadro's hypothesis, Dalton's law, and Graham's law.

40. How are moles, masses, or volumes of gases calculated from one another for a gas at STP?

41. Calculate the number of liters occupied at STP.
   a. 1.7 mol $H_2(g)$
   b. 1.8×10^{-2} mol $N_2(g)$
   c. 2.5×10^2 mol $O_2(g)$

42. How is the partial pressure of a gas in a mixture calculated? How is the rate of effusion of a gas calculated?

43. What is the significance of the volume 22.4 L?

44. At the same temperature, the rates of diffusion of carbon monoxide and nitrogen gas are virtually identical. Explain.

 Chem ASAP! Assessment 12.5 Check your understanding of the important ideas and concepts in Section 12.5.

portfolio project

To estimate the amount of CO_2 in a soft drink, obtain an unopened bottle and a large spherical balloon. Open the bottle and quickly place the balloon over its neck. Fasten the balloon tightly and shake the bottle gently for at least 5 minutes. Use the volume of a sphere to estimate the volume of CO_2. Use the gas laws to find the number of moles of CO_2. Compare different brands. Identify possible sources of error in this experiment.

DIVING CAN BE A GAS

A lot of important work goes on under the ocean's surface, and much of it is done by commercial scuba divers. Divers repair and inspect ships, help build offshore oil platforms, salvage sunken ships, and repair undersea cables and pipelines.

Professional divers often have to do their work at great depths, where the water exerts extreme pressure. How can divers journey safely into this foreign world? Only by bringing with them special breathing equipment and mixtures of gases can they compensate for the effects of high pressure.

If you have ever dived below the surface, you are aware of the pressure exerted by water. The pressure is high enough, even a few meters under water, that if you tried to breathe through a hose connected to the surface you would not be able to. Your lungs would be unable to expand. So how are scuba divers able to breathe at even greater depths?

Divers can breathe deep under water because the gases they take with them are under pressure. A device attached to a diver's air tanks, called a regulator, automatically adjusts the pressure of the air coming out of the tanks and into the diver's lungs. The regulator works to equalize the pressure inside and outside the lungs.

Regulating the pressure of the air they breathe, however, is not divers' main concern. At the high pressures that exist even at moderate depths, more gas can be dissolved in divers' blood than can be dissolved at normal pressures. Any gas present in divers' air tanks, therefore, dissolves in their blood in greater-than-normal concentrations.

The main component of air is molecular nitrogen (N_2). When dissolved nitrogen reaches high concentrations in the blood, it can cause two different problems.

> Divers can breathe deep under water because the gases they take with them are under pressure.

The first is nitrogen narcosis, a condition with effects similar to those produced by ingesting too much alcohol. The second problem arises only when the diver begins to ascend toward the surface. As the pressure is reduced, the nitrogen dissolved in the blood tends to come out of solution and to form tiny bubbles. If this happens, it causes a condition called the bends, which is extremely painful and potentially fatal. Divers prevent the bends by gradually letting the nitrogen come out of the bloodstream at stops during the ascent.

For deep dives, it is especially important to take measures to prevent nitrogen narcosis and the bends. For these dives, commercial divers often use air tanks containing a special blend of gases instead of pressurized air.

One of these blends is a mixture of nitrogen and oxygen, called Nitrox, which has less nitrogen than pressurized air. By breathing Nitrox, a diver reduces the potential for nitrogen-related problems. For very deep dives, a mixture of helium and oxygen, called Heliox, is often used. This mixture eliminates nitrogen's negative effects, but it can lead to high-pressure nervous syndrome, in which the diver shakes uncontrollably. A third combination of gases, called Trimix, is used for extremely deep dives. Trimix is Heliox with a small amount of nitrogen added to prevent the shaking problem.

CHEMISTRY IN CAREERS

COMMERCIAL DIVER
Are you good at working under pressure? Consider being a commercial diver. See page 873.

CHEMIST NEEDED

TAKE IT TO THE NET

Find out more about career opportunities: www.phschool.com

CHEMICAL SPECIALIST
Local food service distributor seeks responsible self-motivated individ

Chapter 12 STUDENT STUDY GUIDE

Take It to the NET
For interactive study and review, go to www.phschool.com

KEY TERMS

- Avogadro's hypothesis *p. 347*
- Boyle's law *p. 333*
- Charles's law *p. 336*
- combined gas law *p. 339*
- compressibility *p. 327*

- Dalton's law of partial pressures *p. 350*
- diffusion *p. 352*
- effusion *p. 352*
- Gay-Lussac's law *p. 338*

- Graham's law of effusion *p. 352*
- ideal gas constant (R) *p. 341*
- ideal gas law *p. 341*
- partial pressure *p. 350*

KEY EQUATIONS

- Boyle's law:

$$P_1 \times V_1 = P_2 \times V_2$$

- Charles's law:

$$\frac{V_1}{T_1} = \frac{V_2}{T_2}$$

- Gay-Lussac's law:

$$\frac{P_1}{T_1} = \frac{P_2}{T_2}$$

- Combined gas law:

$$\frac{P_1 \times V_1}{T_1} = \frac{P_2 \times V_2}{T_2}$$

- Ideal gas law:

$$P \times V = n \times R \times T$$

- Dalton's law:

$$P_{total} = P_1 + P_2 + P_3 + \ldots$$

- Graham's law:

$$\frac{\text{Rate}_A}{\text{Rate}_B} = \frac{\sqrt{\text{molar mass}_B}}{\sqrt{\text{molar mass}_A}}$$

CONCEPT SUMMARY

12.1 The Properties of Gases
- Kinetic molecular theory can be used to explain gas pressure, volume, and temperature.
- The average kinetic energy of a collection of gas particles is directly proportional to the Kelvin temperature of the gas.

12.2 Factors Affecting Gas Pressure
- The collision of gas particles with the walls of the container constitutes gas pressure.
- In general, increasing the volume of a container decreases gas pressure; decreasing the volume of a container increases gas pressure.
- In general, increasing the temperature of a contained gas increases its pressure; decreasing the temperature decreases its pressure.

12.3 The Gas Laws
- The pressure and volume of a fixed mass of gas are inversely related (Boyle's law).
- The volume of a gas at constant pressure is directly related to its Kelvin temperature (Charles's law).

- The pressure of a fixed volume of gas is directly related to its Kelvin temperature (Gay-Lussac's law).

12.4 Ideal Gases
- The ideal gas law relates the moles of a gas to its pressure, temperature, and volume.
- Real gases differ from ideal gases because intermolecular forces tend to reduce the distance between real gas particles and because real gas particles have volume.

12.5 Gas Molecules: Mixtures and Movements
- Avogadro stated that equal volumes of gases, at the same temperature and pressure, contain an equal number of particles.
- The total pressure in a mixture of gases is equal to the sum of the partial pressures of each gas present (Dalton's law).
- Gases diffuse from a region of high gas concentration to one of lower concentration. The smaller the molar mass of a gas, the greater its rate of diffusion (Graham's law).

CHAPTER CONCEPT MAP

Use these terms to construct a concept map that organizes the major ideas of this chapter.

 Chem ASAP! Concept Map 12
Create your Concept Map using the computer.

- Boyle's law
- Charles's law
- partial pressure
- combined gas law
- Avogadro's hypothesis
- diffusion

CONCEPT PRACTICE

45. Heating a contained gas that is held at a constant volume increases its pressure. Why? *12.1*

46. What happens to gas particles when a gas is compressed? *12.1*

47. A metal cylinder contains 1 mol of nitrogen gas at STP. What will happen to the pressure if another mole of gas is added to the cylinder, but the temperature and volume do not change? *12.2*

48. If a gas is compressed from 4 L to 1 L and the temperature remains constant, what happens to the pressure? *12.2*

49. Why is Kelvin temperature specified in calculations that involve gases? *12.2*

50. Describe what happens to the volume of a balloon when it is taken outside on a cold winter day. Explain why this happens. *12.2*

51. The gas in a closed container has a pressure of 3.00×10^2 kPa at 30 °C (303 K). What will the pressure be if the temperature is lowered to −172 °C (101 K)? *12.3*

52. Calculate the volume of a gas (in L) at a pressure of 1.00×10^2 kPa if its volume at 1.20×10^2 kPa is 1.50×10^3 mL. *12.3*

53. A gas with a volume of 4.0 L at 90.0 kPa expands until the pressure drops to 20.0 kPa. What is the new volume if the temperature remains constant? *12.3*

54. A gas with a volume of 3.00×10^2 mL at 150.0 °C is heated until its volume is 6.00×10^2 mL. What is the new temperature of the gas if the pressure remains constant during the heating process? *12.3*

55. Why do aerosol containers display the warning, "Do not incinerate"? *12.3*

56. State the combined gas law. 12.3

57. A sealed cylinder of gas contains nitrogen gas at 1.00×10^3 kPa pressure and a temperature of 20 °C. The cylinder is left in the sun, and the temperature of the gas increases to 50 °C. What is the new pressure in the cylinder? *12.3*

58. Show how Charles's law can be derived from the combined gas law. *12.3*

59. Explain why it is impossible for an ideal gas to exist. *12.4*

60. Describe an ideal gas. *12.4*

61. Explain the reasons why real gases deviate from ideal behavior. *12.4*

62. If 4.50 g of methane gas (CH_4) is introduced into an evacuated 2.00-L container at 35 °C, what is the pressure in the container? *12.4*

63. Calculate the number of liters occupied at STP. *12.5*
  a. 2.5 mol $N_2(g)$
  b. 0.600 g $H_2(g)$
  c. 0.350 mol $O_2(g)$

64. How would the number of particles of two gases compare if their partial pressures in a container were identical? *12.5*

65. Which gas effuses faster: hydrogen or chlorine? How much faster? *12.5*

66. Which gas effuses faster at the same temperature: molecular oxygen or atomic argon? *12.5*

67. Calculate the ratio of the velocity of helium atoms to the velocity of neon atoms at the same temperature. *12.5*

68. Calculate the ratio of the velocity of helium atoms to fluorine molecules at the same temperature. *12.5*

CONCEPT MASTERY

69. What can you conclude about the nature of the relationship between two variables with a quotient that is a constant?

70. A certain gas effuses four times as fast as oxygen (O_2). What is the molar mass of the gas?

71. A 3.50-L gas sample at 20 °C and a pressure of 86.7 kPa expands to a volume of 8.00 L. The final pressure of the gas is 56.7 kPa. What is the final temperature of the gas, in degrees Celsius?

72. During an effusion experiment, it took 75 seconds for a certain number of moles of an unknown gas to pass through a tiny hole. Under the same conditions, the same number of moles of oxygen gas passed through the hole in 30 seconds. What is the molar mass of the unknown gas?

73. Choose the term that best completes the second relationship.

   a. ideal gas : real gas

      fiction :_____

      (1) biography

      (2) novel

      (3) movie

      (4) nonfiction

   b. Charles's law : temperature

      Boyle's law :_____

      (1) pressure

      (2) volume

      (3) ideal mass

      (4) mass

   c. volume : Charles's law

      pressure :_____

      (1) Boyle's law

      (2) combined gas law

      (3) Gay-Lussac's law

      (4) temperature

   d. inverse relationship : Boyle's law

      direct relationship :_____

      (1) absolute zero

      (2) Avagadro's hypothesis

      (3) Charles's law

      (4) ideal gas law

   e. kelvins : degrees Celsius

      kilopascals :_____

      (1) atmospheric pressure

      (2) atmospheres

      (3) pressure

      (4) absolute zero

74. Gases will expand to fill a vacuum. Why do Earth's atmospheric gases not escape into the near-vacuum of space?

75. How does the vacuum used in Thermos™ bottles prevent heat transfer?

76. What real gas comes closest to having the characteristics of an ideal gas? Why?

77. Calculate the molar mass of each substance.

   a. $Ca(CH_3CO_2)_2$

   b. H_3PO_4

   c. $C_{12}H_{22}O_{11}$

   d. $Pb(NO_3)_2$

78. Name each compound.

   a. $SnBr_2$

   b. $BaSO_4$

   c. $Mg(OH)_2$

   d. IF_5

79. An atom of lead-206 weighs 17.16 times as much as an atom of carbon.

   a. What is the molar mass of this isotope of lead?

   b. How many protons, electrons, and neutrons are in this atom of lead?

80. How many kilojoules and kilocalories of heat are required to raise 40.0 g of water from $-12\,°C$ to $130\,°C$?

81. Write a balanced equation for each chemical reaction.

   a. Calcium reacts with water to form calcium hydroxide and hydrogen gas.

   b. Tetraphosphorus decoxide reacts with water to form phosphoric acid.

   c. Mercury and oxygen are prepared by heating mercury(II) oxide.

   d. Aluminum hydroxide and hydrogen sulfide form when aluminum sulfide reacts with water.

82. Classify each of the reactions in Problem 81 based on type.

83. Calculate the molecular formula of each of the following compounds.

   a. The empirical formula is C_2H_4O and the molar mass = 88 g/mol.

   b. The empirical formula is CH and the molar mass = 104 g/mol.

   c. The molar mass = 90 g/mol. The percent composition is 26.7% C, 71.1% O, and 2.2% H.

84. A piece of metal has a mass of 9.92 g and measures 4.5 cm × 1.3 cm × 1.6 mm. What is the density of the metal?

85. Calculate the percent composition of 2-propanol (C_3H_7OH).

86. Aluminum oxide is formed from its elements.

$$Al(s) + O_2(g) \longrightarrow Al_2O_3(s)$$

a. Balance the equation.
b. How many grams of each reactant are needed to form 583 g $Al_2O_3(s)$?

CONCEPT CHALLENGE

87. Oxygen is produced in the laboratory by heating potassium nitrate (KNO_3). Use the data table below, which gives the volume of oxygen produced at STP from varying quantities of KNO_3, to determine the mole ratio by which KNO_3 and O_2 react.

Mass of KNO_3 (g)	Volume of O_2 (cL)
0.84	9.3
1.36	15.1
2.77	30.7
4.82	53.5
6.96	77.3

88. The following reaction takes place in a sealed 40.0-L container at a temperature of 120 °C.

$$4NH_3(g) + 5O_2(g) \longrightarrow 4NO(g) + 6H_2O(g)$$

a. When 34.0 g $NH_3(g)$ reacts with 96.0 g $O_2(g)$, what is the partial pressure of $NO(g)$ in the container?
b. What is the total pressure in the container?

89. A mixture of ethyne (C_2H_2)(g) and methane (CH_4)(g) occupied a certain volume at a total pressure of 16.8 kPa. Upon burning the sample to form $CO_2(g)$ and $H_2O(g)$, the $CO_2(g)$ was collected and its pressure found to be 25.6 kPa in the same volume and at the same temperature as the original mixture. What percentage of the original mixture was methane?

90. A 0.10-L container holds 3.0×10^{20} molecules H_2 at 100 kPa and 0 °C.

a. If the volume of a hydrogen molecule is 6.7×10^{-24} mL, what percentage of the volume of the gas is occupied by its molecules?
b. If the pressure is increased to 100 000 kPa, the volume of the gas is 1×10^{-4} L. What fraction of the total volume do the hydrogen molecules now occupy?

91. Many gases that have small molecules, such as $N_2(g)$ and $O_2(g)$, have the expected molar volume of 22.41 L at STP. However, other gases behave in a very nonideal manner, even if extreme pressures and temperatures are not involved. The molar volumes of $CH_4(g)$, $CO_2(g)$, and $NH_3(g)$ at STP are 22.37 L, 22.26 L, and 22.06 L, respectively. Explain the reasons for these large departures from the ideal.

Select the choice that best answers each question or completes each statement.

1. A gas in a container has a volume of 120.0 mL at −123 °C. What volume does this gas occupy at 27.0 °C?
   a. 60.0 mL
   c. 26.5 mL
   b. 240.0 mL
   d. 546 mL

2. If the Kelvin temperature of a gas is tripled and the volume is doubled, the new pressure will be
   a. 1/6 the original pressure.
   b. 2/3 the original pressure.
   c. 3/2 the original pressure.
   b. 5 times the original pressure.

3. Which of these gases effuses fastest?
   a. Cl_2
   c. NH_3
   b. NO_2
   d. N_2

4. All the oxygen gas from a 10.0-L container at a pressure of 202 kPa is added to a 20.0-L container of hydrogen at a pressure of 505 kPa. After the transfer, what are the partial pressures of oxygen and hydrogen?
   a. oxygen is 101 kPa; hydrogen is 505 kPa
   b. oxygen is 202 kPa; hydrogen is 505 kPa
   c. oxygen is 101 kPa; hydrogen is 253 kPa
   d. oxygen is 202 kPa; hydrogen is 253 kPa

5. Which of the following changes would increase the pressure of a gas in a closed container?
   I. Part of the gas is removed.
   II. The container size is decreased.
   III. Temperature is increased.
   a. I and II only
   b. II and III only
   c. I and III only
   d. I, II, and III

6. A real gas behaves most nearly like an ideal gas
   a. at high pressure and low temperature.
   b. at low pressure and high temperature.
   c. at low pressure and low temperature.
   d. at high pressure and high temperature.

Use this description to answer questions 7 and 8.

A teacher adds a 1 mL of water to an empty metal soda can. The teacher heats the can over a burner and then quickly plunges it upside down in an ice-water bath. The can immediately collapses inward as though crushed in a trash compactor.

7. Use kinetic theory to explain why the can collapsed inward.

8. If the experiment were done with a dry can, would the results be similar? Explain.

Use the graphs to answer questions 9-12. A graph may be used once, more than once, or not at all.

a.

b.

c.

Which graph shows each of the following?
9. directly proportional relationship
10. graph with slope = 0
11. inversely proportional relationship
12. graph with a constant slope

Use the drawing to answer questions 13 and 14.

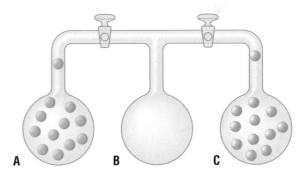

A   B   C

13. Bulbs A and C contain different gases. Bulb B contains no gas. If the valves between the bulbs are opened, how will the particles of gas be distributed when the system reaches equilibrium? For this exercise, assume none of the particles are in the tubes that connect the bulbs.

14. *You Draw it!* Make a similar three-bulb drawing. Place 6 blue spheres in bulb A, 9 green spheres in bulb B, and 12 red spheres in bulb C. Then draw the setup to represent the distribution of gases after the valves are opened and the system reaches equilibrium.

A "neon" sign's colors depend on the gases in its light tubes.

FEATURES

Stay current with **SCIENCE NEWS**
Find out more about electrons in atoms:
www.phschool.com

DISCOVER IT! OBSERVING LIGHT EMISSION FROM WINTERGREEN MINTS

You need 3 different brands of wintergreen mints, a pair of pliers, transparent tape, and a dark room.

1. Break each mint in half.
2. Wrap the jaws of the pliers with transparent tape.
3. Turn off the lights and allow your eyes to adjust to the darkness.
4. Watch the exposed edge of the mint as you carefully crush it between the jaws of the pliers. Note the color and brightness of any emitted light.
5. Repeat Step 4 for the other two mints.

What did you observe when you crushed the mints? Did all the mints emit light? Propose an explanation for your observations. After completing this chapter, return to this activity to revise and expand your explanation.

MODELS OF THE ATOM

Aeronautical engineers use wind tunnels and scale models to simulate and test the aerodynamic drag forces that will act on a proposed design. The scale model shown is a physical model. However, not all models are physical. In fact, several theoretical models of the atom have been developed over the past several hundred years. **What is the current model of the atom, and how was it developed?**

objectives

▸ Summarize the development of atomic theory

▸ Explain the significance of quantized energies of electrons as they relate to the quantum mechanical model of the atom

key terms

▸ energy level
▸ quantum
▸ quantum mechanical model
▸ atomic orbitals

The Evolution of Atomic Models

Thus far, the atomic model presented in this textbook has considered atoms as combinations of protons and neutrons making up a nucleus that is surrounded by electrons. Although this model has worked very well, it has outlived its usefulness because it explains only a few simple properties of atoms. It does not explain, for example, why metals or compounds of metals give off characteristic colors when heated in a flame. A more sophisticated atomic model is needed. As it turns out, the chemical properties of atoms, ions, and molecules are related to the arrangement of the electrons within them. Therefore, in this chapter, models of atomic structure will be expanded, with an emphasis on the electrons in atoms.

For about 50 years past the time of John Dalton (1766–1844), the atom was considered a solid indivisible mass. Dalton's atomic theory was a great advance in explaining the nature of chemical reactions. However, the discovery of subatomic particles shattered every theory scientists had about indivisible atoms.

The discoverer of the electron, J. J. Thomson (1856–1940), realized that the accepted model of an indivisible atom did not take electrons into account. Thomson, therefore, proposed a revised model, referred to as the plum-pudding atom. **Figure 13.2** on the following page shows this and other proposed models of the atom. The plum-pudding atom had negatively charged electrons stuck into a lump of positively charged material, similar to raisins stuck in dough. The plum-pudding model explained some electrical properties of atoms. It said nothing, however, about the number of protons and electrons, their arrangements in the atom, or the ease with which atoms are stripped of electrons to form ions.

Figure 13.1

Each of these scientists contributed to the development of atomic models.

John Dalton
1766–1844

J. J. Thomson
1856–1940

Ernest Rutherford
1871–1937

Niels Bohr
1885–1962

Electrons in Atoms **361**

Figure 13.2

These illustrations show how the atomic model has changed as scientists have learned more about the atom's structure. What would a picture of Dalton's model of the atom look like?

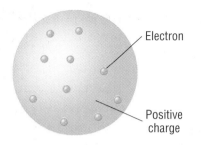

Thomson model
In the nineteenth century, Thomson described the atom as a ball of positive charge containing a number of electrons.

Rutherford model
In the early twentieth century, Rutherford showed that most of an atom's mass is concentrated in a small, positively charged region called the nucleus.

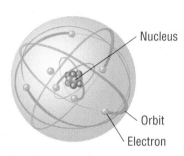

Bohr model
After Rutherford's discovery, Bohr proposed that electrons travel in definite orbits around the nucleus.

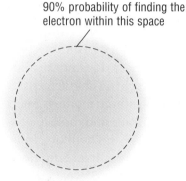

Quantum mechanical model
Modern atomic theory describes the electronic structure of the atom as the probability of finding electrons within certain regions of space.

Based on his discovery of the nucleus, Ernest Rutherford (1871–1937) proposed the nuclear atom, in which electrons surround a dense nucleus. He thought of the rest of the atom as empty space. Later experiments showed that the nuclei of atoms are composed of protons and neutrons. What kind of charge does the nucleus of every atom carry?

As you know, oppositely charged particles attract each other. Thus one could argue that the negative electrons should be drawn into a positive nucleus, causing the atom to collapse. However, this does not occur.

In 1913, Niels Bohr (1885–1962), a young Danish physicist and a student of Rutherford's, came up with a new atomic model. He proposed that electrons are arranged in concentric circular paths, or orbits, around the nucleus. This model, patterned after the motions of the planets around the sun, is often referred to as the planetary model. Bohr answered in a novel way the question of what prevents electrons from falling into the nucleus. He proposed that the electrons in a particular path have a fixed energy; the electrons do not lose energy and cannot fall into the nucleus. The **energy level** of an electron is the region around the nucleus where the electron is likely to be moving.

The fixed energy levels of electrons are analogous to the rungs of a ladder. The lowest rung of the ladder corresponds to the lowest energy level. A person can climb up or down a ladder by going from rung to rung. Similarly, an electron can jump from one energy level to another. A person on a ladder cannot stand between the rungs. Similarly, the electrons in an atom cannot exist between energy levels. To move from one rung to another, a person climbing a ladder must move just the right distance. To move from one energy level to another, an electron must gain or lose just the right amount of energy.

A **quantum** of energy is the amount of energy required to move an electron from its present energy level to the next higher one. The energies of electrons are said to be quantized. The term quantum leap, used to describe an abrupt change, comes from this concept. In general, the higher an electron is on the energy ladder, the farther it is from the nucleus.

The amount of energy gained or lost by an electron is not always the same. Unlike the rungs of a ladder, the energy levels in an atom are not equally spaced. In fact, the energy levels become more closely spaced the farther they are from the nucleus. Instead of a ladder, you might prefer to think of the spacing of energy levels in terms of garden steps like those illustrated in **Figure 13.3.** The steps become closer together as you climb higher. This makes it easier to step off at the top. Similarly, the higher the energy level occupied by an electron, the easier the electron escapes from the atom. Why do you think this is true?

Figure 13.3
These garden steps are analogous to the energy levels in an atom. The higher the energy level occupied by an electron, the more energetic it is, and the farther it usually is from the nucleus.

The Quantum Mechanical Model

In 1926, the Austrian physicist Erwin Schrödinger (1887–1961) took atomic models one step further. He used the new quantum theory to write and solve a mathematical equation describing the location and energy of an electron in a hydrogen atom. The modern description of the electrons in atoms, the **quantum mechanical model,** comes from the mathematical solutions to the Schrödinger equation. Previous models were essentially physical models based on the motion of large objects. In contrast, the quantum mechanical model is primarily mathematical. It has few analogies in the visible world.

Like the Bohr model, the quantum mechanical model of the atom restricts the energy of electrons to certain values. In a radical departure from the Bohr model, however, the quantum mechanical model does not define an exact path an electron takes around the nucleus. Rather, it estimates the probability of finding an electron in a certain position. Probability is a concept that you may know of as chance. If you place three red marbles and one green marble into a box and then pick a marble without looking, the probability, or chance, of picking the green marble is one in four, or 25%. The chance of picking a red marble is three in four, or 75%. What is the chance of picking a red marble after one red marble has already been taken from the box?

In the quantum mechanical model of the atom, the probability of finding an electron within a certain volume of space surrounding the nucleus can be represented as a fuzzy cloud. The cloud is more dense where the probability of finding the electron is high. The cloud is less dense where the probability of finding the electron is low. Although it is unclear where the cloud ends, there is at least a slight chance of finding the electron a considerable distance from the nucleus. Therefore, attempts to show probabilities as a fuzzy cloud are usually limited to the volume in which the electron is found 90% of the time. To visualize an electron probability cloud, imagine that you could mold a sack around the cloud so that the electron was inside the sack 90% of the time. The shape of the sack would then give you a useful picture of the shape of the cloud. Illustrations of electron clouds typically show the shape of the space in which the electron is found 90% of the time.

Atomic Orbitals

As in the Bohr atom, the quantum mechanical model designates energy levels of electrons by means of principal quantum numbers (n). Each principal quantum number refers to a major, or principal, energy level in an atom. These principal energy levels are assigned values in order of increasing energy: $n = 1, 2, 3, 4$, and so forth. The average distance of the electron from the nucleus increases with increasing values of n. Electrons in the third principal energy level have a greater average distance from the nucleus than electrons in the second principal energy level.

Within each principal energy level, the electrons occupy energy sublevels, much as people in theater seats arranged in sections (principal energy levels) occupy rows within those sections (energy sublevels). **Table 13.1** gives the number of sublevels within each principal energy level. Notice that the number of energy sublevels is the same as the principal quantum number. How many energy sublevels would be in the fifth principal energy level?

Where are the electrons in the various sublevels located in relation to the nucleus? You may recall that the quantum mechanical model limits the description of an electron's position to an area within an electron probability cloud. Because the electron is not confined to a fixed circular path, as it is in the Bohr atom, these regions in which electrons are likely to be found

Table 13.1

Summary of Principal Energy Levels, Sublevels, and Orbitals		
Principal energy level	Number of sublevels	Type of sublevel
$n = 1$	1	1s (1 orbital)
$n = 2$	2	2s (1 orbital), 2p (3 orbitals)
$n = 3$	3	3s (1 orbital), 3p (3 orbitals), 3d (5 orbitals)
$n = 4$	4	4s (1 orbital), 4p (3 orbitals), 4d (5 orbitals), 4f (7 orbitals)

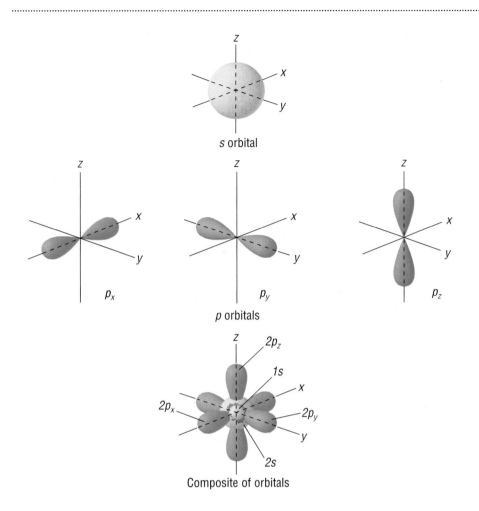

Figure 13.4

The electron probability clouds for the s orbital, the p orbitals, and a composite of one 1s, one 2s, and three 2p orbitals are shown here.

Chem ASAP!

Animation 15
Observe the characteristics of atomic orbitals.

s orbital

p_x

p_y

p_z

p orbitals

$2p_z$

$1s$

$2p_x$

$2p_y$

$2s$

Composite of orbitals

cannot be called orbits. In the quantum mechanical model, these regions are called **atomic orbitals.** Letters denote the atomic orbitals. As **Figure 13.4** shows, *s* orbitals are spherical, and *p* orbitals are dumbbell-shaped. The three kinds of *p* orbitals have different orientations in space. **Figure 13.5** shows the shapes of *d* orbitals. Four of the five kinds of *d* orbitals have clover-leaf shapes. The shapes of *f* orbitals are very complex and hard to visualize. Notice that in *p* orbitals and *d* orbitals there are regions close to the nucleus where the probability of finding the electron is very low. These regions are called nodes.

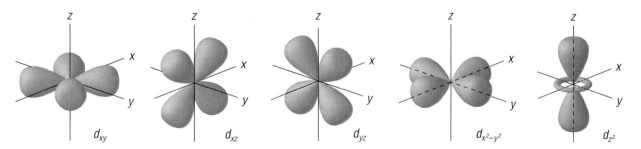

d_{xy}

d_{xz}

d_{yz}

$d_{x^2-y^2}$

d_{z^2}

Figure 13.5

The d orbitals are illustrated here. Four of the five d orbitals have the same shape but different orientations in space. How are the orientations of the d_{xy} and $d_{x^2-y^2}$ orbitals similar? How are they different?

The numbers and kinds of atomic orbitals depend on the energy sublevel. The lowest principal energy level ($n = 1$) has only one sublevel, called 1s. Because an s orbital is spherical, at any given distance from the nucleus, the probability of finding an electron does not vary with direction. This is not true for p, d, or f orbitals.

The second principal energy level ($n = 2$) has two sublevels, 2s and 2p. The 2s orbital is spherical, and the 2p orbitals are dumbbell-shaped. The 2p sublevel is of higher energy than the 2s and consists of three p orbitals of equal energy. The long axis of each dumbbell-shaped p orbital is perpendicular to the other two. It is convenient to label the axes $2p_x$, $2p_y$, and $2p_z$. Thus the second principal energy level has four orbitals: 2s, $2p_x$, $2p_y$, and $2p_z$.

The third principal energy level ($n = 3$) has three sublevels, called 3s, 3p, and 3d. The 3d sublevel consists of five d orbitals of equal energy. Thus the third principal energy level has nine orbitals (one 3s, three 3p, and five 3d orbitals).

The fourth principal energy level ($n = 4$) has four sublevels, called 4s, 4p, 4d, and 4f. The 4f sublevel consists of seven f orbitals of equal energy. The fourth principal energy level, then, has 16 orbitals (one 4s, three 4p, five 4d, and seven 4f orbitals).

As mentioned, the principal quantum number always equals the number of sublevels within that principal energy level. The maximum number of electrons that can occupy a principal energy level is given by the formula $2n^2$, where n is the principal quantum number. The number of electrons allowed in each of the first four energy levels is as follows.

	Increasing energy (increasing distance from nucleus) →			
Energy level n	1	2	3	4
Maximum number of electrons allowed	2	8	18	32

section review 13.1

1. List, in chronological order, a major contribution of each of these scientists to the understanding of the atom: Dalton, Thomson, Bohr, Schrödinger, Rutherford.

2. In general terms, explain how the quantum mechanical model of the atom describes the electron structure of an atom.

3. The energies of electrons are said to be quantized. Explain what this means.

4. How many orbitals are in the following sublevels?
   a. 3p sublevel
   b. 2s sublevel
   c. 4f sublevel
   d. 4p sublevel
   e. 3d sublevel

 Chem ASAP! Assessment 13.1 Check your understanding of the important ideas and concepts in Section 13.1.

ELECTRON ARRANGEMENT IN ATOMS

*D*oes this scene look natural to you? Surprisingly, it is. This structure was formed by natural processes. Arrangements like this are rare in nature because they are unstable. Unstable arrangements, whether the grains of sand in a sandcastle or the rock formation shown here, lose energy in an attempt to become more stable. The tendency to become stable also greatly affects how electrons are arranged in atoms.

What role do energy and stability play in the way in which electrons are configured in an atom?

objectives

▶ Apply the aufbau principle, the Pauli exclusion principle, and Hund's rule in writing the electron configurations of elements

▶ Explain why the electron configurations for some elements differ from those assigned using the aufbau principle

key terms

▶ electron configurations
▶ aufbau principle
▶ Pauli exclusion principle
▶ Hund's rule

Electron Configurations

In most natural phenomena, change proceeds toward the lowest possible energy. High-energy systems are unstable. Unstable systems lose energy to become more stable. In the atom, electrons and the nucleus interact to make the most stable arrangement possible. The ways in which electrons are arranged around the nuclei of atoms are called **electron configurations.**

Three rules—the aufbau principle, the Pauli exclusion principle, and Hund's rule—tell you how to find the electron configurations of atoms. The three rules are as follows.

1. **Aufbau principle:** *Electrons enter orbitals of lowest energy first.* The various orbitals within a sublevel of a principal energy level are always of equal energy. Further, within a principal energy level the *s* sublevel is always the lowest-energy sublevel. Yet the range of energy levels within a principal energy level can overlap the energy levels of an adjacent principal level. Electrons enter the orbitals of lowest energy first. Note

Increasing energy →

7s, 7p, 6d, 5f
6s, 6p, 5d, 4f
5s, 5p, 4d
4s, 4p, 3d
3s, 3p
2s, 2p
1s

~ **Figure 13.6**

This aufbau diagram shows the energy levels of the various atomic orbitals. Orbitals of greater energy are higher on the diagram. Which is of higher energy, a 4d or a 5s orbital?

Chem ASAP!

Simulation 12

Fill atomic orbitals to build the ground states of several atoms.

Electrons in Atoms **367**

that the filling of atomic orbitals does not follow a simple pattern beyond the second energy level. For example, the $4s$ orbital is lower in energy than a $3d$ orbital. This is shown on the aufbau diagram of **Figure 13.6** on the previous page. Each box (☐) represents an atomic orbital. Is a $4f$ orbital higher or lower in energy than a $5d$ orbital?

2. **Pauli exclusion principle:** *An atomic orbital may describe at most two electrons.* For example, either one or two electrons can occupy an *s* orbital or a *p* orbital. To occupy the same orbital, two electrons must have opposite spins; that is, the electron spins must be paired. Spin is a quantum property of electrons and may be clockwise or counter-clockwise. A vertical arrow indicates an electron and its direction of spin ($\uparrow$ or $\downarrow$). An orbital containing paired electrons is written as ⬆⬇.

3. **Hund's rule:** *When electrons occupy orbitals of equal energy, one electron enters each orbital until all the orbitals contain one electron with parallel spins.* For example, three electrons would occupy three orbitals of equal energy as follows: ↑ ↑ ↑. Second electrons then add to each orbital so their spins are paired with the first electrons. Thus each orbital can eventually have two electrons with paired spins.

Consider the electron configurations of atoms of the nine elements in **Table 13.2.** An oxygen atom contains eight electrons. The orbital of lowest energy, $1s$, gets one electron, then a second electron of opposite spin. The next orbital to fill is $2s$. It also gets one electron, then a second electron of opposite spin. One electron then goes into each of the three $2p$ orbitals of equal energy. The remaining electron now pairs with an electron occupying one of the $2p$ orbitals. The other two $2p$ orbitals remain only half filled with one electron each.

Table 13.2

Electron Configurations for Some Selected Elements							
	Orbital filling						Electron configuration
Element	$1s$	$2s$	$2p_x$	$2p_y$	$2p_z$	$3s$	
H	↑	☐	☐	☐	☐	☐	$1s^1$
He	↑↓	☐	☐	☐	☐	☐	$1s^2$
Li	↑↓	↑	☐	☐	☐	☐	$1s^2 2s^1$
C	↑↓	↑↓	↑	↑	☐	☐	$1s^2 2s^2 2p^2$
N	↑↓	↑↓	↑	↑	↑	☐	$1s^2 2s^2 2p^3$
O	↑↓	↑↓	↑↓	↑	↑	☐	$1s^2 2s^2 2p^4$
F	↑↓	↑↓	↑↓	↑↓	↑	☐	$1s^2 2s^2 2p^5$
Ne	↑↓	↑↓	↑↓	↑↓	↑↓	☐	$1s^2 2s^2 2p^6$
Na	↑↓	↑↓	↑↓	↑↓	↑↓	↑	$1s^2 2s^2 2p^6 3s^1$

There is a convenient shorthand method for showing the electron configuration of an atom. This method involves writing the energy level and the symbol for every sublevel occupied by an electron. A superscript indicates the number of electrons occupying that sublevel. For hydrogen, with one electron in a $1s$ orbital, the electron configuration is written $1s^1$. For helium, with two electrons in a $1s$ orbital, the configuration is $1s^2$. For oxygen, with two electrons in a $1s$ orbital, two electrons in a $2s$ orbital, and four electrons in $2p$ orbitals, it is $1s^2 2s^2 2p^4$. Note that the sum of the superscripts equals the number of electrons in the atom.

Sample Problem 13-1

Use **Figure 13.6** to write the electron configurations of these atoms.
    a. phosphorus   **b.** nickel

1. ANALYZE Plan a problem-solving strategy.
Phosphorus has 15 electrons; nickel has 28 electrons. Using **Figure 13.6,** start placing electrons in the orbitals with the lowest energy ($1s$). Remember, there is a maximum of two electrons per orbital. Electrons do not pair up within an energy sublevel (orbitals of equal energy) until each orbital already has one electron.

2. SOLVE Apply the problem-solving strategy.
    a. phosphorus   **b.** nickel

3d

4s

3p

3s

2p

2s

1s

P $1s^2 2s^2 2p^6 3s^2 3p^3$ Ni $1s^2 2s^2 2p^6 3s^2 3p^6 3d^8 4s^2$

3. ANALYZE Do the results make sense?
The superscripts add up to the number of electrons. When the configurations are written, the sublevels within the same principal energy level are written together. This is not always the same order as given on the aufbau diagram. In this case, the $3d$ sublevel is written before the lower-energy $4s$ sublevel.

Practice Problems

5. Write the complete electron configuration for each atom.
    a. carbon
    b. argon
6. Write the electron configuration for each atom. How many unpaired electrons does each atom have?
    a. boron
    b. silicon

Chem ASAP!
Problem-Solving 6
Solve Problem 6 with the help of an interactive guided tutorial.

Figure 13.7
The hood ornament has a high shine and resists corrosion because it is plated with chromium (left). Copper (right) is a good conductor of electricity and is commonly used in electrical wiring.

Exceptional Electron Configurations

You can obtain correct electron configurations for the elements up to vanadium (atomic number 23) by following the aufbau diagram for orbital filling. If you were to continue in that fashion, however, you would assign chromium and copper the following incorrect configurations.

$$\text{Cr } 1s^2 2s^2 2p^6 3s^2 3p^6 3d^4 4s^2$$
$$\text{Cu } 1s^2 2s^2 2p^6 3s^2 3p^6 3d^9 4s^2$$

The correct electron configurations are

$$\text{Cr } 1s^2 2s^2 2p^6 3s^2 3p^6 3d^5 4s^1$$
$$\text{Cu } 1s^2 2s^2 2p^6 3s^2 3p^6 3d^{10} 4s^1$$

These arrangements give chromium a half-filled *d* sublevel and copper a filled *d* sublevel. Filled energy sublevels are more stable than partially filled sublevels. Half-filled levels are not as stable as filled levels, but they are more stable than other configurations. Therefore, chromium atoms and copper atoms are more stable with only one electron in the 4*s* sublevel.

section review 13.2

7. Write the complete electron configuration for each atom.
   a. lithium
   b. fluorine
   c. rubidium

8. Explain why the actual electron configurations for chromium and copper differ from those assigned using the aufbau diagram.

9. Arrange the following sublevels in order of decreasing energy: 2*p*, 4*s*, 3*s*, 3*d*, and 3*p*.

10. Why does one electron in a potassium atom go into the fourth energy level instead of squeezing into the third energy level along with the eight already there?

 Chem ASAP! Assessment 13.2 Check your understanding of the important ideas and concepts in Section 13.2.

portfolio project

Use two bar magnets to model and explain the Pauli exclusion principle. Compare the property that determines whether two magnets attract or repel with the property that determines whether two electrons can occupy the same orbital.

ELECTRON CONFIGURATIONS OF ATOMS AND IONS

SAFETY

Wear safety glasses and follow the standard safety procedures outlined on page 18.

PURPOSE

To make observations of metal ion solutions and relate them to electron configurations.

MATERIALS

- pencil
- paper
- ruler
- reaction surface
- solutions of chemicals shown in Figure A

PROCEDURE

On separate sheets of paper, draw two grids similar to Figure A. Make each square 2 cm on each side. Draw large black **X**s on only one of the grids. Place a reaction surface over the grid with black **X**s and add one drop of each chemical as shown in Figure A. Use the other grid as a data table to record your observations.

NaCl	MgSO$_4$	AlCl$_3$
FeCl$_3$	CaCl$_2$	NiSO$_4$
CuSO$_4$	ZnCl$_2$	AgNO$_3$

Figure A

ANALYSIS

Using your experimental data, record the answers to the following questions below your data table.

1. Write the electron configurations of Na, Mg, and Al.

2. Metal ions form when metal atoms lose valence electrons. The number of electrons lost equals the ion's charge. Write the electron configurations of Na$^+$, Mg^{2+}, and Al^{3+}. What do they have in common?

3. How many electrons does Cl$^-$ have? Write its electron configuration.

4. Transition-metal ions having partially filled *d* orbitals usually have a color. Which solutions contain transition-metal ions with partially filled *d* orbitals? Transition metals usually lose *s* orbital electrons first. Write electron configurations for Fe and Fe^{3+} and Ni and Ni^{2+}.

5. Write the exceptional electron configurations of Cu and Ag.

6. The solutions of both Ag$^+$ and Zn^{2+} ions have no color. What does this suggest about their electron configurations? Write them.

7. Predict which of the following transition metal ions has a color: Cr^{3+}, Cd^{2+}, Hg^{2+}, V^{2+}.

YOU'RE THE CHEMIST

The following small-scale activities allow you to develop your own procedures and analyze the results.

1. **Analyze It!** Predict which of the metal cations in this experiment will form colored precipitates upon the addition of NaOH. Carry out an experiment to find out. What color are the precipitates?

2. **Analyze It!** Predict which of the metal cations in this experiment will form colored precipitates upon the addition of Na$_2$CO$_3$.

3. **Design It!** Design and carry out an experiment to find out which metal ions form precipitates with sodium carbonate. What color are the precipitates?

4. **Analyze It!** Write chemical equations for all the reactions in Steps 1 and 3.

objectives

▶ Calculate the wavelength, frequency, or energy of light, given two of these values
▶ Explain the origin of the atomic emission spectrum of an element

key terms

▶ electromagnetic radiation
▶ amplitude
▶ wavelength (λ)
▶ frequency (ν)
▶ hertz (Hz)
▶ spectrum
▶ atomic emission spectrum
▶ Planck's constant (h)
▶ photons
▶ photoelectric effect
▶ ground state
▶ de Broglie's equation
▶ Heisenberg uncertainty principle

PHYSICS AND THE QUANTUM MECHANICAL MODEL

Neon signs are exciting in more than one sense. In addition to being exciting to see, neon signs contain gas that emits light when its atoms become excited by electricity. **What causes an element such as neon to emit light when excited by an electric current?**

Light and Atomic Spectra

The previous sections in this chapter introduced you to some ideas about atomic structure. You also learned how to write electron configurations for atoms. In the remainder of this chapter, you will backtrack a bit to delve further into the work that led to the development of Schrödinger's equation and the quantum mechanical model of the atom. Rather curiously, this model grew out of the study of light. Isaac Newton (1642–1727) thought of light as consisting of particles. By the year 1900, however, most scientists accepted the idea that light was a wave phenomenon.

According to the wave model, light consists of electromagnetic waves. **Electromagnetic radiation** includes radio waves, microwaves, infrared waves, visible light, ultraviolet waves, x-rays, and gamma rays. **Figure 13.8** shows a typical wave. All electromagnetic waves travel in a vacuum at a speed of 3.0×10^{10} cm/s (3.0×10^{8} m/s). Each complete wave cycle begins at the origin, then returns to the origin. The **amplitude** of a wave is the wave's height from the origin to the crest. The **wavelength** ($\boldsymbol{\lambda}$, the Greek letter lambda) is the distance between the crests. **Frequency** ($\boldsymbol{\nu}$, the Greek letter nu) is the number of wave cycles to pass a given point per unit of time.

The frequency and wavelength of all waves, including light, are inversely related. As the wavelength of light increases, for example, the frequency decreases. **Figure 13.9** shows this relationship. The product of frequency and wavelength always equals a constant (c), the speed of light; that is,

$$c = \lambda \nu$$

The units of frequency are usually cycles per second. The SI unit of cycles per second is called a **hertz (Hz).** A hertz can also be expressed as a reciprocal second (s^{-1}) where the term "cycles" is assumed to be understood. Most problems are easiest to solve when frequency is expressed as s^{-1}.

Figure 13.8

The amplitude of a wave is the height of the wave from the origin to the crest. The wavelength is the distance between crests. How does a change in wavelength affect the amplitude of a wave?

Chem ASAP!

Simulation 13
Explore the properties of electromagnetic radiation.

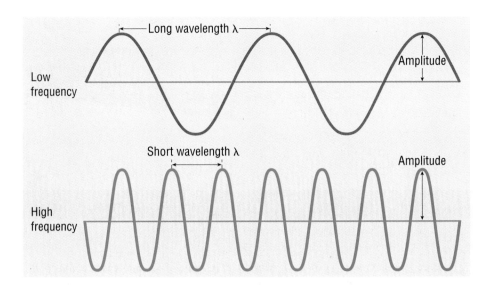

Figure 13.9
The frequency and wavelength of light waves are inversely related. As the wavelength increases, the frequency decreases. The wavelength and frequency do not affect the amplitude.

Sunlight consists of light with a continuous range of wavelengths and frequencies. The wavelength and frequency of each color of light are characteristic of that color. When sunlight passes through a prism, the different wavelengths separate into a **spectrum** of colors. A rainbow is an example of this phenomenon. Each tiny droplet of water acts as a prism to produce a spectrum. Each color blends into the next in the order red, orange, yellow, green, blue, indigo, and violet. In the visible spectrum, as shown in **Figure 13.10,** red light has the longest wavelength and the lowest frequency. Which part of the visible spectrum has the shortest wavelength and highest frequency?

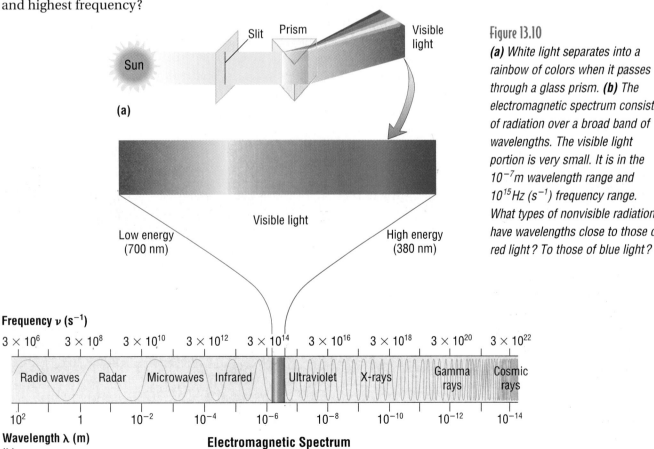

Figure 13.10
(a) White light separates into a rainbow of colors when it passes through a glass prism. (b) The electromagnetic spectrum consists of radiation over a broad band of wavelengths. The visible light portion is very small. It is in the 10^{-7} m wavelength range and 10^{15} Hz (s^{-1}) frequency range. What types of nonvisible radiation have wavelengths close to those of red light? To those of blue light?

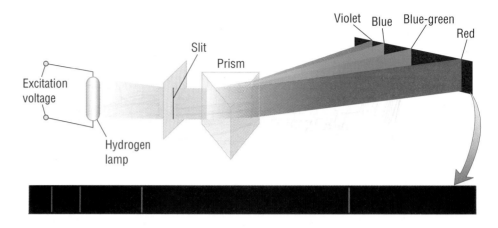

Figure 13.11

The emission spectrum of an element consists of a series of discrete spectral lines that are characteristic of the element. The emission spectrum of atomic hydrogen shown here consists of a series of widely spaced lines, the most prominent of which are violet, blue, blue-green, and red. Which of the bands has the highest frequency?

Chem ASAP!

Animation 16

Learn about atomic emission spectra and about how neon lights work.

Every element emits light when it is excited by the passage of an electric discharge through its gas or vapor. The atoms first absorb energy, then lose the energy as they emit light. Passing the light emitted by an element through a prism gives the **atomic emission spectrum** of the element. The instrument used to obtain the emission spectra is called an emission spectrograph. The emission spectra of elements are quite different from the spectrum of white light. While white light gives a continuous spectrum, atomic emission spectra consist of relatively few lines and are called line spectra or discontinuous spectra. Each line in an emission spectrum corresponds to one exact frequency of light emitted by the atom. Therefore each line corresponds to a specific amount of energy being emitted. **Figure 13.11** shows the visible portion of the emission spectrum of hydrogen.

Sodium light

Mercury light   Nitrogen light

Figure 13.12

Sodium vapor lamps produce a bright yellow light; mercury vapor lamps produce a blue glow; and nitrogen gas gives off a yellowish-orange light.

Figure 13.13

When a noble gas is energized, it gives off light of a characteristic color. Helium produces a pink light, and argon produces lavender. Krypton gives off a whitish light, xenon produces blue, and neon shines orange-red.

The emission spectrum of each element is unique to that element. See **Figure 13.12** and **Figure 13.13.** This makes such spectra extremely useful for the identification of unknown or inaccessible substances. Much of the knowledge of the composition of the universe comes from studying the atomic spectra of the stars, which are hot glowing bodies of gases. A telescope gathers light from the star of interest. This light is then transmitted to an emission spectrograph to record the atomic emission spectrum.

Sample Problem 13-2

Calculate the wavelength of the yellow light emitted by a sodium lamp if the frequency of the radiation is 5.10×10^{14} Hz $(5.10 \times 10^{14} \text{ s}^{-1})$.

1. **ANALYZE List the knowns and the unknown.**

   Knowns:
   - frequency $(\nu) = 5.10 \times 10^{14} \text{ s}^{-1}$
   - $c = 3.00 \times 10^{10}$ cm/s
   - $c = \lambda \nu$

   Unknown:
   - wavelength $(\lambda) = ?$ cm

   Solve the equation $c = \lambda \nu$ for λ, then substitute the known values and solve.

2. **CALCULATE Solve for the unknown.**

   Solving for λ yields
   $$\lambda = \frac{c}{\nu}$$

   Substituting values for c and ν yields
   $$\lambda = \frac{c}{\nu} = \frac{3.00 \times 10^{10} \text{ cm/s}}{5.10 \times 10^{14} \text{ s}^{-1}} = 5.88 \times 10^{-5} \text{ cm}$$

3. **EVALUATE Does the result make sense?**

   The magnitude of the frequency is much larger than the numerical value of the speed of light, so the answer should be much less than 1. The answer has three significant figures, as it should, because the original known value had three significant figures.

Practice Problems

11. What is the wavelength of radiation with a frequency of $1.50 \times 10^{13} \text{ s}^{-1}$? Does this radiation have a longer or shorter wavelength than red light?

12. What frequency is radiation with a wavelength of 5.00×10^{-6} cm? In what region of the electromagnetic spectrum is this radiation?

Chem ASAP!

Problem-Solving 12
Solve Problem 12 with the help of an interactive guided tutorial.

The Discovery of Helium

Sometimes discoveries in one area of science, such as chemistry, become important in solving problems in another, such as astronomy. In 1868,

Pierre Janssen and Joseph Norman Lockyer discovered an emission spectrum from gases on the surface of the sun that was unmatched by any known element on Earth. In 1895, William Ramsay discovered the existence of helium on Earth. The emission spectrum of helium was found to be identical to that of the unknown gas observed by Janssen and Lockyer almost thirty years earlier. Thus by combining two discoveries from different fields of science, a new discovery was made: Earth and the stars have some elements in common.

The Quantum Concept and the Photoelectric Effect

The laws of classical physics state that there is no limit to how small the energy gained or lost by an object may be. According to these laws, when a gaseous or vaporized element is excited by electricity, the spectrum of the emitted light should be continuous. Thus classical physics does not explain the emission spectra of atoms, which consist of lines. The seed of an idea that explained atomic spectra came in 1900 from the German physicist Max Planck (1858–1947).

Planck was trying to describe quantitatively why a body such as a chunk of iron appears to change color as it is heated. First it appears black, then red, yellow, white, and blue as its temperature increases, as shown in **Figure 13.14.** Planck found he could explain the color changes if he assumed that the energy of a body changes only in small discrete units. You can think of these discrete units as bricks used to build a wall—a brick wall can only increase or decrease in size in increments of one or more bricks.

Planck showed mathematically that the amount of radiant energy (E) absorbed or emitted by a body is proportional to the frequency of the radiation (ν).

$$E \propto \nu \quad \text{or} \quad E = h \times \nu$$

The constant *(h)* in the above equation is called **Planck's constant,** which has a value of 6.6262×10^{-34} J $\times$ s (J is the joule, the SI unit of energy). The energy of a quantum equals $h \times \nu$. Any attempt to increase or decrease the energy of a system by a fraction of $h \times \nu$ must fail. The size of an emitted or absorbed quantum depends on the size of the energy change. A small energy change involves the emission or absorption of low-frequency radiation. A large energy change involves the emission or absorption of high-frequency radiation.

Planck's proposal that quanta of energy are absorbed or emitted was revolutionary. Everyday experience had led people to believe that there was no limitation to the smallness of permissible energy changes in a system. It appears, for example, that thermal energy may be continuously supplied to heat liquid water to any temperature between 0 °C and 100 °C. Actually, the water temperature increases by infinitesimally small steps, which occurs as individual molecules absorb quanta of energy. An ordinary thermometer is unable, however, to detect such small changes in temperature. Thus your everyday experience gives you no clue to the fact that energy is quantized.

Figure 13.14

All objects change color when heated. Although the color change of this horseshoe looks like a continuous process, the atoms in the iron are giving off energy in small discrete units.

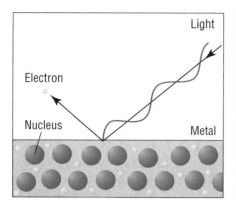

(a) When light strikes a metal surface, electrons are ejected.

(b) If the threshold frequency has been reached, increasing the intensity only increases the number of electrons ejected.

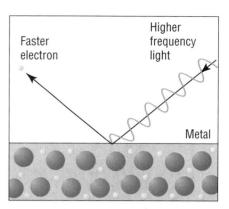

(c) If the frequency is increased, the ejected electrons will travel faster.

In 1905 Albert Einstein, then a patent examiner in Zurich, Switzerland, returned to Newton's idea of particles of light. Einstein proposed that light could be described as quanta of energy that behave as if they were particles. Light quanta are called **photons.** The energy of photons is quantized according to the equation $E = h \times \nu$.

The dual wave–particle behavior of light was difficult for scientists trained in classical physics to accept. However, it was even more difficult to dispute because it provided an explanation for the previously mysterious photoelectric effect. In the **photoelectric effect,** metals eject electrons called photoelectrons when light shines on them. The alkali metals (Li, Na, K, Rb, and Cs) are particularly subject to the effect. Not just any frequency of light will cause the photoelectric effect. Red light ($\nu = 4.3 \times 10^{14}$ s^{-1} to 4.6×10^{14} s^{-1}), for example, will not cause the ejection of photoelectrons from potassium, no matter how intense the light. Yet even a very weak yellow light ($\nu = 5.1 \times 10^{14}$ s^{-1} to 5.2×10^{14} s^{-1}) shining on potassium begins the effect.

The photoelectric effect could not be explained by classical physics, which had no quantum concept. Classical physics correctly viewed light as a form of energy. It assumed, however, that under weak light of any wavelength, an electron in a metal should eventually collect enough energy to be ejected. Obviously, the photoelectric effect presented a serious problem for the classical wave theory of light.

Einstein used his particle theory of light to explain the photoelectric effect, which is demonstrated in **Figure 13.15.** He recognized that there is a threshold value of energy below which the photoelectric effect does not occur. Because $E = h \times \nu$, all the photons in a beam of monochromatic light (light of only one frequency) have the same energy. If the frequency, and therefore the energy, of the photons is too low, then no photoelectrons will be ejected. It does not matter whether a single photon or a steady stream of low-energy photons strikes an electron in the metal. Only if the frequency of light is above the threshold frequency will the photoelectric effect occur. The photoelectric effect has practical applications in photoelectric cells such as in the car shown in **Figure 13.16,** which uses the energy of light to generate electricity. The operation of numerous electronic devices, such as solar-powered calculators, is also based on the photoelectric effect.

Figure 13.15

The photoelectric effect, illustrated here, was explained by Einstein's dual wave-particle theory of light.

Chem ASAP!

Simulation 14

Simulate the photoelectric effect and observe the results as a function of radiation frequency and intensity.

Figure 13.16

Photoelectric cells convert light energy into the electrical energy that will be used to power this car.

Electrons in Atoms **377**

CHEMath

USING CONSTANTS

You have seen many constants in your study of mathematics and chemistry. In this chapter you are introduced to Planck's constant, h. But what exactly are constants and how are they used?

In mathematics, a *constant* is a quantity that never changes. For example, the numbers 2, 10, and π are constants you have used in mathematics and in your everyday life. A constant is distinguished from a *variable,* which is a quantity that can vary. Treat a constant the same as any other numerical value used in a problem.

Some examples of constants are shown in the table below. Notice that some constants include units, but some do not. Constants with units are often expressed in different but equivalent forms. For example, the constant representing the speed of light can be written as 2.998×10^{10} cm/s or 2.998×10^8 m/s—different in form but equivalent in value. When solving a problem involving a constant, always pay attention to the units and use dimensional analysis to ensure that you use the correct form of the constant.

Also pay attention to whether the constant used in a formula is exact or approximate. For example, if you use 3.14 for π or 6.02×10^{23} for Avogadro's number, your approximation is accurate to 3 significant figures. However, a conversion factor such as $\frac{60 \text{ s}}{1 \text{ min}}$ is exact and has an unlimited number of significant figures.

Constant	Description	Approximate value
π	Pi, the ratio of circumference to diameter of a circle	3.1416
N_A	Avogadro's number, the number of representative particles in 1 mole	6.02×10^{23}
m_p	The mass of a proton	1.673×10^{-27} kg
R	Ideal gas constant, used in the ideal gas law: $PV = nRT$	$8.31 \frac{\text{L} \times \text{kPa}}{\text{K} \times \text{mol}}$
c	The speed of light in a vacuum	2.998×10^8 m/s
h	Planck's constant, used to calculate the radiant energy absorbed or emitted by a body: $E = h \times \upsilon$.	6.626×10^{-34} J $\times$ s

Example

Use the formula $A = \pi r^2$ to find the area of a circle with radius 8.43 cm.

Write the formula.	$A = \pi r^2$
Substitute the known values for the constant π and the variable r.	$A = 3.1416 \times (8.43 \text{ cm})^2$
Evaluate and round to 3 significant figures.	$A = 223 \text{ cm}^2$

The area of the circle is 223 cm².

Practice Problems

Prepare for upcoming problems in this chapter by using the constants in the table above to solve each of the following problems.

A. Use the formula $A = \pi r^2$ to calculate the area of a circle with radius $r = 5.36$ cm.

B. Use the formula $t = d/c$ to calculate the time it takes for light to travel from Alpha Centauri to Earth, a distance of $d = 4.1 \times 10^{16}$ meters.

C. Use the formula $E = h \times \upsilon$ to calculate the energy E (in J) of a photon with a frequency of $\upsilon = 8.93 \times 10^{15}$ s^{-1}.

D. Find the mass, in kilograms, of 3.00 moles of protons.

Sample Problem 13-3

Calculate the energy (in J) of a quantum of radiant energy (the energy of a photon) with a frequency of 5.00×10^{15} s^{-1}.

1. **ANALYZE** *List the knowns and the unknown.*

   Knowns:
   - frequency (ν) = 5.00×10^{15} s^{-1}
   - $h = 6.626 \times 10^{-34}$ J $\times$ s

   Unknown:
   - energy (E) = ? J

   Substitute the known values for h and ν into the equation $E = h \times \nu$ and solve.

2. **CALCULATE** *Solve for the unknown.*

   Substitute values for h and ν and calculate E.

   $$E = h \times \nu$$

   $$E = (6.626 \times 10^{-34} \text{ J} \times \cancel{s}) \times (5.00 \times 10^{15} \cancel{s^{-1}})$$

   $$= 3.31 \times 10^{-18} \text{ J}$$

3. **EVALUATE** *Does the result make sense?*

   Individual photons have very small energies, so the answer seems reasonable. The answer has the proper number of significant figures.

Practice Problems

13. What is the energy of a photon of microwave radiation with a frequency of 3.20×10^{11} s^{-1}?

14. The threshold photoelectric effect in tungsten is produced by light of wavelength 260 nm. Give the energy of a photon of this light in joules.

Chem ASAP!

Problem-Solving 14

Solve Problem 14 with the help of an interactive guided tutorial.

An analogous situation to the photoelectric effect occurs when a table-tennis ball strikes a billiard ball. The table-tennis ball simply does not have enough energy to budge the stationary billiard ball. No matter how many times the table-tennis ball collides with the billiard ball, the billiard ball will not move. By contrast, one golf ball moving at the same speed as the table-tennis ball sets the target billiard ball in motion. The golf ball is above the energy threshold. With the photoelectric effect, any excess energy of a photon beyond that needed to eject a photoelectron causes the ejected electron to travel faster. Increasing the intensity of light will increase the number of photons striking the metal and the number of electrons ejected; however, it will not effect the speed of the ejected electrons.

An Explanation of Atomic Spectra

Bohr's application of quantum theory to electron energy levels in atoms resulted in an explanation of the hydrogen spectrum. The lines observed in the spectrum are consistent with the idea that quantization limits the possible energies that an electron in a hydrogen atom can attain. Consider the lone electron of a hydrogen atom in its lowest energy level, or **ground state.** In the ground state, the quantum number (n) is 1. Excitation of the electron raises it to an excited state so that $n = 2, 3, 4, 5,$ or 6, and so forth. If the energy levels are quantized, it takes a quantum of energy ($h \times \nu$) to raise the electron from the ground state to an excited state. The same amount of energy is emitted as a photon when the electron drops from the excited state to the ground state. Only electrons in transition from higher to lower energy levels lose energy and emit light.

Figure 13.17

The three groups of lines in the hydrogen spectrum correspond to the transition of electrons from higher energy levels to lower energy levels. The Lyman series corresponds to the transition to the n = 1 energy level. The Balmer series corresponds to the transition to the n = 2 energy level. The Paschen series corresponds to the transition to the n = 3 energy level.

Figure 13.17 shows the explanation for the three groups of lines observed in the emission spectrum of hydrogen atoms. The lines at the ultraviolet end of the hydrogen spectrum are the Lyman series. These match expected values for the emission due to the transition of electrons from higher energy levels to $n = 1$. The lines in the visible spectrum are the Balmer series. The lines in the Balmer series result from transitions from higher energy levels to $n = 2$. The lines in the infrared spectrum are the Paschen series. They correspond to transitions from higher energy levels to $n = 3$. Spectral lines for the transitions from higher energy levels to $n = 4$ and $n = 5$ also exist. Note that the spectral lines in each group become more closely spaced at increased values of n. This means that the energy difference between any two higher energy levels is smaller than that between two lower levels. There is an upper limit to the frequency of emitted light for each set of lines. The upper limit exists because a very excited electron completely escapes the atom.

Bohr's theory of the atom was only partially satisfactory. It explained only the emission spectra of atoms and ions containing one electron. Moreover, it was of no help in understanding how atoms bond to form molecules. Eventually a new and better model displaced the Bohr model of the atom. The new model is based on the description of the motion of material objects as waves.

Quantum Mechanics

Such strange goings on! Energy absorbed or emitted in packages. Light behaving as waves *and* particles. Stranger things were yet to come. In 1924 Louis de Broglie (1892–1987), a French graduate student, asked an important question: Given that light behaves as waves and particles, can particles of matter behave as waves? De Broglie derived an equation that described the wavelength (λ) of a moving particle:

$$\lambda = \frac{h}{mv}$$

Here h is Planck's constant, m is the mass of the particle, and v is the velocity of the particle. From this equation it is easy to calculate the wavelength of a moving electron. With a mass of 9.11×10^{-28} g and moving at nearly the speed of light, an electron has a wavelength of about 2×10^{-10} cm. How does this value compare with the diameter of a typical atom?

Indeed, **de Broglie's equation** predicts that all matter exhibits wavelike motions. You have certainly seen wave motion in water, as in **Figure 13.18.** Why then are people generally unaware of the wave motion of all matter? As with quanta, the answer is that the motion depends on the size of the object. Wavelengths of objects visible to the unaided eye are too small to measure. Objects with measurable wavelengths cannot be seen by the unaided eye. A 200-g baseball moving at 30 m/s has a wavelength of approximately 10^{-32} cm, which is too small to detect by any experiment that you could perform. By contrast, an electron moving at the same speed has a wavelength of about 2×10^{-3} cm. This distance is large enough to be measured with appropriate scientific instruments.

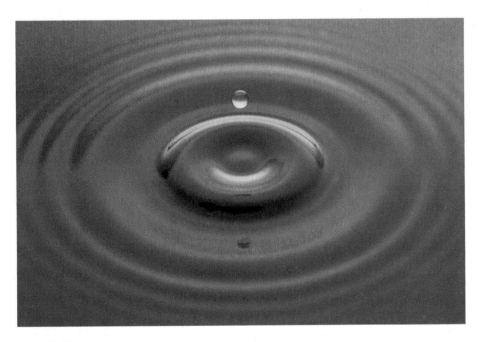

Figure 13.18
De Broglie stated that all matter in motion exhibits wavelike properties. This phenomenon is more apparent in some forms of matter than in others. In what other forms of moving matter do you notice wavelike properties?

De Broglie's prediction that matter would exhibit both wave and particle properties set the stage for an entirely new method of describing the motions of subatomic particles, atoms, and molecules. Because mechanics is the study of the motion of bodies, the new method is called quantum mechanics. Here is a summary of the most important differences between classical mechanics and quantum mechanics.

1. Classical mechanics adequately describes the motions of bodies much larger than the atoms that they comprise. It appears that such a body gains or loses energy in any amount.

2. Quantum mechanics describes the motions of subatomic particles and atoms as waves. These particles gain or lose energy in packages called quanta.

Another feature of quantum mechanics not found in classical mechanics is the uncertainty principle, derived by the German physicist Werner Heisenberg (1901–1976) in 1927. The **Heisenberg uncertainty principle** states that it is impossible to know exactly both the velocity and the position of a particle at the same time. The more precisely the velocity is measured, the less precise the measurement of the position must become. Conversely, if the position of a moving particle is known precisely, the velocity is less precisely known. **Figure 13.19** illustrates and explains the Heisenberg uncertainty principle.

The uncertainty principle is much more obvious with small bodies like electrons than with large objects like baseballs. The uncertainty in the position of a baseball traveling at 30 m/s is only about 10^{-21} cm, which is not measurable. The uncertainty in the position of an electron with a mass of 9.11×10^{-28} g is nearly a billion centimeters! Schrödinger's quantum mechanical description of the electrons in atoms shaped the concept of electron orbitals and configurations and incorporated matter's wavelike motion and the uncertainty principle.

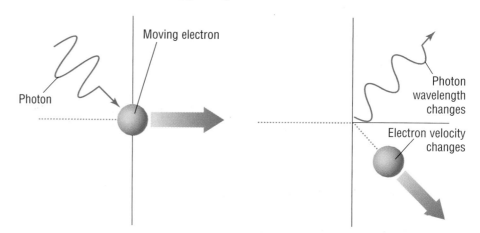

Before collision
The position of an electron can be determined only if it is struck by another particle, such as a photon.

After collision
After the impact, the electron's velocity changes. Thus it is impossible to know both the position and velocity of the electron at the same time.

Figure 13.19

The Heisenberg uncertainty principle, illustrated here, states that it is impossible to know exactly both the velocity and the position of a particle at the same time.

MINI LAB

Flame Tests

PURPOSE

Use the flame test to determine the identity of the cation in an unknown solution based on its characteristic color.

MATERIALS

- Bunsen burner
- small beaker
- 6 small test tubes
- test tube rack
- tongs
- flame test wire (10-cm length of nichrome wire)
- 6M HCl
- 0.1M NaCl
- 0.1M CaCl$_2$
- 0.1M LiCl
- 0.1M CuCl$_2$
- 0.1M BaCl$_2$
- unknown solution

PROCEDURE

1. Make a two-column data table. Label column one Cation. Label column two Flame Color. Enter the name of the cation of each salt solution in column one.

2. Label each of 5 test tubes with the name of a salt solution; label the sixth tube Unknown. Add 1 mL of each salt solution to the appropriately labeled test tube. Add 5 mL HCl to the beaker.

3. Grasp one end of the nichrome wire with the tongs. Clean the wire by alternately heating it in the hot burner flame and dipping it into the hydrochloric acid. Repeat several times until the flame remains almost colorless when the wire is heated.

4. Dip the clean wire into the sodium chloride solution and then hold it in the hot burner flame. Record the color of the flame. Repeat Step 3 to clean the wire.

5. Repeat Step 4 for each of the remaining salt solutions.

6. Perform a flame test with the unknown solution. Note the color of the flame.

ANALYSIS AND CONCLUSIONS

1. What is the identity of the cation in the unknown?

2. Each known salt solution has a unique color. Would you expect this based on the modern view of the atom? Explain.

3. Some commercially available fireplace logs burn with a red and/or green flame. On the basis of your data, what elements could be responsible for these colored flames?

4. Aerial fireworks contain gunpowder and chemicals that produce colors. What elements would you include to produce the following colors?
   a. crimson red   b. yellow

---

section review 13.3

15. A hydrogen lamp emits several lines in the visible region of the spectrum. One of these lines has a wavelength of 6.56×10^{-5} cm. What are the color and frequency of this radiation?

16. Explain the origin of the atomic emission spectrum of an element.

17. Can classical physics explain the photoelectric effect? Explain your answer.

18. Compare the ground state and the excited state of an electron.

19. Arrange the following in order of decreasing wavelength.
   a. infrared radiation from a heat lamp
   b. dental x-rays
   c. signal from a shortwave radio station

 Chem ASAP! Assessment 13.3 Check your understanding of the important ideas and concepts in Section 13.3.

LASERS AT WORK

Once chemists and physicists understood the relationship between electrons and light, they could begin applying this knowledge in practical ways. One of these applications is the laser. When they were first conceived, lasers were described as "death rays" in science fiction stories, but today lasers can be found in a variety of everyday technologies.

What exactly is a laser? It is a device that emits a beam of light very different from ordinary light. Ordinary white light, you will recall, is composed of waves (or photons) of many different wavelengths and frequencies; moreover, all these waves are traveling in different directions, making ordinary light chaotic. In contrast, the waves of light emitted by a laser are all of the same frequency, and they are all traveling parallel to one another. This type of light is called coherent light.

How is a laser able to create a beam of coherent light? The main part of a gas laser is a tube filled with an inert gas, such as neon, argon, or krypton. An electrical current is passed through the tube. The electrical energy excites the electrons of the gas atoms to higher energy states. As the electrons return to their normal energy states, they emit photons of light. The same process is at work in neon signs.

But unlike a neon sign, the gas tube of a laser is not made of glass and it has mirrors at both ends, one of which is semitransparent. Photons that happen to be traveling parallel to the walls of the tube will begin reflecting back and forth between the mirrors. As they do so, they strike already excited gas atoms, causing each of those atoms to emit a photon with the same energy and direction as the original photon. As a result, the number of photons traveling parallel to the walls of the tube increases. At the same time, some of these photons

> **The waves of light emitted by a laser are all of the same frequency, and they are all traveling parallel to one another.**

escape through the semitransparent mirror, forming a laser beam. Because all the photons/waves emerging from the laser are parallel, the laser beam does not spread out and lose intensity with increasing distance from the source, unlike the beam of a flashlight.

The coherent light of a laser has enormous power and possibilities, which is why lasers have many applications in society. One place you will find lasers is the supermarket. Many cash registers now have low-intensity lasers to scan the bar codes on packages and cans. The coherent light of the laser reflects off the bar code clearly enough to be interpreted by an optical reader, which translates the code into a number unique to the product. Lasers are used in a similar way to read the digital code on compact discs.

Lasers of higher intensity can cut through matter with great precision. High-intensity lasers directed by computers are used in the automobile and aircraft industries, for example, to cut metals for parts. Lasers have also proven invaluable in the medical field. Because everything about a laser beam can be finely controlled—its energy, width, and movement—it can be used for surgery. Laser surgery is sometimes called bloodless surgery because the laser burns away small areas, sealing the blood vessels as it goes.

CHEMISTRY IN CAREERS

LASER TECHNICIAN
Assist medical or industrial personnel in the operation of lasers in the workplace.
See page 874.

CHEMIST NEEDED
Envira Lab. GC Must know

TAKE IT TO THE NET

Find out more about career opportunities:
www.phschool.com

CHEMICAL SPECIALIST
Local food service distributor see responsible self-motivated indivi

Chapter 13 STUDENT STUDY GUIDE

Take It to the NET
For interactive study and review, go to www.phschool.com

KEY TERMS

- amplitude *p. 372*
- atomic emission spectrum *p. 374*
- atomic orbital *p. 365*
- aufbau principle *p. 367*
- de Broglie's equation *p. 381*
- electromagnetic radiation *p. 372*
- electron configuration *p. 367*
- energy level *p. 362*

- frequency (ν) *p. 372*
- ground state *p. 379*
- Heisenberg uncertainty principle *p. 382*
- hertz (Hz) *p. 372*
- Hund's rule *p. 368*
- Pauli exclusion principle *p. 368*
- photoelectric effect *p. 377*

- photon *p. 377*
- Planck's constant (*h*) *p. 376*
- quantum *p. 363*
- quantum mechanical model *p. 363*
- spectrum *p. 373*
- wavelength (λ) *p. 372*

KEY EQUATIONS

- $c = \lambda \nu$

- $E = h \times \nu$

- $\lambda = \dfrac{h}{mv}$

CONCEPT SUMMARY

13.1 Models of the Atom

- Rutherford pictured the atom as a dense nucleus surrounded by electrons.
- In the Bohr model of the atom, the electrons move in fixed circular paths around a dense, positively charged nucleus.
- The energies of electrons in an atom are quantized in the modern quantum mechanical model of the atom.
- Current theory predicts the probability of finding an electron in terms of a cloud of negative charge. The atomic orbital, or regions in which electrons are likely to be found, can be calculated from a mathematical expression.

13.2 Electron Arrangement in Atoms

- The ways in which electrons are arranged around the nuclei of atoms are called electron configurations.
- Correct electron configurations for atoms may be written using the aufbau principle, the Pauli exclusion principle, and Hund's rule.

13.3 Physics and the Quantum Mechanical Model

- For all electromagnetic waves, the product of frequency and wavelength always equals the speed of light.
- The concept of quantized electron energy levels in atoms grew out of the study of the interaction of light and matter.
- The line emission spectra of atoms are best explained by quantized energy levels.
- The quantum concept developed in part from Planck's studies of light radiation from heated objects and from Einstein's explanation of the photoelectric effect.
- De Broglie proposed that all matter in motion has wavelike properties.
- Schrödinger devised the most successful of these early quantum mechanical models.
- In de Broglie's equation, the wavelength of an object equals Planck's constant divided by the product of the mass and velocity of the object.

CHAPTER CONCEPT MAP

Use these terms to construct a concept map that organizes the major ideas of this chapter.

 Chem ASAP! Concept Map 13
Create your Concept Map using the computer.

CONCEPT PRACTICE

20. Which subatomic particles did Thomson include in the plum-pudding model of the atom? *13.1*

21. How did Bohr answer the objection that an electron traveling in a circular orbit would radiate energy and fall into the nucleus? *13.1*

22. Describe Rutherford's model of the atom and compare it with the model proposed by his student Niels Bohr. *13.1*

23. What is the significance of the boundary of an electron cloud? *13.1*

24. What is an atomic orbital? *13.1*

25. Sketch 1*s*, 2*s*, and 2*p* orbitals using the same scale for each. *13.1*

26. How many electrons are in the highest occupied energy level of these atoms? *13.2*
  a. barium
  b. sodium
  c. aluminum
  d. oxygen

27. What are the three rules that govern the filling of atomic orbitals by electrons? *13.2*

28. Write electron configurations for the elements that are identified only by these atomic numbers. *13.2*
  a. 15
  b. 12
  c. 9
  d. 18

29. What is meant by $3p^3$? *13.2*

30. Which of these orbital designations are invalid? *13.2*
  a. 4*s*
  b. 3*f*
  c. 2*d*
  d. 3*d*

31. What is the maximum number of electrons that can go into each of the following sublevels? *13.2*
  a. 2*s*
  b. 3*p*
  c. 4*s*
  d. 3*d*
  e. 4*p*
  f. 5*s*
  g. 4*f*
  h. 5*p*

32. How many electrons are in the second energy level of an atom of each element? *13.2*
  a. chlorine
  b. phosphorus
  c. potassium

33. Write electron configurations for atoms of these elements. *13.2*
  a. selenium
  b. vanadium
  c. nickel
  d. calcium

34. List the colors of the visible spectrum in order of increasing wavelength. *13.3*

35. What is meant by the frequency of a wave? What are the units of frequency? Describe the relationship between frequency and wavelength. *13.3*

36. Use a diagram to illustrate each term. *13.3*
  a. wavelength
  b. amplitude
  c. wave cycle

37. Explain the difference between the laws of classical physics and the quantum concept when describing the energy lost or gained by an object. *13.3*

38. What is the energy of a photon of green light with a frequency of 5.80×10^{14} s^{-1}? *13.3*

39. How did Planck influence the development of modern atomic theory? *13.3*

40. What will happen if the following occur? *13.3*
  a. Monochromatic light shining on the alkali metal cesium is just above the threshold frequency.
  b. The intensity of light increases, but the frequency remains the same.
  c. Monochromatic light of a shorter wavelength is used.

41. Explain the difference between a photon and a quantum. *13.3*

42. What happens when a hydrogen atom absorbs a quantum of energy? *13.3*

43. When white light is viewed through sodium vapor in a spectroscope, the spectrum is continuous except for a dark line at 589 nm. How can you explain this observation? *13.3*

44. What is the wavelength of a 2500-kg truck traveling at a rate of 75 km/h? *13.3*

45. Give the symbol for the atom that corresponds to each electron configuration.

    a. $1s^2 2s^2 2p^6 3s^2 3p^6$

    b. $1s^2 2s^2 2p^6 3s^2 3p^6 3d^{10} 4s^2 4p^6 4d^7 5s^1$

    c. $1s^2 2s^2 2p^6 3s^2 3p^6 3d^{10} 4s^2 4p^6 4d^{10} 4f^7$
       $5s^2 5p^6 5d^1 6s^2$

46. Write the electron configuration for an arsenic atom. Calculate the total number of electrons in each energy level and state which energy levels are not full.

47. How many paired electrons are there in an atom of each element?

    a. helium

    b. boron

    c. sodium

    d. oxygen

48. An atom of an element has two electrons in the first energy level and five electrons in the second energy level. Write the electron configuration for this atom and name the element. How many unpaired electrons does an atom of this element have?

49. Suppose your favorite AM radio station broadcasts at a frequency of 1150 kHz. What is the wavelength, in centimeters, of the radiation from the station?

50. A mercury lamp, such as the one below, emits radiation with a wavelength of 4.36×10^{-7} m.

    a. What is the wavelength of this radiation in centimeters?

    b. In what region of the electromagnetic spectrum is this radiation?

    c. Calculate the frequency of this radiation.

51. Calculate the energy of a photon of red light with a wavelength of 6.45×10^{-5} cm. Compare your answer with the answer to Problem 38. Is red light of higher or lower energy than green light?

52. Give the symbol and name of the elements that correspond to these configurations.

    a. $1s^2 2s^2 2p^6 3s^1$

    b. $1s^2 2s^2 2p^3$

    c. $1s^2 2s^2 2p^6 3s^2 3p^2$

    d. $1s^2 2s^2 2p^4$

    e. $1s^2 2s^2 2p^6 3s^2 3p^6 4s^1$

    f. $1s^2 2s^2 2p^6 3s^2 3p^6 3d^2 4s^2$

53. Choose the term that best completes the second relationship.

    a. orbital : energy level

        apartment : _____

        (1) floor   (3) building

        (2) room   (4) stairway

    b. water : container

        electrons : _____

        (1) frequency   (3) nuclei

        (2) sublevel   (4) orbitals

    c. electromagnetic radiation : visible light

        student body : _____

        (1) eleventh graders   (3) teachers

        (2) principal   (4) textbooks

54. Traditional cooking methods make use of infrared radiation (heat). Microwave radiation cooks food faster. Could radio waves be used for cooking? Explain.

55. Think about the currently accepted models of the atom and of light. In what ways do these models seem strange to you? Why are these models not exact or definite?

56. A potassium atom has a diameter of about 0.406 nm. Express this in meters and micrometers. If the measurement is always the same, explain why the two numbers are different.

57. Balance the following chemical equations.

    a. $KNO_3 + H_2SO_4 \longrightarrow K_2SO_4 + HNO_3$

    b. $Cu_2O + H_2 \longrightarrow Cu + H_2O$

    c. $NO + Br_2 \longrightarrow NOBr$

    d. $SnO_2 + CO \longrightarrow Sn + CO_2$

58. Calculate the volume of O_2 at STP required for the complete combustion of 5.00 L of acetylene (C_2H_2) at STP.

$$2C_2H_2(g) + 5O_2 \longrightarrow 4CO_2 + 2H_2O(l)$$

59. Calculate the percent composition of each compound.
   a. SiO_2
   b. $FeCl_3$
   c. H_2O
   d. H_2SO_4
   e. $CaCO_3$

60. Write symbols for the following ions.
   a. iron(III)
   b. mercury(II)
   c. nitride
   d. hydrogen carbonate
   e. oxide
   f. permanganate

61. Give the number of protons and electrons in each of the following.
   a. Cs
   b. Ag^+
   c. Cd^{2+}
   d. Se^{2-}

62. The temperature of a gas at STP is changed to 125 °C at constant volume. Calculate the final pressure of the gas in atmospheres.

63. The density of gold is 19.3 g/cm^3. What is the mass, in grams, of a cube of gold 2.00 cm on each edge? In kilograms?

CONCEPT CHALLENGE

64. The energy of a photon is related to its wavelength and its frequency.
   a. Complete the following table.
   b. Plot the energy of the photon (y-axis) versus the frequency (x-axis).
   c. Determine the slope of the line.
   d. What is the significance of this slope?

Energy of photon (J)	Frequency (s^{-1})	Wavelength (cm)
3.45×10^{-21}		5.77×10^{-3}
2.92×10^{-20}		6.82×10^{-4}
6.29×10^{-20}		3.16×10^{-4}
1.13×10^{-19}		1.76×10^{-4}
1.46×10^{-19}		1.36×10^{-4}
3.11×10^{-19}		6.38×10^{-5}

65. The average distance between Earth and Mars is about 2.08×10^8 km. How long does it take to transmit television pictures from the *Mariner* spacecraft to Earth from Mars?

66. In a photoelectric experiment, a student shines light of greater than the threshold frequency on the surface of a metal. The student observes that after a long time the maximum energy of the ejected electrons begins to decrease. Can you explain why?

67. Bohr's atomic theory can be used to calculate the energy required to remove an electron from an orbit of a hydrogen atom or an ion containing only one electron. This is the ionization energy for that atom or ion. The formula for determining the ionization energy (E) is

$$E = Z^2 \times \frac{k}{n^2}$$

where Z is the atomic number, k is 1312 kJ mol, and n is the energy level. What is the energy required to eject an electron from a hydrogen atom when the electron is in the ground state $(n = 1)$? In the second energy level? How much energy is required to eject a ground state electron from the species Li^{2+}?

Select the choice that best answers each question or completes each statement.

1. Select the correct electron configuration for silicon, atomic number 14.
   a. $1s^2 2s^2 2p^2 3s^2 3p^2 4s^2 3d^2$
   b. $1s^2 2s^2 2p^4 3s^2 3p^4$
   c. $1s^2 2s^6 2p^6$
   d. $1s^2 2s^2 2p^6 3s^2 3p^2$

2. Which pair of orbitals has the same shape?
   a. $2s$ and $2p$
   b. $2s$ and $3s$
   c. $3p$ and $3d$
   d. More than one is correct.

3. Which of these statements characterize the nucleus of every atom?
       I. It has a positive charge.
       II. It is very dense.
       III. It is composed of protons, electrons, and neutrons.
   a. I and II only
   b. II and III only
   c. I and III only
   d. I, II, and III

4. As the wavelength of light increases
   a. the frequency increases.
   b. the speed of light increases.
   c. the energy decreases.
   d. the intensity increases.

5. In the third energy level,
   a. there are two energy sublevels.
   b. the f sublevel has 7 orbitals.
   c. there are three s orbitals.
   d. a maximum of 18 electrons are allowed.

The lettered choices below refer to questions 6–10. A lettered choice may be used once, more than once, or not at all.

    (A) $s^2 p^6$
    (B) $s^2 p^2$
    (C) s^2
    (D) $s^4 p^1$
    (E) $s^2 p^4$

Which configuration is the outer shell electron configuration for each of these elements?

6. sulfur

7. germanium

8. beryllium

9. krypton

10. strontium

Use the atomic models to answer questions 11–13.

a.

c.

b.

d.

11. Which model of the atom most closely resembles a planetary model?

12. Which model was proposed based on data from Rutherford's gold foil experiment?

13. In which model are electrons in orbitals?

Use the drawings to answer questions 14–17. Each drawing represents an electromagnetic wave.

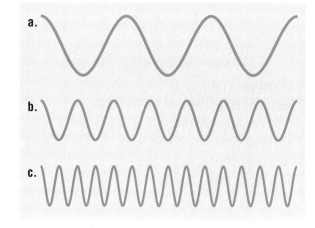

14. The wave has the longest wavelength.

15. The wave has the highest energy,

16. The wave has the lowest frequency.

17. The wave has the highest amplitude.

Write a short essay to answer question 18.

18. Explain the rules that determine how electrons are arranged around the nuclei of atoms.

CHEMICAL PERIODICITY

но въ ней, мнѣ кажется, уже ясно выражается примѣнимость вы ставляемаго мною начала ко всей совокупности элементовъ, пай которыхъ извѣстенъ съ достовѣрностію. На этотъ разъ я и желалъ преимущественно найдти общую систему элементовъ. Вотъ этотъ опытъ:

				Ti=50	Zr=90	?=180.
				V=51	Nb=94	Ta=182.
				Cr=52	Mo=96	W=186.
				Mn=55	Rh=104,4	Pt=197,4
				Fe=56	Ru=104,4	Ir=198.
			Ni=Co=59		Pl=106,6	Os=199.
H=1				Cu=63,4	Ag=108	Hg=200.
	Be=9,4	Mg=24		Zn=65,2	Cd=112	
	B=11	Al=27,4		?=68	Ur=116	Au=197?
	C=12	Si=28		?=70	Sn=118	
	N=14	P=31		As=75	Sb=122	Bi=210
	O=16	S=32		Se=79,4	Te=128?	
	F=19	Cl=35,5		Br=80	I=127	
Li=7	Na=23	K=39		Rb=85,4	Cs=133	Tl=204
		Ca=40		Sr=87,6	Ba=137	Pb=207.
		?=45		Ce=92		
		?Er=56		La=94		
		?Yt=60		Di=95		
		?In=75,6		Th=118?		

This early periodic table was designed by Dmitri Mendeleev.

FEATURES

DISCOVER IT!
Periodic Trends in Physical Properties

SMALL-SCALE LAB
Chemical Properties of the Halides

MINI LAB
Periodic Trends in Atomic Radii

CHEMISTRY SERVING … INDUSTRY
Big Jobs for Little Devices

CHEMISTRY IN CAREERS
Solid State Chemist

LINK TO ASTRONOMY
The Big Bang

LINK TO MUSIC
Newlands's Octaves

Stay current with **SCIENCE NEWS**
Find out more about the periodic table:
www.phschool.com

DISCOVER IT! PERIODIC TRENDS IN PHYSICAL PROPERTIES

You need paper, a pencil, and this textbook.

1. Make a table with five columns. In the first column, list the alkali metals Li, Na, K, Rb, and Cs in order. Title the other four columns Atomic number, Melting point, Boiling point, and Density.

2. Make a similar table, but list the halogens F, Cl, Br, and I in the first column.

3. Complete each table using Table A.1 in Appendix A of this textbook. Include the appropriate units.

4. Make a single histogram graph showing melting point and boiling point versus atomic number of the alkali metals.

5. Repeat Step 4 for the halogens.

For the alkali metals, what are the trends in melting points and boiling points as the atomic number increases? Are the trends the same or different for the halogens? What is the general trend in densities of the alkali metals with increasing atomic number? Although there is a trend in the densities of the halogens, some of the values differ dramatically. Explain. After completing the chapter, return to this activity and provide detailed explanations for the trends you observed.

CLASSIFICATION OF THE ELEMENTS

Chlorine and bromine are used in swimming pools to disinfect the water. Copper and silver, two relatively soft metals, are excellent conductors of heat and electricity. Each of these pairs of elements have similar chemical properties and are listed in the same column on the modern periodic table. This order is not coincidental, but by design. **How is the early periodic table, shown here, similar to the modern periodic table, and what does an element's position on the table indicate about its properties?**

objectives

▶ Explain why you can infer the properties of an element based on those of other elements in the periodic table

▶ Use electron configurations to classify elements as noble gases, representative elements, transition metals, or inner transition metals

key terms

▶ noble gases
▶ representative elements
▶ transition metals
▶ inner transition metals

The Periodic Table Revisited

In the second half of the 1800s, before physicists began to uncover the structure of the atom, chemists were busy exploring the nature of solutions and establishing the basis of kinetic molecular theory. The science of organic chemistry was born, as were the fertilizer, bleaching, glassmaking, dyestuff, and soap industries, to name just a few. Of crucial importance to this growth in chemistry was a tool for organizing the numerous facts being discovered about the behavior of elements. Among the many attempts that were made, the most successful organizing scheme was the one devised by the Russian chemist Dmitri Mendeleev in 1871. As you learned in Chapter 5, Mendeleev arranged all of the then-known elements into a periodic table—the forerunner of the modern periodic table displayed in current chemistry textbooks. Do you recall on what basis Mendeleev ordered the elements in his table? **Figure 14.2,** on the following pages, shows a detailed periodic table of the elements. In addition to the chemical symbol, atomic number, average atomic mass, and physical state of each element, the table includes group numbers, electron configurations, and the recently accepted names and symbols for elements 104 through 109.

The periodic table is probably the most important tool in chemistry. Among other things, it is very useful for understanding and predicting the properties of the elements. For example, if you know the physical and chemical properties of one element in a group or family (vertical column) of the periodic table, you can make a good guess about the physical and chemical properties of the other elements in the same group—and perhaps even of the elements in neighboring groups.

You already know that elements are arranged in the periodic table by order of increasing atomic number. In this chapter, you will learn how the periodic table also relates to atomic structure and trends among the elements.

Classifying Elements by Electron Configuration

Of the three major subatomic particles, the electron plays the most significant role in determining the physical and chemical properties of an element. The arrangement of elements in the periodic table depends on these properties. Thus there should be some relationship between the electron configurations of the elements and their placement in the table.

Figure 14.1

Dmitri Mendeleev proposed the basis for the periodic table that is used today.

Figure 14.2

Periodic Table of the Elements

Legend:
- Hydrogen
- Alkali metals
- Alkaline earth metals
- Transition metals
- Other metals
- Nonmetals
- Noble gases
- Inner transition metals

					18
					O
13 **3A**	14 **4A**	15 **5A**	16 **6A**	17 **7A**	2 2 **He** Helium 4.0026
5 2 3 **B** Boron 10.81	6 2 4 **C** Carbon 12.011	7 2 5 **N** Nitrogen 14.007	8 2 6 **O** Oxygen 15.999	9 2 7 **F** Fluorine 18.998	10 2 8 **Ne** Neon 20.179

10	11 **1B**	12 **2B**	13 2 8 3 **Al** Aluminum 26.982	14 2 8 4 **Si** Silicon 28.086	15 2 8 5 **P** Phosphorus 30.974	16 2 8 6 **S** Sulfur 32.06	17 2 8 7 **Cl** Chlorine 35.453	18 2 8 8 **Ar** Argon 39.948
28 2 8 16 2 **Ni** Nickel 58.71	29 2 8 18 1 **Cu** Copper 63.546	30 2 8 18 2 **Zn** Zinc 65.38	31 2 8 18 3 **Ga** Gallium 69.72	32 2 8 18 4 **Ge** Germanium 72.59	33 2 8 18 5 **As** Arsenic 74.922	34 2 8 18 6 **Se** Selenium 78.96	35 2 8 18 7 **Br** Bromine 79.904	36 2 8 18 8 **Kr** Krypton 83.80
46 2 8 18 18 **Pd** Palladium 106.4	47 2 8 18 1 **Ag** Silver 107.87	48 2 8 18 2 **Cd** Cadmium 112.41	49 2 8 18 3 **In** Indium 114.82	50 2 8 18 4 **Sn** Tin 118.69	51 2 8 18 5 **Sb** Antimony 121.75	52 2 8 18 6 **Te** Tellurium 127.60	53 2 8 18 7 **I** Iodine 126.90	54 2 8 18 8 **Xe** Xenon 131.30
78 2 8 18 17 1 **Pt** Platinum 195.09	79 2 8 18 32 18 1 **Au** Gold 196.97	80 2 8 18 32 18 2 **Hg** Mercury 200.59	81 2 8 18 32 18 3 **Tl** Thallium 204.37	82 2 8 18 32 18 4 **Pb** Lead 207.2	83 2 8 18 32 18 5 **Bi** Bismuth 208.98	84 2 8 18 32 18 6 **Po** Polonium (209)	85 2 8 18 32 18 7 **At** Astatine (210)	86 2 8 18 32 18 8 **Rn** Radon (222)
110 2 8 18 32 32 17 1 *__Uun__ Ununnilium (269)	111 2 8 18 32 32 18 1 *__Uuu__ Unununium (272)	112 2 8 18 32 32 18 2 *__Uub__ Ununbium (277)		114 *__Uuq__ Ununquadium		116 *__Uuh__ Ununhexium		118 *__Uuo__ Ununoctium

*Name not officially assigned.

63 2 8 18 25 8 2 **Eu** Europium 151.96	64 2 8 18 25 9 2 **Gd** Gadolinium 157.25	65 2 8 18 27 8 2 **Tb** Terbium 158.93	66 2 8 18 28 8 2 **Dy** Dysprosium 162.50	67 2 8 18 29 8 2 **Ho** Holmium 164.93	68 2 8 18 30 8 2 **Er** Erbium 167.26	69 2 8 18 31 8 2 **Tm** Thulium 168.93	70 2 8 18 32 8 2 **Yb** Ytterbium 173.04

95 2 8 18 32 25 8 2 **Am** Americium (243)	96 2 8 18 32 25 9 2 **Cm** Curium (247)	97 2 8 18 32 27 8 2 **Bk** Berkelium (247)	98 2 8 18 32 28 8 2 **Cf** Californium (251)	99 2 8 18 32 29 8 2 **Es** Einsteinium (252)	100 2 8 18 32 30 8 2 **Fm** Fermium (257)	101 2 8 18 32 31 8 2 **Md** Mendelevium (258)	102 2 8 18 32 32 8 2 **No** Nobelium (259)

0
2
He
Helium
4.0026
10
Ne
Neon
20.179
18
Ar
Argon
39.948
36
Kr
Krypton
83.80
54
Xe
Xenon
131.30
86
Rn
Radon
(222)

(a)

(b)

(c)

Figure 14.3

(a) Group 0 of the periodic table contains the noble gases. (b) Why do helium-filled balloons rise in air? (c) Passing an electric current through a glass tube filled with any noble gas creates the bright glow of "neon" lights.

Elements can be classified into four categories according to their electron configurations. You will find it useful to refer to **Figure 14.2** as you read about these classifications.

1. **The noble gases.** *These are elements in which the outermost s and p sublevels are filled.* The noble gases belong to Group 0. The elements in this group are sometimes called the inert gases because they do not participate in many chemical reactions. The electron configurations for the first four noble-gas elements are listed below. Notice that these elements have filled outermost *s* and *p* sublevels.

Helium	$1s^2$
Neon	$1s^2 2s^2 2p^6$
Argon	$1s^2 2s^2 2p^6 3s^2 3p^6$
Krypton	$1s^2 2s^2 2p^6 3s^2 3p^6 3d^{10} 4s^2 4p^6$

2. **The representative elements.** *In these elements, the outermost s or p sublevel is only partially filled.* The representative elements are usually called the Group A elements. (Some definitions of the representative elements may also include the noble gases.) Three groups of representative elements that have been named are the Group 1A elements, called the alkali metals; the Group 2A elements, called the alkaline earth metals; and the nonmetallic elements of Group 7A, called the halogens. For any representative element, the group number equals the number of electrons in the outermost energy level. For example, the elements in Group 1A (lithium, sodium, potassium, rubidium, and cesium) have one electron in the outermost energy level.

Lithium	$1s^2 2s^1$
Sodium	$1s^2 2s^2 2p^6 3s^1$
Potassium	$1s^2 2s^2 2p^6 3s^2 3p^6 4s^1$

Carbon, silicon, and germanium, in Group 4A, have four electrons in the outermost energy level.

Carbon	$1s^2 2s^2 2p^2$
Silicon	$1s^2 2s^2 2p^6 3s^2 3p^2$
Germanium	$1s^2 2s^2 2p^6 3s^2 3p^6 3d^{10} 4s^2 4p^2$

How many electrons are in the outermost energy level of the Group 2A elements magnesium and calcium? In the outermost energy level of the Group 5A elements phosphorus and arsenic?

3. **The transition metals.** *These are metallic elements in which the outermost s sublevel and nearby d sublevel contain electrons.* The transition elements, called the Group B elements, are characterized by addition of electrons to the *d* orbitals.

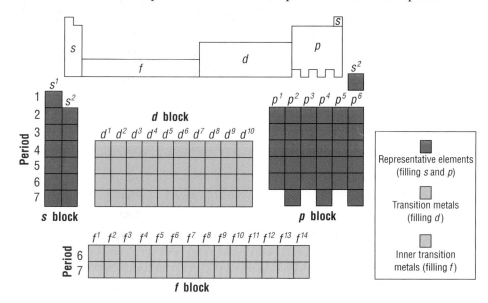

4. **The inner transition metals.** *These are metallic elements in which the outermost s sublevel and nearby f sublevel generally contain electrons.* The inner transition metals are characterized by the filling of *f* orbitals.

If you consider both the electron configurations and the positions of the elements in the periodic table, another pattern emerges. As you can see in **Figure 14.5,** the periodic table can be divided into sections, or blocks, that correspond to the sublevels that are filled with electrons.

The *s* block is the part of the periodic table that contains the elements with s^1 and s^2 outer electron configurations. It is composed of the elements in Groups 1A and 2A and the noble gas helium. The *p* block is composed of the elements in Groups 3A, 4A, 5A, 6A, 7A, and 0 with the exception of helium. The transition metals belong to the *d* block, and the inner transition metals belong to the *f* block.

Electron configurations of elements can be determined by using the periodic table in **Figure 14.5.** Simply read the periodic table as you would read a book, from left to right and top to bottom, until you reach the element of interest. Each period number on the periodic table corresponds to

Figure 14.4

Elements in Groups 1A–7A are called representative elements. **(a)** *Recyclable cans are often made of aluminum.* **(b)** *Pure sodium, a very reactive metal, is so soft that it can be cut with a knife.* **(c)** *The element carbon accounts for 0.08% of the mass of Earth's crust. Graphite, diamond, and buckminsterfullerene are allotropes of carbon.* **(d)** *Sulfur, a Group 6A element, is present in petroleum and coal, causing environmental pollution during combustion of these fossil fuels.*

Figure 14.5

This block diagram identifies groups of elements according to the sublevels filled with electrons. How many electrons are in the p sublevel of every halogen?

the principal energy level. The number of electrons in each sublevel is determined by counting over to the element, again from left to right. For the transition elements, electrons are added to a d sublevel with a principal energy level that is one less than the period number. For the inner transition metals, the principal energy level of the f sublevel is two less than the period number. Following this procedure gives the correct electron configurations for most atoms.

Sample Problem 14-1

Use the periodic table in **Figure 14.5** to write the electron configurations of these elements.

   a. nitrogen   **b.** nickel

1. **ANALYZE** *Plan a problem-solving strategy.*
   Apply the procedure of using position in the periodic table to determine electron configurations of elements. The atomic number equals the number of electrons. The period in which the element is located corresponds to the highest occupied principal energy level. The number of electrons in the highest occupied sublevel is related to the group location.

2. **SOLVE** *Apply the problem-solving strategy.*
   a. Nitrogen has 7 electrons. The periodic table in **Figure 14.5** shows that the first period is $1s^2$ and the second period is $2s^2 2p^3$. There are 3 electrons in the $2p$ sublevel because nitrogen is the third element in the $2p$ block.
   b. Nickel has 28 electrons. From **Figure 14.5,** the first three periods are $1s^2 2s^2 2p^6 3s^2 3p^6$. Next is $4s^2$ and finally $3d^8$. Remember that the principal energy level number for the d block is always one less than the period number. The complete configuration is $1s^2 2s^2 2p^6 3s^2 3p^6 3d^8 4s^2$.

3. **EVALUATE** *Do the results make sense?*
   In each case, the sum of the superscripts equals the total number of electrons in, or the atomic number of, the atom.

Practice Problems

1. Use **Figure 14.5** to write the electron configurations of these elements.
   a. carbon
   b. vanadium
   c. strontium
2. What are the symbols for all the elements that have the following outer configurations?
   a. s^2
   b. $s^2 p^5$
   c. $s^2 d^2$

section review 14.1

3. Why do the elements potassium and sodium have similar chemical and physical properties?

4. Categorize each element as a representative element, a transition metal, or a noble gas.

   a. $1s^2 2s^2 2p^6 3s^2 3p^6 3d^{10} 4s^2 4p^6 4d^{10} 5s^1$ **c.** $1s^2 2s^2 2p^6 3s^2 3p^6 3d^5 4s^1$
   b. $1s^2 2s^2 2p^6 3s^2 3p^6 3d^{10} 4s^2 4p^6$ **d.** $1s^2 2s^2 2p^6 3s^2 3p^2$

5. Which of the following are transition metals: Cu, Sr, Cd, Au, Al, Ge, Co?

 Chem ASAP! **Assessment 14.1** Check your understanding of the important ideas and concepts in Section 14.1.

SMALL-SCALE LAB

CHEMICAL PROPERTIES OF THE HALIDES

SAFETY

Wear safety glasses and follow the standard safety procedures outlined on page 18.

PURPOSE

To observe some properties of halide ions and to use these data to predict trends.

MATERIALS

- pencil
- paper
- reaction surface
- ruler
- chemicals shown in Figure A along with HNO_3 and NaOCl

PROCEDURE

On separate sheets of paper, draw two grids similar to Figure A, one with large Xs and one without. Make each square 2 cm on each side. Place a reaction surface over the grid with the Xs and add the chemicals as shown in Figure A. Use the second grid as a data table to record your observations.

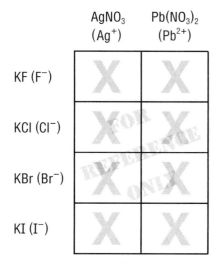

Figure A

ANALYSIS

Using your experimental data, record the answers to the following questions below your data table.

1. List the formulas and charges of each halide ion.

2. Write the electron configuration of each halide ion. What do the electron configurations of all the halide ions have in common?

3. Which halide ions formed precipitates? What color was each precipitate? Write and balance a net ionic equation for each precipitation reaction you observed.

4. Which silver halide did not form a precipitate? This halide is the most soluble. Assuming the solubility of the silver halides follows a group trend, list the silver halides in order of decreasing solubility.

5. Can you make the same sort of prediction about the relative solubilities of the lead halides? Why or why not?

YOU'RE THE CHEMIST

The following small-scale activities allow you to develop your own procedures and analyze the results.

1. **Design It!** Design and carry out an experiment to determine how halide ions react with sodium hypochlorite in the presence of nitric acid. Which halide ions react with NaOCl? Which do not?

2. **Analyze It!** Use your data to predict a trend in reactivity of the halide ions.

3. **Analyze It!** OCl^- reacts with I^- and H^+ to form I_2 according to the following chemical equation.

$$OCl^- + 2H^+ + 2I^- \longrightarrow H_2O + Cl^- + I_2$$

Write a similar equation for the other halide ion that reacts with OCl^-.

4. **Analyze It!** The value of the reduction potential (E^0) is a measure of the relative ease with which halide ions react to form halogens. In general, the more positive the reduction potential, the less likely a halide will form a halogen. Look up the reduction potential values of I_2, Br_2, Cl_2, and F_2 in Section 23.2. Are these reduction potential values consistent with your prediction? Explain.

objectives

▶ Interpret group trends in atomic radii, ionic radii, ionization energies, and electronegativities

▶ Interpret period trends in atomic radii, ionic radii, ionization energies, and electronegativities

key terms

▶ atomic radius
▶ ionization energy
▶ electronegativity

PERIODIC TRENDS

*H*ave you ever noticed physical similarities between relatives at a family reunion? The relatives may have similar-shaped noses or faces, or have lots of freckles. These characteristics generally indicate a relationship among the family members. As you know, the elements also belong to families—chemical families. **What trends in physical and chemical properties exist among the families and periods of the periodic table?**

Trends in Atomic Size

You know from the quantum mechanical model, which you read about in Chapter 13, that an atom does not have a sharply defined boundary that sets the limit of its size. Therefore, the radius of an atom cannot be measured directly. There are, however, several ways to estimate the relative sizes of atoms. If the atoms are in a solid crystalline structure, a technique called x-ray diffraction can provide an estimate of the distance between the nuclei. For elements that exist as diatomic molecules, the distance between the nuclei of the atoms bonded in the molecule can be estimated. The **atomic radius** is one-half of the distance between the nuclei of two like atoms in a diatomic molecule. Look at **Figure 14.7,** which shows the distance between the nuclei in the diatomic molecules of seven elements. The separation between the nuclei in a diatomic bromine molecule (Br_2) is 228 pm (1 pm = 1 picometer = 1×10^{-12} m). As you can see, because the atomic radius is one-half the distance between the nuclei, a value of 114 pm (228/2) is assigned as the radius of the bromine atom. **Figure 14.8** shows atomic radii for most of the representative elements. Remember, the atomic radius of an element indicates its relative size.

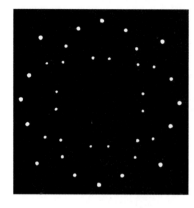

Figure 14.6

Analysis of this x-ray diffraction pattern of NaCl will reveal the distance between the two nuclei in the crystalline structure.

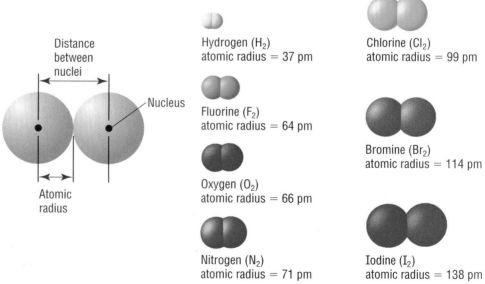

Distance between nuclei

Nucleus

Atomic radius

Hydrogen (H_2)
atomic radius = 37 pm

Fluorine (F_2)
atomic radius = 64 pm

Oxygen (O_2)
atomic radius = 66 pm

Nitrogen (N_2)
atomic radius = 71 pm

Chlorine (Cl_2)
atomic radius = 99 pm

Bromine (Br_2)
atomic radius = 114 pm

Iodine (I_2)
atomic radius = 138 pm

Figure 14.7

Seven elements exist as diatomic molecules. In the bromine molecule (Br_2), the distance between the nuclei is 228 pm and the atomic radius is 114 pm. What is the atomic radius, in meters, of a bromine atom? What is the diameter, in nanometers?

Figure 14.8
Atomic and ionic radii of the representative elements are given here in picometers. Transition metals are omitted from the figure because they show many exceptions to the general trend.

○ Metal atom
● Metal ion
◌ Nonmetal atom
○ Nonmetal ion

152 —— Atomic radius
Li
60 —— Ionic radius

MINI LAB

Periodic Trends in Atomic Radii

PURPOSE

To graph ionic radius versus atomic number for the representative elements in periods 2–5 and to examine the graph for periodic and group trends.

MATERIALS

- graph paper
- pencil

PROCEDURE

Use the information presented in **Figure 14.8** to plot ionic radius versus atomic number.

ANALYSIS AND CONCLUSIONS

1. Comment on the sizes of cations compared with the sizes of anions. How do these sizes compare with those of the atoms?

2. Are the general trends shown for periods 2, 3, 4, and 5 similar or different?

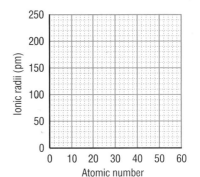

Ionic Radii vs. Atomic Number

3. Describe and explain the shape of each period's portion of the graph.

4. How do the radii for anions and cations change as you go down a group? Explain.

Group Trends Atomic size generally increases as you move down a group of the periodic table. As you descend, electrons are added to successively higher principal energy levels and the nuclear charge increases. The outermost orbital is larger as you move downward. The shielding of the nucleus by electrons also increases with the additional occupied orbitals between the outermost orbital and the nucleus. Although you might expect the increase in charge on the nucleus to attract the outer electrons and shrink the size of the atom, this is not the case. The enlarging effect of the greater distance of the outer electrons from the nucleus overcomes the shrinking effect caused by the increasing charge of the nucleus. Therefore the atomic size increases. The bar graphs in **Figure 14.9** show how atomic size (atomic radius) increases as you go down Group 1A (the alkali metals), Group 2A (the alkaline earth metals), and Group 7A (the halogens).

Periodic Trends Atomic size generally decreases as you move from left to right across a period. As you go across a period, the principal energy level remains the same. Each element has one more proton and one more electron than the preceding element. The electrons are added to the same principal energy level. The effect of the increasing nuclear charge on the outermost electrons is to pull them closer to the nucleus. Atomic size therefore decreases. Plotting atomic radius against atomic number, as in **Figure 14.10,** reveals a periodic trend. The trend is less pronounced in periods where there are more electrons in the occupied principal energy levels

Figure 14.9

*The atomic radii of **(a)** Group 1A, **(b)** Group 2A, and **(c)** Group 7A elements increase as you go down the group, or as the atomic number increases. The ions (cations) in **(a)** and **(b)** are smaller than the neutral atoms. In contrast, the ions (anions) in **(c)** are larger than the neutral atoms. Why is a potassium atom larger than a potassium ion?*

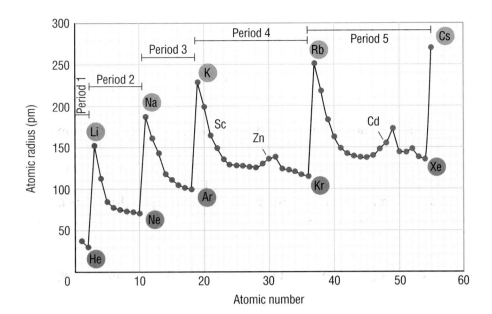

Figure 14.10
This graph of atomic radius versus atomic number shows a periodic trend.

between the nucleus and the outermost electrons. This is because these inner electrons help shield the outermost electrons and the nucleus from each other. In any given period, however, the number of electrons between the nucleus and the outermost electrons is the same for all elements. Consequently, the shielding effect of these electrons on the nucleus is constant within a period.

Figure 14.11 summarizes the group and period trends in atomic size. How would you describe the atomic radius of a period-2 alkaline earth metal compared with that of a period-4 alkaline earth metal?

Trends in Ionization Energy

When an atom gains or loses an electron, it becomes an ion. The energy required to overcome the attraction of the nuclear charge and remove an electron from a gaseous atom is called the **ionization energy.** Removing one electron results in the formation of a positive ion with a 1+ charge.

$$Na(g) \longrightarrow Na^+(g) + e^-$$

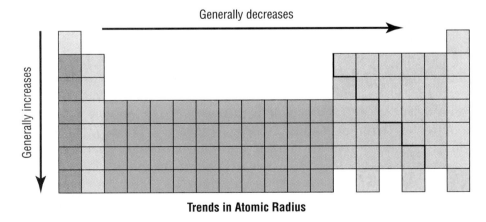

Figure 14.11
Atomic radii generally decrease across periods and increase down groups. Which has the larger atomic radius within the same period: a halogen or an alkali metal?

ASTRONOMY

The Big Bang
Astronomers have evidence that the material universe began with an event of indescribable energy. At the moment of this event, called the Big Bang, the

temperature was many billions of degrees. As a result of the Big Bang, the elements formed. Neutrons, protons, and electrons may have formed within 10^{-4} second after the Big Bang, and the lightest nuclei formed within 3 minutes. At this time, the temperature was still probably 70 times the temperature of Earth's sun. Matter was in the form of plasma, a sea of positive nuclei and negative electrons. It took an estimated 500 000 years for electrons and nuclei to cool enough to form atoms. According to the Big Bang theory, planet Earth, with its wealth of chemical elements, is the debris of supernova explosions. It is this literal star dust that contains all the elements essential for life.

Table 14.1

Ionization Energies of the First 20 Elements			
Symbol of element	Ionization energy (kJ/mol)		
	First	Second	Third
H	1 312		
He (noble gas)	2 371	5 247	
Li	520	7 297	11 810
Be	900	1 757	14 840
B	800	2 430	3 659
C	1 086	2 352	4 619
N	1 402	2 857	4 577
O	1 314	3 391	5 301
F	1 681	3 375	6 045
Ne (noble gas)	2 080	3 963	6 276
Na	495.8	4 565	6 912
Mg	737.6	1 450	7 732
Al	577.4	1 816	2 744
Si	786.2	1 577	3 229
P	1 012	1 896	2 910
S	999.6	2 260	3 380
Cl	1 255	2 297	3 850
Ar (noble gas)	1 520	2 665	3 947
K	418.8	3 069	4 600
Ca	589.5	1 146	4 941

The energy required to remove this first outermost electron is called the first ionization energy. To remove the outermost electron from the gaseous 1+ ion requires an amount of energy called the second ionization energy, and so forth. **Table 14.1** gives the first three ionization energies of the first 20 elements.

You can use the concept of ionization energy to predict ionic charges. Look at the three Group 1A metals in **Table 14.1.** Do you see a large increase in energy between the first and second ionization energies? It is relatively easy to remove one electron from a Group 1A metal to form an ion with a 1+ charge. It is very difficult, however, to remove an additional electron. For the three Group 2A metals, the large increase in ionization energy occurs between the second and third ionization energies. What does this tell you about the relative ease of removing one electron from these metals? Two electrons? Three electrons? You know that aluminum, in Group 3A, forms a 3+ ion. The large increase in ionization energy for aluminum occurs after the third electron is removed.

Group Trends As you can see from **Table 14.1,** the first ionization energy generally decreases as you move down a group of the periodic table. This is because the size of the atoms increases as you descend, so the

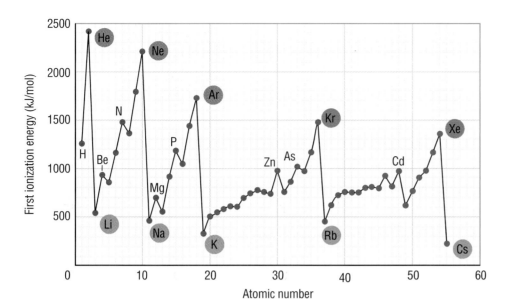

Figure 14.12
This graph of first ionization energy versus atomic number shows a periodic trend. Notice the ease with which Group 1A elements are ionized and the difficulty of ionizing noble gases. What is the group trend for the noble gases?

outermost electron is farther from the nucleus. The outermost electron should be more easily removed, and the element should have a lower ionization energy.

Periodic Trends For the representative elements, the first ionization energy generally increases as you move from left to right across a period. See **Figure 14.12**. The nuclear charge increases and the shielding effect is constant as you move across. A greater attraction of the nucleus for the electron leads to the increase in ionization energy.

Figure 14.13 summarizes the group and periodic trends in first ionization energies. Which element in Group 6A has the highest first ionization energy? In period 2?

Trends in Ionic Size

The atoms of metallic elements have low ionization energies. They form positive ions easily. By contrast, the atoms of nonmetallic elements readily form negative ions. Let's look at how the loss or gain of electrons affects the size of the ion formed.

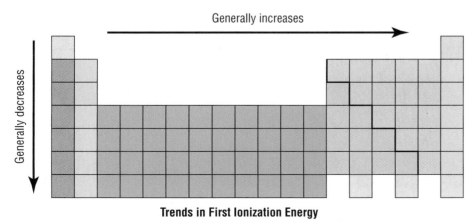

Trends in First Ionization Energy

Figure 14.13
First ionization energies generally increase across periods and decrease down groups.

Figure 14.14

The relative sizes (radii) of atoms and ions for selected metals and nonmetals are given in picometers.

Group Trends Positive ions (cations) are always smaller than the neutral atoms from which they form. This is because the loss of outer-shell electrons results in increased attraction by the nucleus for the fewer remaining electrons. As you can see in **Figure 14.14,** the radius of the Na$^+$ ion (95 pm) is only about one-half that of the Na atom (186 pm). The radius of the Al^{3+} ion is only about one-third that of the Al atom. In contrast, negative ions (anions) are always larger than the neutral atoms from which they form. This is because the effective nuclear attraction is less for an increased number of electrons. The radius of the Cl$^-$ ion (181 pm) is about twice that of the Cl atom (99 pm). The bar graphs in **Figure 14.9** on page 400, which show trends in atomic radii, also give the group trends in ionic size for Group 1A, 2A, and 7A elements.

Periodic Trends A periodic relationship for the ionic radii of the elements is shown in **Figure 14.8** on page 399. Going from left to right across a row, there is a gradual decrease in the size of positive ions. Then beginning with Group 5A, the negative ions, which are much larger, gradually decrease in size as you continue to move right. The ionic radii of both anions and cations increase as you go down each group.

The group and periodic trends in ionic size are summarized in **Figure 14.15.** How does the ionic radius of sodium compare with that of cesium? Boron with that of fluoride?

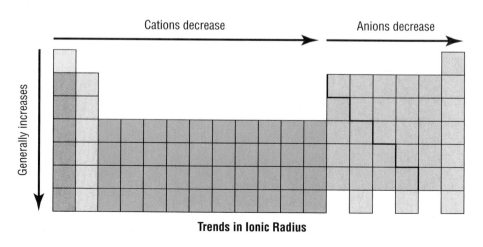

Figure 14.15

Cationic and anionic radii decrease across periods and increase down groups.

Trends in Electronegativity

The **electronegativity** of an element is the tendency for the atoms of the element to attract electrons when they are chemically combined with atoms of another element. Electronegativities have been calculated for the elements and are expressed in arbitrary units on the Pauling electronegativity scale. This numerical scale is based on a number of factors, including the ionization energies of the elements.

The electronegativities of selected elements, arranged in the form of the periodic table, are presented in **Table 14.2.** Note that the noble gases are omitted because they do not form many compounds. With their exception, each element is assigned an electronegativity number in units of Paulings. As you can see, electronegativity generally decreases as you move down a group. As you go across a period from left to right, the electronegativity of the representative elements increases. The metallic elements at the far left of the periodic table have low electronegativities. By contrast, the non-metallic elements at the far right (excluding the noble gases) have high electronegativities. The trends in electronegativities among the transition metals are not so regular; these numbers are not included in the table.

The electronegativity of cesium, the least electronegative element, is 0.7; the electronegativity of fluorine, the most electronegative element, is 4.0. Because fluorine has such a strong tendency to attract electrons, when it is chemically bonded to any other element it either attracts the shared electrons or forms a negative ion. In contrast, cesium has the least tendency to attract electrons. It loses the electron "tug-of-war" and forms a positive ion.

As you will learn in the following chapters on ionic bonding and covalent bonding, electronegativity values help predict the type of bonding that can exist between atoms in compounds.

MUSIC

Newlands's Octaves

Mendeleev's publication of his first periodic table in 1869 was far from the first attempt to organize the elements according to their properties. In 1863, John Newlands (1838–1898), an English chemist, arranged the elements in order of increasing atomic masses. He noted that the properties of the elements repeated when the elements were arranged by increasing atomic mass in groups of eight. For example, the chemical properties of lithium and sodium are very similar. Newlands referred to his arrangement as the law of octaves. This is similar to the musical scale, which repeats every eighth tone. Although the law of octaves fails for elements beyond calcium, Newlands's work was a step in the right direction in the classification of the elements.

Table 14.2

Electronegativity Values for Atoms of Selected Elements						
H 2.1						
Li 1.0	Be 1.5	B 2.0	C 2.5	N 3.0	O 3.5	F 4.0
Na 0.9	Mg 1.2	Al 1.5	Si 1.8	P 2.1	S 2.5	Cl 3.0
K 0.8	Ca 1.0	Ga 1.6	Ge 1.8	As 2.0	Se 2.4	Br 2.8
Rb 0.8	Sr 1.0	In 1.7	Sn 1.8	Sb 1.9	Te 2.1	I 2.5
Cs 0.7	Ba 0.9	Tl 1.8	Pb 1.9	Bi 1.9		

Figure 14.16

Periodic trends vary as you move across and down the periodic table. Properties that show periodic trends include atomic radius, ionic size, ionization energy, nuclear charge, shielding effect, and electronegativity of the elements.

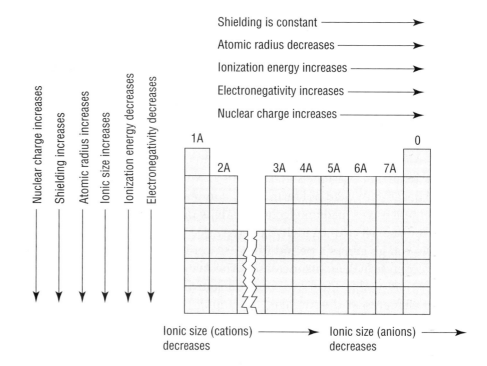

Summary of Periodic Trends

You have now seen that a number of periodic trends exist among the elements and that these trends can be explained by looking at variations in atomic structure. Remember, trends occur within groups and within periods. **Figure 14.16** summarizes the trends in atomic radius, ionization energy, ionic size, and electronegativity that you have just learned about. Which is the only property that shows a decreasing trend as you move from left to right across the periodic table?

section review 14.2

6. For which of these properties does lithium have a larger value than potassium?

    a. first ionization energy

    b. atomic radius

    c. electronegativity

    d. ionic radius

7. Arrange these elements in order of decreasing atomic size: sulfur, chlorine, aluminum, and sodium. Does your arrangement demonstrate a periodic trend or a group trend?

8. How does the ionic radius of a typical anion compare with the radius for the corresponding neutral atom?

9. Which element in each pair has the larger ionization energy?

    a. sodium, potassium

    b. magnesium, phosphorus

 Chem ASAP! **Assessment 14.2** Check your understanding of the important ideas and concepts in Section 14.2.

portfolio project

Research what grades of chemicals are available from suppliers. What is the difference between reagent grade and laboratory grade in terms of purity and cost? How pure are the chemicals that you use for your lab experiments?

BIG JOBS FOR LITTLE DEVICES

In 1946 at the University of Pennsylvania, a team of engineers built the Electronic Numerical Integrator and Calculator (ENIAC). A complex mass of wires and vacuum tubes, ENIAC occupied 2000 square feet of floor space, almost half the size of a basketball court. It was the first electronic computer, designed to perform high-speed calculations for the government.

Although ENIAC was an amazing achievement for its time, it would be outperformed today by a calculator the size of a credit card! Within the small space of the calculator's circuitry is the equivalent of ENIAC's thousands of vacuum tubes and miles of wires. This incredible miniaturization was made possible by semiconductor technology.

Chemically speaking, semiconductors are elements that conduct electricity better than insulators but less well than conductors. The elements silicon (Si), germanium (Ge), and gallium (Ga) are semiconductors.

In their pure forms, semiconductors are not very useful. But when contaminated with atoms of other elements, their properties of conductivity change dramatically. Because of the different ways they can affect the movement of electrons within them, "contaminated" semiconductors can be used to make tiny

An integrated circuit containing millions of components can be placed on a semiconductor wafer smaller than your fingernail!

electronic devices. One such device is the transistor, which amplifies an electrical signal.

A transistor smaller than the size of the period at the end of this sentence can do the work of one of the many four-inch-tall vacuum tubes contained in ENIAC.

The basis of semiconductor technology is the process called doping. In doping, some of the atoms that make up a crystal of pure silicon are replaced with atoms of either arsenic (As) or boron (B). Doping with arsenic creates a donor, or n-type semiconductor. Each atom of arsenic contains five electrons in its outer shell, compared with the four electrons of the neighboring silicon atoms. The extra electron from the arsenic atom is free to move around.

Doping with boron has the opposite effect, creating an acceptor, or p-type semiconductor. Because boron has only three electrons in its outer shell, a positive "hole" is created for every boron atom. These holes can move and thus conduct.

Miniature electronic components are built from different combinations of n-type and p-type semiconductors placed together. Transistors are just one example. Integrated circuits, such as the one shown in the photograph, are another. An integrated circuit containing millions of components can be placed on a semiconductor wafer smaller than your fingernail! The resulting "chip" can control a computer, portable CD player, television, calculator, or automobile fuel system.

Miniature electronic circuits have revolutionized the electronics and computer industries. Electronic equipment is now smaller, more complex, and less expensive than ever. Current research is focusing on finding ways to make even smaller and faster chips.

CHEMISTRY IN CAREERS

☆☆☆☆☆☆☆☆☆☆☆☆☆☆☆☆☆☆☆☆☆

TAKE IT TO THE NET
Find out more about career opportunities:
www.phschool.com

SOLID STATE CHEMIST
Do you have a "solid" understanding of chemistry? If so, consider this career.
See page 874.

CHEMICAL SPECIALIST
Local food service distributor seeks responsible se... motivated individ...

CHEMIST NEEDED
Enviro Lab, GC M...

KEY TERMS

- atomic radius *p. 398*
- electronegativity *p. 405*
- inner transition metal *p. 395*
- ionization energy *p. 401*
- noble gas *p. 394*
- representative element *p. 394*
- transition metal *p. 394*

CONCEPT SUMMARY

14.1 Classification of the Elements

- Elements that have similar properties also have similar electron configurations and are members of the same group.
- The atoms of the noble gas elements have filled outermost *s* and *p* sublevels.
- The outermost *s* and *p* sublevels of the representative elements are only partially filled.
- The outermost *s* and nearby *d* sublevels of transition metals contain electrons.
- The outermost *s* and nearby *f* sublevels of inner transition metals contain electrons.

14.2 Periodic Trends

- Regular changes in the electron configuration of the elements cause gradual changes in both the physical and chemical properties of the elements within a group and within a period.
- Atomic radii generally decrease as you move from left to right in a given period because there is an increase in the nuclear charge while the number of inner electrons, and hence the shielding effect, remains constant.
- Ionization energy, the energy required to remove an electron from an atom, generally increases as you move from left to right across a period. Ionization energy decreases as you move down a group.

- Atomic radii generally increase within a given group because the outer electrons are farther from the nucleus as you go down the group. The attractive force of the increased nuclear charge is unable to overcome the effect of the greater distance, which acts in opposition.
- Ionic radii decrease for cations and anions as you move from left to right across a period and increase as you move down a group.
- Electronegativity measures the ability of a bonded atom to attract electrons to itself. It generally increases as you move from left to right across a period. It decreases as you move down a group.

CHAPTER CONCEPT MAP

Use these terms to construct a concept map that organizes the major ideas of this chapter.

 Chem ASAP! Concept Map 14
Create your Concept Map using the computer.

electronegativity   ionic radius   periodic trends

electron configuration   atomic size

ionization energy   periodic table

CONCEPT PRACTICE

10. What are the noble gases, the representative elements, the transition elements, and the inner transition elements? *14.1*

11. Use **Figure 14.2** to write the electron configuration of these elements. *14.1*
a. boron   **b.** magnesium   **c.** arsenic

12. Which of the following are representative elements: Na, Mg, Fe, Ni, Cl? *14.1*

13. Write the electron configuration of these elements. *14.1*
a. the inert gas in period 3
b. the element in Group 4A, period 4
c. the element in Group 2A, period 6

14. Explain how an element's outer electron configuration is related to its position in the periodic table. *14.1*

15. Use **Figure 14.2** to write the electron configuration of these atoms. *14.1*
a. fluorine   **b.** zinc   **c.** aluminum   **d.** tin

16. What are the symbols for all the elements with the following outer configurations? *14.1*
a. s^1 **b.** s^2p^4 **c.** s^2d^{10}

17. Explain why fluorine has a smaller atomic radius than both oxygen and chlorine. *14.2*

18. Indicate which element in each pair has the greater atomic radius. *14.2*
a. sodium, lithium
b. strontium, magnesium
c. carbon, germanium
d. selenium, oxygen

19. Distinguish between the first and second ionization energy of an atom. *14.2*

20. Indicate which element in each pair has the greater first ionization energy. *14.2*
a. lithium, boron
b. magnesium, strontium
c. cesium, aluminum

21. Would you expect metals or nonmetals to have higher ionization energies? Why? *14.2*

22. Arrange the following elements in order of increasing ionization energy. *14.2*
a. Be, Mg, Sr   **b.** Bi, Cs, Ba   **c.** Na, Al, S

23. Why is there a large increase between the first and second ionization energies of the alkali metals? *14.2*

24. Which particle has the larger radius in each atom/ion pair? *14.2*
a. Na, Na^+ **b.** S, S^{2-} **c.** I, I^- **d.** Al, Al^{3+}

25. How does the ionic radius of a typical metallic atom compare with its atomic radius? *14.2*

26. Explain why the noble gases do not appear in **Table 14.2**. *14.2*

27. Which element is more electronegative? *14.2*
a. Cl, F   **b.** C, N   **c.** Mg, Ne   **d.** As, Ca

CONCEPT MASTERY

28. The Mg^{2+} and Na^+ ions each have ten electrons surrounding the nucleus. Which ion would you expect to have the smaller radius? Why?

29. Explain why it takes more energy to remove a $4s$ electron from zinc than from calcium.

30. The graphs show the relationship between the electronegativities and first ionization energies for period 2 and period 3 elements.
a. State the general trend between these two values in each period.
b. Propose an explanation for this trend.

31. Give the electron configuration of the element found at each location in the periodic table.
    a. Group 1A, period 4
    b. Group 3A, period 3
    c. Group 6A, period 3
    d. Group 2A, period 6

32. In each pair, which ion is larger?
    a. Ca^{2+}, Mg^{2+} b. Cl^-, P^{3-} c. Cu^+, Cu^{2+}

33. Give the names, symbols, and electron configurations for the ten period-4 transition metals.

CRITICAL THINKING

34. Choose the term that best completes the second relationship.

    a. sister : brother   oxygen : _____
       (1) hydrogen   (3) silicon
       (2) sulfur   (4) Group 6A

    b. potassium : cation   sulfur : _____
       (1) anion   (3) yellow
       (2) nonmetal   (4) solid

    c. magnesium : s orbital   zinc : _____
       (1) s orbital   (3) d orbital
       (2) p orbital   (4) f orbital

35. There is a large jump between the second and third ionization energies of magnesium. The corresponding large jump is between the third and fourth ionization energies of aluminum. Explain.

36. The following graph shows how many elements were discovered before 1750 and in each 50-year period since then.
    a. In which 50-year period were the most elements discovered?
    b. How did Mendeleev's work contribute to the discovery of so many elements?
    c. What characteristic do all the elements discovered since 1950 have in common?

37. Atoms and ions with the same number of electrons are called isoelectronic.
    a. Name a cation and an anion that are isoelectronic with krypton.
    b. Is it possible for a cation to be isoelectronic with an anion from the same period? Explain.

CUMULATIVE REVIEW

38. A 2.00-L flask at 27 °C contains 4.40 g of carbon dioxide and 2.00 g of nitrogen gas. What is the pressure (in atm) of each of the two components?

39. Balance the following chemical equations.
    a. $Ag + S \longrightarrow Ag_2S$
    b. $Na_2SO_4 + Ba(OH)_2 \longrightarrow BaSO_4 + NaOH$
    c. $Zn + HNO_3 \longrightarrow Zn(NO_3)_2 + H_2$
    d. $H_2O + SO_2 + O_2 \longrightarrow H_2SO_4$

40. The smelting of iron ore consists of heating the ore with carbon.

$$2Fe_2O_3 + 3C \longrightarrow 4Fe + 3CO_2$$

What mass of iron can be obtained from 100 g of the ore?

41. Write chemical formulas for the following compounds.
    a. lithium sulfate
    b. zinc phosphate
    c. potassium permanganate
    d. strontium carbonate

42. If a gas sample at 25 °C occupies a volume of 2.93 L, what will be the volume at 500 °C if the pressure is unchanged?

CONCEPT CHALLENGE

43. The ions S^{2-}, Cl^-, K^+, Ca^{2+}, and Sc^{3+} have the same total number of electrons as the noble gas argon. How would you expect the radii of these ions to vary? Would you expect to see the same variation in the series O^{2-}, F^-, Na^+, Mg^{2+}, and Al^{3+}, in which each ion has the same total number of electrons as the noble gas neon? Why or why not?

44. Using a chemistry reference book, make a table for the Group 2A elements. Include densities, atomic masses, formulas of the chlorides and oxides, and first ionization energies. Can you justify placing these elements in one group on the basis of these data?

Select the choice that best answers each question or completes each statement.

1. Which of the following properties increases as you move across a period from left to right?
   I. electronegativity
   II. ionization energy
   III. atomic radius
   a. I and II only
   b. I and III only
   c. II and III only
   d. I, II, and III

2. List the symbols for sodium, sulfur, and cesium in order of increasing atomic radii.
   a. Na, S, Cs   **c.** S, Na, Cs
   b. Cs, Na, S   **d.** Cs, S, Na

3. The outer electron configuration for an element in the halogen group is
   a. $s^2 p^6$.   **c.** $s^2 p^4$.
   b. $s^2 p^5$.   **d.** $s^2 p^2$.

4. Which of these does *not* form an ion isoelectronic with krypton?
   a. argon   **c.** strontium
   b. bromine   **d.** selenium

Use the following data to answer questions 5 and 6.
The ionization energies for the removal of the first six electrons in carbon are, starting with the first electron, 1086 kJ/mol, 2352 kJ/mol, 4619 kJ/mol, 6220 kJ/mol, 37 820 kJ/mol, and 47 260 kJ/mol.

5. Make a graph of ionization energy as a function of ionization number. The ionization number indicates which electron is lost.

6. Between which two ionization numbers does the ionization energy have the largest increase? Why is this behavior predictable?

Use the spheres to answer questions 7–9.

7. Which sphere would most likely represent a potassium atom, K?

8. Which sphere would most likely represent a potassium ion, K^+?

9. If the spheres represent an atom and an anion of the same element, which sphere represents the atom and which represents the anion?

Use the data table to answer questions 10–12.

Alkali metal	Atomic radius (pm)	First ionization energy (kJ/mol)	Electronegativity value
Li	152	520	1.0
Na	186	495.8	0.9
K	227	418.8	0.8
Rb	244	250	0.8
Cs	262	210	0.7

10. If you plotted atomic radius versus first ionization energy, would the graph reveal a direct or inverse relationship?

11. If you plotted atomic radius versus electronegativity, would the graph reveal a direct or inverse relationship?

12. If you plotted first ionization energy versus electronegativity, would the graph reveal a direct or inverse relationship?

For each question there are two statements. Decide whether each statement is true or false. Then decide whether Statement II is a correct explanation for Statement I.

Statement I		Statement II
13. A large increase between the first and second ionization energies is characteristic of the alkali metals.	BECAUSE	It takes considerable energy to remove an electron from a completely filled energy level.
14. Nonmetallic elements have higher electronegativity values than do metallic elements.	BECAUSE	Atoms of nonmetals are among the largest atoms.
15. A calcium atom is larger than a calcium ion.	BECAUSE	Ions are always larger than the atoms from which they are formed.
16. The ionization energy of the noble gas is always the smallest of all the elements in a period.	BECAUSE	Within any period, atomic radii tend to decrease moving from right to left.

Chapter 15

IONIC BONDING AND IONIC COMPOUNDS

The arrangement of ions in table salt determines its crystal shape.

FEATURES

Stay current with **SCIENCE NEWS**
Find out more about ionic compounds:
www.phschool.com

DISCOVER IT! SHAPES OF CRYSTALLINE MATERIALS

You need four small disposable cups, distilled water, a ruler, a spoon, sodium chloride (table salt), sucrose (table sugar), sodium hydrogen carbonate (baking soda), magnesium sulfate (Epsom salt), a small clean mirror, and a magnifying glass.

1. Label each cup with the name of one of the solids and pour water into each cup to a depth of 1 cm.

2. Add a spoonful of each solid to its corresponding cup. Swirl each cup for 30 seconds and then let it stand for a few minutes.

3. Swirl the cups at least two more times. Each time, note whether any of the solids completely dissolves. If so, add more of that solid and repeat the swirling. Continue this process until there is some undissolved solid at the bottom of each cup.

4. Set the mirror on a flat surface and place 2 or 3 drops of each liquid onto separate areas of the mirror.

5. Use a magnifying glass to examine each drop of liquid after 15 minutes, and then again after 24 hours.

For each material, did the solids crystallize? Did the crystals form at the same time? Describe the crystals that formed. Revisit this activity later in the chapter when you read about crystalline solids. Add to your notes any relevant information about the crystals you observed.

ELECTRON CONFIGURATION IN IONIC BONDING

objectives
▶ Use the periodic table to infer the number of valence electrons in an atom and draw its electron dot structure
▶ Describe the formation of cations from metals and of anions from nonmetals

key terms
▶ valence electrons
▶ electron dot structures
▶ octet rule
▶ halide ions

*O*ver time, underground salt deposits can rise through layers of sediment to form hollow, spherical structures called salt domes. More than 300 salt domes are found along a 2800-km stretch of the Gulf of Mexico. Some of these domes are more than 18 km deep and can be up to 10 km wide. As seen here, the salt found in salt domes exists as crystals of sodium chloride. **What characteristics of sodium and chlorine atoms allow them to form the stable compound sodium chloride, also known as table salt?**

Valence Electrons

In Chapters 5, 13, and 14, you learned about the electron structure of atoms and the organization of the periodic table. That knowledge will now help you understand the chemical bonding that occurs between atoms. For example, knowing the electron configurations of sodium and chlorine enables you to determine why these atoms combine to make sodium chloride. The configurations also explain why the formula unit for sodium chloride is NaCl and not Na_2Cl or $NaCl_2$. Questions about the properties of many compounds can be answered on the basis of their electron structure. Questions such as "Why does melted sodium chloride conduct electricity?" and "Why is sodium chloride a solid with a high melting point?" will be answered in this chapter.

You may recall that Mendeleev used similarities in the properties of elements to organize his periodic table. Scientists later learned that all of the elements within each group of the periodic table behave similarly because they have the same number of valence electrons. **Valence electrons** are the electrons in the highest occupied energy level of an element's atoms. The number of valence electrons largely determines the chemical properties of an element. One way to determine the number of valence electrons is to look at an element's electron configuration.

The number of valence electrons is also related to the group numbers in the periodic table. To find the number of valence electrons for a representative element, simply look at its group number. For example, the elements of Group 1A (hydrogen, lithium, sodium, potassium, and so forth) all have

Figure 15.1
The sodium chloride in the sea water (left) has crystallized out of solution to form deposits on the rocks (right).

Table 15.1

					Group			
Electron Dot Structures of Some Group A Elements								
Period	1A	2A	3A	4A	5A	6A	7A	0
1	H·							He:
2	Li·	·Be·	·Ḃ·	·Ċ·	·N̈·	:Ö·	:F̈·	:N̈e:
3	Na·	·Mg·	·Al·	·Si·	·P̈·	:S̈·	:Cl·	:Är:
4	K·	·Ca·	·Ga·	·Ge·	·As·	:Se·	:Br·	:Kr:

one valence electron, corresponding to the 1 in 1A. Carbon and silicon, in Group 4A, have four valence electrons. Nitrogen and phosphorus, in Group 5A, have five valence electrons; and oxygen and sulfur, in Group 6A, have six. How many valence electrons do the elements of Group 2A and Group 3A have? The noble gases (Group 0) are the only exceptions to the group-number rule: Helium has two valence electrons, and all of the other noble gases have eight. Why does helium not have eight valence electrons? **Figure 15.2** shows several applications of Group 4A elements.

Valence electrons are usually the only electrons used in chemical bonds. Therefore, as a general rule only the valence electrons are shown in **electron dot structures.** Electron dot structures are diagrams that show valence electrons as dots. The inner electrons and the atomic nuclei are included in the letter symbol for the element being represented. **Table 15.1** shows electron dot structures for atoms of some Group A elements. Notice that all of the elements within a given group (with the exception of helium) have the same number of electron dots in their structures. How many electron dots would the Group 7A element iodine have?

Electron Configurations for Cations

You learned in Chapter 14 that noble gases, such as neon and argon, are unreactive in chemical reactions. In 1916, chemist Gilbert Lewis used this fact to explain why atoms form certain kinds of ions and molecules. He called his explanation the **octet rule:** In forming compounds, atoms tend to achieve the electron configuration of a noble gas. An octet is a set of eight. Recall that each noble gas (except helium) has eight electrons in its highest energy level and a general electron configuration of ns^2np^6. Thus the octet rule takes its name from this fact about noble gases. Atoms of the metallic elements tend to lose their valence electrons, leaving a complete octet in the next-lowest energy level. Atoms of some nonmetallic elements tend to gain electrons or to share electrons with another nonmetallic element to achieve a complete octet. Although there are exceptions, the octet rule applies to most atoms in compounds.

An atom's loss of valence electrons produces a cation, or a positively charged ion. The most common cations are those produced by the loss of valence electrons from metal atoms. Most of these atoms have one to three valence electrons, which are easily removed. Sodium, in Group 1A of the periodic table, is typical. Sodium atoms have a total of eleven electrons,

Carbon (in the form of diamond)

Silicon and germanium

Figure 15.2

This polishing bit (top) consists of carbon in the form of diamond. Silicon and germanium are used in computer chips (bottom). All of these elements are from Group 4A. How many valence electrons do they have?

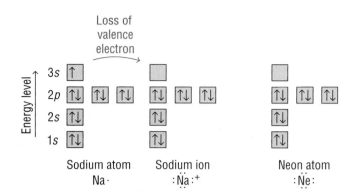

Figure 15.3

A sodium atom can lose an electron to become a positively charged sodium ion. The sodium ion has an electron configuration that is similar to the noble gas neon.

including one valence electron. When forming a compound, a sodium atom loses its one valence electron and is left with an octet (eight electrons) in what is now its highest energy level. Because the number of protons in the sodium nucleus is still eleven, the loss of one unit of negative charge (an electron) produces a sodium ion with a charge of 1+. You can represent the electron loss, or ionization, of the sodium atom by drawing the complete electron configuration of the atom and of the ion formed.

$$\text{Na}\ 1s^2 2s^2 2p^6 3s^1 \xrightarrow{-e^-} \text{Na}^+\ 1s^2 \underbrace{2s^2 2p^6}_{\text{octet}}$$

As you can see in **Figure 15.3,** the electron configuration of the sodium ion is the same as that of the neon atom. How many electrons are in the highest energy levels of Na$^+$ and of Ne?

$$\text{Ne}\ 1s^2 \underbrace{2s^2 2p^6}_{\text{octet}}$$

Both the sodium ion and neon have eight electrons in their valance shells. Using an electron dot structure for the atom can show the ionization more simply.

$$\text{Na·} \xrightarrow[\text{ionization}]{\text{loss of valence electron}} \text{Na}^+\ +\ e^-$$

| Sodium atom (electrically neutral, charge = 0) | Sodium ion (plus sign indicates one unit of positive charge) | electron (minus sign indicates one unit of negative charge) |

Magnesium (atomic number 12) belongs to Group 2A of the periodic table. Therefore it has two valence electrons. A magnesium atom attains the electron configuration of neon by losing both valence electrons. The loss of the valence electrons produces a magnesium cation with twice the positive charge of a sodium ion.

$$\text{·Mg·} \longrightarrow \text{Mg}^{2+}\ +\ 2e^-$$

| Magnesium atom (electrically neutral, charge = 0) | Magnesium ion (2+ indicates two units of positive charge) | (2 in front of e$^-$ indicates two units of negative charge) |

Figure 15.4

Elemental copper's distinctive color is seen in this thirteenth century artifact (left). Basic copper(II) carbonate, containing Cu^{2+} ions, forms the greenish patina on this statue (right).

Copper   Copper(II) carbonate

You have seen that the cations of Group 1A elements always have a charge of 1+. Similarly, the cations of Group 2A elements always have a charge of 2+. This consistency can be explained in terms of the loss of valence electrons by metal atoms: The atoms lose enough electrons to attain the electron configuration of a noble gas. For example, all Group 2A elements have two valence electrons. In losing these two electrons, they form 2+ cations.

For transition metals, the charges of cations may vary. An atom of iron, for example, may lose two or three electrons. In the first case, it forms the iron(II), or ferrous, ion (Fe^{2+}). In the second case, it forms the iron(III), or ferric, ion (Fe^{3+}).

Some ions formed by transition metals do not have noble-gas electron configurations (ns^2np^6) and are therefore exceptions to the octet rule. Silver, with the electron configuration of $1s^22s^22p^63s^23p^63d^{10}4s^24p^64d^{10}5s^1$, is an example. To achieve the structure of krypton, which is the preceding noble gas, a silver atom would have to lose eleven electrons. To acquire the electron configuration of xenon, which is the following noble gas, silver would have to gain seven electrons. Ions with charges of three or greater are uncommon, and these possibilities are extremely unlikely. Thus silver does not achieve a noble-gas configuration. But if it loses its $5s^1$ electron, the configuration that results ($4s^24p^64d^{10}$), with 18 electrons in the outer energy level and all of the orbitals filled, is relatively favorable in compounds. Such a configuration is known as a pseudo noble-gas electron configuration. Silver forms a positive ion (Ag^+) in this way. Other elements that behave similarly to silver are found at the right of the transition metal block. Another example is shown in **Figure 15.5.** Copper(I) (Cu^+), gold(I) (Au^+), cadmium (Cd^{2+}), and mercury(II) (Hg^{2+}) ions all have pseudo noble-gas electron configurations.

Figure 15.5

By losing its lone 4s electron, copper attains a pseudo noble-gas electron configuration. Thus a copper atom can become a copper(I) ion (Cu$^+$).

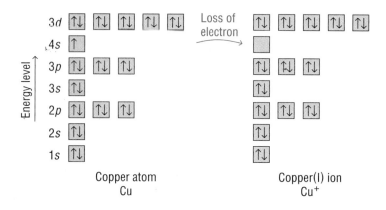

Electron Configurations for Anions

An anion is an atom or a group of atoms with a negative charge. The gain of negatively charged electrons by a neutral atom produces an anion. Because they have relatively full valence shells, atoms of nonmetallic elements attain noble-gas electron configurations more easily by gaining electrons than by losing them. For example, chlorine belongs to Group 7A (the halogen family) and has seven valence electrons. A gain of one electron gives chlorine an octet and converts a chlorine atom into a chloride ion. This ion is an anion with a single negative charge. Chlorine atoms, therefore, need one more valence electron to achieve the electron configuration of the nearest noble gas, argon.

$$\text{Cl} \quad 1s^2 2s^2 2p^6 3s^2 3p^5 \xrightarrow{+e^-} \text{Cl}^- \quad 1s^2 2s^2 2p^6 \underbrace{3s^2 3p^6}_{\text{octet}}$$

The chloride ion has eight electrons, an octet, in its highest energy level, as shown in **Figure 15.6.** The ion has the same electron configuration as the noble gas argon.

$$\text{Ar} \quad 1s^2 2s^2 2p^6 \underbrace{3s^2 3p^6}_{\text{octet}}$$

Electron configuration diagrams can be used to write an equation showing the formation of a chloride ion from a chlorine atom. Compare the electron configuration diagrams in **Figure 15.6** with the corresponding electron dot structures. What is the relationship between the number of electrons in the valence shells in the electron configuration diagrams and the number of dots in the electron dot structures?

$$:\ddot{\text{Cl}}\cdot \ + \ e^- \ \xrightarrow{\substack{\text{gain of one} \\ \text{valence electron}}} \ :\ddot{\text{Cl}}:^-$$

Chlorine atom   Chloride ion (Cl⁻)

The ions that are produced when atoms of chlorine and other halogens gain electrons are called **halide ions.** All halogen ions have seven valence electrons and need to gain only one electron to achieve the electron configuration of a noble gas. Thus all halide ions (F^-, Cl^-, Br^-, and I^-) have a charge of 1−.

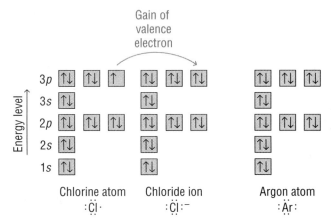

Gain of valence electron

3p   3s   2p   2s   1s

Energy level

Chlorine atom   Chloride ion   Argon atom
$:\ddot{\text{Cl}}\cdot$ $:\ddot{\text{Cl}}:^-$ $:\ddot{\text{Ar}}:$

Figure 15.6

An atom of chlorine can gain an electron to become a negatively charged chloride ion. The chloride ion has an electron configuration similar to the noble gas argon. Both the chloride ion and the argon atom have an octet of electrons.

Table 15.2

Some Common Anions							
1−				2−		3−	
F^-	fluoride	OH^-	hydroxide	O^{2-}	oxide	N^{3-}	nitride
Cl^-	chloride	ClO^-	hypochlorite	S^{2-}	sulfide	P^{3-}	phosphide
Br^-	bromide	NO_3^-	nitrate	SO_4^{2-}	sulfate	PO_4^{3-}	phosphate
I^-	iodide	HCO_3^-	hydrogen carbonate	CO_3^{2-}	carbonate		
		$C_2H_3O_2^-$	acetate				

Look at another example. Oxygen is in Group 6A, and oxygen atoms each have six valence electrons. Oxygen atoms attain the electron configuration of neon by gaining two electrons. The resulting oxide ions have charges of 2− and are written as O^{2-}. **Table 15.2** lists some common anions. How many electrons must a sulfur atom gain to form a sulfide (S^{2-}) ion?

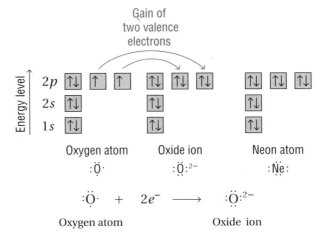

section review 15.1

1. How can the periodic table be used to infer the number of valence electrons in an atom?

2. Why do metals tend to form cations, and nonmetals tend to form anions?

3. How many valence electrons does each atom have?

   a. potassium   c. magnesium

   b. carbon   d. oxygen

4. Write the electron dot structure for each element in question 3.

5. Write electron configurations for the 1+ ion of copper and the 2+ ion of cadmium.

6. How many electrons will each element gain or lose in forming an ion?

   a. calcium (Ca)   c. aluminum (Al)

   b. fluorine (F)   d. oxygen (O)

 Chem ASAP! **Assessment 15.1** Check your understanding of the important ideas and concepts in Section 15.1.

IONIC BONDS

*F*ound naturally in Earth's crust, fluorite is a brittle, glasslike mineral. Although it is not durable enough to be used in fine jewelry, gem collectors often search for pure, colorless forms of fluorite to display as part of their collections. Like other crystalline solids, however, this beautiful crystal is very stable and melts at a very high temperature. **Why are crystalline solids such stable structures?**

objectives
▶ List the characteristics of an ionic bond
▶ Use the characteristics of ionic compounds to explain the electrical conductivity of ionic compounds when melted and when in aqueous solutions

key terms
▶ ionic bonds
▶ coordination number

Formation of Ionic Compounds

Anions and cations have opposite charges. They attract one another by electrostatic forces. The forces of attraction that bind these oppositely charged ions are called **ionic bonds.** Compounds that consist of electrically neutral groups of ions joined by electrostatic forces are called ionic compounds. In any sample of an ionic compound, the total positive charges of the cations must equal the total negative charges of the anions. This same principle of electrical neutrality was used (in Chapter 5) to write formulas of ionic compounds.

Sodium chloride provides a simple example of how ionic bonds are formed. Consider the reaction between a sodium atom and a chlorine atom. Sodium has a single valence electron that it can easily lose. (If the sodium atom loses its valence electron, it achieves the stable electron configuration of neon.) Chlorine has seven valence electrons and can easily gain one. (If the chlorine atom gains a valence electron, it achieves the stable electron configuration of argon.) When sodium and chlorine react to form a compound, the sodium atom gives its one valence electron to a chlorine atom. Thus sodium and chlorine atoms combine in a one-to-one ratio and both ions have stable octets.

$$\text{Na} \cdot \overset{\longrightarrow}{} \cdot \overset{..}{\underset{..}{\text{Cl}}} : \longrightarrow \text{Na}^+ \quad : \overset{..}{\underset{..}{\text{Cl}}} :^-$$

$$\underbrace{1s^2 2s^2 2p^6}_{} \textcircled{$3s^1$} \quad 1s^2 2s^2 2p^6 3s^2 3p^5 \qquad \underbrace{1s^2 2s^2 2p^6}_{\text{octet}} \quad \underbrace{1s^2 2s^2 2p^6 3s^2 3p^6}_{\text{octet}}$$

$$\text{Ne} \qquad\qquad \text{Ar}$$

$$\underbrace{1s^2 2s^2 2p^6}_{\text{octet}} \quad \underbrace{1s^2 2s^2 2p^6 3s^2 3p^6}_{\text{octet}}$$

The chemical formula for sodium chloride (NaCl) represents a formula unit. It indicates the lowest whole-number ratio of cations to anions in any sample of an ionic compound. The formula NaCl, for example, shows that one formula unit of sodium chloride contains one sodium ion and one chloride ion.

Figure 15.7 shows aluminum and bromine reacting to form the compound aluminum bromide. Each aluminum atom has three valence electrons to lose. Each bromine atom has seven valence electrons and readily gains one additional electron. Therefore, when aluminum and bromine react, three bromine atoms combine with each aluminum atom. The formula for aluminum bromide is $AlBr_3$.

Chem ASAP!
Animation 17
Take an atomic level look at the formation of KCl.

Bromine (Br₂)   Aluminum (Al)

Aluminum bromide (AlBr₃)

Figure 15.7
Aluminum metal and the nonmetal bromine combine to form the ionic solid, aluminum bromide. Why do three Br atoms combine with each Al atom?

CHEMath

VISUALIZING MOLECULES

As you have seen by now, molecules can be described in a number of different ways. Each description provides specific information about the molecule.

Chemical Formulas A chemical formula indicates the kinds and numbers of atoms in a molecular compound, but does not give any information about the shape of the molecule. For example, the chemical formula for methane is

$$CH_4$$

Structural Formulas A structural formula indicates which atoms are bonded to each other in a molecule, but does not show the three-dimensional structure of the molecule. One type of structural formula, a Lewis electron-dot structure, use dots to represent each atom's valence electrons. In another type of structural formula, known as bond-line notation, lines are used to represent the covalent bonds in a molecule. Sometimes the bond lines are replaced with wedge-like shapes to provide a simple three-dimensional perspective. Various structural formulas for methane are shown here.

H H:C:H H	H │ H—C—H │ H	H │ C H⟋ ⟍H H
electron-dot structure	bond-line structure	wedge structure

Ball-and-Stick Models A ball-and-stick model uses spheres to represent an atom's nucleus and inner-level electrons, and sticks to represent bonds. A ball-and-stick model shows the three-dimensional shape of a molecule. The ball-and-stick model for methane is shown.

Space-Filling Models A space-filling model of a molecule uses spheres to show both the relative sizes of atoms and the three-dimensional shape of the molecule. The space-filling model does not use sticks to show the bonds. Space-filling models are the most realistic representations of molecules because they are large-scale versions of the actual molecules. The space-filling model for methane is shown.

Examples

Several examples of the various molecular representations used throughout this text book are shown below.

water (H_2O)	:O:H H electron-dot structure	O H⟋ ⟍H bond-line structure	space-filling model

butane (C_4H_{10})	H H H H │ │ │ │ H—C—C—C—C—H │ │ │ │ H H H H bond-line structure	H H H H \\⟋ \\⟋ C C H⟍ ⟋ ⟍ ⟋ ⟍H C C ⟋\\ ⟋\\ H H H H wedge-bond structure	space-filling model

Sample Problem 15-1

Use electron dot structures to predict the formulas of the ionic compounds formed from these elements.
   a. potassium and oxygen
   b. magnesium and nitrogen

1. *ANALYZE Plan a problem-solving strategy.*
   The correct electron dot structure of each atom in the compound must be written. Atoms of metals lose their valence electrons when forming an ionic compound. Atoms of non-metals gain electrons. Enough atoms of each element must be used in the formula so that electrons lost equals electrons gained.

2. *SOLVE Apply the problem-solving strategy.*
   a. Start with the atoms.

$$\text{K·} \quad \text{and} \quad \text{·}\overset{..}{\underset{.}{\text{O}}}\text{:}$$

   In order to have a completely filled valence shell, oxygen requires the addition of two electrons. These electrons come from two potassium atoms, each of which loses one electron.

$$\begin{array}{c} \text{K·} \\ \text{K·} \end{array} + \text{·}\overset{..}{\underset{..}{\text{O}}}\text{:} \longrightarrow \begin{array}{c} \text{K}^+ \\ \text{K}^+ \end{array} \text{:}\overset{..}{\underset{..}{\text{O}}}\text{:}^{2-}$$

   Electrons lost now equals electrons gained. The formula of the compound formed (potassium oxide) is K_2O.

   b. Start with the atoms.

$$\overset{.}{\underset{.}{\text{Mg}}} \quad \text{and} \quad \text{·}\overset{.}{\underset{.}{\text{N}}}\text{:}$$

   Each nitrogen needs three electrons to have an octet, but each magnesium atom can lose only two electrons. Thus three magnesium atoms are needed for every two nitrogen atoms.

$$\begin{array}{c} \overset{.}{\underset{.}{\text{Mg}}} \\ \overset{.}{\underset{.}{\text{Mg}}} \\ \overset{.}{\underset{.}{\text{Mg}}} \end{array} + \begin{array}{c} \text{·}\overset{.}{\underset{.}{\text{N}}}\text{:} \\ \\ \text{·}\overset{.}{\underset{.}{\text{N}}}\text{:} \end{array} \longrightarrow \begin{array}{c} \text{Mg}^{2+} \\ \text{Mg}^{2+} \\ \text{Mg}^{2+} \end{array} \begin{array}{c} \text{:}\overset{..}{\underset{..}{\text{N}}}\text{:}^{3-} \\ \\ \text{:}\overset{..}{\underset{..}{\text{N}}}\text{:}^{3-} \end{array}$$

   The formula of the compound formed (magnesium nitride) is Mg_3N_2.

3. *EVALUATE Do the results make sense?*
   In each example, the number of electrons gained by the nonmetal balances the number of electrons lost by the metal. In addition, division by an integer cannot reduce the formulas of the compounds further. The formulas K_2O and Mg_3N_2 are correct.

Practice Problems

7. Use electron dot structures to determine chemical formulas of the ionic compounds formed when the following elements combine.
   a. potassium and iodine
   b. aluminum and oxygen
8. Name the compounds formed in Practice Problem 7.

Chem ASAP!

Problem-Solving 7
Solve Problem 7 with the help of an interactive guided tutorial.

Chem ASAP!

Simulation 15
Simulate the formation of ionic compounds at the atomic level.

Properties of Ionic Compounds

At room temperature, most ionic compounds are crystalline solids. **Figure 15.8** shows the striking beauty of the crystals of some ionic compounds. The component ions in such crystals are arranged in repeating three-dimensional patterns. The composition of a crystal of sodium chloride is typical. In solid NaCl, each sodium ion is surrounded by six chloride ions, and each chloride ion is surrounded by six sodium ions. In this arrangement, each ion is attracted strongly to each of its neighbors and repulsions are minimized. The large attractive forces result in a very stable structure. This is reflected in the fact that NaCl and ionic compounds in general have high melting temperatures.

Figure 15.8

The beauty of crystalline solids, such as these, comes from the orderly arrangement of their component ions.

Aragonite ($CaCO_3$)

Barite ($BaSO_4$) and calcite ($CaCO_3$)

Beryl ($BeAl_2(SiO_3)_6$)

Franklinite ((Zn,Mn^{2+},Fe^{2+})(Fe^{3+},Mn^{3+})$_2 O_4$)

Pyrite (FeS_2)

Hematite (Fe_2O_3)

Rutile (TiO_2)

Cinnabar (HgS)

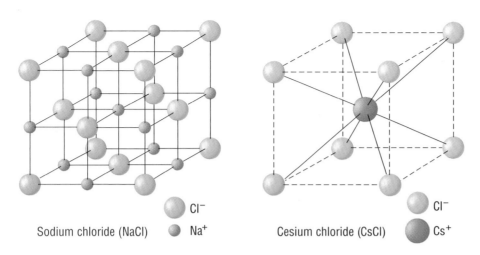

Figure 15.9
Sodium chloride and cesium chloride form clear, colorless cubic crystals. The unit cells of these cubic compounds differ. The unit cell of sodium chloride is face-centered cubic, but that of cesium chloride is simple cubic. The arrangement of the ions in the crystal structure are shown for sodium chloride (left) and cesium chloride (right). How many chloride ions surround each sodium ion? How many chloride ions surround each cesium ion?

The **coordination number** of an ion is the number of ions of opposite charge that surround the ion in a crystal. **Figure 15.9** shows the three-dimensional arrangement of ions in NaCl. Because each Na^+ ion is surrounded by six Cl^- ions, Na^+ has a coordination number of 6. Each Cl^- ion is surrounded by six Na^+ ions and also has a coordination number of 6.

Cesium chloride (CsCl) has a formula unit that is similar to that of NaCl. Both compounds have cubic crystals, but their internal crystal structures are different. Each Cs^+ ion is surrounded by eight Cl^- ions, and each Cl^- ion is surrounded by eight Cs^+ ions. The anion and cation in cesium chloride each have a coordination number of 8.

The crystalline form of titanium dioxide (TiO_2) is called rutile. In this compound, the coordination number for the cation (Ti^{4+}) is 6. Each Ti^{4+} ion is surrounded by six O^{2-} ions. The coordination number of the anion (O^{2-}) is 3. Each O^{2-} ion is surrounded by three Ti^{4+} ions. **Figure 15.10** shows a specimen of a rutile crystal along with an illustration showing how the ions are arranged in the crystal.

Rutile (TiO_2)

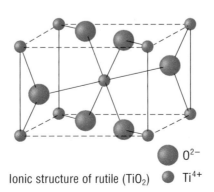

Ionic structure of rutile (TiO_2)

Figure 15.10
The shape of a crystal depends on its unit cell structure. Crystals of the mineral rutile (titanium dioxide) are tetragonal. The ionic structure of rutile is also shown.

Ionic Bonding and Ionic Compounds **423**

Figure 15.11

When sodium chloride melts, the sodium and chloride ions are free to move throughout the molten salt. If a voltage is applied, positive sodium ions move to the negative electrode (the cathode). At the same time, negative chloride ions move to the positive electrode (the anode).

The internal structures of crystals are determined by a technique called x-ray diffraction crystallography. X-rays that pass through a crystal are recorded on film. The pattern on the exposed film shows how ions in the crystal deflect the x-rays. The pattern is used to calculate the positions of ions in the crystal and to define the structure of the crystal.

When melted, ionic compounds can conduct an electric current. When sodium chloride is melted (melting point about 800 °C), the orderly crystal structure breaks down, as shown in **Figure 15.11.** If a voltage is applied across this molten mass, cations migrate freely to one electrode and anions migrate to the other. This ion movement produces a flow of electricity between the electrodes through an external wire. For a similar reason, ionic compounds also conduct electricity if they are dissolved in water. When dissolved, the ions are free to move about in the aqueous solution.

Figure 15.12

This solar facility uses molten NaCl to store thermal energy. Rather than using the compound for its ability to conduct electricity, the facility uses the molten NaCl for its ability to absorb and hold a large quantity of heat.

MINI LAB

Solutions Containing Ions

PURPOSE

To show that ions in solution conduct an electric current.

MATERIALS

- 3 D-cell batteries
- masking tape
- 2 30-cm lengths of bell wire with ends scraped bare
- clear plastic cup
- distilled water
- tap water
- vinegar • sucrose
- sodium chloride
- baking soda
- conductivity probe (optional)

PROCEDURE

 Probe version available in the Probeware Lab Manual.

1. Tape the batteries together so the positive end of one touches the negative end of another. Tape the bare end of one wire to the positive terminal of the battery assembly and the bare end of the other wire to the negative terminal.

2. Half fill the cup with distilled water. Hold the bare ends of the wires close together in the water. Look for the production of bubbles. They are a sign that the solution conducts electricity.

3. Repeat Step 2 with tap water, vinegar, and concentrated solutions of sucrose, sodium chloride, and baking soda (sodium hydrogen carbonate).

ANALYSIS AND CONCLUSIONS

1. Which solutions produced bubbles of gas? Explain.

2. Which samples did not produce bubbles of gas? Explain.

3. Would you expect the same results if you used only one battery? If you used six batteries? Explain your answer.

---

section review 15.2

9. What are the characteristics of ionic bonds?

10. Explain why ionic compounds can conduct electricity when melted and when in aqueous solutions.

11. Write the correct chemical formula (the formula unit) for the compounds formed from each pair of ions.
   a. K^+, S^{2-}
   c. Na^+, SO_4^{2-}
   b. Ca^{2+}, O^{2-}
   d. Al^{3+}, PO_4^{3-}

12. Write formulas for each compound.
   a. potassium nitrate
   b. barium chloride
   c. magnesium sulfate
   d. lithium oxide
   e. ammonium carbonate
   f. calcium phosphate

13. Which pairs of elements are likely to form ionic compounds?
   a. chlorine and bromine
   b. potassium and helium
   c. lithium and chlorine
   d. iodine and sodium

14. What determines the crystal structure of an ionic compound?

 portfolio project

Research x-ray diffraction crystallography. How are the samples prepared? How are the x-rays generated and detected? If possible, visit a site where x-ray crystal diffraction studies are done.

Chem ASAP! Assessment 15.2 Check your understanding of the important ideas and concepts in Section 15.2.

SMALL-SCALE LAB

ANALYSIS OF ANIONS AND CATIONS

SAFETY

Wear safety glasses and follow the standard safety procedures outlined on page 18.

PURPOSE

To develop tests for various ions and use the tests to analyze unknown substances.

MATERIALS

- pencil
- ruler
- cotton swab
- medicine droppers
- chemicals shown in Figures A and B
- paper
- reaction surface
- pipet

PROCEDURE

On one sheet of paper, draw grids similar to Figure A and Figure B. Draw similar grids on a second sheet of paper. Make each square 2 cm on each side. Place a reaction surface over the grids on one of the sheets of paper and add one drop of each solution or one piece of each solid as shown in Figures A and B. Stir each solution by blowing air through an empty pipet. Use the grids on the second sheet of paper as a data table to record your observations for each solution. Absorb the NH_4Cl and $NaOH$ mixture onto a cotton swab and carefully determine its odor.

	Na_2SO_4 (SO_4^{2-})	HNO_3 (NO_3^-)	Na_3PO_4 (PO_4^{3-})
$AgNO_3$	X	X	X
HCl plus 1 piece of Fe(s)	X	X	X
$Pb(NO_3)_2$	X	X	X

Figure A
Anion Analysis

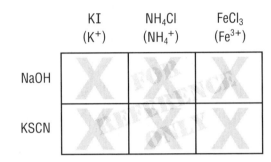

	KI (K^+)	NH_4Cl (NH_4^+)	$FeCl_3$ (Fe^{3+})
NaOH	X	X	X
KSCN	X	X	X

Figure B
Cation Analysis

ANALYSIS

Using your experimental data, record the answers to the following questions below your data table.

1. Carefully examine the reaction of Fe(s) and HCl in the presence of HNO_3. What is unique about this reaction? How can you use it to identify nitrate ion?

2. Which solutions from Figure A are the best for identifying each anion? Explain.

3. Which solutions from Figure B are the best for identifying each cation? Explain.

4. Can your experiments conclusively identify potassium ions? Explain.

YOU'RE THE CHEMIST

The following small-scale activities allow you to develop your own procedures and analyze the results.

1. **Design It!** Obtain a set of unknown anion solutions from your teacher and design and carry out a series of tests that will identify each anion.

2. **Design It!** Obtain a set of unknown cation solutions from your teacher and design and carry out a series of tests that will identify each cation.

3. **Design It!** Obtain a set of unknown solid ionic compounds from your teacher and design and carry out a series of tests that will identify each cation and anion present.

4. **Analyze It!** Obtain an unknown fertilizer sample from your teacher and analyze it for cations and anions.

BONDING IN METALS

The melting point of gallium is only 30°C, which is very low for a metal. Because normal human body temperature is 37°C, gallium melts readily if you hold it in your hand. In both its liquid and solid forms, this metal is a strong con-ductor of electricity and is used in both transistors and solar cells. **What property makes metals good electrical conductors?**

objectives
▶ Use the theory of metallic bonds to explain the physical properties of metals
▶ Describe the arrangements of atoms in some common metallic crystal structures
key term
▶ metallic bonds

Metallic Bonds and Metallic Properties

Metals are made up of closely packed cations rather than neutral atoms. The cations are surrounded by mobile valence electrons, as shown in **Figure 15.13,** which can drift freely from one part of the metal to another. **Metallic bonds** consist of the attraction of the free-floating valence elec-trons for the positively charged metal ions. These bonds are the forces of attraction that hold metals together.

This model of metallic bonding explains many physical properties of metals. For example, metals are good conductors of electrical current because electrons can flow freely in them. As electrons enter one end of a bar of metal, an equal number leave the other end. Metals are ductile—that is, they can be drawn into wires, as shown in **Figure 15.14.** Is copper ductile? How do you know? Metals are also malleable, which means that they can be hammered or forced into shapes. Both the ductility and malleability of met-als can be explained in terms of the mobility of valence electrons. A sea of drifting valence electrons insulates the metal cations from one another. When a metal is subjected to pressure, the metal cations easily slide past one another like ball bearings immersed in oil. In contrast, if an ionic crystal is struck with a hammer, the blow tends to push ions of like charge into con-tact. They repel, and the crystal shatters.

Figure 15.13
The valence electrons of metal atoms pool to form a sea of electrons. The metal is held together by the attractions between these electrons and the metal cations.

Chem ASAP!
Animation 18

See how metallic bonding explains some physical properties of metals.

Figure 15.14
A metal rod can be forced through a narrow opening in a die to pro-duce wire (left). As this occurs, the metal changes shape but remains in one piece (center). If an ionic crystal were forced through the die it would shatter (right). Why is this so?

Figure 15.15
These oranges illustrate a hexagonal close-packed arrangement.

Crystalline Structure of Metals

Often brightly colored and transparent, the shiny crystals of many ionic compounds are among the most beautiful substances known. You may be surprised to learn, however, that metals are also crystalline. In fact, metals that contain just one kind of atom are among the simplest forms of all crystalline solids.

Metal atoms are arranged in very compact and orderly patterns, like tennis balls packed in a box. For spheres of identical size, such as metal atoms, there are several arrangements that give the closest packing possible. **Figure 15.16** shows three such arrangements: body-centered cubic, face-centered cubic, and hexagonal close-packed arrangements. Which of these three arrangements are the least closely packed?

In a body-centered cubic structure, every atom (except those on the surface) has eight neighbors. The metallic elements sodium, potassium, iron, chromium, and tungsten crystallize in a body-centered cubic pattern. In a face-centered cubic arrangement, every atom has twelve neighbors. Among the metals that form a face-centered cubic lattice are copper, silver, gold, aluminum, and lead. In a hexagonal close-packed arrangement, every atom also has twelve neighbors. Because of its hexagonal shape, however, the pattern is different from the face-centered cubic arrangement. Metals that have the hexagonal close-packed crystal structure include magnesium, zinc, and cadmium. These arrangements are not limited strictly to metal atoms however. The next time you visit a grocery store, take a look at how the apples or oranges are stacked. More than likely, they will have a close-packed arrangement, as shown in **Figure 15.15.** What is the purpose of stacking fruit in a hexagonal close-packed arrangement?

Chromium

Body-centered cubic

Gold

Face-centered cubic

Zinc

Hexagonal close-packed

Figure 15.16
The atoms of chromium (top) have a body-centered cubic arrangement. The atoms of gold (center) have a face-centered cubic arrangement. The atoms of zinc (bottom) have a hexagonal close-packed arrangement.

Alloys

Although every day you use metallic items, such as spoons, very few of these objects are pure metals. Instead, most metals you encounter are alloys. Alloys are mixtures composed of two or more elements, at least one of which is a metal. Alloys are generally prepared by melting a mixture of the ingredients and then cooling the mixture. There are many different alloys. Brass, for example, is an alloy of copper and zinc.

Alloys are important because their properties are often superior to those of their component elements. Sterling silver (92.5% silver and 7.5% copper) is harder and more durable than pure silver but still soft enough to be made into jewelry and tableware. Bronze is an alloy generally containing seven parts of copper to one part of tin. Bronze is harder than copper and more easily cast. Nonferrous (noniron) alloys, such as bronze, copper-nickel, and aluminum alloys, are commonly used in coinage. **Figure 15.17** shows examples of alloys.

The most important alloys today are steels. The principal elements in most steel, in addition to iron and carbon, are boron, chromium, manganese, molybdenum, nickel, tungsten, and vanadium. Steels have a wide range of useful properties, such as corrosion resistance, ductility, hardness, and toughness. **Table 15.3** lists the composition of some common alloys.

Alloys can form from their component atoms in different ways. If the atoms of the components in an alloy are about the same size, they can replace each other in the crystal. This type of alloy is called a substitutional alloy. If the atomic sizes are quite different, the smaller atoms can fit into the interstices (spaces) between the larger atoms. Such an alloy is called an interstitial alloy. In the various types of steel, for example, carbon atoms occupy the spaces between the iron atoms. Thus, steels are interstitial alloys.

Table 15.3

Composition of Some Common Alloys	
Name	**Composition (by mass)**
Sterling silver	Ag 92.5% Cu 7.5%
Coinage silver	Ag 90% Cu 10%
Cast iron	Fe 96% C 4%
Stainless steel	Fe 80.6% Cr 18.0% C 0.4% Ni 1.0%
Spring steel	Fe 98.6% Cr 1.0% C 0.4%
Surgical steel	Fe 67% Cr 18% Ni 12% Mo 3%

Figure 15.17

Alloys have many different uses. Chrome-moly, an alloy of steel, is commonly used for bicycle frames. Amalgams are alloys of mercury. Dental amalgam, an alloy of mercury, silver, and zinc, expands as it hardens to fill the cavity in a tooth.

section review 15.3

15. Use metallic bonding theory to explain the physical properties of metals.

16. Describe the arrangement of atoms in metallic crystal structures.

17. In your own words define metallic bond.

18. Describe what is meant by ductile and malleable.

19. Why is it possible to bend metals but not ionic crystals?

 Chem ASAP! Assessment 15.3 Check your understanding of the important ideas and concepts in Section 15.3

WHEN WATER IS HARD TO DEAL WITH

Have you ever found it difficult to get soap to lather? If so, you may have been trying to wash in hard water. Hard water is water that contains a significant concentration of calcium ions (Ca^{2+}) and often ions of magnesium (Mg^{2+}) and iron (Fe^{2+}) as well. These ions usually get into the water while it is underground, when dissolved CO_2 reacts with minerals such as limestone ($CaCO_3$).

The presence of these ions in water gives the water a number of annoying properties. In addition to deactivating soap, these ions can be deposited as a rock-hard "scale" in industrial boilers, hot-water heaters, pipes, and tea kettles. The photo shows an electrode from a hot-water heater that has been corroded by hard water. As a result, families and businesses spend large sums of money every year to replace clogged plumbing and water heaters and to buy extra soap.

To prevent these problems, it is possible to remove the guilty cations from the water. This is done with a home water softener. It works by replacing the calcium, magnesium, and iron ions with sodium ions, which do not give water the hardness property. Water entering a home passes through the water softener before it reaches faucets, the washing machine, or the water heater.

Inside the water softener is a matrix made of a material with negatively charged sites that attract positive cations. The matrix material may be the naturally occurring mineral zeolite (aluminum silicate) or beads of synthetic polystyrene resin. Before a water softener is put into use, the matrix is bathed with a brine solution (sodium chloride). Sodium ions from the brine are attracted and bond to the negatively charged sites on the matrix material.

> When hard water enters the water softener, magnesium, calcium, and iron ions in the hard water exchange places with sodium ions on the matrix material.

When hard water enters the water softener, calcium, magnesium, and iron ions in the hard water exchange places with sodium ions on the matrix material. They can displace sodium ions because they are more strongly attracted than the sodium ions to the negative charges of the matrix material. As hard-water cations leave the water moving through the water softener, sodium cations enter the water. By the time the water leaves the water softener, it has lost nearly all its hard-water cations.

The sodium ions in softened water do not cause hardness, but they do have problems of their own. Drinking water high in sodium is linked to certain forms of high blood pressure. For this reason, health experts recommend that people with home water softeners use some source of unsoftened water for drinking.

The process of ion exchange in the water softener can continue for weeks or months because the matrix material has a huge surface area and many negatively charged sites. Eventually, however, all the sites become filled with hard-water cations and the water softener must be recharged. This is done by pouring a strong sodium chloride solution through the matrix to displace the calcium, magnesium, and iron cations.

CHEMISTRY IN CAREERS

☆ ☆

WASTEWATER ENGINEER
Interested in monitoring water purity and providing safe drinking water?
See page 875.

CHEMIST NEEDED

TAKE IT TO THE NET

Find out more about career opportunities:
www.phschool.com

CHEMICAL SPECIALIST
Local food service distributor see
responsible self-motivated indiv

Take It to the NET
For interactive study and
review, go to www.phschool.com

KEY TERMS

- coordination number *p. 423*
- electron dot structure *p. 414*
- halide ion *p. 417*
- ionic bond *p. 419*
- metallic bond *p. 427*
- octet rule *p. 414*
- valence electron *p. 413*

CONCEPT SUMMARY

15.1 Electron Configuration in Ionic Bonding

- Atoms in compounds are held together by chemical bonds. Chemical bonds result from the sharing or transfer of valence electrons between pairs of atoms.
- Bonded atoms attain the stable electron configuration of a noble gas. The noble gases themselves exist as isolated atoms because that is their most stable condition.
- For the representative elements, the number of valence electrons is equal to the element's group number in the periodic table.
- The transfer of one or more valence electrons between atoms produces positively and negatively charged ions, or cations and anions, respectively.

15.2 Ionic Bonds

- The attraction between an anion and a cation is an ionic bond. A substance with ionic bonds is an ionic compound.
- Nearly all ionic compounds are crystalline solids at room temperature. They generally have high melting points. The total positive charge in an ionic compound is balanced by the total negative charge; thus ionic compounds are electrically neutral.

- Ionic solids consist of positive and negative ions packed in an orderly arrangement. The coordination number of an ion indicates the number of ions of opposite charge that surround the ion in a crystal.
- When melted or in aqueous solution, ionic compounds can conduct electricity because the ions can move freely when a voltage is applied.

15.3 Bonding in Metals

- Metals are like ionic compounds in some ways. They consist of positive metal ions packed together and surrounded by a sea of valence electrons. This arrangement constitutes the metallic bond.
- The valence electrons in metals are mobile and can travel from one end of a piece of metal to the other. This electron mobility accounts for the excellent electrical conductivity of metals and helps explain why metals are malleable and ductile.
- Metals are among the simplest crystalline solids. The metal atoms are commonly packed in a body-centered cubic, a face-centered cubic, or a hexagonal close-packed arrangement.

CHAPTER CONCEPT MAP

Use these terms to construct a concept map that organizes the major ideas of this chapter.

 Chem ASAP! Concept Map 15
Create your Concept Map using the computer.

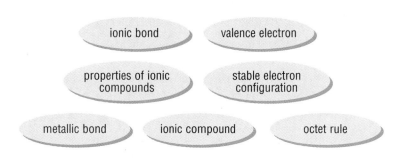

CONCEPT PRACTICE

20. Define valence electrons. *15.1*

21. Name the first four halogens. What group are they in, and how many valence electrons does each have? *15.1*

22. How many electrons does each atom have? What group is each in? *15.1*
 a. nitrogen   **c.** phosphorus
 b. lithium   **d.** barium

23. Write electron dot structures for each of the following elements. *15.1*
 a. Cl   **b.** S   **c.** Al   **d.** Li

24. The atoms of the noble gas elements are stable. Explain. *15.1*

25. How many electrons must each atom lose to attain a noble-gas electron configuration? *15.1*
 a. Ca   **b.** Al   **c.** Li   **d.** Ba

26. Write the formula for the ion formed when each of the following elements loses its valence electrons. *15.1*
 a. aluminum   **c.** barium   **e.** calcium
 b. lithium   **d.** potassium   **f.** strontium

27. Write electron configurations for the tripositive ions (3+) of these elements. *15.1*
 a. chromium   **b.** manganese   **c.** iron

28. Why do nonmetals tend to form anions when they react to form compounds? *15.1*

29. What is the formula of the ion formed when the following elements gain or lose valence electrons and attain noble-gas configurations? *15.1*
 a. sulfur   **c.** fluorine
 b. sodium   **d.** phosphorus

30. How many electrons must be gained by each of the following atoms to achieve a stable electron configuration? *15.1*
 a. N   **b.** S   **c.** Cl   **d.** P

31. Write the formula for the ion formed when each element gains electrons and attains a noble-gas configuration. *15.1*
 a. Br   **b.** H   **c.** As   **d.** Se

32. Write electron configurations for the following and comment on the result. *15.1*
 a. N^{3-} **b.** O^{2-} **c.** F^- **d.** Ne

33. Explain why ionic compounds are electrically neutral. *15.2*

34. Which of the following pairs of elements will not form ionic compounds? *15.2*
 a. sulfur and oxygen
 b. sodium and calcium
 c. sodium and sulfur
 d. oxygen and chlorine

35. Write the formula for the ions in the following compounds. *15.2*
 a. KCl   **b.** $BaSO_4$ **c.** $MgBr_2$ **d.** Li_2CO_3

36. Can you predict the coordination number of an ion from the formula of an ionic compound? Explain. *15.2*

37. Most ionic substances are brittle. Why? *15.2*

38. Explain why molten $MgCl_2$ does conduct an electric current although crystalline $MgCl_2$ does not. *15.2*

39. Explain briefly why metals are good conductors of electricity. *15.3*

40. Name the three crystal arrangements of closely packed metal atoms. Give an example of a metal that crystallizes in each arrangement. *15.3*

41. Name some alloys that you have used or seen today. *15.3*

42. Why aren't the properties of all steels identical? Explain. *15.3*

43. The properties of all samples of brass are not identical. Explain. *15.3*

CONCEPT MASTERY

44. Which of the following substances are most likely not ionic?
 a. H_2O **c.** CO_2 **e.** NH_3
 b. Na_2O **d.** CaS   **f.** SO_2

45. Construct a table that shows the relationship among the group number, valence electrons lost or gained, and the formula of the cation or anion produced for the following metallic and nonmetallic elements: Na, Ca, Al, N, S, Br.

46. Write electron dot formulas for the following atoms.
 a. C   **b.** Be   **c.** O   **d.** F   **e.** Na   **f.** P

47. Show the relationship between the electron dot structure of an element and the location of the element in the periodic table.

48. In terms of electrons, why does a cation have a positive charge?

49. Why does an anion have a negative charge?

50. Metallic cobalt crystallizes in a hexagonal close-packed structure. How many neighbors will a cobalt atom have?

51. Write electron configurations for the dipositive ions (2+) of these elements.
a. Fe **b.** Co **c.** Ni

52. Write electron configurations for these atoms and ions, and comment on the result.
a. Ar **b.** Cl^- **c.** S^{2-} **d.** P^{3-}

53. Explain how hexagonal close-packed, face-centered cubic, and body-centered cubic unit cells are different from one another.

54. The spheres below represent the relative diameters of atoms or ions. Rearrange the sequences in **a.** and **b.** so the relative sizes of the particles correspond to the increasing size of the particles in the illustration.

a. oxygen atom, oxide ion, sulfur atom, sulfide ion
b. sodium atom, sodium ion, potassium atom, potassium ion

55. Write complete electron configurations for the following atoms and ions. For each group, comment on the results.
a. Ar, K^+, Ca^{2+} **b.** Ne, Na^+, Mg^{2+}, Al^{3+}

CRITICAL THINKING

56. Choose the term that best completes the second relationship.

a. cow : horse   ionic bond : _____
(1) anion   (3) chemical bond
(2) cation   (4) covalent bond

b. Cl : Cl^- Mg : _____
(1) Mg^{2+} (3) Al^{3+}
(2) Mg^{2-} (4) Mn

c. pipe : water   metal : _____
(1) ions   (3) electricity
(2) ionic bond   (4) conductor

57. Compare the physical and chemical characteristics of metals and ionic compounds.

CUMULATIVE REVIEW

58. Hydrogen and oxygen react to produce water according to this equation.

$$2H_2 + O_2 \longrightarrow 2H_2O$$

How many liters of hydrogen at STP are needed to produce 0.50 mol H_2O?

59. Distinguish among gases, liquids, and solids with respect to shape, volume, relative density, and motion of particles.

60. What is the volume, in liters, occupied by 8.0 g of oxygen gas at STP?

61. If you raise the temperature of a gas, what actually happens to the gas particles?

62. A gas occupies 750 cm^3 at 27 °C and 1.6 kPa. Find its volume at STP.

63. Explain each of these observations on the basis of the kinetic theory and the forces of attraction that exist between the particles in matter.
a. Water evaporates faster at 40 °C than at 20 °C.
b. A burn from steam at 100 °C is worse than a burn from water at 100 °C.
c. A cap pops off a bottle of root beer that has been kept in the trunk of a car on a hot day.
d. Diethyl ether ($C_4H_{10}O$) has a vapor pressure of 58.9 kPa at 20 °C, whereas the vapor pressure of water at 20 °C is only 2.3 kPa.
e. A melting ice cube cools a glass of tea.
f. Foods are dehydrated (water is removed) by using low pressures rather than high heat.

64. Use the gas laws and kinetic theory to complete these statements. Unless otherwise stated, assume a constant amount of gas.
a. As the volume of a gas increases at constant temperature, its pressure _____ .
b. As the temperature of a gas increases and its pressure decreases, its volume _____ .
c. At constant pressure, a decrease in the volume of a gas is caused by a(n) _____ in its temperature.
d. An increase in the volume and pressure of a gas is caused by a(n) _____ in its temperature.
e. At constant volume, a decrease in the temperature of a gas causes the pressure to _____ .
f. If the volume of a gas is increased while its temperature is increased, the pressure will _____ .

65. A gas mixture contains 1.50 g O_2 and 1.50 g N_2. If the partial pressure of O_2 is 63.3 kPa, what is the total pressure of the mixture?

66. At what temperature will the average kinetic energy of a nitrogen molecule be twice the average kinetic energy of a nitrogen molecule at 25 °C?

67. The reaction of zinc with an acid produces hydrogen gas. The table below lists the amount of hydrogen gas produced at STP when various amounts of zinc are reacted with an excess of hydrochloric acid.

Mass of Zn (g)	Moles of Zn	Volume of H_2 (L)
0.960		0.329
2.44		0.835
4.18		1.43
5.75		1.96

a. Calculate the moles of zinc used.
b. Make a graph of the volume of hydrogen produced (y-axis) versus the moles of zinc reacting (x-axis).
c. Determine the slope of the line. Include the units of the slope.
d. Based on the value of the slope, what can you determine about the moles of hydrogen produced per mole of zinc that reacts?

CONCEPT CHALLENGE

68. The chemically similar alkali metal chlorides NaCl and CsCl have different crystal structures, whereas the chemically different NaCl and MnS have the same crystal structures. Why?

69. Silver crystallizes in a face-centered cubic unit cell. A silver atom is at the edge of each lattice point. The length of the edge of the unit cell is 0.4086 nm. What is the atomic radius of silver?

70. Classify each atom in the following list. Will each atom form a cation or an anion? Or is it chemically unreactive? For the atoms that do form ions during a chemical reaction, write the number of electrons the atom will gain or lose.
a. lithium
b. sodium
c. neon
d. magnesium
e. chlorine

71. Write the IUPAC name of the cation in each transition metal compound.
a. $FeCl_2$
b. Fe_2O_3
c. CuO
d. Cu_2O
e. $CoCl_3$

72. List the elements that are used to make each alloy.
a. brass
b. sterling silver
c. bronze
d. stainless steel
e. surgical steel
f. spring steel

Select the choice that best answers each question or completes each statement.

1. Which of these is not an ionic compound?
   a. KF
   c. SiO_2
   b. Na_2SO_4
   d. Na_2O

2. Which statements are correct when barium and oxygen react to form an ionic compound?
   I. Barium atoms lose 2 electrons and form a cation.
   II. Oxygen atoms form oxide anions (O^{2-}).
   III. In the compound the ions are present in a one-to-one ratio.
   a. I and II only
   b. II and III only
   c. I and III only
   d. I, II, and III

3. How many valence electrons does arsenic have?
   a. 5   **b.** 4   **c.** 3   **d.** 2

4. For which compound name is the *incorrect* formula given?
   a. magnesium iodide, MgI_2
   b. potassium selenide, K_2Se
   c. calcium oxide, Ca_2O_2
   d. aluminum sulfide, Al_2S_3

5. Which electron configuration represents a nitride ion?
   a. $1s^2\,2s^2\,3s^2\,4s^2$
   c. $1s^2\,2s^2\,2p^6$
   b. $1s^2\,2s^2\,2p^3$
   d. $1s^2$

6. When a bromine atom gains an electron
   a. a bromide ion is formed.
   b. the ion formed has a $1-$ charge.
   c. the ion formed is an anion.
   d. all the above are correct.

The lettered choices below refer to questions 7–10. A lettered choice may be used once, more than once, or not at all.

   (A) gains two electron
   (B) loses two electrons
   (C) gains three electrons
   (D) loses one electron
   (E) gains one electron

Which choice describes what happens as each of the following elements forms its ion?

7. iodine

8. magnesium

9. cesium

10. phosphorus

Use the description and the graph to answer questions 11–13.

Lattice energy is the energy required to change one mole of a crystalline, ionic solid to gaseous ions. The graph below shows the lattice energy for ionic compounds formed between selected alkali metals and halogens.

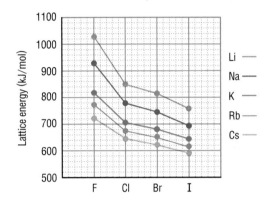

11. For a given alkali metal, what is the trend in lattice energy as the atomic radius of the halogens increases?

12. For a given halogen, what is the trend in lattice energy as the atomic radius of the alkali metals increases?

13. Complete this sentence. "As the atomic radius of either the halogen or the alkali metal increases, the lattice energy _____ ."

Use the atomic windows to answer question 14.

14. How atoms and ions are arranged in crystals is not just dependent on size. The spheres in each window are identical in size. The windows have exactly the same area. In which window are the spheres more closely packed? Explain your reasoning.

a.   **b.**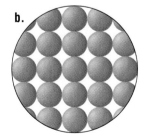

COVALENT BONDING

FEATURES

Stay current with **SCIENCE NEWS**
Find out more about covalent bonding:
www.phschool.com

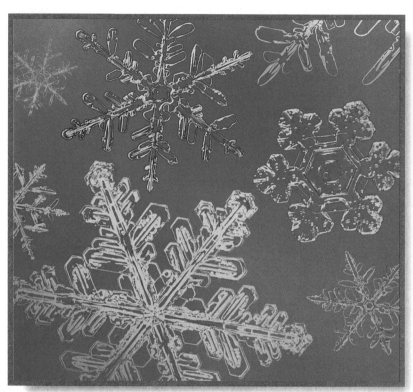

Individual snowflakes can contain 100 snow crystals.

DISCOVER IT! SHAPES OF MOLECULES

You need nine spherical balloons and several short pieces of string.

1. Inflate the nine balloons to approximately the same size and tie them off.

2. Use short pieces of string to tie the ends of two balloons together to form a cluster. Tie the ends of three other balloons together to form a second cluster, and then tie the remaining four balloons to form a third cluster.

3. Arrange the balloons in each cluster so they are as far away from one another as possible. (Note: The balloons will probably be positioned this way already.)

4. Sketch the three-dimensional shape of each balloon cluster.

What are some geometric terms that you can use to describe the shapes? Some of the terms used by chemists to describe these shapes are trigonal planar, tetrahedral, and linear. Can you match each term with one of the shapes you made? After reading about molecular shapes later in this chapter, return to this activity and review your answers.

THE NATURE OF COVALENT BONDING

objectives

▶ Use electron dot structures to show the formation of single, double, and triple covalent bonds

▶ Describe and give examples of coordinate covalent bonding, resonance structures, and exceptions to the octet rule

key terms

▶ single covalent bond
▶ structural formulas
▶ unshared pairs
▶ double covalent bonds
▶ triple covalent bonds
▶ coordinate covalent bond
▶ bond dissociation energy
▶ resonance structures
▶ diamagnetic
▶ paramagnetic

You know that without oxygen to breathe, you could not live. But did you know that oxygen plays another important role in your life? High in the atmosphere, a different kind of oxygen molecule, called ozone, forms a layer that filters out harmful radiation from the sun. **How are the bonds in molecules of ordinary oxygen similar to the bonds in molecules of ozone?**

Single Covalent Bonds

Salts, such as sodium chloride (NaCl), are crystalline solids with high melting points. Other compounds, however, have very different properties. Hydrogen chloride (HCl), for example, is a gas at room temperature. Water (H_2O) is a liquid. These two compounds are so different from salts that you might suspect that electrostatic attraction between ions fails to explain their bonding. Your suspicions would be correct. Such compounds are not ionic. Their atoms do not give up electrons or accept electrons as readily as sodium does in combining with chlorine. Instead, a "tug of war" for electrons takes place between the atoms, ending more or less in a standoff. In this chapter, you will learn about atoms that share electrons to form a different kind of bond, called a covalent bond.

To begin your study of covalent bonding, consider hydrogen (H_2), a very simple molecule. A hydrogen atom has a single valence electron. A pair of hydrogen atoms shares electrons to form a diatomic hydrogen molecule.

$$\text{H·} \quad + \quad \text{·H} \quad \longrightarrow \quad \text{H:H} \qquad \text{shared pair of electrons}$$

Hydrogen atom   Hydrogen atom   Hydrogen molecule

In this molecule, each hydrogen achieves the electron configuration of the noble gas helium, which has two valence electrons. The hydrogen atoms form a **single covalent bond,** a bond in which two atoms share a pair of electrons. **Figure 16.1** shows this process in terms of atomic orbitals.

When writing a formula for a covalent bond, the pair of electrons is represented as a dash, as in H—H for hydrogen. Notations of this type, called **structural formulas,** are chemical formulas that show the arrangement of atoms in molecules and polyatomic ions. Each dash between atoms in structural formulas indicates a pair of shared electrons. Such dashes are never used to show ionic bonds.

By looking at hydrogen (H_2), you can see that there is a difference between the formulas of ionic and covalent compounds. The chemical formulas of ionic compounds describe formula units, while the chemical formulas of covalent compounds describe molecules. Ionic compounds do not have molecular formulas because they are not composed of molecules. Ionic copper(II) oxide, for example, is composed of equal numbers of Cu^{2+} and O^{2-} ions in a crystal lattice. The formula unit, which is written as CuO, shows the lowest whole-number ratio of Cu^{2+} to O^{2-}, which is 1:1. The chemical formula CuO represents the smallest electrically neutral unit that is representative of copper(II) oxide.

Figure 16.1

The bonding electrons in the hydrogen molecule come from the 1s atomic orbitals of the hydrogen atoms. How many electrons do the hydrogen atoms share?

Figure 16.2

Sodium chloride—an ionic compound—and water—a molecular compound—are compared here. How do molecular compounds differ from ionic compounds?

Ionic compound

Molecular compound

Pile of salt crystals

Array of sodium ions and chloride ions

Formula unit of sodium chloride: Na⁺ Cl⁻

Chemical formula: NaCl

Drop of water

Collection of water molecules

Molecule of water: H—O—H

Chemical formula: H_2O

In contrast, individual hydrogen molecules actually do exist. Each contains two hydrogen atoms bonded together. The molecular formula of hydrogen is thus H_2. The correct formulas of molecular compounds reflect the actual number of atoms in each molecule, and their subscripts are not necessarily lowest whole-number ratios. **Figure 16.2** illustrates some essential differences between ionic and covalent compounds, using sodium chloride and water as examples.

Combinations of atoms of the nonmetallic elements in Groups 4A, 5A, 6A, and 7A of the periodic table are likely to form covalent bonds. Chemist Gilbert Lewis summarized this tendency in his formulation of the octet rule for covalent bonding: Sharing of electrons occurs if the atoms involved acquire the electron configurations of noble gases. Often the configurations contain eight valence electrons (an octet). Which covalent compound that has already been discussed in this chapter is a notable exception to this rule?

The halogens form single covalent bonds in their diatomic molecules. Fluorine is one example. Because a fluorine atom has seven valence electrons, it needs one more to attain the electron configuration of a noble gas. By sharing electrons and forming a single covalent bond, two fluorine atoms each achieve the electron configuration of neon. **Figure 16.3** illustrates this process in terms of atomic orbitals.

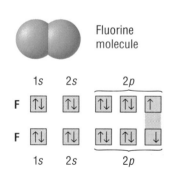

Fluorine molecule

Figure 16.3

The bonding electrons in the fluorine molecule come from the 2p atomic orbitals of the fluorine atoms. How many electrons are needed to form the single covalent bond in the fluorine molecule?

Fluorine atom   Fluorine atom   Fluorine molecule

In the F_2 molecule, each fluorine atom contributes one electron to complete the octet. Notice that the two fluorine atoms share only one pair of valence electrons. Pairs of valence electrons that are not shared between atoms are called **unshared pairs,** also known as lone pairs or nonbonding pairs.

(a) Water molecule

(b) Ammonia molecule

(c) Methane molecule

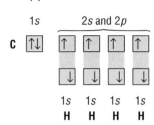

You can write electron dot formulas for molecules of compounds in much the same way that you write them for molecules of diatomic elements. Consider the examples for water, ammonia, and methane, illustrated in **Figure 16.4.**

Water (H_2O) is a triatomic molecule with two single covalent bonds. Two hydrogen atoms share electrons with one oxygen atom. The hydrogen and oxygen atoms attain noble-gas configurations by sharing electrons. As you can see in the electron dot structure below, the oxygen atom in water has two unshared pairs of valence electrons.

$$2H\cdot \quad + \quad :\ddot{O}\cdot \quad \longrightarrow \quad :\ddot{O}:H \quad or \quad :\ddot{O}-H$$
$$\qquad\qquad\qquad\qquad\qquad\qquad\ddot{H}\qquad\qquad\quad |$$
$$\qquad\qquad\qquad\qquad\qquad\qquad\qquad\qquad\quad H$$

Hydrogen atoms   Oxygen atom   Water molecule

You can write the electron dot formula for ammonia (NH_3), a suffocating gas, in a similar way. The ammonia molecule has one unshared pair of electrons.

$$3H\cdot \quad + \quad :\dot{N}\cdot \quad \longrightarrow \quad :\ddot{N}:H \quad or \quad :N-H$$

Hydrogen atoms   Nitrogen atom   Ammonia molecule

Methane (CH_4) contains four single covalent bonds. The carbon atom has four valence electrons and needs four more valence electrons to attain a noble-gas configuration. Each of the four hydrogen atoms contributes one electron to share with the carbon atom, forming four identical carbon-hydrogen bonds. As you can see in the electron dot structure below, methane has no unshared pairs of electrons.

$$4H\cdot \quad + \quad \cdot\dot{C}\cdot \quad \longrightarrow \quad H:\ddot{C}:H \quad or \quad H-C-H$$

Hydrogen atoms   Carbon atom   Methane molecule

Figure 16.4
(a) In a water molecule, two hydrogen atoms form single covalent bonds with one oxygen atom.
(b) In an ammonia molecule, three hydrogen atoms form single covalent bonds with one nitrogen atom.
(c) A methane molecule has four carbon–hydrogen bonds. In each bond, carbon and hydrogen share a 1s electron from the hydrogen and an electron from the carbon. *Why does carbon form four covalent bonds, and not two, with hydrogen?*

When carbon forms bonds with other atoms, it usually forms four bonds. You might not have predicted this based on carbon's electron configuration.

If you tried to form covalent C—H bonds for methane by combining the two 2p electrons of the carbon with two 1s electrons of hydrogen atoms, you would incorrectly predict a molecule with the formula CH_2 (instead of CH_4). The formation of four bonds by carbon can be simply explained. One of carbon's 2s electrons is promoted to the vacant 2p orbital to form the following.

This electron promotion requires only a small amount of energy. As shown in **Figure 16.4c** on the previous page, the promotion provides four electrons of carbon that are capable of forming covalent bonds with four hydrogen atoms. Methane, the carbon compound formed by electron sharing of carbon with four hydrogen atoms, is much more stable than CH_2. The stability of the resulting methane more than compensates for the small energy cost of the electron promotion. Therefore, formation of methane (CH_4) is much preferred to formation of CH_2.

Sample Problem 16-1

Hydrogen chloride (HCl) is a diatomic molecule with a single covalent bond. Draw the electron dot structure for HCl.

1. **ANALYZE Plan a problem-solving strategy.**
In a single covalent bond, a hydrogen and a chlorine atom must share a pair of electrons. Each must contribute one electron to the bond. First, write the electron dot structures for the two atoms. Then show the electron sharing in the compound they produce.

2. **SOLVE Apply the problem-solving strategy.**

$$H\cdot \quad + \quad \cdot \ddot{\underset{\cdot\cdot}{Cl}}: \quad \longrightarrow \quad H\!:\!\ddot{\underset{\cdot\cdot}{Cl}}:$$

Hydrogen   Chlorine   Hydrogen chloride
atom   atom   molecule

3. **EVALUATE Does the result make sense?**
In the electron dot structures, the hydrogen atom and the chlorine atom are each correctly shown to have an unpaired electron. Through electron sharing, the hydrogen and chlorine atoms are shown to attain the electron configurations of the noble gases helium and argon, respectively.

Practice Problems

1. Draw electron dot structures for each molecule.
   a. chlorine
   b. bromine
   c. iodine
2. The following molecules have single covalent bonds. Draw an electron dot structure for each.
   a. H_2O_2
   b. PCl_3

Chem ASAP!

Problem-Solving 2

Solve Problem 2 with the help of an interactive guided tutorial.

CHEMath

LEWIS ELECTRON DOT STRUCTURES

As you have learned, it is the valence electrons of an atom that are involved in chemical bonding. Because valence electrons are significant, it is important to be able to study the valence electrons of atoms and compounds. Chemists use a notation in which valence electrons are identified as dots, and their bonds as dashes. This notation is known as a Lewis electron-dot structure in honor of its founder, Gilbert Lewis.

You were introduced to Lewis electron-dot structures in Chapter 15. Now is a good time to review these structures because they will be used to explain concepts in this and upcoming chapters. Understanding how to read and write electron-dot structures will help you understand how electrons are arranged in molecules, how they rearrange during chemical reactions, and how they contribute to determining the shape of a molecule.

Electron-Dot Structures for Atoms In an electron-dot structure, the symbol for the element represents the nucleus of the atom along with its inner electrons. Dots are placed around the symbol to represent the valence electrons.

To write an electron-dot structure for an atom, use the periodic table to find the number of valence electrons. Iodine, for example, has seven valence electrons. Write the symbol for the atom and then place the dots around the symbol. No more than two dots can be placed on any one side of a chemical symbol. The electron-dot structure for iodine is

Paired electrons / Unpaired electron / Symbol of the element

Electron-Dot Structures for Molecules Follow these basic rules to write the electron-dot structure for molecules.

1. Add up the valence electrons for each atom in the molecule. Use the periodic table to determine the number of valence electrons for each atom. For example, in the case of a water molecule, H_2O,

   (Group 1)   (Group 6)
     H H   O
     1 + 1   +   6   =   8 valence electrons

2. Write the symbols for the atoms in the molecule. In simple molecules, one atom will be the central atom surrounded by the other atoms. The central atom is often the first atom in the formula. Hydrogen can form only one covalent bond, so it cannot be the central atom.

   H O H

3. Draw a dash between each pair of atoms covalently bonded together.

   H—O—H

4. For each dash you drew, subtract 2 from your total number of valence electrons. Then draw the remaining electrons as dots around the atoms. Arrange the dots so that most atoms have eight valence electrons, and hydrogen has two. In the case of water, there are two covalent bonds. So subtract 4 (2 × 2) electrons from the 8 original valence electrons. That leaves 4 valence electrons to add to the structure.

   H—Ö—H

5. If there are not enough electrons to give the atoms eight electrons, shift unbonded electrons as necessary or change single bonds to double or triple bonds. Verify that each atom has a noble gas structure (two electrons for hydrogen and eight for the others).

Practice Problems

Prepare for upcoming problems in this chapter by determining the total number of valence electrons for these compounds. Then draw an electron dot structure for each.

A. HCl   **C.** PCl_3

B. CH_4 **D.** CO_2

Double and Triple Covalent Bonds

Atoms sometimes share more than one pair of electrons to attain stable noble-gas electron configurations. **Double covalent bonds** are bonds that involve two shared pairs of electrons. **Triple covalent bonds** are bonds that involve three shared pairs of electrons.

Oxygen (O_2) is an example of a molecule that may seem as if it should have a double covalent bond according to the octet rule. You might assume that an oxygen atom, which has six valence electrons, would form a double bond by sharing two of its electrons with another oxygen atom.

Oxygen   Oxygen   Oxygen
atom   atom   molecule

Chem ASAP!

Simulation 16
Simulate the covalent bonding between atoms of molecules.

In such an arrangement, all the electrons within the molecule would be paired. Experimental evidence, however, indicates that two of the electrons in O_2 are unpaired. Study **Figure 16.5** and keep oxygen in mind when you read about exceptions to the octet rule later in this section.

In contrast to the exceptional bonding in the oxygen molecule, the nitrogen molecule (N_2) does bond according to the octet rule. As shown in **Figure 16.5**, N_2 contains a triple covalent bond. In the nitrogen molecule, each nitrogen has one unshared pair of electrons. A single nitrogen atom has five valence electrons. How many electrons must each nitrogen atom in the nitrogen molecule acquire to attain the electron configuration of neon?

:N· + ·N: ⟶ :N::N: *or* :N≡N:

Nitrogen   Nitrogen   Nitrogen
atom   atom   molecule

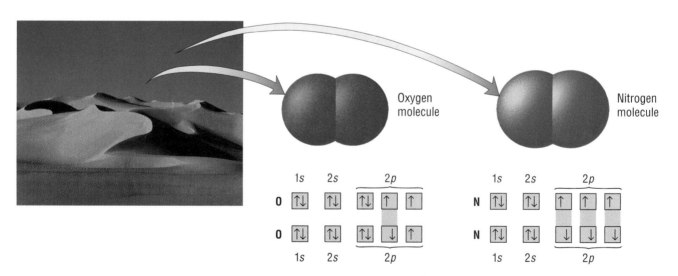

Figure 16.5

Oxygen and nitrogen are the main components of Earth's atmosphere. The oxygen molecule is an exception to the octet rule. It has two unpaired electrons. Three pairs of electrons are shared in a nitrogen molecule.

Table 16.1

The Diatomic Elements			
Name	Chemical formula	Structure	Properties and uses
Fluorine	F_2	:F—F:	Greenish-yellow reactive toxic gas. Compounds of fluorine, a halogen, are added to drinking water and toothpaste to promote healthy teeth.
Chlorine	Cl_2	:Cl—Cl:	Greenish-yellow reactive toxic gas. Chlorine is a halogen used in household bleaching agents.
Bromine	Br_2	:Br—Br:	Dense red-brown liquid with pungent odor. Compounds of bromine, a halogen, are used in the preparation of photographic emulsions.
Iodine	I_2	:I—I:	Dense gray-black solid that produces purple vapors; a halogen. A solution of iodine in alcohol (tincture of iodine) is used as an antiseptic.
Hydrogen	H_2	H—H	Colorless, odorless, tasteless gas. Hydrogen is the lightest known element.
Nitrogen	N_2	:N≡N:	Colorless, odorless, tasteless gas. Air is almost 80% nitrogen by volume.
Oxygen	O_2	:O—O:	Colorless, odorless, tasteless gas that is vital for life. Air is about 20% oxygen by volume.

Up to this point in your textbook, the examples of multiple covalent bonds have all involved diatomic molecules. **Table 16.1** lists the properties and uses of the elements that exist as diatomic molecules. Multiple covalent bonds can also exist between unlike atoms. For example, consider carbon dioxide (CO_2), shown in **Figure 16.6.** The carbon dioxide molecule contains two oxygens, both of which share two electrons with carbon to form two carbon–oxygen double bonds.

$$:O: \ + \ :C: \ + \ :O: \ \longrightarrow \ :O::C::O: \ \textit{or} \ :O=C=O:$$

Oxygen   Carbon   Oxygen   Carbon dioxide
atom   atom   atom   molecule

Carbon dioxide molecule

Figure 16.6

Carbon dioxide gas is soluble in water and is used to carbonate many beverages. A carbon dioxide molecule has two carbon–oxygen double bonds.

Covalent Bonding   **443**

Carbon monoxide molecule

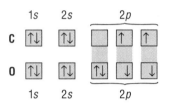

Figure 16.7

In a coordinate covalent compound, one atom contributes both electrons of a bonding pair. In carbon monoxide, which atom contributes two electrons in one of the carbon–oxygen bonds?

Figure 16.8

The polyatomic ammonium ion (NH_4^+), present in ammonium sulfate, is an important component of fertilizer for field crops, home gardens, and potted plants.

Coordinate Covalent Bonds

Carbon monoxide (CO) is an example of a type of covalent-bonding different from that seen in water, ammonia, methane, and carbon dioxide. A carbon atom needs to gain four electrons to attain the electron configuration of neon. An oxygen atom needs two electrons. Yet it is possible for both atoms to achieve noble-gas electron configurations by a type of bonding called coordinate covalent bonding. To see how, begin by looking at the double covalent bond between carbon and oxygen.

$$\ddot{C} \quad + \quad \ddot{O} \colon \longrightarrow \colon C \colon\colon \ddot{O} \colon$$

Carbon   Oxygen
atom   atom

With the double bond in place, the oxygen has a stable configuration but the carbon does not. As shown in **Figure 16.7,** the dilemma is solved if the oxygen also donates one of its unshared pairs of electrons for bonding.

$$\colon C \colon \overset{\curvearrowleft}{\ddot{O}} \colon^{\ominus} \longrightarrow \colon C \colon\colon \ddot{O} \colon$$

Carbon monoxide
molecule

A covalent bond in which one atom contributes both bonding electrons is called a **coordinate covalent bond.** In structural formulas, you can show coordinate covalent bonds as arrows that point from the atom donating the pair of electrons to the atom receiving them. The structural formula of carbon monoxide, with two covalent bonds and one coordinate covalent bond, is C ≝ O. Once formed, a coordinate covalent bond is like any other covalent bond. The only difference is the source of the bonding electrons.

The polyatomic ammonium ion (NH_4^+) has a coordinate covalent bond. This ion forms when a positively charged hydrogen ion (H^+) is attracted to the unshared electron pair of an ammonia molecule (NH_3) and attaches to it. As **Figure 16.8** shows, the ammonium ion is an important component of some nitrogen fertilizers.

unshared electron pair

Hydrogen   Ammonia   Ammonium
ion   molecule   ion
(proton)   (NH_3)   (NH_4^+)

Most polyatomic cations and anions contain covalent and coordinate covalent bonds. **Table 16.2** lists some common examples. Which of these compounds are exceptions to the octet rule?

Table 16.2

Some Common Covalent Compounds			
Name	Chemical formula	Structure	Properties and uses
Carbon monoxide	CO	:C≡O:	Colorless, highly toxic gas. It is a major air pollutant present in cigarette smoke and exhaust.
Carbon dioxide	CO_2	:O=C=O:	Colorless unreactive gas. This normal component of the atmosphere is exhaled in the breath of animals and is essential for plant growth.
Water	H_2O	H—O: \ H	Colorless, odorless, tasteless liquid with melting point of 0 °C and boiling point of 100 °C. The human body is approximately 60% water.
Hydrogen peroxide	H_2O_2	H \ :O—O: \ H	Colorless, unstable liquid when pure. It is used as rocket fuel. A 3% solution is used as a bleach and antiseptic.
Sulfur dioxide	SO_2	:O=S \ :O:	Oxides of sulfur are produced in combustion of petroleum products and coal. They are major air pollutants in industrial areas. Oxides of sulfur can lead to respiratory problems.
Sulfur trioxide	SO_3	:O: / :O=S \ :O:	
Ammonia	NH_3	H—N—H | H	Colorless gas with pungent odor; extremely soluble in water. Household ammonia is a solution of ammonia in water.
Nitric oxide	NO	:O=N·	Oxides of nitrogen are major air pollutants produced by the combustion of fossil fuels in automobile engines. They irritate the eyes, throat, and lungs. Nitrogen dioxide, a dark-brown gas, readily converts to colorless dinitrogen tetroxide.
Nitrogen dioxide	NO_2	:O=N \ :O.	
Dinitrogen tetroxide	N_2O_4	:O: :O: \\ // N—N // \\ :O. O:	
Nitrous oxide	N_2O	:O←N≡N:	Colorless sweet-smelling gas. It is used as an anesthetic commonly called laughing gas.
Hydrogen cyanide	HCN	H—C≡N:	Colorless toxic gas with the smell of almonds.
Hydrogen fluoride	HF	H—F:	Four hydrogen halides, all extremely soluble in water. Hydrogen chloride, a colorless gas with pungent odor, readily dissolves in water to give a solution called hydrochloric acid.
Hydrogen chloride	HCl	H—Cl:	
Hydrogen bromide	HBr	H—Br:	
Hydrogen iodide	HI	H—I:	

The atoms in polyatomic ions are covalently bonded. You can write electron dot structures for these ions. The negative charge of a polyatomic ion shows the number of electrons in addition to the valence electrons of the atoms present. Because a polyatomic ion is part of an ionic compound, the positive charge of the cation of the compound balances these additional electrons.

Sample Problem 16-2

The polyatomic hydronium ion (H_3O^+) contains a coordinate covalent bond. It forms when a hydrogen ion is attracted to an unshared electron pair in a water molecule. Write the electron dot structure of the hydronium ion.

1. *ANALYZE* **Plan a problem-solving strategy.**
H_3O^+ forms by the addition of a hydrogen ion to a water molecule. Write the electron dot structure of the water molecule. Then, add the hydrogen ion. Oxygen must share a pair of electrons with the added hydrogen ion to form a coordinate covalent bond.

2. *SOLVE* **Apply the problem-solving strategy.**

$$H^+ \ + \ \overset{..}{\underset{..}{O}}\!:\!H \longrightarrow \left[H\!:\!\overset{..}{\underset{..}{O}}\!:\!H \right]^+ \quad or \quad \left[H \leftarrow \overset{\overset{\displaystyle H}{\displaystyle |}}{\underset{..}{O}} - H \right]^+$$

| Hydrogen ion (proton) | Water molecule (H_2O) | Hydronium ion (H_3O^+) |

3. *EVALUATE* **Does the result make sense?**
The oxygen in the hydronium ion has eight valence electrons, and each hydrogen shares two valence electrons. This satisfies the needs of both hydrogen and oxygen for valence electrons. The water molecule is electrically neutral, and the hydrogen ion has a positive charge. The combination of these two species must have a charge of 1+, as is found in the hydronium ion.

Practice Problems

3. Draw the electron dot structure of the hydroxide ion (OH^-).
4. Draw the electron dot structure of the polyatomic boron tetra-fluoride anion (BF_4^-).

Chem ASAP!

Problem-Solving 4

Solve Problem 4 with the help of an interactive guided tutorial.

Sample Problem 16-3

Draw the electron dot structure of the sulfite ion (SO_3^{2-}), in which sulfur is the central atom.

1. *ANALYZE* **Plan a problem-solving strategy.**
The formula of the sulfite ion (SO_3^{2-}) is given, as is the information that the oxygen atoms are attached to the sulfur; that is, sulfur is the central atom. Start with the oxygen and sulfur atoms, their valence electrons, and the two extra electrons indicated by the charge.

Sample Problem 16-3 (cont.)

2. SOLVE *Apply the problem-solving strategy.*

Draw the atoms, their valence electrons, and the two extra electrons.

$$:\ddot{O}\cdot \quad \cdot\ddot{S}\cdot \quad \cdot\ddot{O}: \ + \ \cdot\cdot$$
$$\cdot\ddot{O}:$$

Join two of the oxygens to sulfur by single covalent bonds.

$$:\ddot{O}:\ddot{S}:\ \cdot\ddot{O}:$$
$$\cdot\ddot{O}:$$

Join the remaining oxygen by a coordinate covalent bond and add the two extra electrons. Put brackets around the structure and indicate the 2− charge.

$$:\ddot{O}:\ddot{S}:\ddot{O}: \ + \ \cdot\cdot \ \longrightarrow \ \left[:\ddot{O}:\ddot{S}:\ddot{O}:\right]^{2-}$$
$$\cdot\ddot{O}: \qquad\qquad\qquad :\ddot{O}:$$

3. EVALUATE *Does the result make sense?*

Each of the atoms of the completed structure has eight valence electrons, satisfying the octet rule. The two extra electrons were shown to be needed. Without them, the SO_3 grouping would be electrically neutral, and two of the oxygens would be electron-deficient.

Practice Problems

5. Draw the electron dot structures for sulfate (SO_4^{2-}) and carbonate (CO_3^{2-}). Sulfur and carbon are the central atoms, respectively.

6. Draw the electron dot structure for the hydrogen carbonate ion (HCO_3^-). Carbon is the central atom, and hydrogen is attached to oxygen in this polyatomic anion.

Bond Dissociation Energies

A large quantity of heat is liberated when hydrogen atoms combine to form hydrogen molecules. This release of heat suggests that the product is more stable than the reactants. The covalent bond in the hydrogen molecule is so strong that it requires 435 kJ of energy to dissociate 1 mol of hydrogen molecules to hydrogen atoms. The total energy required to break the bond between two covalently bonded atoms is known as the **bond dissociation energy.** Hydrogen molecules have a bond dissociation energy of 435 kJ/mol.

$$\text{H}-\text{H} + 435\,\text{kJ} \longrightarrow \text{H}\cdot + \cdot\text{H}$$

A typical carbon–carbon single covalent bond has a bond dissociation energy of about 347 kJ. The ability of carbon to form strong carbon–carbon bonds helps explain the stability of carbon compounds. Compounds with only C—C and C—H single covalent bonds, such as methane, are quite unreactive chemically. They are unreactive partly because the dissociation energy for each of these bonds is high. **Table 16.3** on the following page gives bond dissociation energies and bond lengths of several representative covalent bonds. What is the strongest bond listed? What is the weakest bond listed?

Table 16.3

	Bond Dissociation Energies and Bond Lengths for Covalent Bonds	
Bond	**Bond energy (kJ/mol)**	**Bond length (pm)**
H—H	435	74
C—H	393	109
C—O	356	143
C=O	736	121
C≡O	1074	113
C—C	347	154
C=C	657	133
C≡C	908	121
C—N	305	147
Cl—Cl	243	199
N—N	209	140
O—H	464	96
O—O	142	132

MINI LAB

Strengths of Covalent Bonds

PURPOSE

To compare and contrast the stretching of rubber bands and the dissociation energy of covalent bonds.

MATERIALS

- 1 170-g (6-oz) can of food
- 2 454-g (16-oz) cans of food
- 3 identical No. 25 rubber bands
- metric ruler
- coat hanger
- plastic grocery bag
- paper clip
- graph paper
- pencil
- motion detector (optional)

PROCEDURE

 Sensor version available in the Probeware Lab Manual.

1. Bend the coat hanger to fit over the top of a door. The hook should hang down on one side of the door. Measure the length of the rubber bands (in cm). Hang a rubber band on the hook created by the coat hanger.

2. Place the 170-g can in the plastic bag. Use a paper clip to fasten the bag to the end of the rubber band. Lower the bag gently until it is suspended from the end of the rubber band. Measure and record the length of the stretched rubber band. Using different food cans, repeat this process three times with the following masses: 454 g, 624 g, and 908 g.

3. Repeat Step 2, first using two rubber bands to connect the hanger and the paper clip, and then using three.

4. Graph the length difference: (stretched rubber band) − (unstretched rubber band) on the y-axis versus mass (kg) on the x-axis for one, two, and three rubber bands. Draw an estimated best-fit straight line through the points for each set of data. (Your graph should have three separate lines.) The x-axis and y-axis intercepts of the lines should pass through zero, and the lines should extend past 1 kg on the x-axis. Determine the slope of each line in cm/kg.

ANALYSIS AND CONCLUSIONS

1. Assuming the rubber bands are models for covalent bonds, what can you conclude about the relative strengths of single, double, and triple bonds?

2. How does the behavior of the rubber bands differ from that of covalent bonds?

Resonance

Consider the two electron dot structures for ozone.

$$:\ddot{O}:\ddot{O}::\ddot{O}: \longleftrightarrow :\ddot{O}::\ddot{O}:\ddot{O}:$$

Notice that the structure on the left can be converted to the one on the right by shifting electron pairs without changing the positions of the oxygen atoms.

As drawn, these electron dot structures suggest that the bonding in ozone consists of one single coordinate covalent bond and one double covalent bond. Because earlier chemists imagined that the electron pairs rapidly flip back and forth, or resonate, between the various electron dot structures, they used double-headed arrows to indicate that two or more structures are in resonance.

Double covalent bonds are usually shorter than single bonds, so it was believed that the bond lengths in ozone were unequal. Experimental measurements show, however, that this is not the case. The two bonds in ozone are the same length. This result can be explained if you assume that the actual bonding in the ozone molecule is the average of the two electron dot structures. The electron pairs do not actually resonate back and forth. The actual bonding is a hybrid, or mixture, of the extremes represented by the resonance forms.

Thus the two electron dot formulas for ozone are examples of what are still referred to as resonance structures. **Resonance structures** are structures that occur when it is possible to write two or more valid electron dot formulas that have the same number of electron pairs for a molecule or ion. Resonance structures are simply a way to envision the bonding in certain molecules. Although no back-and-forth changes occur, double-headed arrows are used to connect resonance structures.

Exceptions to the Octet Rule

As you have seen, the octet rule provides guidance for writing electron dot structures. For some molecules or ions, however, it is impossible to write structures that satisfy the octet rule. This occurs whenever the total number of valence electrons is an odd number. The NO_2 molecule, for example, contains a total of seventeen valence electrons. Each oxygen contributes six electrons and the nitrogen contributes five. **Figure 16.9** illustrates bonding in the nitrogen dioxide molecule.

Figure 16.9
The nitrogen dioxide molecule, a major component of air pollution in some cities, is unusual in that it contains an unpaired electron.

Nitrogen dioxide molecule

Two plausible resonance structures can be written for the NO_2 molecule.

$$\ddot{\text{O}}{=}\dot{\text{N}}{-}\dot{\ddot{\text{O}}}\cdot$$

$$\cdot\ddot{\text{O}}{-}\dot{\text{N}}{=}\ddot{\text{O}}\colon$$

An unpaired electron is present in each of these structures, both of which fail to follow the octet rule. It is impossible to write a Lewis dot structure for NO_2 that satisfies the octet rule for all atoms. Yet, NO_2 does exist as a stable molecule.

The concept of electron pairing is important in understanding the bonding and properties of molecules. You can consider electrons as small, spinning, electric charges. These moving electric charges create magnetic fields, much as the current in an electric motor creates a magnetic field. You can think of paired electrons as spinning in opposite directions. The magnetic effects of paired electrons essentially cancel. Substances in which all of the electrons are paired are **diamagnetic.** Diamagnetic substances are weakly repelled by an external magnetic field. In contrast, **paramagnetic** substances are those that contain one or more unpaired electrons. Such substances show a strong attraction to an external magnetic field. Paramagnetism can be detected by measuring the mass of a compound in the absence and then in the presence of a magnetic field. If the compound is paramagnetic, its mass will appear to be greater in the magnetic field.

Paramagnetism should not be confused with ferromagnetism, the form of magnetism with which you are most familiar. Ferromagnetism is the strong attraction of iron, cobalt, and nickel to magnetic fields. The ions Fe^{2+}, Co^{2+}, and Ni^{2+} all have unpaired electrons. Normally, these ions are randomly dispersed in a sea of electrons throughout their metals. In a magnetic field, the ions line up in an orderly fashion with the field, which creates a strong magnetic attraction. Because the new arrangement of ions remains when the magnetic field is removed, the magnetism is permanent.

As you have learned in this section, it is possible to write a structure for the oxygen molecule in which both oxygen atoms are surrounded by eight electrons and all the electrons are paired. You have also learned, however, that such a structure is incorrect. The experimental evidence for this statement is that oxygen is paramagnetic. Given what you know about the correct structure for O_2, can you explain the paramagnetism of oxygen?

The measured distance between the oxygen atoms in O_2 indicates that the molecule does have some multiple bond character. The idea that the oxygen molecule has some double-bond character is plausible. All this information taken together suggests that oxygen is a hybrid of the following two structures.

$$\ddot{\text{O}}{-}\ddot{\text{O}}\colon$$

$$\ddot{\text{O}}{=}\ddot{\text{O}}\colon$$

Several other molecules, such as some compounds of boron, also do not follow the octet rule. The boron atom in boron trifluoride (BF_3), for example, is deficient by two electrons. Boron trifluoride readily reacts with ammonia to make the compound $BF_3 \cdot NH_3$. In doing so, the boron atom accepts the unshared electron pair from ammonia and completes the octet.

A few atoms, especially phosphorus and sulfur, sometimes expand the octet to include ten or twelve electrons. Consider phosphorus trichloride (PCl_3) and phosphorus pentachloride (PCl_5). Both are stable compounds in which all of the chlorines are bonded to a single phosphorus atom. Covalent bonding in PCl_3 follows the octet rule because all the atoms acquire eight electrons. However, as shown in **Figure 16.10**, the electron dot structure for PCl_5 can be written so that phosphorus has ten valence electrons. How many valence electrons does the sulfur in sulfur hexafluoride (SF_6) have for the structure shown in **Figure 16.10?**

Phosphorus pentachloride   Sulfur hexafluoride

Figure 16.10
Phosphorus pentachloride, a slightly yellow crystalline solid used as a chlorinating and dehydrating agent, and sulfur hexafluoride, a colorless, odorless gas used as an insulator for electrical equipment, are exceptions to the octet rule.

section review 16.1

7. How are single, double, and triple bonds indicated in electron dot structures?

8. Give an example of each of the following
   a. coordinate covalent bonding
   b. resonance structures
   c. exceptions to the octet rule

9. What kinds of information does a structural formula reveal about the compound it represents?

10. Draw electron dot structures for the following molecules, which have only single covalent bonds.
    a. H_2S
    b. PH_3
    c. ClF

11. Draw the resonance structures for sulfur dioxide (SO_2). Sulfur is the central atom.

12. How many kilojoules are required to dissociate all the C—H single bonds in 0.1 mol of methane (CH_4)? Assume that the bond dissociation energy is the same for each bond.

 Chem ASAP! **Assessment 16.1** Check your understanding of the important ideas and concepts in Section 16.1.

 portfolio project

Research how chemists determine bond length in a compound. How might they determine that the two bonds in an ozone molecule have the same length?

▶ Describe the molecular orbital theory of covalent bonding, including orbital hybridization

▶ Use VSEPR theory to predict the shapes of simple covalently bonded molecules

key terms

▶ molecular orbitals
▶ bonding orbital
▶ antibonding orbital
▶ sigma bond
▶ pi bond
▶ tetrahedral angle
▶ VSEPR theory
▶ hybridization

BONDING THEORIES

This car is being painted by a process called electrostatic spray painting. The paint droplets become negatively charged as they exit the spray gun. The negatively charged paint particles are attracted to the positively charged auto body. Painting with attractive and repulsive forces is very efficient, because almost all the paint is applied to the car body and very little is wasted. **How do attractive and repulsive forces influence molecular bonding?**

Molecular Orbitals

The model for covalent bonding that you have been working with so far is based on the assumption that the atomic orbitals of individual atoms are unchanged in bonded atoms. There is a quantum mechanical model of bonding, however, that describes the electrons in molecules by means of orbitals that exist only for groupings of atoms. When two atoms combine, this model assumes that their atomic orbitals overlap to produce **molecular orbitals,** or orbitals that apply to the entire molecule.

Some important parallels exist between atomic orbitals and molecular orbitals. Just as an atomic orbital belongs to a particular atom, a molecular orbital belongs to a molecule as a whole. Each atomic orbital is filled if it contains two electrons. Similarly, two electrons are required to fill a molecular orbital.

The molecular orbital model of bonding requires that the number of molecular orbitals equal the number of overlapping atomic orbitals. When two atomic orbitals overlap, for example, two molecular orbitals are created. One is called a **bonding orbital,** which is a molecular orbital with an energy that is lower than that of the atomic orbitals from which it formed. The other molecular orbital is called an **antibonding orbital,** and its energy is higher than that of the atomic orbitals from which it formed. The following illustration shows the relationship between atomic orbitals and molecular orbitals.

You can use the molecular orbital model of bonding to explain the bonding in the hydrogen molecule (H_2). In the formation of a hydrogen molecule, the 1s atomic orbitals of each of the two hydrogen atoms overlap. Two electrons, one from each hydrogen atom, are available for bonding. The energy of the electrons in the bonding molecular orbital is lower than the energy of the electrons in the atomic orbitals of separate hydrogen atoms. Because electrons seek the lowest energy, they fill the bonding molecular orbital. This makes a stable covalent bond between the hydrogens. Note that the

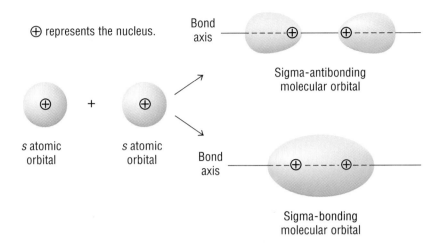

Figure 16.11

In a bonding molecular orbital, the electron density between the nuclei is high. In an antibonding molecular orbital, the electron density between the nuclei is extremely low. Which orbital do the two electrons occupy in a hydrogen molecule?

antibonding orbital is empty. **Figure 16.11** shows the formation of the bonding and antibonding molecular orbitals in a hydrogen molecule.

In the bonding molecular orbital of H_2, there is a high probability of finding the electrons between the nuclei of the bonded atoms. The orbital is symmetrical along the axis between the hydrogen atoms. When two atomic orbitals combine to form a molecular orbital that is symmetrical along the axis connecting two atomic nuclei, a **sigma bond** is formed. The symbol for this bond is the Greek letter sigma (σ).

In general, covalent bonding results from an imbalance between the attractions and repulsions of the nuclei and electrons involved. Being oppositely charged, the nuclei and electrons attract each other. Being similarly charged, nuclei repel other nuclei and electrons repel other electrons. In a hydrogen molecule, the nuclei repel each other, as do the electrons. In a bonding molecular orbital of hydrogen, however, the attractions between the hydrogen nuclei and the electrons are stronger than the repulsions. The balance of all the interactions between the hydrogen atoms is thus tipped in favor of the attractions. The result is a stable diatomic molecule of H_2.

In other cases, attempts to combine two atoms could lead to electron pairs in higher energy, antibonding molecular orbitals. Electrons in antibonding orbitals are not found between the nuclei, and the balance between attractions and repulsions would favor the repulsions. Such destabilizing electron repulsions would occur, for example, if two helium

GEOGRAPHY
....

Topographic Maps

Topographic maps are usually drawn as a series of lines tracing the elevations of a terrain. For example, a line might be drawn for every increase of 10 meters in

elevation. Thus the more closely spaced the lines are, the steeper is the terrain. Scientists who wish to know the positions of atoms in crystals of molecules may use electron densities that are plotted in much the same way that a terrain is shown on a topographic map. From x-ray diffraction data, scientists can map the electron density at any position in a crystal of interest. Where the lines are closest in the map, the electron density of the molecule is greatest. This method allows scientists to pinpoint positions of the atoms in the molecule with great accuracy.

atoms were to combine into an He_2 molecule. Each He atom has two $1s$ electrons, so there would be a total of four electrons in an He_2 molecule. Two of these electrons can go into a low-energy bonding orbital, but the other two must go into a high-energy antibonding orbital.

In this case, the overall repulsions are stronger than the overall attractions. Hence, a theoretical He_2 molecule is unstable compared with two separate helium atoms. For this reason, helium exists as individual atoms in nature.

Not only s orbitals overlap to form molecular orbitals. Atomic p orbitals can overlap as well. A fluorine atom, for example, has a half-filled $2p$ orbital. When two fluorine atoms combine, as shown in **Figure 16.12,** the p orbitals overlap to produce a bonding molecular orbital. There is a high probability of finding a pair of electrons in the bonding molecular orbital between the positively charged nuclei of the two fluorines. The fluorine nuclei are attracted to this region of high electron density. This attraction holds the atoms together in the fluorine molecule (F_2). The overlap of the $2p$ orbitals produces a bonding molecular orbital that is symmetrical when viewed along the F—F bond axis connecting the nuclei. Therefore, the F—F bond is a sigma bond.

In the sigma bond of the fluorine molecule, the p atomic orbitals overlap end-to-end. In some molecules, however, orbitals can overlap side-by-side. As shown in **Figure 16.13,** the side-by-side overlap of atomic p orbitals produces what are called pi molecular orbitals. When a pi molecular orbital is filled with two electrons, a pi bond results. In a **pi bond** (symbolized by the Greek letter π), the bonding electrons are most likely to be found in sausage-shaped regions above and below the bond axis of the bonded atoms. Orbital overlap in pi bonding is not as extensive as it is in sigma bonding. Therefore, pi bonds tend to be weaker than sigma bonds.

⊕ represents the nucleus.

Figure 16.12

Two p atomic orbitals can combine to form a sigma-bonding molecular orbital, as in the case of fluorine (F_2). Notice that the sigma bond is symmetrical along the bond axis connecting the nuclei.

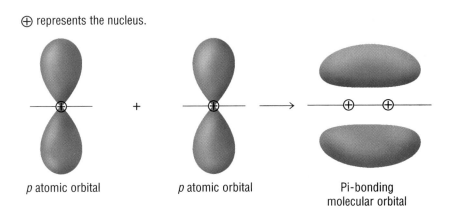

⊕ represents the nucleus.

p atomic orbital   p atomic orbital   Pi-bonding
                                                    molecular orbital

Figure 16.13
*The side-by-side overlap of
two p atomic orbitals produces
a pi-bonding molecular orbital.
Together, the two sausage-
shaped regions in which a
bonding electron pair is most
likely to be found constitute one
pi-bonding molecular orbital.*

VSEPR Theory

A photograph or sketch may fail to do justice to your appearance. Similarly, electron dot structures fail to reflect the three-dimensional shapes of molecules. The electron dot structure and structural formula of methane (CH_4), for example, show the molecule as if it were flat and merely two-dimensional.

Methane
(electron dot structure)

Methane
(structural formula)

In reality, methane molecules are three-dimensional. As **Figure 16.14** shows, the hydrogens in a methane molecule are at the four corners of a geometric solid called a regular tetrahedron. In this arrangement, all of the H—C—H angles are 109.5°, the **tetrahedral angle.**

(a) Methane (CH_4)

(b) Ammonia (NH_3)

Figure 16.14
***(a)** Methane is a good example of
a tetrahedral molecule. The hydrogens in methane are at the four
corners of a regular tetrahedron,
and the bond angles are all 109.5°.
(b) An ammonia molecule is pyramidal. The unshared pair of
electrons repels the bonding pairs.
Are the resulting H—N—H bond
angles larger or smaller than the
tetrahedral angle?*

The valence-shell electron-pair repulsion theory, or VSEPR theory, explains the three-dimensional shape of methane. **VSEPR theory** states that because electron pairs repel, molecular shape adjusts so the valence-electron pairs are as far apart as possible. The methane molecule has four bonding electron pairs and no unshared pairs. The bonding pairs are farthest apart when the angle between the central carbon and its attached hydrogens is 109.5°. This is the H—C—H bond angle found experimentally. Any other arrangement tends to bring two bonding pairs of electrons closer together.

Unshared pairs of electrons are also important when you are trying to predict the shapes of molecules. The nitrogen in ammonia (NH_3) is surrounded by four pairs of valence electrons, so you might predict the tetrahedral angle of 109.5° for the H—N—H bond angle. However, one of the valence-electron pairs is an unshared pair. See **Figure 16.14** on the previous page. No bonding atom is vying for these unshared electrons. Thus they are held closer to the nitrogen than are the bonding pairs. The unshared pair strongly repels the bonding pairs, pushing them closer together than might be expected. The experimentally measured H—N—H bond angle is only 107°. What is the shape of the ammonia molecule?

In a water molecule, oxygen forms single covalent bonds with two hydrogen atoms. The two bonding pairs and the two unshared pairs of electrons form a tetrahedral arrangement around the central oxygen. Thus the water molecule is planar (flat) but bent. With two unshared pairs repelling the bonding pairs, the H—O—H bond angle is compressed in comparison with the H—C—H bond angle in methane. The experimentally measured bond angle in water is about 105°, as shown in **Figure 16.15a.**

In contrast, the carbon in a carbon dioxide molecule has no unshared electron pairs. The double bonds joining the oxygens to the carbon are farthest apart when the O=C=O bond angle is 180°. See **Figure 16.15b.** Thus CO_2 is a linear molecule. A selection of various molecular shapes is shown in **Figure 16.16.**

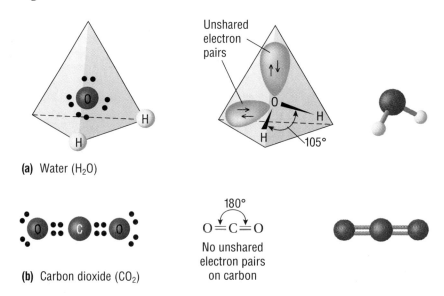

Unshared electron pairs

105°

(a) Water (H_2O)

180°

O=C=O

No unshared electron pairs on carbon

(b) Carbon dioxide (CO_2)

Figure 16.15

(a) The water molecule is bent because the two unshared pairs of electrons on oxygen repel the bonding electrons. (b) In contrast, the carbon dioxide molecule is linear. The carbon atom has no unshared electron pairs.

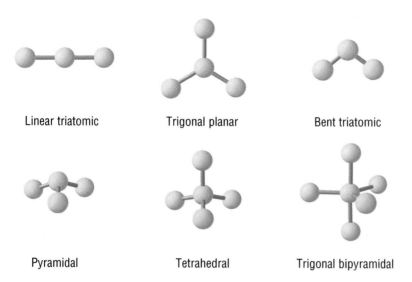

Linear triatomic   Trigonal planar   Bent triatomic

Pyramidal   Tetrahedral   Trigonal bipyramidal

Figure 16.16
Shown here are several common molecular shapes.

Hybrid Orbitals

The VSEPR theory works well when accounting for molecular shapes, but it does not help much in describing the types of bonds formed. Another way to describe molecules, which is informative of both bonding and shape, is orbital hybridization. In **hybridization,** several atomic orbitals mix to form the same total number of equivalent hybrid orbitals.

Orbital hybridization can be used to describe the single covalent bonds of the methane molecule.

$$
\begin{array}{c}
\text{H} \\
| \\
\text{H}-\text{C}-\text{H} \\
| \\
\text{H}
\end{array}
$$

Methane

One $2s$ orbital and three $2p$ orbitals of a carbon atom mix to form four sp^3 hybrid orbitals. These are at the tetrahedral angle of 109.5°. As you can see in **Figure 16.17,** the four sp^3 orbitals of carbon overlap with the $1s$ orbitals of the four hydrogen atoms. The sp^3 orbitals extend farther into space than either s or p orbitals, allowing a great deal of overlap with the hydrogen $1s$ orbitals. The eight available valence electrons fill the molecular orbitals to form four C—H sigma bonds. The extent of overlap results in unusually strong covalent bonds.

1s

1s

sp^3

109.5°

1s

1s

Atomic orbitals of two hydrogen atoms

Hybrid orbitals of a carbon atom

Atomic orbitals of two hydrogen atoms

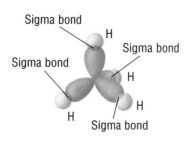

Sigma bond

Sigma bond

Sigma bond

Sigma bond

H

H

H

H

Methane molecule

Figure 16.17
In methane, each of the four sp^3 hybrid orbitals of carbon overlaps with a 1s orbital of hydrogen. What type of bond results: sigma or pi?

Hybridization is also useful in describing double covalent bonds. Ethene is a relatively simple molecule that has one carbon–carbon double bond and four carbon–hydrogen single bonds.

$$\begin{array}{c} H \\ \diagdown \\ \diagup \\ H \end{array} C = C \begin{array}{c} H \\ \diagup \\ \diagdown \\ H \end{array}$$

Ethene

Experimental evidence indicates that the H—C—H bond angles in ethene are about 120°. In ethene, sp^2 hybrid orbitals form from the combination of one $2s$ and two $2p$ atomic orbitals of carbon. As you can see in **Figure 16.18,** each hybrid orbital is separated from the other two by 120°. Two sp^2 hybrid orbitals of each carbon form sigma-bonding molecular orbitals with the four available hydrogen $1s$ orbitals. The third sp^2 orbitals of each of the two carbons overlap to form a carbon–carbon sigma-bonding orbital. The non-hybridized $2p$ carbon orbitals overlap side-by-side to form a pi-bonding orbital. A total of twelve electrons fills six bonding molecular orbitals. Thus five sigma bonds and one pi bond hold the ethene molecule together. The sigma bonds and the pi bond are two-electron covalent bonds. Although they are drawn alike in structural formulas, pi bonds are weaker than sigma bonds. In chemical reactions that involve the cleavage of one bond of a carbon–carbon double bond, would the pi bond or the sigma bond be more likely to break?

A third type of covalent bond is a triple bond, such as is found in ethyne (C_2H_2), also called acetylene.

$$H—C\equiv C—H$$

As with other molecules, the hybrid orbital description of ethyne is guided by an understanding of the properties of the molecule. Ethyne is a linear molecule. The best hybrid orbital description is obtained if a $2s$ atomic orbital of carbon mixes with only one of the three $2p$ atomic orbitals.

Figure 16.18

In an ethene molecule, two sp^2 hybrid orbitals from each carbon overlap with a 1s orbital of hydrogen to form a sigma bond. The other sp^2 orbitals overlap to form a carbon–carbon sigma bond. The p atomic orbitals overlap to form a pi bond. What region of space does the pi bond occupy relative to the carbon atoms?

Ethene molecule

Ethyne molecule

Figure 16.19
In an ethyne molecule, one sp hybrid orbital from each carbon overlaps with a 1s orbital of hydrogen to form a sigma bond. The other sp hybrid orbital of each carbon overlaps to form a carbon–carbon sigma bond. The two p atomic orbitals from each carbon also overlap. What kind of bonds do they form? How many of these bonds do they form?

Chem ASAP!
Simulation 17
Compare the sp, sp^2, and sp^3 hybrid orbitals.

The result is two sp hybrid orbitals for each carbon. See **Figure 16.19.** A carbon–carbon sigma-bonding molecular orbital forms from the overlap of one sp orbital from each carbon. The other sp orbital of each carbon overlaps with the 1s orbital of each hydrogen, also forming sigma-bonding molecular orbitals. The remaining pair of p atomic orbitals on each carbon overlap side-by-side. They form two pi-bonding molecular orbitals that surround the central carbons. The ten available electrons completely fill five bonding molecular orbitals. The bonding of ethyne consists of three sigma bonds and two pi bonds.

section review 16.2

13. Use the molecular orbital theory to describe covalent bonding. What occurs during hybridization?

14. Explain how the VSEPR theory can be used to predict bond angles in the following covalently bonded molecules.

   a. methane

   b. ammonia

   c. water

15. What shape would you expect a simple carbon-containing compound to have if the carbon atom has the following hybridizations.

   a. sp^2 **b.** sp^3 **c.** sp

16. What is a sigma bond? Describe, with the aid of a diagram, how the overlap of two half-filled 1s orbitals produces a sigma bond.

17. How many sigma and how many pi bonds are in an ethyne molecule (C_2H_2)?

18. The BF_3 molecule is planar. The attachment of a fluoride ion to the boron in BF_3, through a coordinate covalent bond, creates the BF_4^- ion. What is the geometric shape of this ion?

Chem ASAP! **Assessment 16.2** Check your understanding of the important ideas and concepts in Section 16.2.

POLAR BONDS AND MOLECULES

*S*now *covers approximately 23 percent of Earth's surface. Each individual snowflake is formed from as many as 100 snow crystals. The size and shape of each crystal depends mainly on the air temperature and amount of water vapor in the air at the time the snow crystal forms.* **How do the polar bonds in water molecules influence the distinctive geometry of snowflakes?**

Bond Polarity

Covalent bonds involve electron sharing between atoms. However, covalent bonds differ in terms of how the bonded atoms share the electrons. The character of the bonds in a given molecule depends on the kind and number of atoms joined together. These features, in turn, determine the molecular properties.

The bonding pairs of electrons in covalent bonds are pulled, as in a tug-of-war, between the nuclei of the atoms sharing the electrons. See **Figure 16.20.** When the atoms in the bond pull equally (as occurs when like atoms are bonded), the bonding electrons are shared equally, and the bond is a **nonpolar covalent bond.** Molecules of hydrogen (H_2), oxygen (O_2), and nitrogen (N_2) have nonpolar covalent bonds. Are diatomic halogen molecules, such as Cl_2, also nonpolar?

When a covalent bond joins two atoms of different elements and the bonding electrons are shared unequally, the bond is a **polar covalent bond,** or simply a **polar bond.** The more electronegative atom will have the stronger electron attraction and will acquire a slightly negative charge. The less electronegative atom will acquire a slightly positive charge. Refer back to **Table 14.2** on page 405 to see the electronegativities of some common elements. The higher the electronegativity value, the greater the ability of an atom to attract electrons to itself.

Shared pair of electrons

Nucleus + ⟷ ⦂ ⟶ + Nucleus

Figure 16.20
The nuclei of atoms pull on the bonding electrons between them, much as a rope is pulled toward opposing sides in a tug-of-war between two groups.

Figure 16.21
This electron-cloud picture of hydrogen chloride shows that the chlorine atom attracts the electron cloud more than the hydrogen atom does. Which atom is more electronegative, a chlorine atom or a hydrogen atom?

Consider the hydrogen chloride molecule (HCl) shown in **Figure 16.21.** Hydrogen has an electronegativity of 2.1 and chlorine has an electronegativity of 3.0. These values are significantly different, so the covalent bond in hydrogen chloride is polar. The chlorine atom acquires a slightly negative charge. The hydrogen atom acquires a slightly positive charge. The lowercase Greek letter delta (δ) shows that atoms involved in the covalent bond acquire only partial charges, much less than 1+ or 1−.

$$\overset{\delta+}{H}-\overset{\delta-}{Cl}$$

The minus sign in this notation shows that chlorine has acquired a slightly negative charge. The plus sign shows that hydrogen has acquired a slightly positive charge. These partial charges are shown as clouds of electron density. The polarity of the bond may also be represented with an arrow pointing to the more electronegative atom, as shown here.

$$\overset{\longrightarrow}{H-Cl}$$

The O—H bonds in the water molecule are also polar. The highly electronegative oxygen partially pulls the bonding electrons away from hydrogen. The oxygen acquires a slightly negative charge. What type of charge do the hydrogens acquire?

As shown in **Table 16.4** on the following page, the size of the electronegativity difference between two atoms is one indicator of the type of bond that the two atoms may form. For each range of electronegativity difference, the table shows the most probable type of bond. When you use the ranges in the table, it is important to remember that the boundary between ionic and covalent bonds is not distinct. As the electronegativity difference between two atoms increases, the polarity of the bond increases. If the electronegativity difference is greater than 2.0, there is a high probability that electrons will be pulled away completely by one of the atoms. In that case, an ionic bond will form.

Table 16.4

Electronegativity Differences and Bond Types		
Electronegativity difference range	Most probable type of bond	Example
0.0–0.4	Nonpolar covalent	H—H (0.0)
0.4–1.0	Moderately polar covalent	$\overset{\delta+}{H}—\overset{\delta-}{Cl}$ (0.9)
1.0–2.0	Very polar covalent	$\overset{\delta+}{H}—\overset{\delta-}{F}$ (1.9)
≥ 2.0	Ionic	Na⁺Cl⁻ (2.1)

Sample Problem 16-4

Which type of bond (nonpolar covalent, moderately polar covalent, very polar covalent, or ionic) will form between each of the following pairs of atoms?

a. N and H   **b.** F and F   **c.** Ca and O   **d.** Al and Cl

1. **ANALYZE** *Plan a problem-solving strategy.*

   In each case, the pairs of atoms involved in the bonding pair are given. The types of bonds formed depend on the electronegativity differences between the bonding elements. Use **Table 14.2** on page 405 to find the electronegativity difference, then use **Table 16.4** to determine the bond type.

2. **SOLVE** *Apply the problem-solving strategy.*

   From **Tables 14.2** and **16.4,** the electronegativities, their differences, and the corresponding bond types are

   a. N (3.0), H (2.1); 0.9; moderately polar covalent
   b. F (4.0), F (4.0); 0.0; nonpolar covalent
   c. Ca (1.0), O (3.5); 2.5; ionic
   d. Al (1.5), Cl (3.0); 1.5; very polar covalent

3. **EVALUATE** *Do the results make sense?*

   The answers are consistent with the magnitudes of the electronegativity differences.

Practice Problems

19. Identify the bonds between atoms of each pair of elements as nonpolar covalent, moderately polar covalent, very polar covalent, or ionic.

   a. H and Br   **d.** Cl and F
   b. K and Cl   **e.** Li and O
   c. C and O   **f.** Br and Br

20. Order the following covalent bonds from least to most polar.

   a. H—Cl   **d.** H—C
   b. H—Br   **e.** F—F
   c. H—S

Polar Molecules

The presence of a polar bond in a molecule often makes the entire molecule polar. In a **polar molecule,** one end of the molecule is slightly negative and the other end is slightly positive. In the hydrogen chloride molecule, for example, the partial charges on the hydrogen and chlorine atoms are electrically charged regions or poles. A molecule that has two poles is called a dipolar molecule, or **dipole.** The hydrogen chloride molecule is a dipole. As shown in **Figure 16.22,** when such molecules are placed in an electric field, they become oriented with respect to the positive and negative plates.

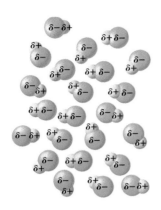

Negative plate   Positive plate

Electric field absent.
Polar molecules oriented randomly.

Electric field on.
Polar molecules line up.

Figure 16.22
When polar molecules, such as HCl, are placed in an electric field, the slightly negative ends of the molecules become oriented toward the positively charged plate and the slightly positive ends of the molecules become oriented toward the negatively charged plate. What would happen if carbon dioxide molecules were placed in such a field? Why?

Chem ASAP!
Animation 19
Learn to distinguish between polar and nonpolar molecules.

The effect of polar bonds on the polarity of an entire molecule depends on the shape of the molecule and the orientation of the polar bonds. A carbon dioxide molecule, for example, has two polar bonds and is linear.

$$\overset{\longleftarrow\!+}{}\overset{+\!\longrightarrow}{}$$
$$O=C=O$$

Note that the carbon and oxygens lie along the same axis. Therefore, the bond polarities cancel because they are in opposite directions. Carbon dioxide is thus a nonpolar molecule, despite the presence of two polar bonds.

The water molecule also has two polar bonds. However, the water molecule is bent rather than linear. Therefore, the bond polarities do not cancel. Is a water molecule polar or nonpolar?

Attractions Between Molecules

Molecules are often attracted to each other by a variety of forces. These intermolecular attractions are weaker than either an ionic or a covalent bond. Nevertheless, you should not underestimate the importance of these forces. Among other things, these attractions are responsible for determining whether a molecular compound is a gas, a liquid, or a solid at a given temperature.

There are several kinds of molecular attractions. The weakest attractions are collectively called **van der Waals forces,** named after the Dutch chemist Johannes van der Waals (1837–1923). Van der Waals forces consist of two possible types: dispersion forces and dipole interactions. **Dispersion forces,** the weakest of all molecular interactions, are caused by the motion of electrons. The strength of dispersion forces generally increases as the number of electrons in a molecule increases. The halogen diatomic molecules are examples of molecules where the major attraction for one another is caused by dispersion forces. Fluorine and chlorine have relatively few electrons and are gases at STP because of their especially weak dispersion forces. The larger number of electrons in bromine generates larger dispersion forces. Bromine molecules are therefore sufficiently attracted to each other to make bromine a liquid at STP. Iodine, with a still larger number of electrons, is a solid at STP.

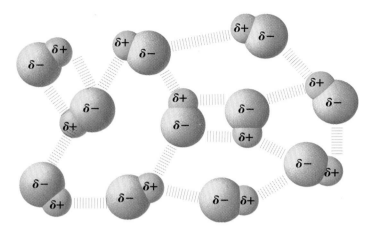

Figure 16.23

Polar molecules are attracted to one another by dipole interactions, a type of van der Waals force.

Molecular Modeling

The widespread availability of fast computers has greatly benefited chemists interested in the shapes of molecules and in the interactions between molecules.

Molecular modeling computer programs, for example, are becoming an important tool in the pharmaceutical industry for designing drugs. These programs allow the creation of models of molecules composed of thousands of atoms. Using a special viewing apparatus, chemists can see three-dimensional representations of complex molecules on the computer monitor. On the monitor, it is possible to turn the molecule over to see the other side, to shrink it, or to cut it in pieces. Through a computer technology called virtual reality, it is likely that a chemist will soon be able to get virtually inside a molecular structure to examine it from every possible angle.

The second type of van der Waals force, **dipole interactions,** occurs when polar molecules are attracted to one another. The electrostatic attractions involved occur between the oppositely charged regions of dipolar molecules, as shown in **Figure 16.23.** The slightly negative region of a polar molecule is weakly attracted to the slightly positive region of another polar molecule. Dipole interactions are similar to but much weaker than ionic bonds.

The dipole interactions in water, for example, result in a weak attraction of water molecules for one another. Each $O-H$ bond in the water molecule is highly polar, and the oxygen acquires a slightly negative charge because of its greater electronegativity. The hydrogens in water acquire a slightly positive charge. The positive region of one water molecule attracts the negative region of another water molecule. The dipolar attraction between the hydrogen of one water molecule and the oxygen of another water molecule is strong relative to other dipolar attractions. This relatively strong interaction, which is also found in hydrogen-containing molecules other than water, is given the special name hydrogen bond.

Hydrogen bonds are attractive forces in which a hydrogen covalently bonded to a very electronegative atom is also weakly bonded to an unshared electron pair of another electronegative atom. This other atom may be in the same molecule or in a nearby molecule. Hydrogen bonding always involves hydrogen—it is the only chemically reactive element with valence electrons that are not shielded from the nucleus by a layer of underlying electrons.

A very polar covalent bond forms when hydrogen bonds to an electronegative atom such as oxygen, nitrogen, or fluorine. This leaves the hydrogen nucleus very electron-deficient. The sharing of a nonbonding electron pair on a nearby electronegative atom compensates for the deficiency. The resulting hydrogen bond has about 5% of the strength of an average covalent bond. Hydrogen bonds are the strongest of the intermolecular forces. They are extremely important in determining the properties of water and biological molecules such as proteins. **Figure 16.24** shows hydrogen bonding between water molecules.

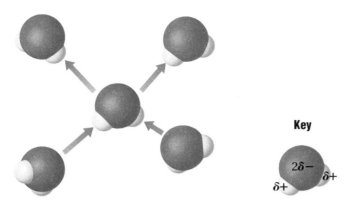

Figure 16.24
The strong hydrogen bonding between water molecules accounts for many properties of water, such as the fact that water is a liquid rather than a gas at ordinary temperatures. Although a hydrogen bond between water molecules has only about 5% of the strength of an average covalent bond, it is much stronger than the dipole interactions characteristic of other polar molecules.

Intermolecular Attractions and Molecular Properties

At room temperature, some compounds are gases, some are liquids, and some are solids. The physical properties of a compound depend on the type of bonding it displays—in particular, on whether it is ionic or covalent. **Table 16.5** summarizes some of the characteristic differences between ionic and covalent (molecular) substances. A great range of physical properties occurs among covalent compounds. This is mainly because of widely varying intermolecular attractions.

The melting and boiling points of most molecular compounds are low compared with those of ionic compounds. In most molecular solids, only the weak attractions between molecules need to be broken. However, a few

Table 16.5

Characteristics of Ionic and Covalent Compounds		
Characteristic	**Ionic compound**	**Covalent compound**
Representative unit	Formula unit	Molecule
Bond formation	Transfer of one or more electrons between atoms	Sharing of electron pairs between atoms
Type of elements	Metallic and nonmetallic	Nonmetallic
Physical state	Solid	Solid, liquid, or gas
Melting point	High (usually above 300 °C)	Low (usually below 300 °C)
Solubility in water	Usually high	High to low
Electrical conductivity of aqueous solution	Good conductor	Poor to nonconducting

Figure 16.25
Liquids tend to form drops because of intermolecular attractions. Molecular substances with weak intermolecular attractions are gases at room temperature. Molecular substances with very strong intermolecular attractions are generally found as solids.

Figure 16.26
Diamond is a network-solid form of carbon. Diamond has a three-dimensional structure, with each carbon at the center of a tetrahedron.

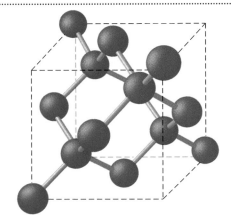

Chem ASAP!
Simulation 18
Relate melting and boiling points to the strength of intermolecular forces.

molecular solids do not melt until the temperature reaches 1000 °C or higher, or they decompose without melting at all. Most of these very stable substances are **network solids** (or network crystals), solids in which all of the atoms are covalently bonded to each other. Diamond is an example of a network solid. As shown in **Figure 16.26,** each carbon atom in a diamond is covalently bonded to four other carbons. Cutting a diamond requires breaking a multitude of these bonds. Diamond does not melt; rather, it vaporizes to a gas at 3500 °C and above. Silicon carbide, with the formula SiC and a melting point of about 2700 °C, is also a network solid. Silicon carbide is so hard that it is used in grindstones and as an abrasive. How do you think the molecular structures of silicon carbide and diamond compare? You can think of samples of diamond, silicon carbide, and other network solids as single molecules. Their melting or decomposition requires that actual covalent bonds be broken.

section review 16.3

21. Explain how you can use electronegativity values to classify a bond as nonpolar covalent, polar covalent, or ionic.

22. Describe the three kinds of weak attractive forces that hold groups of molecules together. Rank these forces from weakest to strongest.

23. Not every molecule with polar bonds is polar. Explain this statement. Use CCl_4 as an example.

24. Draw the electron dot structure for each molecule. Identify polar covalent bonds by assigning slightly positive ($\delta+$) and slightly negative ($\delta-$) symbols to the appropriate atoms.
    a. HOOH   **b.** BrCl   **c.** HBr   **d.** H_2O

25. How does a network solid differ from most other covalent compounds?

26. Which of the following are characteristic of most covalent compounds?
    a. high melting point
    b. shared bonding electrons
    c. low water solubility
    d. existence as molecules
    e. composed of a metal and a nonmetal

 Chem ASAP! Assessment 16.3 Check your understanding of the important ideas and concepts in Section 16.3.

---

portfolio project

RasMol is a free program for viewing the structures of molecules. Search for the RasMol site on the Internet. Download a copy of the RasMol package, which contains the program, documentation, and models of protein molecules. Prepare a demonstration of the software for your class.

PAPER CHROMATOGRAPHY OF FOOD DYES

SAFETY

Use safe and proper laboratory procedures.

PURPOSE

To use paper chromatography to separate and identify food dyes in various samples.

MATERIALS

- pencil
- paper
- ruler
- scissors
- toothpicks
- 4 different colors of food coloring
- plastic cup
- 0.1% NaCl solution
- chromatography paper

PROCEDURE

Cut a 5 cm × 10 cm strip of chromatography paper and label it with a pencil as shown in Figure A. Use a different toothpick to place a spot of each of the four food colors on the Xs on your chromatography paper. Allow the spots to dry for a few minutes. Fill the plastic cup so its bottom is just covered with the solvent (0.1% NaCl solution). Wrap the chromatography paper around a pencil. Remove the pencil and place the chromatography paper, color-spot side down, in the solvent. When the solvent reaches the top of the chromatography paper, remove the paper and allow it to dry.

Figure A

ANALYSIS

Using your experimental data, record the answers to the following questions below your data table.

1. If a food color sample yields a single streak or spot, it is usually a pure compound. Which food colors consist of pure compounds?

2. Which food colors are mixtures of compounds?

3. Food colors often consist of a mixture of three colored dyes: Red No. 40, Yellow No. 5, and Blue No. 1. Read the label on the food color package. Which dyes do your food color samples contain?

4. Identify each spot or streak on your chromatogram as Red No. 40, Yellow No. 5, or Blue No. 1.

5. Paper chromatography separates polar covalent compounds on the basis of their relative polarities. The most polar dyes migrate the fastest and appear at the top of the paper. Which dye is the most polar? The least polar?

YOU'RE THE CHEMIST

The following small-scale activities allow you to develop your own procedures and analyze the results.

1. **Design It!** Design and carry out an experiment to identify the dyes in various colored candies.

2. **Design It!** Design and carry out an experiment to identify the dyes in various colored markers using the paper chromatography method.

3. **Design It!** Design and carry out an experiment to identify the dyes in various colored powdered drinks using the paper chromatography method.

4. **Analyze It!** Use different solvents, such as 2-propanol (rubbing alcohol), vinegar, and ammonia, to separate food colors. Does the solvent affect the results?

5. **Analyze It!** Explore the effect of different papers on your results. Try paper towels, notebook paper, and coffee filters. Report your results. Examine the relative positions of Blue No. 1 and Yellow No. 5. What do you observe?

BLOCKS AND BONDS

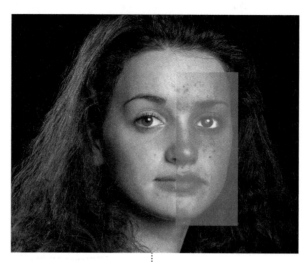

Is sunlight good for you or not? At one time, people thought you should get as much sun as possible. A dark tan was considered a sign of health. Today, however, it is well-known that sunlight can be very harmful, especially for people with light skin. The reason is that the ultraviolet (UV) radiation in sunlight can break covalent bonds in the molecules of your skin cells.

Sunlight, of course, is not all bad. Your skin cells require some sunlight to make vitamin D, a substance necessary for the formation of healthy bones and teeth. But unless they are protected in some way, skin cells are damaged by excessive exposure to UV radiation. In the short term, the damage shows itself as sunburn. Over the long term, skin that has received too much UV radiation becomes wrinkled and may develop cancer.

UV radiation is capable of penetrating your skin to a depth of about 1 mm. When UV radiation penetrates your skin, it can damage the molecules of DNA in your skin cells by breaking the covalent bonds that hold the molecules together. Even slight damage to DNA can be significant, as DNA controls the functions of a cell. When a skin cell's DNA is damaged, it may no longer be able to function normally. One possible result is that it may begin to divide uncontrollably, making more and more cells with abnormal DNA. This uncontrolled cell division is the beginning stage of cancer.

In people with light skin, a suntan is visible evidence that the body is trying to protect itself from harm. The skin responds to UV exposure by making more of the dark pigment melanin. Melanin absorbs some of the damaging radiation and thus protects the molecular structure of the skin. Even with this protective mechanism, however, damage to the skin can occur. People with dark skin can withstand more UV exposure without

Over the long term, skin that has received too much UV radiation becomes wrinkled and may develop cancer.

cell damage because they have larger amounts of melanin, but even they are not immune to the effects of UV exposure.

The ozone layer in the upper atmosphere also helps to block the sun's harmful UV rays. Unfortunately, however, the ozone layer is being diminished by chemical reactions between ozone and pollutants such as chlorofluorocarbons (CFCs). As a result, the worldwide incidence of skin cancer is gradually increasing. Today, UV radiation from the sun must be considered an environmental hazard.

The best way to protect yourself from the effects of UV radiation is to remain out of the sun as much as possible. The next-best way is to use a sunscreen or sunblock on your skin. The covalent bonds of certain compounds in the sunscreen absorb many of the harmful wavelengths of UV radiation, thus protecting the covalent bonds in your skin.

All sunscreens are given a sun protection factor (SPF) value as a measure of their effectiveness. The SPF value indicates the amount of increase in UV protection you receive by using the product. If you use a sunscreen with an SPF of 6, for example, and stay in the sun for six hours, you will receive an amount of UV equivalent to one hour of exposure with no sunscreen. Most doctors recommend that light-skinned people use sunscreens with an SPF of 15 or higher.

CHEMISTRY IN CAREERS

☆ ☆

ONCOLOGIST
Use the latest medical treatments to save lives.
See page 875.

CHEMIST NEEDED
Environment GC. Must know
troubleshooting;

TAKE IT TO THE NET

Find out more about career opportunities:
www.phschool.com

CHEMICAL SPECIALIST
Local food service distributor seek
responsible self-motivated indivic

KEY TERMS

- antibonding orbital *p. 452*
- bond dissociation energy *p. 447*
- bonding orbital *p. 452*
- coordinate covalent bond *p. 444*
- diamagnetic *p. 450*
- dipole *p. 462*
- dipole interaction *p. 464*
- dispersion force *p. 463*
- double covalent bond *p. 442*
- hybridization *p. 457*

- hydrogen bond *p. 464*
- molecular orbital *p. 452*
- network solid *p. 466*
- nonpolar covalent bond *p. 460*
- paramagnetic *p. 450*
- pi bond *p. 454*
- polar bond *p. 460*
- polar covalent bond *p. 460*
- polar molecule *p. 462*
- resonance structure *p. 449*

- sigma bond *p. 453*
- single covalent bond *p. 437*
- structural formula *p. 437*
- tetrahedral angle *p. 455*
- triple covalent bond *p. 442*
- unshared pair *p. 438*
- van der Waals force *p. 463*
- VSEPR theory *p. 456*

CONCEPT SUMMARY

16.1 The Nature of Covalent Bonding

- Atoms form covalent bonds when they share electrons to form an octet.
- A shared pair of valence electrons constitutes a single covalent bond. Sometimes two or three pairs of electrons may be shared to give double or triple covalent bonds.
- Sometimes one atom may contribute both bonding electrons in a covalent bond. This type of bond is called a coordinate covalent bond.
- Resonance structures help to visualize the bonding in molecules when more than one electron dot formula can be written.

16.2 Bonding Theories

- Molecular orbital theory is a logical extension of the quantum mechanical description of the electron structure of atoms. Covalent bonding is described in terms of sigma and pi bonds.
- The valence-shell electron-pair repulsion, or VSEPR, theory of molecular geometry states that, as a general rule, molecules adjust their three-dimensional shapes so the valence-electron pairs are as far apart as possible.

- In some instances, molecular geometry is adequately described by simple overlap of atomic orbitals. In others, a description of molecular shape that better fits experimental results is obtained from hybridized atomic orbitals.

16.3 Polar Bonds and Molecules

- When covalent bonds join like atoms, the bonding electrons are shared equally and the bond is nonpolar. When the atoms in a bond have different electronegativities, the bonding electrons are shared unequally and the bond is polar.
- Hydrogen bonds are attractive forces in which a hydrogen covalently bonded to a very electronegative atom is also weakly bonded to an unshared electron pair of another electronegative atom. Hydrogen bonds are strong relative to other dipole interactions.
- Weak intermolecular forces determine whether a covalent compound will be a solid, liquid, or gas. Weak attractions between molecules are called van der Waals forces and include dispersion forces, dipole interactions, and hydrogen bonds.

CHAPTER CONCEPT MAP

Use these terms to construct a concept map that organizes the major ideas of this chapter.

 ChemASAP! Concept Map 16
Create your Concept Map using the computer.

CONCEPT PRACTICE

27. Explain why neon is monatomic but chlorine is diatomic. *16.1*

28. Classify the following compounds as ionic or covalent. *16.1*
    a. $MgCl_2$ **b.** Na_2S **c.** H_2O **d.** H_2S

29. Describe the difference between an ionic and a covalent bond. *16.1*

30. How many electrons do two atoms in a double covalent bond share? How many in a triple covalent bond? *16.1*

31. Based on the examples given in Section 16.1, state a general rule for determining which atom is the central one in a binary molecular compound. *16.1*

32. Write plausible electron dot structures for the following substances. Each substance contains only single covalent bonds. *16.1*
    a. I_2 **b.** OF_2 **c.** H_2S **d.** NI_3

33. Draw the electron dot structure of each of the following molecules. *16.1*
    a. F_2 **b.** HCl   **c.** HCCH   **d.** HCN

34. Characterize a coordinate covalent bond and give an example. *16.1*

35. Explain why compounds containing C—N and C—O single bonds can form coordinate covalent bonds with H^+ but compounds containing only C—H and C—C single bonds cannot. *16.1*

36. What is true for the electron dot structures of all compounds that exhibit resonance? *16.1*

37. Draw resonance structures for the carbonate ion (CO_3^{2-}). Each oxygen is attached to the carbon. *16.1*

38. Using electron dot structures, draw at least two resonance structures for the nitrite ion (NO_2^-). The oxygens in NO_2^- are attached to the nitrogen. *16.1*

39. How can you experimentally determine whether a substance is paramagnetic? *16.1*

40. Predict whether the following species are diamagnetic or paramagnetic. *16.1*
    a. BF_3 **b.** O_2^- **c.** NO_2 **d.** F_2

41. Which of these compounds would you expect to contain elements that do not follow the octet rule? Explain. *16.1*
    a. NF_3 **b.** PCl_2F_3 **c.** SF_4 **d.** SCl_2

42. Which of the following species would you predict to be diamagnetic? Paramagnetic? *16.1*
    a. NO_3^- **b.** OH^- **c.** H_2O **d.** SO_3

43. What is the relationship between the magnitude of a molecule's bond dissociation energy and its expected chemical reactivity? *16.1*

44. Explain what is meant by bond dissociation energy. *16.1*

45. Assume the total bond energy in a molecule is the sum of the individual bond energies. Calculate the total bond energy in a mole of ethyne (C_2H_2). (*Hint:* Write the electron dot structure to determine the kinds of bonds. Then refer to **Table 16.3**.) *16.1*

46. Draw molecular orbital diagrams for the possible diatomic molecule Li_2. Would you expect Li_2 to exist as a stable molecule? *16.2*

47. What is the total number of sigma bonds and pi bonds in each molecule? *16.2*

    a. $H-C\equiv N$ **b.** $H-\overset{\displaystyle H}{\underset{\displaystyle H}{\overset{|}{\underset{|}{C}}}}-N=C=O$

48. Use VSEPR theory to predict the shapes of the following species. *16.2*
    a. CO_2 **c.** SO_3 **e.** CO
    b. $SiCl_4$ **d.** SCl_2 **f.** H_2Se

49. The molecule CO_2 has two carbon–oxygen double bonds. Describe the bonding in the CO_2 molecule, which involves hybridized orbitals for carbon and oxygen. *16.2*

50. What types of hybrid orbitals are involved in the bonding of the carbon atoms in the following molecules? *16.2*
    a. CH_4 **c.** $HC\equiv CH$
    b. $H_2C=CH_2$ **d.** $N\equiv C-C\equiv N$

51. What must always be true if a covalent bond is to be polar? *16.3*

52. The bonds between the following pairs of elements are covalent. Arrange them according to polarity, naming the most polar bond first. *16.3*
    a. H—Cl   **c.** H—F   **e.** H—H
    b. H—C   **d.** H—O   **f.** S—Cl

53. Arrange the following bonds in order of increasing ionic character. *16.3*
    a. Cl—F   **c.** K—O   **e.** S—O
    b. N—N   **d.** C—H   **f.** Li—F

54. Based on the information about molecular shapes in Section 16.2, which of these molecules would you expect to be polar? *16.3*
  a. SO_2 **c.** CO_2
  b. H_2S **d.** BF_3

55. Depict the hydrogen bonding between two ammonia molecules and between one ammonia molecule and one water molecule. *16.3*

56. Which compound in each pair exhibits the stronger intermolecular hydrogen bonding? *16.3*
  a. H_2S, H_2O **c.** HBr, HCl
  b. HCl, HF   **d.** NH_3, H_2O

57. What is a hydrogen bond? *16.3*

58. Why do compounds with strong intermolecular attractive forces have higher boiling points than compounds with weak intermolecular attractive forces? *16.3*

CONCEPT MASTERY

59. Devise a hybridization scheme for PCl_3 and predict the molecular shape based on this scheme.

60. Write two electron dot structures for the molecule N_2O. Predict the magnetic properties and shape of this molecule.

61. The chlorine and oxygen atoms in thionyl chloride ($SOCl_2$) are bonded directly to the sulfur. Write an acceptable electron dot structure for thionyl chloride.

62. Explain why each electron dot structure is incorrect. Replace each structure with one that is more acceptable.

                   :Cl:

a. $[:C::\ddot{N}:]^-$ **c.** $H:\ddot{C}::O$

b. $:\ddot{F}:P::\ddot{F}:$ **d.**   :$\ddot{F}$:
      :$\ddot{F}$:   :$\ddot{F}$:$\ddot{B}$:$\ddot{F}$:

63. Use VSEPR theory to predict the geometry of each of the following.
  a. $SiCl_4$ **c.** CCl_4
  b. CO_3^{2-} **d.** SCl_2

64. The following graph shows how the percent ionic character of a single bond varies according to the difference in electronegativity between the two elements forming the bond. Answer the following questions, using this graph and **Table 14.2.**

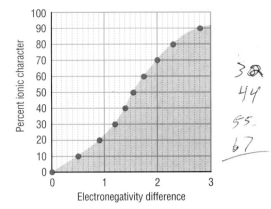

a. What is the relationship between the percent ionic character of single bonds and the electronegativity difference of their elements?
b. What electronegativity difference will result in a bond with a 50% ionic character?
c. Estimate the percent ionic character of the bonds formed between (1) lithium and oxygen, (2) nitrogen and oxygen, (3) magnesium and chlorine, and (4) nitrogen and fluorine.

65. Using bond dissociation energies, estimate ΔH for the following reaction.

$$CO(g) + 2H_2(g) \longrightarrow CH_3OH(g)$$

66. Give the angles between the orbitals of each hybrid.
  a. sp^3 hybrids   **b.** sp^2 hybrids   **c.** sp hybrids

67. Describe the difference between a bonding molecular orbital and an antibonding molecular orbital. How do the energies of these orbitals compare?

CRITICAL THINKING

68. Choose the term that best completes the second relationship.
  a. house : lumber
    bond : _____
    (1) atoms   (3) valence electrons
    (2) molecules   (4) octet rule
  b. globe : Earth
    electron dots : _____
    (1) atoms   (3) valence electrons
    (2) molecules   (4) octet rule

69. Make a list of the elements found in **Table 16.2.** What do the elements that form covalent bonds have in common?

70. Is there a clear difference between a very polar covalent bond and an ionic bond? Explain.

71. Which of the following ions have the same number of electrons as a noble gas?
    a. Al^{3+} **b.** O^{2-} **c.** Br^- **d.** N^{3-}

72. A solution containing 0.10 mol $BaCl_2$ is mixed with a solution containing 0.20 mol Na_2SO_4 to give a precipitate of $BaSO_4$. What is the maximum yield in moles of $BaSO_4$? In grams?

73. Write correct electron configurations for atoms of the following elements.
    a. sodium   **c.** phosphorus
    b. sulfur   **d.** nitrogen

74. Calculate the gram formula mass of each substance.
    a. $CaSO_4$ **c.** NI_3
    b. H_2SO_4 **d.** $FeCl_3$

75. Give the number of representative particles in the following molar quantities.
    a. 2.00 centimoles
    b. 1.54 millimoles
    c. 8.73 nanomoles
    d. 3.00 micromoles

76. Name and give the symbol for the element in the following position in the periodic table.
    a. Group 7B, period 4
    b. Group 3A, period 5
    c. Group 1A, period 7
    d. Group 6A, period 6

77. The electron structure and geometry of the methane molecule (CH_4) can be described by a variety of models, including electron dot structure, simple overlap of atomic orbitals, and orbital hybridization of carbon. Write the electron dot structure of CH_4. Sketch two molecular orbital pictures of the CH_4 molecule. For your first sketch, assume that one of the paired $2s^2$ electrons of carbon has been promoted to the empty $2p$ orbital. Overlap each half-filled atomic orbital of carbon to a half-filled $2s$ orbital of hydrogen. What is the predicted geometry of the CH_4 molecule, using this simple overlap method? In your second sketch, assume hybridization of the $2s$ and $2p$ orbitals of carbon. Now what geometry would you predict for CH_4? Which picture is preferable based on the facts that all $H—C—H$ bond angles in CH_4 are 109.5° and all $C—H$ bond distances are identical?

78. There are some compounds in which one atom has more electrons than the corresponding noble gas. Examples are PCl_5, SF_6, and IF_7. Write the electron dot structures of P, S, and I atoms, and of these compounds. Considering the outer shell configuration of P, S, and I, develop an orbital hybridization scheme to explain the existence of these compounds.

Select the choice that best answers each question or completes each statement.

1. A bond in which two atoms share a pair of electrons is *not*
   a. a coordinate covalent bond.
   b. a polar covalent bond.
   c. an ionic bond.
   d. a nonpolar covalent bond.

2. How many valence electrons are in a molecule of phosphoric acid, H_3PO_4?
   a. 7   b. 16   c. 24   d. 32

3. Which of these molecules can form a hydrogen bond with a water molecule?
   a. N_2 b. NH_3 c. O_2 d. CH_4

4. Which substance contains both covalent and ionic bonds?
   a. NH_4NO_3 c. LiF
   b. CH_3OCH_3 d. $CaCl_2$

5. Which of these bonds is most polar?
   a. H—Cl   c. H—F
   b. H—Br   d. H—I

Use the description and data table below to answer questions 6–9.

Nonbonding pairs of electrons must be considered when predicting shapes of molecules. The table relates molecular shape to the number of bonding and nonbonding electron pairs in molecules.

Bonding pairs	Non-bonding pairs	Arrangement of electron pairs	Molecular shape	Example
4	0	tetrahedral	tetrahedral	CH_4
3	1	tetrahedral	pyramidal	NCl_3
2	2	tetrahedral	bent	H_2S
1	3	tetrahedral	linear	HF

6. Draw the electron dot structure for each example molecule.

7. Explain why the arrangement of electron pairs is tetrahedral in each molecule.

8. H_2S has two hydrogen atoms bonded to a sulfur atom. Why isn't the molecule linear?

9. What is the arrangement of electron pairs in PBr_3? Predict the molecular shape of a PBr_3 molecule.

For questions 10–12, identify the type of inter-molecular bonding represented by the dotted lines in the drawings.

10. H_2O

11. BrCl (bromine chloride)

12. CH_3OH (methanol)

13. *You Draw It!* Draw two different pictures that show hydrogen bonding between a water molecule and a methanol molecule.

For each question there are two statements. Decide whether each statement is true or false. Then decide whether Statement II is a correct explanation for Statement I.

	Statement I		Statement II
14.	Water is a polar molecule.	BECAUSE	The covalent bonds in water are polar.
15.	A carbon monoxide molecule has a triple covalent bond.	BECAUSE	Carbon and oxygen atoms have an unequal number of valence electrons.
16.	Xenon has a lower boiling point than neon.	BECAUSE	Dispersion forces between xenon atoms are stronger than those between neon atoms.
17.	The nitrate ion has three resonance structures.	BECAUSE	The nitrate ion has three single bonds.

Chapter 17

WATER AND AQUEOUS SYSTEMS

Oceans cover about three quarters of Earth's surface.

FEATURES

DISCOVER IT!
Observing Surface Tension

SMALL-SCALE LAB
Electrolytes

MINI LAB
Surfactants

CHEMISTRY SERVING ... THE ENVIRONMENT
It's the Water

CHEMISTRY IN CAREERS
Oceanographer

LINK TO HEALTH
Water and Exercise

LINK TO SANITATION
Wastewater Treatment

Stay current with **SCIENCE NEWS**
Find out more about aqueous systems:
www.phschool.com

DISCOVER IT! OBSERVING SURFACE TENSION

You need waxed paper, a ruler, a teaspoon, a cup, tap water, and liquid dish detergent.

1. Place a 15-cm square of waxed paper on a flat surface.
2. Drop 1/3 teaspoon of water from a height of about 20 cm onto the center of the paper.
3. Add 1 drop of detergent to 1/2 cup of water and stir.
4. Repeat Steps 1 and 2 using the diluted detergent in place of water.
5. You may wish to repeat this activity with squares of aluminum foil, clear wrap, and writing paper.

What do you observe when you drop water onto the waxed paper surface? What do you observe when you use diluted detergent instead of water? Use your results to suggest how the detergent may have changed the physical properties of water. After completing this chapter, review your suggestion and modify it if necessary.

LIQUID WATER AND ITS PROPERTIES

*I*n December of 1968, when the Apollo 8 astronauts first saw their home planet from a distance of thousands of kilometers, they affectionately called it the big blue marble. As you can see in this photograph, water covers about three-quarters of Earth's surface. In addition to making up Earth's oceans, water forms the polar ice caps and cycles through the atmosphere. All life forms with which we are familiar are made mostly of water. **What properties of water make this unique substance essential to life on Earth?**

objectives
▶ Describe the hydrogen bonding that occurs in water
▶ Explain the high surface tension and low vapor pressure of water in terms of hydrogen bonding

key terms
▶ surface tension
▶ surfactant

The Water Molecule

Water is a unique compound. It is the foundation of all life on Earth. Without water neither plant nor animal life as we know it could exist. Liquid water in the form of oceans, lakes, rivers, ponds, and streams covers about three-quarters of Earth's surface. Immense aquifers store water deep underground. Ice, or solid water, dominates the vast polar regions of the globe. Water appears as icebergs in the oceans, and it blankets the temperate zones as snow in winter. Water vapor from the evaporation of surface water and from steam spouted out of geysers and volcanoes is ever-present in Earth's atmosphere.

Water is a simple triatomic molecule. Each O—H covalent bond in the water molecule is highly polar. Because of its greater electronegativity, oxygen attracts the electron pair of the covalent O—H bond and acquires a slightly negative charge. The less electronegative hydrogen atoms acquire a slightly positive charge. The water molecule has an H—O—H bond angle of 105°. Because of this bent shape, the two O—H bond polarities do not cancel, and the water molecule as a whole is polar. The net polarity of the water molecule is illustrated in **Figure 17.2**. The region around the oxygen has a slightly negative charge, and the region around the hydrogens has a slightly positive charge.

Figure 17.1

Water is vital to life. Animals that live on the grasslands depend on watering holes, such as the one shown here.

Polar bonds

Molecule has net polarity.

Figure 17.2

In a water molecule, the bond polarities are equal, but the two dipoles do not cancel each other because a water molecule is bent. There is a net polarity, and the molecule as a whole is polar.

Figure 17.3

(a) Due to their polarity, water molecules attract each other.
(b) They participate in hydrogen bonding. To form a hydrogen bond, what must be true about the hydrogen and the element to which it is hydrogen bonded?

Chem ASAP!

Animation 20

See how hydrogen bonding results in the unique properties of water.

(a)

(b)

Hydrogen bonds

In general, polar molecules are attracted to one another by dipole interactions. In water, however, the attraction is the result of intermolecular hydrogen bonds, as **Figure 17.3** illustrates. Water molecules change position by sliding over one another. But because of hydrogen bonding, most water molecules do not have enough kinetic energy at room temperature to escape the surface of the liquid. Many unique and important properties of water—including its high surface tension, low vapor pressure, high specific heat capacity, high heat of vaporization, and high boiling point—result from hydrogen bonding.

Surface Properties

Have you ever seen a glass so filled with water that the water surface bulges above the rim? Or have you noticed that water forms nearly spherical droplets at the end of a medicine dropper or when sprayed on a greasy surface? Perhaps you have observed that a needle floats if placed on the surface of water, but the needle sinks immediately if it breaks through the surface.

The surface of water acts like a skin. The water strider shown in **Figure 17.4** takes advantage of this skinlike property of water's surface. This phenomenon, called surface tension, is explained by water's ability to form hydrogen bonds. The molecules within the liquid are surrounded by and hydrogen-bonded to adjacent water molecules. At the surface of the

Figure 17.4

Surface tension makes it possible for some insects, such as this water strider, to "walk" on water. The force of gravity pulling the insect downward is less than the forces of attraction between the water molecules.

Chem ASAP!

Animation 21

Discover how some insects can walk on water.

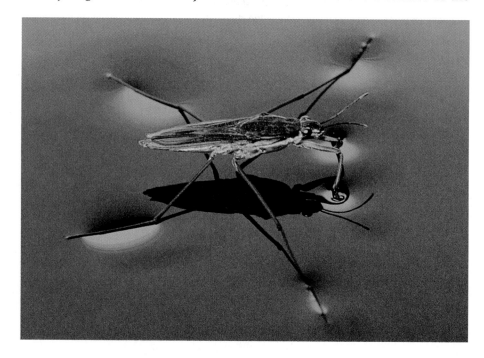

liquid, however, water molecules experience an uneven attraction. As you can see in **Figure 17.5,** the water molecules are hydrogen-bonded on only one side of the drop. The water molecules are not attracted to the air because they cannot form hydrogen bonds with air molecules. As a result, water molecules at the surface tend to be drawn into the body of the liquid. The inward force, or pull, that tends to minimize the surface area of a liquid is called **surface tension.**

The surface tension of a liquid tends to hold a drop of liquid in a spherical shape, as shown in **Figure 17.6.** A sphere has the smallest surface area for a given volume. At the same time, the force of gravity tends to flatten the drop. A liquid that has strong intermolecular attractions has a high surface tension. The higher the surface tension, the more nearly spherical is the drop of that particular liquid.

All liquids have a surface tension, but water's surface tension is higher than most. This is why water tends to bead up on some surfaces rather than to spread out. It is possible to decrease the surface tension of water by adding a **surfactant,** which is a wetting agent such as soap or detergent that gets its name from *surf*ace *act*ive *agent.* When a detergent is added to beads of water on a greasy surface, the detergent molecules interfere with the hydrogen bonding between water molecules. As a result, surface tension is reduced, the beads collapse, and the water spreads out.

Hydrogen bonding between water molecules also explains water's unusually low vapor pressure. As you learned in Section 10.2, the vapor pressure of a liquid is caused by molecules that escape the surface of the liquid and enter the gas phase. Because hydrogen bonds hold water molecules to one another, the tendency of these molecules to escape is low. Imagine what would happen if it were not. All the lakes and oceans, with their large surface areas, would rapidly evaporate!

Air   Drop of water

Figure 17.5

Water molecules at the surface of the water drop experience an uneven attraction. Because they cannot form hydrogen bonds with air molecules, they are drawn into the body of the liquid, producing surface tension. What does each arrow in the figure represent?

Figure 17.6

(a) Surface tension tends to hold drops of liquids in a spherical shape. At the same time, the force of gravity tends to flatten the drops. (b) All the drops shown are of equal volume. From left to right, they are mercury, water, and water with detergent. Which of these three liquids has the least surface tension?

(a)

(b)

LiNK
TO
HEALTH

Water and Exercise
The normal human body contains about 66% water by mass. You lose water through perspiration, as water vapor from breathing, and in your body's waste products—mainly urine.

The loss of water during periods of inactivity is probably 25–100 mL/h. Obviously, you must replace this water to avoid dehydration. Medical experts recommend that you drink at least eight glasses of water every day. When you exercise vigorously for prolonged periods, your water loss through perspiration may increase to as much as 3000 mL/h, which heightens your risk of dehydration. Most sports physiologists agree that athletes should drink water when exercising to maintain good health and maximize performance.

Figure 17.7
Many people flock to the beach in hot weather because the shore is cooler than inland areas. How would you explain this phenomenon in terms of water's heat capacity?

Specific Heat Capacity

As you may recall, it takes 4.18 J (1 cal) of heat energy to raise the temperature of 1 g of water 1 °C. This is the specific heat capacity of water. The specific heat capacity of water is nearly constant at 4.18 J/(g × °C) at temperatures between 0 °C and 100 °C. Because of hydrogen bonding, the specific heat capacity of water is higher than that of most other substances. Iron has a specific heat capacity of 0.447 J/(g × °C). For the same increase in temperature, iron requires only about one-tenth as much heat as does an equal mass of water. On a sunny day, a puddle of water remains relatively cool, but a nearby sewer cover gets hot enough, it is said, to fry an egg. If the same amount of heat energy were added to identical masses of water and iron, how would the increases in temperature compare?

Water's high specific heat capacity helps moderate daily air temperatures around large bodies of water. On a warm day, water absorbs heat from its warmer environment, lowering the air temperature. On a cool night, heat is transferred from the water to its cooler environment, raising the air temperature. Thus water is a good storage medium for solar energy.

section review 17.1

1. Describe the hydrogen bonding between molecules in water.
2. How is hydrogen bonding responsible for the high surface tension and low vapor pressure of water?
3. What is a surfactant? How does it affect the surface tension of water?
4. What is the specific heat capacity of water?

Chem ASAP! **Assessment 17.1** Check your understanding of the important ideas and concepts in Section 17.1.

WATER VAPOR AND ICE

*O*n *October 27, 1915, the British Imperial Trans-Antarctic Expedition ship Endurance was crushed by pack ice and sank, leaving the members of the expedition to float on ice floes for five months. Today, icebreakers are used to open a safe path for navigation through floating pack ice.* **What property of water allows its solid phase, ice, to float in its liquid phase?**

objectives
▶ Account for the high heat of vaporization and the high boiling point of water in terms of hydrogen bonding
▶ Explain why ice floats in water

Evaporation and Condensation

You are probably familiar with several examples of both the evaporation and condensation of water. Have you ever left a glass of water out on the kitchen counter overnight? What happens? What have you noticed about the air you exhale on a very cold winter morning?

Because of hydrogen bonding, water absorbs a large amount of heat as it evaporates or vaporizes. The heat of vaporization is the amount of energy needed to convert 1 g of a substance from a liquid to a gas at the boiling point. It takes 2.26 kJ to convert 1 g of liquid water at 100 °C to 1 g of steam at 100 °C. An extensive network of hydrogen bonds tightly holds the molecules in liquid water together. These bonds must be broken before water changes from the liquid to the vapor state. The heat of vaporization of liquid ammonia, which is less hydrogen-bonded than water, is 1.37 kJ/g. Liquid methane, which has no hydrogen bonding, has a heat of vaporization of only 0.510 kJ/g.

The reverse of vaporization is condensation. When 1 g of steam at 100 °C condenses to 1 g of liquid water at 100 °C, 2.26 kJ of heat is given off. Thus the heat of condensation of water is 2.26 kJ/g. As expected, the heat of condensation of water is equal to the heat of vaporization of water. You can get a severe burn if steam condenses on your skin. Not only is the temperature of steam 100 °C, but the additional heat of condensation is also absorbed by your skin.

Figure 17.8
Mist rising from the rain forest, dew on morning grass, and clouds in the sky are all evidence of evaporation and condensation.

Table 17.1

Melting Points and Boiling Points of Some Substances with Low Molar Mass				
Name of substance	Formula	Molar mass (g/mol)	Melting point (°C)	Boiling point (°C)
Methane	CH_4	16	−183	−164
Ammonia	NH_3	17	−77.7	−33.3
Water	H_2O	18	0	100
Neon	Ne	20	−249	−246
Methanol	CH_3OH	32	−93.9	64.9
Hydrogen sulfide	H_2S	34	−85.5	−60.7

The evaporation and condensation of water are important to regional temperatures on Earth. Temperatures in the tropics would be much higher if water did not absorb heat while evaporating from the surfaces of the surrounding oceans. Temperatures in the polar regions would be much lower if water vapor did not release its heat while condensing out of the air.

Molecular compounds of low molar mass are usually gases or liquids with low boiling points at normal atmospheric pressure. As you can see in **Table 17.1,** ammonia is a typical example of a molecular compound. Ammonia has a molar mass of 17 g/mol and boils at about −33 °C. Water, however, with a molar mass of 18 g/mol, is an important exception. Its boiling point is 100 °C. What do you think accounts for water's high boiling point? You are correct if your answer is hydrogen bonding. Hydrogen bonding is more extensive in water than in ammonia. Therefore it takes much more heat to disrupt the attractions between water molecules than those between ammonia molecules. If the hydrogen bonding in water were as weak as it is in ammonia, water would be a gas at the usual temperatures found on Earth. What do you think this would mean for life as we know it? Compare the molar masses and boiling points of methanol and hydrogen sulfide provided in **Table 17.1.** Which of these two compounds has more extensive hydrogen bonding?

Ice

As a typical liquid cools, it contracts slightly. Its density increases because its volume decreases while its mass stays constant. If the cooling continues, the liquid eventually solidifies. Because the density of a typical solid is greater than that of the corresponding liquid, the solid sinks in its own liquid. For example, lead shot sinks in molten lead.

As water cools, it first behaves like a typical liquid. It contracts slightly and its density gradually increases until the temperature reaches 4 °C. Below 4 °C, however, the density of water starts to decrease. Water no longer behaves like a typical liquid. Ice, which forms at 0 °C, has about 10% greater volume and therefore a lower density than liquid water at 0 °C. See **Table 17.2.** As a result of its lower density, ice floats in liquid water. This is certainly unusual behavior for a solid. Ice is one of only a few solids that float in their own liquid.

Table 17.2

Density of Liquid Water and Ice	
Temperature (°C)	Density (g/cm³)
100 (liquid water)	0.9584
50	0.9881
25	0.9971
10	0.9997
4	1.000*
0 (liquid water)	0.9998
0 (ice)	0.9168

*Most dense

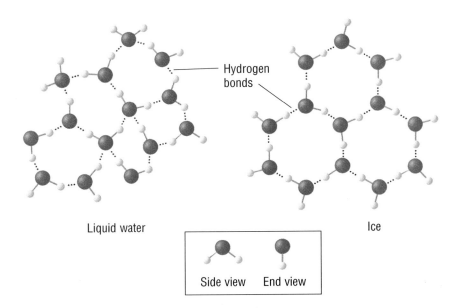

Liquid water   Hydrogen bonds   Ice

Side view   End view

Figure 17.9

The molecules in liquid water are hydrogen bonded but free to move about. Extensive hydrogen bonding in ice holds the water molecules farther apart in a more ordered arrangement than in liquid water. The hexagonal symmetry of snowflakes results from the hydrogen bonding of water molecules in ice.

Why does ice behave so differently? As you can see in **Figure 17.9,** the structure of ice is a very regular open framework of water molecules arranged like a honeycomb. Hydrogen bonding holds the water molecules in place. At low temperatures, the molecules do not have sufficient kinetic energy to break out of this rigid framework. When ice melts, the framework collapses. Consequently, the water molecules pack closer together, making liquid water more dense than ice.

The fact that ice floats has important consequences for organisms. A layer of ice on the top of a pond acts as an insulator for the water beneath, preventing it from freezing solid except under extreme conditions. Because the liquid water at the bottom of an otherwise frozen pond is warmer than 0 °C, aquatic life is able to survive. If ice were more dense than liquid water, bodies of water would tend to freeze solid during the winter months, destroying many types of aquatic life. What are some other phenomena that result from the expansion of water as it freezes to form ice?

Water molecules require a considerable amount of kinetic energy to return to the liquid state from the solid state. Ice melts at 0 °C, a high temperature for a molecule with such a low molar mass. The heat absorbed when 1 g of water changes from a solid to a liquid is 334 J/g. This heat-absorbing property can be used to great advantage, as you can see in **Figure 17.10.** This same amount of energy could also raise the temperature of 1 g of liquid water from 0 °C to 80 °C!

section review 17.2

5. Explain why water has a relatively high boiling point and heat of vaporization.

6. What is the difference between the structure of liquid water and the structure of ice? How does this explain why ice floats in water?

7. How much energy in kilojoules is required to change 47.6 g of ice at 0 °C to liquid water at the same temperature? In kilocalories?

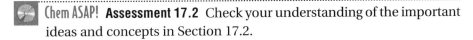

Chem ASAP! Assessment 17.2 Check your understanding of the important ideas and concepts in Section 17.2.

Figure 17.10

Ice packs decrease swelling and pain from an injury. Ice absorbs a large amount of heat as it changes from a solid to a liquid at 0 °C.

Water and Aqueous Systems   **481**

AQUEOUS SOLUTIONS

objectives

▶ Explain the significance of the statement "like dissolves like"

▶ Distinguish among strong electrolytes, weak electrolytes, and nonelectrolytes, giving examples of each

key terms

▶ aqueous solutions
▶ solvent
▶ solute
▶ solvation
▶ electrolytes
▶ nonelectrolytes
▶ weak electrolyte
▶ strong electrolyte
▶ water of hydration
▶ effloresce
▶ hygroscopic
▶ desiccants
▶ deliquescent

*I*s it possible to read by the light of a glowing pickle? *Although it sounds absurd, it is possible! The aqueous solution in a pickle will glow as an electric current is passed through it.* **What kind of solution conducts electricity?**

Solvents and Solutes

Chemically pure water never exists in nature because water dissolves so many substances. Tap water contains varying amounts of dissolved minerals and gases, as does water from ponds, streams, rivers, lakes, and oceans. Water samples containing dissolved substances are called **aqueous solutions.** In a solution, the dissolving medium is called the **solvent,** and the dissolved particles are called the **solute.** When sodium chloride dissolves in water, water is the solvent and sodium chloride is the solute. If you were making lemonade, what would the solvent be? The solutes?

As you may recall, solutions are homogeneous mixtures. They are also stable mixtures. For example, sodium chloride does not settle out when its solutions are allowed to stand, provided other conditions, such as temperature, remain constant. Solute particles can be either ionic or molecular, and their average diameters are usually less than 1.0 nm (10^{-9} m). Therefore, if you filter a solution through filter paper, both the solute and the solvent pass through the filter. See **Figure 17.11.** Solvents and solutes may be gases, liquids, or solids. It might be helpful for you to refer to **Table 2.3** on page 33 to review some common types of solutions.

Substances that dissolve most readily in water include ionic compounds and polar covalent molecules. Nonpolar covalent molecules, such as methane and those in oil, grease, and gasoline, do not dissolve in water. However, oil and grease will dissolve in gasoline. To understand this difference, you must know more about the structural features of the solvent and the solute and the attractions between them.

Figure 17.11

A solution cannot be separated by filtration. The small size of solute particles allows them to pass through filter paper.

The Solution Process

Water molecules are in continuous motion because of their kinetic energy. When a crystal of sodium chloride is placed in water, the water molecules collide with it. The solvent molecules (H_2O) attract the solute ions (Na^+, Cl^-). As individual sodium ions and chloride ions break away from the crystal, the sodium chloride dissolves. **Solvation** is the process that occurs when a solute dissolves. The negatively and positively charged ions become solvated; that is, they become surrounded by solvent molecules. **Figure 17.12** shows a model of the solvation of an ionic solid.

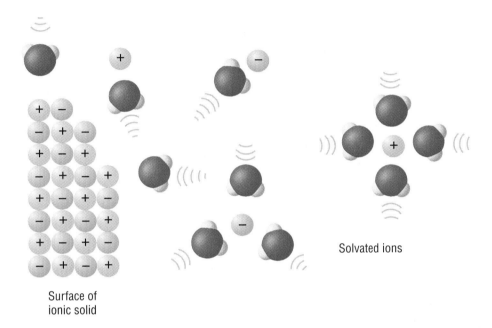

Surface of
ionic solid

Solvated ions

Figure 17.12
When an ionic solid dissolves, the ions become solvated and are surrounded by solvent molecules. Why do the water molecules orient themselves differently around the anions and the cations?

Chem ASAP!
Simulation 19
Explore the nature of solute–solvent interactions.

In some ionic compounds, the attractions between the ions in the crystals are stronger than the attractions exerted by water. These compounds cannot be solvated to any significant extent and are therefore nearly insoluble. Barium sulfate ($BaSO_4$) and calcium carbonate ($CaCO_3$) are examples of nearly insoluble ionic compounds.

What about dissolving oil in gasoline? Both oil and gasoline are composed of nonpolar molecules. They mix to form a solution, not because the solute and solvent are attracted, but because there are no repulsive forces between them. As a rule, polar solvents dissolve ionic compounds and polar molecules; nonpolar solvents dissolve nonpolar compounds. This relationship can be summed up in the expression "like dissolves like." What is the chemistry that explains the saying "oil and water don't mix"?

Figure 17.13
Oil and water do not mix.

Electrolytes and Nonelectrolytes

Compounds that conduct an electric current in aqueous solution or the molten state are called **electrolytes.** All ionic compounds are electrolytes. Sodium chloride, copper(II) sulfate, and sodium hydroxide are typical water-soluble electrolytes. Electrolytes conduct electricity in solution and in the molten state. Barium sulfate is an example of an ionic compound that conducts electricity in the molten state but not in aqueous solution because it is insoluble.

Compounds that do not conduct an electric current in either aqueous solution or the molten state are called **nonelectrolytes.** Because they are not composed of ions, many molecular compounds are nonelectrolytes. Most compounds of carbon, such as cane sugar and rubbing alcohol, are nonelectrolytes.

Some very polar molecular compounds are nonelectrolytes in the pure state, but become electrolytes when they dissolve in water. This occurs because such compounds ionize in solution. For example, neither ammonia (NH_3)(g) nor hydrogen chloride (HCl)(g) is an electrolyte in the pure state. Yet an aqueous solution of ammonia conducts electricity because ammonium ions (NH_4^+) and hydroxide ions (OH^-) form when ammonia dissolves in water.

$$NH_3(g) + H_2O(l) \longrightarrow NH_4^+(aq) + OH^-(aq)$$

Similarly, in aqueous solution, hydrogen chloride produces hydronium ions (H_3O^+) and chloride ions (Cl^-). An aqueous solution of hydrogen chloride conducts electricity and is therefore an electrolyte.

$$HCl(g) + H_2O(l) \longrightarrow H_3O^+(aq) + Cl^-(aq)$$

Not all electrolytes conduct an electric current to the same degree. In a simple conductivity test, shown in **Figure 17.14,** a bulb glows brightly when electrodes attached to it are immersed in a sodium chloride solution. By

Figure 17.14

*The presence of an electrolyte in solution can be determined by a conductivity test. **(a)** Sodium chloride is a strong electrolyte; it dissociates nearly 100% in water. Its ions move in solution and readily conduct a current.*
***(b)** Mercury(II) chloride is a weak electrolyte; it only partially dissociates in water and conducts a small current. **(c)** Glucose is a nonelectrolyte; it does not dissociate in water. Would the molecular compound ethanol (C_2H_5OH) be an electrolyte?*

Chem ASAP!

Simulation 20
Explore the behavior of electrolytes and nonelectrolytes in a circuit and at the atomic level.

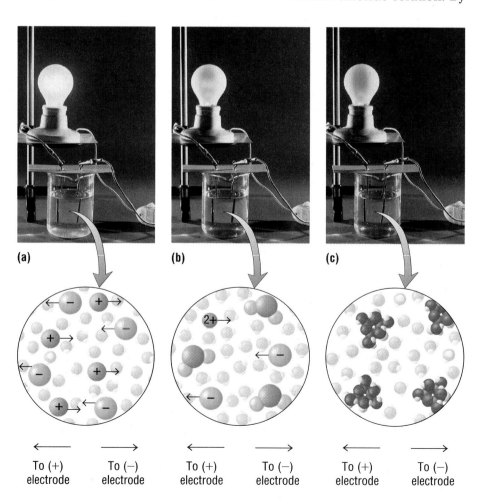

(a)   (b)   (c)

| ← To (+) electrode | → To (−) electrode | ← To (+) electrode | → To (−) electrode | ← To (+) electrode | → To (−) electrode |

contrast, the bulb glows dimly when the electrodes are immersed in a mercury(II) chloride solution. Mercury(II) chloride is a weak electrolyte. When a **weak electrolyte** is in solution, only a fraction of the solute exists as ions. In a solution of mercury(II) chloride, most of the solute exists as un-ionized $HgCl_2$. When a **strong electrolyte** is dissolved, almost all the solute exists as separate ions. Sodium chloride is a strong electrolyte. Nearly all the dissolved sodium chloride in a solution exists as separate Na^+ and Cl^- ions. The ions move in solution and conduct an electric current. In a solution of glucose, a nonelectrolyte, the bulb fails to glow. What is the representative particle of glucose? How does this explain why glucose is a nonelectrolyte? **Table 17.3** lists some common electrolytes and nonelectrolytes.

Table 17.3

Some Examples of Strong Electrolytes, Weak Electrolytes, and Nonelectrolytes		
Strong electrolyte	**Weak electrolyte**	**Nonelectrolyte**
Acids (inorganic)	Heavy metal halides	Most organic compounds
HCl	$HgCl_2$	Glucose
HBr	$PbCl_2$	Glycerol
HI		
HNO_3	Bases (inorganic)	
H_2SO_4	NH_3	
$HClO_4$		
	Acids (organic)	
Bases (inorganic)	acetic acid	
NaOH		
KOH	Bases (organic)	
	aniline	
Soluble salts		
KCl	H_2O (very weak)	
$MgSO_4$		
$KClO_3$		
$CaCl_2$		

Water of Hydration

Water molecules are an integral part of the crystal structure of many substances. The water in a crystal is called the **water of hydration** or water of crystallization. A compound that contains water of hydration is called a hydrate. When an aqueous solution of copper(II) sulfate is allowed to evaporate, deep-blue crystals of copper(II) sulfate pentahydrate are deposited. The chemical formula for this compound is $CuSO_4 \cdot 5H_2O$. In writing the formula of a hydrate, a dot is used to connect the formula of the compound and the number of water molecules per formula unit. Crystals of copper sulfate pentahydrate always contain five molecules of water for each copper and sulfate ion pair. The deep-blue crystals are dry to the touch. They are unchanged in composition or appearance in normally moist air. When heated above 100 °C, however, the crystals lose their water of hydration. As

SANITATION

Wastewater Treatment
Cleaning wastewater protects the environment from the harmful substances it carries. Wastewater treatment also helps recycle water, a resource that is in increasingly short supply. Wastewater treatment begins with the used water from your home, your school, or industry. The water collects in underground pipes called sewers. Gravity moves the wastewater through the sewers to the wastewater treatment plant. Once at the plant, the wastewater undergoes a number of purification stages. The primary treatment stage is mostly a physical process involving filtration and sedimentation. In secondary treatment, large populations of microorganisms convert the remaining dissolved organic matter into solids that separate as a sludge. Sometimes tertiary treatment is needed as well. At this level of treatment, nutrients such as nitrogen compounds and phosphorus compounds that produce unwanted growth of algae are removed.

Figure 17.15

When hydrated copper sulfate (a) is heated, the water is driven off, leaving anhydrous copper sulfate (b).

(a)

(b)

you can see in **Figure 17.15,** the blue crystals crumble to a white anhydrous powder with a formula of $CuSO_4$. If anhydrous copper sulfate is treated with water, the blue pentahydrate is regenerated.

$$CuSO_4 \cdot 5H_2O(s) \underset{-\text{heat}}{\overset{+\text{heat}}{\rightleftharpoons}} CuSO_4(s) + 5H_2O(g)$$

Cobalt(II) chloride is another compound that changes color in the presence of moisture. A piece of filter paper dipped in an aqueous solution of cobalt(II) chloride and dried is blue in color (anhydrous $CoCl_2$). If exposed to moist air, the paper turns pink due to the formation of the hexa-hydrate ($CoCl_2 \cdot 6H_2O$). See **Figure 17.16.** This paper is used to test for the presence of water.

Table 17.4 lists some familiar hydrates. They all contain a fixed quantity of water and have a definite composition. Do you know uses for any of these compounds?

Figure 17.16

Paper treated with anhydrous cobalt(II) chloride is blue. In the presence of moisture the paper turns pink. How could you change the pink paper back to blue?

Table 17.4

Some Common Hydrates		
Formula	**Chemical name**	**Common name**
$MgSO_4 \cdot 7H_2O$	magnesium sulfate heptahydrate	Epsom salt
$Ba(OH)_2 \cdot 8H_2O$	barium hydroxide octahydrate	
$CaCl_2 \cdot 2H_2O$	calcium chloride dihydrate	
$CuSO_4 \cdot 5H_2O$	copper(II) sulfate pentahydrate	blue vitriol
$Na_2SO_4 \cdot 10H_2O$	sodium sulfate decahydrate	Glauber's salt
$KAl(SO_4)_2 \cdot 12H_2O$	potassium aluminum sulfate dodecahydrate	alum
$Na_2B_4O_7 \cdot 10H_2O$	sodium tetraborate decahydrate	borax
$FeSO_4 \cdot 7H_2O$	iron(II) sulfate heptahydrate	green vitriol
$H_2SO_4 \cdot H_2O$	sulfuric acid hydrate (mp 8.6 °C)	

The forces holding the water molecules in hydrates are not very strong, which is apparent from the ease with which water is lost and regained. Because the water molecules are held by weak forces, hydrates often have an appreciable vapor pressure. If a hydrate has a vapor pressure higher than that of the water vapor in air, the hydrate will **effloresce** by losing the water of hydration. For example, $CuSO_4 \cdot 5H_2O$ has a vapor pressure of about 1.0 kPa at room temperature. The average pressure of water vapor at room temperature is usually about 1.3 kPa. This hydrate is stable until the humidity decreases. When the vapor pressure drops below 1.0 kPa, the hydrate effloresces. Washing soda, or sodium carbonate decahydrate ($Na_2CO_3 \cdot 10H_2O$), is efflorescent. As the crystals lose water of hydration, they effloresce and become coated with a white powder of anhydrous sodium carbonate.

Some hydrated salts that have a low vapor pressure remove water from moist air to form higher hydrates. Salts and other compounds that remove moisture from air are **hygroscopic.** Calcium chloride monohydrate is hygroscopic, as are sodium hydroxide and concentrated sulfuric acid.

$$CaCl_2 \cdot H_2O(s) \xrightarrow{\text{moist air}} CaCl_2 \cdot 2H_2O(s)$$

Hygroscopic substances are used as drying agents, or **desiccants.** One familiar example is silica gel, which is used to maintain a dry atmosphere in food packaging containers. Small packets of silica gel are also packaged with electronic equipment to absorb moisture from the air and to prevent damage to the equipment. Some compounds are so hygroscopic that they become wet when exposed to normally moist air. These compounds are deliquescent. **Deliquescent** compounds remove sufficient water from the air to dissolve completely and form solutions. As you can see in **Figure 17.17,** pellets of sodium hydroxide are deliquescent. Deliquescence occurs when the solution formed has a lower vapor pressure than that of the water in the air.

(a)   (b)

Figure 17.17
(a) Dry sodium hydroxide pellets exposed to air will, over time, remove water from the air.
(b) Eventually a solution will be formed. What is this process called?

Sample Problem 17-1

Calculate the percent by mass of water in washing soda, or sodium carbonate decahydrate ($Na_2CO_3 \cdot 10H_2O$).

1. **ANALYZE** *List the known and the unknown.*

Known:
- formula of hydrate = $Na_2CO_3 \cdot 10H_2O$

Unknown:
- percent water = ? %

To determine the percent by mass, determine the mass of the hydrated compound and the mass of the water in the hydrate, then substitute these values into the following equation and solve.

$$\text{percent } H_2O = \frac{\text{mass of water}}{\text{mass of hydrate}} \times 100\%$$

2. **CALCULATE** *Solve for the unknown.*

$$\text{mass of } 10H_2O = 180 \text{ g}$$

$$\text{mass of } Na_2CO_3 \cdot 10H_2O = 286.0 \text{ g}$$

$$\text{percent } H_2O = \frac{1.80 \times 10^2 \text{ g}}{286.0 \text{ g}} \times 100\% = 62.9\%$$

3. **EVALUATE** *Does the result make sense?*

Because the mass of the water accounts for more than half the molar mass of the compound, a percentage greater than 50% should be expected. The answer should have three significant figures.

Practice Problems

8. What is the percent by mass of water in $CuSO_4 \cdot 5H_2O$?

9. Calcium chloride forms a hexahydrate.
   a. Write the equation for the formation of this hydrate from the anhydrous salt.
   b. Calculate the percent by mass of water in the hexahydrate.

Chem ASAP!

Problem-Solving 9

Solve Problem 9 with the help of an interactive guided tutorial.

section review 17.3

10. What is the significance of the statement "like dissolves like"? What does "like" refer to?

11. Distinguish between an electrolyte and a nonelectrolyte. Distinguish between a weak electrolyte and a strong electrolyte. Give an example of each.

12. Identify the solvent and the solute in vinegar, a dilute aqueous solution of acetic acid.

13. Write an equation showing how calcium chloride dissociates in water.

14. Which of the following substances dissolve to a significant extent in water? Explain your answer in terms of polarity.

    a. CH_4 d. $MgSO_4$
    b. KCl   e. sucrose
    c. He   f. $NaHCO_3$

portfolio project

Research and report on which electrolytes are found in sports drinks. What is the biological function of these electrolytes? How does exercise affect the body's electrolyte balance?

 Chem ASAP! **Assessment 17.3** Check your understanding of the important ideas and concepts in Section 17.3.

SMALL-SCALE LAB

ELECTROLYTES

SAFETY

Wear safety glasses and follow the standard safety procedures outlined on page 18.

PURPOSE

To classify compounds as electrolytes by testing their conductivity in aqueous solution.

MATERIALS

- pencil
- paper
- ruler
- conductivity probe (optional)
- reaction surface
- conductivity tester
- chemicals shown in Figure A

PROCEDURE

 Probe version available in the Probeware Lab Manual.

On separate sheets of paper, draw two grids similar to Figure A. Make each square 2 cm on each side. Place a reaction surface over one of the grids and place a few grains of each solid in the indicated places. Test each solid for conductivity. Then add 1 drop of water to each solid and test the wet mixture for conductivity. Be sure to clean and dry the conductivity leads between each test.

$NaCl(s)$	$MgSO_4(s)$
$Na_2CO_3(s)$	Table Sugar
$NaHCO_3(s)$	Cornstarch
$KCl(s)$	$KI(s)$

Figure A

ANALYSIS

Using your experimental data, record the answers to the following questions below your data table.

1. Electrolytes are compounds that conduct electricity in aqueous solution. Which compounds in Figure A are electrolytes? Which are not electrolytes?

2. Do any of these electrolytes conduct electricity in the solid form? Why?

3. The formula for table sugar is $C_{12}H_{22}O_{11}$ and the formula for cornstarch is $(C_6H_{12}O_6)_n$. Are these ionic or covalent compounds? Classify each compound in Figure A as ionic or covalent. For a compound to be an electrolyte, what must happen when it dissolves in water?

YOU'RE THE CHEMIST

The following small-scale activities allow you to develop your own procedures and analyze the results.

1. **Analyze It!** When an ionic solid dissolves in water, water molecules attract the ions, causing them to come apart, or dissociate. The resulting dissolved ions are electrically charged particles that allow the solution to conduct electricity. The following chemical equations represent this phenomenon.

$$NaCl(s) \longrightarrow Na^+(aq) + Cl^-(aq)$$
$$Na_2CO_3(s) \longrightarrow 2Na^+(aq) + CO_3^{2-}(aq)$$

Write a similar chemical equation for each electrolyte in Figure A to illustrate how the ions dissociate in water.

2. **Design It!** Obtain the following aqueous solutions: HCl, H_2SO_4, HNO_3, CH_3COOH, NH_3, NaOH, rubbing alcohol, and distilled water. Design and carry out an experiment to classify each solution as a strong electrolyte (bright light), weak electrolyte (dim light), or nonelectrolyte (no light).

3. **Design It!** Test various liquids for conductivity. Try soft drinks, orange juice, pickle juice, and coffee. Which liquids are electrolytes?

- ▶ Explain how colloids and suspensions differ from solutions
- ▶ Describe the Tyndall effect

key terms
- ▶ suspensions
- ▶ colloids
- ▶ Tyndall effect
- ▶ Brownian motion
- ▶ emulsions

HETEROGENEOUS AQUEOUS SYSTEMS

It wiggles and jiggles. It comes in many colors and flavors. When you pop it in your mouth, it dissolves. It is gelatin, one of the most popular desserts in the United States. In fact, more than a million packages of gelatin are purchased or eaten every day. Gelatin has even traveled into space. In 1996, American astronaut Shannon Lucid shared a gelatin dessert with her Russian crewmates. Gelatin is a type of mixture called a colloid. **What is a colloid, and what are its characteristics?**

Suspensions

So far, the emphasis of this chapter has been on homogeneous mixtures involving water. We will now focus on heterogeneous mixtures, as opposed to mixtures that are true solutions. Two such heterogeneous mixtures are called suspensions and colloids.

Figure 17.18

A suspension is a heterogeneous mixture. Suspended particles can be removed by filtration.

Suspensions are mixtures from which particles settle out upon standing. A piece of clay shaken with water forms a suspension. The clay breaks into fine particles that become suspended in the water, but they start to settle out when shaking stops. A suspension differs from a solution because the component particles of a suspension are much larger. The particles in a typical suspension have an average diameter greater than 100 nm. By contrast, the particle size in a solution is usually about 1 nm. Suspensions are heterogeneous because at least two substances can be clearly identified. In the example just given, the two substances are clay and water. As you can see in **Figure 17.18,** if muddy water is filtered, the suspended clay particles are trapped by the filter, and clear water passes through.

Colloids

Colloids are heterogeneous mixtures containing particles that are intermediate in size between those of suspensions and true solutions. Thus the particles range in size from 1 nm to 100 nm. The particles are the dispersed phase. They are spread throughout the dispersion medium, which can be a solid, liquid, or gas. The first colloids that were identified as such were glues. Other colloids include such mixtures as gelatin desserts, paint, aerosol sprays, and smoke. **Table 17.5** lists some common colloidal systems and gives examples of familiar colloids.

The properties of colloids differ from those of solutions and suspensions. Many colloids are cloudy or milky in appearance when concentrated,

Table 17.5

Some Colloidal Systems				
System				
Dispersed phase	**Dispersion medium**	**Type**	**Example**	
gas	liquid	foam	whipped cream	
gas	solid	foam	marshmallow	
liquid	liquid	emulsion	milk, mayonnaise	
liquid	gas	aerosol	fog, aerosols	
solid	gas	smoke	dust in air	
solid	liquid	sols and gels	egg white, jellies, paint, blood, colloidal gold, starch in water, gelatin	

but they look clear or almost clear when they are very dilute. Intermediate-sized particles in a colloid cannot be retained by filter paper and do not settle out with time.

Colloidal particles exhibit the **Tyndall effect,** which is the scattering of visible light in all directions. You can see a beam of light passed through a colloid just as you see a sunbeam in a dusty room. Colloidal particles scatter light in the same way that dust particles scatter sunlight. Suspensions also exhibit the Tyndall effect, but solutions never do. Particles of solute in a true solution are too small to produce this effect. **Figure 17.19** on the following page summarizes the Tyndall effect with respect to solutions, colloids, and suspensions. Would carbonated mineral water exhibit the Tyndall effect?

(a)

Solution   Colloid   Suspension

(b)

Figure 17.19

(a) Fog is a colloid and thus exhibits the Tyndall effect.
(b) Particles in colloids and suspensions reflect light in all directions. This effect is not observed with true solutions.

Flashes of light, or scintillations, are seen when colloids are studied under a microscope. Colloids scintillate because the particles reflecting and scattering the light move erratically. The chaotic movement of colloidal particles is called **Brownian motion**, which was first observed by the Scottish botanist Robert Brown (1773–1858). While he was studying water samples with a microscope, Brown noticed the random movement of pollen grains suspended in the water. Brownian motion is caused by collisions of the water molecules of the medium with the small, dispersed colloidal particles. These collisions prevent the colloidal particles from settling.

Colloidal particles may also adsorb (collect) ions from the surrounding medium onto their surface. Some colloidal particles can adsorb positively charged ions and become positively charged. Other colloidal particles can adsorb negatively charged ions and become negatively charged. All the particles in a particular colloidal system will have the same charge. The repulsion of the like-charged particles prevents the particles from forming aggregates, which keeps them dispersed throughout the medium. When ions of opposite charge are added to the colloidal system, charged colloidal particles form aggregates and precipitate from the dispersion. **Table 17.6** summarizes the properties of solutions, colloids, and suspensions.

Table 17.6

Properties of Solutions, Colloids, and Suspensions			
Property	**System**		
	Solution	**Colloid**	**Suspension**
Particle type	ions, atoms, small molecules	large molecules or particles	large particles or aggregates
Particle size (approximate)	0.1–1 nm	1–100 nm	100 nm and larger
Effect of light	no scattering	exhibits Tyndall effect	exhibits Tyndall effect
Effect of gravity	stable, does not separate	stable, does not separate	unstable, sediment forms
Filtration	particles not retained on filter	particles not retained on filter	particles retained on filter
Uniformity	homogeneous	borderline	heterogeneous

MINI LAB

Surfactants

PURPOSE

To observe the unusual surface properties of water due to hydrogen bonding.

MATERIALS

- shallow dish or Petri dish
- water
- paper clip
- rubber band, approximately 2 inches in diameter
- vegetable oil
- liquid dish detergent

PROCEDURE

1. Thoroughly clean and dry the dish.

2. Fill the dish most of the way with water. Dry your hands.

3. Being careful not to break the surface, gently place the paper clip on the water. Observe what happens.

4. Repeat Steps 1 and 2.

5. Gently place the open rubber band on the water.

6. Slowly add oil, drop by drop, onto the water encircled by the rubber band until that water is covered with a layer of oil. Observe for 15 seconds.

7. Allow one drop of dish detergent to fall onto the center of the oil layer. Observe the system for 15 seconds.

ANALYSIS AND CONCLUSIONS

1. What happened to the paper clip? Explain.

2. If a paper clip becomes wet, does it float? Explain your answer.

3. What shape did the rubber band take when the water inside it was covered with oil? Why did it take the observed shape?

4. Describe what happened when dish detergent was dropped onto the layer of oil.

Emulsions are colloidal dispersions of liquids in liquids. An emulsifying agent is essential for the formation of an emulsion and for maintaining the emulsion's stability. For example, oils and greases are not soluble in water. However, they readily form a colloidal dispersion if soap or detergent is added to the water. Soap and detergents are emulsifying agents. One end of the large soap or detergent molecule is polar and is attracted to water molecules. The other end of the soap or detergent molecule is nonpolar and is soluble in oil or grease. Soaps and other emulsifying agents thus allow the formation of colloidal dispersions between liquids that do not ordinarily mix.

Figure 17.20
Many salad dressings are liquid-in-liquid colloids, or emulsions. When vinegar and oil are shaken, a temporary emulsion forms. If an emulsifying agent, such as egg yolk, is used and the oil is added slowly to the egg–vinegar mixture, the result is mayonnaise, a stable emulsion of vinegar and oil.

section review 17.4

15. What is the basis for distinguishing among solutions, colloids, and suspensions?

16. What is the Tyndall effect?

17. What is Brownian motion?

18. What are emulsions? How are emulsions stabilized?

 Chem ASAP! **Assessment 17.4** Check your understanding of the important ideas and concepts in Section 17.4.

IT'S THE WATER

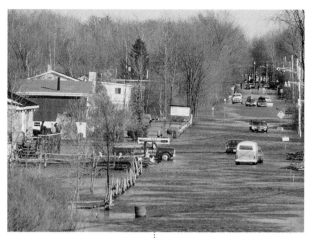

Earth is a watery planet. Oceans cover 72% of Earth's surface, and large amounts of water, in the form of water vapor, exist in Earth's atmosphere. Weather conditions around the planet are mostly the result of complex interactions between the water in Earth's oceans and in the atmosphere.

Large-scale weather patterns around the globe are somewhat stable. Some parts of the world usually receive large amounts of rainfall at certain times; other parts receive very little. These patterns are in part the result of how water in the oceans is heated and circulates around the planet.

Sometimes, for reasons scientists do not understand, water circulation in the oceans shifts away from the norm, causing major changes in the weather over large parts of Earth. One of these shifts, called El Niño, has now been observed and studied many times in the Pacific Ocean. It occurs, on average, every seven years.

El Niño begins in the waters just north of the equator, where the ocean surface water is heated rapidly by the nearly vertical rays of sunlight. Because of water's high heat capacity, this water tends to stay warm, and because warm water is less dense than cold water, it also tends to stay at the surface. Normally, trade winds blow from east to west across the Pacific and push the warm surface water to the west, toward Indonesia. If the trade winds die down, however, the warm water that usually pools in the western Pacific spreads toward the east. This shift is the El Niño effect.

Moving east, the warm water of El Niño reaches the coast of South America. Normally, cold, nutrient-rich waters rise from deep in the Pacific off the western coast of South America. The nutrients in the water fuel the growth of microscopic plants and animals, which are food for large fish populations. But as warmer

At no other time is the ocean's influence on weather more obvious than during El Niño.

waters move east during El Niño, the nutrient-rich colder waters are kept from rising. The microscopic ocean plants and animals have less food, and fish populations suffer.

When an El Niño occurs, among the first people to feel its effects are those who fish off the western coast of South America. They are also the ones who gave El Niño its name. They noted that the changes brought on by El Niño often begin around Christmas, the Christian celebration of the birth of Jesus, who is called "El Niño" (the Child) in South America.

El Niño's effects spread well beyond South America. The warm water bumps up against the South American coast and spreads north to the western coast of North America, affecting the weather and fish populations there. In Indonesia, where the nearby ocean is cooler than normal, there is often a severe drought.

El Niño covers so much of the Pacific that it influences the movement of the jet stream, a high-altitude wind that steers storms through the atmosphere. The effect on the jet stream is unpredictable, but the usual result is wetter-than-normal weather in parts of South America, North America, and Asia, and drier-than-normal weather in other parts of the world. At no other time is the ocean's influence on global weather more obvious than during El Niño.

CHEMISTRY IN CAREERS

☆ ☆ ☆ ☆ ☆ ☆ ☆ ☆ ☆ ☆ ☆ ☆ ☆ ☆ ☆ ☆ ☆ ☆

OCEANOGRAPHER
Study ocean surface-water temperature, salt content, and nutrient levels.
See page 876.

CHEMIST NEEDED
Enviro. Lab. GC Must know

TAKE IT TO THE NET

Find out more about career opportunities:
www.phschool.com

CHEMICAL SPECIALIST
Local food service distributor see responsible self-motivated indiv

Take It to the NET
*For interactive study and
review, go to www.phschool.com*

KEY TERMS

- aqueous solution *p. 482*
- Brownian motion *p. 492*
- colloid *p. 490*
- deliquescent *p. 487*
- desiccant *p. 487*
- effloresce *p. 487*
- electrolyte *p. 483*

- emulsion *p. 493*
- hygroscopic *p. 487*
- nonelectrolyte *p. 484*
- solute *p. 482*
- solvation *p. 483*
- solvent *p. 482*
- strong electrolyte *p. 485*

- surface tension *p. 477*
- surfactant *p. 477*
- suspension *p. 490*
- Tyndall effect *p. 491*
- water of hydration *p. 485*
- weak electrolyte *p. 485*

KEY EQUATION

- $\text{Percent H}_2\text{O} = \dfrac{\text{mass of water}}{\text{mass of hydrate}} \times 100\%$

CONCEPT SUMMARY

17.1 Liquid Water and Its Properties

- Water molecules are polar and they extensively hydrogen-bond with one another.
- Intermolecular hydrogen bonding explains the high freezing point (0 °C) and high boiling point (100 °C) of water.
- Hydrogen bonding is responsible for the high surface tension of water.

17.2 Water Vapor and Ice

- Extensive hydrogen bonding between water molecules explains water's high heat of vaporization.
- Ice floats in liquid water because it is less dense than liquid water.

17.3 Aqueous Solutions

- Aqueous solutions are homogeneous mixtures of ions or molecules in water. The solubility of a solute depends on solute–solvent interactions. A good rule to remember is "like dissolves like."
- Substances that are in solution as ions are electrolytes. A solute that is completely ionized

in solution is a strong electrolyte. A solute that is only partially ionized is a weak electrolyte.

- Many crystals are hydrates; they contain water of hydration, which can be lost through heating. Loss of water of hydration from a hydrate when exposed to air is called efflorescence.
- Hygroscopic substances take up water from moist air. A deliquescent substance takes up so much moisture it forms an aqueous solution.

17.4 Heterogeneous Aqueous Systems

- Particles in a suspension have an average diameter greater than 100 nm and can be kept in suspension if the fluid (water) is kept agitated. Gravity or filtration, however, will separate the suspended particles from the liquid.
- The particles in a colloidal dispersion range in size from 1 nm to 100 nm. In general, they do not settle under gravity, and they pass through ordinary filter paper unchanged.
- Colloids and suspensions scatter light, as evidenced by the Tyndall effect. Colloidal dispersions also exhibit Brownian motion.

CHAPTER CONCEPT MAP

Use these terms to construct a concept map that organizes the major ideas of this chapter.

aqueous solution   nonelectrolyte   solute

electrolyte   solvation   solvent

Chem ASAP! **Concept Map 17**
Create your Concept Map
using the computer.

CONCEPT PRACTICE

19. Explain why water molecules are polar. *17.1*

20. Why do the particles at the surface of a liquid behave differently from those in the bulk of the liquid? *17.1*

21. Describe the origin of the vapor pressure of water. *17.1*

22. Describe some observable effects that can be produced by the surface tension of a liquid. *17.1*

23. What is a surfactant? Explain how it works. *17.1*

24. Does the specific heat capacity of water vary depending on the quantity of water? Explain. *17.1*

25. How many calories are required to heat 256 g of water from 20 °C to 99 °C? How many calories are required to heat the same mass of iron through the same range of temperature? *17.1*

26. How many joules are required to vaporize 5.0 mg of water at its boiling point? *17.2*

27. Why does ammonia have a much higher boiling point (−33 °C) than methane (−164 °C) even though their molar masses are almost the same? *17.2*

28. How many calories are liberated when 24 g of steam at 100 °C condenses to liquid water at 100 °C? *17.2*

29. What characteristic of ice distinguishes it from other solid substances? *17.2*

30. How many kilojoules are required to melt 24 g of ice at 0 °C? *17.2*

31. What would be some of the consequences if ice were denser than water? *17.2*

32. Distinguish between a solution and an aqueous solution. *17.3*

33. Why is water an excellent solvent for most ionic compounds and polar covalent molecules but not for nonpolar compounds? *17.3*

34. Suppose an aqueous solution contains both sugar and salt. Can you separate either of these solutes from the water by filtration? Explain your reasoning. *17.3*

35. Describe how an ionic compound dissolves in water. *17.3*

36. Which of the following substances dissolve appreciably in water? Give reasons for your choice. *17.3*
   a. HCl   **d.** $MgSO_4$ **f.** $CaCO_3$
   b. NaI   **e.** CH_4 **g.** gasoline
   c. NH_3

37. Why does molten sodium chloride conduct electricity? *17.3*

38. What is the main distinction between an aqueous solution of a strong electrolyte and an aqueous solution of a weak electrolyte? *17.3*

39. Describe the water of hydration of a substance. *17.3*

40. Write formulas for these hydrates. *17.3*
   a. sodium sulfate decahydrate
   b. magnesium sulfate heptahydrate
   c. barium hydroxide octahydrate

41. Name each hydrate. *17.3*
   a. $SnCl_4 \cdot 5H_2O$ **c.** $BaBr_2 \cdot 4H_2O$
   b. $FeSO_4 \cdot 7H_2O$ **d.** $FePO_4 \cdot 4H_2O$

42. Epsom salt ($MgSO_4 \cdot 7H_2O$) changes to the monohydrate form at 150 °C. Write an equation for this change. *17.3*

43. Name two ways to distinguish a suspension from a colloid. *17.4*

44. Solutions do not demonstrate the Tyndall effect. Why? *17.4*

45. What makes a colloidal dispersion stable? *17.4*

46. Define Brownian motion. *17.4*

CONCEPT MASTERY

47. Water has its maximum density at 4 °C. Explain why this is so, and discuss the consequences of this fact.

48. From your knowledge of intermolecular forces, arrange these liquids in order of increasing surface tension: water (H_2O), hexane (C_6H_{14}), ethanol (C_2H_5OH).

49. Name these hydrates and determine the percent by mass of water in each.
   a. $Na_2CO_3 \cdot H_2O$ **b.** $MgSO_4 \cdot 7H_2O$

50. If 5.00 g of steam (H_2O)(g) at 100.0 °C condenses to liquid water (H_2O)(l) that is cooled to 50.0 °C, how much heat is liberated in
   a. calories?   **b.** kilocalories?

51. Explain why ions become solvated in aqueous solution.

52. A block of ice at 0 °C has a mass of 176.0 g. How much heat must be added to change 25% of this mass of ice to liquid water at 0 °C? Express your answer in calories, kilocalories, joules, and kilojoules. What is the mass of ice remaining?

53. You have a solution containing either sugar or salt dissolved in water.
　a. Can you tell which it is by visual inspection?
　b. Give two ways by which you could easily tell which it is.

54. Water is a polar solvent; gasoline is a nonpolar solvent. Decide which compounds are more likely to dissolve in water and which are more likely to dissolve in gasoline.
　a. sucrose ($C_{12}H_{22}O_{11}$)　**c.** methane (CH_4)
　b. Na_2SO_4　　　　　　**d.** KCl

55. Match each term with the following descriptions. A description may apply to more than one term.
　a. true solution　　　**c.** suspension
　b. colloidal
　　(1) does not settle out on standing
　　(2) heterogeneous mixture
　　(3) particle size less than 1.0 nm
　　(4) particles can be filtered out
　　(5) demonstrates Tyndall effect
　　(6) particles are invisible to the unaided eye
　　(7) homogenized milk
　　(8) salt water
　　(9) jelly

56. Explain which properties of water are responsible for these occurrences.
　a. Water in tiny cracks in rocks helps break up the rocks when it freezes.
　b. Water beads up on a newly waxed car.
　c. As you exercise and your body temperature increases, your body cools itself by producing sweat.
　d. Temperatures below 28 °F damage grapevines. When severe frost is predicted, grape growers spray a mist of water on their vines.
　e. An efficient way of heating a large building is to generate steam in a boiler and circulate it through pipes to radiators throughout the building.

57. Explain why ethanol (C_2H_5OH) will dissolve in both gasoline and water.

58. A 25.0 m × 10.0 m swimming pool is filled with fresh water to a depth of 1.7 m. The water temperature is initially 25 °C. How much heat must be removed from the water to change it all to ice at 0 °C? Express your answer in kilocalories and kilojoules.

59. Are all liquids soluble in each other? Explain.

60. Write equations to show how these substances ionize or dissociate in water.
　a. NH_4Cl　　　**c.** $HC_2H_3O_2$
　b. $Cu(NO_3)_2$　**d.** $HgCl_2$

61. The following graph shows the density of water over the temperature range 0 °C to 20 °C.

　a. What is the maximum density of water?
　b. At what temperature does the maximum density of water occur?
　c. Would it be correct to extend the smooth curve of the graph below 0 °C?

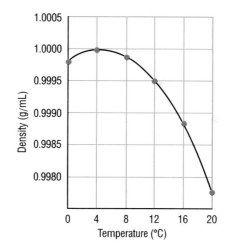

CRITICAL THINKING

62. Choose the term that best completes the second relationship.
　a. plant : green　　　water molecule : _____
　　(1) polar　　　　　(3) frozen
　　(2) ionic　　　　　(4) vapor
　b. east : west　　　condensation : _____
　　(1) boiling　　　　(3) vaporization
　　(2) vapor pressure　(4) freezing
　c. colloid : emulsion　cat : _____
　　(1) dog　　　　　　(3) poodle
　　(2) Siamese　　　　(4) fox

63. When the humidity is low and the temperature high, humans must take in large quantities of water or face serious dehydration. Why do you think water is so important for the proper functioning of your body?

64. Describe as specifically as possible what would happen if a nonpolar molecular liquid were added to water. What would form if you shook this mixture vigorously?

CUMULATIVE REVIEW

65. A cylindrical vessel, 28.0 cm in height and 3.00 cm in diameter, is filled with water at 50 °C. The density of water is 0.988 g/cm³ at this temperature. Express the mass of water in the vessel in the following units.
    a. grams   b. milligrams   c. kilograms

66. The temperature of 1 L of steam at constant volume and 1.00 atm pressure is increased from 100 °C to 200 °C. Calculate the final pressure of the steam in atmospheres, assuming the volume does not change.

67. How do the following changes in the pressure on the surface of water affect the water's boiling point?
    a. an increase in pressure
    b. a decrease in pressure

68. The decomposition of hydrogen peroxide is given by this equation.

    $$2H_2O_2(l) \longrightarrow 2H_2O(l) + O_2\,(g)$$

    Calculate the mass of water (in grams) and the volume of oxygen at STP formed when 2.00×10^{-3} mol of hydrogen peroxide is decomposed.

69. How many grams each of hydrogen and oxygen are required to produce 4.50 mol of water?

70. Calculate the mass of water produced in the complete combustion of 8.00 L of propane (C_3H_8) at STP, given the unbalanced equation

    $$C_3H_8 + O_2 \longrightarrow CO_2 + H_2O$$

71. Acetaldehyde (C_2H_4O) is produced commercially by the reaction of acetylene (C_2H_2) with water, as shown by the equation

    $$C_2H_2 + H_2O \longrightarrow C_2H_4O$$

    How many grams of C_2H_4O can be produced from 2.60×10^2 g H_2O, assuming sufficient C_2H_2 is present?

CONCEPT CHALLENGE

72. Cobalt chloride test paper is blue. This paper is made by soaking strips of paper in an aqueous solution of $CoCl_2 \cdot 6H_2O$. These paper strips are then dried in an oven.

    $$CoCl_2 \cdot 6H_2O \text{ (pink)} + \text{heat} \longrightarrow$$
    $$CoCl_2 \text{ (blue)} + 6H_2O$$

    a. When cobalt(II) chloride hexahydrate is dissolved in water, what is the color of the solution?
    b. What is the color of wet cobalt chloride paper?
    c. What is the color of dry cobalt chloride paper?
    d. What is the percent by mass of water in the hexahydrate?
    e. What does cobalt chloride test paper test for?

73. A graph of boiling point versus molar mass for the noble gases is given below.
    a. Make a statement summarizing the observed trend relating these two physical properties.
    b. How does a doubling of the molar mass (from Ne to Ar) affect the boiling point?

74. What relationships exist between the following volumes?
    a. 1 g of ice at 0 °C and 1 g of liquid water at 0 °C
    b. 1 g of liquid water at 100 °C and 1 g of steam at 100 °C

75. A mixture of 40 cm³ of oxygen gas and 60 cm³ of hydrogen gas at STP is ignited.
    a. Which gas is the limiting reagent, oxygen or hydrogen?
    b. What is the mass of water produced?
    c. Which gas remains after reaction?
    d. What is the volume, at STP, of the remaining gas?

Select the choice that best answers each question or completes each statement.

1. When a sugar cube completely dissolves in a glass of water, it forms
   a. a colloid.
   c. a suspension.
   b. an emulsion.
   d. a solution.

2. How many water molecules are tied up per formula unit of a compound that is an octahydrate?
   a. nine
   c. seven
   b. eight
   d. six

3. Which property is characteristic of water?
   a. relatively low boiling point
   b. relatively low vapor pressure
   c. relatively low surface tension
   d. relatively low heat of vaporization

4. Which statement is *false*?
   a. If less than 1% of an acid is ionized in water, the acid is a weak electrolyte.
   b. A weak electrolyte can become a strong electrolyte with the addition of more solute.
   c. Because melted wax does not conduct an electrical current, it is a nonelectrolyte.
   d. $(NH_4)_3PO_4(aq)$ is a strong electrolyte.

Use this description and the data table in the next column to answer questions 5–7.

A student used a conductivity meter to measure the ability of several aqueous solutions to conduct electric current. The magnitude of the conductivity value is proportional to the number of ions in the solution. The SI conductivity unit is the microsiemens/cm (μS/cm). The table gives the results reported by the student who tested six solutions plus distilled water. Each solution had a concentration of $0.02M$.

Solution	Conductivity (μS/cm)
potassium chloride, KCl	2050
aluminum chloride, $AlCl_3$	4500
calcium chloride, $CaCl_2$	3540
sodium hydroxide, NaOH	2180
ethanol, C_2H_5OH	0
magnesium bromide, $MgBr_2$	3490
distilled water	0

5. Why do distilled water and the ethanol solution have zero conductivity?

6. Explain why two pairs of conducting solutions have similar conductivities.

7. The $AlCl_3$ solution has a conductivity that is about twice that of the KCl solution. Offer an explanation for this ratio.

Use the atomic windows to answer question 8.

8. Atomic window (a) represents solute particles in a given volume of solution. Which window represents the solute particles in the same volume of solution when the amount of solvent is doubled?

For each question there are two statements. Decide whether each statement is true or false. Then decide whether Statement II is a correct explanation for Statement I.

Statement I		Statement II
9. Water has a relatively high surface tension.	BECAUSE	Water molecules form strong hydrogen bonds with other water molecules.
10. Methanol, CH_3OH, is a strong electrolyte.	BECAUSE	Methanol molecules can form hydrogen bonds with water.
11. Particles in a colloid settle out faster than particles in a solution.	BECAUSE	Particles in a colloid are larger than particles in a solution.
12. Water molecules are polar.	BECAUSE	The bond between hydrogen and oxygen atoms in a water molecule is polar.

SOLUTIONS

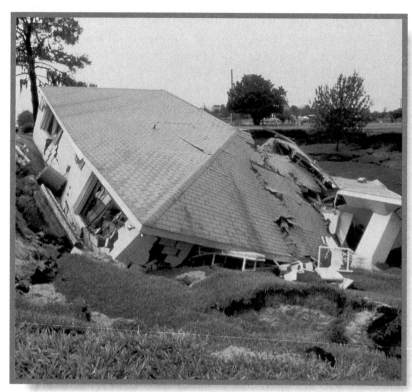

A sinkhole can form when groundwater dissolves limestone.

FEATURES

DISCOVER IT!
Salt and the Freezing Point of Water

SMALL-SCALE LAB
Making a Solution

MINI LAB
Solutions and Colloids

CHEMISTRY SERVING ... SOCIETY
A Solution for Kidney Failure

CHEMISTRY IN CAREERS
Nephrology Nurse

LINK TO AGRICULTURE
Fertilizer Runoff

LINK TO NURSING
Intravenous Solutions

Stay current with **SCIENCE NEWS**
Find out more about solutions:
www.phschool.com

DISCOVER IT! SALT AND THE FREEZING POINT OF WATER

You need a plastic plate, a 20-cm piece of string or narrow ribbon, water, an ice cube, and some table salt (sodium chloride).

1. Remove an ice cube from the freezer and place it on the plate.

2. Moisten the string or ribbon with water and place it in a straight line across the ice cube.

3. Sprinkle some salt along the length of the string on the ice.

4. Wait 1–2 minutes and then slowly lift the ends of the string, which should raise the ice cube off the plate.

5. If you are not successful in lifting the cube with the string, repeat Steps 3 and 4.

What effect does the salt have on the water/ice? Can you name some practical instances of salt being used to affect the freezing point of water? Do you think sugar or baking soda would work equally well? Try it! When you read about solution properties later in this chapter, look back at your findings and try to explain them.

PROPERTIES OF SOLUTIONS

*I*t was there one minute and gone the next! An entire house—front yard and back yard included—swallowed up by the earth. A victim of a natural phenomenon of moving groundwater, the house had disappeared into a sinkhole! Groundwater, or the water that soaks into the ground from rain and melted snow, can have a significant effect on the rocks beneath the soil surface. As groundwater moves through layers of limestone, it can dissolve huge amounts over time. This process creates beautiful limestone caves, as well as destructive sinkholes. A sinkhole forms when an overlying layer of limestone, often the roof of a cave, weakens from being dissolved and suddenly collapses. One recorded sinkhole swallowed a house, several other buildings, five cars, and a swimming pool! **How does the solution process occur and what influences it?**

objectives
▶ Identify the factors that determine the rate at which a solute dissolves
▶ Calculate the solubility of a gas in a liquid under various pressure conditions

key terms
▶ saturated solution
▶ solubility
▶ unsaturated
▶ miscible
▶ immiscible
▶ Henry's law
▶ supersaturated solution

Solution Formation

If you have ever made ice cream, you know that salt is added to the ice–water mixture surrounding the ice-cream container. But do you know why the salt is needed? You may also have noticed that granulated sugar dissolves faster than sugar cubes in iced tea, and that both will dissolve faster in hot tea or with stirring. See **Figure 18.1.** You will be able to explain each of these observations once you have gained an understanding of the properties of solutions.

Recall that solutions are homogeneous mixtures that may be solid, liquid, or gaseous. In this chapter, you will study the formation of solutions and ways to express their composition. You will also examine how the properties of solutions change when the number of particles dissolved in them is changed.

Figure 18.1

The process by which a solute dissolves takes place at the surface of the solid. The photograph showing a sugar cube suspended in water illustrates this. The sugar particles near the cube's surface are dissolving. Agitation and heat increase the rate at which a solute dissolves. (a) A cube of sugar in cold tea dissolves slowly. (b) Granulated sugar dissolves in cold water more quickly than a sugar cube, especially with stirring. (c) Granulated sugar dissolves very quickly in hot tea.

(a)

(b)

(c)

AGRICULTURE

Fertilizer Runoff

Most farmers use fertilizers that contain salts of one or more of three elements essential to plant growth: potassium, nitrogen, and phosphorus. When more fertilizer is applied than the soil can absorb, rain washes off the excess salts. Not only is this economically wasteful, it is also hazardous to the environment. The water containing these dissolved salts flows into streams and rivers. The dissolved nutrients contribute to the eutrophication of these waters. Eutrophied waters are rich in nutrients but deficient in dissolved oxygen. Signs of eutrophication include overgrowth of water plants, algal blooms, and bad odors resulting from the growth of bacteria that do not need oxygen. In recent years, the problem of fertilizer runoff has lessened with the introduction of slow-release nitrogenous fertilizers. Many farmers have adopted new fertilizer application cycles and cultivation methods to reduce runoff.

One factor that affects whether a substance will dissolve is the nature of the solvent and of the solute. Do you remember the definition of solvent and solute? Several other factors determine how fast the substance dissolves. These factors are stirring (agitation), temperature, and surface area. Each factor involves the contact of the solute with the solvent. If a few sodium chloride crystals are placed in a flask of water, for example, the crystals will dissolve slowly. If the flask and its contents are shaken, however, the crystals dissolve quickly. The agitation has this effect because the dissolving process is a surface phenomenon. It occurs faster if fresh solvent is brought into contact with the surface of the solute, which is what occurs during shaking. This is why people stir coffee after they have added sugar. It is important to realize, however, that agitation affects only the rate at which a solute dissolves. It cannot influence the amount of solute that dissolves. An insoluble substance remains undissolved regardless of how vigorously or for how long the system is agitated.

Temperature is another factor that influences the rate at which solutes dissolve. Sugar dissolves much more rapidly in hot tea than in iced tea because the kinetic energy of the water molecules is greater at the higher temperature. This increase in kinetic energy leads to an increased frequency and force of collisions between water molecules and the surfaces of the sugar crystals.

Another factor that determines the rate at which a solute dissolves is its particle size. A fine powder dissolves more rapidly than do larger crystals, because finer particles expose a greater surface area to the colliding water molecules. Here again, the dissolving process is a surface phenomenon, and the more surface of the solute that is exposed, the faster is the rate of dissolving. Can you think of an example of how particle size affects the rate of dissolving?

Solubility

If you add 36.0 g of sodium chloride to 100 g of water at 25 °C, all 36.0 g of salt dissolves. But if you add one more gram of salt and stir, no matter how vigorously or for how long, only 0.2 g of the last portion goes into solution. Why do crystals of salt remain out of solution? According to the kinetic theory, water molecules are in continuous motion. Therefore, they should continue to bombard the excess solid, removing and solvating the ions. As ions are solvated, they dissolve in the water. Based on this information, you might expect all of the sodium chloride to dissolve eventually. That does not happen, however, because an exchange process is occurring. New particles from the solid are solvated and enter into solution, but at the same time an equal number of already dissolved particles come out of solution. These particles become desolvated and are deposited as a solid. As ions in solution are desolvated, they crystallize. The mass of undissolved crystals remains constant.

Thus the particles move from the solid to the solvated state and back to the solid again. Yet there is no net change in the overall system. As shown in **Figure 18.2,** a state of dynamic equilibrium exists between the solution and the undissolved solute, provided that the temperature remains constant. Such a solution is said to be saturated. A **saturated solution** contains the maximum amount of solute for a given amount of solvent at a constant temperature. For example, 36.2 g of sodium chloride in 100 g of water produces a saturated solution at 25 °C. The **solubility** of a substance is the amount that dissolves in a given quantity of a solvent at a given temperature to produce a saturated solution. Solubility is often expressed in grams of solute per 100 g of solvent. A solution that contains less solute than a saturated solution is said to be **unsaturated.**

Figure 18.2
In a saturated solution, a state of dynamic equilibrium exists between the solution and the excess solute. At these conditions, the rate of solvation (dissolving) equals the rate of crystallization, so the total amount of dissolved solute remains constant.

Two liquids are said to be **miscible** if they dissolve in each other. Some liquids—for example, water and ethanol—are infinitely soluble in each other. Any amount of ethanol will dissolve in a given volume of water, and vice versa. Such a pair of liquids is said to be completely miscible. Liquids that are slightly soluble in each other—for example, water and diethyl ether—are partially miscible. Liquids that are insoluble in each other are **immiscible.** As you can see in **Figure 18.3,** oil and vinegar are immiscible, as are oil and water. Why? (*Hint:* Remember from Chapter 17 that like dissolves like.)

Factors Affecting Solubility

As you have just read, the solubility of sodium chloride in water at 25 °C is 36.2 g per 100 g of water. At 100 °C, the solubility increases to 39.2 g NaCl per 100 g of water. As shown in **Figure 18.4** on the following page, the solubility of most solid substances increases as the temperature of the solvent increases. For a few substances, however, the reverse occurs. For example,

Figure 18.3
Vinegar, which is water-based, and oil are immiscible. The less-dense oil floats on the water phase. Light produces a rainbow of colors as it is reflected off an oil film on the surface of water.

Figure 18.4

Changing the temperature may affect the solubility of a substance. Notice that increasing the temperature greatly increases the solubility of KNO_3 but decreases the solubility of $Yb_2(SO_4)_3$.

the solubility of ytterbium sulfate, $Yb_2(SO_4)_3$, in water drops from 44.2 g per 100 g of water at 0 °C to 5.8 g per 100 g of water at 90 °C. Which of the solids has the lowest solubility at 40 °C? Which has the highest? **Table 18.1** lists the solubilities of some common substances at various temperatures.

Note that the solubilities of the gases listed in the table are greater in cold water than in hot water. You are probably familiar with this fact if you have ever heated water and observed bubbles forming before the water has reached its boiling point. These bubbles are dissolved atmospheric gases escaping from solution. As **Figure 18.5** shows, the two main components of

Table 18.1

Solubilities of Some Substances in Water at Various Temperatures					
Substance	Formula	Solubility (g/100 g H_2O)			
		0 °C	20 °C	50 °C	100 °C
Barium hydroxide	$Ba(OH)_2$	1.67	31.89	—	—
Barium sulfate	$BaSO_4$	0.00019	0.00025	0.00034	—
Calcium hydroxide	$Ca(OH)_2$	0.189	0.173	—	0.07
Lead(II) chloride	$PbCl_2$	0.60	0.99	1.70	—
Lithium carbonate	Li_2CO_3	1.5	1.3	1.1	0.70
Potassium chlorate	$KClO_3$	4.0	7.4	19.3	56.0
Potassium chloride	KCl	27.6	34.0	42.6	57.6
Sodium chloride	$NaCl$	35.7	36.0	37.0	39.2
Sodium nitrate	$NaNO_3$	74	88.0	114.0	182
Aluminum chloride	$AlCl_3$	30.84	31.03	31.60	33.32
Silver nitrate	$AgNO_3$	122	222.0	455.0	733
Lithium bromide	$LiBr$	143.0	166	203	266.0
Sucrose (cane sugar)	$C_{12}H_{22}O_{11}$	179	230.9	260.4	487
Hydrogen*	H_2	0.00019	0.00016	0.00013	0.0
Oxygen*	O_2	0.0070	0.0043	0.0026	0.0
Carbon dioxide*	CO_2	0.335	0.169	0.076	0.0

* Gas at 101 kPa total pressure

air—oxygen and nitrogen—become less soluble in water as the temperature of the solution rises. When an industrial plant takes cool water from a lake and dumps the resulting heated water back into the lake, the temperature of the entire lake increases. Such a change in temperature is known as thermal pollution. Because the temperature increase lowers the concentration of dissolved oxygen in the lake water, aquatic animal and plant life can be severely affected.

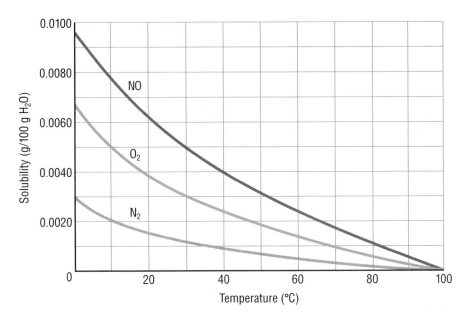

The solubility of a gas is also affected by pressure. Gas solubility increases as the partial pressure of the gas above the solution increases. Carbonated beverages are a good example of this principle. These drinks contain large amounts of carbon dioxide (CO_2) dissolved in water. (It is dissolved CO_2 that makes the liquid fizz and your mouth tingle.) The drinks are bottled under a high pressure of CO_2 gas, which forces large amounts of CO_2 into solution. When a carbonated-beverage bottle is opened, the partial pressure of CO_2 above the liquid decreases, and the concentration of dissolved CO_2 decreases. Bubbles of CO_2 form in the liquid and escape from the open bottle, as shown in **Figure 18.6.** If the bottle is left open, the drink becomes flat as the solution loses its CO_2.

Figure 18.5

Gases have different solubilities in water at different temperatures. In general, as the temperature increases, the solubilities of gases decrease. Notice on the graph that nitrogen, oxygen, and nitric oxide become virtually insoluble as the temperature approaches 100 °C. Can you use the kinetic theory to explain this solubility behavior of gases?

Chem ASAP!

Simulation 21
Observe the effect of temperature on the solubility of solids and gases in water.

(a)   (b)   (c)

Figure 18.6

(a) When a carbonated-beverage bottle is sealed, the pressure of CO_2 above the liquid is high and the concentration of CO_2 in the liquid is also high. (b) When the cap is removed, the equilibrium is disturbed; the pressure of CO_2 gas above the liquid becomes low. (c) Carbon dioxide bubbles out of the carbonated beverage.

Solutions **505**

Figure 18.7

A supersaturated solution before a seed crystal is added (left). The same solution after the addition of the seed crystal (center). The seed crystal causes the excess solute to crystallize rapidly (right). How would you characterize the solution once crystallization has ceased?

Henry's law states that at a given temperature the solubility (S) of a gas in a liquid is directly proportional to the pressure (P) of the gas above the liquid. In other words, as the pressure of the gas above the liquid increases, the solubility of the gas increases. Similarly, as the pressure of the gas decreases, the solubility of the gas decreases. You can write this relationship in mathematical form as follows.

$$\frac{S_1}{P_1} = \frac{S_2}{P_2}$$

When the temperature of a saturated solution in contact with a small excess of solid solute is raised, some or all of the excess solid generally dissolves. If the solution is then slowly cooled to its original temperature, the excess solute may not always immediately crystallize out of solution. A solution that contains more solute than it should theoretically continue to hold at a given temperature is called a **supersaturated solution.** Crystallization in a supersaturated solution can be initiated if a very small crystal, called a seed crystal, of the solute is added. The rate at which excess solute deposits upon the surface of a seed crystal can be very rapid, as shown in **Figure 18.7.** Crystallization can also occur if the inside of the container is scratched. The water of the hot spring in **Figure 18.8** is saturated with minerals. As the solution of minerals cools, it becomes supersaturated. The rocks over which the solution flows act as seed crystals that speed the formation of mineral deposits. Another example of crystallization in a supersaturated solution is the production of rock candy. The solution is supersaturated with sugar. Seed crystals cause the sugar to crystallize out of solution onto a string for you to enjoy!

Figure 18.8

Mineral deposits form around the edges of this hot spring because the hot water is saturated with minerals. As the water cools at the surface, some of the minerals crystallize because they are less soluble at the lower temperature.

Figure 18.9
Clouds can be seeded with silver iodide to produce water droplets, causing rain to fall.

You may have heard of clouds being seeded to make them produce rain. Scientific rainmaking is done by seeding clouds, which contain masses of air supersaturated with water vapor. Tiny silver iodide (AgI) crystals are dusted onto a cloud to seed it, as shown in **Figure 18.9**. Water molecules are attracted to the ionic AgI particles and come together, forming droplets that act as seeds for other water molecules. The water droplets grow and eventually fall as rain when they are large enough.

Sample Problem 18-1

If the solubility of a gas in water is 0.77 g/L at 3.5 atm of pressure, what is its solubility (in g/L) at 1.0 atm of pressure? (The temperature is held constant at 25 °C.)

1. **ANALYZE** *List the knowns and the unknown.*

   Knowns:
   - P_1 = 3.5 atm
   - S_1 = 0.77 g/L
   - P_2 = 1.0 atm

   - Henry's law: $\dfrac{S_1}{P_1} = \dfrac{S_2}{P_2}$

   Unknown:
   - S_2 = ? g/L

2. **CALCULATE** *Solve for the unknown.*
   Solving Henry's law for S_2 yields
   $$S_2 = \frac{S_1 \times P_2}{P_1}$$
   Substituting the known values and calculating yields
   $$S_2 = \frac{0.77 \text{ g/L} \times 1.0 \text{ atm}}{3.5 \text{ atm}} = 0.22 \text{ g/L}$$

3. **EVALUATE** *Does the result make sense?*
   The pressure is reduced (from 3.5 atm to 1.0 atm), so the solubility of the gas should decrease, which it is shown to do. Because the new pressure is approximately one-third of the original pressure, the new solubility should be approximately one-third of the original, which it is. The answer is correctly expressed to two significant figures.

Practice Problems

1. The solubility of a gas in water is 0.16 g/L at 104 kPa of pressure. What is the solubility when the pressure of the gas is increased to 288 kPa? Assume the temperature remains constant.

2. A gas has a solubility in water at 0 °C of 3.6 g/L at a pressure of 1.0 atm. What pressure is needed to produce an aqueous solution containing 9.5 g/L of the same gas at 0 °C?

Chem ASAP!
Problem-Solving 2
Solve Problem 2 with the help of an interactive guided tutorial.

MINI LAB

Solutions and Colloids

PURPOSE

To classify mixtures as solutions or colloids using the Tyndall effect.

MATERIALS

- sodium hydrogen carbonate
- cornstarch
- distilled water (or tap water)
- flashlight
- masking tape
- 3 jars with parallel sides
- teaspoon
- cup

PROCEDURE

1. In a cup, make a paste by mixing $\frac{1}{2}$ teaspoon cornstarch with 4 teaspoons water.

2. Fill one of the jars with water. Add $\frac{1}{2}$ teaspoon sodium hydrogen carbonate to a second jar and fill with water. Stir to mix. Add the cornstarch paste to the third jar and fill with water. Stir to mix.

3. Turn out the lights in the room. Shine the beam of light from the flashlight at each of the jars and record your observations.

ANALYSIS AND CONCLUSIONS

1. In which of the jars was it possible to see the path of the beam of light?

2. What made the light beam visible?

3. If a system that made the light beam visible were filtered, would the light beam be visible in the filtrate?

The Tyndall effect

4. Predict what you would observe if you were to replace the sodium hydrogen carbonate with sucrose (cane sugar) or sodium chloride (table salt).

5. Predict what you would observe if you were to replace the cornstarch with flour or diluted milk.

6. Explain how you could use this method to distinguish a colloid from a suspension.

---

section review 18.1

3. Name three factors that influence the rate at which a solute dissolves in a solvent.

4. How can you calculate the solubility of a gas in a liquid under different pressure conditions?

5. What mass of NaCl can be dissolved in 7.50×10^2 g of water at 25 °C?

6. What could you do to change

   a. a saturated solution to an unsaturated solution?

   b. an unsaturated solution to a saturated solution?

7. Use the solid substances listed in **Table 18.1** on page 504 to make a general statement that relates a change in solubility of a solid to a change in temperature.

 Chem ASAP! **Assessment 18.1** Check your understanding of the important ideas and concepts in Section 18.1.

A supply of clean drinking water is important for all communities. What constitutes clean water? The federal government, along with state governments, has set standards limiting the amount of contaminants allowed in drinking water. These contaminants include metals, pesticides, bacteria, and even the byproducts of water treatment. Water must be tested continuously to ensure that the concentrations of these contaminants do not exceed established limits. **How is the concentration of a solute in a solvent calculated?**

objectives
▸ Solve problems involving the molarity of a solution
▸ Describe how to prepare dilute solutions from more concentrated solutions of known molarity
▸ Explain what is meant by percent by volume (% (v/v)) and percent by mass (% (m/v)) solutions

key terms
▸ concentration
▸ dilute solution
▸ concentrated solution
▸ molarity (*M*)

Molarity

So far, you have learned that at a certain set of conditions a particular substance dissolves to some extent in a particular solvent to form a solution. This section focuses on ways to express the actual extent of dissolving. The **concentration** of a solution is a measure of the amount of solute that is dissolved in a given quantity of solvent. A **dilute solution** is one that contains only a low concentration of solute. By contrast, a **concentrated solution** contains a high concentration of solute. An aqueous solution of sodium chloride containing 1 g NaCl per 100 g H_2O might be described as dilute compared with an NaCl solution containing 30 g NaCl per 100 g H_2O, but concentrated compared with another solution containing only 0.01 g NaCl per 100 g H_2O. The terms concentrated and dilute are thus only qualitative descriptions of the amount of a solute in solution.

There are ways to express concentration quantitatively. The most important unit of concentration in chemistry is molarity. **Molarity (*M*)** is the number of moles of a solute dissolved per liter of solution. Molarity is also known as molar concentration and when accompanying a numerical value is read as "molar." Note that the volume involved is the total volume of the resulting solution, not the volume of the solvent alone. **Figure 18.10** demonstrates how a solution with a molarity of 0.5 (or a 0.5-molar solution) can be made. **Figure 18.11** on the following page shows 1-mol samples of some common compounds.

Figure 18.10

To make a 0.5-molar (0.5M) solution, (a) add 0.5 mol of solute to a 1-L volumetric flask half filled with distilled water. (b) Swirl the flask carefully to dissolve the solute. (c) Then fill the flask with water exactly to the 1-L mark.

(a)

(b)

(c)

Figure 18.11
If 1 mol of a compound is dissolved in 1 L of a solution, it has a 1-molar (1M) concentration. These are 1-mol samples of several compounds.

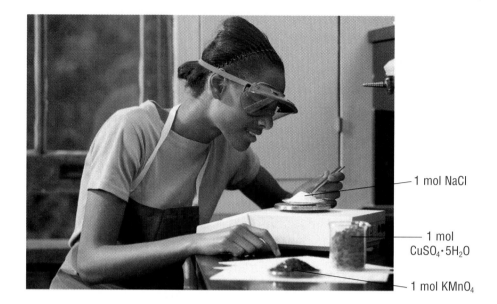

1 mol NaCl

1 mol $CuSO_4 \cdot 5H_2O$

1 mol $KMnO_4$

NURSING

Intravenous Solutions
A patient in a hospital is often administered an intravenous (IV) drip containing an aqueous solution. The patient may need the solution to prevent dehydration

or to administer nutrients or medicines. Great care must be taken when fluids are introduced into the bloodstream. The balance of dissolved electrolytes inside and outside of the tissue cells could be disturbed. The effects of an imbalance in electrolytes and water can be harmful or could even cause the death of the patient. Aqueous solutions containing 0.85%–0.9% (mass/volume) of sodium chloride or 5% (mass/volume) of glucose prevent undesired changes in the electrolyte balance.

To determine the molarity of any solution, calculate the number of moles in 1 L of the solution, using the following equation.

$$\text{Molarity } (M) = \frac{\text{moles of solute}}{\text{liters of solution}}$$

For example, to calculate the molarity when 2 mol of glucose is dissolved in 5 L of solution, divide the number of moles by the volume in liters.

$$\frac{2 \text{ mol glucose}}{5 \text{ L solution}} = 0.4 \text{ mol/L} = 0.4M$$

In some problems, the number of moles of solute dissolved in a given volume of solution needs to be determined. This can be done if the molarity of the solution is known. For example, how many moles are in 2.00 L of 2.5M lithium chloride? Rearranging the formula to solve for number of moles gives the following equation.

$$\begin{aligned} \text{Moles of solute} &= \text{liters of solution} \times \text{molarity } (M) \\ &= 2.00 \text{ L} \times 2.5M = 2.00 \, \cancel{L} \times 2.5 \text{ mol}/\cancel{L} \\ &= 5.0 \text{ mol} \end{aligned}$$

Sample Problem 18-2

A saline solution contains 0.90 g NaCl in exactly 100 mL of solution. What is the molarity of the solution?

1. ANALYZE *List the knowns and the unknown.*
Knowns:
• solution concentration = 0.90 g NaCl/100 mL
• molar mass NaCl = 58.5 g/mol
Unknown:
• solution concentration = ?M

Convert the concentration from g/100 mL to mol/L. The sequence is g/100 mL → mol/100 mL → mol/L.

Sample Problem 18-2 (cont.)

2. **CALCULATE** *Solve for the unknown.*

First use the molar mass to convert g NaCl/100 mL to mol NaCl/100 mL. Then use the conversion factor between milliliters and liters to convert to mol/L, which is molarity.

$$\frac{0.90 \text{ g NaCl}}{100 \text{ mL}} \times \frac{1 \text{ mol NaCl}}{58.5 \text{ g NaCl}} \times \frac{1000 \text{ mL}}{1 \text{ L}}$$

$$= 0.15 \text{ mol/L} = 0.15M$$

3. **EVALUATE** *Does the result make sense?*

An answer less than $1M$ should be expected because a concentration of 0.90 g/100 mL is the same as 9.0 g/1000 mL (9.0 g/1 L), and 9.0 g is less than 1 mol NaCl. The answer is correctly expressed to two significant figures.

Practice Problems

8. A solution has a volume of 2.0 L and contains 36.0 g of glucose. If the molar mass of glucose is 180 g/mol, what is the molarity of the solution?

9. A solution has a volume of 250 mL and contains 0.70 mol NaCl. What is its molarity?

Sample Problem 18-3

How many moles of solute are present in 1.5 L of $0.24M$ Na_2SO_4?

1. **ANALYZE** *List the knowns and the unknown.*

Knowns:
- volume of solution = 1.5 L
- solution concentration = $0.24M$ Na_2SO_4

Unknown:
- moles solute = ? mol

The conversion is volume of solution → moles of solute. Molarity has the units mol/L and is a conversion factor between moles of solute and volume of solution. Multiply the given volume by the molarity, expressed in mol/L.

2. **CALCULATE** *Solve for the unknown.*

$$1.5 \text{ L} \times \frac{0.24 \text{ mol NaCl}}{1 \text{ L}} = 0.36 \text{ mol NaCl}$$

3. **EVALUATE** *Does the result make sense?*

An answer less than 1 mol should be expected because the solution concentration is less than 0.25 mol/L and the volume is less than 2 L. The answer is correctly expressed to two significant figures.

Practice Problems

10. How many moles of ammonium nitrate are in 335 mL of $0.425M$ NH_4NO_3?

11. How many moles of solute are in 250 mL of $2.0M$ $CaCl_2$? How many grams of $CaCl_2$ is this?

Chem ASAP!

Problem-Solving 11
Solve Problem 11 with the help of an interactive guided tutorial.

Making Dilutions

Solutions of certain standard molarities are usually available in the laboratory. However, you may need a dilute solution of a different concentration. You can make a solution less concentrated by diluting it with solvent.

Figure 18.12

A concentrated solution contains a relatively large amount of solute for a given quantity of solution. A dilute solution contains a relatively small amount of solute. A concentrated solution has more solute particles per unit volume than does a dilute solution. Adding solvent to a concentrated solution lowers the concentration, but the total number of moles of solute present remains the same.

● Solute particle
● Solvent particle   Concentrated solution   Dilute solution

The dilution in **Figure 18.12** reduces the moles of solute per unit volume; however, the total moles of solute in solution does not change. Thus

Moles of solute before dilution = moles of solute after dilution

Rearranging the definition of molarity gives an expression for moles of solute in terms of molarity and volume.

$$\text{Molarity } (M) = \frac{\text{moles of solute}}{\text{liters of solution}}$$

Moles of solute = molarity $(M) \times$ liters of solution (V)

The total number of moles of solute remains unchanged upon dilution, so you can write

$$\text{Moles of solute} = M_1 \times V_1 = M_2 \times V_2$$

where M_1 and V_1 are the initial solution's molarity and volume, and M_2 and V_2 are the final solution's molarity and volume. Volumes can be in liters or milliliters, as long as the same units are used for both V_1 and V_2. Sample Problem 18-4 shows how to calculate the volume needed in preparing a dilute solution. **Figure 18.13** shows a solution being diluted.

Figure 18.13

To prepare 100 mL of 0.40M MgSO₄ from a stock solution of 2.0M MgSO₄, transfer 20 mL of the stock solution to a 100-mL volumetric flask. Carefully add water to make 100 mL of solution.

Sample Problem 18-4

How many milliliters of a stock solution of 2.00M $MgSO_4$ would you need to prepare 100.0 mL of 0.400M $MgSO_4$?

1. ANALYZE *List the knowns and the unknown.*

Knowns:
- M_1 = 2.00M $MgSO_4$
- M_2 = 0.400M $MgSO_4$
- V_2 = 100.0 mL of 0.400M $MgSO_4$
- $M_1 \times V_1 = M_2 \times V_2$

Unknown:
- V_1 = ? mL of 2.00M $MgSO_4$

2. CALCULATE *Solve for the unknown.*

Solving for V_1 yields:

$$V_1 = \frac{M_2 \times V_2}{M_1}$$

$$= \frac{0.400M \times 100.0 \text{ mL}}{2.00M}$$

$$= 20.0 \text{ mL}$$

Thus 20.0 mL of the initial solution must be diluted by adding enough water to raise the volume to 100.0 mL.

3. EVALUATE *Does the result make sense?*

The concentration of the initial (stock) solution is five times larger than the concentration of the solution to be prepared. Because the moles of solute in each solution are identical, it makes sense that the volume of the stock solution to be diluted should be one-fifth the final volume of the diluted solution. The answer is correctly expressed to three significant figures.

Practice Problems

12. How many milliliters of a stock solution of 4.00M KI would you need to prepare 250.0 mL of 0.760M KI?

13. Suppose you need 250 mL of 0.20M NaCl, but the only supply of sodium chloride you have is a solution of 1.0M NaCl. How do you prepare the required solution? Assume that you have the appropriate volume-measuring devices on hand.

Problem-Solving 12
Solve Problem 12 with the help of an interactive guided tutorial.

You may have a variety of volume-measuring devices available to you in the laboratory. Your choice of which to use in a given dilution depends on how accurate the concentration of the solution you are making must be. Suppose the solution in Sample Problem 18-4 must be prepared very accurately. You might measure 20.0 mL of the 2.00M $MgSO_4$ with a 20-mL volumetric pipet and transfer the solution to a 100-mL volumetric flask. (You can also use a buret to measure volumes accurately.) You would then add distilled water to the flask up to the etched line and mix well. This dilutes the contents to exactly 100.0 mL of 0.400M $MgSO_4$.

Percent Solutions

If both the solute and the solvent are liquids, a convenient way to make a solution is to measure volumes. The concentration of the solute is then expressed as a percent of the solution by volume. For example, if 20 mL of pure alcohol is diluted with water to a total volume of 100 mL, the final solution is 20% alcohol by volume. The concentration can be expressed as

Figure 18.14

Many product labels give the amounts of their ingredients by percent. Without units, however, you cannot be certain how the percent composition was determined. What are the two kinds of percent solutions?

20 percent (volume/volume), or 20% (v/v). The relationship between percent by volume and the volumes of solute and solution is

$$\text{Percent by volume (\% (v/v))} = \frac{\text{volume of solute}}{\text{solution volume}} \times 100\%$$

A commonly used relationship for solutions of solids dissolved in liquids is percent (mass/volume). It is usually convenient to weigh the solute in grams and to measure the volume of the resulting solution in milliliters. Percent (mass/volume) is the number of grams of solute per 100 mL of solution. For example, a solution containing 7 g of sodium chloride in 100 mL of solution is 7 percent (mass/volume), or 7% (m/v). The relationship among percent (mass/volume), solute mass, and solution volume is

$$\text{Percent (mass/volume) (\% (m/v))} = \frac{\text{mass of solute (g)}}{\text{solution volume (mL)}} \times 100\%$$

Because there are two kinds of percent solutions, information expressed as percent composition, such as on food labels, can often be misleading unless the units are given. See **Figure 18.14.** For example, a label stating that a candy bar contains 5% glucose is not conveying clear information. The number expressed is probably specifying percent (mass/mass), but this is not certain because the units are not given. When you use percentages to express concentration, be sure to state the units.

Sample Problem 18-5

What is the percent by volume of ethanol (C_2H_6O), or ethyl alcohol, in the final solution when 85 mL of ethanol is diluted to a volume of 250 mL with water?

1. **ANALYZE** *List the knowns and the unknown.*

   Knowns:
   - volume of ethanol = 85 mL
   - volume of solution = 250 mL
   - % (v/v) = $\dfrac{\text{volume of solute}}{\text{volume of solution}} \times 100\%$

   Unknown:
   - % ethanol (v/v) = ? %

2. **CALCULATE** *Solve for the unknown.*

   Substitute the known values into the equation and solve for the unknown.

   $$\% \text{ (v/v)} = \frac{\text{volume of solute}}{\text{volume of solution}} \times 100\%$$

   $$= \frac{85 \text{ mL ethanol}}{250 \text{ mL solution}} \times 100\%$$

   $$= 34\% \text{ ethanol (v/v)}$$

3. **EVALUATE** *Does the result make sense?*

   The volume of the solute is about one-third the volume of the solution, so the answer is reasonable. The answer is correctly expressed to two significant figures.

Practice Problems

14. If 10 mL of pure acetone is diluted with water to a total solution volume of 200 mL, what is the percent by volume of acetone in the solution?

15. A bottle of hydrogen peroxide antiseptic is labeled 3.0% (v/v). How many mL H_2O_2 are in a 400.0-mL bottle of this solution?

Chem ASAP!

Problem-Solving 15

Solve Problem 15 with the help of an interactive guided tutorial.

Sample Problem 18-6

How many grams of glucose ($C_6H_{12}O_6$) would you need to prepare 2.0 L of 2.8% glucose (m/v) solution?

....

1. **ANALYZE** *List the knowns and the unknown.*

   Knowns:
   • volume of solution = 2.0 L
   • concentration of solution (% (m/v)) = 2.8% $C_6H_{12}O_6$ (m/v)

   Unknown:
   • mass of solute = ? g $C_6H_{12}O_6$

   In a 2.8% glucose (m/v) solution, each 100 mL of the solution contains 2.8 g of glucose. Convert the given volume to milliliters, then use the concentration term to convert from milliliters of solution to grams of glucose:

   liters of solution → milliliters of solution → grams of solute

....

2. **CALCULATE** *Solve for the unknown.*

$$2.0 \, \cancel{L} \times \frac{1000 \, \cancel{mL}}{1 \, \cancel{L}} \times \frac{2.8 \, g}{100 \, \cancel{mL}} = 56 \, g \, C_6H_{12}O_6$$

....

3. **EVALUATE** *Does the result make sense?*

   Because one-tenth of a liter of solution contained 2.8 g, 1 L of solution should contain ten times as much solute (28 g) and 2 L should contain twice as much again (56 g of solute). The answer is correctly expressed to two significant figures.

Practice Problems

16. Calculate the grams of solute required to make 250 mL of 0.10% $MgSO_4$ (m/v).

17. A solution contains 2.7 g $CuSO_4$ in 75 mL of solution. What is the percent (mass/volume) of the solution?

---

section review 18.2

18. How are problems involving solution molarity solved?

19. Describe how dilute solutions are prepared from more concentrated solutions of known molarity.

20. Distinguish between percent (v/v) and percent (m/v) solutions.

21. Calculate the molarity of each solution.

   a. 400 g $CuSO_4$ in 4.00 L of solution

   b. 0.060 mol $NaHCO_3$ in 1500 mL of solution

22. You have the following stock solutions available: 2.00*M* NaCl, 4.0*M* KNO_3, and 0.50*M* $MgSO_4$. Calculate the volumes you must dilute to make the following solutions.

   a. 500.0 mL of 0.500*M* NaCl   c. 50.0 mL of 0.20*M* KNO_3

   b. 2.0 L of 0.20*M* $MgSO_4$

23. What is the concentration, in percent (m/v), of a solution with 75 g K_2SO_4 in 1500 mL of solution?

portfolio project

Write a report comparing the concentration of fruit juice in different types of juice drinks. Is the percent of fruit juice given by volume or by mass? Can the way these concentrations are reported be confusing or misleading?

 Chem ASAP! **Assessment 18.2** Check your understanding of the important ideas and concepts in Section 18.2.

SMALL-SCALE LAB

MAKING A SOLUTION

SAFETY

Wear safety glasses and follow the standard safety procedures outlined on page 18.

PURPOSE

To make a solution and use carefully measured data to calculate the solution's concentration in various units.

MATERIALS

- solid NaCl
- water
- 50-mL plastic volumetric bottle
- balance

PROCEDURE

Weigh a clean, dry, plastic volumetric bottle. Add solid NaCl to approximately the 5-mL mark on the bottle. Weigh the bottle again. Half fill the bottle with water and shake it gently until all the NaCl dissolves. Fill the bottle with water to the 50-mL mark and weigh it again.

ANALYSIS

Using your experimental data, record the answers to the following questions below your data table.

1. Percent by mass tells how many grams of solute are present in 100 g of solution.

$$\% \text{ by mass} = \frac{\text{mass of solute}}{\text{mass of solute} + \text{solvent}} \times 100\%$$

   a. Calculate the mass of the solute (NaCl).

   b. Calculate the mass of the solvent (water).

   c. Calculate the percent by mass of NaCl in the solution.

2. Mole fraction tells how many moles of solute are present for every 1 mol of total solution.

$$\text{Mole fraction} = \frac{\text{mol NaCl}}{\text{mol NaCl} + \text{mol H}_2\text{O}}$$

   a. Calculate the moles of NaCl solute. Molar mass NaCl = 58.5 g/mol

   b. Calculate the moles of water.
      Molar mass H_2O = 18 g/mol

   c. Calculate the mole fraction of your solution.

3. Molality (m) tells how many moles of solute are present in 1 kg of solvent.

$$m = \frac{\text{mol NaCl}}{\text{kg H}_2\text{O}}$$

Calculate the molality of your solution.

4. Molarity (M) tells how many moles of solute are dissolved in 1 L of solution.

$$M = \frac{\text{mol NaCl}}{\text{L solution}}$$

   a. Calculate the liters of solution. 1000 mL = 1 L

   b. Calculate the molarity of the NaCl solution.

5. Density tells how many grams of solution are present in 1 mL of solution.

$$\text{Density} = \frac{\text{g solution}}{\text{mL solution}}$$

Calculate the density of the solution.

YOU'RE THE CHEMIST

The following small-scale activities allow you to develop your own procedures and analyze the results.

1. **Analyze It!** Use a small-scale pipet to extract a sample of your NaCl solution and deliver it to a pre-weighed empty plastic bottle. Weigh the bottle again and then fill the bottle with water to the 50-mL line. Weigh the bottle a third time and calculate the concentration of this dilute solution using the same units you used to calculate the concentration of the NaCl solution.

2. **Design It!** Design and carry out an experiment to make a solution of table sugar quantitatively. Calculate the concentration of the table sugar solution using the same units you used to calculate the concentration of the NaCl solution.

COLLIGATIVE PROPERTIES OF SOLUTIONS

*T*he wood frog is a remarkable creature because it can survive being frozen. Scientists believe that a substance in the cells of this frog acts as a natural antifreeze, which prevents the cells from freezing. Although fluids surrounding the frog's cells may freeze, the cells themselves do not. **How can a solute change the freezing point of a solvent?**

objectives
▶ Explain on a particle basis why a solution has a lower vapor pressure than the pure solvent of that solution
▶ Explain on a particle basis why a solution has an elevated boiling point and a depressed freezing point compared with the pure solvent

key terms
▶ colligative properties
▶ boiling-point elevation
▶ freezing-point depression

Decrease in Vapor Pressure

The physical properties of a solution differ from those of the pure solvent used to make the solution. Some of these differences are due to the mere presence of solute particles in the solution, rather than to the specific identity of the solute. Such properties, which depend only on the number of particles dissolved in a given mass of solvent, are called **colligative properties.** Three important colligative properties of solutions are vapor-pressure lowering, boiling-point elevation, and freezing-point depression.

Recall that vapor pressure is the pressure exerted by a vapor that is in dynamic equilibrium with its liquid in a closed system. A solution that contains a solute that is nonvolatile (not easily vaporized) always has a lower vapor pressure than the pure solvent. Glucose, a molecular compound, and sodium chloride, an ionic compound, are examples of nonvolatile solutes. Both glucose and sodium chloride would lower the vapor pressure of a pure solvent. Consider an aqueous sodium chloride solution as an example. Sodium ions and chloride ions are dispersed throughout the liquid water. Both within the liquid and at the surface, the ions are surrounded by layers of shells of associated water, or shells of water of solvation. The formation of these shells of water of solvation reduces the number of solvent molecules that have enough kinetic energy to escape as vapor. See **Figure 18.15.** As a result, the solution has a lower vapor pressure than the pure solvent (water) would have on its own.

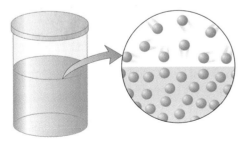

Pure solvent   **(a)** Higher vapor pressure

Solution containing nonvolatile solute   **(b)** Lower vapor pressure

● Solute particle
● Solvent particle

Figure 18.15

The vapor pressure of a solution of a nonvolatile solute is less than the vapor pressure of a pure solvent. (a) Equilibrium is established between the liquid and the vapor in the pure solvent. (b) The equilibrium is disrupted when solute is added. Solvent particles form shells around the solute particles, thus reducing the number of free solvent particles able to escape the liquid. Equilibrium is eventually re-established at a lower vapor pressure.

The decrease in the vapor pressure is proportional to the number of particles the solute makes in solution. A solute such as sodium chloride, which dissociates into several particles, has a greater effect on the vapor pressure than a nondissociating solute such as glucose. For example, the vapor-pressure lowering caused by 0.1 mol of sodium chloride in 1000 g of water is twice that caused by the same number of moles of glucose in the same quantity of water. This is because each formula unit of the ionic compound sodium chloride produces two particles in solution: a sodium ion and a chloride ion, as illustrated in **Figure 18.16.** In contrast, when glucose dissolves, the molecules do not dissociate. In the same way, 0.1 mol $CaCl_2$ in 1000 g of water produces three times the vapor-pressure lowering as 0.1 mol of glucose in the same quantity of water. This is because each formula unit of calcium chloride produces three particles in solution. How many particles in solution are produced by each formula unit of aluminum bromide?

(a) Glucose in solution

(b) Sodium chloride in solution

(c) Calcium chloride in solution

⬣ Glucose   ⚬ Na$^+$ ⚬ Cl$^-$ • Ca^{2+}

Figure 18.16

*Particle concentrations for dissolved covalent and ionic compounds in water differ depending on the number of particles formed per formula unit. **(a)** When 3 mol of glucose is dissolved in water, there are 3 mol of solute particles because glucose does not dissociate. **(b)** When 3 mol of sodium chloride is dissolved in water, there are 6 mol of solute particles because each formula unit of NaCl dissociates into two ions. **(c)** When 3 mol of calcium chloride dissolves in water, there are 9 mol of particles because each formula unit of $CaCl_2$ dissociates into three ions. How many moles of particles would 3 mol Na_3PO_4 give in solution?*

Boiling-Point Elevation

The boiling point of a substance is the temperature at which the vapor pressure of the liquid phase equals the atmospheric pressure. As you just learned, adding a nonvolatile solute to a liquid solvent decreases the vapor pressure of the solvent. Because of the decrease in vapor pressure, additional kinetic energy must be added to raise the vapor pressure of the liquid phase of the solution to atmospheric pressure. Thus the boiling point of the solution is higher than the boiling point of the pure solvent. The **boiling-point elevation** is the difference in temperature between the boiling point of a solution and that of the pure solvent.

You can also think about boiling-point elevation in terms of particles. Attractive forces exist between the solvent and solute particles. It takes additional kinetic energy for the solvent particles to overcome the attractive forces that keep them in the liquid. Thus the presence of a solute elevates the boiling point of the solvent. The magnitude of the boiling-point elevation is proportional to the number of solute particles dissolved in the solvent. For example, the boiling point of water increases by 0.512 °C for every mole of particles that the solute forms when dissolved in 1000 g of water. Thus boiling-point elevation is a colligative property: It depends on the concentration of particles, not on their identity.

Freezing-Point Depression

When a substance freezes, the particles of the solid take on an orderly pattern. The presence of a solute in water disrupts the formation of this pattern because of the shells of water of solvation. As a result, more kinetic energy must be withdrawn from a solution than from pure solvent for it to solidify. The **freezing-point depression** is the difference in temperature between the freezing point of a solution and that of the pure solvent. The magnitude of the freezing-point depression is proportional to the number of solute particles dissolved in the solvent and does not depend upon their identity. Freezing-point depression is a colligative property.

The addition of 1 mol of solute particles to 1000 g of water lowers the freezing point by 1.86 °C. For example, if you add 1 mol (180 g) of glucose to 1000 g of water, the solution freezes at −1.86 °C. However, if you add 1 mol (58.5 g) of sodium chloride to 1000 g of water, the solution freezes at −3.72 °C. This is because 1 mol NaCl produces 2 mol of particles, and thus doubles the freezing-point depression. What is the freezing point of a solution that contains 1 mol of calcium chloride in 1000 g of water? You take advantage of the freezing-point depression of aqueous solutions when you sprinkle salt on icy sidewalks to make the ice melt. The ice melts and forms a solution with a lower freezing point than that of pure water. **Figure 18.17** shows another application of the freezing-point depression of an aqueous solution.

Figure 18.17
Temperatures below 0 °C are needed to make ice cream. Rock salt is added to ice in an ice-cream maker to produce a freezing-point depression. The temperature of the ice–water–rock salt mixture decreases to a few degrees below 0 °C. What kind of property is freezing-point depression?

section review 18.3

24. Why does a solution have a lower vapor pressure than the pure solvent of that solution?

25. Why does a solution have an elevated boiling point and a depressed freezing point compared with the pure solvent?

26. Would a dilute or a concentrated sodium fluoride solution have a higher boiling point? Explain.

27. An equal number of moles of KI and MgF_2 are dissolved in equal volumes of water. Which solution has the higher
    a. boiling point?
    b. vapor pressure?
    c. freezing point?

 Chem ASAP! **Assessment 18.3** Check your understanding of the important ideas and concepts in Section 18.3.

portfolio project

Salt is often spread on icy streets and highways. Research the environmental problems this causes. Find out what alternative approaches are available.

CALCULATIONS INVOLVING COLLIGATIVE PROPERTIES

▸ Calculate the molality and mole fraction of a solution

▸ Calculate the molar mass of a molecular compound from the freezing-point depression or boiling-point elevation of a solution of the compound

key terms

▸ molality (*m*)

▸ mole fraction

▸ molal boiling-point elevation constant (K_b)

▸ molal freezing-point depression constant (K_f)

*C*ooking instructions for a wide variety of foods—from dried pasta to packaged beans to frozen fruits to fresh vegetables—often call for the addition of a small amount of salt to the cooking water. Most people like the flavor of food cooked with salt. What other effect can adding salt have on the cooking process? Recall that dissolved salt elevates the boiling point of water. Suppose you added a teaspoon of salt to 2 liters of water. A teaspoon of salt has a mass of about 20 g. Would the resulting boiling point increase be enough to shorten the time required for cooking? **How is the boiling-point elevation of an aqueous solution calculated?**

Molality and Mole Fraction

Colligative properties depend only on solute concentration, or the ratio of the number of solute particles to solvent particles. There are two convenient ways of expressing this ratio: in molality and in mole fractions. **Molality (*m*)** is the number of moles of solute dissolved per kilogram (1000 g) of solvent. Molality is also known as molal concentration.

$$\text{Molality} = \frac{\text{moles of solute}}{\text{kilogram of solvent}} = \frac{\text{moles of solute}}{1000 \text{ g solvent}}$$

Note that molality is not the same as molarity. Molality refers to moles per kilogram of solvent rather than per liter of solution. In the case of water as the solvent, 1000 g equals a volume of 1000 mL, or 1 L.

You can prepare a solution that is 1.00 molal (1*m*) in glucose, for example, by adding 1.00 mol (180 g) of glucose to 1000 g of water. A solution prepared by dissolving 0.500 mol (29.25 g) of sodium chloride in 1.000 kg (1000 g) of water is 0.500 molal (0.500*m*) in NaCl. See **Figure 18.18.**

Figure 18.18

To make a 0.500m solution of NaCl, use a balance to measure 1.000 kg of water and add 0.500 mol (29.3 g) NaCl. What would be the molality if only 0.500 kg of water were used?

0.500 mol
(29.3 g)
NaCl

1.000 kg
H₂O

Sample Problem 18-7

How many grams of potassium iodide must be dissolved in 500.0 g of water to produce a 0.060 molal KI solution?

1. ANALYZE List the knowns and the unknown.

Knowns:
- mass of water = 500.0 g
- solution concentration = $0.060m$
- molar mass KI = 166.0 g/mol

Unknown:
- mass of solute = ? g KI

According to the definition of molal, the final solution must contain 0.060 mol KI per 1000 g H_2O. Use the molality as a conversion factor to convert from mass of water to moles of the solute (KI). Then use the molar mass of KI to convert from mol KI to g KI. The steps are mass of $H_2O \rightarrow$ mol KI $\rightarrow$ g KI.

2. CALCULATE Solve for the unknown.

$$500.0 \text{ g } H_2O \times \frac{0.060 \text{ mol KI}}{1000 \text{ g } H_2O} \times \frac{166.0 \text{ g KI}}{1 \text{ mol KI}} = 5.0 \text{ g KI}$$

3. EVALUATE Does the result make sense?

A 1 molal KI solution is made by dissolving a molar mass of KI (166.0 g) in 1000 g of water. The desired molal concentration ($0.060m$) is about $\frac{1}{20}$ of that value, so it should be expected that the mass of KI would be much less than the molar mass. The answer is correctly expressed to two significant figures.

Practice Problems

28. How many grams of sodium fluoride are needed to prepare a $0.400m$ NaF solution that contains 750.0 g of water?

29. Calculate the molality of a solution prepared by dissolving 10.0 g NaCl in 600 g of water.

Solution concentration can be expressed in yet another way. The ratio of the moles of solute in solution to the total number of moles of solvent and solute is the **mole fraction** of that solute. In a solution containing n_A mol of solute A and n_B mol of solvent B, the mole fraction of solute (X_A) and mole fraction of solvent (X_B) can be expressed as follows.

$$X_A = \frac{n_A}{n_A + n_B} \qquad X_B = \frac{n_B}{n_A + n_B}$$

Sample Problem 18-8

Compute the mole fraction of each component in a solution of 1.25 mol of ethylene glycol (EG) and 4.00 mol of water.

1. ANALYZE List the knowns and the unknowns.

Knowns:
- moles of ethylene glycol (n_{EG}) = 1.25 mol
- moles of water (n_{H_2O}) = 4.00 mol H_2O

Unknowns:
- mole fraction EG (X_{EG}) = ?
- mole fraction H_2O (X_{H_2O}) = ?

Figure 18.19

The mole fraction is the ratio of the number of moles of one substance to the total number of moles of all substances in the solution. Ethylene glycol (EG) is often added to water in a car radiator as an antifreeze. What is the sum of all mole fractions in a solution?

1.25 mol
EG

4.00 mol
H_2O

Total moles = (A) + (B) = 5.25 mol

$$\text{Mole fraction EG} = \frac{\text{A}}{\text{A} + \text{B}} = \frac{1.25}{5.25}$$

$$\text{Mole fraction } H_2O = \frac{\text{B}}{\text{A} + \text{B}} = \frac{4.00}{5.25}$$

Sample Problem 18-8 (cont.)

The mole fraction of ethylene glycol (X_{EG}) in the solution is the number of moles of ethylene glycol divided by the total number of moles in solution:

$$X_{EG} = \frac{n_{EG}}{n_{EG} + n_{H_2O}}$$

Similarly, the mole fraction of water (X_{H_2O}) is the number of moles of water divided by the total number of moles in solution:

$$X_{H_2O} = \frac{n_{H_2O}}{n_{EG} + n_{H_2O}}$$

2. CALCULATE Solve for the unknowns.

$$X_{EG} = \frac{n_{EG}}{n_{EG} + n_{H_2O}} = \frac{1.25 \text{ mol}}{1.25 \text{ mol} + 4.00 \text{ mol}} = 0.238$$

$$X_{H_2O} = \frac{n_{H_2O}}{n_{EG} + n_{H_2O}} = \frac{4.00 \text{ mol}}{1.25 \text{ mol} + 4.00 \text{ mol}} = 0.762$$

3. EVALUATE Do the results make sense?

Note that mole fraction is a dimensionless quantity. The sum of the mole fractions of all the components in a solution equals unity, or one, as should be expected. Each answer is correctly expressed to three significant figures.

Practice Problems

30. What is the mole fraction of each component in a solution made by mixing 300 g of ethanol (C_2H_5OH) and 500 g of water?

31. A solution contains 50.0 g of carbon tetrachloride (CCl_4) and 50.0 g of chloroform ($CHCl_3$). Calculate the mole fraction of each component in the solution.

Chem ASAP!

Problem-Solving 31

Solve Problem 31 with the help of an interactive guided tutorial.

Boiling-Point Elevation and Freezing-Point Depression

Elevations of boiling points and depressions of freezing points are usually quite small. Thus they can be measured accurately only with thermometers that measure temperature changes as small as 0.001 °C.

The boiling point of a solvent is raised by the addition of a nonvolatile solute, as shown in **Figure 18.20**. The magnitude of the boiling-point elevation (ΔT_b) is directly proportional to the molal concentration (*m*), assuming the solute is molecular, not ionic.

$$\Delta T_b \propto m$$

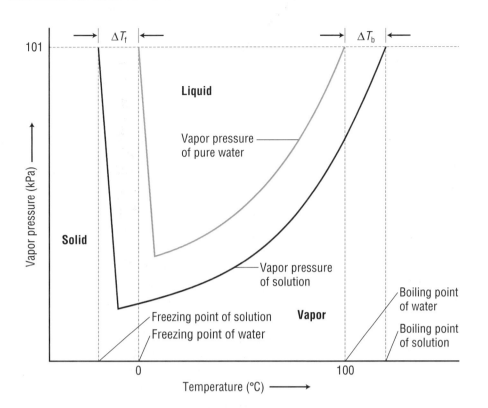

Figure 18.20
The addition of a nonvolatile solute to water lowers the water's vapor pressure. This results in an increase in the normal boiling point of the water and a decrease in the normal freezing point of the water.

Chem ASAP!
Simulation 22
Discover the principle underlying the colligative properties of solutions.

The change in the boiling temperature (ΔT_b) is the elevation of the boiling point of the solvent. It is the boiling point of the solution minus the boiling point of the pure solvent. The term m is the molal concentration of the solution. Adding a proportionality constant (K_b) to this relationship makes it an equality.

$$\Delta T_b = K_b \times m$$

This constant is the **molal boiling-point elevation constant (K_b),** which is equal to the change in boiling point for a 1-molal solution of a nonvolatile molecular solute. K_b is dependent on the solvent, and its units are °C/m. **Table 18.2** lists the K_b values for water and some other solvents.

The boiling-point elevation for ionic solids depends on the number of ions produced by each formula unit. This number is used to calculate the effective molality. Which aqueous solution would have the larger boiling-point elevation: $1m$ KCl or $1m$ CaBr$_2$?

Table 18.2

K_b Values for Some Common Solvents	
Solvent	K_b (°C/m)
Water	0.512
Ethanol	1.19
Benzene	2.53
Cyclohexane	2.79
Acetic acid	3.07
Phenol	3.56
Nitrobenzene	5.24
Camphor	5.95

Sample Problem 18-9

What is the boiling point of a 1.50m NaCl solution?

1. **ANALYZE** *List the knowns and the unknown.*

Knowns:
* solution concentration (m) = 1.50m NaCl
* K_b for H$_2$O = 0.512 °C/m
* $\Delta T_b = K_b \times m$

Unknown:
* boiling point = ? °C

Sample Problem 18-9 (cont.)

Each formula unit of NaCl is ionized into two particles.

$$NaCl(s) \rightarrow Na^+(aq) + Cl^-(aq)$$

Therefore, the molality of total particles is $2 \times 1.50m = 3.00m$. Calculate the boiling-point elevation and then add it to 100 °C.

2. CALCULATE *Solve for the unknown.*

$$\Delta T_b = K_b \times m$$
$$= 0.512 \,°C/m \times 3.00m$$
$$= 1.54 \,°C$$

The boiling point of this solution is

$$100 \,°C + 1.54 \,°C = 101.54 \,°C$$

3. EVALUATE *Does the result make sense?*

The boiling point increases about 0.5 °C for each mole of solute particles, so the total change is reasonable. The answer is correctly expressed to hundredths of a degree. Because the boiling point of water is defined as exactly 100 °C, this value does not limit the number of significant figures in the solution of the problem.

Practice Problems

32. What is the boiling point of a solution that contains 1.25 mol $CaCl_2$ in 1400 g of water?

33. What mass of NaCl would have to be dissolved in 1.000×10^3 g of water to raise the boiling point by 2.00 °C?

Chem ASAP!

Problem-Solving 33
Solve Problem 33 with the help of an interactive guided tutorial.

You can also calculate the freezing-point depression of a solution. To do so use the equation

$$\Delta T_f = K_f \times m$$

The change in the freezing temperature (ΔT_f) represents the freezing-point depression. The molality is m. The **molal freezing-point depression constant** (K_f) is equal to the change in the freezing point for a 1-molal solution of a nonvolatile molecular solute. The units of K_f are °C/m. Table 18.3 gives the values of the constant K_f for some common solvents.

Table 18.3

K_f Values for Some Common Solvents	
Solvent	K_f (°C/m)
Water	1.86
Acetic acid	3.90
Benzene	5.12
Nitrobenzene	7.00
Phenol	7.40
Cyclohexane	20.2
Camphor	37.7

Molar Mass

You can use the changes in boiling and freezing points to determine the molar mass of a substance. To do this, you would first add a known mass of solute to a known mass of solvent that has a known molal boiling-point elevation constant (K_b) or molal freezing-point depression constant (K_f). Next you would measure the change in the boiling or freezing point. Finally, you would calculate the molar mass for the solute. Sample Problem 18-10 illustrates this strategy.

Sample Problem 18-10

A solution of 7.50 g of a nonvolatile compound in 22.60 g of water boils at 100.78 °C at 760 mm Hg. What is the molar mass of the solute? Assume that the solute exists as molecules, not ions.

Sample Problem 18-10 (cont.)

1. ANALYZE List the knowns and the unknown.

Knowns:
- mass of water = 22.60 g
- mass of solute = 7.50 g
- boiling-point elevation (ΔT_b) = (100.78 °C − 100 °C) = 0.78 °C
- K_b for H_2O = 0.512 °C/m
- $\Delta T_b = K_b \times m$

Unknown:
- molar mass = ? g/mol

2. CALCULATE Solve for the unknown.

Solve $\Delta T_b = K_b \times m$ for m and substitute the known values.

$$m = \frac{\Delta T_b}{K_b} = \frac{0.78\,°C}{0.512\,°C/m} = 1.5m = 1.5\,\frac{\text{mol solute}}{\text{kg water}}$$

Calculate moles of solute.

$$22.60\,\text{g water} \times \frac{1\,\text{kg water}}{1000\,\text{g water}} \times \frac{1.5\,\text{mol solute}}{1\,\text{kg water}}$$
$$= 0.034\,\text{mol solute}$$

$$\text{Molar mass of solute} = \frac{\text{mass of solute}}{\text{moles of solute}}$$
$$= \frac{7.50\,\text{g}}{0.034\,\text{mol}} = 2.2 \times 10^2\,\text{g/mol}$$

3. EVALUATE Does the result make sense?

A molality of 1.5 is reasonable because the boiling point was increased about 1.5 times K_b. The amount of water is about $\frac{1}{50}$ of a kilogram and the solution is 1.5m, so it makes sense that the moles of solute should be greater than $\frac{1}{50}$ of a mole. The actual number of moles was about $\frac{1}{30}$ of a mole, so the molar mass should be about 30 times the mass of the solute.

Practice Problems

34. The freezing point of the water is lowered to −0.390 °C when 3.90 g of a nonvolatile molecular solute is dissolved in 475 g of water. Calculate the molar mass of the solute.

35. A solution containing 16.9 g of a nonvolatile molecular compound in 250 g of water has a freezing point of −0.744 °C. What is the molar mass of the substance?

section review 18.4

36. How many kilograms of water must be added to 9.0 g of oxalic acid ($H_2C_2O_4$) to prepare a 0.025m solution?

37. One mole of a compound of iron and chlorine is dissolved in 1 kg of water. The boiling point of this aqueous solution is 102.05 °C. The freezing point of this aqueous solution is −7.44 °C. What is the formula of the solute compound?

38. How are boiling-point elevation and freezing-point depression related to molality?

39. Estimate the freezing point of a solution of 12.0 g of carbon tetrachloride dissolved in 750 g of benzene (which has a freezing point of 5.48 °C).

 Chem ASAP! Assessment 18.4 Check your understanding of the important ideas and concepts in Section 18.4.

A SOLUTION FOR KIDNEY FAILURE

Your blood is a solution, a colloid, and a suspension all at the same time. Blood contains gases, ions, and nutrient molecules in solution. It also contains biologically important particles—protein molecules in colloidal dispersion and cells in suspension.

For your body to function properly, the blood's solutes must be kept at the right concentrations. Many of your organs participate in this process. Your liver and pancreas, for example, are responsible for regulating the concentration of sugar in your blood.

Similarly, your kidneys have the important but often under-appreciated job of keeping the concentration of dissolved waste products in your blood at a minimum. As part of their normal functioning, all of your body's cells continuously produce waste products and dump these wastes into the blood. If they were not removed from your blood, the dissolved waste products would build up and become toxic to your body.

The work of filtering waste products from your blood is done by thousands of small units in your kidneys called nephrons. Blood enters a nephron through a tiny blood vessel. Everything except blood cells and very large molecules can then pass out of the blood through a semipermeable membrane into a long collecting tube. As the fluid travels through this tube, all the necessary components of your blood—water, ions, and other solutes—pass through the walls of the tube and back into the blood. Waste products, however, remain in the tube. By the time the tube exits the nephron, it contains only urine. Blood that leaves the nephron has all its necessary components—minus the waste products in the urine.

What happens if the kidneys fail to function correctly? Many people suffer from kidney failure and must have their blood "cleaned" in some other way.

> For your body to function properly, the blood's solutes must be kept at the right concentrations. Many of your organs participate in this process.

Many of these people rely on the process called hemodialysis, a way of filtering the blood outside the body.

The hemodialysis machine is an artificial kidney. Blood leaves a patient's artery through a tube and enters the dialysis machine. Inside the machine, the blood passes through a semipermeable membrane similar to the one shown in the photograph. The membrane is submersed in a solution containing the same ions and other solutes as in human blood at the same concentrations. This solution, called dialysate, contains no waste products, so the waste products in the blood readily move out of the blood, across the dialyzing membrane, and into the dialysate. During the process of hemodialysis, the dialysate is continuously recirculated to prevent the return of wastes to the blood. After cleaning the blood, the machine returns it to the body through a vein.

The process of cleaning a person's entire blood supply takes several hours. The process is effective, but as soon as the patient is disconnected from the machine, waste products once again begin building up in the blood. For this reason, several visits to the dialysis clinic are needed every week. Today, a dialysis machine represents life-giving technology for those suffering from kidney failure.

CHEMISTRY IN CAREERS

NEPHROLOGY NURSE
Work in a hospital or treatment facility to care for patients with various types of renal disease. See page 876.

CHEMIST NEEDED

TAKE IT TO THE NET

Find out more about career opportunities: www.phschool.com

CHEMICAL SPECIALIST
Local food service distributor see responsible self-motivated indivi

Take It to the NET
For interactive study and
review, go to www.phschool.com

KEY TERMS

- boiling-point elevation *p. 518*
- colligative property *p. 517*
- concentrated solution *p. 509*
- concentration *p. 509*
- dilute solution *p. 509*
- freezing-point depression *p. 519*
- Henry's law *p. 506*

- immiscible *p. 503*
- miscible *p. 503*
- molal boiling-point elevation constant (K_b) *p. 523*
- molal freezing-point depression constant (K_f) *p. 524*
- molality (*m*) *p. 520*

- molarity (*M*) *p. 509*
- mole fraction *p. 521*
- saturated solution *p. 502*
- solubility *p. 503*
- supersaturated solution *p. 506*
- unsaturated *p. 503*

KEY EQUATIONS

- Henry's law: $\dfrac{S_1}{P_1} = \dfrac{S_2}{P_2}$

- Molarity = $\dfrac{\text{moles of solute}}{\text{liters of solution}}$

- $M_1 \times V_1 = M_2 \times V_2$

- Percent by volume = $\dfrac{\text{volume of solute}}{\text{solution volume}} \times 100\%$

- Percent (mass/volume) = $\dfrac{\text{mass of solute (g)}}{\text{solution volume (mL)}} \times 100\%$

- Molality = $\dfrac{\text{moles of solute}}{\text{kilogram of solvent}} = \dfrac{\text{moles of solute}}{1000 \text{ g solvent}}$

- Mole fractions: $X_A = \dfrac{n_A}{n_A + n_B}$ $X_B = \dfrac{n_B}{n_A + n_B}$

- $\Delta T_b = K_b \times m$

- $\Delta T_f = K_f \times m$

CONCEPT SUMMARY

18.1 Properties of Solutions
- The rate at which a solute dissolves is influenced by a number of factors, including the temperature of the solvent, the particle size of the solute, and stirring of the solution.
- Two liquids are said to be miscible if they dissolve in each other; immiscible if they do not.
- Changes in temperature and pressure of a system affect the solubility of a solute.

18.2 Concentrations of Solutions
- The relative amounts of solute and solvent in a solution are described by molar concentration, percent composition, molal concentration, and mole fraction.

18.3 Colligative Properties of Solutions
- Colligative properties include vapor-pressure lowering, freezing-point depression, and boiling-point elevation.

18.4 Calculations Involving Colligative Properties
- The magnitude of every colligative property is directly proportional to the number of solute molecules or ions present.
- Molality is moles of solute per kilogram of solvent. The mole fraction of a substance in solution is equal to the number of moles of the substance divided by the total number of moles of all substances in the solution.

CHAPTER CONCEPT MAP

Use these terms to construct a concept map that organizes the major ideas of this chapter.

 Chem ASAP! Concept Map 18
Create your Concept Map using the computer.

CONCEPT PRACTICE

40. Name and distinguish between the two components of a solution. *18.1*

41. Explain why the dissolved component does not settle out of a solution. *18.1*

42. Explain miscible and immiscible. *18.1*

43. Define solubility, saturated solution, and unsaturated solution. *18.1*

44. What mass of $AgNO_3$ can be dissolved in 250 g of water at 20 °C? *18.1*

45. If a saturated solution of sodium nitrate is cooled, what change might you observe? *18.1*

46. Can a solution with undissolved solute be supersaturated? Explain. *18.1*

47. What is the effect of pressure on the solubility of gases in liquids? *18.1*

48. The solubility of methane, the major component of natural gas, in water at 20 °C and 1.00 atm pressure is 0.026 g/L. If the temperature remains constant, what will be the solubility of this gas at the following pressures? *18.1*
    a. 0.60 atm
    b. 1.80 atm

49. Having a measure of the molarity of a solution is more meaningful than knowing whether a solution is dilute or concentrated. Explain. *18.2*

50. Calculate the molarity of each solution. *18.2*
    a. 1.0 mol KCl in 750 mL of solution
    b. 0.50 mol $MgCl_2$ in 1.5 L of solution

51. Define molarity. *18.2*

52. Calculate the moles and grams of solute in each solution. *18.2*
    a. 1.0 L of $0.50M$ NaCl
    b. 5.0×10^2 mL of $2.0M$ KNO_3
    c. 250 mL of $0.10M$ $CaCl_2$
    d. 2.0 L of $0.30M$ Na_2SO_4

53. Calculate the grams of solute required to make the following solutions. *18.2*
    a. 2.5 L of normal saline solution (0.90% NaCl (m/v))
    b. 50.0 mL of 4.0% $MgCl_2$ (m/v)

54. What is the concentration (in % (m/v)) of the following solutions? *18.2*
    a. 20.0 g KCl in 0.60 L of solution
    b. 32 g $NaNO_3$ in 2.0 L of solution

55. What is the boiling point of each solution? *18.4*
    a. 0.50 mol glucose in 1000 g H_2O
    b. 1.50 mol NaCl in 1000 g H_2O

56. Describe how you would make an aqueous solution of methanol (CH_3OH) in which the mole fraction of methanol is 0.40. *18.4*

57. Distinguish between a $1M$ solution and a $1m$ solution. *18.4*

58. What is the freezing point of each solution? *18.4*
    a. 1.40 mol Na_2SO_4 in 1750 g H_2O
    b. 0.060 mol $MgSO_4$ in 100 g H_2O

59. Determine the freezing points of each $0.20m$ aqueous solution. *18.4*
    a. K_2SO_4
    b. $CsNO_3$
    c. $Al(NO_3)_3$

60. What laboratory measurements must be made to find the molar mass of a solute in a boiling-point elevation experiment? *18.4*

CONCEPT MASTERY

61. Varying numbers of moles of two different solutes, A and B, were added to identical quantities of water. The graph shows the freezing point of each of the solutions formed with various amounts of solutes.
    a. Explain the relative slopes of the two lines between 0 and 2 mol of solute added.
    b. Why does the freezing point for solution A not continue to drop as amounts of solute A are added beyond 2.4 mol?

62. Calculate the freezing- and boiling-point changes for a solution containing 12.0 g of naphthalene ($C_{10}H_8$) in 50.0 g of benzene.

63. Describe how you would prepare an aqueous solution of acetone (CH_3COCH_3) in which the mole fraction of acetone is 0.25.

64. The solubility of sodium hydrogen carbonate ($NaHCO_3$) in water at 20 °C is 9.6 g/100 g H_2O. What is the mole fraction of $NaHCO_3$ in a saturated solution? What is the molality of the solution?

65. A solution is labeled 0.150m NaCl. What are the mole fractions of the solute and solvent in this solution?

66. You are given a clear aqueous solution containing KNO_3. How would you determine experimentally if the solution is unsaturated, saturated, or supersaturated?

67. A mixture of ethylene glycol (EG) and water is used as antifreeze in automobile engines. The freezing point and specific gravity of the mixture vary with the percent by mass of (EG) in the mixture. On the following graph, point A represents 20% (EG) by mass; point B, 40%; and point C, 60%.

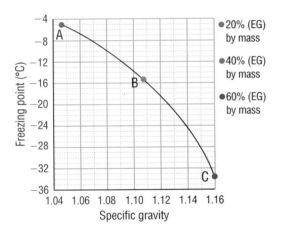

a. What is the specific gravity of the antifreeze mixture that freezes at −25 °C?
b. What is the freezing point of a mixture that has a specific gravity of 1.06?
c. Estimate the freezing point of a mixture that is 30% by mass (EG).

68. Calculate the freezing point and the boiling point of a solution that contains 15.0 g of urea (CH_4N_2O) in 250 g of water. Urea is a covalently bonded compound.

69. Calculate the mole fractions in a solution that is made of 25.0 g of ethanol (C_2H_5OH) and 40.0 g of water.

70. Estimate the freezing point of an aqueous solution of 20.0 g of glucose ($C_6H_{12}O_6$) dissolved in 500.0 g of water.

71. Plot a graph of solubility versus temperature for the three gases listed in **Table 18.1.**

72. The solubility of KCl in water is 34.0 g KCl/100 g H_2O at 20 °C. A warm solution containing 50.0 g KCl in 130 g H_2O is cooled to 20 °C.
a. How many grams of KCl remain dissolved?
b. How many grams came out of solution?

73. How many moles of ions are present when 0.10 mol of each compound is dissolved in water?
a. K_2SO_4
b. $Fe(NO_3)_3$
c. $Al_2(SO_4)_3$
d. $NiSO_4$

74. Complete the following table for aqueous solutions of glucose ($C_6H_{12}O_6$).

Mass solute	Moles solute	Volume of solution	Molarity
12.5 g		219 mL	
	1.08		0.519
		1.62 L	1.08

75. A solution contains 26.5 g NaCl in 75.0 g H_2O at 20 °C. Determine if the solution is unsaturated, saturated, or supersaturated. (The solubility of NaCl at 20 °C is 36.0 g/100 g H_2O.)

76. An aqueous solution freezes at −2.47 °C. What is its boiling point?

77. Hydrogen peroxide is often sold commercially as a 3.0% (m/v) aqueous solution.
a. If you buy a 250-mL bottle of 3.0% H_2O_2 (m/v), how many grams of hydrogen peroxide have you purchased?
b. What is the molarity of this solution?

78. How many grams of $NaNO_3$ will precipitate if a saturated solution of $NaNO_3$ in 200 g H_2O at 50 °C is cooled to 20 °C?

79. What is the molar mass of a nondissociating compound if 5.76 g of the compound in 750 g of benzene gives a freezing-point depression of 0.460 °C?

80. The molality of an aqueous solution of sugar ($C_{12}H_{22}O_{11}$) is 1.62m. Calculate the mole fractions of sugar and water.

81. Choose the term that best completes the second relationship.

    a. volume : liter   concentration : ____

    (1) moles   (3) solution
    (2) volume   (4) molarity

    b. molarity : L of solution   molality : _____

    (1) kg of solvent   (3) concentration
    (2) L of solvent   (4) mol of solute

82. Why is molarity measured in moles per liter of solution instead of in grams per liter?

83. Why might calcium chloride spread on icy roads be more effective at melting ice than sodium chloride?

CUMULATIVE REVIEW

84. Indicate by simple equations how the following substances ionize or dissociate in water.

    a. NH_4Cl c. HNO_3 e. Na_2SO_4
    b. $Cu(NO_3)_2$ d. $HC_2H_3O_2$ f. $HgCl_2$

85. What relationship exists between surface tension and intermolecular attractions in a liquid?

86. The solubility of hydrogen chloride gas in the polar solvent water is much greater than its solubility in the nonpolar solvent benzene. Why?

87. Discuss the effect that hydrogen bonding has on the boiling points of compounds that have low formula mass.

88. When soap is shaken with water, do you get a solution, a suspension, or a colloid? Explain.

89. Explain each term as it applies to solutions.

    a. solute   e. supersaturated
    b. solvent   f. nonelectrolyte
    c. saturated   g. weak electrolyte
    d. unsaturated   h. strong electrolyte

CONCEPT CHALLENGE

90. When an excess of zinc is added to 800 mL of a hydrochloric acid solution, the solution evolves 1.21 L of hydrogen gas measured over water at 21 °C and 747.5 mm Hg. What was the molarity of the acid? The vapor pressure of water at 21 °C is 18.6 mm Hg.

91. How many milliliters of 1.50M HNO_3 contain enough nitric acid to dissolve an old copper penny with a mass of 3.94 g?

$$3Cu + 8HNO_3 \longrightarrow 3Cu(NO_3)_2 + 2NO + 4H_2O$$

92. One way to express the solubility of a compound is in terms of moles of compound that will dissolve in 1 kg of water. Solubility depends on temperature. Plot a graph of the solubility of potassium nitrate (KNO_3) from the following data.

Temperature (°C)	Solubility (mol/kg)
0	1.61
20	2.80
40	5.78
60	11.20
80	16.76
100	24.50

From your graph estimate
a. the solubility of KNO_3 at 76 °C and at 33 °C.
b. the temperature at which its solubility is 17.6 mol/kg of water.
c. the temperature at which the solubility is 4.24 mol/kg of water.

93. A 250-mL sample of Na_2SO_4 is reacted with an excess of $BaCl_2$. If 5.28 g $BaSO_4$ is precipitated, what is the molarity of the Na_2SO_4 solution?

94. The following table lists the most abundant ions in sea water and their molal concentrations.

Ion	Molality (m)
Chloride	0.568
Sodium	0.482
Magnesium	0.057
Sulfate	0.028
Calcium	0.011
Potassium	0.010
Hydrogen carbonate	0.002

Calculate the mass (in g) of each component ion contained in 5.00 L of sea water. The density of sea water is 1.024 g/mL.

Select the choice that best answers each question or completes each statement.

1. An aqueous solution is 65% (v/v) rubbing alcohol. How many milliliters of water are in a 95-mL sample of this solution?
   a. 62 mL
   b. 1.5 mL
   c. 33 mL
   d. 30 mL

2. Which of these actions will cause more sugar to dissolve in a saturated sugar water solution?
   I. Add more sugar while stirring.
   II. Add more sugar and heat the solution.
   III. Grind the sugar to a powder; then add while stirring.
   a. I only
   b. II only
   c. III only
   d. I and II only
   e. II and III only

3. How many moles of sodium nitrate are in 650 mL of a $0.28M$ NaNO$_3$ solution?
   a. 0.18 mol
   b. 2.3 mol
   c. 0.43 mol
   d. 18 mol

4. Compared to pure water, an aqueous solution of potassium bromide has a
   a. higher boiling point and freezing point.
   b. lower vapor pressure and higher boiling point.
   c. lower freezing point and higher vapor pressure.
   d. lower boiling point and vapor pressure.

5. When 2.0 mol of methanol is dissolved in 45 g of water, the mole fraction of methanol is
   a. 0.44.
   b. 0.043.
   c. 2.25.
   d. 0.55.

The lettered choices below refer to questions 6–9. A lettered choice may be used once, more than once, or not at all.

(A) moles/liter of solution
(B) grams/mole
(C) moles/kilogram of solvent
(D) °C/molal
(E) no units

Which of the above units is appropriate for each measurement?

6. molality
7. mole fraction
8. molar mass
9. molarity

Use the description and the data table to answer questions 10–13.

A student measured the freezing points of three different aqueous solutions at five different concentrations. The data table summarizes the data the student collected.

Molarity (M)	Freezing Point Depression (°C)		
	NaCl	CaCl$_2$	C$_2$H$_5$OH
0.5	1.7	2.6	0.95
1.0	3.5	5.6	2.0
1.5	5.3	8.3	3.0
2.0	7.2	11.2	4.1
2.5	9.4	14.0	5.3

10. Graph the data for all three solutes on the same graph, using molarity as the independent variable.

11. Summarize the relationship between molarity and freezing point depression.

12. Compare the slopes of the three lines and explain any difference.

13. If you collected similar data for KOH and added a fourth line to your graph, which existing line would the new line approximate?

Use the atomic windows to answer questions 14–16. The windows show water and two aqueous solutions with different concentrations. The purple spheres represent the solute particles; the blue spheres represent water.

a. b. c.

14. Which system has the highest vapor pressure?
15. Which system has the lowest vapor pressure?
16. Which solution has the lowest boiling point?

Write a brief essay to answer question 17.

17. Describe how you would prepare 100 mL of $0.50M$ KCl starting with a stock solution that is $2.0M$ KCl.

REACTION RATES AND EQUILIBRIUM

FEATURES

DISCOVER IT!
Temperature and Reaction Rates

SMALL-SCALE LAB
Enthalpy and Entropy

MINI LAB
Does Steel Burn?

CHEMath
Balancing Equations

CHEMISTRY SERVING … THE CONSUMER
Don't Let Good Food Go Bad!

CHEMISTRY IN CAREERS
FDA Inspector

LINK TO AUTO SHOP
Auto Body Repair

LINK TO GEOLOGY
Weathering of Rocks

Stay current with **SCIENCE NEWS**
Find out more about reaction rates:
www.phschool.com

The energy stored in oil is wasted during uncontrolled combustion.

DISCOVER IT! TEMPERATURE AND REACTION RATES

You need masking tape, four plastic cups, hot and cold tap water, ice, a thermometer, four effervescent antacid tablets, a clock or watch with a second hand, graph paper, and a pen or pencil.

1. Mark an A, B, C, or D on four separate pieces of masking tape. Label each plastic cup with one of the lettered pieces of tape.

2. Fill each cup three-quarters full as follows: (A) cold tap water plus some ice, (B) cold tap water, (C) half-and-half mixture of cold tap water and hot tap water, (D) hot tap water.

3. Measure and record the temperature of the water in each cup.

4. Drop a tablet into cup A and measure the time it takes for the reaction to go to completion. Repeat this procedure using the remaining three cups.

5. Draw a line or bar graph of temperature versus reaction time.

Do the tablets react faster at higher temperatures? Explain why or why not. What results would you expect if you crushed the tablets into a powder before adding them to the water? Explain your prediction. If time permits, check this prediction experimentally. As you read this chapter, return to this activity and revise your explanations on the basis of the new information.

RATES OF REACTION

Although corrosion can damage many different types of metal objects, the process can be useful to hungry soldiers, truck drivers, and others who want a hot meal but do not have a place to cook it. Products now on the market use the heat given off by the corrosion reaction of an iron-magnesium alloy with salt water to produce a hot meal. Normally the reaction takes place at a very slow rate, so that the heat generated has ample time to dissipate. But when the rate is increased, as it is in this case by the addition of salt water, heat is produced very rapidly. **What are some ways the rate of a reaction can be increased?**

objectives

▶ Explain what is meant by the rate of a chemical reaction

▶ Using collision theory, explain how the rate of a chemical reaction is influenced by the reaction conditions

key terms

▶ rates
▶ collision theory
▶ activation energy
▶ activated complex
▶ transition state
▶ catalyst
▶ inhibitor

Collision Theory

The amount of time required for a chemical reaction to come to completion can vary tremendously, depending on the reaction. When you strike a match, it seems to erupt into flame almost instantaneously. Many other reactions, however, occur much more slowly. Did you know that coal is produced from dead plants by a process involving heat and pressure that takes millions of years? In this chapter, you will examine the factors that make chemical reactions proceed at different speeds.

When exposed to damp air, iron turns to rust. However, you know the reverse process does not readily occur. Bringing a rusty chair in out of the damp weather cannot make it look like new again. In this chapter, you will learn why some substances react readily, whereas others seem inert.

The concept of speed is probably already familiar to you. A fast sprinter may cover 100 meters in about 11.5 seconds; a slower sprinter may take 15.0 seconds to cover the same distance. On average, the first sprinter covers 100 meters in 11.5 seconds, or runs at a speed of 8.70 m/s. The second sprinter covers 100 meters in 15.0 seconds, or runs at a speed of 6.67 m/s. Both 8.70 m/s and 6.67 m/s express rates of travel. **Rates** measure the speed of any

Figure 19.1

A rate tells you how much something changes in a specified amount of time. Speeds are measured as changes of distance in a given interval of time. A world-class sprinter might cover 100 meters in 11.5 seconds; the speed, or rate, is 100 m/11.5 s = 8.70 m/s.

Start   Distance (m)   Finish

$$\text{Rate} = \frac{\text{Distance (m)}}{\text{Time (s)}} = ? \frac{m}{s}$$

Figure 19.2

(a) Burning, (b) rusting, (c) aging, and (d) ripening are four processes. Which occurs fastest (that is, at the highest rate) and which occurs slowest?

(a)

(b)

(c)

(d)

change that occurs within an interval of time. The interval of time may range from fractions of a second to centuries. **Figure 19.2** shows some familiar examples of rates of change. In chemistry, rates of chemical change usually are expressed as the amount of reactant changing per unit time. The rate at which an iron plate containing 1 mol of iron rusts might be expressed as 0.5 mol/yr. **Figure 19.3** illustrates the progress of a typical reaction.

Visible changes caused by chemical reactions are related to changes in the properties of individual atoms, ions, or molecules. For example, atoms of shiny silver-colored sodium metal react with molecules of yellow-green chlorine gas to produce colorless crystals of sodium chloride. The properties of sodium atoms and chlorine molecules are different from the

Figure 19.3

As time passes, the amount of reactant (red squares) decreases and the amount of product (blue spheres) increases. Rates of chemical reactions are often measured as a change in the number of moles during a given interval of time.

Time ⟶

Reaction:

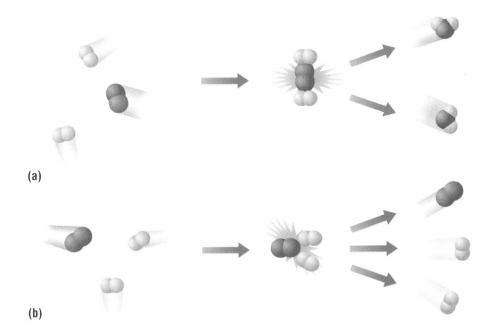

Figure 19.4

If colliding particles have enough kinetic energy and collide at the right orientation, they can react to form a new product. **(a)** *An effective collision of reactant molecules produces product molecules.* **(b)** *An ineffective collision of reactant molecules produces no reaction, and the reactants bounce apart unchanged.*

properties of sodium ions and chloride ions in sodium chloride. Rates of chemical reactions are related to the properties of atoms, ions, and molecules through a model called collision theory. According to **collision theory,** atoms, ions, and molecules can react to form products when they collide, provided that the particles have enough kinetic energy. Particles lacking the necessary kinetic energy to react bounce apart when they collide. This process is illustrated in **Figure 19.4.**

You can use two balls of soft modeling clay to illustrate further the concept of collision theory. If you throw the balls of clay together gently, they do not stick to each other, which is analogous to a lack of reaction between colliding particles of low energy. The same balls of clay thrown together with great force, however, stick tightly to each other, which is analogous to the chemical combination of two particles that collide with sufficient energy.

You can also use modeling clay to illustrate another point about chemical reactions. If you roll the clay into a rope and vigorously shake one end, the clay rope will eventually break. Similarly, the bonds holding molecules together can break apart. Substances supplied with enough energy decompose to simpler substances or reorganize themselves into new substances. The minimum amount of energy that particles must have in order to react is called the **activation energy.** In a sense, activation energy is a barrier that reactants must cross to be converted to products, as shown in **Figure 19.5.** During a reaction, particles that are neither reactants nor products form momentarily if there is sufficient

Figure 19.5

The activation-energy barrier must be crossed before reactants are converted to products. The activated complex is a temporary arrangement of particles that has sufficient energy to become either reactants or products.

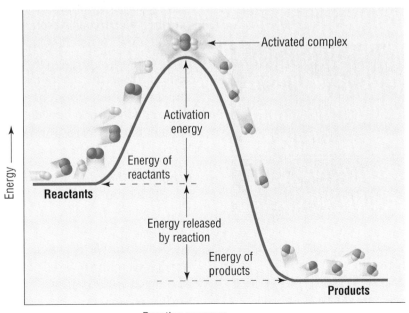

energy and if the atoms are oriented properly. An **activated complex** is the arrangement of atoms at the peak of the activation-energy barrier. The lifetime of an activated complex is typically about 10^{-13} s. The very unstable activated complex is as likely to re-form reactants as it is to form products. Thus the activated complex is sometimes called the **transition state.** Can you explain why?

Collision theory explains why some naturally occurring reactions are immeasurably slow at room temperature. For example, carbon and oxygen react when charcoal burns, but this reaction has a high activation energy. At room temperature, the collisions of oxygen and carbon molecules are not energetic enough to break the O—O and C—C bonds. These bonds must be broken to form the activated complex. Thus the reaction rate of carbon with oxygen at room temperature is essentially zero.

Factors Affecting Reaction Rates

Every chemical reaction proceeds at its own rate. Some reactions are naturally fast and some are naturally slow under the same conditions. However, by varying the conditions of the reaction, the rate of almost any reaction can be modified. Collision theory helps explain why these rate changes occur and how they depend on conditions such as temperature, concentration, and particle size.

Temperature Usually, raising the temperature speeds up reactions, while lowering the temperature slows down reactions. At higher temperatures, the motions of the reactant particles are faster and more chaotic than they are at lower temperatures. The main effect of increasing the temperature is to increase the number of particles that have enough kinetic energy to react when they collide. At high temperatures, more colliding particles are energetic enough to slip over the activation-energy barrier to become products. The frequency of high-energy collisions between reactant particles also increases. An increase in temperature, therefore enables products to form faster.

A familiar example of the effect of temperature on reaction rate is the burning of charcoal. At room temperature, charcoal does not burn at a measurable rate. If the charcoal is supplied with enough energy in the form of heat, however, the result is dramatic. When a starter flame touches the charcoal, atoms of the reactants (carbon and oxygen) collide with higher energy and greater frequency. Some collisions are at a high enough energy to form the product (carbon dioxide). The heat released by the reaction then supplies enough energy to get more carbon and oxygen over the activation-energy barrier. When the starter flame is removed, the reaction continues.

Concentration The number of reacting particles in a given volume also affects the rate at which reactions occur. Cramming more particles into a fixed volume increases the concentration of reactants, the collision frequency, and therefore the reaction rate. The lighted splint in **Figure 19.6** vividly illustrates this effect. Such a splint glows in air, which is 20% oxygen. A glowing splint plunged into pure oxygen, however, immediately bursts into flame because the increased concentration of oxygen greatly speeds up the combustion reaction. This is why smoking is forbidden in areas where bottled oxygen is in use.

(a)

(b)

Figure 19.6
*Why will a glowing splint **(a)** burst into flame **(b)** if it is placed in a bottle of pure oxygen?*

Particle Size The smaller the particle size, the larger is the surface area for a given mass of particles. The total surface area of a solid or liquid reactant has an important effect on the reaction rate: An increase in surface area increases the amount of the reactant exposed for reaction, which further increases the collision frequency and the reaction rate. Why would a bundle of kindling burn faster than a single log of equal mass?

One way to increase the surface area of solid reactants is to dissolve them. This process separates the particles and makes them more accessible to other reactants. Another way to increase the surface area is to grind solids into a fine powder. Small dustlike particles, however, can be very dangerous. As coal miners know, large chunks of coal pose very little hazard, but coal dust suspended in the air is potentially very reactive and presents an explosion hazard. The same is true of dust in a flour mill, as the dramatic photograph in **Figure 19.7** shows.

Figure 19.7
In 1932, an explosion destroyed this Chicago grain elevator. The minute size of the reactant particles (grain dust), and the mixture of the grain dust with oxygen in the air caused the reaction to be explosive.

Catalysts An increase in temperature is not always the best way to increase the rate of a reaction. A catalyst, if one can be found, is often better. A **catalyst** is a substance that increases the rate of a reaction without being used up itself during the reaction. Catalysts permit reactions to proceed at a lower energy than is normally required. **Figure 19.8** on the following page shows how catalysts lower the activation-energy barrier. With a lower activation-energy barrier, more reactants can form products within a given time. For instance, the reaction rate of hydrogen and oxygen at room temperature is negligible. With a trace of catalyst added, however, the reaction is rapid. Finely divided platinum (Pt) catalyzes this reaction, as illustrated in the following equation.

$$2H_2(g) + O_2(g) \xrightarrow{\text{Pt}} 2H_2O(l)$$

Because catalysts are not consumed during a reaction, they do not appear as reactants or products in the chemical equation. To convey this information, without suggesting that the catalyst is chemically altered, catalysts are often written above the yield arrow, as in the preceding equation.

Figure 19.8
A catalyst increases the rate of a reaction by lowering the activation-energy barrier.

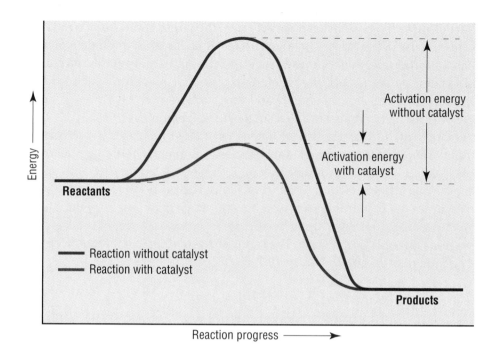

Reactants

Energy

Activation energy
without catalyst

Activation energy
with catalyst

——— Reaction without catalyst
——— Reaction with catalyst

Products

Reaction progress ⟶

AUTO SHOP

Auto Body Repair
Auto body repair technicians often repair rust-damaged automobiles. Rust damage usually occurs where water is able to catalyze the reaction of oxygen

with iron to produce iron(III) oxide, or rust. Removing the rust and repainting the damaged area is effective for small repairs, but extensive damage may require the replacement of body panels. Due to the extensive use of galvanized steel and noncorroding plastics in newer automobiles, body rust is much less common today than it was in the past.

Catalysts are crucial for many life processes. Your body temperature is only 37 °C and cannot be raised significantly without danger. Without catalysts, few reactions in the body would proceed fast enough at that temperature. Enzymes, biological catalysts, increase the rates of biological reactions. You could not live without enzymes to catalyze these reactions. When you eat a meal containing protein, enzymes in your digestive tract break down the protein molecules in a few hours. Without enzymes, the digestion of protein at 37 °C would take many years!

An **inhibitor** is a substance that interferes with the action of a catalyst. Some inhibitor molecules work by reacting with, or "poisoning," the catalyst itself. Thus the inhibitor reduces the amount of functional catalyst available. Reactions slow or even stop when a catalyst is poisoned.

section review 19.1

1. What is meant by the rate of a chemical reaction?

2. How does each factor affect the rate of a chemical reaction?
   a. temperature
   b. concentration
   c. particle size
   d. an inhibitor

3. Does every collision between reacting particles lead to products? Explain.

4. Suppose a thin sheet of zinc containing 0.2 mol of the metal is completely converted in air to zinc oxide (ZnO) in one month. How would you express the rate of conversion of the zinc?

5. Refrigerated food stays fresh for long periods. The same food stored at room temperature quickly spoils. Why?

 Chem ASAP! Assessment 19.1 Check your understanding of the important ideas and concepts in Section 19.1.

REVERSIBLE REACTIONS AND EQUILIBRIUM

For years, scientists tried to produce nitrogen compounds that would be useful as fertilizers. Unfortunately, none of these efforts produced compounds in quantities sufficient to be commercially successful. Finally, in the early 1900s, two German chemists, Fritz Haber and Karl Bosch refined the process of making ammonia for use as a fertilizer. Their success came from controlling the temperature and pressure under which the ammonia synthesis reaction takes place. **How can changing the reaction conditions influence the yield of a chemical reaction?**

objectives
▶ Predict changes in the equilibrium position due to changes in concentration, temperature, and pressure
▶ Write the equilibrium-constant expression for a reaction and calculate its value from experimental data

key terms
▶ reversible reactions
▶ chemical equilibrium
▶ equilibrium position
▶ Le Châtelier's principle
▶ equilibrium constant (K_{eq})

Reversible Reactions

From the previous discussions of chemical reactions, you may have inferred that chemical reactions go completely from reactants to products as written. This is not always the case, however. Some reactions are reversible. In **reversible reactions,** the reactions occur simultaneously in both directions. One example of a reversible reaction is the reaction of sulfur dioxide with oxygen to give sulfur trioxide. The double arrows in the equation below show that the reaction is reversible.

$$2SO_2(g) + O_2(g) \rightleftharpoons 2SO_3(g)$$

Sulfur dioxide   Oxygen   Sulfur trioxide

Figure 19.9 shows that this equation represents two opposite reactions. In the first reaction, which is read from left to right, sulfur dioxide and oxygen produce sulfur trioxide. In the second reaction, which is read from right to left, sulfur trioxide decomposes into oxygen and sulfur dioxide. The first reaction is called the forward reaction. The second reaction is called the reverse reaction.

Consider what happens when sulfur dioxide and oxygen gases are mixed in a sealed chamber. Initially, there is no sulfur trioxide. The rate of the reverse process—formation of sulfur dioxide and oxygen from sulfur trioxide—is zero. Sulfur trioxide, the product of the forward reaction, then

Chem ASAP!
Animation 23
Take a close look at a generalized reversible reaction.

Figure 19.9
Molecules of SO_2 and O_2 react to give SO_3. Molecules of SO_3 decompose to give SO_2 and O_2. At equilibrium, all three types of molecules are present in the mixture.

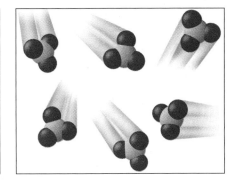

SO₂ and O₂
(not at equilibrium)

$2SO_2 + O_2 \rightleftharpoons 2SO_3$
(at equilibrium)

SO₃
(not at equilibrium)

Figure 19.10

*These graphs show the variation with time of the concentration of O_2, SO_2, and SO_3. **(a)** Initially, SO_2 concentration is twice that of O_2; SO_3 is absent. At equilibrium, a mixture of all three gases is obtained. **(b)** Initially only SO_3 is present. At equilibrium, the amounts of O_2, SO_2, and SO_3 are the same as in the equilibrium shown in **(a)**.*

(a)

(b)

Figure 19.11

If the rate at which shoppers move from the first floor to the second is equal to the rate at which shoppers move from the second floor to the first, then the number of shoppers on each floor will remain constant, although not necessarily equal to each other. The two populations of shoppers will be in a state of dynamic equilibrium.

begins to form. As the sulfur trioxide concentration increases, a small amount slowly reverts to sulfur dioxide and oxygen by the reverse reaction. As the concentration of sulfur trioxide becomes higher and higher, the reverse reaction speeds up. The forward reaction is simultaneously slowing down because sulfur dioxide and oxygen are being used up. As you can see in **Figure 19.10,** eventually sulfur trioxide decomposes to sulfur dioxide and oxygen as fast as sulfur dioxide and oxygen form sulfur trioxide. At equilibrium, what substance has the highest concentration? The reaction has reached **chemical equilibrium,** a state in which the forward and reverse reactions take place at the same rate. At chemical equilibrium, there is no net change in the actual amounts of the components of the system.

Although the rates of the forward and reverse reactions are equal at chemical equilibrium, the concentrations of the components on both sides of the chemical equation are not necessarily the same. In fact, they can be dramatically different. The escalators in **Figure 19.11** are like the double arrows in a dynamic equilibrium equation. The number of people using the up escalator must equal the number of people using the down escalator for the number of people on each floor to remain constant.

The **equilibrium position** of a reaction is given by the relative concentrations of the system's components at equilibrium. The equilibrium position indicates whether the components on the left or right side of a reversible reaction are at a higher concentration. If A reacts to give B and the equilibrium mixture contains significantly more of B—say 1% A and 99% B—then the formation of B is said to be favored.

$$A \; \rightleftharpoons \; B$$
$$1\% \qquad\qquad 99\%$$

On the other hand, if the mixture contains 99% A and 1% B at equilibrium, then the formation of A is favored.

$$A \; \rightleftharpoons \; B$$
$$99\% \qquad\qquad 1\%$$

Note that the longer of the two double arrows indicates the favored direction of a reaction.

In principle, almost all reactions are reversible to some extent under the right conditions. In practice, one set of components is often so favored at equilibrium that the other set cannot be detected. If one set of components (reactants) is completely converted to new substances (products), you can say that the reaction has gone to completion or is irreversible. When you mix chemicals expecting to get a reaction but no products can be detected, you can say there is no reaction. Reversible reactions occupy a middle ground between the theoretical extremes of irreversibility and no reaction.

A catalyst speeds up forward and reverse reactions equally because the reverse reaction is exactly the opposite of the forward reaction. Therefore, the catalyst reduces the energy needed for the reaction by the same amount in both the forward and reverse directions. Catalysts do not affect the amounts of reactants and products present at equilibrium; they simply decrease the time it takes to establish equilibrium.

Factors Affecting Equilibrium: Le Châtelier's Principle

A delicate balance exists in a system at equilibrium. Changes of almost any kind can disrupt this balance. A system whose equilibrium has been disturbed makes adjustments to restore equilibrium. When equilibrium has been restored, however, the position of equilibrium is different from its original position; that is, the amount of products or reactants may have increased or decreased. Such a difference is called a shift in the position of equilibrium.

The French chemist Henri Le Châtelier (1850–1936) studied shifts in the position of equilibrium that result from changing conditions. He proposed **Le Châtelier's principle:** If a stress is applied to a system in dynamic equilibrium, the system changes to relieve the stress. Stresses that upset the equilibrium of a chemical system include changes in the concentration of reactants or products, changes in temperature, and changes in pressure.

The following examples of applications of Le Châtelier's principle all involve reversible reactions. Therefore, the product of the forward reaction is the reactant of the reverse reaction, and vice versa. For simplicity and clarity, however, the components to the left of the reaction arrow will be considered the reactants and the components to the right of the reaction arrow will be considered the products. Blue arrows indicate the shifts resulting from additions to or removals from the system. The arrows always point in the direction of the resulting shift in the equilibrium position— that is, toward the favored side. In each case, the equilibrium shift compensates for the disturbance that caused it.

Concentration Changing the amount, or concentration, of any reactant or product in a system at equilibrium disturbs the equilibrium. The system adjusts to minimize the effects of the change. Consider an equilibrium involving carbonic acid (H_2CO_3) in aqueous solution, which decomposes to form carbon dioxide and water. At equilibrium the amount of carbonic acid is less than 1%.

$$H_2CO_3(aq) \underset{\underset{\text{Direction of shift} \rightarrow}{\text{Remove } CO_2}}{\overset{\overset{\text{Add } CO_2}{\leftarrow \text{Direction of shift}}}{\rightleftharpoons}} CO_2(aq) + H_2O(l)$$

$< 1\%$ $\qquad\qquad\qquad\qquad\qquad\qquad > 99\%$

Adding more carbon dioxide disturbs the equilibrium. For example, at the instant of the addition, the added carbon dioxide changes the ratio of carbon

Figure 19.12

The rapid exhalation of CO_2 during and after vigorous exercise helps reestablish the body's correct CO_2:H_2CO_3 equilibrium. This keeps the acid concentration in the blood within a safe range.

dioxide to carbonic acid (CO_2:H_2CO_3) from 99:1 to 99.5:0.5. Although the change in the ratio may look small, the amount of carbon dioxide has doubled from the original 99:1 ratio to a ratio of 199:1 (99.5/0.5 = 199:1). As soon as the carbon dioxide is added, however, it reacts with water to form more carbonic acid. The system shifts to the left to use up some of the added CO_2 and thus minimize the stress. The ratio shifts toward the original 99:1. What occurs is typical of such shifts in equilibrium—adding a product always pushes a reversible reaction in the direction of reactants.

If, on the other hand, carbon dioxide is removed, the CO_2:H_2CO_3 ratio momentarily decreases to less than 99:1. Carbonic acid decomposes to minimize the imposed stress, and the system readjusts itself toward a CO_2:H_2CO_3 ratio of 99:1. Removing a product always pulls a reversible reaction in the direction of products.

Removal of products is often used to increase the yield of a desired product. As products are removed from a reaction mixture, the system continually changes to restore equilibrium by producing more products. Because the products are being removed as fast as they form, however, the reaction never builds up enough of them to reestablish an equilibrium. The system continues readjusting, and the reaction continues to give products until the reactants are completely used up. Farmers use a similar technique to increase the yield of eggs laid by hens. Hens lay eggs and then proceed to hatch them. When the eggs are removed after they are laid (removing the product), the hen will lay more eggs (increasing the yield). Another example of this concept is found in the body. Blood contains dissolved carbonic acid in equilibrium with carbon dioxide and water. The body uses the removal of products to keep carbonic acid at low, safe concentrations in the blood. When the athletes in **Figure 19.12** exhale carbon dioxide, the equilibrium shifts toward carbon dioxide and water, thus reducing the amount of carbonic acid and keeping the acid concentration of the blood within a safe range. The same principle applies to adding or removing reactants. When a reactant is added to a system at equilibrium, the reaction shifts in the direction of the formation of products. When a reactant is removed, the reaction shifts in the direction of formation of reactants.

Temperature Increasing the temperature causes the equilibrium position of a reaction to shift in the direction that absorbs heat. The heat absorption reduces the applied temperature stress. For example, consider the following exothermic reaction that occurs when SO_3 is produced from the reaction of SO_2 and O_2.

$$2SO_2(g) + O_2(g) \underset{\underset{\text{Direction of shift} \longrightarrow}{\text{Remove heat (cool)}}}{\overset{\overset{\text{Add heat}}{\longleftarrow \text{Direction of shift}}}{\rightleftharpoons}} 2SO_3(g) + \text{heat}$$

The heat can be considered to be a product, just like SO_3. Heating the reaction mixture at equilibrium pushes the equilibrium position to the left, which favors the reactants. As a result, the product yield decreases. Cooling, or removing heat, pulls the equilibrium to the right, and the product yield increases.

Pressure A change in the pressure on a system affects only an equilibrium that has an unequal number of moles of gaseous reactants and products. An example is the equilibrium established between ammonia gas and the gaseous elements from which it forms. Imagine those gases are at equilibrium in a cylinder that has a piston attached to a plunger, similar to a bicycle pump with the hose sealed. A catalyst has been included to speed up the reaction. What happens to the pressure when you push the plunger down? The pressure on the gases momentarily increases because the same number of molecules is contained in less than the original volume. The system can relieve some of the pressure increase by reducing the number of gas molecules. For every two molecules of ammonia made, four molecules of the reactants are used up (three molecules of hydrogen and one of nitrogen). Therefore, the equilibrium position shifts to make more ammonia. There are then fewer molecules in the system. The pressure decreases, although it will not decrease all the way to the original pressure. As you can see in **Figure 19.13,** increasing the pressure on the system results in a shift in the equilibrium position that favors the formation of product. What will happen to the equilibrium position when the pressure is restored to its initial value?

$$N_2(g) + 3H_2(g) \underset{\underset{\longleftarrow \text{ Direction of shift}}{\text{Reduce pressure}}}{\overset{\overset{\text{Increase pressure}}{\text{Direction of shift} \longrightarrow}}{\rightleftharpoons}} 2NH_3(g)$$

Chem ASAP!

Simulation 24
Simulate Le Châtelier's principle for the synthesis of ammonia.

Figure 19.13
Pressure affects a mixture of nitrogen, hydrogen, and ammonia in equilibrium. (a) The system is in equilibrium. (b) Equilibrium is disturbed by an increase in pressure. (c) A new equilibrium condition is created, more hydrogen and nitrogen have reacted and formed ammonia, reducing the total number of molecules and partially offsetting the pressure increase in the cylinder.

(a) Initial equilibrium condition (11 gas molecules)

(b) Pressure increased, equilibrium disturbed

(c) New equilibrium condition at increased pressure (9 gas molecules)

Ammonia molecule (NH_3)

Hydrogen molecule (H_2)

Nitrogen molecule (N_2)

The equilibrium position for this reaction can be made to favor the reactants instead of the product. Imagine pulling the plunger of the piston device back up so the volume containing the gases increases. This increase of volume decreases the pressure on the system. To restore the higher starting pressure, the system needs more gas molecules, which are produced by decomposition of some of the ammonia molecules. Decomposition of two molecules of gaseous ammonia produces a total of four molecules of reactants (three molecules of hydrogen and one molecule of nitrogen). Pressure at the new equilibrium is higher than when the pressure was first decreased, although it is not as high as it was at the starting equilibrium. Lowering the pressure on the system thus results in a shift of equilibrium to favor the reactants.

Sample Problem 19-1

What effect do each of the following changes have on the equilibrium position for this reversible reaction?

$$PCl_5(g) + heat \rightleftharpoons PCl_3(g) + Cl_2(g)$$

a. addition of Cl_2
b. increase in pressure
c. removal of heat
d. removal of PCl_3 as it forms

1. *ANALYZE Plan a problem-solving strategy.*
   a.–d. In each part of the problem, the stress placed on the system is known. The effect of the stress is unknown. By Le Châtelier's principle, the equilibrium system will shift in a direction that minimizes the imposed stress. Analyze the effect of each change on the reaction.

2. *SOLVE Apply the problem-solving strategy.*
   a. The addition of Cl_2, a product, shifts the equilibrium to the left, forming more PCl_5.
   b. The equation shows 2 mol of gaseous product and 1 mol of gaseous reactant. The increase in pressure is relieved if the equilibrium shifts to the left because a decrease in the number of moles of gaseous substances gives a decrease in pressure.
   c. The removal of heat causes the equilibrium to shift to the left because the reverse reaction is heat-producing.
   d. The removal of PCl_3 causes the equilibrium to shift to the right to produce more PCl_3.

3. *EVALUATE Do the results make sense?*
   The answers follow Le Châtelier's principle: If a stress is applied to a system in a dynamic equilibrium, the system changes to relieve the stress.

Practice Problems

6. How is the equilibrium position of this reaction affected by the following changes?
$$C(s) + H_2O(g) + heat \rightleftharpoons CO(g) + H_2(g)$$
   a. lowering the temperature
   b. increasing the pressure
   c. removing H_2
   d. adding H_2

7. What effect does each change have on the equilibrium position of this reaction?
$$N_2(g) + 3H_2(g) \rightleftharpoons 2NH_3(g) + 92 \text{ kJ}$$
   a. addition of heat
   b. increase in pressure
   c. addition of catalyst
   d. removal of heat

Chem ASAP!

Problem-Solving 7

Solve Problem 7 with the help of an interactive guided tutorial.

Equilibrium Constants

Chemists generally express the position of equilibrium in terms of numerical values. These values relate the amounts of reactants to products at equilibrium. Consider the hypothetical reaction in which a mol of reactant A and b mol of reactant B react to give c mol of product C and d mol of product D at equilibrium.

$$aA + bB \rightleftharpoons cC + dD$$

The **equilibrium constant** (K_{eq}) is the ratio of product concentrations to reactant concentrations at equilibrium, with each concentration raised to a power equal to the number of moles of that substance in the balanced chemical equation. Thus the equilibrium-constant expression has the general form

$$K_{eq} = \frac{[C]^c \times [D]^d}{[A]^a \times [B]^b}$$

The exponents in the equilibrium-constant expression are the coefficients from the balanced chemical equation. The square brackets indicate the concentrations of substances in moles per liter (mol/L). The value of K_{eq} for a reaction depends on the temperature. If the temperature changes, the value of K_{eq} also changes.

Equilibrium constants provide valuable chemical information. Among other things, they show whether products or reactants are favored at equilibrium. Because an equilibrium constant is always written as a ratio of products to reactants, a value of K_{eq} greater than 1 means that products are favored over reactants. Conversely, a value of K_{eq} less than 1 means that reactants are favored over products. In short,

$$K_{eq} > 1, \text{ products favored at equilibrium}$$

$$K_{eq} < 1, \text{ reactants favored at equilibrium}$$

● Nitrogen dioxide (NO_2)

■ Dinitrogen tetroxide (N_2O_4)

Figure 19.14
Dinitrogen tetroxide is a colorless gas, whereas nitrogen dioxide is brown. The flask on the left is in a dish of hot water; the flask on the right is in ice. How does temperature affect the equilibrium of a mixture of these gases?

Sample Problem 19-2

Dinitrogen tetroxide (N_2O_4), a colorless gas, and nitrogen dioxide (NO_2), a dark-brown gas, exist in equilibrium with each other, as shown in **Figure 19.14.**

$$N_2O_4(g) \rightleftharpoons 2NO_2(g)$$

A liter of the gas mixture at 10 °C at equilibrium contains 0.0045 mol N_2O_4 and 0.030 mol NO_2. Write the expression for the equilibrium constant and calculate the equilibrium constant (K_{eq}) for the reaction.

....

1. **ANALYZE** *List the knowns and the unknowns.*

   Knowns:
   - $[N_2O_4] = 0.0045$ mol/L
   - $[NO_2] = 0.030$ mol/L
   - $K_{eq} = \dfrac{[C]^c \times [D]^d}{[A]^a \times [B]^b}$

   Unknowns:
   - K_{eq} (algebraic expression) = ?
   - K_{eq} (numerical value) = ?

Practice Problems

8. Analysis of an equilibrium mixture of nitrogen, hydrogen, and ammonia contained in a 1-L flask at 300 °C gives the following results: hydrogen, 0.15 mol; nitrogen, 0.25 mol; ammonia, 0.10 mol. Calculate K_{eq} for the reaction
   $$N_2(g) + 3H_2(g) \rightleftharpoons 2NH_3(g)$$

Sample Problem 19-2 (cont.)

2. CALCULATE Solve for the unknowns.

At equilibrium, there is no net change in the amount of N_2O_4 or NO_2 at any given instant. The only product of the reaction is NO_2, which has a coefficient of 2 in the balanced equation. According to the rule for writing the equilibrium-constant expression, the concentration of NO_2, raised to the second power, is placed in the numerator. The only reactant is N_2O_4, with a coefficient of 1. The concentration of this substance, raised to the first power, is placed in the denominator. The equilibrium-constant expression and its calculated value are

$$K_{eq} = \frac{[NO_2]^2}{[N_2O_4]}$$

$$= \frac{(0.030 \text{ mol/L})^2}{0.0045 \text{ mol/L}}$$

$$= \frac{(0.030 \text{ mol/L} \times 0.030 \text{ mol/L})}{0.0045 \text{ mol/L}}$$

$$= 0.20 \text{ mol/L}$$

3. EVALUATE Do the results make sense?

Each concentration is raised to the correct power. The numerical value of the constant is correctly rounded to two significant figures.

Practice Problems (cont.)

9. Assume you have the mixture described in Problem 8 with the same volume, temperature, and equilibrium concentrations.

a. Calculate K_{eq} for the reaction $2NH_3(g) \rightleftharpoons 3H_2(g) + N_2(g)$

b. Based on your answers to Problem 8 and Problem 9a, how is the K_{eq} for a forward reaction related to the K_{eq} for a reverse reaction?

Chem ASAP!

Problem-Solving 8

Solve Problem 8 with the help of an interactive guided tutorial.

Sample Problem 19-3

One mol of colorless hydrogen gas and 1 mol of violet iodine vapor are sealed in a 1-L flask and allowed to react at 450 °C. At equilibrium, 1.56 mol of colorless hydrogen iodide is present, together with some of the reactant gases. Calculate K_{eq} for the reaction.

$$H_2(g) + I_2(g) \rightleftharpoons 2HI(g)$$

1. ANALYZE List the knowns and the unknowns.

Knowns:
- $[H_2]$ (initial) = 1 mol/L
- $[I_2]$ (initial) = 1 mol/L
- $[HI]$ (equilibrium) = 1.56 mol/L
- $K_{eq} = \dfrac{[C]^c \times [D]^d}{[A]^a \times [B]^b}$

Unknowns:
- K_{eq} (algebraic expression) = ?
- K_{eq} (numerical value) = ?

Practice Problems

10. Suppose the following system reaches equilibrium at a high temperature.

$$N_2(g) + O_2(g) \rightleftharpoons 2NO(g)$$

An analysis of the equilibrium mixture in a 1-L flask gives the following results: nitrogen, 0.50 mol; oxygen, 0.50 mol; nitrogen monoxide, 0.020 mol. Calculate K_{eq} for the reaction.

Sample Problem 19-3 (cont.)

2. CALCULATE Solve for the unknowns.

The balanced equation indicates that 1.00 mol of hydrogen and 1.00 mol of iodine are needed to form 2.00 mol of hydrogen iodide. Making 1.56 mol of hydrogen iodide, therefore, consumes $\frac{1}{2} \times 1.56$ mol of each: 0.78 mol of hydrogen and 0.78 mol of iodine. First, calculate how much H_2 and I_2 remain in the flask at equilibrium.

$$\text{mol } H_2 = \text{mol } I_2 = (1.00 \text{ mol} - 0.78 \text{ mol}) = 0.22 \text{ mol}$$

Write the expression for K_{eq}.

$$K_{eq} = \frac{[HI]^2}{[H_2] \times [I_2]}$$

Now substitute the concentrations of the reactants and products into the equation for K_{eq}.

$$K_{eq} = \frac{(1.56 \text{ mol/L})^2}{0.22 \text{ mol/L} \times 0.22 \text{ mol/L}} = \frac{1.56 \text{ mol/L} \times 1.56 \text{ mol/L}}{0.22 \text{ mol/L} \times 0.22 \text{ mol/L}}$$

$$= 5.0 \times 10^1$$

3. EVALUATE Do the results make sense?

Each concentration is raised to the correct power. The numerical value of the constant is correctly rounded to two significant figures. Note that because $K_{eq} > 1$, the product (HI) is favored at equilibrium.

Practice Problems (cont.)

11. At 750 °C the following reaction reaches equilibrium in a 1-L container.

$$H_2(g) + CO_2(g) \rightleftharpoons H_2O(g) + CO(g)$$

An analysis of the equilibrium mixture gives the following results: hydrogen, 0.053 mol; carbon dioxide, 0.053 mol; water vapor, 0.047 mol; carbon monoxide, 0.047 mol. Calculate K_{eq} for the reaction.

Sample Problem 19-4

Bromine chloride (BrCl) decomposes to form chlorine and bromine.

$$2BrCl(g) \rightleftharpoons Cl_2(g) + Br_2(g)$$

At a certain temperature, the equilibrium constant for the reaction is 11.1, and the equilibrium mixture contains 4.00 mol Cl_2. How many moles of Br_2 and BrCl are present in the equilibrium mixture? Assume that initially only pure BrCl existed and that the container has a volume of 1 L.

1. ANALYZE List the knowns and the unknowns.

Knowns:
- $K_{eq} = 11.1$
- quantity of Cl_2 (at equilibrium) = 4.00 mol
- $K_{eq} = \dfrac{[C]^c \times [D]^d}{[A]^a \times [B]^b}$

Unknowns:
- $[Br_2]$ = ? mol/L
- $[BrCl]$ = ? mol/L

Practice Problems

12. The decomposition of hydrogen iodide at 450 °C in a 1-L container produces an equilibrium mixture that contains 0.50 mol of hydrogen. The equilibrium constant is 0.020 for the reaction. How many moles of iodine and of hydrogen iodide are present in the equilibrium mixture? The equation is

$$2HI(g) \rightleftharpoons H_2(g) + I_2(g)$$

Sample Problem 19-4 (cont.)

2. CALCULATE Solve for the unknowns.

The equilibrium expression that corresponds to the chemical equation is

$$K_{eq} = \frac{[Cl_2] \times [Br_2]}{[BrCl]^2}$$

According to the equation, when BrCl breaks down, equal numbers of moles of Cl_2 and Br_2 form. The measured equilibrium quantity of Cl_2 was given as 4.00 mol. Thus there must also be 4.00 mol Br_2 in the equilibrium mixture. The volume of the container is 1 L, so $[Br_2]$ and $[Cl_2]$ are each 4.00 mol/L. Substitute the known values in the equilibrium expression for the reaction.

$$11.1 = \frac{(4.00 \text{ mol/L}) \times (4.00 \text{ mol/L})}{[BrCl]^2}$$

Rearrange the equation to solve for $[BrCl]^2$, and then for $[BrCl]$.

$$[BrCl]^2 = \frac{(4.00 \text{ mol/L}) \times (4.00 \text{ mol/L})}{11.1}$$

$$= \frac{16.0 \text{ mol}^2/\text{L}^2}{11.1} = 1.44 \text{ mol}^2/\text{L}^2$$

$$[BrCl] = \sqrt{1.44 \text{ mol}^2/\text{L}^2} = 1.20 \text{ mol/L}$$

3. EVALUATE Do the results make sense?

Each concentration is raised to the correct power. The result has the proper units and is correctly rounded to three significant figures. Note that $K_{eq} > 1$; the products Cl_2 and Br_2 are slightly favored at equilibrium.

Practice Problems (cont.)

13. Write the expression for the equilibrium constant for each.
a. $2HBr(g) \rightleftharpoons H_2(g) + Br_2(g)$
b. $2SO_3(g) \rightleftharpoons 2SO_2(g) + O_2(g)$
c. $CO_2(g) + H_2(g) \rightleftharpoons$
$\qquad\qquad CO(g) + H_2O(g)$
d. $4NH_3(g) + 5O_2(g) \rightleftharpoons$
$\qquad\qquad 6H_2O(g) + 4NO(g)$

Chem ASAP!

Problem-Solving 12
Solve Problem 12 with the help of an interactive guided tutorial.

section review 19.2

14. How can changes in the equilibrium position be predicted from changes in concentration, temperature, and pressure?

15. How can a balanced chemical equation and experimental data be used to write an equilibrium-constant expression and to calculate its value?

16. What is the significance of double arrows in an equation?

17. How do the amounts of reactants and products change once a reaction has achieved chemical equilibrium?

18. Can a pressure change shift the equilibrium position in every reversible reaction? Explain your answer.

19. Imagine you have determined the following equilibrium constants for several reactions. In which of these reactions are the products favored over the reactants? Why?

a. $K_{eq} = 1 \times 10^2$ **c.** $K_{eq} = 3.5$
b. $K_{eq} = 0.003$ **d.** $K_{eq} = 6 \times 10^{-4}$

 Chem ASAP! Assessment 19.2 Check your understanding of the important ideas and concepts in Section 19.2.

DETERMINING WHETHER A REACTION WILL OCCUR

*F*ires in homes, barns, and other places sometimes appear to start on their own, without heat applied from an external source. These types of fires are caused by spontaneous combustion. Inside a pile of oily rags or a stack of hay that has not been thoroughly dried, oxidation causes heat to build up. If the existing conditions do not allow the heat to escape, the temperature can build up enough to cause a fire. **What are the conditions that will produce a spontaneous chemical reaction?**

Free Energy and Spontaneous Reactions

Many chemical and physical processes release energy that can be used to bring about other changes. For example, some of the energy liberated in a reaction can be harnessed to do work, such as driving the pistons of an internal-combustion engine. **Free energy** is energy that is available to do work. Just because free energy is available to do work, however, does not mean it can be used efficiently. The internal-combustion engine in a car is only about 30% efficient; that is, only about 30% of the free energy released by burning gasoline is used to propel the car. The remaining 70% is lost as friction and waste heat. Efforts to conserve energy include attempts to increase the efficiency of engines and other mechanical devices. There are limits to such efficiency increases, however. No process can be made 100% efficient. Even in living things, which are among the most efficient users of free energy, processes are seldom more than 70% efficient. The temperature of the human body is maintained at 37 °C by the available free energy that is wasted as heat.

In addition to energy efficiency, there is another complication. Energy can be obtained from a reaction only if the reaction actually—rather than theoretically—occurs. In other words, although a balanced equation can

Figure 19.15
Fireworks displays are the result of highly favored spontaneous reactions. A large quantity of free energy is released.

be written for a chemical system, it does not mean the reaction will really take place. For example, you can write an equation for the decomposition of carbon dioxide to carbon and oxygen.

$$CO_2(g) \longrightarrow C(s) + O_2(g)$$

This equation, which represents the reverse of combustion, is balanced. However, experience tells you that the reaction represented by the equation does not tend to occur. Carbon and oxygen burn to make carbon dioxide, not the reverse. So the world of balanced chemical equations is really divided into two groups. One group contains equations representing reactions that actually occur; the other contains equations representing reactions that do not tend to occur, or at least not efficiently. The first group involves processes that are spontaneous. **Spontaneous reactions** are reactions that occur naturally and that favor the formation of products at the specified conditions. In other words, spontaneous reactions actually give substantial amounts of products at equilibrium. All spontaneous reactions release free energy. The colorful fireworks display shown in **Figure 19.15** on the previous page is due to spontaneous reactions. In contrast, **nonspontaneous reactions** are reactions that do not favor the formation of products at the specified conditions. Nonspontaneous reactions do not give substantial amounts of products at equilibrium.

Consider again the reversible decomposition of carbonic acid in water.

$$H_2CO_3(aq) \; \rightleftharpoons \; CO_2(g) + H_2O(l)$$
$$< 1\% \qquad\qquad\qquad > 99\%$$

Carbonic acid is the reactant of the forward reaction. If you could start with pure carbonic acid in water and let the system come to equilibrium, more than 99% of the reactant would be converted to the products carbon dioxide and water. These products are highly favored at equilibrium. There is a natural tendency for carbonic acid to decompose to carbon dioxide and water. Thus the forward reaction is spontaneous and releases free energy. In the reverse reaction, carbon dioxide and water are the reactants, and carbonic acid is the product. If you permit a solution of carbon dioxide in water to come to equilibrium, less than 1% of the reactants combines to form carbonic acid. There is little natural tendency for the reactants to go to products. Does this mean that the combination of carbon dioxide and water to form carbonic acid is spontaneous or nonspontaneous? In nearly all reversible reactions, one reaction is favored over the other.

Another example, shown in **Figure 19.16,** is the spontaneous reaction of aqueous cadmium nitrate with aqueous sodium sulfide to produce aqueous sodium nitrate and solid yellow cadmium sulfide. Cadmium sulfide is highly favored in this equilibrium. The reverse reaction, or the production of cadmium nitrate and sodium sulfide from cadmium sulfide and sodium nitrate, is nonspontaneous.

$$Cd(NO_3)_2(aq) + Na_2S(aq) \; \rightleftharpoons \; CdS(s) + 2NaNO_3(aq)$$

It is important to note that the terms spontaneous and nonspontaneous do not refer to how fast reactants go to products. Some spontaneous reactions go so slowly that they appear to be nonspontaneous. The reaction

Figure 19.16

A yellow precipitate of cadmium sulfide (CdS) forms spontaneously when clear colorless solutions of sodium sulfide (Na₂S) and cadmium nitrate (Cd(NO₃)₂) are mixed.

of sugar and oxygen, for example, produces carbon dioxide and water. However, a bowl of sugar on a table does nothing, and you might assume that the equilibrium among sugar, oxygen, carbon dioxide, and water greatly favors the sugar and oxygen. The equilibrium does favor the products, but at room temperature this reaction is so slow that it takes thousands of years to reach equilibrium. When you supply energy in the form of heat, the reaction is fast. Only then is it obvious that, at equilibrium, the formation of carbon dioxide and water is highly favored. The combustion of the sugar goes to completion.

Some reactions that are nonspontaneous at one set of conditions may be spontaneous at other conditions. Changing the temperature or pressure, for example, may determine whether or not a reaction is spontaneous. The nonspontaneous photosynthesis reaction summarized in **Figure 19.17** could not be driven to completion without the energy supplied by sunlight.

Sometimes a nonspontaneous reaction can be made to occur if it is coupled to a spontaneous reaction—a reaction that releases free energy. Coupled reactions are a common feature of the complex biological processes that take place in living organisms. Within cells, a series of spontaneous reactions release the energy stored in glucose. As you will learn in Chapter 27, there are molecules in a cell that can capture and transfer free energy to nonspontaneous reactions, such as the formation of proteins.

$$6CO_2 + 6H_2O \xrightarrow{\text{light energy}} C_6H_{12}O_6 + 6O_2$$

Figure 19.17
Many nonspontaneous reactions are required for a plant to grow. Nonspontaneous reactions can occur when they are coupled with spontaneous reactions.

Entropy

You may recall that heat (enthalpy) changes accompany most chemical and physical processes. The combustion of carbon, for example, is exothermic and spontaneous. The heat released during this reaction is 393.5 kJ for each mole of carbon (graphite) burned.

$$C(s, \text{graphite}) + O_2(g) \longrightarrow CO_2(g) + 393.5 \text{ kJ/mol}$$

You might expect that only exothermic reactions would be spontaneous. Some processes, however, may be spontaneous even though they absorb heat. For example, consider the physical process of melting ice to water. As it turns from a solid to a liquid, 1 mol of ice at 25 °C absorbs 6.0 kJ of heat from its surroundings.

$$H_2O(s) + 6.0 \text{ kJ/mol} \longrightarrow H_2O(l)$$

Ice melts spontaneously at 25 °C, even though the water produced contains more heat than the ice from which it forms. Considering only heat changes, the energy of the water seems higher than the energy of the ice. That would seem to violate the rule that in spontaneous processes, the direction of the change in energy is from higher energy to lower energy; that is, free energy is released. Yet this process occurs anyway. Some factor other than the heat change must help determine whether a physical or chemical process is spontaneous.

Figure 19.18

The entropy of a recently cleaned and orderly room is low. However, over time a room tends to become disorderly. Entropy has a tendency to increase.

The other factor is related to order. You are probably familiar with everyday ideas about order and disorder. For example, a handful of marbles is relatively ordered in the sense that all the marbles are collected in one place. It is improbable that when permitted to fall the marbles will end up in the same neat arrangement. Instead, the marbles will scatter on the ground. The marbles will become disordered. The disorder of a system is measured as **entropy.** Scattered marbles have a higher entropy than gathered marbles.

The concept that physical and chemical systems attain the lowest possible energy has a companion idea called the law of disorder. The **law of disorder** states that processes move in the direction of maximum disorder or randomness. You already know something about this natural tendency toward disorder. More than likely, your bedroom is neat and clean at the beginning of the week. But unless you clean it regularly, your room probably becomes messy by the end of the week. Do the photographs in **Figure 19.18** look familiar to you? The law of disorder also operates at the level of atoms and molecules. On an atomic and molecular scale, the following information can be applied.

(a) For a given substance, the entropy of the gas is greater than the entropy of the liquid or the solid. Similarly, the entropy of the liquid is greater than that of the solid. Thus entropy increases in reactions in which solid reactants form liquid or gaseous products. Entropy also increases when liquid reactants form gaseous products.

Figure 19.19

Entropy is a measure of the disorder of a system. (a) The entropy of a solid is less than the entropy of the corresponding liquid, which is less than the corresponding gas. (b) Entropy increases when a substance is divided into parts. (c) Entropy tends to increase in reactions in which the number of molecules increases. (d) Entropy also increases with an increase in temperature.

Increasing entropy

Solid   Liquid   Gas

(b) Entropy increases when a substance is divided into parts. For instance, entropy increases when a crystalline ionic compound, such as sodium chloride, dissolves in water. This is because the solute particles—sodium ions and chloride ions—are more separated in solution than they are in the crystal form. What happens to the entropy of sodium and chloride ions when a solution of salt water evaporates?

Increasing entropy

(c) Entropy tends to increase in chemical reactions in which the total number of product molecules is greater than the total number of reactant molecules.

Increasing entropy

Electricity

Electricity

$$2H_2O(l) \xrightarrow{\text{Electricity}} 2H_2(g) + O_2(g)$$

Electrolysis of water

(d) Entropy tends to increase when temperature increases. As the temperature increases, the molecules move faster and faster, which increases the disorder.

Increasing entropy

Heat, Entropy, and Free Energy

The size and direction of heat (enthalpy) changes and entropy changes together determine whether a reaction is spontaneous; that is, whether it favors products and releases free energy. An exothermic, or heat-releasing, reaction accompanied by an increase in entropy, or an increase in disorder, is definitely spontaneous because both factors are favorable. The combustion of carbon, for example, is exothermic. The entropy also increases as solid carbon is converted to gaseous carbon dioxide. Because both factors are favorable, the reaction must be spontaneous. The reverse reaction—production of carbon and oxygen from carbon dioxide—is nonspontaneous; neither the heat nor the entropy change is favorable.

A reaction will also be spontaneous if a decrease in entropy is offset by a large release of heat. Similarly, an endothermic, or heat-absorbing, reaction will be spontaneous if an entropy increase offsets the heat absorption. For example, heat change and entropy change work in opposition when ice melts. The melting of ice is endothermic but is still spontaneous above 0 °C. At such temperatures, the absorption of heat is more than offset by a favorable entropy change. Why is the freezing of water to ice a nonspontaneous process at 10 °C?

Table 19.1 summarizes how entropy and heat changes affect the spontaneity of chemical reactions. Notice that either of the two variables, but not both, can be unfavorable for a spontaneous process. **Figure 19.20** summarizes the relationship among heat, entropy, and free-energy changes for spontaneous reactions.

A nonspontaneous reaction, one in which the products are not favored, has heat changes, entropy changes, or both working against it. The desired reaction might not be able to overcome a large decrease in entropy and might also be highly endothermic. In that case, both these changes work against the formation of products. On the other hand, a nonspontaneous reaction may be exothermic but involve a decrease in entropy large enough to offset the favorable heat change. Alternatively, an increase in entropy might be too small to overcome an endothermic heat change. **Figure 19.20** also summarizes the relationships for nonspontaneous reactions.

Table 19.1

How Changes in Heat and Entropy Affect Reaction Spontaneity		
Heat change	**Entropy**	**Spontaneous reaction?**
Decreases (exothermic)	Increases (more disorder in products than in reactants)	Yes
Increases (endothermic)	Increases	Only if unfavorable heat change is offset by favorable entropy change
Decreases (exothermic)	Decreases (less disorder in products than in reactants)	Only if unfavorable entropy change is offset by favorable heat change
Increases (endothermic)	Decreases	No

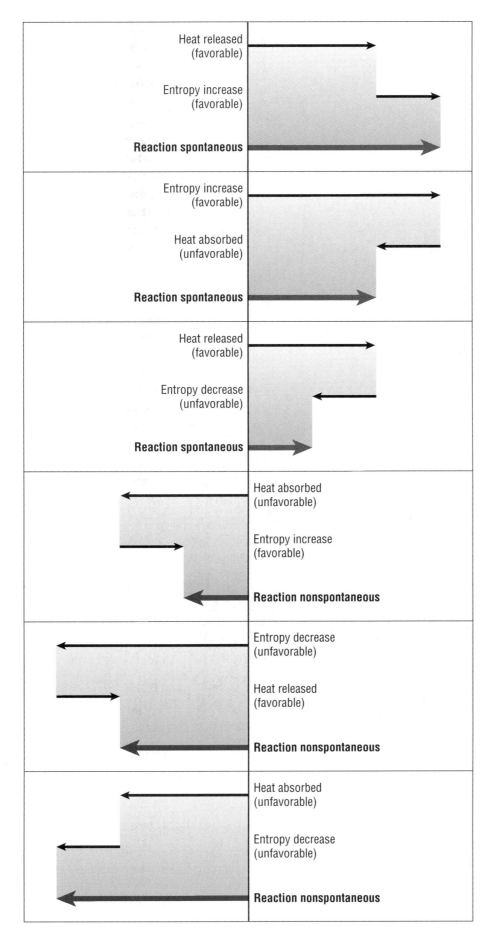

Figure 19.20
Free energy is released in sponta-neous reactions. The reaction may be exothermic, the entropy of the system may increase, or both may occur. A reaction may be non-spontaneous because the reaction is endothermic or the entropy of the system decreases, or both may occur.

MINI LAB

Does Steel Burn?

PURPOSE

To determine whether steel will burn.

MATERIALS

- 0000 steel wool pad
- tissue paper
- tongs
- Bunsen burner
- heat-resistant pad
- pencil and paper

PROCEDURE

1. Roll a small piece of steel wool into a very tight, pea-sized ball. Use the tissue paper to protect your fingers from small steel fibers while handling the steel wool.

2. Holding the ball with tongs, heat the steel wool for no longer than 10 seconds in the blue-tip flame of the burner. In this and subsequent steps, place pieces of heated steel wool on the heat-resistant pad to cool. Observe all appropriate safety precautions when working with the burner and the heated materials. Record your observations.

3. Gently roll a second piece of steel wool into a loose, pea-sized ball. Holding the loose ball with the tongs, heat the wool for no longer than 10 seconds in the burner flame. Record your observations.

4. Pull a few individual fibers of steel wool from the pad. Hold one end of the loose fibers with the tongs and heat them for no longer than 10 seconds in the flame of the burner. Again record your observations.

ANALYSIS AND CONCLUSIONS

1. What differences did you observe when the tight ball, the loose ball, and the loose fibers were heated in the flame? Give a reason for any differences you observed.

2. Write the balanced equation for any chemical reaction you may have observed (assume that the steel wool is composed mainly of iron).

3. How do your results differ from those observed in the rusting of an automobile body?

4. Explain why steel wool is a hazard in shops where there are hot plates, open flames, or sparking motors.

---

section review 19.3

20. Explain what is meant by the following:

   a. entropy

   b. free energy

   c. spontaneous reaction

   d. nonspontaneous reaction

21. What two factors determine whether a reaction is spontaneous?

22. Where does lost free energy typically end up? Does free energy lost as heat ever serve a useful function? Explain.

23. What can change a reaction from nonspontaneous to spontaneous?

24. Suppose the products in a spontaneous process are more ordered than the reactants. Is the entropy change favorable or unfavorable?

 Chem ASAP! Assessment 19.3 Check your understanding of the important ideas and concepts in Section 19.3.

ENTHALPY AND ENTROPY

SAFETY

Wear safety glasses and follow the standard safety procedures outlined on page 18.

PURPOSE

To observe and measure energy changes during the formation of a solution and to describe and explain these changes in terms of entropy and enthalpy.

MATERIALS

- alcohol thermometer
- four 1-oz plastic cups
- solid chemicals shown in Figure A
- plastic spoon
- crushed ice
- water

PROCEDURE

Place two level spoonfuls of water in a plastic cup and measure the temperature (T_1) of the water. Add one level spoonful of solid NaCl to the cup, stir gently, and measure the highest or lowest temperature (T_2). Record this information on a separate sheet of paper in a table similar to Figure A. Repeat the experiment twice more, substituting NaCl with NH_4Cl the first time and $CaCl_2$ the second time. Record the temperatures.

Mixture	T_1	T_2	ΔT
a. $NaCl(s) + H_2O(l)$			
b. $NH_4Cl(s) + H_2O(l)$			
c. $CaCl_2(s) + H_2O(l)$			

Figure A

ANALYSIS

Using your experimental data, record the answers to the following questions in or below your data table.

1. Calculate ΔT for each mixture. $\Delta T = T_2 - T_1$.

2. An exothermic process gives off heat (warms up). An endothermic process absorbs heat (cools off). Which solutions are endothermic and which are exothermic? What is the sign of ΔH in each case?

3. Which solution(s) had little or no change in temperature?

4. When sodium chloride dissolves in water, the ions dissociate.

$$NaCl(s) \longrightarrow Na^+(aq) + Cl^-(aq)$$

Write two ionic equations, similar to the one above, that describe how NH_4Cl and $CaCl_2$ each dissociate as they dissolve in water. Include heat as a reactant or product in each equation.

5. Which solids in this experiment rapidly dissolved in water? Does the dissolving process usually occur with an increase or decrease in entropy? What is the sign of ΔS in each case?

6. Consider the equation $\Delta G = \Delta H - T\Delta S$. For each dissolving process, substitute the sign of ΔS and ΔH into the equation and determine the sign of ΔG. For which process might ΔG be either positive or negative?

YOU'RE THE CHEMIST

The following small-scale activities allow you to develop your own procedures and analyze the results.

1. **Analyze It!** Mix a tablespoon of ice (solid water) with a tablespoon of solid NaCl. Stir gently, then measure and record the lowest temperature reached. Compare this mixture with the mixture of solid NaCl and liquid water. What is the difference in temperature?

2. **Analyze It!** Is the process of melting ice exothermic or endothermic? Does this explain the difference in temperature in Activity 1? Explain.

3. **Design It!** What effect does mixing other salts with crushed ice have on temperature? Try substituting different salts in Activity 1.

4. **Design It!** What effect does dissolving other salts in liquid water have on temperature? Try dissolving the following salts in liquid water: potassium chloride (KCl), sodium hydrogen carbonate ($NaHCO_3$), sodium carbonate (Na_2CO_3), and sodium phosphate (Na_3PO_4).

objectives

▶ Calculate the standard entropy changes that accompany chemical and physical processes
▶ Calculate the free-energy changes that accompany chemical and physical processes

key terms

▶ standard entropy (S^0)
▶ Gibbs free-energy change (ΔG)

CALCULATING ENTROPY AND FREE ENERGY

*E*nergy, in the form of heat, is required to cook a hot dog. Would you want to use a welding torch to cook your hot dog? A reaction that releases the same amount of energy over a longer period of time, such as the combustion of charcoal in a barbeque grill, might be more appropriate. **How do chemists calculate the amount of energy that a chemical reaction will release?**

Entropy Calculations

Entropy is a quantitative measure of the disorder of a system. The symbol for the entropy of a substance is S, with units of J/K. When entropy (S) is given per mole of substance, it has units of J/(K × mol), which is also written as J/K·mol. The **standard entropy** of a liquid or solid substance at 25 °C is designated S^0. The pressure at S^0 for gaseous substances is 101.3 kPa. The theoretical entropy of a perfect crystal at 0 K is zero. Other substances have positive entropies, even at absolute zero. **Table 19.2** lists standard entropies for some common substances.

Standard entropy change (ΔS^0) can be calculated from standard entropies using the following equation.

$$\Delta S^0 = S^0(\text{products}) - S^0(\text{reactants})$$

Table 19.2

Standard Entropies (S^0) at 25 °C and 101.3 kPa			
Substance	S^0 (J/K·mol)	Substance	S^0 (J/K·mol)
$Al_2O_3(s)$	50.99	$HCl(g)$	186.7
$Br_2(g)$	245.3	$H_2S(g)$	205.6
$Br_2(l)$	152.3	$I_2(g)$	260.6
C(s, diamond)	2.439	$I_2(s)$	117
C(s, graphite)	5.694	$N_2(g)$	191.5
$CH_4(g)$	186.2	$NH_3(g)$	192.5
$CO(g)$	197.9	$NO(g)$	210.6
$CO_2(g)$	213.6	$NO_2(g)$	240.5
$CaCO_3(s)$	88.7	$Na_2CO_3(s)$	136
$CaO(s)$	39.75	$NaCl(s)$	72.4
$Cl_2(g)$	223.0	$O_2(g)$	205.0
$F_2(g)$	203	$O_3(g)$	238
$Fe(s)$	27.2	P(s, white)	44.4
$Fe_2O_3(s)$	90.0	P(s, red)	29
$H_2(g)$	130.6	S(s, rhombic)	31.9
$H_2O(g)$	188.7	S(s, monoclinic)	32.6
$H_2O(l)$	69.94	$SO_2(g)$	248.5
$H_2O_2(l)$	92	$SO_3(g)$	256.2

CHEMath

BALANCING EQUATIONS

You will find that many of the problems in this chapter rely on properly balanced chemical equations. This page offers a review of the skills needed to balance these equations. For a more thorough review, see Chapter 8. Balancing an equation is the process of inserting coefficients into a skeleton equation so that each side of the equation has the same number of atoms of each element. A correctly balanced equation is consistent with the principle that atoms are neither created nor destroyed in a chemical reaction, they are just rearranged into new groupings.

Balancing equations is largely a matter of logical thinking combined with trial and error.

1. Write a skeleton equation in the form

$$\text{reactants} \longrightarrow \text{products}$$

using chemical formulas separated by plus signs. Leave space for coefficients.

2. Choose one element or polyatomic ion to balance. It is best to start with elements that appear only once on each side of the equation. Adjust the coefficients as necessary so the number of atoms of the chosen element is the same on both sides of the equation. When no coefficient is written, it is assumed to be 1.

3. Repeat Step 2, choosing different elements until all the elements are balanced.

4. Check your work by making sure each element is balanced. This step is very important because the elements that you balance in the early steps can become "unbalanced" as you continue your work. Then make sure the coefficients are in the lowest possible ratio; that is, they should have a greatest common factor of 1.

Example 1

Balance the equation $Na(s) + Cl_2(g) \longrightarrow NaCl(s)$.

Sodium is balanced (1 atom on each side), but chlorine is not (2 on the left, 1 on the right). Balance the chlorine:

$$Na(s) + Cl_2(g) \longrightarrow \mathbf{2}NaCl(s)$$

Now chlorine is balanced (2 atoms on each side), but sodium is not (1 on the left, 2 on the right). Balance the sodium:

$$\mathbf{2}Na(s) + Cl_2(g) \longrightarrow 2NaCl(s)$$

Check:
Sodium is balanced (2 atoms on each side).
Chlorine is balanced (2 atoms on each side).

The equation is $2Na(s) + Cl_2(g) \longrightarrow 2NaCl(s)$.

Example 2

Balance the equation

$$NaOH(aq) + H_2SO_4(aq) \longrightarrow Na_2SO_4(aq) + H_2O(l)$$

Note that the polyatomic ion SO_4 appears on each side of the equation, so count it as a single unit. Balance the sodium:

$$\mathbf{2}NaOH(aq) + H_2SO_4(aq) \longrightarrow Na_2SO_4(aq) + H_2O(l)$$

Oxygen is not balanced (2 on the left, 1 on the right, not counting the SO_4). Balance the oxygen:

$$2NaOH(aq) + H_2SO_4(aq) \longrightarrow Na_2SO_4(aq) + \mathbf{2}H_2O(l)$$

The equation appears to be balanced. Check:
Na is balanced (2 atoms on each side).
O is balanced (2 atoms on each side).
H is balanced (4 atoms on each side).
SO_4 is balanced (1 ion on each side).

Practice Problems

Practice balancing chemical equations by writing a balanced equation for each reaction.

A. $Zn(s) + HCl(aq) \longrightarrow ZnCl_2(aq) + H_2(g)$

B. $CaCO_3(s) + HCl(aq) \longrightarrow H_2CO_3(aq) + CaCl_2(aq)$

C. $PbCl_2(aq) + K_2SO_4(aq) \longrightarrow PbSO_4(s) + KCl(aq)$

D. $C_4H_{10}(g) + O_2(g) \longrightarrow CO_2(g) + H_2O(g)$

E. Solid iron metal reacts with oxygen gas to produce solid iron(III) oxide (rust).

F. Solid tungsten(VI) oxide reacts with hydrogen gas to produce solid tungsten metal and water vapor.

Sample Problem 19-5

Calculate the standard entropy change (ΔS^0) that occurs when 1 mol $H_2O(g)$ at 25 °C and 101.3 kPa condenses to 1 mol $H_2O(l)$ at the same temperature.

1. **ANALYZE** *List the knowns and the unknown.*
   Knowns (from Table 19.2):
   - $H_2O(g)$ $S^0 = 188.7$ J/K·mol
   - $H_2O(l)$ $S^0 = 69.94$ J/K·mol

   Unknown:
   - ΔS^0(condensation) = ?

   $$\Delta S^0 = S^0\text{(products)} - S^0\text{(reactants)}$$

   The change in physical state is $H_2O(g) \rightarrow H_2O(l)$. Substitute the known values into the equation and solve for the unknown.

2. **CALCULATE** *Solve for the unknown.*
   Only 1 mol of each reactant and product is involved; therefore,
   $$\Delta S^0 = 69.94 \text{ J/K·mol} - 188.7 \text{ J/K·mol} = -118.8 \text{ J/K·mol}$$
   The negative sign indicates that entropy decreases.

3. **EVALUATE** *Does the result make sense?*
   As would be expected, the condensation of 1 mol of water vapor to liquid water at 25 °C results in a large decrease in entropy. The result is expressed in the proper units.

Practice Problem

25. The standard entropies for some substances at 25 °C are
    $KBrO_3(s)$ $S^0 = 149.2$ J/K·mol
    $KBr(s)$ $S^0 = 96.4$ J/K·mol
    $O_2(g)$ $S^0 = 205.0$ J/K·mol
    Calculate ΔS^0 for the reaction
    $$KBrO_3(s) \longrightarrow KBr(s) + \tfrac{3}{2}O_2(g)$$

Chem ASAP!

Problem-Solving 25

Solve Problem 25 with the help of an interactive guided tutorial.

Sample Problem 19-6

$NO(g)$ reacts with O_2 to form $NO_2(g)$. What is the standard change in entropy for this reaction when reactants and products are in the specified physical states at 101.3 kPa and 25 °C?
$$NO(g) + O_2(g) \longrightarrow NO_2(g)$$

1. **ANALYZE** *List the knowns and the unknown.*
   Knowns (from Table 19.2):
   - reactants, $NO(g)$ and $O_2(g)$
   - product, NO_2
   - $NO(g)$ $S^0 - 210.6$ J/K·mol
   - $O_2(g)$ $S^0 = 205.0$ J/K·mol
   - $NO_2(g)$ $S^0 = 240.5$ J/K·mol
   - $\Delta S^0 = S^0\text{(products)} - S^0\text{(reactants)}$

   Unknown:
   - ΔS^0(reaction) = ?

   First, balance the chemical equation. Obtain S^0 for the reactants, then substitute the known S^0 values into the ΔS^0 equation and solve.

Sample Problem 19-6 (cont.)

2. **CALCULATE** *Solve for the unknown.*
Balancing the chemical equation yields:

$$2NO(g) + O_2(g) \longrightarrow 2NO_2(g)$$

Sum the S^0 of the reactants, taking into account the number of moles.

S^0 for NO_2 = 2 mol NO × 210.6 J/K·mol NO = 421.2 J/K
S^0 for O_2 = 1 mol O_2 × 205.0 J/K·mol O_2 = 205.0 J/K
$\qquad\qquad\qquad\qquad S^0\text{(reactants)}$ = 626.2 J/K

Calculate the S^0 of the products.

S^0 for NO_2 = 2 mol NO_2 × 240.5 J/K·mol NO_2 = 481.0 J/K

Calculate the change in entropy by subtracting.

$$\Delta S^0 = S^0\text{(products)} - S^0\text{(reactants)}$$
$$= (481.0 \text{ J/K}) - (626.2 \text{ J/K}) = -145.2 \text{ J/K}$$

3. **EVALUATE** *Does the result make sense?*
The entropy decreases as expected because three reactant molecules are reorganized to only two product molecules.

Practice Problem

26. Based on the data in **Table 19.2,** calculate ΔS^0 for converting the monoclinic form of sulfur to the rhombic form.

Figure 19.21
What characteristics of an explosion would lead you to think that an increase in entropy is occurring?

Free-Energy Calculations

You may recall that in every spontaneous process, some energy becomes available to do work. This energy, called the **Gibbs free-energy change (ΔG),** is the maximum amount of energy that can be coupled to another process to do useful work. The change in Gibbs free energy is related to the change in entropy (ΔS) and the change in enthalpy (ΔH) of the system by the free-energy equation

$$\Delta G = \Delta H - T\Delta S,$$

where temperature (T) is in kelvins.

GEOLOGY

Weathering of Rocks

The weathering of rock usually occurs so slowly that the process is imperceptible over many human lifetimes. In spite of its low rate, the weathering

of rocks has shaped, and continues to shape, Earth's surface. Chemical and physical processes induced by water produce much of the weathering. Some mountains in the United States show the effects of weathering over long periods of time. The relatively new Rocky Mountains (100 million years) are high and craggy. By contrast, the old southern Appalachians (345 million years) are low and smooth because of an additional 245 million years of weathering!

All spontaneous processes release free energy. The numerical value of ΔG is negative in spontaneous processes because the system loses free energy. Nonspontaneous processes require that work be expended to make them go forward at the specified conditions. Therefore, the numerical value of ΔG is positive for a nonspontaneous process.

You can calculate the standard free-energy change (ΔG^0) to determine whether a chemical reaction is spontaneous when ΔH^0 and ΔS^0 are known. The following equation is used to calculate the standard free-energy change.

$$\Delta G^0 = \Delta H^0 - T\Delta S^0$$

Alternatively, you can determine ΔH^0 or ΔS^0 for a reaction if the other two quantities in the equation are known. **Table 19.3** lists values of ΔG^0 for some common reactions.

When ΔH^0 and ΔS^0 are unknown, you can use ΔG_f^0, the standard free-energy change for the formation of substances from their elements, to calculate ΔG^0 for a given reaction.

$$\Delta G^0 = \Delta G_f^0(\text{products}) - \Delta G_f^0(\text{reactants})$$

This is similar to how standard heats of formation (ΔH_f^0) are used to calculate heats of reaction. For what other kind of change have you calculated the value in a similar way?

Table 19.4 lists values of ΔG_f^0 for some spontaneous processes. Note that $\Delta G_f^0 = 0$ for elemental substances. If you calculate ΔG^0 to determine whether a reaction is spontaneous, the result applies only to reactants and products in their standard states. Also, a reaction that is nonspontaneous under one set of conditions may be spontaneous under another set of conditions. Why does bromine gas (Br_2) have a greater free energy than bromine liquid?

Table 19.3

Free Energy Values (ΔG^0) for Some Spontaneous Processes at 25 °C		
	Free energy	
Reaction	Kilocalories	Kilojoules
$H_2(g) + Cl_2(g) \longrightarrow 2HCl(g)$ Hydrogen Chlorine Hydrogen chloride	−45.6	−191
$S(s) + O_2(g) \longrightarrow SO_2(g)$ Sulfur Oxygen Sulfur dioxide	−71.7	−300
$2N_2O_5(s) \longrightarrow 4NO_2(g) + O_2(g)$ Dinitrogen pentoxide Nitrogen dioxide Oxygen	−7.2	−30
$C_6H_{12}O_6(s) + 6O_2(g) \longrightarrow 6CO_2(g) + 6H_2O(l)$ Glucose Oxygen Carbon dioxide Water	−686.0	−2868

Table 19.4

Standard Gibbs Free Energies of Formation (ΔG_f^0) at 25 °C and 101.3 kPa			
Substance	ΔG_f^0 (kJ/mol)	Substance	ΔG_f^0 (kJ/mol)
$Al_2O_3(s)$	−1576.4	$HCl(g)$	−95.27
$Br_2(g)$	3.14	$H_2S(g)$	−33.02
$Br_2(l)$	0.0	$I_2(g)$	19.4
C(s, diamond)	2.866	$I_2(s)$	0.0
C(s, graphite)	0.0	$N_2(g)$	0.0
$CH_4(g)$	−50.79	$NH_3(g)$	−16.64
$CO(g)$	−137.3	$NO(g)$	86.69
$CO_2(g)$	−394.4	$NO_2(g)$	51.84
$CaCO_3(s)$	−1127.7	$Na_2CO_3(s)$	−1048
$CaO(s)$	−604.2	$NaCl(s)$	−384.03
$Cl_2(g)$	0.0	$O_2(g)$	0.0
$F_2(g)$	0.0	$O_3(g)$	163.4
$Fe(s)$	0.0	P(s, white)	0.0
$Fe_2O_3(s)$	−741.0	P(s, red)	−14
$H_2(g)$	0.0	S(s, rhombic)	0.0
$H_2O(g)$	−228.6	S(s, monoclinic)	0.096
$H_2O(l)$	−237.2	$SO_2(g)$	−300.4
$H_2O_2(l)$	−114.0	$SO_3(g)$	−370.4

It may be helpful to consider a real chemical reaction to see the effect of temperature on the spontaneity of a reaction. Solid calcium carbonate decomposes to give calcium oxide and carbon dioxide.

CaCO₃ (formula unit) ⟶ CaO (formula unit) + CO₂ (molecule)

Decomposition reaction

In this reaction, the entropy increases because one of the products formed from the solid reactant is a gas. The entropy increase is not great enough, however, for the reaction to be spontaneous at ordinary temperatures because the reaction is endothermic. The enthalpy of the reactants is lower than that of the products. The effect of an entropy increase, however, is magnified as the temperature increases. At temperatures above 850 °C, the favorable entropy–temperature term $T\Delta S^0$ outweighs the unfavorable enthalpy term ΔH^0. Under these conditions, the identical reaction then becomes spontaneous.

Sample Problem 19-7

Using values for ΔH and S^0, determine whether this reaction is spontaneous at 25 °C.

$$C(s, \text{graphite}) + O_2(g) \longrightarrow CO_2(g)$$

1. **ANALYZE List the knowns and the unknown.**

Knowns at 25 °C (from **Tables 11.6** *and* **19.2***):*

Substance	ΔH_f^0 (kJ/mol)	S^0 (J/K·mol)
C(s, graphite)	0.0	5.69
$O_2(g)$	0.0	205
$CO_2(g)$	−393.5	214

Unknown:
- $\Delta G^0(\text{reaction}) = ?$

2. **CALCULATE Solve for the unknown.**

The S^0 values listed in **Table 19.2** are in J/K·mol. Convert them to kJ/K·mol to match the units of ΔH_f^0.

$$C(s, \text{graphite}) \; S^0 = 5.7 \frac{J}{K \cdot mol} \times \frac{1 \, kJ}{1000 \, J} = 0.0057 \, kJ/K \cdot mol$$

$$O_2(g) \; S^0 = 205 \frac{J}{K \cdot mol} \times \frac{1 \, kJ}{1000 \, J} = 0.205 \, kJ/K \cdot mol$$

$$CO_2(g) \; S^0 = 214 \frac{J}{K \cdot mol} \times \frac{1 \, kJ}{1000 \, J} = 0.214 \, kJ/K \cdot mol$$

Calculate the change in entropy (ΔS^0).

$$\Delta S^0 = S^0(\text{products}) - S^0(\text{reactants})$$

$$= 0.214 \frac{kJ}{K \cdot mol} - (0.0057 + 0.205) \frac{kJ}{K \cdot mol} = 0.003 \frac{kJ}{K \cdot mol}$$

Calculate the standard enthalpy change for the reaction in a similar way.

$$\Delta H^0 = \Delta H_f^0(\text{products}) - \Delta H_f^0(\text{reactants})$$

$$\Delta H^0 = -393.5 \, kJ/mol - (0.0 \, kJ/mol + 0.0 \, kJ/mol)$$

$$= -393.5 \, kJ/mol$$

Calculate the value of ΔG^0 from the changes in enthalpy and the changes in entropy.

$$\Delta G^0 = \Delta H^0 - T\Delta S^0$$

where $T = 273.15 + 25 \,°C = 298.15 \, K$

$$\Delta G^0 = -393.5 \, kJ/mol - \left(298.15 \, K \times 0.003 \frac{kJ}{K \cdot mol} \right)$$

$$= -394.4 \, kJ/mol$$

3. **EVALUATE Does the result make sense?**

The reaction is spontaneous due to the decrease in ΔH^0 and the increase in entropy when solid graphite is converted to gaseous CO_2. In other words, both enthalpy and entropy changes work in favor of reaction spontaneity.

Practice Problem

27. When gaseous nitrogen and hydrogen are converted to gaseous ammonia, $\Delta G^0 = -16.64 \, kJ/mol$.
The chemical equation is
$$N_2(g) + 3H_2(g) \longrightarrow 2NH_3(g)$$
Using the S^0 values in **Table 19.2**, calculate the ΔH_f^0 for the formation of ammonia.

Chem ASAP!

Problem-Solving 27

Solve Problem 27 with the help of an interactive guided tutorial.

Sample Problem 19-8

Using the ΔG_f^0 for the reactants and products, determine whether the reaction in Sample Problem 19-7 is spontaneous.

1. ANALYZE List the knowns and the unknown.

Knowns (from **Table 19.4**):
- C(s, graphite) $\Delta G_f^0 = 0$ kJ/mol
- $O_2(g)$ $\Delta G_f^0 = 0$ kJ/mol
- $CO_2(g)$ $\Delta G_f^0 = -394.4$ kJ/mol
- $\Delta G^0 = \Delta G_f^0$ (products) $- \Delta G_f^0$ (reactants)

Unknown:
- ΔG_f^0 (reaction) = ?

The chemical equation is C(s, graphite) $+ O_2(g) \rightarrow CO_2(g)$.

2. CALCULATE Solve for the unknown.

Sum the ΔG_f^0 of the reactants and sum the ΔG_f^0 of the products.

$$\Delta G_f^0 \text{(reactants)} = 0.0 \text{ kJ/mol}$$

$$\Delta G_f^0 \text{(products)} = -394.4 \text{ kJ/mol}$$

The ΔG_f^0 for the reaction is the difference between the ΔG_f^0 of the products and the ΔG_f^0 of the reactants.

$$\Delta G^0 = \Delta G_f^0 \text{(products)} - \Delta G_f^0 \text{(reactants)}$$

$$\Delta G^0 = -394.4 \text{ kJ/mol} - 0.0 \text{ kJ/mol}$$

$$= -394.4 \text{ kJ/mol}$$

3. EVALUATE Does the result make sense?

The results obtained in this problem and Sample Problem 19-7 are identical, as they should be. The reaction is spontaneous, with a large release of free energy. This is consistent with experience—charcoal, which is primarily carbon, does burn readily.

Practice Problems

28. Use the data in **Table 19.4** to calculate the standard free-energy change for each reaction. Is the reaction spontaneous or nonspontaneous?

a. $Cl_2(g) + H_2O(g) \longrightarrow 2HCl(g) + \frac{1}{2}O_2(g)$

b. $4NH_3(g) + 7O_2(g) \longrightarrow 4NO_2(g) + 6H_2O(g)$

29. Use the data in **Table 19.4** to calculate the standard free-energy change for each reaction. Is the reaction spontaneous or nonspontaneous?

a. $2CO_2(g) \longrightarrow 2CO(g) + O_2(g)$

b. $H_2S(g) \longrightarrow H_2(g) + S(s, \text{rhombic})$

Chem ASAP!

Problem-Solving 29

Solve Problem 29 with the help of an interactive guided tutorial.

---

section review 19.4

30. Calculate the change in entropy for these reactions.

a. $CaCO_3(s) \longrightarrow CaO(s) + CO_2(g)$

b. $2H_2(g) + O_2(g) \longrightarrow 2H_2O(l)$

c. $H_2(g) + Cl_2(g) \longrightarrow 2HCl(g)$

d. $CH_4(g) + 2O_2(g) \longrightarrow CO_2(g) + 2H_2O(g)$

31. How does the magnitude of the standard entropy of an element in the gaseous state compare with the standard entropy of the same element in the liquid state?

32. Determine whether the following reactions are spontaneous. Assume all substances are at 25 °C and 101.3 kPa.

a. $2Na(s) + Cl_2(g) \longrightarrow 2NaCl(s)$

b. $4Al(s) + 3O_2(g) \longrightarrow 2Al_2O_3(s)$

 Chem ASAP! Assessment 19.4 Check your understanding of the important ideas and concepts in Section 19.4.

objectives

▶ Interpret experimental rate data to deduce the rate laws for simple chemical reactions

▶ Given an energy diagram for a reaction, analyze the mechanism for the reaction

key terms

▶ rate law
▶ specific rate constant
▶ first-order reaction
▶ elementary reaction
▶ reaction mechanism
▶ intermediate

THE PROGRESS OF CHEMICAL REACTIONS

*T*he Tour de France is one of the most famous bicycle races in the world. It is held from mid-July to early August. During the course of the race, cyclists travel almost 4000 kilometers and cross steep mountains at heights of 1600 meters or more. To cross these high mountains requires extra amounts of energy. A chemical reaction can be thought of as a process involving peaks and valleys also. **What are the energy requirements for a chemical reaction to progress from initial reactants to final products?**

Rate Laws

The rate of a reaction depends in part on the concentrations of the reactants. For a reaction in which reactant A reacts to form product B in one step, you can write a simple equation. A one-step reaction is a reaction with only one activated complex between the reactants and products.

$$A \longrightarrow B$$

The rate at which A transforms to B is the change in concentration of A with time. Mathematically, you can express the rate as the change in A (ΔA) with respect to the change in time (Δt).

$$\text{Rate} = \frac{\Delta A}{\Delta t}$$

The rate of disappearance of A is proportional to the molar concentration of A.

$$\frac{\Delta A}{\Delta t} \propto [A]$$

The proportionality can be expressed as a constant (k) multiplied by [A].

$$\text{Rate} = \frac{\Delta A}{\Delta t} = k \times [A]$$

This equation is an example of a **rate law,** an expression relating the rate of a reaction to the concentration of reactants. The **specific rate constant** (k) for a reaction is a proportionality constant relating the concentrations of reactants to the rate of the reaction. The magnitude of the specific rate constant depends on the conditions at which the reaction is conducted. If reactant A reacts to form product B quickly, the value of k will be large. If reactant A reacts to form product B slowly, the value of k will be small.

The order of a reaction is the power to which the concentration of a reactant must be raised to give the experimentally observed relationship between concentration and rate. In a **first-order reaction,** the reaction rate is directly proportional to the concentration of only one reactant. The conversion of A to B in a one-step reaction is an example of a first-order reaction; the reaction rate is proportional to the concentration of A raised to the first power: $[A]^1 = [A]$. As a first-order reaction progresses, the rate of reaction decreases, as shown in **Figure 19.22.** This decrease occurs because the concentration of reactant decreases. On a graph, the rate ($\Delta A/\Delta t$) at any point equals the slope of the tangent to the curve at that point. For a first-order reaction, a halving of [A] results in a halving of the reaction rate.

In some kinds of reactions, such as double-replacement, two substances react to give products. The coefficients in the equation for such a reaction are represented by lowercase letters.

$$a\text{A} + b\text{B} \longrightarrow c\text{C} + d\text{D}$$

For a one-step reaction of A with B, the rate of reaction is dependent on the concentrations of both A and B.

$$\text{Rate} = k[\text{A}]^a[\text{B}]^b$$

When each of the exponents a and b in the above rate law equals 1, the reaction is said to be first-order in A, first-order in B, and second-order overall. The overall order of a reaction is the sum of the exponents for the individual reactants.

For any one-step reaction, the experimentally determined exponents in the rate law will be the same as the coefficients a and b in the chemical equation. However, the exponents in the rate law and the coefficients in the equation do not correspond in most real reactions because most reactions are more complex than the one-step reactions used in the examples. Remember, the actual kinetic order of a reaction must be determined by experiment. There is not necessarily a relationship between the kinetic order and the coefficients in the overall chemical equations for complex reactions.

Figure 19.22

The rate of a first-order reaction decreases in direct proportion to the concentration of one reactant. The curved line shows the decrease in concentration of reactant A with time. The short colored lines illustrate the reaction rates at two distinct points of time.

Chem ASAP!

Animation 24
Observe the characteristics of a first-order reaction.

Sample Problem 19-9

The rate law for the one-step reaction $a\text{A} \rightarrow \text{B}$ is of the form Rate $= k[\text{A}]^a$. From the data in the following table, find the kinetic order of the reaction with respect to A and the overall order of the reaction.

Initial concentration of A (mol/L)	Initial rate (mol/L·s)
0.050	3.0×10^{-4}
0.10	12×10^{-4}
0.20	48×10^{-4}

Sample Problem 19-9 (cont.)

1. **ANALYZE** *Plan a problem-solving strategy.*
The initial concentration, the initial rate data, and the form of the rate law are given. This is a one-step reaction. Use these data to find the desired kinetic orders by inspection.

2. **SOLVE** *Apply the problem-solving strategy.*
If a reaction is first-order in A, then $a = 1$ in the rate equation. In that case, the initial rate would be directly proportional to the initial [A]. However, the reaction cannot be first-order in A because a doubling of A causes the rate to increase by four times. This suggests that $a = 2$, because $2^2 = 4$. Increasing [A] fourfold should, therefore, increase the rate sixteenfold ($4^2 = 16$). When the initial concentration of A is increased from 0.050 mol/L to 0.20 mol/L, the initial rate increases from 3.0×10^{-4} mol/L·s to 48×10^{-4} mol/L·s, which is a sixteenfold increase. The reaction is thus second-order in A; it must be second-order overall because A is the only reactant.

3. **EVALUATE** *Does the result make sense?*
The hypothetical reaction given in this problem represents a special case, in that it is a one-step reaction. Remember, for a one-step reaction, the experimentally determined exponents in the rate law are the same as the coefficients a and b in the chemical equation. That is not generally true for most real reactions. For reactions in general, determine the kinetic order from the kinetic data and not from the coefficients in the chemical equation.

Practice Problems

33. Show that the unit of k for a first-order reaction is a reciprocal unit of time, such as a reciprocal second (s^{-1}).

34. Suppose a first-order reaction initially proceeds at a rate of 0.5 mol/L·s. What will be the rate when half the starting material remains? When one-fourth of the starting material remains?

Problem-Solving 34
Solve Problem 34 with the help of an interactive guided tutorial.

Reaction Mechanisms

If enough information were available, you could graph all the energy changes that occur as reactants are converted to products in a chemical reaction. Such a graph would constitute a reaction progress curve. The simplest reaction progress curve would be obtained for an **elementary reaction,** one in which reactants are converted to products in a single step (a one-step reaction). Such a reaction has only one activated complex between reactants and products and thus only one activation-energy peak. Most chemical reactions, however, consist of a number of elementary reactions. A **reaction mechanism** includes all the elementary reactions of a complex reaction. For a complex reaction, the reaction progress curve resembles a series of hills and valleys. Study **Figure 19.23.** The hills correspond to the energies of the activated complexes. Each valley corresponds to the energies of an **intermediate** product, or a product of a reaction that becomes a reactant of another reaction. Intermediates have a significant lifetime compared with an activated complex. They have real ionic or molecular structures and some stability. They are reactive enough, however, to react further to give the final product of the reaction.

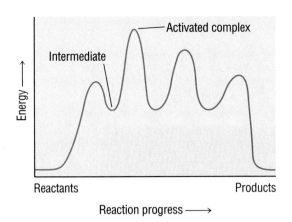

Figure 19.23
A reaction progress curve shows an activation-energy peak for each elementary reaction. Valleys indicate the formation of intermediates. How many elementary reactions are part of this reaction? How many intermediates are formed?

Intermediates do not appear in the overall chemical equation for a reaction. The decomposition of nitrous oxide (N_2O), for example, is believed to occur in two elementary steps:

$$N_2O(g) \longrightarrow N_2(g) + O(g)$$
$$\underline{N_2O(g) + O(g) \longrightarrow N_2(g) + O_2(g)}$$
$$2N_2O(g) \longrightarrow 2N_2(g) + O_2(g)$$

Notice that oxygen atoms are intermediates in this reaction. They disappear when the individual reactants are summed to give the final chemical equation. This illustrates an important general point: The overall chemical equation for a complex reaction gives no information about the reaction mechanism.

section review 19.5

35. Ammonium ions and nitrite ions react in water to form nitrogen gas.

$$NH_4^+(aq) + NO_2^-(aq) \longrightarrow N_2(g) + 2H_2O(l)$$

From the following data, decide the kinetic order of the reaction with respect to NH_4^+, NO_2^-, and the overall order of the reaction.

Initial concentration of NO_2^- (mol/L)	Initial concentration of NH_4^+ (mol/L)	Initial rate (mol/L·s)
0.0100	0.200	5.4×10^{-7}
0.0200	0.200	10.8×10^{-7}
0.0400	0.200	21.5×10^{-7}
0.0600	0.200	32.3×10^{-7}
0.200	0.0202	10.8×10^{-7}
0.200	0.0404	21.6×10^{-7}
0.200	0.0606	32.4×10^{-7}
0.200	0.0808	43.3×10^{-7}

36. Define each term as it applies to chemical reactions.

    a. elementary reaction   **c.** reaction mechanism

    b. intermediate

37. How can an energy diagram be used to analyze a reaction mechanism?

Research and report on the reaction mechanisms for the depletion of ozone in the stratosphere caused by the presence of CFCs.

 Chem ASAP! Assessment 19.5 Check your understanding of the important ideas and concepts in Section 19.5.

DON'T LET GOOD FOOD GO BAD!

The practice of preserving food is not new. For tens of thousands of years, people have salted or smoked meats and have dried fruits and vegetables to preserve them. Food preservation keeps food from spoiling and allows it to be stored for later use. Today, methods for preserving food also include the addition of preservatives, which are inhibitors of chemical and physical processes that cause food to spoil.

Food preservatives are classified into two basic groups—antimicrobials and antioxidants. Antimicrobials prevent the growth of bacteria, yeast, and molds. Antioxidants keep food from oxidizing. When food oxidizes, or reacts with oxygen, it becomes rancid and turns brown. Antioxidants also help reduce the decay of some essential amino acids and the loss of some vitamins.

Preservatives enable food to be produced, transported, purchased by the consumer, and used before it goes bad. Many foods are grown or produced in one location and then sent across the country or even overseas. Without preservatives, these foods would spoil long before they reached their destinations.

The Food and Drug Administration (FDA), a branch of the federal government, is responsible for approving the safety and use of preservatives. As part of the approval process, the manufacturer must demonstrate to the FDA that the chemical is safe. The FDA considers factors such as the quantity to be added to food, the long-term effects of the additive, and the potential toxicity. If the preservative is deemed safe, it is approved for use. If, at some later time, the preservative is found to be dangerous, the FDA can suspend its use.

The FDA requires that manufacturers include preservatives in the list of ingredients on food labels. Some

> Food preservatives are classified into two basic groups— antimicrobials and antioxidants.

common preservatives are BHT, BHA, sulfites, sulfur dioxide, and benzoic acid. BHT (butylated hydroxytoluene) and BHA (butylated hydroxyanisole) are often found in foods that are high in fats and oils. These two antioxidants slow the oxidation reactions that cause undesired flavors, odors, or colors in fats and oils. BHT and BHA are used in foods at a concentration of up to 0.02% of the fat or oil content. For example, if food has 1 g of fat, it can contain only 0.2 mg of either BHT or BHA.

Sulfites and sulfur dioxide have been used in foods for thousands of years. The ancient Egyptians and Romans used these compounds as preservatives. Sulfites and sulfur dioxide are antioxidants and antimicrobials, used mostly on fruit and in fruit juices to prevent discoloration from oxidation and to inhibit the growth of microbes. Sulfites can appear as many different compounds on food labels. Common sulfites include sulfur dioxide, sodium sulfite, sodium bisulfite, potassium bisulfite, sodium metabisulfite, and potassium metabisulfite.

Some people are allergic or sensitive to preservatives. It is especially important for these people to read food labels and avoid foods that have certain preservatives.

CHEMISTRY IN CAREERS

☆☆☆☆☆☆☆☆☆☆☆☆☆☆☆☆☆☆☆☆

FDA INSPECTOR
Help prevent outbreaks of food-borne illnesses.
See page 877.

CHEMIST NEEDED
Enviro. Lab. GC. Must know FDA methods, troubleshooting;

TAKE IT TO THE NET

Find out more about career opportunities:
www.phschool.com

CHEMICAL SPECIALIST
Local food service distributor seek responsible self-motivated indivic

Take It to the NET
For interactive study and
review, go to www.phschool.com

KEY TERMS

- activated complex *p. 536*
- activation energy *p. 535*
- catalyst *p. 537*
- chemical equilibrium *p. 540*
- collision theory *p. 535*
- elementary reaction *p. 568*
- entropy *p. 552*
- equilibrium constant (K_{eq}) *p. 545*
- equilibrium position *p. 540*

- first-order reaction *p. 566*
- free energy *p. 549*
- Gibbs free-energy change (ΔG) *p. 561*
- inhibitor *p. 538*
- intermediate *p. 568*
- law of disorder *p. 552*
- Le Châtelier's principle *p. 541*
- nonspontaneous reaction *p. 550*

- rate *p. 533*
- rate law *p. 566*
- reaction mechanism *p. 568*
- reversible reaction *p. 539*
- specific rate constant *p. 566*
- spontaneous reaction *p. 550*
- standard entropy (S^0) *p. 558*
- transition state *p. 536*

KEY EQUATIONS

- $K_{eq} = \dfrac{[C]^c \times [D]^d}{[A]^a \times [B]^b}$

- $\Delta G^0 = \Delta H^0 - T\Delta S^0$

- $\Delta S^0 = S^0(\text{products}) - S^0(\text{reactants})$

- $\Delta G^0 = \Delta G_f^0(\text{products}) - \Delta G_f^0(\text{reactants})$

CONCEPT SUMMARY

19.1 Rates of Reaction
- The rate at which a chemical reaction proceeds is determined by the number of collisions between reacting particles and the energy with which the particles collide.

19.2 Reversible Reactions and Equilibrium
- In principle, all reactions are reversible. Reactants go to products in the forward direction and products go to reactants in the reverse direction.
- The point at which the rates of conversion of reactants to products and of products to reactants are equal is the equilibrium position.
- Changes in the equilibrium position can be predicted by applying Le Châtelier's principle.

19.3 Determining Whether a Reaction Will Occur
- The natural tendency for all things to go to lower heat content (enthalpy) and greater randomness (entropy) determines whether a reaction will occur (is spontaneous).

19.4 Calculating Entropy and Free Energy
- Standard entropy and free-energy changes can be calculated from standard entropies (S^0), standard enthalpies of formation (H_f^0), and standard free energies of formation (G_f^0).

19.5 The Progress of Chemical Reactions
- The rate of a chemical reaction is dependent on the rate constant (k) and the kinetic order of the reaction.

CHAPTER CONCEPT MAP

Use these terms to construct a concept map that organizes the major ideas of this chapter.

 Chem ASAP! Concept Map 19
Create your Concept Map using the computer.

reaction rate

equilibrium

collision theory

factors affecting rate

reaction mechanism

spontaneous reaction

free energy

rate law

entropy

reversible reaction

heat (enthalpy)

CONCEPT PRACTICE

38. Explain the collision theory of reactions. *19.1*

39. How is the activation energy of a reaction like a wall or barrier? *19.1*

40. Where is the formula of a catalyst written in a chemical equation? Why? *19.1*

41. How is the rate of a reaction influenced by a catalyst? How do catalysts make this possible? *19.1*

42. Which of these statements is true? *19.1*
   a. All chemical reactions can be sped up by increasing the temperature.
   b. Once a chemical reaction gets started, the reacting particles no longer have to collide for products to form.
   c. Enzymes are biological catalysts.

43. When the gas to a stove is turned on, the gas does not burn unless lit by a flame. Once lit, however, the gas burns until turned off. Explain these observations in terms of the effect of temperature on reaction rate. *19.1*

44. In your own words, define a reversible reaction. *19.2*

45. A reversible reaction has reached a state of dynamic chemical equilibrium. What does this information tell you? *19.2*

46. How do the rates of the forward and reverse reactions compare at a state of dynamic chemical equilibrium? *19.2*

47. What is Le Châtelier's principle? Use it to explain why carbonated drinks go flat when their containers are left open. *19.2*

48. Give the equilibrium-constant expression for the formation of ammonia from hydrogen and nitrogen. *19.2*

$$N_2(g) + 3H_2(g) \rightleftharpoons 2NH_3(g)$$

49. Write the expression for the equilibrium constant for each reaction. *19.2*
   a. $4H_2(g) + CS_2(g) \rightleftharpoons CH_4(g) + 2H_2S(g)$
   b. $PCl_5(g) \rightleftharpoons PCl_3(g) + Cl_2(g)$
   c. $2NO(g) + O_2(g) \rightleftharpoons 2NO_2(g)$
   d. $CO(g) + H_2O(g) \rightleftharpoons H_2(g) + CO_2(g)$

50. Comment on the favorability of product formation in each reaction. *19.2*
   a. $H_2(g) + F_2(g) \rightleftharpoons 2HF(g)$; $K_{eq} = 1 \times 10^{13}$
   b. $SO_2(g) + NO_2(g) \rightleftharpoons NO(g) + SO_3(g)$; $K_{eq} = 1 \times 10^2$

51. What is free energy? How can knowing the free energy of a reaction help predict whether the reaction will be spontaneous? *19.3*

52. The reaction of hydrogen and oxygen gas proceeds with a large decrease of free energy. The reaction is very slow at room temperature but occurs with explosive rapidity in the presence of a flame or ignition wire. Explain. *19.3*

53. The products in a spontaneous process are more ordered than the reactants. Is this entropy change favorable or unfavorable? *19.3*

54. What is the meaning of entropy? *19.3.*

55. Which system has the lower entropy? *19.3*
   a. completed jigsaw puzzle or separate jigsaw pieces
   b. 50 mL of liquid water or 50 mL of ice
   c. 10 g of sodium chloride crystals or a solution containing 10 g of sodium chloride

56. Predict the direction of the entropy change in each reaction. *19.3*
   a. $CaCO_3(s) \longrightarrow CaO(s) + CO_2(g)$
   b. $NH_3(g) + HCl(g) \longrightarrow NH_4Cl(s)$
   c. $2NaHCO_3(s) \longrightarrow$
   $$Na_2CO_3(s) + H_2O(g) + CO_2(g)$$
   d. $CaO(s) + CO_2(g) \longrightarrow CaCO_3(s)$

57. Is it true that all spontaneous processes are exothermic? Explain your answer. *19.3*

58. At normal atmospheric pressure, steam condenses to liquid water even though this is an unfavorable entropy change. Explain. *19.3*

59. What two factors together determine whether a reaction is spontaneous? *19.3*

60. For the decomposition of $CaCO_3(s)$ to $CaO(s)$ and $CO_2(g)$ at 298 K the ΔH_f^0 is 178.5 kJ/mol and the ΔS^0 is 161.6 J/K·mol. Is the reaction spontaneous or nonspontaneous at this temperature? *19.4*

61. What is meant by each term? *19.5*
   a. specific rate constant
   b. first-order reaction
   c. rate law

62. The rate law for the reaction
   $$NO(g) + O_3(g) \longrightarrow NO_2(g) + O_2(g)$$
   is first-order in NO and O_3, and second-order overall. Write the complete rate law for this reaction. *19.5*

63. Half of the reactant in a first-order reaction has disappeared in 50 minutes. How many minutes are required for this particular reaction to be 75% complete? *19.5*

64. Sketch a potential-energy diagram for the overall reaction with the following mechanism.

$$2NO(g) \longrightarrow N_2O_2(g) \text{ (fast)}$$
$$N_2O_2(g) + O_2(g) \longrightarrow 2NO_2(g) \text{ (slow)}$$

Write the balanced equation for the overall reaction. *19.5*

CONCEPT MASTERY

65. Consider the decomposition of N_2O_5 in carbon tetrachloride (CCl_4) at 45 °C.

$$2N_2O_5(soln) \rightleftharpoons 4NO_2(g) + O_2(g)$$

The reaction is first-order in N_2O_5, with the specific rate constant 6.08×10^{-4}/s. Calculate the reaction rate at these conditions.
   a. $[N_2O_5] = 0.200$ mol/L
   b. $[N_2O_5] = 0.319$ mol/L

66. Which pieces of information are sufficient to determine whether a reaction will be spontaneous?
   a. The reaction is exothermic.
   b. Entropy is increased in the reaction.
   c. Free energy is released in the reaction.

67. For the reaction $A + B \rightleftharpoons C$, the activation energy of the forward reaction is 5 kJ and the total energy change is −20 kJ. What is the activation energy of the reverse reaction?

68. A large box is divided into two compartments with a door between them. Equal quantities of two different monatomic gases are placed in the compartments, as shown in **(a).** The door between the compartments is opened and the gas particles immediately start to mix. See **(b).** Why would it be highly unlikely for the situation in **(b)** to progress to the situation shown in **(c)?**

(a)

(b)

(c)

69. Would you expect the entropy to increase in each of the following reactions?
   a. $C(s) + O_2(g) \longrightarrow CO_2(g)$
   b. $Al_2O_3(s) \longrightarrow 2Al(s) + \frac{3}{2}O_2(g)$
   c. $2N(g) \longrightarrow N_2(g)$
   d. $N_2(g) \longrightarrow 2N(g)$

70. What would be the effect on the equilibrium position if the volume is decreased in each reaction?
   a. $4HCl(g) + O_2(g) \rightleftharpoons 2Cl_2(g) + 2H_2O(g)$
   b. $CO_2(s) \rightleftharpoons CO_2(g)$
   c. $CaCO_3(s) \rightleftharpoons CaO(s) + CO_2(g)$

71. A mixture at equilibrium at 827 °C contains 0.552 mol CO_2, 0.552 mol H_2, 0.448 mol CO, and 0.448 mol H_2O. The balanced equation is $CO_2(g) + H_2(g) \rightleftharpoons CO(g) + H_2O(g)$. What is the value of K_{eq}?

72. Write the equilibrium-constant expression for each reaction.
   a. $I_2(g) + Cl_2(g) \rightleftharpoons 2ICl(g)$
   b. $2NO_2(g) \rightleftharpoons 2NO(g) + O_2(g)$
   c. $2SO_2(g) + O_2(g) \rightleftharpoons 2SO_3(g)$
   d. $Cl_2(g) + PCl_3(g) \rightleftharpoons PCl_5(g)$

73. The freezing of liquid water at 0 °C can be represented as follows.

$$H_2O(l, d = 1.00 \text{ g/cm}^3) \rightleftharpoons$$
$$H_2O(s, d = 0.92 \text{ g/cm}^3)$$

Explain why the application of pressure causes ice to melt.

74. Sketch an energy profile curve for this gas-phase reaction.

$$F(g) + H_2(g) \rightleftharpoons HF(g) + H(g)$$

The reaction has an activation energy of 22 kJ, and the total energy change is −103 kJ.

75. The reaction between diamond (carbon) and oxygen is spontaneous. What can you say about the speed of this reaction?

$$C(s, \text{diamond}) + O_2(g) \longrightarrow CO_2(g)$$

76. Predict what will happen if a catalyst is added to a slow reversible reaction. What happens to the equilibrium position?

77. Use the standard entropy data of **Table 19.2** to calculate the standard entropy change (ΔS^0) for this reaction.

$$2NO(g) + 3H_2O(g) \longrightarrow 2NH_3(g) + \frac{5}{2}O_2(g)$$

CRITICAL THINKING

78. Choose the term that best completes the second relationship.

   a. reaction : intermediate   life span : _____
     (1) birth   (3) adolescence
     (2) products   (4) 75 years

   b. catalyst : inhibitor   sunshine : _____
     (1) clouds   (3) wind
     (2) photosynthesis   (4) energy

79. An increase in temperature raises the energy of the collisions between reactant molecules. An increase in the concentration of reactants increases the number of collisions. What is the effect of a catalyst on the collisions between molecules?

80. Make a list of five things you did today that resulted in an increase in entropy.

CUMULATIVE REVIEW

81. Name each ion and identify it as an anion or a cation.
   a. F^- **c.** P^{3-} **e.** Na^+ **g.** O^{2-}
   b. Cu^{2+} **d.** H^+ **f.** I^- **h.** Mg^{2+}

82. Explain how crystalline and amorphous substances differ.

83. What is wrong with saying that solid potassium chloride is composed of KCl molecules?

84. Name the following compounds and give the charge on the anion for each.
   a. $NaClO_4$ **c.** $Ca_3(PO_4)_2$ **e.** Na_2SO_4
   b. $KMnO_4$ **d.** $MgCO_3$ **f.** $K_2Cr_2O_7$

85. List some properties that are typical of ionic compounds.

86. Write electron configurations and draw electron dot structures for the following elements.
   a. Ge   **b.** Ca   **c.** O   **d.** Ar   **e.** Br   **f.** P

87. Write the formula for each ionic compound using electron dot structures.
   a. LiBr   **b.** $AlCl_3$ **c.** MgF_2 **d.** Na_2S

88. Write the electron configuration and draw the electron dot structure for each.
   a. Ca^{2+} **b.** Li^+ **c.** Br^- **d.** S^{2-}

89. Which atoms from the following list would you expect to form positive ions, and which would you expect to form negative ions?
   a. Cl   **c.** P   **e.** Cu   **g.** K   **i.** N
   b. Ca   **d.** Se   **f.** Sn   **h.** Fe   **j.** Ni

CONCEPT CHALLENGE

90. Is eating sugar candy really bad for your teeth? Tooth decay is the result of the dissolving of tooth enamel ($Ca_5(PO_4)_3OH$). In the mouth the following equilibrium is established.

$$Ca_5(PO_4)_3OH(s) \rightleftharpoons$$
$$5Ca^{2+}(aq) + 3PO_4{}^{3-}(aq) + OH^-(aq)$$

When sugar ferments on the teeth, H^+ is produced. What effect does this increased H^+ have on tooth enamel?

91. The following data were collected for the decomposition of compound AB into its elements. The reaction is first-order in AB.

[AB] (mol/L)	Time (s)
0.300	0
0.246	50
0.201	100
0.165	150
0.135	200
0.111	250
0.090	300
0.075	350

   a. Make a graph of concentration (*y*-axis) versus time (*x*-axis).
   b. Determine the rate of this reaction at $t = 100$ seconds and $t = 250$ seconds.

92. When table sugar, or sucrose, is dissolved in an acidic solution, the sucrose slowly decomposes into two simpler sugars: fructose and glucose. Use the graph to answer these questions.

   a. How many grams of sucrose decompose in the first 30 minutes?
   b. How many grams of sucrose decompose in the 30-minute interval between 90 and 120 minutes?

Select the choice that best answers each question or completes each statement.

1. Which reaction is represented by the following expression for an equilibrium constant?

$$K_{eq} = \frac{[CO]^2 \times [O_2]}{[CO_2]^2}$$

   a. $2CO_2 \rightleftharpoons O_2 + 2CO$
   b. $CO_2^2 \rightleftharpoons O_2 + 2CO^2$
   c. $O_2 + 2CO \rightleftharpoons 2CO_2$
   d. $O_2 + CO_2 \rightleftharpoons CO_2^2$

2. In which process is there an entropy increase?
   a. Dry ice sublimes.
   b. Liquid wax solidifies.
   c. Dew forms from water vapor.
   d. Liquid water forms from gaseous hydrogen and oxygen.

3. Based on the equilibrium equation, which change will *not* increase the production of $CH_3OH(g)$?
   $$CO(g) + 2H_2(g) \rightleftharpoons CH_3OH(g) + heat$$
   a. adding heat
   b. removing CH_3OH
   c. adding CO
   d. increasing the pressure

4. Which of the following statements is true?
   a. A rate law relates the rate of a reaction to the concentration of the reactants.
   b. A reaction with a very large activation energy will occur very rapidly.
   c. When a reaction reaches equilibrium, the forward reaction stops.
   d. Any reactant particles that collide will react to form product.

Use the table to answer questions 5 and 6.

ΔS	ΔH	ΔG	Spontaneous?
+	−	(a)	Yes
+	(b)	+ or −	At high T
(c)	+	+	No
−	−	(d)	At low T

5. The value of ΔG depends on the enthalpy (ΔH) and entropy (ΔS) terms for a reaction. The value of ΔG also varies as a function of temperature. Use the data in the table to identify the missing entries (a), (b), (c), and (d).

6. Which of these reactions would you expect to be spontaneous at relatively low temperatures? At relatively high temperatures?
   (1) $H_2O(l) \longrightarrow H_2O(s)$
   (2) $H_2O(g) \longrightarrow H_2O(l)$
   (3) $H_2O(s) \longrightarrow H_2O(l)$

Use the atomic windows to answer question 7.

7. The atomic windows represent different degrees of entropy. Arrange the windows in order of increasing entropy.

For each question there are two statements. Decide whether each statement is true or false. Then decide whether Statement II is a correct explanation for Statement I.

Statement I		Statement II
8. A catalyst lowers the activation energy for a reaction.	BECAUSE	A catalyst makes a reaction more exothermic.
9. An exothermic reaction is always a spontaneous reaction.	BECAUSE	Exothermic reactions release heat to the surroundings.
10. The entropy of ice is greater than the entropy of steam.	BECAUSE	The density of ice is greater than the density of steam.
11. The rate of a chemical reaction is affected by a change in temperature.	BECAUSE	The kinetic energy of particles is related to the temperature.
12. A very large value for an equilibrium constant indicates that products are favored at equilibrium.	BECAUSE	The ratio of products to reactants at equilibrium is always > 1.

Chapter 20 ACIDS AND BASES

FEATURES

DISCOVER IT!
Effect of Foods on Baking Soda

SMALL-SCALE LAB
Ionization Constants of Weak Acids

MINI LAB
Indicators from Natural Sources

CHEMath
Using Logarithms

CHEMISTRY SERVING ...
THE ENVIRONMENT
Rain Like Vinegar

CHEMISTRY IN CAREERS
Stone Conservator

LINK TO LIBRARY SCIENCE
Chemistry Rescues Crumbling Books

LINK TO HEALTH
Tooth Decay

Stay current with **SCIENCE NEWS**
Find out more about acids and bases:
www.phschool.com

These tart-tasting fruits contain a weak acid called citric acid.

DISCOVER IT!

EFFECT OF FOODS ON BAKING SODA

You need baking soda (sodium hydrogen carbonate, $NaHCO_3$), a large paper plate, a knife, paper towels, and a variety of fruits and vegetables (e.g., a celery stalk, a banana, a grape, a tomato, a lemon, an apple, an orange, a grapefruit).

1. Carefully cut the fruits and vegetables into small pieces and place them on the plate. Make sure the pieces are well separated from each other. Be sure to wipe any juice off the knife after cutting each fruit.

2. Sprinkle a pinch of baking soda on each sample.

What do you observe? Is there any relationship between what you observe and which foods you know from experience have a sour taste? After reading about acids and bases, provide an explanation for what you observed.

DESCRIBING ACIDS AND BASES

Some ants can give painful stings when threatened or disturbed. Certain ant species called formicines have poison glands that produce venom containing formic acid. Formicines protect themselves by spraying this venom on their predators. Formic acid can stun or even kill the ants' most common enemies. A formicine attack on a human, however, is much less severe, usually resulting only in blistered skin. **What are some of the properties of acids?**

objectives
- ▶ List the properties of acids and bases
- ▶ Name an acid or base when given the formula

key terms
- ▶ acid
- ▶ base

Properties of Acids and Bases

Did you know that acids and bases play a central role in much of the chemistry that affects your daily life? Most manufacturing processes use acids or bases. Your body needs acids and bases to function properly. Vinegar, carbonated drinks, and foods such as citrus fruits contain acids. The electrolyte in a car battery is an acid. Bases are present in many commercial products, including antacid tablets and household cleaning agents. **Figure 20.1** shows some of the many products that contain acids and bases. As you read this chapter, you will learn about the qualitative and quantitative aspects of acids and bases. You will see how these two classes of compounds ionize or dissociate in water. And you will learn how pH is used to describe the concentrations of acidic and basic solutions.

Figure 20.1

All of these items contain acids or bases, or produce acids or bases upon dissolving in water. Tomatoes contain ascorbic acid; tea contains tannic acid. The base calcium hydroxide is a component of mortar, which was used to build the Great Wall of China. Antacids use a variety of bases to neutralize excess stomach acid.

As you just read and perhaps already knew, many common items contain acids. Acids have several distinctive properties with which you are probably familiar. Acidic compounds give foods a tart or sour taste. For example, vinegar contains ethanoic acid, sometimes called acetic acid. Lemons, which taste sour enough to make your mouth pucker, contain citric acid. What type of acid do you think limes contain?

Aqueous solutions of acids are electrolytes. Recall from Chapter 17 that electrolytes conduct electricity. Some acid solutions are strong electrolytes and others are weak electrolytes. Acids cause certain chemical dyes, called indicators, to change color. Many metals, such as zinc and magnesium, react with aqueous solutions of acids to produce hydrogen gas. Acids react with compounds containing hydroxide ions to form water and a salt.

(a)

(b)

Figure 20.2

(a) *Carbonated soft drinks contain carbonic acid (H₂CO₃), and many also contain phosphoric acid (H₃PO₄). These two acids give a drink its fizz and sharp, tangy taste.* **(b)** *Sodium hydroxide (NaOH) is used to prepare wood pulp for the manufacture of paper.*

Bases are compounds that react with acids to form water and a salt. Milk of magnesia (a suspension of magnesium hydroxide in water) is a base used to treat the problem of excess stomach acid. Aqueous solutions of bases taste bitter and feel slippery. Like acids, bases will change the color of an acid–base indicator and can be strong or weak electrolytes.

Names and Formulas of Acids and Bases

An **acid** is a compound that produces hydrogen ions when dissolved in water. Therefore, the chemical formulas of acids are of the general form HX, where X is a monatomic or polyatomic anion. When the compound $HCl(g)$ (hydrogen chloride) dissolves in water to form $HCl(aq)$, it is named as an acid. How, then, is an acid named? To illustrate the naming of an acid, consider the following three rules as applied to the acid HX dissolved in water. Notice that the rules focus on the name of the anion, in particular the suffix of the anion name. **Table 20.1** summarizes these rules.

1. When the name of the anion (X) ends in *-ide*, the acid name begins with the prefix *hydro-*. The stem of the anion has the suffix *-ic* and is followed by the word *acid*. Therefore, $HCl(aq)$ (X = chloride) is named *hydrochloric acid*. $H_2S(aq)$ (X = sulfide) is named *hydrosulfuric acid*.
2. When the anion name ends in *-ite*, the acid name is the stem of the anion with the suffix *-ous*, followed by the word *acid*. Thus $H_2SO_3(aq)$ (X = sulfite) is named *sulfurous acid*.
3. When the anion name ends in *-ate*, the acid name is the stem of the anion with the suffix *-ic*, followed by the word *acid*. Thus $HNO_3(aq)$ (X = nitrate) is named *nitric acid*.

These rules can be used in reverse fashion to write the formulas of acids when given their names. For example, what is the formula of chloric acid? According to Rule 3, chloric acid (*-ic* ending) must be a combination of hydrogen ion (H^+) and chlor*ate* ion (ClO_3^-). The formula of chloric acid is $HClO_3$. What is the formula of hydrobromic acid? Following Rule 1, hydrobromic acid (*hydro-* prefix and *-ic* suffix) must be a combination of hydrogen ion and bromide ion (Br^-). The formula of hydrobromic acid is HBr. What is the formula for phosphorous acid? Using Rule 2, hydrogen ion and phosphite ion (PO_3^{3-}) must be the components of phosphorous acid. The formula of phosphorous acid is H_3PO_3. (*Note:* Do not confuse *phosphorous* with *phosphorus*, the element name.)

Table 20.1

Naming Acids			
Anion ending	Example	Acid name	Example
-ide	Cl⁻ chloride	*hydro-*(stem)*-ic acid*	*hydrochloric acid*
-ite	SO_3^{2-} sulf*ite*	(stem)*-ous acid*	sulfur*ous acid*
-ate	NO_3^- nit*rate*	(stem)*-ic acid*	nit*ric acid*

A **base** is a compound that produces hydroxide ions when dissolved in water. Ionic compounds that are bases are named in the same way as any other ionic compound—the name of the cation followed by the name of the anion. For example, NaOH, a base used in making paper pulp, detergents, and soap, is called sodium hydroxide. What would you call $Ca(OH)_2$? You write the formulas for bases by balancing the ionic charges, just as you do for any ionic compound.

Sample Problem 20-1

Name these compounds as acids.
 a. HClO   **b.** HCN   **c.** H_3PO_4

1. *ANALYZE Plan a problem-solving strategy.*
   The rules for naming acids can be applied because the formulas of the acids are given.

2. *SOLVE Apply the problem-solving strategy.*
   a. Use Rule 2. The anion name (hypochlorite) ends in *-ite,* so add the suffix *-ous* to the anion stem, followed by the word *acid*. The correct name is hypochlorous acid.
   b. Use Rule 1. The anion name (cyanide) ends in *-ide,* so this acid name begins with the prefix *hydro-* and ends with the suffix *-ic,* followed by the word *acid*. The correct name is hydrocyanic acid.
   c. Use Rule 3. The anion name (phosphate) ends in *-ate.* So add the suffix *-ic* to the anion stem (in this case, modified slightly to *phosphor*), followed by the word *acid*. The correct name is phosphoric acid.

3. *EVALUATE Do the results make sense?*
   The names are consistent with the indicated rules.

Practice Problems

1. Name each acid or base.
   a. HF   **c.** KOH
   b. HNO_3 **d.** H_2SO_4
2. Write formulas for each acid or base.
   a. chromic acid
   b. iron(II) hydroxide
   c. hydriodic acid
   d. lithium hydroxide

Chem ASAP!

Problem-Solving 2
Solve Problem 2 with the help of an interactive guided tutorial.

---

section review 20.1

3. Identify each property as applying to an acid, a base, or both.
   a. bitter taste   **c.** indicator color change
   b. electrolyte   **d.** sour taste

4. Write the formula for each acid or base.
   a. barium hydroxide   **c.** rubidium hydroxide
   b. hydrobromic acid   **d.** hydroselenic acid

5. Name each acid or base.
   a. HF   **c.** H_2CO_3
   b. $HClO_3$ **d.** $Al(OH)_3$

 Chem ASAP! Assessment 20.1 Check your understanding of the important ideas and concepts in Section 20.1.

HYDROGEN IONS AND ACIDITY

objectives

▶ Given the hydrogen-ion or hydroxide-ion concentration, classify a solution as neutral, acidic, or basic
▶ Convert hydrogen-ion concentrations into values of pH and hydroxide-ion concentrations into values of pOH

key terms

▶ hydroxide ion (OH⁻)
▶ hydronium ion (H_3O^+)
▶ self-ionization
▶ neutral solution
▶ ion-product constant for water (K_w)
▶ acidic solution
▶ basic solution
▶ alkaline solutions
▶ pH

A patient is brought to a hospital unconscious and with a fruity odor on his breath. The doctor suspects the patient has fallen into a diabetic coma. To confirm her diagnosis, she orders several tests, including one of the acidity of the patient's blood. The results from this test will be expressed in units of pH, not molar concentration. **How is the pH scale used to indicate the acidity of a solution, and why is this scale used?**

Hydrogen Ions from Water

As you already know, water molecules are highly polar and are in continuous motion, even at room temperature. Occasionally, the collisions between water molecules are energetic enough to transfer a hydrogen ion from one water molecule to another. See **Figure 20.3.** A water molecule that loses a hydrogen ion becomes a negatively charged **hydroxide ion (OH⁻).** A water molecule that gains a hydrogen ion becomes a positively charged **hydronium ion (H_3O^+).**

$$H_2O \quad + \quad H_2O \quad \longrightarrow \quad H_3O^+ \quad + \quad OH^-$$

Water molecule · Water molecule · Hydronium ion · Hydroxide ion

Figure 20.3

What is the name and formula of the particle that results when a water molecule gains a hydrogen ion? How is a hydroxide ion formed from a water molecule?

The reaction in which two water molecules produce ions is called the **self-ionization** of water. This reaction can also be written as a simple dissociation.

$$H_2O(l) \rightleftharpoons H^+(aq) \quad + \quad OH^-(aq)$$

Hydrogen ion   Hydroxide ion

In water or aqueous solution, hydrogen ions (H^+) are always joined to water molecules as hydronium ions (H_3O^+). The hydronium ions are themselves solvated to form species such as $H_9O_4^+$. Hydrogen ions in aqueous solution have several names. Some chemists call them protons. Others prefer to call them hydrogen ions, hydronium ions, or solvated protons. In this textbook, either H^+ or H_3O^+ is used to represent hydrogen ions in aqueous solution.

The self-ionization of water occurs to a very small extent. In pure water at 25 °C, the concentration of hydrogen ions ($[H^+]$) and the concentration of hydroxide ions ($[OH^-]$) are each only $1.0 \times 10^{-7}M$. This means that the concentrations of H^+ and OH^- are equal in pure water. Any aqueous solution in which $[H^+]$ and $[OH^-]$ are equal is described as a **neutral solution.**

In any aqueous solution, $[H^+]$ and $[OH^-]$ are interdependent. In other words, when $[H^+]$ increases, $[OH^-]$ decreases. When $[H^+]$ decreases, $[OH^-]$ increases. Le Châtelier's principle, which you learned about in Chapter 19, applies here. If additional ions (either hydrogen ions or hydroxide ions) are added to a solution, the equilibrium shifts. The concentration of the other type of ion decreases. More water molecules are formed in the process.

$$H^+(aq) + OH^-(aq) \rightleftharpoons H_2O(l)$$

For aqueous solutions, the product of the hydrogen-ion concentration and the hydroxide-ion concentration equals 1.0×10^{-14}.

$$[H^+] \times [OH^-] = 1.0 \times 10^{-14}$$

The product of the concentrations of the hydrogen ions and hydroxide ions in water is called the **ion-product constant for water** (K_w).

$$K_w = [H^+] \times [OH^-] = 1.0 \times 10^{-14}$$

Not all solutions are neutral. When some substances dissolve in water, they release hydrogen ions. For example, when hydrogen chloride dissolves in water, it forms hydrochloric acid. How does hydrochloric acid differ from hydrogen chloride?

$$HCl(g) \xrightarrow{H_2O} H^+(aq) + Cl^-(aq)$$

In such a solution, the hydrogen-ion concentration is greater than the hydroxide-ion concentration. The hydroxide ions are present from the self-ionization of water. An **acidic solution** is one in which $[H^+]$ is greater than $[OH^-]$. Therefore, the $[H^+]$ of an acidic solution is greater than $1.0 \times 10^{-7}M$.

When sodium hydroxide dissolves in water, it forms hydroxide ions in solution.

$$NaOH(s) \xrightarrow{H_2O} Na^+(aq) + OH^-(aq)$$

In such a solution, the hydrogen-ion concentration is less than the hydroxide-ion concentration. The hydrogen ions are present from the self-ionization of water. A **basic solution** is one in which $[H^+]$ is less than $[OH^-]$. Therefore, the $[H^+]$ of a basic solution is less than $1.0 \times 10^{-7}M$. Basic solutions are also known as **alkaline solutions.** Look at **Figure 20.4.** What are the names of the acids and bases shown?

Figure 20.4

(a) One of these two chemical reagents is an acid and the other is a base. Which of these reagents would increase the hydrogen-ion concentration when added to an aqueous solution? Which would increase the hydroxide-ion concentration? *(b)* Unrefined hydrochloric acid, commonly known as muriatic acid, is used to clean stone buildings and swimming pools. *(c)* Sodium hydroxide, or lye, is commonly used as a drain cleaner.

(a)

(b)

(c)

Sample Problem 20-2

If the $[H^+]$ in a solution is $1.0 \times 10^{-5}M$, is the solution acidic, basic, or neutral? What is the $[OH^-]$ of this solution?

1. **ANALYZE** *List the knowns and the unknowns.*

Knowns:
- $[H^+] = 1.0 \times 10^{-5}M$
- Ion-product constant for water:
  $K_w = [H^+] \times [OH^-] = 1 \times 10^{-14}$

Unknowns:
- solution = acidic, basic, or neutral?
- $[OH^-] = ?M$

2. **CALCULATE** *Solve for the unknowns.*
$[H^+] = 1.0 \times 10^{-5}M$. Because this is greater than $1.0 \times 10^{-7}M$, the solution is acidic. By definition, $K_w = [H^+] \times [OH^-]$.

Therefore, $[OH^-] = \dfrac{K_w}{[H^+]}$.

Substituting the known numerical values, $[OH^-]$ is computed as follows.

$$[OH^-] = \frac{1.0 \times 10^{-14}}{1.0 \times 10^{-5}M} = 1.0 \times 10^{-9}M$$

3. **EVALUATE** *Do the results make sense?*
If $[H^+]$ is greater than $1.0 \times 10^{-7}M$, then $[OH^-]$ must be less than $1.0 \times 10^{-7}M$. At $1 \times 10^{-9}M$, $[OH^-]$ is less than $1 \times 10^{-7}M$. Notice that when the concentration of the acid is 1.0×10^{-x} and the concentration of the base is 1.0×10^{-y}, $x + y = 14$. In this special case, you can easily find the value of $[H^+]$ when you know $[OH^-]$, or vice versa. To do so, subtract the exponent of the known, either $[H^+]$ or $[OH^-]$, from 14. For example, if

$$[H^+] = 1.0 \times 10^{-9}M,$$
$$\text{then } [OH^-] = 1.0 \times 10^{-(14-9)}M$$
$$= 1.0 \times 10^{-5}M.$$

Practice Problems

6. If the hydroxide-ion concentration of an aqueous solution is $1.0 \times 10^{-3}M$, what is the $[H^+]$ in the solution? Is the solution acidic, basic, or neutral?

7. Classify each solution as acidic, basic, or neutral.
   a. $[H^+] = 6.0 \times 10^{-10}M$
   b. $[OH^-] = 3.0 \times 10^{-2}M$
   c. $[H^+] = 2.0 \times 10^{-7}M$
   d. $[OH^-] = 1.0 \times 10^{-7}M$

The pH Concept

Expressing hydrogen-ion concentration in molarity is cumbersome. A more widely used system for expressing $[H^+]$ is the pH scale, proposed in 1909 by the Danish scientist Søren Sørensen (1868–1939). On the pH scale, which ranges from 0 to 14, neutral solutions have a pH of 7. A pH of 0 is strongly acidic. What is a solution with a pH of 14? Calculating the pH of a solution is straightforward. The **pH** of a solution is the negative logarithm of the hydrogen-ion concentration. The pH may be represented mathematically using the following equation.

$$pH = -\log[H^+]$$

In a neutral solution, $[H^+] = 1 \times 10^{-7}M$. The pH of a neutral solution is 7.0.

$$\begin{aligned} pH &= -\log(1 \times 10^{-7}) \\ &= -(\log 1 + \log 10^{-7}) \\ &= -(0.0 + (-7.0)) \\ &= 7.0 \end{aligned}$$

To summarize, the pH of pure water or a neutral aqueous solution is 7.0. A solution in which $[H^+]$ is greater than $1 \times 10^{-7}M$ has a pH less than 7.0 and is acidic. A solution with a pH greater than 7 is basic and has a $[H^+]$ of less than $1 \times 10^{-7}M$. See **Figure 20.5** for a visual representation of this information.

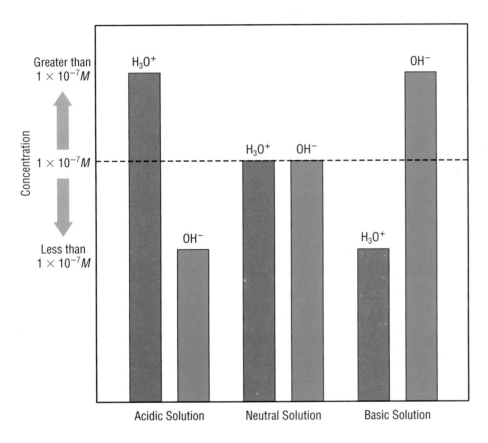

Figure 20.5
In acidic solutions, [H⁺] is greater than [OH⁻]. In basic solutions, [OH⁻] is greater than [H⁺]. Neutral solutions are those in which [H⁺] is equal to [OH⁻].

- Acidic solution: pH < 7.0 $[H^+]$ greater than $1 \times 10^{-7}M$

- Neutral solution: pH = 7.0 $[H^+]$ equals $1 \times 10^{-7}M$

- Basic solution: pH > 7.0 $[H^+]$ less than $1 \times 10^{-7}M$

The pH values of several common aqueous solutions are listed in **Table 20.2** on the following page. The table also summarizes the relationship among $[H^+]$, $[OH^-]$, and pH. You may notice that pH can sometimes be read from the value of $[H^+]$. If $[H^+]$ is written in scientific notation and has a coefficient of 1, then the pH of the solution equals the exponent, with the sign changed from minus to plus. For example, a solution with $[H^+] = 1 \times 10^{-2}M$ has a pH of 2.0. What is the pH of a solution with $[H^+] = 1 \times 10^{-4}M$?

Table 20.2

Relationship among [H⁺], [OH⁻], and pH			
$[H^+]$ (mol/L)	$[OH^-]$ (mol/L)	pH	Aqueous system

In a definition similar to that of pH, the pOH of a solution equals the negative logarithm of the hydroxide-ion concentration.

$$pOH = -\log[OH^-]$$

A neutral solution has a pOH of 7. A solution with a pOH less than 7 is basic. A solution with a pOH greater than 7 is acidic. A simple relationship between pH and pOH makes it easy to find either one when the other is known.

$$pH + pOH = 14$$
$$pH = 14 - pOH$$
$$pOH = 14 - pH$$

For pH calculations, you should express the hydrogen-ion concentration in scientific notation. For example, a hydrogen-ion concentration of $0.0010M$, rewritten as $1.0 \times 10^{-3}M$ in scientific notation, has two significant figures. The pH of this solution is 3.00, with the two numbers to the right of the decimal point representing the two significant figures in the concentration. A solution with a pH of 3.00 is acidic, as shown in **Figure 20.6.** How many significant figures are indicated in a pH of 7.61?

Figure 20.6

The pH scale shows the relationship between pH and the hydrogen-ion concentration. Notice that acids have lower pHs than bases.

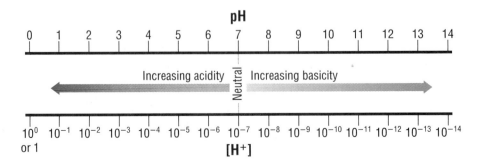

CHEMath

USING LOGARITHMS

Logarithms are used throughout mathematics and science. Examples include the decibel scale for loudness, the Richter scale for earthquakes, and the pH scale for acidity. Because the pH scale is a logarithmic scale, it allows a tremendous range of values (from 1 to 10^{-14}) to be expressed as a number between 1 and 14.

The common logarithm of a number is the exponent to which ten must be raised to produce the given number: $\log x = y$ if $x = 10^y$. Thus $\log 0.01 = -2$ because $0.01 = 10^{-2}$, and $\log 10\ 000 = 4$ because $10\ 000 = 10^4$. The common logarithm is also known as the base-10 logarithm. Logarithms can have other bases, but this textbook only uses common logarithms.

Logarithms of numbers between 1 and 10 can be evaluated directly using **Table B.1** in Appendix B of this textbook. For example, $\log 7.21 = 0.8579$, as shown below.

x	0	1	2
7.1	.8513	.8519	.8525
7.2	.8573	.8579	.8585
7.3	.8633	.8639	.8645

To find the logarithm of a number that is less than 1 or greater than 10, write the number in scientific notation and use the formulas below. See Example 1.

$\log (a \times b) = \log a + \log b$, and $\log (10^x) = x$

A logarithm is rounded so that its number of decimal places equals the number of significant figures in the original number.

The antilog of a number x is the number y whose logarithm is x. Because $\log y = x$ means $y = 10^x$, the antilog of x is the same as 10^x. Antilogs of numbers between 0 and 1 can be found directly from **Table B.1.** To find the antilog of any number, write it as a sum of its decimal part (between 0 and 1) and its integer part (less than or equal to the given number). Then use the formula $10^{a+b} = 10^a \times 10^b$. See Example 2.

Many calculators can be used to find logarithms and antilogs. In general, use [LOG] for a logarithm, or [10ˣ] for an antilog. The exact keystrokes depend on your calculator. Do not confuse the [LOG] key with the [LN] key. The [LN] key gives another kind of logarithm, called the natural logarithm, whose base is the constant $e = 2.718$.

Example 1

Evaluate $\log 0.0000721$.

$$\begin{aligned}
\log 0.0000721 &= \log (7.21 \times 10^{-5}) \\
&= \log 7.21 + \log (10^{-5}) \\
&= 0.8579 + (-5) \\
&= -4.1421
\end{aligned}$$

The original number had 3 significant figures, so the result should be rounded to 3 decimal places.

$$\log 0.0000721 = -4.142$$

Example 2

Find the antilog of -8.375.

Write -8.375 as a sum. Note that the decimal part is 0.625, not -0.375 or 0.375.

$$-8.375 = (-8.375 + 9) + (-9) = 0.625 + (-9)$$

In **Table B.1,** the number nearest to 0.625 is 0.6253, and its antilog is 4.22. So,

$$\begin{aligned}
\text{antilog}\,(-8.375) &= 10^{-8.375} = 10^{0.625 + (-9)} \\
&= 10^{0.625} \times 10^{-9} \\
&= 4.22 \times 10^{-9}
\end{aligned}$$

Practice Problems

Prepare for upcoming problems in this chapter by using **Table B.1** in Appendix B to evaluate the following expressions. Then check your work using a calculator.

A. $\log 1.68$
B. $\log (3.57 \times 10^4)$
C. $\log (2.18 \times 10^{-8})$

D. antilog -8
E. antilog 0.969
F. antilog $(-5 + 0.782)$

G. $\log 17\ 800$
H. $\log 0.0067$
I. $\log 0.0000738$

J. antilog 6.281
K. antilog (-3.192)
L. antilog (-5.936)

Sample Problem 20-3

What is the pH of a solution with a hydrogen-ion concentration of $1.0 \times 10^{-10}M$?

1. *ANALYZE* List the knowns and the unknown.

Knowns:
- $[H^+] = 1.0 \times 10^{-10}M$
- $pH = -\log[H^+]$

Unknown:
- $pH = ?$

2. *CALCULATE* Solve for the unknown.

$$pH = -\log[H^+]$$
$$= -\log(1.0 \times 10^{-10})$$
$$= -(\log 1.0 + \log 10^{-10})$$
$$= -(0.00 + (-10.00))$$
$$= -(-10.00)$$
$$= 10.00$$

3. *EVALUATE* Does the result make sense?

$[H^+]$ is three orders of magnitude (1000 times) less than $1 \times 10^{-7}M$ (pH 7). Each order-of-magnitude decrease in $[H^+]$ equals an increase of 1 pH unit, so the unknown solution should have a pH of $7 + 3 = 10$. This problem can also be solved by inspection. The coefficient of $[H^+]$ is 1.0; therefore, the pH is the value of the exponent (-10) with the sign changed from minus to plus. However, the answer based on experimental data must be reported as 10.00 to show the two significant figures of the original value of $[H^+]$.

Practice Problems

8. Find the pH of each solution.
   a. $[H^+] = 1.0 \times 10^{-4}M$
   b. $[H^+] = 0.0010M$
   c. $[H^+] = 1.0 \times 10^{-9}M$
9. What are the pH values of the following three solutions, based on their hydrogen-ion concentrations?
   a. $[H^+] = 1.0 \times 10^{-12}M$
   b. $[H^+] = 0.010M$
   c. $[H^+] = 1.0 \times 10^{-4}M$

Chem ASAP!

Problem-Solving 9

Solve Problem 9 with the help of an interactive guided tutorial.

Sample Problem 20-4

The pH of an unknown solution is 6.00. What is its hydrogen-ion concentration?

1. *ANALYZE* List the knowns and the unknown.

Knowns:
- $pH = 6.00$
- $pH = -\log[H^+]$

Unknown:
- $[H^+] = ?M$

2. *CALCULATE* Solve for the unknown.

First, rearrange the equation for the definition of pH to solve for the unknown.

$$-\log[H^+] = pH$$

Next, substitute the value of pH.

$$-\log[H^+] = 6.00$$

Sample Problem 20-4 (cont.)

Change the signs on both sides of the equation.

$$\log[H^+] = -6.00$$

Finally, determine the number that has a log of -6.00. The antilog of -6.00 is 1.0×10^{-6}. Therefore,

$$[H^+] = 1.0 \times 10^{-6}M.$$

3. **EVALUATE** *Does the result make sense?*
This problem can be solved by inspection. Any integral value of pH, such as 3.00, 5.00, and so forth, can easily be converted to $[H^+]$. The sign of the pH value is changed from plus to minus and is used as the exponent in the numerical expression of $[H^+]$. A decimal point and zeros are attached to the coefficient (1) to obtain the proper number of significant figures. For example, for pH 4.00, $[H^+] = 1.0 \times 10^{-4}M$; for pH 11.00, $[H^+] = 1.0 \times 10^{-11}M$.

Practice Problems

10. Calculate $[H^+]$ for each solution.
    a. pH = 5.00   **c.** pH = 6.00
    b. pH = 7.00   **d.** pH = 3.00
11. What are the hydrogen-ion concentrations for solutions with the following pH values?
    a. 4.00   **b.** 11.00   **c.** 8.00

Calculating pH Values

Most pH values are not whole numbers. For example, **Table 20.2** on page 584 shows that milk of magnesia has a pH of 10.5. Using the definition of pH, this means that $[H^+]$ must equal $1 \times 10^{-10.5}M$. Thus $[H^+]$ must be less than $1 \times 10^{-10}M$ (pH 10.0), but greater than $1 \times 10^{-11}M$ (pH 11.0).

If $[H^+]$ is written in scientific notation but its coefficient is not 1, then you need a table of common logarithms or a hand calculator with a log function key to calculate pH. A four-place table of common logarithms is provided in Appendix B. Sample Problem 20-5 shows how to make such a pH calculation.

Sample Problem 20-5

What is the pH of a solution if $[OH^-] = 4.0 \times 10^{-11}M$?

1. **ANALYZE** *List the knowns and the unknown.*

   Knowns:
   - $[OH^-] = 4.0 \times 10^{-11}M$
   - $K_w = [OH^-] \times [H^+] = 1 \times 10^{-14}$
   - $pH = -\log[H^+]$

   Unknown:
   - pH = ?

2. **CALCULATE** *Solve for the unknown.*
   To calculate pH, first calculate $[H^+]$ by using the definition of K_w.

   $$K_w = [OH^-] \times [H^+]$$

   $$[H^+] = \frac{K_w}{[OH^-]} = \frac{1.0 \times 10^{-14}}{4.0 \times 10^{-11}M}$$

   $$= 0.25 \times 10^{-3}M$$

   $$= 2.5 \times 10^{-4}M$$

Practice Problems

12. Calculate the pH of each solution.
   a. $[H^+] = 5.0 \times 10^{-6}M$
   b. $[H^+] = 8.3 \times 10^{-10}M$
   c. $[H^+] = 2.7 \times 10^{-7}M$
13. Calculate the pH of each solution.
   a. $[OH^-] = 4.3 \times 10^{-5}M$
   b. $[OH^-] = 2.0 \times 10^{-5}M$
   c. $[OH^-] = 4.5 \times 10^{-11}M$

Chem ASAP!

Problem-Solving 13
Solve Problem 13 with the help of an interactive guided tutorial.

Sample Problem 20-5 (cont.)

With the value of $[H^+]$ determined, use the definition of pH to solve for the pH.

$$pH = -\log[H^+]$$
$$= -\log(2.5 \times 10^{-4})$$
$$= -(\log 2.5 + \log 10^{-4})$$

A log table or calculator indicates that $\log 2.5 = 0.40$, and $\log 10^{-4} = -4$. Insert these values to find the pH.

$$pH = -(0.40) - (-4)$$
$$= -0.40 + 4$$
$$= 3.60$$

3. **EVALUATE** *Does the result make sense?*
A solution in which $[OH^-]$ is less than $1 \times 10^{-7}M$ would be acidic because $[H^+]$ would be greater than $1 \times 10^{-7}M$. $[OH^-]$ is less than $10^{-10}M$ but greater than $10^{-11}M$. Therefore, the solution is somewhere between pOH 10 and pOH 11. Because pOH + pH = 14, the pH should be less than 4 and greater than 3.

You can calculate the hydrogen-ion concentration of a solution if you know the pH. For example, if the solution has a pH of 3.00, then $[H^+] = 1.0 \times 10^{-3}M$. When the pH is not a whole number, you will need log tables or a calculator with a y^x function key to calculate the hydrogen-ion concentration. For example, if the pH is 3.70, the hydrogen-ion concentration must be greater than $1.0 \times 10^{-4}M$ (pH 4.0) and less than $1.0 \times 10^{-3}M$ (pH 3.0). To get an accurate value, use log tables or a calculator.

Sample Problem 20-6

What is $[H^+]$ of a solution if the pH $= 3.70$?

1. **ANALYZE** *List the knowns and the unknown.*
   Knowns:
   • pH = 3.70
   • pH = $-\log[H^+]$
   Unknown:
   • $[H^+] = ?M$

2. **CALCULATE** *Solve for the unknown.*
   First rearrange the equation pH $= -\log[H^+]$.

$$\log[H^+] = -pH = -3.70$$

A log table cannot be used directly to find a number that has a negative log. To avoid this problem, add and then subtract the whole number that is closest to and larger than the negative log. In this case, the negative log is 3.70, and the whole number is 4.

Sample Problem 20-6 (cont.)

$$\log[H^+] = (-3.70 + 4) - 4$$
$$= 0.30 - 4$$
$$[H^+] = 10^{(0.30-4)}$$
$$= 10^{0.30} \times 10^{-4}$$

From the log table, the number with a log of 0.30 is 2.0; the antilog of 0.30 is thus 2.0. The number with a log of -4 is 10^{-4}. Therefore, $[H^+] = 2.0 \times 10^{-4}M$. A calculator with a y^x function key can be used because $[H^+] = 10^{-pH}$; that is, $[H^+]$ is of the form y^x. Thus change the sign of the given pH, in this case to -3.70. Enter $y = 10$, $x = -3.70$, and press the y^x key in the order required by the calculator. The readout gives 1.995×10^{-4}. Rounded to two significant figures, $[H^+] = 2.0 \times 10^{-4}M$.

3. **EVALUATE Does the result make sense?**
A solution of pH 3.70 should have a $[H^+]$ between $1 \times 10^{-4}M$ (pH 4) and $1 \times 10^{-3}M$ (pH 3), as found. Because $[H^+]$ is greater than $1 \times 10^{-7}M$, the solution is acidic.

Practice Problems

14. What is the molarity of $[H^+]$ in each solution?
   a. pH = 7.30   **c.** pH = 7.05
   b. pH = 1.80   **d.** pH = 6.70
15. Calculate the value of $[OH^-]$ in each solution in Practice Problem 14.

Measuring pH

People need to be able to measure the pH of the solutions they use. From maintaining the correct acid–base balance in a swimming pool, to creating soil conditions ideal for plant growth, to making medical diagnoses, pH measurement has valuable applications. For preliminary pH measurements and for small-volume samples, indicators such as the ones shown in **Figure 20.7** are often used. For precise and continuous measurements, a pH meter is preferred.

Methyl red

Phenolphthalein

Bromthymol blue

Figure 20.7
Acid–base indicators respond to pH changes over a specific range. Methyl red (left) changes from red to yellow at pH 5–7. Phenolphthalein (center) changes from colorless to pink at pH 7–9. Bromthymol blue (right) changes from yellow to blue at pH 5–7.

Acid–Base Indicators An indicator (In) is an acid or a base that undergoes dissociation in a known pH range. An indicator is a valuable tool for measuring pH because its acid form and base form have different colors in solution. The following generalized equation represents the dissociation of an indicator (HIn)

$$HIn(aq) \underset{H^+}{\overset{OH^-}{\rightleftharpoons}} H^+(aq) + In^-(aq)$$

Acid form   Base form

The acid form dominates the dissociation equilibrium at low pH (high $[H^+]$), and the base form dominates the equilibrium at high pH (high $[OH^-]$). For each indicator, the change from dominating acid form to dominating base form occurs in a narrow range of approximately two pH units. Within this narrow range, the color of the solution is a mixture of the colors of the acid and the base forms. Knowing the pH range over which this color change occurs can give you a rough estimate of the pH of a solution. At all pH values below this range, you would see only the color of the acid form. At all pH values above this range, you would observe only the color of the base form. You could eventually zero in on a more precise estimate of the pH of the solution by repeating the experiment with indicators that have different pH ranges for their color changes. Many different indicators are needed to span the entire pH spectrum. **Figure 20.8** shows the pH ranges of some commonly used indicators.

Figure 20.8

Each indicator changes color at a different pH. Which indicator would you choose to show that a reaction solution has changed from pH 3 to pH 4?

(a)

(b)

Figure 20.9
*You can determine the approximate pH of a substance by testing it with pH indicator and comparing the color with standards. **(a)** Universal indicator solution has been added to solutions of known pH in the range from 1 to 12 to produce a set of reference colors. **(b)** Universal indicator has been added to samples of some familiar household products: vinegar, soda water, and ammonia solution. Use the colors in **(a)** to assign pH values to the items in **(b)**.*

Although indicators are useful tools, they do have certain characteristics that limit their usefulness. The listed pH values of indicators are usually given for 25 °C. At other temperatures, an indicator may change color at a different pH. If the solution being tested is not colorless, the color of the indicator may be distorted. Dissolved salts in a solution may also affect the indicator's dissociation. Often, using indicator strips can help overcome these problems. An indicator strip is a piece of paper or plastic impregnated with an indicator. The paper is dipped into an unknown solution and compared with a color chart to measure the pH. Some indicator paper is impregnated with multiple indicators that give a palette of colors over a wide pH range. See **Figure 20.9.**

pH Meters A pH meter is used to make rapid, accurate pH measurements. Most chemistry laboratories have a pH meter. If a pH meter is connected to a computer or chart recorder, it can be used to make a continuous recording of pH changes.

Figure 20.10 shows a pH meter. The combination electrode—a glass electrode and a reference electrode—is connected to a millivoltmeter.

(a)

(b)

(c)

Figure 20.10

(a) A pH meter is used to measure hydrogen ion concentrations. The instrument gives the user a direct reading of pH. For continuous monitoring, the pH meter may be connected to a strip-chart recorder. (b) The pH of vinegar, a dilute aqueous solution of ethanoic (acetic) acid, is about 3. (c) The pH of milk of magnesia, an aqueous suspension of magnesium hydroxide, is 10.5. In which of the test solutions is $[H^+] < 1 \times 10^{-7}M$?

The reference electrode has a constant voltage. The voltage of the glass electrode changes with the $[H_3O^+]$ of the solution in which it is dipped. The pH meter makes an electrical measurement of pH by measuring the voltage between the two electrodes. As you can see in **Figure 20.10** on the previous page, the pH meter gives a direct readout of pH. Would you describe the two common household items shown in this figure as acidic or basic?

Before you use a pH meter, you must first calibrate it by immersing the electrodes in a solution of known pH. With the electrodes in the solution, you adjust the readout of the millivoltmeter to this known pH. Then rinse the electrodes with distilled water and dip them into the solution of unknown pH. To make continuous pH readings, you can leave the electrodes in the solution.

A pH meter is a valuable instrument. In many situations it is easier to use than liquid indicators or indicator strips. Measurements of pH obtained with a pH meter are typically accurate to within 0.01 pH unit of the true pH. The color and cloudiness of the unknown solution do not affect the accuracy of the pH value obtained. Hospitals use pH meters to find small but meaningful changes of pH in blood and other body fluids. Sewage and industrial effluents and soil pH are also easily monitored with a pH meter.

(a)

(b)   (c)

Figure 20.11

(a) Altering soil pH can affect the development of plants. In acidic soils, hydrangeas produce blue flowers. In basic soils, they produce pink flowers. (b) Spreading lime on lawns and gardens neutralizes acidic soils. (c) Blood pH is used to help diagnose illness.

MINI LAB

Indicators from Natural Sources

PURPOSE

To measure the pH of various household materials by using a natural indicator to make an indicator chart.

MATERIALS

- red cabbage leaves
- white vinegar (CH₃COOH)
- household ammonia
- baking soda (NaHCO₃)
- 1-cup measure
- 10 clear plastic cups
- 2 jars
- tape
- knife
- pencil
- teaspoon
- ruler
- clean white cloth

- hot water
- 3 sheets of plain white paper
- medicine dropper
- clear plastic wrap
- rubber band
- various household items listed in Step 5

PROCEDURE

1. Put ½ cup of finely chopped red cabbage leaves in a jar and add ½ cup of hot water. Stir and crush the leaves with a spoon. Continue the extraction until the water is distinctly colored.

2. Strain the extract through a piece of cloth into a clean jar. This liquid is your natural indicator.

3. Tape three sheets of paper end to end. Draw a line along the center and label it at 5 cm intervals with the numbers 1 to 14. This is your pH scale.

4. Pour your indicator to about 1 cm depth into each of three plastic cups. To one cup, add several drops of

vinegar, to the second add a pinch of baking soda, and to the third add several drops of ammonia. The resulting colors indicate pH values of about 3, 9, and 11, respectively. Place these colored positions on your pH scale.

5. Repeat Step 4 for household items such as table salt, borax, milk, lemon juice, laundry detergent, dish detergent, milk of magnesia, mouthwash, toothpaste, shampoo, and carbonated beverages.

ANALYSIS AND CONCLUSIONS

1. What was the color of the indicator at acidic, neutral, and basic conditions?

2. What chemical changes were responsible for the color changes?

3. Label the materials you tested as acidic, basic, or neutral.

4. Which group contains items used for cleaning or for personal hygiene?

---

section review 20.2

16. What is true about the relative concentrations of hydrogen ions and hydroxide ions in each kind of solution?

   a. basic   **b.** acidic   **c.** neutral

17. Determine the pH of each solution.

   a. $[H^+] = 1.0 \times 10^{-6}M$ **d.** $[OH^-] = 1.0 \times 10^{-11}M$

   b. $[H^+] = 0.00010M$

   c. $[OH^-] = 1.0 \times 10^{-2}M$

18. What are the hydroxide-ion concentrations for solutions with the following pH values?

   a. 6.00   **b.** 9.00   **c.** 12.00

 Chem ASAP! **Assessment 20.2** Check your understanding of the important ideas and concepts in Section 20.2.

ACID–BASE THEORIES

objectives

▶ Compare and contrast acids and bases as defined by the theories of Arrhenius, Brønsted-Lowry, and Lewis

▶ Identify conjugate acid–base pairs in acid–base reactions

key terms

▶ monoprotic acids
▶ diprotic acids
▶ triprotic acids
▶ hydrogen-ion donor
▶ hydrogen-ion acceptor
▶ conjugate acid
▶ conjugate base
▶ conjugate acid–base pair
▶ amphoteric
▶ Lewis acid
▶ Lewis base

*B*racken Cave, near San Antonio, Texas, is home to twenty to forty million bats, which is probably the largest colony of mammals in the world. Visitors to the cave must wear protective goggles and respirators to protect themselves from the dangerous levels of ammonia in the cave. Ammonia is a by-product of the bats' urine. **Why is ammonia considered a base?**

Arrhenius Acids and Bases

In Section 20.1, you learned the definition of an acid and of a base. Although chemists had recognized the properties of these two groups of compounds for many years, they were not able to explain the chemical theory of this behavior. Then, in 1887, the Swedish chemist Svante Arrhenius (1859–1927) proposed a revolutionary way of defining and thinking about acids and bases. He said that acids are hydrogen-containing compounds that ionize to yield hydrogen ions (H^+) in aqueous solution. He also said that bases are compounds that ionize to yield hydroxide ions (OH^-) in aqueous solution.

Table 20.3 lists some common acids. Acids that contain one ionizable hydrogen, such as nitric acid (HNO_3), are called **monoprotic acids.** Acids that contain two ionizable hydrogens, such as sulfuric acid (H_2SO_4), are called **diprotic acids.** Acids that contain three ionizable hydrogens, such as phosphoric acid (H_3PO_4), are called **triprotic acids.** Not all compounds that contain hydrogen are acids, however. Also, not all the hydrogens in an acid may be released as hydrogen ions. Only the hydrogens in very polar bonds are ionizable. In such bonds, hydrogen is joined to a very electronegative element. When a compound that contains such bonds dissolves in water, it releases hydrogen ions because the hydrogen ions are stabilized by solvation. An example is the hydrogen chloride molecule, shown in **Figure 20.13.** Hydrogen chloride is a polar covalent molecule. It ionizes to form hydrochloric acid in aqueous solution. Is hydrochloric acid a monoprotic, diprotic, or triprotic acid?

Table 20.3

Some Common Acids	
Name	**Formula**
Hydrochloric acid	HCl
Nitric acid	HNO_3
Sulfuric acid	H_2SO_4
Phosphoric acid	H_3PO_4
Ethanoic acid	CH_3COOH
Carbonic acid	H_2CO_3

$$\overset{\delta+}{H}—\overset{\delta-}{Cl}(g) \xrightarrow{H_2O} H^+(aq) + Cl^-(aq)$$

Hydrogen chloride   Hydrogen ion   Chloride ion

(hydrochloric acid)

Figure 20.12

Sea slugs (left) contain diprotic H_2SO_4, which discourages predators. Some products that can keep rust spots on a car (center) from rusting further contain a triprotic acid, phosphoric acid. Monoprotic lactic acid builds up in muscles during prolonged exercise (right).

HCl   H₂O   H₃O⁺   Cl⁻
Hydrogen chloride Water   Hydronium ion   Chloride ion

Figure 20.13

Hydrochloric acid is actually an aqueous solution of hydrogen chloride. The hydrogen forms hydronium ions, making this compound an acid.

In contrast, the four hydrogens in methane (CH_4) are attached by weakly polar C—H bonds. Methane has no ionizable hydrogens and is not an acid. Ethanoic (acetic) acid (CH_3COOH), used in the manufacture of plastics, pharmaceuticals, and photographic chemicals, is different. Although this molecule contains four hydrogens, ethanoic acid is a mono-protic acid. The structural formula shows why.

$$\begin{array}{ccc} & H & O \\ & | & \| \\ H- & C-C & -O-H \\ & | & \\ & H & \end{array}$$

Ethanoic acid
(CH_3COOH)

The three hydrogens attached to the carbon are in weakly polar bonds. They do not ionize. Only the hydrogen attached to the highly electronegative oxygen is able to be ionized. As you gain more experience looking at written formulas for acids, you will be able to recognize which hydrogen atoms can be ionized.

Table 20.4 lists some common bases. The base with which you are perhaps most familiar is sodium hydroxide (NaOH). Sodium metal reacts violently with water to form sodium hydroxide. The following equation illustrates the reaction of sodium metal with water.

$$2Na(s) + 2H_2O(l) \longrightarrow 2NaOH(aq) + H_2(g)$$

Sodium   Water   Sodium   Hydrogen
metal   hydroxide

Because of its extremely caustic nature, sodium hydroxide, commonly known as lye, is a major component of consumer products used to clean clogged drains.

Table 20.4

Some Common Bases		
Name	Formula	Solubility in water
Potassium hydroxide	KOH	High
Sodium hydroxide	NaOH	High
Calcium hydroxide	Ca(OH)₂	Very low
Magnesium hydroxide	Mg(OH)₂	Very low

Chemistry Rescues Crumbling Books

Millions of books printed since the mid-nineteenth century slowly decay as they sit on library shelves. Their pages are so fragile, they crumble at a touch. The cause is the acidity of the paper, which originates from alum (aluminum sulfate). For the past 150 years, alum has been used to prevent inks from soaking into paper. Libraries throughout the world are working with chemists to find ways to stop the acid deterioration of books. One process, carried out in a vacuum chamber, is called mass deacidification. After the air is pumped out of the chamber and most of the moisture is removed from the books, the gas diethyl zinc is introduced. The gas penetrates the closed pages of the books and completely neutralizes any acid that is present. The gas also forms zinc oxide, which protects the paper against future acid attack. For an estimated cost of $6 to $10 per book, hundreds of volumes can be treated at once. If books had to be treated page by page, deacidification could cost $1000 per book!

Potassium metal reacts vigorously with water to produce potassium hydroxide (KOH). Both sodium hydroxide and potassium hydroxide are ionic solids. What happens to the ions in these compounds when they dissolve in water?

$$NaOH(s) \xrightarrow{H_2O} Na^+(aq) + OH^-(aq)$$

Sodium hydroxide   Sodium ion   Hydroxide ion

Sodium and potassium are Group 1A elements. Elements in Group 1A, the alkali metals, react with water to produce alkaline solutions. Metal oxides also react with water to produce alkaline solutions. Both sodium hydroxide and potassium hydroxide are very soluble in water. Concentrated solutions of these compounds can be readily prepared. Such solutions, like other basic solutions, would have a bitter taste and slippery feel. Note, however, that they are extremely caustic to the skin and can cause deep, painful, slow-healing wounds if not immediately washed off.

Calcium hydroxide ($Ca(OH)_2$) and magnesium hydroxide ($Mg(OH)_2$) are hydroxides of Group 2A metals. These hydroxides are not very soluble in water. Consequently, their solutions are always very dilute, even when saturated. The concentration of hydroxide ions in such solutions is correspondingly low. A saturated solution of calcium hydroxide contains only 0.165 g $Ca(OH)_2$ per 100 g of water. Magnesium hydroxide is much less soluble than calcium hydroxide. A saturated solution contains only 0.0009 g $Mg(OH)_2$ per 100 g of water. Suspensions of magnesium hydroxide in water contain low concentrations of hydroxide ion. People take these suspensions internally as milk of magnesia, which is an antacid and a mild laxative.

Brønsted-Lowry Acids and Bases

The Arrhenius definition of acids and bases is not a very comprehensive one. It defines acids and bases rather narrowly and does not include certain substances that have acidic or basic properties. For example, aqueous solutions of ammonia (NH_3)(aq) and sodium carbonate (Na_2CO_3)(aq) are basic. Neither of these compounds is a hydroxide, however, and neither would be classified as a base under the Arrhenius definition. In 1923, the Danish chemist Johannes Brønsted (1879–1947) and the English chemist Thomas Lowry (1874–1936) independently proposed a new definition. The Brønsted-Lowry theory defines an acid as a **hydrogen-ion donor.** Similarly, a Brønsted-Lowry base is a **hydrogen-ion acceptor.** All the acids and bases included in the Arrhenius theory are also acids and bases according to the Brønsted-Lowry theory. Some compounds not included in the Arrhenius theory are classified as bases in the Brønsted-Lowry theory.

The behavior of ammonia as a base can be understood by using the Brønsted-Lowry theory. Ammonia gas is very soluble in water. When ammonia dissolves in water, it acts as a base because it accepts a hydrogen ion from water.

$$NH_3(aq) + H_2O(l) \rightleftharpoons NH_4^+(aq) + OH^-(aq)$$

Ammonia (hydrogen-ion acceptor, Brønsted-Lowry base)   Water (hydrogen-ion donor, Brønsted-Lowry acid)   Ammonium ion   Hydroxide ion (makes the solution basic)

NH_3
Ammonia

H_2O
Water

NH_4^+
Ammonium ion

OH^-
Hydroxide ion

Figure 20.14
Ammonia dissolves in water to form ammonium ions and hydroxide ions. In this reaction, the water molecule donates a hydrogen ion to the ammonia molecule. Why is ammonia not classified as an Arrhenius base?

In this reaction, ammonia is the hydrogen-ion acceptor. Therefore, it is a Brønsted-Lowry base. Water, the hydrogen-ion donor, is a Brønsted-Lowry acid. Hydrogen ions are transferred from water to ammonia, as is shown in **Figure 20.14.** This causes the hydroxide-ion concentration to be greater than it is in pure water. As a result, solutions of ammonia are basic.

Heating an aqueous solution of ammonia releases ammonia gas. Do not try this at home, however; ammonia is a poisonous gas! As ammonia gas leaves the solution, the equilibrium in the equation shifts to the left. The ammonium ion (NH_4^+) reacts with OH^- to form NH_3 and H_2O. When the reaction goes from right to left, NH_4^+ gives up a hydrogen ion; it acts as a Brønsted-Lowry acid. The hydroxide ion accepts an H^+; it acts as a Brønsted-Lowry base. Overall, then, this equilibrium has two acids and two bases.

$$NH_3(aq) + H_2O(l) \rightleftharpoons NH_4^+(aq) + OH^-(aq)$$

Base   Acid   Conjugate   Conjugate
                            acid   base

When ammonia dissolves, NH_4^+ is the conjugate acid of the base NH_3. A **conjugate acid** is the particle formed when a base gains a hydrogen ion. Similarly, OH^- is the conjugate base of the acid water. A **conjugate base** is the particle that remains when an acid has donated a hydrogen ion. Conjugate acids and bases are always paired with a base or an acid, respectively. A **conjugate acid–base pair** consists of two substances related by the loss or gain of a single hydrogen ion. The ammonia molecule and ammonium ion are a conjugate acid–base pair. The water molecule and hydroxide ion are also a conjugate acid–base pair.

$$NH_3(aq) + H_2O(l) \rightleftharpoons NH_4^+(aq) + OH^-(aq)$$

Base   Acid   Conjugate   Conjugate
                            acid   base

The Brønsted-Lowry theory also applies to acids. Consider the ionization of hydrogen chloride in water.

$$HCl(g) + H_2O(l) \rightleftharpoons H_3O^+(aq) + Cl^-(aq)$$

Acid   Base   Conjugate   Conjugate
                            acid   base

Table 20.5

Several Conjugate Acid–Base Pairs	
Acid $\xrightarrow{\text{lose } H^+}$ $\xleftarrow{\text{gain } H^+}$	**Base**
HCl	Cl^-
H_2SO_4	HSO_4^-
H_3O^+	H_2O
HSO_4^-	SO_4^{2-}
CH_3COOH	H_3COO^-
H_2CO_3	HCO_3^-
HCO_3^-	CO_3^{2-}
NH_4^+	NH_3
H_2O	OH^-

Figure 20.15
When sulfuric acid dissolves in water, it forms hydronium ions and hydrogen sulfate ions. Which ion is the conjugate acid and which is the conjugate base?

H_2SO_4	H_2O	H_3O^+	HSO_4^-
Sulfuric acid	Water	Hydronium ion	Hydrogen sulfate ion

In this reaction, hydrogen chloride is the hydrogen-ion donor. Thus it is a Brønsted-Lowry acid. Water is the hydrogen-ion acceptor. It is a Brønsted-Lowry base. The chloride ion is the conjugate base of the acid HCl. The hydronium ion is the conjugate acid of the base water. Compare this reaction with what happens when sulfuric acid dissolves in water, as illustrated in **Figure 20.15.**

Sometimes water accepts a hydrogen ion. At other times, it donates a hydrogen ion. A substance that can act as both an acid and a base is said to be **amphoteric.** Water is amphoteric. In the reaction with HCl, water accepts a proton and is therefore a base. In the reaction with NH_3, is water an acid or a base?

Lewis Acids and Bases

A third theory of acids and bases was proposed by Gilbert Lewis (1875–1946). In his definition, Lewis focused on the donation or acceptance of a pair of electrons during a reaction. This concept is more general than either the Arrhenius theory or the Brønsted-Lowry theory. A **Lewis acid** is a substance that can accept a pair of electrons to form a covalent bond. A **Lewis base** is a substance that can donate a pair of electrons to form a covalent bond. A hydrogen ion (Brønsted-Lowry acid) can accept a pair of electrons in forming a bond. A hydrogen ion, therefore, is also a Lewis acid. A Brønsted-Lowry base, or a substance that accepts a hydrogen ion, must have a pair of electrons available and, therefore, is also a Lewis base. Consider the reaction of H^+ and OH^-.

$$H^+ \; + \; ^-\!\!:\!\ddot{O}\!-\!H \; \longrightarrow \; \underset{H \qquad H}{\overset{\ddot{O}}{\diagdown}}$$

Lewis   Lewis
acid   base

Chem ASAP!

Animation 25
Compare the three important definitions of acids and bases.

In this reaction, a hydroxide ion is a Lewis base. It is also a Brønsted-Lowry base. The hydrogen ion is both a Lewis acid and a Brønsted-Lowry acid. The Lewis definition also includes some compounds not classified as Brønsted-Lowry acids or bases.

Table 20.6

Acid–Base Definitions		
Type	**Acid**	**Base**
Arrhenius	H^+ producer	OH^- producer
Brønsted-Lowry	H^+ donor	H^+ acceptor
Lewis	electron-pair acceptor	electron-pair donor

Sample Problem 20-7

Identify the Lewis acid and the Lewis base in this reaction.

$$
\begin{array}{c}
\ \ \overset{\displaystyle H}{|}\ \ \overset{\displaystyle F}{|} \\
H-N\!:\,+\,B-F \\
\ \ \underset{\displaystyle H}{|}\ \ \underset{\displaystyle F}{|}
\end{array}
\longrightarrow
\begin{array}{c}
\overset{\displaystyle H}{|}\ \ \overset{\displaystyle F}{|} \\
H-N-B-F \\
\underset{\displaystyle H}{|}\ \ \underset{\displaystyle F}{|}
\end{array}
$$

---

1. **ANALYZE** *Plan a problem-solving strategy.*
   The Lewis acid–Lewis base definitions, which are to be used in solving the problem, are based on the acceptance and donation of a pair of electrons.

---

2. **SOLVE** *Apply the problem-solving strategy.*
   Ammonia is donating a pair of electrons. Boron trifluoride is accepting a pair of electrons. Lewis bases donate electrons, so ammonia is acting as a Lewis base. Lewis acids accept electrons, so boron trifluoride is acting as a Lewis acid.

---

3. **EVALUATE** *Does the result make sense?*
   In this reaction, ammonia and boron trifluoride fit the definitions of Lewis bases and Lewis acids, respectively.

Practice Problems

19. Would you predict PCl_3 to be a Lewis acid or a Lewis base in typical reactions? Explain your prediction.
20. Identify the Lewis acid and Lewis base in each reaction
    a. $H^+ +$ $\ \ \ddot{O}\ \ \longrightarrow H_3O^+$
       $\ \diagup\ \diagdown$
       $\ H\ \ \ H$
    b. $AlCl_3 + Cl^- \longrightarrow AlCl_4^-$

section review 20.3

21. **a.** How are acids and bases defined by the Brønsted-Lowry theory?

    b. What advantage does this theory have in terms of accounting for the properties of compounds such as ammonia?

    c. How do the Arrhenius and Brønsted-Lowry theories compare with the Lewis theory of acids and bases?

22. What is a conjugate acid–base pair?

23. Write equations for the ionization of HNO_3 in water and the reaction of CO_3^{2-} with water. For each equation, identify the hydrogen-ion donor and hydrogen-ion acceptor. Then label the conjugate acid–base pairs in each equation.

24. Identify the following acids as monoprotic, diprotic, or triprotic. Explain your reasoning.
    a. H_2CO_3
    b. H_3PO_4
    c. HCl
    d. H_2SO_4

25. Write a balanced equation for each reaction.
    a. Potassium metal reacts with water.
    b. Calcium metal reacts with water.

 portfolio project

Household drain cleaners contain pellets of sodium hydroxide (NaOH) and small metal particles. Use the library or Internet to find out how drain cleaners work. Include the identity of the metal particles in your written report.

 Chem ASAP! **Assessment 20.3** Check your understanding of the important ideas and concepts in Section 20.3.

STRENGTHS OF ACIDS AND BASES

objectives

▸ Define strong acids and weak acids

▸ Calculate an acid dissociation constant (K_a) from concentration and pH measurements

▸ Arrange acids by strength according to their acid dissociation constants (K_a)

▸ Arrange bases by strength according to their base dissociation constants (K_b)

key terms

▸ strong acids

▸ weak acids

▸ acid dissociation constant (K_a)

▸ strong bases

▸ weak bases

▸ base dissociation constant (K_b)

*L*emons and grapefruits have a sour taste because they contain citric acid. When you make lemonade, or cut up a grapefruit, you probably do not wear safety goggles or chemical-resistant clothing even though you are working with an acid. However, some acids require just such precautions. For example, sulfuric acid is a widely used, industrial chemical that can quickly cause severe burns if it comes into contact with the skin. **What makes some acids weak acids and other acids strong acids?**

Strong and Weak Acids and Bases

Acids are classified as strong or weak depending on the degree to which they ionize in water. For practical purposes, **strong acids** are completely ionized in aqueous solution. Hydrochloric acid and sulfuric acid are strong acids.

$$HCl(g) + H_2O(l) \longrightarrow H_3O^+(aq) + Cl^-(aq) \text{ (100\% ionized)}$$

Weak acids ionize only slightly in aqueous solution. The ionization of ethanoic acid (acetic acid), a typical weak acid, is not complete.

$$CH_3COOH(aq) + H_2O(l) \rightleftharpoons H_3O^+(aq) + CH_3COO^-(aq)$$

| Ethanoic acid | Water | Hydronium ion | Ethanoate ion |

Fewer than 1% of ethanoic acid molecules are ionized at any instant. **Table 20.7** gives the relative strength of some common acids and bases. Which is the weakest acid in the table? The weakest base?

Table 20.7

Relative Strengths of Common Acids and Bases		
Substance	**Formula**	**Relative Strength**
Hydrochloric acid	HCl ⎫	
Nitric acid	HNO_3 ⎬	Strong acids
Sulfuric acid	H_2SO_4 ⎭	
Phosphoric acid	H_3PO_4	
Ethanoic acid	CH_3COOH	↑
Carbonic acid	H_2CO_3	Increasing strength of acid
Hydrosulfuric acid	H_2S	
Hypochlorous acid	HClO	
Boric acid	H_3BO_3	
		Neutral solution
Sodium cyanide	NaCN	
Ammonia	NH_3	Increasing strength of base
Methylamine	CH_3NH_2	
Sodium silicate	Na_2SiO_3	
Calcium hydroxide	$Ca(OH)_2$ ⎫	↓
Sodium hydroxide	NaOH ⎬	Strong bases
Potassium hydroxide	KOH ⎭	

You can write the equilibrium-constant expression from a balanced chemical equation. What is the general equation for setting up an equilibrium constant? Using this equation, the equilibrium-constant expression for ethanoic acid is

$$K_{eq} = \frac{[H_3O^+] \times [CH_3COO^-]}{[CH_3COOH] \times [H_2O]}$$

For dilute solutions, the concentration of water is a constant. It can be combined with K_{eq} to give an acid dissociation constant. An **acid dissociation constant** (K_a) is the ratio of the concentration of the dissociated (or ionized) form of an acid to the concentration of the undissociated (nonionized) form. The dissociated form includes both the H^+ and the anion.

$$K_{eq} \times [H_2O] = K_a = \frac{[H^+] \times [CH_3COO^-]}{[CH_3COOH]}$$

Strong Acid

HA(aq) + H₂O(l) ⟶ H₃O⁺(aq) + A⁻(aq)

Weak Acid

HA(aq) + H₂O(l) ⇌ H₃O⁺(aq) + A⁻(aq)

Very Weak Acid

HA(aq) + H₂O(l) ⇌ H₃O⁺(aq) + A⁻(aq)

Figure 20.16

Dissociation of an acid (HA) in water yields H_3O^+ and A^-. The bar graphs compare the extent of dissociation of strong and weak acids. A strong acid completely dissociates in water; $[H_3O^+]$ is high. Weak acids remain largely undissociated; $[H_3O^+]$ is low. Give the name and formula for a strong acid, a weak acid, and a very weak acid. For each example, give the name and formula for the anion that results from the dissociation reaction.

The acid dissociation constant (K_a) reflects the fraction of an acid in the ionized form. For this reason, dissociation constants are sometimes called ionization constants. If the value of the dissociation constant is small, then the degree of dissociation or ionization of the acid in the solution is small. Weak acids have small K_a values. A larger value of K_a means the dissociation or ionization of the acid is more complete. The stronger an acid is, the larger is its K_a value. For example, nitrous acid has a K_a of 4.4×10^{-4}, whereas ethanoic acid (acetic acid) has a K_a of 1.8×10^{-5}. This means that nitrous acid is more ionized in solution than ethanoic acid. Nitrous acid is a stronger acid than ethanoic acid.

Diprotic and triprotic acids lose their hydrogens one at a time. Each ionization reaction has a separate dissociation constant. Thus phosphoric acid (H_3PO_4) has three dissociation constants to go with its three ionizable hydrogens. **Table 20.8** shows the ionization reactions and dissociation constants of some common weak acids, ranked by the value of the first dissociation constant of each acid. What is the second dissociation constant for the ionization of phosphoric acid?

Table 20.8

Dissociation Constants of Weak Acids		
Acid	**Ionization**	**K_a (25 °C)**
Oxalic acid	$HOOCCOOH(aq) \rightleftharpoons H^+(aq) + HOOCCOO^-(aq)$	5.6×10^{-2}
	$HOOCCOO^-(aq) \rightleftharpoons H^+(aq) + OOCCOO^{2-}(aq)$	5.1×10^{-5}
Phosphoric acid	$H_3PO_4(aq) \rightleftharpoons H^+(aq) + H_2PO_4^-(aq)$	7.5×10^{-3}
	$H_2PO_4^-(aq) \rightleftharpoons H^+(aq) + HPO_4^{2-}(aq)$	6.2×10^{-8}
	$HPO_4^{2-}(aq) \rightleftharpoons H^+(aq) + PO_4^{3-}(aq)$	4.8×10^{-13}
Methanoic acid	$HCOOH(aq) \rightleftharpoons H^+(aq) + HCOO^-(aq)$	1.8×10^{-4}
Benzoic acid	$C_6H_5COOH(aq) \rightleftharpoons H^+(aq) + C_6H_5COO^-(aq)$	6.3×10^{-5}
Ethanoic acid	$CH_3COOH(aq) \rightleftharpoons H^+(aq) + CH_3COO^-(aq)$	1.8×10^{-5}
Carbonic acid	$H_2CO_3(aq) \rightleftharpoons H^+(aq) + HCO_3^-(aq)$	4.3×10^{-7}
	$HCO_3^-(aq) \rightleftharpoons H^+(aq) + CO_3^{2-}(aq)$	4.8×10^{-11}

Just as there are strong acids and weak acids, there are also strong bases and weak bases. All the hydroxides in **Table 20.4** on page 595 are classified as strong bases. **Strong bases** dissociate completely into metal ions and hydroxide ions in aqueous solution. Some strong bases, such as calcium hydroxide and magnesium hydroxide, are not very soluble in water. The small amounts of these bases that do dissolve dissociate completely. **Table 20.7** on page 600 lists the relative strengths of some bases.

Weak bases react with water to form the hydroxide ion and the conjugate acid of the base. Ammonia is an example of a weak base.

$$NH_3(aq) + H_2O(l) \rightleftharpoons NH_4^+(aq) + OH^-(aq)$$

Ammonia   Water   Ammonium   Hydroxide
                        ion   ion

The equilibrium of this equation greatly favors the reverse reaction. Only about 1% of the ammonia is present as NH_4^+, the conjugate acid of NH_3. The concentrations of NH_4^+ and OH^- are low and equal. Interestingly, the compound ammonium hydroxide (NH_4OH) cannot be isolated from solutions of aqueous ammonia. To isolate NH_4OH, you would need to remove the NH_3 and H_2O. If you began to remove the ammonia first, the equilibrium would shift even further in the reverse direction (to the left) to compensate for the loss of NH_3. What principle does this demonstrate? This cycle of loss of NH_3 and reduction of the amount of NH_4^+ and OH^- would continue until all the ammonia had been removed from the water. An attempt to remove the water first or the ammonia and water together would also fail to isolate any NH_4OH. Bottles of aqueous ammonia used in laboratories are sometimes labeled ammonium hydroxide, but this compound has never been isolated. The equilibrium-constant expression for the reaction of ammonia with water is

$$K_{eq} = \frac{[NH_4^+] \times [OH^-]}{[NH_3] \times [H_2O]}$$

As you just learned in the discussion of K_a, the concentration of water is constant in dilute solutions. It can be combined with K_{eq} to give a base dissociation constant (K_b).

$$K_b = \frac{[NH_4^+] \times [OH^-]}{[NH_3]}$$

In general, the **base dissociation constant (K_b)** is the ratio of the concentration of the conjugate acid times the concentration of the hydroxide ion to the concentration of the conjugate base. The following is the general form of this equation.

$$K_b = \frac{[\text{conjugate acid}] \times [OH^-]}{[\text{conjugate base}]}$$

The magnitude of K_b indicates the ability of a weak base to compete with the very strong base OH^- for hydrogen ions. Because bases such as ammonia are weak relative to the hydroxide ion, K_b for such bases is usually small. The K_b for ammonia is 1.8×10^{-5}. The smaller the value of K_b, the weaker is the base.

The words concentrated and dilute indicate how much of an acid or base is dissolved in solution. These terms refer to the number of moles of the acid or base in a given volume. The words strong or weak refer to the extent of ionization or dissociation of an acid or base. They indicate how many of the particles ionize or dissociate into ions. Hydrochloric acid (HCl)(*aq*) is a strong acid; it is completely dissociated into ions. Gastric juice in the stomach is a dilute solution of hydrochloric acid. A relatively small number of HCl molecules are present in a given volume of gastric juice, but they are all dissociated into ions. A sample of hydrochloric acid added to a large volume of water becomes more dilute, but it is still a strong acid. Vinegar is a dilute solution of a weak acid, ethanoic acid. Pure ethanoic acid (glacial acetic acid) is still a weak acid, even though it is highly concentrated. Solutions of ammonia can be dilute or concentrated, depending on the amount of ammonia dissolved in a given volume of

Table 20.9

Concentrations of Some Common Laboratory Acids and Bases		
Acid or base	Concentration	
	Moles/liter (molarity)	Grams/liter
Concentrated hydrochloric acid	12	438
Dilute hydrochloric acid	6	219
Concentrated sulfuric acid	18	1764
Dilute sulfuric acid	6	588
Concentrated phosphoric acid	15	1470
Concentrated nitric acid	16	1008
Dilute nitric acid	6	378
Ethanoic acid, glacial	17	1020
Ethanoic acid, dilute	6	360
Dilute sodium hydroxide	6	240
Concentrated aqueous ammonia	15	255
Dilute aqueous ammonia	6	102

water. In any solution of ammonia, however, whether concentrated or dilute, ammonia will be a weak base because the amount of ionization will be small. **Table 20.9** lists the concentrations of acids and bases commonly found in the laboratory. Identify each acid and base in **Table 20.9** as either weak or strong.

Calculating Dissociation Constants

You can calculate the acid dissociation constant (K_a) of a weak acid from experimental data. To do this, you need to measure the equilibrium concentrations of all the substances present at equilibrium. For a weak acid, you can determine these concentrations experimentally if you know two conditions. First, you must know the initial molar concentration of the acid. Second, you must know the pH (or $[H^+]$) of the solution at equilibrium.

Sample Problem 20-8

A 0.1000M solution of ethanoic acid is only partially ionized. From measurements of the pH of the solution, $[H^+]$ is determined to be $1.34 \times 10^{-3}M$. What is the acid dissociation constant (K_a) of ethanoic acid?

1. ANALYZE *List the knowns and the unknown.*

Knowns:
- [ethanoic acid] = 0.1000M
- $[H^+] = 1.34 \times 10^{-3}M$
- $CH_3COOH(aq) \rightleftharpoons H^+(aq) + CH_3COO^-(aq)$
- $K_a = \dfrac{[H^+] \times [CH_3COO^-]}{[CH_3COOH]}$

Unknown:
- $K_a = ?$

Sample Problem 20-8 (cont.)

2. CALCULATE Solve for the unknown.

Each molecule of CH_3COOH that ionizes gives an H^+ and a CH_3COO^- ion. Therefore, at equilibrium $[H^+] = [CH_3COO^-] = 1.34 \times 10^{-3}M$. The equilibrium concentration of CH_3COOH is the initial concentration minus the concentration of the ionized acid or $(0.1000 - 0.00134)M = 0.0987M$. The following table summarizes these data. (All concentrations are in M.)

Concentration	$[CH_3COOH]$	$[H^+]$	$[CH_3COO^-]$
Initial	0.1000	0	0
Change	-1.34×10^{-3}	1.34×10^{-3}	1.34×10^{-3}
Equilibrium	0.0987	1.34×10^{-3}	1.34×10^{-3}

The equilibrium values can now be substituted into the expression for K_a.

$$K_a = \frac{[H^+] \times [CH_3COO^-]}{[CH_3COOH]}$$

$$= \frac{(1.34 \times 10^{-3}) \times (1.34 \times 10^{-3})}{0.0987}$$

$$= 1.82 \times 10^{-5}$$

3. EVALUATE Does the result make sense?

The value of K_a is consistent with that of a weak acid.

Practice Problems

26. For a solution of methanoic acid (formic acid) exactly $0.1M$, $[H^+] = 4.2 \times 10^{-3}M$. Calculate the K_a of methanoic acid.

27. For a solution of a monoprotic weak acid exactly $0.2M$, $[H^+] = 9.86 \times 10^{-4}M$.
    a. What is the pH of this solution?
    b. What is the value of K_a for this acid?

Chem ASAP!

Problem-Solving 27
Solve Problem 27 with the help of an interactive guided tutorial.

section review 20.4

28. What is the definition of a strong acid? A weak acid? Based on the first ionization constant, which acid in **Table 20.8** on page 602 is the strongest? Which is the weakest?

29. A $0.18M$ solution of monoprotic chloroacetic acid ($CH_2ClCOOH$) has a pH of 1.80. Calculate the acid dissociation constant for this acid. Is this a strong or weak acid?

30. Which acid in **Table 20.7** on page 600 would you expect to have the lowest ionization constant?

31. Acid HX has a very small value of K_a. How do the relative amounts of H^+ and HX compare at equilibrium?

32. Write the equations for the ionization or dissociation of the following acids and bases in water.
    a. nitric acid   c. ammonia
    b. ethanoic acid   d. magnesium hydroxide

33. Compare strong/weak and concentrated/dilute as they pertain to acids and bases.

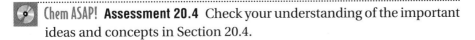

Chem ASAP! Assessment 20.4 Check your understanding of the important ideas and concepts in Section 20.4.

IONIZATION CONSTANTS OF WEAK ACIDS

SAFETY

Wear safety glasses and follow the standard safety procedures outlined on page 18.

PURPOSE

To measure ionization constants of weak acids such as bromocresol green (BCG).

MATERIALS

- pencil
- paper
- ruler
- reaction surface
- chemicals shown in Figure A

PROCEDURE

On separate sheets of paper, draw two grids similar to Figure A. Make each square 2 cm on each side. Place a reaction surface over one of the grids and place one drop of BCG in each square. Place one drop of pH buffer in each square corresponding to its pH value. Use the second grid as a data table to record your observations for each solution.

1 drop pH buffer + 1 drop BCG

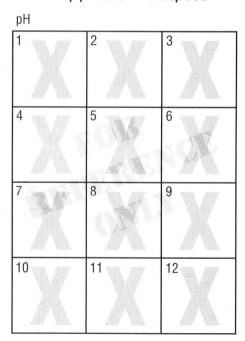

Figure A

ANALYSIS

Using your experimental data, record the answers to the following questions below your data table.

1. What is the color of the lowest pH solutions?

2. What is the color of the highest pH solutions?

3. At which pH does the bromcresol green change from one color to the other? At which pH does an intermediate color exist?

An acid–base indicator is usually a weak acid with a characteristic color. Because bromcresol green is an acid, it is convenient to represent its rather complex formula as HBCG. HBCG ionizes in water according to the following equation.

$$HBCG + H_2O = BCG^- + H_3O^+$$
(yellow)   (blue)

The K_a expression is

$$K_a = \frac{[BCG^-] \times [H_3O^+]}{[HBCG]}$$

When $[BCG^-] = [HBCG]$, $K_a = [H_3O^+]$.

4. What color is the conjugate acid of BCG^-?

5. What color is the conjugate base of HBCG?

6. What color is an equal mixture of the conjugate acid and conjugate base of bromcresol green? At what pH does this equal mixture occur?

YOU'RE THE CHEMIST

The following small-scale activities allow you to develop your own procedures and analyze the results.

1. **Design It!** Design and carry out an experiment to measure the K_a of several more acid–base indicators. Record the colors of the conjugate acids (low pH) and the conjugate bases (high pH). Determine the K_a for each acid.

2. **Analyze It!** Explain in your own words how to measure the K_a of a colored acid–base indicator. Explain what you would do and how you would interpret your results.

Chemistry Serving...the Environment

RAIN LIKE VINEGAR

In Canada and the eastern part of the United States, lakes once full of fish and frogs are now nearly lifeless. Acres and acres of pines and other forest trees are dying in the Appalachian Mountains. In Rome and Athens, ancient carved stonework has been weathered so badly that the details of the carvings have been erased. All this damage has a single cause—acid rain.

Acid rain is rain with a pH lower than that of "normal" precipitation. Normal precipitation is itself mildly acidic, with a pH of about 5.6. This mild acidity comes from small amounts of carbon dioxide in the atmosphere that dissolve in tiny water droplets to form carbonic acid (H_2CO_3). The acidity of normal rainfall poses no problems because it is so mild and because animals and plants have adapted to it. But when the pH of rainfall gets significantly lower than 5.6, negative effects begin to appear. The rain from a 1981 storm in Baltimore was measured at pH 2.7, about the same pH as vinegar! Where it occurs, acid rain causes enormous damage to stone structures, paint, metal, and the environment. It leaches nutrients from the soil and may even be a direct threat to human health.

What causes acid rain? Acid rain results when oxides of sulfur (SO_x) and oxides of nitrogen (NO_x) are emitted into the atmosphere. Although there are some natural sources of these pollutants (such as volcanoes), most of them come from human sources, such as coal- and oil-fired power plants. In the atmosphere, sulfur oxides form sulfuric acid (H_2SO_4), and nitrogen oxides form nitric acid (HNO_3). Eventually, these acids fall to Earth in raindrops or snowflakes.

Fortunately, acid rain can be prevented, and chemistry is playing a big part in the effort. Because power plants are one of the main sources of SO_x and NO_x, chemists have focused on developing devices called scrubbers that remove these pollutants from power plant smoke before it leaves the smokestack.

In one type of scrubber now in common use, the smoke passes through an aqueous suspension of lime (CaO). The lime reacts with the gaseous SO_2 to make calcium sulfite ($CaSO_3$), a solid that can be disposed of. To remove NO_x, a process called Selective Catalytic Reduction (SCR) is often used. In an SCR chamber, ammonia (NH_3) is sprayed onto a surface covered with a mixture of catalysts. As the smoke passes through the chamber, NO and NO_2 in the smoke react with the ammonia and oxygen to form harmless nitrogen gas (N_2) and water (H_2O).

To eliminate the need for separate scrubbers for SO_x and NO_x, researchers have also developed ways of removing the two types of oxides from power plant smoke at the same time. In one technique, the smoke is passed through an alkaline suspension of yellow phosphorus. A variety of chemical reactions occur that convert almost all the SO_x and NO_x into valuable by-products, including some of the important plant nutrients that make up fertilizers.

The use of scrubbers at fossil-fuel-burning power plants has begun to have an impact on the pH of rainfall in many parts of the world, but much more remains to be done to solve the acid rain problem.

> The rain from a 1981 storm in Baltimore was measured at pH 2.7, about the same pH as vinegar!

Take It to the NET
For interactive study and review, go to www.phschool.com

KEY TERMS

- acid *p. 578*
- acid dissociation constant (K_a) *p. 601*
- acidic solution *p. 581*
- alkaline solution *p. 581*
- amphoteric *p. 598*
- base *p. 579*
- base dissociation constant (K_b) *p. 603*
- basic solution *p. 581*
- conjugate acid *p. 597*

- conjugate acid–base pair *p. 597*
- conjugate base *p. 597*
- diprotic acid *p. 594*
- hydrogen-ion acceptor *p. 596*
- hydrogen-ion donor *p. 596*
- hydronium ion (H_3O^+) *p. 580*
- hydroxide ion (OH^-) *p. 580*
- ion-product constant for water (K_w) *p. 581*
- Lewis acid *p. 598*
- Lewis base *p. 598*

- monoprotic acid *p. 594*
- neutral solution *p. 580*
- pH *p. 582*
- self-ionization *p. 580*
- strong acid *p. 600*
- strong base *p. 602*
- triprotic acid p. 594
- weak acid *p. 600*
- weak base *p. 602*

KEY EQUATIONS AND RELATIONSHIPS

- $K_w = [H^+] \times [OH^-] = 1.0 \times 10^{-14} M^2$
- $pH = -\log[H^+]$

- $pOH = -\log[OH^-]$
- $pH + pOH = 14$

CONCEPT SUMMARY

20.1 Describing Acids and Bases

- Acids taste sour, are electrolytes, react with active metals to produce hydrogen, react with bases to form water and salts, and cause indicators to change color.
- Bases taste bitter, are electrolytes, react with acids to form water and salts, and cause indicators to change color.

20.2 Hydrogen Ions and Acidity

- Water molecules dissociate into hydrogen ions (H^+) and hydroxide ions (OH^-).
- On the pH scale, 0 is strongly acidic, 14 is strongly basic, and 7 is neutral. Pure water at 25 °C has a pH of 7.

20.3 Acid–Base Theories

- A Brønsted-Lowry acid is a proton donor, and a Brønsted-Lowry base is a proton acceptor.

- An Arrhenius acid yields hydrogen ions in aqueous solution. An Arrhenius base yields hydroxide ions in aqueous solution.
- A Lewis acid is an electron-pair acceptor, and a Lewis base is an electron-pair donor.
- A conjugate acid–base pair consists of two substances related by the loss or gain of a single hydrogen ion.

20.4 Strengths of Acids and Bases

- The strength of an acid or a base is determined by its degree of ionization in solution. The acid dissociation constant (K_a) is a quantitative measure of acid strength.
- The base dissociation constant (K_b) is a quantitative measure of base strength.

CHAPTER CONCEPT MAP

Use these terms to construct a concept map that organizes the major ideas of this chapter.

Chem ASAP! Concept Map 20
Create your Concept Map using the computer.

CONCEPT PRACTICE

34. Write formulas for these compounds. *20.1*
   a. nitrous acid
   b. aluminum hydroxide
   c. hydroselenic acid
   d. strontium hydroxide
   e. phosphoric acid
   f. ethanoic acid

35. Write an equation showing the ionization of water. *20.2*

36. What are the concentrations of H^+ and OH^- in pure water at 25 °C? *20.2*

37. How is the pH of a solution calculated? *20.2*

38. Why is the pH of pure water at 25 °C equal to 7.00? *20.2*

39. Calculate the pH for the following solutions and indicate whether each solution is acidic or basic. *20.2*
   a. $[H^+] = 1.0 \times 10^{-2}M$
   b. $[OH^-] = 1.0 \times 10^{-2}M$
   c. $[OH^-] = 1.0 \times 10^{-8}M$
   d. $[H^+] = 1.0 \times 10^{-6}M$

40. What are the hydroxide-ion concentrations for solutions with the following pH values? *20.2*
   a. 4.00
   b. 8.00
   c. 12.00

41. Calculate the pH or $[H^+]$ for each solution. *20.2*
   a. $[H^+] = 2.4 \times 10^{-6}M$
   b. $[H^+] = 9.1 \times 10^{-9}M$
   c. pH = 13.20
   d. pH = 6.70

42. A soft drink has a pH of 3.80. What is the hydrogen-ion concentration in the drink? *20.2*

43. Write the reaction for the dissociation of each compound in water. *20.3*
   a. potassium hydroxide
   b. magnesium hydroxide

44. How did Arrhenius describe acids and bases? *20.3*

45. Classify each as an Arrhenius acid or an Arrhenius base. *20.3*
   a. $Ca(OH)_2$ **d.** C_2H_5COOH
   b. HNO_3 **e.** HBr
   c. KOH   **f.** H_2SO_4

46. Identify each acid in Problem 45 as monoprotic, diprotic, or triprotic. *20.3*

47. Write balanced equations for the reaction of each metal with water. *20.3*
   a. lithium
   b. barium

48. Identify each reactant in the following equations as a hydrogen-ion donor (acid) or a hydrogen-ion acceptor (base). *20.3*
   a. $HNO_3 + H_2O \rightleftharpoons H_3O^+ + NO_3^-$
   b. $CH_3COOH + H_2O \rightleftharpoons H_3O^+ + CH_3COO^-$
   c. $NH_3 + H_2O \rightleftharpoons NH_4^+ + OH^-$
   d. $H_2O + CH_3COO^- \rightleftharpoons CH_3COOH + OH^-$

49. Label the conjugate acid–base pairs in each equation in Problem 48. *20.3*

50. What is an amphoteric substance? *20.3*

51. What is a Lewis acid? A Lewis base? In what sense is the Lewis theory more general than the Arrhenius and Brønsted-Lowry theories? *20.3*

52. Identify each compound as a strong or weak acid or base. *20.4*
   a. NaOH
   b. HCl
   c. NH_3
   d. H_2SO_4

53. Would a strong acid have a large or a small K_a? Explain. *20.4*

54. Why are $Mg(OH)_2$ and $Ca(OH)_2$ considered to be strong bases even though their saturated solutions are only mildly basic? *20.4*

55. Write the expression for K_a for each acid. Assume only one hydrogen is ionized. *20.4*
   a. HF
   b. H_2CO_3

56. A $0.0250M$ solution of $KHCrO_4$ has a pH of 3.50. Calculate the K_a for the equilibrium between $HCrO_4^-$ and CrO_4^{2-}. *20.4*

CONCEPT MASTERY

57. Is it possible to have a concentrated weak acid? Explain.

58. Write equations showing that the hydrogen phosphate ion (HPO_4^{2-}) is amphoteric.

59. The pH of a $0.50M$ HNO_2 solution is 1.83. What is the K_a of this acid?

60. Write the formula and name of the conjugate base of each Brønsted-Lowry acid.
   a. HCO_3^- **c.** NH_4^+
   b. HI   **d.** H_2SO_3

61. Write the formula and name of the conjugate acid of each Brønsted-Lowry base.
   a. ClO_2^- c. H_2O
   b. $H_2PO_4^-$ d. NH_3

62. You have determined that 1.40% of a 0.080M solution of a weak acid is ionized. Calculate the K_a for this acid.

63. Calculate the $[OH^-]$ or pH of each solution.
   a. pH = 4.60   c. $[OH^-] = 1.8 \times 10^{-2}M$
   b. pH = 9.30   d. $[OH^-] = 7.3 \times 10^{-9}M$

64. Write the three equations for the stepwise ionization of phosphoric acid.

65. Use the Brønsted-Lowry and Lewis definitions of acids and bases to identify each reactant as an acid or a base.
   a. $KOH + HBr \rightleftharpoons KBr + H_2O$
   b. $HCl + H_2O \rightleftharpoons Cl^- + H_3O^+$

CRITICAL THINKING

66. Choose the term that best completes the second relationship.
   a. sky : blue   acid : _____
      (1) metallic   (3) sour
      (2) basic   (4) bitter
   b. animals : carbon dioxide   base : _____
      (1) electrons   (3) bitter
      (2) hydroxide ions   (4) protons
   c. thermometer : degrees   indicator : _____
      (1) pH   (3) H^+
      (2) acid   (4) base

67. Arrhenius, Brønsted-Lowry, and Lewis all developed theories to explain acids and bases.
   a. Which theory is easiest for you to understand?
   b. How can all three theories be accepted by chemists?

68. Prove the relationship pH + pOH = 14. (*Hint:* Use the expression for K_w.)

69. Which quantity might correspond to the y-axis: $[H^+]$, pH, $[OH^-]$, or pOH? Explain your answer.

[HCl]

70. How would you prepare 400.0 mL of a 0.680M KOH solution?

71. How many liters of 8.0M HCl are needed to prepare 1.50 L of 2.5M HCl?

72. How would each change affect the position of equilibrium of this reaction?

$$2H_2(g) + O_2(g) \rightleftharpoons 2H_2O(g) + heat$$

   a. increasing the pressure
   b. adding a catalyst
   c. increasing the concentration of $H_2(g)$
   d. cooling the reaction mixture
   e. removing water vapor from the container

73. Write an equilibrium-constant expression for each equation.
   a. $2CO_2(g) \rightleftharpoons 2CO(g) + O_2(g)$
   b. $N_2(g) + 3H_2(g) \rightleftharpoons 2NH_3(g)$

CONCEPT CHALLENGE

74. Calculate the pH of a 0.010M solution of sodium cyanide (NaCN). The K_b of CN^- is 2.1×10^{-5}.

75. Show that for any conjugate acid–base pair $K_a \times K_b = K_w$.

76. The K_w of water varies with temperature, as indicated in the table below.

Temperature (°C)	K_w	pH
0	1.137×10^{-15}	
10	2.917×10^{-15}	
20	6.807×10^{-15}	
30	1.469×10^{-14}	
40	2.917×10^{-14}	
50	5.470×10^{-14}	

   a. Find the pH of water for each temperature in the table. Use these data to prepare a graph of pH versus temperature.
   b. Using the graph, estimate the pH of water at 5 °C.
   c. At what temperature is the pH of water approximately 6.85?

77. Suppose you slowly add 0.1M NaOH to 50.0 mL of 0.1M HCl. What volume of NaOH must be added for the resulting solution to become neutral (pH = 7)? Explain your reasoning.

Select the choice that best answers each question or completes each statement.

1. An acid has a measured K_a of 3×10^{-6}.
   a. The acid is a strong acid.
   b. An aqueous solution of the acid would have a pH < 7.
   c. The acid is a strong electrolyte.
   d. All of the above are correct

2. The pH of a sample of orange juice is 3.5. A sample of tomato juice has a pH of 4.5. Compared to the $[H^+]$ of orange juice, the $[H^+]$ of tomato juice is
   a. 1.0 times higher.
   c. 10 times higher.
   b. 10 times lower.
   d. 1.0 times lower.

3. Which species is the conjugate base of an ammonium ion, $NH_4{}^+$?
   a. H_2O
   c. NH_3
   b. OH^-
   d. H_3O^+

4. A solution with a hydrogen ion concentration of $2.3 \times 10^{-8}M$ has a pH between
   a. 2 and 3.
   c. 7 and 8.
   b. 3 and 4.
   d. 8 and 9.

Use the description and data table to answer questions 5–8.

Ethanoic acid (acetic acid) is a weak acid with a K_a of 1.8×10^{-5} at room temperature. A student measured the pH of ethanoic acid solutions at different concentrations. She used the pH values to calculate the percent of ethanoic acid molecules that were ionized in each solution.

Concentration of ethanoic acid (M)	Percent of molecules ionized
0.050	1.9
0.040	2.1
0.030	2.5
0.020	3.1
0.010	4.0

5. Write the equilibrium equation for the ionization of ethanoic acid in water.

6. Use the data in the table to construct a graph. Make the molarity of ethanoic acid the independent variable.

7. Does the relationship between the variables make sense in terms of Le Châtelier's principle? Explain your answer.

8. Use the graph to estimate the percent of molecules ionized at a concentration of 0.015M.

Use the drawings to answer questions 9–11. They show what happens when acids form aqueous solutions. Water molecules have been omitted from the solution windows.

Undissociated acid   Conjugate base   Hydronium ion

a.

b.

c.

9. Put the acids in order of increasing strength.

10. How many of the acids are strong acids?

11. Which acid is dissociated about 10%?

Write a few sentences in response to each of the statements in questions 12–14.

12. Indicators such as methyl red provide accurate and precise measurements of pH.

13. According to the Arrhenius definition of acids and bases, ammonia qualifies as a base.

14. The strength of an acid or base changes as its concentration changes.

Carbon dioxide forms when antacid tablets are dropped in water.

FEATURES

Stay current with **SCIENCE NEWS**
Find out more about neutralization:
www.phschool.com

DISCOVER IT!   REACTION OF AN ACID WITH AN EGG

You need an egg, a small container, white vinegar, paper, a pen or pencil, and a clock.

1. Carefully place the egg in the container.
2. Pour vinegar into the container so that the vinegar level is about 3 cm above the egg.
3. Note the time.
4. Observe the system periodically over 24 hours. Record the elapsed time and your observations.

When did you first notice something happening to the egg? What did you observe? How long did it take for the reaction to cease? Describe the condition of the egg after 24 hours. Hypothesize about what has occurred. After completing the chapter, review your hypothesis and suggest ways in which it might be modified.

NEUTRALIZATION REACTIONS

*N*early all of the adult population suffers from acid indigestion at some time. Although hydrochloric acid is always present in the stomach, an excess can cause heartburn and a feeling of nausea. A common way to relieve the pain of acid indigestion is to take antacids to neutralize the stomach acid. The active ingredient in many antacids is sodium hydrogen carbonate, aluminum hydroxide, or magnesium hydroxide. **What is a neutralization reaction?**

objectives
▶ Explain how acid–base titration is used to calculate the concentration of an acid or a base
▶ Explain the concept of equivalence in neutralization reactions

key terms
▶ neutralization reactions
▶ standard solution
▶ titration
▶ end point
▶ equivalent (equiv)
▶ gram equivalent mass
▶ normality (*N*)
▶ equivalence point

Acid–Base Reactions

In general, the reaction of an acid with a base produces water and one of a class of compounds called salts. When you hear the word salt, you may think of the substance that flavors your french fries or scrambled eggs. Indeed, table salt (sodium chloride) is an example of this class of compounds, but there are many more. Salts are compounds consisting of an anion from an acid and a cation from a base.

The properties of acids, bases, and salts help explain many diverse phenomena. The usefulness of antacids, for example, depends on the process of acid–base neutralization. Farmers use a similar process to control the pH of soil. The formation of caves and of stalactites in caves is caused by changes in the solubilities of salts. Within the human body, the formation of kidney stones from salts is also related to solubility. Neutralization reactions and the solubilities of salts are the topics of this chapter.

If you mix a solution of a strong acid containing hydronium (hydrogen) ions with a solution of a strong base that has an equal number of hydroxide ions, a neutral solution results. The final solution has properties that are characteristic of neither an acidic nor a basic solution. Consider these examples:

$$HCl(aq) + NaOH(aq) \longrightarrow NaCl(aq) + H_2O(l)$$

$$H_2SO_4(aq) + 2KOH(aq) \longrightarrow K_2SO_4(aq) + 2H_2O(l)$$

Figure 21.1

Geodes, such as this amethyst specimen (left), begin as cavities in limestone. Carbonic acid in ground water dissolves silicate minerals in rock. The silicate-rich water fills the cavities. Over time, the silicates in solution deposit as crystals of silicon dioxide, or quartz. Amethyst consists of quartz crystals containing traces of manganese. For fish and other aquatic animals to survive (right), the water in which they live must be maintained at the proper pH.

Hydronium ion
H_3O^+
+
Hydroxide ion
OH^-
⟶
Water
H_2O
+
Water
H_2O

Figure 21.2

In a neutralization reaction, hydronium ions (H_3O^+) combine with hydroxide ions (OH^-) to form neutral water.

In each example, a strong acid reacts with a strong base. If solutions of these substances are mixed in the mole ratios specified by the balanced equation, neutral solutions will result. Similar reactions of weak acids and/or weak bases do not usually produce neutral solutions. In general, however, reactions in which an acid and a base react in an aqueous solution to produce a salt and water are called **neutralization reactions. Figure 21.2** illustrates the formation of water in a neutralization reaction. All neutralization reactions are double-replacement reactions.

Neutralization reactions are one way to prepare pure samples of salts. You could prepare potassium chloride, for example, by mixing equal molar quantities of hydrochloric acid and potassium hydroxide. An aqueous solution of potassium chloride would result. You could heat the solution to evaporate the water, leaving the salt potassium chloride. **Table 21.1** lists some common salts and their applications. What acid and base could you mix to make sodium sulfate? To make lithium nitrate?

Table 21.1

Some Salts and Their Applications		
Name	**Formula**	**Applications**
Ammonium sulfate	$(NH_4)_2SO_4$	Fertilizer
Barium sulfate	$BaSO_4$	Gastrointestinal studies; white pigment
Calcium chloride	$CaCl_2$	De-icing roadways and sidewalks
Calcium sulfate dihydrate (gypsum)	$CaSO_4 \cdot 2H_2O$	Plasterboard
Copper sulfate pentahydrate (blue vitriol)	$CuSO_4 \cdot 5H_2O$	Dyeing, fungicide
Calcium sulfate hemihydrate	$CaSO_4 \cdot \frac{1}{2} H_2O$	Plaster casts
Potassium chloride	KCl	Sodium-free salt substitute
Potassium permanganate	$KMnO_4$	Disinfectant and fungicide
Silver nitrate	$AgNO_3$	Cauterizing agent
Silver bromide	AgBr	Photographic emulsions
Sodium hydrogen carbonate (baking soda)	$NaHCO_3$	Antacid
Sodium carbonate decahydrate (washing soda)	$Na_2CO_3 \cdot 10H_2O$	Glass manufacture; water softener
Sodium chloride (table salt)	NaCl	Body electrolyte; chlorine manufacture
Sodium thiosulfate (hypo)	$Na_2S_2O_3$	Fixing agent in photographic process

MINI LAB

The Neutralizing Power of Antacids

PURPOSE

To measure the effectiveness of antacids at neutralizing excess stomach acid.

MATERIALS

- several brands of antacids
- mortar and pestle
- paper towels
- measuring teaspoon
- clear plastic cups
- dropper
- universal indicator
- white vinegar (5% ethanoic acid)
- sodium hydrogen carbonate
- pH sensor (optional)

PROCEDURE

 Sensor version available in the Probeware Lab Manual.

1. Using the mortar and pestle, grind a brand of antacid tablet into powder. Place the powder on a paper towel labeled with the brand name. Repeat this process for each brand of tablet.

2. Put 2 teaspoons of vinegar in a plastic cup to represent excess stomach acid.

3. Add 5 drops of indicator to the vinegar. Note the color.

4. Add small amounts of sodium hydrogen carbonate until the system is neutral; the indicator will be blue.

5. Estimate how much sodium hydrogen carbonate was needed to neutralize the acid. This is your reference standard.

6. Repeat Steps 2, 3, and 4, but substitute various antacid powders for the sodium hydrogen carbonate.

7. Compare the estimated amounts of each brand of antacid required to neutralize the vinegar with your reference standard.

ANALYSIS AND CONCLUSIONS

1. List the antacid brands tested and indicate their effectiveness with respect to the reference standard.

2. Which ingredients listed on antacid packages neutralize stomach acid?

3. What is the purpose of the non-neutralizing components?

4. Write a balanced equation for the neutralization of ethanoic acid, CH_3COOH, by $NaHCO_3$.

5. As described, this activity will give you only qualitative results. Explain what this means. Design your own activity to give quantitative results.

Titration

Acids and bases sometimes, but not always, react in a 1:1 mole ratio.

$$HCl(aq) + NaOH(aq) \longrightarrow NaCl(aq) + H_2O(l)$$
$$\text{1 mol} \qquad \text{1 mol} \qquad \text{1 mol} \qquad \text{1 mol}$$

When sulfuric acid reacts with sodium hydroxide, however, the ratio is 1:2. Two moles of the base sodium hydroxide are required to neutralize one mole of H_2SO_4.

$$H_2SO_4(aq) + 2NaOH(aq) \longrightarrow Na_2SO_4(aq) + 2H_2O(l)$$
$$\text{1 mol} \qquad \text{2 mol} \qquad \text{1 mol} \qquad \text{2 mol}$$

Similarly, hydrochloric acid and calcium hydroxide react in a 2:1 ratio.

$$2HCl(aq) + Ca(OH)_2(aq) \longrightarrow CaCl_2(aq) + 2H_2O(l)$$
$$\text{2 mol} \qquad \text{1 mol} \qquad \text{1 mol} \qquad \text{2 mol}$$

Sample Problem 21-1

How many moles of sulfuric acid are required to neutralize 0.50 mol of sodium hydroxide?

1. **ANALYZE** *List the knowns and the unknown.*

   Knowns:
   - mol NaOH = 0.50 mol
   - $H_2SO_4(aq) + 2NaOH(aq) \longrightarrow Na_2SO_4(aq) + 2H_2O(l)$
   - $\dfrac{\text{mol } H_2SO_4}{\text{mol NaOH}} = \dfrac{1}{2}$ (from the balanced equation)

   Unknown:
   - mol H_2SO_4 = ? mol

2. **CALCULATE** *Solve for the unknown.*

   The mole ratio of H_2SO_4 to NaOH is 1:2. The necessary number of moles of H_2SO_4 is calculated using this ratio.

   $$0.50 \text{ mol NaOH} \times \frac{1 \text{ mol } H_2SO_4}{2 \text{ mol NaOH}} = 0.25 \text{ mol } H_2SO_4$$

3. **EVALUATE** *Does the result make sense?*

   Because the mole ratio of H_2SO_4 to NaOH is 1:2, the expected number of moles of H_2SO_4 should be half the given number of moles of NaOH. The answer should have two significant figures.

Practice Problems

1. How many moles of potassium hydroxide are needed to completely neutralize 1.56 mol of phosphoric acid?
2. How many moles of sodium hydroxide are required to neutralize 0.20 mol of nitric acid?

Problem-Solving 1

Solve Problem 1 with the help of an interactive guided tutorial.

The concentration of acid (or base) in a solution can be determined by performing a neutralization reaction. An appropriate acid–base indicator is used to show when neutralization has occurred. As you can see in **Figure 21.3,** the juice of the red cabbage is an acid–base indicator. In the laboratory, phenolphthalein is often the preferred indicator for acid–base neutralization reactions. Solutions that contain phenolphthalein turn from colorless to deep pink as the pH of the solution changes from acidic to basic. In slightly basic solutions, the indicator is very faintly pink. What is the color of phenolphthalein at pH = 3?

Figure 21.3

The juice of a red cabbage can be used as an acid–base indicator. When a solution is highly acidic, the juice turns red. As the acidity of the solution decreases, or as the solution becomes more basic, the color changes from red to violet to green to yellow. Would the yellow solution have a high or low pH?

(a) **(b)** **(c)**

Figure 21.4

The titration of an acid with a base is shown here. (a) A known volume of an acid (plus a few drops of phenolphthalein indicator) in a flask is placed beneath a buret filled with a base of known concentration. (b) Base is slowly added from the buret to the acid while the flask is gently swirled. (c) A change in the color of the indicator signals that neutralization has occurred.

Chem ASAP!

Simulation 26

Titrate several acids and bases and observe patterns in the pH at equivalence.

The steps in a neutralization reaction are as follows.

1. A measured volume of an acid solution of unknown concentration is added to a flask.
2. Several drops of the indicator are added to the solution.
3. Measured volumes of a base of known concentration are mixed into the acid until the indicator just barely changes color.

The solution of known concentration is called the **standard solution.** The standard solution is added using a buret. This process of adding a known amount of solution of known concentration to determine the concentration of another solution is called **titration.** A titration is continued until the indicator shows that neutralization has just occurred. The point at which the indicator changes color is the **end point** of the titration. The titration of an acid of unknown concentration with a standard base is shown in **Figure 21.4.** A similar procedure could be used to find the concentration of a base using a standard acid.

Figure 21.5

In this titration of a strong acid with a strong base, 0.10M NaOH is slowly added from a buret to 50.0 mL of 0.10M HCl in the beaker. The pH of the solution is measured with a pH meter and is recorded as a function of the volume of NaOH added. The equivalence point, the midpoint on the vertical portion of the pH titration curve, occurs at 50.0 mL of NaOH added. The pH at the equivalence point is 7, which is the pH of a neutral solution. What is true concerning $[H^+]$ and $[OH^-]$ at the equivalence point?

Figure 21.5 on the previous page shows how the pH of a solution changes during the titration of a strong acid with a strong base. The pH of the initial acid solution is low. As the base is added, the pH increases because some of the acid is neutralized. As the titration approaches the point of neutralization, at a pH of 7, the pH increases dramatically as hydrogen ions are used up. Once past the point of neutralization, additional base produces a further increase of pH. The point of neutralization is the end point of the titration. At this point, the contents of the beaker consist of only H_2O and $NaCl$, which is the salt derived from the strong acid HCl and the strong base $NaOH$, plus a trace of indicator.

Sample Problem 21-2

A 25-mL solution of H_2SO_4 is completely neutralized by 18 mL of $1.0M$ NaOH using phenolphthalein as an indicator. What is the concentration of the H_2SO_4 solution?

1. ANALYZE *List the knowns and the unknown.*

Knowns:
- molarity base = $1.0M$ NaOH
- volume base = 18 mL = 0.018 L
- volume acid = 25 mL = 0.025 L
- $H_2SO_4(aq) + 2NaOH(aq) \longrightarrow Na_2SO_4(aq) + 2H_2O(l)$
- mole ratio = $\dfrac{1 \text{ mol } H_2SO_4}{2 \text{ mol NaOH}}$

Unknown:
- molarity acid = $?M$ H_2SO_4

The conversion steps are

$$\text{L NaOH} \longrightarrow \text{mol NaOH} \longrightarrow \text{mol } H_2SO_4 \longrightarrow M\ H_2SO_4$$

2. CALCULATE *Solve for the unknown.*

First convert the volume of base to the number of moles of base, using the molarity. Then use the mole ratio to find moles of H_2SO_4. Finally, calculate the molarity by dividing the moles of H_2SO_4 by the liters of H_2SO_4.

$$0.018 \text{ L NaOH} \times \frac{1.0 \text{ mol NaOH}}{1 \text{ L NaOH}} \times \frac{1 \text{ mol } H_2SO_4}{2 \text{ mol NaOH}}$$

$$= 0.0090 \text{ mol } H_2SO_4$$

$$\text{molarity} = \frac{\text{moles}}{\text{liters}} = \frac{0.0090 \text{ mol}}{0.025 \text{ L}} = 0.36M$$

The $[H_2SO_4]$ is $0.36M$.

3. EVALUATE *Does the result make sense?*

Because H_2SO_4 has two ionizable hydrogens, the concentration of the acid should be half that of the base if equal volumes of the reactants were used in the neutralization. Because the volume of acid was greater than the volume of base, the concentration is less than $0.5M$. The answer should have two significant figures.

Practice Problems

3. How many milliliters of $0.45M$ hydrochloric acid must be added to 25.0 mL of $1.00M$ potassium hydroxide to make a neutral solution?

4. What is the molarity of phosphoric acid if 15.0 mL of the solution is completely neutralized by 38.5 mL of $0.150M$ NaOH?

Chem ASAP!

Problem-Solving 4
Solve Problem 4 with the help of an interactive guided tutorial.

Equivalents

In any neutralization reaction, one mole of hydrogen ions reacts with one mole of hydroxide ions. This does not mean, however, that one mole of any acid will neutralize one mole of any base. Why? For some acids, one mole of the acid gives one mole of hydrogen ions. HCl, HNO_3, and CH_3COOH are such acids.

$$HCl \longrightarrow H^+ + Cl^-$$
$$HNO_3 \longrightarrow H^+ + NO_3^-$$
$$CH_3COOH \longrightarrow H^+ + CH_3COO^-$$

For other acids, one mole of the acid gives two or more moles of hydrogen ions. One mole of H_2SO_4, for example, gives two moles of hydrogen ions.

$$H_2SO_4 \longrightarrow 2H^+ + SO_4^{2-}$$

One mole of H_3PO_4 gives three moles of hydrogen ions.

$$H_3PO_4 \longrightarrow 3H^+ + PO_4^{3-}$$

The same is true for the number of hydroxide ions given by bases. The bases $Ca(OH)_2$ and $Al(OH)_3$, for example, give two and three moles of hydroxide ions, respectively, for each mole of base.

$$Ca(OH)_2 \longrightarrow Ca^{2+} + 2OH^-$$
$$Al(OH)_3 \longrightarrow Al^{3+} + 3OH^-$$

Calculating the amount of acid needed to neutralize a given amount of base is made simpler by the existence of a unit called an equivalent. One **equivalent (equiv)** is the amount of acid (or base) that will give one mole of hydrogen (or hydroxide) ions.

One mole of HCl is one equivalent of HCl. One mole of H_2SO_4 is two equivalents of H_2SO_4. One mole of NaOH is one equivalent of NaOH. How many equivalents of $Ca(OH)_2$ is one mole of $Ca(OH)_2$? One mole of HCl will neutralize one mole of NaOH. This is because one mole of each compound is also one equivalent.

$$HCl(aq) + NaOH(aq) \longrightarrow NaCl(aq) + H_2O(l)$$

One mole of HCl will not neutralize one mole of $Ca(OH)_2$. Two moles of the acid are required to neutralize one mole of this base because two moles of HCl contain two equivalents of acid, and one mole of $Ca(OH)_2$ contains two equivalents of base.

$$2HCl(aq) + Ca(OH)_2(aq) \longrightarrow CaCl_2(aq) + 2H_2O(l)$$

In any neutralization reaction, the equivalents of acid must equal the equivalents of base. How many equivalents of base are in 2 mol $Ca(OH)_2$?

The mass of one equivalent of a substance is its **gram equivalent mass.** One mole of HCl is one equivalent of HCl. Its gram equivalent mass is equal to its molar mass (36.5 g/mol). One mole of H_2SO_4 is two equivalents of H_2SO_4. Its gram equivalent mass is only half of its molar mass (98.1 g/mol), or roughly 49.0 g/equiv.

COSMETOLOGY

Neutral Curls from Permanent Waves

Curly hair from a permanent wave involves an acid–base neutralization reaction. The waving solution is basic and has a pH of about 9.20. The active ingredient in the waving solution is often an ammonium compound that is applied once the hair has been rolled. After a specified time, the hair is rinsed to remove the excess base. Then a neutralizer is applied. The neutralizer is an acidic solution that has a pH range of 2 to 6. If the hair is exposed to the waving solution for too long a period of time, the hair's texture and appearance are damaged.

Sample Problem 21-3

What is the mass of 1 equivalent of calcium hydroxide?

1. **ANALYZE List the known and the unknown.**
   Known:
   - molar mass $Ca(OH)_2$ = 74 g/mol
   Unknown:
   - gram equivalent mass $Ca(OH)_2$ = ? g/equiv

   To find the gram equivalent mass, the molar mass must be divided by the number of equivalents/mole.

2. **CALCULATE Solve for the unknown.**
   Because each formula unit of $Ca(OH)_2$ gives two hydroxide ions, the molar mass must be divided by 2 equiv/mol to find the gram equivalent mass.

   $$\text{gram equivalent mass } Ca(OH)_2 = \frac{74 \text{ g/mol}}{2 \text{ equiv/mol}} = 37 \text{ g/equiv}$$

3. **EVALUATE Does the result make sense?**
   Because 1 mol of calcium hydroxide is 2 equiv/mol, the equivalent mass is half the molar mass.

Practice Problems

5. What is the mass of 1 equivalent of each compound?
   a. H_3PO_4
   b. NaOH
6. Determine the gram equivalent mass of each compound.
   a. $Mg(OH)_2$
   b. CH_3COOH

Sample Problem 21-4

How many equivalents is 14.6 g of sulfuric acid?

1. **ANALYZE List the knowns and the unknown.**
   Knowns:
   - mass H_2SO_4 = 14.6 g H_2SO_4
   - molar mass H_2SO_4 = 98.1 g/mol
   Unknown:
   - equivalents H_2SO_4 = ? equiv

   Because H_2SO_4 has two ionizable hydrogens, its equivalent mass is half its molar mass. This relationship is the conversion factor used to convert mass to equivalents.

2. **CALCULATE Solve for the unknown.**

   $$\text{gram equivalent mass } H_2SO_4 = \frac{98.1 \text{ g/mol}}{2 \text{ equiv/mol}} = 49.1 \text{ g/equiv}$$

   $$14.6 \text{ g } H_2SO_4 \times \frac{1 \text{ equiv } H_2SO_4}{49.1 \text{ g } H_2SO_4} = 0.297 \text{ equiv } H_2SO_4$$

3. **EVALUATE Does the result make sense?**
   Because the equivalent mass of H_2SO_4 is approximately 50 g, and 14.6 is about one-third of 50, the given number of grams should be approximately one-third the mass of an equivalent.

Practice Problems

7. How many equivalents are in each sample of compound?
   a. 20 g NaOH
   b. 7.4 g $Ca(OH)_2$
8. Determine the number of equivalents in each sample.
   a. 9.8 g H_3PO_4
   b. 19.6 g H_2SO_4

Chem ASAP!

Problem-Solving 8
Solve Problem 8 with the help of an interactive guided tutorial.

Normality

As you have learned, the concentrations of acids and bases can be stated in terms of molarity. However, it is often more useful to know how many equivalents of acid or base a solution contains. An older, non-SI unit used to express the equivalents of acids and bases is normality. A solution containing 1.0 equivalent of an acid or base per liter has a normality of 1.0. That is, the solution is 1.0 normal (1.0N). The **normality** *(N)* of a solution is the concentration expressed as the number of equivalents of solute in one liter of solution.

$$\text{Normality } (N) = \text{equiv/L}$$

The numerical values of normality and molarity are equal for acids and bases that give 1 equivalent of H^+ or OH^- per mole. A solution containing 1 mole of NaOH per liter, for example, is 1M and also 1N. A solution containing 1 mole of H_2SO_4 per liter is 1M, but is 2N because H_2SO_4 contains 2 equivalents per mole. What is the normality of a 0.015M $Ca(OH)_2$ solution? What is the normality of a 1.0M solution of phosphoric acid (H_3PO_4)?

The number of equivalents of an acid or base in a known volume of a solution of known normality can be calculated as follows.

$$\text{Number of equivalents} = \text{volume (liters)} \times \text{normality of solution}$$

$$\text{equiv} = V \text{ (L)} \times N$$

1M HCl
contains
1 equiv HCl/L

1M H_2SO_4
contains
2 equiv H_2SO_4/L

1M H_3PO_4
contains
3 equiv H_3PO_4/L

Figure 21.6
Color intensity is used to show the relationship between molarity and equivalents in monoprotic, diprotic, and triprotic acids.

Sample Problem 21-5

How many equivalents are in 2.5 L of 0.60N H_2SO_4?

1. **ANALYZE** *List the knowns and the unknown.*
   Knowns:
   - normality H_2SO_4 = 0.60N H_2SO_4
   - volume H_2SO_4 = 2.5 L
   - equiv = V (L) $\times$ N

   Unknown:
   - equivalents H_2SO_4 = ? equiv

2. **CALCULATE** *Solve for the unknown.*
   Substitute the given volume and normality (equiv/L) into the equation to calculate the number of equivalents.
   $$\text{equiv} = 2.5 \text{ L} \times 0.60N$$
   $$= 2.5 \text{ L} \times \frac{0.60 \text{ equiv}}{\text{L}}$$
   $$= 1.5 \text{ equiv}$$

3. **EVALUATE** *Does the result make sense?*
   Because 2 L of a 0.5N solution is 1 equiv, an answer of greater than 1 should be expected. The answer should have two significant figures.

Practice Problems

9. How many equivalents are in the following?
   a. 0.55 L of 1.8N NaOH
   b. 1.6 L of 0.50N H_3PO_4
   c. 250 mL of 0.28N H_2SO_4
10. What is the normality of each solution?
    a. 20.0 g NaOH in 1.0 L of solution
    b. 4.9 g H_2SO_4 in 500 mL of solution
    c. 15.0 g HCl in 0.400 L of solution
    d. 88.0 g H_3PO_4 in 1.50 L of solution

Figure 21.7

A solution with a given normality can be diluted to make a solution with a lower normality. The standard solution in the beaker contains 1.00 mole HCl per liter. The solution contains 1.00 equivalent of acid per liter. What is the normality of the acid? A volumetric pipet was used to transfer 10 mL of the standard solution to each of three volumetric flasks. How many equivalents of acid were added to each flask? The contents of each flask were then diluted with distilled water to their marks—100 mL, 50 mL, and 25 mL, respectively. How many equivalents of acid are in each flask? What is the normality of HCl in each flask?

Solutions of known normality can be made less concentrated by diluting them with water. As you can see in **Figure 21.7,** a solution of known normality is used to make three solutions, each of known normality. The changes in concentration can be calculated by using the following relationship.

$$N_1 \times V_1 = N_2 \times V_2$$

Here N_1 and V_1 are the normality and volume of the initial (standard) solution, and N_2 and V_2 are the normality and volume of the final solution.

Titration calculations are often accomplished more easily using normality instead of molarity because normality takes into account the number of ionizable hydrogens in an acid, whereas molarity does not. In a titration, the point of neutralization is called the **equivalence point.** At the equivalence point, the number of equivalents of acid and base are equal. It is thus possible to calculate the number of equivalents of acid or base in an unknown sample. If N_A and N_B represent the normalities of the acid and base solutions, and V_A and V_B represent the volumes of the acid and base solutions required to give a neutral solution, then

$$\text{Equivalents of acid} = N_A \times V_A$$

$$\text{Equivalents of base} = N_B \times V_B$$

And because the number of equivalents of acid and base are equal at the equivalence point,

$$N_A \times V_A = N_B \times V_B$$

Sample Problem 21-6

You need to make 250 mL of 0.10N sodium hydroxide from a stock solution that is 2.0N sodium hydroxide. How many milliliters of the stock solution must you dilute to 250 mL to get the required solution?

1. ANALYZE List the knowns and the unknown.

Knowns:
- $N_1 = 2.0N$
- $N_2 = 0.10N$
- $V_2 = 250$ mL
- $N_1 \times V_1 = N_2 \times V_2$

Unknown:
- $V_1 = ?$ mL

2. CALCULATE Solve for the unknown.

To find V_1, rearrange the equation and then substitute the values of N_1, N_2, and V_2.

$$V_1 = \frac{N_2 \times V_2}{N_1} = \frac{0.10N \times 250 \text{ mL}}{2.0N} = 13 \text{ mL}$$

Dilute 13 mL of 2.0N NaOH to 250 mL to make 0.10N NaOH.

3. EVALUATE Does the result make sense?

Because the concentration decreases by a factor of 20, the volume of the stock solution (initial solution) to be diluted should be about one-twentieth of the volume of the final solution. The answer should have two significant figures.

Practice Problems

11. How many milliliters of 3.0N KOH are needed to prepare 870 mL of 0.20N KOH?

12. How would you prepare 500 mL of 0.20N sulfuric acid from a stock solution of 4.0N sulfuric acid?

Chem ASAP!

Problem-Solving 11

Solve Problem 11 with the help of an interactive guided tutorial.

Sample Problem 21-7

If 35.0 mL of 0.20N hydrochloric acid are needed to neutralize 25.0 mL of an unknown base, what is the normality of the base?

1. ANALYZE List the knowns and the unknown.

Knowns:
- $V_A = 35.0$ mL
- $N_A = 0.20N$
- $V_B = 25.0$ mL
- $N_A \times V_A = N_B \times V_B$

Unknown:
- $N_B = ?N$

2. CALCULATE Solve for the unknown.

To solve for N_B, rearrange the equation and then substitute the values of V_A, N_A, and V_B.

$$N_B = \frac{V_A \times N_A}{V_B} = \frac{35.0 \text{ mL} \times 0.20N}{25.0 \text{ mL}} = 0.28N$$

3. EVALUATE Does the result make sense?

Because a smaller volume of the base is required, the normality of the base must be larger than the normality of the acid.

Practice Problems

13. If you need 50.0 mL of 0.152N hydrochloric acid to neutralize 29.2 mL Ca(OH)$_2$, what is the normality of the base?

14. What is the normality of a solution of a base if 25 mL is neutralized by 75 mL of 0.40N acid?

Chem ASAP!

Problem-Solving 14

Solve Problem 14 with the help of an interactive guided tutorial.

Sample Problem 21-8

How many milliliters of 0.500N sulfuric acid are needed to neutralize 50.0 mL of 0.200N potassium hydroxide?

1. **ANALYZE** *List the knowns and the unknown.*

   Knowns:
   - V_B = 50.0 mL
   - N_B = 0.200N
   - N_A = 0.500N
   - $N_A \times V_A = N_B \times V_B$

   Unknown:
   - V_A = ? mL

2. **CALCULATE** *Solve for the unknown.*

   To solve for V_A, rearrange the equation and then substitute the values of N_B, V_B, and N_A.

   $$V_A = \frac{V_B \times N_B}{N_A} = \frac{50.0 \text{ mL} \times 0.200N}{0.500N} = 20.0 \text{ mL}$$

3. **EVALUATE** *Does the result make sense?*

   The normality of the acid is more than twice the normality of the base, so the volume of the acid needed for neutralization should be less than half the volume of base. The answer should have three significant figures.

Practice Problems

15. How many milliliters of 0.850N hydrochloric acid would you need to neutralize 25.0 mL of 0.480N sodium hydroxide?

16. How many milliliters of 1.05N NaOH are needed to neutralize 50.0 mL of 0.620N H$_2$SO$_4$?

section review 21.1

17. How is acid–base titration used to calculate the concentration of an acid or a base?

18. Write complete balanced equations for these acid–base reactions. Give the names of the salts produced.

    a. $H_2SO_4(aq) + KOH(aq) \longrightarrow$

    b. $HCl(aq) + LiOH(aq) \longrightarrow$

    c. $H_3PO_4(aq) + Ca(OH)_2(aq) \longrightarrow$

    d. $HNO_3(aq) + Mg(OH)_2(aq) \longrightarrow$

19. How many moles of hydrochloric acid are required to neutralize aqueous solutions of these bases?

    a. 0.2 mol NaOH

    b. 2 mol NH_3

    c. 0.1 mol $Ca(OH)_2$

20. What is an equivalent? How is it related to normality?

21. Why are equivalents of acid and equivalents of base always equal in a neutralization reaction?

22. How many milliliters of 0.20N sodium hydroxide must be added to 75 mL of 0.050N hydrochloric acid to make a neutral solution?

portfolio project

Hypochlorite salts are used to disinfect swimming pools. Hypochlorite ions react with water.

$OCl^-(aq) + H_2O(l) \rightleftharpoons$

$HOCl(aq) + OH^-(aq)$

Hypochlorous acid, HOCl, prevents the growth of algae and bacteria. Research and prepare a report describing how the pH of pool water is regulated to maintain the necessary concentration of HOCl.

 Chem ASAP! **Assessment 21.1** Check your understanding of the important ideas and concepts in Section 21.1.

SMALL-SCALE LAB

SMALL-SCALE TITRATIONS

SAFETY

Wear safety glasses and follow the standard safety procedures outlined on page 18.

PURPOSE

To measure and compare the molar concentrations of acids using various titration techniques.

MATERIALS

- plastic cup
- well strip
- 2 pipets
- NaOH
- HCl
- phenolphthalein
- pH sensor (optional)

PROCEDURE

Sensor version available in the Probeware Lab Manual.

1. Perform a simple titration of HCl with NaOH.

   a. Add 5 drops of HCl to a clean, dry plastic cup. Add 1 drop of phenolphthalein to the cup.

   b. Slowly add NaOH to the cup, counting the number of drops that you add. As you titrate, swirl the cup gently. Continue to slowly add NaOH to the cup until the solution turns a very pale pink. Stop and record the total number of drops you added.

   c. Carefully repeat the experiment to verify your answer.

2. Perform another titration. This time account for the differences in drop size.

   a. Hold an HCl pipet vertically, expel the air bubble, and count the number of drops required to fill one well in a well strip. Repeat this procedure until you obtain consistent results.

   b. Repeat the above step using a NaOH pipet.

   c. Add 10 drops of HCl to a clean, dry plastic cup. Then add one drop of phenolphthalein to the cup.

d. Slowly add NaOH to the cup while counting the number of drops added. As you titrate, swirl the cup gently. Add NaOH slowly until the solution turns a very pale pink. Record the number of drops added. Repeat the procedure until you obtain consistent results.

3. Perform a mass titration.

   a. Determine the mass of a clean, dry cup to which a drop of phenolphthalein has been added.

   b. Add about $\frac{1}{3}$ of a pipet of HCl to the cup and determine its mass.

   c. Slowly add NaOH from a pipet to the HCl until the solution turns a very pale pink. Determine the mass of the cup and its contents.

   d. Clean and dry the same cup and repeat steps **a** through **d** until you obtain consistent results.

ANALYSIS

Using your experimental data, record the answers to the following questions below your data table.

1. Calculate the molar concentration (M) of HCl from the data in Step 1.

   $$M \, HCl = 0.5M \times \frac{b}{a}$$

2. Calculate the molar concentration of HCl using the data from Step 2.

   $$M \, HCl = 0.5M \times \frac{d}{c} \times \frac{a}{b}$$

3. Calculate the molar concentration of HCl from the data in Step 3.

   $$M \, HCl = 0.5M \times \frac{c - b}{b - a}$$

YOU'RE THE CHEMIST!

The following small-scale activity allows you to develop your own procedures and analyze the results.

1. **Analyze It!** For each equation you used to calculate the molar concentration of HCl, what were the assumptions that allowed you to cancel all units except molar concentration?

SALTS IN SOLUTION

objectives
▶ Demonstrate with equations how buffers resist changes in pH
▶ Calculate the solubility product constant of a slightly soluble salt

key terms
▶ salt hydrolysis
▶ buffers
▶ buffer capacity
▶ solubility product constant (K_{sp})
▶ common ion
▶ common ion effect

The internal pH of most living cells is close to 7. Because the chemical processes of the cell are very sensitive to pH levels, even a slight change in pH can be harmful. Human blood, for example, normally maintains a pH very close to 7.4. A person cannot survive for more than a few minutes if the blood pH drops to 6.8 or rises to 7.8. **What chemical process helps ensure that blood is kept at the appropriate pH?**

Salt Hydrolysis

As you learned in Section 21.1, a salt consists of an anion from an acid and a cation from a base, and it forms as a result of a neutralization reaction. Although solutions of many salts are neutral, there are some that are acidic and others that are basic. Solutions of sodium chloride and of potassium sulfate are neutral. A solution of ammonium chloride is acidic. A solution of sodium ethanoate (sodium acetate) is basic. Look at **Figure 21.8.** The titration curve **(a)** was obtained by adding a solution of sodium hydroxide, a strong base, to a solution of ethanoic (acetic) acid, a weak acid. An aqueous solution of sodium ethanoate exists at the equivalence point.

$$CH_3COOH(aq) + NaOH(aq) \longrightarrow CH_3COONa(aq) + H_2O(l)$$

| Ethanoic acid | Sodium hydroxide | Sodium ethanoate | Water |

The pH at the equivalence point is 8.7—basic. For a strong acid–strong base titration, the pH at the equivalence point was 7, or neutral. (Refer to **Figure 21.5** on page 617.) Why does this difference exist? The answer lies in the fact that some salts promote hydrolysis. In **salt hydrolysis,** the cations or anions of the dissociated salt remove hydrogen ions from or donate hydrogen ions to water. Depending on the direction of the hydrogen-ion transfer, solutions containing hydrolyzing salts may be either acidic or basic. Hydrolyzing salts are usually derived from a strong acid and a weak base, or from a weak acid and a strong base. What distinguishes a strong acid from a weak acid?

Figure 21.8

*The titration curve for a weak acid and a strong base **(a)** is compared with the titration curve for a strong acid and a strong base **(b).** In the weak acid–strong base titration, 0.10M NaOH is added slowly from a buret to 50.0 mL of 0.10M CH₃COOH. The pH of the solution is measured with a pH meter and recorded as a function of the volume of NaOH added. The equivalence point occurs at 50.0 mL of NaOH added. The pH at the equivalence point is 8.7, which is the pH of a basic solution, which means that [OH⁻] > [H⁺]. Note that for the strong acid–strong base titration, the pH is 7 at the equivalence point, and [H⁺] is equal to [OH⁻].*

(a) —— Weak acid–strong base
(b) —— Strong acid–strong base

Sodium ethanoate (CH_3COONa) is the salt of a weak acid (ethanoic acid, CH_3COOH) and a strong base (sodium hydroxide, $NaOH$). In solution, the salt is completely ionized.

$$CH_3COONa(aq) \longrightarrow CH_3COO^-(aq) + Na^+(aq)$$

Sodium ethanoate   Ethanoate ion   Sodium ion

The ethanoate ion is a Brønsted-Lowry base, which means it is a hydrogen-ion acceptor. It establishes an equilibrium with water, forming electrically neutral ethanoic acid and negative hydroxide ions.

$$CH_3COO^-(aq) + H_2O(l) \rightleftharpoons CH_3COOH(aq) + OH^-(aq)$$

(hydrogen-ion acceptor, Brønsted-Lowry base)   (hydrogen-ion donor, Brønsted-Lowry acid)   (makes the solution basic)

This process is called hydrolysis because it splits a hydrogen ion off a water molecule. The resulting solution contains a hydroxide-ion concentration greater than the hydrogen-ion concentration. Thus the solution is basic.

Ammonium chloride (NH_4Cl) is the salt of a strong acid (hydrochloric acid, HCl) and a weak base (ammonia, NH_3). It is completely ionized in solution.

$$NH_4Cl(aq) \longrightarrow NH_4^+(aq) + Cl^-(aq)$$

The ammonium ion (NH_4^+) is a strong enough acid to donate a hydrogen ion to a water molecule, although the equilibrium is strongly to the left.

$$NH_4^+(aq) + H_2O(l) \rightleftharpoons NH_3(aq) + H_3O^+(aq)$$

(hydrogen-ion donor, Brønsted-Lowry acid)   (hydrogen-ion acceptor, Brønsted-Lowry base)   (makes the solution acidic)

This process is also called hydrolysis. It results in the formation of un-ionized ammonia and hydronium (hydrogen) ions. The $[H_3O^+]$ is greater than the $[OH^-]$. Thus a solution of ammonium chloride is acidic. Look at **Figure 21.10** and remember the following rules:

Strong acid + Strong base $\longrightarrow$ Neutral solution

Strong acid + Weak base $\longrightarrow$ Acidic solution

Weak acid + Strong base $\longrightarrow$ Basic solution

Figure 21.9
Vapors of the strong acid HCl(aq) and the weak base NH_3(aq) combine to form the acidic white salt ammonium chloride (NH_4Cl).

Figure 21.10
A few drops of universal indicator solution have been added to each of these 0.10M aqueous salt solutions. The color of the indicator shows that ammonium chloride (NH_4Cl), at left, is acidic (pH about 5.3); sodium chloride (NaCl), center, is neutral (pH 7); and sodium ethanoate (CH_3COONa), at right, is basic (pH about 8.7).

Neutralization   **627**

Figure 21.11

(a) The universal indicator shows that the buffered solution on the left and the unbuffered solution on the right are basic—pH about 8.
(b) After the addition of 1.0 mL of 0.01M HCl solution, the pH of the buffered solution shows no visible change. The pH of the unbuffered solution, however, is now about 3—the solution is acidic.

(a)

(b)

Chem ASAP!

Animation 26

Discover the chemistry behind buffer action.

BIOLOGY

Blood Buffers

Your body functions properly only when the pH of your blood lies between 7.35 and 7.45. A blood pH outside these narrow limits can be life-threatening! To keep your blood at the proper pH, your blood contains buffers. The most important blood buffer consists of carbonic acid and hydrogen carbonate ions. Hydrogen ions produced by chemical reactions in your body are the main threat to your blood's pH. This buffer maintains the desired blood pH by removing excess hydrogen ions.

$$HCO_3^-(aq) + H^+(aq) \rightleftharpoons H_2CO_3(aq)$$
Hydrogen   Hydrogen   Carbonic
carbonate ion   ion   acid

As long as there are hydrogen carbonate ions available, the excess hydrogen ions are removed, and the pH of the blood changes very little.

Buffers

The addition of 10 mL of 0.10M sodium hydroxide to 1 L of pure water increases the pH by 4.0 pH units (from 7.0 to 11.0). A solution containing 0.20 mol/L each of ethanoic acid and sodium ethanoate has a pH of 4.76. When moderate amounts of either acid or base are added to this solution, however, the pH changes little. The addition of 10 mL of 0.10M sodium hydroxide to 1 L of this solution, for example, increases the pH by only 0.01 pH unit, from 4.76 to 4.77. Another example of this behavior is illustrated in **Figure 21.11.**

The solution of ethanoic acid and sodium ethanoate is an example of a typical buffer. **Buffers** are solutions in which the pH remains relatively constant when small amounts of acid or base are added. A buffer is a solution of a weak acid and one of its salts, or a solution of a weak base and one of its salts.

A buffer solution is better able to resist drastic changes in pH than is pure water. **Figure 21.12** illustrates how a buffer works. Ethanoic acid (CH_3COOH) and its anion (CH_3COO^-) act as reservoirs of neutralizing power. They react with any hydroxide ions or hydrogen ions added to the solution. For example, consider the buffer solution in which the sodium ethanoate (CH_3COONa) is completely ionized.

$$CH_3COONa(aq) \longrightarrow CH_3COO^-(aq) + Na^+(aq)$$
Sodium   Ethanoate   Sodium
ethanoate   ion   ion

When an acid is added to the solution, the ethanoate ions (CH_3COO^-) act as a hydrogen-ion "sponge." This creates ethanoic acid, which does not ionize extensively in water; thus the pH does not change appreciably.

$$CH_3COO^-(aq) + H^+(aq) \rightleftharpoons CH_3COOH(aq)$$
Ethanoate   Hydrogen   Ethanoic acid
ion   ion

A base is a source of hydroxide ions. When a base is added to the solution, the ethanoic acid and the hydroxide ions react to produce water and the ethanoate ion.

$$CH_3COOH(aq) + OH^-(aq) \rightleftharpoons CH_3COO^-(aq) + H_2O(l)$$
Ethanoic acid   Hydroxide   Ethanoate   Water
ion   ion

The ethanoate ion is not a strong enough base to accept hydrogen ions from water extensively. Again, the pH does not change very much.

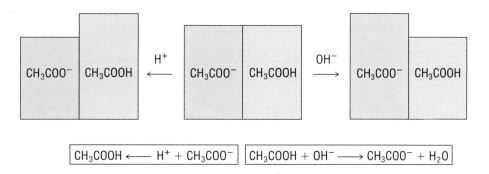

$$\boxed{CH_3COOH \longleftarrow H^+ + CH_3COO^-} \quad \boxed{CH_3COOH + OH^- \longrightarrow CH_3COO^- + H_2O}$$

Figure 21.12

The buffer described here is made of ethanoic acid (CH_3COOH) and sodium ethanoate, which is the source of ethanoate ions (CH_3COO^-). To begin, the concentrations of ethanoic acid and ethanoate ions are equal. When H^+ is added, it combines with CH_3COO^- to form CH_3COOH. The [CH_3COO^-] decreases and the [CH_3COOH] increases. When OH^- is added, it reacts with CH_3COOH to produce CH_3COO^- and H_2O. The [CH_3COOH] decreases and the [CH_3COO^-] increases. In both situations, the ratio of [CH_3COOH] to [CH_3COO^-] changes very little and, consequently, the pH changes very little.

An ethanoate buffer solution cannot control the pH when too much acid is added, because no more ethanoate ions are present to accept hydrogen ions. The ethanoate buffer also becomes ineffective when too much base is added. Do you know why this is so? When too much base is added, no more ethanoic acid molecules are present to donate hydrogen ions. When too much acid or base is added, the buffer capacity of a solution is exceeded. The **buffer capacity** is the amount of acid or base that can be added to a buffer solution before a significant change in pH occurs.

Two buffer systems are crucial in maintaining human blood pH within a very narrow range (pH 7.35–7.45). One is the carbonic acid–hydrogen carbonate buffer system. The other is the dihydrogen phosphate–monohydrogen phosphate buffer system. **Table 21.2** lists several important buffer systems.

Figure 21.13

This device measures the pH of human blood. Changes in blood pH are minimized by very effective blood buffering systems.

Table 21.2

Important Buffer Systems		
Buffer name	**Buffer species**	**Buffer pH (components 0.1M)**
Ethanoic acid–ethanoate ion	CH_3COOH/CH_3COO^-	4.76
Dihydrogen phosphate ion–hydrogen phosphate ion	$H_2PO_4^-/HPO_4^{2-}$	7.20
Carbonic acid–hydrogen carbonate (solution saturated with CO_2)	H_2CO_3/HCO_3^-	6.46
Ammonium ion–ammonia	NH_4^+/NH_3	9.25

Sample Problem 21-9

Show how the carbonic acid–hydrogen carbonate buffer can "mop up" added hydrogen ions and hydroxide ions.

1. **ANALYZE** *Plan a problem solving strategy.*

   The definition of a buffer, in terms of its ability to act as a reservoir of neutralizing power, should be illustrated. One component in a buffer can react with H^+; this component is a proton acceptor. Another component can react with OH^-; this component is a proton donor.

2. **CALCULATE** *Apply the problem-solving strategy.*

   The carbonic acid–hydrogen carbonate buffer is a solution of carbonic acid (H_2CO_3) and hydrogen carbonate ions (HCO_3^-). When a base is added to this buffer, it reacts with H_2CO_3 (a proton donor) to produce neutral water. The pH changes very little.

   $$H_2CO_3(aq) + OH^-(aq) \rightleftharpoons HCO_3^-(aq) + H_2O(l)$$

   Carbonic acid   Hydroxide ion   Hydrogen carbonate ion   Water

   When an acid is added to the buffer, it reacts with HCO_3^- (a proton acceptor) to produce un-ionized carbonic acid. Again, the pH changes very little.

   $$HCO_3^-(aq) + H^+(aq) \rightleftharpoons H_2CO_3(aq)$$

   Hydrogen carbonate ion   Hydrogen ion   Carbonic acid

3. **EVALUATE** *Does the result make sense?*

   The carbonic acid–hydrogen carbonate system is a good buffer solution because it can neutralize small quantities of strong acid or strong base.

Practice Problems

23. Write reactions to show what happens when the following occur.
    a. Acid is added to a solution of HPO_4^{2-}.
    b. Base is added to a solution of $H_2PO_4^-$.
24. Write an equation that shows what happens when acid is added to the ethanoic acid–ethanoate buffer.

The Solubility Product Constant

Salts differ in their solubilities. In general, compounds of the alkali metals are soluble in water. More than 35 g of sodium chloride, for example, will dissolve in only 100 mL of water. Many classes of ionic compounds, however, are insoluble. For example, many compounds that contain phosphate, sulfide, sulfite, or carbonate ions are insoluble. Exceptions are compounds in which these ions are combined with ammonium ions or alkali metal ions. **Table 21.3** summarizes the solubilities of many ionic compounds in water. Would you expect copper(II) hydroxide to be very soluble?

Most insoluble salts will actually dissolve to some extent in water. These salts are said to be slightly, or sparingly, soluble in water. For example, **Figure 21.14** shows what happens when the "insoluble" salt silver chloride is mixed with water.

Table 21.3

Solubilities of Ionic Compounds in Water		
Compounds	**Solubility**	**Exceptions**
Salts of Group 1A metals and ammonia	Soluble	Some lithium compounds
Ethanoates, nitrates, chlorates, and perchlorates	Soluble	Few exceptions
Sulfates	Soluble	Compounds of Pb, Ag, Hg, Ba, Sr, and Ca
Chlorides, bromides, and iodides	Soluble	Compounds of Ag and some compounds of Hg and Pb
Sulfides and hydroxides	Most are insoluble	Alkali metal sulfides and hydroxides are soluble. Compounds of Ba, Sr, and Ca are slightly soluble.
Carbonates, phosphates, and sulfites	Insoluble	Compounds of the alkali metals and of ammonium ions

When silver chloride is mixed with water a very small amount of silver chloride dissolves in the water.

$$AgCl(s) \rightleftharpoons Ag^+(aq) + Cl^-(aq)$$

You can write an equilibrium expression for this process.

$$K_{eq} = \frac{[Ag^+][Cl^-]}{[AgCl]}$$

Figure 21.14
Silver chloride is slightly soluble in water. Would adding solid silver chloride to this test tube disturb the equilibrium?

Table 21.4

Solubility Product Constants (K_{sp}) at 25 °C							
Salt	K_{sp}	Salt	K_{sp}	Salt	K_{sp}		
Halides		**Sulfates**		**Hydroxides**			
AgCl	1.8×10^{-10}	$PbSO_4$	6.3×10^{-7}	$Al(OH)_3$	3.0×10^{-34}		
AgBr	5.0×10^{-13}	$BaSO_4$	1.1×10^{-10}	$Zn(OH)_2$	3.0×10^{-16}		
AgI	8.3×10^{-17}	$CaSO_4$	2.4×10^{-5}	$Ca(OH)_2$	6.5×10^{-6}		
$PbCl_2$	1.7×10^{-5}	**Sulfides**		$Mg(OH)_2$	7.1×10^{-12}		
$PbBr_2$	2.1×10^{-6}	NiS	4.0×10^{-20}	$Fe(OH)_2$	7.9×10^{-16}		
PbI_2	7.9×10^{-9}	CuS	8.0×10^{-37}	**Carbonates**			
PbF_2	3.6×10^{-8}	Ag_2S	8.0×10^{-51}	$CaCO_3$	4.5×10^{-9}		
CaF_2	3.9×10^{-11}	ZnS	3.0×10^{-23}	$SrCO_3$	9.3×10^{-10}		
Chromates		FeS	8.0×10^{-19}	$ZnCO_3$	1.0×10^{-10}		
$PbCrO_4$	1.8×10^{-14}	CdS	1.0×10^{-27}	Ag_2CO_3	8.1×10^{-12}		
Ag_2CrO_4	1.2×10^{-12}	SnS	1.3×10^{-26}	$BaCO_3$	5.0×10^{-9}		
		PbS	3.0×10^{-28}				

As long as some undissolved (solid) AgCl is present, the concentration of the AgCl is a constant. Thus the concentration of AgCl can be combined with the equilibrium constant to form a new constant.

$$K_{eq} \times [AgCl] = [Ag^+] \times [Cl^-] = K_{sp}$$

This new constant, called the **solubility product constant (K_{sp})**, equals the product of the concentration terms each raised to the power of the coefficient of the substance in the dissociation equation. The coefficients for the dissociation of silver chloride are each 1. The value of K_{sp} for silver chloride at 25 °C is 1.8×10^{-10}.

$$K_{sp} = [Ag^+] \times [Cl^-]$$
$$= 1.8 \times 10^{-10}$$

The solubility product constants for some common sparingly soluble salts are given in **Table 21.4**. Although most compounds of barium are highly toxic, barium sulfate is so insoluble ($K_{sp} = 1.1 \times 10^{-10}$) that it is routinely used by physicians for gastrointestinal examinations. See **Figure 21.15**.

Figure 21.15

Barium sulfate is used for making x-ray images of the digestive tract. Barium sulfate absorbs the x-rays, thereby producing light areas on the developed x-ray film. Barium sulfate can be used safely for this procedure because it is insoluble in body fluids. Soluble barium salts are highly toxic.

CHEMath

ALGEBRA AND K_{sp}

The solubility product constant K_{sp} is closely related to K_{eq}, the equilibrium constant introduced in Chapter 19. This page offers a review of the math skills needed to solve problems involving K_{eq} and K_{sp}.

Consider the slightly soluble salt AB, which partially dissociates into A^+ and B^- ions.

$$AB(s) \rightleftharpoons A^+(aq) + B^-(aq)$$

The general formula for calculating K_{sp} is

$$K_{sp} = [A]^x [B^-]^y$$

where [A] and [B] are concentrations, and x and y are their respective coefficients from the dissociation equation. Thus K_{sp} for the dissociation of AB is

$$K_{sp} = [A^+][B^-]$$

When silver chloride (AgCl) dissolves in water, one Ag^+ ion forms for every Cl^- ion, thus $x = 1$ and $y = 1$.

$$AgCl(s) \rightleftharpoons Ag^+(aq) + Cl^-(aq) \qquad K_{sp} = [Ag^+][Cl^-]$$

When lead fluoride (PbF_2) dissolves in water, one Pb^{2+} ion forms for every two F^- ions, thus $x = 1$ and $y = 2$.

$$PbF_2(s) \rightleftharpoons Pb^{2+}(aq) + 2F^-(aq) \qquad K_{sp} = [Pb][F]^2$$

Without knowing the actual concentration of either ion in solution, you can use algebra to relate the relative concentrations of the ions. You can then write an equation involving a known value of K_{sp} to calculate each ion's exact concentration. This is done by substituting x for the concentration of one of the ions and using the dissociation equation to write the other ion's concentration, also in terms of x. Solving the equation then usually involves the use of square roots or cube roots.

Example

What are the concentrations of nickel and sulfide ions in a saturated solution of nickel sulfide (NiS) at 25 °C? ($K_{sp} = 4.0 \times 10^{-20}$)

First, write the dissociation equation.

$$NiS(s) \rightleftharpoons Ni^{2+}(aq) + S^{2-}(aq)$$

Note that one Ni^{2+} ion forms for every S^{2-} ion. Recall the general equations for K_{sp}.

$$K_{sp} = [A^+]^x[B^-]^y, \text{ thus } K_{sp} = [Ni^{2+}][S^{2-}]$$

Substituting the known value for K_{sp} yields,

$$4.0 \times 10^{-20} = [Ni^{2+}][S^{2-}]$$

Set $x = [Ni^{2+}]$. Because $[Ni^{2+}]$ and $[S^{2-}]$ are equal, x also equals $[S^{2-}]$. Substituting for $[Ni^{2+}]$ and $[S^{2-}]$ yields

$$4.0 \times 10^{-20} = (x)(x)$$
$$4.0 \times 10^{-20} = x^2$$

Taking the square root of both sides of the equation yields,

$$\sqrt{4.0 \times 10^{-20}} = \sqrt{x^2}$$
$$2.0 \times 10^{-10} = x$$

Going back to a relationship between x and ion concentrations yields

$$[Ni^{2+}] = [S^{2-}] = 2.0 \times 10^{-10} M$$

Note that for a dissociation that yields two A ions for every one B ion, algebra can still be used to relate the concentrations. In this case, x equals the concentration of B, $x = [B]$, and $2x$ equals the concentration of A, $2x = [A]$. Substituting these x values into the K_{sp} equation, the ion concentrations can be calculated.

Practice Problems

Prepare for upcoming problems in this chapter by using solubility products to calculate the following concentrations.

A. Write the solubility product expression for the salts CuS, $ZnCO_3$, and $PbCrO_4$.

B. What are the concentrations of silver and bromide ions in a saturated solution of silver bromide (AgBr) at 25 °C? $K_{sp} = 5 \times 10^{-13}$

C. What is the concentration of iodide ions in a saturated solution of lead iodide (PbI_2) at 25.0 °C? $K_{sp} = 7.9 \times 10^{-9}$

Sample Problem 21-10

What is the concentration of silver ions and chloride ions in a saturated silver chloride solution at 25 °C? ($K_{sp} = 1.8 \times 10^{-10}$)

1. **ANALYZE** *List the knowns and the unknowns.*

Knowns:
- $K_{sp} = 1.8 \times 10^{-10}$
- $K_{sp} = [Ag^+] \times [Cl^-]$
- $AgCl(s) \rightleftharpoons Ag^+(aq) + Cl^-(aq)$

Unknowns:
- $[Ag^+] = ?M$
- $[Cl^-] = ?M$

The equation shows that for each Ag^+ ion formed, one Cl^- ion is formed.

2. **CALCULATE** *Solve for the unknowns.*

$$K_{sp} = [Ag^+] \times [Cl^-] = 1.8 \times 10^{-10}$$

At equilibrium $[Ag^+] = [Cl^-]$, so $[Ag^+]$ can be substituted for $[Cl^-]$ in the expression for K_{sp}. This gives an equation with one unknown.

$$K_{sp} = [Ag^+] \times [Ag^+] = 1.8 \times 10^{-10}$$

Solving for $[Ag^+]$:

$$[Ag^+]^2 = 1.8 \times 10^{-10}$$

$$[Ag^+] = 1.3 \times 10^{-5}M$$

The equilibrium concentration of Cl^- is also $1.3 \times 10^{-5}M$, because $[Ag^+] = [Cl^-]$.

3. **EVALUATE** *Do the results make sense?*

The product $[Ag^+] \times [Cl^-]$ is very close to the value of K_{sp}. The answer should have two significant figures.

Practice Problems

25. Lead(II) sulfide (PbS) has a K_{sp} of 3×10^{-28}. What is the concentration of lead(II) ions in a saturated solution of PbS?

26. What is the concentration of calcium and carbonate ions in a saturated calcium carbonate solution at 25 °C? ($K_{sp} = 4.5 \times 10^{-9}$)

Chem ASAP!

Problem-Solving 26

Solve Problem 26 with the help of an interactive guided tutorial.

Sample Problem 21-11

Calcium fluoride has a K_{sp} of 3.9×10^{-11} at 25 °C. What is the fluoride-ion concentration at equilibrium?

1. **ANALYZE** *List the knowns and the unknowns.*

Knowns:
- $K_{sp} = 3.9 \times 10^{-11}$
- $CaF_2 \rightleftharpoons Ca^{2+}(aq) + 2F^-(aq)$
- $K_{sp} = [Ca^{2+}] \times [F^-]^2$

Unknowns:
- $[Ca^{2+}] = ?M$
- $[F^-] = ?M$

There are twice as many F^- ions as Ca^{2+} ions formed when CaF_2 dissociates. To determine the $[F^-]$, the $[Ca^{2+}]$ must also be determined.

Sample Problem 21-11 (cont.)

2. *CALCULATE* Solve for the unknowns.

When the $[Ca^{2+}]$ is x, the $[F^-]$ is $2x$. If these terms are substituted into the K_{sp} expression, the expression can be solved for x.

$$K_{sp} = (x)(2x)^2 = 3.9 \times 10^{-11}$$

$$4x^3 = 3.9 \times 10^{-11}$$

$$x^3 = 9.8 \times 10^{-12}$$

$$x = 2.1 \times 10^{-4}$$

The $[Ca^{2+}] = 2.1 \times 10^{-4}M$. The $[F^-]$ is twice the $[Ca^{2+}]$. Thus $[F^-] = 4.2 \times 10^{-4}M$.

3. *EVALUATE* Do the results make sense?

The concentrations are reasonable because 10^{-4} cubed (10^{-12}) is close to the value for K_{sp}. The answers should have two significant figures.

Practice Problems

27. The K_{sp} of silver sulfide (Ag_2S) is 8×10^{-51}.
  a. What is the silver-ion concentration of a saturated solution of silver sulfide?
  b. What is the sulfide-ion concentration of the same solution?

28. Write the solubility product expression for each salt.
  a. $PbCl_2$
  b. Ag_2CrO_4

The Common Ion Effect

In a saturated solution of lead(II) chromate, an equilibrium is established between the solid lead(II) chromate and its ions.

$$PbCrO_4(s) \rightleftharpoons Pb^{2+}(aq) + CrO_4^{2-}(aq) \qquad K_{sp} = 1.8 \times 10^{-14}$$

What do you think would happen if you added some lead nitrate to this solution? Immediately after the addition, the product of $[Pb^{2+}]$ and $[CrO_4^{2-}]$ would be greater than K_{sp}. Applying Le Châtelier's principle (Section 19.2), the stress of the additional Pb^{2+} can be relieved if the reaction shifts to the left. As you can see in **Figure 21.16**, lead ions would combine with chromate ions in solution to form additional solid $PbCrO_4$. In fact, $PbCrO_4$ will precipitate until the product of $[Pb^{2+}]$ and $[CrO_4^{2-}]$ once again equals 1.8×10^{-14}.

(a) $PbCrO_4(s) \rightleftharpoons Pb^{2+}(aq) + CrO_4^{2-}$

(b) $PbCrO_4(s) \rightleftharpoons Pb^{2+}(aq) + CrO_4^{2-}$
(more Pb^{2+} added)

Figure 21.16

(a) Lead(II) chromate, a bright-yellow compound, is only slightly soluble in water. A saturated solution of this compound is very pale yellow due to the presence of $CrO_4^{2-}(aq)$, as shown in the equilibrium expression. (b) When a few drops of lead nitrate ($Pb(NO_3)_2$) are added to the clear, pale-yellow solution, more lead(II) chromate precipitates. The amount of lead(II) chromate ($PbCrO_4$)(s) increases because its solubility is lower in the presence of the common ion (Pb^{2+}).

In this example, the lead ion is called a common ion. A **common ion** is an ion that is common to both salts. Adding lead nitrate to a saturated solution of $PbCrO_4$ causes the solubility of $PbCrO_4$ to be decreased. The solubility of $PbCrO_4$ is less in the presence of a solution of $Pb(NO_3)_2$ than it is in pure water. The lowering of the solubility of a substance by the addition of a common ion is called the **common ion effect.**

Adding sodium chromate would also produce the common ion effect in this example. The additional chromate ion, a different common ion, would cause the reaction to shift to the left. More $PbCrO_4$ would be formed and the solubility of $PbCrO_4$ would again decrease until the K_{sp} equaled 1.8×10^{-14}. Sample Problem 21-12 illustrates how to use the common ion effect to predict the iodide-ion concentration of a solution of silver iodide when silver nitrate solution is added. In this case, silver is the common ion.

Sample Problem 21-12

The K_{sp} of silver iodide is 8.3×10^{-17}. What is the iodide-ion concentration of a 1.00-L saturated solution of AgI to which 0.020 mol $AgNO_3$ is added?

1. ANALYZE List the knowns and the unknown.

Knowns:
- $K_{sp} = 8.3 \times 10^{-17}$
- mol $AgNO_3$ added = 0.020 mol
- $AgI(s) \rightleftharpoons Ag^+(aq) + I^-(aq)$
- $K_{sp} = [Ag^+] \times [I^-]$

Unknown:
- $[I^-] = ?\ M$

If the equilibrium concentration of iodide ion from the dissociation is x, then the equilibrium concentration of silver ion is $x + 0.020$.

2. CALCULATE Solve for the unknown.

Because of the small value of K_{sp}, x will be small compared with 0.020. Therefore the $[Ag^+]$ at equilibrium equals $0.020M$. Substitute these values into the K_{sp} expression.

$$K_{sp} = [Ag^+] \times [I^-]$$
$$8.3 \times 10^{-17} = (0.020)(x)$$
$$x = \frac{8.3 \times 10^{-17}}{0.020}$$
$$x = 4.2 \times 10^{-15}$$

The equilibrium concentration of iodide ion is $4.2 \times 10^{-15} M$.

3. EVALUATE Does the result make sense?

Because $[Ag^+]$ is so high, it is to be expected that $[I^-]$ will be very low, approaching the numerical value for K_{sp}. The answer should have two significant figures.

Practice Problems

29. What is the concentration of sulfide ion in a 1.0-L solution of iron(II) sulfide to which 0.04 mol of iron(II) nitrate has been added? The K_{sp} of FeS is 8×10^{-19}.
30. The K_{sp} of $SrSO_4$ is 3.2×10^{-7}. What is the equilibrium concentration of sulfate ion in a 1.0-L solution of strontium sulfate to which 0.10 mol $Sr(CH_3COO)_2$ has been added?

The solubility product (K_{sp}) can be used to predict whether a precipitate will form when solutions are mixed. If the ion-product concentration of two ions in the mixture is greater than the K_{sp} of the compound formed from the ions, a precipitate will form. If the ion-product concentration of two ions is less than the K_{sp}, no precipitate will form, and the solution will be unsaturated. What do you think will happen if the ion-product concentration of two ions equals K_{sp}?

Sample Problem 21-13

Predict whether barium sulfate will precipitate when 0.50 L of 0.002M Ba(NO$_3$)$_2$ mixes with 0.50 L of 0.008M Na$_2$SO$_4$ to form 1.00 L of solution. The K_{sp} of BaSO$_4$ is 1.1×10^{-10}.

1. ANALYZE *List the knowns and the unknown.*

Knowns:
- $K_{sp} = 1.1 \times 10^{-10}$
- 0.50 L of 0.002M Ba(NO$_3$)$_2$
- 0.50 L of 0.008M Na$_2$SO$_4$

Unknown:
- [Ba^{2+}] × [SO$_4{}^{2-}$] > K_{sp}?

Precipitation will occur if the product of the concentrations of the two ions exceeds the K_{sp} of BaSO$_4$.

2. CALCULATE *Solve for the unknown.*

Halve the concentration of each ion because the volume is doubled when the original solutions mix. So in the final solution, [Ba^{2+}] = 0.001M and [SO$_4{}^{2-}$] = 0.004M. After mixing, the ion product is

$$[Ba^{2+}] \times [SO_4{}^{2-}] = (0.001M) \times (0.004M)$$
$$= 4 \times 10^{-6}$$

This number is larger than the K_{sp}.

3. EVALUATE *Does the result make sense?*

Because the ion-product concentration of the two ions exceeds K_{sp}, BaSO$_4$ will precipitate.

Practice Problems

31. Predict whether calcium carbonate will precipitate when 0.5 L of 0.001M Ca(NO$_3$)$_2$ is mixed with 0.5 L of 0.0008M Na$_2$CO$_3$ to form 1.0 L of solution. The K_{sp} of CaCO$_3$ is 4.5×10^{-9}.

32. A student prepares a solution by combining 0.025 mol CaCl$_2$ and 0.015 mol Pb(NO$_3$)$_2$ and adding water to make 1.0 L of solution. Will a precipitate of PbCl$_2$ form in this solution?

Chem ASAP!

Problem-Solving 32
Solve Problem 32 with the help of an interactive guided tutorial.

---

section review 21.2

33. Using equations, show what happens when acid is added to an ammonium ion–ammonia buffer. What happens when base is added?

34. What is the K_{sp} of nickel(II) sulfide if the equilibrium concentrations of a saturated solution of Ni^{2+} and S^{2-} are each $2 \times 10^{-10}M$?

35. Would precipitation occur when 500 mL of a 0.02M solution of AgNO$_3$ is mixed with 500 mL of a 0.001M solution of NaCl? Explain.

Chem ASAP! **Assessment 21.2** Check your understanding of the important ideas and concepts in Section 21.2.

EXTREME ORGANISMS' VALUABLE ENZYMES

You probably would not want to jump into the pool of water shown in this photo. Even if you could survive the near-boiling temperature, the pH might begin to eat away at your skin. Although an environment like this is inhospitable to human life, it is not necessarily lifeless. Scientists have discovered that a variety of extreme environments on Earth support living organisms. These environments include boiling hot springs, frozen glaciers, lagoons much saltier than the ocean, highly alkaline soda lakes, and acidic mine pits.

The organisms that live in these extreme environments are called extremophiles. Most of these organisms are very simple, primitive bacteria. Recently, scientists have found that the chemical tricks extremophiles use to survive in their harsh habitats may have many useful applications in industry.

In particular, scientists are interested in the enzymes that extremophiles produce for carrying out their life processes. Enzymes are biological catalysts. Like the synthetic catalysts you have already learned about, enzymes greatly speed up chemical reactions without themselves being altered. Enzymes are very important in many industrial processes today. But most enzymes cannot function under extreme conditions. Heat destroys them, cold inactivates them, and extremes of pH break them down. In contrast, the enzymes produced by extremophiles—called extremozymes—are able to survive harsh conditions such as these. Therefore they have the potential for being used where typical enzymes cannot.

Two types of extremophiles of interest to scientists are acidophiles and alkaliphiles. Acidophiles live in very acidic environments (pH < 5), and alkaliphiles live

> The chemical tricks extremophiles use to survive in their harsh habitats may have many useful applications in industry.

in very basic environments (pH > 9). Some of the extremozymes produced by acidophiles work to break down food outside the organism so it can be absorbed or ingested. These extremozymes could be used to increase the digestibility of animal feed. When added to the feed, these enzymes would work in the acid environment of animals' stomachs to help break down inexpensive grains that would normally be only partially digested. Other acid-tolerant extremozymes could be used as catalysts for producing compounds that must be synthesized under acidic conditions.

The alkaline-tolerant enzymes produced by alkaliphiles also have many possible uses. Detergent makers, for example, are very interested in the ability of alkaliphiles to remove food stains from clothes. Certain typical enzymes work well as stain removers because they help break down the proteins and fats that make up the stains. But these enzymes are destroyed in the highly alkaline environment created by detergents. Alkaline-tolerant versions of these enzymes would solve this problem, allowing detergent makers to create powerful stain-fighting detergents that would be of value to many people.

CHEMISTRY IN CAREERS

Take It to the NET
For interactive study and
review, go to www.phschool.com

KEY TERMS

- buffer *p. 628*
- buffer capacity *p. 629*
- common ion *p. 636*
- common ion effect *p. 636*
- end point *p. 617*

- equivalence point *p. 622*
- equivalent (equiv) *p. 619*
- gram equivalent mass *p. 619*
- neutralization reaction *p. 614*
- normality (*N*) *p. 621*

- salt hydrolysis *p. 626*
- solubility product constant (K_{sp}) *p. 632*
- standard solution *p. 617*
- titration *p. 617*

KEY EQUATIONS AND RELATIONSHIPS

- Acid + base $\longrightarrow$ salt + water

- Gram equivalent mass $= \dfrac{\text{molar mass}}{\text{number of ionizable hydrogens}}$

- Normality (*N*) = equiv/L
- $N_1 \times V_1 = N_2 \times V_2$
- $N_A \times V_A = N_B \times V_B$
- For a slightly soluble salt (MX), $K_{sp} = [M^+] \times [X^-]$

CONCEPT SUMMARY

21.1 Neutralization Reactions

- In the reaction of an acid with a base, hydrogen ions and hydroxide ions react to produce a salt and water. This reaction, called neutralization, is usually carried out by titration.
- The end point in a titration is the point at which the indicator changes color. An indicator is chosen so the solution reaches the end point very near the point of neutralization.
- An equivalent of an acid is the mass of the acid that provides one mole of hydrogen ions in solution.
- A solution that contains one equivalent of an acid or a base in a single liter of solution is a one-normal (1*N*) solution.
- At the equivalence point of a titration, the number of equivalents of acid equals the number of equivalents of base.

21.2 Salts in Solution

- A salt consists of an anion from an acid and a cation from a base and forms when an acid is neutralized by a base.
- Salts of strong acid–strong base reactions produce neutral solutions in water.
- Salts formed from weak acids or weak bases hydrolyze water and produce basic or acidic solutions.
- Solutions that resist changes in pH are called buffer solutions. Within limits, components of a buffer can react with hydrogen and hydroxide ions and minimize changes in pH.
- The solubility product constant (K_{sp}) is the equilibrium constant for the reaction between an ionic solid and its ions in solution.
- The solubility of a salt is decreased by the addition of a common ion.

CHAPTER CONCEPT MAP

Use these terms to construct a concept map that organizes the major ideas of this chapter.

equivalence point   equivalent   neutralization

end point   titration   normality

Chem ASAP! **Concept Map 21**
Create your Concept Map using the computer.

CONCEPT MASTERY

36. Write a general word equation for a neutralization reaction. *21.1*

37. Identify the products and write balanced equations for each neutralization reaction. *21.1*
a. $HNO_3(aq) + KOH(aq) \longrightarrow$
b. $HCl(aq) + Ca(OH)_2(aq) \longrightarrow$
c. $H_2SO_4(aq) + NaOH(aq) \longrightarrow$

38. What is characteristic of the end point of a titration? *21.1*

39. What is the molarity of sodium hydroxide if 20.0 mL of the solution is neutralized by each of the following 1.00M solutions? *21.1*
a. 28.0 mL of HCl   **b.** 17.4 mL of H_3PO_4

40. Determine the gram equivalent mass and the equivalents per mole for each compound. *21.1*
a. KOH   **b.** HCl   **c.** H_2SO_4

41. How many equivalents is each compound? *21.1*
a. 3.7 g $Ca(OH)_2$ **c.** 9.8 g H_3PO_4
b. 189 g H_2SO_4

42. How is the normality of a solution calculated? *21.1*

43. What is the normality of each solution? *21.1*
a. 1M NaOH   **c.** 0.2M KOH
b. 2M HNO_3 **d.** 0.1M H_2SO_4

44. Determine the normality of each solution. *21.1*
a. 250 mL of solution containing 10 g NaOH
b. 750 mL of solution containing 4.9 g H_2SO_4
c. 270 mL of solution containing 0.74 g HCl
d. 2.80 L of solution containing 18.6 g HNO_3
e. 7.3 g HCl in 250 mL of solution
f. 18.4 g HNO_3 in 1250 mL of solution

45. A student titrated several solutions of unknown concentration with various standard solutions to the point of neutralization. The volume of each unknown solution and the volume and normality of the standard solution used are given below. Calculate the normality for each unknown. *21.1*
a. 25.0 mL H_2SO_4 required 15.0 mL of 0.100N NaOH
b. 10.0 mL NaOH required 20.0 mL of 0.200N HCl
c. 17.5 mL NaOH required 25.0 mL of 0.120N HNO_3
d. 50.0 mL CH_3COOH required 39.6 mL of 0.0950N KOH

46. What kinds of salts hydrolyze water? *21.2*

47. Write an equation showing why an aqueous solution of sodium hydrogen carbonate is basic. *21.2*

48. Explain why solutions of salts that hydrolyze water do not have a pH of 7. *21.2*

49. Predict whether an aqueous solution of each salt will be acidic, basic, or neutral. *21.2*
a. $NaHCO_3$ **d.** Na_2CO_3
b. NH_4NO_3 **e.** Na_2SO_4
c. KCl   **f.** NH_4Cl

50. A buffered solution cannot absorb an unlimited amount of acid or base. Explain. *21.2*

51. Would a solution of HCl and NaCl be a good buffer? Explain. *21.2*

52. Write the solubility product expression for each salt. *21.2*
a. NiS   **b.** $BaCO_3$

53. What does the solubility product constant (K_{sp}) represent? *21.2*

54. Use **Table 21.4** on page 632 to rank these salts from most soluble to least soluble. *21.2*
a. CuS   **c.** $SrCO_3$
b. $BaSO_4$ **d.** AgI

55. How does the addition of a common ion affect the solubility of another substance? *21.2*

CONCEPT MASTERY

56. The graph shows the number of millimoles (mmol) of water formed by the dropwise addition of 1.0N HCl to a 25.0-mL sample of NaOH of unknown concentration.
a. Write an equation for the reaction.
b. Estimate the concentration of NaOH.

Millimoles of Water vs. Volume of 1.0N HCl

57. What must be true about the concentration of two ions if precipitation occurs when solutions of the two ions are mixed?

58. How many equivalents are in each solution?
   a. 5.8 L of 0.55N HCl
   b. 330 mL of 1.4N H_3PO_4
   c. 0.14 L of 0.22N KOH

59. Use the phosphate buffer (H_2PO_4/HPO_4^{2-}) to illustrate how a buffer system works. Show, by means of equations, how the pH of a solution can be kept almost constant when small amounts of acid or base are added.

60. Find the normality of each solution.
   a. 86.3 g $Mg(OH)_2$ in 2.5 L of solution
   b. 5.6 g HBr in 450 mL of solution
   c. 49.4 g H_2SO_3 in 1.5 L of solution

61. The following data were collected from a titration of 50.00 mL of ethanoic acid (CH_3COOH) of unknown concentration with 0.100N NaOH. Plot these data (pH on the y-axis) to obtain a titration curve.

Volume of NaOH (mL)	pH	Volume of NaOH (mL)	pH
0		50.00	8.73
10.00	4.15	50.01	8.89
25.00	4.76	51.00	11.00
40.00	5.36	60.00	11.96
49.00	6.45	75.00	12.30
49.99	8.55	100.00	12.52

   a. What is the pH at the end point of this titration?
   b. Use **Figure 20.8** on page 590 to identify one or more indicators that could be used to determine the end point in this titration.

62. Write an equation for the reaction of each antacid with hydrochloric acid.
   a. magnesium hydroxide
   b. calcium carbonate
   c. aluminum hydroxide

63. How many milliliters of 2.00N NaOH would you need to dilute with water to make 250 mL of 0.100N NaOH?

64. What is the concentration of hydroxide ions in a saturated solution of each salt?
   a. $Zn(OH)_2$
   b. $Ca(OH)_2$
   c. $Al(OH)_3$

65. How would the equilibrium between hypochlorous acid and the hypochlorite ion be affected by the addition of each?
   $$HOCl(aq) + OH^-(aq) \rightleftharpoons OCl^-(aq) + H_2O(l)$$
   a. HCl   **b.** NaOH

66. Write an equation to show that an aqueous solution of sodium ethanoate will be basic.

67. Arrange these solutions in order of decreasing acidity.
   a. 0.1N NaOH
   b. 0.1N HCl
   c. 0.1M ammonium chloride
   d. 0.1M sodium ethanoate

68. What is the equilibrium concentration of barium ion in a 1.0-L saturated solution of barium carbonate to which 0.25 mol K_2CO_3 has been added?

CRITICAL THINKING

69. Choose the term that best completes the second relationship.
   a. animal : dog   indicator : _____
      (1) pH   (3) titration
      (2) phenolphthalein   (4) end point
   b. molarity : moles   normality : _____
      (1) normals   (3) equivalents
      (2) concentration   (4) ions

70. It is important for the pH of blood to be maintained in the range of 7.35 to 7.45. The hydrogen carbonate ion–carbonic acid buffer system is the most important of three buffer systems in the blood that help maintain this pH range. This system is represented by the following equation.

$$H_2O(l) + CO_2(g) \overset{\text{Lungs}}{\rightleftharpoons} H_2CO_3(aq) \overset{\text{Blood}}{\rightleftharpoons} H^+(aq) + HCO_3^-(aq)$$

Given this equation, explain how abnormal breathing patterns can lead to acid–base imbalances in the blood that are called respiratory acidosis (abnormally low pH) and respiratory alkalosis (abnormally high pH). Too-rapid and too-deep breathing, a condition called hyperventilation, leads to respiratory alkalosis. Why? Conversely, hypoventilation, the result of too-shallow breathing, can cause respiratory acidosis. Explain.

71. The following equilibria are involved in the solubility of carbon dioxide in water.

$$CO_2(g) \rightleftharpoons CO_2(aq)$$

$$CO_2(aq) + H_2O(l) \rightleftharpoons H_2CO_3(aq)$$

$$H_2CO_3(aq) \rightleftharpoons H^+(aq) + HCO_3^-(aq)$$

$$HCO_3^-(aq) \rightleftharpoons H^+(aq) + CO_3^{2-}(aq)$$

If sea water is slightly alkaline, would you expect the concentration of dissolved CO_2 to be higher or lower than in pure water? Explain.

CUMULATIVE REVIEW

72. These beakers contain the same solution. Bromocresol green has been added to the beaker on the left, and phenolphthalein has been added to the beaker on the right.

a. What is the approximate pH of the solution?
b. How could you determine the pH more accurately?

73. Calculate the pH of solutions with the following hydrogen-ion concentrations.
   a. $4.6 \times 10^{-6}M$ **c.** $3.0 \times 10^{-1}M$
   b. $5.0 \times 10^{-12}M$ **d.** $9.8 \times 10^{-10}M$

74. How many grams of potassium chloride are in 45.0 mL of a 5.00% (by mass) solution?

75. Write the formula for the conjugate base of each acid.
   a. H_2SO_4 **b.** HCN   **c.** H_2O **d.** NH_4^+

76. In each pair, which has the higher entropy?
   a. NaCl(s) or NaCl(aq)
   b. $CO_2(s)$ or $CO_2(g)$
   c. $H_2O(l)$ at 60 °C or $H_2O(l)$ at 25 °C

77. What is the molarity of the salt in a solution that results from mixing 200 mL of $1.00M$ NaOH with 200 mL of $1.00M$ HCl?

CONCEPT CHALLENGE

78. What is the normality of an H_2SO_4 solution if 80.0 mL of the solution reacts completely with 0.424 g Na_2CO_3?

$$H_2SO_4(aq) + Na_2CO_3(aq) \longrightarrow$$
$$H_2O(l) + CO_2(aq) + Na_2SO_4(aq)$$

79. An impure sample of $AgNO_3$ weighing 0.340 g was dissolved in water. After the addition of 10.0 mL of $0.200N$ HCl, 0.213 g AgCl was recovered. Calculate the percentage of $AgNO_3$ in the sample.

80. Use the cyanate buffer HOCN /OCN⁻ to illustrate how a buffer system works. Show, by means of equations, how the pH of a solution can be kept almost constant when small amounts of acid or base are added.

Select the choice that best answers each question or completes each statement.

1. How many moles of NaOH are required to neutralize 2.4 mol H_2SO_4?
   a. 1.2 mol
   c. 3.6 mol
   b. 2.4 mol
   d. 4.8 mol

2. The net ionic equation for the neutralization reaction between solutions of potassium hydroxide and hydrochloric acid is
   a. $H^+(aq) + OH^-(aq) \longrightarrow H_2O(l)$
   b. $KOH(aq) + HCl(aq) \longrightarrow H_2O(l) + KCl(aq)$
   c. $K^+(aq) + Cl^-(aq) \longrightarrow KCl(aq)$
   d. $K^+(aq) + OH^-(aq) + H^+(aq)$
      $+ Cl^-(aq) \longrightarrow KCl(aq) + H_2O(l)$

3. Calculate the molarity of an HCl solution if 25.0 mL of the solution is neutralized by 15.5 mL of 0.800M NaOH.
   a. 0.248M
   c. 1.29M
   b. 0.496M
   d. 0.645M

4. At 25 °C, zinc sulfide has a K_{sp} of 3.0×10^{-23}, zinc carbonate has a K_{sp} of 1.0×10^{-10}, and silver iodide has a K_{sp} of 8.3×10^{-17}. Order these salts from most soluble to least soluble.
   a. zinc carbonate, zinc sulfide, silver iodide
   b. silver iodide, zinc carbonate, zinc sulfide
   c. zinc carbonate, silver iodide, zinc sulfide
   d. zinc sulfide, silver iodide, zinc carbonate

5. Which combination of compound and ion would *not* make a useful buffer solution?
   a. ammonium ion and ammonia
   b. hydrogen carbonate ion and carbonic acid
   c. sulfate ion and sulfuric acid
   d. ethanoate ion and ethanoic acid

The lettered choices below refer to questions 6–9. A lettered choice may be used once, more than once, or not at all

   (A) PQ
   (B) P_2Q_3
   (C) PQ_3
   (D) P_3Q
   (E) PQ_2

Which of the choices is the general formula for the salt formed in each of the following neutralization reactions? P is a cation; Q is an anion.

6. $HCl + Ca(OH)_2 \longrightarrow$

7. $H_3PO_4 + NaOH \longrightarrow$

8. $H_2SO_4 + Mg(OH)_2 \longrightarrow$

9. $HNO_3 + Al(OH)_3 \longrightarrow$

A student titrated three different acids with three different bases. He then used the experimental data to produce three titration curves. Use the graphs to answer questions 10–12.

a.

b.

c.

Match each graph with one acid–base pair.

10. aqueous ammonia + hydrochloric acid

11. sulfuric acid + potassium hydroxide

12. sodium hydroxide + ethanoic acid

Use the atomic windows to answer question 13.

13. Window (a) represents an aqueous solution of a weak acid, HA, and its sodium salt, Na^+A^-. For simplicity, the sodium ions (Na^+) and water molecules have been omitted. Which window shows the system after two OH^- ions are added?

a.

 A^- HA

b.

c.

d.

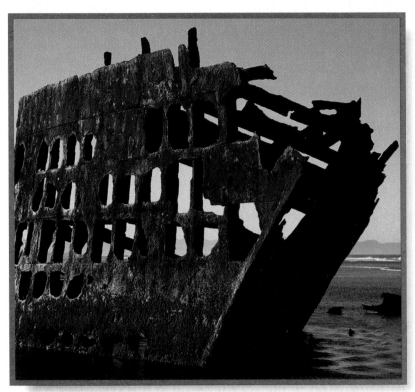

Salt water increased the rate at which this ship's hull rusted.

FEATURES

DISCOVER IT!
Rusting

SMALL-SCALE LAB
Half-Reactions

MINI LAB
Bleach It! Oxidize the Color Away

CHEMISTRY SERVING ... SOCIETY
Just Add Cold Water for a Hot Meal on the Go

CHEMISTRY IN CAREERS
Mechanical Engineer

LINK TO PHOTOGRAPHY
Redox in Photography

LINK TO BIOLOGY
Bioluminescence

Stay current with **SCIENCE NEWS**
Find out more about redox reactions:
www.phschool.com

DISCOVER IT! RUSTING

You need seven iron finishing nails (approximately 6 cm long), pliers, scissors, copper wire, zinc strip, fine sandpaper, plastic wrap, a saucer, water, table salt, petroleum jelly, and paper towels.

1. Use sandpaper to polish seven nails. Wipe them clean with a paper towel.

2. Place two wet paper towels on the saucer.

3. Nail 1: Using pliers, bend into a U shape. Nail 2: Wrap one end with copper wire. Nail 3: Wrap one end with a strip of zinc. Nail 4: Cover the entire nail with a thin coat of petroleum jelly. Nail 5: Moisten with water and sprinkle with salt. Nail 6: Leave untreated. Nail 7: Leave untreated.

4. Place nails 1 through 6 on the wet paper towel. Make sure the nails do not touch. Cover them with a piece of plastic wrap. Place nail 7 (the control) on top of the plastic wrap. During a 24-hour period, record your observations in a table.

THE MEANING OF OXIDATION AND REDUCTION

During winter in cold climates, salt is often used on roads to prevent the buildup of slippery ice. Although salt may make driving safer, it can cause the metallic parts of cars to corrode or rust relatively quickly. This problem is often so severe that people will not drive their newer cars in winter because they fear that their car will end up looking as rusty as this ship.

What property causes metal to corrode?

objectives
- ▶ Define oxidation and reduction in terms of the loss or gain of oxygen or hydrogen and the loss or gain of electrons
- ▶ State the characteristics of a redox reaction, and identify the oxidizing agent and reducing agent

key terms
- ▶ oxidation
- ▶ reduction
- ▶ oxidation–reduction reactions
- ▶ redox reactions
- ▶ reducing agent
- ▶ oxidizing agent

Oxygen in Redox Reactions

The combustion of gasoline in an automobile engine and the burning of wood in a fireplace produce energy. So does the metabolism of food by your body. Such reactions are among the principal sources of energy on Earth, and all involve a process called oxidation. What do you think of when you hear that term? If you answered "oxygen," you are thinking along the same lines as most early chemists.

Oxidation originally meant the combination of an element with oxygen to produce oxides. As you will soon learn, the term also has a more modern, and wider, meaning. When gasoline or wood burns in air, it oxidizes and produces carbon dioxide. So does coal, as shown in **Figure 22.1.** Methane (CH_4), a component of natural gas, also burns in air. Methane oxidizes to form oxides of carbon and hydrogen.

Not all oxidation processes involve burning, however. Bleaching is an example of oxidation that does not involve burning. Bleaches are substances that remove stains or unwanted color from fabrics and other

Figure 22.1

When coal, which is mostly carbon, is burned in air, carbon dioxide and heat are produced.

$C(s)$ $+$ $O_2(g)$ $\longrightarrow$ $CO_2(g)$

Figure 22.2

A Bunsen burner oxidizes the methane in natural gas to carbon dioxide and water. This reaction releases a great deal of heat.

$$CH_4(g) \quad + \quad 2O_2(g) \quad \longrightarrow \quad CO_2(g) \quad + \quad 2H_2O(g)$$

materials. Common liquid household bleaches contain sodium hypochlorite (NaClO). Powder bleaches may contain calcium hypochlorite ($Ca(ClO)_2$) or sodium perborate ($NaBO_3$).

Hydrogen peroxide (H_2O_2) is another good oxidizing agent. Common household peroxide is both a bleach and a mild antiseptic that kills bacteria by oxidizing them. Notice that, in keeping with the original definition of oxidation, all these substances have one thing in common: They all contain oxygen.

Another familiar example of an oxidation process that does not involve burning is rusting. When elemental iron turns to rust, it slowly oxidizes to compounds such as iron(III) oxide (Fe_2O_3).

Figure 22.3

When items made of iron are exposed to moist air, the Fe atoms react with O_2 molecules. The iron rusts; it is oxidized to compounds such as iron(III) oxide (Fe_2O_3).

$$4Fe(s) \quad + \quad 3O_2(g) \quad \longrightarrow \quad 2Fe_2O_3(s)$$

Figure 22.4
These iron objects (left) were made in ancient times. The iron was obtained by reduction of iron ore with charcoal. A similar process is carried out in a modern-day blast furnace (right).

A process called reduction is the opposite of oxidation. Originally, **reduction** meant the loss of oxygen from a compound. The reduction of iron ore to metallic iron involves the removal of oxygen from iron(III) oxide. The reduction is accomplished by heating the ore with charcoal. A large decrease in volume occurs during the reduction of a metal oxide to metal. Can you explain how reduction got its name? The equation for the reduction of iron ore is

$$2Fe_2O_3(s) + 3C(s) \longrightarrow 4Fe(s) + 3CO_2(g)$$

| Iron(III) oxide | Carbon | Iron | Carbon dioxide |

The artifacts in **Figure 22.4** show that ancient people reduced iron ore to iron in the early Iron Age, more than 2500 years ago!

The equation for the reduction of iron also includes an oxidation process. Oxidation and reduction always occur simultaneously. As iron oxide is reduced to iron by losing oxygen, carbon is oxidized to carbon dioxide by gaining oxygen. No oxidation occurs without reduction, and no reduction occurs without oxidation. Reactions that involve these processes are therefore called **oxidation–reduction reactions.** Oxidation–reduction reactions are also known as **redox reactions.**

Electron Transfer in Redox Reactions

Today, the concepts of oxidation and reduction have been extended to include many reactions that do not even involve oxygen. Redox reactions are understood to involve a shift of electrons between reactants. **Oxidation** is redefined to mean complete or partial loss of electrons or gain of oxygen. **Reduction** is complete or partial gain of electrons or loss of oxygen.

Oxidation	**Reduction**
Loss of electrons	Gain of electrons
Gain of oxygen	Loss of oxygen

"*LEO* the lion goes *GER*" may help you remember the definitions of oxidation and reduction. *LEO* stands for *L*osing *E*lectrons is *O*xidation; *GER* stands for *G*aining *E*lectrons is *R*eduction.

Some examples will illustrate these redefined concepts. Consider reactions between a metal and a nonmetal. Electrons are transferred from atoms of the metal to atoms of the nonmetal. For example, the ionic compound magnesium sulfide is produced when magnesium metal is heated with the nonmetal sulfur. See **Figure 22.5.**

$$\text{Mg} + \text{S} \longrightarrow \text{Mg}^{2+} + \text{S}^{2-}$$

| Magnesium | Sulfur | Magnesium | Sulfide |
| atom | atom | ion | ion |

The result of this reaction is the transfer of two electrons from a magnesium atom to a sulfur atom. Because it loses electrons, the magnesium atom is said to be oxidized to a magnesium ion. How many electrons does the magnesium atom lose? Simultaneously, the sulfur atom gains two

Magnesium (ribbon)

Sulfur

Magnesium sulfide

$\text{Mg}(s)$ + $\text{S}(s)$ $\xrightarrow{\text{Heat}}$ $\text{MgS}(s)$

Figure 22.5

When magnesium and sulfur are heated together, they undergo an oxidation–reduction reaction to form magnesium sulfide. The magnesium atoms become more stable by the loss of electrons (oxidation). The sulfur atoms become more stable by the gain of electrons (reduction).

electrons and is reduced to a sulfide ion. The overall process is represented as the two component processes below.

Oxidation: $\cdot Mg \cdot \longrightarrow Mg^{2+} + 2e^-$ (loss of electrons)

Reduction: $\cdot \ddot{S} : + 2e^- \longrightarrow : \ddot{S} :^{2-}$ (gain of electrons)

The substance in a redox reaction that loses electrons is called the **reducing agent.** By losing electrons to sulfur, magnesium reduces the sulfur. Magnesium is thus the reducing agent. The substance in a redox reaction that accepts electrons is called the **oxidizing agent.** By accepting electrons from magnesium, sulfur oxidizes the magnesium. Sulfur is thus the oxidizing agent.

$$Mg(s) + S(s) \longrightarrow MgS(s)$$

| Magnesium (reducing agent) | Sulfur (oxidizing agent) | Magnesium sulfide |

Sample Problem 22-1

What is oxidized and what is reduced in this single-replacement reaction? What is the oxidizing agent? The reducing agent?

$$2AgNO_3(aq) + Cu(s) \longrightarrow Cu(NO_3)_2(aq) + 2Ag(s)$$

1. **ANALYZE Plan a problem-solving strategy.**
   Begin by rewriting the equation and showing the ions. Determine what loses electrons (is oxidized) and what gains electrons (is reduced).

2. **SOLVE Apply the problem-solving strategy.**
   The rewritten equation showing the ions is:

   $$2Ag^+ + 2NO_3^- + Cu \longrightarrow Cu^{2+} + 2NO_3^- + 2Ag$$

   In this reaction, two electrons have been lost from a copper atom (Cu) because it becomes a Cu^{2+} ion. These electrons are gained by two silver ions (Ag^+), which become neutral silver atoms.

   Oxidation: $Cu \longrightarrow Cu^{2+} + 2e^-$ (loss of electrons)
   Reduction: $2Ag^+ + 2e^- \longrightarrow 2Ag$ (gain of electrons)

   The Cu is oxidized and is therefore the reducing agent. The Ag^+ is reduced and is therefore the oxidizing agent.

3. **EVALUATE Does the result make sense?**
   Ag^+, the oxidizing agent, gained electrons and is thus reduced. Cu, the reducing agent, lost electrons and is thus oxidized. The definitions of oxidation and reduction have been correctly applied.

Practice Problems

1. Determine what is oxidized and what is reduced in each reaction. Identify the oxidizing agent and reducing agent in each case.
   a. $2Na(s) + S(s) \longrightarrow Na_2S(s)$
   b. $4Al(s) + 3O_2(g) \longrightarrow 2Al_2O_3(s)$
2. Identify these processes as either oxidation or reduction.
   a. $Li \longrightarrow Li^+ + e^-$
   b. $2I^- \longrightarrow I_2 + 2e^-$
   c. $Zn^{2+} + 2e^- \longrightarrow Zn$
   d. $Br_2 + 2e^- \longrightarrow 2Br^-$

<u>Chem ASAP!</u>
Problem-Solving 1
Solve Problem 1 with the help of an interactive guided tutorial.

PHOTOGRAPHY

Redox in Photography

Black-and-white photography involves oxidation–reduction reactions. Exposing black-and-white film to light activates very fine grains of silver bromide in the film. The film is developed by placing it in a developing solution that is actually a reducing agent. The developer, usually an organic chemical such as hydroquinone ($C_6H_4(OH)_2$), reduces the activated silver bromide to finely divided, black metallic silver. Any silver bromide that remains unactivated is removed from the film by using a solvent called a fixer. Sodium thiosulfate, commonly called hypo, is used for this purpose. The areas of the film exposed to the most light appear darkest because they have the highest concentration of metallic silver. The reversed image, called a negative, is used to produce a positive print, the black-and-white photograph, of the image.

It is easy to identify complete transfers of electrons in ionic reactions such as those just examined. But what about reactions that produce covalent compounds; that is, compounds in which complete electron transfer does not occur? Consider the reaction of hydrogen and oxygen.

$$2H_2(g) + O_2(g) \longrightarrow 2H_2O(l)$$

According to the older definition of oxidation as a combination with oxygen, it is clear that the hydrogen is oxidized to water. The newer definition involving electron transfer will also provide the same answer. Consider what happens to the bonding electrons in the formation of a water molecule. The bonding electrons in each reactant hydrogen molecule are shared equally between the hydrogen atoms. In water, however, the bonding electrons are pulled toward oxygen because it is much more electronegative than hydrogen. The result is a shift of bonding electrons away from hydrogen, even though there is not a complete transfer.

$$H—H \quad \text{electrons shared equally} \qquad \overset{\longleftarrow}{H—O}\underset{H}{|} \quad \text{shift of bonding electrons away from hydrogen}$$

Hydrogen is oxidized because it undergoes a partial loss of electrons. Thus the old gain-of-oxygen and the newer loss-of-electron definitions of oxidation agree that it is the hydrogen that is oxidized when the water forms.

What about oxygen, the other reactant? The bonding electrons are shared equally between oxygen atoms in the reactant oxygen molecule, but there is a shift of electrons toward oxygen in water. Oxygen is thus reduced because it undergoes a partial gain of electrons.

$$O—O \quad \text{electrons shared equally} \qquad \overset{\longleftarrow}{H—O}\underset{H}{|} \quad \text{shift of bonding electrons toward oxygen}$$

In every redox reaction, including those that produce covalent products, there is an oxidizing agent and a reducing agent. In the reaction of hydrogen and oxygen to produce water, hydrogen is the reducing agent because it is oxidized. Oxygen is the oxidizing agent because it is reduced. This redox reaction is highly exothermic—that is, it releases a great deal of energy, as shown in **Figure 22.6.**

In some reactions involving covalent products, the partial electron shifts are less obvious. Some general guidelines are thus helpful. For example, for carbon compounds, the addition of oxygen or the removal of hydrogen is always oxidation. **Table 22.1** lists processes that constitute oxidation and reduction. The last entry in the table identifies oxidation numbers, which are another way to describe oxidation and reduction. You will learn more about oxidation numbers in Section 22.2.

Figure 22.6

This artist uses an oxyhydrogen torch to cut and weld steel to make a sculpture. When hydrogen burns in oxygen, the redox reaction generates temperatures of about 2600 °C.

Table 22.1

Processes Leading to Oxidation and Reduction	
Oxidation	**Reduction**
Complete loss of electrons (ionic reactions)	Complete gain of electrons (ionic reactions)
Shift of electrons *away* from an atom in a covalent bond	Shift of electrons *toward* an atom in a covalent bond
Gain of oxygen	Loss of oxygen
Loss of hydrogen by a covalent compound	Gain of hydrogen by a covalent compound
Increase in oxidation number	Decrease in oxidation number

Corrosion

Billions of dollars are spent yearly to prevent and to repair damage caused by the corrosion of metals. Iron, a common construction metal often used in the form of the alloy steel, corrodes by being oxidized to ions of iron by oxygen. Water in the environment accelerates the rate of corrosion. Oxygen, the oxidizing agent, is reduced to oxide ions (in compounds such as Fe_2O_3) or to hydroxide ions. The following equations describe the corrosion of iron to iron hydroxides at moist conditions.

$$2Fe(s) + O_2(g) + 2H_2O(l) \longrightarrow 2Fe(OH)_2(s)$$

$$4Fe(OH)_2(s) + O_2(g) + 2H_2O(l) \longrightarrow 4Fe(OH)_3(s)$$

Corrosion occurs more rapidly in the presence of salts and acids. These substances produce conducting solutions that make electron transfer easier. The corrosion of some metals can be a desirable feature, as **Figure 22.7** shows.

Not all metals corrode easily. Gold and platinum are called noble metals because they are very resistant to losing their electrons by corrosion. Other metals lose electrons easily but are protected from extensive corrosion by the oxide coating formed on their surface. For example, aluminum oxidizes quickly in air to form a coating of very tightly packed aluminum oxide particles. This coating protects the aluminum object from further corrosion, as

Figure 22.7

Oxidation–reduction reactions cause corrosion. The copper on this roof reacted with water vapor, carbon dioxide, and other substances in the air to form a patina. This patina consists of a pale-green film of basic copper(II) carbonate. Because patinas enhance the surface appearance of objects, they are valued by architects and artists.

Water Aluminum oxide Oxygen

Aluminum

(a)

Iron(III) oxide

Water Oxygen

Iron

(b)

Figure 22.8

Oxidation causes the complete corrosion of some metals. Aluminum, however, resists such corrosion because it forms a protective coating of aluminum oxide. How does the aluminum oxide on aluminum (a) differ from the iron(III) oxide formed on corroding iron (b)?

shown in **Figure 22.8.** Iron also forms a coating when it corrodes, but the coating of iron oxide that forms is not tightly packed. Water in the air can penetrate the coating and attack the iron metal below it. The corrosion continues until the iron object becomes only a pile of rust.

The corrosion of objects such as shovels or knives is a common problem but not usually a serious one. In contrast, the corrosion of a steel support pillar of a bridge or the hull of an oil tanker is much more serious and costly to repair! To prevent corrosion in such cases, the metal surface may be coated with oil, paint, plastic, or another metal, as shown in **Figure 22.9.** These coatings exclude air and water from the surface, thus preventing corrosion. If the coating is scratched or worn away, however, the exposed metal will begin to corrode.

In another method of corrosion control, one metal is used to save a second metal. For example, to protect an iron object, a piece of magnesium may be placed in electrical contact with the iron. When oxygen and water attack the iron object, the iron atoms lose electrons as the iron begins to be oxidized. However, because magnesium is a better reducing agent than iron and is more easily oxidized, the magnesium immediately transfers electrons to the iron ions, reducing them back to neutral iron atoms.

Figure 22.9

Painting a surface (left) protects it from the effects of the environment. Chromium metal also serves as a protective coating and imparts an attractive, mirrorlike finish (right). Like aluminum, chromium forms a corrosion-resistant oxide film on its surface.

Sacrificial zinc and magnesium blocks are sometimes attached to piers and ship hulls to prevent corrosion damage in areas submerged in water, as shown in **Figure 22.10.** Underground pipelines and storage tanks may be connected to magnesium blocks for protection. Obviously, it is easier and cheaper to replace a block of magnesium or zinc than to replace a bridge or a pipeline.

Figure 22.10
Zinc blocks, the white strips in the photograph, are attached to the steel hull of this ship to protect the steel from corrosion. The zinc blocks oxidize (corrode) and release electrons. The steel hull consumes the electrons supplied by the zinc, preventing it from corroding.

section review 22.1

3. Define oxidation and reduction in terms of
   a. gain or loss of electrons.
   b. gain or loss of hydrogen (in a covalent bond).
   c. gain or loss of oxygen.
   d. shift of electrons (in a covalent bond).

4. State the characteristics of a redox reaction, and explain how to identify the oxidizing agent and the reducing agent.

5. Which of the following would most likely be oxidizing agents and which would most likely be reducing agents? (*Hint:* Think in terms of tendencies to lose or gain electrons.)
   a. Cl_2 **b.** K   **c.** Ag^+

6. Refer to the electronegativity values in **Table 14.2** on page 405 to determine which reactant is oxidized and which reactant is reduced in each reaction. Also determine which reactant is the reducing agent and which is the oxidizing agent.
   a. $H_2(g) + Cl_2(g) \longrightarrow 2HCl(g)$
   b. $S(s) + Cl_2(g) \longrightarrow SCl_2(g)$
   c. $N_2(g) + 2O_2(g) \longrightarrow 2NO_2(g)$
   d. $2Li(s) + F_2(g) \longrightarrow 2LiF(s)$
   e. $H_2(g) + S(s) \longrightarrow H_2S(g)$

7. Use electron transfer or electron shift to identify what is oxidized and what is reduced in each reaction. Make use of electronegativity values, as needed, for molecular compounds.
   a. $2Na(s) + Br_2(l) \longrightarrow 2NaBr(s)$
   b. $N_2(g) + 3H_2(g) \longrightarrow 2NH_3(g)$
   c. $S(s) + O_2(g) \longrightarrow SO_2(g)$
   d. $Mg(s) + Cu(NO_3)_2(aq) \longrightarrow Mg(NO_3)_2(aq) + Cu(s)$

8. Why would a metal corrode more quickly in salt water than in distilled water?

 Chem ASAP! Assessment 22.1 Check your understanding of the important ideas and concepts in Section 22.1.

 portfolio project

Shipwrecks of Spanish galleons often contain gold or silver treasures. Why is the recovered gold hardly changed while the silver has turned black? Research and write a report on how the thick layers of tarnish are removed from silver artifacts.

OXIDATION NUMBERS

objectives
▶ Determine the oxidation number of an atom of any element in a pure substance
▶ Define oxidation and reduction in terms of a change in oxidation number, and identify atoms being oxidized or reduced in redox reactions

key term
▶ oxidation number

Did you know that the different colors produced by fireworks are the result of various elements and compounds being burned? Burning sodium produces yellow light. Burning barium and copper compounds produces green light and blue-green light, respectively. The fireworks shown here are called red stars—their beautiful crimson glow coming from the burning of strontium compounds. As elements burn, their oxidation state often changes. **How are oxidation numbers assigned, and how are they used to analyze redox reactions?**

Assigning Oxidation Numbers

An **oxidation number** is a positive or negative number assigned to an atom according to a set of rules. Oxidation numbers can be thought of as a chemical bookkeeping device. As you will learn in Section 22.3, complex redox equations can be balanced by the use of oxidation-number changes. As a general rule, a bonded atom's oxidation number is the charge that it would have if the electrons in the bond were assigned to the atom of the more electronegative element. In binary ionic compounds, such as NaCl and $CaCl_2$, the oxidation numbers of the atoms equal their ionic charges. The compound sodium chloride is composed of sodium ions (Na^{1+}) and chloride ions (Cl^{1-}). Thus the oxidation number of sodium is +1, and that of chlorine is −1. Notice that when oxidation numbers are written, the sign is put before the number. Sodium in NaCl has an ionic charge of 1+ and an oxidation number of +1. What are the oxidation numbers of calcium and of fluorine in calcium fluoride (CaF_2)?

Because water is a molecular compound, no ionic charges are associated with its atoms. As you learned in Section 22.1, however, oxygen is reduced in the formation of water. Oxygen is more electronegative than

Figure 22.11
The oxidation number of any element in the free or uncombined state is zero. The elements shown here (left to right) are white phosphorus (stored under water), sulfur, potassium (stored under oil), carbon, and bromine liquid. The potassium and phosphorus are stored under a liquid to prevent them from reacting with oxygen in the air.

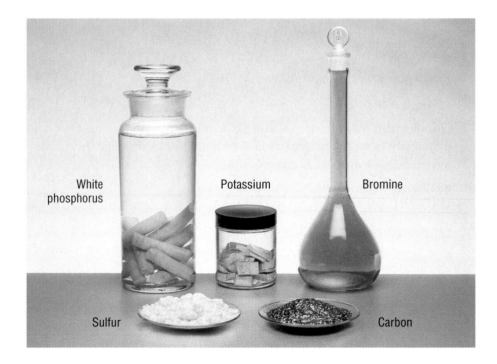

White phosphorus

Potassium

Bromine

Sulfur

Carbon

Figure 22.12

Yellow potassium chromate (K_2CrO_4) and orange potassium dichromate ($K_2Cr_2O_7$) each have a chromium-containing polyatomic ion. What are the formulas of the chromate ion and the dichromate ion?

hydrogen. In water, the two shared electrons in the H—O bond are shifted toward oxygen and away from hydrogen. Imagine that the electrons contributed by the hydrogen atoms are completely transferred to the oxygen. The charges that would result from this transfer are the oxidation numbers of the bonded elements. The oxidation number of oxygen is −2. The oxidation number of each hydrogen is +1. Oxidation numbers are often written above the chemical symbols in a formula. For example, water can be represented as

$$\overset{+1\ -2}{H_2O}$$

The following set of rules should help you determine oxidation numbers.

Rules for Assigning Oxidation Numbers

1. The oxidation number of a monatomic ion is equal in magnitude and sign to its ionic charge. For example, the oxidation number of the bromide ion (Br^{1-}) is −1; that of the Fe^{3+} ion is +3.

2. The oxidation number of hydrogen in a compound is +1, except in metal hydrides, such as NaH, where it is −1.

3. The oxidation number of oxygen in a compound is −2, except in peroxides, such as H_2O_2, where it is −1.

4. The oxidation number of an atom in uncombined (elemental) form is 0. For example, the oxidation number of the potassium atoms in potassium metal (K) or of the nitrogen atoms in nitrogen gas (N_2) is 0. See **Figure 22.11.**

5. For any neutral compound, the sum of the oxidation numbers of the atoms in the compound must equal 0.

6. For a polyatomic ion, the sum of the oxidation numbers must equal the ionic charge of the ion.

The last two rules can be used together to determine the oxidation number of atoms not covered in the first four rules. The yellow crystals and the orange crystals in **Figure 22.12** are both compounds of chromium. What is the oxidation number of chromium in each compound?

Sample Problem 22-2

What is the oxidation number of each kind of atom in the following compounds?

a. SO_2 **b.** CO_3^{2-} **c.** K_2SO_4

1. **ANALYZE** *Plan a problem-solving strategy.*

   a.–c. Use the set of rules you just learned to assign oxidation numbers and to calculate unknown ones.

2. **SOLVE** *Apply the problem-solving strategy.*

   a. There are two oxygen atoms and the oxidation number of each oxygen is -2 (rule 3). You also know that the sum of the oxidation numbers for the neutral compound must be 0 (rule 5). Therefore the oxidation number of sulfur is $+4$, because $+4 + (2 \times (-2)) = 0$.

   $$\overset{+4\,-2}{SO_2}$$

   b. The oxidation number of oxygen is -2 (rule 3).

   $$\overset{?\,-2}{CO_3^{2-}}$$

   The sum of the oxidation numbers of the carbon and oxygen atoms must equal the ionic charge, $2-$ (rule 6). The oxidation number of carbon must be $+4$, because $+4 + (3 \times (-2)) = -2$.

   $$\overset{+4\,-2}{CO_3^{2-}}$$

   c. The oxidation number of the potassium ion is the same as its ionic charge, $+1$ (rule 1). The oxidation number of oxygen is -2 (rule 3).

   $$\overset{+1\ \ ?\,-2}{K_2SO_4}$$

   For the sum of the oxidation numbers in the compound to be 0 (rule 5), the oxidation number of sulfur must be $+6$, because $(2 \times (+1)) + (+6) + (4 \times (-2)) = 0$.

   $$\overset{+1\,+6\,-2}{K_2SO_4}$$

3. **EVALUATE** *Do the results make sense?*

The results are consistent with the rules for determining oxidation numbers. Rule 1 was used to find the oxidation number of potassium in K_2SO_4. Rule 3 was used to find the oxidation number of oxygen in all three compounds. Rule 5 was used to find the oxidation number of sulfur in SO_2 and K_2SO_4. Rule 6 was used to find the oxidation number of carbon in CO_3^{2-}. Also, addition of the oxidation numbers correctly gives the final overall charge for the ion and the two neutral compounds.

Practice Problems

9. Determine the oxidation number of each element in these substances.

   a. S_2O_3 **b.** O_2 **c.** $Al_2(SO_4)_3$
   d. Na_2O_2

10. Find the oxidation number of each kind of atom in the following.

   a. P_2O_5 **b.** NH_4^+
   c. $Na_2Cr_2O_7$ **d.** $Ca(OH)_2$

Figure 22.13
When a copper wire is placed in a colorless silver nitrate solution (left), crystals of silver coat the wire (right). The solution slowly turns blue as a result of the formation of copper(II) nitrate. What change occurs in the oxidation number of the silver? How does the oxidation number of the copper change?

Oxidation-Number Changes in Chemical Reactions

An increase in the oxidation number of an atom indicates oxidation. A decrease in the oxidation number of an atom indicates reduction. Look again at the equation in Sample Problem 22-1 on page 649 and at **Figure 22.13.** Can you identify what is being oxidized and what is being reduced on the basis of oxidation-number changes? Here is the equation with oxidation numbers added:

$$\overset{+1\ +5\ -2}{2AgNO_3}(aq) + \overset{0}{Cu}(s) \longrightarrow \overset{+2\ +5\ -2}{Cu(NO_3)_2}(aq) + \overset{0}{2Ag}(s)$$

In this reaction, the oxidation number of silver decreases from +1 to 0, which indicates reduction: Silver ions (Ag^{1+}) reduce to silver metal (Ag^0). Copper is oxidized in this reaction. Its oxidation number increases from 0 to +2 as copper metal oxidizes from Cu^0 to Cu^{2+}. Note that these results agree with those obtained by analyzing the electron transfers that occur in the reaction. **Figure 22.14** illustrates a redox reaction that shows what occurs when a shiny iron nail is dipped into a solution of copper(II) sulfate.

Figure 22.14
An iron nail dipped in a copper(II) sulfate solution (left) becomes coated with metallic copper (right). The iron reduces Cu^{2+} ions in solution and is simultaneously oxidized to Fe^{2+}. Write the balanced ionic equation for this redox reaction.

Sample Problem 22-3

Use the changes in oxidation number to identify which atoms are oxidized and which are reduced in each reaction.

a. $Cl_2(g) + 2HBr(aq) \longrightarrow 2HCl(aq) + Br_2(l)$

b. $C(s) + O_2(g) \longrightarrow CO_2(g)$

c. $Zn(s) + 2MnO_2(s) + 2NH_4Cl(aq) \longrightarrow$
$$ZnCl_2(aq) + Mn_2O_3(s) + 2NH_3(g) + H_2O(l)$$

1. **ANALYZE** *Plan a problem-solving strategy.*

Use the rules to assign an oxidation number to each atom on both sides of the equation. Note the increases and decreases in oxidation numbers. On the basis of these changes, identify the atoms oxidized and those reduced. A decrease in oxidation number indicates reduction. An increase in oxidation number indicates oxidation.

2. **SOLVE** *Apply the problem-solving strategy.*

$$\overset{0}{Cl_2}(g) + 2\overset{+1-1}{HBr}(aq) \longrightarrow 2\overset{+1-1}{HCl}(aq) + \overset{0}{Br_2}(l)$$

a.

The element chlorine is reduced because its oxidation number decreases (0 to −1). The bromide ion is oxidized because its oxidation number increases (−1 to 0).

$$\overset{0}{C}(s) + \overset{0}{O_2}(g) \longrightarrow \overset{+4-2}{CO_2}(g)$$

b.

The element carbon is oxidized (0 to +4). The element oxygen is reduced (0 to −2).

$$\overset{0}{Zn}(s) + 2\overset{+4\ -2}{MnO_2}(s) + 2\overset{-3+1\ -1}{NH_4Cl}(aq) \longrightarrow$$
$$\overset{+2\ -1}{ZnCl_2}(aq) + \overset{+3\ -2}{Mn_2O_3}(s) + 2\overset{-3+1}{NH_3}(g) + \overset{+1\ -2}{H_2O}(l)$$

c.

The element zinc is oxidized (0 to +2). The manganese ion is reduced (+4 to +3).

3. **EVALUATE** *Do the results make sense?*

Checking the results reveals that the assignments of oxidation numbers are correct; that is, the rules for assigning oxidation numbers have been correctly applied. In each case, a decrease in oxidation number has correctly been used to indicate reduction, and an increase in oxidation number has been used to indicate oxidation.

Recall that in every redox reaction there is an oxidizing agent and a reducing agent. The element that is oxidized is the reducing agent, and the element that is reduced is the oxidizing agent. Thus once you have identified the elements that are oxidized and the elements that are reduced in a reaction, you can use this information to identify the oxidizing agent and the reducing agent. This is illustrated in Sample Problem 22-4.

Practice Problem

11. Use the changes in oxidation numbers to identify which atoms are oxidized and which are reduced in each reaction.

a. $2H_2(g) + O_2(g) \longrightarrow 2H_2O(l)$

b. $2KNO_3(s) \longrightarrow$
$$2KNO_2(s) + O_2(g)$$

c. $NH_4NO_2(s) \longrightarrow$
$$N_2(g) + 2H_2O(g)$$
(*Hint:* Consider each N in NH_4NO_2 separately.)

d. $PbO_2(aq) + 4HI(aq) \longrightarrow$
$$I_2(aq) + PbI_2(s) + 2H_2O(l)$$

Problem-Solving 11
Solve Problem 11 with the help of an interactive guided tutorial.

Sample Problem 22-4

Identify the oxidizing agent and the reducing agent in each equation in Sample Problem 22-3.

1. **ANALYZE** *Plan a problem-solving strategy.*
   a.–c. Use the following facts to solve the problem: The substance oxidized in a reaction is the reducing agent, and the substance reduced is the oxidizing agent.

2. **SOLVE** *Apply the problem-solving strategy.*
   a. Chlorine is reduced, so Cl_2 is the oxidizing agent. Bromide (in HBr) is oxidized, so Br^- is the reducing agent.
   b. Carbon is oxidized, so C is the reducing agent. Oxygen is reduced, so O_2 is the oxidizing agent.
   c. Zinc is oxidized, so Zn is the reducing agent. Manganese (in MnO_2) is reduced, so Mn^{4+} is the oxidizing agent.

3. **EVALUATE** *Do the results make sense?*
   It makes sense that what is oxidized in a chemical reaction is the reducing agent because it loses electrons—it becomes the agent by which the atom that is reduced gains electrons. Conversely, it makes sense that what is reduced in a chemical reaction is the oxidizing agent because it gains electrons—it is the agent by which the atom that is oxidized loses electrons. These facts were correctly applied in solving the problem.

Practice Problem

12. Identify the oxidizing agent and the reducing agent in each equation in Practice Problem 11.

section review 22.2

13. **a.** What is the oxidation number of nitrogen in nitrogen gas (N_2)? Explain.

    b. How would you determine the oxidation numbers of the elements in a compound?

    c. How is charge used to assign oxidation numbers to the elements in a polyatomic ion?

14. How are oxidation numbers determined and used?

15. Use the changes in oxidation numbers to identify which atoms are oxidized and which are reduced in each reaction.

    a. $2Na(s) + Cl_2(g) \longrightarrow 2NaCl(s)$

    b. $2HNO_3(aq) + 6HI(aq) \longrightarrow 2NO(g) + 3I_2(s) + 4H_2O(l)$

    c. $3H_2S(aq) + 2HNO_3(aq) \longrightarrow 3S(s) + 2NO(g) + 4H_2O(l)$

    d. $2PbSO_4(s) + 2H_2O(l) \longrightarrow Pb(s) + PbO_2(s) + 2H_2SO_4(aq)$

16. Identify the oxidizing agent and the reducing agent in each reaction in Problem 15.

 Chem ASAP! **Assessment 22.2** Check your understanding of the important ideas and concepts in Section 22.2.

BALANCING REDOX EQUATIONS

objectives

▶ Use the oxidation-number–change method to balance redox equations

▶ Break a redox equation into oxidation and reduction half-reactions, and then use the half-reaction method to balance the equation

key terms

▶ oxidation-number–change method

▶ half-reactions

▶ half-reaction method

*T*he unattainable, but long pursued, goal of alchemists was to change common metals, such as lead or copper, into gold. One tool that the alchemists employed in their quest was aqua regia, which means "royal water." Aqua regia is a mixture of concentrated hydrochloric (HCl) and nitric (HNO_3) acids that is capable of dissolving gold. When gold is added to aqua regia, oxidation and reduction reactions produce gaseous nitrogen monoxide (NO) and stable $AuCl_4^-$ ions.

How can a balanced chemical equation for this redox reaction be written?

Identifying Redox Reactions

In general, all chemical reactions can be assigned to one of two classes. In oxidation–reduction (redox) reactions, electrons are transferred from one reacting species to another. In all other reactions, no electron transfer occurs. For example, double-replacement reactions and acid–base reactions are not redox reactions. Many single-replacement reactions, combination reactions, decomposition reactions, and combustion reactions, however, are redox reactions. Can you write a balanced equation for each reaction shown in **Figure 22.15**?

Figure 22.15

(a) Potassium metal reacts violently with water to produce hydrogen gas (which ignites) and potassium hydroxide. Is this a redox reaction? Explain. *(b)* Zinc metal reacts vigorously with hydrochloric acid to produce hydrogen gas and zinc chloride. Is this a redox reaction? Explain.

(a)

(b)

You can determine whether a reaction is a redox reaction by using oxidation numbers to keep track of electrons. If the oxidation number of an element in a reacting species changes, then that element has undergone either oxidation or reduction. Therefore the reaction as a whole must be a redox reaction. Consider this example: During an electrical storm, oxygen molecules and nitrogen molecules in the air react to form nitrogen(II) oxide. The equation for the reaction is

$$N_2(g) + O_2(g) \longrightarrow 2NO(g)$$

Is this a redox reaction? How can you tell? Does the oxidation number of either reacting species change? If so, what is that change?

Figure 22.16

A color change can signal a redox reaction. When a colorless solution containing bromide ions is added to a solution containing permanganate ions, the distinctive purple color of the permanganate ion (MnO_4^-) is replaced by the pale brown color of bromine. What is the oxidation-number change in manganese and bromine?

Various other changes often signal that an oxidation–reduction reaction has taken place. One such change is a change in color. For example, look at **Figure 22.16.** When a colorless aqueous solution of bromide ions (Br^-) is added to a purple aqueous solution of permanganate ions (MnO_4^-), the solution changes from purple to pale brown. As the following unbalanced equation shows, bromide ions are oxidized to bromine, and permanganate ions are reduced to manganese(II) ions.

$$MnO_4^-(aq) \ + \ Br^-(aq) \ \longrightarrow \ Mn^{2+}(aq) \ + \ Br_2(aq)$$

| Permanganate ion (purple) | Bromide ion (colorless) | Manganese(II) ion (colorless) | Bromine (brown) |

Color changes can do more than signal that a redox reaction has taken place. They can help obtain quantitive information about concentrations in redox reactions. The titration of reducing agents and oxidizing agents is similar to the titration of acids and bases, which you learned about in Section 21.1. For example, the titration of the reducing agent oxalic acid ($H_2C_2O_4$) with a solution of unknown concentration of the oxidizing agent potassium permanganate ($KMnO_4$) is illustrated in **Figure 22.17.** To obtain a quantitative result in such a titration, a balanced equation of the redox reaction is required. A known mass of colorless oxalic acid, the reducing

Figure 22.17

In this redox titration, the oxidizing agent in the buret (purple aqueous potassium permanganate) serves as the indicator. A known mass of the reducing agent, colorless oxalic acid, is dissolved in dilute sulfuric acid in the flask. As permanganate is added slowly to the contents of the flask, it immediately loses its purple color (left). When all the oxalic acid in the flask is oxidized, the next drop of permanganate remains unreacted, and the solution in the flask turns light purple (right). That is the end point of the redox titration.

agent, is dissolved in dilute sulfuric acid in the reaction flask. The concentration of the purple potassium permanganate solution can be calculated from the volume added to reach the end point, which is reached when all the oxalic acid is oxidized and the next drop of purple $KMnO_4$ remains unreacted. The net ionic equation for the reaction can be written. From this equation, the oxidation-number changes for the oxidized and reduced species can be determined. The full balanced equation for the reaction is

$$2KMnO_4(aq) + 5H_2C_2O_4(aq) + 3H_2SO_4(aq) \longrightarrow$$
$$2MnSO_4(aq) + K_2SO_4(aq) + 10CO_2(g) + 8H_2O(l)$$

Sample Problem 22-5

Use the change in oxidation number to identify whether each reaction is a redox reaction or a reaction of some other type. If a reaction is a redox reaction, identify the element reduced, the element oxidized, the reducing agent, and the oxidizing agent.

a. $N_2O_4(g) \longrightarrow 2NO_2(g)$
b. $Cl_2(g) + 2NaBr(aq) \longrightarrow 2NaCl(aq) + Br_2(g)$
c. $PbCl_2(aq) + K_2SO_4(aq) \longrightarrow 2KCl(aq) + PbSO_4(s)$
d. $2NaOH(aq) + H_2SO_4(aq) \longrightarrow Na_2SO_4(aq) + 2H_2O(l)$

1. **ANALYZE** *Plan a problem-solving strategy.*

a.–d. Use the rules to assign oxidation numbers to each element. Note whether there are any changes in oxidation number. If there are, the reaction is a redox reaction. The element with an oxidation number that increases is oxidized and is the reducing agent. The element with an oxidation number that decreases is reduced and is the oxidizing agent.

2. **SOLVE** *Apply the problem-solving strategy.*

a. $\overset{+4-2}{N_2O_4}(g) \longrightarrow 2\overset{+4-2}{NO_2}(g)$

This is a decomposition reaction. Neither oxygen nor nitrogen changes in oxidation number. Therefore the reaction is not a redox reaction.

b. $\overset{0}{Cl_2}(g) + 2\overset{+1\ -1}{NaBr}(aq) \longrightarrow 2\overset{+1\ -1}{NaCl}(aq) + \overset{0}{Br_2}(g)$

This is a single-replacement reaction. The chlorine is reduced. The bromide ion is oxidized. This is a redox reaction. Chlorine is the oxidizing agent; bromide ion is the reducing agent.

c. $\overset{+2\ -1}{PbCl_2}(aq) + \overset{+1+6-2}{K_2SO_4}(aq) \longrightarrow 2\overset{+1-1}{KCl}(aq) + \overset{+2+6-2}{PbSO_4}(s)$

This is a double-replacement reaction. None of the elements changes in oxidation number. This is not a redox reaction.

Practice Problems

17. Identify which of the following are oxidation–reduction reactions. If a reaction is a redox reaction, name the element oxidized and the element reduced.

a. $BaCl_2(aq) + 2KIO_3(aq) \longrightarrow$
$Ba(IO_3)_2(s) + 2KCl(aq)$

b. $H_2CO_3(aq) \longrightarrow$
$H_2O(l) + CO_2(g)$

c. $Mg(s) + Br_2(l) \longrightarrow$
$MgBr_2(s)$

d. $NH_4NO_2(s) \longrightarrow$
$N_2(g) + 2H_2O(l)$

e. $2KClO_3(s) \longrightarrow$
$2KCl(s) + 3O_2(g)$

Sample Problem 22-5 (cont.)

$$\overset{+1\ -2+1}{} \quad \overset{+1+6-2}{} \quad \overset{+1\ +6-2}{} \quad \overset{+1\ -2}{}$$
d. $2NaOH(aq) + H_2SO_4(aq) \longrightarrow Na_2SO_4(aq) + 2H_2O(l)$

This is an acid–base (neutralization) reaction. None of the elements changes in oxidation number. This is not a redox reaction.

---

3. *EVALUATE* *Do the results make sense?*
Only in redox reactions do the oxidation numbers of reactants change as products form. Only reaction **b.** represents a redox reaction. In **b.**, each chlorine atom (Cl) accepts an electron from a bromide ion (Br^-). The chlorine molecule is reduced to two chloride ions (Cl^-); therefore, it is the oxidizing agent in the reaction. That makes sense because chlorine is more electronegative than bromine (see **Table 14.2**) and thus more apt to gain electrons. Because the bromide ions are oxidized to molecular bromine (Br_2), the bromide ions are the reducing agent.

Practice Problems (cont.)

18. Identify which of the following are oxidation–reduction reactions. If a reaction is a redox reaction, name the element oxidized and the element reduced.
 a. $CaCO_3(s) + 2HCl(aq) \longrightarrow$
 $CaCl_2(aq) + H_2O(l) + CO_2(g)$
 b. $CuO(s) + H_2(g) \longrightarrow$
 $Cu(s) + H_2O(l)$

Problem-Solving 18
Solve Problem 18 with the help of an interactive guided tutorial.

As you know, the ability to write a correctly balanced equation that accurately represents what happens in a chemical reaction is essential to chemists and chemical engineers. Many oxidation–reduction reactions are too complex to be balanced by trial and error. Fortunately, two systematic methods are available. These methods, described below, are based on the fact that the total number of electrons gained in reduction must equal the total number of electrons lost in oxidation. One method uses oxidation-number changes, and the other uses half-reactions.

Using Oxidation-Number Changes

In the **oxidation-number–change method,** a redox equation is balanced by comparing the increases and decreases in oxidation numbers. To use this method, start with a skeleton equation for the redox reaction. The reduction of iron ore is used here as an example.

$$Fe_2O_3(s) + CO(g) \longrightarrow Fe(s) + CO_2(g) \text{ (unbalanced)}$$

Step 1. Assign oxidation numbers to all the atoms in the equation. Write the numbers above the atoms.

$$\overset{+3\ -2}{Fe_2O_3(s)} + \overset{+2-2}{CO(g)} \longrightarrow \overset{0}{Fe(s)} + \overset{+4-2}{CO_2(g)}$$

Note that the oxidation number is stated as the charge per atom. So although the total positive charge of Fe ions in Fe_2O_3 is 6+, the oxidation number of each Fe ion is +3.

Step 2. Identify which atoms are oxidized and which are reduced. In this reaction, iron decreases in oxidation number from +3 to 0, a change of −3. Therefore iron is reduced. Carbon increases in oxidation number from +2 to +4, a change of +2. Thus carbon is oxidized. Oxygen does not change in oxidation number.

Figure 22.18

Potassium dichromate, shown on the left, is an orange crystalline substance. It reacts with water and sulfur to form chromium(III) oxide, the green compound shown on the right. What are the other products?

Step 3. Use one bracketing line to connect the atoms that undergo oxidation and another such line to connect those that undergo reduction. Write the oxidation-number change at the midpoint of each line.

$$\overset{+3\ \ -2}{Fe_2O_3}(s) + \overset{+2-2}{CO}(g) \longrightarrow \overset{0}{Fe}(s) + \overset{+4-2}{CO_2}(g)$$

(with +2 bracket above CO → CO₂, and −3 bracket below Fe₂O₃ → Fe)

Step 4. Make the total increase in oxidation number equal to the total decrease in oxidation number by using appropriate coefficients. In this example, the oxidation-number increase should be multiplied by 3 and the oxidation-number decrease should be multiplied by 2, which gives an increase of +6 and a decrease of −6. This can be done in the equation by placing the coefficient 2 in front of Fe on the right side and the coefficient 3 in front of both CO and CO_2. The formula Fe_2O_3 does not need a coefficient because the formula already indicates 2 Fe.

$$\overset{3 \times (+2) = +6}{Fe_2O_3(s) + 3CO(g)} \longrightarrow 2Fe(s) + 3CO_2(g)$$

$$2 \times (-3) = -6$$

Step 5. Finally, make sure that the equation is balanced for both atoms and charge. If necessary, the remainder of the equation can be balanced by inspection.

$$Fe_2O_3(s) + 3CO(g) \longrightarrow 2Fe(s) + 3CO_2(g)$$

Sample Problem 22-6

Balance this redox equation by using the oxidation-number–change method. Samples of the initial and final chromium-containing compounds for this reaction are shown in **Figure 22.18.**

$$K_2Cr_2O_7(aq) + H_2O(l) + S(s) \longrightarrow$$
$$KOH(aq) + Cr_2O_3(s) + SO_2(g)$$

1. ANALYZE Plan a problem-solving strategy.
Apply the five steps of the oxidation-number–change method to balance the equation.

2. SOLVE Apply the problem-solving strategy.
Step 1. Assign oxidation numbers.

$$\overset{+1\ +6\ -2}{K_2Cr_2O_7}(aq) + \overset{+1\ -2}{H_2O}(l) + \overset{0}{S}(s) \longrightarrow$$

$$\overset{+1-2+1}{KOH}(aq) + \overset{+3\ -2}{Cr_2O_3}(s) + \overset{+4-2}{SO_2}(g)$$

Step 2. Identify which atoms are oxidized and which atoms are reduced. Cr is reduced because its oxidation number decreases, while S is oxidized because its oxidation number increases.

Practice Problems

19. Balance each redox equation using the oxidation-number–change method.
a. $KClO_3(s) \longrightarrow$
$$KCl(s) + O_2(g)$$
b. $HNO_2(aq) + HI(aq) \longrightarrow$
$$NO(g) + I_2(s) + H_2O(l)$$
c. $As_2O_3(s) + Cl_2(g) + H_2O(l)$
$$\longrightarrow H_3AsO_4(aq) + HCl(aq)$$

Sample Problem 22-6 (cont.)

Step 3. Connect the atoms that change in oxidation number. Indicate the signs and magnitudes of the changes.

$$\overset{+6}{K_2}\overset{}{Cr_2}O_7(aq) + H_2O(l) + \overset{0}{S}(s) \longrightarrow KOH(aq) + \overset{+3}{Cr_2}O_3(s) + \overset{+4}{S}O_2(g)$$

$$-3$$
$$+4$$

Step 4. Balance the increase and decrease in oxidation numbers. Four chromium atoms must be reduced ($4 \times (-3) = -12$ decrease) for each three sulfur atoms that are oxidized ($3 \times (+4) = +12$ increase). Put the coefficient 3 in front of S and SO_2 and the coefficient 2 in front of $K_2Cr_2O_7$ and Cr_2O_3,

$$(4)(-3) = -12$$
$$2\overset{+6}{K_2}Cr_2O_7(aq) + H_2O(l) + 3\overset{0}{S}(s) \longrightarrow KOH(aq) + 2\overset{+3}{Cr_2}O_3(s) + 3\overset{+4}{S}O_2(g)$$
$$(3)(+4) = +12$$

Step 5. Check the equation and finish balancing by inspection if necessary. The coefficient 4 in front of KOH balances potassium. The coefficient 2 in front of H_2O balances hydrogen and oxygen. The final equation is

$$2K_2Cr_2O_7(aq) + 2H_2O(l) + 3S(s) \longrightarrow$$
$$4KOH(aq) + 2Cr_2O_3(s) + 3SO_2(g)$$

3. EVALUATE Does the result make sense?
Inspection reveals that the equation is correctly balanced.

Practice Problems (cont.)

20. Use the oxidation-number–change method to balance each redox equation.
  a. $Bi_2S_3(s) + HNO_3(aq) \longrightarrow$
  $Bi(NO_3)_3(aq) + NO(g) + S(s) + H_2O(l)$
  b. $MnO_2(s) + H_2SO_4(aq) + H_2C_2O_4(aq) \longrightarrow MnSO_4(aq) + CO_2(g) + H_2O(l)$
  c. $SbCl_5(aq) + KI(aq) \longrightarrow$
  $SbCl_3(aq) + KCl(aq) + I_2(s)$

Chem ASAP!

Problem-Solving 20
Solve Problem 20 with the help of an interactive guided tutorial.

Using Half-Reactions

You have just learned about the oxidation-number–change method, one of two methods often used to balance redox equations. A second method involves the use of **half-reactions,** or equations showing either the reduction or the oxidation of a species in an oxidation–reduction reaction. The **half-reaction method** is used to balance redox equations by balancing the oxidation and reduction half-reactions. The procedure is different, but the outcome is the same as with the oxidation-number–change method. The half-reaction method is particularly useful in balancing equations for ionic reactions.

The oxidation of sulfur by nitric acid in aqueous solution is one example of a redox reaction that can be balanced by the half-reaction method.

$$S(s) + HNO_3(aq) \longrightarrow SO_2(g) + NO(g) + H_2O(l) \text{ (unbalanced)}$$

The following steps show how to balance this equation using the half-reaction method.

Step 1. Write the unbalanced equation in ionic form. In this case, only HNO_3 is ionized. The products are covalent compounds.

$$S(s) + H^+(aq) + NO_3^-(aq) \longrightarrow SO_2(g) + NO(g) + H_2O(l)$$

Table 22.2

Oxidation Numbers of Sulfur in Different Compounds	
Compound	Oxidation Number
H_2SO_4	$+6$
SO_3	$+6$
H_2SO_3	$+4$
SO_2	$+4$
$Na_2S_2O_3$	$+2$
SCl_2	$+2$
S_2Cl_2	$+1$
S	0
H_2S	-2

Step 2. Write separate half-reactions for the oxidation and reduction processes. As you can see from **Table 22.2**, which shows the oxidation numbers of sulfur in various compounds, sulfur is oxidized in this reaction because its oxidation number increases from 0 to 4. Nitrogen is reduced because its oxidation number decreases from +5 to +2.

$$\text{Oxidation half-reaction:} \quad S(s) \longrightarrow SO_2(g)$$
$$\text{Reduction half-reaction:} \quad NO_3^-(aq) \longrightarrow NO(g)$$

Step 3. Balance the atoms in the half-reactions.

a. *Balance the oxidation half-reaction.* This reaction takes place in acid solution. In such cases, H_2O and H^+ can be used to balance oxygen and hydrogen as needed. Sulfur is already balanced in the half-reaction. Add two molecules of H_2O on the left to balance the oxygen in the half-reaction.

$$2H_2O(l) + S(s) \longrightarrow SO_2(g)$$

Oxygen is now balanced, but four hydrogen ions ($4H^+$) must be added to the right to balance the hydrogen on the left.

$$2H_2O(l) + S(s) \longrightarrow SO_2(g) + 4H^+(aq)$$

This half-reaction is now balanced in terms of atoms. Note that it is not balanced for charge. The charges will be balanced in Step 4.

b. *Balance the reduction half-reaction.* Nitrogen is already balanced. Add two molecules of H_2O on the right to balance the oxygen.

$$NO_3^-(aq) \longrightarrow NO(g) + 2H_2O(l)$$

Oxygen is balanced, but four hydrogen ions ($4H^+$) must be added to the left to balance hydrogen.

$$4H^+(aq) + NO_3^-(aq) \longrightarrow NO(g) + 2H_2O(l)$$

This half-reaction is now balanced in terms of atoms, but not for charge.

Step 4. Add sufficient electrons to one side of each half-reaction to balance the charges. Four electrons are needed on the right side in the oxidation half-reaction.

$$\text{Oxidation:} \quad 2H_2O(l) + S(s) \longrightarrow SO_2(g) + 4H^+(aq) + 4e^-$$

Three electrons are needed on the left side in the reduction half-reaction.

$$\text{Reduction:} \quad 4H^+(aq) + NO_3^-(aq) + 3e^- \longrightarrow NO(g) + 2H_2O(l)$$

Each half-reaction is now balanced with respect to both atoms and charge.

Step 5. Multiply each half-reaction by an appropriate number to make the numbers of electrons equal in both. In any redox reaction, the number of electrons lost in oxidation must equal the number of electrons gained in reduction. In this case, the oxidation half-reaction is multiplied by 3 and the reduction half-reaction is multiplied by 4. Therefore the number of electrons lost in oxidation and the number of electrons gained in reduction both equal 12.

$$\text{Oxidation:} \quad 6H_2O(l) + 3S(s) \longrightarrow 3SO_2(g) + 12H^+(aq) + 12e^-$$
$$\text{Reduction:} \quad 16H^+(aq) + 4NO_3^-(aq) + 12e^- \longrightarrow 4NO(g) + 8H_2O(l)$$

Step 6. Add the half-reactions to show an overall equation. Then subtract terms that appear on both sides of the equation. The equation is

$$6H_2O(l) + 3S(s) + 16H^+(aq) + 4NO_3^-(aq) + 12e^- \longrightarrow$$
$$3SO_2(g) + 12H^+(aq) + 12e^- + 4NO(g) + 8H_2O(l)$$

Subtracting terms that are on both the left and right produces

$$3S(s) + 4H^+(aq) + 4NO_3^-(aq) \longrightarrow 3SO_2(g) + 4NO(g) + 2H_2O(l)$$

Step 7. Add the spectator ions and balance the equation. Recall from Chapter 8 that like the spectators at an athletic event, spectator ions are present but do not participate in or change during a reaction. Because none of the ions in the reactants appear in the products, there are no spectator ions in this particular example. The balanced equation above is thus correct. However, it can be written to show the HNO_3 as un-ionized.

$$3S(s) + 4HNO_3(aq) \longrightarrow 3SO_2(g) + 4NO(g) + 2H_2O(l)$$

Sample Problem 22-7

Use the half-reaction method to balance the equation for the following redox reaction.

$$KMnO_4(aq) + HCl(aq) \longrightarrow$$
$$MnCl_2(aq) + Cl_2(g) + H_2O(l) + KCl(aq)$$

1. **ANALYZE** *Plan a problem-solving strategy.*
   Follow the seven steps of the half-reaction method to balance the equation.

2. **SOLVE** *Apply the problem-solving strategy.*
   Step 1. Write the unbalanced equation in ionic form.
   $$K^+(aq) + MnO_4^-(aq) + H^+(aq) + Cl^-(aq) \longrightarrow$$
   $$Mn^{2+}(aq) + 2Cl^-(aq) + Cl_2(g) + H_2O(l) + K^+(aq) + Cl^-(aq)$$
   Step 2. Write separate half-reactions for the oxidation and reduction processes. Use oxidation numbers to determine the oxidation process and the reduction process.
   Oxidation: $Cl^- \longrightarrow Cl_2$
   Reduction: $MnO_4^- \longrightarrow Mn^{2+}$

   Step 3. Balance the atoms in the half-reactions. Because the solution is acidic, use H_2O and H^+ to balance the oxygen and hydrogen if necessary. (If the solution were basic, H_2O and OH^- would be used.)
   Oxidation: $2Cl^-(aq) \longrightarrow Cl_2(g)$ (atoms balanced)
   Reduction: $MnO_4^-(aq) + 8H^+(aq) \longrightarrow Mn^{2+}(aq) + 4H_2O(l)$
   (atoms balanced)

   Step 4. Add electrons to balance the charges.
   Oxidation: $2Cl^-(aq) \longrightarrow Cl_2(g) + 2e^-$ (charges balanced)
   Reduction: $MnO_4^-(aq) + 8H^+(aq) + 5e^- \longrightarrow$
   $Mn^{2+}(aq) + 4H_2O(l)$ (charges balanced)

BIOLOGY

Bioluminescence
Some organisms produce light by means of oxidation–reduction reactions in a process known as bioluminescence. Light is given off when one of a class of

compounds called luciferins is oxidized by combination with oxygen. A product of these reactions is energy in the form of light. Bioluminescence serves different functions in different organisms. For example, fireflies use bioluminescence to attract mates, while some squids release a glowing cloud of "ink" to confuse and escape from their predators.

Sample Problem 22-7 (cont.)

Step 5. Make the numbers of electrons equal. Multiply the oxidation half-reaction by 5 and the reduction half-reaction by 2, so that 10 electrons are lost in oxidation and 10 electrons are gained in reduction.

Oxidation: $10Cl^-(aq) \longrightarrow 5Cl_2(g) + 10e^-$

Reduction: $2MnO_4^-(aq) + 16H^+(aq) + 10e^- \longrightarrow$
$$2Mn^{2+}(aq) + 8H_2O(l)$$

Step 6. Add the half-reactions and subtract terms that appear on both sides of the equation.

$10Cl^-(aq) + 2MnO_4^-(aq) + 16H^+(aq) + \cancel{10e^-} \longrightarrow$
$$5Cl_2(g) + \cancel{10e^-} + 2Mn^{2+}(aq) + 8H_2O(l)$$

The equation, after subtracting terms that appear on both sides, is

$10Cl^-(aq) + 2MnO_4^-(aq) + 16H^+(aq) \longrightarrow$
$$5Cl_2(g) + 2Mn^{2+}(aq) + 8H_2O(l)$$

Step 7. Add the spectator ions and balance the equation. In the example, the permanganate ions come from $KMnO_4$. The chloride ions come from HCl. K^+ ions, which appear on both sides of the unbalanced ionic equation in Step 1, come from $KMnO_4$ and must equal the number of MnO_4^- ions (given the formula, $KMnO_4$). The K^+ ions are spectator ions as are some of the Cl^- ions from the HCl—namely, those that are still present as products combined with Mn^{2+} and K^+.

The number of spectator Cl^- ions combined with Mn^{2+} must be twice the number of Mn^{2+} ions (given the formula, $MnCl_2$). The number of spectator Cl^- ions combined with K^+ must equal the number of K^+ ions (given the formula, KCl). The spectator ions are now added to the equation and balanced. Spectator ions are shown in blue.

$10Cl^- + 2MnO_4^- + 2K^+ + 16H^+ + 6Cl^- \longrightarrow$
$$5Cl_2 + 2Mn^{2+} + 4Cl^- + 8H_2O + 2K^+ + 2Cl^-$$

Summing spectator and nonspectator Cl^- on each side gives

$16Cl^-(aq) + 2MnO_4^-(aq) + 2K^+(aq) + 16H^+(aq) \longrightarrow$
$$5Cl_2(g) + 2Mn^{2+}(aq) + 6Cl^-(aq) + 8H_2O(l) + 2K^+(aq)$$

The equation is balanced for atoms and charge. To show it balanced for the substances given in the question (rather than for ions), rewrite it as

$2KMnO_4(aq) + 16HCl(aq) \longrightarrow$
$$2MnCl_2(aq) + 5Cl_2(g) + 8H_2O(l) + 2KCl(aq)$$

3. EVALUATE Does the result make sense?
The equation is correctly balanced for atoms and charge.

Practice Problems

21. Write balanced ionic equations for the following reactions, which occur in acid solution. Use the half-reaction method.
    a. $Sn^{2+}(aq) + Cr_2O_7^{2-}(aq) \longrightarrow$
    $$Sn^{4+}(aq) + Cr^{3+}(aq)$$
    b. $CuS(s) + NO_3^-(aq) \longrightarrow$
    $$Cu(NO_3)_2(aq) + NO_2(g) + SO_2(g)$$
    c. $I^-(aq) + NO_3^-(aq) \longrightarrow$
    $$I_2(s) + NO(g)$$

22. The following reactions take place in basic solution. Use the half-reaction method to write a balanced ionic equation for each.
    a. $MnO_4^-(aq) + I^-(aq) \longrightarrow$
    $$MnO_2(s) + I_2(s)$$
    b. $NiO_2(s) + S_2O_3^{2-}(aq) \longrightarrow$
    $$Ni(OH)_2(s) + SO_3^{2-}(aq)$$
    c. $Zn(s) + NO_3^-(aq) \longrightarrow$
    $$NH_3(aq) + Zn(OH)_4^{2-}(aq)$$

Chem ASAP!

Problem-Solving 22
Solve Problem 22 with the help of an interactive guided tutorial.

MINI LAB

Bleach It! Oxidize the Color Away

PURPOSE

To test the effect of oxidizing agents on stains and dyes.

MATERIALS

- spot plate
- medicine dropper
- water
- colorimeter (optional)

Oxidizing agents

- liquid chlorine bleach (5% (m/v) sodium hypochlorite)
- powder bleach
- oxalic acid solution (1% (m/v))
- sodium thiosulfate solution (hypo) (0.2M $Na_2S_2O_3$)

- hydrogen peroxide (3% (v/v) H_2O_2)

Samples

- iodine solution (1% I_2 in 2% (m/v) KI)
- potassium permanganate solution (0.05M $KMnO_4$)
- grape juice
- rusty water
- piece of colored fabric
- colored flower petals
- grass stain on piece of white fabric

PROCEDURE

 Sensor version available in the Probeware Lab Manual.

1. Place samples on a spot plate. Use 4 drops of each liquid or a small piece of each solid.

2. Describe the color and appearance of each sample in Step 1.

3. Add a few drops of the first oxidizing agent to each sample.

4. Describe any immediate change in appearance and any further change after 15 minutes.

5. Repeat Steps 2–4 with each oxidizing agent.

ANALYSIS AND CONCLUSIONS

1. Make a grid and record your observations.

2. Compare the oxidizing power of the oxidizing agents.

3. How do you know that chemical changes have occurred?

---

section review 22.3

23. Balance each redox equation, using the oxidation-number–change method.

a. $ClO_3^-(aq) + I^-(aq) \longrightarrow Cl^-(aq) + I_2(aq)$ [acid solution]

b. $C_2O_4^{2-}(aq) + MnO_4^-(aq) \longrightarrow Mn^{2+}(aq) + CO_2(g)$ [acid solution]

c. $Br_2(l) + SO_2(g) \longrightarrow Br^-(aq) + SO_4^{2-}(aq)$ [acid solution]

24. Use the half-reaction method to write a balanced ionic equation for each reaction.

a. $MnO_4^-(aq) + ClO_2^-(aq) \longrightarrow MnO_2(s) + ClO_4^-(aq)$ [basic solution]

b. $Cr^{3+}(aq) + ClO^-(aq) \longrightarrow CrO_4^{2-}(aq) + Cl^-(aq)$ [basic solution]

c. $Mn^{3+}(aq) + I^-(aq) \longrightarrow Mn^{2+}(aq) + IO_3^-(aq)$ [basic solution]

 Chem ASAP! **Assessment 22.3** Check your understanding of the important ideas and concepts in Section 22.3.

SMALL-SCALE LAB

HALF-REACTIONS

PURPOSE

To observe redox reactions and to write half-reactions that describe them.

MATERIALS

- pencil
- paper
- ruler
- reaction surface
- chemicals shown in Figure A

PROCEDURE

On separate sheets of paper, draw two grids similar to Figure A. Make each square 2 cm on each side.

Figure A

Place a reaction surface over one of the grids and add one drop of each acid solution to one piece of each metal, as shown in Figure A. Use the second grid as a data table to record your observations for each solution.

ANALYSIS

Using your experimental data, record the answers to the following questions below your data table.

1. Which metal is the most reactive? On what observation do you base your answer? Which metal did not react with any of the acids? List the metals in order of decreasing reactivity.

2. What is the chemical formula of the gas produced in each reaction?

3. An active metal reacts with an acid to produce hydrogen gas and a salt. Write equations and net ionic equations to describe the reactions you observed. Are all of these redox reactions? Explain.

4. The half-reaction for the oxidation of Zn is
$$Zn(s) \longrightarrow Zn^{2+}(aq) + 2e^-$$
Write the oxidation half-reaction for the other metals that react.

5. The half-reaction for the reduction of H^+ from the acid is
$$2H^+ + 2e^- \longrightarrow H_2(g)$$
Notice that this half-reaction is the same for all the acids. Demonstrate how adding this half-reaction to each oxidation half-reaction results in the overall net ionic equations.

YOU'RE THE CHEMIST

The following small-scale activities allow you to develop your own procedures and analyze the results.

1. **Analyze It!** Pennies minted after 1982 are made of zinc with a thin copper coating. Find a penny that has been damaged so that a portion of the zinc shows through. Carry out experiments to compare the reactivity of the zinc and the copper toward various acids. What are your results?

2. **Design It!** Many household products, such as toilet-bowl cleaners and vinegar, contain acids. Design and carry out experiments to find out if these products also dissolve metals. When using these household products in your home, what precautions should you take?

Chemistry Serving...Society

JUST ADD COLD WATER FOR A HOT MEAL ON THE GO

People spend a considerable amount of time and energy trying to prevent or inhibit the simple redox reaction called corrosion. Many metals oxidize when exposed to the oxygen in air. To keep them from corroding or rusting, the metals can be painted, plated with chromium, or galvanized with zinc. But corrosion is not all bad.

Because the oxidation of metal is generally an exothermic reaction, it can be used to generate useful heat—as long as the oxidation takes place quickly enough to release the heat energy in a short span of time.

Researchers working for the U.S. Army have put corrosion to work to solve a long-standing problem: how to provide soldiers with hot meals when there is no time to cook. They developed the Flameless Ration Heater (FRH), a simple way of heating precooked, packaged meal rations. All a soldier has to do is put a meal pouch in an FRH and add water. After about 15 minutes, the food has been heated to a warm 60 °C. Already proven in the battlefield, the FRH can also be used by forest firefighters, emergency crews, and other people who need quick, warm food under demanding conditions.

> **Researchers working for the U.S. Army have put corrosion to work to solve a long-standing problem: how to provide soldiers with hot meals when there is no time to cook.**

The Flameless Ration Heater is based on the reaction in which magnesium metal is oxidized by water to yield magnesium hydroxide, hydrogen, and heat.

$$Mg + 2H_2O \rightarrow Mg(OH)_2 + H_2 + heat$$

Just 24 grams of magnesium (1 mol) releases 355 000 joules (85 kcal) of heat, enough energy to boil approximately one liter of water.

But developing the FRH was not as simple as packaging a few grams of magnesium in a box. When exposed to air, magnesium oxidizes to magnesium oxide (MgO), which forms a thin film on the metal's surface. This film prevents further oxidation of the metal, either by air or by water. So the researchers had to find a way of letting water get through the MgO film.

They discovered that adding common table salt (NaCl) and powdered iron to the magnesium would do the trick. When water is added to this mixture, the chloride ions (Cl^-) react with the MgO film to form MgOHCl, which eats away at the remaining MgO.

Once the MgO film is gone, the water can react directly with the magnesium metal. The powdered iron seems to help this reaction take place more rapidly than it normally would. The researchers do not understand exactly how the iron helps, but they theorize that it assists in the transfer of electrons between the water and the magnesium. In any case, with the iron present, the reaction occurs rapidly and vigorously. As a result of putting corrosion to work, the energy stored in the chemical bonds of the reactants is released in just a few minutes—and you have a hot meal!

CHEMISTRY IN CAREERS

☆☆☆☆☆☆☆☆☆☆☆☆☆☆☆☆☆☆☆☆☆

TAKE IT TO THE NET
Find out more about career opportunities:

www.phschool.com

CHEMICAL SPECIALIST
Local food service distributor seeks responsible self-motivated individ-

MECHANICAL ENGINEER
Use redox reactions to invent new electrical technology.
See page 878.

CHEMIST NEEDED
Enviro. Lab. GC Must know EPA methods, troubleshoot-

Chapter 22 STUDENT STUDY GUIDE

Take It to the NET
For interactive study and review, go to www.phschool.com

KEY TERMS

▶ half-reaction *p. 665*
▶ half-reaction method *p. 665*
▶ oxidation *pp. 645, 647*
▶ oxidation number *p. 654*

▶ oxidation-number–change method *p. 663*
▶ oxidation–reduction reaction *p. 647*

▶ oxidizing agent *p. 649*
▶ redox reaction *p. 647*
▶ reducing agent *p. 649*
▶ reduction *p. 647*

KEY RELATIONSHIPS

X loses electron(s).
X is oxidized.
X is the reducing agent.
X increases oxidation number.

Y gains electron(s).
Y is reduced.
Y is the oxidizing agent.
Y decreases oxidation number.

CONCEPT SUMMARY

22.1 The Meaning of Oxidation and Reduction

• Oxidation is the gain of oxygen or the loss of electrons. Reduction is the loss of oxygen or the gain of electrons.

• An oxidation process is always accompanied by a reduction process. The substance that does the oxidizing is called an oxidizing agent. The substance that does the reducing is called a reducing agent.

22.2 Oxidation Numbers

• Oxidation numbers help to keep track of electrons in redox reactions. An oxidation-number increase is oxidation. An oxidation-number decrease is reduction.

• The oxidation number of an element in an uncombined state is zero. The oxidation number of a monatomic ion is the same in magnitude and sign as its ionic charge. The sum of the oxidation numbers of the elements in a neutral compound is zero.

22.3 Balancing Redox Equations

• The oxidation-number–change method for balancing redox equations involves determining the oxidation-number change of the substances that are oxidized and reduced. Coefficients are used to make the increase in oxidation number equal to the decrease.

• In the half-reaction method, which is another way to write a balanced equation for a redox reaction, the net ionic equation is first divided into two half-reactions. One is for the oxidation and the other is for the reduction. Each half-reaction is balanced independently for atoms. H^+, OH^-, H_2O are added as needed. The charge on both sides is balanced by adding electrons. The half-reactions are then multiplied by factors to make the number of electrons lost equal to the number of electrons gained. Finally, the half-reactions are added.

CHAPTER CONCEPT MAP

Use these terms to construct a concept map that organizes the major ideas of this chapter.

 ChemASAP! Concept Map 22
Create your Concept Map using the computer.

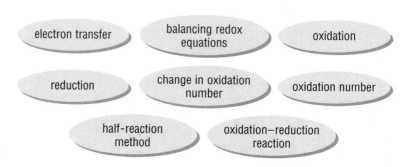

CONCEPT PRACTICE

25. What chemical process must always accompany a reduction process? *22.1*

26. Balance each redox equation. *22.1*
   a. $Ba(s) + O_2(g) \longrightarrow BaO(s)$
   b. $CaO(s) + Al(s) \longrightarrow Al_2O_3(s) + Ca(s)$
   c. $C_2H_5OH(l) + O_2(g) \longrightarrow CO_2(g) + H_2O(l)$

27. Balance each redox equation. *22.1*
   a. $C_2H_4(g) + O_2(g) \longrightarrow CO_2(g) + H_2O(l)$
   b. $KClO_3(s) \longrightarrow KCl(s) + O_2(g)$
   c. $CuO(s) + H_2(g) \longrightarrow Cu(s) + H_2O(l)$
   d. $H_2(g) + O_2(g) \longrightarrow H_2O(l)$

28. In redox reactions, a reduction is a gain. Explain. *22.2*

29. How do electrons lost and electrons gained compare in every redox reaction? *22.3*

30. Balance each redox equation. *22.3*
   a. $Al(s) + Cl_2(g) \longrightarrow AlCl_3(s)$
   b. $Al(s) + Fe_2O_3(s) \longrightarrow Al_2O_3(s) + Fe(s)$
   c. $Cl_2(g) + KOH(aq) \longrightarrow$
   $ KClO_3(aq) + KCl(aq) + H_2O(l)$
   d. $HNO_3(aq) + H_2S(g) \longrightarrow$
   $ S(s) + NO(g) + H_2O(l)$
   e. $KIO_4(aq) + KI(aq) + HCl(aq) \longrightarrow$
   $ KCl(aq) + I_2(s) + H_2O(l)$

31. Name some general types of reactions that are typically redox reactions. *22.3*

32. Identify which of these unbalanced equations represent redox reactions. *22.3*
   a. $Li(s) + H_2O(l) \longrightarrow LiOH(aq) + H_2(g)$
   b. $K_2Cr_2O_7(aq) + HCl(aq) \longrightarrow$
   $ KCl(aq) + CrCl_3(aq) + H_2O(l) + Cl_2(g)$
   c. $Al(s) + HCl(aq) \longrightarrow AlCl_3(aq) + H_2(g)$
   d. $P_4(s) + S_8(s) \longrightarrow P_2S_5(s)$

33. Which of these unbalanced equations represent redox reactions? *22.3*
   a. $MnO(s) + PbO_2(s) \longrightarrow$
   $ MnO_4^-(aq) + Pb^{2+}(aq)$ [acidic]
   b. $Cl_2(g) + H_2O(l) \longrightarrow$
   $ HCl(aq) + HClO(aq)$
   c. $I_2O_5(s) + CO(g) \longrightarrow I_2(s) + CO_2(g)$
   d. $H_2O(l) + SO_3(g) \longrightarrow H_2SO_4(aq)$

34. For each redox equation in Problem 32, identify the oxidizing agent and reducing agent. *22.3*

35. For each redox equation in Problem 33, identify the oxidizing agent and reducing agent. *22.3*

CONCEPT MASTERY

36. Balance the equations in Problem 32 by an appropriate method.

37. Balance the equations in Problem 33 by an appropriate method.

38. Determine the oxidation number of phosphorus in each substance.
   a. P_4O_8 **c.** P_2O_5 **e.** $H_2PO_4^-$
   b. PO_4^{3-} **d.** P_4O_6 **f.** PO_3^{3-}

39. Sodium chlorite is a powerful bleaching agent used in the paper and textile industries. It is prepared by this reaction.

$4NaOH(aq) + Ca(OH)_2(aq) + C(s) + 4ClO_2(g)$
$ \longrightarrow 4NaClO_2(aq) + CaCO_3(s) + 3H_2O(l)$

   a. Identify the element oxidized in this reaction.
   b. What is the oxidizing agent?

40. Identify the element oxidized, the element reduced, the oxidizing agent, and the reducing agent in each unbalanced redox equation.
   a. $MnO_2(s) + HCl(aq) \longrightarrow$
   $ MnCl_2(aq) + Cl_2(g) + H_2O(l)$
   b. $Cu(s) + HNO_3(aq) \longrightarrow$
   $ Cu(NO_3)_2(aq) + NO_2(g) + H_2O(l)$
   c. $P(s) + HNO_3(aq) + H_2O(l) \longrightarrow$
   $ NO(g) + H_3PO_4(aq)$
   d. $Bi(OH)_3(s) + Na_2SnO_2(aq) \longrightarrow$
   $ Bi(s) + Na_2SnO_3(aq) + H_2O(l)$

41. Balance each redox equation in Problem 40 by using the oxidation-number–change method.

CRITICAL THINKING

42. Choose the term that best completes the second relationship.
   a. oxidation : reduction
      fill up : _____
      (1) empty   (3) dry out
      (2) overflow   (4) splash
   b. oxidizing agent : Group 7A
      reducing agent : _____
      (1) Group 6A   (3) Group 0
      (2) Group 1A   (4) Group 4A

43. Many decomposition, single-replacement, combination, and combustion reactions are also redox reactions. Why is a double-replacement reaction never a redox reaction?

44. Calculate the pH of solutions with the following hydrogen-ion or hydroxide-ion concentrations.
a. $[H^+] = 0.000\ 010M$
b. $[OH^-] = 1.0 \times 10^{-4}M$
c. $[OH^-] = 1.0 \times 10^{-1}M$
d. $[H^+] = 3.0 \times 10^{-7}M$

45. Classify each solution in Problem 44 as acidic, basic, or neutral.

46. Identify the conjugate acid–base pairs in each equation.
a. $NH_4^+(aq) + H_2O(l) \longrightarrow$
$$NH_3(aq) + H_3O^+(aq)$$
b. $H_2SO_3(aq) + NH_2^-(aq) \longrightarrow$
$$HSO_3^-(aq) + NH_3(aq)$$
c. $HNO_3(aq) + I^-(aq) \longrightarrow HI(aq) + NO_3^-(aq)$

47. How many milliliters of a $4.00M$ KOH solution are needed to neutralize 45.0 mL of $2.50M$ H_2SO_4 solution?

48. What is the hydrogen-ion concentration of solutions with the following pH?
a. 2.00   **b.** 11.00   **c.** 8.80

49. What is the normality of the solution prepared by dissolving 46.4 g H_3PO_4 in enough water to make 1.25 L of solution?

50. The K_{sp} of lead(II) bromide ($PbBr_2$) at 25 °C is 2.1×10^{-6}. What is the solubility of $PbBr_2$ (in mol/L) at this temperature?

51. Bottles containing $0.1M$ solutions of Na_2SO_4, $BaCl_2$, and NaCl have had their labels accidentally switched. To discover which bottle contains the NaCl, you set up the following test. You place a clear saturated solution of $BaSO_4$ ($K_{sp} = 1.1 \times 10^{-10}$) into three test tubes. To each test tube you add a few drops of each mislabeled solution. The results are shown below. To which tube was NaCl added? Explain.

Test tube A   Test tube B   Test tube C

52. How would you make 440 mL of $1.5M$ HCl solution from a stock solution of $6.0M$ HCl?

53. The complete combustion of hydrocarbons involves the combination of both carbon and hydrogen atoms with oxygen. Carbon combines with oxygen to form carbon dioxide, and hydrogen combines with oxygen to form water. The following table lists the moles of O_2 used and the moles of CO_2 and moles of H_2O produced when a series of hydrocarbons called alkanes are burned.

Alkane burned	O_2 used (mol)	CO_2 produced (mol)	H_2O produced (mol)
CH_4	2	1	2
C_2H_6	3.5	2	3
C_3H_8	5	3	4
C_4H_{10}			
C_5H_{12}			
C_6H_{14}			

a. Complete the table.
b. Based on the data, write a balanced generalized equation for the complete combustion of any alkane. Use the following form, and write the coefficients in terms of x and y:

$$C_xH_y + \underline{\quad} O_2 \longrightarrow \underline{\quad} CO_2 + \underline{\quad} H_2O$$

CONCEPT CHALLENGE

54. How many grams of copper are needed to reduce completely the silver ions in 85.0 mL of $0.150M$ $AgNO_3(aq)$ solution?

55. How many milliliters of $0.280M$ $K_2Cr_2O_7(aq)$ solution are needed to oxidize 1.40 g of sulfur? First balance the equation.

$$K_2Cr_2O_7(aq) + H_2O(l) + S(s) \longrightarrow$$
$$SO_2(g) + KOH(aq) + Cr_2O_3(aq)$$

56. Carbon monoxide can be removed from the air by passing it over solid diiodine pentoxide.

$$CO(g) + I_2O_5(s) \longrightarrow I_2(s) + CO_2(g)$$

a. Balance the equation.
b. Identify the element being oxidized and the element being reduced.
c. How many grams of carbon monoxide can be removed from the air by 0.55 g of diiodine pentoxide (I_2O_5)?

Select the choice that best answers each question or completes each statement.

1. Which of these processes is *not* an oxidation?
   a. a decrease in oxidation number
   b. a complete loss of electrons
   c. a gain of oxygen
   d. a loss of hydrogen by a covalent molecule

2. In which of these pairs of nitrogen-containing ions and compounds is the oxidation number of nitrogen in the ion higher than in the nitrogen compound?
   I. N_2H_4 and NH_4^+
   II. NO_3^- and N_2O_4
   III. N_2O and NO_2^-
   a. I only
   b. I and II only
   c. I and III only
   d. II and III only
   e. I, II, and III

3. Identify the elements oxidized and reduced in this reaction.
   $$ClO^- + H_2 + 2e^- \longrightarrow Cl^- + 2OH^-$$
   a. Cl is oxidized; H is reduced
   b. H is oxidized; Cl is reduced
   c. Cl is oxidized; O is reduced
   d. O is oxidized; Cl is reduced

4. Which of these half-reactions represents a reduction?
   I. $Fe^{2+} \longrightarrow Fe^{3+}$
   II. $Cr_2O_7^{2-} \longrightarrow Cr^{3+}$
   III. $MnO_4^- \longrightarrow Mn^{2+}$
   a. I and II only
   b. II and III only
   c. I and III only
   d. I, II, and III

5. Which of these general types of reactions is *not* a redox reaction?
   a. single replacement
   b. double replacement
   c. combustion
   d. combination

6. What is the reducing agent in this unbalanced redox reaction?
   $$MnO_4^- + SO_2 \longrightarrow Mn^{2+} + SO_4^{2-}$$
   a. SO_2 c. Mn^{2+}
   b. SO_4^{2-} d. MnO_4^-

Use the table to answer questions 7–11.

Metal		Metal ion
	K	K^+
3	Ca	Ca^{2+}
	Na	Na^+
	Mg	Mg^{2+}
	Al	Al^{3+}
	Zn	Zn^{2+}
1 4	Fe	Fe^{2+} 2
	Ni	Ni^{2+}
	Sn	Sn^{2+}
	Pb	Pb^{2+}
	Cu	Cu^{2+}
5	Hg	Hg^{2+}
	Ag	Ag^+
	Au	Au^{3+}

7. Which arrow indicates increasing ease of oxidation? Of reduction?

8. Which numbered group of metals are the strongest reducing agents?

9. Which numbered group of metals are the most difficult to oxidize?

10. Which is a stronger oxidizing agent, Na or Ni?

11. Which is a stronger reducing agent, Mg or Hg?

Use this diagram to answer questions 12 and 13. It shows the formation of an ion from an atom.

Atom   Ion

12. Does the diagram represent an oxidation or a reduction? Does the oxidation number increase or decrease when the ion forms?

13. *You Draw It!* Draw a diagram showing the formation of a sulfide ion from a sulfur atom. Make the relative sizes of the atom and ion realistic. Does your drawing represent an oxidation or a reduction?

This squid emits energy in the form of light.

DISCOVER IT! A LEMON BATTERY

You need a whole lemon, a copper strip (1 cm × 3 cm), a zinc strip (1 cm × 3 cm), fine sandpaper, and a voltmeter (optional).

1. Polish the copper and zinc strips with sandpaper.

2. Push the zinc strip into the lemon. Leave about 1.5 cm of the zinc strip sticking out of the lemon.

3. Push the copper strip into the lemon about 1 cm away from the zinc strip. It should not make contact with the zinc strip. Leave about 1.5 cm of the copper strip sticking out of the lemon.

4. Briefly touch both metal strips at the same time with your tongue and observe what happens.

5. If you have a voltmeter, measure the voltage of your lemon battery.

Describe the sensation you felt on your tongue. Do you think you would feel the same sensation using two copper strips or two zinc strips? Try it! What would you expect to happen if, in place of the lemon, you were to use an orange? If you connected 12 lemon batteries together in series, you would generate a voltage of about 12 V. Could you use this assembly to start a car? Explain your answer. As you read about electrochemical cells in this chapter, refer back to this activity and explain what occurred.

FEATURES

DISCOVER IT!
A Lemon Battery

SMALL-SCALE LAB
Electrolysis of Water

MINI LAB
Tarnish Removal

**CHEMISTRY SERVING ...
THE ENVIRONMENT**
How Many Kilometers per Charge?

CHEMISTRY IN CAREERS
Electrochemist

LINK TO METALLURGY
Anodizing

Stay current with **SCIENCE NEWS**
Find out more about electrochemistry:
www.phschool.com

ELECTROCHEMICAL CELLS

On a summer evening, fireflies glow to attract their mates. In the ocean depths, anglerfish emit light to attract prey. Luminous shrimp, squid, jellyfish, and even bacteria also exist. These organisms, and others, are able to give off energy in the form of light as a result of redox reactions. **How does the transfer of electrons in a redox reaction produce energy?**

objectives

▶ Describe how redox reactions interconvert electrical energy and chemical energy

▶ Explain the structure of a dry cell and identify the substances that are oxidized and reduced

key terms

▶ electrochemical process
▶ electrochemical cell
▶ voltaic cells
▶ half-cell
▶ salt bridge
▶ electrode
▶ anode
▶ cathode
▶ dry cell
▶ battery
▶ fuel cells

The Nature of Electrochemical Cells

As you have learned, chemical processes can either release energy or absorb energy. The energy can sometimes be in the form of electricity. Electrochemistry has many applications in the home as well as in industry. Flashlight and automobile batteries are familiar examples of devices used to generate electrochemical energy. The manufacture of sodium and aluminum metals and the silverplating of tableware involve the use of electricity. Biological systems also use electrochemistry to carry nerve impulses. In this chapter, you will learn about the relationship between redox reactions and electrochemistry.

When a strip of zinc metal is dipped into an aqueous solution of blue copper sulfate, the zinc becomes copper-plated, as shown in **Figure 23.1**. The net ionic equation involves only zinc and copper.

$$Zn(s) + Cu^{2+}(aq) \longrightarrow Zn^{2+}(aq) + Cu(s)$$

Electrons are transferred from zinc atoms to copper ions. This is a redox reaction that occurs spontaneously. As the reaction proceeds, zinc atoms lose electrons as they are oxidized to zinc ions. The zinc metal slowly dissolves. At the same time, copper ions in solution gain the electrons lost by

Figure 23.1

A spontaneous redox reaction occurs when a zinc strip is immersed in a solution of copper sulfate (left). As the redox reaction proceeds, copper plates out on the zinc (the copper appears black because it is finely divided), and the zinc strip is corroded. Slowly, the blue copper sulfate solution is replaced by a solution of zinc sulfate (right). The blue color of the original copper sulfate gradually diminishes, and eventually the solution becomes colorless as zinc sulfate replaces copper sulfate. At the atomic level, each Zn atom loses two electrons, which are picked up by a Cu^{2+} ion. What substance is oxidized? Reduced?

Electrochemistry **677**

Table 23.1

Activity Series of Metals, with Half-Reactions for Oxidation Processes		
	Element	Oxidation half-reactions
Most active and most easily oxidized	Lithium	$Li(s) \longrightarrow Li^+(aq) + e^-$
	Potassium	$K(s) \longrightarrow K^+(aq) + e^-$
	Barium	$Ba(s) \longrightarrow Ba^{2+}(aq) + 2e^-$
	Calcium	$Ca(s) \longrightarrow Ca^{2+}(aq) + 2e^-$
	Sodium	$Na(s) \longrightarrow Na^+(aq) + e^-$
	Magnesium	$Mg(s) \longrightarrow Mg^{2+}(aq) + 2e^-$
Decreasing activity	Aluminum	$Al(s) \longrightarrow Al^{3+}(aq) + 3e^-$
	Zinc	$Zn(s) \longrightarrow Zn^{2+}(aq) + 2e^-$
	Iron	$Fe(s) \longrightarrow Fe^{2+}(aq) + 2e^-$
	Nickel	$Ni(s) \longrightarrow Ni^{2+}(aq) + 2e^-$
	Tin	$Sn(s) \longrightarrow Sn^{2+}(aq) + 2e^-$
	Lead	$Pb(s) \longrightarrow Pb^{2+}(aq) + 2e^-$
	Hydrogen*	$H_2(g) \longrightarrow 2H^+(aq) + 2e^-$
	Copper	$Cu(s) \longrightarrow Cu^{2+}(aq) + 2e^-$
	Mercury	$Hg(s) \longrightarrow Hg^{2+}(aq) + 2e^-$
Least active and least easily oxidized	Silver	$Ag(s) \longrightarrow Ag^+(aq) + e^-$
	Gold	$Au(s) \longrightarrow Au^{3+}(aq) + 3e^-$

*Hydrogen is included for reference purposes.

the zinc. They are reduced to copper atoms and are deposited as metallic copper. As the copper ions in solution are gradually replaced by zinc ions, the blue color of the solution fades. Balanced half-reactions for this redox reaction can be written as follows.

$$\text{Oxidation:} \quad Zn(s) \longrightarrow Zn^{2+}(aq) + 2e^-$$

$$\text{Reduction:} \quad Cu^{2+}(aq) + 2e^- \longrightarrow Cu(s)$$

If you look at the activity series of metals in **Table 23.1,** you will see that zinc is higher on the list than copper. For any two metals in the table, the metal that is the higher of the two is the more readily oxidized. As **Figure 23.1** shows, zinc is more readily oxidized than copper because when dipped into a copper sulfate solution, zinc becomes plated with copper. In contrast, when a copper strip is dipped into a solution of zinc sulfate, the copper does not spontaneously become zinc-plated. This is because copper metal is not oxidized by zinc ions.

When a zinc strip is dipped into a copper sulfate solution, electrons are transferred from zinc metal to copper ions. This flow of electrons is an electric current. Thus the zinc-metal–copper-ion system is an example of the conversion of chemical energy into electrical energy. Any conversion between chemical energy and electrical energy is an **electrochemical process.** All electrochemical processes involve redox reactions.

If a redox reaction is to be used as a source of electrical energy, the two half-reactions must be physically separated. In the case of the zinc-metal–copper-ion reaction, the electrons released by zinc must pass through an external circuit to reach the copper ions if useful electrical energy is to be produced. In that situation, the system serves as an electrochemical cell. Alternatively, an electric current can be used to produce a chemical change. That system, too, serves as an electrochemical cell. An **electrochemical cell** is any device that converts chemical energy into electrical energy or electrical energy into chemical energy. Redox reactions occur in electrochemical cells.

Voltaic Cells

The Italian physicist Alessandro Volta (1745–1827) invented the first electrochemical cell. In 1800, Volta designed and built a cell that could be used to generate a direct electric current (DC). **Figure 23.2** shows a photograph of Volta's illustration of one of his early cells. **Voltaic cells** (not surprisingly named after their inventor) are electrochemical cells used to convert chemical energy into electrical energy. The energy is produced by spontaneous redox reactions within the cell. You use a voltaic cell every time you turn on a flashlight or a battery-powered calculator.

A **half-cell** is one part of a voltaic cell in which either oxidation or reduction occurs. A half-cell consists of a metal rod or strip immersed in a solution of its ions. **Figure 23.3** on the following page shows a voltaic cell that makes use of the zinc–copper reaction. In this cell, one half-cell is a zinc rod immersed in a solution of zinc sulfate. The other half-cell is a copper rod immersed in a solution of copper sulfate. The half-cells are separated by a **salt bridge**—a tube containing a strong electrolyte, often potassium sulfate (K_2SO_4). Salt bridges usually are made of agar, a gelatinous substance. A porous plate may be used instead of a salt bridge. The porous plate allows ions to pass from one half-cell to the other but prevents the solutions from mixing completely. A wire carries the electrons in the external circuit from the zinc rod to the copper rod. A voltmeter or light bulb can be connected in the circuit. The driving force of such a voltaic cell is the spontaneous redox reaction between zinc metal and copper(II) ions in solution. Is the zinc metal oxidized or reduced?

Figure 23.2

Volta built his electrochemical cell using piles of copper and zinc plates separated by cardboard soaked in salt water. He used his cell to obtain an electrical current. A working voltaic cell can be constructed using strips of copper and zinc and a lemon.

Figure 23.3

In all electrochemical cells, oxidation occurs at the anode and reduction occurs at the cathode. In this voltaic cell, the electrons generated from the oxidation of Zn to Zn^{2+} pass up the zinc strip and flow through the external circuit (the wire) into the copper strip. These electrons reduce the surrounding Cu^{2+} to Cu. As electrons flow from left to right in the external circuit, anions flow from right to left in the salt bridge to maintain neutrality in the electrolytes.

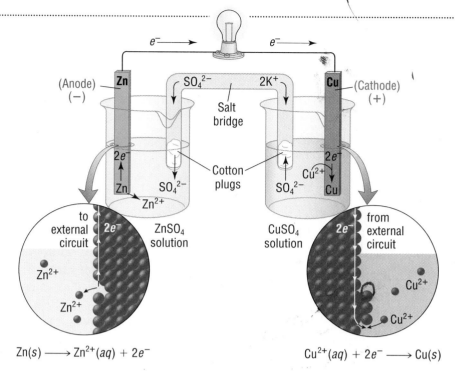

$$Zn(s) \longrightarrow Zn^{2+}(aq) + 2e^-$$

$$Cu^{2+}(aq) + 2e^- \longrightarrow Cu(s)$$

The zinc and copper rods in this voltaic cell are the electrodes. An **electrode** is a conductor in a circuit that carries electrons to or from a substance other than a metal. The reaction at the electrode determines whether the electrode is labeled as an anode or a cathode. The electrode at which oxidation occurs is called the **anode**. Because electrons are produced at the anode, it is labeled the negative electrode. The electrode at which reduction occurs is called the **cathode**. Electrons are consumed at the cathode. As a result, the cathode is labeled the positive electrode. Neither electrode is really charged, however. All parts of the voltaic cell remain balanced in terms of charge at all times. The moving electrons balance any charge that might build up as oxidation and reduction occur.

The electrochemical process that occurs in a zinc–copper voltaic cell can best be described in a number of steps. These steps actually occur at the same time.

1. Electrons are produced at the zinc rod according to the oxidation half-reaction.

$$Zn(s) \longrightarrow Zn^{2+}(aq) + 2e^-$$

Because it is oxidized, the zinc rod is the anode, or negative electrode.

2. The electrons leave the zinc anode and pass through the external circuit to the copper rod. (If a bulb is in the circuit, the electron flow will cause it to light. If a voltmeter is present, it will indicate a voltage.)

3. Electrons enter the copper rod and interact with copper ions in solution. There the following reduction half-reaction occurs.

$$Cu^{2+}(aq) + 2e^- \longrightarrow Cu(s)$$

Because copper ions are reduced at the copper rod, the copper rod is the cathode, or positive electrode, in the voltaic cell.

4. To complete the circuit, both positive and negative ions move through the aqueous solutions via the salt bridge. The two half-reactions can be summed to show the overall cell reaction. Note that the electrons in the overall reaction must cancel.

$$Zn(s) \longrightarrow Zn^{2+}(aq) + 2e^-$$

$$Cu^{2+}(aq) + 2e^- \longrightarrow Cu(s)$$

$$Zn(s) + Cu^{2+}(aq) \longrightarrow Zn^{2+}(aq) + Cu(s)$$

You can use a shorthand method to represent an electrochemical cell. For example, you can write the zinc–copper voltaic cell as follows.

$$Zn(s) \mid ZnSO_4(aq) \parallel CuSO_4(aq) \mid Cu(s)$$

The single vertical lines indicate boundaries of phases that are in contact. The zinc rod $(Zn)(s)$ and the zinc sulfate solution $(ZnSO_4)(aq)$, for example, are separate phases in physical contact. The double vertical lines represent the salt bridge or porous partition that separates the anode compartment from the cathode compartment. The half-cell that undergoes oxidation (the anode) is written first, to the left of the double vertical lines. When the zinc sulfate and copper(II) sulfate solutions in the voltaic half-cells are both 1.0M, the cell generates an electrical potential of 1.10 volts (V). If different metals are used for the electrodes in the cell, the voltage will differ. Would different solution concentrations affect the voltage as well?

Dry Cells

Although the zinc–copper voltaic cell is of historical importance, it is no longer used commercially. Nevertheless, this cell is a convenient model to use when describing the production of electrical energy from a chemical change. Today, the more practical and compact dry cell is usually chosen when a portable electrical energy source is required. A **dry cell** is a voltaic cell in which the electrolyte is a paste. A type of dry cell that is very familiar to you is the common flashlight battery, which, despite the name, is not a true battery. In such a dry cell, a zinc container is filled with a thick, moist electrolyte paste of manganese(IV) oxide (MnO_2), zinc chloride ($ZnCl_2$), ammonium chloride (NH_4Cl), and water (H_2O). As shown in **Figure 23.4a,** a graphite rod is embedded in the paste. The zinc container is the anode and the graphite rod is the cathode. The thick paste and its surrounding paper liner prevent the contents of the cell from freely mixing, so a salt bridge is not needed. The half-reactions for this cell are shown on the following page.

Figure 23.4

Many devices—including portable radios, toys, and flashlights—are powered by voltaic cells such as dry cells and alkaline batteries.
(a) A common dry cell is a single electrochemical cell that produces about 1.5 V. Although inexpensive, it has a short shelf-life and suffers from voltage drop when in use. What is oxidized in this cell and what is reduced? (b) The alkaline battery is an improved dry cell. Although more expensive than the common dry cell, it has a longer shelf-life and does not suffer from voltage drop. Both of these batteries have many uses.

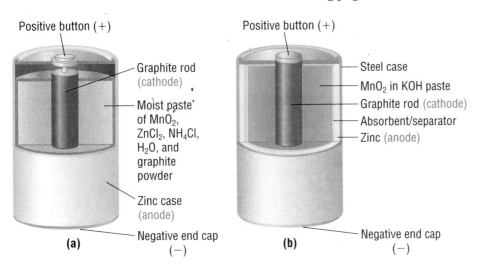

Positive button (+)

Graphite rod (cathode)

Moist paste of MnO_2, $ZnCl_2$, NH_4Cl, H_2O, and graphite powder

Zinc case (anode)

Negative end cap (−)

(a)

Positive button (+)

Steel case

MnO_2 in KOH paste

Graphite rod (cathode)

Absorbent/separator

Zinc (anode)

Negative end cap (−)

(b)

Electrochemistry **681**

Oxidation: $Zn(s) \longrightarrow Zn^{2+}(aq) + 2e^-$ (anode reaction)

Reduction: $2MnO_2(s) + 2NH_4^+(aq) + 2e^- \longrightarrow$
$Mn_2O_3(s) + 2NH_3(aq) + H_2O(l)$ (cathode reaction)

In this cell, the graphite rod serves only as a conductor and does not undergo reduction, even though it is the cathode. The manganese in MnO_2 is the species that is actually reduced. The electrical potential of this cell starts out at 1.5 V but decreases steadily during use to about 0.8 V. Dry cells of this type are not rechargeable.

The alkaline battery, shown in **Figure 23.4b** on the previous page, is an improved dry cell used for the same purposes. In the alkaline battery, the reactions are similar to those in the common dry cell, but the electrolyte is a basic KOH paste. This change in design eliminates the buildup of ammonia gas and maintains the Zn electrode, which corrodes more slowly under alkaline conditions. What is oxidized in an alkaline battery?

Lead Storage Batteries

A **battery** is a group of cells connected together. People depend on lead storage batteries to start their cars. A 12-V car battery consists of six voltaic cells connected together. Each cell produces about 2 V and consists of lead grids, as shown in **Figure 23.5.** One set of grids, the anode, is packed with spongy lead. The other set, the cathode, is packed with lead(IV) oxide (PbO_2). The grids are immersed in an electrolyte of concentrated sulfuric acid. The half-reactions are as follows.

Oxidation: $Pb(s) + SO_4^{2-}(aq) \longrightarrow PbSO_4(s) + 2e^-$

Reduction: $PbO_2(s) + 4H^+(aq) + SO_4^{2-}(aq) + 2e^- \longrightarrow$
$PbSO_4(s) + 2H_2O(l)$

When a lead storage battery discharges, it produces the electric power needed to start a car. The overall spontaneous redox reaction that occurs is the sum of the oxidation and reduction half-reactions.

$$Pb(s) + PbO_2(s) + 2H_2SO_4(aq) \longrightarrow 2PbSO_4(s) + 2H_2O(l)$$

This equation shows that during discharge, lead sulfate forms. The sulfate slowly builds up on the plates, and the concentration of sulfuric acid decreases.

The reverse reaction occurs when a lead storage battery is recharged. This reaction occurs whenever the car's generator is running.

$$2PbSO_4(s) + 2H_2O(l) \longrightarrow Pb(s) + PbO_2(s) + 2H_2SO_4(aq)$$

This reaction is nonspontaneous. To make it go, a direct current must be passed through the cell in a direction opposite that of the current flow during discharge. In theory, a lead storage battery can be discharged and recharged indefinitely, but in practice its lifespan is limited. This is because small amounts of lead sulfate fall from the electrodes and collect on the bottom of the cell. Eventually, the electrodes lose so much lead sulfate that the recharging process is ineffective or the cell is shorted out. The battery must then be replaced. The processes that occur during the discharge and recharge of a lead–acid battery are summarized in **Figure 23.6.**

Dilute sulfuric acid (H_2SO_4)(aq) electrolyte

Lead grid filled with lead(IV) oxide (PbO_2) (cathode)

Lead grid filled with spongy lead (Pb) (anode)

Figure 23.5

A 12-V lead storage battery, such as those used in cars, consists of six 2-V cells in series. One such cell is illustrated here. The cells do not need to be in separate compartments, but if they are, performance is improved. While the battery is producing a current, lead at the anode and lead(IV) oxide at the cathode are both converted to lead sulfate. These processes decrease the sulfuric acid concentration in the battery. Reversing the reaction recharges the battery.

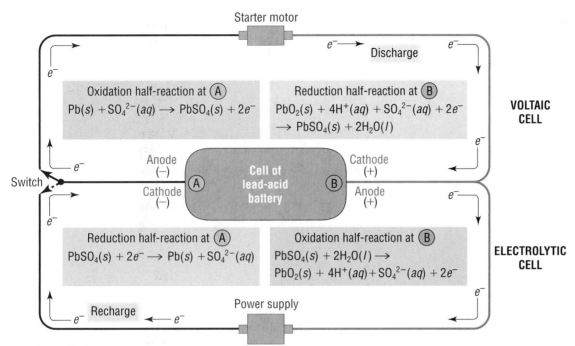

Figure 23.6
Turning a car's ignition causes energy from the battery to activate the starter motor, which starts the car's engine. During this process, the lead–acid battery is discharging and acts as a voltaic cell (top). The anode (terminal A) is negative and the cathode (terminal B) is positive. When the engine is running, some of the power it generates is used to recharge the battery. When the battery is recharging, it acts as an electrolytic cell (bottom) with a positive anode (terminal B) and a negative cathode (terminal A). You will learn more about electrolytic cells in Section 23.3.

Fuel Cells

To overcome the disadvantages associated with lead storage batteries, cells with renewable electrodes have recently been developed. Such cells, called **fuel cells,** are voltaic cells in which a fuel substance undergoes oxidation and from which electrical energy is continuously obtained. Fuel cells do not have to be recharged. They can be designed to emit no air pollutants and to operate more quietly and more cost-effectively than a conventional electrical generator.

Perhaps the simplest fuel cell is the hydrogen–oxygen fuel cell, which is shown in **Figure 23.7** on the following page. In this fuel cell, there are three compartments separated from one another by two electrodes made of porous carbon. Oxygen (the oxidizer) is fed into the cathode compartment. Hydrogen (the fuel) is fed into the anode compartment. The gases diffuse slowly through the electrodes. The electrolyte in the central compartment is a hot, concentrated solution of potassium hydroxide. Electrons from the oxidation half-reaction at the anode pass through an external circuit to enter the reduction half-reaction at the cathode.

Oxidation: $2H_2(g) + 4OH^-(aq) \longrightarrow 4H_2O(l) + 4e^-$ (anode)

Reduction: $O_2(g) + 2H_2O(l) + 4e^- \longrightarrow 4OH^-(aq)$ (cathode)

The overall reaction is the oxidation of hydrogen to form water.

$$2H_2(g) + O_2(g) \longrightarrow 2H_2O(l)$$

Figure 23.7

The hydrogen–oxygen fuel cell is a clean source of power. Such cells are often used in spacecraft. What waste products, if any, are produced?

Other fuels, such as methane (CH_4) and ammonia (NH_3), can be used in place of hydrogen. Other oxidizers, such as chlorine (Cl_2) and ozone (O_3), can be used in place of oxygen. Fuel cells are currently being built as auxiliary power sources for submarines and other military vehicles. At present, however, they are too expensive for general use. Hydrogen–oxygen fuel cells with a mass of approximately 100 kg each were used in the Apollo spacecraft missions. Can you name a benefit of producing energy with a hydrogen–oxygen fuel cell on an extended space mission?

section review 23.1

1. How do redox reactions interconvert electrical energy and chemical energy?

2. What is the source of the electrical energy produced in a voltaic cell?

3. Describe the structure of a dry cell. Identify the substance oxidized and the substance reduced in this type of cell. Include a diagram in your description.

4. Represent the electrochemical reaction of a flashlight battery using the shorthand method.

5. Predict the result when a strip of copper is dipped into a solution of iron(II) sulfate.

6. Describe the composition of the anode, cathode, and electrolyte in a fully charged lead storage battery.

7. Based on the half-reactions for the hydrogen–oxygen fuel cell, would KOH be consumed in such a cell? Explain.

 Chem ASAP! Assessment 23.1 Check your understanding of the important ideas and concepts in Section 23.1.

 portfolio project

Design an experiment to test different brands of batteries for longevity. Should all the batteries be the same type, for example, D cells or AA cells? If your teacher approves your design, perform the experiment. Make a graph illustrating your results.

B*atteries provide current to power lights, electronic devices, and even toys—such as the robot shown here. One type of battery most people use is a car battery. The potential difference between the negative and positive terminals of a* car battery is 12 V. Other common batteries are the ones used to power flashlights, television remote controls, radios, and CD players. They are commonly known as AA, AAA, C, and D batteries. The potential difference in these batteries is 1.5 V. **How can electrical potential be calculated?**

objectives
▶ Define standard cell potential and standard reduction potential
▶ Use standard reduction potentials to calculate standard cell potential

key terms
▶ electrical potential
▶ reduction potential
▶ cell potential
▶ standard cell potential
▶ standard hydrogen electrode

Electrical Potential

The **electrical potential** of a voltaic cell is a measure of the cell's ability to produce an electric current. Electrical potential is usually measured in volts (V). The potential of an isolated half-cell cannot be measured. For example, you cannot measure the electrical potential of a zinc half-cell or of a copper half-cell separately. When these two half-cells are connected to form a voltaic cell, however, the difference in potential can be measured. The electrical potential of a $1M$ zinc–copper cell is $+1.10$ V.

The electrical potential of a cell results from a competition for electrons between the two half-cells. The half-cell that has a greater tendency to acquire electrons will be the one in which reduction occurs. Oxidation occurs in the other half-cell as there is a loss of electrons. The tendency of a given half-reaction to occur as a reduction is called the **reduction potential.** The half-cell in which reduction occurs has a greater reduction potential than the half-cell in which oxidation occurs. The difference between the reduction potentials of the two half-cells is called the **cell potential.**

$$\text{cell potential} = \left(\begin{array}{c}\text{reduction potential}\\\text{of half-cell in which}\\\text{reduction occurs}\end{array}\right) - \left(\begin{array}{c}\text{reduction potential}\\\text{of half-cell in which}\\\text{oxidation occurs}\end{array}\right)$$

$$or \quad E^0_{cell} = E^0_{red} - E^0_{oxid}$$

Standard Cell Potential

The **standard cell potential** (E^0_{cell}) is the measured cell potential when the ion concentrations in the half-cells are $1M$, any gases are at a pressure of 101 kPa, and the temperature is 25 °C. The symbols E^0_{red} and E^0_{oxid} represent the standard reduction potentials for the reduction and oxidation half-cells, respectively. The relationship between these values follows the general relationship for cell potential given above.

$$E^0_{cell} = E^0_{red} - E^0_{oxid}$$

Because half-cell potentials cannot be measured, scientists have chosen an arbitrary electrode to serve as a reference. The **standard hydrogen electrode** is used with other electrodes so the reduction potentials of the other cells can be measured. The standard reduction potential of the hydrogen electrode has been assigned a value of 0.00 V. The standard hydrogen

Figure 23.8

The standard hydrogen electrode is arbitrarily assigned a standard reduction potential of 0.00 V at 25 °C.

Chem ASAP!

Simulation 27

Simulate the operation of voltaic cells.

electrode, which is illustrated in **Figure 23.8,** consists of a platinum electrode immersed in a solution with a hydrogen-ion concentration of 1*M*. The solution is at 25 °C. The electrode itself is a small square of platinum foil coated with finely divided platinum, known as platinum black. Hydrogen gas at a pressure of 101 kPa is bubbled around the platinum electrode. The half-cell reaction that occurs at the platinum black surface is as follows.

$$2H^+(aq, 1M) + 2e^- \rightleftharpoons H_2(g, 101 \text{ kPa}) \qquad E^0_{H^+} = 0.00 \text{ V}$$

The symbol $E^0_{H^+}$ represents the standard reduction potential of H^+. The standard reduction potential of H^+ is the tendency of H^+ ions to acquire electrons and be reduced to $H_2(g)$. What is the significance of the double arrows in this reaction? Whether this half-cell reaction occurs as a reduction or as an oxidation is determined by the reduction potential of the half-cell to which the standard hydrogen electrode is connected.

Standard Reduction Potentials

A voltaic cell can be made by connecting a standard hydrogen half-cell to a standard zinc half-cell, as shown in **Figure 23.9.** To determine the overall reaction for this cell, first identify the half-cell in which reduction takes place. In all electrochemical cells, reduction takes place at the cathode and oxidation takes place at the anode. A voltmeter gives a reading of +0.76 V when the zinc electrode is connected to the negative terminal and the hydrogen electrode is connected to the positive terminal. The zinc is oxidized, which means that it is the anode. Hydrogen ions are reduced, which means that the hydrogen electrode is the cathode. You can now write the half-reactions and the overall cell reaction.

Figure 23.9

This voltaic cell consists of zinc and hydrogen half-cells. Where does reduction occur, and what is reduced in this cell?

Oxidation: $Zn(s) \longrightarrow Zn^{2+}(aq) + 2e^-$ (at anode)

Reduction: $2H^+(aq) + 2e^- \longrightarrow H_2(g)$ (at cathode)

Cell reaction: $Zn(s) + 2H^+(aq) \longrightarrow Zn^{2+}(aq) + H_2(g)$

Use of a standard hydrogen electrode allows you to calculate the standard reduction potential for the zinc half-cell according to the equation for standard cell potential just developed.

$$E^0_{cell} = E^0_{red} - E^0_{oxid}$$

Therefore,

$$E^0 = E^0_{H^+} - E^0_{Zn^{2+}}$$

The cell potential (E^0_{cell}) was measured at $+0.76$ V. The reduction potential of the hydrogen half-cell is a defined standard: $E^0_{H^+}$ always equals 0.00 V. Substituting these values into the preceding equation will give the standard reduction potential for the zinc half-cell.

$$+0.76 \text{ V} = 0.00 \text{ V} - E^0_{Zn^{2+}}$$

$$E^0_{Zn^{2+}} = -0.76 \text{ V}$$

The standard reduction potential for the zinc half-cell is -0.76 V. The value is negative because the tendency of zinc ions to be reduced to zinc metal in this cell is less than the tendency of hydrogen ions to be reduced to hydrogen gas (H_2). Consequently, the zinc ions are not reduced. Instead, the opposite occurs: Zinc metal is oxidized to zinc ions.

Many different half-cells can be paired with the hydrogen half-cell in a similar manner. Using this method, the standard reduction potential for each half-cell can be obtained. For a standard copper half-cell, for example, the measured standard cell potential is $+0.34$ V. Copper is the cathode (the positive electrode), and Cu^{2+} ions are reduced to Cu metal when the cell operates. The hydrogen half-cell is the anode (the negative electrode), and H_2 gas is oxidized to H^+ ions. You can calculate the standard reduction potential for copper as follows.

$$E^0_{cell} = E^0_{red} - E^0_{oxid}$$

$$E^0_{cell} = E^0_{Cu^{2+}} - E^0_{H^+}$$

$$+0.34 \text{ V} = E^0_{Cu^{2+}} - 0.00$$

$$E^0_{Cu^{2+}} = +0.34 \text{ V}$$

These calculations show that the standard reduction potential of copper is $+0.34$ V. The value is positive because the tendency of copper ions to be reduced in this cell is greater than the tendency of hydrogen ions to be reduced.

Table 23.2 on the following page lists some standard reduction potentials at 25 °C. The half-reactions are arranged in increasing order of their tendency to occur in the forward direction—that is, as a reduction. Thus the half-reactions at the top of the table have the least tendency to occur as reductions. The half-reactions at the bottom of the table have the greatest tendency to occur as reductions. For example, lithium ions (at the top) have very little tendency to be reduced to lithium metal. Which substance has the greatest tendency to be reduced?

Table 23.2

Reduction Potentials at 25 °C with 1*M* Concentrations of Aqueous Species		
Electrode	**Half-reaction**	**E^0 (V)**
Li^+/Li	$Li^+ + e^- \longrightarrow Li$	−3.05
K^+/K	$K^+ + e^- \longrightarrow K$	−2.93
Ba^{2+}/Ba	$Ba^{2+} + 2e^- \longrightarrow Ba$	−2.90
Ca^{2+}/Ca	$Ca^{2+} + 2e^- \longrightarrow Ca$	−2.87
Na^+/Na	$Na^+ + e^- \longrightarrow Na$	−2.71
Mg^{2+}/Mg	$Mg^{2+} + 2e^- \longrightarrow Mg$	−2.37
Al^{3+}/Al	$Al^{3+} + 3e^- \longrightarrow Al$	−1.66
H_2O/H_2	$2H_2O + 2e^- \longrightarrow H_2 + 2OH^-$	−0.83
Zn^{2+}/Zn	$Zn^{2+} + 2e^- \longrightarrow Zn$	−0.76
Cr^{3+}/Cr	$Cr^{3+} + 3e^- \longrightarrow Cr$	−0.74
Fe^{2+}/Fe	$Fe^{2+} + 2e^- \longrightarrow Fe$	−0.44
H_2O/H_2 (pH 7)	$2H_2O + 2e^- \longrightarrow H_2 + 2OH^-$	−0.42
Cd^{2+}/Cd	$Cd^{2+} + 2e^- \longrightarrow Cd$	−0.40
$PbSO_4/Pb$	$PbSO_4 + 2e^- \longrightarrow Pb + SO_4^{2-}$	−0.36
Co^{2+}/Co	$Co^{2+} + 2e^- \longrightarrow Co$	−0.28
Ni^{2+}/Ni	$Ni^{2+} + 2e^- \longrightarrow Ni$	−0.25
Sn^{2+}/Sn	$Sn^{2+} + 2e^- \longrightarrow Sn$	−0.14
Pb^{2+}/Pb	$Pb^{2+} + 2e^- \longrightarrow Pb$	−0.13
Fe^{3+}/Fe	$Fe^{3+} + 3e^- \longrightarrow Fe$	−0.036
H^+/H_2	$2H^+ + 2e^- \longrightarrow H_2$	0.000
$AgCl/Ag$	$AgCl + e^- \longrightarrow Ag + Cl^-$	+0.22
Hg_2Cl_2/Hg	$Hg_2Cl_2 + 2e^- \longrightarrow 2Hg + 2Cl^-$	+0.27
Cu^{2+}/Cu	$Cu^{2+} + 2e^- \longrightarrow Cu$	+0.34
O_2/OH^-	$O_2 + 2H_2O + 4e^- \longrightarrow 4OH^-$	+0.40
Cu^+/Cu	$Cu^+ + e^- \longrightarrow Cu$	+0.52
I_2/I^-	$I_2 + 2e^- \longrightarrow 2I^-$	+0.54
Fe^{3+}/Fe^{2+}	$Fe^{3+} + e^- \longrightarrow Fe^{2+}$	+0.77
Hg_2^{2+}/Hg	$Hg_2^{2+} + 2e^- \longrightarrow 2Hg$	+0.79
Ag^+/Ag	$Ag^+ + e^- \longrightarrow Ag$	+0.80
O_2/H_2O (pH 7)	$O_2 + 4H^+ + 4e^- \longrightarrow 2H_2O$	+0.82
Hg^{2+}/Hg	$Hg^{2+} + 2e^- \longrightarrow Hg$	+0.85
Br_2/Br^-	$Br_2 + 2e^- \longrightarrow 2Br^-$	+1.07
O_2/H_2O	$O_2 + 4H^+ + 4e^- \longrightarrow 2H_2O$	+1.23
MnO_2/Mn^{2+}	$MnO_2 + 4H^+ + 2e^- \longrightarrow Mn^{2+} + 2H_2O$	+1.28
$Cr_2O_7^{2-}/Cr^{3+}$	$Cr_2O_7^{2-} + 14H^+ + 6e^- \longrightarrow 2Cr^{3+} + 7H_2O$	+1.33
Cl_2/Cl^-	$Cl_2 + 2e^- \longrightarrow 2Cl^-$	+1.36
PbO_2/Pb^{2+}	$PbO_2 + 4H^+ + 2e^- \longrightarrow Pb^{2+} + 2H_2O$	+1.46
MnO_4^-/Mn^{2+}	$MnO_4^- + 8H^+ + 5e^- \longrightarrow Mn^{2+} + 4H_2O$	+1.51
$PbO_2/PbSO_4$	$PbO_2 + 4H^+ + SO_4^{2-} + 2e^- \longrightarrow PbSO_4 + 2H_2O$	+1.69
F_2/F^-	$F_2 + 2e^- \longrightarrow 2F^-$	+2.87

Calculating Standard Cell Potentials

To function, a cell must be constructed of two half-cells. The half-cell reaction having the more positive (or less negative) reduction potential occurs as a reduction in the cell. With this in mind, it is possible to write cell reactions and calculate cell potentials for cells without actually assembling them. You can simply use the known standard reduction potentials for the various half-cells (from **Table 23.2**) to predict the half-cells in which reduction and oxidation will occur. This information can then be used to find the resulting E^0_{cell} value.

If the cell potential for a given redox reaction is positive, then the reaction is spontaneous. If the cell potential is negative, then the reaction is nonspontaneous. This latter reaction will be spontaneous in the reverse direction, however, and the cell potential will then have a numerically equal but positive value.

Sample Problem 23-1

Determine the cell reaction, the standard cell potential, and the half-cell that acts as the cathode for a voltaic cell composed of the following half-cells.

$$Fe^{3+}(aq) + e^- \longrightarrow Fe^{2+}(aq) \quad E^0_{Fe^{3+}} = +0.77 \text{ V}$$
$$Ni^{2+}(aq) + 2e^- \longrightarrow Ni(s) \quad\quad E^0_{Ni^{2+}} = -0.25 \text{ V}$$

1. ANALYZE *List the knowns and the unknowns.*

Knowns:
- $E^0_{Fe^{3+}} = +0.77$ V
- $E^0_{Ni^{2+}} = -0.25$ V

Unknowns:
- cell reaction = ?
- E^0_{cell} = ? V
- cathode = ?

The half-cell with the more positive reduction potential is the one in which reduction occurs (the cathode). That means the oxidation reaction occurs at the anode. Add the half-reactions, making certain that the number of electrons lost equals the number of electrons gained. Then calculate the standard cell potential using the following equation.

$$E^0_{cell} = E^0_{red} - E^0_{oxid}$$

---

2. CALCULATE *Solve for the unknowns.*

In this cell, Fe^{3+} is reduced and Ni is oxidized. Because reduction takes place in the Fe^{3+} half-cell, this half-cell is the cathode. The half-cell reactions, written in the direction in which they actually occur, are as follows.

Oxidation: $Ni(s) \longrightarrow Ni^{2+}(aq) + 2e^-$ (at anode)

Reduction: $Fe^{3+}(aq) + e^- \longrightarrow Fe^{2+}(aq)$ (at cathode)

Practice Problems

8. A voltaic cell is constructed using the following half-reactions.

$$Cu^{2+}(aq) + 2e^- \longrightarrow Cu(s)$$
$$E^0_{Cu^{2+}} = +0.34 \text{ V}$$
$$Al^{3+}(aq) + 3e^- \longrightarrow Al(s)$$
$$E^0_{Al^{3+}} = -1.66 \text{ V}$$

Determine the cell reaction and calculate the standard cell potential.

Sample Problem 23-1 (cont.)

Before adding the half-reactions, be sure that the electrons cancel—that is, that they are present in equal number on both sides of the equation. Because Ni loses two electrons as it is oxidized, while Fe^{3+} gains only one electron as it is reduced, you must multiply the iron equation by 2.

$$Ni(s) \longrightarrow Ni^{2+}(aq) + 2e^-$$
$$\underline{2[Fe^{3+}(aq) + e^- \longrightarrow Fe^{2+}(aq)]}$$
$$Ni(s) + 2Fe^{3+}(aq) \longrightarrow Ni^{2+}(aq) + 2Fe^{2+}(aq)$$

The standard cell potential can now be calculated.

$$E^0_{cell} = E^0_{red} - E^0_{oxid}$$
$$= E^0_{Fe^{3+}} - E^0_{Ni^{2+}}$$
$$= +0.77 \text{ V} - (-0.25 \text{ V})$$
$$= +1.02 \text{ V}$$

Note that the E^0 of a half-cell is not multiplied by any number even if one or both of the equations is multiplied by a coefficient to make the electrons cancel.

....

3. **EVALUATE** *Does the result make sense?*

The equations are properly set up and added, and the calculation is correct. If the reduction potential of the reduction is positive and the reduction potential of the oxidation is negative, the E^0_{cell} will always be positive. This is because subtracting a negative number is the same as adding the same positive value.

Practice Problems (cont.)

9. A voltaic cell is constructed using the following half-reactions.

$$Ag^+(aq) + e^- \longrightarrow Ag(s)$$
$$E^0_{Ag^+} = +0.80 \text{ V}$$
$$Cu^{2+}(aq) + 2e^- \longrightarrow Cu(s)$$
$$E^0_{Cu^{2+}} = +0.34 \text{ V}$$

Determine the cell reaction and the standard cell potential.

Problem-Solving 9
Solve Problem 9 with the help of an interactive guided tutorial.

Sample Problem 23-2

Calculate E^0_{cell} to determine whether the following redox reaction is spontaneous as written.

$$Ni(s) + Fe^{2+}(aq) \longrightarrow Ni^{2+}(aq) + Fe(s)$$

....

1. **ANALYZE** *List the knowns and the unknowns.*

Knowns (from **Table 23.2**):
- $E^0_{Ni^{2+}} = -0.25 \text{ V}$
- $E^0_{Fe^{2+}} = -0.44 \text{ V}$

Unknowns:
- reaction spontaneous = ?
- $E^0_{cell} = ? \text{ V}$

The redox reaction is spontaneous if the standard cell potential is positive.

Sample Problem 23-2 (cont.)

2. CALCULATE *Solve for the unknowns.*

Write each half-reaction with its standard reduction potential. Find the standard cell potential, using $E^0_{cell} = E^0_{red} - E^0_{oxid}$. The half-reactions from the given equation are as follows.

$$\text{Oxidation: } Ni(s) \longrightarrow Ni^{2+}(aq) + 2e^-$$
$$\text{Reduction: } Fe^{2+}(aq) + 2e^- \longrightarrow Fe(s)$$

The standard reduction potentials for the half-cells, both written as reductions, are given in **Table 23.2** as

$$Ni^{2+}(aq) + 2e^- \longrightarrow Ni(s) \qquad E^0_{Ni^{2+}} = -0.25 \text{ V}$$
$$Fe^{2+}(aq) + 2e^- \longrightarrow Fe(s) \qquad E^0_{Fe^{2+}} = -0.44 \text{ V}$$

The equation given was written with the nickel half-cell as the oxidation half-cell and the iron half-cell as the reduction half-cell. The standard cell potential is thus the difference of the potentials of the iron half-cell and the nickel half-cell.

$$E^0_{cell} = E^0_{red} - E^0_{oxid} = E^0_{Fe^{2+}} - E^0_{Ni^{2+}}$$
$$= -0.44 \text{ V} - (-0.25 \text{ V}) = -0.19 \text{ V}$$

Because the calculated standard cell potential is a negative number, the redox reaction is nonspontaneous as written. Energy would have to be applied to make the reaction proceed. Without such an energy input, the reverse reaction would be the one that occurs.

3. EVALUATE *Does the result make sense?*

Because iron is above nickel in the activity series of metals, it makes sense that iron ions would not be reduced by nickel ions. Instead, iron would be oxidized in the presence of nickel ions and would reduce Ni^{2+} ions to nickel metal.

Practice Problems

10. Calculate the standard cell potential to determine whether this redox reaction will occur spontaneously.

$$3Zn^{2+}(aq) + 2Cr(s) \longrightarrow$$
$$3Zn(s) + 2Cr^{3+}(aq)$$

11. Is this redox reaction spontaneous as written?

$$Co^{2+}(aq) + Fe(s) \longrightarrow$$
$$Fe^{2+}(aq) + Co(s)$$

<u>Chem ASAP!</u>

Problem-Solving 10
Solve Problem 10 with the help of an interactive guided tutorial.

section review 23.2

12. What is the difference between standard cell potential and standard reduction potential?

13. How can standard reduction potentials be used to determine standard cell potentials?

14. What is the standard cell potential for the zinc–copper voltaic cell?

$$Zn(s) \mid ZnSO_4(aq) \parallel CuSO_4(aq) \mid Cu(s)$$

15. What is the purpose of using the standard hydrogen electrode as a reference electrode?

16. The standard reduction potential for a cadmium half-cell is -0.40 V. What does this mean?

 Chem ASAP! **Assessment 23.2** Check your understanding of the important ideas and concepts in Section 23.2.

ELECTROLYTIC CELLS

objectives

▶ Distinguish between electrolytic and voltaic cells, and list some possible uses of electrolytic cells

▶ Identify the products of the electrolysis of brine, molten sodium chloride, and water

key terms

▶ electrolysis

▶ electrolytic cell

*D*VDs are used to store all types of data, from multimedia computer programs to the latest popular movie. DVDs have made it possible to store large amounts of data in a very small space. To manufacture a DVD, a laser is used to transfer all the necessary data to the master DVD. Then, metal is deposited on the master using electricity. Once the metal disc is removed from the master, it is used to stamp out the duplicates sold to the public. **How can metal be deposited on objects by using electricity?**

Electrolysis of Water

In Section 23.1, you learned how a spontaneous chemical reaction can be used to generate a flow of electrons (an electric current). In this section, you will learn how an electric current can be used to make a nonspontaneous redox reaction go forward. The process in which electrical energy is used to bring about such a chemical change is called **electrolysis.** Although you may not have realized it, you are already familiar with some results of electrolysis: silverplated dishes and utensils, gold-plated jewelry, and chrome-plated automobile parts are a few examples.

The apparatus in which electrolysis is carried out is an electrolytic cell. An **electrolytic cell** is an electrochemical cell used to cause a chemical change through the application of electrical energy. An electrolytic cell uses electrical energy (DC current) to make a nonspontaneous redox reaction proceed to completion. The vast array of electrolytic cells shown in **Figure 23.10** are used for the commercial production of chlorine and sodium hydroxide from brine, a concentrated aqueous solution of sodium chloride. What are some uses of chlorine and sodium hydroxide?

In both voltaic and electrolytic cells, electrons flow from the anode to the cathode in the external circuit. As shown in **Figure 23.11,** for both types of cells, the electrode at which reduction occurs is the cathode. The electrode at which oxidation occurs is the anode. The difference between the

Figure 23.10

To produce chlorine and sodium hydroxide in electrolytic cells, electricity is passed through brine, a sodium chloride solution. The products have many uses, such as disinfecting water, cleaning drains, manufacturing soap, and producing paper pulp.

Voltaic Cell   **Electrolytic Cell**

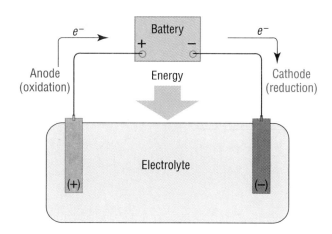

- Energy is released from a spontaneous redox reaction.
- System (cell) does work on the surroundings (light bulb).

- Energy is absorbed to drive a nonspontaneous redox reaction.
- Surroundings (battery or power supply) do work on the system (cell).

Figure 23.11

Voltaic cells and electrolytic cells share some features. In both cells, reduction occurs at the cathode, and oxidation occurs at the anode. Also, in both cells, electrons flow from the anode to the cathode in the external circuit. However, the charges on the anode and cathode differ for the two kinds of cells. The redox process in the voltaic cell is spontaneous. The redox process in the electrolytic cell is nonspontaneous. What would make a nonspontaneous redox process go?

two cells is that in a voltaic cell the flow of electrons is the result of a spontaneous redox reaction, whereas in an electrolytic cell electrons are pushed by an outside power source such as a battery. Electrolytic and voltaic cells also differ in the assignment of charge to the electrodes. In an electrolytic cell, the cathode is considered to be the negative electrode. This is because it is connected to the negative electrode of the battery. (Remember that in a voltaic cell, the anode is the negative electrode and the cathode is the positive electrode.) The anode in the electrolytic cell is considered to be the positive electrode because it is connected to the positive electrode of the battery. It is important to remember these conventions about the two kinds of cells.

When a current is applied to two electrodes immersed in pure water, nothing happens. There is no current flow and no electrolysis. However, when an electrolyte such as H_2SO_4 or KNO_3 in low concentration is added to the pure water, the solution conducts electricity and electrolysis occurs. This process is illustrated in **Figure 23.12** on the following page. The products of the electrolysis of water are hydrogen gas and oxygen gas. Water is reduced to hydrogen at the cathode according to the following reduction half-reaction.

Reduction: $2H_2O(l) + 2e^- \longrightarrow H_2(g) + 2OH^-(aq)$ (at cathode)

Water is oxidized at the anode according to the following oxidation half-reaction.

Oxidation: $2H_2O(l) \longrightarrow O_2(g) + 4H^+(aq) + 4e^-$ (at anode)

Figure 23.12
When an electric current is passed through water, the water decomposes into oxygen gas and hydrogen gas. At which electrode is hydrogen gas produced? Which gas results from the oxidation process?

The region around the cathode turns basic due to the production of OH^- ions. The region around the anode turns acidic due to an increase in H^+ ions. The overall cell reaction is obtained by adding the half-reactions (after doubling the first one to balance electrons).

Reduction: $2[2H_2O(l) + 2e^- \longrightarrow H_2(g) + 2OH^-(aq)]$

Oxidation: $2H_2O(l) \longrightarrow O_2(g) + 4H^+(aq) + 4e^-$

Overall cell reaction: $6H_2O(l) \longrightarrow 2H_2(g) + O_2(g) + 4H^+(aq) + 4OH^-(aq)$

The ions produced tend to recombine to form water.

$$4H^+(aq) + 4OH^-(aq) \longrightarrow 4H_2O(l)$$

For that reason they are not included in the net reaction.

$$2H_2O(l) \xrightarrow{\text{electrolysis}} 2H_2(g) + O_2(g)$$

Electrolysis of Brine

If the electrolyte in an aqueous solution is more easily oxidized or reduced than water, then the products of electrolysis will be substances other than hydrogen and oxygen. An example is the electrolysis of brine, a concentrated aqueous solution of sodium chloride, which simultaneously produces three important industrial chemicals: chlorine gas, hydrogen gas, and sodium hydroxide. The electrolytic cell for this process is shown in **Figure 23.13.**

During electrolysis, chloride ions are oxidized to produce chlorine gas at the anode. Water is reduced to produce hydrogen gas at the cathode. Sodium ions are not reduced to sodium metal in the process because water molecules are more easily reduced than are sodium ions. The reduction of water produces hydroxide ions as well as hydrogen gas. Thus the electrolyte in solution becomes sodium hydroxide (NaOH). The half-reactions are

Oxidation: $2Cl^-(aq) \longrightarrow Cl_2(g) + 2e^-$ (at anode)

Reduction: $2H_2O(l) + 2e^- \longrightarrow H_2(g) + 2OH^-(aq)$ (at cathode)

The overall ionic equation is the sum of the two half-reactions.

$$2Cl^-(aq) + 2H_2O(l) \longrightarrow Cl_2(g) + H_2(g) + 2OH^-(aq)$$

The spectator ion Na^+ can be included in the equation (as part of NaCl and of NaOH) to show the formation of sodium hydroxide during the electrolytic process.

$$2NaCl(aq) + 2H_2O(l) \longrightarrow Cl_2(g) + H_2(g) + 2NaOH(aq)$$

When the sodium hydroxide solution is about 10% (m/v), it is removed from the cell and processed further.

Electrolysis of Molten Sodium Chloride

Both sodium and chlorine are commercially important. Sodium is used in sodium vapor lamps and as the coolant in some nuclear reactors. Chlorine, a toxic greenish-yellow gas, is used to sterilize drinking water and is important in the manufacture of polyvinyl chloride and various pesticides. These two elements are produced when pure molten sodium chloride, rather than an aqueous solution of NaCl, is electrolyzed. Chlorine gas comes off at the anode and molten sodium collects at the cathode. The sodium, with a melting point of 97.8 °C, remains in liquid form, floating on the more dense molten sodium chloride. The electrolytic cell in which this commercial process is carried out is called the Downs cell and is shown in **Figure 23.14** on the following page. The design of the Downs cell allows fresh sodium chloride to be added as required. The design also separates the products so they will not recombine to re-form sodium chloride. The half-reactions and overall cell reaction for this electrolysis are as follows.

Oxidation: $2Cl^-(l) \longrightarrow Cl_2(g) + 2e^-$ (at anode)

Reduction: $2Na^+(l) + 2e^- \longrightarrow 2Na(l)$ (at cathode)

Overall cell reaction: $2NaCl(l) \longrightarrow 2Na(l) + Cl_2(g)$

LINK TO METALLURGY

Anodizing

Anodizing is an electrolytic process for applying a corrosion-resistant oxide coating to aluminum and certain other metals. When an electric current flows through an electrolytic cell

containing an aluminum anode, a thin coat of aluminum oxide forms on the surface of the aluminum. Immersion of the aluminum object in pure boiling water permanently seals the film against corrosion. Dyeing of anodized aluminum can produce metallic red, metallic blue, and a host of other metallic colors on the metal surface. Also, the high porosity of the oxide coating permits it to absorb pigments and lubricants.

Figure 23.14

The Downs cell produces sodium metal and chlorine gas from the electrolysis of molten NaCl. The cell operates at a temperature of 801 °C to maintain the salt in a molten state. A perforated iron screen separates the circular cathode from the anode. The liquid sodium floats to the top of the molten salt and is drawn off. The chlorine gas is collected after it bubbles up and out of the molten salt.

Recharge of NaCl

$Cl_2(g)$

Na(l)

Molten NaCl

Molten Na

Steel cathode (−)

Iron screen

Graphite anode (+)

Chem ASAP!

Animation 27

Take an atomic-level look at how electricity can bring about a chemical change.

Electroplating and Related Processes

Electroplating is the deposition of a thin layer of a metal on an object in an electrolytic cell. The process has many important applications. An object may be electroplated to protect the surface of the base metal from corrosion or to make it more attractive. The layer of the deposited metal is very thin, usually from 5×10^{-5} cm to 1×10^{-3} cm thick. Metals commonly used for electroplating include gold, silver, copper, nickel, and chromium. An object that is to be silverplated is made the cathode in an electrolytic cell. The anode is the metallic silver that is to be deposited, and the electrolyte is a solution of a silver salt, such as silver cyanide. When a DC current is applied, silver ions move from the anode to the object to be plated. What happens to the silver ions at the cathode?

$$\text{Reduction:} \quad Ag^+(aq) + e^- \xrightarrow{\text{electrolysis}} Ag(s) \text{ (at cathode)}$$

The net result is that silver transfers from the silver electrode to objects being plated, like those shown in **Figure 23.15**. Controlling this reaction is a fine art. Many factors contribute to the quality of the metal coating that forms. In the plating solution, the concentration of the cations to be reduced must be carefully controlled. The solution must contain compounds to control the acidity and to increase the conductivity. Some solutions contain compounds that form complex ions with the cation to be reduced. Other compounds may be used to make the metal coating brighter or smoother. In many plating cells, the anode must be shaped like the object at the cathode in order to plate all parts of the cathode evenly.

Figure 23.15

Electroplating is the coating of an object with a thin layer of metal in an electrolytic cell. Pure silver was electroplated onto steel to produce this silverplated tea service.

Several useful processes involve the depositing of metal at the cathode of a cell. In electroforming, an object is reproduced by making a metal mold of it at the cathode. A phonograph record, for example, can be coated with metal so it will conduct electricity. It is then electroplated to obtain a thick coating of metal. This coating can then be stripped off and used as a mold to produce copies of the record. In another process, called electrowinning, impure metals can be purified in electrolytic cells. The cations of molten salts or aqueous solutions are reduced at the cathode to give very

MINI LAB

TARNISH REMOVAL

PURPOSE
To remove tarnish from silver.

MATERIALS
- baking soda (sodium hydrogen carbonate)
- water
- hot plate
- saucepan
- tablespoon
- shallow dish (glass or plastic)
- aluminum foil
- tarnished silver item
- tongs

PROCEDURE
1. Mix 1 tablespoon of baking soda with about 1 quart of water. Heat the solution in the saucepan until it is hot but not boiling. **CAUTION:** Be careful when using the heat source and handling the hot solution.

2. Place the aluminum foil on the bottom of the shallow dish.

3. Place the tarnished item on the foil, making sure the item is in contact with the foil.

4. Carefully pour the hot solution from the saucepan into the dish so the solution covers the tarnished item.

5. After 5–10 minutes, use tongs to remove the item and rinse with water.

6. Optional: Try to retarnish the silver item by smearing egg yolk over one part of it and letting it sit for 30 minutes.

ANALYSIS AND CONCLUSIONS
1. How did the tarnished item differ in appearance before and after its treatment?

2. What do you think would have happened if the treatment solution had been cold?

3. The tarnish on silver is usually a film of the ionic compound Ag_2S. Use information from **Table 23.1** to explain how this layer of Ag_2S is removed. What is the purpose of the baking-soda solution?

---

pure metals. Electrowinning from molten salts is the only method for obtaining pure sodium and other very reactive metals. In the process of electrorefining, a piece of impure metal is made the anode of the cell. It is oxidized to the cation and then reduced to the pure metal at the cathode. This technique is used to obtain ultrapure silver, lead, and copper.

Other electrolytic processes are centered on the anode rather than the cathode. In electropolishing, for example, the surface of an object at the anode is dissolved selectively to give it a high polish. In electromachining, a piece of metal at the anode is partially dissolved until the remaining portion is an exact copy of the object at the cathode.

section review 23.3

17. Describe the difference between an electrolytic cell and a voltaic cell. Name several uses for electrolytic cells.

18. What are the products of the electrolysis of the following?

   a. brine   **b.** molten sodium chloride   **c.** water

19. What process occurs at the anode of an electrolytic cell? At the cathode?

 Chem ASAP! Assessment 23.3 Check your understanding of the important ideas and concepts in Section 23.3.

SMALL-SCALE LAB

ELECTROLYSIS OF WATER

SAFETY

Wear safety glasses and follow the standard safety procedures outlined on page 18.

PURPOSE

To electrolyze solutions and interpret your observations in terms of chemical reactions and equations.

MATERIALS

- pencil
- paper
- ruler
- reaction surface
- electrolysis device
- chemicals shown in Figure A

PROCEDURE

On separate sheets of paper, draw two grids similar to Figure A. Make each square 2 cm on each side. Place a reaction surface over one of the grids and add one drop of each solution as shown in Figure A. Apply the leads of the electrolysis device to each solution. Be sure to clean the leads between each experiment. Look carefully at the cathode (negative lead) and the anode (positive lead). Use the second grid as a data table to record your observations for each solution.

H_2O	Na_2SO_4	Na_2SO_4 + BTB

Figure A

ANALYSIS

Using your experimental data, record the answers to the following questions below your data table.

1. Explain why pure water does not conduct electricity and does not undergo electrolysis.

2. Explain why water with sodium sulfate conducts electricity and undergoes electrolysis.

3. The cathode (negative lead) provides electrons to water and the following half-reaction occurs.

$$2H_2O + 2e^- \longrightarrow H_2(g) + 2OH^-$$

Explain how your observations correspond to the products shown in this reaction.

4. The anode (positive lead) takes away electrons from water and the following half-reaction occurs.

$$H_2O \longrightarrow \frac{1}{2} O_2(g) + 2H^+ + 2e^-$$

Explain how your observations correspond to the products shown in this reaction.

5. Add the two half-reactions to obtain the overall reaction for the electrolysis of water. Simplify the result by adding the OH^- and H^+ to get HOH, and then canceling anything that appears on both sides of the equation.

YOU'RE THE CHEMIST

The following small-scale activities allow you to develop your own procedures and analyze the results.

1. **Analyze It!** Perform the above experiment using the chemicals shown in Figure B. Record your results. The cathode and anode reactions are

$$2H_2O + 2e^- \longrightarrow H_2(g) + 2OH^- \text{ (at cathode)}$$
$$2I^- \longrightarrow I_2(aq) + 2e^- \text{ (at anode)}$$

Explain how your observations correspond to the products shown in these half-reactions.

KI	KI + starch	KI + BTB

Figure B

2. **Design It!** Design an experiment to explore what happens when you electrolyze NaCl, KBr, and $CuSO_4$ with and without BTB. Use half-reactions to predict your results.

3. **Analyze It!** For each half-reaction listed above, look up the E^0 values in Section 23.2. Show that the E^0 values are consistent with what happens in each case.

HOW MANY KILOMETERS PER CHARGE?

Imagine this: After breakfast, you open your garage, unplug your car and drive off to school. After school, you take some friends to the football game at a school in the next town. Later you pick up your aunt at the airport. You have logged 150 kilometers on the road, but you have not burned a drop of gasoline or emitted a gram of pollutants from your tailpipe. Actually, you do not even have a tailpipe because your car runs on electricity.

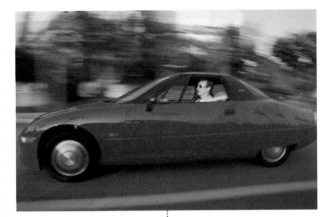

This scenario is not a vision of the future: Electric cars are here! Most of the major automakers now offer an electric vehicle, or EV, for lease or sale. EVs are hard to distinguish from gasoline-powered models because they have many of the same features. The main advantage EVs have over gasoline-powered cars is that they are environmentally friendly. They do not produce air pollutants and are therefore classified as zero-emission vehicles.

But EVs have a major drawback: Their distance range is limited. Current models can go only 150 to 200 kilometers on a single charge of their batteries, a problem that stems from the energy-storage capacity of the batteries. Improving battery technology, therefore, is the central problem for electric-car designers.

The most common type of battery used in EVs is an improved version of the lead–acid battery, which has

Improving battery technology is the central problem for electric-car designers.

been used in gasoline-fueled vehicles for nearly 100 years. Despite its improvements, this type of battery is a poor choice for storing energy in a vehicle. For the amount of electrical energy it can store, a lead–acid battery is very heavy. And it is an established fact that the greater the mass of a vehicle, the poorer its performance and efficiency. Consider the fact that 100 kilograms of lead–acid batteries are needed to store the energy contained in only 1 kilogram of gasoline!

Other types of more-efficient batteries are being used in EVs. These include nickel-metal hydride batteries and lithium-ion batteries, which can store more energy than lead–acid batteries. However, they are considerably more expensive because large-scale production has only just begun.

Researchers are developing other types of batteries that can store more energy in less mass. One promising technology is the sodium–sulfur battery in which sodium atoms supply electrons to the electric motor. For the battery to work, the sodium and sulfur must be molten, which requires temperatures of 300 °C or more. This type of battery has the potential to store more than four times as much energy as a lead–acid battery of the same mass. However, keeping the battery hot enough when not in use remains an unresolved problem to date.

The long-term goal for battery designers is to have batteries that are relatively inexpensive, long lasting (more than 10 years), and able to power an EV for more than 300 kilometers. Once such batteries become a reality, EVs may be on their way to replacing gasoline-powered cars. Such progress would undoubtedly benefit the environment by reducing air pollution.

CHEMISTRY IN CAREERS

Take It to the NET
For interactive study and review, go to www.phschool.com

KEY TERMS

- anode *p. 680*
- battery *p. 682*
- cathode *p. 680*
- cell potential *p. 685*
- dry cell *p. 681*
- electrical potential *p. 685*
- electrochemical cell *p. 679*

- electrochemical process *p. 678*
- electrode *p. 680*
- electrolysis *p. 692*
- electrolytic cell *p. 692*
- fuel cell *p. 683*
- half-cell *p. 679*
- reduction potential *p. 685*

- salt bridge *p. 679*
- standard cell potential *p. 685*
- standard hydrogen electrode *p. 685*
- voltaic cell *p. 679*

KEY EQUATIONS AND RELATIONSHIPS

- Representing electrochemical cells:

$$\text{Zn}(s) \mid \text{ZnSO}_4(aq) \parallel \text{CuSO}_4(aq) \mid \text{Cu}(s)$$

    Oxidation   Reduction
     (anode)   (cathode)

- $E^0_{cell} = E^0_{red} - E^0_{oxid}$

CONCEPT SUMMARY

23.1 Electrochemical Cells

- Spontaneous redox equations can be used to generate electrical energy in voltaic cells.
- In an electrochemical cell, oxidation occurs at the anode and reduction occurs at the cathode.
- In a voltaic cell the cathode is the positively charged electrode and the anode is the negatively charged electrode.
- The half-cells are separated by a porous plate or salt bridge that prevents the contents of the two half-cells from mixing but permits the passage of ions between the half-cells.
- The half-cell with the higher reduction potential undergoes reduction; the other half-cell undergoes oxidation.
- A dry cell is not rechargeable. The lead storage battery is rechargeable.
- Fuel cells do not have to be recharged because the fuels they consume are fed into the cell continuously.

23.2 Half-Cells and Cell Potentials

- The cell potential is the difference between the reduction potentials of the half-cells.
- The reduction potential of an isolated half-cell is determined by comparison to the standard hydrogen electrode, which is assigned a reduction potential of 0.00 V.
- Half-cells more easily reduced than the reference electrode have positive reduction potentials. Half-cells less easily reduced have negative reduction potentials.

23.3 Electrolytic Cells

- In electrolysis, reduction occurs at the cathode (negatively charged) and oxidation occurs at the anode (positively charged).
- In an electrolytic cell, electrical energy is used to bring about desired redox reactions.
- Electrolytic cells are used in electroplating, in the refining of metals, and in the production of important chemicals.

CHAPTER CONCEPT MAP

Use these terms to construct a concept map that organizes the major ideas of this chapter.

 Chem ASAP! **Concept Map 23**
Create your Concept Map using the computer.

CONCEPT PRACTICE

20. What is meant by the term half-reaction? Write the half-reactions that occur when a strip of aluminum is dipped into a solution of copper(II) sulfate. *23.1*

21. What would you expect to happen when a strip of lead is placed in an aqueous solution of magnesium nitrate? *23.1*

22. For each pair of metals listed below, decide which metal is more readily oxidized. *23.1*
a. Hg, Cu   **c.** Ni, Mg   **e.** Pb, Zn
b. Ca, Al   **d.** Sn, Ag   **f.** Cu, Al

23. At which electrode in a voltaic cell does reduction always occur? *23.1*

24. Explain the function of the salt bridge in a voltaic cell. *23.1*

25. In a typical flashlight battery, what material is used for the anode? For the cathode? *23.1*

26. Explain why the specific gravity of the electrolyte in a lead storage battery decreases during the discharge process. *23.1*

27. Use the shorthand method to represent the electrochemical reaction in a car battery. *23.1*

28. Fuel cells can be designed to generate electrical energy while emitting no air pollutants, yet they are not widely used. Explain. *23.1*

29. List the advantages of a fuel cell over a lead storage battery. *23.1*

30. How was the standard reduction potential of the hydrogen electrode determined? *23.2*

31. What is the electric potential of a cell? *23.2*

32. How does the order of the metals in **Table 23.1** compare with the order in **Table 23.2?** Why? *23.2*

33. Explain how to determine the standard reduction potential for the aluminum half-cell. *23.2*

34. Determine whether these redox reactions will occur spontaneously. Calculate the standard cell potential in each case. *23.2*
a. $Cu(s) + 2H^+(aq) \longrightarrow Cu^{2+}(aq) + H_2(g)$
b. $2Ag(s) + Fe^{2+}(aq) \longrightarrow 2Ag^+(aq) + Fe(s)$

35. Use the information in **Table 23.2** to calculate standard cell potentials for these voltaic cells. *23.2*
a. $Ni \mid Ni^{2+} \parallel Cl_2 \mid Cl^-$
b. $Sn \mid Sn^{2+} \parallel Ag^+ \mid Ag$

36. Why is direct current, not alternating current, used in the electroplating of metals? *23.3*

37. Describe briefly how you would electroplate a teaspoon with silver. *23.3*

CONCEPT MASTERY

38. Distinguish between voltaic and electrolytic cells.

39. Why is it not possible to measure the potential of an isolated half-cell?

40. Describe the composition of the anode, cathode, and electrolyte in a fully discharged lead storage battery.

41. Predict what will happen, if anything, when an iron nail is dipped into a solution of copper sulfate. Write the oxidation and reduction half-reactions for this process and the balanced equation for the overall reaction.

42. Calculate E^0_{cell} and write the overall cell reaction for these cells.
a. $Sn \mid Sn^{2+} \parallel Pb^{2+} \mid Pb$
b. $H_2 \mid H^+ \parallel Br_2 \mid Br^-$

43. What property do lead(II) sulfate and lead dioxide have that makes salt bridges unnecessary in a lead storage battery?

44. Complete this data table for the electrolysis of water.

	H_2O used	H_2 formed	O_2 formed
a.	2.0 mol	____ mol	____ mol
b.	____ g	____ g	16.0 g
c.	____ mL	10.0 g	____ g
d.	44.4 g	____ g	____ g
e.	____ g	8.80 L (STP)	____ L (STP)
f.	66.0 mL	____ g	____ L (STP)

CRITICAL THINKING

45. Gold is not included in **Table 23.2.** In what part of the table does gold belong?

46. Lead storage batteries can be recharged. Why are dry cells not rechargeable?

47. For any voltaic cell, chemists consider the electrode that produces electrons to be negative, and they call it the anode. Most dictionaries, however, define the anode as the positively charged electrode. Explain.

48. Choose the term that best completes the second relationship.

a. battery : cells
herd : _____
(1) birds　　　　(3) trees
(2) sheep　　　　(4) fuel cells

b. river : water
electrode : _____
(1) electrons　　(3) salt bridge
(2) anode　　　　(4) ions

c. anode : electrons
fire hydrant : _____
(1) fire　　　　　(3) dogs
(2) firefighter　　(4) water

49. Describe the process that is occurring in the following illustration.

50. Which plot is characteristic of a dry cell? Explain.

(a)

(c)

(b)

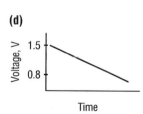

(d)

CUMULATIVE REVIEW

51. A sample of oxygen gas has a volume of 425 mL at 30 °C. What is the new volume of the gas if the temperature is raised to 60 °C while the pressure is kept constant?

52. Balance each equation.
a. $H_2S(g) + HNO_3(aq) \longrightarrow$
　　　　　$S(s) + NO(g) + H_2O(l)$
b. $AgNO_3(aq) + Pb(s) \longrightarrow$
　　　　　$Pb(NO_3)_2(aq) + Ag(s)$
c. $Cl_2(g) + NaOH(aq) \longrightarrow$
　　　　$NaCl(aq) + NaClO_3(aq) + H_2O(l)$

53. Concentrated nitric acid is $16M$. How would you prepare 500 mL of $1.0M$ HNO_3?

54. What is the oxidation number of the italicized element in each formula?
a. $K_2Cr_2O_7$
b. KIO_3
c. MnO_4^-
d. $FeCl_3$

CONCEPT CHALLENGE

55. Write the overall cell reactions and calculate E^0_{cell} for voltaic cells composed of the following sets of half-reactions.
a. $AgCl(s) + e^- \longrightarrow Ag(s) + Cl^-(aq)$
　　$Ni^{2+}(aq) + 2e^- \longrightarrow Ni(s)$
b. $Al^{3+}(aq) + 3e^- \longrightarrow Al(s)$
　　$Cl_2(g) + 2e^- \longrightarrow 2Cl^-(aq)$

56. Impure copper is purified in an electrolytic cell. Design an electrolytic cell, with H_2SO_4 as electrolyte, that will allow you to carry out this process. Give the oxidation and reduction half-reactions and a balanced equation for the overall reaction.

57. This spontaneous redox reaction occurs in the voltaic cell illustrated below.

$$Ni^{2+}(aq) + Fe(s) \longrightarrow Ni(s) + Fe^{2+}(aq)$$

a. Identify the anode and the cathode.

b. Assign charges to the electrodes.

c. Write the half-reactions.

d. Calculate the standard cell potential when the half-cells are at standard conditions.

Select the choice that best answers each question or completes each statement.

1. Which statement describes electrolysis?
   a. Reduction occurs at the anode.
   b. Energy is produced.
   c. Oxidation occurs at the cathode.
   d. Positive ions move to the cathode.

2. Which of these statements about rusting is true?
       I. Iron is oxidized.
       II. Oxygen is the oxidizing agent.
       III. Iron atoms gain electrons.
   a. I and II only
   b. II and III only
   c. I only
   d. I, II, and III

3. The energy source for an ordinary flashlight is a
   a. dry cell.
   b. voltaic cell.
   c. battery.
   d. all of the above

4. Magnesium metal is prepared by the electrolysis of molten $MgCl_2$. One half-reaction is $Mg^{2+}(l) + 2e^- \longrightarrow Mg(l)$.
   a. This half-reaction occurs at the cathode.
   b. Magnesium ions are oxidized.
   c. Chloride ions are reduced at the anode.
   d. Chloride ions gain electrons during this process.

5. If the cell potential for a redox reaction is positive,
   a. the redox reaction is spontaneous.
   b. the redox reaction is not spontaneous.
   c. the reaction only occurs during electrolysis.
   d. More than one statement is correct.

Use this table to answer questions 6–12. Hydrogen is included as a reference point for the metals.

Activity Series of Selected Metals	
Element	**Oxidation half-reaction**
Lithium	$Li(s) \longrightarrow Li^+(aq) + e^-$
Potassium	$K(s) \longrightarrow K^+(aq) + e^-$
Sodium	$Na(s) \longrightarrow Na^{2+}(aq) + 2e^-$
Aluminum	$Al(s) \longrightarrow Al^{3+}(aq) + 3e^-$
Zinc	$Zn(s) \longrightarrow Zn^{2+}(aq) + 2e^-$
Iron	$Fe(s) \longrightarrow Fe^{2+}(aq) + 2e^-$
Hydrogen	$H_2(g) \longrightarrow 2H^+(aq) + 2e^-$
Copper	$Cu(s) \longrightarrow Cu^{2+}(aq) + 2e^-$

6. Which metal will more easily lose an electron, sodium or potassium?

7. Which metal is more easily oxidized, copper or aluminum?

8. What is the relationship between ease of oxidation and the activity of a metal?

9. Describe what would happen if you placed a clean strip of aluminum in a solution of copper(II) sulfate. Explain your answer.

10. Would a copper strip placed in a solution containing zinc ions react spontaneously with the zinc ions? Explain your reasoning.

11. Based on the positions of zinc and iron in the table, explain how attaching zinc blocks to a steel ship hull protects the steel from corrosion.

12. Write the half-reaction for the reduction of aluminum ions.

Use the diagram to answer questions 13–15.

13. Write an equation for the decomposition of water by electrolysis.

14. At which electrode, A or B, is hydrogen produced?

15. The equation for the electrolysis of brine is
    $2NaCl(aq) + 2H_2O(l) \longrightarrow$
    $$Cl_2(g) + H_2(g) + 2NaOH(aq)$$
    How would you modify the electrolysis diagram to make it quantitatively represent the formation of hydrogen and chlorine?

Use complete sentences in response to question 16.

16. What do voltaic cells and electrolytic cells have in common? How do they differ?

Chapter 24

THE CHEMISTRY OF METALS AND NONMETALS

FEATURES

DISCOVER IT!
Tempering of Metals

SMALL-SCALE LAB
Complex Ions

MINI LAB
Decomposition of Hydrogen Peroxide

CHEMath
Classification

CHEMISTRY SERVING … INDUSTRY
Diamonds Are an Engineer's Best Friend

CHEMISTRY IN CAREERS
Gemologist

LINK TO OCEANOGRAPHY
Deep-Sea Minerals

LINK TO ENVIRONMENTAL AWARENESS
Radon Gas

Stay current with **SCIENCE NEWS**
Find out more about elements:
www.phschool.com

Among the gems on this crown are rubies (Al_2O_3) and pearls ($CaCO_3$).

DISCOVER IT! TEMPERING OF METALS

You need four metal hairpins, pliers or tweezers, a glass of cold water, heatproof gloves, a heat-resistant surface, and a gas burner.

1. Wearing heatproof gloves, use the pliers to hold a hairpin by the open end. Heat the bend of the hairpin red-hot over the burner. Set the hairpin aside on the heat-resistant surface to cool.

2. Heat the bend of another hairpin red-hot, remove it from the flame, and immediately plunge it into the glass of cold water.

3. Repeat Step 1 with a third hairpin. After cooling, gently reheat it but do not let it get red-hot. Allow it to cool slowly in the air.

4. Try bending each of the three hairpins you heated, as well as a fourth hairpin that was not heated.

Tempering is the control of the hardness and flexibility of a metal by heating. Compare the flexibility of the three hairpins that were heated with the flexibility of the fourth hairpin, which serves as a control. Which has the most flexibility? The least? How does slow cooling affect the flexibility? After completing this chapter, return to this activity and explain the results.

THE s-BLOCK ELEMENTS: ACTIVE METALS

*T*he Bonneville Salt Flats, which stretch over 30 000 acres, are one of the most barren, inhospitable, and unique natural features in Utah. Part of the Great Basin, this dazzling white plain, along with the Great Salt Lake, is a remnant of ancient Lake Bonneville, which nearly 15 000 years ago covered one-third of present-day Utah and parts of neighboring states. Wind and water combine to create the flat surface of salt that has made Bonneville a world-famous destination for high-speed auto racers. Since 1896, when its potential for racing was first recognized, vehicles have hurtled along at record-breaking speeds, currently topping 600 miles per hour! The Bonneville Salt Flats are rich in salts of lithium, sodium, potassium, magnesium—metals of Groups 1A and 2A. **What are the properties of these active metals?**

objectives
▶ List sources, properties, and uses for the alkali metals (Group 1A) and their compounds
▶ Describe the preparation and properties of the alkaline-earth metals (Group 2A) and give uses for their compounds

key terms
▶ lime
▶ slaked lime

The Alkali Metals

You know from Chapter 14 that the representative elements occupy the *s* and *p* blocks in the periodic table because the outermost electrons of those elements are in the *s* and *p* sublevels. You also know that the transition elements occupy the *d* block and that the inner transition elements occupy the *f* block. About three-quarters of the more than 100 known elements are metals. The metals occupy all of the *s*, *d*, and *f* blocks and about half of the *p* block. The nonmetals occupy the remainder of the *p* block, in the upper-right corner of the periodic table. This chapter describes, block by block, some of the distinctive features of metals and nonmetals and their practical applications.

The alkali metals are the Group 1A elements. Rich deposits of alkali metal salts are found all over the world. The Bonneville Salt Flats in Utah and deposits at Searles Lake, California, contain huge quantities of sodium chloride and other alkali salts. The evaporation of ancient seas left large alkali metal salt deposits that are now underground near the Gulf Coast shores of Texas and Louisiana. Alkali metal salts are very soluble in water. Rain water leaches them out of the soil, and rivers carry them to the sea. Sea water is about 3% by mass alkali metal salts. As **Figure 24.1** shows, sea water is a source of table salt.

Figure 24.1
Large amounts of sodium chloride (table salt) are produced by the evaporation of sea water.

Table 24.1

Some Physical Properties of the Alkali Metals				
Element	Melting point (°C)	Boiling point (°C)	Density (g/cm³)	Atomic radius (nm)
Lithium	179	1336	0.53	0.123
Sodium	98	883	0.97	0.157
Potassium	64	758	0.86	0.203
Rubidium	39	700	1.53	0.216
Cesium	28	670	1.90	0.235

The metals of Group 1A are the most reactive known. Because of their reactivity, alkali metals are not found free in nature but are typically combined with nonmetals as alkali salts. Within the group, cesium and rubidium are the most reactive. Each alkali metal reacts violently with cold water, producing hydrogen gas and a solution of the alkali metal hydroxide (simply known as an alkali or base). Sodium, for example, reacts with cold water, forming sodium hydroxide and releasing hydrogen gas.

$$2Na(s) + 2H_2O(l) \longrightarrow 2NaOH(aq) + H_2(g)$$

The reaction of alkali metals with water is so rapid and exothermic that the hydrogen often burns as it is produced. Alkali metals will also react vigorously with the moisture in skin and should never be handled with bare hands. The alkali metals are usually stored under oil or kerosene to keep them from reacting with oxygen and moisture in the air.

The alkali metals have low densities, low melting points, and high electrical conductivity. **Table 24.1** lists some physical properties of the alkali metals. If you had a 10-g sample of each alkali metal listed in the table, which sample would have the largest volume? Why? These metals have the consistency of stiff modeling clay and are soft enough to be cut with a knife, as shown in **Figure 24.2**. The freshly cut surface is shiny, with the typical silvery luster of a metal. The surface quickly dulls on exposure to air, however, due to rapid reaction with oxygen and moisture.

Sodium is the only alkali metal manufactured on a large scale. To produce the free metal, sodium ions must be reduced. Metallic sodium is generally produced by the electrolysis of molten sodium chloride. Chlorine gas is a valuable by-product of this process.

Sodium is used as the light source in sodium vapor lamps and in the production of many chemicals. Liquid sodium is an excellent conductor of heat, and because of this it can be used in nuclear reactors to remove heat from the reactor core.

Sodium hydroxide is an ingredient in common household products used to clear clogged drains. Another compound of sodium is a popular type of bleach. An aqueous solution of sodium hypochlorite (NaClO) is an alternative to hydrogen peroxide. Do you know what important compound of sodium is present on most dining tables? What sodium compound is known commonly as baking soda?

Figure 24.2

Sodium is shiny when it is first cut, but it quickly reacts with oxygen and moisture in the air to become dull.

CHEMath

CLASSIFICATION

As you study chemistry, you will encounter more than 100 different chemical elements. In this chapter you learn how the elements are organized, or classified, into groups in the periodic table. A classification system, such as the periodic table, is a plan for organizing a large number of items into smaller groups.

Classification systems are not limited to chemistry, and they do not have to be complex. For example, do you keep your shirts, pants, and socks in different drawers? If so, you have classified your clothing.

The key to classifying anything is to divide large sets of items into smaller subsets according to similarities among items. In the case of clothes, the large set might include all of your clothes. Shirts, pants, and socks might be subsets. You can make even more subsets, such as long pants and short pants, tee shirts and sweatshirts, and so on.

Keep in mind that there is no single correct classification system. The same items can be classified in more than one way. Can you think of another way to classify your clothes? Perhaps by color, by the season in which you wear them, or by whether you wear them during the day or at night.

Biologists also use a classification system. They need to organize the more than two million different types of living things in existence. One common classification system divides living things into five major groups, called kingdoms. For example, animals are in one kingdom and plants are in another. The kingdoms are then divided into smaller groups by more specific characteristics. Animals, for example, can be divided according to whether or not they have a backbone. The more specific the characteristic, the fewer items there are in the group.

In chemistry, the elements are easier to study if they are classified into groups. Elements can be classified according to properties such as atomic size, ionic size, ionization energy, and electronegativity. Becoming familiar with how the elements are classified will help you better understand chemical concepts.

Example 1

Classify the following items according to their use.

paper clip	clothespin
pen	staple
pencil	marker

Things that hold something together:
paper clip, clothespin, staple

Things to write with:
pen, pencil, marker

Example 2

Classify the following elements according to their positions in the periodic table.

helium	beryllium
lithium	potassium
calcium	xenon

Group 1A: lithium, potassium
Group 2A: beryllium, calcium
Group 8A: helium, xenon

Practice Problems

A. Develop a classification system for all of the motor vehicles parked in the school parking lot. Compare your classification system with those of your classmates and determine the strengths and weaknesses of each.

B. Classify the items in each of the following sets and identify the characteristic you used to classify them.

1. dog, cat, shark, elephant, guppy, whale

2. book, newspaper, calculator, adding machine, letter

3. lead, tungsten, bromine, chlorine, zinc, iodine

s block

The Alkaline Earth Metals

The alkaline earth metals are the elements of Group 2A. Alkaline earth metal salts are less soluble in water than are the corresponding alkali metal salts. Nevertheless, the sea is a rich source of the ions of magnesium and calcium, two alkaline earth metals. Calcium ions in sea water are used by shellfish in building their calcium carbonate shells and by coral animals in forming reefs.

Some of the alkaline earth carbonates and sulfates are insoluble enough to resist weathering and the leaching action of rainwater. The most common mineral form of calcium carbonate is limestone. Other forms that occur naturally are shown in **Figure 24.3.** The White Cliffs of Dover, on the southern coast of England, are another form of calcium carbonate. There, the shells of microscopic marine animals have been pressed into a natural chalk.

Calcite

Limestone

Marble

Stalactites

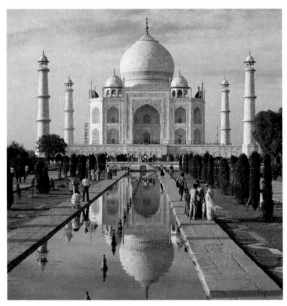

Figure 24.3

Calcium carbonate (CaCO₃) occurs naturally in several forms. The Taj Mahal in India is built of marble, one form of CaCO₃.

The alkaline earth metals react with water to produce basic, or alkaline, solutions. Their compounds are extracted from the minerals that since early times have been called "earths." The term "earths" has its origin with the alchemists of the Middle Ages who used the word to describe substances that are unchanged by fire, notably calcium oxide (CaO) and magnesium oxide (MgO). Although the alkaline earth metals are not found uncombined in nature, they are chemically less reactive than the alkali metals in Group 1A. Therefore they need not be stored under oil. Barium is the most reactive element in the group. As **Figure 24.4** shows, calcium reacts with cold water to produce hydrogen, but it does so more slowly than Group 1A metals do. Beryllium and magnesium react only with hot water or steam.

The alkaline earth metals are harder than the alkali metals. They have a gray-white luster but tarnish quickly in air to form a tough, thin oxide coating. The coating protects the metals, particularly beryllium and magnesium, from further oxidation. This property allows alloys of these metals to be used as low-density structural materials. **Table 24.2** lists some physical properties of the alkaline earth metals. What is the trend in the atomic radii of the alkaline earth metals? Why?

Table 24.2

Some Physical Properties of the Alkaline Earth Metals				
Element	Melting point (°C)	Boiling point (°C)	Density (g/cm³)	Atomic radius (nm)
Beryllium	1280	1500	1.86	0.089
Magnesium	651	1107	1.75	0.136
Calcium	851	1487	1.55	0.174
Strontium	800	1366	2.60	0.191
Barium	850	1537	3.59	0.198

Figure 24.4
Alkaline earth metals are less reactive than alkali metals. Here, calcium reacts slowly with water.

Calcium and magnesium are the two most important alkaline earth metals. Calcium is produced by the electrolysis of molten calcium chloride in a reaction similar to that used to produce sodium. Magnesium is prepared from sea water, as illustrated in **Figure 24.5**. Magnesium is an important structural material and is the chief component in a number of high-tensile-strength, low-density alloys. These properties make the alloys valuable in aircraft and spacecraft construction. Magnesium is also present in asbestos, which is shown in **Figure 24.6** on the following page. Because asbestos is a

Figure 24.5
Sea water is the main source of magnesium compounds, with each ton of sea water yielding about 3 kg of magnesium. Calcium carbonate from oyster shells is converted to lime, which reacts with the Mg^{2+} in the sea water. Most commercial magnesium is prepared electrolytically from magnesium chloride, which is produced at a later stage of the process.

The Chemistry of Metals and Nonmetals **709**

Figure 24.6
Magnesium is present in asbestos, which is a fibrous form of the mineral serpentine (left). Asbestos was used as an insulation material until it was discovered that inhalation of its fibers causes lung cancer. As a result, most asbestos is being removed from the sites where it was installed (right).

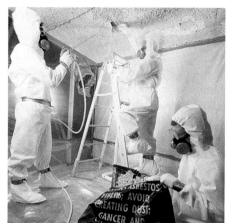

very poor conductor of heat, it was once commonly used as an insulator. This use has been discontinued because it is now known that asbestos fibers cause lung cancer.

Calcium oxide, commonly called **lime** or quicklime, is an important industrial chemical. Calcium oxide is produced by the high-temperature decomposition of limestone in a lime kiln.

$$CaCO_3(s) \xrightarrow{900\,°C} CaO(s) + CO_2(g)$$

Limestone   Lime

The reaction of lime with water is called slaking. The process is exothermic and the product is **slaked lime,** or calcium hydroxide.

$$CaO(s) + H_2O(l) \longrightarrow Ca(OH)_2(aq) + \text{heat}$$

Lime   Slaked lime

Slaked lime is used to make plaster and mortar and to neutralize acidic soils. The setting process for mortar involves the conversion of slaked lime back to calcium carbonate (limestone) by the action of atmospheric carbon dioxide.

$$Ca(OH)_2(aq) + CO_2(g) \longrightarrow CaCO_3(s) + H_2O(g)$$

portfolio project

Some caves are created when underground limestone deposits are dissolved. Prepare a report or poster display on the chemistry of such caves. Find out the identity and source of the acid that dissolves the limestone. Include an explanation for the formation of stalagmites and stalactites.

section review 24.1

1. List the properties of the alkali metals, their main sources, and their uses.

2. How are alkaline earth metals prepared? What are their properties and main uses?

3. Why are alkali metals stored under kerosene or mineral oil?

4. Which alkaline earth metals react with cold water and which do not? Write a typical equation that shows such a reaction.

5. Write an equation for the reaction of potassium with water.

6. Would you expect to find pure samples of alkali metals in Earth's crust? Explain.

7. How does the reactivity of the Group 2A metals compare with that of the Group 1A metals?

 Chem ASAP! **Assessment 24.1** Check your understanding of the important ideas and concepts in Section 24.1.

COMPLEX IONS

Wear safety glasses and follow the standard safety procedures outlined on page 18.

PURPOSE

To observe some chemical reactions of metal ions to form complex ions.

MATERIALS

- pencil
- ruler
- paper
- reaction surface
- chemicals shown in Figure A

PROCEDURE

On separate sheets of paper, draw two grids similar to Figure A. Draw one with Xs and one without. Make each square 2 cm on a side. Place a reaction surface over the grid with Xs and add one drop of each chemical as shown in Figure A. Use the grid without Xs as a data table to record your observations for each reaction.

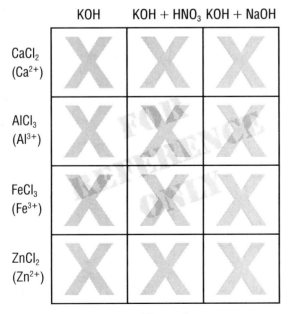

Figure A

ANALYSIS

Using your experimental data, record the answers to the following questions below your data table.

1. An amphoteric compound is one that behaves as a base under a certain set of conditions and as an acid under a different set of conditions. An amphoteric compound reacts with both an acid and a base. Which compounds in this experiment are amphoteric?

2. Hydroxide ions commonly form precipitates with metal ions. For example, copper(II) ion reacts with hydroxide ion to produce copper(II) hydroxide.

$$Cu^{2+}(aq) + 2OH^-(aq) \longrightarrow Cu(OH)_2(s)$$

Write the net ionic equations that describe each precipitation reaction you observed.

3. Hydroxide precipitates dissolve readily in acid solution. For example, copper(II) hydroxide reacts with acid to form copper(II) ions and water.

$$Cu(OH)_2(s) + 2H^+(aq) \longrightarrow Cu^{2+}(aq) + 2H_2O(l)$$

Write the net ionic equations that describe each neutralization reaction you observed.

4. When hydrogen ions are added, do the hydroxide precipitates act as bases or acids? Explain your answer.

5. Some hydroxide precipitates dissolve in excess NaOH. For example, aluminum hydroxide reacts with excess hydroxide ions to produce an aluminum hydroxide complex ion.

$$Al(OH)_3(s) + OH^-(aq) \longrightarrow Al(OH)_4^-(aq)$$

Which other hydroxide precipitate(s) reacted with excess sodium hydroxide? Write the net ionic equations that describe the formation of these complex ions.

6. When a base is added in excess, do the hydroxide precipitates act as acids or bases? Explain your answer.

7. Which hydroxide precipitates in this experiment are amphoteric?

objectives
▶ Describe properties and uses of *p*-block metals and nonmetals
▶ Explain methods for obtaining specific *p*-block metals and nonmetals from their compounds and minerals

THE *p*-BLOCK ELEMENTS: METALS AND NONMETALS

*H*ow much do you value aluminum objects such as containers and cans? Probably not enough to consider them a treasure or to store them in a safety-deposit box. However, there are some objects made partially of aluminum that are quite valuable indeed. Some of the jewels shown in this photo actually contain compounds of aluminum. Aluminum is an element in the p block of the periodic table. **What are the properties of the metals and nonmetals that make up the groups in the *p* block?**

p block

Aluminum and Group 3A

Boron is the first element in Group 3A. Boron occurs naturally in borate minerals. Although not widespread, large deposits of the borate mineral borax are found in the arid regions of the United States, particularly the Mojave Desert and Death Valley, California. Borax was once hauled from Death Valley by teams of mules, as shown in **Figure 24.7.**

Purified borax, or sodium tetraborate decahydrate ($Na_2B_4O_7 \cdot 10H_2O$), is soft, colorless, and crystalline. Borax is found in glass, in glazes used to decorate ceramics, and in fertilizers. Borax is used to soften water, to disinfect, or as a flux to help solder flow between pieces of metal.

Pure boron is black, lustrous, and extremely hard but brittle. It is also a metalloid, or semiconductor. Boron can be prepared by the reaction of its oxide with magnesium metal.

$$B_2O_3(s) + 3Mg(s) \longrightarrow 2B(s) + 3MgO(s)$$

One important compound of boron, boron carbide (B_4C), is a ceramic material approaching diamond in hardness. Boron carbide is used in the fabrication of machine tools and for other applications in which wear-resistance is important.

The elements that follow boron in Group 3A are the metals aluminum, gallium, indium, and thallium. Aluminum is the most abundant metal in Earth's crust. Although it does not exist in the uncombined state in nature, it is a major component of many rocks and minerals, especially in the form of bauxite (Al_2O_3). Aluminum is commonly found as the very hard mineral

Figure 24.7

Borax is a borate mineral. Large mule teams were once used to transport mined borax out of Death Valley, California.

Figure 24.8

Corundum is a mineral form of aluminum oxide. Rubies are corundum in which a few of the aluminum ions are replaced by chromium ions. Blue sapphires are corundum with traces of iron and titanium ions. What are the formulas for aluminum oxide and chromium(III) oxide?

corundum (impure aluminum oxide). Cut forms of corundum with trace amounts of other elements are the commonly known gemstones ruby and sapphire, shown in **Figure 24.8.** Corundum, in its less exotic form, is used as the abrasive in emery powder and grinding wheels.

As a pure metal, aluminum has strength and ductility in addition to low density, high electrical conductivity, and corrosion resistance. These properties make it a valuable structural and manufacturing metal. When aluminum is exposed to air, a tough film of oxide quickly forms, protecting it from further corrosion by oxygen and water.

Until the end of the nineteenth century, aluminum sold for the same price as silver. Aluminum was so expensive because there was no practical way to produce it. Paul Héroult, a Frenchman, and Charles Hall, an American, almost simultaneously invented the first commercial process for the production of aluminum. Hall's chemistry professor challenged his class to find an inexpensive way to produce aluminum. After graduation, Hall set up a laboratory in a woodshed. He found that cryolite (Na_3AlF_6) dissolves aluminum oxide, forming a low melting point solution, from which aluminum could be obtained by electrolysis. This process is essentially the method used for aluminum production today. Aluminum is widely used as a lightweight structural material in aircraft production, as shown in **Figure 24.9,** and in the manufacture of cookware. What is another everyday item made from aluminum?

The other Group 3A elements—gallium, indium, and thallium—are quite rare. One interesting use of gallium is in thermometers because of its extraordinarily wide liquid temperature range. Gallium has a melting point of 30 °C and a boiling point of 1980 °C. Because gallium is a semiconductor, it is also used in the manufacture of some electronic components.

Figure 24.9

Aluminum is particularly useful in the construction of aircraft because it is lightweight and very strong. It also reacts with oxygen to form a thin protective coating of aluminum oxide that will not react with water and that resists further corrosion.

p block

Carbon and Group 4A

Two of the most important elements on Earth, carbon and silicon, are in Group 4A. Carbon is the fundamental element in the molecules of all living things. Silicon is the fundamental element of the geologic world.

The two familiar allotropes of carbon are diamond and graphite. Diamond, the hardest material known, behaves like a typical nonmetal. It is transparent and an electric insulator—that is, a nonconductor of electricity. Graphite, however, is soft, black, and opaque and is a good conductor of electricity. In the late 1980s, a third allotrope of carbon, the soccer ball shaped buckminsterfullerene, was isolated from soot. **Figure 24.10**

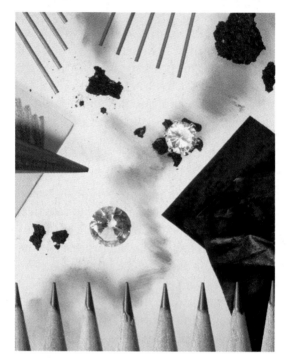

shows examples of the three allotropes of carbon. In general, carbon-containing compounds, which number at least 10 million, are called organic compounds. Organic compounds are the basis of all living things.

Silicon is the second-most-abundant element in Earth's crust. It occurs in nature in the combined state as silicon dioxide (SiO_2) in quartz, an essential component of sand, and as silicates in rocks, soils, and clays. Silicon and germanium, the third element in Group 4A, are semiconductors. At low temperatures, both substances are insulators. At high temperatures, however, they conduct electricity. These two elements, when highly purified, form the foundation of transistor technology. A silicon computer chip is shown in **Figure 24.11.** Silicon and germanium are also used in photocells for solar power units.

Tin and lead are the remaining elements in Group 4A. Both are fairly unreactive metals. Therefore, tin and lead have many uses as free metals. Tin, a soft, silvery metal that can be rolled into thin sheets to make tin foil, is usually found in nature as its oxide (SnO_2). In tin cans, a tin coating protects the iron underneath against the corroding effect of acidic foods. Tin has been used for centuries in various alloys, such as bronze (an alloy of tin and copper) and solder (an alloy of tin and lead). One tin compound, stannous fluoride (SnF_2), is an important ingredient in some toothpastes.

Lead has a low melting point (327 °C) and is easily obtained from the sulfide mineral galena (PbS). Lead was known to the Egyptians as early as 3000 B.C., and since Roman times it has been used in plumbing. Lead's toxicity is a major health concern, and its use in certain products is now regulated. For example, plumber's solder, which was once an alloy of tin and lead, is now lead free, and the manufacture of leaded gasoline has been phased out. Currently, the largest commercial use for lead is for the electrodes in lead storage batteries.

Figure 24.10 ▶

Diamond, graphite, and the recently isolated buckminster-fullerene (also called buckyballs) are three allotropes of carbon.

Figure 24.11

The size of a present-day computer chip is shown here relative to a penny. Each chip may contain millions of transistors.

Nitrogen and Group 5A

The first Group 5A element, nitrogen, is a nonmetal and is a gas at room temperature. In descending order, the next elements are phosphorus (a solid nonmetal) and arsenic and antimony, which are metalloids. The last element, bismuth, is a metal.

Nitrogen is essential to living organisms. Although 80% of the air you breathe is nitrogen, your body cannot use the element in that form. Fortunately, bacteria in the soil and in the root nodules of peas, beans, and other legumes, fix atmospheric nitrogen into a usable form. Plants can use the fixed nitrogen compounds to synthesize proteins and other biologically important nitrogen-containing compounds.

Nitrogen is isolated commercially from air by two processes. In one method, the nitrogen is fractionally distilled from liquefied air. Because liquid nitrogen, shown in **Figure 24.12,** boils at a lower temperature than liquid oxygen does, nitrogen distills off first from the mixture. In the second method of isolating nitrogen, air is moved over red-hot coke, which is almost pure carbon. The carbon combines with oxygen to form carbon dioxide while the nitrogen remains unchanged.

Elemental nitrogen is a colorless, odorless, tasteless gas, composed of diatomic molecules (N_2). It is slightly soluble in water. Its melting point is $-210\,°C$ and its boiling point is $-196\,°C$.

The most important industrial uses of atmospheric nitrogen are in the manufacture of two compounds: ammonia (by the Haber-Bosch process, illustrated in the flowchart in **Figure 24.13**) and nitric acid (by the Ostwald method).

Figure 24.12

Extremely cold liquid nitrogen boils away quickly when poured from an insulated flask into a beaker at room temperature. The smokelike effect is caused by the condensation of water vapor in the air.

Figure 24.13

In the Haber-Bosch process, nitrogen and hydrogen combine to form ammonia. The hydrogen is derived from the reaction of steam with methane. What is the source of the nitrogen?

Figure 24.14

Pure liquid ammonia is called anhydrous ammonia. It is used extensively as a fertilizer and is injected directly into the ground.

In the Haber-Bosch process, nitrogen and hydrogen gases are heated to 500 °C at 6×10^4 kPa (600 atm) in the presence of an iron catalyst.

$$N_2(g) + 3H_2(g) \xrightleftharpoons{\text{Fe}} 2NH_3(g)$$

The ammonia gas produced is easily liquefied by cooling and is separated from the reactants by liquefaction.

Ammonia, which is very soluble in water, is a colorless gas with a strong, irritating odor with which you are probably familiar. Aqueous ammonia is weakly basic and is a component of many cleaning products. Liquid ammonia, aqueous ammonia, and several ammonium salts are used as fertilizers. Liquid ammonia, also called anhydrous ammonia, is sometimes applied under pressure directly to soil, as shown in **Figure 24.14.** Liquid ammonia is also used as a refrigerant, particularly in the frozen-food industry. Ammonium nitrate is the most important solid fertilizer in the world today.

About one-quarter of all ammonia produced is made into nitric acid. Nitric acid is made commercially from ammonia by the Ostwald method, a process invented by Wilhelm Ostwald (1853–1932), a German chemist. Nitric acid is used in etching processes and in the production of fertilizers and dyes. It is also an important raw material in the manufacture of explosives.

Like nitrogen, phosphorus is essential to living organisms. Phosphorus is present in the double strands of DNA, in bones, and in teeth. It is also part of ATP (adenosine triphosphate), which is the principal energy-transfer molecule in living systems. Phosphorus occurs mainly in the form of phosphate rock. As shown in **Figure 24.15,** pure phosphorus is prepared in a white form and a red form. The white form is very reactive. Red phosphorus is a less active form used in the manufacture of matches. Why do you think white phosphorus is usually stored under water?

The other Group 5A elements—arsenic, antimony, and bismuth—occur in nature mainly in the form of sulfide minerals. They are not essential to living organisms. Because they expand as they solidify, alloys containing antimony and bismuth are used in making metal type characters

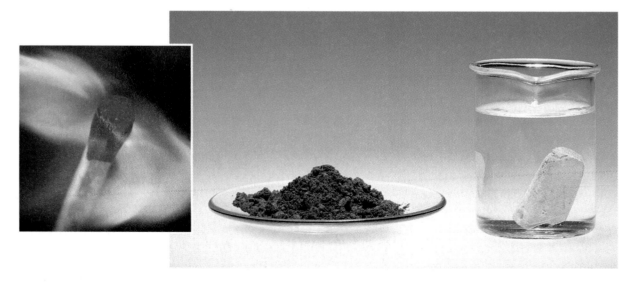

Figure 24.15

White (or yellow) phosphorus is very reactive and must be stored under water (right). Red phosphorus is much more stable, and is used to make matches (left).

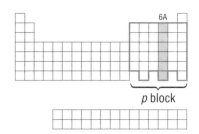

for traditional press printing. Because characters of type must be identical, the metals used to manufacture them must expand to fill the type molds completely.

Oxygen and Group 6A

The Group 6A elements include oxygen, sulfur, selenium, tellurium, and polonium. Oxygen is a gas and a nonmetal. Sulfur is a nonmetal that occurs free in nature as a brittle yellow solid. Selenium and tellurium are both solids and metalloids, with properties intermediate to those of metals and nonmetals. Polonium is a radioactive metal that occurs only in trace quantities in radium-containing minerals.

Oxygen is Earth's most abundant element. It accounts for 50% by mass of Earth's crust, 60% by mass of the human body, and 20% by volume of the air you breathe. Most oxygen is combined in the silicate rocks of Earth's crust.

The primary source of commercial oxygen (O_2) is air. Relatively pure oxygen is obtained by liquefying air and then fractionally distilling the liquid. Oxygen distills off at $-183\,°C$. When cooled, oxygen condenses to a clear blue liquid that freezes at $-218\,°C$. In liquid form, oxygen can be held between the poles of a magnet, as shown in **Figure 24.16.** This property, called paramagnetism, is caused by the presence of unpaired electrons in the oxygen molecule. The major commercial use of oxygen is in the basic oxygen process for the manufacture of steel.

Medical emergency teams administer oxygen to victims of smoke inhalation, electrical shock, or drowning, as shown in **Figure 24.17.** For certain medical conditions, such as pneumonia, emphysema, or gas poisoning, a patient may need to breathe air enriched with oxygen for long periods of time. Why are tanks of oxygen carried in airplanes for use at high altitudes?

Ozone (O_3) is an allotrope of oxygen. Ozone is produced during electrical storms, as well as in Earth's upper atmosphere—the ozone layer—by the action of ultraviolet light on oxygen. Ozone is also produced near high-voltage generators. The ozone layer protects living things from excess ultraviolet light from the sun. In the 1970s, it was discovered that chlorofluorocarbons (CFCs), used as refrigerants and as propellants in aerosol cans, had begun to destroy the ozone layer. In 1985, a hole was found in the ozone layer over Antarctica. The nations of the world have since agreed to reduce production of CFCs and hope for 100% elimination in a few years.

Figure 24.16
When liquid oxygen is poured between the poles of a magnet, the magnet attracts and holds the oxygen. What property of oxygen does this demonstrate?

Figure 24.17
Oxygen is often administered to medical patients who have difficulty breathing.

Ozone is a pale-blue gas with a characteristic odor. When cooled to −112 °C, it condenses to a deep-blue, explosive liquid. Ozone is a strong oxidizing agent. It is used commercially to bleach flour, oil, and delicate fabrics and to sterilize water. Because ozone is unstable, it must be generated where it will be used. It is prepared by passing air through an electrical discharge.

When substances combine chemically with oxygen, the process is called oxidation. The product of an oxidation reaction is an oxide. Oxides of all elements, except the noble gases and a few inactive metals, can be prepared simply by heating the elements in the presence of oxygen. In general, oxides of metals are solids, and many react with water to form bases. Oxides of nonmetals may be solid, liquid, or gas, and many react with water to form acids.

Sulfur is a pale-yellow, tasteless, odorless, water-insoluble, brittle solid that has been known about since ancient times. Sulfur occurs in the elemental state in large underground deposits. Some of the world's richest deposits of elemental sulfur are on the Gulf Coast in Louisiana and Texas. These deposits are not easily mined, however, because they are buried under several hundred feet of quicksand. A German-American engineer, Herman Frasch (1851–1914), devised an ingenious method for getting this sulfur out of the ground. The method takes advantage of sulfur's low melting point (119 °C). The Frasch process produces 80% of the world's sulfur output.

In the Frasch process, wells are drilled into the sulfur bed. Then an arrangement of three concentric tubes (with 2.5-cm, 7.5-cm, and 15-cm diameters) is installed, as shown in **Figure 24.18.** Superheated water (180 °C) under pressure is pumped down the outside tube to melt the sulfur. Compressed air is pumped down the center tube. A frothy mixture of air, water, and molten sulfur rises up the third tube. The molten sulfur, 99.5% pure, is pumped into large storage vats, where it cools and solidifies into huge blocks. The blocks may be as much as 130 m long, 70 m wide, and 30 m high. For shipping, the sulfur is loosened by dynamite blasting and loaded into freight cars.

Figure 24.18

Sulfur deposits deep underground are mined by the Frasch process. The sulfur, melted by hot water and whipped into a froth by compressed air, rises to the surface. After being mined, the sulfur is dried and stored in huge blocks until it is shipped.

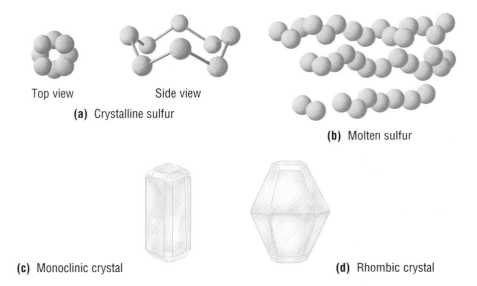

(a) Crystalline sulfur

Top view   Side view

(b) Molten sulfur

(c) Monoclinic crystal   **(d)** Rhombic crystal

Figure 24.19

*Crystalline sulfur exists as S_8 molecules **(a)**. Above the melting point, the S_8 rings of sulfur break and form chains of sulfur atoms. Near the boiling point, the chains break into smaller groups and individual atoms **(b)**. As the sulfur cools, the needlelike monoclinic crystals **(c)** gradually change to the stable rhombic form **(d)**.*

Large amounts of sulfur are also obtained from hydrogen sulfide, a poisonous gas. Hydrogen sulfide is a product of petroleum refining and can be present up to 40% in natural gas. To obtain pure sulfur, some of the hydrogen sulfide is burned in air to make sulfur dioxide. The sulfur dioxide is then treated with more hydrogen sulfide to produce elemental sulfur. This reaction can be summarized in a single equation.

$$2H_2S(g) + SO_2(g) \longrightarrow 2H_2O(l) + 3S(s)$$

Sulfur occurs in several allotropic forms. When molten sulfur cools below 119 °C, it forms crystals of monoclinic sulfur. This allotrope contains eight-membered rings of covalently bonded sulfur atoms (S_8) arranged in monoclinic crystals. Below 95.5 °C, the sulfur changes to rhombic sulfur, which is also composed of S_8 units. The crystal forms of sulfur are shown in **Figure 24.19.** A third form of sulfur is the dark-brown, rubberlike allotrope known as amorphous or plastic sulfur. It can be produced by pouring molten sulfur, near its boiling point, into cold water, as shown in **Figure 24.20.** Amorphous solids do not have a distinct crystal form. Within hours, the amorphous sulfur loses its elasticity as it is converted to rhombic crystals. Sulfur can be purified by boiling it and condensing the vapor. Tiny rhombic crystals form in flowerlike patterns on the walls of the condensation chamber. This powder is called flowers of sulfur.

Figure 24.20

Sulfur in the liquid state after being heated over a flame (left). When the liquid sulfur is poured into water, it forms an amorphous solid (right).

OCEANOGRAPHY

Deep-Sea Minerals

Minerals have been found in the developing undersea ridges of the Pacific Ocean near Hawaii. Where the tectonic plates of Earth's crust are separating,

sea water comes into contact with liquid magma of the underlying volcanic rocks. This superheated water, with recorded temperatures as high as 500 °C, extracts minerals from crust material and deposits these minerals in immense underwater fields on the ocean floor. In one area of the Pacific Ocean, there is an extensive field of potato-sized manganese nodules. Rich deposits of chromium, cobalt, copper, gold, iron, nickel, and zinc have also been found.

When heated with metals (except gold and platinum), sulfur forms compounds called sulfides. Hydrogen sulfide gas, which smells like rotten eggs, is prepared by the action of an acid on a sulfide.

$$FeS(s) + 2HCl(aq) \longrightarrow FeCl_2(aq) + H_2S(g)$$

Sulfur is an extremely important raw material in the chemical industry. It is used in the preparation of paints, plastics, drugs, and dyes, but its major uses are in the vulcanization of rubber and the manufacture of sulfuric acid.

The annual production of sulfuric acid in North America is in excess of 50 million metric tons. Practically every industry makes some use of sulfuric acid. Almost half of the world's production goes into the manufacture of fertilizers, such as ammonium sulfate and superphosphate. Large amounts of sulfuric acid are used in the metal industry for pickling iron and steel. Pickling involves putting a metal in a chemical bath to remove oxides on the metal surface. Sulfuric acid is also essential to many of the processes in petroleum refining.

Today, sulfuric acid is produced mainly by the contact process. In this process, sulfur is first burned in air to produce sulfur dioxide, an irritating toxic gas. Then the sulfur dioxide is oxidized to sulfur trioxide in the presence of a vanadium(V) oxide catalyst.

$$2SO_2(g) + O_2(g) \xrightarrow{V_2O_5} 2SO_3(g)$$

The addition of sulfur trioxide to water gives sulfuric acid.

$$SO_3(g) + H_2O(l) \longrightarrow H_2SO_4(l)$$

The entire process is called the contact process because the key reaction takes place when the reactants are in contact with the surface of the solid catalyst.

Pure, anhydrous sulfuric acid is a dense, colorless, syrupy liquid. The concentrated acid generally used in laboratories is 98% H_2SO_4 and 2% H_2O. Sulfuric acid has the chemical properties of a typical acid. The dilute acid reacts with metals, oxides, hydroxides, or carbonates to form salts called sulfates. The reaction with metals also releases hydrogen gas. Sulfuric acid displaces other acids from their salts. For example, hydrogen chloride can be produced from sulfuric acid and sodium chloride according to the following equation.

$$H_2SO_4(l) + 2NaCl(s) \longrightarrow Na_2SO_4(s) + 2HCl(g)$$

When dissolved in water, the gaseous hydrogen chloride that is produced forms hydrochloric acid.

Concentrated sulfuric acid dissolves readily in water, liberating a large amount of heat. Is such a process endothermic or exothermic? Its strong affinity for water makes sulfuric acid a powerful dehydrating agent. Thus it must be handled with great care. When the concentrated acid is added to sugar, a vigorous dehydration reaction takes place. A large volume of charred material is produced as the acid removes water from the sugar, leaving only carbon, as shown in **Figure 24.21.**

$$C_{12}H_{22}O_{11}(s) \xrightarrow{H_2SO_4(l)} 12C(s) + 11H_2O(g)$$

Figure 24.21
When concentrated sulfuric acid is added to sucrose (cane sugar), water is removed. The reaction releases a great deal of heat. The water turns to steam and the residual carbon expands to a porous mass. What kind of an agent is concentrated sulfuric acid in this reaction? Why?

Hot concentrated sulfuric acid is an oxidizing agent. For example, it reacts with certain metals to generate sulfur dioxide.

$$2H_2SO_4(aq) + Cu(s) \longrightarrow CuSO_4(aq) + SO_2(g) + 2H_2O(l)$$

Selenium, another Group 6A element, is a semiconductor. It is a poor conductor of electricity in the dark, but its conductivity increases greatly in the light. Because of that property, selenium is used in photoelectric cells, in exposure meters for cameras, and in light-sensitive switches. The xerographic process of photocopying also depends on the photoconductivity of selenium.

Tellurium is one of the rarest elements. Its compounds are toxic. The element itself plays no known role in living organisms.

The Halogens

The halogens, Group 7A, do not exist in nature in the uncombined state, but their compounds are fairly abundant. The salts sodium chloride, sodium bromide, and sodium iodide are found in sea water and salt beds. Calcium fluoride is found in the form of the mineral fluorspar.

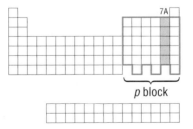

The halogens are fluorine, chlorine, bromine, iodine, and astatine. All of the halogens are nonmetals. The first two elements, fluorine and chlorine, are yellowish or yellowish-green gases at room temperature and normal atmospheric pressure. Bromine is a dark-red liquid, while iodine is a purple-black crystalline solid with a metallic sheen. The last element, astatine, is a rare radioactive solid that has not been well investigated. The colors of chlorine, bromine, and iodine vapors are shown in **Figure 24.22** on the following page. Also evident in this figure is an important property of the free halogens—free halogens are very reactive and must be handled with extreme caution. **Figure 24.22** illustrates the reactivity of chlorine gas with steel wool.

The Chemistry of Metals and Nonmetals **721**

Figure 24.22

(a) *Iodine, chlorine, and bromine (left to right) are very different in color and in physical state.*
(b) *A heated piece of steel wool reacts vigorously with chlorine gas. The smokelike cloud that appears is actually made up of fine particles of iron(III) chloride. Would the reaction be more or less vigorous in bromine? In fluorine?*

(a) (b)

Compounds of fluorine, chlorine, and iodine are essential to your well-being and must be included in your diet. Why is fluoride ion added to many municipal water supplies? Chlorine, as chloride ions, is an important component of the blood and other body fluids. Iodine, as iodide ions, is necessary to prevent goiter, an enlargement of the thyroid gland. For this reason sodium iodide is commonly added to table salt. Thus the iodized table salt you eat contains a small amount of NaI.

The halogens and their compounds have many other uses. A dilute solution of chlorine is used as a bleaching and disinfecting agent. Light-sensitive silver chloride and silver bromide are used to make photographic film. Fluorine is used in the manufacture of nonstick PTFE (*polytetrafluoroethylene*) coatings, which are applied to frying pans and a variety of other cookware, as shown in **Figure 24.23.**

Most of the compounds of halogens are soluble in water. Halide ions are abundant in sea water and in salt beds formed by the evaporation of salt water. **Table 24.3** lists the typical concentrations of halide ions found in sea water.

Fluorine was known in compounds long before it was isolated as an element. In 1886, French chemist Henri Moissan made pure fluorine by electrolyzing an ice-cold solution of potassium fluoride in hydrogen fluoride. Fluorine is still made this way today.

Chlorine gas is made commercially by the electrolysis of brine, a concentrated solution of sodium chloride. In a separate process, the hydrogen also produced in the electrolysis is burned in the chlorine to make hydrogen chloride gas—an important source of hydrochloric acid.

Bromine is obtained commercially from sea water and salt-well brines. Sodium chloride in the water is allowed to crystallize, leaving a solution containing the more soluble bromides. Chlorine gas, which is more electronegative than bromine, is then used to displace bromide ions from the solution as free bromine.

$$2NaBr(aq) + Cl_2(g) \longrightarrow 2NaCl(aq) + Br_2(l)$$

Figure 24.23

One nonstick coating commonly used is a heat-resistant polymer composed of fluorine and carbon.

At one time, iodine was extracted from the ashes of certain seaweeds that concentrate iodine from sea water. Now it is produced commercially from sodium iodate ($NaIO_3$), which occurs as an impurity in deposits of sodium nitrite.

$$2NaIO_3(aq) + 5NaHSO_3(aq) \longrightarrow$$
$$2Na_2SO_4(aq) + 3NaHSO_4(aq) + H_2O(l) + I_2(s)$$

Fluorine is the most chemically reactive of all the nonmetals. Where do you think fluorine ranks on the electronegativity scale? Fluorine, the strongest elemental oxidizing agent known, forms compounds with all elements except helium, neon, and argon. The reactivity of the other halogens decreases as their atomic size and atomic mass increase. Thus iodine is the least reactive of the common halogens.

With the exception of hydrogen fluoride, the hydrogen halides are highly ionized in water, forming strong acids. Hydrofluoric acid is a weak acid; that is, it is weakly ionized in water. Hydrogen fluoride molecules are very polar and are strongly hydrogen-bonded to one another. The other hydrogen halides exhibit this effect to a much lesser degree. Hydrofluoric acid is used to etch designs in glass and to frost light bulbs. For many years, hydrofluoric acid had to be stored in wax containers. Today, plastic bottles are used instead.

The enrichment of uranium is another important use of fluorine. In the process for separating the isotopes of uranium, the metal is converted to uranium hexafluoride (UF_6), a gas. The diffusion of this gas allows the separation of uranium-235 (the fissionable isotope) from uranium-238 (the nonfissionable isotope).

Large amounts of chlorine are used in the purification of city water supplies, swimming pools, and sewage. Because chlorine in solution is a powerful oxidizing agent, it kills disease-causing bacteria. Chlorine is also used in the synthesis of vinyl chloride ($CH_2{=}CHCl$), which reacts to form polyvinyl chloride (PVC). PVC, a plastic, is used for floor coverings and other vinyl products.

Table 24.3

Concentration of Halide Ions in Sea Water	
Ion	g/L
F^-	1.3×10^{-3}
Cl^-	1.9×10^{1}
Br^-	6.5×10^{-2}
I^-	5.0×10^{-5}

section review 24.2

8. Describe some properties of p-block elements from the various groups of the periodic table.

9. Describe how several p-block elements are obtained from their compounds or minerals.

10. Why is aluminum so resistant to corrosion?

11. Aluminum is produced by electrolysis. Write the electrode reactions for the process.

12. Which of the Group 4A elements are used in electronic equipment?

13. In what form is nitrogen present in Earth's atmosphere?

14. What are some important uses of sulfuric acid?

15. What are the halogens? Describe some properties and uses of each.

portfolio project

Both Joseph Priestly, the discoverer of oxygen, and Antoine Lavoisier, who gave oxygen its name, were persecuted for their political beliefs. Prepare a written report describing their scientific accomplishments and their political fates.

 Chem ASAP! Assessment 24.2 Check your understanding of the important ideas and concepts in Section 24.2.

objectives

▶ List the properties of specific transition metals
▶ Describe the chemical diversity shown by the transition metals and inner transition metals

key terms

▶ ores
▶ metallurgy
▶ Monel metal
▶ inner transition elements

d block

THE *d*- AND *f*-BLOCK ELEMENTS: TRANSITION AND INNER TRANSITION METALS

What do broken bones and aircraft engines have in common?
The same metal that is strong enough to withstand the forces inside a jet engine is also lightweight and corrosion-resistant enough to be used to repair broken bones and replace joints. **What is this versatile metal?**

Overview

Most metals come from mineral deposits in Earth. Minerals used for the commercial production of metals are called **ores. Metallurgy** is the use of various procedures to separate metals from their ores. Many of these techniques were developed over the centuries by trial and error. Three basic steps are involved: concentrating the ore, chemically reducing the ore to the metal, and refining and purifying the metal.

Figure 24.24 shows aqueous solutions of some transition-metal compounds. You can see from the periodic table that these metals make up ten columns, extending from Group 3B on the left, through 7B and the three columns that together make up Group 8B, and finally to Groups 1B and 2B. Among the transition metals, as atomic number increases, there is an increase in the number of electrons in the second-to-highest energy level. The transition metals exhibit typical metallic properties. In general, they are ductile, malleable, and good conductors of heat and electricity. With the exception of copper and gold, they have a silvery luster.

Table 24.4 lists some important uses of the transition metals. Tungsten, a hard, brittle solid with a melting point of 3400 °C, is used in light-bulb filaments. At the other end of the scale is mercury, with a melting point of −38 °C. Mercury is used in making thermometers. The production of copper wire in enormous quantities attests to the high electrical conductivity of copper. Adding small amounts of cobalt, copper, chromium, nickel, or vanadium to iron makes alloy steels with widely different characteristics.

Figure 24.24

These aqueous solutions contain cations of transition metals. Note that many of the solutions have a distinctive color.

Table 24.4

Common Transition Metals and Their Uses	
Metal	**Uses**
Cadmium (Cd)	Batteries; control rods for nuclear reactors
Chromium (Cr)	Plating; making stainless steel
Cobalt (Co)	Alloys; treatment of cancer (Cobalt-60 only)
Copper (Cu)	Electrical wiring; plumbing; coinage
Gold (Au)	Jewelry; ornaments; standard of wealth
Iron (Fe)	Steel; magnets
Manganese (Mn)	Steel; nonferrous alloys
Mercury (Hg)	Lamps; switches; thermometers; barometers
Nickel (Ni)	Hardening steel; plating; catalyst
Platinum (Pt)	Catalyst; electronics; lab-ware; jewelry
Silver (Ag)	Mirrors; jewelry; photography; coins
Tantalum (Ta)	Surgery; corrosion-resistant equipment
Titanium (Ti)	Combustion chambers for rockets and jets
Tungsten (W)	Filaments for light bulbs; alloys
Vanadium (V)	Shock-resistant steel alloys; catalyst
Zinc (Zn)	Galvanized iron; brass; dry cell batteries

Figure 24.25

Most metals are refined from ores. Those shown here are (clockwise from the top): vanadinite (vanadium), hematite (iron), wulfenite (lead, molybdenum), sphalerite (zinc), galena (lead), and malachite with azurite (copper) in the center.

Your body needs some transition metals to function normally. Iron is required in the production of hemoglobin. Cobalt is part of vitamin B_{12} molecules. Zinc and copper are necessary components of many enzymes.

The transition metals vary greatly in their chemical reactivity. The elements scandium, yttrium, and lanthanum are similar to the Group 1A and 2A metals in that they are easily oxidized on exposure to air and react with water to liberate hydrogen. In contrast, platinum and gold are extremely unreactive and resist oxidation.

Figure 24.26

The transition-metal oxyanions that produced the colored solutions (left) are VO_4^{3-}, $Cr_2O_7^{2-}$, and MnO_4^-, respectively. Because the solid compounds (right) contain transition metal ions, they display a wide range of characteristic colors.

One of the most characteristic chemical properties of the transition metals is the occurrence of multiple oxidation states. **Figure 24.26** on the previous page shows the colorful aqueous solutions of oxyanions of vanadium, chromium, and manganese in their highest oxidation states. In addition to the characteristically colored aqueous solutions, solid compounds of the transition metals also produce a striking range of colors.

d block

4B 6B   2B

Titanium, Chromium, and Zinc

Figure 24.27 shows some uses of the metals titanium, chromium, and zinc. Titanium is an important structural metal. It is strong and corrosion-resistant. Moreover, its density is only about half that of iron. Titanium alloys are used in high-performance aircraft engines and missiles. Each engine of a 747 jetliner contains almost 1500 kg of titanium alloys. Titanium alloys are also used for joint replacements, such as hips and knees, and as screws to repair broken bones. What is an everyday application of titanium? The most familiar and important compound of titanium is its dioxide (TiO_2). Titanium dioxide, or, more correctly, titanium(IV) oxide, is an opaque, white compound used as a pigment in white paint, paper, and other consumer items, such as sunscreen. Titanium is widely distributed in Earth's crust; the major ore is rutile, which is impure TiO_2.

Although relatively rare, chromium has many important uses. It is a hard, brittle metal with a luster. Its extreme resistance to corrosion makes it an ideal coating for iron and steel objects. It retains its bright surface by developing an invisible oxide coating. Chromium is an important ingredient in stainless steel. Typical stainless steel contains about 18% chromium and 8% nickel, with trace amounts of carbon, manganese, and phosphorus. The remaining percentage consists of iron.

Figure 24.27
The transition metals titanium, chromium, and zinc have many important uses. For example, titanium is used in paints and pigments. Chromium is used to produce a shiny, corrosion-resistant coating. Zinc is used to galvanize steel to help prevent rusting.

Like most transition metals, chromium has more than one oxidation state. The most common oxidation states of chromium are +2, +3, and +6. Chromium has an oxidation number of +6 in two polyatomic ions: chromate (CrO_4^{2-}) and dichromate ($Cr_2O_7^{2-}$). All compounds in which chromium is in the +6 oxidation state are powerful oxidizing agents.

Zinc is one of industry's most useful metals. Zinc is obtained from the sulfide ore zinc blend (sphalerite), which is shown in **Figure 24.25** on page 725. Large amounts of zinc are used to produce galvanized steel, which is iron coated with a thin layer of zinc to protect the iron from rusting. Zinc forms the case in dry-cell batteries and is alloyed with copper to form brass.

Iron, Cobalt, and Nickel

Iron, cobalt, and nickel share a number of common properties. Their densities are similar, as are their melting and boiling points. Their most striking physical property, however, is magnetism. Iron is the most strongly magnetic and nickel is the least magnetic of the three metals.

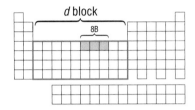

Making up about 5% of Earth's crust, iron is the second-most-abundant metal on Earth. (Aluminum is the most abundant.) Iron is the cheapest metal and, in the form of steel, the most useful. Common iron minerals are Fe_2O_3 (the red oxide hematite) and Fe_3O_4 (magnetite). Millions of tons of iron are produced annually in the United States by the reaction of Fe_2O_3 with coke (pure carbon). This reaction is carried out in a blast furnace, similar to the one shown in **Figure 24.28.** A modern blast furnace produces about 5000 tons of iron daily.

Figure 24.28

A blast furnace is about 30 m high and 10 m in diameter. Iron ore, limestone, and coke (a form of carbon) are added at the top. During the process, carbon, the reducing agent, is oxidized to CO_2. The limestone converts sand in the ore to silicate slag. What is reduced in the blast furnace?

Figure 24.29
The transition metal iron, like cobalt and nickel, is attracted by magnets.

There are two types of steels: carbon steels and alloy steels. Both types actually contain carbon, but carbon steels contain no metal other than iron. About 90% of all steels produced are carbon steels. Carbon steel with less than 0.2% carbon is called mild steel. Mild steel, which is malleable and ductile, is used when load-bearing ability is not important. Medium steels, which contain from 0.2% to 0.6% carbon, are used for structural materials, such as beams and girders. High-carbon steels contain between 0.8% and 1.5% carbon and are used to make drill bits, knives, and other items for which hardness is important.

Alloy steels contain other transition metals in small amounts. Different metals give different properties to the alloy steels. Chromium improves hardness and resistance to corrosion, manganese improves resistance to wear, molybdenum and tungsten increase resistance to heat, nickel adds toughness, and vanadium adds springiness. The wide ranging properties of alloy steels make them useful in many industrial applications.

The alloy steels called stainless steels contain high percentages of chromium and nickel. Stainless steels resist corrosion. What are some uses of stainless steel? The most common stainless steel contains 18% chromium and 8% nickel.

The world's largest nickel and cobalt deposits are in Ontario, Canada. The two metals occur as sulfide ores, together with copper, silver, iron, platinum, palladium, and iridium. Most of the nickel and cobalt produced today is used in the manufacture of steels. Nickel makes steel more ductile and corrosion resistant and adds toughness. Why are these properties essential to steel? One isotope of cobalt, cobalt-60, is radioactive and is used in the treatment of certain cancers.

Unlike iron, nickel and cobalt are resistant to atmospheric corrosion. Nickel is often used to electroplate iron and steel objects before they are plated with chromium. **Monel metal,** a strong, corrosion-resistant alloy of nickel and copper, is used to make the propeller shafts of seagoing vessels. Both cobalt and nickel are used as catalysts in industrial processes. For example, finely divided nickel catalyzes the hydrogenation of vegetable oils in the manufacture of butter substitutes.

Copper, Silver, and Gold

Copper, silver, and gold have low chemical reactivity and often occur naturally in the free state, as shown in **Figure 24.30.** These elements are called the coinage metals and were the first metals collected and worked by humans. In areas of the Middle East, copper and gold artifacts dating to about 7000 B.C. have been found.

Copper occurs occasionally as the free metal and was probably the first metal to be reduced from its naturally occurring ores. Some of the most important copper ores are chalcopyrite ($CuFeS_2$), chalcocite (Cu_2S), and cuprite (Cu_2O). The crushed ores are processed into copper of high purity by reduction and electrolytic refining. Electrolytic refining produces 99.99% pure copper.

Copper is the most widely used metal for electrical wiring. Only silver is a better conductor of electricity. Copper is also widely used in plumbing for pipes that carry hot or cold water. **Figure 24.31** illustrates some applications of copper.

Copper (Cu)

Silver (Ag)

Gold (Au)

Figure 24.30
Shown above are samples of native copper, silver, and gold.

Brass is an alloy of copper with zinc, and bronze is an alloy of copper with tin. Brass and bronze are among the earliest known alloys. Brass usually contains about 35% zinc and has high ductility and strength. It is used for piping, nozzles, marine equipment, ornaments and jewelry. Bronze usually contains about 5% to 10% tin and is very corrosion resistant. It is used for casting, to make marine equipment and spark-resistant tools, and in fine-arts work.

Silver occurs as the free metal and as the sulfide ore argentite (Ag_2S). Most commercial silver is produced as a by-product in the processing of other ores such as copper, lead, and zinc. Silver is recovered from the muddy layers that collect on the bottom of the electrolysis tanks used in copper refining. Because of its high luster, silver reflects light extremely well and has long been used to coat the backs of mirrors. Silver is an excellent conductor of both electricity and heat. Perhaps you have had the painful experience of using a silver spoon to eat hot soup! What are some uses of silver that are familiar to you? The light-sensitive silver halides are also used in photographic processes.

Figure 24.31
Copper is still a common coinage metal, though modern pennies are only copper plated. Copper is also used for crush washers or gaskets that deform under large forces to create tight seals. The colorful patina that forms when copper is exposed to weather makes it useful to artists, architects, and designers.

The Chemistry of Metals and Nonmetals **729**

Figure 24.32

Because of its high luster, metallic silver is used to plate mirrors, such as the ones shown here.

Unfortunately, silver is a metal that tarnishes easily. You have probably seen tarnish and possibly even cleaned it off a variety of silver-plated objects such as knives, forks, spoons, jewelry, and picture frames. Tarnish is black silver sulfide (Ag_2S) that forms on the shiny surface of a silver object as a result of a redox reaction that is a form of corrosion. The reaction involves silver combining with hydrogen sulfide (H_2S) in the air. Is silver oxidized or reduced in the reaction?

Gold has been used for thousands of years to make jewelry and ornate artifacts. The gold mask of the Egyptian King Tutankhamen, shown in **Figure 24.33,** was fashioned in about 1350 B.C. Gold occurs chiefly as small particles of the free metal in veins of quartz. Typically, about 5 grams of gold is produced per metric ton of gold-bearing rock. Gold is also recovered as a by-product of copper refining.

Gold is the most malleable and ductile of all metals and can be pounded into sheets so thin that they transmit light. These thin sheets, called gold leaf, are used in decorative lettering and other forms of ornamentation. Corrosion resistance coupled with high electrical and thermal conductivity make gold valuable in high-technology industries. Gold is used to plate the contacts in microcircuits, also shown in **Figure 24.33,** and to cover the external surfaces of satellite components. Gold alloys are used extensively in dentistry, and certain compounds of gold have useful therapeutic applications; for example, salts of Au^+ are used to treat certain kinds of rheumatoid arthritis. Pure gold is soft and is often alloyed to make it harder. A karat system, based on 24 karat = 100%, is used to express the purity of gold. Pure gold is 24 karat. Coinage gold is 22 karat, or $22/24 \times 100 = 92\%$ gold. White gold, which is used in jewelry, is an alloy of gold, nickel, and other metals. What percentage of gold does 14-karat gold contain?

Figure 24.33

In the past, gold was often used to adorn the burial artifacts of the dead. Gold is now commonly used for the contacts on computer chips and other electronic devices. What properties make gold well-suited for this task?

Lanthanides and Actinides

Below the main body of the periodic table is a row of 14 lanthanides, ranging from cerium (Ce, atomic number 58) through lutetium (Lu, atomic number 71). Below that row is another row consisting of 14 actinides, ranging from thorium (Th, atomic number 90) through lawrencium (Lw, atomic number 103). The lanthanides and actinides are called the **inner transition elements** because their seven inner 4*f* and 5*f* orbitals, respectively, are being filled.

The lanthanides are often called the rare-earth elements because it was once believed that they existed only in small quantities. Actually, they are not rare. For example, the lanthanide cerium (Ce) is about five times more abundant than lead. All the lanthanides are silvery, high-melting (800 °C to 1600 °C) metals. The chemical properties of the inner transition elements are so similar that nineteenth-century chemists had great difficulty in separating the metals individually from their ores. Several of the lanthanide oxides are used for tinting sunglasses and welder's goggles and in the manufacture of high-quality camera lenses.

The actinides are radioactive with similar chemical properties. Except for technetium (Tc, 43) and promethium (Pr, 61), elements up to and including uranium (atomic number 92) occur in nature. Elements with atomic numbers greater than 92 are called transuranium elements. These elements are synthesized in particle accelerators, but usually in very small amounts—in some cases, only a few atoms!

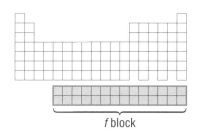

f block

Figure 24.34

Lanthanide oxides are sometimes used to make tinted sunglasses, such as these, as well as certain camera lenses. Compounds of europium and ytterbium are used in the picture tubes of color televisions. High-power lasers use neodymium.

section review 24.3

16. Name five transition metals and describe their properties.

17. Describe the range of chemical diversity shown by the transition metals and inner transition metals.

18. Suggest reasons why copper, silver, and gold are valued for the manufacture of electronic devices. Why is copper preferred to silver and gold for home wiring?

19. What is an ore? What are hematite and magnetite?

20. What are the properties and uses of nickel? Of titanium?

 Chem ASAP! **Assessment 24.3** Check your understanding of the important ideas and concepts in Section 24.3.

HYDROGEN AND NOBLE GASES

objectives
▶ Show how hydrogen is unique among the elements
▶ Explain why the noble gases, Group 0, are important even though they are chemically unreactive

You might expect the fuel used in the main engines of a space shuttle to have a complicated molecular formula that only a rocket scientist would understand. In fact, these engines burn a mixture of hydrogen (the simplest element) and oxygen. **What properties of hydrogen make it so useful as a rocket fuel?**

Hydrogen—A Group by Itself

Hydrogen is the most abundant element in the universe. Free (or elemental) hydrogen is very rare on Earth, but compounds of hydrogen are common. They account for about 1% of Earth's crust. Water is the most abundant hydrogen-containing compound on Earth. Combined with carbon and oxygen, hydrogen is present in all sugars, starches, fats, and proteins. Proteins also contain nitrogen. These complex compounds are abundant in living tissues. Coal, natural gas, and petroleum products, such as gasoline, kerosene, and lubricating oils, also contain hydrogen. **Figure 24.35** shows a wide range of hydrogen-containing items.

Naturally occurring hydrogen and its compounds are composed of three isotopes. The most abundant of the isotopes is protium, commonly referred to simply as hydrogen. Protium (hydrogen-1) and deuterium (hydrogen-2) account for approximately 99.98% and 0.02% of naturally occurring hydrogen samples, respectively. Tritium (hydrogen-3), an unstable (radioactive) form of hydrogen, is present in extremely small amounts.

Hydrogen usually appears at the top of Group 1A in the periodic table. Unlike the true Group 1A elements, however, hydrogen is not a metal nor is it a good conductor of heat or electricity. Like the alkali metals, however, hydrogen does react with the halogens. In some periodic tables, hydrogen appears at the top of Group 7A as well as at the top of Group 1A. There is some justification for placing it in Group 7A because, like the halogens, hydrogen has one fewer valence electron than the noble gas it precedes. Like the halogens, it reacts with the alkali metals and takes on an oxidation number of −1. Thus hydrogen is unique in this regard, behaving like both an alkali metal and a halogen.

Figure 24.35
Hydrogen is seldom found free in nature but is present in a large number of compounds. All of these items contain compounds of hydrogen.

Hydrogen combines directly with a number of metallic and nonmetallic elements. With chlorine, it forms hydrogen chloride (HCl); with calcium, it forms calcium hydride (CaH_2); with nitrogen, it forms ammonia (NH_3). Hydrogen loses its single electron easily. Does this make it a good oxidizing agent or a good reducing agent?

The major use of hydrogen is in the manufacture of ammonia. Large volumes of hydrogen are also used in the conversion of vegetable oils, such as peanut and coconut oil, into solid fats. This process, called hydrogenation, involves treating the oils with hydrogen at high temperature and pressure in the presence of a catalyst. Finely divided nickel or platinum is commonly used. Solid shortenings and margarine are produced in this way. Liquid hydrogen is an important rocket fuel because of its high chemical energy and the fact that it is lightweight. Hydrogen gas was once used to fill lighter-than-air balloons and dirigibles, sometimes with disastrous results, as you can see in **Figure 24.36.** Helium, a nonflammable gas, is now used instead.

The electrolysis of water can produce very pure hydrogen. This method is practical, however, only in small-scale operations. Although the raw material, water, is cheap and plentiful, the cost of the electricity makes the process expensive.

Hydrogen can be prepared commercially from water by the Bosch process. In this method, steam is passed over red-hot iron filings. The iron combines with the oxygen in the steam, and hydrogen gas is liberated.

$$3Fe(s) + 4H_2O(g) \longrightarrow Fe_3O_4(s) + 4H_2(g)$$

More than half of the hydrogen produced in North America is produced by the reaction between steam and natural gas (methane), in a process called steam reforming. Methane reacts with the steam over a finely divided nickel catalyst at 700 °C to 1000 °C.

$$CH_4(g) + H_2O(g) \xrightarrow{\text{catalyst}} CO(g) + 3H_2(g)$$

The carbon monoxide that forms is removed by cooling and compressing the mixture of gases. Hydrogen remains a gas after the carbon monoxide liquefies out of the mixture.

Radon Gas

In the 1970s, the noble gas radon generated concern as an environmental hazard. At first, radon was found in homes built on the tailings of uranium and phosphate mines. Further research has shown that there are measurable amounts of radon in most regions of the United States. The highest radon levels are recorded in regions where the bedrock is granite. Radon is a natural product of the decay of radioactive minerals that contain uranium-238. It seeps through cracks in basement floors, and because it is denser than air, it tends to collect in the lower levels of a house. The danger of radon is that high levels in the lungs may increase the risk of lung cancer. Testing homes for radon can be done easily. High levels of radon are reduced by improved ventilation in basements and in closed areas where it collects.

The Noble Gases

When compared with all other elements, the Group 0 elements helium, neon, argon, krypton, xenon, and radon are extremely unreactive. There-fore, these elements are now called noble gases. This name emphasizes their tendency to exist as separate atoms rather than in combination with other atoms.

The name rare gases was originally used to describe the Group 0 elements because they occur in the atmosphere in only very small amounts. Early chemists also called these elements inert gases because they were thought to be completely unable to combine with other elements. In 1962, however, a Canadian chemist named Neil Bartlett prepared xenon tetra-fluoride (XeF_4), a compound of xenon. Since that time, compounds of krypton, radon, and argon have also been prepared, but scientists have been unable to react helium and neon.

Despite their low reactivity, the noble gases have many uses. Helium is used to fill weather balloons. Both helium and neon are mixed with oxygen for use in artificial atmospheres, such as those required in deep-sea diving. An artificial atmosphere is preferred to air because decompression sickness, or the bends, is less likely to occur than when nitrogen (a more soluble gas) is present. Argon, krypton, and xenon are used to produce the inert atmospheres needed for photographic flashbulbs and aluminum welding. The noble gases are also used to fill gas discharge tubes for neon signs.

Figure 24.37

Underwater research facilities commonly have an artificial atmosphere consisting primarily of oxygen and a noble gas. Noble gases are also used in advertising signs and light bulbs. Why are light bulbs filled with noble gases rather than with air?

MINI LAB

Decomposition of Hydrogen Peroxide

PURPOSE

To prepare and identify a gas evolved during the decomposition of hydrogen peroxide.

MATERIALS

- hydrogen peroxide (3% solution from drugstore)
- manganese dioxide
- toothpicks
- candle
- matches
- test tube
- cork to fit test tube (or plastic film wrap)
- tongs

PROCEDURE

1. Fill a test tube about one-third full with the hydrogen peroxide solution.

2. Using the flat end of a toothpick as a spatula, add a small portion of manganese dioxide to the hydrogen peroxide solution.

3. When the bubbling and foaming have stopped, cork the test tube.

4. Hold a toothpick with tongs and light it from a candle flame. When the toothpick is burning well, blow it out, uncork the test tube, and plunge the glowing end of the toothpick into the gas above the liquid in the test tube.

ANALYSIS AND CONCLUSIONS

1. What happened to the glowing toothpick when it was plunged into the gas above the liquid in the test tube?

2. What must be the gas that is released from the hydrogen peroxide solution? Write an equation for this decomposition of hydrogen peroxide.

3. Does the manganese dioxide undergo any apparent change during the reaction?

4. What is the role of manganese dioxide in the decomposition reaction?

---

section review 24.4

21. In what sense is hydrogen unique among the elements?

22. Why are the noble gases important to industry despite their chemical unreactivity?

23. What are the names, atomic symbols, and mass numbers of the isotopes of hydrogen?

24. The elements in Group 0 have been called rare, inert, and noble. Explain the origin of each of these terms. Are any of these terms misleading based on what you know?

25. What is the largest industrial use of hydrogen? Write an equation for the preparation of hydrogen by the Bosch process.

26. Describe what happens to hydrogen when it combines with chlorine. With calcium. With nitrogen. What common compounds are formed in these reactions?

27. Name an advantage and a disadvantage of producing hydrogen through electrolysis of water.

 ChemASAP! Assessment 24.4 Check your understanding of the important ideas and concepts in Section 24.4.

Chemistry Serving...Industry

DIAMONDS ARE AN ENGINEER'S BEST FRIEND

Diamond—one of the three allotropes of carbon—is the hardest material known. This property makes it extremely valuable for certain industrial applications, such as cutting, grinding, or shaping other materials. Naturally occurring diamond, however, is rare and very costly. It is formed hundreds of kilometers beneath Earth's surface under conditions of extreme temperature and pressure. Only chance geologic events bring it close enough to the surface to be mined.

Fortunately, scientists have discovered ways of producing synthetic diamond. This material, chemically identical to natural diamond, is used in industry more extensively than natural diamond is.

In one sense, creating synthetic diamond is simple because diamond is made of only carbon, and carbon is extremely easy to obtain. In practice, however, getting carbon atoms to arrange themselves in the tightly packed tetrahedral arrangement of diamond is very difficult.

Thermodynamically, graphite is favored over diamond. If diamond is heated in the absence of air to 1200 °C, its very stable sp^3 bonds will be broken and rearranged into the sp^2 bonds of graphite. To reverse this reaction—or to make diamond from graphite—even higher temperatures and very high pressures are required.

The first attempt to create the necessary conditions for forming diamond from graphite was a failure. Researchers created a chamber that could maintain a pressure of 1.5 million pounds per square inch and a temperature of 2500 °C. This temperature, however, was not high enough to melt the graphite.

Then the researchers tried another approach: They added small amounts of a metal with a melting point below 2500 °C. The graphite dissolved in the molten metal and then crystallized out as diamond. The

Diamond's hardness makes it extremely valuable for certain industrial applications, such as cutting, grinding, or shaping other materials.

diamond crystals were only about 1 mm in size, but they were as hard as natural diamonds. Today, this high-pressure, high-temperature (HPHT) method is still used to make large quantities of synthetic diamond, mostly for use as industrial abrasives.

After the first synthetic diamonds were created, researchers explored other ways of growing diamonds. One method that has become very important in industry involves using carbon vapor to grow films of diamond. The carbon can come from various sources, including methane (CH_4) or graphite. The carbon is vaporized with intense heat or with the energy from microwaves, laser beams, or electric discharges. The vaporized carbon is then deposited as an ice-like film on diamond "seeds" or on other substances such as quartz or silicon.

Diamond films have many uses. A diamond coating can make a lens durable and scratch-proof. Cutting tools coated with diamond never need sharpening. Diamond's unmatched ability to conduct heat also makes diamond films useful in many other applications, such as in the manufacture of extremely fast computer chips.

Natural diamonds may always be consumers' choice for adornment, but synthetic diamonds are the preference of industry.

CHEMISTRY IN CAREERS

☆☆☆☆☆☆☆☆☆☆☆☆☆☆☆☆☆☆☆☆

GEMOLOGIST
Grade the quality of valuable gems using your knowledge of crystal structure.
See page 879.

CHEMIST NEEDED
Enviro Lab GC Must know

TAKE IT TO THE NET

Find out more about career opportunities:
www.phschool.com

CHEMICAL SPECIALIST
Local food service distributor seeks responsible self-motivated individ-

Take It to the NET
For interactive study and review, go to www.phschool.com

KEY TERMS

▸ inner transition element *p. 731*
▸ lime *p. 710*

▸ metallurgy *p. 724*
▸ Monel metal *p. 728*

▸ ore *p. 724*
▸ slaked lime *p. 710*

KEY EQUATIONS

▸ Preparation of sulfuric acid:
$$2SO_2(g) + O_2(g) \xrightleftharpoons{catalyst} 2SO_3(g)$$
$$SO_3(g) + H_2O(l) \longrightarrow H_2SO_4(aq)$$

▸ Bosch process:
$$3Fe(s) + 4H_2O(g) \longrightarrow Fe_3O_4(s) + 4H_2(g)$$

▸ Haber-Bosch process:
$$N_2(g) + 3H_2(g) \xrightleftharpoons{Fe} 2NH_3(g)$$

CONCEPT SUMMARY

24.1 The *s*-Block Elements: Active Metals

• The alkali and alkaline earth metals have low ionization energies and high reactivities.
• Metallic sodium is produced by electrolysis. It is used in sodium vapor lamps and in the production of many chemicals.
• Calcium is produced by electrolysis. Calcium oxide, or lime, is an industrial chemical.
• Magnesium is produced from sea water. It is an important structural material.

24.2 The *p*-Block Elements: Metals and Nonmetals

• Aluminum is the most abundant metal in Earth's crust. It is not found as a free metal. Its value in industry derives from its corrosion resistance and high electrical conductivity.
• Carbon and silicon are the basic elements of life and minerals, respectively. Tin and lead have numerous uses as both free metals and in alloys such as bronze and solder.
• Nitrogen exists as N_2. It makes up 80% of the air by volume. Two important nitrogen compounds are ammonia and nitric acid.
• Oxygen is the most abundant element in Earth's crust. It exists in the atmosphere mainly as O_2.

• Sulfur readily forms compounds with most metals and nonmetals. Sulfuric acid is an important industrial chemical.
• The halogens exist in nature as halide ions found in sea water and salt beds.

24.3 The *d*- and *f*-Block Elements: Transition and Inner Transition Metals

• Many transition metals are used to make alloys. Monel metal is a corrosion-resistant alloy of copper and nickel. Copper, silver, and gold are excellent conductors.
• The lanthanides and actinides are the inner transition metals. The lanthanides are silvery, high-melting metals. The actinides are radioactive.

24.4 Hydrogen and Noble Gases

• Free hydrogen is rare on Earth. The three isotopes of hydrogen are protium, deuterium, and tritium. Hydrogen is used as a reducing agent, in ammonia production, and in the hydrogenation of vegetable oils.
• The noble gases are chemically unreactive. They are used in weather balloons, artificial atmospheres, and gas discharge tubes.

CHAPTER CONCEPT MAP

Use these terms to construct a concept map that organizes the major ideas of this chapter.

 Chem ASAP! **Concept Map 24**
Create your Concept Map using the computer.

alkali metal

halogen

Group 5A

Group 3A

Group 4A

alkaline earth metal

Group 6A

noble gas

CONCEPT PRACTICE

28. When sodium is exposed to oxygen, it forms a peroxide. A solution of sodium hydroxide can be obtained by adding sodium to water. Write balanced equations for these two reactions. *24.1*

29. What are the group names for the elements in Group 1A and Group 2A? *24.1*

30. What is lime? How is lime made from calcium carbonate ($CaCO_3$)? *24.1*

31. Why do the alkaline-earth metals as a group have higher densities than the alkali metals? *24.1*

32. Give the equations for two reactions by which $Ca(OH)_2$ can be made. *24.1*

33. Name an aluminum ore rich in Al_2O_3. *24.2*

34. Describe the physical properties of aluminum that make it a commercially valuable metal. *24.2*

35. Name the three allotropes of carbon. *24.2*

36. Give four physical properties of ammonia. *24.2*

37. What are three uses of nitric acid? *24.2*

38. What are two forms of elemental phosphorus? How do they differ in their reactivity with oxygen? *24.2*

39. Why is atmospheric nitrogen not directly useful to plants? What makes it possible for nitrogen to be used by plants? *24.2*

40. List major uses of ammonia in industry. *24.2*

41. What are the three conditions of the Haber-Bosch process that make the commercial production of ammonia possible? *24.2*

42. Give the names and formulas of two nitrogen-containing substances used as fertilizers. *24.2*

43. Name at least one industrial use of each. *24.2*
    a. oxygen   **b.** sulfur   **c.** selenium

44. Give three physical properties of each of the following substances. *24.2*
    a. oxygen   **b.** ozone   **c.** sulfur

45. List some uses of hydrogen peroxide. *24.2*

46. In what three major forms is oxygen present on Earth? *24.2*

47. What is the volume percentage of oxygen in Earth's atmosphere? *24.2*

48. Explain paramagnetism. Use liquid oxygen as your example. *24.2*

49. What is the largest industrial use of oxygen? *24.2*

50. Where is ozone produced naturally? *24.2*

51. Complete and balance these equations. *24.2*
    a. $Mg(s) + O_2(g) \longrightarrow$
    b. $H_2(g) + O_2(g) \longrightarrow$
    c. $S(s) + O_2(g) \longrightarrow$

52. Describe the common allotrope of sulfur that is stable at room temperature. *24.2*

53. What are some uses of sulfur? *24.2*

54. Give the names and molecular formulas of the halogens. *24.2*

55. Why is chlorine added to drinking water and swimming pools? *24.2*

56. How is chlorine gas normally prepared for commercial use? *24.2*

57. Describe how iodine is obtained commercially. *24.2*

58. What process is used to make fluorine? *24.2*

59. Give colors and physical states at STP of chlorine, bromine, and iodine. *24.2*

60. Write formulas for the oxides of iron. *24.3*

61. Nickel is an important metal. Why? What is Monel metal? *24.3*

62. Copper, silver, and gold are among the few metals that have been used for thousands of years. Explain why. *24.3*

63. Reduction—not oxidation—is required to convert the metal in a compound to the free metal. Why? *24.3*

64. Name three practical uses of various noble gases. *24.4*

65. Explain how superheated water and compressed air are used in sulfur recovery by the Frasch process. What conditions prevent sulfur from being mined in the same way coal is? *24.4*

66. Large volumes of hydrogen are used in the hydrogenation of vegetable oils. Describe the process, and comment on its commercial value. *24.4*

CONCEPT MASTERY

67. Calculate the mass percent of aluminum in cryolite (Na_3AlF_6).

68. At which electrode is the free metal produced in the electrolysis of a metal compound? Explain your answer.

69. The following data table shows the quantities of iron ore (Fe_2O_3) and coke (C) that react in a blast furnace to produce pig iron.

Mass of Fe_2O_3 (kg)	Amount of Fe_2O_3 (mol)	Mass of C (kg)	Amount of C (mol)
8.65×10^4		1.95×10^4	
1.26×10^5		2.84×10^4	
2.01×10^5		4.54×10^4	
6.56×10^5		1.48×10^5	
9.61×10^5		2.17×10^5	

a. Complete the table.
b. Plot moles of iron ore (y-axis) versus moles of carbon (x-axis).
c. From the slope of the line, determine the mole ratio by which iron reacts with carbon in a blast furnace.

70. A commercially important source of titanium is ilmenite ($FeTiO_3$). Calculate the percent by mass of titanium in ilmenite.

71. Calculate the percent by mass of cobalt in cobaltite (CoAsS). How many kilograms of cobalt would be contained in 1.00×10^3 kg of an ore containing 72.6% CoAsS by mass.

72. Describe the process used to obtain aluminum from its natural source.

73. Name the two allotropic forms of the element oxygen. Describe one method of preparation for each.

74. Distinguish between oxygen and ozone.

75. Write a balanced equation for the reaction of hydrogen with these elements.
a. nitrogen   **b.** chlorine   **c.** calcium

76. List the halogens in order of increasing electronegativity.

77. List some of the major uses of sulfuric acid.

78. The following data table lists the melting and boiling points of the halogens.

Element	Melting point (°C)	Boiling point (°C)
F	−219	−188
Cl	−107	−34
Br	−7	58
I	113	184

a. Describe the trends you observe.
b. Explain these trends. Are they likely to occur with other groups in the periodic table?

79. Explain why ammonia exhibits many waterlike properties.

80. Name a nonmetallic oxide that reacts with water to form a base and a metallic oxide that reacts with water to form an acid. Write a balanced equation for each reaction.

CRITICAL THINKING

81. Choose the term that best completes the second relationship.
a. sister : brother
beryllium : _____
(1) cesium   (3) barium
(2) lead   (4) sodium
b. protium : deuterium
nitrogen-14 : _____
(1) isotope   (3) carbon-14
(2) tritium   (4) nitrogen-15

82. Hydrogen and helium are by far the most abundant elements in the universe. Why are helium and the free, or elemental, form of hydrogen very rare on Earth?

83. Compare the methods used to produce hydrogen. What are the disadvantages of each for producing hydrogen as a fuel?

84. What advantage does the recycling of aluminum have over the production of aluminum from its minerals?

85. The period of human history called the Bronze Age began about 3000 B.C. and was followed by the Iron Age. Why was bronze widely used for tools and weapons before iron?

86. The histogram below classifies chlorides of Pb, Cu, Co, Ni, Mn, Ca, and Fe by percent chloride composition. Give the chemical formula for each compound shown.

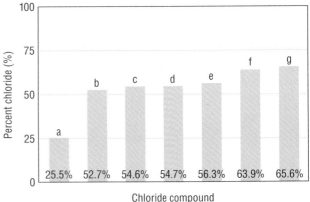

The Chemistry of Metals and Nonmetals   **739**

87. Write the formula of each compound.
    a. calcium oxide
    b. mercury(II) oxide
    c. carbon monoxide
    d. aluminum oxide
    e. sulfur dioxide
    f. sodium peroxide

88. Calculate the mass percent of iron in each mineral compound.
    a. Fe_3O_4 b. Fe_2O_3

89. Write complete electron configurations for each.
    a. Fe   c. Ag   e. Cu   g. Zn
    b. V   d. Fe^{3+} f. Ni^{2+} h. Ag^+

90. A sample of spring water contains 46.0 mg of magnesium ions per liter.
    a. What is the molarity of Mg^{2+} in the sample?
    b. What volume of this water contains 1.00 mol Mg^{2+}?

91. What ions are produced when each substance is dissolved in water?
    a. LiBr   b. $Ca(OH)_2$ c. KI   d. $CdBr_2$

92. Classify each compound as a nonelectrolyte, a weak electrolyte, or a strong electrolyte.
    a. CH_3COCH_3 (acetone)   d. KNO_3
    b. C_2H_5OH (ethyl alcohol)   e. Na_2SO_4
    c. CH_3COOH (acetic acid)   f. $CaCl_2$

93. Determine the oxidation number of nitrogen in each.
    a. N_2 b. NO_3^- c. NO_2 d. N_2O e. NO_2^-

94. Identify the oxidizing agent and the reducing agent in the following reaction.
$$I_2O_5(s) + 5CO(g) \longrightarrow 5CO_2(g) + I_2(s)$$

95. Calcium carbonate is used as an antacid to neutralize HCl in the stomach. Write the equation for the neutralization reaction.

CONCEPT CHALLENGE

96. Calculate the mass, in kilograms, of sulfur dioxide produced in the roasting of 1000 kg of chalcocite ore containing 7.2% Cu_2S, 0.6% Ag_2S, and no other sulfur compounds.

97. A 0.50-g sample of metallic sodium is converted to NaCl by reaction with chlorine gas. What volume of Cl_2 at 20 °C and 98.6 kPa will be required to react completely with the sodium?

98. Azurite, a dark-blue copper mineral, has the following composition: Cu 55.3%, C 6.97%, O 37.1%, H 0.585%. Determine the simplest formula of this mineral.

99. Use this equation to answer the questions.
$$Mg(OH)_2 + 2HCl \longrightarrow MgCl_2 + 2H_2O$$
    a. How many moles of H^+ are required to react with 3.20 g $Mg(OH)_2$?
    b. What volume of 3.00M HCl is required to react with 3.20 g $Mg(OH)_2$?

100. Barium peroxide decomposes above 700 °C, according to this equation.
$$2BaO_2(s) \longrightarrow 2BaO(s) + O_2(g)$$
The oxygen liberated when 20.0 g of barium peroxide is heated is collected in a 1-L flask at 25 °C. Calculate the pressure in the flask.

101. How many kilograms of Br^- are in a cubic mile of sea water?

102. What mass of sulfur dioxide is produced when 2.00×10^2 g of sulfur is burned in oxygen?

103. Hydrogen peroxide decomposes according to the equation:
$$2H_2O_2(l) \longrightarrow 2H_2O(l) + O_2(g)$$
A solution is 3.00% H_2O_2 by volume. The density of H_2O_2 is 1.44 g/cm^3. How many liters of oxygen gas, measured at STP, are produced when 1 L of 3.00% H_2O_2 is decomposed?

104. In the following graph, the SO_2 emissions of coal-burning electric plants in a recent year are shown to vary according to generating capacity and plant age. In the year shown, all coal-burning electric plants emitted approximately 13 million tons of SO_2.

    a. What are the three types of plants with the largest SO_2 emissions?
    b. Approximately what percent of the year's emissions were due to the three types of plants identified in question a?

Select the choice that best answers each question or completes each statement.

1. The *s*-block elements are the
   a. halogens and noble gases.
   b. alkali metals and alkaline earth metals.
   c. alkaline earth metals and transition metals.
   d. transition metals and inner transition metals.

2. Which of these metals would react most vigorously with water?
   a. aluminum   c. cesium
   b. zirconium   d. magnesium

3. The most reactive nonmetallic element is
   a. helium.   c. chlorine.
   b. oxygen.   d. fluorine.

4. Variations in ionic charge are found in the
   a. noble gases.
   b. transition metals.
   c. alkali metals.
   d. alkaline earth metals.

5. The elements known for their limited chemical reactivity are the
   a. inner transition metals.
   b. halogens.
   c. noble gases.
   d. *d*-block elements.

6. An allotrope of which element protects Earth from ultraviolet radiation?
   a. oxygen   c. sulfur
   b. carbon   d. helium

Questions 7–9 describe three different elements labeled X, Y, and Z, respectively. Use the descriptions to identify the elements.

7. Element X has several allotropes. Herman Frasch devised a method for mining underground deposits of element X. An oxide of element X reacts to produce an acid used in almost every industry.

8. Element Y often is found uncombined in nature. It is an excellent conductor of both electricity and heat. Element Y darkens when it reacts with hydrogen sulfide gas. Light-sensitive halides of element Y are used to coat photographic film.

9. Element Z is the second most abundant element in Earth's crust. It is an insulator at low temperatures and a conductor at high temperatures. A highly pure form of element Z is used to make computer chips.

The lettered choices below refer to questions 10–13. A lettered choice may be used once, more than once, or not at all.
   (A) alkaline earth metal
   (B) noble gas
   (C) halogen
   (D) transition metal
   (E) alkali metal

Which of the above element types describes each of the following elements?

10. potassium

11. iodine

12. xenon

13. molybdenum

Use the atomic windows to answer question 14.

14. Ammonia is produced by the Haber-Bosch process. The overall equation is
$$N_2(g) + 3H_2(g) \longrightarrow 2NH_3(g)$$
Which of the windows shows the correct result when 3 molecules of nitrogen react with 11 molecules of hydrogen?

Methane gas (CH₄) reacts with steam at a high temperature to produce carbon monoxide gas and hydrogen gas. Use this information to answer questions 15 and 16.

15. Write a balanced equation for the reaction.

16. *You Draw It!* Using the equation from question 15 and the symbols provided below, draw the atomic window that shows the result of reacting 2 molecules of methane with 3 molecules of steam.

$$CH_4 \quad + \quad H_2O \quad \longrightarrow \quad CO \quad + \quad H_2$$

HYDROCARBON COMPOUNDS

FEATURES

DISCOVER IT!
What Dissolves What?

SMALL-SCALE LAB
Hydrocarbon Isomers

MINI LAB
Structural Isomers of Heptane

CHEMISTRY SERVING ...
THE CONSUMER
A Number You Can't Knock

CHEMISTRY IN CAREERS
Organic Chemist

LINK TO ECOLOGY
Oil Spills

Stay current with **SCIENCE NEWS**
Find out more about hydrocarbons:
www.phschool.com

This painting shows Saturn's moon, Titan, as a place to refuel in space.

DISCOVER IT! WHAT DISSOLVES WHAT?

You need candle wax, vegetable oil, petroleum jelly, rubbing alcohol, mineral oil, water, three saucers, and nine toothpicks.

1. Place 3 pea-sized portions of petroleum jelly 10 cm apart on a saucer.

2. Add 5 drops of rubbing alcohol to one portion of the petroleum jelly, 5 drops of mineral oil to another, and 5 drops of water to the third.

3. Use a clean toothpick to mix each as completely as possible. Observe whether the substances appear to dissolve.

4. On a second saucer, repeat steps 1 through 3 using pea-sized portions of candle wax.

5. On a third saucer, repeat steps 1 through 3 using pea-sized portions of vegetable oil.

How did the solubility of these three materials (petroleum jelly, candle wax, and vegetable oil) in water compare with their solubility in mineral oil? Was the solubility of these substances in rubbing alcohol more like that in water or in mineral oil? Use your observations to develop a statement about solubility trends (similarities and differences). When you have completed the chapter, return to your statement to see if it is correct.

HYDROCARBONS

*P*eople use fuels such as gasoline and diesel fuel every day—in cars and trucks, trains, airplanes and lawnmowers, and many other machines. These fuels and others contain a mixture of many compounds called hydrocarbons. **What are hydrocarbons, and why are there so many compounds?**

objectives
▶ Describe the bonding in hydrocarbons
▶ Distinguish between straight-chain and branched-chain alkanes

key terms
▶ hydrocarbons
▶ alkanes
▶ straight-chain alkanes
▶ homologous series
▶ condensed structural formulas
▶ substituent
▶ alkyl group
▶ branched-chain alkane

Organic Chemistry and Hydrocarbons

Fewer than 200 years ago, it was thought that the carbon compounds found in nature could be synthesized, or built, only by living organisms. From the word *organism* came the classification of these carbon compounds as organic and the chemistry of carbon compounds as organic chemistry. The prevailing theory held that the formation of carbon compounds was directed by a mysterious vital force. The German chemist Friedrich Wöhler (1800–1882) refuted this theory in 1828 when he synthesized urea from inorganic materials. Urea is a carbon-containing compound found in urine.

Today, organic chemistry includes the chemistry of virtually all carbon compounds, regardless of their origin. Carbon compounds number more than a million, with a dazzling array of valuable properties. One of the reasons carbon compounds are so numerous is carbon's unique bonding ability. Your study of organic chemistry starts with the simplest organic compounds, the hydrocarbons.

Organic compounds that contain only carbon and hydrogen are called **hydrocarbons.** The simplest hydrocarbons are the **alkanes,** which contain only single covalent bonds. Methane is the simplest alkane. It is the major component of natural gas. Methane is sometimes called marsh gas because it is formed by the action of bacteria on decaying vegetation in swamps and other marshy areas. Livestock and termites also emit substantial quantities of methane.

Chem ASAP!

Animation 28
Get a glimpse of the staggering variety of hydrocarbon compounds.

Figure 25.1

Bacteria feeding on decaying vegetation produce methane. Termites produce methane as a byproduct of digestion. Methane is the main component of natural gas, used for cooking and heating.

The methane molecule, which consists of four hydrogen atoms and one carbon atom, is a good example of carbon–hydrogen bonding. As you will recall (or a glance at the periodic table will remind you), a carbon atom has four valence electrons. Four hydrogen atoms, each with one valence electron, form four covalent carbon–hydrogen bonds. This combination is a molecule of methane.

$$\dot{\underset{\displaystyle \cdot}{C}}\cdot \; + \; 4H\cdot \; \longrightarrow \; H\!:\!\!\overset{\displaystyle H}{\underset{\displaystyle H}{\ddot{C}}}\!\!:\!H$$

Carbon   Hydrogen   Methane
atom   atoms   molecule

The carbon–hydrogen bonding in methane illustrates an important principle: Because a carbon atom contains four valence electrons, it always forms four covalent bonds. Remembering this principle will help you to write complete and correct structures for organic molecules.

For simplicity, the structural formulas you learned to write in Chapter 16 will be used here to represent organic molecules. Remember, the line between the atomic symbols represents two bonding electrons.

$$\begin{array}{c} H \\ | \\ H - C - H \\ | \\ H \end{array}$$

Line represents
shared electron pair

Methane
molecule

Structural formulas are convenient to write on a page, but keep in mind that they are only two-dimensional representations of three-dimensional molecules. Molecular models represent the shapes of molecules more accurately. Throughout this chapter and the next, ball-and-stick molecular models and space-filling molecular models will be used with structural formulas to represent the shapes of organic molecules more accurately. These shapes are predicted by VSEPR theory and hybrid orbital theory. For example, methane has a tetrahedral shape shown in **Figure 25.2.**

Figure 25.2

The tetrahedral shape of the methane molecule is illustrated in the ball-and-stick model (a) and the space-filling model (b).

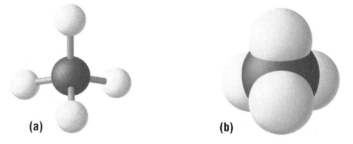

(a)   (b)

Carbon has the unique ability to make stable carbon–carbon bonds and to form chains. This is the major reason for the vast number of organic molecules. Silicon also forms chains, but they are unstable in an oxygen environment.

Ethane (C_2H_6) is the simplest alkane containing a carbon–carbon bond. Similar to methane, ethane is a gas at standard temperature and pressure. When ethane is formed from carbon and hydrogen, two carbon atoms share a pair of electrons. A carbon–carbon covalent bond is formed. The remaining six valence electrons form bonding pairs with the electrons from six hydrogen atoms.

$$2 \cdot \dot{C} \cdot + 6H \cdot \longrightarrow \cdot \dot{C} - \dot{C} \cdot + 6H \cdot \longrightarrow H - \underset{\underset{H}{|}}{\overset{\overset{H}{|}}{C}} - \underset{\underset{H}{|}}{\overset{\overset{H}{|}}{C}} - H$$

Carbon Hydrogen
atoms   atoms

Ethane
molecule

(a)

(b)

Figure 25.3
A ball-and-stick model (a) and a space-filling model (b) of ethane.

Straight-Chain Alkanes

Straight-chain alkanes contain any number of carbon atoms, one after the other, in a chain. To draw a structural formula for a straight-chain alkane, write the symbol for carbon as many times as necessary to get the proper chain length. Then fill in with hydrogens and lines representing covalent bonds. Remember that carbon forms four covalent bonds. **Table 25.1** shows the straight-chain alkanes containing up to ten carbons. Note that the names of alkanes always end with *-ane*. According to **Table 25.1**, what is the name of the straight-chain alkane with six carbons? Eight carbons? How many carbons does butane have?

The straight-chain alkanes are an example of a homologous series. A group of compounds forms a **homologous series** if there is a constant increment of change in molecular structure from one compound in the series to the next. The $-CH_2-$ group is the increment of change in straight-chain alkanes. This change can be traced in the structural formulas in **Table 25.1**.

Table 25.1

The First Ten Straight-Chain Alkanes			
Name	**Molecular formula**	**Structural formula**	**Boiling point (°C)**
Methane	CH_4	CH_4	−161.0
Ethane	C_2H_6	CH_3CH_3	−88.5
Propane	C_3H_8	$CH_3CH_2CH_3$	−42.0
Butane	C_4H_{10}	$CH_3CH_2CH_2CH_3$	0.5
Pentane	C_5H_{12}	$CH_3CH_2CH_2CH_2CH_3$	36.0
Hexane	C_6H_{14}	$CH_3CH_2CH_2CH_2CH_2CH_3$	68.7
Heptane	C_7H_{16}	$CH_3CH_2CH_2CH_2CH_2CH_2CH_3$	98.5
Octane	C_8H_{18}	$CH_3CH_2CH_2CH_2CH_2CH_2CH_2CH_3$	125.6
Nonane	C_9H_{20}	$CH_3CH_2CH_2CH_2CH_2CH_2CH_2CH_2CH_3$	150.7
Decane	$C_{10}H_{22}$	$CH_3CH_2CH_2CH_2CH_2CH_2CH_2CH_2CH_2CH_3$	174.1

Butane

Propane

Figure 25.4

Pressurized tanks of propane are used to fuel the burners in hot-air balloons. Butane serves as the fuel for many lighters.

Figure 25.4 shows some common uses for these two hydrocarbons. As the number of carbons in the straight-chain alkanes increases, so does the boiling point. This is also true of the melting point.

Complete structural formulas show all the atoms and bonds in a molecule. Sometimes, however, shorthand or condensed structural formulas work just as well. **Condensed structural formulas** leave out some bonds and/or atoms from the structural formula. Although they do not appear, you must understand that these bonds and atoms are there. The following illustrates several ways to draw condensed structural formulas for butane.

C_4H_{10}	Molecular formula
(complete structural formula of butane with H—C—C—C—C—H and H atoms)	Complete structural formula
$CH_3 - CH_2 - CH_2 - CH_3$	Condensed structural formula; C—H bonds understood
$CH_3CH_2CH_2CH_3$	Condensed structural formula; C—H and —C—C— bonds understood
$CH_3(CH_2)_2CH_3$ Methylene units — Subscript	Condensed structural formula; all bonds understood; parentheses indicate CH_2 units are linked together in a continuous chain (the —CH_2— unit is called a methylene group); subscript 2 to the right of parenthesis indicates there are two methylene units linked together
$C - C - C - C$	Carbon skeleton; all hydrogens and C—H bonds understood

The names of the straight-chain alkanes listed in **Table 25.1** are recommended by the International Union of Pure and Applied Chemistry (IUPAC). As you can see, all the names end with the suffix *-ane*. The root part of an

Sample Problem 25-1

Draw complete structural formulas for the straight-chain alkanes that have three and four carbons.

1. **ANALYZE** *Plan a problem-solving strategy.*

   Apply the rules for carbon–hydrogen and carbon–carbon bonding. Because these are straight-chain alkanes, the appropriate number of carbons will be written in a straight line and then connected to each other by single bonds. The chain will then be filled in with hydrogen atoms so that each carbon forms four covalent bonds.

2. **SOLVE** *Apply the problem-solving strategy.*

   A three-carbon straight-chain alkane has three carbon atoms connected to each other in a straight line. This gives the center carbon two covalent bonds, so it needs two hydrogen atoms bonded to it. The two end carbons each need three hydrogen atoms bonded to them. A four-carbon straight-chain alkane has four carbon atoms connected to each other in a straight line. The two center carbons each need two hydrogen atoms, and the two end carbons each need three hydrogen atoms to give each carbon atom four single covalent bonds. The correct structural formulas are shown below.

$$
\begin{array}{cccc}
 & H & H & H \\
 & | & | & | \\
H- & C- & C- & C-H \\
 & | & | & | \\
 & H & H & H
\end{array}
\qquad
\begin{array}{ccccc}
 & H & H & H & H \\
 & | & | & | & | \\
H- & C- & C- & C- & C-H \\
 & | & | & | & | \\
 & H & H & H & H
\end{array}
$$

3. **EVALUATE** *Do the results make sense?*

   The carbon chains have three and four carbons. Each carbon atom forms a total of four single covalent bonds with carbon and hydrogen atoms.

Practice Problems

1. Draw complete structural formulas for the straight-chain alkanes with five and six carbons.
2. How many single bonds are in a propane molecule?

alkane's name indicates how many carbon atoms it contains. For example, *meth-* means one carbon atom, *prop-* means three carbon atoms, *pent-* means five carbon atoms, and *dec-* means ten carbon atoms. You may find it helpful to learn these names now. They are the basis of a precise, internationally accepted system of naming organic compounds called the IUPAC system. As precise as the IUPAC system is, however, organic chemists still rely on a combination of systematic, semisystematic, and common names to identify organic compounds.

Many organic compounds are best known by their common names. Although these names bear no relation to IUPAC names or to the molecular structure of the compounds, they have been used for a long time. In most instances, common names are simpler than IUPAC names, which can be long and cumbersome. Like any living language, the language of science is constantly changing. IUPAC, semisystematic, and common names are used in this textbook.

Figure 25.5
Many organic compounds isolated from nature have common names that reflect their origins. For example, penicillin, a common antibiotic, is named for the mold it is derived from, Penicillium notatum (shown here).

Hydrocarbon Compounds **747**

Branched-Chain Alkanes

Hydrogen atoms are not the only atoms that can bond to the carbon atoms in a hydrocarbon. The halogens and groups of atoms including carbon, hydrogen, oxygen, nitrogen, sulfur, or phosphorus may take the place of a hydrogen atom. An atom or group of atoms that can take the place of a hydrogen atom on a parent hydrocarbon molecule is called a **substituent.**

$$\text{Substituent} \quad \text{Substituents}$$

$$
\begin{array}{ccc}
& C & \\
& | & \\
C - C - C & \\
\text{Parent alkane (propane)} &
\end{array}
\qquad
\begin{array}{ccccc}
C & C & C & & \\
| & | & | & & \\
C - C - C - C - C - C & & & \\
\text{Parent alkane (hexane)} & & &
\end{array}
$$

A hydrocarbon substituent is called an **alkyl group.** An alkyl group can be one carbon or several carbons long. Three common alkyl groups are the methyl group (CH_3—), the ethyl group (CH_3CH_2—), and the propyl group ($CH_3CH_2CH_2$—). As you can see, an alkyl group consists of an alkane with one hydrogen removed. Alkyl groups are sometimes referred to as radicals. They are named by removing the -*ane* ending from the parent hydrocarbon name and adding -*yl*. What is the name of the alkyl group with the formula $CH_3CH_2CH_2CH_2CH_2$—?

When a substituent alkyl group is added to a straight-chain hydrocarbon, branches are formed. An alkane with one or more alkyl groups is called a **branched-chain alkane.** The IUPAC rules for naming branched-chain alkanes are quite straightforward. The following compound can be used as an example.

$$
\begin{array}{ccccccc}
7 & 6 & 5 & 4 & 3 & 2 & 1 \\
CH_3 - & CH_2 - & CH_2 - & CH - & CH - & CH - & CH_3 \\
& & & | & | & | & \\
& & & CH_2 & CH_3 & CH_3 & \\
& & & | & & & \\
& & & CH_3 & & &
\end{array}
$$

1. Find the longest chain of carbons in the molecule. This chain is considered the parent structure. In the example, the longest chain contains seven carbon atoms. Therefore, the parent hydrocarbon structure is heptane.

2. Number the carbons in the main chain in sequence. To do this, start at the end that will give the groups attached to the chain the smallest numbers. This has already been done in the example. As you can see, the numbers go from right to left, which places the substituent groups at carbon atoms 2, 3, and 4. If the chain were numbered from left to right, the groups would be at positions 4, 5, and 6. These are higher numbers and therefore violate the rule.

3. Add numbers to the names of the substituent groups to identify their positions on the chain. These numbers become prefixes to the name of the parent alkane. In this example the substituents and positions are 2-methyl, 3-methyl, and 4-ethyl.

4. Use prefixes to indicate the appearance of a group more than once in the structure. Common prefixes are *di-* (twice), *tri-* (three times), *tetra-*

(four times), and *penta-* (five times). This example has two methyl substituents. Thus the word *dimethyl* will be part of the complete name.

5. List the names of alkyl substituents in alphabetical order. For purposes of alphabetizing, ignore the prefixes *di-, tri-,* and so on. In this example, the 4-ethyl group is listed before the 2-methyl and 3-methyl groups (which are combined as 2,3-dimethyl in the name).

6. Use proper punctuation. This is very important in writing the names of organic compounds in the IUPAC system. Commas are used to separate numbers. Hyphens are used to separate numbers and words. The entire name is written without any spaces.

According to the IUPAC rules, the name of this compound is 4-ethyl-2,3-dimethylheptane. Note that the name of the parent alkane, heptane, follows directly after the final prefix, dimethyl. (4-ethyl-2,3-dimethyl heptane would be incorrect.) A ball-and-stick model and a space-filling model of this compound are shown in **Figure 25.6.**

(a)

(b)

Figure 25.6
A ball-and-stick model (a) and a space-filling model (b) of 4-ethyl-2,3-dimethylheptane.

Sample Problem 25-2

Name these compounds using the IUPAC system. Notice that the longest chain is not written in a straight line in molecule **a.**

a.
$$CH_3 - CH_2 - \overset{\overset{\textstyle CH_3}{|}}{\underset{\underset{\textstyle CH_2}{|}}{\overset{}{C}}} - CH_3$$
$$\underset{\underset{\textstyle CH_3}{|}}{CH_2}$$

b.
$$CH_3 - \overset{\overset{\textstyle CH_3}{|}}{\underset{\underset{\textstyle CH_3}{|}}{C}} - CH_2 - \overset{\overset{\textstyle CH_3}{|}}{\underset{\underset{\textstyle CH_3}{|}}{C}} - CH_3$$

1. ANALYZE Plan a problem-solving strategy.

For each compound, follow the IUPAC rules. Find the longest chain of carbon atoms, or the parent structure, and name it. Number the carbons in the main chain in sequence, making sure that the carbons to which the alkyl substituents are attached have the lowest numbers possible. These location numbers become part of the name as prefixes. If a substituent appears more than once in a structure, another appropriate prefix must be used. List the names of the alkyl substituents in alphabetical order. Separate numbers with commas; separate numbers and words with hyphens.

Practice Problems

3. Name the following alkanes.

a.
$$H - \overset{\overset{\textstyle H}{|}}{\underset{\underset{\textstyle H}{|}}{C}} - \overset{\overset{\textstyle H}{|}}{\underset{\underset{\textstyle H}{|}}{C}} - \overset{\overset{\textstyle H}{|}}{\underset{\underset{\textstyle H}{|}}{C}} - H$$

b.
$$H - \overset{\overset{\textstyle H}{|}}{\underset{\underset{\textstyle H}{|}}{C}} - \overset{\overset{\textstyle H}{|}}{\underset{\underset{\textstyle H}{|}}{C}} - \overset{\overset{\textstyle H}{|}}{\underset{\underset{\textstyle H}{|}}{C}} - \overset{\overset{\textstyle H}{|}}{\underset{\underset{\textstyle H}{|}}{C}} - \overset{\overset{\textstyle H}{|}}{\underset{\underset{\textstyle H}{|}}{C}} - H$$

c.
$$H - \overset{\overset{\textstyle H}{|}}{\underset{\underset{\textstyle H}{|}}{C}} - \overset{\overset{\textstyle H}{|}}{\underset{\underset{\textstyle H}{|}}{C}} - \overset{\overset{\textstyle H}{|}}{\underset{\underset{\textstyle H}{|}}{C}} - \overset{\overset{\textstyle H}{|}}{\underset{\underset{\textstyle H}{|}}{C}} - \overset{\overset{\textstyle H}{|}}{\underset{\underset{\textstyle H}{|}}{C}} - \overset{\overset{\textstyle H}{|}}{\underset{\underset{\textstyle H}{|}}{C}} - H$$

Sample Problem 25-2 (cont.)

2. **SOLVE** *Apply the problem-solving strategy.*

   a. The longest carbon chain in the molecule is hexane (six carbons). There are two methyl substituents on carbon 3, so the prefix is 3,3-dimethyl. The correct IUPAC name is 3,3-dimethylhexane.

   b. The longest carbon chain in the molecule is pentane (five carbons). There are two methyl substituents each on carbon 2 and on carbon 4. The prefix is 2,2,4,4-tetramethyl, and the correct IUPAC name is 2,2,4,4-tetramethylpentane.

3. **EVALUATE** *Do the results make sense?*

   The names of the parent structures conform to the longest chains. The substituents are given the lowest numbers and the correct names. Prefixes are used to indicate the appearance of the substituents, if they appear more than once. Numbers are separated by commas, and numbers are separated from words by hyphens.

Practice Problems (cont.)

4. Name these compounds according to the IUPAC system.

   a. $CH_3-CH_2-CH-CH_3$

                       |

                       CH_3

   b. $CH_2-CH_2-CH-CH_2-CH_3$

     | |

     CH_3 CH_2

                      |

                      CH_3

Chem ASAP!

Problem-Solving 4

Solve Problem 4 with the help of an interactive guided tutorial.

With an alkane name and knowledge of the IUPAC rules, it is easy to reconstruct the structural formula.

1. Find the root word (ending in *-ane*) in the hydrocarbon name. Then write the longest carbon chain to create the parent structure.
2. Number the carbons on this parent carbon chain.
3. Identify the substituent groups. Attach the substituents to the numbered parent chain at the proper positions.
4. Add hydrogens as needed.

Sample Problem 25-3

Draw complete structural formulas for each of the following compounds.

   a. 3-ethylhexane
   b. 2,2,4-trimethylpentane

---

1. **ANALYZE** *Plan a problem-solving strategy.*

   Work backward from each name to arrive at the structure. The prefix indicates the types of alkyl substituents, the number of times each appears, and the carbon to which each is attached. The root word in the hydrocarbon name, the word that ends in *-ane,* is the parent structure. The carbons on the parent chain are numbered to give the carbons bonded to the alkyl substituents the lowest numbers. Hydrogens are added as needed.

Practice Problems

5. Draw the structural formula for the compound 2,3-dimethyl-hexane.

Sample Problem 25-3 (cont.)

2. **SOLVE** *Apply the problem-solving strategy.*
   a. The parent structure is a straight chain of six carbon atoms (hexane). An ethyl substituent is found on carbon 3. There are a total of 13 additional hydrogens added to the parent chain.

$$
\begin{array}{c}
\quad\quad\quad CH_3 \\
\quad\quad\quad | \\
\quad\quad\quad CH_2 \\
\quad\quad\quad | \\
CH_3 - CH_2 - CH - CH_2 - CH_2 - CH_3 \\
\;\;1 \quad\;\; 2 \quad\;\; 3 \quad\;\; 4 \quad\;\; 5 \quad\;\; 6
\end{array}
$$

   b. The parent structure is a five-carbon straight chain (pentane) with three methyl substituents—two on carbon 2 and one on carbon 4. A total of nine hydrogens are added to the parent chain.

$$
\begin{array}{c}
\quad\quad CH_3 \quad\quad CH_3 \\
\quad\quad | \quad\quad\quad\; | \\
CH_3 - C - CH_2 - CH - CH_3 \\
\;\;1 \quad\; 2\,| \quad 3 \quad\; 4 \quad\; 5 \\
\quad\quad CH_3
\end{array}
$$

3. **EVALUATE** *Do the results make sense?*
   Chains of the proper length are written and numbered. Substituents are placed on the carbons indicated by the names. The correct number of hydrogens is present.

Practice Problems (cont.)

6. Draw structural formulas for these compounds.
   a. 3-ethylpentane
   b. 4-ethyl-2,3,4-trimethyloctane

Chem ASAP!
Problem-Solving 6
Solve Problem 6 with the help of an interactive guided tutorial.

Properties of Alkanes

The electron pair in a carbon–hydrogen or a carbon–carbon bond is shared about equally by the nuclei of the atoms involved. Therefore, hydrocarbon molecules such as alkanes are nonpolar. The nonpolar attractions between hydrocarbon molecules are the very weak van der Waals forces, which you learned about in Chapter 16. Thus hydrocarbons of low molar mass tend to be gases or low-boiling liquids.

Nonpolar organic molecules such as hydrocarbons are not attracted to water. For example, oil (a hydrocarbon) and water do not mix. A good rule of thumb is that "like dissolves like." This means that two nonpolar compounds will form a solution as will two polar compounds. But a nonpolar compound and a polar compound will not form a solution.

Figure 25.7
The nonpolar molecules in this oil spill are not attracted to the polar water molecules in the ocean. The insoluble oil from an oil spill remains on the surface of the water because oil has a lower density than water.

section review 25.1

7. Describe the bonding in hydrocarbons.

8. Differentiate between a straight-chain and a branched-chain alkane.

9. What is a homologous series? Why are the alkanes such a series?

10. Explain why alkane molecules are nonpolar.

 Chem ASAP! Assessment 25.1 Check your understanding of the important ideas and concepts in Section 25.1.

UNSATURATED HYDROCARBONS

objectives
▶ Explain the difference between unsaturated and saturated hydrocarbons
▶ Differentiate between the structures of alkenes and alkynes

key terms
▶ alkenes
▶ unsaturated compounds
▶ saturated compounds
▶ alkynes

*R*oach traps are filled with pheromones, chemicals which are given off by many insects to attract mates. When a roach senses the pheromones inside the trap, it crawls in and is stuck on sticky paper. Unsaturated hydrocarbons form the basis for the molecular structures of many pheromones.

How do unsaturated hydrocarbons differ from alkanes?

Alkenes

As you just learned, the carbon–carbon bonds in alkanes are single covalent bonds. But single covalent bonds are not the only kind of carbon–carbon bond to be found in hydrocarbons. Multiple bonds between carbons also exist. Hydrocarbons containing carbon–carbon double covalent bonds are called **alkenes.** This is the carbon–carbon double bond found in alkenes.

$$\diagdown_{C=C}\diagup$$

Organic compounds that contain double or triple carbon–carbon bonds are called **unsaturated compounds.** The compounds have this name because they contain fewer than the maximum number of hydrogens in their structure. The alkanes, which contain the maximum number of hydrogens, are called **saturated compounds.**

To name an alkene by the IUPAC system, find the longest chain in the molecule that contains the double bond. This chain is the parent alkene. It gets the root name of the alkane with the same number of carbons plus the ending -*ene.* The chain is numbered so that the carbon atoms of the double bond get the lowest possible numbers. Substituents on the chain are named and numbered in the same way they are for the alkanes. Ethene and propene are the simplest alkenes. They are often called by the common names ethylene and propylene. Some examples of the structures and IUPAC names of simple alkenes are shown below.

Figure 25.8
Ethene, the simplest alkene, stimulates the growth of plants and the ripening of their fruits.

$$\underset{H}{\overset{H}{\diagdown}}C=C\underset{H}{\overset{H}{\diagup}}$$

Ethene
(ethylene, the simplest alkene)

$$CH_3-\underset{\underset{H}{|}}{\overset{\overset{H}{|}}{C}}=\overset{\overset{H}{|}}{C}-H$$

Propene
(propylene)

$$CH_2=CH-CH_2-CH_3$$

1-butene

$$CH_3-\overset{\overset{H}{|}}{C}=\overset{\overset{H}{|}}{C}-CH_3$$

2-butene

$$CH_3-\overset{\overset{CH_3}{|}}{CH}-\overset{\overset{H}{|}}{C}=\overset{\overset{H}{|}}{C}-CH_3$$

4-methyl-2-pentene

Figure 25.9 shows the ball-and-stick and space-filling models of ethene. Notice that the four hydrogens that project from the double-bonded carbons lie in a plane and are 120° apart. Try to imagine freely rotating each CH_2 group around the double bond. It is impossible. The same is true of the double bond in real alkene molecules. No rotation occurs about a carbon–carbon double bond.

Alkynes

Hydrocarbons containing carbon–carbon triple covalent bonds are called **alkynes.** Like alkenes, alkynes are unsaturated compounds. This is the carbon–carbon triple bond found in alkynes.

$$-C \equiv C-$$

Alkynes are not plentiful in nature. The simplest alkyne is the gas ethyne (C_2H_2). The common name for ethyne is acetylene. Acetylene is the fuel burned in oxyacetylene torches used in welding. **Figure 25.10** shows that the single bonds that extend from the carbons in the carbon–carbon triple bond of ethyne are separated by the maximum angle of 180°. This makes ethyne a linear molecule.

The major attractions between alkane molecules, alkene molecules, or alkyne molecules are weak van der Waals forces. As a result, the introduction of a double or triple bond into a hydrocarbon does not have a dramatic effect on physical properties such as boiling point. See **Table 25.2.**

Figure 25.9
The six atoms of ethene lie in one plane. Can rotation occur about the double bond?

Table 25.2

Boiling Points of Homologous Alkanes, Alkenes, and Alkynes		
Name	**Molecular structure**	**Boiling point (°C)**
C_2		
Ethane	CH_3-CH_3	−88.5
Ethene	$CH_2=CH_2$	−103.9
Ethyne	$CH \equiv CH$	−81.8
C_3		
Propane	$CH_3CH_2CH_3$	−42.0
Propene	$CH_3CH=CH_2$	−47.0
Propyne	$CH_3C \equiv CH$	−23.3
C_4		
Butane	$CH_3CH_2CH_2CH_3$	−0.5
1-Butene	$CH_3CH_2CH=CH_2$	−6.3
1-Butyne	$CH_3CH_2C \equiv CH$	8.6
C_5		
Pentane	$CH_3CH_2CH_2CH_2CH_3$	36.0
1-Pentene	$CH_3CH_2CH_2CH=CH_2$	30.0
1-Pentyne	$CH_3CH_2CH_2C \equiv CH$	40.0

Figure 25.10
The triple bond in ethyne is rigid, so rotation about this bond does not occur. Ethyne is the simplest alkyne. The common name for ethyne is acetylene.

---

section review 25.2

11. Differentiate between unsaturated and saturated hydrocarbons.

12. Write electron dot structures for ethene and ethyne. Describe the shape of each.

13. Draw and name all the alkenes with the molecular formula C_4H_8.

 Chem ASAP! Assessment 25.2 Check your understanding of the important ideas and concepts in Section 25.2.

ISOMERISM

objectives
▶ Distinguish among structural, geometric, and stereoisomers
▶ Identify the asymmetric carbon or carbons in stereoisomers
key terms
▶ structural isomers
▶ *trans* configuration
▶ *cis* configuration
▶ geometric isomers
▶ asymmetric carbon
▶ stereoisomers

*R*etinal is a molecule in your eyes that has a hydrocarbon skeleton. The first step in the process of vision occurs when a ray of light enters your eye and strikes retinal, causing its hydrocarbon skeleton to rearrange to a different form called an isomer. **What is an isomer and what types of isomerization are possible?**

Structural Isomers

You may have noticed that the structures of some hydrocarbons are similar, differing only in the positions of the substituent groups or of the multiple bonds in their molecules. Compounds that have the same molecular formula but different molecular structures are called **structural isomers.** For example, two different molecules having the formula C_4H_{10} are shown below. One molecule is butane; the other molecule is 2-methylpropane. They are structural isomers of each other.

$$CH_3-CH_2-CH_2-CH_3$$

Butane (C_4H_{10})
(bp $-0.5\,°C$)

$$CH_3-\overset{\overset{\displaystyle CH_3}{\displaystyle |}}{CH}-CH_3$$

2-Methylpropane (C_4H_{10})
(bp $-10.2\,°C$)

Structural isomers differ in physical properties such as boiling point and melting point. They also have different chemical reactivity. In general, the more highly branched the hydrocarbon structure, the lower its boiling point compared with its other structural isomers. For example, 2-methylpropane has a lower boiling point than butane has.

Geometric Isomers

The lack of rotation around carbon–carbon double bonds has an important structural implication. Look at the structure of 2-butene in **Figure 25.11.** Two arrangements are possible for the methyl groups with respect to the rigid double bond. In the ***trans* configuration,** the substituted groups are on opposite sides of the double bond. In the ***cis* configuration,** the substituted groups are on the same side of the double bond. *Trans*-2-butene and *cis*-2-butene are geometric isomers. **Geometric isomers** differ only in the geometry of their substituted groups. Like other structural isomers, isomeric 2-butenes are distinguishable by their physical and chemical

Figure 25.11

These are the two geometric isomers of 2-butene. How does the trans configuration (a) differ from the cis configuration (b)?

(a)   (b)

properties. The groups on the carbons of the double bond do not need to be the same. Geometric isomerism is possible whenever each carbon of the double bond has at least one substituent. Why does 2-methyl-1-butene have no *cis, trans* isomers?

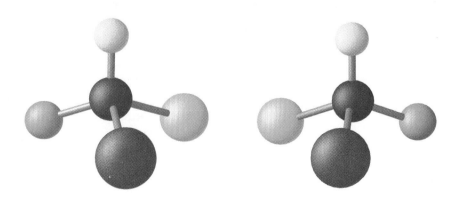

trans-2-Pentene   cis-2-Pentene   2-Methyl-1-butene
                                                 (no *cis, trans* isomers)

Stereoisomers

The structures that you have drawn up until now have ignored the fact that molecules are really three-dimensional. Could two molecules that look the same on paper differ in the third dimension—the positions of their atoms in space? They can, if the molecules are nonsuperimposable mirror images of each other. Placing an object in front of a mirror can give two different results. If the object is symmetrical, like a ball, then its mirror image is superimposable. That is, the appearance of the ball and its reflection are indistinguishable. By contrast, a pair of hands is distinguishable even though the hands consist of identical parts. The right hand reflects as a left hand and the left hand reflects as a right hand. Your hands are examples of nonsuperimposable mirror images. They are mirror images that cannot be placed on top of each other to obtain a match. Many pairs of ordinary objects, such as ears, feet, shoes, and bird wings, are similarly related.

You learned earlier that four groups attached to a carbon by single covalent bonds form a tetrahedron with the carbon at the center. In **Figure 25.12**, the carbon atom has four different groups attached: F, H, Cl, and Br. A carbon with four different groups attached is called an **asymmetric carbon**. Compounds with molecules that contain an asymmetric carbon have handedness. For these compounds, two kinds of molecules exist that are related to each other in much the same way as a pair of hands. **Figure 25.12** shows the mirror images of CHFClBr. Like hands, these mirror images are nonsuperimposable. Unless bonds are broken, these molecules cannot be superimposed. The four atoms attached to the carbon will not all match at once. **Stereoisomers** are molecules of the same molecular structure that differ only in the arrangement of the atoms in space. The mirror images of CHFClBr are stereoisomers.

Chem ASAP!
Simulation 28
Play the isomer game of "Pick the Pairs."

Figure 25.12
These ball-and-stick models illustrate the stereoisomers of CHFClBr. Stereoisomers are mirror-image molecules that cannot be superimposed on each other. Build models from toothpicks and clay to prove to yourself that these two isomers cannot be superimposed.

Sample Problem 25-4

Which of the following compounds have an asymmetric carbon?

a. CH_3CHCH_3
      |
     OH

c. CH_3CHCHO
      |
     OH

b. $CH_3CHCH_2CH_3$
      |
     OH

1. **ANALYZE** *Plan a problem-solving strategy.*

Use the definition of an asymmetric carbon to analyze the structures: An asymmetric carbon has four different groups attached.

2. **SOLVE** *Apply the problem-solving strategy.*

Draw the structures in a more complete form to determine the presence of a carbon atom with four different groups attached.

a. The central carbon has one H, one OH, and two CH_3 groups attached. It is not asymmetric.

$$CH_3-\overset{\overset{\displaystyle H}{|}}{\underset{\underset{\displaystyle OH}{|}}{C}}-CH_3$$

b. The central carbon has one H, one OH, one CH_3, and one CH_2CH_3 group attached. Because these four groups are different, the central carbon is asymmetric. It can be marked with an asterisk. None of the other carbons in this molecule is asymmetric.

$$CH_3-\overset{\overset{\displaystyle H}{|}}{\underset{\underset{\displaystyle OH}{|}}{\overset{*}{C}}}-CH_2CH_3$$

c. This molecule also has an asymmetric carbon because the central carbon has four different groups attached: H, OH, CH_3, CHO. The asymmetric carbon is marked with an asterisk.

$$CH_3-\overset{\overset{\displaystyle H}{|}}{\underset{\underset{\displaystyle OH}{|}}{\overset{*}{C}}}-CHO$$

3. **EVALUATE** *Do the results make sense?*

Only the two carbons with four different groups attached have been correctly identified as asymmetric. All other carbons shown have three or fewer different groups attached. The molecule that does not include an asymmetric carbon has a superimposable image.

Practice Problems

14. Identify the asymmetric carbon, if any, in each of the following structures.

a. CH_3CH_2CHO

c. CH_3CHOH
         |
       CH_3

b. CH_3CHCHO
      |
     Cl

15. For which of the following molecular formulas can mirror image molecules be drawn? Why?

a. CH_2Cl_2

b. $HS-\overset{\overset{\displaystyle F}{|}}{\underset{\underset{\displaystyle F}{|}}{C}}-OH$

c. $CH_3CF_2CH_3$

d. $CH_3CH_2-\overset{\overset{\displaystyle CH_3}{|}}{\underset{\underset{\displaystyle F}{|}}{C}}-Br$

MINI LAB

Structural Isomers of Heptane

PURPOSE

To build ball-and-stick models and name the nine structural isomers of heptane (C_7H_{16}).

MATERIALS

- ball-and-stick molecular model kit

PROCEDURE

1. Build a model for the straight-chain molecule of C_7H_{16}. Draw the structural formula and write the IUPAC name for this compound.

2. Move one carbon atom from the end of the chain and use it as a methyl substituent, making a new compound. Draw the structural formula and name this structural isomer.

3. Move the methyl group to a new position on the chain and draw and name this third structural isomer. Is there a third position that this methyl group can be moved to on the chain of six carbons, giving yet another compound?

4. Make other structural isomers by shortening the longest continuous chain and using the removed carbons as substituents. Draw the structural formulas and name each compound.

ANALYSIS AND CONCLUSIONS

1. What are structural isomers?

2. What are the names of the nine structural isomers of C_7H_{16}?

3. What was the shortest continuous chain?

4. Did each structural isomer have its own unique name? Should it?

---

section review 25.3

16. How do geometric isomers differ from structural isomers?

17. How do geometric isomers differ from stereoisomers?

18. Draw structural formulas for the following alkenes. If a compound has geometric isomers, draw both the *cis* and *trans* forms.

  a. 1-pentene

  b. 2-hexene

  c. 2-methyl-2-hexene

  d. 2,3-dimethyl-2-butene

19. How can an asymmetric carbon be identified? Why does the presence of an asymmetric carbon produce stereoisomers?

 Chem ASAP! **Assessment 25.3** Check your understanding of the important ideas and concepts in Section 25.3.

HYDROCARBON ISOMERS

SAFETY

Use safe and proper laboratory procedures.

PURPOSE

To draw line-angle formulas and name some of the isomers in gasoline.

MATERIALS

- pencil
- paper
- toothpicks
- modeling clay

PROCEDURE

Gasoline is a complex mixture of hydrocarbon molecules. Each molecule contains between five and nine carbon atoms. Study the formulas and names of the isomers of C_5H_{12} in Figure A. Make a model of each isomer using toothpicks and modeling clay. Compare the models and make accurate drawings on your paper.

Various Formulas Representing Isomers of C_5H_{12}

Condensed	Line-angle	Space-filling
$CH_3CH_2CH_2CH_2CH_3$ pentane		
$CH_3CHCH_2CH_3$ $\|$ CH_3 2-methylbutane		
CH_3 $\|$ CH_3CCH_3 $\|$ CH_3 2, 2-dimethylpropane		

Figure A

ANALYSIS

Using your experimental data, record the answers to the following questions below your drawings.

1. Expanded structural formulas represent all chemical bonds in a molecule as short lines. Draw the expanded structural formulas for each isomer of C_5H_{12} in Figure A.

2. In a line-angle formula, each line represents a C—C bond. Each end of a line, as well as the intersection of lines, represents a carbon atom. All hydrogen atoms are implied. Knowing that carbon always forms four bonds in organic compounds, explain how to determine the number of hydrogen atoms bonded to each carbon in a line-angle formula.

3. Because of its volatility, butane is used in the formulations of gasolines in cold climates during winter. Draw the condensed structural formulas, the line-angle formulas, and the space-filling formulas for the two isomers of butane (C_4H_{10}). Make models of each isomer.

YOU'RE THE CHEMIST

The following small-scale activities allow you to develop your own procedures and analyze the results.

1. **Analyze It!** Gasoline contains isomers of hexane. Draw the line-angle formulas and name the five isomers of C_6H_{14}. Make a model of one isomer and convert that model into the other four.

2. **Analyze It!** There are nine isomers of C_7H_{16}. Draw their line-angle formulas and name them.

3. **Analyze It!** There are eighteen isomers of C_8H_{18}. Draw their line-angle formulas and name them.

4. **Analyze It!** See how many isomers of C_9H_{20} you can draw and name.

5. **Analyze It!** Gasoline also contains cyclic alkanes. Draw the line-angle formulas and name several isomers of C_5H_{10} and C_6H_{12}.

HYDROCARBON RINGS

*N*ot everyone loves carrots, but you have probably heard about how good they are for you. One reason carrots are a healthful food choice is that they contain betacarotene, an important nutrient for vision. Betacarotene also gives carrots their orange color. The hydrocarbon skeleton of betacarotene contains hydrocarbon rings. **What is a hydrocarbon ring?**

objectives

▶ Identify common cyclic ring structures

▶ Explain resonance in terms of the aromatic ring of benzene

key terms

▶ cyclic hydrocarbons
▶ aliphatic compounds
▶ arenes
▶ aromatic compound

Cyclic Hydrocarbons

So far, you have seen a wide variety of short and long carbon chains; chains containing single, double, and triple covalent bonds between carbon atoms; and chains containing a number of different substituents. What if the ends of these chains linked up to form rings?

In some hydrocarbon compounds, the two ends of a carbon chain are attached to form a ring. Compounds that contain a hydrocarbon ring are called **cyclic hydrocarbons.** The structures of some cyclic hydrocarbons are shown in **Figure 25.13.** Rings containing from 3 to 20 carbons are found in nature. Five- and six-membered rings are the most abundant. Hydrocarbon compounds that do not contain rings are known as **aliphatic compounds.** They include compounds with both short and long carbon chains. The hydrocarbon compounds you have learned about in the previous sections are aliphatic compounds.

Aromatic Hydrocarbons

A special group of unsaturated cyclic hydrocarbons are known as **arenes.** These compounds contain single rings or groups of rings. The arenes were originally called aromatic compounds because many of them have pleasant odors. Benzene (C_6H_6) is the simplest arene. Today the term **aromatic compound** is applied to any substance in which the bonding is like that of benzene.

Figure 25.13 ▶

Molecular structures for a series of cycloalkanes are shown in the left column. The middle column shows a convenient way to represent cyclic rings. In these minimal structures, each intersection of lines represents a carbon atom and the hydrogens bonded to it. The space-filling models in the right column show the shapes of the rings. Cycloalkenes can be drawn similarly but are not shown here.

Cyclopropane
(bp −34.4 °C)

Cyclobutane
(bp −13 °C)

Cyclopentane
(bp 49.5 °C)

Cyclohexane
(bp 81.4 °C)

Cycloheptane
(bp 118 °C)

Figure 25.14
A space-filling model of benzene.

The benzene molecule has a six-membered carbon ring with one hydrogen attached to each carbon. This leaves one electron from each carbon free to participate in a double bond. Two different structures with double bonds can be written for benzene.

These structural formulas show only the extremes in electron sharing between any two adjacent carbons in benzene. One extreme is a normal single bond. The other extreme is a normal double bond. When two or more equally valid structures can be drawn for a molecule, resonance occurs. The benzene molecule exhibits resonance. Benzene and other molecules that exhibit resonance are more stable than similar molecules that do not exhibit resonance. Thus benzene is not as reactive as six-carbon alkenes.

The inscribed circle is a good way to represent the nature of resonance bonding. However, it does not show the number of electrons involved. For this reason, the traditional structure, which is the structure shown on the right, is used in this textbook.

Compounds containing substituents attached to the benzene ring are named as derivatives of benzene. Sometimes the benzene ring is named as a substituent on an alkane. In such instances the C_6H_5— group is called a phenyl group.

Methylbenzene (toluene)

3-Phenylhexane

Ethylbenzene

Figure 25.15
Part of the molecule that produces the distinctive aroma of vanilla beans is derived from aromatic hydrocarbons. Portions of many dyes are also derived from aromatic hydrocarbons.

Some derivatives of benzene have two substituents. These derivatives are called disubstituted benzenes. Three different structural isomers occur for the liquid aromatic compound dimethylbenzene ($C_6H_4(CH_3)_2$). Once again, the physical properties of structural isomers are different, as indicated by their boiling points.

1,2-dimethylbenzene
(*o*-dimethylbenzene,
o-xylene)
(bp 144 °C)

1,3-dimethylbenzene
(*m*-dimethylbenzene,
m-xylene)
(bp 139 °C)

1,4-dimethylbenzene
(*p*-dimethylbenzene,
p-xylene)
(bp 138 °C)

In the IUPAC naming system, the possible positions of two substituents in disubstituted benzene are designated as 1,2; 1,3; or 1,4. Common names for disubstituted benzenes use the terms *ortho, meta,* and *para* (abbreviated *o, m,* and *p*) in place of numbers. The dimethylbenzenes are also called xylenes.

section review 25.4

20. Name the following compounds.

a.

c.

b. CH_2CH_3 / $CH_2CH_2CH_3$

d. CH_2CH_3

21. Using structures, explain why benzene exhibits resonance. How does resonance affect stability?

22. The molecules of both cyclohexane and benzene have six carbon atoms bonded in a ring. What are some differences between these two compounds?

23. Name the following compounds.

a. $CH_2CH_2CH_3$

b. $CH_3-CH-CH_3$

 Chem ASAP! Assessment 25.4 Check your understanding of the important ideas and concepts in Section 25.4.

portfolio project

Research the origin of the International Union of Pure and Applied Chemistry (IUPAC). Find out when, where, and why the first international congress was held. Present your findings in a written report.

HYDROCARBONS FROM THE EARTH

objectives

▶ Identify three important fossil fuels and describe their origins
▶ Name some products obtained from natural gas, petroleum, and coal

key term

▶ cracking

*N*eed a fill-up? If you were traveling near Saturn's moon, Titan, you might easily fill up your tank with some of the many hydrocarbons in Titan's atmosphere. But here on Earth, hydrocarbon fuels are more difficult to obtain.
What are the sources of hydrocarbons on Earth, and how do they form?

Natural Gas

You have learned quite a lot about hydrocarbons. But one question that has yet to be answered is where hydrocarbons come from. To explore the origins of hydrocarbons, you will need to look back into Earth's past, back before the age of dinosaurs.

Much of the world's energy is supplied by burning fossil fuels. Fossil fuels are organic because they are derived from the decay of organisms in geologic history. Millions of years ago, marine life settled on the ocean floors and became buried in ocean sediments. Heat, pressure, and the action of bacteria changed this residue into petroleum and natural gas, which are two important fossil fuels. Petroleum and natural gas contain mostly aliphatic, or straight-chain, hydrocarbons. **Figure 25.16** illustrates how natural gas is often found overlying oil deposits or in separate pockets in rock.

Natural gas is an important source of alkanes of low molar mass. Typically, natural gas is composed of about 80% methane, 10% ethane, 4%

Figure 25.16

Natural gas and oil are typically found in dome-shaped geological formations. Petroleum prospectors drill oil wells to tap into the gas and oil. Sometimes the gas is under pressure and will force the oil up the well pipe, but pumping is usually required.

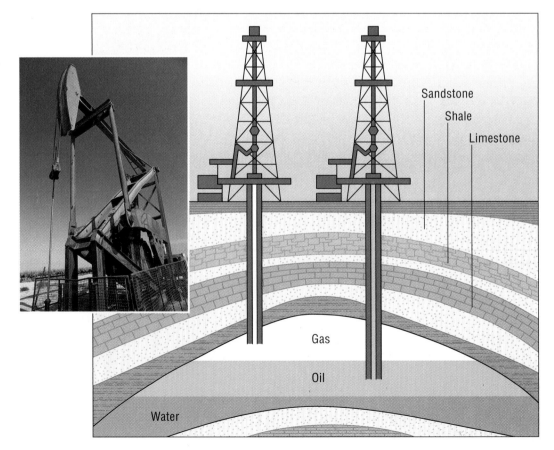

Sandstone
Shale
Limestone

Gas

Oil

Water

propane, and 2% butane. The remaining 4% consists of nitrogen and higher molar mass hydrocarbons. Natural gas also contains a small amount of the noble gas helium and is one of its major sources. Methane, the major constituent of natural gas, is especially prized for combustion because it burns with a hot, clean flame.

$$CH_4(g) + 2O_2(g) \longrightarrow CO_2(g) + 2H_2O(g) + heat$$

Propane and butane, which are separated from the other gases by liquefaction, are also good heating fuels. They are sold in liquid form in pressurized tanks as liquid petroleum gas (LPG).

A sufficient supply of oxygen is necessary to oxidize a hydrocarbon fuel completely and to obtain the greatest amount of heat. Complete combustion of a hydrocarbon gives a blue flame. Incomplete combustion gives a yellow flame. This is due to the formation of small, glowing carbon particles that are deposited as soot when they cool. Carbon monoxide, a toxic gas, is also formed along with carbon dioxide and water during incomplete combustion.

Petroleum

The organic compounds found in petroleum, or crude oil, are more complex than those in natural gas. Most of the hydrocarbons in petroleum are straight-chain and branched-chain alkanes. Petroleum also contains small amounts of aromatic compounds and sulfur-, oxygen-, and nitrogen-containing organic compounds.

Humans have known about petroleum for centuries; ancient peoples found it seeping from the ground in certain areas. In the late 1850s, a vast deposit of petroleum was discovered in Pennsylvania when a well was drilled to obtain petroleum for use as a fuel. Within decades, petroleum deposits had also been found in the Middle East, Europe, and the East Indies. Petroleum has since been found in other parts of the world as well.

Crude oil must be refined before it is commercially useful. The refining process consists of distilling crude oil to divide it into fractions according to boiling point. A schematic of a petroleum refining distillation tower is shown in **Figure 25.17.** Each distillation fraction contains several different hydrocarbons. The fractions, which have a variety of uses, are listed in **Table 25.3.**

Fractionating Column

Figure 25.17

Petroleum is refined by fractional distillation. The crude oil is heated so that it vaporizes and rises through the fractionating column. Compounds with the highest boiling points condense first near the bottom. Compounds with the lowest boiling points condense last near the top.

Table 25.3

Fractions Obtained from Crude Oils			
Fraction	Composition of carbon chains	Boiling range (°C)	Percent of crude oil
Natural gas	C_1 to C_4	Below 20	10%
Petroleum ether (solvent)	C_5 to C_6	30 to 60	
Naphtha (solvent)	C_7 to C_8	60 to 90	
Gasoline	C_6 to C_{12}	40 to 175	40%
Kerosene	C_{12} to C_{15}	150 to 275	10%
Fuel oils, mineral oil	C_{15} to C_{18}	225 to 400	30%
Lubricating oil, petroleum jelly, greases, paraffin wax, asphalt	C_{16} to C_{24}	Over 400	10%

Oil Spills

Spilled oil from oil tankers can destroy fragile marine ecosystems. Because cleaning up oil spills is difficult and expensive, researchers are developing new cleanup technologies and safer transportation methods. Most current cleanup methods involve containing the oil and either pumping it away or soaking it up with absorbent materials. Some of the new developments include the genetic engineering of bacteria to "eat" up the oil spill and the design of double-hulled tankers that are less likely to spill their oil in a collision.

The fractions containing compounds of higher molar mass can be "cracked" to produce the more useful short-chain components of gasoline and kerosene. **Cracking** is a controlled process by which hydrocarbons are broken down or rearranged into smaller, more useful molecules. Hydrocarbons are cracked with the aid of a catalyst and with heat. By this process, petroleum is the principal source of raw materials for the organic chemicals industry. For example, low-molar-mass alkanes are starting materials for the manufacture of paints and plastics.

Coal

Geologists believe that coal had its origin some 300 million years ago when huge tree ferns and mosses grew abundantly in swampy tropical regions. When the plants died, they formed thick layers of decaying vegetation. Layer after layer of soil and rock eventually covered the decaying vegetation, which caused a buildup of intense pressure. This pressure, together with heat from Earth's interior, slowly turned the plant remains into coal.

The first stage in the formation of coal is an intermediate material known as peat. Peat is a soft, brown, spongy, fibrous material rather like decayed and compressed garden refuse. When first dug out of a peat bog, it has a very high water content. After it has been allowed to dry, it produces a low-cost but smoky fuel. If peat is left in the ground, it continues to change. After a long period of time, it loses most of its fibrous texture and becomes lignite, or brown coal. Lignite is much harder than peat and has a higher carbon content (about 50%). The water content, however, is still high. Continued pressure and heat slowly change lignite to bituminous, or soft coal. Bituminous coal has a lower water content and higher carbon content

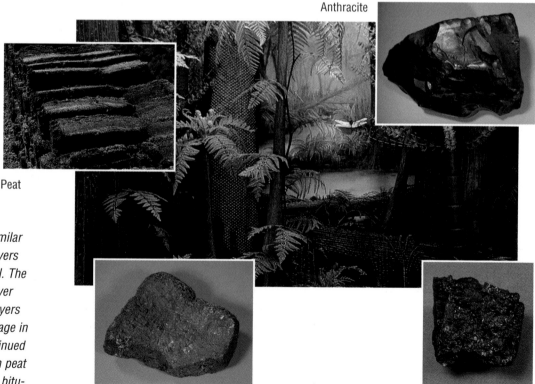

Peat

Anthracite

Lignite

Bituminous

Figure 25.18
Coal formed when plants similar to these died and formed layers of decaying organic material. The material was compressed over millions of years between layers of soil and rock. The first stage in coal formation is peat. Continued pressure and heat transform peat into forms of coal—lignite, bituminous, and anthracite.

Figure 25.19
Coal is mined from both surface mines, shown here, and underground mines. Underground coal seams may be thin and wandering, making mining difficult and hazardous. Modern machinery is reducing the number of miners who have to work underground.

(70–80%) than lignite. In some regions of Earth's crust, even greater pressures have been exerted. In those places, such as eastern Pennsylvania, soft coal has been changed into anthracite, or hard coal. Anthracite has a carbon content that exceeds 80%, making it an excellent fuel source.

Coal, which is usually found in seams from 1 to 3 meters thick, is obtained from both underground and surface mines. In North America, coal mines are usually less than 100 meters underground. Much of the coal is so close to the surface that it is strip-mined. By contrast, many coal mines in Europe and other parts of the world extend 1000 to 1500 meters below Earth's surface.

Coal consists largely of condensed ring compounds of extremely high molar mass. These compounds have a very high proportion of carbon compared with hydrogen. Due to the high proportion of these aromatic compounds, coal leaves more soot upon burning than do the more aliphatic fuels obtained from petroleum. The majority of the coal once burned in North America contained about 7% sulfur, which burns to form the major air pollutants SO_2 and SO_3.

Coal may be distilled to obtain a variety of products: coal gas, coal tar, coke, and ammonia. Coal gas consists mainly of hydrogen, methane, and carbon monoxide, all of which are flammable. Coal tar can be distilled further into benzene, toluene, naphthalene, phenol, and pitch. Coke is used as a fuel in many industrial processes. Because it is almost pure carbon, coke produces intense heat and little or no smoke when it burns. The ammonia from distilled coal is converted to ammonium sulfate for use as a fertilizer.

section review 25.5

24. What are the three major fossil fuels? How did each form?

25. What is the source of methane? Of aliphatic hydrocarbons? Of aromatic hydrocarbons?

26. Write a balanced equation for the complete combustion of pentane. What other products would be formed if combustion were incomplete?

27. Define petroleum refining and cracking.

 Chem ASAP! Assessment 25.5 Check your understanding of the important ideas and concepts in Section 25.5.

portfolio project

Research the structures that petroleum geologists use to locate oil. Prepare a poster with labeled diagrams showing each type of geologic structure. Explain what the structures have in common that makes them good indicators for oil deposits.

A NUMBER YOU CAN'T KNOCK

When you buy gas for your car, you have a choice of fuels with different octane numbers, usually from 87 to 93. What do these numbers mean? Because higher octane gasoline costs more, many people believe that octane is an indicator of fuel quality—that higher octane fuel will give them better performance. But this belief is not quite accurate. The octane number is actually a measurement of the fuel's ability to resist engine "knock", which occurs when the fuel ignites by itself in the engine cylinder.

Engine knock has been a problem in internal combustion gasoline engines since they began to be widely used at the beginning of the twentieth century. Knocking throws off the engine's rhythm, causing overheating, loss of power, and engine damage. It is influenced by two main variables.

The first variable is engine compression—the degree to which the gas-air mixture in the cylinder is compressed prior to ignition by the spark plug. The higher the compression, the more power delivered by the ignition of the fuel. But higher compression also means greater likelihood of engine knock.

The second variable is the chemical structure of the hydrocarbons that make up the fuel. Straight-chain alkanes are more prone to knocking than are branched-chain alkanes, cycloalkanes, and aromatic hydrocarbons.

In practice, these two variables mean that engine compression—and thus performance—is limited by the composition of the gasoline used. In the early part of the twentieth century, this was a problem for automobile engineers. They could design an engine with any compression ratio, but they could not be sure of the quality of the fuel the engine would burn. They needed a method for measuring each fuel's resistance to knocking. The octane rating system was born out of this need.

> **Knocking throws off the engine's rhythm, causing overheating, loss of power, and engine damage.**

The designers of the octane system developed a way of testing fuels in a special, one-cylinder engine with a variable compression ratio. For each fuel tested, they could increase the compression until the engine began to knock. Then they chose two pure fuels as standards against which to measure others: isooctane (2,2,4-trimethylpentane) and heptane. These two hydrocarbons had similar physical properties, but isooctane was very resistant to knocking, and heptane was very prone to it. The designers arbitrarily assigned the heptane an octane rating of 0 and the isooctane a rating of 100. Every fuel tested could then be assigned an octane number relative to these. An octane rating of 89, for example, meant that a fuel performed the same in the special test engine as a mixture that was 89 parts isooctane and 11 parts heptane.

This fuel rating system is still in use today. The major modification is that two somewhat different testing methods are used. One, called the motor octane rating (M), tests the fuel under conditions that approximate high-speed driving with heavy loads. The other, called the research octane rating (R), uses conditions that simulate more normal driving. Usually, the octane number assigned to gasolines is an average of the numbers given by these two methods. You can see this indicated on gasoline pumps as (R + M) / 2.

CHEMISTRY IN CAREERS

ORGANIC CHEMIST
Does synthesizing organic compounds match your career interests?
See page 880.

CHEMIST NEEDED
~~Entire Lab GC Must know~~

TAKE IT TO THE NET

Find out more about career opportunities:
www.phschool.com

CHEMICAL SPECIALIST
Local food service distributor seek responsible self-motivated individ

Chapter 25 STUDENT STUDY GUIDE

Take It to the NET
For interactive study and
review, go to **www.phschool.com**

KEY TERMS

- aliphatic compound *p. 759*
- alkane *p. 743*
- alkene *p. 752*
- alkyl group *p. 748*
- alkyne *p. 753*
- arene *p. 759*
- aromatic compound *p. 759*
- asymmetric carbon *p. 755*

- branched-chain alkane *p. 748*
- *cis* configuration *p. 754*
- condensed structural formula *p. 746*
- cracking *p. 764*
- cyclic hydrocarbon *p. 759*
- geometric isomer *p. 754*
- homologous series *p. 745*

- hydrocarbons *p. 743*
- saturated compound *p. 752*
- stereoisomer *p. 755*
- straight-chain alkane *p. 745*
- structural isomer *p. 754*
- substituent *p. 748*
- *trans* configuration *p. 754*
- unsaturated compound *p. 752*

CONCEPT SUMMARY

25.1 Hydrocarbons
- Carbon makes stable covalent bonds with other carbons to form chain and ring compounds.
- Hydrocarbons are compounds containing only carbon and hydrogen. Alkanes contain only carbon–carbon single bonds.
- Straight-chain hydrocarbons contain carbon atoms in a chain, one after another. Branched-chain hydrocarbons are formed when one or more substituent alkyl groups are added to a straight-chain hydrocarbon.

25.2 Unsaturated Hydrocarbons
- Alkenes are unsaturated hydrocarbons containing at least one carbon–carbon double bond.
- Alkynes are unsaturated hydrocarbons containing at least one carbon–carbon triple bond.

25.3 Isomerism
- Structural isomers have the same molecular formula but different molecular structures.
- Alkenes may exhibit geometric isomerism according to whether substituents are on the same side or on opposite sides of the double bond.

- Stereoisomers can occur if four different groups are attached to a single carbon atom.

25.4 Hydrocarbon Rings
- Aromatic hydrocarbons, or arenes, are related to the hydrocarbon benzene.
- As a result of resonance, the interior bonds of the benzene ring are somewhere between ordinary single bonds and double bonds. Benzene is less reactive than ordinary alkenes because of this unusual bonding.

25.5 Hydrocarbons from the Earth
- The fossil fuels—coal, petroleum, and natural gas—had their origin in marine life buried in ocean sediments millions of years ago and subjected to the effects of heat, pressure, and bacteria.
- Aliphatic hydrocarbons come mainly from natural gas and petroleum. Aromatic hydrocarbons come mainly from coal.
- The molecular structures of the hydrocarbons present in natural petroleum can be broken down into other useful products by cracking.

CHAPTER CONCEPT MAP

Use these terms to construct a concept map that organizes the major ideas of this chapter.

 Chem ASAP! **Concept Map 25**
Create your Concept Map using the computer.

CONCEPT PRACTICE

28. Draw condensed structural formulas for pentane and hexane. Assume that the C—H and C—C bonds are understood. *25.1*

29. Name the alkanes that have the following molecular or structural formulas. *25.1*

   a. $CH_3CH_2CH_3$

   b. $CH_3(CH_2)_6CH_3$

   c.
$$H-\underset{\underset{H}{|}}{\overset{\overset{H}{|}}{C}}-\underset{\underset{H}{|}}{\overset{\overset{H}{|}}{C}}-\underset{\underset{H}{|}}{\overset{\overset{H}{|}}{C}}-\underset{\underset{H}{|}}{\overset{\overset{H}{|}}{C}}-\underset{\underset{H}{|}}{\overset{\overset{H}{|}}{C}}-H$$

30. Draw structures for the alkyl groups derived from methane, ethane, and propane. *25.1*

31. Why are the following names incorrect? What are the correct names? *25.1*

   a. 2-dimethylpentane

   b. 1,3-dimethylpropane

   c. 3-methylbutane

   d. 3,4-dimethylbutane

32. Give the IUPAC name for each compound. *25.1*

   a. $CH_3-\underset{\underset{CH_3}{|}}{CH}-\underset{\underset{CH_3}{|}}{CH_2}$

   b. $CH_3-\underset{\underset{CH_3}{|}}{CH}-\underset{\underset{CH_3}{|}}{CH}-CH_3$

   c. $CH_3-\underset{\underset{CH_2}{\underset{\underset{CH_3}{|}}{|}}}{CH}-CH_2-\underset{\underset{CH_3}{|}}{CH_2}$

33. Why are alkane molecules nonpolar? *25.1*

34. You cannot draw a structural formula for methene. Explain. *25.2*

35. Give a systematic name for these alkenes. *25.2*

   a. $CH_3CH=CH_2$

   b. $\underset{H}{\overset{CH_3}{>}}C=C\underset{CH_2CH_3}{\overset{H}{<}}$

   c. $CH_3\underset{\underset{CH_3}{|}}{CH}CH_2CH=CH_2$

   d. $\underset{CH_3}{\overset{CH_3}{>}}C=C\underset{CH_2CH_3}{\overset{CH_2CH_3}{<}}$

   e. $CH_2=CHCH_2\underset{\underset{CH_2CH_3}{|}}{CH_2}$

36. Draw a structural formula for each alkene with the molecular formula C_5H_{10}. Name each compound. *25.2*

37. Draw all the structural isomers with the molecular formula C_6H_{14}. Name each one. (For convenience, you may wish to draw only the carbon skeleton for each structure.) *25.3*

38. Draw one structural isomer of each compound. *25.3*

   a. $CH_3-\underset{\underset{CH_3}{|}}{\overset{\overset{CH_3}{|}}{CH}}-CH_3$

   b. $CH_3-\underset{\underset{CH_2}{\underset{\underset{CH_3}{|}}{|}}}{\overset{\overset{CH_3}{|}}{CH}}-CH-CH_3$

   c. $CH_3-\overset{\overset{CH_3}{|}}{CH}-CH_2-\underset{\underset{CH_2}{\underset{\underset{CH_3}{|}}{|}}}{CH}-\underset{\underset{CH_2}{\underset{\underset{CH_3}{|}}{|}}}{\overset{\overset{CH_3}{|}}{CH}}$

39. Draw a structural formula or carbon skeleton for each of the following alkenes. Include both *cis* and *trans* forms if the compound has geometric isomers. *25.3*

   a. 2-pentene

   b. 2-methyl-2-pentene

   c. 3-ethyl-2-pentene

40. Show how lack of rotation about a carbon–carbon double bond leads to geometric isomerism. Use the isomers of 2-pentene to illustrate your answer. *25.3*

41. Do all molecules have stereoisomers? Explain. *25.3*

42. Can you draw a structural isomer of hexane (C_6H_{14}) that has an asymmetric carbon? *25.3*

43. Draw a structure for each compound. *25.4*
   a. *p*-diethylbenzene
   b. 2-methyl-3-phenylpentane
   c. *p*-xylene
   d. toluene

44. Explain why both of these structures represent 1,2-diethylbenzene. *25.4*

45. Write an equation for the complete combustion of octane (C_8H_{18}). *25.5*

46. Rank these materials in order of increasing hardness: bituminous coal, peat, lignite, and anthracite coal. *25.5*

47. Discuss the chemical structure of coal. *25.5*

48. How does the amount of sulfur in coal affect its potential use? *25.5*

CONCEPT MASTERY

49. For each hydrocarbon pictured below, identify the type of bonding and name the compound.

(a)

(b)

(c)

50. Write structural formulas for the following compounds.
   a. propyne
   b. cyclohexane
   c. 2-phenylpropane
   d. 2,2,4-trimethylpentane
   e. 2,3-dimethylpentane
   f. 1,1-diphenylhexane

51. Name the next three higher homologs of ethane.

52. Draw electron dot structures for each compound.
   a. ethene   c. ethyne
   b. propane   d. cyclobutane

53. Compare these three molecular structures. Which would you expect to be most stable? Why?

54. The seven organic chemicals produced in the largest amounts in the United States in a recent year are listed in the table below. Answer the following questions based on the data given.

Chemical	Amount produced (billions of kg)
Ethylene	15.9
Propylene	8.4
Urea	6.8
Ethylene dichloride	6.3
Benzene	5.3
Ethyl benzene	4.3
Vinyl chloride	3.7

   a. How many billion kilograms of aromatic compounds were produced?
   b. Of the total mass of all seven compounds produced, what percent by mass was made up of aliphatic compounds?

55. Are these two structures geometric isomers? Explain.

56. Choose the term that best completes the second relationship.
   a. tree:branch

   hydrocarbon chain:_____
   (1) alkyl substituent   (3) isomer
   (2) methane   (4) double bond
   b. cyclic:aliphatic

   circle:_____
   (1) oval   (3) square
   (2) parallelogram   (4) line
   c. propane:three

   hexene:_____
   (1) seven   (3) five
   (2) six   (4) four

57. Why do most cyclic hydrocarbons have higher boiling points than alkanes with the same number of carbons?

CUMULATIVE REVIEW

58. What are the pH values for aqueous solutions containing each of the following hydroxide-ion concentrations?
   a. $1.0 \times 10^{-4}M$
   b. $3.9 \times 10^{-7}M$
   c. $0.010M$
   d. $0.0050M$

59. Give the oxidation number of each element in the following compounds.
   a. $CaCO_3$ **c.** $LiIO_3$
   b. Cl_2 **d.** Na_2SO_3

60. Draw electron dot structures and predict the shapes of the following molecules.
   a. PH_3 **b.** CO **c.** CS_2 **d.** CF_4

61. Write equilibrium constant expressions for the following reactions.
   a. $Cl_2(g) + I_2(g) \rightleftharpoons 2ICl(g)$
   b. $2HBr(g) \rightleftharpoons H_2(g) + Br_2(g)$
   c. $2S_2Cl_2(g) + 2H_2O(g) \rightleftharpoons$
          $\qquad 4HCl(g) + 3S(g) + SO_2(g)$
   d. $N_2(g) + 3H_2(g) \rightleftharpoons 2NH_3(g)$

62. Identify any incorrect formulas among the following compounds.
   a. H_2O_2 **c.** SrO **e.** $CaHPO_4$
   b. $NaIO_4$ **d.** CaS_2 **f.** $BaOH$

63. A colorless solution of unknown pH turns blue when tested with the acid-base indicator bromthymol blue. It remains colorless when tested with phenolphthalein.
   a. What is the approximate pH of the solution?
   b. How could you determine the pH more accurately?

CONCEPT CHALLENGE

64. Use the data in **Table 25.1** to make a graph of boiling point versus number of carbons for the first ten straight-chain alkanes. Does the graph describe a straight line? On the basis of this graph, what would you predict to be the boiling point of undecane, the straight-chain alkane containing eleven carbons? Use a chemistry handbook to find the actual boiling point of undecane. Compare this boiling point with your prediction.

65. Fossil fuels such as oil and natural gas are the raw materials for many consumer products. Do you believe it is wise to continue to use the limited supplies of fossil fuels as an energy source?

66. The graph shows the number of structural isomers for alkanes with three through ten carbon atoms.

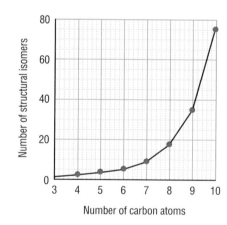

   a. According to the graph, how many structural isomers are there for the C_6, C_7, C_8, C_9, and C_{10} alkanes?
   b. The difference between the number of isomers for C_7 and C_8 is 9. The difference between the number of isomers for C_9 and C_{10} is 40. In each case, one additional carbon atom is added to the molecule. Why is the change in the number of isomers so different?

Select the choice that best answers each question or completes each statement.

1. What is the name of the compound with the following structural formula?

$$
\begin{array}{ccc}
& CH_3 \ \ H \ \ CH_3 & \\
& | \quad | \quad | & \\
CH_3 - & C - C - C & - CH_3 \\
& | \quad | \quad | & \\
& H \ \ \ H \ \ \ H &
\end{array}
$$

  a. 1,2,3,3-tetramethylpropane
  b. heptane
  c. 2,4-dimethylpentane
  d. 1,5-demethylbutane

2. Which of these are characteristic of all alkenes?
    I. unsaturated
    II. carbon-carbon double bond
    III. stereoisomers
  a. I and II only
  b. II and III only
  c. I and III only
  d. I, II, and III

3. How many carbon atoms are in a molecule of 4,5-diethyloctane?
  a. 10   **c.** 14
  b. 12   **d.** 16

4. *Cis-trans* geometric isomerism is possible in
  a. 2-pentene.   **c.** propyne.
  b. 2-butane.   **d.** benzene.

5. A structural isomer of heptane is
  a. methylbenzene.
  b. 3,3-dimethylpentane.
  c. cycloheptane.
  d. 3-methylhexene.

6. Which molecule has stereoisomers?
  a. CH_4 **c.** $CFClBrI$
  b. CF_2H_2 **d.** CF_2Cl

Use the space-filling models of pentane isomers to answer questions 7 and 8.

7. Write structural formulas for three structural isomers of pentane, C_5H_{12}. Name each isomer.

8. *You Draw It!* Write structural formulas for the four structural isomers of cyclopentane. Draw ball-and-stick models of the isomers.

The lettered choices below refer to questions 9–12. A lettered choice may be used once, more than once, or not at all.

  (A) alkene
  (B) arene
  (C) alkyne
  (D) alkane

In which of the above classes of hydrocarbons does each of the following compounds belong?

9. C_7H_{16}
10. C_5H_8
11. C_6H_6
12. C_8H_{16}

Use the molecular structures below to answer questions 13–16. A molecular structure may be used once, more than once, or not at all.

(A)
$$
\begin{array}{cc}
CH_3 & \quad H \\
\ \ \diagdown & \diagup \\
& C = C \\
\diagup & \ \ \diagdown \\
H & \quad CH_3
\end{array}
$$
(B) $CH_2 = CH - CH = CH_2$

(C)
$$
\begin{array}{cc}
H & \quad H \\
\ \ \diagdown & \diagup \\
& C = C \\
\diagup & \ \ \diagdown \\
CH_3 & \quad CH_3
\end{array}
$$
(D)

13. Which structure is a cycloalkane?
14. Which structure is a saturated hydrocarbon?
15. Which structure is a *cis*-isomer?
16. Which structure is a *trans*-isomer?

Use the labeled features in the molecular structure below to answer questions 17–21.

$$
\begin{array}{c}
(2) \\
(1) \qquad CH_3CH_2CH_2 \\
C_6H_5 \diagdown \qquad \qquad \diagup H \\
\qquad \qquad \qquad \qquad (3) \\
(5)\,CH_3 \qquad \qquad CH = CH_2 \\
\diagdown \qquad \diagup \\
Cl - C - Br \\
| \\
F \\
(4)
\end{array}
$$

17. Which label identifies a double bond?
18. Which label identifies a phenyl group?
19. Which label identifies a methyl group?
20. Which label identifies an asymmetric carbon?
21. Which label identifies a propyl group?

Chapter 26

FUNCTIONAL GROUPS AND ORGANIC REACTIONS

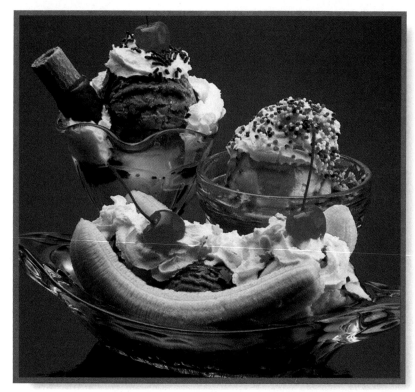

Many desserts owe their flavors to organic aldehydes and esters.

FEATURES

DISCOVER IT!
Making the Slimiest Polymer

SMALL-SCALE LAB
Polymers

MINI LAB
Testing for an Aldehyde

CHEMISTRY SERVING ... THE CONSUMER
The Sweet Smell of Functional Groups

CHEMISTRY IN CAREERS
Flavor Developer

LINK TO POLLUTION
Alternative Fuels

LINK TO GENETICS
Scientists Growing Flavors

Stay current with **SCIENCE NEWS**
Find out more about organic reactions:
www.phschool.com

DISCOVER IT! MAKING THE SLIMIEST POLYMER

You need white paper glue, borax, two large glasses, four paper or foam cups, a spoon, a 10-mL graduated cylinder, and a 100-mL graduated cylinder.

1. Mix 60 mL (about 2 oz) of white paper glue with 60 mL of water in a glass.

2. Pour 30 mL of this mixture into each of the four cups.

3. Make a borax solution by stirring 5 g of borax into 100 mL of water in the other glass.

4. Add 5 mL of borax solution to the first cup of glue, 10 mL to the second, 15 mL to the third, and 20 mL to the fourth. Stir the mixture in each cup and knead it with your fingers until it is smooth.

5. Take the contents of the cup with 5 mL of borax and slowly stretch it into a long strand. Repeat for the other three cups.

Which amount of borax allowed you to pull the longest strand? Do you think adding less than 5 mL or more than 20 mL of the borax solution would allow you to pull a longer strand? Would the results be different if you did not add water to the glue initially? Try it! After you complete this chapter, try to determine what polymer you made.

INTRODUCTION TO FUNCTIONAL GROUPS

*T*he lights dim and the audience chatter subsides as the musicians enter the hall. All the musicians wear black, and from a distance they look nearly identical. But their differences become apparent when they pick up their instruments. As the conductor signals the beginning of the piece, a single flute is heard. The warm sounds of the stringed instruments join in, and soon each musician contributes a unique sound to the music. In a similar way, one hydrocarbon is nearly identical to another until it picks up a functional group. **How do functional groups determine the character of organic compounds?**

Functional Groups

In Chapter 25, you learned about hydrocarbon chains and rings—the essential components of every organic compound. Yet in most chemical reactions involving organic molecules, the saturated hydrocarbon skeletons of the molecules are chemically inert. How, then, can there be hundreds of different kinds of organic reactions?

Most organic chemistry involves substituents, which are groups attached to hydrocarbon chains. The substituents of organic molecules often contain oxygen, nitrogen, sulfur, or phosphorus. They are called functional groups because they are the chemically functional parts of the molecules. A **functional group** is a specific arrangement of atoms in an organic compound that is capable of characteristic chemical reactions. Most organic chemistry is functional-group chemistry. Organic compounds can be classified according to their functional groups. The symbol R represents any carbon chains or rings attached to the functional group. Because the double and triple bonds of alkenes and alkynes are chemically reactive, they are considered functional groups. **Table 26.1** on the following page lists the other functional groups that you will learn about in this chapter and in Chapter 27. What do most of the functional groups in **Table 26.1** have in common? You will find it helpful to refer to this table throughout the chapter.

Figure 26.1
A wide array of consumer products contains hydrocarbon derivatives. The hydrocarbon skeletons in these products are chemically similar. Functional groups give each product unique properties and uses.

Table 26.1

Organic Compounds Classified by Functional Group		
Compound type	Compound structure	Functional group
Halocarbon	$R-X$ (X = F, Cl, Br, I)	Halogen
Alcohol	$R-OH$	Hydroxyl
Ether	$R-O-R$	Ether
Aldehyde	$R-\overset{\displaystyle O}{\overset{\displaystyle \|}{C}}-H$	Carbonyl
Ketone	$R-\overset{\displaystyle O}{\overset{\displaystyle \|}{C}}-R$	Carbonyl
Carboxylic acid	$R-\overset{\displaystyle O}{\overset{\displaystyle \|}{C}}-OH$	Carboxyl
Ester	$R-\overset{\displaystyle O}{\overset{\displaystyle \|}{C}}-O-R$	Ester
Amine	$R-NH_2$	Amino
Amide	$R-\overset{\displaystyle O}{\overset{\displaystyle \|}{C}}-\overset{\displaystyle H}{\overset{\displaystyle \|}{N}}-R$	Amido

Halogen Substituents

Halocarbons are a class of organic compounds containing covalently bonded fluorine, chlorine, bromine, or iodine. The IUPAC rules for naming halocarbons are based on the name of the parent hydrocarbon. The halogen groups are added as substituents. Examples of IUPAC names for several simple halocarbons along with their structural formulas are given below. (Common names are in parentheses.)

CH₃—Cl

Chloromethane
(methyl chloride)

Chloroethene
(vinyl chloride)

Chlorobenzene
(phenyl chloride)

Common names of halocarbons consist of two parts. The first part names the hydrocarbon portion of the molecule as an alkyl group, such as methyl, ethyl, butyl, or phenyl. The second part gives the halogen with an -*ide* ending. Methyl chloride (CH₃Cl) is an example. Remember, however, that the bonding in a halocarbon is covalent, not ionic.

On the basis of their common names, halocarbons in which a halogen attaches to a carbon of an aliphatic chain are called **alkyl halides**. **Table 26.2** lists the names of alkyl groups other than methyl, ethyl, and propyl. Halocarbons in which a halogen attaches to a carbon of an arene ring are called **aryl halides**.

(a)

(b)

(c)

Figure 26.2
Space-filling models of chloromethane (a), chloroethene (b), and chlorobenzene (c).

Table 26.2

Names of Some Common Alkyl Groups		
Name	**Alkyl group**	**Remarks**
Isopropyl	$CH_3-\overset{\overset{\displaystyle CH_3}{\displaystyle \vert}}{\underset{\underset{\displaystyle H}{\displaystyle \vert}}{C}}-$	The prefix *iso-* is used when there is a methyl group on the carbon second from the unsubstituted end of the longest chain.
Isobutyl	$CH_3-\overset{\overset{\displaystyle CH_3}{\displaystyle \vert}}{CH}-CH_2-$ primary carbon	The carbon joining this alkyl group to another group is bonded to one other carbon; it is a primary carbon.
Secondary butyl (*sec*-butyl)	$CH_3-CH_2-\underset{\vert}{CH}-CH_3$ secondary carbon	The carbon joining this alkyl group to another group is bonded to two other carbons; it is a secondary carbon.
Tertiary butyl (*tert*-butyl)	$CH_3-\overset{\overset{\displaystyle CH_3}{\displaystyle \vert}}{\underset{\underset{\displaystyle CH_3}{\displaystyle \vert}}{C}}-$ tertiary carbon	The carbon joining this alkyl group to another group is bonded to three carbons; it is a tertiary carbon.
Vinyl	$\overset{H}{\underset{H}{}}C=C\overset{}{\underset{H}{}}$	When used as an alkyl group in giving compounds common names, this group is called vinyl.
Phenyl	(benzene ring)	Phenyl is derived from benzene.

The attractions between halocarbon molecules are primarily the result of the weak van der Waals interactions called dispersion forces. These attractions increase with the degree of halogen substitution. Thus more highly halogenated organic compounds have higher boiling points, as illustrated in **Table 26.3**.

Table 26.3

Molecular Masses and Boiling Points of the Chloromethanes			
Molecular structure	**Name**	**Molar mass**	**Boiling point (°C)**
CH_4^*	Methane	16	-161
CH_3Cl	Chloromethane (methyl chloride)	50.5	-24
CH_2Cl_2	Dichloromethane (methylene chloride)	85.0	40
$CHCl_3$	Trichloromethane (chloroform)	119.5	61
CCl_4	Tetrachloromethane (carbon tetrachloride)	154	74

* Included for purposes of comparison.

Figure 26.3
Halothane (2-bromo-2-chloro-1,1,1-trifluoroethane) is used as an anesthetic. Is this molecule fully halogenated?

Very few halocarbons are found in nature, but they are readily prepared and used for many purposes. For example, halothane is used as an anesthetic. Hydrofluorocarbons are used as refrigerants in automobile air-conditioning systems.

Substitution Reactions

Organic reactions often proceed more slowly than the reactions of inorganic molecules and ions. This is because reactions of organic molecules commonly involve the breaking of relatively strong covalent bonds. Chemists are therefore constantly seeking new catalysts and improved procedures for conducting organic reactions. Many organic reactions are complex, often producing a mixture of products. The desired product must then be separated by distillation, crystallization, or other means. A common type of organic reaction is a **substitution reaction,** in which an atom or group of atoms replaces another atom or group of atoms.

A halogen can replace a hydrogen on an alkane to produce a halocarbon. The symbol X stands for a halogen in this generalized equation.

$$R-H \ + \ X_2 \ \longrightarrow \ R-X \ + \ HX$$

Alkane Halogen   Halocarbon Hydrogen halide

Sunlight or another source of ultraviolet radiation is usually a sufficient catalyst for this reaction. From the generalized equation, you can write a specific one.

$$CH_4 \ + \ Cl_2 \ \xrightarrow{\text{UV light}} \ CH_3Cl \ + \ HCl$$

Methane Chlorine   Chloromethane Hydrogen chloride

Even under controlled conditions, this simple halogenation reaction produces a mixture of mono-, di-, tri-, and tetrachloromethanes.

Treating benzene with a halogen in the presence of a catalyst causes the substitution of a ring hydrogen. Iron compounds are often used as catalysts for aromatic substitution reactions. Even a rusty nail dropped in the reaction flask acts as a catalyst.

Figure 26.4
Space-filling models can be used to represent this substitution reaction visually.

Halogens on carbon chains are readily displaced by hydroxide ions to produce an alcohol and a salt. The general reaction is as follows.

$$R-X \ + \ OH^- \ \xrightarrow[\text{100 °C}]{H_2O} \ R-OH \ + \ X^-$$

Halocarbon Hydroxide ion   Alcohol Halide ion

Chemists usually use aqueous solutions of sodium or potassium hydroxide as the source of hydroxide ions. The chemical equations for two specific examples are shown below.

$$CH_3-I(l) + KOH(aq) \xrightarrow[100\,°C]{H_2O} CH_3-OH(l) + KI(aq)$$

| Iodomethane (methyl iodide) | Potassium hydroxide | | Methanol | Potassium iodide |

$$CH_3CH_2Br(l) + NaOH(aq) \xrightarrow[100\,°C]{H_2O} CH_3CH_2OH(l) + NaBr(aq)$$

| Bromoethane (ethyl bromide) | Sodium hydroxide | | Ethanol | Sodium bromide |

How do KOH, KI, NaOH, and NaBr occur in aqueous solution? Fluoro groups are not easily displaced. Thus fluorocarbons are seldom, if ever, used to make alcohols.

section review 26.1

1. What is a functional group?

2. Identify the functional group in each structure.

   a. CH_3-OH

   b. $CH_3-CH_2-NH_2$

   c.

$$\begin{array}{c} -C-OH \\ \| \\ O \end{array}$$

   d. $CH_3-CH_2-CH_2-Br$

   e. $CH_3-CH_2-O-CH_2-CH_3$

3. What is a halocarbon? Write IUPAC names for each halocarbon.

   a. (benzene ring with) Br

   b. CH_3CH_2Cl

   c. $CH_3CHCH=CH_2$
      $|$
      Cl

4. Give the structural formula for each compound.

   a. isopropyl chloride

   b. 1-iodo-2,2-dimethylpentane

   c. *p*-bromotoluene

5. What is a substitution reaction? Give the general equations for the substitution of an alkane to form a halocarbon and the substitution of a halocarbon to form an alcohol.

6. Write the names of all possible dichloropropanes that could form from the chlorination of propane.

 Chem ASAP! **Assessment 26.1** Check your understanding of the important ideas and concepts in Section 26.1.

ALCOHOLS AND ETHERS

objectives

▶ Describe the structures and naming of alcohols and ethers
▶ Define an addition reaction and give several examples
▶ Compare the properties of alcohols and ethers

key terms

▶ alcohols
▶ hydroxyl group
▶ fermentation
▶ denatured alcohol
▶ addition reaction
▶ hydration reaction
▶ hydrogenation reaction
▶ ethers

*P*rior to the 1840s, patients had to endure surgery while they were fully conscious. Today, when having major surgery, a patient often receives a general anesthetic. In addition to causing the patient to lose consciousness, a general anesthetic also causes the patient's muscles to become relaxed. The major benefit of a general anesthetic is that the patient does not experience pain during surgery. The earliest anesthetics belonged to a class of chemical compounds called ethers. **What are the chemical characteristics of ethers?**

Alcohols

When you hear the word alcohol, what do you think of? Probably not a general class of thousands of organic compounds! **Alcohols** are organic compounds with an —OH group.

$$\ddot{\text{O}}$$
$$R \diagdown \diagup H$$

Alcohol molecule

The —OH functional group in alcohols is called a **hydroxyl group** or hydroxy function. How does a hydroxyl group differ from a hydroxide ion? (If you need to review the structure of a hydroxide ion, refer back to Section 20.2.) Aliphatic alcohols can be arranged into structural categories according to the number of R groups attached to the carbon with the hydroxyl group. If one R group is attached, the alcohol is a primary alcohol; if two R groups, a secondary alcohol; if three R groups, a tertiary alcohol. This nomenclature is summarized below.

Primary alcohol	$R-CH_2-OH$	Only one R group is attached to C—OH of a primary (abbreviated 1°) alcohol.
Secondary alcohol	$\underset{\displaystyle R}{\overset{\displaystyle R}{R-CH-OH}}$	Two R groups are attached to C—OH of a secondary (2°) alcohol.
Tertiary alcohol	$R-\overset{\displaystyle R}{\underset{\displaystyle R}{C}}-OH$	Three R groups are attached to C—OH of a tertiary (3°) alcohol.

Both IUPAC and common names are used for alcohols. When using the IUPAC system to name continuous-chain and substituted alcohols, drop the -*e* ending of the parent alkane name and add the ending -*ol*. The parent alkane is the longest continuous chain of carbons that includes the carbon attached to the hydroxyl group. In numbering the longest continuous chain, the position of the hydroxyl group is given the lowest possible number. Alcohols containing two, three, and four —OH substituents are named diols, triols, and tetrols, respectively.

Common names of aliphatic alcohols are written in the same way as those of the halocarbons. The alkyl group methyl, for example, is named and followed by the word alcohol, as in methyl alcohol. Compounds with more than one —OH substituent are called glycols. The structural formulas for some simple aliphatic alcohols along with their IUPAC and common names are shown below.

CH_3—OH
Methanol
(methyl alcohol)

CH_3—CH_2—OH
Ethanol
(ethyl alcohol)

CH_3—CH_2—CH_2—OH
1-propanol
(propyl alcohol)

OH
|
CH_3—CH—CH_3
2-propanol
(isopropyl alcohol)

CH_3
|
CH_3—CH—CH_2—OH
2-methyl-1-propanol
(isobutyl alcohol)

CH_3—CH_2—CH—CH_3
|
OH
2-butanol
(sec-butyl alcohol)

CH_3
|
CH_3—C—CH_3
|
OH
2-methyl-2-propanol
(tert-butyl alcohol)

CH_2—CH_2
| |
OH   OH
1,2-ethanediol
(ethylene glycol)

CH_3—CH—CH_2
| |
OH   OH
1,2-propanediol
(propylene glycol)

CH_2—CH—CH_2
| | |
OH   OH   OH
1,2,3-propanetriol
(glycerol)

Figure 26.5
Ethanol is a common component of household products.

Phenols are compounds in which a hydroxyl group is attached directly to an aromatic ring. Phenol is the parent compound. Cresol is the common name for the *o*, *m*, and *p* structural isomers of methylphenol.

Properties of Alcohols

Like water, alcohols are capable of intermolecular hydrogen bonding. Alcohols, therefore, boil at a higher temperature than do alkanes and halocarbons containing comparable numbers of atoms.

Because alcohols are derivatives of water (the hydroxyl group is part of a water molecule), you might expect them to be soluble in water. To a point, you would be correct. Alcohols of up to four carbons are soluble in water in all proportions. The solubility of alcohols with four or more carbons in the chain is usually much lower. The explanation for this solubility difference is that alcohols consist of two parts: the carbon chain and the hydroxyl group. The carbon chain is nonpolar and is not attracted to water. The hydroxyl group is polar and strongly interacts with water through hydrogen bonding.

Figure 26.6

The alcohols contain one, two, or three hydroxyl groups. Which space-filling model depicts a diol? A triol?

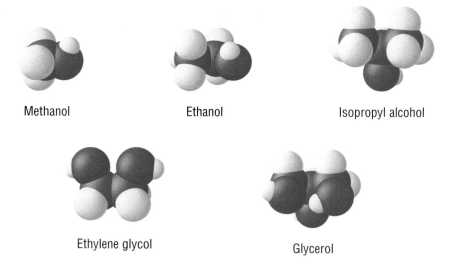

Methanol   Ethanol   Isopropyl alcohol

Ethylene glycol   Glycerol

For alcohols of up to four carbons, the polarity of the hydroxyl group is more significant than the nonpolarity of the carbon chain. Thus these alcohols are soluble in water. As the number of carbon atoms increases above four, however, the nonpolarity of the chain becomes more significant and the solubility decreases.

Many aliphatic alcohols are used in laboratories, clinics, and industry. Isopropyl alcohol (IUPAC: 2-propanol), which is more familiarly known as rubbing alcohol, is a colorless, nearly odorless liquid (bp 82 °C) used as an antiseptic. It is also used as a base for perfumes, creams, lotions, and other cosmetics. Ethylene glycol (IUPAC: 1,2-ethanediol) is the principal ingredient of certain antifreezes. Its boiling point is 197 °C. Its advantages over other liquids with high boiling points are its solubility in water and a freezing point of −17.4 °C. If water is added to ethylene glycol, the mixture freezes at an even lower temperature: A 50% (v/v) aqueous solution of ethylene glycol freezes at −36 °C. Glycerol (IUPAC: 1,2,3-propanetriol) is a viscous, sweet-tasting, water-soluble liquid used as a moistening agent in cosmetics, foods, and drugs. Glycerol is also an important component of fats and oils, which you will learn about in Chapter 27.

Figure 26.7

Many cosmetic products contain glycerol (left). Isopropyl alcohol is an effective antiseptic (center). Ethylene glycol is the main ingredient in antifreeze (right). How does this poisonous substance keep the water in a car's radiator from freezing at 0 °C and boiling at 100 °C?

Ethyl alcohol (IUPAC: ethanol), which has a boiling point of 78.5 °C, is also called grain alcohol. It is an important industrial chemical. Some ethanol is still produced by yeast fermentation of sugar. **Fermentation** is the production of ethanol from sugars by the action of yeast or bacteria. The enzymes of the yeast or bacteria serve as catalysts for the transformation. The breakdown of the sugar glucose ($C_6H_{12}O_6$) is an important fermentation reaction.

$$C_6H_{12}O_6(aq) \longrightarrow 2CH_3CH_2OH(aq) + 2CO_2(g)$$
$$\text{Glucose} \qquad \text{Ethanol} \qquad \text{Carbon dioxide}$$

Ethanol is the intoxicating substance in alcoholic beverages. It is a depressant that can be fatal if taken in large doses at once. Over time, continuous abuse of alcoholic beverages can damage the liver, which can lead to death.

The ethanol used in industrial applications is denatured. **Denatured alcohol** is ethanol with an added substance to make it toxic (poisonous). That added substance, or denaturant, is often methyl alcohol (IUPAC: methanol). Methyl alcohol is sometimes called wood alcohol because prior to 1925 it was prepared by the distillation of wood. Wood alcohol is extremely toxic: As little as 10 mL has been reported to cause permanent blindness and as little as 30 mL has been known to cause death.

Figure 26.8
Cracker and bread dough alike are made primarily of flour and water, but bread dough also contains yeast. Carbon dioxide, a product of sugar fermentation by yeast, causes bread to rise. What happens to the ethanol that is also produced?

Addition Reactions

As you already know, carbon–carbon single bonds are not easy to break. However, one of the bonds in an alkene double bond is somewhat weaker and thus easier to break than a carbon–carbon single bond. So it is sometimes possible for a compound of general structure X—Y to add to a double bond. In an **addition reaction,** a substance is added at the double or triple bond of an alkene or alkyne. Addition reactions are an important method of introducing new functional groups into organic molecules. In the general reaction shown below, X and Y stand for the two parts of the compound that are added.

$$\underset{/}{\overset{\backslash}{C}}=\underset{\backslash}{\overset{/}{C}} + X-Y \longrightarrow -\underset{|}{\overset{\overset{\displaystyle X}{|}}{C}}-\underset{|}{\overset{\overset{\displaystyle Y}{|}}{C}}-$$

The addition of water to an alkene is a **hydration reaction.** Hydration reactions usually occur when the alkene and water are heated to about 100 °C in the presence of a trace of strong acid. The acid, usually hydrochloric acid or sulfuric acid, serves as a catalyst for the reaction. The addition of water to ethene, the equation for which is shown below, is a typical hydration reaction. The parts of ethanol that come from the addition of water are shown in blue.

$$\underset{H}{\overset{H}{\backslash}}C=C\underset{H}{\overset{H}{/}} + H-OH \xrightarrow[100°C]{H^+} H-\underset{\overset{|}{H}}{\overset{\overset{H}{|}}{C}}-\underset{\overset{|}{H}}{\overset{\overset{OH}{|}}{C}}-H$$
$$\text{Ethene} \qquad\qquad \text{Water} \qquad\qquad \text{Ethanol}$$

When the reagent X—Y is a halogen molecule such as chlorine or bromine, the product of the reaction is a disubstituted halocarbon. The addition of bromine to ethene to form the disubstituted halocarbon 1,2-dibromoethane is an example.

Ethene   Bromine   1,2-dibromoethane
(colorless)   (brownish   (colorless)
                  orange)

The addition of bromine to carbon–carbon multiple bonds is often used as a chemical test for unsaturation in an organic molecule. Bromine has a brownish-orange color, but most organic compounds of bromine are colorless. The test for unsaturation is performed by adding a few drops of a 1% solution of bromine in carbon tetrachloride (CCl_4) to the suspected alkene. As **Figure 26.9** shows, the loss of the orange color is a positive test for unsaturation. If the orange color remains, what would you conclude about the sample?

Hydrogen halides, such as HBr or HCl, can also add to a double bond. Because the product contains only one substituent, it is called a monosubstituted halocarbon. The addition of hydrogen chloride to ethene is an example.

Ethene   Hydrogen   Chloroethane
(ethylene)   chloride   (ethyl chloride)

The addition of hydrogen to a carbon–carbon double bond to produce an alkane is a **hydrogenation reaction.** A hydrogenation reaction usually requires a catalyst. Finely divided platinum (Pt) or palladium (Pd) is often used. A common application of a hydrogenation reaction is the manufacture of margarine from unsaturated vegetable oils.

Figure 26.9
When a few drops of orange bromine solution (top) are added to an unsaturated organic compound (center), the bromine reacts to form a colorless halocarbon (bottom). Bromine can be used to identify unsaturated compounds.

Ethene   Hydrogen   Ethane
(ethylene)

Cyclohexene   Hydrogen   Cyclohexane

The hydrogenation of a double bond is a reduction reaction. In the examples on the previous page, ethene is reduced to ethane, and cyclohexene is reduced to cyclohexane.

Under normal conditions, benzene resists hydrogenation. It also resists the addition of a halogen or a hydrogen halide. Under conditions of high temperatures and high pressures of hydrogen, however, three molecules of hydrogen reduce one molecule of benzene to cyclohexane. What property of benzene distinguishes it from alkenes and causes it to be less reactive?

$$\text{Benzene} \quad + \quad 3H-H \xrightarrow{Pt} \quad \text{Cyclohexane}$$

Benzene   Hydrogen   Cyclohexane

Ethers

Another class of organic compounds may sound familiar to you—ethers. **Ethers** are compounds in which oxygen is bonded to two carbon groups. The general structure of an ether is R—O—R. Ethers are easy to name. The alkyl groups attached to the ether linkage are named in alphabetical order and are followed by the word ether.

$$R \overset{\ddot{O}}{\diagup\diagdown} R \qquad CH_3CH_2-O-CH_3 \qquad CH_3-O-\text{(phenyl)}$$

Ether molecule   Ethylmethyl ether   Methylphenyl ether
(anisole)

Some ethers, such as ethylmethyl ether and methylphenyl ether, are nonsymmetric. This is because the R groups attached to the ether oxygen are different. When both R groups are the same, the ether is symmetric. Symmetric ethers are named by using the prefix *di-*. Sometimes, however, the prefix *di-* is dropped and a compound such as diethyl ether is simply called ethyl ether.

$$CH_3CH_2-O-CH_2CH_3 \qquad \text{(phenyl)}-O-\text{(phenyl)}$$

Diethyl ether   Diphenyl ether
(ethyl ether)   (phenyl ether)

Diethyl ether, a volatile liquid (bp 35 °C), was the first reliable general anesthetic. (An anesthetic is a substance that produces a loss of sensation.) Originally reported in 1842 by Crawford W. Long, an American physician, diethyl ether was used by doctors for more than a century. It has been replaced by other anesthetics because it is highly flammable and often causes nausea. An anesthetic used today is halothane, a halocarbon you read about in Section 26.1.

(a)

(b)

Figure 26.10
*Ethylmethyl ether **(a)** is an example of a nonsymmetric ether, and diphenyl ether **(b)** is an example of a symmetric ether.*

Ethers usually have lower boiling points than alcohols of comparable molar mass. They have higher boiling points than comparable hydrocarbons and halocarbons. Ethers are more soluble in water than hydrocarbons and halocarbons, but less soluble than alcohols. The reason for this is that the oxygens in ethers are hydrogen acceptors. However, ethers have no hydroxyl hydrogens to donate in hydrogen bonding. Ethers, therefore, form more hydrogen bonds than hydrocarbons and halocarbons but fewer hydrogen bonds than alcohols.

section review 26.2

7. Write general structural formulas for an alcohol and an ether. How would you name these molecules?

8. What is an addition reaction? Give examples of a hydration reaction and a hydrogenation reaction.

9. How does the solubility of alcohols compare with that of ethers? The boiling points? Explain your answers.

10. Give the following alcohols IUPAC names and classify each as primary, secondary, or tertiary.

    a. $CH_3CH_2CH_2CH_2OH$

    b. $CH_3\overset{\overset{\displaystyle CH_3}{|}}{C}HOH$

    c. $CH_3CH_2\overset{\overset{\displaystyle CH_3}{|}}{C}HCH_2OH$

11. Write the common names for the following compounds.

    a. $CH_3CH_2\underset{\underset{\displaystyle OH}{|}}{C}HCH_3$

    b. $CH_3\underset{\underset{\displaystyle CH_3}{|}}{C}HCH_2OH$

    c. $CH_3CH_2OCH_2CH_3$

    d. $CH_3CH_2CH_2OCH_2CH_2CH_2CH_3$

12. Give the structure for the expected organic product from each of the following reactions.

    a. $\underset{H}{\overset{CH_3}{\diagdown}}C{=}C\underset{CH_3}{\overset{H}{\diagup}}$ + HBr $\longrightarrow$

    b. ⬡ + Cl_2 $\xrightarrow{\text{catalyst}}$

    c. ⬡ + $3H_2$ $\xrightarrow[\text{pressure}]{\text{catalyst}}$

 Chem ASAP! **Assessment 26.2** Check your understanding of the important ideas and concepts in Section 26.2.

*W*hat is your favorite flavor, benzaldehyde or vanillin? Although these flavors might sound like they belong in the foods of a science-fiction movie, the chances are good that you have eaten these organic molecules, called aldehydes, on many occasions. Aldehydes and many other carbonyl compounds have important everyday uses—even though they may have unfamiliar names. **What properties are associated with carbonyl compounds?**

objectives

▶ Distinguish among the carbonyl groups of aldehydes, ketones, carboxylic acids, and esters

▶ Describe the reactions of compounds that contain the carbonyl functional group

key terms

▶ carbonyl group
▶ aldehydes
▶ ketones
▶ carboxylic acids
▶ carboxyl group
▶ fatty acids
▶ esters
▶ dehydrogenation reaction
▶ Benedict's test
▶ Fehling's test

Aldehydes and Ketones

You have now learned that in an alcohol, an oxygen atom is bonded to a carbon group and a hydrogen atom. In an ether, an oxygen atom is bonded to two carbon groups. An oxygen atom can also be bonded to a single carbon atom by a double covalent bond. Such an arrangement is called a carbonyl group. A **carbonyl group** consists of a carbon atom and an oxygen atom joined by a double bond. It is the functional group in aldehydes and ketones.

Aldehydes are organic compounds in which the carbon of the carbonyl group is always joined to at least one hydrogen. The general formula for an aldehyde is RCHO.

Ketones are organic compounds in which the carbon of the carbonyl group is joined to two other carbons. The general formula for a ketone is RCOR.

$$\begin{array}{cc} \overset{\displaystyle O}{\underset{\displaystyle R-C-H}{\|}} \leftarrow \text{Carbonyl group} & \overset{\displaystyle O}{\underset{\displaystyle R-C-R}{\|}} \leftarrow \text{Carbonyl group} \\ \text{Aldehyde} & \text{Ketone} \end{array}$$

The IUPAC system may be used for naming aldehydes and ketones. For either class of compounds, you must first identify the longest hydrocarbon chain that contains the carbonyl group. The *-e* ending of the hydrocarbon is replaced by *-al* to designate an aldehyde. In the IUPAC system, the continuous-chain aldehydes are named methanal, ethanal, propanal, butanal, and so forth.

Ketones are named by changing the ending of the longest continuous carbon chain that contains the carbonyl group from *-e* to *-one*. **Table 26.4** on the following page illustrates the naming of some common aldehydes and ketones. If the carbonyl group of a ketone could occur at several places on the chain, then its position is designated by the lowest possible number. Why is it unnecessary to use a number prefix when naming an aldehyde?

Aldehydes and ketones can form weak hydrogen bonds between the carbonyl oxygen and the hydrogens of water. The lower members of the series—methanal (formaldehyde), ethanal (acetaldehyde), and propanone (acetone)—are soluble in water in all proportions. As the length of the hydrocarbon chain increases, however, water solubility decreases. When the carbon chain exceeds five or six carbons, solubility of both aldehydes and ketones is very low. As might be expected, all aldehydes and ketones are soluble in nonpolar solvents.

(a)

(b)

(c)

Figure 26.11
*The low-molar-mass carbonyl-group compounds methanal **(a)**, ethanal **(b)**, and propanone **(c)** are completely soluble in water.*

Table 26.4

Some Common Aldehydes and Ketones			
Condensed formula	**Structural formula**	**IUPAC name**	**Common name**
Aldehydes			
HCHO		Methanal	Formaldehyde
CH_3CHO		Ethanal	Acetaldehyde
C_6H_5CHO		Benzaldehyde	Benzaldehyde
$C_6H_5CH=CHCHO$		3-phenyl-2-propenal	Cinnamaldehyde
$CH_3O(OH)C_6H_3CHO$		4-hydroxy-3-methoxybenzaldehyde	Vanillin
Ketones			
CH_3COCH_3		Propanone	Acetone (dimethyl ketone)
$C_6H_5COC_6H_5$		Diphenylmethanone	Benzophenone (diphenyl ketone)

Aldehydes and ketones cannot form intermolecular hydrogen bonds because they lack hydroxyl (—OH) groups. Consequently, they have boiling points lower than those of the corresponding alcohols. Aldehydes and ketones can attract each other, however, through polar–polar interactions of their carbonyl groups. As a result, their boiling points are higher than those of the corresponding alkanes. These attractive forces account for the fact that nearly all aldehydes and ketones are either liquids or solids at room temperature. The exception is methanal, which is an irritating, pungent gas. **Table 26.5** compares the boiling points of alkanes, aldehydes, and alcohols of similar molar mass.

A wide variety of aldehydes and ketones have been isolated from plants and animals. Many of them, particularly those with high molar masses, have fragrant or penetrating odors. They are usually known by their common names, which can indicate their natural sources or perhaps a characteristic property. Aromatic aldehydes are often used as flavoring

Table 26.5

Boiling Points of Some Compounds with One and Two Carbons				
Compound	Formula	Molar mass	Boiling point (°C)	Comments
One carbon				
Methane	CH_4	16	−161	No hydrogen-bonding or polar-polar interactions
Methanal	HCHO	30	−21	Polar-polar interactions
Methanol	CH_3OH	32	65	Hydrogen bonding
Two carbons				
Ethane	C_2H_6	30	−89	No hydrogen-bonding or polar-polar interactions
Ethanal	CH_3CHO	44	20	Polar-polar interactions
Ethanol	CH_3CH_2OH	46	78	Hydrogen bonding

agents. Benzaldehyde is the simplest aromatic aldehyde. Also known as oil of bitter almond, benzaldehyde is a constituent of almonds. It is a colorless liquid with a pleasant almond odor. Cinnamaldehyde imparts the characteristic odor of oil of cinnamon. Vanillin, which is responsible for the popular vanilla flavor, was at one time obtainable only from the podlike capsules of certain climbing orchids, such as those shown in **Figure 26.12.** Today much vanillin is synthetically produced.

The simplest aldehyde is methanal, which is also called formaldehyde. Methanal is very important industrially, having its greatest use in the manufacture of synthetic resins, but it is inconvenient to handle in the gaseous state. Methanal is usually available as a 40% aqueous solution, known as formalin. Formalin is used to preserve biological specimens. The methanal in solution combines with protein in tissues to make the tissues hard and insoluble in water. This process prevents the specimen from decaying. Today, formalin is used infrequently as a preservative because it is a carcinogen, or cancer-causing agent.

The most important industrial ketone is propanone, also called acetone. It is a colorless, volatile liquid that boils at 56 °C. Propanone is used as a solvent for resins, plastics, and varnishes and is often found in nail-polish removers. Propanone is miscible with water in all proportions. Can you suggest a reason why propanone is used in nail-polish removers?

Figure 26.12
Vanilla beans, the seed pods from this orchid, are the natural source of vanilla flavor for ice cream and other foods. What is the IUPAC name for vanillin?

787

Carboxylic Acids

Carboxylic acids are compounds with a carboxyl group. A **carboxyl group** consists of a carbonyl group attached to a hydroxyl group.

$$
\underset{\substack{\text{Carboxyl group}\\ \text{(also written } -CO_2H \text{ or } -COOH\text{)}}}{R-\overset{\overset{\displaystyle O}{\|}}{C}-OH}
$$

Carbonyl group

Hydroxyl group

The general formula for a carboxylic acid is RCOOH. Carboxylic acids are weak acids because they ionize only slightly in solution to give a carboxylate ion and a hydrogen ion.

$$
\underset{\substack{\text{Carboxylic}\\ \text{acid}}}{R-\overset{\overset{\displaystyle O}{\|}}{C}-OH} \rightleftharpoons \underset{\substack{\text{Carboxylate}\\ \text{ion}}}{R-\overset{\overset{\displaystyle O}{\|}}{C}-O^-} + \underset{\substack{\text{Hydrogen ion}\\ \text{(proton)}}}{H^+}
$$

In the IUPAC system, carboxylic acids are named by replacing the *-e* ending of the parent alkane with the ending *-oic acid*. Remember, the parent alkane is the hydrocarbon with the longest continuous carbon chain containing the carboxyl group.

Carboxylic acids are abundant and widely distributed in nature. Many have common names derived from a Greek or Latin word describing their natural sources. For example, the common name for ethanoic acid is acetic acid, which comes from the Latin word *acetum,* meaning vinegar. Acetic acid is produced when wine turns sour and becomes vinegar. The pungent aroma of vinegar comes from acetic acid. Common household vinegar contains about 5% (v/v) acetic acid. Many continuous-chain carboxylic acids were first isolated from fats and are called **fatty acids.** Propionic acid, the three-carbon acid, literally means first fatty acid. Common names are used more often than IUPAC names for carboxylic acids. **Table 26.6** lists the names and formulas of some common aliphatic carboxylic acids. What relationship do you notice between the number of carbon atoms and the melting point for the fatty acids?

The low-molar-mass members of the aliphatic carboxylic acid series are colorless, volatile liquids. They have sharp, unpleasant odors. The smells of rancid butter and dirty feet are due in part to butyric acid, the four-carbon acid. The higher members of the series are nonvolatile, waxy solids with low melting points. Stearic acid, an 18-carbon acid obtained from beef fat, is used to make inexpensive wax candles. Stearic acid and other long-chain fatty acids have very little odor.

Like alcohols, carboxylic acids can form intermolecular hydrogen bonds. As a result, carboxylic acids have higher boiling points and higher melting points than other compounds of similar molar mass. All aromatic carboxylic acids are crystalline solids at room temperature.

The carboxyl group in carboxylic acids is polar and readily forms hydrogen bonds with water molecules. This should indicate an important

Figure 26.13

Carboxylic acids give a variety of foods—spoiled as well as fresh—a distinctive sour taste.

Table 26.6

Saturated Aliphatic Carboxylic Acids				
Formula	Carbon atoms	IUPAC name	Common name	Melting point (°C)
$HCOOH$	1	Methanoic acid	Formic acid	8
CH_3COOH	2	Ethanoic acid	Acetic acid	17
CH_3CH_2COOH	3	Propanoic acid	Propionic acid	−22
$CH_3(CH_2)_2COOH$	4	Butanoic acid	Butyric acid	−6
$CH_3(CH_2)_4COOH$	6	Hexanoic acid	Caproic acid	−3
$CH_3(CH_2)_6COOH$	8	Octanoic acid	Caprylic acid	16
$CH_3(CH_2)_8COOH$	10	Decanoic acid	Capric acid	31
$CH_3(CH_2)_{10}COOH$	12	Dodecanoic acid	Lauric acid	44
$CH_3(CH_2)_{12}COOH$	14	Tetradecanoic acid	Myristic acid	58
$CH_3(CH_2)_{14}COOH$	16	Hexadecanoic acid	Palmitic acid	63
$CH_3(CH_2)_{16}COOH$	18	Octadecanoic acid	Stearic acid	70

property of some carboxylic acids. Methanoic, ethanoic, propanoic, and butanoic acids are completely miscible with water. The solubility of carboxylic acids of higher molar mass drops sharply, however. Most carboxylic acids dissolve in organic solvents such as ethanol or propanone.

Figure 26.14
Ethanoic acid, shown in this space-filling model, is a colorless, volatile liquid. Is it soluble in water? Why?

Esters

Esters are probably the most pleasant and delicious organic compounds to study. **Esters** are derivatives of carboxylic acids in which the —OH of the carboxyl group has been replaced by an —OR from an alcohol. Thus esters contain a carbonyl group and an ether link to the carbonyl carbon. Many esters have pleasant, fruity odors. Esters give blueberries, pineapples, apples, pears, bananas, and many other fruits their characteristic odors. They are also responsible for giving some perfumes their fragrances.

The general formula for a carboxylate ester is RCOOR. The R group can be a short-chain or long-chain aliphatic (alkyl) or aromatic (aryl) group, saturated or unsaturated.

Simple esters are neutral substances. Although the molecules are polar, they cannot form hydrogen bonds with one another because they do not contain hydrogen attached to oxygen or another electronegative atom. As a result, only weak attractions hold ester molecules to one another. As you might expect, esters have much lower boiling points than the strongly hydrogen-bonded carboxylic acids from which they are derived. The low-formula-mass esters are somewhat soluble in water, but esters containing more than four or five carbons have very limited solubility.

Figure 26.15

Esters impart the characteristic odors and flavors of many flowers and fruits.

If an ester is heated with water for several hours, usually very little happens. In strong acid or base solutions, however, the ester breaks down. An ester is hydrolyzed by the addition of water to produce a carboxylic acid and an alcohol. The reaction is rapid in acidic solution. How might you explain this?

$$CH_3-\overset{\overset{\displaystyle O}{\|}}{C}-OCH_2CH_3 + H-OH \underset{}{\overset{H^+}{\rightleftharpoons}} CH_3-\overset{\overset{\displaystyle O}{\|}}{C}-OH + HOCH_2CH_3$$

Ethyl ethanoate   Ethanoic acid   Ethanol

Hydroxide ions also promote this reaction. The usual agent for ester hydrolysis is an aqueous solution of sodium hydroxide or potassium hydroxide. Because many esters do not dissolve in water, a solvent such as ethanol is added to make the solution homogeneous. The reaction mixture is usually heated. All of the ester is converted to products. The carboxylic acid product is in solution as its sodium or potassium salt.

$$CH_3-\overset{\overset{\displaystyle O}{\|}}{C}-OCH_2CH_3 + NaOH \longrightarrow CH_3-\overset{\overset{\displaystyle O}{\|}}{C}-O^-Na^+ + HOCH_2CH_3$$

Ethyl ethanoate   Sodium ethanoate   Ethanol

If the reaction mixture is acidified, the carboxylic acid forms.

$$CH_3-\overset{\overset{\displaystyle O}{\|}}{C}-O^-Na^+ + HCl \longrightarrow CH_3-\overset{\overset{\displaystyle O}{\|}}{C}-OH + NaCl$$

Sodium ethanoate   Ethanoic acid

Esters may be prepared from an acid and an alcohol. Esterification is the formation of an ester from a carboxylic acid and an alcohol. The reactants, usually a carboxylic acid and a primary or secondary alcohol, are heated with a trace of mineral acid as a catalyst. The reaction is reversible.

$$R-\overset{\overset{\displaystyle O}{\diagup\!\!\!\!\diagdown}}{C}_{\diagdown OH} + RO-H \overset{H^+}{\rightleftharpoons} R-\overset{\overset{\displaystyle O}{\diagup\!\!\!\!\diagdown}}{C}_{\diagdown OR} + H-OH$$

Carboxylic   Alcohol   Carboxylate   Water
acid   ester

TO

GENETICS

Scientists Growing Flavors

Scientists are learning how to grow flavor molecules and other naturally occurring compounds in plant cell cultures and genetically altered yeast cells. For example, Japanese scientists are using a tissue culture technique called root culture to produce ginseng for teas and medicines and for a red pigment used in cosmetics. In the United States, scientists are obtaining vanilla flavor from cells surgically removed from a vanilla orchid and cultured in a glass bioreactor. Prior to any commercial production, a patent application is usually filed, and manufacturers must seek approval from the Food and Drug Administration to use the prepared flavor molecules in food products.

The formation of the ester ethyl ethanoate from ethanoic acid and ethanol is an example of esterification.

$$CH_3-C \underset{OH}{\overset{O}{\lessgtr}} \ + \ CH_3CH_2O-H \ \underset{}{\overset{H^+}{\rightleftharpoons}} \ CH_3-C \underset{OCH_2CH_3}{\overset{O}{\lessgtr}} \ + \ H_2O$$

| Ethanoic acid | Ethanol | | Ethyl ethanoate | Water |

Figure 26.16
Ethyl ethanoate, shown in this space-filling model, is a low-molar-mass ester.

Oxidation–Reduction Reactions

All the classes of organic compounds you have just studied are related by oxidation and reduction reactions. Before you explore this concept further, it would probably be helpful to review the definitions of these reactions. As you have learned, oxidation is the gain of oxygen, loss of hydrogen, or loss of electrons. Reduction is the reverse: loss of oxygen, gain of hydrogen, or gain of electrons. Oxidation and reduction reactions are coupled: One does not occur without the other.

In organic chemistry, the number of oxygens and hydrogens attached to carbon indicates the degree of oxidation of a compound. The fewer the number of hydrogens on a carbon–carbon bond, the more oxidized the bond. Thus a triple bond (characteristic of an alkyne) is more oxidized than a double bond (an alkene) and a single bond (an alkane). Expressed another way, an alkane can be oxidized to an alkene and then to an alkyne. For example, ethane (an alkane) can be oxidized to ethene (an alkene) and then to ethyne (an alkyne).

The loss of hydrogen is a **dehydrogenation reaction.** Strong heating and a catalyst are usually necessary to make dehydrogenation reactions occur. The loss of each molecule of hydrogen involves the loss of two electrons from the organic molecule. The remaining carbon electrons pair to make a second or third bond, as shown below.

$$H-\overset{\overset{\displaystyle H}{|}}{\underset{\underset{\displaystyle H}{|}}{C}}-\overset{\overset{\displaystyle H}{|}}{\underset{\underset{\displaystyle H}{|}}{C}}-H \quad \xrightarrow[\text{oxidation}]{\substack{\text{loss of hydrogen} \\ \text{(dehydrogenation)}}} \quad \overset{H}{\underset{H}{>}}C=C\overset{H}{\underset{H}{<}} \quad \xrightarrow[\text{oxidation}]{\substack{\text{loss of hydrogen} \\ \text{(dehydrogenation)}}} \quad H-C\equiv C-H$$

Least oxidized (most reduced)   Most oxidized (least reduced)

These reactions are reversible. Alkynes can be reduced to alkenes, and alkenes can be reduced to alkanes by the addition of hydrogen to a double bond.

$$H-C\equiv C-H \quad \xrightarrow[\text{reduction}]{\substack{\text{gain of} \\ \text{hydrogen}}} \quad \overset{H}{\underset{H}{>}}C=C\overset{H}{\underset{H}{<}} \quad \xrightarrow[\text{reduction}]{\substack{\text{gain of} \\ \text{hydrogen}}} \quad H-\overset{\overset{\displaystyle H}{|}}{\underset{\underset{\displaystyle H}{|}}{C}}-\overset{\overset{\displaystyle H}{|}}{\underset{\underset{\displaystyle H}{|}}{C}}-H$$

Most oxidized (least reduced)   Most reduced (least oxidized)

Oxidation in organic chemistry also involves the number and degree of oxidation of oxygens attached to carbon. For example, methane, a saturated hydrocarbon, can be oxidized in steps to carbon dioxide. This occurs if it alternately gains oxygens and loses hydrogens. Methane is oxidized to methanol, then to methanal, then to methanoic acid, and finally to carbon dioxide. The same sequence of oxidations occurs for other alkanes. Each series consists of an alkane, alcohol, aldehyde (or ketone), carboxylic acid, and carbon dioxide. The carbon dioxide is most oxidized or least reduced, and the alkane is least oxidized or most reduced.

$$H-\underset{\underset{H}{|}}{\overset{\overset{H}{|}}{C}}-H \xrightarrow[\text{oxidation}]{\text{gain of oxygen}} H-\underset{\underset{H}{|}}{\overset{\overset{OH}{|}}{C}}-H \xrightarrow[\text{oxidation}]{\text{loss of hydrogen}} H-\overset{\overset{O}{\|}}{C}-H \xrightarrow[\text{oxidation}]{\text{gain of oxygen}} H-\overset{\overset{O}{\|}}{C}-OH \xrightarrow[\text{oxidation}]{\text{loss of hydrogen}} O=C=O$$

| Methane (most energetic molecule) | Methanol (methyl alcohol) | Methanal (formaldehyde) | Methanoic acid (formic acid) | Carbon dioxide (least energetic molecule) |

The more reduced a carbon compound, the more energy it can release upon its complete oxidation to carbon dioxide. Are oxidation reactions endothermic or exothermic? The energy-releasing properties of oxidation reactions are extremely important for energy production in living systems. They also explain why the combustion of hydrocarbons such as methane is a good source of energy. **Figure 26.17** shows examples of energy production by oxidation reactions.

Primary alcohols can be oxidized to aldehydes, and secondary alcohols can be oxidized to ketones.

$$R-\underset{\underset{H}{|}}{\overset{\overset{OH}{|}}{C}}-H \xrightarrow[-2H]{\text{oxidation}} R-\overset{\overset{O}{\|}}{C}-H \qquad R-\underset{\underset{H}{|}}{\overset{\overset{OH}{|}}{C}}-R \xrightarrow[-2H]{\text{oxidation}} R-\overset{\overset{O}{\|}}{C}-R$$

| Primary alcohol | Aldehyde | Secondary alcohol | Ketone |

Tertiary alcohols, however, cannot be oxidized because there is no hydrogen present on the carbon bearing the hydroxyl group. A comparison of the structure of primary, secondary, and tertiary alcohols is shown below.

$$H-\underset{\underset{H}{|}}{\overset{\overset{H}{|}}{C}}-\underset{\underset{H}{|}}{\overset{\overset{H}{|}}{C}}-\underset{\underset{H}{|}}{\overset{\overset{H}{|}}{C}}-OH \qquad H-\underset{\underset{H}{|}}{\overset{\overset{H}{|}}{C}}-\underset{\underset{OH}{|}}{\overset{\overset{H}{|}}{C}}-\underset{\underset{H}{|}}{\overset{\overset{H}{|}}{C}}-H \qquad H-\underset{\underset{H}{|}}{\overset{\overset{H}{|}}{C}}-\underset{\underset{OH}{|}}{\overset{\overset{CH_3}{|}}{C}}-\underset{\underset{H}{|}}{\overset{\overset{H}{|}}{C}}-H$$

| Primary alcohol | Secondary alcohol | Tertiary alcohol |

Figure 26.17

These soccer players are energized by oxidation reactions. Much of the world relies on hydrocarbon combustion as a source of energy.

The primary alcohols methanol and ethanol can be oxidized to aldehydes by warming them at about 50 °C with acidified potassium dichromate ($K_2Cr_2O_7$). In these reactions, methanol produces formaldehyde, and ethanol produces acetaldehyde.

$$\underset{\substack{\text{Methanol}\\ \text{(methyl alcohol)}\\ \text{(bp 65 °C)}}}{\text{H}-\overset{\overset{\displaystyle \text{OH}}{|}}{\underset{\underset{\displaystyle \text{H}}{|}}{\text{C}}}-\text{H}} \;\xrightarrow[\text{H}_2\text{SO}_4]{\text{K}_2\text{Cr}_2\text{O}_7}\; \underset{\substack{\text{Methanal}\\ \text{(formaldehyde)}\\ \text{(bp }-21\text{ °C)}}}{\text{H}-\overset{\overset{\displaystyle \text{O}}{\|}}{\text{C}}-\text{H}} \qquad \underset{\substack{\text{Ethanol}\\ \text{(ethyl alcohol)}\\ \text{(bp 78 °C)}}}{\text{CH}_3-\overset{\overset{\displaystyle \text{OH}}{|}}{\underset{\underset{\displaystyle \text{H}}{|}}{\text{C}}}-\text{H}} \;\xrightarrow[\text{H}_2\text{SO}_4]{\text{K}_2\text{Cr}_2\text{O}_7}\; \underset{\substack{\text{Ethanal}\\ \text{(acetaldehyde)}\\ \text{(bp 21 °C)}}}{\text{CH}_3-\overset{\overset{\displaystyle \text{O}}{\|}}{\text{C}}-\text{H}}$$

Preparing an aldehyde by this method is often a problem because aldehydes are easily oxidized to carboxylic acids.

$$\underset{\text{Aldehyde}}{\text{R}-\overset{\overset{\displaystyle \text{O}}{\|}}{\text{C}}-\text{H}} \;\xrightarrow[\text{H}_2\text{SO}_4]{\text{K}_2\text{Cr}_2\text{O}_7}\; \underset{\text{Carboxylic acid}}{\text{R}-\overset{\overset{\displaystyle \text{O}}{\|}}{\text{C}}-\text{OH}}$$

However, further oxidation of aldehydes that have low boiling points, such as acetaldehyde, is not a problem. Why is this?

Oxidation of the secondary alcohol 2-propanol by warming it with acidified potassium dichromate produces acetone.

$$\underset{\substack{\text{2-Propanol}\\ \text{(isopropyl alcohol)}}}{\text{CH}_3-\overset{\overset{\displaystyle \text{OH}}{|}}{\underset{\underset{\displaystyle \text{H}}{|}}{\text{C}}}-\text{CH}_3} \;\xrightarrow[\text{H}_2\text{SO}_4]{\text{K}_2\text{Cr}_2\text{O}_7}\; \underset{\substack{\text{Propanone}\\ \text{(acetone)}}}{\text{CH}_3-\overset{\overset{\displaystyle \text{O}}{\|}}{\text{C}}-\text{CH}_3}$$

Unlike aldehydes, ketones are resistant to further oxidation, so there is no need to remove them from the reaction mixture during the course of the reaction.

Chemists have taken advantage of the ease with which an aldehyde can be oxidized to develop several tests for their detection. **Benedict's test** and **Fehling's test** are commonly used for aldehyde detection. Benedict's and Fehling's reagents are deep-blue alkaline solutions of copper(II) sulfate of slightly differing composition. **Figure 26.18** illustrates Fehling's test for an aldehyde. When an aldehyde is oxidized with Benedict's or Fehling's reagent, a red precipitate of copper(I) oxide (Cu_2O) is obtained. The aldehyde is oxidized to its acid, and copper(II) ions (Cu^{2+}) are reduced to copper(I) ions (Cu^+).

Figure 26.18

When an aldehyde is mixed with Fehling's reagent (left) and heated, the blue copper(II) ions in Fehling's reagent are reduced to form Cu_2O, a red precipitate (right). What is the oxidation state of copper in the product?

$$\underset{\text{Ethanal}}{\text{CH}_3-\overset{\overset{\displaystyle \text{O}}{\|}}{\text{C}}-\text{H}(aq)} + \underset{\substack{\text{Copper(II) ion}\\ \text{complex}\\ \text{(blue solution)}}}{2\text{Cu}^{2+}(aq)} + 5\text{OH}^-(aq) \longrightarrow \underset{\substack{\text{Ethanoic acid}\\ \text{(as ethanoate ion)}}}{\text{CH}_3-\overset{\overset{\displaystyle \text{O}}{\|}}{\text{C}}-\text{O}^-(aq)} + \underset{\substack{\text{Copper(I)}\\ \text{oxide (red}\\ \text{precipitate)}}}{\text{Cu}_2\text{O}(s)} + 3\text{H}_2\text{O}(l)$$

MINI LAB

Testing for an Aldehyde

PURPOSE

To distinguish an aldehyde from an alcohol or a ketone using Tollens's reagent.

MATERIALS

- 1M sodium hydroxide
- 6M aqueous ammonia
- 5% silver nitrate
- 4 small test tubes
- test tube rack
- plastic eyedroppers
- methanal
- propanone
- ethanol

PROCEDURE

1. Add 1 drop of 1M sodium hydroxide to 2 mL of 5% silver nitrate in a test tube. Add 6M aqueous ammonia drop by drop, shaking after each addition until the brownish precipitate dissolves. This will be your Tollens's reagent.

2. Place 10 drops of Tollens's reagent in each of three clean, labeled test tubes.

3. To test tube 1, add 2 drops of methanal solution. To test tube 2, add 2 drops of propanone. To test tube 3, add 2 drops of ethanol. Shake the test tubes to mix the contents.

4. Observe the test tubes, leaving them undisturbed for at least 5 minutes.

ANALYSIS AND CONCLUSIONS

1. What evidence of a chemical reaction did you observe in test tube 1? In test tube 2? In test tube 3?

2. Write the equation for any chemical reaction you observed.

3. If you observed a chemical reaction in one or more of the test tubes, what practical uses might the reaction have?

---

section review 26.3

13. What is a carbonyl group? Describe the carbonyl groups that are characteristic of aldehydes, ketones, carboxylic acids, and esters.

14. What reactants are needed to make the ester propyl ethanoate?

15. What is dehydrogenation? What products are expected when the following compounds are oxidized?

a. $CH_3CH_2CH_2CH_2OH$

b. $CH_3CH_2\overset{\overset{\displaystyle OH}{|}}{\underset{\underset{\displaystyle CH_3}{|}}{C}}CH_3$

c. $CH_3CH_2\overset{\overset{\displaystyle OH}{|}}{C}HCH_3$

16. Give the IUPAC name for aldehyde and ketone.

a. CH_3CH_2CHO

c. $CH_3CH_2\overset{\overset{\displaystyle CH_3}{|}}{C}HCH_2CHO$

b. $CH_3CH_2CH_2\overset{\overset{\displaystyle O}{\|}}{C}CH_2CH_3$

d. $CH_3\overset{\overset{\displaystyle O}{\|}}{C}CH_2CH_3$

 Chem ASAP! **Assessment 26.3** Check your understanding of the important ideas and concepts in Section 26.3.

POLYMERIZATION

The base of the Tower of the Americas in San Antonio, Texas, is actually hundreds of feet tall! The restaurant at the top was built and then elevated as the section below it was constructed. This section was then pushed upward as the next section was put into place. In this fashion, the entire tower was established by piecing together unit after unit until the original base ended up at the top. Chemical compounds called polymers are very much like this tower. **What are some characteristics of polymers and monomers?**

Addition Polymers

Most of the reactions that you have learned about so far involve reactants and products of low molar mass. Some of the most important organic compounds that exist, however, are giant molecules called polymers. Each day, you see many different polymers. For example, the materials you know as plastics are polymers. The kinds and uses of plastics are numerous indeed!

A **polymer** is a large molecule formed by the covalent bonding of repeating smaller molecules. The smaller molecules that combine to form a polymer are called **monomers.** Some polymers contain only one type of monomer. Others contain two or more types of monomers. Polymerization is the reaction that joins monomers to form a polymer. Most polymerization reactions require a catalyst.

An addition polymer forms when unsaturated monomers react to form a polymer. Ethene undergoes addition polymerization. The ethene molecules bond to one another to form the long-chain polymer polyethylene.

$$x \quad \overset{H}{\underset{H}{>}}C=C\overset{H}{\underset{H}{<}} \quad \longrightarrow \quad H \!+\! CH_2 \!-\! CH_2 \!+_x H$$

x is number of ethylene units that combine to form long chain

Ethene (ethylene)

Polyethylene

x is number of repeating $-CH_2-CH_2-$ units in polymer; parentheses identify the repeating unit

Polyethylene, which is chemically resistant and easy to clean, is an important industrial product. It is used to make refrigerator dishes, plastic milk bottles, plastic wrappings, and many other familiar items found in the home. The physical properties of polyethylene can be controlled by shortening or lengthening the carbon chains. Polyethylene containing relatively short chains ($x = 100$) has the consistency of paraffin wax. Polyethylene with long chains ($x = 1000$) is harder and more rigid.

Polymers of substituted ethenes are also useful. Polypropylene is prepared by the polymerization of propene.

$$x CH_2 = \overset{\overset{\textstyle CH_3}{|}}{CH} \quad \longrightarrow \quad +CH_2 - \overset{\overset{\textstyle CH_3}{|}}{CH} +_x$$

Propene (propylene)

Polypropylene

Polypropylene, a stiffer polymer than polyethylene, is used extensively in utensils and containers. Polystyrene is prepared by the polymerization of styrene. Polystyrene in the form of a rigid foam is a poor heat conductor, which makes it useful for insulating homes and for manufacturing molded items such as coffee cups and picnic coolers. What brand name is commonly used to describe this substance?

$$x CH_2 = CH \longrightarrow -(CH_2 - CH)_x$$

Styrene
(vinyl benzene)

Polystyrene

Many halocarbon polymers, including polyvinyl chloride, have useful properties. Vinyl chloride is the monomer of polyvinyl chloride.

$$\overset{Cl}{\underset{|}{}}\quad\quad\overset{Cl}{\underset{|}{}}$$
$$x CH_2 = CH \longrightarrow -(CH_2 - CH)_x$$

Chloroethene
(vinyl chloride)

Polyvinyl chloride
(PVC)

Polyvinyl chloride (PVC) is used for pipes in plumbing. It is also produced in sheets, sometimes with a fabric backing, for use as a tough plastic upholstery covering. Polytetrafluoroethene (Teflon™ or PTFE) is the product of

(a) $H-(CH_2 - CH_2)_x H$

Polyethylene

(b) $\overset{CH_3}{\underset{|}{}}$
$-(CH - CH_2)_x$

Polypropylene

(c) $\overset{Cl}{\underset{|}{}}$
$-(CH_2 - CH)_x$

Polyvinyl chloride
(PVC)

Figure 26.19

*These common polymers are used for various applications: **(a)** Polyethylene is shown here as it is formed into a film. This film is commonly used to wrap food. **(b)** Polypropylene is used in the manufacture of a variety of items, such as these whistles. **(c)** Polyvinyl chloride is used for pipes in plumbing.*

Figure 26.20 ▶
PTFE is used to coat cookware and to insulate wires, cables, motors, and generators. It is also suspended in motor oils as a friction-reducing agent.

the polymerization of tetrafluoroethene monomers. PTFE is very resistant to heat and chemical corrosion. You are probably familiar with this polymer as the coating on nonstick cookware. Because PTFE is very durable and slick, it is formed into bearings and bushings used in chemical reactors.

$$x CF_2 = CF_2 \longrightarrow (CF_2 - CF_2)_x$$

$\quad\quad$ Tetrafluoroethene $\quad\quad\quad\quad\quad$ Teflon (PTFE)

Polyisoprene is the polymer that constitutes natural rubber. It is used in the manufacture of boots, tires, and rubber tubing.

$$x CH_2 = CCH = CH_2 \longrightarrow$$
$$\quad\quad\quad | \quad\quad\quad\quad\quad\quad\quad\quad\quad\quad (CH_2 \quad\quad CH_2)_x$$
$$\quad\quad\quad CH_3 \quad\quad\quad\quad\quad\quad\quad\quad C = C$$
$$\quad\quad\quad\quad\quad\quad\quad\quad\quad\quad\quad CH_3 \quad\quad H$$

$\quad\quad\quad$ Isoprene $\quad\quad\quad\quad\quad\quad$ Polyisoprene

Figure 26.21
Natural rubber is used in a variety of products. What is the source of this polyisoprene?

Condensation Polymers

Condensation polymers are formed by the head-to-tail joining of monomer units. This is usually accompanied by the loss of water from the reacting monomers and the formation of water as a reaction product; thus the name condensation polymers. What is the opposite of a condensation reaction? The formation of polyesters is an example of condensation polymerization. Polyesters are polymers consisting of many repeating units of dicarboxylic acids and dihydroxy alcohols joined by ester bonds. The formation of a polyester is represented by a block diagram, which shows only the functional groups involved in the polymerization reaction. The squares and circles represent unreactive parts of the organic molecules.

Condensation polymerization requires that there be two functional groups on each monomer molecule.

$$x\text{HO}-\overset{\text{O}}{\overset{\|}{\text{C}}}-\boxed{}-\overset{\text{O}}{\overset{\|}{\text{C}}}-\text{OH} + x\text{HO}-\bigcirc-\text{OH} \longrightarrow \left(\overset{\text{O}}{\overset{\|}{\text{C}}}-\boxed{}-\overset{\text{O}}{\overset{\|}{\text{C}}}-\text{O}-\bigcirc-\text{O}\right)_{x} + 2x\text{H}_2\text{O}$$

Dicarboxylic acid   Dihydroxy alcohol   Representative polymer unit of a polyester

The polyester polyethylene terephthalate (PET) is formed from terephthalic acid and ethylene glycol.

$$\text{HO}-\overset{\text{O}}{\overset{\|}{\text{C}}}-\!\!\!\bigcirc\!\!\!-\overset{\text{O}}{\overset{\|}{\text{C}}}-\text{OH} + \text{HO}-\text{CH}_2\text{CH}_2-\text{OH} \longrightarrow \left(\overset{\text{O}}{\overset{\|}{\text{C}}}-\!\!\!\bigcirc\!\!\!-\overset{\text{O}}{\overset{\|}{\text{C}}}-\text{O}-\text{CH}_2\text{CH}_2-\text{O}\right)_{x} + 2x\text{H}_2\text{O}$$

Terephthalic acid   Ethylene glycol   Representative polymer unit of
polyethylene terephthalate (PET)

PET fibers form when the compound is melted and forced through tiny holes in devices called spinnerettes. The fibers, sold as Dacron™, Fortrel®, or Terylene (depending on the manufacturer), are used for tire cord and permanent-press clothing. The fibers are often blended with cotton to make garments that are more comfortable on hot, humid days than those containing 100% polymer. These garments retain the wrinkle resistance of 100% polyester. PET melts may be forced through a narrow slit to produce sheets of Mylar™, a polymer used extensively as magnetic tape for tape recorders and computers. Can you think of another common use of Mylar?

Figure 26.22
Woven Dacron tubing can be used to replace major blood vessels.

Many important polymers are formed by the reaction of carboxylic acids and amines. The amines used to make polymers generally contain the amino functional group $-NH_2$. The condensation of a carboxylic acid and an amine produces an amide.

$$R-\overset{\overset{\displaystyle O}{\|}}{C}-OH \ + \ H-\overset{\overset{\displaystyle H}{|}}{N}-R \ \longrightarrow \ R-\overset{\overset{\displaystyle O}{\|}}{C}-\overset{\overset{\displaystyle H}{|}}{N}-R \ + \ HO-H$$

Carboxylic acid   Amine   Amide   Water

Polyamides are polymers in which the carboxylic acid and amine monomer units are linked by amide bonds. Various types of nylon are polyamides. You are probably familiar with a range of nylon products. Nylon polymer has a molar mass of about 1×10^4 g/mol and a melting point of 250 °C. The representative polymer unit of nylon is derived from 6-aminohexanoic acid, a compound that contains carboxylic acid and amino functional groups. The long polymer chain is formed by the successive attachment of the carboxyl group of one molecule of the acid to the amino group of the next by the formation of an amide bond.

$$x H_2N-CH_2 \!+\! CH_2 \!\overset{}{\underset{4}{\longrightarrow}}\! \overset{\overset{\displaystyle O}{\|}}{C}-OH \ \xrightarrow{\text{heat}} \ \left(CH_2 \!+\! CH_2 \!\overset{}{\underset{4}{\longrightarrow}}\! \overset{\overset{\displaystyle O}{\|}}{C}-\overset{\overset{\displaystyle H}{|}}{N} \right)_{\!x} + \ x H_2O$$

6-Aminohexanoic acid   Representative polymer
                                               unit of nylon

The melted polymer can be spun into very fine, yet very strong fibers. Nylon fibers are used for carpeting, tire cord, fishing lines, and textiles. They have replaced natural silk in sheer hosiery. Nylon is also molded into gears, bearings, and zippers. Can you think of additional uses of nylon?

Figure 26.23
Nylon fishing lines are lightweight, yet very strong. Flame-resistant clothing is made of Nomex™, a polyamide with aromatic rings.

Polyamides that contain aromatic rings are extremely tough and flame resistant. The aromatic rings make the resulting fiber stiffer and tougher. Nomex™ is a polyamide with a carbon skeleton consisting of aromatic rings derived from isophthalic acid and *m*-phenylenediamine.

Isophthalic acid   *m*-Phenylenediamine   Representative unit of Nomex

Like nylon, Nomex is a poor conductor of electricity. Because it is more rigid than nylon, it is used to make parts for electrical fixtures. Nomex is also used in the manufacture of flame-resistant clothing for race-car drivers and fire-fighters and in the fabrication of flame-resistant building materials.

Kevlar™ has a structure similar to that of Nomex. It is a polyamide made from terephthalic acid and *p*-phenylenediamine. What type of reaction do these components undergo to form Kevlar?

Terephthalic acid   *p*-Phenylenediamine   Representative unit of Kevlar

Kevlar is used extensively where strength and flame resistance are needed. You can see one application of Kevlar in **Figure 26.24.** A properly constructed vest made of Kevlar is strong enough to stop high-speed bullets, yet light and flexible enough to be worn under normal clothing.

Proteins, which are polyamides of naturally occurring amino acids, rank among the most important of all biological molecules. You will learn about these essential polymers in more detail in Chapter 27.

Figure 26.24
Bulletproof vests are made of Kevlar.

section review 26.4

17. What is a polymer? A monomer?

18. Describe addition and condensation polymerization. Give an example of each type of polymer.

19. Give names and uses for three types of polymers.

Chem ASAP! **Assessment 26.4** Check your understanding of the important ideas and concepts in Section 26.4.

SMALL-SCALE LAB

POLYMERS

SAFETY

Wear safety glasses and follow the standard safety proceedures outlined on page 18.

PURPOSE

To cross-link some polymers and examine their properties.

MATERIALS

- $3\frac{1}{2}$-oz plastic cup
- plastic spoon
- soda straw
- 4% borax solution
- powdered guar gum
- pipet

PROCEDURE

1. Half fill a $3\frac{1}{2}$-oz cup with water.

2. Use a soda straw as a measuring scoop to obtain approximately 2 cm of powdered guar gum. Gently sprinkle the guar gum powder into the water while stirring with a plastic spoon. Add the guar gum powder slowly to prevent it from clumping. Stir the mixture well.

3. While stirring, add one full pipet (about 4 mL) of borax solution. Continue to stir until a change occurs.

ANALYSIS

Using your experimental data, record the answers to the following questions below your observations.

1. Describe the polymer you just made. Is it a liquid or a solid? What special characteristics does it have?

2. Guar gum is a carbohydrate, or a polymer with many repeating alcohol functional groups (—OH). Draw a zig-zag line to represent a crude polymer chain.

3. Add —OH groups along the chain to represent the alcohol functional groups.

4. Borate ions combine with alcohol to form water and borate complexes of the alcohol.

$$HO \underset{^-O}{\overset{OH}{\diagdown} B \diagup} OH + R{-}OH \longrightarrow HO \underset{^-O}{\overset{OH}{\diagdown} B \diagup} OR + HOH$$

Write a similar equation that replaces all of the —OH groups on the borate with —OR groups.

5. If two polymer chains each contain two nearby —OH groups, borate will cross-link the polymer chains by forming a complex with two alcohols on each chain. Draw a structure similar to the one you drew for Question 4, but replace your four R groups with two polymer chains.

YOU'RE THE CHEMIST

The following small-scale activities allow you to develop your own procedures and analyze the results.

1. **Design It!** Try using borax to cross-link other common carbohydrate polymers, such as corn starch or liquid laundry starch. For each polymer, half fill a $3\frac{1}{2}$-oz cup with the chosen carbohydrate polymer and add enough water to bring the liquid to within about 1 cm of the rim. Stir carefully and thoroughly. Add one full pipet (about 4 mL) of borax solution while stirring. Describe the similarities and differences between this cross-linked polymer and the polymer you made previously. Compare the properties of these polymers.

2. **Analyze It!** Cut a 1 cm × 15 cm strip of paper and use a drop of glue or a stapler to fasten one end of the strip of paper to the other end to form a ring. Now cut out some identical-sized strips of paper and glue or staple them together into an interlocking chain of paper rings. Explain how this chain is like a polymer. Now make another paper ring that links your chain to one of your classmate's chains. Explain how these linked chains are like cross-linked polymers.

THE SWEET SMELL OF FUNCTIONAL GROUPS

What happens when you smell good food cooking? The scent of a freshly mowed lawn? The salt air of the ocean? If you are like most people, smells have the power to change the way you feel and to evoke memories of the past.

The power of smell has always led human beings to find ways to capture and produce certain scents that are particularly pleasing or meaningful. Long ago, people burned the wood and leaves of aromatic plants to release their scents, often as part of religious practices. Oils from the scent glands of certain animals, such as the musk deer, were also used for their compelling odors. Applied to the body, these oils became the first perfumes.

Attempts to capture a wider variety of odors in a concentrated, storable form led to the beginnings of perfumery. From its earliest days up to the present, perfumery has been an art—but it has also always involved quite a bit of chemistry.

Most of the fragrances that have enchanted people throughout the ages, such as jasmine, patchouli, lavender, and myrrh, come from the essential oils found in plants. These oils, containing the organic compounds that give each plant its characteristic scent, are found in a variety of plant parts, including flowers, bark, roots, seeds, and fruits. The oils must be extracted from the plant parts to be used in perfume.

The ancient Egyptians were perhaps the first to extract the essential oils of plant parts. They soaked flower petals in liquid fat, which dissolved the essential oils. Then they mixed the fat with ethanol. The essential oils were more soluble in ethanol than in fat, and dissolved in the ethanol, resulting in a strongly scented solution that could be stored and applied to the body.

From its earliest days up to the present, perfumery has been an art—but it has also always involved quite a bit of chemistry.

Since the time of the Egyptians, various other extraction methods have been developed. Some are similar to the Egyptians' method but employ a variety of different solvents. Other methods take advantage of differences in boiling point between essential oils and solvents by using distillation to concentrate the oils.

During the past century, advances in chemistry techniques have revolutionized the perfume industry. Natural essential oils are still extracted from plants, but most perfumes are made mostly from synthetic compounds.

The synthetic compounds used in perfumes are either identical or similar to compounds in natural essential oils. To make such a compound, chemists first have to identify the active compound in the essential oil and learn its structure. Then they can find ways of synthesizing it from more common substances.

Analysis of essential oils has revealed that many of the scents that please human noses are produced by alcohols, aldehydes, and esters. And in many, the carbon backbone of the molecule contains a benzene ring or one or more carbon–carbon double bonds. Scientists believe that molecules such as these have their effect on our noses because of their shapes and the functional groups they contain.

CHEMISTRY IN CAREers

FLAVOR DEVELOPER
Put your money where your mouth is! Learn the art of making new flavors and scents for various industries. **See page 880.**

TAKE IT TO THE NET

Find out more about career opportunities:
www.phschool.com

CHEMICAL SPECIALIST
Local food service distributor seek responsible self-motivated individ

Take It to the NET
For interactive study and review, go to www.phschool.com

KEY TERMS

- addition reaction *p. 781*
- alcohol *p. 778*
- aldehyde *p. 785*
- alkyl halide *p. 774*
- aryl halide *p. 774*
- Benedict's test *p. 793*
- carbonyl group *p. 785*
- carboxyl group *p. 788*
- carboxylic acid *p. 788*

- dehydrogenation reaction *p. 791*
- denatured alcohol *p. 781*
- ester *p. 789*
- ether *p. 783*
- fatty acid *p. 788*
- Fehling's test *p. 793*
- fermentation *p. 781*
- functional group *p. 773*
- halocarbon *p. 774*

- hydration reaction *p. 781*
- hydrogenation reaction *p. 782*
- hydroxyl group *p. 778*
- ketone *p. 785*
- monomer *p. 795*
- polymer *p. 795*
- substitution reaction *p. 776*

CONCEPT SUMMARY

26.1 Introduction to Functional Groups

- Saturated hydrocarbons undergo few useful reactions. The chemical reactions of most organic compounds involve functional groups.
- A functional group is a specific arrangement of atoms in an organic compound capable of characteristic chemical reactions.
- A substitution reaction occurs when an atom or group of atoms replaces another atom or group of atoms.

26.2 Alcohols and Ethers

- An alcohol is an organic compound with a hydroxyl group. An ether is a compound in which oxygen is bonded to two carbon groups.
- A common functional group is the carbon–carbon double bond of an alkene. Alkenes undergo addition of water to form alcohols. Alkenes can add a hydrogen halide or a halogen to form halocarbons. They can add hydrogen to form alkanes.
- A benzene ring usually undergoes a substitution reaction rather than addition.

26.3 Carbonyl Compounds

- Common functional groups containing oxygen include alcohols, ethers, aldehydes, ketones, carboxylic acids, and esters. The latter four types of functional groups contain a carbon–oxygen double bond, or carbonyl group.
- Alcohols may be oxidized to aldehydes or ketones. Aldehydes may be oxidized to carboxylic acids. Fehling's and Benedict's solutions can be used to detect the presence of aldehydes.
- Esters result from the combination of carboxylic acids and alcohols. Hydrolysis of an ester produces these components.

26.4 Polymerization

- Alkenes can undergo addition polymerization to form useful materials such as the long-chain polymer polyethylene.
- Condensation polymerization of monomer units containing hydroxyl and carboxyl groups in the same molecule produces polyesters.

CHAPTER CONCEPT MAP

Use these terms to construct a concept map that organizes the major ideas of this chapter.

 Chem ASAP! **Concept Map 26**
Create your Concept Map using the computer.

functional group • ether • ketone • halocarbon • carboxylic acid • polymer • alcohol • aldehyde • ester

CONCEPT PRACTICE

20. What does R in the formula R—CH_2Cl represent? *26.1*

21. Write a structural formula for each compound. *26.1*
  a. 1,2,2-trichlorobutane
  b. 1,3,5-tribromobenzene
  c. 1,2-dichlorocyclohexane

22. Name the following halocarbons. *26.1*
  a. CH_2=$CHCH_2Cl$

  b. $\overset{\overset{\displaystyle CH_3}{|}}{CH_3CHCH_2}\overset{\overset{\displaystyle Cl}{|}}{CHCH_2Cl}$

  c.

23. Write structural formulas and give IUPAC names for all the isomers of the following compounds. *26.1*
  a. $C_3H_6Cl_2$
  b. C_4H_9Br

24. What organic products are formed in the following reactions? *26.1*

  a. ⬡—Br + NaOH $\xrightarrow{\text{heat}}$ _____ + NaBr

  b. ⬡—Cl + NaOH ⟶ _____ + NaCl

  c. $CH_3\overset{\overset{\displaystyle CH_3}{|}}{CHCl}$ + NaOH ⟶ _____ + NaCl

  d. ⬡ + Br_2 $\xrightarrow{\text{catalyst}}$ _____ + HBr

25. Write the structure for the expected product from each reaction. *26.2*
  a. CH_2=$CHCH_2CH_3$ + Br_2 ⟶
  b. CH_3CH=$CHCH_3$ + I_2 ⟶
  c. CH_3CH=$CHCH_3$ + H_2 ⟶

  d. ⬡ + Cl_2 ⟶

26. Write structures and names of the products obtained upon addition of each of the following reagents to ethene. *26.2*
  a. HBr   **d.** H_2
  b. Cl_2 **e.** HCl
  c. H_2O

27. Name the following ethers. *26.2*
  a. $CH_3OCH_2CH_3$

  b. ⬡—O—CH_2CH_3

  c. CH_2=$CHOCH$=CH_2

  d. $CH_3\overset{\overset{\displaystyle CH_3}{|}}{CHOCH}\overset{\overset{\displaystyle CH_3}{|}}{CH_3}$

28. Explain why diethyl ether is more soluble in water than dihexyl ether is. Would you expect propane or diethyl ether to be more soluble in water? Why? *26.2*

29. Explain why 1-butanol has a higher boiling point than diethyl ether has. Which compound would you expect to be more soluble in water? Why? *26.2*

30. Name these aldehydes and ketones. *26.3*

  a. $CH_3\overset{\overset{\displaystyle O}{||}}{C}CH_3$

  b. $CH_3\overset{\overset{\displaystyle CH_3}{|}}{CH}CH_2CHO$

  c. ⬡—CH_2CHO

  d. ⬡—$\overset{\overset{\displaystyle O}{||}}{C}$—⬡

  e. CH_3CHO

  f. $CH_3CH_2\overset{\overset{\displaystyle O}{||}}{C}CH_2CH_2CH_3$

31. How would you expect the boiling points of propane, propanol, and propanal to compare? *26.3*

32. Propane ($CH_3CH_2CH_3$) and acetaldehyde (CH_3CHO) have the same molar mass, but propane boils at $-42\ °C$ and acetaldehyde boils at $20\ °C$. Account for this difference. *26.3*

33. How would you expect the water solubility of ethanoic and decanoic acids to compare? *26.3*

34. What are the products of each reaction? *26.3*
   a. HCOOH + KOH $\longrightarrow$
   b. CH$_3$CH$_2$COOH + NaOH $\longrightarrow$
   c. CH$_3$COOH + NaOH $\longrightarrow$

35. Give common names for each carboxylic acid. *26.3*
   a. HCOOH
   b. CH$_3$COOH
   c. CH$_3$CH$_2$COOH
   d. CH$_3$(CH$_2$)$_{16}$COOH

36. Give the name and structure of the alcohol that must be oxidized to make the following compounds. *26.3*
   a. CH$_3$CH$_2$CHO

   b. CH$_3$CH$_2$$\overset{\overset{\text{O}}{\|}}{\text{C}}CH_3$

   c. CH$_3$CH$_2$$\overset{\overset{\text{CH}_3}{|}}{\text{CH}}$CHO

37. Complete the reactions by writing the structure of the expected products. *26.3*
   a. CH$_3$CH$_2$OH $\xrightarrow{\text{K}_2\text{Cr}_2\text{O}_7}$

   b. CH$_3$CH$_2$CHO $\xrightarrow{\text{K}_2\text{Cr}_2\text{O}_7}$

   c. CH$_3$CH$_2$$\overset{\overset{\text{}}{|}}{\underset{\text{CH}_3}{\text{CHOH}}}$ $\xrightarrow{\text{K}_2\text{Cr}_2\text{O}_7}$

   d. ⬡—CH$_2$CHO $\xrightarrow{\text{K}_2\text{Cr}_2\text{O}_7}$

   e. CH$_3$CH$_2$$\overset{\overset{\text{O}}{\|}}{\text{C}}CH_3$ $\xrightarrow{\text{K}_2\text{Cr}_2\text{O}_7}$

38. Write the name and structure for the alcohol that must be oxidized to make each carbonyl compound. *26.3*
   a. HCHO
   b. CH$_3$$\overset{\overset{\text{O}}{\|}}{\text{C}}CH_3$
   c. CH$_3$$\overset{\overset{\text{CH}_3}{|}}{\text{CH}}$CHO
   d. ⬡=O

39. Write the structures of the expected products for these reactions. *26.3*

a. CH$_3$CH$_2$COOCH$_2$CH$_3$ $\xrightarrow{\text{NaOH}}$

b. CH$_3$COO—⬡ $\xrightarrow{\text{KOH}}$

c. CH$_3$CH$_2$COOCH$_2$$\overset{\overset{\text{}}{|}}{\underset{\text{CH}_3}{\text{CHCH}_3}}$ $\xrightarrow{\text{HCl}}$

40. Complete the following reactions by writing the structures of the expected products and by naming the reactants and products. *26.3*
   a. CH$_3$COOCH$_3$ + H$_2$O $\xrightarrow{\text{HCl}}$

   b. CH$_3$CH$_2$CH$_2$COOCH$_2$CH$_2$CH$_3$ + H$_2$O $\xrightarrow{\text{NaOH}}$

   c. HCOOCH$_2$CH$_3$ + H$_2$O $\xrightarrow{\text{KOH}}$

41. Write the structure and name of the ester that could be produced from each reaction. *26.3*
   a. formic acid + methanol $\longrightarrow$
   b. butyric acid + ethanol $\longrightarrow$
   c. acetic acid + propanol $\longrightarrow$

42. Different samples of a polymer such as polyethylene can have different properties. Explain. *26.4*

43. What is the structure of the repeating units in a polymer that has the following monomers? *26.4*
   a. 1-butene
   b. 1,2-dichloroethene

CONCEPT MASTERY

44. Write a general structure for each type of compound.
   a. halocarbon   **c.** ester
   b. ketone   **d.** amide

45. Predict which compound has the highest boiling point. Molar masses are given in parentheses.
   a. CH$_3$CHO (44)
   b. CH$_3$CH$_2$OH (46)
   c. CH$_3$CH$_2$CH$_3$ (44)

46. Write the structure and name of the expected products for each reaction.
   a. CH$_3$COOH + CH$_3$OH $\xrightarrow{\text{H}^+}$

   b. CH$_3$CH$_2$CH$_2$COOCH$_2$CH$_3$ + H$_2$O $\xrightarrow{\text{NaOH}}$

   c. CH$_3$CH$_2$OH $\xrightarrow{\text{K}_2\text{Cr}_2\text{O}_7}$

47. Explain why a carbon–carbon double bond is nonpolar, but a carbon–oxygen double bond is very polar.

48. Classify each compound as an alcohol, a phenol, or an ether.

a.

b. (diphenyl ether structure with O)

c. (benzene ring with —CH₂OH)

d. (benzene ring with OH)

e. CH_3CH_2CHOH
        |
        CH_3

49. Write the structural formulas for the products of these reactions.

a. $CH_3CH_2CH=CH_2 + Cl_2 \longrightarrow$

b. $CH_3CH_2CH=CH_2 + Br_2 \longrightarrow$

c. (cyclohexene) $+ HBr \longrightarrow$

50. For each compound pictured, identify the functional group and name the compound. The red atoms represent oxygen.

a.   c.

b.   d.

CRITICAL THINKING

51. Benzene is poisonous and a proven carcinogen. Yet many compounds containing benzene rings, such as benzaldehyde, are common in the foods you eat. Why are some organic compounds with phenyl groups safe to eat?

CUMULATIVE REVIEW

52. A solution is made by diluting 250 mL of $0.210M$ $Ca(NO_3)_2$ solution with water to a final volume of 450 mL. Calculate the molarity of $Ca(NO_3)_2$ in the diluted solution.

53. In a saturated solution containing undissolved solute, the solute is continually dissolving, but the solution concentration remains constant. Explain.

54. What is the maximum number of orbitals in the p sublevel of an atom?
a. 1
b. 3
c. 5
d. 9

55. Using electron dot structures, illustrate the formation of F^- from a fluorine atom and a hydroxide ion from atoms of hydrogen and oxygen.

56. Calculate the mass, in grams, of one liter of SO_2 at standard temperature and pressure.

CONCEPT CHALLENGE

57. Cholesterol is a compound in your diet and is also synthesized in the liver. Sometimes it is deposited on the inner walls of blood vessels, causing hardening of the arteries. Describe the structural features and functional groups of this important molecule.

(cholesterol structure)

58. Hydrocarbons from petroleum are an important source of raw material for the chemical industry. Using reactions covered in this chapter and any required inorganic chemicals, propose a scheme for the manufacture of ethylene glycol, a major component of antifreeze, from petrochemical ethene.

Select the choice that best answers each question or completes each statement.

1. Which type of organic compound is associated with the odors of fruits?
   a. alcohols   c. esters
   b. amines   d. ethers

2. The acid-catalyzed hydrolysis of an ester gives a carboxylic acid and
   a. an amine.   c. an alcohol.
   b. an ether.   d. an alkene.

3. Ethane, methanal, and methanol have similar molar masses. Which series lists the compounds in order of increasing boiling point?
   a. ethane, methanal, methanol
   b. methanal, methanol, ethane
   c. methanol, methanal, ethane
   d. ethane, methanol, methanal

4. A carbonyl group is characterized by a
   a. carbon-carbon double bond.
   b. carbon-oxygen double bond.
   c. carbon-nitrogen single bond.
   d. carbon-oxygen single bond.

The lettered choices below refer to questions 5–8. A lettered choice may be used once, more than once, or not at all.

   (A) alcohol
   (B) ketone
   (C) carboxylic acid
   (D) ether
   (E) aldehyde

To which class of organic compounds does each of the following compounds belong?

5. CH_3CH_2COOH

6. $CH_3CH_2OCH_3$

7. $CH_3CH_2CH_2OH$

8. CH_3COCH_3

Use the space-filling models with questions 9 and 10.

a.   b.   c.

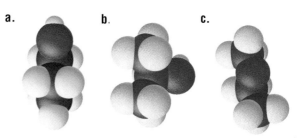

9. Using the space-filling models as a guide, draw ball-and-stick models of the three compounds that have the formula C_3H_8O. Name each compound.

10. *You Draw It!* There are two compounds with a carbonyl group that have the molecular formula C_3H_6O. Write a complete structural formula and draw a ball-and-stick model for each compound. Name each compound.

Characterize the reactions in questions 11–15 as addition, esterification, oxidation, polymerization, or substitution reactions.

11. $CH_3CHO \xrightarrow[H_2SO_4]{K_2Cr_2O_7} CH_3COOH$

12. $CH_2{=}CH_2 + HCl \longrightarrow CH_3CH_2Cl$

13. $CH_3CO_2H + CH_3CH_2OH \xrightarrow{H^+}$
    $CH_3COOCH_2CH_3 + H_2O$

14. $xCH_2{=}CH_2 \longrightarrow H{-}(CH_2{-}CH_2)_x{-}H$

15. ⬡ $+ Br_2 \xrightarrow{catalyst}$ ⬡—Br $+ HBr$

For each question there are two statements. Decide whether each statement is true or false. Then decide whether Statement II is a correct explanation for Statement I.

Statement I		Statement II
16. The addition of hydrogen to an alkene is a reduction reaction.	BECAUSE	The addition of hydrogen to any molecule is a reduction reaction.
17. Aldehydes react readily with oxidizing agents.	BECAUSE	Oxidation of aldehydes produces alcohols.
18. Ethanol (CH_3CH_2OH) is immiscible in water in all proportions.	BECAUSE	Ethanol molecules can form hydrogen bonds with other ethanol molecules.
19. The hydrogenation of benzene is easier than the hydrogenation of ethene.	BECAUSE	The benzene ring is stabilized by resonance.

THE CHEMISTRY OF LIFE

FEATURES

Stay current with **SCIENCE NEWS**
Find out more about biochemistry:
www.phschool.com

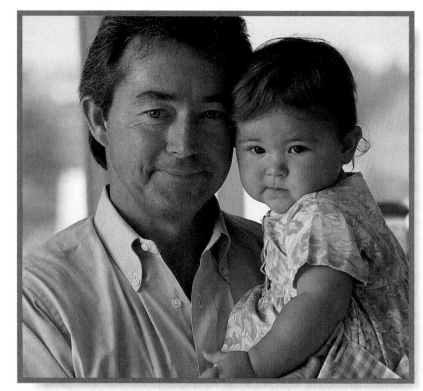

Children resemble their biological parents because of inherited DNA.

DISCOVER IT! BIOLOGICAL CATALYSIS

You need a small piece of raw red meat, such as ground beef, a similar-size piece of the same kind of meat that has been cooked, two plates, a small amount of 3% hydrogen peroxide, and a medicine dropper.

1. Place the two meat samples on separate plates. Add a few drops of hydrogen peroxide solution to the raw and the cooked meat samples. Both samples should be at room temperature.

2. Observe the samples for about five minutes.

Do you observe any difference in the appearance of the hydrogen peroxide placed on the raw meat and on the cooked meat? What do you think causes the difference in the appearance of the hydrogen peroxide on the raw and cooked meats? What can you conclude from this experiment? Return to your results as you read about chemical processes in this chapter and try to explain what you have observed.

A STRATEGY FOR LIFE

The air you breathe is composed mainly of oxygen (O_2) and nitrogen (N_2). A hypothesis regarding Earth's early atmosphere suggests, however, that the air was very different and most inhospitable to life. It is thought that the atmosphere changed over time as a result of photosynthesis, a process carried out by certain living organisms. One of the products of photosynthesis is oxygen, which began to accumulate in the atmosphere, changing its composition. **What are the reactants and products of photosynthesis, and in what organisms does the process occur?**

objectives
▸ Describe the structure of a typical eukaryotic cell
▸ Explain the relationship between photosynthesis and all life on Earth

key term
▸ photosynthesis

The Structure of Cells

Life! You are certainly familiar with it, but what does it really mean? Until recently, life has been defined as the ability of an organism to grow and to reproduce its own kind. However, recent discoveries made at the fringes of life seem to blur this simple definition. As difficult as it is to define life, you can generally regard tiny structures called cells as the fundamental units of life. In this section, you will learn some basic ideas about the construction of cells and about the chemistry that cells use to obtain the energy they need to sustain life.

Organisms are composed of as few as one cell or as many as billions of cells. Two major cell designs occur in nature. Prokaryotic cells are the cells of bacteria. The cells of all other organisms, including green plants and humans, are called eukaryotic cells. The prokaryotic cell is the more ancient of the two. Microscopic examination of fossilized remains shows that prokaryotic cells were present on Earth at least 3 billion years ago. Eukaryotic cells did not appear until about 1 billion years ago. **Figure 27.1** shows both types of cells.

Chromosome

Cell membrane

Cell wall

Nucleus

Endoplasmic reticulum

Mitochondrion

Lysosome

Cell membrane

Cytoplasm

Prokaryotic cell

├────── 1.0 to 10.0 micrometers (μm) ──────┤

Eukaryotic cell

├────── 10.0 to 100.0 micrometers (μm) ──────┤

Figure 27.1

The structures of a typical prokaryotic cell and a typical eukaryotic cell are shown here. Note that only the eukaryotic cell has a nucleus.

Both types of cells include the chemicals necessary for life, encased in a cell membrane. The cell membrane is a sack that holds the contents of a cell and that acts as a selective barrier for the passage of substances into and out of the cell. Eukaryotic cells are considerably larger and more complicated than prokaryotic cells, but the chemical processes carried out by both types of cells are very similar, and both are extremely efficient chemical factories. One major feature that distinguishes eukaryotic cells is the presence of certain organelles, which means little organs. Organelles are small, usually membrane-enclosed, structures suspended in the interior cellular fluid, or cytoplasm. The organelles are the sites of many specialized functions in eukaryotic cells.

The nucleus, one structure that is important in eukaryotic cell reproduction, is not present in prokaryotic cells. Mitochondria (singular: mitochondrion), are the source of cellular energy in eukaryotic cells that use oxygen. Mitochondria are often referred to as the powerhouses of the cell. Lysosomes are the sites for the digestion of substances taken into a cell. Yet another membrane-encased structure in eukaryotic cells is the highly folded, netlike endoplasmic reticulum (ER). Among its various functions, the ER serves as an attachment site for ribosomes. The ribosomes, small organelles that are not membrane-encased, are the sites where essential substances called proteins are made.

Energy and Carbon Cycle

Organisms must have energy to survive. Sunlight is the source of all energy obtained by organisms. **Photosynthesis** is the process by which cells directly capture and use solar energy to make food. Chloroplasts, which are specialized organelles in the cells of green plants, and some algae contain a light-capturing system that converts light energy into chemical energy. Photosynthetic organisms also absorb carbon dioxide from the atmosphere. The energy obtained from sunlight is used to reduce the carbon dioxide to compounds that contain C—H bonds, mainly in the form of the sugar glucose ($C_6H_{12}O_6$).

$$6CO_2 \; + \; 6H_2O \; + \; \text{Energy} \; \longrightarrow \; C_6H_{12}O_6 \; + \; 6O_2$$

| Carbon dioxide (carbon in more oxidized state) | Water | from sunlight | Glucose (carbon in more reduced state) | Oxygen |

Figure 27.2 illustrates the relationship between photosynthesis and the carbon compounds used by all organisms. In the energy and carbon cycle, photosynthetic organisms produce necessary carbon compounds. Animals, which do not carry out photosynthesis, get those carbon compounds by eating plants or by eating animals that feed on plants. Animals get energy by unleashing the energy stored in the chemical bonds of these carbon compounds. The nutrients are oxidized back to carbon dioxide and water in the process.

$$C_6H_{12}O_6 \; + \; 6O_2 \; \longrightarrow \; 6CO_2 \; + \; 6H_2O \; + \; \text{Energy}$$

| Glucose (carbon in more reduced state) | Oxygen | Carbon dioxide (carbon in more oxidized state) | Water | |

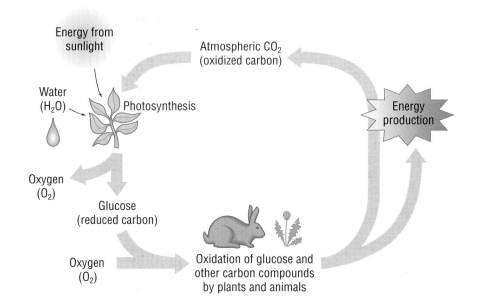

Figure 27.2
In the energy and carbon cycle, the processes of photosynthesis and the oxidation of glucose are responsible for the major trans-formations and movements of carbon.

Thus, although plant life could survive without animals, animal life could never survive without plants. Without photosynthesis the supply of carbon compounds needed by animals for energy production would not exist.

Oxygen is also an important product of photosynthesis. Photosynthetic organisms produce the oxygen found in Earth's atmosphere. The oxygen is necessary for most organisms to sustain life. The importance of photosynthetic organisms in producing carbon compounds and oxygen is a major reason for the concern about the loss of such organisms through the destruction of rain forests, shown in **Figure 27.3,** and the pollution of the oceans.

All biological processes, including photosynthesis, are based on certain essential kinds of chemical substances. Surprisingly, the great complexity of life arises from just a few types of biological molecules. In the remainder of this chapter, you will learn about the molecular structures of the great classes of biological molecules. You will also learn about the roles they play.

Chem ASAP!
Animation 29
Explore the complexity of chemicals essential to all life.

Figure 27.3
Plants, such as these rain forest trees, release essential oxygen into the atmosphere through photosynthesis. The destruction of these trees raises serious concerns about the future of Earth's atmosphere.

section review 27.1

1. Describe the structure of a eukaryotic cell.

2. Explain how the existence of life on Earth depends on photosynthesis.

3. Write an equation that summarizes the process of photosynthesis.

 Chem ASAP! **Assessment 27.1** Check your understanding of the important ideas and concepts in Section 27.1.

CARBOHYDRATES

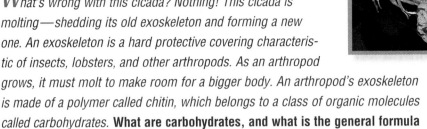

*W*hat's wrong with this cicada? Nothing! This cicada is molting—shedding its old exoskeleton and forming a new one. An exoskeleton is a hard protective covering characteristic of insects, lobsters, and other arthropods. As an arthropod grows, it must molt to make room for a bigger body. An arthropod's exoskeleton is made of a polymer called chitin, which belongs to a class of organic molecules called carbohydrates. **What are carbohydrates, and what is the general formula of these compounds?**

Monosaccharides

Long-distance runners often prepare for a big race by eating a great deal of food such as bread and pasta, a process known as carbohydrate loading. Breads and pastas are excellent sources of the family of important molecules called carbohydrates. **Carbohydrates** are monomers and polymers of aldehydes and ketones that have numerous hydroxy groups attached; they are made up of carbon, hydrogen, and oxygen. The name carbohydrate comes from the early observation that many of these compounds have the general formula $C_n(H_2O)_n$ and, as a result, appear to be hydrates of carbon. (They are not, in fact, true hydrates.)

You would probably call a diet based mainly on bread and pasta a starchy diet. You would be correct. Such foods contain carbohydrates called starches. In this section, you will learn about the similarities and differences among some well-known types of carbohydrates.

Carbohydrates are present in most foods, as **Figure 27.4** shows. The simplest carbohydrate molecules are called simple sugars, or **monosaccharides.** Examples of simple sugars are glucose and fructose, which are also structural isomers, because they both have the molecular formula $C_6H_{12}O_6$. However, glucose has an aldehyde functional group, whereas fructose has a ketone functional group. They both undergo many of the same reactions as ordinary aldehydes and ketones.

Figure 27.4

Carbohydrates are the most abundant sources of energy in food. The foods in the photograph on the left contain simple carbohydrates called sugars. The foods in the photograph on the right are good sources of complex carbohydrates called starches.

In aqueous solution, simple sugars such as glucose and fructose exist in dynamic equilibrium in straight-chain and cyclic forms. The cyclic form predominates. Glucose is abundant in plants and animals. Depending on the source, glucose has also been called corn sugar, grape sugar, or blood sugar. Fructose occurs in a large number of fruits and in honey. Here are the structures for each sugar in its two forms:

Straight-chain and cyclic forms of glucose   Straight-chain and cyclic forms of fructose

Note the aldehyde functional group ($-CHO$) on the straight-chain glucose, and the ketone functional group ($-\overset{\overset{\textstyle O}{\|}}{C}-$) on the straight-chain fructose. What difference do you notice between the cyclic form of glucose and the cyclic form of fructose?

Disaccharides and Polysaccharides

The cyclic forms of two simple sugars can be linked with the loss of water. The linking of glucose and fructose by means of such a condensation reaction gives sucrose, or common table sugar. Sugars that form from two monosaccharides in this way are known as **disaccharides.** Sucrose is thus an example of a disaccharide. The reaction by which it forms is as follows.

Sucrose is obtained commercially mainly from the juice of sugarcane and sugar beets. The world's production from these sources exceeds 7×10^9 metric tons per year.

Figure 27.5

Starch and cellulose are similar polymers made up of hundreds of glucose monomers. They differ in the orientation of the bond between the glucose units. Because of this difference, starch is readily digestible, but cellulose is indigestible by most organisms. What organisms can digest cellulose?

Starch

Cellulose

The formation of a disaccharide is sometimes the first step in a condensation polymerization that produces extremely large molecules. The polymers produced by the linkage of many monosaccharide monomers are called **polysaccharides.** Starches, the major storage form of glucose in plants, are polysaccharide polymers consisting of glucose monomers. **Figure 27.5a** shows a portion of a starch molecule. A typical linear starch molecule contains hundreds of glucose monomers. Some starches are branched molecules, each branch containing about a dozen glucose units. Glycogen, the starchlike polysaccharide produced by animals, is a source of stored energy for animals and is more highly branched than plant starches. Molecules of glycogen are stored in the liver and muscles of animals.

Cellulose is probably the most abundant biological molecule. As **Figure 27.5b** shows, cellulose is also a polymer of glucose. The orientation of the bond that links the glucose monomers in cellulose is different, however, from the orientation in starch. Starch is digestible by most organisms and is partially soluble in water. Cellulose, however, can be digested by only a few kinds of microorganisms, such as those that live in the digestive tracts of cattle and termites. Cellulose is insoluble in water and is an important structural polysaccharide that provides form, hardness, and rigidity in plants. Plant cell walls, such as those in wood, are made of cellulose. Cotton is about 80% cellulose.

section review 27.2

4. Describe the main characteristics of monosaccharides, disaccharides, and polysaccharides.

5. Give a source for each.

    a. starch   **b.** cellulose   **c.** glycogen

6. Glycogen and cellulose have different properties, but both are composed of glucose units. Explain what makes them different.

7. Distinguish between the important structural features of sucrose, glucose, and fructose.

 Chem ASAP! **Assessment 27.2** Check your understanding of the important ideas and concepts in Section 27.2.

*M*any people are lactose intolerant, meaning they cannot digest milk or products containing milk. These people cannot digest milk products because their bodies do not produce enough of the enzyme lactase to digest lactose, the sugar found in milk. The undigested lactose causes bloating and stomach upset. Some people with lactose intolerance can enjoy milk products if they take a pill containing the enzyme lactase before eating. **What are enzymes, and what function do they serve in the body?**

objectives

▸ Write a general formula for an amino acid, and describe the bonding between amino acids in peptides and proteins
▸ Describe the effect of enzymes on biochemical reactions

key terms

▸ amino acid
▸ peptide
▸ peptide bond
▸ amino acid sequence
▸ polypeptide
▸ protein
▸ enzymes
▸ substrates
▸ active site
▸ enzyme–substrate complex
▸ coenzymes

Amino Acids

Many biological compounds contain nitrogen in addition to carbon, oxygen, and hydrogen. Plants obtain nitrogen through nitrogen fixation, a process in which atmospheric nitrogen (N_2) is reduced to ammonia (NH_3). Legumes, a family of plants that includes beans, peas, and alfalfa, carry out most nitrogen fixation. The ammonia produced by nitrogen fixation is incorporated into biological molecules. This section will introduce you to the amino acids, a very important class of nitrogen-containing molecules. In fact, the polymers of amino acids, which you will also learn about, make up more than one half of the dry weight of your body.

An **amino acid** is any compound that contains amino ($-NH_2$) and carboxylic acid ($-COOH$) groups in the same molecule. For chemists and biochemists, however, the term is usually reserved for amino acids that are formed and used in living organisms. All 20 amino acids common in nature have a skeleton consisting of a carboxylic acid group and an amino group, both of which are covalently bonded to a central carbon atom. The remaining two groups on the central carbon atom are hydrogen and an R group that constitutes the amino acid side chain.

Because the central carbon of the amino acids is asymmetric, these compounds can exist as stereoisomers. As you may recall from Section 25.3, stereoisomers may be right- or left-handed. Nearly all the amino acids found in nature are of the left-handed, or L form. What is the major difference in the composition of amino acids and carbohydrates?

The chemical nature of the side-chain group accounts for the differences in properties among the 20 amino acids. In some cases, the side chains are nonpolar aliphatic or aromatic hydrocarbons. In other cases, the side chains are neutral but polar. In still other cases, the side chains are acidic or basic. **Table 27.1** gives the names of the amino acids with their three-letter abbreviations. What is the three-letter abbreviation for the amino acid phenylalanine? For aspartic acid?

Table 27.1

Abbreviations for Amino Acids	
Amino acid	**Abbreviation**
Alanine	Ala
Arginine	Arg
Asparagine	Asn
Aspartic acid	Asp
Cysteine	Cys
Glutamine	Gln
Glutamic acid	Glu
Glycine	Gly
Histidine	His
Isoleucine	Ile
Leucine	Leu
Lysine	Lys
Methionine	Met
Phenylalanine	Phe
Proline	Pro
Serine	Ser
Threonine	Thr
Tryptophan	Trp
Tyrosine	Tyr
Valine	Val

Peptides

A **peptide** is any combination of amino acids in which the amino group of one acid is united with the carboxylic acid group of another. The amide bond between the carbonyl group of one amino acid and the nitrogen of the next amino acid in the peptide chain is called a **peptide bond.** The bonds between the amino acids always involve the central amino and central carboxylic acid groups. The side chains are not involved in the bonding.

$$H_2N - \underset{\underset{H}{|}}{\overset{\overset{R}{|}}{C}} - \overset{\overset{O}{||}}{C} - OH \; + \; H - \underset{\underset{H}{|}}{\overset{\overset{R}{|}}{N}} - \underset{\underset{H}{|}}{\overset{\overset{O}{||}}{C}} - OH \longrightarrow H_2N - \underset{\underset{H}{|}}{\overset{\overset{R}{|}}{C}} - \overset{\overset{O}{||}}{C} - \underset{\underset{H}{|}}{\overset{R}{N}} - \underset{\underset{H}{|}}{\overset{\overset{R}{|}}{C}} - \overset{\overset{O}{||}}{C} - OH + H_2O$$

Peptide bond

Amino acid   Amino acid   Peptide

BIOLOGY

Ethnobiology

Often exploring the remotest jungles and forests, ethnobiologists search for information about plants, fungi, and even insects that people use as medicine.

These scientists carefully interview local specialists, who administer or use the remedies; collect samples of the remedies; and send these samples to laboratories for analysis of their chemical components. Ethnobiologists carry out an important task—fewer than 3% of the flowering plants on Earth have been examined for medicinal value, but about 40% of medicines in use today come from plant sources.

Note that a free amino group remains at one end of the resulting peptide. The convention is to write the formula of the peptide so that this free amino group is at the left end. There is also a free carboxylic acid group, which appears at the right end.

More amino acids may be added to the peptide in the same fashion to form long chains by condensation polymerization. The order in which the amino acids of a peptide molecule are linked is called the **amino acid sequence** of that molecule. The amino acid sequence of a peptide is conveniently expressed using the three-letter abbreviations for the amino acids. For example, Asp—Glu—Gly represents a peptide containing three amino acids. This tripeptide contains aspartic acid, glutamic acid, and glycine, in that order, with the free amino group assumed to be on the left end (on the Asp) and the free carboxyl group on the right end (on the Gly). Note that Asp—Glu—Gly is a different peptide from Gly—Glu—Asp, because the order of amino acids is reversed, and thus the free amino group and free carboxyl group are on different amino acids.

Proteins

In theory, the process of adding amino acids to a peptide chain may continue indefinitely. Any peptide with more than ten amino acids is called a **polypeptide.** A peptide with more than about 100 amino acids is called a **protein.** On average, a molecule of 100 amino acids has a molar mass of about 10 000 amu. Proteins are an important class of biomolecules. Your skin, hair, nails, muscles, and the hemoglobin molecules in your blood are made of protein. Why is it so important to include protein in your diet?

Differences in the chemical and physiological properties of peptides and proteins result from differences in the amino acid sequence. The number of ways in which 20 amino acids can be linked in a protein molecule is enormous. For example, as many as 20^{100} amino acid sequences are possible for a protein of 100 amino acids containing a combination of the 20 different amino acids.

The long peptide chains of proteins, shown in **Figure 27.6a,** can fold into relatively stable shapes. **Figure 27.6b** shows how sections of peptide chain may coil into a regular spiral, known as a helix. Peptide chains may also be arranged side by side to form a wavy sheet, as shown in **Figure 27.6c.**

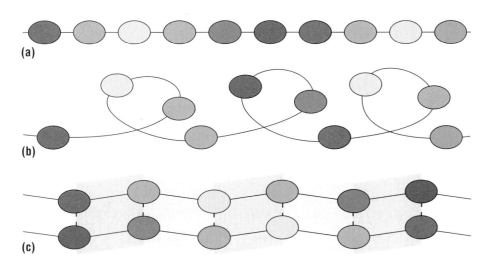

Figure 27. 6
(a) This is a representation of amino acids in a peptide chain.
(b) The chain may fold into a helix.
(c) Two peptide chains may become arranged in a sheetlike structure.

Irregular folding of the chains can also occur. Three-dimensional protein shape is determined by interactions between the amino acids of its peptide chains. Protein shape is partly maintained by hydrogen bonds between adjacent parts of the folded chains. Covalent bonds also form between sulfur atoms in the side-chain groups of cysteine monomers that are folded near each other. In that way, separate polypeptide chains may be joined into a single protein. **Figure 27.7** traces the shape of myoglobin, a protein that stores oxygen in muscle cells. As is shown in the figure, the peptide chains of most of the myoglobin molecule are twisted into helixes.

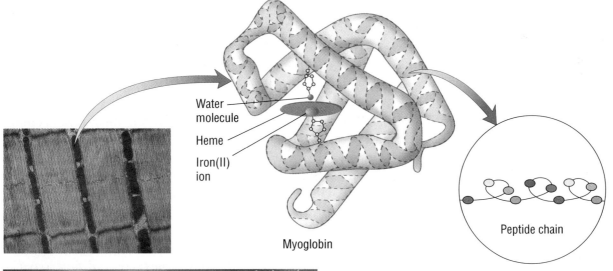

Water molecule
Heme
Iron(II) ion
Myoglobin
Peptide chain

Figure 27.7
(a) The three-dimensional structure of myoglobin, the oxygen storage protein of muscle, is shown here. Most of the peptide chain of myoglobin is wound into helixes. Myoglobin also contains a nonprotein structure called heme. The heme group is shown as a disk in the myoglobin structure. Heme contains four linked rings with an iron(II) ion (Fe^{2+}) at the center. Molecular oxygen binds to the heme iron. **(b)** Dolphins and other marine animals have a large concentration of myoglobin in their muscles. This allows them to store oxygen during long dives.

Enzymes

Enzymes are proteins that act as biological catalysts. Enzymes increase the rates of chemical reactions in living things. In 1926, the American chemist James B. Sumner reported the first isolation and crystallization of an enzyme. The enzyme he isolated was urease, which is able to hydrolyze urea, a constituent of urine, into ammonia and carbon dioxide. The strong ammonia smell of dirty diapers allowed to stand for a time is the result of the action of bacteria that contain this enzyme. The reaction is shown here.

$$H_2N - \overset{\overset{\displaystyle O}{\|}}{C} - NH_2(aq) \ + \ H_2O(l) \ \xrightarrow{\text{urease}} \ 2NH_3(g) \ + \ CO_2(g)$$

| Urea | Water | Ammonia | Carbon dioxide |

Since the discovery of urease, hundreds of enzymes have been isolated and structurally characterized as proteins.

In addition to being able to promote reactions, enzymes have two other properties of true catalysts. First, they are unchanged by the reaction they catalyze. Second, they do not change the normal equilibrium position of a chemical system. The same amount of product is eventually formed whether or not an enzyme is present. Few reactions in cells ever reach equilibrium, however. The products tend to rapidly convert to another substance in a subsequent enzyme-catalyzed reaction. According to Le Châtelier's principle, such removal of a product pulls the reaction toward completion.

Enzymes catalyze most of the chemical changes that occur in the cell. **Substrates** are the molecules on which an enzyme acts. **Figure 27.8** shows how substrates are transformed into products by bond-making and bond-breaking processes. In an enzymatic reaction, the substrate interacts with side chains of the amino acids on the enzyme. These interactions cause the making and breaking of bonds. A substrate molecule must make contact with and bind to an enzyme molecule before the substrate can be transformed into product. The **active site** is the place on an enzyme where processes that convert substrates to products occur. The active site is usually a pocket or crevice formed by folds in the peptide chains of the enzyme protein. The peptide chain of an enzyme is folded in a unique way to accommodate the substrate at the active site. **Figure 27.9** shows this folding for an enzyme called the HIV protease. The HIV protease, which is produced by the virus that causes AIDS, allows the replicated virus to package itself for release from an infected cell.

Figure 27.8

A substrate fits into a distinctively shaped active site on an enzyme. Bond-breaking occurs at the active site to produce the products of the reaction. What would happen if access to the active site were blocked by another molecule?

Substrate — Bond to be broken — Active site — Enzyme ⇌ Enzyme–substrate complex ⇌ Product — Bond broken — Product — Enzyme

Figure 27.9
The scanning electron micrograph shows HIV infecting a human white blood cell. The illustration models the enzyme HIV protease. The ribbons trace the two peptide chains of the enzyme. A substrate molecule is embedded in the active site formed between the two peptide chains.

The active site of each enzyme has a distinctive shape. This allows only one specific substrate molecule to fit into the enzyme, much as only one key will fit into a certain lock. Each enzyme catalyzes only one chemical reaction, with only one substrate. An **enzyme–substrate complex** is formed when an enzyme molecule and a substrate molecule are joined.

To get an idea of the tremendous efficiency of enzymes, consider the action of an enzyme called carbonic anhydrase. It catalyzes only one reaction, the reversible breakdown of carbonic acid to water and carbon dioxide.

$$H_2CO_3(aq) \xrightleftharpoons{\text{carbonic anhydrase}} CO_2(g) + H_2O(l)$$

Carbonic acid   Carbon dioxide   Water

A single molecule of carbonic anhydrase can catalyze the breakdown of about 36 million molecules of carbonic acid in one minute!

Some enzymes can directly catalyze the transformation of biological substrates without assistance from other substances. Other enzymes need nonprotein coenzymes, also called cofactors, to assist the transformation. **Coenzymes** are metal ions or small organic molecules that must be present for an enzyme-catalyzed reaction to occur. Many water-soluble vitamins, such as B vitamins, are coenzymes. Metal ions that act as cofactors include the cations of magnesium, potassium, iron, and zinc. The enzyme catalase, for example, includes an iron(III) ion in its molecular structure. Catalase catalyzes the decomposition of hydrogen peroxide to water and oxygen.

$$2H_2O_2(aq) \xrightarrow{\text{catalase}} 2H_2O(l) + O_2(g)$$

section review 27.3

8. Write the general formula for an amino acid, and describe the bonding between such acids in peptides and proteins.

9. Describe how enzymes affect biochemical reactions.

10. What is meant by the amino acid sequence of a protein?

11. Describe three properties of enzymes.

 Chem ASAP! Assessment 27.3 Check your understanding of the important ideas and concepts in Section 27.3.

THE EGG: A BIOCHEMICAL STOREHOUSE

SAFETY

Use safe and proper laboratory procedures.

PURPOSE

To explore some physical and chemical properties of a chicken egg.

MATERIALS

- chicken egg
- pencil
- paper
- ruler
- balance

PROCEDURE

Obtain a chicken egg. Examine the egg's shape and measure its length and width in centimeters. Measure the mass of the egg. Make an accurate, life-size sketch of your egg and record all your data on the sketch.

ANALYSIS

Using your experimental data, record the answers to the following questions below your drawing.

1. A common way to compare the shapes of eggs is by using the shape index. The shape index is the width of an egg expressed as a percentage of its length.

$$\text{Shape index} = \frac{\text{width}}{\text{length}} \times 100\%$$

   Calculate the shape index of your egg.

2. The volume, original mass (when freshly laid), and surface area of an egg can easily be estimated by using the following equations.

$$V = (0.5236)(lw^2) \quad M = (0.5632)(lw^2)$$
$$A = (3.138)(lw^2)^{2/3}$$

   V = volume M = original mass
   A = surface area l = length w = width

   Use your data to calculate the volume, original mass, and surface area of your egg. Show your work and record your results.

3. Compare your measured mass of the egg with your calculated mass. Which is greater? Suggest why the mass of an egg might change over time.

4. Using your measured mass and your calculated volume, calculate the density of your egg. Compare this value with the density of a freshly laid egg ($d = 1.075$ g/cm^3).

YOU'RE THE CHEMIST

The following small-scale activities allow you to develop your own procedures and analyze the results.

1. **Design It!** Design an experiment to answer the following question: Does the mass of an egg change over time?

2. **Analyze It!** Using your measured mass, your calculated original mass, and your experiments on the mass loss of an egg over time, estimate the age of your egg. What assumptions must you make?

3. **Design It!** Design and carry out an experiment to measure the volume of your egg. Write down what you did and what you found.

4. **Design It!** Carry out a series of experiments, or consult with your classmates and use their data, to determine if and how the shape index varies with the size of the egg (small, medium, large, extra large, jumbo).

5. **Analyze It!** Determine how the mass of an egg varies with its size (small, medium, large, extra large, jumbo).

6. **Analyze It!** An eggshell contains a calcium carbonate matrix with a protein cuticle. Place one drop of HCl on an eggshell and observe what happens. Write a chemical equation for this reaction.

7. **Analyze It!** Proteins can be detected by adding aqueous solutions of copper(II) sulfate and sodium hydroxide to a sample. A violet color indicates the presence of protein. Test powdered milk and an eggshell for protein. What are your results?

8. **Design It!** Design and carry out an experiment to answer the following question. Does temperature affect the mass of an egg over time?

LIPIDS

*C*andles were an early invention of ancient civilizations. Candlesticks that date to at least 5000 years ago have been found with other artifacts from the civilizations of ancient Egypt and Crete. Before the invention of electric lighting, candles were the major source of illumination in homes. **What type of molecules make up waxes such as candle wax?**

objectives
▶ Characterize the molecular structures of triglycerides, phospholipids, and waxes
▶ Describe the functions of phospholipids and proteins in cell membranes

key terms
▶ lipids
▶ triglycerides
▶ saponification
▶ phospholipids
▶ waxes

Triglycerides

Experts recommend that your fat intake make up less than 30% of your daily caloric intake of food. Although excessive dietary fat is harmful, you do need some fat in your diet to stay healthy. Fat provides an efficient way for your body to store energy. It is also needed to keep your cell membranes healthy. Fats, oils, and other water-insoluble compounds are called **lipids.** In this section, you will learn about the chemical composition and biological uses of lipids.

Lipids tend to dissolve readily in organic solvents, such as ether and chloroform, rather than in highly polar solvents such as water. This property sets them apart from biological substances such as carbohydrates and proteins. Natural **triglycerides** are fats and oils that are triesters of glycerol with fatty acids, which are long-chain carboxylic acids (C_{12} through C_{24}). Triglycerides are important as the long-term storage form of energy in the human body. The following equation shows the general reaction for the formation of triglycerides.

$$
\begin{array}{c}
\underset{\text{Glycerol}}{
\begin{array}{l}
CH_2OH \\[4pt]
\;\;\;| \\[4pt]
CHOH \\[4pt]
\;\;\;| \\[4pt]
CH_2OH
\end{array}}
\;+\;
\underset{\substack{\text{3 Fatty acid}\\\text{molecules}}}{
\begin{array}{l}
HO-\overset{\displaystyle O}{\overset{\|}{C}}-R \\[10pt]
HO-\overset{\displaystyle O}{\overset{\|}{C}}-R \\[10pt]
HO-\overset{\displaystyle O}{\overset{\|}{C}}-R
\end{array}}
\;\longrightarrow\;
\underset{\substack{\text{Triglyceride}\\\text{(triester of glycerol)}}}{
\begin{array}{l}
CH_2-O-\overset{\displaystyle O}{\overset{\|}{C}}-R \\[10pt]
CH-O-\overset{\displaystyle O}{\overset{\|}{C}}-R \\[10pt]
CH_2-O-\overset{\displaystyle O}{\overset{\|}{C}}-R
\end{array}}
\;+\;
\underset{\text{Water}}{3H_2O}
\end{array}
$$

The difference between fats and oils is simply that fats are solid at room temperature and oils are liquid. Most fats, such as lard, are obtained from animals. The fats from palm kernels and coconuts, however, are exceptions. Most oils, such as olive oil, are plant products. From the organic chemist's point of view, however, fats and oils are both esters. Like other esters, they are easily hydrolyzed in the presence of acids and bases. The hydrolysis of oils or fats by boiling with an aqueous solution of an alkali-metal hydroxide is called **saponification.** Saponification is a process used to make soap. Soaps are thus the alkali metal (Na, K, or Li) salts of fatty acids. A typical saponification reaction is shown at the top of the following page. Which alkali metal hydroxide is used in this saponification reaction?

Figure 27.10
Moderate levels of dietary fats and oils are essential to health.

$$CH_2-O-\overset{\overset{\textstyle O}{\|}}{C}-(CH_2)_{16}CH_3$$
$$CH-O-\overset{\overset{\textstyle O}{\|}}{C}-(CH_2)_{16}CH_3 \quad + \quad 3NaOH \quad \longrightarrow \quad CHOH \quad + \quad 3CH_3(CH_2)_{16}-\overset{\overset{\textstyle O}{\|}}{C}-O^-Na^+$$
$$CH_2-O-\overset{\overset{\textstyle O}{\|}}{C}-(CH_2)_{16}CH_3$$

Tristearin
(triester of glycerol
and stearic acid)

CH₂OH

CHOH

CH₂OH

Glycerol

Sodium stearate
(a soap)

Figure 27.11

These photographs illustrate soap-making. Once the soap is formed, it is poured into molds. Later it may be milled, or shredded, with scent or color added, and then remolded to produce a finished product.

As shown in **Figure 27.11**, soap can be made by heating a fat, such as beef tallow or coconut oil, with an excess of sodium hydroxide. When sodium chloride is added to the saponified mixture, the sodium salts of the fatty acids separate as a thick curd of crude soap. Glycerol is an important by-product of saponification reactions. It is recovered by evaporating the water layer. The crude soap is then purified. Coloring agents and perfumes are added according to market demands.

Phospholipids

Phospholipids, or lipids that contain phosphate groups, are abundant in cells. **Figure 27.12** shows a typical phospholipid lecithin molecule. The lecithin molecule has a hydrophilic (water-loving) ionic head and an oily or hydrophobic (water-hating) hydrocarbon tail. You know the solubility rule, "Like dissolves like." In water, lecithin, which is only partly hydrophobic and only partly hydrophilic, behaves like both an insoluble hydrocarbon and a soluble ionic compound. In water, the hydrophobic carbon chains aggregate to exclude water. The hydrophilic part is drawn to water, which can solvate it. This results in the spontaneous formation of a spherical double layer of phospholipid called a lipid bilayer. **Figure 27.13** shows a lipid bilayer. Where are the hydrophobic tails located in a lipid bilayer?

Hydrophilic head   Hydrophobic tail

Figure 27.12

A space-filling model of lecithin is shown here. In the simplified representation, the hydrophilic head is shown as a sphere and the hydrophobic tails as wavy lines.

Cell membranes consist primarily of lipid bilayers. The lipid bilayer of a cell membrane is a barrier against the passage of molecules and ions into and out of the cell. However, cells do need to take in certain ions and molecules, such as nutrients, while excluding other materials. Selective absorption is accomplished by the protrusion of protein molecules through the lipid bilayer. These proteins form channels through which specific ions

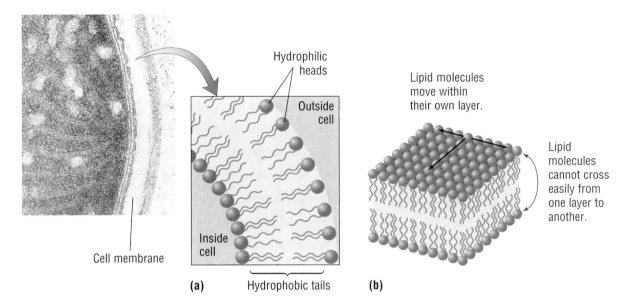

(a) Hydrophilic heads

Outside cell

Inside cell

(b)

Hydrophobic tails

Cell membrane

Lipid molecules move within their own layer.

Lipid molecules cannot cross easily from one layer to another.

and molecules can selectively pass. Not all membrane proteins extend all the way through the membrane. Proteins, such as enzymes, may be bound to the interior surface of the membrane. Many membrane proteins have attached carbohydrate molecules. The carbohydrate portion is on the exterior of the lipid bilayer, where it can hydrogen-bond with water. The protein portion is on the interior of the lipid bilayer, so it does not contact the water.

Waxes

Waxes are also part of the lipid family. **Waxes** are esters of long-chain fatty acids and long-chain alcohols. The hydrocarbon chains for both the acid and the alcohol usually contain from 10 to 30 carbon atoms. Waxes are low-melting, stable solids that occur in both plants and animals. In many plants, a wax coat protects the surfaces of leaves from water loss and attack by microorganisms. For example, carnauba wax, a major ingredient in car wax and floor polish, is found on the leaves of a South American palm tree. In many animals, waxes coat the skin, hair, and feathers and are used to help keep these structures pliable and waterproof. Beeswax, shown in **Figure 27.14,** is largely myricyl palmitate, the ester of myricyl alcohol and palmitic acid.

$$CH_3(CH_2)_{14} - \overset{\overset{\displaystyle O}{\|}}{C} - O(CH_2)_{29}CH_3$$

Myricyl palmitate

Figure 27.13

(a) A cell membrane typically includes a lipid bilayer. (b) The lipid molecules move easily within their own layer but do not readily move to the other layer. In such a lipid bilayer, the hydrophilic heads are in contact with water, but the hydrophobic tails are not.

Figure 27.14

Bees construct their honeycomb from beeswax. Waxes are esters of long-chain fatty acids and long-chain alcohols.

section review 27.4

12. Describe the molecular structures of the three main types of lipids.

13. What role do phospholipids and proteins play in cell membranes?

14. Name the two classes of organic compounds produced when waxes are hydrolyzed.

 Chem ASAP! Assessment 27.4 Check your understanding of the important ideas and concepts in Section 27.4.

- ▶ Describe the structural components of nucleotides and nucleic acids, including DNA
- ▶ Give simple examples of genetic mutations
- ▶ Explain what is meant by recombinant DNA technology

key terms

- ▶ nucleic acids
- ▶ nucleotides
- ▶ gene
- ▶ genetic code

NUCLEIC ACIDS

Maybe people have told you that you have your mother's eyes or your father's nose. Although this is not literally true (your eyes and nose are your own), you do inherit the instructions for assembling the proteins of your body from your parents. **What are these instructions called, and how do they code for proteins?**

DNA and RNA

More than 100 years ago, a Swiss biochemist discovered a class of nitrogen-containing compounds in the nuclei of cells. The nuclei were first obtained from dead white blood cells in the pus of infected wounds. The eventual understanding of the biological role of the compounds has led to a revolution in biochemistry.

These nitrogen-containing compounds, called **nucleic acids,** are polymers found primarily in cell nuclei. They are indispensable components of every living thing. Two kinds of nucleic acids are found in cells—*deoxyribo*nucleic *a*cid (DNA) and *ribo*nucleic *a*cid (RNA). DNA stores the information needed to make proteins and governs the reproduction and growth of cells and new organisms. RNA has a key role in the transmission of the information stored in DNA.

The monomers that make up the DNA and RNA polymers are called **nucleotides.** Nucleic acids are therefore polynucleotides. As shown below, each nucleotide consists of a phosphate group, a five-carbon sugar, and a nitrogen-containing unit called a nitrogen base.

The sugar unit in the nucleotides of DNA is the five-carbon monosaccharide known as deoxyribose. The nitrogen bases may be any one of four compounds—adenine, guanine, thymine, and cytosine. Adenine and guanine are each composed of a double ring. Thymine and cytosine are each composed of a single ring. These four bases are abbreviated A, G, T, and C, respectively, and are shown in a short segment of a DNA molecule in **Figure 27.16**. Ribose, which has one more oxygen than deoxyribose, is the sugar in the nucleotide monomers of RNA. The base thymine is never found in RNA. Instead, it is replaced by a fifth nitrogen base, uracil, abbreviated U.

Chemists studying nucleic acids discovered that the amount of adenine in DNA always equals the amount of thymine (A = T). Similarly, the amount of guanine always equals the amount of cytosine (G = C). The significance of this fact was not apparent until 1953. At that time, two scientists—James Watson and Francis Crick—proposed that DNA molecules consist of two polynucleotide chains wrapped into a spiral shape, as shown in **Figure 27.17**. This is the famous double helix of DNA. For the nitrogen bases to fit neatly into the double helix, every double-ringed base

Figure 27.15

This photo shows strands of DNA extracted from cellular material.

Figure 27.16
The nucleotide monomers of DNA are linked together through their phosphate groups.

Adenine

Cytosine

Guanine

Thymine

Nitrogen base
Simple sugar
Phosphate group

Figure 27.17
This is a space-filling model of a segment of the DNA double helix.

on one strand must be matched with a single-ringed base on the opposing strand. The pairing of A with T and G with C not only provides the best possible fit, it also gives the maximum number of hydrogen bonds between the opposing bases, as **Figure 27.18** shows. Thus the pairing of A with T (two hydrogen bonds between the opposing bases) and of G with C (three hydrogen bonds) makes for the most stable arrangement in the double helix.

Thymine   Adenine

T＝A

Cytosine   Guanine

C≡G

Phosphate group
Simple sugar

Figure 27.18
The two DNA strands in a double helix are held together by many hydrogen bonds; two hydrogen bonds between each thymine (T) and adenine (A) and three hydrogen bonds between each cytosine (C) and guanine (G).

Chem ASAP!
Simulation 29
Construct a portion of a DNA molecule.

The Chemistry of Life **825**

MINI LAB

A Model of DNA

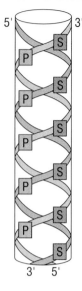

PURPOSE

To construct a model of double-stranded DNA.

MATERIALS

- cardboard tube from paper-towel roll
- 10 toothpicks
- felt-tip markers (two colors)
- thumbtack
- metric ruler

PROCEDURE

1. The typical tube has a seam that when viewed from one end describes a spiral that moves away from the observer. This spiral is a helix. Outline the spiral seam with a colored marker.

2. Using a different-colored marker, draw a second spiral midway between the lines of the first. These two spirals represent the two strands of double-stranded DNA.

3. Measure along the tube and mark a dot on each spiral every 5 cm. Label each dot with the letter S to indicate a sugar unit. Make a hole in the spirals at each S mark with the thumbtack. Move down each spiral and mark a letter P to indicate a phosphate group halfway between each two S dots.

4. Color each toothpick along half its length with a marker. A toothpick represents a base pair in the DNA molecule.

5. Starting at the top of the tube, insert a toothpick in one hole at an S label and guide it so it emerges through the hole in the S on the opposite side of the tube. Repeat the process for the other holes.

ANALYSIS AND CONCLUSIONS

1. Are the bases on the interior or the exterior of the double helix? Are they randomly arranged or neatly stacked?

2. Are the phosphate groups on the exterior or the interior of the DNA structure?

3. Are the sugar groups on the interior or the exterior of the DNA molecule?

The Genetic Code

An organism contains many peptides and proteins characteristic of that organism. The proteins of cats are different from the proteins of pine trees, which are different from the proteins of people. How do cells in a given kind of organism know which proteins to make? The cells use the instructions contained in DNA. A **gene** is a segment of DNA that codes for one kind of protein. Thus the products of genes are the peptides and proteins found in an organism.

You can think of DNA as a reference manual that stores the instructions for building proteins. The instructions are written in a simple language that has 4 "letters"—the bases A, T, G, and C. Experimental data shows that each "word" in a DNA manual is exactly three letters in length. The three-letter base sequences, or triplets, are the code words for 20 common amino acids. Some triplets are synonyms. The arrrangement of the code words in DNA is called the **genetic code.** The code words are strung together to form segments of DNA called genes, which specify proteins. Three bases of

DNA arranged in a specific sequence are required to specify one amino acid in a peptide or protein chain.

Table 27.2 provides the DNA code words for the 20 common amino acids. For example, you can see that the DNA code word for the amino acid phenylalanine is AAA and that the DNA code word for the amino acid alanine is CGA. An amino acid may be specified by more than one code word, but a code word never specifies more than one amino acid. With DNA code words of three letters, 900 bases arranged in a specific sequence would be required to code for a protein made up of 300 amino acids arranged in a specific sequence.

Three code words (ATT, ATC, and ACT) are reserved as end, or termination, code words. The translation of a gene sequence of DNA to the amino acid sequence of a protein begins after one termination code word and runs continuously until another termination code word is reached. The termination code word signals a stop to the addition of amino acids to the protein, which is thus completed. You can think of a termination code as being similar to the period at the end of a sentence.

The molar masses of DNA molecules reach into the millions and possibly billions. Even with only four bases, the number of possible sequences of nucleotides in a DNA chain is enormous. The sequence of the nitrogen bases A, T, G, and C in the DNA of an organism constitutes the genetic plan, or blueprint, for that organism. This genetic plan is inherited from parents and passed to offspring. Differences in the number and order of the bases in DNA ultimately are responsible for the great diversity of living creatures found on Earth.

Table 27.2

Three-Letter DNA Code Words for the Amino Acids									
		Second Letter in Code Word							
		A		G		T		C	
A	AAA Phe	AGA Ser	ATA Tyr	ACA Cys	A
	AAG Phe	AGG Ser	ATG Tyr	ACG Cys	G
	AAT Leu	AGT Ser	ATT End	ACT End	T
	AAC Leu	AGC Ser	ATC End	ACC Trp	C
G	GAA Leu	GGA Pro	GTA His	GCA Arg	A
	GAG Leu	GGG Pro	GTG His	GCG Arg	G
	GAT Leu	GGT Pro	GTT Gln	GCT Arg	T
	GAC Leu	GGC Pro	GTC Gln	GCC Arg	C
T	TAA Ile	TGA Thr	TTA Asn	TCA Ser	A
	TAG Ile	TGG Thr	TTG Asn	TCG Ser	G
	TAT Ile	TGT Thr	TTT Lys	TCT Arg	T
	TAC Met	TGC Thr	TTC Lys	TCC Arg	C
C	CAA Val	CGA Ala	CTA Asp	CCA Gly	A
	CAG Val	CGG Ala	CTG Asp	CCG Gly	G
	CAT Val	CGT Ala	CTT Glu	CCT Gly	T
	CAC Val	CGC Ala	CTC Glu	CCC Gly	C

First Letter in Code Word

Third Letter in Code Word

Gene Mutations

Substitutions, additions, or deletions of one or more nucleotides in the DNA molecule are called gene mutations. The effect of the deletion of a single base from a gene can be illustrated by starting with a string of letters of the alphabet. Suppose the string goes as follows.

PATTHEBADCAT

The letters may not make sense at first glance. However, if you separate them into three-letter words, they form a perfectly sensible statement.

PAT THE BAD CAT

Now remove the first letter, and again separate the string into three-letter segments.

ATT HEB ADC AT

This last sequence is nonsensical. Similarly, the deletion of a base in the DNA genetic code can turn the code into nonsense. A sequence that once may have coded for the proper sequence of amino acids in a necessary protein may be replaced by a code that produces a useless or damaging amino acid sequence. The same sort of harmful effect may be obtained by mutations involving substitutions or additions of nucleotides.

Such mutations might result in the production of a faulty protein or of no protein at all. Diseases that result from gene mutations are called inborn errors or molecular diseases. More than 200 such molecular diseases are known. For example, sickle cell anemia, which affects mainly people of African descent, is due to a mutation in the peptide chain of hemoglobin, the oxygen-carrying protein of blood. **Figure 27.19** shows the three-dimensional structure of hemoglobin. The defective hemoglobin reduces the oxygen supply to the tissues, triggering the painful episodes of the disease. In methemoglobinemia, another molecular disease, iron in some of the hemoglobin is in the oxidized iron(III) state rather than the normal reduced iron(II) state. A faulty hemoglobin chain permits the undesirable oxidation of the iron(II) to occur.

Figure 27.19

(a) The abbreviated molecular structure of hemoglobin, the oxygen-transporting protein of blood, is shown here. The hemoglobin molecule consists of four peptide chains, each containing a heme group. (b) In the molecular disease called sickle cell anemia, defective hemoglobin causes red blood cells to take on a distorted shape. (c) Normal red blood cells have a donut-like shape.

Heme

Figure 27.20
This scientist is comparing DNA fingerprints. DNA fingerprinting is an important tool in the identification of people.

Not all gene mutations are harmful, however. Some can result in the synthesis of a protein that can perform its function better than the version that previously existed. Such a mutation could thus be beneficial to the survival of an organism.

DNA Fingerprinting

Only about 5% of the DNA of human beings is used for coding information for the synthesis of proteins. The remaining 95% of DNA consists of repeating, noncoding base sequences that separate or sometimes interrupt gene coding sequences. The role of these stretches of noncoding DNA is unclear. The noncoding sequences are similar for members of the same family but are slightly different for almost every individual. Differences also exist in the coding portions of DNA. The base sequences of DNA are different for different individuals, except for identical twins.

The variation in the DNA of individuals forms the basis of a method for identifying a person from samples of their hair, skin cells, or body fluid. Because DNA sequences, like fingerprints, are unique for each individual, the DNA method is called DNA fingerprinting. To construct a DNA fingerprint, scientists first isolate the DNA in the sample. Only a tiny sample is needed because a method is available to amplify the amount of DNA in a sample by many millions of times. Enzymes that cut DNA chains between specific base sequences are used to cleave the DNA chains in the sample, thus providing a large number of DNA fragments. The fragments are of different lengths and base compositions for different individuals and can be separated and visualized. The pattern, or DNA fingerprint, that emerges can then be compared with the DNA of a sample from a known individual, as **Figure 27.20** shows.

If the DNA fingerprints are identical, it can be stated with a high degree of certainty that the DNA in the unknown sample is from the known individual. The chance in favor of a DNA fingerprint being unique to one individual can be as high as 1×10^{19} to 1—a high degree of certainty, given that the world's population is only about 6×10^9 people. In practice, however, the chance of positively identifying an individual from a DNA sample is generally lower and is often subject to interpretation. For example, a person claiming to be the long-lost heir to a family fortune would have a DNA fingerprint that contains DNA fragments that are characteristic of his or her father and mother but that would not be identical to that of the father or the mother.

Questions about the certainty of identification by means of DNA fingerprints are often at issue in criminal cases. DNA fingerprints can be obtained from evidence left at the scene of a crime, such as blood, but there is no standard for absolute determination of innocence or guilt from DNA fingerprinting, nor is there likely to be. Juries must decide whether the evidence is convincing. Evidence based on DNA fingerprints is permitted in more than half of the states in the U.S.

Recombinant DNA Technology

Scientists have learned to manipulate genes by various methods. Recombinant DNA technology consists of methods for cleaving a DNA chain, inserting a new piece of DNA into the gap created by the cleavage, and resealing the chain. **Figure 27.21** illustrates such a method.

The first practical application of recombinant DNA technology was to insert the gene for making human insulin into bacteria. Most people naturally make insulin, a polypeptide that controls levels of blood sugar, but insufficient insulin production results in diabetes, a potentially deadly disease. The symptoms of diabetes can often be controlled by insulin injections. In the past, human insulin was not available for this purpose. Pig insulin, which is quite similar in structure to human insulin, was used as a substitute. Some patients, however, were allergic to pig insulin. Today, diabetic patients use the human form of insulin produced by the bacteria altered by recombinant DNA technology. Such bacteria can produce large amounts of insulin in very pure form. Use of this insulin removes the need for the potentially dangerous use of pig insulin.

Other proteins produced by recombinant DNA technology are used as medicinal drugs. For example, an enzyme called tissue plasminogen activator is used to dissolve blood clots in patients who have suffered heart attacks. Another protein, interferon, is thought to alleviate or delay some of the debilitating effects of multiple sclerosis. Many other proteins produced by recombinant DNA technology are in use, under investigation, or on

Figure 27.21

Included here are the elements of an experiment involving recombinant DNA. In this experiment, DNA from one organism is inserted into the DNA of a different organism.

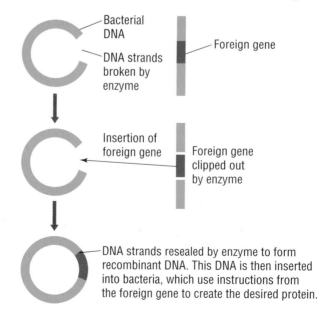

Bacterial DNA

DNA strands broken by enzyme

Foreign gene

Insertion of foreign gene

Foreign gene clipped out by enzyme

DNA strands resealed by enzyme to form recombinant DNA. This DNA is then inserted into bacteria, which use instructions from the foreign gene to create the desired protein.

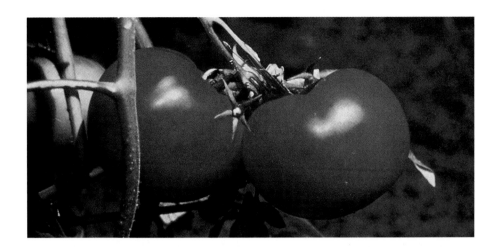

Figure 27.22
These genetically engineered tomatoes were altered to increase the period it takes them to ripen.

their way to eventual approval for human use. Recombinant DNA technology is also being applied to the cure of molecular diseases.

In agriculture, new recombinant DNA techniques can make plants resistant to pests and weed killers and produce fruits and vegetables that are better suited for shipping and storage. **Figure 27.22** shows genetically altered tomatoes that have a longer ripening period, which prevents spoilage and allows for their year-round availability. Genetically altered organisms have many potential benefits, but some people have concerns about the possibility of mistakes or misuse.

Ethical concerns were raised recently when Scottish scientists announced the birth of a lamb named Dolly, shown in **Figure 27.23.** In normal animal reproduction, an offspring is a genetic mixture of the characteristics of both parents; however, Dolly was a clone, an offspring of a single individual. A clone is an exact genetic copy of its parent because it is formed using the DNA of only that parent. The birth of Dolly has raised the question of whether human beings might eventually be cloned. Many people are horrified by some of the possible outcomes of cloning identical individuals. These reactions are one aspect of more general concerns about the uniqueness of life. Human cloning experiments have been outlawed in several countries for such reasons.

Figure 27.23
The sheep Dolly has no father. She was cloned from a single cell taken from her mother.

section review 27.5

15. Describe the structure of a nucleotide and of the nucleic acid DNA.

16. What are some types of gene mutations?

17. What is recombinant DNA technology?

18. Why do you think recombinant DNA research is controversial? What are your personal thoughts on this matter?

 Chem ASAP! Assessment 27.5 Check your understanding of the important ideas and concepts in Section 27.5.

METABOLISM

- Describe the role of ATP in energy production and energy use in the cell
- Define metabolism and explain the relationship between catabolism and anabolism

key terms

- adenosine triphosphate
- metabolism
- catabolism
- anabolism

The body's metabolic rate is controlled by a hormone called thyroxine that is released by the thyroid gland. When a person's diet does not contain adequate iodine, the thyroid gland is unable to produce and release thyroxine, and the gland begins to swell, forming a goiter. **What kind of metabolic reactions break down biomolecules in a person's diet?**

ATP

Adenosine triphosphate (ATP), shown in **Figure 27.24,** is the molecule that transmits the energy needed by cells of all living things. The function of ATP can be compared with a belt connecting an electric motor to a pump. The motor generates energy capable of operating the pump. But if a belt does not connect the motor to the pump, the energy produced by the motor is wasted. You can think of ATP as the belt that couples the production and use of energy by cells as shown in **Figure 27.25.**

Recall that oxidation reactions, such as the combustion of methane in a furnace or the oxidation of glucose in a living cell, produce energy. Energy is also captured when adenosine diphosphate (ADP) condenses with a molecule of phosphoric acid and becomes ATP. The addition of a phosphate group, called phosphorylation, occurs during certain biochemical oxidation reactions.

$$\text{Adenosine}-\overset{\overset{\displaystyle O}{\|}}{\underset{\underset{\displaystyle OH}{|}}{P}}-O-\overset{\overset{\displaystyle O}{\|}}{\underset{\underset{\displaystyle OH}{|}}{P}}-OH \; + \; HO-\overset{\overset{\displaystyle O}{\|}}{\underset{\underset{\displaystyle OH}{|}}{P}}-OH \longrightarrow \text{Adenosine}-\overset{\overset{\displaystyle O}{\|}}{\underset{\underset{\displaystyle OH}{|}}{P}}-O-\overset{\overset{\displaystyle O}{\|}}{\underset{\underset{\displaystyle OH}{|}}{P}}-O-\overset{\overset{\displaystyle O}{\|}}{\underset{\underset{\displaystyle OH}{|}}{P}}-OH \; + \; H_2O$$

Adenosine diphosphate (ADP)   Inorganic phosphate (P_i)   Adenosine triphosphate (ATP)   Water

The formation of ATP efficiently captures energy produced by the oxidation reactions in living cells. Every mole of ATP produced by the phosphorylation of ADP stores about 30.5 kJ of energy. The reverse happens when ATP is hydrolyzed back to ADP: Every mole of ATP hydrolyzed back to ADP releases about 30.5 kJ of energy. Cells use this released energy to drive processes that would ordinarily be nonspontaneous. Because of its ability to capture energy from one process and transmit it to another,

Figure 27.24

ATP is ADP that has been phosphorylated. ATP is important because it occupies an intermediate position in the energetics of the cell.

$$^-O-\overset{\overset{\displaystyle O}{\|}}{\underset{\underset{\displaystyle O^-}{|}}{P}}-O-\overset{\overset{\displaystyle O}{\|}}{\underset{\underset{\displaystyle O^-}{|}}{P}}-O-\overset{\overset{\displaystyle O}{\|}}{\underset{\underset{\displaystyle O^-}{|}}{P}}-O-CH_2$$

Triphosphate

NH₂ — Adenine

Adenosine

Ribose

OH   OH

Energy released
by cells

Energy used
by cells

Cellular work

ATP is sometimes referred to as a high-energy compound; however, the energy produced by the breakdown of ATP to ADP is not particularly high for the breaking of a covalent bond. ATP is important because it occupies an intermediate position in the energetics of the cell. It can be formed by using the energy obtained from a few higher-energy oxidation reactions. The energy conserved in ATP is then used to drive other cellular processes.

Catabolism

Metabolism is the entire set of chemical reactions carried out by an organism. In metabolism, food and unneeded cellular components are degraded to simpler compounds by chemical reactions collectively called **catabolism.** The degradation of complex biological molecules (carbohydrates, lipids, proteins, and nucleic acids) during catabolism provides building blocks for the construction of new compounds needed by the cell.

Through the formation of ATP, catabolic reactions provide the energy for such needs as body motion and the transport of nutrients to cells where they are required. The oxidation reactions of catabolism also provide energy in the form of heat. These reactions help keep your body temperature constant at 37 °C.

The complete oxidation of glucose to carbon dioxide and water is one of the most important energy-yielding processes of catabolism. Study **Figure 27.26,** which summarizes the major steps in the degradation of glucose to six molecules of carbon dioxide. The complete oxidation actually involves many reactions, which are not shown. As you can see, the major carbon-containing reactants and products are named, and they are also referred to according to the number of carbons they contain.

The combustion of 1 mol of glucose to carbon dioxide and water, whether by fire or by oxidation by a living organism, produces 2.82×10^3 kJ of energy.

EXERCISE PHYSIOLOGY

Training Energy Pathways
In the human body, glycogen is stored in skeletal muscles and the liver. Liver glycogen is used to maintain a normal blood sugar level. Muscle glycogen, however, is used solely for muscle work. Large amounts of carbohydrates, including glycogen, are used by the body during athletic events that require power or speed. The carbohydrates provide the necessary energy. Interval training, a technique that alternates rest and work phases, is designed as much to train biochemical energy pathways as to train the muscles used in an athletic activity. Proper training and diet can actually increase the amount of glycogen stored after a training session by more than a thousandfold.

Glucose (6-carbon chain)

2 Pyruvate ions, $CH_3COCO_2^-$
(3-carbon fragments)

2 Acetate
ions, $CH_3CO_2^-$
(2-carbon fragments)

2 Carbon dioxide
molecules, CO_2
(1-carbon fragments)

4 Carbon dioxide
molecules

Figure 27.26
The oxidation of glucose to carbon dioxide and water is one of the most important energy-yielding processes of catabolism.

The Chemistry of Life **833**

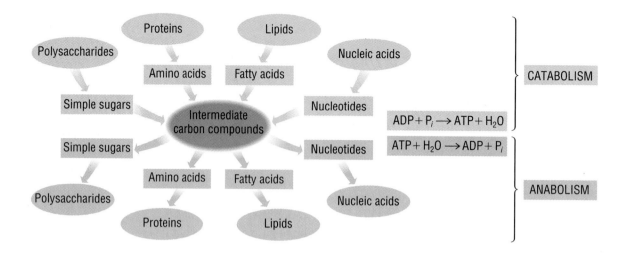

Figure 27.27

Simple compounds produced by catabolism are used in the synthesis reactions of anabolism. Catabolism produces energy, whereas anabolism uses energy.

Cells that use oxygen may produce up to 38 mol of ATP by capturing the energy produced by the complete oxidation of a single mole of glucose! How many kilojoules of energy are produced per mole of ATP produced? The large amount of ATP produced from the oxidation of glucose makes it the likeliest mode of energy production for most kinds of cells. In fact, if glucose is available, brain cells use no other source of carbon compounds for energy production.

Anabolism

Some of the simple compounds produced by catabolism are used to synthesize more-complex biological molecules (carbohydrates, lipids, proteins, and nucleic acids) necessary for the health and growth of an organism. The synthesis reactions of metabolism are called **anabolism.** Unlike catabolism, which produces energy, anabolism uses energy.

Figure 27.27 gives an overview of the relationship between catabolism and anabolism. As you have learned, nutrients and unneeded cell components are degraded to simpler components by the reactions of catabolism. The oxidative reactions of catabolism yield energy captured in the formation of ATP. In anabolism, the products and the energy of catabolism are used to make new cell parts and compounds needed for cellular life and growth. You already know that energy produced by physical and chemical processes is of little value unless the energy can be captured to do work. If it is not captured, the energy is lost as heat. The chemical energy produced by catabolism must have some means of being used for the chemical work of anabolism. As you read earlier in this section, the ATP molecule is that means of transmitting energy.

portfolio project

Prepare a written report on human basal metabolism. Define basal metabolism and discuss how it varies with the age, weight, and gender of an individual. Include the units of basal metabolism.

section review 27.6

19. Discuss the function of ATP in cellular metabolism.

20. Define metabolism, catabolism, and anabolism.

21. How many moles of ATP are formed from the complete oxidation of 1 mol of glucose in a cell that uses oxygen?

 Chem ASAP! **Assessment 27.6** Check your understanding of the important ideas and concepts in Section 27.6.

FAKE FAT

What are your favorite foods? If you are like most people, the list probably includes a number of foods that are high in fat, such as cheeseburgers, pizza, french fries, and chocolate. Although they taste good, foods like these may not be good for your health if you eat them often. Medical research shows that a diet high in fat greatly increases the risk of heart disease, cancer, diabetes, and other health problems. For these reasons, the Food and Drug Administration (FDA) recommends that no more than 30% of your daily caloric intake come from fat.

But limiting your intake of fat can be very difficult. One reason is that much of the food available is either cooked in fat or has fat added to it. Try looking at the ingredients list next time you eat potato chips, a candy bar, or crackers—you will find that some kind of vegetable oil or animal fat is among the first ingredients listed. Another reason it is hard to cut down on fat is that it tastes good.

Now, thanks to biochemical research, fatty-food lovers have another option other than avoiding their favorite foods. They can eat foods containing Olestra™, a fat substitute with none of the drawbacks of real fat (but perhaps some of its own). Olestra has the same properties as fats and oils, but because of its

Eating a 1-ounce serving of Olestra potato chips instead of regular potato chips will cut about 11 grams of fat out of your diet.

chemical structure, it is not digested or absorbed by the body.

Biochemists spent many years designing the Olestra molecule. It is made up of six to eight fatty acid groups connected to a sucrose base. A normal fat molecule, in contrast, is a triglyceride, which is an organic compound made up of three fatty acid groups attached to a glycerol base. Olestra is similar enough to fat to share its properties, but the substitution of the sucrose for the glycerol base fools the body's digestive enzymes. When you ingest real fat molecules, digestive enzymes bind to them and act as catalysts in the hydrolysis of the bonds between the glycerol and the fatty acids. These same enzymes, however, are unable to bind to Olestra molecules. Olestra, therefore, passes through the digestive system unchanged.

But Olestra has drawbacks that will likely restrict its total replacement of fat in foods. It can tie up fat-soluble vitamins, which include vitamins A, D, E, and K. If foods containing these vitamins are cooked with Olestra, the vitamins will dissolve in the Olestra just as they would in a triglyceride fat. Because the body cannot digest the Olestra, it cannot absorb the vitamins dissolved in the Olestra. Olestra can also cause digestive problems in certain people.

In January 1998, the FDA approved Olestra for use in snack foods such as chips and crackers. Snack foods are an ideal candidate for Olestra because they are not an important source of fat-soluble vitamins. At the same time they are often very high in fat. Eating a 1-ounce serving of Olestra potato chips instead of regular potato chips will cut about 11 grams of fat out of your diet.

Olestra will never completely replace fat, but eating high-fat foods may become a little more guilt free.

CHEMISTRY IN CAREERS

☆ ☆

TAKE IT TO THE NET
Find out more about career opportunities:

www.phschool.com

CHEMICAL SPECIALIST
Local food service distributor seeks responsible self-motivated individ-

BIOCHEMIST
Study and manipulate the molecules of living organisms. Identify enzymes and biochemical pathways.
See page 881.

CHEMIST NEEDED

Take It to the NET
For interactive study and review, go to www.phschool.com

KEY TERMS

- active site *p. 818*
- adenosine triphosphate (ATP) *p. 832*
- amino acid *p. 815*
- amino acid sequence *p. 816*
- anabolism *p. 834*
- carbohydrate *p. 812*
- catabolism *p. 833*
- coenzyme *p. 819*
- disaccharide *p. 813*

- enzyme *p. 818*
- enzyme–substrate complex *p. 819*
- gene *p. 826*
- genetic code *p. 826*
- lipid *p. 821*
- metabolism *p. 833*
- monosaccharide *p. 812*
- nucleic acid *p. 824*
- nucleotide *p. 824*
- peptide *p. 816*

- peptide bond *p. 816*
- phospholipid *p. 822*
- photosynthesis *p. 810*
- polypeptide *p. 816*
- polysaccharide *p. 814*
- protein *p. 816*
- saponification *p. 821*
- substrate *p. 818*
- triglyceride *p. 821*
- wax *p. 823*

KEY EQUATIONS

- Photosynthesis:

$$6CO_2 + 6H_2O + Energy \longrightarrow C_6H_{12}O_6 + 6O_2$$

- Oxidation of glucose:

$$C_6H_{12}O_6 + 6O_2 \longrightarrow 6CO_2 + 6H_2O + Energy$$

CONCEPT SUMMARY

27.1 A Strategy for Life

- Photosynthetic organisms use the sun's energy during photosynthesis to reduce carbon dioxide to glucose. Plants and animals use glucose as an energy source.

27.2 Carbohydrates

- Carbohydrates are made up of carbon, hydrogen, and oxygen and are often found in nature as simple molecules containing one or a few sugar units called monosaccharides.
- Condensation polymers called polysaccharides contain hundreds of thousands of sugar units.

27.3 Amino Acids and Their Polymers

- Peptides and proteins are condensation polymers of amino acids.
- Enzymes, which are proteins, serve as catalysts of biological reactions.

27.4 Lipids

- Lipids, which include fats and oils, are water-insoluble substances.
- Phospholipids, lipids that contain phosphate groups, make up cell membranes.

27.5 Nucleic Acids

- Nucleic acids are polymers of nucleotides.
- Alterations in base sequences are gene mutations, which can cause errors in protein production.

27.6 Metabolism

- ATP is the molecule that stores and transmits the energy needed by cells of all living things.
- Metabolism is the sum of all the reactions carried out by an organism.
- The energy and compounds generated by catabolism are used for anabolism, the non-spontaneous synthesis reactions.

CHAPTER CONCEPT MAP

Use these terms to construct a concept map that organizes the major ideas of this chapter.

 Chem ASAP! Concept Map 27
Create your Concept Map using the computer.

lipid   carbohydrate   protein

enzyme   amino acid   substrate

photosynthesis   genetic code   nucleic acid

CONCEPT PRACTICE

22. Explain what happens in photosynthesis. *27.1*

23. Where do biological molecules originate? *27.1*

24. Write a balanced equation for the complete oxidation of glucose. *27.2*

25. Name two important monosaccharides. *27.2*

26. Give sources for glucose and fructose. *27.2*

27. How does the carbonyl functional group differ in glucose and fructose? *27.2*

28. Which monosaccharides are combined to form the disaccharide sucrose? *27.2*

29. What is the product of the complete hydrolysis of each polysaccharide? *27.2*
    a. starch
    b. glycogen

30. What is the name given to the bond connecting two amino acids in a peptide chain? *27.3*

31. Consider the tripeptide Ser—Gly—Phe. How many peptide bonds does this molecule have? *27.3*

32. Describe what an enzyme does. *27.3*

33. Describe two common patterns found in the folding of protein chains. *27.3*

34. What is the meaning of each abbreviation? Are the structures of these tripeptides the same? Explain. *27.3*
    a. Ala—Ser—Gly
    b. Gly—Ser—Ala

35. Distinguish between a fat and an oil. *27.4*

36. What is a triglyceride? *27.4*

37. What is a soap? *27.4*

38. Draw structural formulas for the products of complete hydrolysis of tristearin. *27.4*

39. Draw a simple representation of a lipid bilayer. *27.4*

40. Name two functions of membrane proteins. *27.4*

41. Cells contain two types of nucleic acids. What are they called? *27.5*

42. What are the components of a nucleotide? *27.5*

43. What is the structural difference between the sugar unit in RNA and the sugar unit in DNA? *27.5*

44. What type of bonding helps hold a DNA double helix together? *27.5*

45. Does every code word in DNA specify an amino acid in protein synthesis? Explain. *27.5*

46. Which of the following base pairs are found in a DNA molecule? *27.5*
    a. A—A   c. C—G   e. A—U
    b. A—T   d. G—A   f. T—U

47. What causes a gene mutation? *27.5*

48. An average adult expends about 8400 kJ of energy every day. How many moles of ATP must be converted to ADP to provide this amount of energy? *27.6*

49. Where do the complex biomolecules your body degrades during catabolism come from? *27.6*

50. Write an abbreviated, balanced equation for the hydrolysis of ATP to ADP. *27.6*

51. Compare and contrast catabolism and anabolism. *27.6*

52. Some experts recommend that complex carbohydrates provide 50–55% of dietary calories. What is the relationship between energy production and complex carbohydrates? *27.6*

CONCEPT MASTERY

53. What is glycogen? How does it differ from starch?

54. What is cellulose and where is it found?

55. Give the names and structures of the compounds produced by the hydrolysis of sucrose.

56. What is an enzyme–substrate complex?

57. What is the active site of an enzyme?

58. What role do coenzymes play?

59. The formula for palmitic acid is $CH_3(CH_2)_{14}CO_2H$. A popular soap is mostly sodium palmitate. Write the structure of sodium palmitate.

60. Which part of a phospholipid molecule can interact favorably with water?

61. Consider the following segment of DNA.
    G—C—C—C—C—A—A—C—G—T—T—A

    a. Using abbreviations for the amino acids from **Table 27.2,** write the amino acid sequence formed by translation of this information into a peptide.
    b. What amino acid sequence would result from the substitution of adenine (A) for the second cytosine (C)?

62. Use **Table 27.2** to write a base sequence for DNA that codes for the tripeptide Ala—Gly—Ser.

63. Determine the amino acid sequence of a peptide if the corresponding base sequence on DNA is

T—A—C—G—C—A—C—A—T—A—T—A

64. A segment of a DNA strand has the following base sequence.

C—G—A—T—C—C—A

Write the base sequence that appears on its opposing strand in the double helix.

65. What is a molecular disease? Name two such diseases.

66. What are some outcomes of recombinant DNA research?

67. Describe a possible use of gene therapy.

68. What is the oxidation state of iron in the following?
   a. normal hemoglobin
   b. methemoglobinemia

69. What are the possible consequences of an error in a DNA sequence?

70. How is the catabolism carried out in brain cells different from that in other body cells?

71. Why is it necessary to breathe deeply during vigorous exercise?

72. The complete oxidation of glucose releases 2.82×10^3 kJ/mol of energy, and the formation of ATP from ADP requires 30.5 kJ/mol. What percent of the energy released in the complete oxidation of glucose is captured in the formation of ATP?

CRITICAL THINKING

73. Choose the term that best completes the second relationship.
   a. animals : carbon dioxide   plants : _____
      (1) oxygen   (3) methanol
      (2) ethanol   (4) sugar
   b. polymer : monomer   protein : _____
      (1) monosaccharide   (3) fatty acid
      (2) nucleic acid   (4) amino acid

74. Interpret this statement: "Carbon dioxide is an energy-poor molecule, but glucose is an energy-rich molecule."

75. In the DNA double helix, are the base pairs part of the backbone structure, inside the double helix, or outside the double helix? What must happen before the protein-making machinery of the cell can recognize the DNA bases?

CUMULATIVE REVIEW

76. Write a molecular formula for each compound.
   a. methyl acetate   **c.** 5-methyl-3-hexene
   b. heptane   **d.** butanal

77. What must be true at the end point of an acid–base titration?

78. How many carbon atoms are in 2.00 mol of ethanol?

79. Name the four structural isomers of C_4H_9Cl.

80. How many electrons are in each ion?
   a. Fe^{3+} **b.** S^{2-} **c.** As^{3-} **d.** V^{5+}

81. Identify the oxidizing agent in each reaction.
   a. xenon + fluorine $\longrightarrow$ xenon tetrafluoride
   b. sulfur + oxygen $\longrightarrow$ sulfur trioxide
   c. gaseous chlorine + aqueous sodium bromide $\longrightarrow$ aqueous bromine + aqueous sodium chloride

82. Calculate the pH of each solution.
   a. $[H^+] = 7.0 \times 10^{-5} M$
   b. $[OH^-] = 1.8 \times 10^{-9} M$
   c. $[OH^-] = 6.1 \times 10^{-2} M$
   d. $[H^+] = 4.4 \times 10^{-11} M$

83. What is a necessary condition for a molecule to have stereoisomers?

CONCEPT CHALLENGE

84. Explain why a lack of nutrients stops cell growth.

85. The following compound is hydrolyzed by boiling with sodium hydroxide.

$$
\begin{array}{c}
\overset{\textstyle O}{\overset{\textstyle \|}{}} \\
CH_2-O-C-(CH_2)_{14}CH_3 \\
| \\
\overset{\textstyle O}{\overset{\textstyle \|}{}} \\
CH-O-C-(CH_2)_{12}CH_3 \\
| \\
\overset{\textstyle O}{\overset{\textstyle \|}{}} \\
CH_2-O-C-(CH_2)_{16}CH_3
\end{array}
$$

What are the saponification products?

86. What causes the spontaneous formation of lipid bilayers?

Select the choice that best answers each question or completes each statement.

1. What phrase best describes ATP?
   a. energy producer
   b. energy consumer
   c. energy transmitter
   d. energy pump

2. Which element is *not* found in amino acids?
   a. phosphorus
   b. nitrogen
   c. carbon
   d. oxygen
   e. hydrogen

3. For any enzyme to function, the substrate must bind to the
   a. product.
   b. cofactor.
   c. active site.
   d. peptide.

Use the paragraph to answer questions 4–6.

Because an amino acid contains both a carboxylic acid group and an amino group, it is amphoteric, that is, it can act as either an acid or a base. Crystalline amino acids have some properties— relatively high melting points and high water solubilities—that are more characteristic of ionic substances than molecular substances.

4. Write an equation showing glycine acting as an acid in a reaction with water.

5. Write an equation showing glycine acting as a base in a reaction with water.

6. It is possible for glycine to undergo an internal Brønsted-Lowry acid–base neutralization reaction. Write the resulting structural formula. Explain how this reaction would account for the ionic properties of glycine.

Use the photo to answer question 7.

7. The photo shows three DNA fingerprints. The DNA in sample E was taken from a crime scene. The DNA in samples S1 and S2 were taken from suspects. Based on the DNA evidence, which suspect did not commit the crime?

For questions 8–11, name the category of organic compounds most closely identified with each biological molecule.

8. proteins
9. nucleic acids
10. lipids
11. carbohydrates

Use these models to answer question 12.

12. *You Draw It!* Glycine, which is the simplest amino acid, can form hydrogen bonds with water. Draw a glycine molecule with at least two water molecules bonded to each end of the glycine molecule.

For each question there are two statements. Decide whether each statement is true or false. Then decide whether Statement II is a correct explanation for Statement I.

Statement I		Statement II
13. Lipids tend to be insoluble in water.	BECAUSE	Lipid molecules have mainly nonpolar bonds.
14. Starch and cellulose are both digestible by most organisms.	BECAUSE	Glucose is the monomer in both starch and cellulose.
15. Many of the reactions in catabolism are oxidation reactions.	BECAUSE	Oxidation reactions tend to be energy-producing reactions.
16. The sequence of bases in DNA contains the code for making proteins.	BECAUSE	Each pair of bases in DNA codes for a specific amino acid.

Chapter 28

NUCLEAR CHEMISTRY

A bubble chamber can detect ionizing radiation.

FEATURES

DISCOVER IT!
Simulating Radioactive Decay

SMALL-SCALE LAB
Radioactivity and Half-Lives

MINI LAB
Studying Inverse-Square Relationships

CHEMath
Calculating Half-Life

CHEMISTRY SERVING …
THE ENVIRONMENT
Nuclear Waste: Storage, Disposal, and Containment

CHEMISTRY IN CAREERS
Nuclear Physician

LINK TO PHYSICS
Particle Accelerators

LINK TO ARCHAEOLOGY
Carbon Dating

Stay current with **SCIENCE NEWS**
Find out more about nuclear chemistry:
www.phschool.com

DISCOVER IT!   SIMULATING RADIOACTIVE DECAY

You need a small container with a lid, 128 pennies, a flat table or desk surface, a scientific calculator, loose-leaf paper, graph paper, and a pen or pencil.

1. Make a two-column data table with the headings "Trial" and "Number of heads."

2. Put 128 pennies in the container and shake them.

3. Carefully pour the pennies onto a flat surface.

4. Pick up, count, and set aside those pennies that are turned heads up. In the table, enter the number of heads for Trial 1.

5. Return the remaining pennies (those that were tails) to the container and repeat Steps 3–5 for a total of five trials.

6. If time permits, repeat the entire experiment four more times and average your data or the data collected by the class.

Prepare a graph of the number of heads (*y*-axis) versus the trial number (*x*-axis). Is the result a straight line or a curve? Add a third column titled "Log of number of heads" to the data table, and use your calculator to complete the table. Prepare a graph of the data in Column 3 (*y*-axis) versus trial number (*x*-axis). Is the result a straight line or a curve? After you have read this chapter, relate the results of this activity to radioactive decay and half-life.

NUCLEAR RADIATION

*M*arie Curie was a Polish scientist whose research led to many discoveries about radiation and radioactive elements. In 1903 she and her husband Pierre won the Nobel Prize for physics. She was also awarded the Nobel Prize for chemistry in 1911 for her research on radioactive elements. Marie Curie's research was invaluable to the understanding and use of newly discovered radioactive elements. In 1934 she died from leukemia caused by her long-term exposure to radiation. **What types of radiation are there, and how harmful are they?**

objectives

▶ Discuss the processes of radioactivity and radioactive decay

▶ Characterize alpha, beta, and gamma radiation in terms of composition and penetrating power

key terms

▶ radioisotopes
▶ radioactivity
▶ radiation
▶ radioactive decay
▶ alpha radiation
▶ alpha particles
▶ beta radiation
▶ beta particles
▶ gamma radiation

Radioactivity

In the preceding chapters, you read about chemical reactions. In such reactions, atoms tend to attain stable electron configurations. This chapter deals with nuclear reactions, reactions in which the nuclei of unstable isotopes, called **radioisotopes,** gain stability by undergoing changes. These changes are always accompanied by the emission of large amounts of energy. Unlike chemical reactions, nuclear reactions are not affected by changes in temperature, pressure, or the presence of catalysts. They are also unaffected by the compounds in which the unstable isotopes are present, and they cannot be slowed down, speeded up, or turned off.

In 1896, the French chemist Antoine Henri Becquerel (1852–1908) made an interesting accidental discovery. He was studying the ability of uranium salts that had been exposed to sunlight to fog photographic film plates. During a period of bad weather in Paris, Becquerel realized that even uranium salts not exposed to the sun caused the same result in the film, as shown in **Figure 28.1.** At that time, two of Becquerel's associates were Marie Curie (1867–1934) and Pierre Curie (1859–1906). The Curies were able to show that the fogging of the plates was caused by rays emitted by the uranium atoms in the ore. Marie Curie named the process by which materials give off such rays **radioactivity.** The penetrating rays and particles emitted by a radioactive source are called **radiation.** Pierre Curie assisted his wife in the isolation of several radioactive elements. Together with Becquerel, they won the Nobel Prize in physics in 1903 for their work.

Figure 28.1

Uranium salts, which are radioactive, can fog a photographic plate like this one. This effect was discovered by the French chemist Antoine Henri Becquerel.

Table 28.1

Characteristics of Some Ionizing Radiations			
Property	**Alpha radiation**	**Beta radiation**	**Gamma radiation**
Composition	Alpha particle (helium nucleus)	Beta particle (electron)	High-energy electro-magnetic radiation
Symbol	α, ^4_2He	β, $^0_{-1}e$	γ
Charge	2+	1−	0
Mass (amu)	4	1/1837	0
Common source	Radium-226	Carbon-14	Cobalt-60
Approximate energy	5 MeV*	0.05 to 1 MeV	1 MeV
Penetrating power	Low (0.05 mm body tissue)	Moderate (4 mm body tissue)	Very high (penetrates body easily)
Shielding	Paper, clothing	Metal foil	Lead, concrete (incompletely shields)

*(1 MeV = 1.60×10^{-13} J)

The discovery of radioactivity dealt a deathblow to Dalton's theory of indivisible atoms. A radioactive atom, or radioisotope, undergoes drastic changes as it emits radiation. Such radioisotopes have unstable nuclei. The stability of a nucleus depends on the relative proportion of neutrons to protons in the nucleus as well as on the overall size of the nucleus. The presence of too many or too few neutrons, relative to the number of protons, leads to an unstable nucleus. An unstable nucleus loses energy by emitting radiation during the process of **radioactive decay.** Eventually, unstable radioisotopes of one element are transformed into stable (nonradioactive) isotopes of a different element. Radioactive decay is spontaneous and does not require any input of energy.

Types of Radiation

Several types of radiation can be emitted during radioactive decay. **Table 28.1** summarizes the characteristics of three of these types of radiation. The different types of radiation from a radioactive source can be separated by an electric or magnetic field, as shown in **Figure 28.2**.

Figure 28.2

An electric field has different effects on these three types of radiation. Alpha particles and beta particles are deflected in opposite directions—alpha particles toward the negative plate and beta particles toward the positive plate. Gamma rays are undeflected.

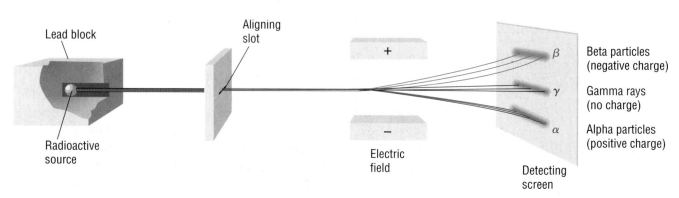

Lead block
Radioactive source
Aligning slot
+
−
Electric field
Detecting screen

β Beta particles (negative charge)
γ Gamma rays (no charge)
α Alpha particles (positive charge)

A type of radiation called **alpha radiation** consists of helium nuclei that have been emitted from a radioactive source. These emitted particles, called **alpha particles,** contain two protons and two neutrons and have a double positive charge. In nuclear equations, an alpha particle is written $_2^4\text{He}$ or α. The electric charge is generally omitted.

The radioisotope uranium-238 releases alpha radiation and is transformed into another radioisotope, thorium-234. **Figure 28.3** illustrates this transformation.

$$_{92}^{238}\text{U} \xrightarrow[\text{decay}]{\text{Radioactive}} {}_{90}^{234}\text{Th} + {}_2^4\text{He } (\alpha \text{ emission})$$

Uranium-238   Thorium-234   Alpha particle

Note that this nuclear equation is balanced. The sum of the mass numbers (superscripts) on the right equals the sum on the left. How does the sum of the atomic numbers (subscripts) on the right compare with the sum on the left?

When an atom loses an alpha particle, the atomic number of the product atom is lower by two and its mass number is lower by four. Because of their large mass and charge, alpha particles do not tend to travel very far and are not very penetrating. They are easily stopped by a sheet of paper or by the surface of your skin. However, radioisotopes that emit alpha particles are dangerous when ingested. The particles do not have to travel far to penetrate soft tissue and cause damage.

Beta radiation consists of fast-moving electrons formed by the decomposition of a neutron in an atom. The neutron decomposes into a proton, which remains in the nucleus, and an electron, which is released.

$$_0^1\text{n} \longrightarrow {}_1^1\text{H} + {}_{-1}^0\text{e}$$

Neutron   Proton   Electron (beta particle)

The fast-moving electrons released by a nucleus are called **beta particles.** The fact that they are negatively charged is reflected in the subscript -1 where atomic number is generally written. Their virtual lack of mass is represented by the superscript 0, corresponding to mass number.

Carbon-14 emits a beta particle as it undergoes radioactive decay to form nitrogen-14. **Figure 28.4** shows this beta emission.

$$_6^{14}\text{C} \longrightarrow {}_7^{14}\text{N} + {}_{-1}^0\text{e } (\beta \text{ emission})$$

Carbon-14 (radioactive)   Nitrogen-14 (stable)   Beta particle

The mass number of the nitrogen-14 atom produced is the same as that of carbon-14. Its atomic number has increased by 1. The nucleus now contains an additional proton and one fewer neutron. Note that the nuclear equation is balanced. The sum of the atomic numbers on the right $(7 + (-1))$ equals the sum of the atomic numbers on the left (6). The mass numbers are also balanced (14 on each side). Beta particles have less charge and much less mass than alpha particles. Consequently, they are more penetrating. Beta particles are stopped by aluminum foil or thin pieces of wood.

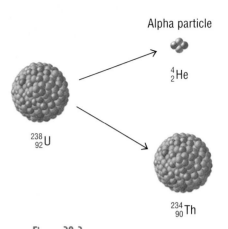

Alpha particle

$_2^4\text{He}$

$_{92}^{238}\text{U}$

$_{90}^{234}\text{Th}$

Figure 28.3
Uranium-238 is shown undergoing alpha decay to form thorium-234. What particle is emitted during this decay process?

Beta particle

$_{-1}^0\text{e}$

$_6^{14}\text{C}$

$_7^{14}\text{N}$

Figure 28.4
Carbon-14 is shown undergoing beta decay to form nitrogen-14. What particle is emitted during this decay process?

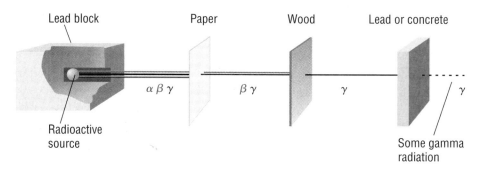

Figure 28.5
Because of their large mass and charge, alpha particles (red) have the least penetrating power of the three main types of radiation. Gamma rays (black) have no mass or charge and are the most penetrating.

PHYSICS

Particle Accelerators
Since the 1930s, physicists have used particle accelerators to probe the mysteries of the atom. In a particle accelerator, a beam of subatomic particles traveling near the speed of light collides with a nucleus, smashing it into fragments. Using a detection device called a bubble chamber, the path that these fragments take may be traced. Researchers have discovered evidence that suggests that protons and neutrons consist of even smaller particles called quarks. Quarks are thought to be held together by other particles, called gluons.

Gamma radiation is high-energy electromagnetic radiation given off by a radioisotope. Visible light, or the light you see, is also electromagnetic radiation, but of much lower energy. Gamma rays are often emitted along with alpha or beta radiation by the nuclei of disintegrating radioactive atoms. The following examples demonstrate this process.

$$\ce{^{230}_{90}Th} \longrightarrow \ce{^{226}_{88}Ra} + \ce{^{4}_{2}He} + \gamma$$

Thorium-230   Radon-226   Alpha   Gamma
                                    particle   ray

$$\ce{^{234}_{90}Th} \longrightarrow \ce{^{234}_{91}Pa} + \ce{^{0}_{-1}e} + \gamma$$

Thorium-234   Protactinium-234   Beta   Gamma
                                      particle   ray

Gamma rays have no mass and no electrical charge. Thus the emission of gamma radiation in itself does not alter the atomic number or mass number of an atom.

X-radiation, or x-rays, behave essentially the same as gamma rays, but their origin is different. X-rays are not emitted during radioactive decay. They are produced as excited electrons in certain metals lose their energy. X-rays are extremely penetrating and potentially very dangerous. Both gamma rays and x-rays pass easily through paper, wood, and the human body. They can be stopped, although not completely, by several meters of concrete or several centimeters of lead, as shown in **Figure 28.5.** Why does your dentist place a heavy apron over your torso before taking an x-ray?

section review 28.1

1. Explain what is meant by radioactivity and radioactive decay.

2. Distinguish among alpha, beta, and gamma radiation on the basis of the following.

   a. mass   **b.** charge   **c.** penetrating power

3. What part of an atom undergoes change during radioactive decay?

 Chem ASAP! **Assessment 28.1** Check your understanding of the important ideas and concepts in Section 28.1.

NUCLEAR TRANSFORMATIONS

*A*lthough weather stripping and insulation help conserve energy, thus lowering heating and cooling bills, such efforts can prevent an ample exchange of fresh air. As a result, radioactive substances such as radon gas can accumulate and pose a health risk. Radon-222 is a radioactive isotope that is present naturally in the soil in some areas. It has a constant rate of decay. **How is the decay rate of a radioactive substance expressed?**

objectives
▶ Use half-life information to determine the amount of a radioisotope remaining at a given time
▶ Give examples of equations for the synthesis of transuranium elements by transmutation

key terms
▶ band of stability
▶ positron
▶ half-life
▶ transmutation
▶ transuranium elements

Nuclear Stability and Decay

About 1500 different nuclei are known. Of those, only 264 are stable and do not decay or change with time. As mentioned earlier, the stability of a nucleus depends on its neutron-to-proton ratio. For elements of low atomic number (below about 20), the ratio for stability is about 1. That means the stable nuclei have roughly equal numbers of neutrons and protons. For example, the isotopes $^{12}_{6}C$, $^{14}_{7}N$, and $^{16}_{8}O$ are stable. Above atomic number 20, stable nuclei have more neutrons than protons. The neutron-to-proton ratio reaches about 1.5 for heavy elements. The lead isotope $^{206}_{82}Pb$, for example, with 124 neutrons and 82 protons, is stable. Its ratio is $\frac{124}{82} \approx 1.5$.

Figure 28.6 shows a plot of the number of neutrons versus the number of protons for all the known stable nuclei. The stable nuclei on a neutron-versus-proton plot are located in a region called the **band of stability.** Unstable nuclei undergo spontaneous radioactive decay. The type of decay that occurs depends on the neutron-to-proton ratio of the unstable nucleus.

Figure 28.6

A neutron-versus-proton plot of all the known stable nuclei forms a pattern called the band of stability (shown in red). For isotopes of low atomic number, the stability ratio is about 1:1; for the heavier isotopes, the ratio increases to about 1.5:1.

A nucleus may be unstable for several reasons. Some nuclei have too many neutrons relative to the number of protons. These nuclei decay by turning a neutron into a proton and by emitting a beta particle (an electron) from the nucleus.

$$_{0}^{1}n \longrightarrow {}_{1}^{1}H + {}_{-1}^{0}e$$

This process is known as beta decay or beta emission. It produces a simultaneous increase in the number of protons and a decrease in the number of neutrons. Here are the nuclear equations for several isotopes that undergo beta emission.

$$_{29}^{66}Cu \longrightarrow {}_{30}^{66}Zn + {}_{-1}^{0}e$$

$$_{6}^{14}C \longrightarrow {}_{7}^{14}N + {}_{-1}^{0}e$$

Other nuclei are unstable because they have too few neutrons relative to the number of protons. These nuclei increase their stability by converting a proton to a neutron. As seen in the following examples, an electron is captured by a nucleus during this process.

$$_{28}^{59}Ni + {}_{-1}^{0}e \longrightarrow {}_{27}^{59}Co$$

$$_{18}^{37}Ar + {}_{-1}^{0}e \longrightarrow {}_{17}^{37}Cl$$

A **positron** is a particle with the mass of an electron but a positive charge. Its symbol is $_{+1}^{0}e$. A positron may be emitted as a proton changes to a neutron, as in the following cases.

$$_{5}^{8}B \longrightarrow {}_{4}^{8}Be + {}_{+1}^{0}e$$

$$_{8}^{15}O \longrightarrow {}_{7}^{15}N + {}_{+1}^{0}e$$

When a proton is converted to a neutron, the atomic number decreases by 1 and the number of neutrons increases by 1. How does this change affect the mass number?

All nuclei with atomic number greater than 83 are radioactive. These nuclei lie in the upper end of the band of stability, and are especially heavy. They have both too many neutrons and too many protons to be stable. Therefore they undergo decay. Most of them emit alpha particles. Alpha emission results in an increase in the neutron-to-proton ratio, which tends to increase the stability of the nucleus.

$$_{82}^{204}Pb \longrightarrow {}_{80}^{200}Hg + {}_{2}^{4}He$$

$$_{88}^{226}Ra \longrightarrow {}_{86}^{222}Rn + {}_{2}^{4}He$$

$$_{90}^{232}Th \longrightarrow {}_{88}^{228}Ra + {}_{2}^{4}He$$

In alpha emission, the mass number decreases by four and the atomic number decreases by two. If the masses of the reactants and products of a nuclear reaction could be determined with a sufficiently sensitive balance, you would find that mass is not conserved! In fact, an infinitesimally small quantity of mass is lost. The lost mass is converted to energy associated with radiation.

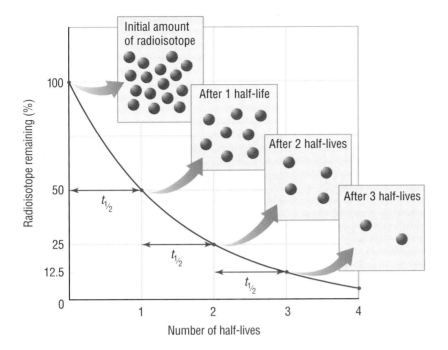

Half-Life

Every radioisotope has a characteristic rate of decay measured by its half-life. A **half-life** $(t_{1/2})$ is the time required for one-half of the nuclei of a radioisotope sample to decay to products. After one half-life, half of the original radioactive atoms have decayed into atoms of a new element. The other half are still unchanged at that point, as demonstrated in **Figure 28.7**. After a second half-life, only one-quarter of the original radioactive atoms remain.

Half-lives may be as short as a fraction of a second or as long as billions of years. **Table 28.2** shows the half-lives of some naturally occurring radioisotopes. Scientists use the half-lives of some naturally occurring radioisotopes to determine the age of ancient artifacts. Many artificially produced radioisotopes have very short half-lives, a feature that is a great advantage in nuclear medicine. The rapidly decaying isotopes do not pose long-term biological radiation hazards to the patient.

Table 28.2

Half-Lives and Radiation of Some Naturally Occurring Radioisotopes		
Isotope	Half-life	Radiation emitted
Carbon-14	5.73×10^3 years	β
Potassium-40	1.25×10^9 years	β, γ
Radon-222	3.8 days	α
Radium-226	1.6×10^3 years	α, γ
Thorium-230	7.54×10^4 years	α, γ
Thorium-234	24.1 days	β, γ
Uranium-235	7.0×10^8 years	α, γ
Uranium-238	4.46×10^9 years	α

Figure 28.7
This decay curve for a radioactive element shows that by the end of each half-life, half of the remaining original radioactive atoms have decayed into atoms of another element.

ARCHAEOLOGY

Carbon Dating
Carbon-14, which has a half-life of 5730 years, is used extensively to date artifacts that are made of organic material. All living organisms contain carbon-12

and carbon-14 in a fixed ratio. After an organism dies, however, the ratio of carbon-12 to carbon-14 changes as the carbon-14 decays to nitrogen-14. An object that was made of plant fibers might now have a carbon-14 concentration of one-half its original value. This object must therefore be about 5730 years old (one half-life). Carbon-14 dating can be used to determine the ages of objects between 200 and 50 000 years old. The Dead Sea Scrolls, for example, were determined to be 1940 ± 70 years old.

CALCULATING HALF-LIFE

This CHEMath feature provides more detailed information about half-life. With this information, you will have the skills needed to write the exponential decay function for a radioactive element. The table shows the amount of radioactive isotope remaining after 0, 1, and 2 half-lives if the initial amount is A_0.

Do you see the pattern? After n half-lives, the amount remaining is $A = A_0 \times \left(\frac{1}{2}\right)^n$. Since n is the time elapsed divided by the half-life, this equation can be written as $A = A_0 \times \left(\frac{1}{2}\right)^{t/T}$, where t is time and T is the half-life (using the same units). This type of equation is known as an exponential decay function.

Number of Half-Lives	Amount Remaining	Exponential Form
0	A_0	$A_0 \times \left(\frac{1}{2}\right)^0$
1	$A_0 \times \frac{1}{2}$	$A_0 \times \left(\frac{1}{2}\right)^1$
2	$A_0 \times \frac{1}{2} \times \frac{1}{2}$	$A_0 \times \left(\frac{1}{2}\right)^2$

Logarithms can be used to algebraically calculate half-lives. You will use the formula $\log (a^b) = b \times \log a$, and you will want to use a calculator. See Example 2.

Example 1

Iodine-131 has a half-life of 8 days. Write and graph an equation for the amount (A) of iodine-131 after t days if the sample initially contains 80 g iodine-131.
Using $A = A_0 \times \left(\frac{1}{2}\right)^{t/T}$, the equation is $A = 80 \times \left(\frac{1}{2}\right)^{t/8}$.
The graph includes the points listed below.

t (days)	0	8	16	24	32
A (grams)	80	40	20	10	5

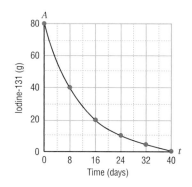

Example 2

A sample initially contains 100.0 g of thorium-234. After 16.0 days, the sample contains 63.1 g of thorium-234. Calculate the half-life.

Use the formula $A = A_0 \times \left(\frac{1}{2}\right)^{t/T}$.

$$63.1 \text{ g} = (100 \text{ g}) \times \left(\frac{1}{2}\right)^{(16.0 \text{ days})/T}$$

$$\frac{63.1}{100} = \left(\frac{1}{2}\right)^{(16.0 \text{ days})/T}$$

$$0.631 = 0.5^{(16.0 \text{ days})/T}$$

$$\log 0.631 = \log \left(0.5^{(16.0 \text{ days})/T}\right)$$

$$\log 0.631 = \frac{(16.0 \text{ days})}{T} \times \log 0.5$$

$$T = (16.0 \text{ days}) \times \frac{\log 0.5}{\log 0.631} = 24.1 \text{ days}$$

The half-life of thorium-234 is 24.1 days.

Practice Problems

Practice writing and using exponential decay functions by solving each of the following.

A. Technetium-104 has a half-life of 18 minutes. Write and graph an equation for the amount A of technetium-104 after t minutes if the sample initially contains 64 g of technetium-104.

B. A sample initially contains 248 g of strontium-90, which has a half-life of 29 years. Write an equation for the amount A of strontium-90 after t years. What is the amount of strontium-90 at $t = 52$ years?

C. A sample initially contains 50.0 g of cobalt-60. After 2.00 years, the sample contains 38.4 g of cobalt-60. Calculate the half-life of cobalt-60. What is the amount of cobalt-60 at $t = 8.00$ years?

Figure 28.8
Uranium-238 decays through a complex series of radioactive intermediates, including radon gas (Rn). What is the stable end-product of this series?

Chem ASAP!
Simulation 30
Simulate the decay of several radioisotopes.

One isotope that has a long half-life is uranium-238, which decays through a complex series of radioactive intermediates to the stable isotope lead-206. **Figure 28.8** illustrates this process. The age of uranium-containing minerals can be estimated by measuring the ratio of uranium-238 to lead-206. Because the half-life of uranium-238 is 4.5×10^9 years, it is possible to use this method to date rocks nearly as old as the solar system.

Sample Problem 28-1

Nitrogen-13 emits beta radiation and decays to carbon-13 with a half-life $(t_{1/2})$ of 10 min. Assume a starting mass of 2.00 g of nitrogen-13.

a. How long is three half-lives?

b. How many grams of the isotope will still be present at the end of three half-lives?

1. **ANALYZE** *List the knowns and the unknowns.*

Knowns:
- $(t) = 10$ min
- initial mass = 2.00 g
- number of half-lives = 3

Unknowns:
- 3 half-lives = ? min
- mass after 3 half-lives = ? g

Calculate the time required for three half-lives by multiplying the length of each half-life by the number of half-lives (3). Determine the mass remaining by multiplying the original mass by $\frac{1}{2}$ for each half-life.

Practice Problems

4. Manganese-56 is a beta emitter with a half-life of 2.6 h. What is the mass of manganese-56 in a 1.0-mg sample of the isotope at the end of 10.4 h?

Sample Problem 28-1 (cont.)

2. CALCULATE *Solve for the unknowns.*
a. 3×10 min $= 30$ min
b. The initial mass of nitrogen-13, 2.00 g, is cut by one-half for each half-life, so for three half-lives

$$2.00 \text{ g} \times \frac{1}{2} \times \frac{1}{2} \times \frac{1}{2} = 0.250 \text{ g}$$

3. EVALUATE *Do the results make sense?*
The mass of nitrogen-13 after three half-lives is expected to be much lower than the original mass. The final answer has the proper units and the proper number of significant figures.

Transmutation Reactions

The conversion of an atom of one element to an atom of another element is called **transmutation.** As you have learned, radioactive decay is one way in which transmutation occurs. A transmutation can also occur when high-energy particles bombard the nucleus of an atom. The high-energy particles may be protons, neutrons, or alpha particles.

Many transmutations occur in nature. The production of carbon-14 from naturally occurring nitrogen-14, for example, takes place in the upper atmosphere. Another naturally occurring isotope, uranium-238, undergoes 14 transmutations before reaching a stable isotope, as was shown in **Figure 28.8.** Many other transmutations are done in laboratories or in nuclear reactors. The earliest artificial transmutation was performed in 1919 by Ernest Rutherford (1871–1937). He bombarded nitrogen gas with alpha particles to produce an unstable isotope of fluorine. The results of this reaction are shown in **Figure 28.9.** The reaction is

$$^{14}_{7}\text{N} \quad + \quad ^{4}_{2}\text{He} \quad \longrightarrow \quad ^{18}_{9}\text{F}$$

Nitrogen-14   Alpha particle   Fluorine-18

The fluorine isotope quickly decomposes to a stable isotope of oxygen and a proton.

$$^{18}_{9}\text{F} \quad \longrightarrow \quad ^{17}_{8}\text{O} \quad + \quad ^{1}_{1}\text{H}$$

Fluorine-18   Oxygen-17   Proton

Figure 28.9
In 1919, Ernest Rutherford carried out the first artificial transmutation when he bombarded nitrogen gas with alpha particles. What particles were formed?

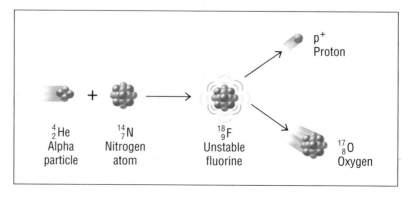

Rutherford's experiment eventually helped lead to the discovery of the proton. James Chadwick's discovery of the neutron in 1932 also involved a transmutation experiment. Neutrons were produced when beryllium-9 was bombarded with alpha particles.

$$^{9}_{4}\text{Be} \quad + \quad ^{4}_{2}\text{He} \longrightarrow \quad ^{12}_{6}\text{C} \quad + \quad ^{1}_{0}\text{n}$$

Beryllium-9   Alpha   Carbon-12   Neutron
              particle

The elements in the periodic table with atomic numbers above 92, called the **transuranium elements,** all undergo transmutation. None of them occurs in nature, and all of them are radioactive. These elements have been synthesized in nuclear reactors and nuclear accelerators, one of which is shown in **Figure 28.10.** Such devices accelerate bombarding particles to very high speeds. When uranium-238 is bombarded with relatively slow neutrons from a nuclear reactor, some uranium nuclei capture neutrons to produce uranium-239.

$$^{238}_{92}\text{U} + ^{1}_{0}\text{n} \longrightarrow ^{239}_{92}\text{U}$$

Uranium-239 is radioactive and emits a beta particle. The product is an isotope of the artificial radioactive element neptunium (atomic number 93).

$$^{239}_{92}\text{U} \longrightarrow ^{239}_{93}\text{Np} + ^{0}_{-1}\text{e}$$

Neptunium is unstable and decays to produce a second artificial element, plutonium (atomic number 94). What particle is emitted in this reaction?

$$^{239}_{93}\text{Np} \longrightarrow ^{239}_{94}\text{Pu} + ^{0}_{-1}\text{e}$$

Plutonium and neptunium are both transuranium elements and do not occur naturally. These first artificial elements were synthesized in 1940 by scientists in Berkeley, California. Since that time, more than 20 additional transuranium elements have been synthesized.

Figure 28.10
The Stanford Linear Accelerator Center is operated by Stanford University in California. This research facility houses a linear accelerator that is two miles long.

section review 28.2

6. How is half-life used to determine the amount of a radioisotope remaining at a given time?

7. Give two examples of equations for the synthesis of transuranium elements by transmutation.

8. Complete and balance the equations for the following nuclear reactions.

  a. $^{27}_{13}\text{Al} + ^{4}_{2}\text{He} \longrightarrow ^{30}_{14}\text{Si} + ?$ **c.** $^{27}_{14}\text{Si} \longrightarrow ^{0}_{-1}\text{e} + ?$

  b. $^{214}_{83}\text{Bi} \longrightarrow ^{4}_{2}\text{He} + ?$ **d.** $^{66}_{29}\text{Cu} \longrightarrow ^{66}_{30}\text{Zn} + ?$

9. Explain the process of transmutation. Write at least three nuclear equations to illustrate your answer.

10. The mass of cobalt-60 in a sample is found to have decreased from 0.800 g to 0.200 g in a period of 10.5 years. From this information, calculate the half-life of cobalt-60.

portfolio project

Research the methods used by archeologists to date materials such as pottery, coral, and stone. Prepare a poster display on the radioisotopes used, their half-lives, and their limitations.

Chem ASAP! **Assessment 28.2** Check your understanding of the important ideas and concepts in Section 28.2.

RADIOACTIVITY AND HALF-LIVES

SAFETY

Use safe and proper laboratory procedures.

PURPOSE

To simulate the chemical conversion of a reactant over time and to graph the data and relate it to radioactive decay and half-lives.

MATERIALS

- pencil
- ruler
- penny
- paper
- graph paper

PROCEDURE

On a sheet of paper, draw a grid similar to Figure A. Flip a penny 100 times and, in your grid, record the total number of heads that result. Now flip the penny the same number of times as the number of heads that you obtained in the first 100 flips. Record the total number of flips and the number of heads that result. Continue this procedure until you obtain no more heads. Record all your data in Figure A.

Trial #	Number of flips	Number of heads
1	100	
2		
3		
4		
5		
6		
7		

Figure A

ANALYSIS

Using your experimental data, record the answers to the following questions below your data table.

1. Use graph paper to plot the number of flips (*y*-axis) versus the trial number (*x*-axis). Draw a smooth line through the points.

2. Examine your graph. Is the rate of the number of heads produced over time linear or nonlinear? Is the rate constant over time or does it change?

3. Why does each trial reduce the number of heads by approximately one-half?

4. A half-life is the time required for one-half of the atoms of a radioisotope to emit radiation and to decay to products. What value represents one half-life for the process of flipping coins?

YOU'RE THE CHEMIST

The following small-scale activities allow you to develop your own procedures and analyze the results.

1. **Design It!** Design and carry out an experiment using a single die to model radioactive decay. Plot your data.

2. **Analyze It!** Many radioisotopes undergo alpha decay. They emit an alpha particle (helium nucleus $_2^4\text{He}$). For example,

$$_{86}^{222}\text{Rn} \longrightarrow {}_{84}^{218}\text{Po} + {}_2^4\text{He}$$

Write similar balanced nuclear equations for the alpha decay of each of the following.

a. Pa-231   c. Ra-226

b. Am-241   d. Es-252

3. **Analyze It!** Other radioisotopes undergo beta decay, emitting a beta particle (electron $_{-1}^0\text{e}$). For example,

$$_6^{14}\text{C} \longrightarrow {}_7^{14}\text{N} + {}_{-1}^0\text{e}$$

Write similar balanced nuclear equations for the beta decay of each of the following.

a. H-3   c. I-131

b. Mg-28   d. Se-75

FISSION AND FUSION OF ATOMIC NUCLEI

The sun appears as a fiery ball in the sky—so bright it should never be looked at with unprotected eyes. Although its surface temperature is about 5800 K, the sun is not actually burning. If the energy given off by the sun were the product of a combustion reaction, the sun would have burned out approximately 2000 years after it was formed, long before today. **How is the energy given off by the sun produced?**

objectives
▶ Compare nuclear fission and nuclear fusion, and comment on their potential as sources of energy
▶ Describe the methods used in nuclear power plants to produce and control fission reactions
▶ Explain the issues involved in storage, containment, and disposal of nuclear waste.

key terms
▶ fission
▶ neutron moderation
▶ neutron absorption
▶ fusion

Nuclear Fission

When the nuclei of certain isotopes are bombarded with neutrons, they undergo **fission,** the splitting of a nucleus into smaller fragments. Uranium-235 and plutonium-239 are fissionable materials. As shown in **Figure 28.11,** a fissionable atom, such as uranium-235, breaks into two fragments of roughly the same size when struck by a slow-moving neutron. At the same time, more neutrons are released by the fission. These neutrons strike the nuclei of other uranium-235 atoms, continuing the fission by a chain reaction. In a chain reaction, some of the neutrons produced react with other fissionable atoms, producing more neutrons, which react with still more fissionable atoms. This process is similar to the toppling of dominoes shown in **Figure 28.11**.

Nuclear fission can unleash enormous amounts of energy. The fission of 1 kg of uranium-235, for example, releases an amount of energy equal to that generated in the explosion of 20 000 tons of dynamite. In an uncontrolled nuclear chain reaction, the total energy release is nearly instantaneous. The entire reaction takes only fractions of a second. Atomic bombs are devices that start uncontrolled nuclear chain reactions.

Chem ASAP!
Animation 30
Take a close look at a nuclear fission chain reaction.

Figure 28.11

In nuclear fission, uranium-235 breaks into two fragments. What is produced? The released neutrons can split other uranium-235 atoms, creating a chain reaction. The toppling dominoes shown in the photograph illustrate the idea of a chain reaction.

Figure 28.12

The illustration shows the basic components of a nuclear reactor. Heat produced in the reactor by the fission process is removed by circulating coolant. The removed heat is used to power a steam-driven turbine, which generates electricity.

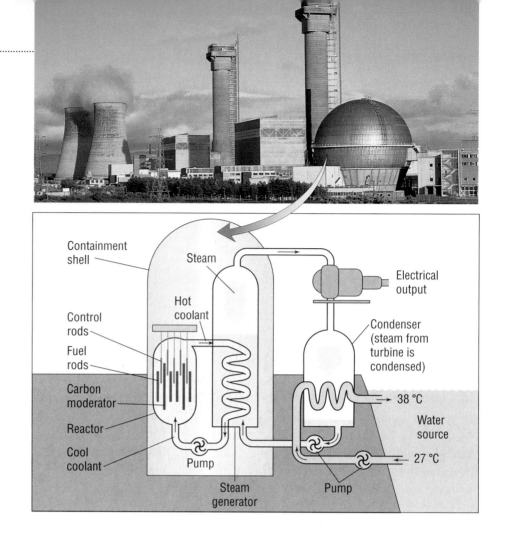

Fission can be controlled so energy is released more slowly. Nuclear reactors, such as the one diagrammed in **Figure 28.12,** use controlled fission to produce useful energy. In the controlled fission reaction within a nuclear reactor, much of the energy generated is in the form of heat. A suitable coolant fluid, usually liquid sodium or water, removes the heat from the reactor core. The heat is used to generate steam, which drives a turbine that in turn generates electricity. The control of fission in a nuclear reactor involves two steps.

1. **Neutron moderation** is a process that reduces the speed of neutrons so they can be captured by the reactor fuel (usually uranium-235 or plutonium-239) in order to continue the chain reaction. Moderation is necessary because most of the neutrons produced move so fast that they will pass right through a nucleus without being absorbed. Water and carbon are good moderators because they slow the neutrons so the chain reaction can be sustained.

2. **Neutron absorption** is a process that decreases the number of slow moving neutrons. To prevent the chain reaction from going too fast, some of the slowed neutrons must be trapped before they hit fissionable atoms. Neutron absorption is carried out by control rods made of a material, such as cadmium, that absorbs neutrons. When the control rods extend almost all the way into the reactor core, they absorb many neutrons, and fission occurs slowly. As the rods are pulled out, they absorb fewer neutrons and the fission process speeds up. If the chain reaction were to go too fast, heat might be produced faster than

it could be removed by the coolant. In this case, the reactor core would overheat, which could lead to mechanical failure and release of radioactive materials into the atmosphere. Ultimately, a meltdown of the reactor core might occur.

Despite other dangers, a nuclear reactor cannot produce a nuclear explosion. The fuel elements are widely separated and cannot physically connect to produce the critical mass required. Once a nuclear reactor is started, however, it remains highly radioactive for many generations. Shields protect the reactor structure from radiation damage. Walls of high-density concrete are also designed to protect the operating personnel.

Nuclear Waste

Fuel rods from nuclear power plants are one major source of nuclear waste. The fuel rods are made from a fissionable isotope, either uranium-235 or plutonium-239. The fuel rods are long and narrow—typically 3 meters long with a 0.5-cm diameter. Three hundred fuel rods are bundled together to form an assembly and one hundred assemblies are arranged to form the reactor core. During fission, the amount of fissionable isotope in each fuel rod decreases. There comes a time when there is no longer enough fuel in the rods to ensure that the output of the power station remains constant. The isotope-depleted, or spent, fuel rods must be removed and replaced with new fuel rods.

Spent fuel rods are classified as high-level nuclear waste. They contain the remainder of the fissionable isotope along with the fission products, a complex mixture of highly radioactive isotopes. Some of these fission products have very short half-lives, on the order of fractions of seconds. Others have half-lives of hundreds or thousands of years. All nuclear power plants have holding tanks, or swimming pools, for spent fuel rods. These pools, which are typically 12 meters deep, are filled with water as shown in **Figure 28.13.** Storage racks at the bottom of these pools are designed to hold the spent fuel assemblies. There are two reasons fuel assemblies are stored in water. Water cools the rods, which continue to produce heat for years after their removal from the core. Water also acts as a radiation shield to reduce the radiation levels from the spent fuel rods.

The assemblies of spent fuel rods may spend a decade or more in a holding pool. Plant operators expected used fuel rods to be reprocessed to recover the remaining fissionable isotope, which would be recycled in the manufacture of new fuel rods. However, with large deposits of uranium ore available—many in the United States—it is less expensive to mine new fuel than to reprocess depleted fuel. At some nuclear plants, there is no space left in the storage pool. In order to keep these plants open, their fuel rods must be moved to off-site storage facilities.

The number of years a nuclear plant can operate is limited. Eventually the plant must be decommissioned and dismantled. Because the plant is usually contaminated with radioactive materials, dismantling produces thousands of tons of low-level nuclear waste. Low-level waste is taken to licensed burial sites that are monitored and controlled by the Department of Transportation (DOT) and the Nuclear Regulatory Commission (NRC). For more information on nuclear waste, see the feature on page 862.

Figure 28.13

The racks at the bottom of this pool contain spent fuel rods.

Figure 28.14
Figure 28.14
Thermonuclear fusion reactions occurring in the sun have provided Earth with energy for billions of years.

$$4\,{}^{1}_{1}\text{H} \quad + \quad 2\,{}^{0}_{-1}\text{e} \quad \longrightarrow \quad {}^{4}_{2}\text{He} \quad + \quad \text{Energy}$$

hydrogen nuclei   beta particles   helium nucleus

Nuclear Fusion

The sun is an extraordinary energy source. The energy released by the sun results from a thermonuclear reaction, or nuclear fusion. **Fusion** occurs when nuclei combine to produce a nucleus of greater mass. In solar fusion, hydrogen nuclei (protons) fuse to make helium nuclei. **Figure 28.14** shows that the reaction also requires two beta particles. Fusion reactions tend to release more energy than do fusion reactions. However, fusion reactions occur only at very high temperatures—in excess of 40 000 000 °C.

The use of controlled nuclear fusion as an energy source on Earth is appealing. The potential fuels are inexpensive and readily available, and the fusion products are usually not radioactive. One reaction that scientists are studying is the combination of a deuterium (hydrogen-2) nucleus and a tritium (hydrogen-3) nucleus to form a helium nucleus.

$$\,{}^{2}_{1}\text{H} + \,{}^{3}_{1}\text{H} \longrightarrow \,{}^{4}_{2}\text{He} + \,{}^{1}_{0}\text{n} + \text{energy}$$

The problems with fusion lie in achieving the high temperatures necessary to start the reaction, and in containing the reaction once it has started. The high temperatures required to initiate fusion reactions have been achieved by using a fission bomb. Such a bomb is the triggering device used for setting off a hydrogen bomb, which is an uncontrolled-fusion device. Such a process is clearly of no use, however, as a controlled generator of power.

At the very high temperatures involved in fusion, matter exists as a plasma, a high-energy state in which ions exist in a gaslike form. To contain a plasma is a formidable task. No known structural material can withstand the hot, corrosive plasma. Scientists are experimenting with magnetic fields to contain plasma.

section review 28.3

11. Compare nuclear fission and fusion. Evaluate the reliability of each as a source of energy.

12. Describe how a nuclear fission power plant operates.

13. Explain what happens in a nuclear chain reaction.

14. Identify two types of nuclear waste produced by nuclear power plants.

15. Assuming technical problems could be overcome, what are some advantages to producing electricity in a fusion reactor?

 Chem ASAP! **Assessment 28.3** Check your understanding of the important ideas and concepts in Section 28.3.

RADIATION IN YOUR LIFE

*T*he Scottish physicist C.T.R Wilson wanted to study the formation of clouds, so he built a chamber in which he could duplicate cloud formation. In the chamber, water in the air condensed on dust particles, forming clouds. When Wilson used dust-free air, clouds continued to condense, provided the air was saturated enough. He hypothesized that clouds condensed on ions in the air. To test his hypothesis, Wilson exposed his chamber to ionizing radiation. The radiation left trails of condensed water droplets. When Wilson finished his work in 1912, his chamber had become a radiation detector used by many scientists of the day. **What are some other devices used to detect radiation, and how do they function?**

objectives
▶ Describe three methods of detecting radiation
▶ List some applications of radioisotopes in research and medicine

key terms
▶ ionizing radiation
▶ Geiger counter
▶ scintillation counter
▶ film badge

Detecting Radiation

X-rays and the radiation emitted by radioisotopes are called ionizing radiation. **Ionizing radiation** is radiation with enough energy to knock electrons off some atoms of the bombarded substance to produce ions. You cannot detect ionizing radiation with any of your senses. Instead, various instruments and monitoring devices are used for this purpose. One such device, called a **Geiger counter,** uses a gas-filled metal tube to detect radiation. **Figure 28.15** shows the construction of a Geiger counter. The tube has a central wire electrode that is connected to a power supply. When ionizing radiation penetrates a thin window at one end of tube, the gas inside the tube becomes ionized. Because of the ions and free electrons produced, the gas becomes an electrical conductor. Each time a Geiger tube is exposed to radiation, current flows. The bursts of current drive electronic counters or cause audible clicks from a built-in speaker. Geiger counters are used primarily to detect beta radiation. Alpha particles cannot pass through the end window. Most gamma rays and x-rays pass directly through the gas, causing few ionizations.

Figure 28.15
Radiation cannot be seen, heard, felt, or smelled. Thus warning signs and radiation-detection instruments must be used to alert people to the presence of radiation and to monitor its level. The Geiger counter is one such instrument that is widely used. What type of radiation does a Geiger counter primarily detect?

Counter or audio device
DC power supply
Ionization of fill gas takes place along track of radiation
Metal tube (negatively charged)
Window
Ionizing radiation path
Atoms or molecules of fill gas
Central wire electrode (positively charged)
e^-

MINI LAB

Studying Inverse-Square Relationships

Flashlight

1 cm × 1 cm
square opening

Duct tape

PURPOSE

To demonstrate the relationship between radiation intensity and the distance from the radiation source.

MATERIALS

- flashlight
- strips of duct tape
- scissors
- poster board, white (50 cm × 50 cm)
- meter ruler or tape measure
- flat surface, long enough to hold the meter ruler
- loose-leaf paper
- graph paper
- pen or pencil
- light sensor (optional)

PROCEDURE

 Sensor version available in the Probeware Lab Manual.

1. Measure and record the distance (*A*) from the bulb filament to the front surface of the flashlight.

2. Cover the end of a flashlight with tape. Leave a 1-cm × 1-cm square hole in the center for light to pass through.

3. Place the flashlight on its side on a flat, horizontal surface. Turn on the flashlight. Darken the room.

4. Mount a large piece of white poster board directly in front of the flashlight, perpendicular to the horizontal surface.

5. Move the flashlight backward from the vertical board in short increments. At each position you select, record the distance (*B*) from the flashlight to the vertical board and the length (*L*) of one side of the square image projected on the board.

6. On a sheet of graph paper, plot *L* on the *y*-axis versus *A* + *B* on the *x*-axis. On another sheet, plot *L*² on the *y*-axis versus *A* + *B* on the *x*-axis.

ANALYSIS AND CONCLUSIONS

1. As the flashlight is moved away from the vertical board, what do you notice about the intensity of the light in the illuminated square? Use your graphs to demonstrate the relationship between intensity and distance.

2. When the distance of the flashlight from the board is doubled and tripled, what can you say about the areas and intensities of the illuminated squares?

A **scintillation counter** is a device that uses a specially coated phosphor surface to detect radiation. Ionizing radiation striking the phosphor surface produces bright flashes of light, or scintillations. The number of flashes and their respective energies are detected electronically. The information is then converted into electronic pulses, which are measured and recorded. Scintillation counters have been designed to detect all types of ionizing radiation. Such devices are similar to television screens coated with zinc sulfide (ZnS) as the phosphor. Inside a television, electrons are shot at a phosphor screen, producing scintillations. The pattern of these scintillations produces the television picture.

Film badges are important radiation detectors for persons who work near radiation sources. A **film badge**, shown in **Figure 28.16,** consists of several layers of photographic film covered with black lightproof paper, all encased in a plastic or metal holder. The badge is worn the entire time the person is at work. At specific intervals, with the frequency depending on the type of work involved, the film is removed and developed. The strength and type of radiation exposure are determined from the darkening of the film.

Figure 28.16
People who work with ionizing radiation wear film badge detectors. The film inside such a badge is exposed in proportion to the amount and type of radiation it receives.

Records are kept of the results. Film badges do not protect a person from radiation exposure. They merely serve as precautionary monitoring devices. Protection against radiation is achieved by keeping a safe distance from the source and by using adequate shielding.

Using Radiation

Although radiation can be harmful and should always be handled with care, it can be used safely and is important in many scientific procedures. Neutron activation analysis is a procedure used to detect trace amounts of elements in samples. In this procedure, a sample of interest is bombarded with neutrons from a radioactive source, which causes some atoms in the sample to become radioactive. The half-life and type of radiation emitted by the radioisotopes are detected, and this information is processed by a computer. Because this information is characteristic for each element, scientists can determine what radioisotopes were produced and what elements were originally present in the sample. This is a sensitive technique used to detect trace amounts of elements. It is capable of measuring 10^{-9} g of an element in a sample. Neutron activation analysis is used by museums to detect art forgeries, and by crime laboratories to analyze gunpowder residues.

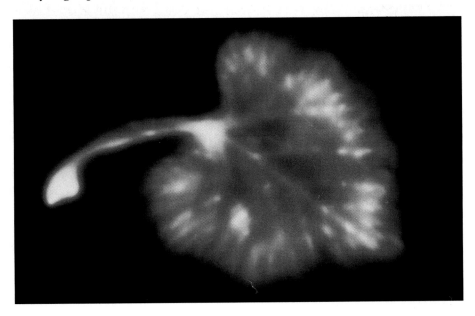

Figure 28.17
A radioactive tracer is used to determine where an absorbed pesticide or fertilizer is taken up by a plant.

Radioisotopes called tracers are used to study chemical reactions and molecular structures. During this procedure, one of the reactants is labeled with a radioisotope and added to the reaction mixture. After the reaction is complete, the radiation of the product is measured to determine the uptake of the tracer. By comparing this amount with the amount originally added, much can be learned about the reaction mechanism. Reactions with many steps can be studied using this method.

Radioisotope tracers are also used in agricultural research to test the effects of herbicides, pesticides, and fertilizers. During this procedure, the tracer is first introduced into the substance being tested to make the substance radioactive. Next, plants are treated with the radioactively labeled substance. Then, the radioactivity of the plants is measured to determine the location of the substance, as shown in **Figure 28.17** on the previous page. Often, the tracer is also monitored in animals that consume the plants, in water, and in soil. This information helps scientists determine the effects of using the substance.

Radioisotopes can even be used to diagnose some diseases. Iodine-131, for example, is used to detect thyroid problems. The thyroid gland extracts iodide ions from the bloodstream and uses them to make the hormone thyroxine. To diagnose thyroid disease, the patient is given a drink containing a small amount of the radioisotope iodine-131. After about two hours, the amount of iodide uptake is measured by scanning the patient's throat with a radiation detector. **Figure 28.18** shows the results of such a scan. In a similar way, the radioisotope technetium-99m is used to detect brain tumors and liver disorders. Phosphorus-32 is used to detect skin cancer.

Radiation has become a routine part of the treatment of some cancers. Cancer is a disease in which abnormal cells in the body are produced at a rate far beyond the rate for normal cells. The mass of cancerous tissue resulting from this runaway growth is called a tumor. Radiation therapy is often used to treat cancer because the fast-growing cancer cells are more susceptible to damage by high-energy radiation such as gamma rays than are the healthy cells. The cancerous area can be treated with radiation to kill the cancer cells. Some normal cells are also killed, however, and cancer cells at the center of the tumor may be resistant to the radiation. Therefore, the benefits of the treatment and the risks to the patient must be carefully evaluated before radiation treatment begins.

Figure 28.18

This scanned image of a thyroid gland shows where radioactive iodine-131 has been absorbed. Doctors use these images to identify thyroid disorders.

Figure 28.19
Radiation therapy is commonly used to treat cancer. The unit shown here emits a narrow, intense beam of radiation that destroys the ability of cells to reproduce. Cells are most vulnerable to the radiation when they are dividing. Why are cancer cells generally more sensitive to radiation than are normal cells?

In a technique called teletherapy, a narrow beam of high-intensity gamma radiation is directed at cancerous tissue. A radiation therapy unit used for teletherapy is shown in **Figure 28.19.** Cobalt-60 and cesium-137 are commonly used as the radiation sources. To minimize damage to healthy tissue, the patient is positioned so that only the cancerous region is within the radiation beam at all times. The unit rotates so that the radiation dose to the skin and surrounding normal tissue is minimized and distributed in a belt that extends all the way around the patient.

Salts of radioisotopes can also be sealed in gold tubes and directly implanted in tumors. These seeds emit beta and gamma rays that kill the surrounding cancer cells. Because the radioisotope is in a sealed container, it is prevented from traveling throughout the body.

Pharmaceuticals containing radioisotopes of gold, iodine, or phosphorus are sometimes given in radiation therapy. For example, a dose of iodine-131 larger than that used simply to detect thyroid diseases can be given to treat the diseased thyroid. The radioactive iodine accumulates in the thyroid and emits beta and gamma rays to provide therapy.

section review 28.4

16. Describe several methods of detecting radiation.

17. Describe several applications of radioisotopes in scientific research and in medicine.

18. Name an advantage of a scintillation counter over a Geiger counter.

19. Suppose that a radioactive solution containing an alpha emitter accidentally gets on your hands. You wash your hands with soap and water and then check them with a Geiger counter for residual radioactive contamination. The Geiger counter does not register any radioactivity. Are your hands definitely free from radioactive contamination? Explain.

20. What are some uses of radioactive tracers?

21. What is an advantage of using a radioactive seed to treat a cancerous tumor?

 Chem ASAP! Assessment 28.4 Check your understanding of the important ideas and concepts in Section 28.4.

portfolio project

Research and report on the use of technetium-99m to diagnose diseases and disorders of the liver or gallbladder. Explain how doctors use this technique to pinpoint the source of a problem without surgery.

NUCLEAR WASTE: STORAGE, DISPOSAL, AND CONTAINMENT

The proper disposal of chemical wastes, which can pollute air, land, and water, is an ongoing issue for society. Nuclear waste offers an even greater challenge because the ionizing radiation it emits can harm both existing organisms and future generations. Nuclear waste began accumulating in the 1940s at nuclear weapons facilities, which no longer operate. Today, nuclear waste is created by power plants and sectors of society such as hospitals that use radioisotopes. The nuclear waste accumulated in the last fifty years has been in temporary storage awaiting sites and methods for permanent disposal.

Transuranic waste is low- to mid-level waste contaminated with alpha-emitting radioisotopes with half-lives greater than 20 years and atomic numbers greater than 92. This waste consists of disposable items such as tools, clothing, and debris.

The photograph shows the interior of the Waste Isolation Pilot Plant (WIPP) near Carlsbad, New Mexico. The plant is located on unpopulated, federally owned land near the site where more than 900 nuclear tests were conducted. WIPP is a network of underground excavations in an ancient bed of rock salt about 660 meters beneath the desert. WIPP is an example of a geologic repository, which is a storage facility located in rock deep underground. WIPP is the world's first geologic repository for the permanent disposal of defense-generated transuranic waste. It is vital to the Department of Energy's (DOE) long-range environmental cleanup plan.

WIPP is designed to store thousands of tons of transuranic waste. The plant is expected to receive more than 35 000 loads of transuranic waste from 23 DOE sites for a period of about 35 years. The waste must be contained before shipment. Liquid waste will

be solidified. All waste will be packed in 55-gallon drums.

In 1982, the United States Congress passed the Nuclear Waste Policy Act, which set policy guidelines for the disposal of all high-level nuclear waste. This waste consists of spent fuel rods from commercial nuclear reactors and high-level waste from the production of nuclear weapons.

The high-level waste will be vitrified and packed in corrosion-resistant containers. Vitrification is the technical term for the production of glass. The contained waste will then be transported for permanent burial in a geologic repository.

Choosing a site for the repository is difficult because it takes more than 600 years for the fission product strontium-90 and more than 20 000 years for plutonium-239 to decay to safe levels. The site must meet health and safety standards over thousands of years. For more than a decade, studies have been done at Yucca Mountain, Nevada. Approval by the President and Congress, licensing by the Nuclear Regulatory Commission, and construction by the Department of Energy could take another decade. Meanwhile spent fuel rods will remain in their on-site or off-site temporary storage facilities.

> Nuclear waste has been in temporary storage awaiting sites and methods for permanent disposal.

Take It to the NET
*For interactive study and
review, go to www.phschool.com*

KEY TERMS

- alpha particle *p. 843*
- alpha radiation *p. 843*
- band of stability *p. 845*
- beta particle *p. 843*
- beta radiation *p. 843*
- film badge *p. 858*
- fission *p. 853*
- fusion *p. 855*

- gamma radiation *p. 844*
- Geiger counter *p. 857*
- half-life *p. 847*
- ionizing radiation *p. 857*
- neutron absorption *p. 854*
- neutron moderation *p. 854*
- positron *p. 846*
- radiation *p. 841*

- radioactive decay *p. 842*
- radioactivity *p. 841*
- radioisotope *p. 841*
- scintillation counter *p. 858*
- transmutation *p. 850*
- transuranium elements *p. 851*

KEY EQUATIONS

- $^{238}_{92}\text{U} \xrightarrow[\text{decay}]{\text{Radioactive}} {}^{234}_{90}\text{Th} + {}^{4}_{2}\text{He}$

- $^{230}_{90}\text{Th} \longrightarrow {}^{226}_{88}\text{Ra} + {}^{4}_{2}\text{He} + \gamma$

- $^{14}_{6}\text{C} \longrightarrow {}^{14}_{7}\text{N} + {}^{0}_{-1}\text{e}$

CONCEPT SUMMARY

28.1 Nuclear Radiation

- Isotopes with unstable nuclei are radioactive and are called radioisotopes. The nuclei of radioisotopes emit radiation as they decay to stable nuclei.
- The radiation may be alpha (positively charged helium nuclei), beta (electrons), or gamma (electromagnetic radiation).

28.2 Nuclear Transformations

- When a radioactive nucleus emits an alpha particle, its atomic number decreases by 2 and its mass number decreases by 4. For beta emission, the atomic number increases by 1 and the mass number stays the same. The atomic number and the mass number stay the same for gamma emission.
- Every radioisotope decays at a characteristic rate. A half-life is the time required for one-half of the nuclei in a radioisotope to decay.

28.3 Fission and Fusion of Atomic Nuclei

- In nuclear fission, fissionable isotopes split when bombarded with neutrons. The isotopes release neutrons that cause a chain reaction.
- Nuclear power plants control fission through neutron moderation and neutron absorption. These plants generate electricity and high-level nuclear waste. Spent fuel rods removed from nuclear cores are stored in on-site pools.
- In nuclear fusion, light nuclei fuse to make more massive nuclei.

28.4 Radiation in Your Life

- Radiation may be detected with a Geiger counter or a scintillation counter. A film badge monitors radiation exposure of individuals who work with radioactive materials.
- Radioactivity and radiation are used extensively in agricultural research, in medical diagnosis, and in the treatment of some diseases.

CHAPTER CONCEPT MAP

Use these terms to construct a concept map that organizes the major ideas of this chapter.

 Chem ASAP! **Concept Map 28**
Create your Concept Map using the computer.

alpha particle · fission · radioactive decay · applications · fusion · stability · beta particle · gamma radiation · half-life

CONCEPT PRACTICE

22. Explain the difference between an isotope and a radioisotope. *28.1*

23. The disintegration of the radioisotope radium-226 produces an isotope of the element radon and alpha radiation. The atomic number of radium (Ra) is 88; the atomic number of radon (Rn) is 86. Write a balanced equation for this transformation. *28.1*

24. A radioisotope of the element lead (Pb) decays to an isotope of the element bismuth (Bi) by emission of a beta particle. Complete the equation for the decay process by supplying the missing atomic number and mass number. *28.1*

$$^{210}\text{Pb} \longrightarrow {}_{83}\text{Bi} + {}_{-1}^{0}\text{e}$$

25. Write the symbol and charge for each. *28.1*
    a. alpha particle
    b. beta particle
    c. gamma ray

26. Alpha radiation is emitted during the disintegration of the following isotopes. Write balanced nuclear equations for their decay processes. Name the element produced in each case. *28.1*
    a. uranium-238 ($^{238}_{92}\text{U}$)
    b. thorium-230 ($^{230}_{90}\text{Th}$)
    c. uranium-235 ($^{235}_{92}\text{U}$)
    d. radon-222 ($^{222}_{86}\text{Rn}$)

27. The following radioisotopes are beta emitters. Write balanced nuclear equations for their decay processes. *28.1*
    a. carbon-14 ($^{14}_{6}\text{C}$)
    b. strontium-90 ($^{90}_{38}\text{Sr}$)
    c. potassium-40 ($^{40}_{19}\text{K}$)
    d. nitrogen-13 ($^{13}_{7}\text{N}$)

28. How are the mass number and atomic number of a nucleus affected by the loss of the following? *28.1*
    a. beta particle
    b. alpha particle
    c. gamma ray

29. The following radioactive nuclei decay by emitting alpha particles. Write the product of the decay process for each. *28.1*
    a. $^{238}_{94}\text{Pu}$ c. $^{210}_{84}\text{Po}$
    b. $^{210}_{83}\text{Bi}$ d. $^{230}_{90}\text{Th}$

30. What happens to an atom with a nucleus that falls outside the band of stability? *28.2*

31. Write an equation for the radioactive decay of fluorine-17 by positron emission. *28.2*

32. Identify the more stable isotope in each pair. *28.2*
    a. $^{14}_{6}\text{C}$, $^{13}_{6}\text{C}$
    b. $^{3}_{1}\text{H}$, $^{1}_{1}\text{H}$
    c. $^{16}_{8}\text{O}$, $^{18}_{8}\text{O}$
    d. $^{14}_{7}\text{N}$, $^{15}_{7}\text{N}$

33. Name the elements represented by the following symbols and indicate which of them would have no stable isotopes. *28.2*
    a. Pt   e. Xe
    b. Th   f. Cf
    c. Fr   g. V
    d. Tc   h. Pd

34. Why is it important that radioactive isotopes used internally for diagnosis or treatment have relatively short half-lives? *28.2*

35. Explain half-life. *28.2*

36. A patient is administered 20 mg of iodine-131. How much of this isotope will remain in the body after 40 days if the half-life for iodine-131 is 8 days? *28.2*

37. What is the difference between natural and artificial radioactivity? *28.2*

38. What are the transuranium elements? Why are they unusual? *28.2*

39. Describe the process of nuclear fission and define a nuclear chain reaction. *28.3*

40. Why are spent fuel rods removed from a reactor core? What do they contain? What happens to them after they are removed? *28.3*

41. Fusion reactions produce enormous amounts of energy. Why is fusion not used to generate electrical power? *28.3*

42. Why are x-rays and the radiation emitted by radioisotopes called ionizing radiation? *28.4*

43. What is the purpose of wearing a film badge when working with ionizing radiation sources? *28.4*

44. Explain how iodine-131 is used in both the diagnosis and treatment of thyroid disease. *28.4*

CONCEPT MASTERY

45. Write nuclear equations for these conversions.

a. $^{30}_{15}P$ to $^{30}_{14}Si$

b. $^{13}_{6}C$ to $^{14}_{6}C$

c. $^{131}_{53}I$ to $^{131}_{54}Xe$

46. What is the difference between the nuclear reactions taking place in the sun and the nuclear reactions taking place in a nuclear reactor?

47. Complete these nuclear equations.

a. $^{32}_{15}P \longrightarrow$ ____ $+ {}^{0}_{-1}e$

b. ____ $\longrightarrow {}^{14}_{7}N + {}^{0}_{-1}e$

c. $^{238}_{92}U \longrightarrow {}^{234}_{90}Th +$ ____

d. $^{141}_{56}Ba \longrightarrow$ ____ $+ {}^{0}_{-1}e$

e. ____ $\longrightarrow {}^{181}_{77}Ir + {}^{4}_{2}He$

48. Write nuclear equations for the beta decay of the following isotopes.

a. $^{90}_{38}Sr$

b. $^{14}_{6}C$

c. $^{137}_{55}Cs$

d. $^{239}_{93}Np$

e. $^{50}_{22}Ti$

49. The following graph shows the radioactive decay curve for thorium-234. Use the graph to answer the questions.

a. What percent of the isotope remains after 60 days?

b. How many grams of a 250-g sample of thorium-234 would remain after 40 days had passed?

c. How many days would pass while 44 g of thorium-234 decayed to 4.4 g of thorium-234?

d. What is the half-life of thorium-234?

50. Write a nuclear equation for each word equation.

a. Radon-222 emits an alpha particle to form polonium-218.

b. Radium-230 is produced when thorium-234 emits an alpha particle.

c. When polonium-210 emits an alpha particle, the product is lead-206.

51. Describe the various contributions the following people made to the fields of nuclear and radiation chemistry.

a. Marie Curie

b. Antoine Henri Becquerel

c. James Chadwick

d. Ernest Rutherford

CRITICAL THINKING

52. Choose the term that best completes the second relationship.

a. decomposition : combination

fission : _____

(1) energy　　　　　(3) radioactivity

(2) nuclei　　　　　(4) fusion

b. anion : cation

electron : _____

(1) positron　　　　(3) beta particle

(2) neutron　　　　(4) alpha particle

c. umbrella : rain

wood : _____

(1) radioactive decay　(3) beta radiation

(2) gamma radiation　(4) x-radiation

53. Compare the half-life of an element to a single-elimination sports tournament.

54. Why does the relatively large mass and charge of an alpha particle limit its penetrating power?

55. Why might radioisotopes of C, N, and O be especially harmful to living creatures?

CUMULATIVE REVIEW

56. What is the Pauli exclusion principle? What is Hund's rule?

57. Balance the following equations.

a. $Ca(OH)_2 + HCl \longrightarrow CaCl_2 + H_2O$

b. $Fe_2O_3 + H_2 \longrightarrow Fe + H_2O$

c. $NaHCO_3 + H_2SO_4 \longrightarrow$

$Na_2SO_4 + CO_2 + H_2O$

d. $C_2H_6 + O_2 \longrightarrow CO_2 + H_2O$

58. You have a 0.30M solution of sodium sulfate. What volume (in mL) must be measured to give 0.0020 mol of sodium sulfate?

59. How many protons, neutrons, and electrons are in an atom of each isotope?
    a. iron-59
    b. uranium-235
    c. chromium-52

60. Identify the bonds between each pair of atoms as ionic or covalent.
    a. carbon and silicon
    b. calcium and fluorine
    c. sulfur and nitrogen
    d. bromine and cesium

61. How many cubic centimeters of hydrogen gas (at STP) will be produced when 10.00 g of magnesium metal reacts with an excess of sulfuric acid? How many moles is this?

CONCEPT CHALLENGE

62. The radioisotope cesium-137 has a half-life of 30 years. A sample decayed at the rate of 544 counts per minute (cpm) in the year 1985. In what year will the decay rate be 17 cpm?

63. Describe the process depicted in the following graph.

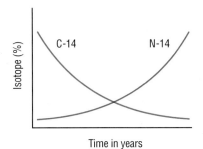

64. Bismuth-211 is a radioisotope. It decays by alpha emission to yield another radioisotope, which emits beta radiation as it decays to a stable isotope. Write equations for the nuclear reactions and name the decay products.

65. What isotope remains after three beta particles and five alpha particles are lost from a thorium-234 isotope? (Refer to the uranium-238 decay series to check your answer.)

66. Write a paragraph analyzing the overall logic of the reasoning in the following argument.
    (1) Radiation kills fast-growing cells.
    (2) Cancer cells are fast-growing.
    (3) Therefore, radiation kills only cancer cells.

Select the choice that best answers each question or completes each statement.

1. If a radioisotope undergoes beta emission,
 a. the atomic number changes.
 b. the number of neutrons remains constant.
 c. the isotope loses a proton.
 d. the mass number changes.

2. The radioisotope radon-222 has a half-life of 3.8 days. How much of an initial 20.0-g sample of radon-222 would remain after 15.2 days?
 a. 5.00 g   **c.** 1.25 g
 b. 12.5 g   **d.** 2.50 g

3. Spent fuel rods
 a. are no longer radioactive.
 b. are stored under water for at least a decade.
 c. contain only one isotope of uranium, ^{238}U.
 d. remain radioactive for less than 100 years.

4. What particle is needed to balance this equation?
$$^{27}_{13}\text{Al} + ^{4}_{2}\text{He} \longrightarrow \underline{\hspace{1cm}} + ^{30}_{15}\text{P}$$
 a. alpha   **c.** proton
 b. electron   **d.** neutron

For each nuclear equation in questions 5–8, name the particle that is being emitted or captured.

5. $^{59}_{26}\text{Fe} \longrightarrow ^{59}_{27}\text{Co} + ^{0}_{-1}\text{e}$

6. $^{185}_{79}\text{Au} \longrightarrow ^{181}_{77}\text{Ir} + ^{4}_{2}\text{He}$

7. $^{59}_{27}\text{Co} + ^{1}_{0}\text{n} \longrightarrow ^{60}_{27}\text{Co}$

8. $^{118}_{54}\text{Xe} \longrightarrow ^{118}_{53}\text{I} + ^{0}_{+1}\text{e}$

Use the graph to answer question 9.

9. Use the graph to determine whether neon-21, zirconium-90, and neodymium-130 have nuclei that are stable.

Use the graph to answer questions 10–12.

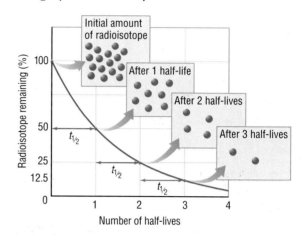

Estimate the percent remaining of the radioisotope after the given number of half-lives.

10. 0.5 $t_{1/2}$

11. 1.25 $t_{1/2}$

12. 3.75 $t_{1/2}$

Use the drawings of atomic nuclei to answer questions 13 and 14.

a.   **b.**   **c.**

● Proton   ● Neutron

13. Write the name and symbol for each isotope.

14. Which isotope is radioactive?

The lettered choices below refer to questions 15–19. A lettered choice may be used once, more than once, or not at all.

 (A) film badge
 (B) radioactive tracer
 (C) radiation therapy
 (D) neutron activation analysis
 (E) Geiger counter

Which of the above items or processes is best described by each of the following applications?

15. treating some cancers

16. detect ionizing radiation

17. monitoring exposure to radiation

18. diagnosing some diseases

19. detecting art forgeries

CHEMIST

The job descriptions of a chemist are very diverse. Some chemists solve problems that help make industrial processes more efficient. These industrial chemists perform quality control to ensure that the highest production standards are met. Other chemists conduct research in which they isolate new chemicals from a dazzling array of sources. Research chemists may invent processes that earn patents, or they may discover new chemicals that they get to name. Other chemists measure levels of chemicals in the environment, solve crimes, analyze the nutritional content of food, or invent new flavors.

Most chemists begin their careers by earning an undergraduate degree in chemistry. Many go on to get advanced degrees in fields such as analytical chemistry, forensic chemistry, biochemistry, organic chemistry, or nuclear chemistry. Throughout this textbook, you will have the opportunity to explore many of the career possibilities in chemistry.

MATERIALS SCIENTIST

Some scientists work solely with solid state materials. Some examples of solid state materials are safety glass, synthetic gems, superconductors, and ceramics. Materials scientists study properties such as heat conduction, strength-to-density ratios, electrical resistance, crystalline structure, and chemical reactivity. The fundamental knowledge gained by materials scientists is used to develop materials for specific applications.

A scientist who develops and describes solid state materials must be a physicist as well as a chemist. These scientists must know how a solid's crystal structure is formed and what it is made of. Such information is important if the scientist wants to describe how and where the different atoms in the solid are located. One way to map the crystalline structure of a solid is by using x-rays to probe a sample of the substance. This technique is called x-ray diffraction (XRD). When a sample is bombarded with x-rays, the x-rays scatter in a characteristic pattern, providing information on how the sample's atoms are arranged.

In addition to courses in general chemistry and physics, courses in the electronic structure of solids, the movement of heat, and applied mathematics are also recommended. A four- year degree can cover the basics of materials science if your courses are chosen with care. You also may pursue graduate studies in specialty

areas such as superconductivity, ceramics, corrosion resistance, and composite materials.

ANALYTICAL CHEMIST

Analytical chemists focus on making quantitative measurements. They must be familiar with many analytical techniques to work successfully on a wide variety of tasks. As an analytical chemist, you would spend your time making measurements and calculations to solve laboratory and math-based research problems. You could, for example, be involved in analyzing the composition of biomolecules. Pharmaceutical companies need people to analyze the composition of medicines and research new combinations of compounds to use as drugs. As an analytical chemist, you must be able to think creatively and develop new means for finding solutions.

Many exciting new fields, such as biomedicine and biochemistry, are now hiring analytical chemists. More traditional areas, including industrial manufacturers, also employ analytical chemists. The educational background you need to enter this field is quite extensive. You would need advanced chemical training, including organic chemistry and quantitative chemistry, as well as some training in molecular biology and computer operation. A master's degree in chemistry may be required, and certain positions require a Ph.D.

MEDICAL LABORATORY TECHNICIAN

When you go to a doctor's office for a physical examination, you typically provide a urine sample and have some blood drawn by a medical laboratory technician (MLT). Medical laboratory technicians are part medical aide and part chemist. These health care professionals perform standard laboratory tests that are used in the detection and treatment of human diseases and disorders. Typical tasks of an MLT may include collecting blood samples, classifying blood by type, and counting the different types of cells in a blood sample. They also measure the levels of enzymes and ions in the blood to detect abnormalities. MLTs prepare slides of tissues and fluids and examine them under a microscope. They isolate and identify microorganisms from samples such as urine and throat swabs. Working as part of a team with doctors, nurses, and other health care workers, MLTs help to maintain their patients' health. And knowledge of chemistry can go a long way in this endeavor!

To become an MLT, you must complete an accredited medical laboratory technician program. Such programs are offered by many community colleges and some hospitals. High school courses in biology, chemistry, computer science, and mathematics are recommended. MLTs are employed by hospitals, clinics, and public and private laboratories.

ARCHAEOLOGIST

Archaeologists are detectives of the past, sifting for clues that uncover secrets of past civilizations. Archaeologists excavate ancient cities and dwellings looking for artifacts that indicate what kinds of foods ancient people ate, how they built their homes, what types of tools they used, and how they interacted with one another as a society. Often, archaeologists must draw conclusions based on indirect evidence.

Knowing when an event occurred or when an artifact was made can provide important information. To obtain such information, archaeologists use radiometric-dating techniques such as carbon dating. This method tells them the age of a sample within a certain range, and is used with the greatest accuracy for samples that are not more than 10 000 years old. Carbon dating is often used in conjunction with other kinds of evidence, such as the types of tools or pottery present.

Archaeologists also perform chemical tests on samples of artifacts to determine their composition. For example, archaeologists might analyze the glazes used on pottery, or the dyes and fabrics used for clothing. Archaeologists may also use chemicals to preserve artifacts that have been unearthed so that the artifacts can be handled and examined without being damaged.

Archaeology requires a background in both history and science. Archaeologists often spend as much time in the laboratory studying their finds as they do out in the field excavating sites. Archaeologists take courses in archaeological techniques, biology, anatomy, chemistry, math, and history.

PHARMACIST

Pharmacists work in pharmacies where they dispense prescription drugs to customers. Pharmacists also advise people on how and when they should take medicine, describe any side effects they might experience, and answer any other questions the customers might have. Pharmacists also make sure that physicians have not prescribed a medicine or dosage that could harm the patient. Although pharmacists are trained to mix chemicals to prepare drugs, they usually dispense medicines prepared by large pharmaceutical companies.

Many pharmacists obtain a degree in pharmacology from college. This degree usually takes about five years to complete. Pharmacists must study chemistry, biology, mathematics, and statistics. They also take courses about the biological effects of drugs and drug interactions. After obtaining a degree, pharmacists have to pass a state test to obtain a license to dispense drugs. To complete the licensing procedure, they must work for a specified period of time under the supervision of another pharmacist.

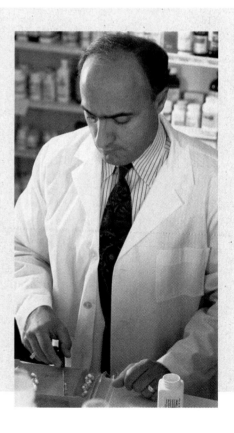

ECOLOGIST

Ecologists study relationships between the living and nonliving aspects of ecosystems. By experiment and observation, ecologists can determine how healthy an ecosystem is and pinpoint potential problems facing the system. As a water ecologist, you would work with water ecosystems such as ponds, rivers, and streams.

Water ecologists use chemistry as they study biology. One of the most important tools water ecologists use is called a dissolved gas test. Dissolved gas tests can be used to check the amounts of dissolved carbon dioxide and dissolved oxygen in different locations of a body of water, such as pools, riffles (areas of moving water),

shaded regions, and full-sun regions. The amount of gases found in these areas helps the ecologist understand where life can exist and whether this life is more likely to be plant or animal. Water ecologists may dredge up the bottom of a body of water to uncover specimens of invertebrates and vertebrates living there. They may also map the land around bodies of water, noting plant and animal species as well as possible sources of pollution or human disturbance to the water.

As a water ecologist, you must be skilled in designing and carrying out experiments, working in the field, analyzing data, recognizing different species of aquatic life, and collecting specimens. A bachelor's degree in

biology or chemistry is required as well as training in water chemistry and in invertebrate, vertebrate, and plant classification.

FIREFIGHTER

If you are courageous, mentally alert, team-oriented, and have a strong sense of public service, you may wish to consider a career as a firefighter. Firefighters respond to fires, medical emergencies, and hazardous chemical spills. In responding to a fire, firefighters must know what types of chemicals can be used on different classes of fires. Having knowledge of the requirements of different chemical fires and spills enables firefighters to put out, rather than feed fires. In addition to these tasks, firefighters clean and maintain equipment, write reports, practice drills, and conduct fire inspections. Firefighters also engage in physical fitness activities to build stamina and improve agility and coordination. Regular reviews of fire science literature keep firefighters up

to date on current technological developments and policy changes.

Although the job is hazardous and includes unpredictable hours, competition for jobs is relatively high. To become a firefighter, you must be at least 18 years of age with a high school education or equivalent. Selection for positions in fire departments often depends on passing a written test as well as a medical examination that includes drug screening and a physical fitness test. Once hired, training consists of instruction in firefighting and rescue techniques, the use of fire and rescue tools, emergency medical procedures, basic chemistry of fires and firefighting, and instruction in local building codes and fire prevention methods. Promotion within the department often depends on further training and education,

such as college-level courses in fire engineering and fire science. Higher positions may require a master's degree in administration.

QUALITY CONTROL CHEMIST

A quality control chemist is responsible for seeing that products meet manufacturing standards. The consistent quality of many products you use is due to the work of a quality control chemist. They work in a wide variety of industries, including those that manufacture airbags for automobiles. They are involved in every aspect of producing the product. They contribute to the original research and development of the product, and help refine its manufacturing process. They then develop methods to test the product, or to determine why it has failed to perform for the consumer.

Quality control chemists must know how to make and interpret measurements. Experience in analytical

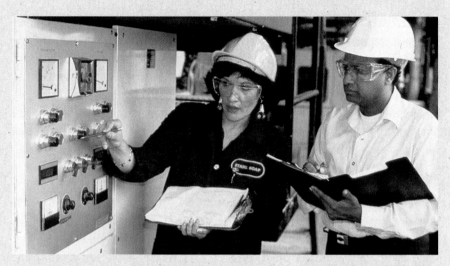

chemistry and the ability to develop new analytical methods are particularly important. The specific requirements for the job depend on the industry and company that employs the quality control chemist.

A good quality control chemist assures that his or her company's customers receive the highest-quality products.

CLIMATOLOGIST

If you want to know what tomorrow's weather will be, you may watch a television weather forecast. What if you wanted to know what the weather will be like fifty years from now? A climatologist is a scientist who studies patterns of weather change and uses them to make such predictions.

A climatologist might use complex computer programs, called forecast models, that take into account many atmospheric variables, such as temperature, wind speed, and pressure. These programs help climatologists make long-term predictions. For example, a forecast model might indicate that an increase in the level of greenhouse gases in the atmosphere will result in an increase in the level of Earth's oceans. A climatologist would use this forecast model to help governments develop plans to minimize the adverse effects that a rise in greenhouse gases would have on such areas as biodiversity, agriculture, and health.

Climatologists also study what Earth's climate was like thousands, or even millions, of years ago. They can

use such data to learn how weather has changed over time and predict how it may change in the future. For example, climatologists study ancient ice core samples. The chemical composition of the gases trapped in the ice can be determined, indicating the makeup of the atmosphere at the time the ice formed.

A climatologist needs training in many scientific and mathematical areas, including physical chemistry, meteorology, physics, statistics, and ecology. A bachelor's or master's degree in meteorology or a related science is required. A climatologist may work in field areas, in a laboratory, or at a computer terminal. Research and computer skills are required.

SOLAR ENGINEER

A solar engineer is responsible for evaluating the performance of photovoltaic cells and modules made of different types, and percentages of, semiconducting materials. Photovoltaic cells are devices that convert the sun's energy into electricity. A solar engineer works with the consumer in mind, seeking to increase the safety, performance levels, and reliability of photovoltaic devices while keeping costs low. The engineer seeks to improve the function of the photovoltaic mechanism: converting sunlight directly into electricity.

Photovoltaic cells and modules are used for a wide variety of tasks. They power the emergency call boxes that are seen along most interstate highways, as well as street lights, solar calculators, and some traffic signals. A solar engineer is responsible for designing and conducting experiments in the field and in the laboratory. The engineer must be able to analyze and draw conclusions from experimental data. He or she must also understand the basics of solar energy, and have a working knowledge of designing and building photovoltaic devices and systems. A bachelor's degree in physics or a related field is usually required, as well as experience with photovoltaics.

COMMERCIAL DIVER

Commercial divers work under tremendous pressure: pressure not only from needing to do a difficult job correctly, but also from working under water. Underwater pressures can exceed ten atmospheres. Commercial divers work as welders and general construction workers. They also perform underwater inspections of dams, pilings, cables and pipelines, bridge and pier foundations, and ship hulls. Sometimes they have to spend many hours undergoing decompression for doing just five minutes of work.

Commercial divers work in a wide variety of jobs. They undergo specialized training in the underwater techniques of construction, welding, and demolition. They take courses that train them to use air and other specialized gases for underwater breathing purposes. It is important for divers to understand the chemistry of gases, as proper blood levels of the dissolved gases oxygen and nitrogen are critical to the divers' safety. In addition, divers must be aware of possible hazardous reactions from materials they use to perform various underwater repair and demolition tasks. Commercial divers need to understand important principles of mathematics, physics, and chemistry to perform their jobs.

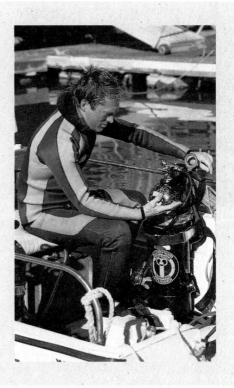

LASER TECHNICIAN

As lasers become a more commonly used tool in many industries, there will be a greater demand for people who know how to operate and maintain them. These jobs often belong to laser technicians. One type of laser technician, a medical laser specialist (MLS), is responsible for maintaining medical laser equipment and for supervising the operation of the lasers. The MLS prepares the laser equipment for use by a surgeon, makes suggestions about settings and adjustments, and operates the controls while the surgeon performs a medical procedure. The MLS is also responsible for the safety of the staff and patients while the laser is in use, and must keep surgeons up to date on new equipment and procedures.

Another type of laser technician is an industrial laser technician (ILT). An ILT is responsible for setting up and maintaining industrial laser equipment, such as laser cutting and welding devices. The ILT must be able to program laser equipment to perform specific tasks and to train other personnel in the proper use of the laser. ILTs are often responsible for the maintenance and repair of the laser equipment, as well as maintaining laser safety in the workplace.

Laser technicians usually have a two-year Associate of Applied Science degree in laser technology from a community or technical college. Laser technicians must complete courses in math and science to understand how lasers work and how to operate them safely.

SOLID STATE CHEMIST

By now you are familiar with chemical reactions in aqueous solutions and the gaseous state. But did you know that chemical reactions can also take place in solids, without the addition of a liquid or a gas? The process of doping semiconductors, for example, involves reactions that take place in the solid state. Manufacturing semiconductors is not the only application for solid state chemistry, however. The lighter on a gas grill, for example, is made of a type of ceramic called a piezoelectric. Devices that operate on the piezoelectric effect produce a voltage when they are subjected to mechanical pressure. Solid photopolymers are now used in place of gelatin in some photographic processes. Even the darkening process used in photosensitive lenses is a solid state chemical reaction.

Solid state chemists are interested in the study of crystal structures, superconductors, semiconductors, and electrical, magnetic, and optical properties of solid compounds. They often work at major universities, teaching and performing basic research, or for corporations, doing research or developing applications for new discoveries in this field. Companies in the petroleum, electronic, and computer industries are just a few of the places a solid state chemist might be employed. To work in this field usually requires an undergraduate or graduate degree in chemistry or chemical engineering. Courses studied include chemistry, physics, and mathematics.

WASTEWATER ENGINEER

Wastewater must be physically and chemically treated before it is returned to the environment or recycled for human use. A wastewater engineer is responsible for monitoring this process. These engineers control the amount of water treated, the level of treatment, and the quality of water produced. When water is received at a treatment plant, a wastewater engineer oversees primary treatment that involves filtering the water for solids and debris. The engineer then adds microorganisms to the water that convert the remaining dissolved organic matter into solids that can be removed as sludge. If this water is to be released into a river or stream, the engineer then tests the water for levels of remaining organic compounds. If amounts of these compounds fall below recommended levels, the water is safe to be released. Production of drinking water often requires additional steps. The engineer must test the water for nitrogen and phosphorus compounds that would need to be removed. The engineer then disinfects the water using chlorine, ozone, or other disinfectants, and might possibly add fluoride to strengthen consumers' teeth.

A wastewater engineer must be able to test water for very small amounts of ions, disease-causing organisms, and other unwanted chemicals or microbes. Interpreting

the results of such tests requires experience and an understanding of the entire chemical, and often biological, environment. Wastewater engineers usually have a degree in engineering. They must take courses in water toxicology, organic chemistry, and environmental biology.

ONCOLOGIST

If helping others and studying cells interests you, a career as a cancer specialist, or oncologist, may be for you. An oncologist diagnoses the various forms and stages of cancer and determines the appropriate treatment. Perhaps you will surgically remove abnormal cancerous skin cells or give your patients the latest anticancer drugs developed by biotechnology. You may have to combine surgery and chemotherapy to maximize the destruction of the cancerous cells. Radiation therapy is another often-used treatment. Application of radiation to the affected area kills cancer cells and shrinks tumors by breaking bonds and damaging cell structures. Unfortunately, radiation also damages healthy cells, so you must carefully balance the benefits of radiation treatment with the damaging side effects. As a cancer specialist, you must be aware of the latest medical techniques and drugs, and the potential side effects of treatments. You must also have a strong knowledge of patient care and disease statistics.

As there are many new cancer cases diagnosed every day in the United States, being an oncologist is a valuable profession. Hospitals, medical research centers, and pharmaceutical and biotechnology companies employ oncologists. Becoming an oncologist requires an undergraduate background in chemistry and biology, a four-year medical degree, and several additional years of specialized training.

OCEANOGRAPHER

Oceanography is the study of oceans. Because oceans are complex systems, oceanography is broken down into several interrelated subfields.

Physical oceanographers study the movement of seawater by waves, currents, and tides, and the interactions between the ocean and the atmosphere. Chemical oceanographers are concerned with the composition of seawater and the interactions between seawater and the organic and inorganic material in it. Geological oceanographers study the structure, features, and evolution of the ocean floor. Biological oceanographers study the diverse plants and animals of the sea and their relationship to their environment.

Oceanographers use many different tools to explore the oceans. Some use submersible vehicles to observe conditions in and take samples from the deepest parts of the ocean. Others wear scuba gear and visit the ocean floor. Oceanographers also use aircraft and satellites to study water temperatures and wave heights. When they are not in the field, oceanographers use computers to analyze data and create theoretical models.

Most oceanographers have advanced degrees. They begin their college education by obtaining a bachelor's degree in biology, marine biology, chemistry, or geology. They then obtain a master's degree or doctorate in a more specialized field, such as marine geology, meteorology, marine biology, or aquatic chemistry.

NEPHROLOGY NURSE

Because renal disease (disease of the kidneys) can be so debilitating to patients who have it, caring for these patients is an important task. Nephrology nurses are health-care professionals who specialize in the treatment and care of renal disease patients. The word nephrology comes from nephron, the name given to each of the more than one million tiny blood-processing units contained in each kidney. Once a patient has been diagnosed with renal disease, a nephrology nurse will assist the patient's doctor in assessing the disease's impact on the patient. Nephrology nurses are often the health-care professionals who help patients during hemodialysis. A major goal of nephrology nurses is to help patients regain the highest level of functioning while undergoing lengthy dialysis treatments. Duties include connecting patients to the dialysis machine, answering questions about treatment and progress, and providing moral support to patients who must endure hours of treatment. Nephrology nurses also assist in renal surgery such as kidney transplants.

Nephrology nurses are usually registered nurses (RNs) who specialize in nephrology. This level of certification requires an undergraduate degree in nursing plus special training in nephrology. Many vocational nurses are also involved in nephrology, and must undergo several years of training after high school.

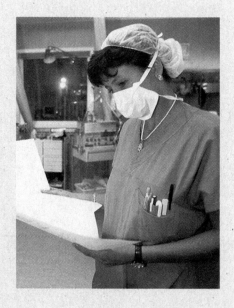

FDA INSPECTOR

The Food and Drug Administration (FDA) touches the lives of most Americans every day. It is the FDA's job to see that the food we eat is safe and wholesome, that the cosmetics we use will not harm us, and that the medicines we take are safe and effective. The FDA also ensures that these products are labeled accurately with the information that people need to use them properly.

FDA is a public health agency with approximately 1100 inspectors who visit more than 15 000 facilities every year. FDA inspectors are responsible for conducting inspections of the procedures and products related to the manufacture of cosmetics, dietary supplements, and food additives. They also do investigative work related to biotechnology and to food-borne illnesses. Inspecting and regulating food labeling and nutrition information, as well as the import and export of foods, are other responsibilities of FDA inspectors. FDA inspectors also test food for pesticides and chemical contaminants. Because of the extensive range of job tasks, FDA inspectors tend to specialize in only one area.

FDA inspectors usually have college degrees in biology, microbiology, chemistry, or food and nutrition science. They also take courses in law, economics, mathematics, and statistics. FDA inspectors have years of on-the-job training, and they take annual courses in regulatory changes.

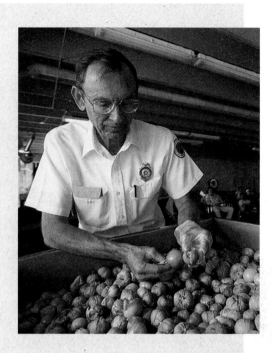

STONE CONSERVATOR

As more is learned about the damaging effects of airborne pollutants, such as acid rain, there is a growing concern to preserve historic buildings and pieces of sculpture from damage. Stone conservators work to both prevent and repair the damage to stone used in buildings and sculpture.

Stone conservators must clean statues properly to remove pollution deposits. One method they use is to apply a thin, clay mudpack to the stone's surface to pull out the deposits. Lasers are also used to remove pollution from stone. When making repairs, stone conservators sometimes use surgical microscopes to examine the surfaces of statues. If the stone was originally painted, the original paint is chemically analyzed to determine its composition. New paint is then produced that closely matches the original paint's composition. In addition, conservators research and apply methods to preserve the stone once it has been repaired. One preservation technique is to seal the stone to prevent water, which carries dissolved gases and salts, from seeping into the pores of the stone.

Stone conservators often work for museums, universities, or private companies that specialize in the cleaning and restoration of stone objects. They must have a knowledge of both chemistry and art because they often work closely with both chemists and museum personnel. A stone conservator's level of education may range from a bachelor's degree to a doctorate.

MICROBIOLOGIST

Microbiologists generally work with microscopic organisms, or organisms that are too small to be seen with the unaided eye. These organisms include bacteria, molds, protozoans, and algae. Microbiologists study the structure and function of these organisms, looking for ways in which these tiny life forms can benefit humans in fields such as industry and medicine.

For example, in the mining industry, microbiologists have discovered several different species of bacteria that can be used to retrieve specific metals from ores. These types of bacteria usually convert a chemical compound in the ore into a different compound, which is then extracted from the bacteria. The bacteria-formed compound then undergoes a third reaction to yield the pure metal. Currently, bacteria are used in the mining of copper, and research is being done on the use of bacteria in the mining of zinc and lead.

In medicine, microbiologists have developed ways to use bacteria to produce human proteins. This is done by inserting a human gene with the genetic code for a specific protein into the DNA of a bacterium. The bacterium will then produce the desired protein. Using this technique, genetically engineered bacteria are used to produced insulin, an important human hormone. People with diabetes do not produce enough insulin in their own bodies and must rely on daily insulin injections to survive.

Microbiologists usually have at least a bachelor's degree in microbiology, which requires some courses in chemistry and mathematics. Jobs involving higher-level research generally require a master's or doctorate degree.

MECHANICAL ENGINEER

Redox reactions can be used to produce heat, such as in the Flameless Ration Heater; they can also be used in fuel cells to create electricity. Fuel cells may be supplying your electrical needs in the future, but proving that a concept is theoretically workable is a far cry from putting it to practical use in people's homes.

Mechanical engineers work as part of a large team of scientists and other engineers who design not only fuel cells that can be produced easily and affordably, but also the components that complement such technology. For example, engineers must also design power grids to distribute the electricity produced by fuel cells.

Mechanical engineering is certainly not limited to the field of fuel-cell technology. Because mechanical engineers help to design all types of machines, they are employed in any industry that involves the manufacture or use of machinery. To be successful in their career, mechanical engineers must be knowledgeable about the interactions of different types of materials: Strength, corrosiveness, and a variety of other properties must be considered in the design.

A mechanical engineer typically has a bachelor's degree with college courses in mathematics, chemistry, physics, and computer science. Good communication skills are also important to a mechanical engineer because oral or written expression of ideas is an essential element of the job.

ELECTROCHEMIST

Electrochemistry provides a variety of valuable applications. Some electrochemists are interested in developing high-energy batteries that convert chemical energy to electrical power. These batteries can be used to power electric vehicles. The goal is to make batteries that can hold a charge longer and still be small enough to use in a car. Along with batteries, electrochemists investigate the function and design of high-performance fuel cells. Among other things, they are interested in the effects of temperature variation on the performance of these cells, because of their use in space and other hostile environments.

Electrochemists are also interested in designing instruments that will detect minute levels of environmental pollutants, such as carcinogens. Other electrochemists study corrosion. They want to know how to slow down or

completely stop the oxidation of metal used to build bridges and roadways, the hulls of ships, and the components of space vehicles. Metal refining and purification is another area of interest to electrochemists.

Electrochemists are employed by universities to teach and work in research laboratories. They can also find work in the computer and electronics industries. Steel companies

and the space program also hire electrochemists. Degrees in electrochemistry can be obtained at all levels, from a bachelor's degree to a doctorate. Electrochemists can also have degrees in materials science and chemical engineering. During the course of study, a prospective electrochemist may be required to take classes in physics and math, in addition to chemistry.

GEMOLOGIST

A gemologist grades gemstones on the basis of their color, clarity, and the presence or absence of flaws. Some gemologists specialize in cutting gemstones, which is an art that requires years of practice to perfect. Cutting gemstones brings out the crystal characteristics that make the gemstones sparkle. Other gemologists specialize in matching gemstones with jewelry settings.

Becoming a gemologist requires years of specialized training. Gemologists learn about different gemstones and their chemical composition. They must study crystal structure and

understand how it enhances a gem. They must be familiar with compounds of transition elements that produce the different colors and shades of the gems. And they must know how these chemical features relate to value.

Gemologists undergo training in gem appraisal and cutting. This training involves examining many different gemstones to become familiar with identifying the unique characteristics of each gem. Gemologists usually specialize in one or a few types of gemstones. Gemologists are often employed in jewelry stores, insurance companies, and gem mines.

ORGANIC CHEMIST

Organic chemists work with carbon-containing compounds. Most organic chemists create and analyze new chemicals made from these carbon-containing building blocks. You use these compounds in just about every part of your life, from medicine to cosmetics, to food. An organic chemist might be best described as part inventor and part detective. Organic chemists make use of both scientific theories and techniques to build specific molecules that react in certain ways. To confirm the identity of these new molecules, organic chemists use many advanced technologies. Infrared (IR) spectrophotometry and nuclear magnetic resonance (NMR) spectrometry are two of the most common techniques for characterizing a chemical sample.

To become an organic chemist, you will need at least an undergraduate education in chemistry. You must have a firm background in physical, inorganic, and analytical chemistry in addition to courses in organic chemistry. If you are interested in the computer-aided design of bioactive molecules, such as new drugs, biochemistry and computer training are also important. An organic chemist must know how to use laboratory equipment and must be aware of safety guidelines for handling dangerous substances.

FLAVOR DEVELOPER

Do you love ice cream? Could you create flavor after flavor after flavor? If so, then the job of flavor developer could be for you. But don't be fooled! Flavor chemistry is not as easy as it sounds. A flavor developer needs to be familiar with the tools of instrumental and sensory analysis. You will also need to know the basics of biochemistry, chromatography, flavor compound isolation and characterization, and flavor model design. Knowledge of organometallics, a class of compounds used in flavor chemistry, would also be beneficial.

As a flavor chemist, you may find yourself working on a variety of projects beyond basic flavor development. For example, you may face the task of reducing the bitterness of a compound, or of replacing a fatty acid with a synthetic component. You may be involved in researching new ways to make flavor compounds, or ways to use esters or aromatic aldehydes to enhance a product's fragrance. You may even be hired to use the 9000 taste buds in your mouth to check ice cream (or other foods) for taste quality and consistency.

To get a job in flavor chemistry, you will need either a bachelor's degree or a master's degree in food science, biochemistry, or chemistry.

BIOCHEMIST

Biochemists study the molecules that make up organisms and that participate in biological processes. Biochemists identify enzymes and determine reaction mechanisms for biochemical reactions. Some biochemists specialize in food chemistry and digestion processes. They develop new foods, flavors, and preservatives, and study how vitamins and minerals are used in the body. Other biochemists work with DNA and RNA to identify organisms and their evolutionary relationships. Biochemists also work for pharmaceutical companies, where they develop new drugs and study their effects.

Biochemists usually earn either a master's degree or a doctorate after obtaining a bachelor's degree in either biology or chemistry. During their studies, biochemists take courses in mathematics, statistics, genetics, and physics in addition to courses in biology and chemistry. When obtaining an advanced degree, they usually specialize in one area, such as the biochemistry of nutrients, cellular processes, or genetics.

NUCLEAR PHYSICIAN

Nuclear physicians are medical doctors who specialize in the use of radiation and radioisotopes to diagnose, manage, treat, and prevent serious diseases. Nuclear physicians are often involved in nuclear imaging of the body, which is a safe and highly effective method of studying the structure and function of organs.

One use of isotopes is to inject them into the body. Different organs take up the isotope in different amounts. By recording the amount of radiation emitted and the concentration of the isotope at different points in the body, nuclear physicians can determine the size and shape of irregularities present in an organ. Nuclear physicians have found that different isotopes have a tendency to localize in certain organs. For example, iodine-131 concentrates in the thyroid and, therefore, can be useful in diagnosing defects in that organ. Also, carbon-14 can be used to study diabetes. Nuclear physicians also administer small and safe doses of radioisotopes to treat certain diseases.

A nuclear physician must first earn a medical degree and specialize in a specific field; then at least three years of postdoctoral training is necessary to become a licensed nuclear physician. Nuclear physicians must take courses in biology, chemistry, mathematics, physics, and computer science before entering a medical school program. Entrance into medical school is highly competitive, so care must be taken to maintain a high grade-point average.

Table A.1 Some Properties of the Elements

Element	Symbol	Atomic number	Atomic mass	Melting point (°C)	Boiling point (°C)	Density (g/cm³) (gases at STP)	Major oxidation states
Actinium	Ac	89	(227)	1050	3200	10.07	+3
Aluminum	Al	13	26.98154	660.37	2467	2.6989	+3
Americium	Am	95	243	994	2607	13.67	+3, +4, +5, +6
Antimony	Sb	51	121.75	630.74	1950	6.691	−3, +3, +5
Argon	Ar	18	39.948	−189.2	−185.7	0.0017837	
Arsenic	As	33	74.9216	817	613	5.73	−3, +3, +5
Astatine	At	85	(210)	302	337	—	
Barium	Ba	56	137.33	725	1640	3.5	+2
Berkelium	Bk	97	(247)	986	—	14.78	
Beryllium	Be	4	9.01218	1278	2970	1.848	+2
Bismuth	Bi	83	208.9804	271.3	1560	9.747	+3, +5
Bohrium	Bh	107	(264)	—	—	—	
Boron	B	5	10.81	2079	3675	2.34	+3
Bromine	Br	35	79.904	−7.2	58.78	3.12	−1, +1, +5
Cadmium	Cd	48	112.41	320.9	765	8.65	+2
Calcium	Ca	20	40.08	839	1484	1.55	+2
Californium	Cf	98	(251)	900	—	14	
Carbon	C	6	12.011	3550	4827	2.267	−4, +2, +4
Cerium	Ce	58	140.12	799	3426	6.657	+3, +4
Cesium	Cs	55	132.9054	28.40	669.3	1.873	+1
Chlorine	Cl	17	35.453	−100.98	−34.6	0.003214	−1, +1, +5, +7
Chromium	Cr	24	51.996	1857	2672	7.18	+2, +3, +6
Cobalt	Co	27	58.9332	1495	2870	8.9	+2, +3
Copper	Cu	29	63.546	1083.4	2567	8.96	+1, +2
Curium	Cm	96	(247)	1340	—	13.51	+3
Dubnium	Db	105	(262)	—	—	—	
Dysprosium	Dy	66	162.50	1412	2562	8.550	+3
Einsteinium	Es	99	(252)	—	—	—	
Erbium	Er	68	167.26	159	2863	9.066	+3
Europium	Eu	63	151.96	822	1597	5.243	+2, +3
Fermium	Fm	100	(257)	—	—	—	
Fluorine	F	9	18.998403	−219.62	−188.54	0.001696	−1
Francium	Fr	87	(223)	27	677	—	+1
Gadolinium	Gd	64	157.25	1313	3266	7.9004	+3
Gallium	Ga	31	69.72	29.78	2403	5.904	+3
Germanium	Ge	32	72.59	937.4	2830	5.323	+2, +4
Gold	Au	79	196.9665	1064.43	3080	19.3	+1, +3
Hafnium	Hf	72	178.49	2227	4602	13.31	+4
Hassium	Hs	108	(265)	—	—	—	
Helium	He	2	4.00260	−272.2	−268.934	0.001785	
Holmium	Ho	67	164.9304	1474	2695	8.795	+3
Hydrogen	H	1	1.00794	−259.14	−252.87	0.00008988	+1
Indium	In	49	114.82	156.61	2080	7.31	+1, +3
Iodine	I	53	126.9045	113.5	184.35	4.93	−1, +1, +5, +7
Iridium	Ir	77	192.22	2410	4130	22.42	+3, +4
Iron	Fe	26	55.847	1535	2750	7.874	+2, +3
Krypton	Kr	36	83.80	−156.6	−152.30	0.003733	
Lanthanum	La	57	138.9055	921	3457	6.145	+3
Lawrencium	Lr	103	(262)	—	—	—	+3
Lead	Pb	82	207.2	327.502	1740	11.35	+2, +4
Lithium	Li	3	6.941	180.54	1342	0.534	+1
Lutetium	Lu	71	174.967	1663	3395	9.840	+3
Magnesium	Mg	12	24.305	648.8	1090	1.738	+2
Manganese	Mn	25	54.9380	1244	1962	7.32	+2, +3, +4, +7
Meitnerium	Mt	109	(268)	—	—	—	

Element	Symbol	Atomic number	Atomic mass	Melting point (°C)	Boiling point (°C)	Density (g/cm^3) (gases at STP)	Major oxidation states
Mendelevium	Md	101	257	—	—	—	+2, +3
Mercury	Hg	80	200.59	−38.842	356.58	13.55	+1, +2
Molybdenum	Mo	42	95.94	2617	4612	10.22	+6
Neodymium	Nd	60	144.24	1021	3068	6.90	+3
Neon	Ne	10	20.179	−248.67	−246.048	.0008999	
Neptunium	Np	93	(237)	640	3902	20.25	+3, +4, +5, +6
Nickel	Ni	28	58.69	1453	2732	8.902	+2, +3
Niobium	Nb	41	92.9064	2468	4742	8.57	+3, +5
Nitrogen	N	7	14.0067	−209.86	−195.8	.0012506	−3, +3, +5
Nobelium	No	102	(259)	—	—	—	+2, +3
Osmium	Os	76	190.2	3045	5027	22.57	+3, +4
Oxygen	O	8	15.9994	−218.4	−182.962	.001429	−2
Palladium	Pd	46	106.42	1554	2970	12.02	+2, +4
Phosphorus	P	15	30.97376	44.1	280	1.82	−3, +3, +5
Platinum	Pt	78	195.08	1772	3827	21.45	+2, +4
Plutonium	Pu	94	(244)	641	3232	19.84	+3, +4, +5, +6
Polonium	Po	84	(209)	254	962	9.32	+2, +4
Potassium	K	19	39.0982	63.25	760	.862	+1
Praseodymium	Pr	59	140.9077	931	3512	6.64	+3
Promethium	Pm	61	(145)	1168	2460	7.22	+3
Protactinium	Pa	91	231.0359	1560	4027	15.37	+4, +5
Radium	Ra	88	(226)	700	1140	5.5	+2
Radon	Rn	86	(222)	−71	−61.8	.00973	
Rhenium	Re	75	186.207	3180	5627	21.02	+4, +6, +7
Rhodium	Rh	45	102.9055	1966	3727	12.41	+3
Rubidium	Rb	37	85.4678	38.89	686	1.532	+1
Ruthenium	Ru	44	101.07	2310	3900	12.41	+3
Rutherfordium	Rf	104	(261)	—	—	—	
Samarium	Sm	62	150.36	1077	1791	7.520	+2, +3
Scandium	Sc	21	44.9559	1541	2831	2.989	+3
Seaborgium	Sg	106	(263)	—	—	—	
Selenium	Se	34	78.96	217	684.9	4.79	−2, +4, +6
Silicon	Si	14	28.0855	1410	2355	2.33	−4, +2, +4
Silver	Ag	47	107.8682	961.93	2212	10.50	+1
Sodium	Na	11	22.98977	97.81	882.9	0.971	+1
Strontium	Sr	38	87.62	769	1384	2.54	+2
Sulfur	S	16	32.06	112.8	444.7	2.07	−2, +4, +6
Tantalum	Ta	73	180.9479	2996	5425	16.654	+5
Technetium	Tc	43	(98)	2172	4877	11.50	+4, +6, +7
Tellurium	Te	52	127.60	449.5	989.8	6.24	−2, +4, +6
Terbium	Tb	65	158.9254	1356	3123	8.229	+3
Thallium	Tl	81	204.383	303.5	1457	11.85	+1, +3
Thorium	Th	90	232.0381	1750	4790	11.72	+4
Thulium	Tm	69	168.9342	1545	1947	9.321	+3
Tin	Sn	50	118.69	231.968	2270	7.31	+2, +4
Titanium	Ti	22	47.88	1660	3287	4.54	+2, +3, +4
Tungsten	W	74	183.85	3410	5660	19.3	+6
Ununbium	Uub	112	(277)	—	—	—	
Ununhexium	Uuh	116	—	—	—	—	
Ununnilium	Uun	110	(269)	—	—	—	
Ununoctium	Uuo	118	—	—	—	—	
Ununquadium	Uuq	114	—	—	—	—	
Unununium	Uuu	111	(272)	—	—	—	
Uranium	U	92	238.0289	1132.3	3818	18.95	+3, +4, +5, +6
Vanadium	V	23	50.9415	1890	3380	6.11	+2, +3, +4, +5
Xenon	Xe	54	131.29	−111.9	−107.1	.005887	
Ytterbium	Yb	70	173.04	819	1194	6.965	+2, +3
Yttrium	Y	39	88.9059	1522	3338	4.469	+3
Zinc	Zn	30	65.38	419.58	907	7.133	+2
Zirconium	Zr	40	91.22	1852	4377	6.506	+4

	Elements	1s	2s	2p	3s	3p	3d	4s	4p	4d	4f	5s	5p	5d	5f	6s	6p	6d	7s	7p
1	hydrogen	1																		
2	helium	2																		
3	lithium	2	1																	
4	beryllium	2	2																	
5	boron	2	2	1																
6	carbon	2	2	2																
7	nitrogen	2	2	3																
8	oxygen	2	2	4																
9	fluorine	2	2	5																
10	neon	2	2	6																
11	sodium	2	2	6	1															
12	magnesium	2	2	6	2															
13	aluminum	2	2	6	2	1														
14	silicon	2	2	6	2	2														
15	phosphorus	2	2	6	2	3														
16	sulfur	2	2	6	2	4														
17	chlorine	2	2	6	2	5														
18	argon	2	2	6	2	6														
19	potassium	2	2	6	2	6		1												
20	calcium	2	2	6	2	6		2												
21	scandium	2	2	6	2	6	1	2												
22	titanium	2	2	6	2	6	2	2												
23	vanadium	2	2	6	2	6	3	2												
24	chromium	2	2	6	2	6	5	1												
25	manganese	2	2	6	2	6	5	2												
26	iron	2	2	6	2	6	6	2												
27	cobalt	2	2	6	2	6	7	2												
28	nickel	2	2	6	2	6	8	2												
29	copper	2	2	6	2	6	10	1												
30	zinc	2	2	6	2	6	10	2												
31	gallium	2	2	6	2	6	10	2	1											
32	germanium	2	2	6	2	6	10	2	2											
33	arsenic	2	2	6	2	6	10	2	3											
34	selenium	2	2	6	2	6	10	2	4											
35	bromine	2	2	6	2	6	10	2	5											
36	krypton	2	2	6	2	6	10	2	6											
37	rubidium	2	2	6	2	6	10	2	6			1								
38	strontium	2	2	6	2	6	10	2	6			2								
39	yttrium	2	2	6	2	6	10	2	6	1		2								
40	zirconium	2	2	6	2	6	10	2	6	2		2								
41	niobium	2	2	6	2	6	10	2	6	4		1								
42	molybdenum	2	2	6	2	6	10	2	6	5		1								
43	technetium	2	2	6	2	6	10	2	6	5		2								
44	ruthenium	2	2	6	2	6	10	2	6	7		1								
45	rhodium	2	2	6	2	6	10	2	6	8		1								
46	palladium	2	2	6	2	6	10	2	6	10										
47	silver	2	2	6	2	6	10	2	6	10		1								
48	cadmium	2	2	6	2	6	10	2	6	10		2								
49	indium	2	2	6	2	6	10	2	6	10		2	1							
50	tin	2	2	6	2	6	10	2	6	10		2	2							
51	antimony	2	2	6	2	6	10	2	6	10		2	3							
52	tellurium	2	2	6	2	6	10	2	6	10		2	4							
53	iodine	2	2	6	2	6	10	2	6	10		2	5							
54	xenon	2	2	6	2	6	10	2	6	10		2	6							
55	cesium	2	2	6	2	6	10	2	6	10		2	6			1				
56	barium	2	2	6	2	6	10	2	6	10		2	6			2				
57	lanthanum	2	2	6	2	6	10	2	6	10		2	6	1		2				

Elements		1s	2s	2p	3s	3p	3d	4s	4p	4d	4f	5s	5p	5d	5f	6s	6p	6d	7s	7p
58	cerium	2	2	6	2	6	10	2	6	10	2	2	6			2				
59	praseodymium	2	2	6	2	6	10	2	6	10	3	2	6			2				
60	neodymium	2	2	6	2	6	10	2	6	10	4	2	6			2				
61	promethium	2	2	6	2	6	10	2	6	10	5	2	6			2				
62	samarium	2	2	6	2	6	10	2	6	10	6	2	6			2				
63	europium	2	2	6	2	6	10	2	6	10	7	2	6			2				
64	gadolinium	2	2	6	2	6	10	2	6	10	7	2	6	1		2				
65	terbium	2	2	6	2	6	10	2	6	10	9	2	6			2				
66	dysprosium	2	2	6	2	6	10	2	6	10	10	2	6			2				
67	holmium	2	2	6	2	6	10	2	6	10	11	2	6			2				
68	erbium	2	2	6	2	6	10	2	6	10	12	2	6			2				
69	thulium	2	2	6	2	6	10	2	6	10	13	2	6			2				
70	ytterbium	2	2	6	2	6	10	2	6	10	14	2	6			2				
71	lutetium	2	2	6	2	6	10	2	6	10	14	2	6	1		2				
72	hafnium	2	2	6	2	6	10	2	6	10	14	2	6	2		2				
73	tantalum	2	2	6	2	6	10	2	6	10	14	2	6	3		2				
74	tungsten	2	2	6	2	6	10	2	6	10	14	2	6	4		2				
75	rhenium	2	2	6	2	6	10	2	6	10	14	2	6	5		2				
76	osmium	2	2	6	2	6	10	2	6	10	14	2	6	6		2				
77	iridium	2	2	6	2	6	10	2	6	10	14	2	6	7		2				
78	platinum	2	2	6	2	6	10	2	6	10	14	2	6	9		1				
79	gold	2	2	6	2	6	10	2	6	10	14	2	6	10		1				
80	mercury	2	2	6	2	6	10	2	6	10	14	2	6	10		2				
81	thallium	2	2	6	2	6	10	2	6	10	14	2	6	10		2	1			
82	lead	2	2	6	2	6	10	2	6	10	14	2	6	10		2	2			
83	bismuth	2	2	6	2	6	10	2	6	10	14	2	6	10		2	3			
84	polonium	2	2	6	2	6	10	2	6	10	14	2	6	10		2	4			
85	astatine	2	2	6	2	6	10	2	6	10	14	2	6	10		2	5			
86	radon	2	2	6	2	6	10	2	6	10	14	2	6	10		2	6			
87	francium	2	2	6	2	6	10	2	6	10	14	2	6	10		2	6		1	
88	radium	2	2	6	2	6	10	2	6	10	14	2	6	10		2	6		2	
89	actinium	2	2	6	2	6	10	2	6	10	14	2	6	10		2	6	1	2	
90	thorium	2	2	6	2	6	10	2	6	10	14	2	6	10		2	6	2	2	
91	protactinium	2	2	6	2	6	10	2	6	10	14	2	6	10	2	2	6	1	2	
92	uranium	2	2	6	2	6	10	2	6	10	14	2	6	10	3	2	6	1	2	
93	neptunium	2	2	6	2	6	10	2	6	10	14	2	6	10	4	2	6	1	2	
94	plutonium	2	2	6	2	6	10	2	6	10	14	2	6	10	6	2	6		2	
95	americium	2	2	6	2	6	10	2	6	10	14	2	6	10	7	2	6		2	
96	curium	2	2	6	2	6	10	2	6	10	14	2	6	10	7	2	6	1	2	
97	berkelium	2	2	6	2	6	10	2	6	10	14	2	6	10	9	2	6		2	
98	californium	2	2	6	2	6	10	2	6	10	14	2	6	10	10	2	6		2	
99	einsteinium	2	2	6	2	6	10	2	6	10	14	2	6	10	11	2	6		2	
100	fermium	2	2	6	2	6	10	2	6	10	14	2	6	10	12	2	6		2	
101	mendelevium	2	2	6	2	6	10	2	6	10	14	2	6	10	13	2	6		2	
102	nobelium	2	2	6	2	6	10	2	6	10	14	2	6	10	14	2	6		2	
103	lawrencium	2	2	6	2	6	10	2	6	10	14	2	6	10	14	2	6	1	2	
104	rutherfordium	2	2	6	2	6	10	2	6	10	14	2	6	10	14	2	6	2	2	
105	dubnium	2	2	6	2	6	10	2	6	10	14	2	6	10	14	2	6	3	2	
106	seaborgium	2	2	6	2	6	10	2	6	10	14	2	6	10	14	2	6	4	2	
107	bohrium	2	2	6	2	6	10	2	6	10	14	2	6	10	14	2	6	5	2	
108	hassium	2	2	6	2	6	10	2	6	10	14	2	6	10	14	2	6	6	2	
109	meitnerium	2	2	6	2	6	10	2	6	10	14	2	6	10	14	2	6	7	2	
110	ununnilium	2	2	6	2	6	10	2	6	10	14	2	6	10	14	2	6	9	1	
111	unununium	2	2	6	2	6	10	2	6	10	14	2	6	10	14	2	6	10	1	
112	ununbium	2	2	6	2	6	10	2	6	10	14	2	6	10	14	2	6	10	2	
114	ununquadium	2	2	6	2	6	10	2	6	10	14	2	6	10	14	2	6	10	2	2
116	ununhexium	2	2	6	2	6	10	2	6	10	14	2	6	10	14	2	6	10	2	4
118	ununoctium	2	2	6	2	6	10	2	6	10	14	2	6	10	14	2	6	10	2	6

Table A.3 Symbols of Common Elements

Ag	silver	Cu	copper	O	oxygen
Al	aluminum	F	fluorine	P	phosphorus
As	arsenic	Fe	iron	Pb	lead
Au	gold	H	hydrogen	Pt	platinum
Ba	barium	Hg	mercury	S	sulfur
Bi	bismuth	I	iodine	Sb	antimony
Br	bromine	K	potassium	Sn	tin
C	carbon	Mg	magnesium	Sr	strontium
Ca	calcium	Mn	manganese	Ti	titanium
Cl	chlorine	N	nitrogen	U	uranium
Co	cobalt	Na	sodium	W	tungsten
Cr	chromium	Ni	nickel	Zn	zinc

Table A.4 Symbols of Common Polyatomic Ions

$C_2H_3O_2^-$	acetate	$Cr_2O_7^{2-}$	dichromate	NO_3^-	nitrate
ClO^-	hypochlorite	HCO_3^-	hydrogen carbonate	NO_2^-	nitrite
ClO_2^-	chlorite	H_3O^+	hydronium	O_2^{2-}	peroxide
ClO_3^-	chlorate	HPO_4^{2-}	hydrogen phosphate	OH^-	hydroxide
ClO_4^-	perchlorate	HSO_3^-	hydrogen sulfite	PO_4^{3-}	phosphate
CN^-	cyanide	HSO_4^-	hydrogen sulfate	SiO_3^{2-}	silicate
CO_3^{2-}	carbonate	MnO_4^-	permanganate	SO_3^{2-}	sulfite
CrO_4^{2-}	chromate	NH_4^+	ammonium	SO_4^{2-}	sulfate

Table A.5 Other Symbols and Abbreviations

α	alpha rays	gmm	gram molecular mass	m	mass
β	beta rays	H	enthalpy	m	molality
γ	gamma rays	H_f	heat of formation	mL	milliliter (*volume*)
Δ	change in	h	hour	mm	millimeter (*length*)
$\delta+, \delta-$	partial ionic charge	h	Planck's constant	mol	mole (*amount*)
λ	wavelength	Hz	hertz (*frequency*)	mp	melting point
π	pi bond	J	joule (*energy*)	N	normality
σ	sigma bond	K	kelvin (*temperature*)	n^0	neutron
ν	frequency	K_a	acid dissociation constant	n	number of moles
amu	atomic mass unit	K_b	base dissociation constant	n	principal quantum number
(*aq*)	aqueous solution	K_b	molal boiling point	P	pressure
atm	atmosphere (*pressure*)		elevation constant	p^+	proton
bp	boiling point	K_{eq}	equilibrium constant	Pa	pascal (*pressure*)
°C	degree Celsius (*temperature*)	K_f	molal freezing point	R	ideal gas constant
c	speed of light in a vacuum		depression constant	S	entropy
cm	centimeter (*length*)	K_w	ion product constant	s	second
D	density		for water	(*s*)	solid
E	energy	K_{sp}	solubility product constant	SI	International System
e^-	electron	kcal	kilocalorie (*energy*)		of Units
fp	freezing point	kg	kilogram (*mass*)	STP	standard temperature
G	Gibb's free energy	kPa	kilopascal (*pressure*)		and pressure
g	gram (*mass*)	L	liter (*volume*)	T	temperature
(*g*)	gas	(*l*)	liquid	$t_{\frac{1}{2}}$	half-life
gam	gram atomic mass	M	molarity	V	volume
gfm	gram formula mass	m	meter (*length*)	v	velocity, speed

Table A.6 Physical Constants

Atomic mass unit	$1 \text{ amu} = 1.6605 \times 10^{-24} \text{ g}$
Avogadro's number	$N = 6.0221 \times 10^{23} \dfrac{\text{particles}}{\text{mole}}$
Gas constant	$R = 8.31 \dfrac{\text{L} \times \text{kPa}}{\text{K} \times \text{mol}}$
Ideal gas molar volume	$V_m = 22.414 \dfrac{\text{L}}{\text{mol}}$
Masses of fundamental particles	
Electron (e^-)	$m_e = 0.0005486 \text{ amu}$ $\quad\;\; = 9.1096 \times 10^{-28} \text{ g}$
Proton (p^+)	$m_p = 1.007277 \text{ amu}$ $\quad\;\; = 1.67261 \times 10^{-24} \text{ g}$
Neutron (n^0)	$m_n = 1.008665 \text{ amu}$ $\quad\;\; = 1.67492 \times 10^{-24} \text{ g}$
Speed of light (in vacuum)	$c = 2.997925 \times 10^8 \dfrac{\text{m}}{\text{s}}$

Table A.7 Solubilities of Compounds at 25 °C and 101.3 kPa

	acetate	bromide	carbonate	chlorate	chloride	hydroxide	iodide	nitrate	oxide	perchlorate	phosphate	sulfate	sulfide
aluminum	S	S	—	S	S	I	S	S	I	S	I	S	d
ammonium	S	S	S	S	S	S	S	S	—	S	S	S	S
barium	S	S	I	S	S	S	S	S	sS	S	I	I	d
calcium	S	S	I	S	S	S	S	S	sS	S	I	sS	I
copper(II)	S	S	—	S	S	I	S	S	I	S	I	S	I
iron(II)	S	S	I	S	S	I	S	S	I	S	I	S	I
iron(III)	S	S	—	S	S	I	S	S	I	S	I	sS	d
lithium	S	S	sS	S	S	S	S	S	S	S	sS	S	S
magnesium	S	S	I	S	S	I	S	S	S	S	S	S	S
potassium	S	S	S	S	S	S	S	S	S	S	S	S	S
silver	sS	I	I	S	I	—	I	S	I	S	I	sS	I
sodium	S	S	S	S	S	S	S	S	S	S	S	S	S
strontium	S	S	I	S	S	S	S	S	S	S	I	I	I
zinc	S	S	I	S	S	I	S	S	I	S	I	S	I

Key:	S = soluble	d = decomposes in water
	sS = slightly soluble	— = no such compound
	I = insoluble	

B.1 Graphing

The relationship between two variables in an experiment is often determined by graphing the experimental data. A graph is a "picture" of the data. Once a graph is constructed, additional information can be derived about the variables.

In constructing a graph, you must first label the axes. The independent variable is plotted on the *x-axis (abscissa)*. This is the horizontal axis. The independent variable is generally controlled by the experimenter. When the independent variable is changed, a corresponding change in the dependent variable is measured. The dependent variable is plotted on the *y-axis (ordinate)*. This is the vertical axis. The label on each axis should include the unit of the quantity being graphed.

Before data can be plotted on a graph, each axis must be scaled. The scale must take into consideration the smallest and largest values of each quantity. Each interval (square on the graph paper) on the scale must represent the same amount. To make it easy to find numbers along the scale, the interval chosen is usually a multiple of 1, 2, 5, or 10. Although each scale can start at zero, this is not always practical.

Data are plotted by putting a point at the intersection of corresponding values of each pair of measurement. Once the data have been plotted, the points are connected by a smooth curve. This is not the same as "connecting-the-dots," which is an incorrect approach to drawing a line. A smooth curve comes as close as possible to all the plotted points. It may, in fact, not touch any of them.

Depending on the relationship between two variables, the curve may or may not be a straight line. Two common curves are shown in Graphs A and B.

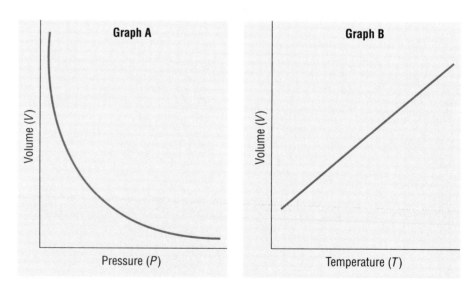

Graphs similar to these are found in Chapter 12 of this textbook. Graph A is typical of an inverse proportionality. As the independent variable (P) increases, the dependent variable (V) decreases. The product of the two variables at any point on the curve of an inverse proportionality is a constant. For graph A, $V \times P$ = constant.

The straight line in graph B is typical of a direct proportionality. As the independent variable (T) increases, there is a corresponding increase in the dependent variable (V). A straight line is represented by this general equation.

$$y = mx + b$$

Here y and x are the variables plotted on the vertical and horizontal axes, respectively; m is the slope of the line; and b is the intercept on the y-axis.

The y intercept, b, is the value of y when x is zero. The slope, m, is the ratio of the change in y (Δy) for a corresponding change in x (Δx). This relationship is often symbolized as follows:

$$m = \frac{\Delta y}{\Delta x}$$

As an example, consider these data about a bicyclist's trip. Assume that the bicyclist rode at a constant speed.

Distance from home (km)	15	25	35	50	75
Time (h)	1	2	3	4.5	7

Graph these data using time as the independent variable, and then use the graph to answer the following questions.

a. How far from home was the bicyclist at the start of the trip?

b. How many hours did it take the bicyclist to get 40 km from home?

c. What was the bicyclist's average speed, in kilometers per hour, on the trip?

The plotted points are shown in Figure 1. Each point was plotted by finding the value of time on the x-axis, then moving up vertically to the value of the other variable (distance). A smooth curve, which in this case happens to be a straight line, has been drawn through the points.

Figure 1

a. The graph in Figure 2 shows that the bicyclist started the trip 5 km from home. This is the value of the vertical axis (distance) when the time elapsed is zero (point *a* on the graph).

b. Find the given value, 40 km, on the vertical axis in Figure 2. Move to the right (horizontally) in the graph until you reach the line. Drop down vertically and read the value of time at this point (point *b*). It takes the bicyclist 3.5 h to get 40 km from home. As another, similar example, how far is the bicyclist from home after riding 5 h? Using the graph in Figure 2, start at 5 h and go up to the line. Then move horizontally to the left. The distance, point *c*, is 55 km.

c. Speed is distance/time. The average speed of the bicyclist is the slope of the line. Calculate the slope using the values for time and distance discussed in the previous paragraph (**b**).

$$m = \frac{\Delta y}{\Delta x} = \frac{55 \text{ km} - 40 \text{ km}}{5 \text{ h} - 3.5 \text{ h}} = \frac{15 \text{ km}}{1.5 \text{ h}} = 10 \text{ km/h}$$

The equation for this line shows the relationship between time and distance traveled by the bicyclist.

$$\text{Distance} = (10 \text{ km/h})(\text{time}) + 5 \text{ km}$$

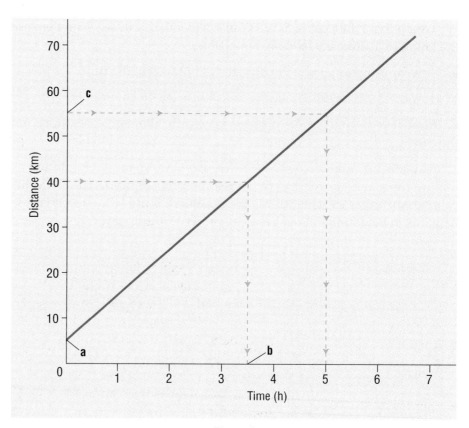

Figure 2

B.2 Logarithms

A logarithm is the exponent to which a fixed number (base) must be raised in order to produce a given number. Common logarithms use 10 as the base. A logarithm to the base 10 of a number is the exponent to which 10 must be raised to obtain the number. If $x = 10^y$, then $\log x = y$. Here x is the number and y is the logarithm of x to the base 10. Common logarithms must not be confused with natural logarithms, which use base e, where $e = 2.71828$. When base 10 is used, logarithm is abbreviated $\log_{10}$, or often simply log. When the base e is used, logarithm is abbreviated ln.

The logarithm of a number has two parts, the characteristic, or whole-number part, and the mantissa, or decimal part. In the example log $421.6 = 2.6249$, the characteristic is 2 and the mantissa is 0.6249. For numbers written in standard exponential form, the characteristic corresponds to the exponent of 10.

$$\log 10^1 = 1, \ \log 10^2 = 2, \ \log 10^3 = 3, \ \log 10^{-2} = -2$$

The mantissa is the decimal part of a logarithm and can be looked up in a log table. The number of significant figures in a logarithm is the number of figures in the mantissa. The logarithm of 176 is found as follows.

1. Write 176 in exponential notation as 1.76×10^2.
2. Locate the number 1.7 in the column labeled N; then under the column headed 6 read the mantissa as 0.2455.
3. Because 1.76×10^2 contains only three significant figures, the mantissa is rounded to three digits. Thus the mantissa is 0.246.
4. The characteristic is the exponent, 2.
5. The logarithm of 176 is 2.246 or log $176 = 2.246$.

Logarithms can also be found using the log key of a calculator. Simply enter the number and press the log key.

The reverse process of converting a logarithm into a number is referred to as obtaining the antilogarithm. The antilogarithm of the logarithm of a number is the number itself. Here x represents any number.

$$\text{antilog} (\log x) = x$$

Antilogarithms can be obtained from a table of common logarithms. They also can be obtained with a calculator by using the antilog key, the 10^x key, or the inverse key in conjunction with the log key. For example, what is the antilog of the logarithm 4.618? Look in the body of the log table for the mantissa, 0.618. This value is found in the row with an N of 4.1 and in the column labeled 5. Thus the antilog of 0.618 is 4.15. The characteristic is 4. This corresponds to an exponential term of 10^4. The number whose log is 4.618 is 4.15×10^4.

There are rules based on the laws of exponents that must be followed when using logarithms for calculations. The logarithm of the product of two numbers is the sum of their logs.

$$\log(a \times b) = \log a + \log b$$

The log of the ratio of two numbers is the log of the numerator minus the log of the denominator.

$$\log(a/b) = \log a - \log b$$

Table B.1 Common Logarithms

x	0	1	2	3	4	5	6	7	8	9
1.0	.0000	.0043	.0086	.0128	.0170	.0212	.0253	.0294	.0334	.0374
1.1	.0414	.0453	.0492	.0531	.0569	.0607	.0645	.0682	.0719	.0755
1.2	.0792	.0828	.0864	.0899	.0934	.0969	.1004	.1038	.1072	.1106
1.3	.1139	.1173	.1206	.1239	.1271	.1303	.1335	.1367	.1399	.1430
1.4	.1461	.1492	.1523	.1553	.1584	.1614	.1644	.1673	.1703	.1732
1.5	.1761	.1790	.1818	.1847	.1875	.1903	.1931	.1959	.1987	.2014
1.6	.2041	.2068	.2095	.2122	.2148	.2175	.2201	.2227	.2253	.2279
1.7	.2304	.2330	.2355	.2380	.2405	.2430	.2455	.2480	.2504	.2529
1.8	.2553	.2577	.2601	.2625	.2648	.2672	.2695	.2718	.2742	.2765
1.9	.2788	.2810	.2833	.2856	.2878	.2900	.2923	.2945	.2967	.2989
2.0	.3010	.3032	.3054	.3075	.3096	.3118	.3139	.3160	.3181	.3201
2.1	.3222	.3243	.3263	.3284	.3304	.3324	.3345	.3365	.3385	.3404
2.2	.3424	.3444	.3464	.3483	.3502	.3522	.3541	.3560	.3579	.3598
2.3	.3617	.3636	.3655	.3674	.3692	.3711	.3729	.3747	.3766	.3784
2.4	.3802	.3820	.3838	.3856	.3874	.3892	.3909	.3927	.3945	.3962
2.5	.3979	.3997	.4014	.4031	.4048	.4065	.4082	.4099	.4116	.4133
2.6	.4150	.4166	.4183	.4200	.4216	.4232	.4249	.4265	.4281	.4298
2.7	.4314	.4330	.4346	.4362	.4378	.4393	.4409	.4425	.4440	.4456
2.8	.4472	.4487	.4502	.4518	.4533	.4548	.4564	.4579	.4594	.4609
2.9	.4624	.4639	.4654	.4669	.4683	.4698	.4713	.4728	.4742	.4757
3.0	.4771	.4786	.4800	.4814	.4829	.4843	.4857	.4871	.4886	.4900
3.1	.4914	.4928	.4942	.4955	.4969	.4983	.4997	.5011	.5024	.5038
3.2	.5051	.5065	.5079	.5092	.5105	.5119	.5132	.5145	.5159	.5172
3.3	.5185	.5198	.5211	.5224	.5237	.5250	.5263	.5276	.5289	.5307
3.4	.5315	.5328	.5340	.5353	.5366	.5378	.5391	.5403	.5416	.5428
3.5	.5441	.5453	.5465	.5478	.5490	.5502	.5514	.5527	.5539	.5551
3.6	.5563	.5575	.5587	.5599	.5611	.5623	.5635	.5647	.5658	.5670
3.7	.5682	.5694	.5705	.5717	.5729	.5740	.5752	.5763	.5775	.5786
3.8	.5798	.5809	.5821	.5832	.5843	.5855	.5866	.5877	.5888	.5899
3.9	.5911	.5922	.5933	.5944	.5955	.5966	.5977	.5988	.5999	.6010
4.0	.6021	.6031	.6042	.6053	.6064	.6075	.6085	.6096	.6107	.6117
4.1	.6128	.6138	.6149	.6160	.6170	.6180	.6191	.6201	.6212	.6222
4.2	.6232	.6243	.6253	.6263	.6274	.6284	.6294	.6304	.6314	.6325
4.3	.6335	.6345	.6355	.6365	.6375	.6385	.6395	.6405	.6415	.6425
4.4	.6435	.6444	.6454	.6464	.6474	.6484	.6493	.6503	.6513	.6522
4.5	.6532	.6542	.6551	.6561	.6571	.6580	.6590	.6599	.6609	.6618
4.6	.6628	.6637	.6646	.6656	.6665	.6675	.6684	.6693	.6702	.6712
4.7	.6721	.6730	.6739	.6749	.6758	.6767	.6776	.6785	.6794	.6803
4.8	.6812	.6821	.6830	.6839	.6848	.6857	.6866	.6875	.6884	.6893
4.9	.6902	.6911	.6920	.6928	.6937	.6946	.6955	.6964	.6972	.6981
5.0	.6990	.6998	.7007	.7016	.7024	.7033	.7042	.7050	.7059	.7067
5.1	.7076	.7084	.7093	.7101	.7110	.7118	.7126	.7135	.7143	.7152
5.2	.7160	.7168	.7177	.7185	.7193	.7202	.7210	.7218	.7226	.7235
5.3	.7243	.7251	.7259	.7267	.7275	.7284	.7292	.7300	.7308	.7316
5.4	.7324	.7332	.7340	.7348	.7356	.7364	.7372	.7380	.7388	.7396

x	0	1	2	3	4	5	6	7	8	9
5.5	.7404	.7412	.7419	.7427	.7435	.7443	.7451	.7459	.7466	.7474
5.6	.7482	.7490	.7497	.7505	.7513	.7520	.7528	.7536	.7543	.7551
5.7	.7559	.7566	.7574	.7582	.7589	.7597	.7604	.7612	.7619	.7627
5.8	.7634	.7642	.7649	.7657	.7664	.7672	.7679	.7686	.7694	.7701
5.9	.7709	.7716	.7723	.7731	.7738	.7745	.7752	.7760	.7767	.7774
6.0	.7782	.7789	.7796	.7803	.7810	.7818	.7825	.7832	.7839	.7846
6.1	.7853	.7860	.7868	.7875	.7882	.7889	.7896	.7903	.7910	.7917
6.2	.7924	.7931	.7938	.7945	.7952	.7959	.7966	.7973	.7980	.7987
6.3	.7993	.8000	.8007	.8014	.8021	.8028	.8035	.8041	.8048	.8055
6.4	.8062	.8069	.8075	.8082	.8089	.8096	.8102	.8109	.8116	.8122
6.5	.8129	.8136	.8142	.8149	.8156	.8162	.8169	.8176	.8182	.8189
6.6	.8195	.8202	.8209	.8215	.8222	.8228	.8235	.8241	.8248	.8254
6.7	.8261	.8267	.8274	.8280	.8287	.8293	.8299	.8306	.8312	.8319
6.8	.8325	.8331	.8338	.8344	.8351	.8357	.8363	.8370	.8376	.8382
6.9	.8388	.8395	.8401	.8407	.8414	.8420	.8426	.8432	.8439	.8445
7.0	.8451	.8457	.8463	.8470	.8476	.8482	.8488	.8494	.8500	.8506
7.1	.8513	.8519	.8525	.8531	.8537	.8543	.8549	.8555	.8561	.8567
7.2	.8573	.8579	.8585	.8591	.8597	.8603	.8609	.8615	.8621	.8627
7.3	.8633	.8639	.8645	.8651	.8657	.8663	.8669	.8675	.8681	.8686
7.4	.8692	.8698	.8704	.8710	.8716	.8722	.8727	.8733	.8739	.8745
7.5	.8751	.8756	.8762	.8768	.8774	.8779	.5785	.8791	.8797	.8802
7.6	.8808	.8814	.8820	.8825	.8831	.8837	.8842	.8848	.8854	.8859
7.7	.8865	.8871	.8876	.8882	.8887	.8893	.8899	.8904	.8910	.8915
7.8	.8921	.8927	.8932	.8938	.8943	.8949	.8954	.8960	.8965	.8971
7.9	.8976	.8982	.8987	.8993	.8998	.9004	.9009	.9015	.9020	.9025
8.0	.9031	.9036	.9042	.9047	.9053	.9058	.9063	.9069	.9074	.9079
8.1	.9085	.9090	.9096	.9101	.9106	.9112	.9117	.9122	.9128	.9133
8.2	.9138	.9143	.9149	.9154	.9159	.9165	.9170	.9175	.9180	.9186
8.3	.9191	.9196	.9201	.9206	.9212	.9217	.9222	.9227	.9232	.9238
8.4	.9243	.9248	.9253	.9258	.9263	.9269	.9274	.9279	.9284	.9289
8.5	.9294	.9299	.9304	.9309	.9315	.9320	.9325	.9330	.9335	.9340
8.6	.9345	.9350	.9355	.9360	.9365	.9370	.9375	.9380	.9385	.9390
8.7	.9395	.9400	.9405	.9410	.9415	.9420	.9425	.9430	.9435	.9440
8.8	.9445	.9450	.9455	.9460	.9465	.9469	.9474	.9479	.9484	.9489
8.9	.9494	.9499	.9504	.9509	.9513	.9518	.9523	.9528	.9533	.9538
9.0	.9542	.9547	.9552	.9557	.9562	.9566	.9571	.9576	.9581	.9586
9.1	.9590	.9595	.9600	.9605	.9609	.9614	.9619	.9624	.9628	.9633
9.2	.9638	.9643	.9647	.9652	.9657	.9661	.9666	.9671	.9675	.9680
9.3	.9685	.9689	.9694	.9699	.9703	.9708	.9713	.9717	.9722	.9727
9.4	.9731	.9736	.9741	.9745	.9750	.9754	.9759	.9763	.9768	.9773
9.5	.9777	.9782	.9786	.9791	.9795	.9800	.9805	.9809	.9814	.9818
9.6	.9823	.9827	.9832	.9836	.9841	.9845	.9850	.9854	.9859	.9863
9.7	.9868	.9872	.9877	.9881	.9886	.9890	.9894	.9899	.9903	.9908
9.8	.9912	.9917	.9921	.9926	.9930	.9934	.9939	.9943	.9948	.9952
9.9	.9956	.9961	.9965	.9969	.9974	.9978	.9983	.9987	.9991	.9996

APPENDIX C   ANSWERS TO SELECTED PROBLEMS

CHAPTER 1

17. Chemistry is the study of matter and its changes for the sake of understanding them; chemical technology is the application of this knowledge to attain specific goals.

19. a. 2   **b.** 5   **c.** 1   **d.** 6   **e.** 3   **f.** 4

21. The ozone layer protects Earth from harmful ultraviolet rays.

23. Experiments are used to test hypotheses.

25. If you are certain that your experiment is not flawed, you must revise your hypothesis.

27. A language uses its vocabulary to express thoughts about anything—food, politics, religion, and so forth. The vocabulary of the sciences is used to express concepts and facts about the workings of the material world.

29. Students' diagrams should show one string that is threaded through both holes at A and C. The string at hole B is a separate thread from the string passing through holes A and C.

31. The experiment may be flawed; if not, the results are evidence that the theory may need to be revised.

33. a. 1   **b.** 3   **c.** 1

35. No; for any discovery to take place, the discoverer must have the knowledge to recognize the significance of the observation or data.

37. a. The textbook contains all of the major content and concepts covered in the course. The visuals, reading/studying guides, and practice/review features are essential elements in learning and understanding chemistry.
b. (false statement) Chemistry concepts are interwoven and are best understood as parts of a big picture. Seeing connections and building a framework imply understanding, not memorization.
c. Learning in small chunks is more effective. Studying on a regular basis helps build a big picture of chemistry into which individual facts can be placed. It assures understanding rather than memorization.
d. An exchange of ideas and perspectives is valuable.
e. Talking about chemistry aids understanding and retention.

CHAPTER 2

5. the attraction of iron, but not salt, to a magnet; the solubility of salt, but not iron, in water

6. a. heterogeneous   **d.** homogeneous
b. homogeneous   **e.** homogeneous
c. heterogeneous

13. The liquid was not an element because a solid was left when the liquid evaporated. Evaporation is a way to physically separate a mixture. Compounds cannot be separated by physical means such as evaporation.

25. a. solid   **c.** gas   **e.** liquid
b. liquid   **d.** solid   **f.** liquid

27. a vapor; The term "vapor" refers to the gaseous state of a substance that normally exists as a liquid or solid at room temperature.

29. chlorine, mercury, bromine, and water; Chlorine condenses, and mercury, bromine and water all freeze when the temperature drops within the stated range.

31. one; A solution is a system with uniform composition and properties. Solutions are homogeneous mixtures, consisting of a single phase.

33. a. nitrogen, hydrogen, chlorine
b. potassium, manganese, oxygen
c. carbon, hydrogen, oxygen
d. calcium, iodine

35. a. physical   **c.** chemical
b. chemical   **d.** physical

37. As the wax burns, the chemical composition of the wax changes, producing the products water and carbon dioxide, which are released into the surrounding air.

39. Mixtures in both cases.

41. a. homogeneous mixture
b. homogeneous mixture
c. heterogeneous mixture
d. homogeneous mixture
e. heterogeneous mixture
f. compound
g. homogeneous mixture
h. heterogeneous mixture

43. a. color and odor change, irreversible
b. gas is produced
c. formation of a precipitate (solid), not easily reversed
d. color change, not easily reversed, change in texture
e. release of energy; change in odor and color; irreversible

45. In gases, particles are far apart; in liquids, particles are in contact; in solids, particles are tightly packed.

47. a. Yes; because the graph is a straight line, the proportion of iron to oxygen is a constant, which is true for a compound.
b. No; plotting these values on the graph would not give a point on the line indicating that the mass ratio of iron to oxygen is different from the other four samples.

49. a. two, mercury and sulfur
b. Sulfur melts at 113 °C and boils at 445 °C. Between 113 °C and 445 °C, it exists as a liquid. Mercury melts at −39 °C, and boils at 357 °C. In between these temperatures, it exists as a liquid.
c. Possibilities include: by color, alphabetically, by increasing boiling point, by increasing density.

CHAPTER 3

5. **a.** 4   **b.** 4   **c.** 2   **d.** 5

6. **a.** 3   **b.** 2   **c.** 4   **d.** 4

7. **a.** 8.71×10^1 m   **d.** 9.01×10^3 m
   b. 4.36×10^8 m   **e.** 1.78×10^{-3} m
   c. 1.55×10^{-2} m   **f.** 6.30×10^2 m

8. **a.** 9×10^1 m   **d.** 9×10^3 m
   b. 4×10^8 m   **e.** 2×10^{-3} m
   c. 2×10^{-2} m   **f.** 6×10^2 m

9. **a.** 79.2 m   **b.** 7.33 m   **c.** 11.53 m   **d.** 17.3 m

10. 23.8 grams

11. **a.** 1.8×10^1 m^2 **b.** 6.75×10^2 m   **c.** 5.87×10^{-1} min

12. 1.3×10^3 m^3

23. 2.50 g/cm^3; no

24. 6.5 cm^3

30. −196 °C

31. melting point: 1234 K; boiling point: 2485 K

37. **a.** precision   **c.** precision   **e.** accuracy
   b. accuracy   **d.** precision   **f.** accuracy

39. Lissa: inaccurate and imprecise
Lamont: accurate and precise
Leigh Anne: inaccurate but precise

41. **a.** infinite   **c.** infinite   **e.** infinite
   b. infinite   **d.** 4   **f.** 3

43. **a.** 9.85×10^1 L   **d.** 1.22×10^1 °C
   b. 7.63×10^{-4} cg   **e.** 7.50×10^1 mm
   c. 5.70×10^1 m   **f.** 1.76×10^3 mL

45. **a.** 4.3×10^1 g   **d.** 9.20×10^1 kg
   b. 7.3×10^0 cm^2 **e.** 3.24×10^1 m^3
   c. 2.258×10^2 L   **f.** 1.04×10^2 m^3

47. The absolute value of the error is used.

49. 23.9 g

51. **a.** second, s   **c.** kelvin, K
   b. meter, m   **d.** kilogram, kg

53. **a.** 2.4 mm   **b.** 17.6 cm   **c.** 27.6 cm

55. 7.9×10^2 cm^3

57. **a.** 0.01 g   **b.** 0.000 001 g   **c.** 1000 g   **d.** 0.001 g

59. **a.** 1   **b.** 4   **c.** 2   **d.** 3

61. No; the density of the metal bar is 12 g/cm^3, but the density of gold is 19 g/cm^3.

63. **a.** 2.70   **b.** 13.6   **c.** 0.917

65. germanium

67. **e., d., c., f., a., b.**

69. °F = 1.8 °C + 32

71. The digit to the right of the last significant figure is dropped if it is less than five.

73. Yes; an object can change position such that the force of gravity acting on it changes, causing its weight to change.

75. **a.** 2   **b.** 1

77. You do not change your estimate. The extra 15 ducks are negligible compared to 850 000 ducks.

79. to understand the world around us

81. **a.** chemical   **c.** physical   **e.** chemical
   b. physical   **d.** chemical   **f.** physical

83. The components of a homogeneous mixture can be separated by physical means; a compound must be chemically broken apart into its components. A homogeneous mixture has a variable composition; a compound has a definite composition.

85. volume of iron = 45.1 cm^3; mass of lead = 514 g Pb

87. The slope of the line yields: density of sulfur = 2.1 g/cm^3

CHAPTER 4

1. 27.0 cm^3

2. 269 °C

9. 67 students

10. 86.4 °F

11. **a.** 44 m   **c.** 89 dm
   b. 4.6×10^{-3} g   **d.** 10.7 cg

12. **a.** 1.5×10^{-2} L   **c.** 6.7×10^2 ms
   b. 7.38×10^{-3} kg   **d.** 9.45×10^7 µg

13. **a.** 6.32 cm^3 **b.** 5.0 g   **c.** 0.342 cm^3

14. See answers for problem 13.

20. 2.27×10^{-8} cm

21. 1.3×10^8 dm

22. 10 080 min

23. 144 000 s

24. 1.93×10^4 kg/m^3

25. 7.0×10^{12} RBC/L

33. 155.3 g

35. one

37. They must equal one another.

39. The unit of the conversion factor in the denominator must be identical to the unit in the given measurement.

41. Estimate an answer to see if your calculator answer makes sense and round the answer off to the correct number of significant figures.

43. **a.** 1.57 s   **d.** 6.5×10^2 dm
   b. 4.27×10^4 mL   **e.** 6.42×10^{-3} kg
   c. 2.61×10^{-4} mm   **f.** 8.25×10^9 µg

45. 10^6 mL

47. 31.1 m/s

49. 3.6 min lost

51. **a.** $C_2 = -90$ °C, $C_4 = 0$ °C, $C_6 = 70$ °C, $C_8 = 125$ °C
   b. C_1 through C_4
   c. three
   d. Over the range C_1 through C_9, the increase is about 38 °C/additional carbon. Over the range C_3 through C_9, the increase is about 32 °C/additional carbon.

53. 73 g

55. 24.0 kg of water

57. Answers will vary.

59. The mass of fuel plus the mass of oxygen must equal the mass of ash plus gaseous products.

61. **a.** mixture   **c.** compound
    b. mixture   **d.** element

63. **a.** centigram   **d.** cubic decimeter
    b. kiloliter   **e.** micrometer
    c. millisecond

65. **a.** 3   **b.** 4   **c.** 2   **d.** 4   **e.** 5   **f.** 4

67. 8.0 g Sr

69. 32 cm

71. **a.** 85 g   **b.** 1.3 g/mL

CHAPTER 5

7. **a.** 9,9   **b.** 13, 13   **c.** 20, 20

8. K: 19; B: 5, 5; S:16, 16; V: 23, 23

9. **a.** 8   **b.** 16   **c.** 61   **d.** 45   **e.** 125

10. **a.** $_6^{12}C$ **b.** $_9^{19}F$ **c.** $_4^9Be$

11. **a.** 8   **b.** 16   **c.** 47   **d.** 35   **e.** 82

12. $_8^{16}O$, $_8^{17}O$, $_8^{18}O$

13. 26, 28, 29

14. boron–11

15. Silicon–28 must be by far the most abundant. The others must be present in only small amounts.

16. 63.6 amu

17. 79.90 amu

33. Dalton would agree with all four statements because they all fit his atomic theory.

35. repel

37. Every atomic nucleus is positively charged.

39. number of protons in the nucleus

41. The atomic number is the number of protons. The mass number is the sum of the number of protons and number of neutrons.

43. mass numbers, atomic masses, number of neutrons, relative abundance

45. which isotopes exist, their masses, and their natural percent abundance

47. Answers will vary.

49. **a.** C   **c.** B, Ne, P, Br   **e.** Bi
    b. La   **d.** Hg, Br

51. five protons and six neutrons in the nucleus; five electrons outside the nucleus

53. 207 amu

55. Atoms are the smallest particle of an element that retains the properties of that element.

57. **a.** 3   **b.** 1   **c.** 4

59. The following are reasonable hypotheses: The space in an individual atom is large relative to the volume of the atom, but very small relative to an object the size of a hand. There are many layers of atoms in a wall or a desk. The space that exists is distributed evenly throughout the solid, similar to the distribution of air pockets in foam insulation.

61. Answers will vary.

63. **a.** 4   **b.** 3   **c.** 3   **d.** 4

65. 4.84×10^5 cm^3

67. **a.** element   **c.** mixture   **e.** mixture
    b. mixture   **d.** mixture   **f.** mixture

69. 92.5%

CHAPTER 6

1. **a.** sulfide ion (S^{2-})
    b. aluminum ion (Al^{3+})
    c. calcium ion (Ca^{2+})

2. **a.** 2 lost   **b.** 3 gained   **c.** 2 lost

10. 2:1

11. No; the ratio in the compound is 1.62:1 rather than 1.75:1, or 7:4.

16. **a.** 2–   **b.** 2+   **c.** 1+   **d.** 3–

17. **a.** 3 lost   **b.** 2 gained   **c.** 1 lost   **d.** 2 lost

18. **a.** selenide ion, anion
    b. barium ion, cation
    c. cesium ion, cation
    d. phosphide ion, anion

19. **a.** iron(III) or ferric ion
    b. oxide ion
    c. copper(I) or cuprous ion
    d. cadmium ion

24. **a.** BaS   **b.** Li_2O **c.** Ca_3N_2 **d.** CuI_2

25. **a.** NaI   **b.** $SnCl_2$ **c.** K_2S **d.** CaI_2

26. **a.** zinc sulfide
    b. potassium chloride
    c. barium oxide
    d. copper(II) or cupric bromide

27. **a.** calcium oxide
    b. copper(I) or cuprous selenide
    c. iron(II) or ferrous sulfide
    d. aluminum fluoride

28. **a.** $(NH_4)_2SO_3$ **c.** $Al(NO_3)_3$
    b. $Ca_3(PO_4)_2$ **d.** K_2CrO_4

29. **a.** $LiHSO_4$ **c.** $HgBr_2$
    b. $Cr(NO_2)_3$ **d.** $(NH_4)_2Cr_2O_7$

30. **a.** calcium oxalate
    b. potassium hypochlorite
    c. potassium permanganate
    d. lithium sulfite

31. **a.** aluminum hydroxide
    b. sodium chlorate
    c. tin(II) or stannous phosphate
    d. sodium chromate

37. a. oxygen difluoride
b. dichlorine octoxide
c. sulfur trioxide

38. a. NF_3 **b.** S_2Cl_2 **c.** N_2O_4

45. Ions are formed when atoms lose electrons or gain electrons.

47. a. bromide ion, anion   **d.** calcium ion, cation
b. sodium ion, cation   **e.** copper(I) ion, cation
c. arsenide ion, anion   **f.** hydride ion, anion

49. a. ionic   **c.** ionic   **e.** ionic
b. molecular   **d.** molecular   **f.** molecular

51. a. carbon 6, hydrogen 8, oxygen 6
b. carbon 5, hydrogen 8, oxygen 4, sodium 1
c. carbon 12, hydrogen 22, oxygen 11
d. carbon 7, hydrogen 5, nitrogen 3, oxygen 6
e. nitrogen 2, hydrogen 4, oxygen 3

53. a. O^{2-} **c.** Li^+ **e.** Cu^{2+}
b. Pb^{2+} **d.** N^{3-} **f.** F^-

55. cyanide (CN^-) and hydroxide (OH^-)

57. The net ionic charge is zero. Ionic compounds are electrically neutral and thus have no net ionic charge.

59. Knowing the number of each ion in the formula and the ionic charge of the anion, the charge of the cation must be such that the net ionic charge is zero.

61. a. $CaCO_3$ **c.** $LiClO$
b. $Ba(HCO_3)_2$ **d.** $Sn(Cr_2O_7)_2$

63. two nonmetals

65. a. hydrochloric acid   **c.** H_2SO_4
b. nitric acid   **d.** $HC_2H_3O_2$

67. a. sodium chlorate   **e.** tin(IV) oxide
b. mercury(I) bromide   **f.** iron(III) acetate
c. potassium chromate   **g.** potassium hydrogen sulfate
d. aluminum iodide   **h.** calcium hydride

69. a. lithium perchlorate   **e.** barium phosphate
b. dichlorine monoxide   **f.** iodine
c. mercury(II) fluoride   **g.** strontium sulfate
d. calcium oxide   **h.** copper(I) acetate

71. a. magnesium permanganate   **e.** lithium hydroxide
b. beryllium nitrate   **f.** barium fluoride
c. potassium carbonate   **g.** phosphorus triiodide
d. dinitrogen tetrahydride   **h.** zinc oxide

73. a. $CaBr_2$ **d.** NO_2 **g.** $Sr(C_2H_3O_2)_2$
b. $AgCl$ **e.** $Sn(CN)_4$ **h.** Na_2SiO_3
c. Al_4C_3 **f.** LiH

75. A molecular formula shows the number of each kind of atom in a molecule of the compound. The formula unit shows the lowest whole-number ratio of ions in a compound.

77. Common names would vary in different languages and might even vary in the same language.

79. Possible answers include: cations always come before anions; when a cation has more than one ionic charge, the charge is indicated by a Roman numeral; monatomic anions use an -ide ending.

81. a. 12 protons, 10 electrons
b. 35 protons, 36 electrons
c. 38 protons, 36 electrons
d. 16 protons, 18 electrons

83. 0.538 g/cm^3

85. a. Potassium carbonate has a much greater water solubility than $CaCO_3$.
b. Copper compound is blue; iron compound is white.
c. Because of differences in solubilities, water could be added to dissolve the NH_4Cl. The resulting solution could be filtered leaving the insoluble $BaSO_4$.
d. chlorine (nonmetal), sulfur (nonmetal), bromine (nonmetal), barium (metal), iodine (nonmetal), mercury (metal)
e. barium sulfate, calcium carbonate, potassium carbonate, copper(II) sulfate pentahydrate, iron(II) sulfate pentahydrate, ammonium chloride
f. 639 g
g. 7.54 cm^3
h. Color, density, melting point, and boiling point could all be used to distinguish among the halogens.

CHAPTER 7

1. 5.0 kg

2. 672 seeds

3. 4.65 mol Si

4. 2.17×10^{23} molecules H_2O

5. 2.75×10^{24} atoms

6. 7.72 mol NO_2

7. a. 30.0 g   **b.** 137.5 g   **c.** 60.0 g   **d.** 108.0 g

8. a. 71.0 g   **b.** 46.0 g   **c.** 331.6 g   **d.** 60.1 g

9. a. 94.2 g   **b.** 136.2 g   **c.** 317.3 g

10. a. 175.3 g   **c.** 84.0 g
b. 139.6 g   **d.** 294.3 g

16. a. 1.30×10^2 g   **b.** 1.27 g   **c.** 1.55 g

17. a. 355 g   **b.** 225 g

18. a. 3.43×10^{-2} mol B
b. 0.343 mol TiO_2
c. 8.82 mol $(NH_4)_2CO_3$

19. a. 0.987 mol N_2O_3
b. 2.68 mol N_2
c. 1.21 mol Na_2O

20. a. 7.17×10^{-2} L   **b.** 21.5 L   **c.** 82.9 L

21. a. 3.00 mol SO_2
b. 3.93×10^{-2} mol He
c. 44.6 mol C_2H_6

22. 80.2 g/mol

23. 3.74 g/L

29. a. 72.2% Mg, 27.8% N   **b.** 87.1% Ag, 12.9% S

30. 93.0% Hg, 7.0% O

31. a. 80.0% C, 20% H
b. 19.2% Na, 0.83% H, 26.7% S, 53.3% O
c. 26.2% N, 7.5% H, 66.4% Cl

32. a. 46.7% N   **b.** 82.4% N   **c.** 35.0% N

33. a. 70 g H   **b.** 0.17 g H   **c.** 0.16 g H

34. a. 58.4 g N   **b.** 103 g N   **c.** 43.8 g N

35. a. OH   **b.** CH_3 **c.** $HgSO_4$ **d.** C_2HNO_3

36. C_3H_8N

37. a. $C_2H_6O_2$ **b.** $C_6H_4Cl_2$

38. a

45. a. molecule **b.** formula unit **c.** molecule **d.** atom

47. All contain 6.02×10^{23} molecules.

49. a. 1.81×10^{24} atoms Sn
b. 2.41×10^{23} formula units KCl
c. 4.52×10^{24} molecules SO_2
d. 2.89×10^{21} formula units NaI

51. a. 60.1 g **b.** 28.0 g **c.** 106.8 g **d.** 63.5 g

53. 71.0 g Cl_2

55. a. 0.258 mol SiO_2 **d.** 0.106 mol KOH
b. 4.80×10^{-4} mol AgCl **e.** 5.93 mol $Ca(C_2H_3O_2)_2$
c. 1.12 mol Cl_2 **f.** 2.00×10^{-2} mol Ca

57. a. 1.7×10^2 L Ar **b.** 9.9 L C_2H_6 **c.** 26.9 L O_2

59. a. 234 L SO_3
b. 2.99×10^{-22} g $C_9H_8O_4$
c. 3.13×10^{25} atoms

61. a. 3.33 g S **b.** 5.65 g N **c.** 40.6 g Mg **d.** 152 g P

63. H_2O_2

65. a. $C_3H_6O_3$ **b.** Hg_2Cl_2 **c.** $C_6H_{10}O_4$

67. You can measure the mass of 22.4 L of the compound at STP; this is the molar volume of the gas. The mass of the molar volume is the molar mass.

69. a. A molecule is composed of two or more atoms.
b. A compound has a gram molecular mass; not a gram atomic mass.
c. 1 mol CO_2 has 3 times Avogadro's number of atoms.

71. 24.5 g

73. a. 27 amu **b.** aluminum

75. a. $CuBr_2$ **b.** CH_3

77. A molecular formula is a whole number multiple of its empirical formula.

79. Gas molecules are separated by so much empty space, their own volumes are insignificant when considering how much space a certain quantity of gas occupies.

81. 1.59 mol Pt

83. a. 4.72×10^3 mg **b.** 97 km/hr **c.** 4.4×10^{-2} dm

85. a. KNO_3 **b.** CuO **c.** Mg_3N_2 **d.** AgF

87. 21.9 cm^3

89. a.

b. 22.4 L/mol **c.** 24.6 g/mol **d.** 2.5 g/L

91. 6.025×10^{23} formula units/mol

CHAPTER 8

1. a. $S(s) + O_2(g) \longrightarrow SO_2(g)$
b. $KClO_3(s) \xrightarrow{MnO_2,\Delta} KCl(s) + O_2(g)$

2. a. Mixing aqueous potassium hydroxide and aqueous sulfuric acid produces water and aqueous potassium sulfate.
b. When solid sodium is added to water, aqueous sodium hydroxide and hydrogen gas are produced.

3. a. $2AgNO_3 + H_2S \longrightarrow Ag_2S + 2HNO_3$
b. $MnO_2 + 4HCl \longrightarrow MnCl_2 + 2H_2O + Cl_2$
c. $3Zn(OH)_2 + 2H_3PO_4 \longrightarrow Zn_3(PO_4)_2 + 6H_2O$

4. a. $H_2 + S \longrightarrow H_2S$
b. $2FeCl_3 + 3Ca(OH)_2 \longrightarrow 2Fe(OH)_3 + 3CaCl_2$

5. $3CO + Fe_2O_3 \longrightarrow 2Fe + 3CO_2$

6. $2C + O_2 \longrightarrow 2CO$

7. a. $FeCl_3 + 3NaOH \longrightarrow Fe(OH)_3 + 3NaCl$
b. $CS_2 + 3Cl_2 \longrightarrow CCl_4 + S_2Cl_2$
c. $CH_4 + Br_2 \longrightarrow CH_3Br + HBr$

8. a. $2Na + 2H_2O \longrightarrow 2NaOH + H_2$
b. $Ca(OH)_2 + H_2SO_4 \longrightarrow CaSO_4 + 2H_2O$

13. a. $2Be + O_2 \longrightarrow 2BeO$
b. $SO_2 + H_2O \longrightarrow H_2SO_3$

14. a. $Sr + I_2 \longrightarrow SrI_2$
b. $3Mg + N_2 \longrightarrow Mg_3N_2$

15. a. $2HI \longrightarrow H_2 + I_2$
b. $Mg(ClO_3)_2 \longrightarrow MgCl_2 + 3O_2$

16. a. HBr **b.** NaCl

17. a. $Fe(s) + Pb(NO_3)_2(aq) \longrightarrow Fe(NO_3)_2(aq) + Pb(s)$
b. $Cl_2(g) + 2NaI(aq) \longrightarrow 2NaCl(aq) + I_2(s)$
c. $Ca(s) + 2H_2O(l) \longrightarrow Ca(OH)_2(aq) + H_2(g)$

18. a. $3NaOH + Fe(NO_3)_3 \longrightarrow Fe(OH)_3 + 3NaNO_3$
b. $3Ba(NO_3)_2 + 2H_3PO_4 \longrightarrow Ba_3(PO_4)_2 + 6HNO_3$

19. a. $3KOH + H_3PO_4 \longrightarrow K_3PO_4 + 3H_2O$
b. $3H_2SO_4 + 2Al(OH)_3 \longrightarrow Al_2(SO_4)_3 + 6H_2O$

20. a. $2HCOOH + O_2 \longrightarrow 2CO_2 + 2H_2O$
b. $C_7H_{16} + 11O_2 \longrightarrow 7CO_2 + 8H_2O$

21. $C_6H_{12}O_6 + 6O_2 \longrightarrow 6CO_2 + 6H_2O$

25. a. $PB^{2+}(aq) + 2I^-(aq) \longrightarrow PbI_2(s)$
b. $Zn(s) + 2H^+(aq) \longrightarrow Zn_2^+(aq) + H_2(g)$
c. $H^+(aq) + OH^-(aq) \longrightarrow H_2O(l)$

26. $Pb^{2+}(aq) + 2Cl^-(aq) \; PbCl_2(s)$

27. $Fe^{3+}(aq) + 3NO_3^-(aq) + 3Na^+(aq) + 3OH^-(aq) \longrightarrow$
$\qquad\qquad\qquad Fe(OH)_3(s) + 3Na^+(aq) + 3NO_3^-(aq)$
$Fe^{3+}(aq) + 3OH^-(aq) \longrightarrow Fe(OH)_3(s)$

33. Dalton said that the atoms of reactants are rearranged to form new substances as products.

35. a. Gaseous ammonia and oxygen react in the presence of platinum to produce nitrogen monoxide gas and water vapor.
b. Aqueous solutions of sulfuric acid and barium chloride are mixed to produce a precipitate of barium sulfate and aqueous hydrochloric acid.
c. The gas dinitrogen trioxide reacts with water to produce an aqueous solution of nitrous acid.

37. a. $C + 2F + 2G \longrightarrow CF_2G_2$
b. $F + 3W + S + 2P \longrightarrow FW_3SP_2$

39. a. $2PbO_2 \longrightarrow 2PbO + O_2$
b. $2Fe(OH)_3 \longrightarrow Fe_2O_3 + 3H_2O$
c. $(NH_4)_2CO_3 \longrightarrow 2NH_3 + H_2O + CO_2$
d. $2NaCl + H_2SO_4 \longrightarrow Na_2SO_4 + 2HCl$
e. $4H_2 + Fe_3O_4 \longrightarrow 3Fe + 4H_2O$
f. $2Al + 3CuSO_4 \longrightarrow Al_2(SO_4)_3 + 3Cu$

41. Use ionic charges to write an electrically neutral formula.

43. a. $2Mg + O_2 \longrightarrow 2MgO$
b. $4P + 5O_2 \longrightarrow 2P_2O_5$
c. $Ca + S \longrightarrow CaS$
d. $2Fe + O_2 \longrightarrow 2FeO$
e. $N_2O_5 + H_2O \longrightarrow 2HNO_3$

45. a single reactant

47. a. no reaction
b. $Zn(s) + 2AgNO_3(aq) \longrightarrow Zn(NO_3)_2(aq) + 2Ag(s)$
c. $2Al(s) + 3H_2SO_4(aq) \longrightarrow Al_2(SO_4)_3(aq) + 3H_2(g)$
d. no reaction
e. $2Al(s) + 3CuSO_4(aq) \longrightarrow Al_2(SO_4)_3(aq) + 3Cu(s)$

49. oxygen

51. a. $3Hf + 2N_2 \longrightarrow Hf_3N_4$; combination
b. $Mg + H_2SO_4 \longrightarrow MgSO_4 + H_2$; single-replacement
c. $2C_2H_6 + 7O_2 \longrightarrow 4CO_2 + 6H_2O$; combustion
d. $Pb(NO_3)_2 + 2NaI \longrightarrow PbI_2 + 2NaNO_3$; double-replacement
e. $3Fe + 2O_2 \longrightarrow Fe_3O_4$; combination
f. $2Pb(NO_3)_2 \longrightarrow 2PbO + 4NO_2 + O_2$; decomposition
g. $Hg(NO_3)_2 + 2NH_4SCN \longrightarrow Hg(SCN)_2 + 2NH_4NO_3$; double-replacement
h. $(NH_4)_2SO_4 + 2NaOH \longrightarrow 2NH_3 + 2H_2O + Na_2SO_4$; double-replacement, then decomposition

53. an ion that does not participate in the reaction

55. a. $Cl_2(g) + 2KI(aq) \longrightarrow I_2(s) + 2KCl(aq)$
b. $2Fe(s) + 6HCl(aq) \longrightarrow 2FeCl_3(aq) + 3H_2(g)$
c. $P_4O_{10}(s) + 6H_2O(l) \longrightarrow 4H_3PO_4(aq)$
d. $2Ag_2O(s) \xrightarrow{\Delta} 4Ag(s) + O_2(g)$
e. $I_2(s) + 3Cl_2(g) \longrightarrow 2ICl_3(s)$
f. $4HgS(s) + 4CaO(s) \xrightarrow{\Delta} 4Hg(l) + 3CaS(s) + CaSO_4(s)$

57. a. $Na_2O(s) + H_2O(l) \longrightarrow 2NaOH(aq)$
b. $H_2(g) + Br_2(g) \longrightarrow 2HBr(g)$
c. $Cl_2O_7(l) + H_2O(l) \longrightarrow 2HClO_4(aq)$

59. a. A
b. $2Na(s) + 2H_2O(l) \longrightarrow 2NaOH(aq) + H_2(g)$; single-replacement

61. a. $2Al_2O_3 \xrightarrow{\text{energy}} 4Al + 3O_2$
b. $Sn(OH)_4 \xrightarrow{\Delta} SnO_2 + 2H_2O$
c. $Ag_2CO_3 \xrightarrow{\Delta} Ag_2O + CO_2$

63. a. 4   **b.** 2   **c.** 1

65. a. $C_5H_{12} + 8O_2 \longrightarrow 5CO_2 + 6H_2O$
$C_9H_{20} + 14O_2 \longrightarrow 9CO_2 + 10H_2O$
b. $2C_{12}H_{26} + 37O_2 \longrightarrow 24CO_2 + 26H_2O$
$C_{17}H_{36} + 26O_2 \longrightarrow 17CO_2 + 18H_2O$
c. $n = CO_2$; $(n + 1) = H_2O$

67. 425 g Au

69. a.

$CaCl_2$ (mol)	H_2O (mol)
0.156	0.312
0.439	0.878
1.12	2.24
3.03	6.06

b.

c. Two molecules of water are absorbed by each formula unit of $CaCl_2$.

71. a. 1.01 g/mol protons, 5.48×10^{-4} g/mol electrons
b. 1.84×10^3 electrons/protons

CHAPTER 9

1. 288 seats, 864 wheels, 576 pedals

2. Answers will vary but should include the correct number of "parts" to make the product.

3. 2 molecules H_2 + 1 molecule $O_2 \longrightarrow$ 2 molecules H_2O
2 mol H_2 + 1 mol $O_2 \longrightarrow$ 2 mol H_2O
44.8 L H_2 + 22.4 L $O_2 \longrightarrow$ 44.8 L H_2O

4. 2 mol C_2H_2 + 5 mol $O_2 \longrightarrow$ 4 mol CO_2 + 2 mol H_2O
44.8 L C_2H_2 + 112 L $O_2 \longrightarrow$ 89.6 L CO_2
212 g reactants $\longrightarrow$ 212 g products

9. a. $\dfrac{4 \text{ mol Al}}{3 \text{ mol } O_2}$ $\dfrac{3 \text{ mol } O_2}{4 \text{ mol Al}}$ $\dfrac{4 \text{ mol Al}}{2 \text{ mol } Al_2O_3}$

$\dfrac{2 \text{ mol } Al_2O_3}{4 \text{ mol Al}}$ $\dfrac{2 \text{ mol } Al_2O_3}{3 \text{ mol } O_2}$ $\dfrac{3 \text{ mol } O_2}{2 \text{ mol } Al_2O_3}$
b. 7.4 mol

10. a. 11.1 mol   **b.** 0.52 mol

11. 2.03 g C_2H_2

12. 1.36 mol CaC_2

13. 4.82×10^{22} molecules O_2

14. 11.5 g NO_2

15. 1.93 L O_2

16. 0.28 L PH_3

17. 18.6 mL SO_2

18. 1.9 dL CO_2

23. a. 8.10 mol O_2 required; O_2 is the limiting reagent.
b. 4.20 mol H_2O

24. a. 5.40 mol O_2 required; C_2H_4 is the limiting reagent.
b. 5.40 mol H_2O

25. a. HCl   **b.** 0.16 g H_2

26. 43.2 g H_2O

27. 91.6%

28. 83.5%

33. **a.** Two formula units $KClO_3$ decompose to form 2 formula units KCl and 3 molecules O_2.
  b. Four molecules NH_3 react with 6 molecules NO to form 5 molecules N_2 and 6 molecules H_2O.
  c. Four atoms K react with 1 molecule O_2 to form 2 formula units K_2O.

35. **a.** 245.2 g   **b.** 248.0 g   **c.** 188.4 g
  All obey the law of conservation of mass.

37. **a.** 0.54 mol   **c.** 0.984 mol
  b. 13.6 mol   **d.** 236 mol

39. **a.** 372 g F_2 **b.** 1.32 g NH_3 **c.** 123 g N_2F_4

41. **a.** 51.2 g H_2O
  b. 5.71×10^{23} molecules NH_3
  c. 23.2 g Li_3N

43. To identify the limiting reagent (the reagent that determines how much product is formed), express quantities of reactants as moles and compare to the mole ratios from the balanced equation.

45. **a.** 3.5 mol $AlCl_3$ **c.** 0.96 mol H_3PO_4
  b. 6.4 mol H_2O **d.** 7.20 mol P_2O_5

47. 91.5%

49. The efficiency of a reaction; the actual yield/theoretical yield expressed as a percent.

51. **a.** 2.36 g H_3PO_4 **b.** 1.89 g CO_2

53. **a.** 7.0×10^2 L N_2 **b.** no reagent in excess

55. 10.7 kg $CaSO_4$

57. **a.** 2   **b.** 4

59. Yes; a net ionic equation is balanced and thus obeys the law of conservation of mass.

61. **a.** $2Pb(NO_3)_2 \longrightarrow 2PbO + 4NO_2 + O_2$
  b. $2C_3H_7OH + 9O_2 \longrightarrow 6CO_2 + 8H_2O$
  c. $2Al + 3FeO \longrightarrow 3Fe + Al_2O_3$

63. **a.** 1, 1, 1, 2   **b.** 1, 3, 3, 1   **c.** 1, 1, 1, 2

65. **a.** sodium ion and nitrate ion
  b. aluminum ion and nitrate ion
  c. magnesium ion and sulfate ion

67. 1.30×10^{-22} g C_6H_6

69. $C_2H_2O_4$

71. 13 days

73. 87.4% $CaCO_3$

CHAPTER 10

1. 51.3 kPa, 0.507 atm

2. 33.7 kPa is greater than 0.25 atm.

21. pascal (Pa), millimeter of mercury (mm Hg), atmosphere (atm); Pa is the SI unit.

23. **a.** 25 kPa   **b.** 0.25 atm

25. The kinetic energy of the particles and the absolute temperature are directly proportional.

27. standard temperature and pressure, 0 °C and 1 atm

29. The average kinetic energy of particles at absolute zero is zero.

31. A liquid is condensed in the sense that its volume is minimally affected by an increase in pressure.

33. In both cases, particles with sufficient kinetic energy move from the liquid to the vapor phase. A dynamic equilibrium is set up between a contained liquid and its vapor; this is not possible with an uncontained liquid.

35. A larger percentage of molecules have enough energy to escape attractions within the liquid.

37. It increases the kinetic energy, which increases the vapor pressure.

39. **a.** ~55 mm Hg
  b. T~93 °C
  c. The vapor pressure is 760 mm Hg, which is standard pressure.

41. about 35 kPa

43. Answers will vary, but should include the fact that ionic compounds have crystalline structures with relatively high melting points.

45. The forces between the molecules of molecular solids are weaker.

47. The molecules escaping the liquid remove the added heat. The average kinetic energy of the liquid remains the same.

49. 77 °C

51. There is a continual exchange of particles, though net amounts of vapor molecules and liquid molecules remain constant.

53. It increases.

55. The substance has sufficient average kinetic energy so that the forces holding the solid crystal together are disrupted.

57. Possible answers include: odors will travel through a room; ink will move throughout a beaker of water.

59. No; collisions between objects other than at the atomic level involve the transformation of kinetic energy into heat energy.

61. Some compounds have stronger intermolecular forces than others.

63. 3.74 g/L = 0.003 74 g/cm³

65. **a.** 13.9 mol SO_2
  b. 0.0472 mol NH_3
  c. 0.021 mol CO_2

67. Vapor pressure depends only on the kinetic energy of the escaping molecules.

69. **a.** orthorhombic
  b. rhombohedral
  c. tetragonal
  d. triclinic
  e. cubic

CHAPTER 11

1. $2.0 \text{ J}/(\text{g} \times {}^\circ\text{C})$

2. $0.511 \text{ J}/(\text{g} \times {}^\circ\text{C})$

3. 1.8 kJ

11. 1.5 kJ

12. 150 J

13. 6.63 kJ

14. 89.4 kJ

20. 1.20 g

21. 3.34 kJ

22. 144 kJ

23. 0.19 kJ

24. 301 kJ

25. $3.42 \text{ mol NH}_4\text{NO}_3(s)$

30. **a.** -30.91 kJ **b.** 178.4 kJ **c.** -113.0 kJ

31. CO is a compound.

37. Heat flows from the object at the higher temperature to the object at the lower temperature.

39. the chemical composition of the substance and its mass

41. **a.** $8.50 \times 10^{-1} \text{ Calorie}$
    b. $1.86 \times 10^3 \text{ J}$
    c. $1.8 \times 10^3 \text{ J}$
    d. $1.1 \times 10^2 \text{ cal}$

43. A negative sign is given to heat flow from the system to the surroundings. A positive sign is given to heat flow to the system from the surroundings.

45. **a.** exothermic   **c.** exothermic
    b. endothermic   **d.** endothermic

47. A calorimeter is an instrument used to measure heat changes in physical or chemical processes.

49. bomb calorimeter

51. amount of heat released or absorbed in the chemical change at constant pressure

53. **a.** $-2.10 \times 10^1 \text{ kJ}$
    b. $-1.8 \times 10^1 \text{ kJ}$
    c. $-5.56 \times 10^2 \text{ kJ}$
    d. 6.5 kJ

55. It allows the calculation of the enthalpy of a reaction from the known enthalpies of two or more other reactions.

57. $3.02 \times 10^1 \text{ kJ}$

59. $-1.259 \times 10^2 \text{ kJ}$

61. This statement is true, because stability implies lower energy. The greater the release of heat, the more stable is the compound relative to its elements (all of which have $\Delta H_\text{f}^0 = 0$).

63. ΔH_f^0 for the formation of one mole of a compound from its elements

65. $4.00 \times 10^1 \text{ g water}$; $9.60 \times 10^2 \text{ g ice}$

67. $2.44 \times 10^4 \text{ cal}$; $1.02 \times 10^5 \text{ J}$

69. **a.** $-2.21 \times 10^2 \text{ kJ}$
    b. $-1.96 \times 10^2 \text{ kJ}$
    c. $-9.046 \times 10^2 \text{ kJ}$

71. $2.36 \times 10^1 \text{ kJ}$

73. $2.38 \times 10^2 \text{ kJ}$

75. $6.72 \times 10^1 \text{ kJ}$

77. The region denoted by ΔH_fus represents the coexistence of solid and liquid. The region denoted by ΔH_vap represents the coexistence of liquid and vapor.

79. $1.20 \times 10^{24} \text{ H}_2$ molecules

81. $1.18 \times 10^1 \text{ g O}_2$

83. $-1.37 \times 10^2 \text{ kJ}$

85. $45.4 \, {}^\circ\text{C}$

CHAPTER 12

10. 6.48 L

11. $6.83 \times 10 \text{ kPa}$

12. 3.39 L

13. 8.36 L

14. 2.58 kPa

15. $341 \text{ K}, 68 \, {}^\circ\text{C}$

16. $3.42 \times 10^{-1} \text{ L}$

17. $1.29 \times 10^2 \text{ kPa}$

22. $2.51 \times 10^2 \text{ mol He}(g)$

23. $1.71 \times 10^3 \text{ kPa}$

24. 2.5 g air

25. $1.76 \times 10^1 \text{ L O}_2(g)$

31. 5.60 L

32. $1.66 \times 10^1 \text{ L}$

33. 1.38×10^{23} nitrogen molecules

34. $1.50 \text{ L He}(g)$

35. 4.48 L

36. $7.67 \times 10^1 \text{ L}$

37. $9.34 \times 10^1 \text{ kPa}$

38. 3.3 kPa

45. The increased kinetic energy of the gas particles causes collisions to occur with more force.

47. The pressure doubles.

49. Temperatures measured on the Kelvin scale are always positive and directly proportional to the average kinetic energy of the gaseous particles.

51. $1.00 \times 10^2 \text{ kPa}$

53. $1.8 \times 10^1 \text{ L}$

55. High temperatures can sufficiently increase the pressure of the gas remaining in the container to cause it to explode.

57. 1.10×10^3 kPa

59. Gas particles have a finite volume and are attracted to one another, especially at low temperatures.

61. At lower temperatures, gas particles are attracted to one another; the finite volume of gas particles is significant at high pressures.

63. **a.** 5.6×10^1 L   **b.** 6.7 L   **c.** 7.84 L

65. At any temperature, hydrogen gas diffuses faster than chlorine gas by an approximate factor of six.

67. 2.25:1

69. The variables are directly proportional.

71. 165 °C

73. **a.** (4)   **b.** (1)   **c.** (1)   **d.** (3)   **e.** (2)

75. A vacuum contains no matter to allow the transfer of kinetic energy between molecules.

77. **a.** 1.58×10^2 g   **c.** 3.42×10^2 g
   b. 9.80×10^1 g   **d.** 3.31×10^2 g

79. **a.** 2.06×10^2 g
   b. 82 protons, 82 electrons, 124 neutrons

81. **a.** $Ca + 2H_2O \longrightarrow Ca(OH)_2 + H_2$
   b. $P_4O_{10} + 6H_2O \longrightarrow 4H_3PO_4$
   c. $2HgO \longrightarrow 2Hg + O_2$
   d. $Al_2S_3 + 6H_2O \longrightarrow 2Al(OH)_3 + 3H_2S$

83. **a.** $C_4H_8O_2$ **b.** C_8H_8 **c.** $C_2H_2O_4$

85. 60.0% C, 13.3% H, 26.7% O

87. 2 mol KNO_3 for each 1 mol O_2

89. 46% CH_4

91. Because attractions between molecules in gases such as nitrogen and oxygen are insignificant, these gases have the molar volume of an ideal gas—22.41 L at STP. Based on their molar volumes at STP, attractions between molecules increase in strength and effect from methane to carbon dioxide to ammonia.

CHAPTER 13

5. **a.** $1s^2 2s^2 2p^2$ **b.** $1s^2 2s^2 2p^6 3s^2 3p^6$

6. **a.** $1s^2 2s^2 2p^1$; 1 unpaired electron
   b. $1s^2 2s^2 2p^6 3s^2 3p^2$; 2 unpaired electrons

11. 2.00×10^{-3} cm; longer wavelength than red light

12. $6.00 \times 10^{15}\ s^{-1}$; ultraviolet

13. 2.12×10^{-22} J

14. 7.6×10^{-17} J

21. Electrons have fixed energies. To move from one energy level to another, they must emit or absorb specific amounts of energy, called quanta.

23. 90% of the time an electron is found inside this boundary.

25. The $1s$ orbital is spherical. The $2s$ orbital is spherical with a diameter larger than that of the $1s$ orbital. The $2p$ orbital is dumbbell shaped and reaches beyond the diameter of the $2s$ orbital.

27. The Aufbau principle states that electrons occupy the lowest possible energy levels. The Pauli exclusion principle states that an atomic orbital can hold at most two electrons. Hund's rule states that before any pairing of electrons occurs, one electron occupies each of a set of orbitals with equal energies.

29. The p orbitals in the third quantum level have three electrons.

31. **a.** 2   **b.** 6   **c.** 2   **d.** 10   **e.** 6   **f.** 2   **g.** 14   **h.** 6

33. **a.** $1s^2 2s^2 2p^6 3s^2 3p^6 3d^{10} 4s^2 4p^4$ **c.** $1s^2 2s^2 2p^6 3s^2 3p^6 3d^8 4s^2$
   b. $1s^2 2s^2 2p^6 3s^2 3p^6 3d^3 4s^2$ **d.** $1s^2 2s^2 2p^6 3s^2 3p^6 4s^2$

35. Frequency is the number of wave cycles that pass a given point per unit time. Frequency units are cycles, reciprocal seconds (s^{-1}), or hertz. Frequency and wavelength are inversely related; the speed of light divided by the wavelength of the light equals the frequency.

37. Classical physics viewed energy changes as continuous and occurring in any quantity. In the quantum concept, energy changes occur in tiny discrete units called quanta.

39. Planck showed that radiation is emitted and absorbed in quanta, dependent on the frequency of radiation.

41. A photon is a quantum of light energy. A quantum is a discrete amount of energy.

43. The outermost electron of sodium absorbs photons of wavelength 589 nm as it jumps to a higher orbital.

45. **a.** Ar   **b.** Ru   **c.** Gd

47. **a.** 2   **b.** 4   **c.** 10   **d.** 6

49. 2.61×10^4 cm

51. 3.08×10^{-19} J; lower energy

53. **a.** 1   **b.** 4   **c.** 1

55. The model of the atom uses the abstract idea of probability; light is considered a particle and a wave at the same time. Atoms and light cannot be compared with familiar objects or observations because humans cannot experience atoms or photons directly and because matter and energy behave differently at the atomic level than at the level humans can observe directly.

57. **a.** 2, 1, 1, 2   **b.** 1, 1, 2, 1   **c.** 2, 1, 2   **d.** 1, 2, 1, 2

59. **a.** 46.8% Si, 53.2% O   **c.** 11.1% H, 88.9% O
   b. 34.4% Fe, 65.6% Cl   **d.** 2.1% H, 32.7% S, 65.2% O
   e. 40% Ca, 12% C, 48% O

61. **a.** 55 p$^+$, 55 e$^-$ **c.** 48 p$^+$, 46 e$^-$
   b. 47 p$^+$, 46 e$^-$ **d.** 34 p$^+$, 36 e$^-$

63. 154 g; 0.154 Kg

65. 6.93×10^2 s

67. H: 1312 kJ/mol ($n = 1$); 328 kJ ($n = 2$);
   Li^{2+}: 1.18×10^4 kJ ($n = 1$).

CHAPTER 14

1. **a.** $1s^2 2s^2 2p^2$
   b. $1s^2 2s^2 2p^6 3s^2 3p^6 3d^3 4s^2$
   c. $1s^2 2s^2 2p^6 3s^2 3p^6 3d^{10} 4s^2 4p^6 5s^2$

2. **a.** He, Be, Mg, Ca, Sr, Ba, Ra
   b. F, Cl, Br, I, At
   c. Ti, Zr, Hf, Rf

11. **a.** $1s^22s^22p^1$
    b. $1s^22s^22p^63s^2$
    c. $1s^22s^22p^63s^23p^63d^{10}4s^24p^3$

13. **a.** Ar: $1s^22s^22p^63s^23p^6$
    b. Ge: $1s^22s^22p^63s^23p^63d^{10}4s^24p^2$
    c. Ba: $1s^22s^22p^63s^23p^63d^{10}4s^24p^64d^{10}5s^25p^66s^2$

15. **a.** $1s^22s^22p^5$
    b. $1s^22s^22p^63s^23p^63d^{10}4s^2$
    c. $1s^22s^22p^63s^23p^1$
    d. $1s^22s^22p^63s^23p^63d^{10}4s^24p^64d^{10}5s^25p^2$

17. Fluorine has a smaller atomic radius than oxygen because fluorine has one more nuclear charge. Fluorine has a smaller radius than chlorine because fluorine has eight fewer electrons.

19. The first ionization energy is the energy needed to remove the outermost electron. The second ionization energy is the energy needed to remove the second-outermost electron.

21. nonmetals; The nuclear charge increases, but the shielding effect is the same, thus creating greater electron attraction.

23. An atom of an alkali metal becomes stable by losing one electron. Removing the second electron involves removing an electron from an ion that has a stable noble-gas configuration. This requires much more energy.

25. The radius of a cation is smaller than the atom from which it forms.

27. **a.** F   **b.** N   **c.** Mg   **d.** As

29. Zinc has more protons than calcium, thus attracting the $4s$ electrons more.

31. **a.** potassium, K, $[Ar]4s^1$ **c.** sulfur, S, $[Ne]3s^23p^4$
    b. aluminum, Al, $[Ne]3s^23p^1$ **d.** barium, Ba, $[Kr]6s^2$

33. scandium, Sc, $[Ar]3d^14s^2$
    titanium, Ti, $[Ar]3d^24s^2$
    vanadium, V, $[Ar]3d^34s^2$
    chromium, Cr, $[Ar]3d^54s^1$
    manganese, Mn, $[Ar]3d^54s^2$
    iron, Fe, $[Ar]3d^64s^2$
    cobalt, Co, $[Ar]3d^74s^2$
    nickel, Ni, $[Ar]3d^84s^2$
    copper, Cu, $[Ar]3d^{10}4s^1$
    zinc, Zn, $[Ar]3d^{10}4s^2$

35. Magnesium achieves a stable electron configuration by losing two electrons; aluminum achieves a stable electron configuration by losing three electrons.

37. **a.** Possible cations are Rb^+ and Sr^{2+}; possible anions are Br^-, Se^{2-}, and As^{3-}.
    b. No; a cation is isoelectronic with the noble gas in the preceding period; an anion is isoelectronic with the noble gas in the same period.

39. **a.** $2Ag + S \longrightarrow Ag_2S$
    b. $Na_2SO_4 + Ba(OH)_2 \longrightarrow BaSO_4 + 2NaOH$
    c. $Zn + 2HNO_3 \longrightarrow Zn(NO)_2 + H_2$
    d. $2H_2O + 2SO_2 + O_2 \longrightarrow 2H_2SO_4$

41. **a.** Li_2SO_4 **b.** $Zn_3(PO_4)_2$ **c.** $KMnO_4$ **d.** $SrCO_3$

43. The ionic radii decrease from S^{2-}, Cl^-, Ar, K^+, Ca^{2+}, to Sc^{3+} as the number of protons increases. The radii decrease from O^{2-}, F^-, Ne, Na^+, Mg^{2+}, to Al^{3+} for the same reason.

CHAPTER 15

7. **a.** KI   **b.** Al_2O_3

8. **a.** potassium iodide   **b.** aluminum oxide

21. fluorine (F), chlorine (Cl), bromine (Br), iodine (I); Group 7A; seven valence electrons

23. **a.** :C̈l·   **b.** :S̈:   **c.** ·Ȧl·   **d.** Li·

25. **a.** 2   **b.** 3   **c.** 1   **d.** 2

27. **a.** $1s^22s^22p^63s^23p^63d^3$
    b. $1s^22s^22p^63s^23p^63d^4$
    c. $1s^22s^22p^63s^23p^63d^5$

29. **a.** S^{2-} **b.** Na^+ **c.** F^- **d.** P^{3-}

31. **a.** Br^- **b.** H^- **c.** As^{3-} **d.** Se^{2-}

33. The positive charges of the cations equal the negative charges of the anions.

35. **a.** K^+Cl^- **c.** $Mg^{2+}Br^-$
    b. $Ba^{2+}SO_4^{2-}$ **d.** $Li^+CO_3^{2-}$

37. Their network of electrostatic attractions and repulsions forms a rigid structure.

39. They have many mobile valence electrons. Electrons in the current replace the electrons leaving the metal.

41. Answers will vary and could include tableware, steel in cars and buses, high-speed dental drill bits, solder in stereos and televisions, and structural steel in buildings.

43. Brass is a mixture of copper and zinc. The properties of a particular sample of brass will vary with the relative proportions of the two metals.

45.

Group number	Valence electrons lost or gained	Ion formula
1A	1	Na^+
2A	2	Ca^{2+}
3A	3	Al^{3+}
5A	3	N^{3-}
6A	2	S^{2-}
7A	1	Br^-

47. For the representative elements, the number of electrons in the electron dot structure is the group number.

49. It has gained valence electrons.

51. **a.** $1s^22s^22p^63s^23p^63d^6$
    b. $1s^22s^22p^63s^23p^63d^7$
    c. $1s^22s^22p^63s^23p^63d^8$

53. Hexagonal closest-packed unit cells have 12 neighbors for every atom or ion. Face-centered cubic unit cells also have 12 neighbors for every atom or ion, with an atom or ion in the center of each face. Body-centered cubic units cells have 8 neighbors for every atom or ion, with an atom or ion at the center of each cube.

55. **a.** $1s^22s^22p^63s^23p^6$ **b.** $1s^22s^22p^6$

Each has a noble-gas electron configuration.

57. Both are composed of ions and are held together by electrostatic bonds. Metals always conduct electricity, but ionic compounds conduct only when melted or in aqueous solution. Ionic compounds are composed of cations and anions, but metals are composed of cations and free-floating valence electrons. Metals are malleable, but ionic compounds are brittle.

59. Gases and liquids assume the shapes of their containers. Solids have a definite shape. Liquids and solids have a definite volume; gases do not. Gases have a low density; liquids have an intermediate density; solids have a high density. The molecules in a gas move freely and randomly. The molecules of a liquid flow. The molecules of a solid vibrate and rotate around a fixed position.

61. The average kinetic energy and the speed of the gas molecules increase.

63. a. At 40 °C more water molecules have energies that allow them to overcome intermolecular attractions than at 20 °C.
b. Steam at 100 °C has more potential energy.
c. The molecules' kinetic energy has increased, creating a greater vapor pressure.
d. Because water molecules require more energy to evaporate than do ether molecules, the attractions between water molecules must be greater than those between ether molecules.
e. Ice absorbs energy from the tea. The kinetic energy of the tea decreases.
f. The goal is to change liquid water to water vapor without destroying chemical bonds by heating; lowering the external pressure lowers the temperature at which liquid water molecules have enough energy to vaporize.

65. 1.36×10^2 kPa

67. a. 0.0147
0.0373
0.0639
0.0879

b.

c. 22.4 L/mol
d. 1:1 ratio

69. 0.1445 nm

71. a. iron(II); Fe^{2+} **d.** copper(I); Cu^+
b. iron(III); Fe^{3+} **e.** cobalt(III); Co^{3+}
c. copper(II); Cu^{2+}

CHAPTER 16

1. a. :C̈l:C̈l: **b.** :B̈r:B̈r: **c.** :Ï:Ï:

2. a. H:Ö:Ö:H **b.** :C̈l:P̈:C̈l:
:C̈l:

3. [H:Ö:]⁻

4. [F:B̈:F]⁻ with F above and F below

5. [:Ö:S:Ö:]²⁻ [:Ö:C:Ö]²⁻

6. [H:Ö:C:Ö]⁻ with O above and :Ö: below

19. a. moderately polar covalent
b. ionic
c. moderately to very polar covalent
d. moderately to very polar covalent
e. ionic
f. nonpolar covalent

20. In order of increasing polarity: e, c, d, b, a

27. Neon has an octet of valence electrons. A chlorine atom achieves an octet by sharing an electron with another chlorine atom.

29. Ionic bonds depend on electrostatic attraction between ions. Covalent bonds depend on electrostatic attraction between shared electrons and nuclei of combining atoms.

31. The element of which there is only one atom is the central atom of the molecule.

33. a. :F̈:F̈: **b.** H:C̈l: **c.** H:C::C:H **d.** H:C::N:

35. An unshared pair of electrons is needed for a coordinate covalent bond. There are no unshared pairs in C—H or C—C bonds.

37. [:Ö::C:Ö:]²⁻ ⟷ [:Ö:C::Ö:]²⁻ ⟷ [:Ö:C:Ö:]²⁻
:Ö: :Ö: :Ö:

39. The measured mass of a paramagnetic substance appears greater when measured in the presence of a magnetic field than when measured in the absence of a magnetic field.

41. (b) and (c); assuming only single bonds the P and S atoms each have 10 valence electrons.

43. Increasing bond dissociation energy is linked to lower chemical reactivity.

45. H:C:::C:H   1694 kJ/mol
2H:C 2×393 kJ/mol = 786 kJ/mol
C:::C   908 kJ/mol

47. a. 2 sigma, 2 pi **b.** 6 sigma, 2 pi

49. The 2s and the 2p orbitals form two sp^2 hybrid orbitals in the carbon atom. One sp^2 hybrid orbital from each oxygen atom forms a sigma bond with the carbon atom. Pi bonds between each oxygen atom and the carbon are formed by the unhybridized 2p orbitals.

51. The two atoms involved must have different electronegativities.

53. b., d., e., a., c., f.

55.

57. A hydrogen bond is formed by an electrostatic attraction between a hydrogen atom covalently bonded to a more electronegative atom and an unshared electron pair of a nearby atom.

59. The $3s$ and three $3p$ orbitals of phosphorus hybridize to form four sp^3 hybrid orbitals. The resulting shape is pyramidal with a bond angle of 107° between the sigma bonds.

61. :Cl:S:Cl:
        ::O:

63. **a.** tetrahedral, 109.5° **c.** tetrahedral, 109.5°
        b. trigonal planar, 120° **d.** bent, 105°

65. $\Delta H = -55$ kJ/mol

67. An antibonding orbital has a higher energy because the atomic orbitals overlap on opposite sides of the nuclei, not between them.

69. C, O, H, S, N, F, Cl, I, Br; These elements are all nonmetals.

71. a., b., c., d.

73. **a.** $1s^2 2s^2 2p^6 3s^1$ **c.** $1s^2 2s^2 2p^6 3s^2 3p^3$
        b. $1s^2 2s^2 2p^6 3s^2 3p^4$ **d.** $1s^2 2s^2 2p^3$

75. **a.** 1.20×10^{22} **c.** 5.26×10^{15}
        b. 9.27×10^{20} **d.** 1.81×10^{18}

77.

H:C:H (with H above and below central C)   90° 90° H—C H below with H   109.5° 109.5° H C H with H 109.5° 109.5°

The first sketch is tetrahedral. The second sketch is a tetrahedron. The bond angles in the first sketch are not all the same, with some being 90°. The bond angles in the second sketch are all 109.5°. The second sketch is correct. (Note: The wedge-shaped lines come out of the page; the dotted lines recede into the page.)

CHAPTER 17

8. 36.1%

9. **a.** $CaCl_2 + 6H_2O \rightarrow CaCl_2 \cdot 6H_2O$
      b. 49.3%

19. Oxygen is more electronegative than hydrogen. Because the water molecules are bent, the bond polarities do not cancel.

21. Some water molecules have sufficient energy to leave the surface of the liquid. Vapor pressure is the pressure of the water vapor above the liquid.

23. It physically interferes with hydrogen bonding and reduces surface tension.

25. water, 2.0×10^4 cal; iron, 2.2×10^3 cal

27. Ammonia molecules form hydrogen bonds, whereas methane molecules do not. Substances whose molecules form hydrogen bonds tend to have higher boiling points.

29. Ice floats in liquid water. Solids generally sink in their liquids because a substance is generally more dense in the solid state.

31. Bodies of water would freeze from the bottom up. This would kill many forms of aquatic life.

33. The polar water molecules electrostatically attract ions and polar covalent molecules. Polar compounds will dissolve but nonpolar compounds are unaffected because they have no charges.

35. The positive ions are attracted by the negatively charged end of the polar water molecule; the negative ions are attracted by the positively charged end. As the ions are pulled away from the crystal, they are surrounded by the water molecules.

37. Its ions are free to move toward an electrode.

39. water in the crystal structure of a substance

41. **a.** tin(IV) chloride pentahydrate
        b. iron(II) sulfate heptahydrate
        c. barium bromide tetrahydrate
        d. iron(III) phosphate tetrahydrate

43. A suspension is a mixture with large particles that settle on standing. A colloid is a mixture with particles of intermediate size that do not settle.

45. the random motion of the dispersion medium molecules

47. Water molecules at 4 °C are tightly packed and have maximum density. Below 4 °C the water molecules arrange in a regular network because of the attractions between them. As a result, ice has a lower density than water and floats.

49. **a.** sodium carbonate monohydrate, 14.5% H_2O
        b. magnesium sulfate heptahydrate, 51.1% H_2O

51. Ions in solution are surrounded by water molecules. Negative ions are attracted to the hydrogen atoms and positive ions are attracted to the oxygen atoms.

53. **a.** no
        b. drying to examine the crystals, testing for electrical conductivity, doing a flame test

55. **1.** a, b   **3.** a   **5.** b, c   **7.** b   **9.** b
        2. b, c   **4.** c   **6.** a, b   **8.** a

57. Ethanol has a polar hydroxyl end (−OH) that dissolves in water, and a nonpolar hydrocarbon end (C_2H_5−) that dissolves in gasoline.

59. No; nonpolar molecules do not dissolve in polar molecules.

61. **a.** 1.00 g/mL   **b.** 4 °C
        c. No; the density of ice is 0.917 g/mL at 0 °C. There would be a break in the curve at 0 °C as liquid water at 0 °C changes to solid water (ice) at 0 °C.

63. The blood and all of the body's cells contain large amounts of water. Most of the important chemical reactions of life take place in aqueous solution inside cells.

65. **a.** 195 g   **b.** 1.95×10^5 mg   **c.** 0.195 kg

67. **a.** raises the boiling point
        b. lowers the boiling point

69. 9.00 g H_2, 72.0 g O_2

71. 636 g C_2H_4O

73. a. As the molar mass increases, the boiling point increases.
   b. The boiling point more than doubles.

75. a. hydrogen   **c.** oxygen
   b. 4.9×10^{-2} g H_2O **d.** 10 cm^3 O_2

CHAPTER 18

1. 0.44 g/L

2. 2.6 atm

8. 0.10M

9. 2.8M

10. 0.142 mol

11. 0.50 mol $CaCl_2$; 56 g $CaCl_2$

12. 47.5 mL

13. Use a pipet to transfer 50 mL of the 1.0M solution to a 250-mL volumetric flask. Then add distilled water up to the 250-mL mark.

14. 5% (v/v)

15. 12 mL

16. 0.25 g $MgSO_4$

17. 3.6% $CuSO_4$ (m/v)

28. 12.6 g

29. 0.285m NaCl

30. $X_{C_2H_5OH} = 0.190$; $X_{H_2O} = 0.810$

31. $X_{CCl_4} = 0.437$; $X_{CHCl_3} = 0.563$

32. 101.37 °C

33. 114 g NaCl

34. 39.2 g/mol

35. 169 g/mol

41. Random collisions of the solvent molecules with the solute molecules or ions provide enough force to overcome gravity.

43. Solubility is the amount of solute dissolved in a given amount of solvent to make a saturated solution at a given temperature. A saturated solution has the maximum amount of solute that can be dissolved in a given amount of solvent at a given temperature. An unsaturated solution has less dissolved solute than a saturated solution.

45. Particles of solute crystallize.

47. Increasing pressure increases the solubility.

49. Molarity gives you the exact number of moles of solute per liter of solution. Dilute and concentrated are relative terms and are not quantitative.

51. the number of moles of solute dissolved in one liter of solution

53. a. 23 g NaCl   **b.** 2.0 g $MgCl_2$

55. a. 100.26 °C   **b.** 101.54 °C

57. A 1M solution has 1 mol of solute dissolved in 1 L of solution. A 1m solution has 1 mol of solute dissolved in 1000 g of solvent.

59. a. −1.1 °C   **b.** −0.74 °C   **c.** −1.5 °C

61. a. Because the freezing-point depression is twice as great for solute B compared with solute A, solute B must give twice as many particles in solution compared with solute A.
   b. Solute A forms a saturated solution in this quantity of water when 2.4 mol of A is added.

63. Each gram of acetone requires 0.93 g of water.

65. The mole fraction of NaCl is 0.00269; the mole fraction of H_2O is 0.997.

67. a. about 1.14   **b.** about −7.2 °C   **c.** about −9.5 °C

69. $X_{C_2H_5OH} = 0.20$; $X_{H_2O} = 0.80$

71.

73. a. 0.30 mol   **b.** 0.40 mol   **c.** 0.50 mol   **d.** 0.20 mol

75. unsaturated

77. a. 7.5 g H_2O_2 **b.** 0.88M

79. 85.5 g/mol

81. a. 4   **b.** 1

83. 1 mol of calcium chloride dissolves into 3 mol of particles, and 1 mol of sodium chloride dissolves into 2 mol of particles; freezing-point depression is proportional to the number of particles of solute.

85. The stronger the intermolecular attractions in a liquid, the greater is the surface tension.

87. raises the boiling points

89. a. the substance that is dissolved
b. the substance used for dissolving
c. No additional solute can be dissolved.
d. More solute can be dissolved.
e. The solution contains more solute than a saturated solution.
f. a solute that cannot conduct electricity
g. a solute that conducts a small amount of electricity
h. a solute that can conduct electricity well

91. 1.10×10^2 mL HNO_3

93. $0.090M$ Na_2SO_4

CHAPTER 19

6. a. reactants favored **c.** products favored
   b. reactants favored **d.** reactants favored

7. a. favors reactants **c.** no effect
   b. favors products **d.** favors products

8. $K_{eq} = 12$

9. a. $K_{eq} = 0.084$ or 8.4×10^{-2}
   b. One is the inverse of the other.

10. $K_{eq} = 1.6 \times 10^{-3}$

11. $K_{eq} = 0.79$

12. 3.5 mol HI and 0.50 mol I_2

13. a. $K_{eq} = \dfrac{[H_2] \times [Br_2]}{[HBr]^2}$ **c.** $K_{eq} = \dfrac{[CO] \times [H_2O]}{[CO_2] \times [H_2]}$

   b. $K_{eq} = \dfrac{[SO_2]^2 \times [O_2]}{[SO_3]^2}$ **d.** $K_{eq} = \dfrac{[H_2O]^6 \times [NO]^4}{[NH_3]^4 \times [O_2]^5}$

25. 254.7 J/K•mol

26. −0.7 J/K•mol

27. −46.2 kJ/mol

28. a. 38.1 kJ; nonspontaneous
   b. −1097.7 kJ; spontaneous

29. a. 514.2 kJ; nonspontaneous
   b. 33.02 kJ; nonspontaneous

33. Rate = k[A]; rate is moles per liter per second. [A] is moles per liter. k = rate/[A]. $k = 1/s = s^{-1}$

34. 0.25 mol/L•s; 0.125 mol/L•s

39. Reactant particles must have a certain minimum amount of energy to react to form product, just as it takes a certain minimum amount of energy to climb over a wall or barrier.

41. A catalyst increases the rate of reactions by providing an alternative reaction mechanism with a lower activation energy.

43. Gas molecules and oxygen molecules mix readily but do not have enough energy to react at room temperature. The flame raises the temperature and the energy of collisions, so the reaction rate is increased. The heat released by the reaction maintains the high temperature, and the reaction continues spontaneously.

45. The rate of formation of products from reactants and the rate of formation of reactants from products are equal.

47. A system in dynamic equilibrium changes to relieve the stress applied to it. Carbonated drinks in closed containers have achieved a state of dynamic equilibrium between the carbon dioxide in the liquid and gas states. When the containers are opened, carbon dioxide gas escapes. Carbon dioxide from the liquid goes into the gas state in an attempt to re-establish equilibrium.

49. a. $K_{eq} = \dfrac{[H_2S]^2 \times [CH_4]}{[H_2]^4 \times [CS_2]}$ **c.** $K_{eq} = \dfrac{[NO_2]^2}{[NO]^2 \times [O_2]}$

   b. $K_{eq} = \dfrac{[PCl_3] \times [Cl_2]}{[PCl_5]}$ **d.** $K_{eq} = \dfrac{[H_2] \times [CO_2]}{[CO] \times [H_2O]}$

51. the energy in a system available to do work; a spontaneous reaction has a negative free energy

53. unfavorable

55. a. completed jigsaw puzzle
   b. 50 mL of ice
   c. sodium chloride crystals

57. No; some endothermic processes are spontaneous because of their favorable change in entropy.

59. In combination, the change in heat content (enthalpy) and the change in entropy determine whether a process is spontaneous.

61. a. the proportionality constant relating the concentrations of the reactants to the reaction rate
   b. a chemical reaction with a rate proportional to the concentration of one reactant
   c. an equation relating the reaction rate to the concentrations of the reactants

63. 100 minutes

65. a. 1.22×10^{-4} mol/(L · s) **b.** 1.94×10^{-4} mol/(L · s)

67. 25 kJ

69. a. yes **b.** yes **c.** no **d.** yes

71. $K_{eq} = 0.659$

73. Increasing pressure tends to reduce volume and increase density, so the system responds by favoring production of the liquid, which has the greater density.

75. The reaction is slow (activation energy is high).

77. −89.8 J/K

79. A catalyst increases the efficiency of the collisions; a greater number of collisions results in the formation of the product.

81. a. fluoride ion (anion) **e.** sodium ion (cation)
   b. copper(II) ion (cation) **f.** iodide ion (anion)
   c. phosphide ion (anion) **g.** oxide ion (anion)
   d. hydrogen ion (cation) **h.** magnesium ion (cation)

83. Solid potassium chloride is an ionic compound of K^+ and Cl^-, not of KCl molecules. Each ion is surrounded by six ions of opposite charge in a simple cubic unit cell crystal.

85. crystalline solids, high melting points; insulators when solid but conductors when molten; not malleable or ductile; often soluble in water

87. a. $Li^+\ddot{B}r\!:^-$　　**c.** $^-\!\!:\!\ddot{F}\!:Mg^{2+}:\ddot{F}\!:^-$

b. $^-\!:\!\ddot{C}l\!:\!Al^{3+}\!:\!\ddot{C}l\!:^-$ with $:\!\ddot{C}l\!:^-$ above　　**d.** $Na^+\!:\!\ddot{S}\!:^{2-}Na^+$

89. positive ions: **b.**, **e.**, **f.**, **g.**, **h.**, and **j.**; negative ions: **a.**, **c.**, **d.**, and **i.**

91. a.

Time (s) / [AB] (mol/L) graph

b. The rate when $t = 100$ is 8×10^{-4} mol/L·s. The rate when $t = 250$ is 4×10^{-4} mol/L·s.

CHAPTER 20

1. a. hydrofluoric acid　　**c.** potassium hydroxide
b. nitric acid　　**d.** sulfuric acid

2. a. H_2CrO_4　　**c.** HI
b. $Fe(OH)_2$　　**d.** LiOH

6. $1.0 \times 10^{-11}M$; basic

7. a. basic　　**c.** acidic
b. basic　　**d.** neutral

8. a. 4.00　　**b.** 3.00　　**c.** 9.00

9. a. 12.00　　**b.** 2.00　　**c.** 4.00

10. a. $1.0 \times 10^{-5}M$　　**c.** $1.0 \times 10^{-6}M$
b. $1.0 \times 10^{-7}M$　　**d.** $1.0 \times 10^{-3}M$

11. a. $1.0 \times 10^{-4}M$
b. $1.0 \times 10^{-11}M$
c. $1.0 \times 10^{-8}M$

12. a. 5.30　　**b.** 9.08　　**c.** 6.57

13. a. 9.63　　**b.** 9.30　　**c.** 3.65

14. a. $5.0 \times 10^{-8}M$　　**c.** $8.9 \times 10^{-8}M$
b. $1.6 \times 10^{-2}M$　　**d.** $2.0 \times 10^{-7}M$

15. a. $2.0 \times 10^{-7}M$　　**c.** $1.1 \times 10^{-7}M$
b. $6.3 \times 10^{-13}M$　　**d.** $5.0 \times 10^{-8}M$

19. Lewis base; it has a nonbonding pair of electrons, which it can donate.

20. a. H^+ is the Lewis acid; H_2O is the Lewis base.

b. $AlCl_3$ is the Lewis acid; Cl^- is the Lewis base.

26. $K_a = 1.8 \times 10^{-4}$

27. a. pH = 3.006　　**b.** $K_a = 4.89 \times 10^{-6}$

35. $H_2O \rightleftharpoons H^+ + OH^-$

37. the negative logarithm of the hydrogen-ion concentration

39. a. pH = 2.00, acidic　　**c.** pH = 6.00, acidic
b. pH = 12.00, basic　　**d.** pH = 6.00, acidic

41. a. 5.62　　**b.** 8.04　　**c.** $6.3 \times 10^{-14}M$　　**d.** $2.0 \times 10^{-7}M$

43. a. $KOH \longrightarrow K^+ + OH^-$
b. $Mg(OH)_2 \longrightarrow Mg^{2+} + 2OH^-$

45. a. base　　**c.** base　　**e.** acid
b. acid　　**d.** acid　　**f.** acid

47. a. $2Li + 2H_2O \longrightarrow 2LiOH + H_2$
b. $Ba + 2H_2O \longrightarrow Ba(OH)_2 + H_2$

49. a. HNO_3 with NO_3^-, H_2O with H_3O^+
b. CH_3COOH with CH_3COO^-, H_2O with H_3O^+
c. H_2O with OH^-, NH_3 with NH_4^+
d. H_2O with OH^-, CH_3COO^- with CH_3COOH

51. A Lewis acid accepts a pair of electrons to form a covalent bond. A Lewis base donates a pair of electrons to form a covalent bond. The Lewis theory includes as acids or bases many substances that do not donate or accept hydrogen ions.

53. A strong acid is completely dissociated; K_a must be large.

55. a. $K_a = \dfrac{[H^+][F^-]}{[HF]}$　　**b.** $K_a = \dfrac{[H^+][HCO_3^-]}{[H_2CO_3]}$

57. Yes; acids such as acetic acid dissolve well but ionize poorly.

59. $4.5 \times 10^{-4}M$

61. a. $HClO_2$, chlorous acid　　**c.** H_3O^+, hydronium ion
b. H_3PO_4, phosphoric acid　　**d.** NH_4^+, ammonium ion

63. a. $[OH^-] = 4.0 \times 10^{-10}M$　　**c.** pH = 12.26
b. $[OH^-] = 2.0 \times 10^{-5}M$　　**d.** pH = 5.86

65. a. KOH is the base; HBr is the acid.
b. HCl is the acid; H_2O is the base.

67. Answers will vary; students are likely to consider the Arrhenius theory the easiest to understand. All three theories provide definitions and describe accepted behavior of a certain group of compounds. Because it is more general, the Brønsted–Lowry theory includes a greater number of compounds than the Arrhenius theory. The Lewis theory includes the greatest number of compounds because it is the most general. Each theory has advantages in certain circumstances.

69. The y-axis might correspond to $[H^+]$ or pOH because HCl is a strong acid.

71. 0.47 L

73. a. $K_{eq} = \dfrac{[CO]^2[O_2]}{[CO_2]^2}$　　**b.** $K_{eq} = \dfrac{[NH_3]^2}{[H_2]^3[N_2]}$

75. $K_w = K_aK_b = \dfrac{[H^+][A^-]}{[HA]} \times \dfrac{[HA][OH^-]}{[A^-]} = [H^+][OH^-]$

77. 50.0 mL; The pH = 7 when $[H^+] = [OH^-]$. Because HCl is a strong acid that supplies one hydrogen ion per formula unit and NaOH is a strong base that supplies one hydroxide ion per formula unit, $[H^+] = [OH^-]$ when equal volumes of solutions of the same molarity are combined.

CHAPTER 21

1. 4.68 mol KOH

2. 0.20 mol NaOH

3. 56 mL HCl

4. 0.128M

5. **a.** 32.7 g   **b.** 40.0 g

6. **a.** 29.2 g/equiv   **b.** 60.0 g/equiv

7. **a.** 0.50 equiv   **b.** 0.20 equiv

8. **a.** 0.30 equiv   **b.** 0.40 equiv

9. **a.** 0.99 equiv   **b.** 0.80 equiv   **c.** 0.070 equiv

10. **a.** 0.50N **b.** 0.20N **c.** 1.03N **d.** 1.79N

11. 58 mL of 3.0N KOH

12. Dilute 25 mL of 4.0N H_2SO_4 to 500 mL.

13. 0.260N base

14. 1.2N base

15. 14.1 mL

16. 29.5 mL

23. **a.** $HPO_4^{2-} + H^+ \rightleftharpoons H_2PO_4^-$
    b. $H_2PO_4^- + OH^- \rightleftharpoons HPO_4^{2-} + H_2O$

24. $CH_3COO^- + H^+ \rightleftharpoons CH_3COOH$

25. $2 \times 10^{-14}M$

26. $6.7 \times 10^{-5}M$

27. **a.** $2 \times 10^{-17}M$ **b.** $1 \times 10^{-17}M$

28. **a.** $[Pb^{2+}][Cl^-]^2$ **b.** $[Ag^+]^2[CrO_4^{2-}]$

29. $2 \times 10^{-17}M$

30. $3.2 \times 10^{-6}M$

31. It will.

32. Yes

37. **a.** $HNO_3 + KOH \longrightarrow KNO_3 + H_2O$
    b. $2HCl + Ca(OH)_2 \longrightarrow CaCl_2 + 2H_2O$
    c. $H_2SO_4 + 2NaOH \longrightarrow Na_2SO_4 + 2H_2O$

39. **a.** 1.40M **b.** 2.61M

41. **a.** 0.10 equiv   **b.** 3.86 equiv   **c.** 0.30 equiv

43. **a.** 1N **b.** 2N **c.** 0.2N **d.** 0.2N

45. **a.** 0.0600N **c.** 0.171N
    b. 0.400N **d.** 0.0752N

47. $HCO_3^-(aq) + H_2O(l) \rightleftharpoons H_2CO_3(aq) + OH^-(aq)$

49. **a.** basic   **c.** neutral   **e.** neutral
    b. acidic   **d.** basic   **f.** acidic

51. No; HCl is a strong acid.

53. the product of the ion concentrations raised to the power of their coefficients

55. lowers the solubility

57. The product of the concentrations of the two ions is greater than the solubility product constant of the precipitate.

59. $H_2PO_4^- + OH^- \rightleftharpoons H_2O + HPO_4^{2-}$
    $HPO_4^{2-} + H^+ \rightleftharpoons H_2PO_4^-$
    Added OH^- is neutralized by $H_2PO_4^-$ and added acid is neutralized by HPO_4^{2-}.

61. **a.** 8.73
    b. phenolphthalein or thymol blue

63. 12.5 mL

65. **a.** shift to the left   **b.** shift to the right

67. **b., c., d., a.**

69. **a.** 2   **b.** 3

71. CO_2 concentration is higher in pure water. Less CO_2 becomes carbonate because pure water does not have the OH^- ions needed to reduce H^+ concentration.

73. **a.** 5.34   **b.** 11.30   **c.** 0.52   **d.** 9.01

75. **a.** HSO_4^- **b.** CN^- **c.** OH^- **d.** NH_3

77. 0.5M NaCl

79. 74.4% $AgNO_3$

CHAPTER 22

1. **a.** Na: oxidized (reducing agent);
    S: reduced (oxidizing agent)

   b. Al: oxidized (reducing agent);
    O_2: reduced (oxidizing agent)

2. **a.** oxidation   **c.** reduction
    b. oxidation   **d.** reduction

9. **a.** S: +3; O: −2   **c.** Al: +3; S: +6; O: −2
    b. O: 0   **d.** Na: +1; O: −1

10. **a.** P: +5; O: −2   **c.** Na: +1; Cr: +6; O: −2
    b. N: −3; H: +1   **d.** Ca: +2; O: −2; H: +1

11. **a.** H_2 oxidized, O_2 reduced
    b. K unchanged, N reduced, O oxidized
    c. N in NH_4^+ oxidized, H unchanged, N in NO_2^- reduced, O unchanged
    d. Pb reduced, O unchanged, H unchanged, I oxidized

12. **a.** H_2, reducing agent; O_2, oxidizing agent
    b. N in NO_3^-, oxidizing agent;
    O in NO_3^-, reducing agent
    c. N in NH_4^+, reducing agent;
    N in NO_2^-, oxidizing agent
    d. Pb, oxidizing agent; I, reducing agent

17. The following are redox reactions: **c.** Mg is oxidized; Br_2 is reduced. **d.** Nitrogen in NO_2^- is oxidized; nitrogen in NH_4^+ is reduced. **e.** Oxygen is oxidized; chlorine is reduced.

18. **b.** is an oxidation-reduction reaction; Cu is reduced; H_2 is oxidized.

19. **a.** 2, 2, 3
    b. 2, 2, 2, 1, 2
    c. 1, 2, 5, 2, 4

20. **a.** 1, 8, 2, 2, 3, 4
    b. 1, 1, 1, 1, 2, 2
    c. 1, 2, 1, 2, 1

21. **a.** $3Sn^{2+} + 14H^+ + Cr_2O_7^{2-} \longrightarrow 3Sn^{4+} + 2Cr^{3+} + 7H_2O$
    b. $CuS + 8NO_3^- + 8H^+ \longrightarrow Cu(NO_3)_2 + SO_2 + 6NO_2 + 4H_2O$
    c. $6I^- + 2NO_3^- + 8H^+ \longrightarrow 3I_2 + 2NO + 4H_2O$

22. **a.** $6I^- + 2MnO_4^- + 4H_2O \longrightarrow 3I_2 + 2MnO_2 + 8OH^-$
    b. $S_2O_3^{2-} + 2NiO_2 + 2OH^- + H_2O \longrightarrow 2SO_3^{2-} + 2Ni(OH)_2$
    c. $4Zn + NO_3^- + 6H_2O + 7OH^- \longrightarrow 4Zn(OH)_4^{2-} + NH_3$

25. oxidation

27. **a.** $C_2H_4(g) + 3O_2(g) \longrightarrow 2CO_2(g) + 2H_2O(l)$
    b. $2KClO_3(s) \longrightarrow 2KCl(s) + 3O_2(g)$
    c. $CuO(s) + H_2(g) \longrightarrow Cu(s) + H_2O(l)$
    d. $2H_2(g) + O_2(g) \longrightarrow 2H_2O(l)$

29. Must be equal.

31. single-replacement, combustion, combination, and decomposition

33. **a.**, **b.**, **c.**

35. **a.** Mn, reducing agent; Pb, oxidizing agent
    b. Cl, oxidizing agent; Cl, reducing agent
    c. I, oxidizing agent; C, reducing agent

37. **a.** $2MnO(s) + 5PbO_2(s) + 8H^+ \longrightarrow$
    $2MnO_4^-(aq) + 5Pb^{2+}(aq) + 4H_2O(l)$
    b. $Cl_2(g) + H_2O(l) \longrightarrow HCl(aq) + HClO(aq)$
    c. $I_2O_5(s) + 5CO(g) \longrightarrow I_2(s) + 5CO_2(g)$
    d. $H_2O(l) + SO_3(g) \longrightarrow H_2SO_4(aq)$

39. **a.** C   **b.** Cl

41. **a.** $MnO_2(s) + 4HCl(aq) \longrightarrow$
    $MnCl_2(aq) + Cl_2(g) + 2H_2O(l)$
    b. $Cu(s) + 4HNO_3(aq) \longrightarrow$
    $Cu(NO_3)_2(aq) + 2NO_2(g) + 2H_2O(l)$
    c. $3P(s) + 5HNO_3(aq) + 2H_2O(l) \longrightarrow$
    $5NO(g) + 3H_3PO_4(aq)$
    d. $2Bi(OH)_3(s) + 3Na_2SnO_2(aq) \longrightarrow$
    $2Bi(s) + 3Na_2SnO_3(aq) + 3H_2O(l)$

43. Double-replacement reactions never involve the transfer of electrons; instead, they involve the exchange of positive ions in aqueous solution.

45. **a.** acidic   **b.** basic   **c.** basic   **d.** acidic

47. 56.3 mL KOH

49. $1.14N$ H_3PO_4

51. Test tube B has the NaCl added to it. Due to the common-ion effect, the addition of either sulfate ion or barium ion to a saturated solution of $BaSO_4$ will cause the solubility product of $BaSO_4$ to be exceeded, and barium sulfate will precipitate, as shown in test tubes A and C.

53. **a.**

Alkane burned	O_2 used (mol)	CO_2 produced (mol)	H_2O produced (mol)
C_4H_{10}	6.5	4	5
C_5H_{12}	8	5	6
C_6H_{14}	9.5	6	7

   b. $C_xH_y + \left[x + \left(\dfrac{y}{4}\right)\right]O_2 \longrightarrow xCO_2 + \left(\dfrac{y}{2}\right)H_2O$

55. 104 mL $K_2Cr_2O_7$

CHAPTER 23

8. $2Al(s) + 3Cu^{2+}(aq) \longrightarrow 2Al^{3+}(aq) + 3Cu(s)$; $E^0_{cell} = +2.00$ V

9. $E^0_{cell} = +0.46$ V

10. nonspontaneous: $E^0_{cell} = -0.02$ V

11. Yes; $E^0_{cell} = +0.16$ V

21. nothing

23. cathode

25. anode: zinc; cathode: carbon (graphite)

27. $Pb(s) \mid PbSO_4(s) \parallel PbO_2(s) \mid PbSO_4(s)$

29. A fuel cell needs no recharging and does not produce toxic wastes if the fuel is hydrogen gas.

31. the ability of a voltaic cell to produce a current

33. The aluminum half-cell is connected to a standard hydrogen half-cell and a voltmeter is used. The aluminum half-cell has the indicated voltage.

35. **a.** +1.61 V   **b.** +0.94 V

37. The teaspoon is the cathode in an electrolytic cell with silver cyanide as the electrolyte. When the DC current flows, the silver ions deposit on the teaspoon.

39. Two half-cells are needed because oxidation or reduction cannot occur in isolation. One half-cell gains electrons and one loses them, producing an electric current.

41. Some of the iron dissolves and the nail becomes coated with copper.

   $Fe(s) + CuSO_4(aq) \longrightarrow FeSO_4(aq) + Cu(s)$

   oxidation: $Fe \longrightarrow Fe^{2+} + 2e^-$

   reduction: $Cu^{2+} + 2e^- \longrightarrow Cu$

43. Lead(II) sulfate and lead dioxide are very insoluble in sulfuric acid.

45. Gold belongs near the bottom, below silver, because it is one of the least active metals.

47. The chemists' definition focuses on the electrons that are produced by oxidation at the anode of a voltaic cell; the dictionary definition is probably based on an electrolytic cell, whose electrodes are defined by the battery terminals to which they are attached.

49. The baby shoe is being plated with copper.

51. 467 mL O_2

53. Dilute 31 mL of 16M acid to a total volume of 500 mL.

55. a. 2AgCl + Ni $\longrightarrow$ 2Ag + NiCl$_2$
$E^0_{cell} = +0.47$ V
b. 3Cl$_2$ + 2Al $\longrightarrow$ 2AlCl$_3$
$E^0_{cell} = +3.02$ V

57. a. The iron electrode is the anode; the nickel electrode is the cathode.
b. The anode is negative; the cathode is positive.
c. anode: Fe(s) $\longrightarrow$ Fe^{2+}(aq) + 2e$^-$
cathode: Ni^{2+}(aq) + 2e$^-$ $\longrightarrow$ Ni(s)
d. $E^0_{cell} = +0.19$ V

CHAPTER 24

29. Group 1A: alkali metals; Group 2A: alkaline-earth metals

31. Their atomic diameters are smaller.

33. bauxite

35. diamond, graphite, and buckminsterfullerene

37. Nitric acid is used in dye and fertilizer manufacture, etching, and the production of explosives.

39. Plants cannot directly incorporate atmospheric nitrogen (N$_2$) into their tissues. Nitrogen-fixing bacteria must first transform it into nitrogen compounds.

41. The three conditions are a temperature of 500°C, a pressure of 10^5 kPa, and an iron oxide catalyst.

43. a. manufacturing of steel
b. to produce sulfuric acid
c. to produce photoelectric cells and other light-sensitive instruments

45. Hydrogen peroxide is used as a bleach and an antiseptic.

47. 20%

49. the manufacture of steel

51. a. 2Mg(s) + O$_2$(g) $\longrightarrow$ 2MgO(s)
b. 2H$_2$(g) + O$_2$(g) $\longrightarrow$ 2H$_2$O(g)
c. S(s) + O$_2$(g) $\longrightarrow$ SO$_2$(g)

53. Sulfur is used mostly for the production of sulfuric acid, which is used extensively in manufacturing fertilizers, in the steel industry, in petroleum refining, and in many other industries.

55. Chlorine in solution is a strong oxidizing agent that kills disease-causing bacteria.

57. Iodine is obtained by reacting sodium iodate with sodium hydrogen sulfite solution to precipitate iodine crystals.

59. Cl$_2$: yellow-green gas; Br$_2$: dark-red liquid;
I$_2$: purple-black crystalline solid

61. Nickel is used to electroplate iron and steel and to catalyze industrial reactions. Monel metal is a strong, corrosion-resistant alloy of nickel and copper.

63. Reduction converts positively charged metal ions in a compound to the free metal.

65. Superheated water and compressed air are sent down two tubes into the sulfur beds. A third tube brings sulfur froth to the surface. Sulfur is not mined because it is found under quicksand.

67. 12.9% Al

69. a. Amounts of Fe$_2$O$_3$: 5.42 × 10^5, 7.89 × 10^5, 1.26 × 10^6, 4.11 × 10^6, 6.02 × 10^6
Amounts of C: 1.63 × 10^6, 2.36 × 10^6, 3.78 × 10^6, 1.23 × 10^7, 1.81 × 10^7

b.

c. slope = 1 mol Fe$_2$O$_3$/3 mol C

71. 35.5% Co in CoAsS; 2.58 × 10^2 kg Co

73. O$_2$ and O$_3$; oxygen gas (O$_2$) is obtained from liquid air by fractional distillation. Ozone (O$_3$) is made by passing an electrical discharge through oxygen gas.

75. a. 3H$_2$(g) + N$_2$(g) $\longrightarrow$ 2NH$_3$(g)
b. H$_2$(g) + Cl$_2$ (g) $\longrightarrow$ 2HCl(g)
c. H$_2$(g) + Ca(s) $\longrightarrow$ CaH$_2$(s)

77. Sulfuric acid is used to prepare fertilizers and to pickle iron and steel. It is also used in petroleum refining and in many other industries.

79. Ammonia is a small, polar molecule with hydrogen bonding. It is covalently bonded, with bond angles similar to those in water.

81. a. 3   **b.** 4

83. All the processes require an input of energy, either electricity or heat. Steam reforming produces poisonous carbon monoxide and requires the use of a nonrenewable resource, natural gas. The method using steam and white-hot coke produces carbon dioxide, which contributes to global warming.

85. Bronze is an alloy mostly of copper and tin. The technology for producing copper and tin was developed relatively easily. The separation of iron from its ore, however, requires much greater heat and more-advanced technology.

87. a. CaO   **c.** CO   **e.** SO$_2$
b. HgO   **d.** Al$_2$O$_3$ **f.** Na$_2$O$_2$

89. a. [Ar]3$d^6$4s^2 **d.** [Ar]3$d^5$4s^2 **g.** [Ar]3d^{10}4s^2
b. [Ar]3$d^3$4s^2 **e.** [Ar]3d^{10}4s^1 **h.** [Kr]4d^{10}
c. [Kr]4d^{10}5s^1 **f.** [Ar]3$d^8$4s^2

91. a. Li$^+$, Br$^-$ **b.** Ca^{2+}, OH$^-$ **c.** K$^+$, I$^-$ **d.** Cd^{2+}, Br$^-$

93. a. 0   **b.** +5   **c.** +4   **d.** +1   **e.** +3

95. CaCO$_3$(s) + 2HCl(aq) $\longrightarrow$ CaCl$_2$(aq) + H$_2$O(l) + CO$_2$(g)

97. 2.7 × 10^{-1} L Cl$_2$

99. a. 1.10 × 10^{-1} mol H$^+$ **b.** 3.67 × 10^1 mL

101. 2.8 × 10^8 kg Br$^-$

103. 1.42 × 10^1 L O$_2$

CHAPTER 25

1.

$$H-\overset{\overset{\displaystyle H}{|}}{\underset{\underset{\displaystyle H}{|}}{C}}-\overset{\overset{\displaystyle H}{|}}{\underset{\underset{\displaystyle H}{|}}{C}}-\overset{\overset{\displaystyle H}{|}}{\underset{\underset{\displaystyle H}{|}}{C}}-\overset{\overset{\displaystyle H}{|}}{\underset{\underset{\displaystyle H}{|}}{C}}-\overset{\overset{\displaystyle H}{|}}{\underset{\underset{\displaystyle H}{|}}{C}}-H \qquad H-\overset{\overset{\displaystyle H}{|}}{\underset{\underset{\displaystyle H}{|}}{C}}-\overset{\overset{\displaystyle H}{|}}{\underset{\underset{\displaystyle H}{|}}{C}}-\overset{\overset{\displaystyle H}{|}}{\underset{\underset{\displaystyle H}{|}}{C}}-\overset{\overset{\displaystyle H}{|}}{\underset{\underset{\displaystyle H}{|}}{C}}-\overset{\overset{\displaystyle H}{|}}{\underset{\underset{\displaystyle H}{|}}{C}}-\overset{\overset{\displaystyle H}{|}}{\underset{\underset{\displaystyle H}{|}}{C}}-H$$

2. 10

3. a. propane   **b.** pentane   **c.** hexane

4. a. 2-methylbutane   **b.** 3-ethylhexane

5.

$$CH_3CHCHCH_2CH_2CH_3$$

with CH_3 above and CH_3 below

6. a.

$$CH_3-CH_2-\underset{\underset{\displaystyle CH_2}{|}}{CH}-CH_2-CH_3$$
with CH_3 above the CH_2

b.

$$CH_3-\underset{\underset{\displaystyle CH_3}{|}}{CH}-\underset{\underset{\displaystyle CH_3}{|}}{CH}-\underset{\underset{\underset{\displaystyle CH_3}{|}}{CH_2}}{\overset{\overset{\displaystyle CH_3}{|}}{C}}-CH_2-CH_2-CH_2-CH_3$$

14. Molecule **b** has an asymmetric carbon, which is marked with an asterisk in the answer.

$$CH_3-\overset{\overset{\displaystyle H}{|}}{\underset{\underset{\displaystyle Cl}{|}}{\overset{*}{C}}}-CHO$$

15. Molecule **d** has an asymmetric carbon; molecules **a, b,** and **c** do not have nonsuperimposable, mirror images because they have no asymmetric carbons.

29. a. propane   **b.** octane   **c.** pentane

31. a. The prefix *di-* means two methyl groups are bonded to the parent chain. Locations of both groups must be identified by a number.
   b. pentane; The longest carbon chain is misidentified.
   c. 2-methylbutane; Lowest numbering for substituent is not followed.
   d. 3-methylpentane; The longest carbon chain is misidentified.

33. The bonds between carbons are nonpolar and carbon-hydrogen bonds are very weakly polar; thus alkanes are nonpolar.

35. a. propene (or 1-propene)
   b. *trans*-2-pentene
   c. 4-methyl-1-pentene
   d. 3-ethyl-2-methyl-2-pentene
   e. 1-hexene

37. Five structural isomers of molecular formula C_6H_{14} exist.

$$C-C-C-C-C-C$$
hexane

$$C-\underset{\underset{\displaystyle C}{|}}{\overset{\overset{\displaystyle C}{|}}{C}}-C-C$$
2, 2-dimethylbutane

$$C-\underset{\underset{\displaystyle C}{|}}{C}-C-C-C$$
2-methylpentane

$$C-\underset{\underset{\displaystyle C}{|}}{C}-\underset{\underset{\displaystyle C}{|}}{C}-C$$
2, 3-dimethylbutane

$$C-C-\underset{\underset{\displaystyle C}{|}}{C}-C-C$$
3-methylpentane

39. a.

trans-2-pentene   *cis*-2-pentene

b.

2-methyl-2-pentene

c.

3-ethyl-2-pentene

41. No; only molecules with a least one asymmetric carbon have stereoisomers.

43. a.

b.

$$CH_3-CH-CH-CH_2-CH_3$$

c.

CH_3- ⬡ $-CH_3$

d.

⬡ $-CH_3$

45. $2C_8H_{18} + 25O_2 \longrightarrow 16CO_2 + 18H_2O$

47. Coal is mostly large aromatic rings.

49. a. single bonds and triple bond; ethyne (acetylene)
   b. single bonds; propane
   c. single bonding within substituents and between substituents and ring; aromatic bonding (alternating single and double bonds) within the ring; methylbenzene

51. propane, butane, pentane

53. The middle structure is most stable due to resonance within its ring.

55. No; The structures are identical; one has been flipped over.

57. Cyclic hydrocarbons are more structurally rigid, so their van der Waals forces are stronger. Thus, it takes more energy (a higher temperature) to liberate these molecules from the liquid state.

59. a. Ca, +2; C, +4; O, −2   **c.** Li, +1; I, +5; O, −2
   b. Cl, 0   **d.** Na, +1; S, +4; O, −2

61. a. $K_{eq} = \dfrac{[ICl]^2}{[I_2][Cl_2]}$ **c.** $K_{eq} = \dfrac{[HCl]^4[S]^3[SO_2]}{[S_2Cl_2]^2[H_2O]^2}$

   b. $K_{eq} = \dfrac{[H_2][Br_2]}{[HBr]^2}$ **d.** $K_{eq} = \dfrac{[NH_3]^2}{[N_2][H_2]^3}$

63. a. ~8   **b.** Use a pH meter.

65. Answers will vary.

CHAPTER 26

21. a. $ClCH_2\overset{\displaystyle Cl}{\underset{\displaystyle Cl}{CCH_2CH_3}}$ **b.**   **c.** (cyclohexane with Cl, Cl on adjacent carbons)

23. a. $\overset{\displaystyle Cl}{\underset{\displaystyle Cl}{CH}}-CH_2-CH_3$
1, 1-dichloropropane

b. $CH_3-CH_2-CH_2-\overset{\displaystyle Br}{CH_2}$
1-bromobutane

$\overset{\displaystyle Cl}{CH_2}-\overset{\displaystyle Cl}{CH}-CH_3$
1, 2-dichloropropane

$CH_3-CH_2-\overset{\displaystyle Br}{CH}-CH_3$
2-bromobutane

$\overset{\displaystyle Cl}{CH_2}-CH_2-\overset{\displaystyle Cl}{CH_2}$
1, 3-dichloropropane

$CH_3-\overset{\displaystyle CH_3}{CH}-\overset{\displaystyle Br}{CH_2}$
1-bromo-2-methylpropane

$CH_3-\overset{\displaystyle Cl}{\underset{\displaystyle Cl}{C}}-CH_3$
2, 2-dichloropropane

$CH_3-\overset{\displaystyle CH_3}{\underset{\displaystyle Br}{C}}-CH_3$
2-bromo-2-methylpropane

25. a. $\overset{\displaystyle Br\ Br}{CH_2CHCH_2CH_3}$ **c.** $\overset{\displaystyle H\ \ H}{CH_3CHCHCH_3}$

b. $\overset{\displaystyle I\ \ I}{CH_3CHCHCH_3}$ **d.** (cyclohexane with Cl, Cl on adjacent carbons)

27. a. ethylmethyl ether
b. ethylphenyl ether
c. divinyl ether or vinyl ether
d. diisopropyl ether or isopropyl ether

29. The alcohol molecules form hydrogen bonds with one another, resulting in a higher boiling point. They also form hydrogen bonds with water molecules, causing 1-butanol to be more soluble than diethyl ether. (Although diethyl ether is polar, l-butanol has greater polarity.)

31. in order of increasing boiling point: propane, propanal, and propanol

33. The short-chain ethanoic acid has a higher water solubility.

35. a. formic acid   **c.** propionic acid
b. acetic acid   **d.** stearic acid

37. a. $CH_3CH_2OH \xrightarrow{K_2Cr_2O_7} CH_3-\overset{\displaystyle O}{\overset{\|}{C}}-H$

b. $CH_3CH_2CHO \xrightarrow{K_2Cr_2O_7} CH_3-CH_2-\overset{\displaystyle O}{\overset{\|}{C}}-OH$

c. $CH_3CH_2\underset{\displaystyle CH_3}{CHOH} \xrightarrow{K_2Cr_2O_7} CH_3-CH_2-\overset{\displaystyle O}{\overset{\|}{C}}-CH_3$

d. (phenyl)$-CH_2CHO \xrightarrow{K_2Cr_2O_7}$ (phenyl)$-CH_2-\overset{\displaystyle O}{\overset{\|}{C}}-OH$

e. $CH_3CH_2\overset{\displaystyle O}{\overset{\|}{C}}CH_3 \xrightarrow{K_2Cr_2O_7}$ no reaction

39. a. $CH_3CH_2COO^-Na^+$, CH_3CH_2OH

b. $CH_3COO^-K^+$, (phenyl)$-OH$

c. CH_3CH_2COOH, $CH_3\underset{\displaystyle CH_3}{CH}CH_2OH$

41. a. $H-\overset{\displaystyle O}{\overset{\|}{C}}-O-CH_3$
methyl methanoate
(methyl formate)

c. $CH_3-\overset{\displaystyle O}{\overset{\|}{C}}-O-CH_2CH_2CH_3$
propyl ethanoate
(propyl acetate)

b. $CH_3CH_2CH_2-\overset{\displaystyle O}{\overset{\|}{C}}-O-CH_2CH_3$
ethyl butanoate
(ethyl butyrate)

43. a. $-CH_2-\underset{\displaystyle \underset{\displaystyle CH_3}{CH_2}}{CH}-$ **b.** $-\overset{}{\underset{\displaystyle Cl}{CH}}-\overset{}{\underset{\displaystyle Cl}{CH}}-$

45. b. CH_3CH_2OH (46) has the highest boiling point.

47. Both atoms in a carbon–carbon double bond have the same electronegativity, so the bond is nonpolar. Because oxygen is more electronegative than carbon, a carbon–oxygen double bond is very polar.

49. a. $CH_3CH_2\overset{\displaystyle Cl}{CH}-\overset{\displaystyle Cl}{CH_2}$ **b.** $CH_3CH_2\overset{\displaystyle Br}{CH}-\overset{\displaystyle Br}{CH_2}$ **c.** (cyclohexane with H and Br)

51. The chemical properties (and toxicity) of organic compounds are determined by the compound as a whole. As a substituent in a molecule, a phenyl group ring does not have the same properties as benzene.

53. At any given moment, the rate of dissolving of solute is equal to the rate of precipitation of solute. As a result, the concentration of the solution remains constant.

55. a. $:\!\dot{F}\!: + e^- \longrightarrow \ :\!\ddot{F}\!:^-$ **b.** $H\cdot + :\!\dot{O}\!: + e^- \longrightarrow (:\!\ddot{O}\!:H)^-$

57. Cholesterol is an alcohol with a hydroxyl group on a cycloalkane. It has four nonaromatic rings. It has a double bond on one of its rings, as well as a large alkyl group, making it nonpolar.

23. The glucose produced during photosynthesis is used by both plants and animals to fuel the synthesis of more complex biomolecules.

25. Glucose and fructose are two important monosaccharides.

27. Glucose contains an aldehyde functional group; fructose contains a ketone functional group.

29. a. glucose   **b.** glucose

31. Ser—Gly—Phe contains two peptide bonds.

33. Peptide chains commonly fold into spiral shapes called helixes and into sheets in which peptide chains lie side by side.

35. Fats are solid at room temperature and oils are liquid; most fats are animal products, and most oils are plant products.

37. A soap is the alkali metal salt of a fatty acid.

39.

41. deoxyribonucleic acid (DNA) and ribonucleic acid (RNA)

43. Ribose, the sugar unit in RNA, has one more oxygen than deoxyribose, the sugar in DNA.

45. No; there are termination code words that signal the end of a peptide chain in protein synthesis; they do not specify an amino acid.

47. The addition, deletion, or substitution of one or more bases of DNA causes a gene mutation.

49. These complex biomolecules are either the carbohydrates, lipids, and proteins in your diet, or they are the carbohydrates, lipids, and proteins of your own body.

51. Catabolism and anabolism are complementary sets of reactions of metabolism. In catabolism, large biomolecules are broken down and energy is captured in the production of ATP. In anabolism, the products and energy from catabolism are used to make cell parts and other compounds.

53. Glycogen, a polysaccharide produced by animals, is more highly branched than are plant starches.

55. Sucrose gives glucose and fructose when hydrolyzed. The structures are

$$
\begin{array}{cc}
\text{CHO} & \text{CH}_2\text{OH} \\
\text{H}-\text{C}-\text{OH} & \text{C}=\text{O} \\
\text{HO}-\text{C}-\text{H} & \text{HO}-\text{C}-\text{H} \\
\text{H}-\text{C}-\text{OH} & \text{H}-\text{C}-\text{OH} \\
\text{H}-\text{C}-\text{OH} & \text{H}-\text{C}-\text{OH} \\
\text{CH}_2\text{OH} & \text{CH}_2\text{OH} \\
\text{Glucose} & \text{Fructose}
\end{array}
$$

57. The active site is the physical location on an enzyme molecule where the substrate binds and is converted to products.

59.
$$
\underset{\text{Sodium palmitate}}{CH_3(CH_2)_{14} - \overset{\displaystyle O}{\overset{\|}{C}} - O^-Na^+}
$$

61. a. Arg—Gly—Cys—Asn   **b.** Arg—Gly—Cys—Asn

63. The peptide is Met—Arg—Val—Tyr.

65. Molecular diseases result from faulty genes. Sickle cell anemia, methemoglobinemia, and alcaptonuria are examples of molecular diseases.

67. In theory, gene therapy could be used to transplant a normal gene into an individual who has a faulty version of that gene, thereby curing a molecular disease.

69. Gene mutations will occur. The mutations may be beneficial, harmful, or neutral to the individual and to the species.

71. Deep breathing provides a large supply of oxygen for energy-producing cell processes and rids the body of excess carbon dioxide.

73. a. (1) oxygen   **b.** (4) amino acid

75. Base pairs are inside the double helix; strands must unwind for the bases to be recognized.

77. The equivalents of acid must equal the equivalents of base.

79. 1-chlorobutane, 2-chlorobutane, 1-chloro-2-methylpropane, 2-chloro-2-methylpropane

81. a. fluorine   **b.** oxygen   **c.** chlorine

83. The molecule must have at least one asymmetric carbon.

85.
$$
\begin{array}{ll}
CH_2OH & CH_3(CH_2)_{14} - \overset{\displaystyle O}{\overset{\|}{C}} - O^-Na^+ \\
| & \\
CHOII \; + & CH_3(CH_2)_{12} - \overset{\displaystyle O}{\overset{\|}{C}} - O^-Na^+ \\
| & \\
CH_2OH & CH_3(CH_2)_{16} - \overset{\displaystyle O}{\overset{\|}{C}} - O^-Na^+ \\
\text{Glycerol} & \text{Sodium salts of three} \\
& \text{fatty acid molecules}
\end{array}
$$

CHAPTER 28

4. 0.063 mg Mn-56

5. No; one fourth of the sample will remain.

23. $^{226}_{88}Ra \longrightarrow ^{222}_{86}Rn + ^{4}_{2}He$

25. a. α, 2+   **b.** β, 1−   **c.** γ, 0

27. a. $^{14}_{6}C \longrightarrow ^{14}_{7}N + ^{0}_{-1}e$
  b. $^{90}_{38}Sr \longrightarrow ^{90}_{39}Y + ^{0}_{-1}e$
  c. $^{40}_{19}K \longrightarrow ^{40}_{20}Ca + ^{0}_{-1}e$
  d. $^{13}_{7}N \longrightarrow ^{13}_{8}O + ^{0}_{-1}e$

29. a. $^{234}_{92}U$ **b.** $^{206}_{81}Tl$ **c.** $^{206}_{82}Pb$ **d.** $^{226}_{88}Ra$

31. $^{17}_{9}F \longrightarrow ^{17}_{8}O + ^{0}_{+1}e$

33. a. platinum   **d.** technetium   **g.** vanadium
  b. thorium   **e.** xenon   **h.** palladium
  c. francium   **f.** californium

  Francium (**c**), technetium (**d**), and californium (**f**) have no stable isotopes.

35. One half-life is the time required for one-half of the atoms of a radioisotope to emit radiation and decay.

37. Natural radioactivity comes from radioactive elements present in nature. Artificial radioactivity comes from elements created in nuclear reactors and accelerators.

39. The nuclei of certain isotopes are bombarded with neutrons. The nuclei break into two fragments and release more neutrons. The released neutrons hit other nuclei to start a chain reaction that releases large amounts of energy.

41. Fusion requires extremely high temperatures, which would destroy any container.

43. The film badge measures radiation exposure; an exposed film badge indicates how much radiation a worker has received.

45. a. $^{30}_{15}P + ^{0}_{-1}e \longrightarrow ^{30}_{14}Si$
  b. $^{13}_{6}C + ^{1}_{0}n \longrightarrow ^{14}_{6}C$
  c. $^{131}_{53}I \longrightarrow ^{131}_{54}Xe + ^{0}_{-1}e$

47. a. $^{32}_{16}S$ **b.** $^{14}_{6}C$ **c.** $^{4}_{2}He$ **d.** $^{141}_{57}La$ **e.** $^{185}_{79}Au$

49. a. about 20%
  b. about 85 g
  c. about 83 days
  d. 25 days

51. a. Named radioactivity and discovered several radioactive elements.
  b. Discovered natural radioactivity from uranium ores.
  c. Discovered the neutron.
  d. Transmuted elements.

53. In every round of the tournament, one-half the teams are eliminated; in every half-life, one-half of the substance decays. In the tournament a single team eventually emerges as the winner and the tournament stops, but radioactive decay continues (almost) indefinitely.

55. Radioactive isotopes of these elements can be incorporated into the body tissues of organisms. When the isotopes decay, they can damage tissues very easily.

57. a. $Ca(OH)_2 + 2HCl \longrightarrow CaCl_2 + 2H_2O$
  b. $Fe_2O_3 + 3H_2 \longrightarrow 2Fe + 3H_2O$
  c. $2NaHCO_3 + H_2SO_4 \longrightarrow Na_2SO_4 + 2CO_2 + 2H_2O$
  d. $2C_2H_6 + 7O_2 \longrightarrow 4CO_2 + 6H_2O$

59. a. 26 p$^+$, 26 e$^-$, 33 n
  b. 92 p$^+$, 92 e$^-$, 143 n
  c. 24 p$^+$, 24 e$^-$, 28 n

61. 9216 cm^3 H$_2$; 0.4114 mol H$_2$

63. This graph shows the radioactive decay of carbon-14, along with the increase of the nitrogen product.

65. Bismuth-214 remains.

GLOSSARY

A

absolute zero the zero point on the Kelvin temperature scale, equivalent to −273.15 °C; all molecular motion theoretically stops at this temperature. *3.5*

accepted value a quantity used by general agreement of the scientific community. *3.2*

accuracy the closeness of a measurement to the true value of what is being measured. *3.2*

acid a compound that produces hydrogen ions in solution, is a hydrogen-ion donor, or an electron-pair acceptor. *20.1*

acid dissociation constant (K_a) the ratio of the concentration of the dissociated form of an acid to the undissociated form; stronger acids have larger K_a values than weaker acids. *20.4*

acidic solution any solution in which the hydrogen-ion concentration is greater than the hydroxide-ion concentration. *20.2*

activated complex an unstable arrangement of atoms that exists momentarily at the peak of the activation-energy barrier; an intermediate or transitional structure formed during the course of a reaction. *19.1*

activation energy the minimum energy colliding particles must have in order to react. *19.1*

active site a groove or pocket in an enzyme molecule into which the substrate (reactant molecule) fits; where the substrate is converted to products. *27.3*

activity series of metals a table listing metals in order of decreasing activity. *8.2*

actual yield the amount of product that forms when a reaction is carried out in the laboratory. *9.3*

addition reaction a reaction in which a substance is added at the double bond of an alkene or at the triple bond of an alkyne. *26.2*

adenosine triphosphate (ATP) a molecule that transmits the energy needed by cells of all living things. *27.6*

alcohol an organic compound having an —OH (hydroxyl) group; the general structure is R—OH. *26.2*

aldehyde an organic compound in which the carbon of the carbonyl group is joined to at least one hydrogen; the general formula is RCHO. *26.3*

aliphatic compound a hydrocarbon compound that does not contain a ring structure. *25.4*

alkali metal any metal in Group 1A of the periodic table. *5.4*

alkaline earth metal any metal in Group 2A of the periodic table. *5.4*

alkaline solution a basic solution. *20.2*

alkane a hydrocarbon containing only single covalent bonds; alkanes are saturated hydrocarbons. *25.1*

alkene a hydrocarbon containing one or more carbon–carbon double bonds; alkenes are unsaturated hydrocarbons. *25.2*

alkyl group a hydrocarbon substituent; the methyl group (—CH_3) is an alkyl group. *25.1*

alkyl halide a halocarbon in which one or more halogen atoms are attached to the carbon atoms of an aliphatic chain. *26.1*

alkyne a hydrocarbon containing a carbon–carbon triple bond; alkynes are unsaturated hydrocarbons. *25.2*

allotrope one of two or more different molecular forms of an element in the same physical state; oxygen (O_2) and ozone (O_3) are allotropes of the element oxygen. *10.3*

alpha particle a positively charged particle emitted from certain radioactive nuclei; it consists of two protons and two neutrons and is identical to the nucleus of a helium atom. *28.1*

alpha radiation alpha particles emitted from a radioactive source. *28.1*

amino acid an organic compound having amino (—NH_2) and carboxylic acid (—COOH) groups in the same molecule; proteins are made from the 20 naturally occurring amino acids. *27.3*

amino acid sequence the order in which amino acids are linked in a peptide or protein molecule. *27.3*

amorphous solid a term used to describe a solid that lacks an ordered internal structure; denotes a random arrangement of atoms. *10.3*

amphoteric a substance that can act as both an acid and a base; water is amphoteric. *20.3*

amplitude the height of a wave from the origin to the crest. *13.3*

anabolism synthetic processes in the metabolism of cells; which usually require the expenditure of energy. *27.6*

analytical chemistry the study of the composition of substances. *1.1*

anion any atom or group of atoms with a negative charge. *6.1*

anode the electrode at which oxidation occurs. *23.1*

antibonding orbital a molecular orbital with an energy that is higher than that of the atomic orbitals from which it is formed. *16.2*

aqueous solution (*aq*) a solution in which the solvent is water. *17.3*

arene any member of a special group of unsaturated cyclic hydrocarbons. *25.4*

aromatic compound a name originally given to the arenes because many of them have pleasant odors; any compound with bonding like that of benzene. *25.4*

aryl halide a halocarbon in which one or more halogens are attached to the carbon atoms of an arene ring. *26.1*

asymmetric carbon a carbon atom that has four different groups attached. *25.3*

atmospheric pressure the pressure exerted by air molecules in the atmosphere surrounding Earth, resulting from collisions of air molecules with objects. *10.1*

atom the smallest particle of an element that retains the properties of that element. *5.1*

atomic emission spectrum the pattern of frequencies obtained by passing light emitted by atoms of an element in the gaseous state through a prism; the emission spectrum of each element is unique to that element. *13.3*

atomic mass the weighted average of the masses of the isotopes of an element. *5.3*

atomic mass unit (amu) a unit of mass equal to one-twelfth the mass of a carbon-12 atom. *5.3*

atomic number the number of protons in the nucleus of an atom of an element. *5.3*

atomic orbital a region in space around the nucleus of an atom where there is a high probability of finding an electron. *13.1*

atomic radius one-half the distance between the nuclei in a molecule consisting of identical atoms. *14.2*

Aufbau principle electrons enter orbitals of lowest energy first. *13.2*

Avogadro's hypothesis equal volumes of gases at the same temperature and pressure contain equal numbers of particles. *12.5*

Avogadro's number the number of representative particles contained in one mole of a substance; equal to 6.02×10^{23} particles. *7.1*

B

balanced equation a chemical equation in which mass is conserved; each side of the equation has the same number of atoms of each element. *8.1*

band of stability the location of stable nuclei on a neutron-vs-proton plot. *28.2*

barometer an instrument used to measure atmospheric pressure. *10.1*

base a compound that produces hydroxide ions in solution, is a hydrogen-ion acceptor, or an electron-pair donor. *20.1*

base dissociation constant (K_b) the ratio of the concentration of the dissociated form of a base to the undissociated form. *20.4*

basic solution any solution in which the hydroxide-ion concentration is greater than the hydrogen-ion concentration. *20.2*

battery a group of voltaic cells that are connected to one another. *23.1*

Benedict's test a test commonly used to detect the presence of aldehydes. *26.3*

beta particle a fast-moving electron emitted from certain radioactive nuclei; it is formed when a neutron decomposes into a proton and an electron. *28.1*

beta radiation fast-moving electrons (beta particles) emitted from a radioactive source. *28.1*

binary compound a compound composed of two elements; NaCl and Al_2O_3 are binary compounds. *6.4*

biochemistry the study of the composition and behavior of substances in living organisms. *1.1*

boiling point (bp) the temperature at which the vapor pressure of a liquid is just equal to the external pressure on the liquid. *10.2*

boiling-point elevation the difference in temperature between the boiling point of a solution and of the pure solvent. *18.3*

bond dissociation energy the amount of energy required to break a covalent bond between atoms; this value is usually expressed in kJ per mol of substance. *16.1*

bonding orbital a molecular orbital whose energy is lower than that of the atomic orbitals from which it is formed. *16.2*

Boyle's law for a fixed mass of gas at constant temperature, the volume of the gas varies inversely with pressure. *12.3*

branched-chain alkane an alkane with one or more alkyl groups attached. *25.1*

Brownian motion the chaotic movement of colloidal particles, caused by collision with particles of the solvent in which they are dispersed. *17.4*

buffer a solution in which the pH remains relatively constant when small amounts of acid or base are added; a buffer can be either a solution of a weak acid and the salt of a weak acid or a solution of a weak base with the salt of a weak base. *21.2*

buffer capacity a measure of the amount of acid or base that may be added to a buffer solution before a significant change in pH occurs. *21.2*

C

calorie (cal) the quantity of heat that raises the temperature of 1 g of pure water 1 °C. *11.1*

calorimeter a device for measuring heat changes. *11.2*

calorimetry the measurement of heat changes for physical and chemical processes. *11.2*

carbohydrate the name given to monomers and polymers of aldehydes and ketones that have numerous hydroxyl groups; sugars and starches are carbohydrates. *27.2*

carbonyl group a functional group having a carbon atom and an oxygen atom joined by a double bond;

it is found in aldehydes, ketones, esters, and amides. *26.3*

carboxyl group a functional group consisting of a carbonyl group attached to a hydroxyl group;

it is found in carboxylic acids. *26.3*

carboxylic acid an organic acid containing a carboxyl group; the general formula is RCOOH. *26.3*

catabolism the reactions in living cells in which substances are broken down and energy is produced. *27.6*

catalyst a substance that increases the rate of reaction by lowering the activation-energy barrier; the catalyst is not used up. *8.1, 19.1*

cathode the electrode at which reduction occurs. *23.1*

cathode ray a stream of electrons produced at the negative electrode (cathode) of a tube containing a gas at low pressure. *5.2*

cation any atom or group of atoms with a positive charge. *6.1*

cell membrane the partition made of phospholipids and proteins that forms the outermost edge of the cell; it is the barrier between the cell and its environment. *27.1*

cell potential the difference between the reduction potentials of two half-cells. *23.2*

Celsius scale the temperature scale on which the freezing point of water is 0 °C and the boiling point is 100 °C. *3.5*

Charles's law the volume of a fixed mass of gas is directly proportional to its Kelvin temperature if the pressure is kept constant. *12.3*

chemical equation an expression representing a chemical reaction; the formulas of the reactants (on the left) are connected by an arrow with the formulas for the products (on the right). *8.1*

chemical equilibrium a state of balance in which forward and reverse reactions are taking place at the same rate; no net change in the amounts of reactants and products occurs in the chemical system. *19.2*

chemical formula shows the number and type of atoms present in the smallest representative unit of a substance; the chemical formula of ammonia, with one nitrogen and three hydrogens, is NH_3. *6.2*

chemical potential energy energy stored within the structural units of chemical substances. *11.1*

chemical property the ability of a substance to undergo chemical reactions and to form new substances. *2.4*

chemical reaction the changing of substances to other substances by the breaking of bonds in reactants and the formation of bonds in products. *2.4*

chemical symbol a one or two letter representation of an element. *2.3*

chemistry the study of the structure, properties, and composition of substances, and the changes that substances undergo. *1.1*

cis configuration a term applied to geometric isomers; it denotes an arrangement in which the substituted groups are on the same side of the double bond. *25.3*

coefficient a small whole number that appears in front of a formula in a balanced chemical equation. *8.1*

coenzyme a small organic molecule or metal ion necessary for an enzyme's biological activity. *27.3*

colligative properties a property of a solution that depends only on the number of the solute particles; boiling-point elevation, freezing-point depression, and vapor-pressure lowering are colligative properties. *18.3*

collision theory atoms, ions, and molecules can react to form products when they collide, provided that the particles have enough kinetic energy. *19.1*

colloid a mixture whose particles are intermediate in size between those of a suspension and a solute solution. *17.4*

combination reaction a chemical change in which two or more substances react to form a single new substance; also called a synthesis reaction. *8.2*

combined gas law a relationship describing the behavior of gases that combines Boyle's law, Charles's law, and Gay-Lussac's law. *12.3*

combustion reaction a chemical change in which oxygen reacts with another substance, often producing energy in the form of heat and light. *8.2*

common ion an ion that is common to both salts in a solution; in a solution of silver nitrate and silver chloride, Ag^+ would be a common ion. *21.2*

common ion effect a decrease in the solubility of a substance caused by the addition of a common ion. *21.2*

complete ionic equation an equation for a reaction in solution showing all strong electrolytes as ions. *8.3*

compound a substance that can be separated into simpler substances (elements or other compounds) only by chemical reactions. *2.3*

compressibility a measure of how much the volume of matter decreases under pressure. *12.1*

concentrated solution a solution containing a large amount of solute. *18.2*

concentration a measurement of the amount of solute that is dissolved in a given quantity of solvent; usually expressed as mol/L. *18.2*

condensed structural formula a structural formula that leaves out some bonds and/or atoms; the presence of these atoms or bonds is understood. *25.1*

conjugate acid the particle formed when a base gains a hydrogen ion; NH_4^+ is the conjugate acid of the base NH_3. *20.3*

conjugate acid-base pair two substances that are related by the loss or gain of a single hydrogen ion. Ammonia (NH_3) and the ammonium ion (NH_4^+) are a conjugate acid-base pair. *20.3*

conjugate base the particle that remains when an acid has donated a hydrogen ion; OH^- is the conjugate base of the acid water. *20.3*

conversion factor a ratio of equivalent measurements used to convert a quantity from one unit to another. *4.2*

coordinate covalent bond a covalent bond formed when one atom contributes both bonding electrons. *16.1*

coordination number the number of ions of opposite charge that surround each ion in a crystal. *15.2*

cracking the controlled process by which hydrocarbons are broken down or rearranged into smaller, more useful molecules. *25.5*

crystal a substance in which the atoms, ions, or molecules are arranged in an orderly, repeating, three-dimensional pattern called a crystal lattice. *10.3*

cyclic hydrocarbon an organic compound that contains a hydrocarbon ring. *25.4*

D

Dalton's atomic theory the first theory to relate chemical changes to events at the atomic level. *5.1*

Dalton's law of partial pressures at constant volume and temperature, the total pressure of a mixture of gases is the sum of the partial pressures of all the gases present. *12.5*

de Broglie's equation an equation that describes the wavelength of a moving particle; it predicts that all matter exhibits wavelike motions. *13.3*

decomposition reaction a chemical change in which a single compound is broken down into two or more simpler products. *8.2*

dehydrogenation reaction a reaction in which hydrogen is lost. *26.3*

deliquescent a term describing a substance that removes sufficient water from the air to form a solution; the solution formed has a lower vapor pressure than that of the water in the air. *17.3*

denatured alcohol ethanol to which a poisonous substance has been added to make it unfit to drink. *26.2*

density the ratio of the mass of an object to its volume. *3.4*

desiccant a hygroscopic substance used as a drying agent. *17.3*

diamagnetic a substance that is weakly repelled by a magnetic field. *16.1*

diffusion the tendency of molecules and ions to move toward areas of lower concentration until the concentration is uniform throughout the system. *12.5*

dilute solution a solution that contains a small amount of solute. *18.2*

dimensional analysis a technique of problem-solving that uses the units that are part of a measurement to help solve the problem. *4.2*

dipole a molecule that has two electrically charged regions, or poles. *16.3*

dipole interaction a weak intermolecular force resulting from the attraction of oppositely charged regions of polar molecules. *16.3*

diprotic acid any acid that contains two ionizable protons (hydrogen ions); sulfuric acid (H_2SO_4) is a diprotic acid. *20.3*

disaccharide a carbohydrate formed from two monosaccharide units; common table sugar (sucrose) is a disaccharide. *27.2*

dispersion force the weakest kind of intermolecular attraction; this attraction is thought to be caused by the motion of electrons. *16.3*

distillation a purification process in which a liquid is evaporated and then condensed again to a liquid; used to separate dissolved solids from liquids or liquids from liquids according to boiling point. *2.2*

double covalent bond a covalent bond in which two pairs of electrons are shared by two atoms. *16.1*

double-replacement reaction a chemical change that involves an exchange of positive ions between two compounds. *8.2*

dry cell a commercial voltaic cell in which the electrolyte is a moist paste; despite their name, the compact, portable batteries used in flashlights are dry cells. *23.1*

E

effloresce to lose water of hydration; the process occurs when the hydrate has a vapor pressure higher than that of water vapor in the air. *17.3*

effusion a process that occurs when a gas escapes through a tiny hole in its container. *12.5*

electrical potential the ability of a voltaic cell to produce an electric current. *23.2*

electrochemical cell any device that converts chemical energy into electrical energy or electrical energy into chemical energy. *23.1*

electrochemical process the conversion of chemical energy into electrical energy or electrical energy into chemical energy; all electrochemical processes involve redox reactions. *23.1*

electrode a conductor in a circuit that carries electrons to or from a substance other than a metal. *23.1*

electrolysis a process in which electrical energy is used to bring about a chemical change; the electrolysis of water produces hydrogen and oxygen. *23.3*

electrolyte a compound that conducts an electric current in aqueous solution or in the molten state; all ionic compounds are electrolytes, but most covalent compounds are not. *17.3*

electrolytic cell an electrochemical cell used to cause a chemical change through the application of electrical energy. *23.3*

electromagnetic radiation a series of energy waves that travel in a vacuum at 3.0×10^{10} cm/s; includes radio waves, microwaves, visible light, infrared and ultraviolet light, x-rays, and gamma rays. *13.3*

electron a negatively charged subatomic particle. *5.2*

electron configuration the arrangement of electrons around the nucleus of an atom in its ground state. *13.2*

electron dot structure a notation that depicts valence electrons as dots around the atomic symbol of the element; the symbol represents the inner electrons and atomic nucleus; also called Lewis dot structures. *15.1*

electronegativity the tendency for an atom to attract electrons to itself when it is chemically combined with another element. *14.2*

element a substance that cannot be changed into simpler substances under normal laboratory conditions. *2.3*

elementary reaction a reaction in which reactants are converted to products in a single step. *19.5*

empirical formula a formula with the lowest whole-number ratio of elements in a compound; the empirical formula of hydrogen peroxide (H_2O_2) is HO. *7.3*

emulsion the colloidal dispersion of one liquid in another. *17.4*

endothermic process a heat-absorbing process. *11.1*

end point the point in a titration at which neutralization is achieved. *21.1*

energy the capacity for doing work; it exists in several forms, including chemical, nuclear, electrical, radiant, mechanical, and thermal energies. *11.1*

energy level a region around the nucleus of an atom where an electron is likely to be moving. *13.1*

enthalpy (H) the heat content of a system at constant pressure. *11.2*

entropy (S) a measure of the disorder of a system; systems tend to go from a state of order (low entropy) to a state of maximum disorder (high entropy). *19.3*

enzyme proteins that act as biological catalysts; most of the reactions that occur in cells require catalysts. *27.3*

enzyme–substrate complex the structure formed when a substrate molecule joins an enzyme at its active site. *27.3*

equilibrium constant (K_{eq}) the ratio of product concentrations to reactant concentrations at equilibrium with each concentration raised to a power equal to the number of moles of that substance in the balanced chemical equation. *19.2*

equilibrium position the relative concentrations of reactants and products of a reaction that has reached equilibrium; indicates whether the reactants or products are favored in the reversible reaction. *19.2*

equivalence point the point in a titration at which the number of equivalents of acid and base are equal. *21.1*

equivalent (equiv) one equivalent is the amount of an acid (or base) that can give one mole of hydrogen (or hydroxide) ions. *21.1*

error the difference between the accepted value and the experimental value. *3.2*

ester a derivative of a carboxylic acid in which the —OH of the carbonyl group has been replaced by the —OR from an alcohol; the general formula is RCOOR. *26.3*

ether an organic compound in which oxygen is bonded to two carbon groups; the general formula is R—O—R. *26.2*

evaporation vaporization that occurs at the surface of a liquid that is not boiling. *10.2*

excess reagent a reagent present in a quantity that is more than sufficient to react with a limiting reagent; any reactant that remains after the limiting reagent is used up in a chemical reaction. *9.3*

exothermic process a heat-dissipating process. *11.1*

experiment a carefully controlled, repeatable procedure for gathering data to test a hypothesis. *1.3*

experimental value a quantitative value measured during an experiment. *3.2*

F

fatty acid the name given to continuous-chain carboxylic acids that were first isolated from fats. *26.3*

Fehling's test a test used to detect aldehydes. *26.3*

fermentation the production of ethanol from sugars by the action of yeast or bacteria. *26.2*

film badge a small radiation detector worn by persons who work near radiation sources; it consists of several layers of photographic film covered with black lightproof paper encased in a plastic or metal holder. *28.4*

first-order reaction a reaction in which the reaction rate is proportional to the concentration of only one reactant. *19.5*

fission the splitting of a nucleus into smaller fragments, accompanied by the release of neutrons and a large amount of energy. *28.3*

formula unit the lowest whole-number ratio of ions in an ionic compound; in magnesium chloride, the ratio of magnesium ions to chloride ions is 1:2 and the formula unit is $MgCl_2$. *6.2*

free energy the energy available to do work. *19.3*

freezing-point depression the difference in temperature between the freezing point of a solution and of the pure solvent. *18.3*

frequency (v) the number of wave cycles that pass a given point per unit of time; there is an inverse relationship between the frequency and wavelength of a wave. *13.3*

fuel cell a voltaic cell that does not need to be recharged; the fuel is oxidized to produce a continuous supply of electrical energy. *23.1*

functional group a specific arrangement of atoms in an organic compound that is capable of characteristic chemical reactions; the chemistry of an organic compound is determined by its functional groups. *26.1*

fusion a reaction in which two light nuclei combine to produce a nucleus of heavier mass, accompanied by the release of a large amount of energy. *28.3*

G

gamma radiation high energy electromagnetic radiation emitted by certain radioactive nuclei; gamma rays have no mass or electrical charge. *28.1*

gas matter that has no definite shape or volume; it adopts the shape and volume of its container. *2.1*

gas pressure the force exerted by a gas per unit surface area of an object; due to collisions of gas particles with the object. *10.1*

Gay-Lussac's law the pressure and Kelvin temperature of a gas are directly proportional at constant volume. *12.3*

Geiger counter a gas-filled metal tube used to detect the presence of beta radiation. *28.4*

gene a segment of DNA that codes for a single protein; any alteration in the base sequence (a mutation) affects protein synthesis. *27.5*

genetic code the arrangement of code words in DNA; there are 61 triplet code words used to specify the amino acids in protein synthesis plus 3 triplet code words that signal "stop" after the protein synthesis is complete. *27.5*

geometric isomer an organic compound that differs from another compound only in the geometry of their substituted groups. *25.3*

Gibbs free energy change (ΔG) the maximum amount of energy that can be coupled to another process to do useful work. *19.4*

glass the optically transparent fusion product of inorganic materials that have cooled to a rigid state without crystallizing. *10.3*

Graham's laws of effusion the rate of effusion of a gas is inversely proportional to the square root of its molar mass; this relationship is also true for the diffusion of gases. *12.5*

gram (g) a metric mass unit equal to the mass of 1 cm^3 of water at 4 °C. *3.3*

gram atomic mass (gam) the mass, in grams, of one mole of atoms in a monatomic element; it is numerically equal to the atomic mass in amu. *7.1*

gram equivalent mass the mass of one equivalent of a substance. *21.1*

gram formula mass (gfm) the mass of one mole of an ionic compound. *7.1*

gram molecular mass (gmm) the mass, in grams, of one mole of a molecular substance. *7.1*

ground state the lowest energy level occupied by an electron when an atom is in its most stable energy state. *13.3*

group a vertical column of elements in the periodic table; the constituent elements of a group have similar chemical and physical properties. *5.4*

H

half-cell the part of a voltaic cell in which either oxidation or reduction occurs; it consists of a single electrode immersed in a solution of its ions. *23.1*

half-life ($t_{\frac{1}{2}}$) the time required for one-half of the atoms of a radioisotope to emit radiation and decay to products. *28.2*

half-reaction an equation showing either the reduction or the oxidation of a species in an oxidation–reduction reaction. *22.3*

half-reaction method a method of balancing a redox equation by balancing the oxidation and reduction half-reactions. *22.3*

halide ion a negative ion formed when a halogen atom gains an electron. *15.1*

halocarbon any member of a class of organic compounds containing covalently bonded fluorine, chlorine, bromine, or iodine. *26.1*

halogen any member of the nonmetallic elements in Group 7A of the periodic table. *5.4*

heat (q) the energy that is transferred from one body to another because of a temperature difference. *11.1*

heat capacity the quantity of heat required to change an object's temperature by exactly 1 °C. *11.1*

heat of combustion the heat released during a chemical reaction in which one mole of a substance is completely burned. *11.2*

heat of reaction the heat released or absorbed during a chemical reaction; equivalent to h, the change in enthalpy. *11.2*

Heisenberg uncertainty principle it is impossible to know both the velocity and the position of a particle at the same time. *13.3*

Henry's law at a given temperature the solubility of a gas in a liquid is directly proportional to the pressure of the gas above the liquid. *18.1*

hertz (Hz) the SI unit of frequency, equal to one cycle per second. *13.3*

Hess's law of heat summation in going from a particular set of reactants to a particular set of products, the enthalpy change is the same whether the reaction takes place in one step or in a series of steps. *11.4*

heterogeneous mixture a mixture that is not uniform in composition; its components are readily distinguished. *2.2*

homogeneous mixture a mixture that is completely uniform in composition; its components are not readily distinguished. *2.2*

homologous series a group of compounds in which there is a constant increment of change in molecular structure from one compound in the series to the next. *25.1*

Hund's rule when electrons occupy orbitals of equal energy, one electron enters each orbital until all orbitals contain one electron with their spins parallel. *13.2*

hybridization a process in which several atomic orbitals (such as *s* and *p* orbitals) mix to form the same number of equivalent hybrid orbitals. *16.2*

hydration reaction a reaction in which water is added to an alkene. *26.2*

hydrocarbon an organic compound that contains only carbon and hydrogen. *25.1*

hydrogenation reaction a reaction in which hydrogen is added to a carbon–carbon double bond to give an alkane. *26.2*

hydrogen bond a relatively strong intermolecular force in which a hydrogen atom that is covalently bonded to a very electronegative atom is also weakly bonded to an unshared electron pair of another electronegative atom in the same molecule or one nearby. *16.3*

hydrogen-ion acceptor a base, according to the Brønsted-Lowry theory; ammonia acts as a base when it accepts hydrogen ions from water. *20.3*

hydrogen-ion donor an acid, according to the Brønsted-Lowry theory. *20.3*

hydrometer a device used to measure the specific gravity of a liquid. *3.4*

hydronium ion (H_3O^+) the positive ion formed when a water molecule gains a hydrogen ion; all hydrogen ions in aqueous solution are present as hydronium ions. *20.2*

hydroxide ion (OH^-) the negative ion formed when a water molecule loses a hydrogen ion. *20.2*

hydroxyl group the —OH functional group present in alcohols. *26.2*

hygroscopic a term describing salts and other compounds that remove moisture from the air. *17.3*

hypothesis a proposed explanation for observations. *1.3*

I

ideal gas constant (R) a term in the ideal gas law, which has the value 8.31 (L × kPa)/(K × mol). *12.4*

ideal gas law the relationship $P \times V = n \times R \times T$, which describes the behavior of an ideal gas. *12.4*

immiscible describes liquids that are insoluble in one another; oil and water are immiscible. *18.1*

inhibitor a substance that interferes with the action of a catalyst. *19.1*

inner transition element *see* inner transition metal. *24.3*

inner transition metal an element in the lanthanide and actinide series; characterized by addition of electrons to *f* orbitals. *5.4, 14.1*

inorganic chemistry primarily the study of substances that do not contain carbon. *1.1*

intermediate a product of a reaction that immediately becomes a reactant of another reaction. *19.5*

International System of Units (SI) the revised version of the metric system, adopted by international agreement in 1960. *3.3*

ion an atom or group of atoms that has a positive or negative charge; cations are ions with a positive charge, and anions are ions with a negative charge. *6.1*

ionic bond the electrostatic attraction that binds oppositely charged ions together. *15.2*

ionic compound a compound composed of positive and negative ions. *6.1*

ionization energy the energy required to remove an electron from a gaseous atom. *14.2*

ionizing radiation radiation with enough energy to produce ions by knocking electrons off some atoms of a bombarded substance. *28.4*

ion-product constant for water (K_w) the product of the hydrogen ion and hydroxide ion concentrations in water; it is 1×10^{-14} at 25 °C. *20.2*

isotopes atoms of the same element that have the same atomic number but different atomic masses due to a different number of neutrons. *5.3*

J

joule (j) the SI unit of energy; 4.184 J equal one calorie. *11.1*

K

Kelvin scale the temperature scale in which the freezing point of water is 273 K and the boiling point is 373 K; 0 K is absolute zero. *3.5*

ketone an organic compound in which the carbon of the carbonyl group is joined to two other carbons; the general formula is RCOR. *26.3*

kilogram (kg) the mass of 1 L of water at 4 °C; it is the base unit of mass in SI. *3.3*

kinetic energy the energy an object has because of its motion. *10.1*

kinetic theory a theory explaining the states of matter, based on the concept that the particles in all forms of matter are in constant motion. *10.1*

L

law of conservation of energy energy is neither created nor destroyed in an ordinary chemical or physical process. *11.1*

law of conservation of mass mass can be neither created nor destroyed in an ordinary chemical or physical process. *2.4*

law of definite proportions in any sample of a chemical compound, the elements are always combined in the same proportion by mass. *6.2*

law of disorder it is a natural tendency of systems to move in the direction of maximum chaos or disorder. *19.3*

law of multiple proportions whenever two elements form more than one compound, the different masses of one element that combine with the same mass of the other element are in the ratio of small whole numbers. *6.2*

Le Châtelier's principle when stress is applied to a system at equilibrium, the system changes to relieve the stress. *19.2*

Lewis acid any substance that can accept a pair of electrons to form a covalent bond. *20.3*

Lewis base any substance that can donate a pair of electrons to form a covalent bond. *20.3*

lime calcium oxide (CaO); it is sometimes called quicklime. *24.1*

limiting reagent any reactant that is used up first in a chemical reaction; it determines the amount of product that can be formed in the reaction. *9.3*

lipid a member of a large class of relatively water-insoluble organic compounds; fats, oils, and waxes are lipids. *27.4*

liquid a form of matter that flows, has a fixed volume, and takes the shape of its container. *2.1*

liter (L) the volume of a cube measuring 10 centimeters on each edge (1000 cm^3); it is the common unprefixed unit of volume in the metric system. *3.3*

M

mass the amount of matter that an object contains; the SI base unit of mass is the kilogram. *2.1*

mass number the total number of protons and neutrons in the nucleus of an atom. *5.3*

matter anything that takes up space and has mass. *2.1*

melting point (mp) the temperature at which a substance changes from solid to a liquid; the melting point of water is 0 °C. *10.3*

metabolism all the chemical reactions carried out by an organism; includes energy-producing (catabolism) reactions and energy-absorbing (anabolism) reactions. *27.6*

metal one of a class of elements that includes a large majority of the known elements; metals are characteristically lustrous, malleable, ductile, and good conductors of heat and electricity. *5.4*

metallic bond the force of attraction that holds metals together; it consists of the attraction of free-floating valence electrons for positively charged metal ions. *15.3*

metalloid one of a class of elements having properties intermediate to metals and nonmetals. *5.4*

metallurgy the various procedures used to separate metals from their ores. *24.3*

meter (m) the base unit of length in SI. *3.3*

miscible describes liquids that dissolve in each other. *18.1*

mixture a physical blend of two or more substances that are not chemically combined. *2.2*

molal boiling-point elevation constant (K_b) the change in boiling point for a 1-molal solution of a nonvolatile molecular solute. *18.4*

molal freezing-point depression constant (K_f) the change in freezing point for a 1-molal solution of a nonvolatile molecular solute. *18.4*

molality (m) the concentration of solute in a solution expressed as the number of moles of solute dissolved in 1 kilogram (1000 g) of solvent. *18.4*

molar heat of condensation the heat, in joules or calories, released by 1 mole of a substance as it changes from a vapor to a liquid at the liquid's boiling point. *11.3*

molar heat of fusion the energy, in kilojoules, required to melt 1 mole of a solid. *11.3*

molar heat of solidification the heat, in joules or calories, released by 1 mole of a substance as it changes from a liquid to a solid at the solid's melting point. *11.3*

molar heat of solution the heat, in joules or calories, released or absorbed by 1 mole of a substance as it dissolves in water to produce 1 liter of a 1 molar solution. *11.3*

molar heat of vaporization the energy, in kilojoules, required to vaporize 1 mole of a liquid. *11.3*

molarity (M) the concentration of solute in a solution expressed as the number of moles of solute dissolved in 1 liter of solution. *18.2*

molar mass a general expression used to refer to the mass of a mole of any substance unless a more specific term is needed to avoid confusion. *7.2*

molar volume the volume occupied by 1 mole of a gas at standard temperature and pressure (STP); 22.4 L. *7.2*

mole (mol) the amount of a substance that contains 6.02×10^{23} representative particles of that substance. *7.1*

molecular compound a compound that is composed of molecules. *6.1*

molecular formula a chemical formula that shows the actual number and kinds of atoms present in a molecule of a compound. *6.2*

molecular orbital an orbital resulting from the overlapping of atomic orbitals when two atoms combine. *16.2*

molecule a neutral chemically bonded group of atoms that act as a unit. *6.1*

mole fraction the ratio of the moles of solute in solution to the total number of moles of both solvent and solute. *18.4*

monatomic ion a single atom with a positive or negative charge as a result of losing or gaining valence electrons. *6.3*

Monel metal a strong, corrosion-resistant alloy of nickel and copper. *24.3*

monomer a simple molecule that repeatedly combines to form a polymer. *26.4*

monoprotic acid any acid that contains one ionizable proton (hydrogen ion); nitric acid (HNO_3) is a monoprotic acid. *20.3*

monosaccharide a carbohydrate consisting of one sugar unit; it is also called a simple sugar. *27.2*

N

net ionic equation an equation for a reaction in solution showing only those particles that are directly involved in the chemical change. *8.3*

network solid a substance in which all of the atoms are covalently bonded to each other. *16.3*

neutralization reaction a reaction in which an acid and a base react in an aqueous solution to produce a salt and water. *21.1*

neutral solution an aqueous solution in which the concentrations of hydrogen and hydroxide ions are equal, that is, 1.0×10^{-7} mol/L; it has a pH of 7.0. *20.2*

neutron a subatomic particle with no charge and a mass of 1 amu; found in the nucleus of the atom. *5.2*

neutron absorption a process used in a nuclear reactor to slow the chain reaction by decreasing the number of moving neutrons; this is done with control rods made of a material such as cadmium that absorbs neutrons. *28.3*

neutron moderation a process used in a nuclear reactor to slow the neutrons so they can be captured by the reactor fuel to continue the chain reaction; water and carbon are good moderators. *28.3*

noble gas any member of a group of gaseous elements in Group 0 of the periodic table; the *s* and *p* sublevels of their outermost energy level are filled. *5.4, 14.1*

nonelectrolyte a compound that does not conduct an electric current in aqueous solution or in the molten state. *17.3*

nonmetal one of a class of elements that are not lustrous and are generally poor conductors of heat and electricity; nonmetals are grouped on the right side of the periodic table. *5.4*

nonpolar covalent bond a bond formed when the atoms in a molecule are alike and the bonding electrons are shared equally. *16.3*

nonspontaneous reaction a reaction that does not favor the formation of products at the specified conditions. *19.3*

normal boiling point the boiling point of a liquid at a pressure of 1 atmosphere. *10.2*

normality (*N*) the concentration of a solution expressed as the number of equivalents of solute in 1 liter of solution. *21.1*

nucleic acid a polymer of ribonucleotides (RNA) or deoxyribonucleotides (DNA) found primarily in cell nuclei; nucleic acids play an important role in the transmission of hereditary characteristics, protein synthesis, and the control of cell activities. *27.5*

nucleotide one of the monomers that make up DNA and RNA; it consists of a nitrogen-containing base (a purine or pyrimidine), a sugar (ribose or deoxyribose), and a phosphate group. *27.5*

nucleus the dense central portion of an atom, composed of protons and neutrons. *5.2*

O

observation information obtained through the senses; observation in science often involves a measurement. *1.3*

octet rule atoms react by gaining or losing electrons so as to acquire the stable electron structure of a noble gas, usually eight valence electrons. *15.1*

ore a mineral used for commercial production of a metal. *24.3*

organic chemistry the study of compounds that contain the element carbon. *1.1*

oxidation a process that involves complete or partial loss of electrons or a gain of oxygen; it results in an increase in the oxidation number of an atom. *22.1*

oxidation number a positive or negative number assigned to a combined atom according to a set of arbitrary rules; generally it is the charge an atom would have if the electrons in each bond were assigned to the atoms of the more electronegative element. *22.2*

oxidation-number-change method a method of balancing a redox equation by comparing the increases and decreases in oxidation numbers. *22.3*

oxidation–reduction reaction a reaction that involves the transfer of electrons between reactants. *22.1*

oxidizing agent the substance in a redox reaction that accepts electrons; in the reaction, the oxidizing agent is reduced. *22.1*

P

paramagnetic a term used to describe a substance that shows a relatively strong attraction to an external magnetic field; these substances have molecules containing one or more unpaired electrons. *16.1*

partial pressure the pressure exerted by each gas in a gaseous mixture. *12.5*

pascal (Pa) the SI unit of pressure. *10.1*

Pauli exclusion principle no more than two electrons can occupy an atomic orbital; these electrons must have opposite spins. *13.2*

peptide an organic compound formed by a combination of amino acids in which the amino group of one acid is united with the carboxylic group of another through an amide bond. *27.3*

peptide bond the bond between the carbonyl group of one amino acid and the nitrogen of the next amino acid in the peptide chain; the structure is

$$\begin{array}{cc} O & H \\ \| & | \\ -C- & N- \end{array}$$

27.3

percent composition the percent by mass of each element in a compound. *7.3*

percent error the percent that a measured value differs from the accepted value. *3.2*

percent yield the ratio of the actual yield to the theoretical yield for a chemical reaction expressed as a percentage; a measure of the efficiency of a reaction. *9.3*

period a horizontal row of elements in the periodic table. *5.4*

periodic law when the elements are arranged in order of increasing atomic number, there is a periodic repetition of their physical and chemical properties. *5.4*

periodic table an arrangement of elements into rows and columns according to similarities in their properties. *5.4*

pH a number used to denote the hydrogen-ion concentration, or acidity, of a solution; it is the negative logarithm of the hydrogen-ion concentration of a solution. *20.2*

phase any part of a system with uniform composition and properties. *2.2*

phase diagram a diagram showing the conditions at which a substance exists as a solid, liquid, or vapor. *10.4*

phospholipid a lipid that contains a phosphate group; because phospholids have hydrophilic heads and hydrophobic tails, they form the lipid bilayers found in cell membranes. *27.4*

photoelectric effect electrons are ejected by certain metals when they absorb light with a frequency above a threshold frequency. *13.3*

photon a quantum of light; a discrete bundle of electromagnetic energy that behaves as a particle. *13.3*

photosynthesis the process by which green plants and algae use radiant energy from the sun to synthesize glucose from carbon dioxide and water. *27.1*

physical change an alteration of a substance that does not affect its chemical composition. *2.1*

physical chemistry the study of the theoretical basis of chemical behavior, relying on mathematics and physics. *1.1*

physical property a quality of a substance that can be observed or measured without changing the substance's chemical composition. *2.1*

pi bond (π bond) a bond in which the bonding electrons are most likely to be found in the sausage-shaped regions above and below the nuclei of the bonded atoms. *16.2*

Planck's constant (h) a number used to calculate the radiant energy (*E*) absorbed or emitted by a body based on the frequency of radiation. *13.3*

polar bond a bond formed when two different atoms are joined by a covalent bond and the bonding electrons are shared unequally. *16.3*

polar covalent bond *see* polar bond. *16.3*

polar molecule a molecule, like water, in which one or more atoms is slightly negative and one or more is slightly positive, unless molecular geometry causes the polarities to cancel each other out. *16.3*

polyatomic ion a tightly bound group of atoms that behaves as a unit and carries a charge. *6.3*

polymer a very large molecule formed by the covalent bonding of repeating small molecules, known as monomers. *26.4*

polypeptide a peptide with more than 10 amino acids. *27.3*

polysaccharide a complex carbohydrate polymer formed by the linkage of many monosaccharide monomers; starch, glycogen, and cellulose are polysaccharides. *27.2*

positron a particle that has the same mass as an electron but that has a positive charge. *28.2*

precision describes the closeness, or reproducibility, of a set of measurements taken under the same conditions. *3.2*

product a substance formed in a chemical reaction. *2.4*

protein any peptide with more than 100 amino acids. *27.3*

proton a positively charged subatomic particle found in the nucleus of an atom. *5.2*

Q

qualitative measurement a measurement that gives descriptive, nonnumeric results. *3.1*

quantitative measurement a measurement that gives definite, usually numeric results. *3.1*

quantum the amount of energy needed to move an electron from its present energy level to the next higher one. *13.1*

quantum mechanical model the modern description, primarily mathematical, of the behavior of electrons in atoms. *13.1*

R

radiation the penetrating rays and particles emitted by a radioactive source. *28.1*

radioactive decay the spontaneous emission of radiation by an unstable nucleus; the rate of decay is unaffected by temperature, pressure, or catalysts. *28.1*

radioactivity the processes by which unstable atomic nuclei achieve stability. *28.1*

radioisotope an isotope that has an unstable nucleus and undergoes radioactive decay. *28.1*

rate describes the speed of change over an interval of time. *19.1*

rate law an expression relating the rate of a reaction to the concentration of the reactants. *19.5*

reactant a starting substance in a chemical reaction. *2.4*

reaction mechanism a series of elementary reactions that take place during the course of a complex reaction. *19.5*

redox reaction another name for an oxidation–reduction reaction. *22.1*

reducing agent the substance in a redox reaction that donates electrons; in the reaction, the reducing agent is oxidized. *22.1*

reduction a process that involves a complete or partial gain of electrons or the loss of oxygen; it results in a decrease in the oxidation number of an atom. *22.1*

reduction potential a measure of the tendency of a given half-reaction to occur as a reduction (gain of electrons) in an electrochemical cell. *23.2*

representative element Group A element on the periodic table; together, these elements, which have only partially filled outermost *s* and *p* sublevels, illustrate the entire range of chemical properties. *5.4, 14.1*

representative particle the smallest unit into which a substance can be broken down without a change in composition; the term refers to whether a substance commonly exists as atoms, ions, or molecules. *7.1*

resonance structure one of two or more equally valid electron dot structures for a molecule or polyatomic ion; the actual bonding is a hybrid, or mixture, of the resonance structures. *16.1*

reversible reaction a reaction in which the conversion of reactants into products and the conversion of products into reactants occur simultaneously. *19.2*

S

salt bridge a tube containing a conducting solution used to connect half-cells in a voltaic cell; it allows the passage of ions from one compartment to another but prevents the solutions from mixing completely. *23.1*

salt hydrolysis a process in which the cations or anions of a dissociated salt accept hydrogen ions from water or donate hydrogen ions to water; solutions containing hydrolyzed salts may be either acidic or basic. *21.2*

saponification the process used to make soap; it involves the hydrolysis of fats or oils by a hot aqueous alkali-metal hydroxide. *27.4*

saturated compound an organic compound in which all carbon atoms are joined by single covalent bonds; it contains the maximum number of hydrogen atoms. *25.2*

saturated solution a solution containing the maximum amount of solute for a given amount of solvent at a constant temperature and pressure; an equilibrium exists between undissolved solute and ions in solution. *18.1*

scientific law a concise statement that summarizes the results of many observations and experiments. *1.3*

scientific method a method of inquiry involving observation, experiments, hypotheses, and broad explanations called theories. *1.3*

scientific notation expression of numbers in the form $n \times 10^n$ where n is equal to or greater than 1 and less than 10 and n is an integer. *3.1*

scintillation counter a device that uses a surface coated with a phosphor to detect radiation; ionizing radiation striking the phosphor surface produces bright flashes of light (scintillations). *28.4*

self-ionization a term describing the reaction in which two water molecules react to produce ions. *20.2*

sigma bond (σ bond) a bond formed when two atomic orbitals combine to form a molecular orbital that is symmetrical along the axis connecting the two atomic nuclei. *16.2*

significant figures all the digits that can be known precisely in a measurement, plus a last estimated digit. *3.2*

single covalent bond a bond formed when a pair of electrons is shared between two atoms. *16.1*

single-replacement reaction a chemical change in which one element replaces a second element in a compound; also called a displacement reaction. *8.2*

skeleton equation a chemical equation that does not indicate the relative amounts of reactants and products. *8.1*

slaked lime calcium hydroxide ($Ca(OH)_2$). *24.1*

solid matter that has a definite shape and volume. *2.1*

solubility the amount of a substance that dissolves in a given quantity of solvent at specified conditions of temperature and pressure to produce a saturated solution. *18.1*

solubility product constant (K_{sp}) an equilibrium constant that can be applied to the solubility of electrolytes; it is equal to the product of the concentration terms each raised to the power of the coefficient of the substance in the dissociation equation. *21.2*

solute dissolved particles in a solution. *17.3*

solution a homogeneous mixture. *2.2*

solvation a process that occurs when an ionic solute dissolves; in solution, the ions are surrounded by solvent molecules. *17.3*

solvent the dissolving medium in a solution. *17.3*

specific gravity the ratio of the density of a substance to that of a standard substance (usually water). *3.4*

specific heat (c) the quantity of heat, in joules or calories, required to raise the temperature of 1 g of a substance 1 °C. *11.1*

specific heat capacity *see* specific heat. *11.1*

specific rate constant a proportionality constant relating the concentrations of reactants to the rate of the reaction. *19.5*

spectator ion an ion that is not directly involved in a chemical reaction; an ion that does not change oxidation number or composition during a reaction. *8.3*

spectrum range of wavelengths of electromagnetic radiation; wavelengths of visible light are separated when a beam of white light passes through a prism. *13.3*

spontaneous reaction a reaction that favors the formation of products at the specified conditions; spontaneity depends on enthalpy and entropy changes. *19.3*

standard atmosphere (atm) a unit of pressure; it is the pressure required to support 760 mm of mercury in a mercury barometer at 25 °C; this is the average atmospheric pressure at sea level. *10.1*

standard cell potential the measured cell potential when the ion concentration in the half-cells are 1.00 M at 1 atm of pressure and 25 °C. *23.2*

standard entropy (S^0) the entropy of a substance in its stable state at 25 °C and 1 atm. *19.4*

standard heat of formation (H_f^0) the change in enthalpy for a reaction in which one mole of a compound is formed from its constituent elements. *11.4*

standard hydrogen electrode an arbitrary reference electrode (half-cell) used with another electrode (half-cell) to measure the standard reduction potential of that cell; the standard reduction potential of the hydrogen electrode is assigned a value of 0.00 V. *23.2*

standard solution a solution of known concentration used in carrying out a titration. *21.1*

standard temperature and pressure (STP) the conditions under which the volume of a gas is usually measured; standard temperature is 0 °C and standard pressure is 1 atmosphere (atm). *7.2*

stereoisomer an organic molecule having the same molecular structure as another molecule, but differing in the arrangement of atoms in the space. *25.3*

stoichiometry that portion of chemistry dealing with numerical relationships in chemical reactions; the calculation of quantities of substances involved in chemical equations. *9.1*

straight-chain alkane a saturated open-chain hydrocarbon in which all carbons are arranged consecutively; that is, there is no branching. *25.1*

strong acid an acid that is completely (or almost completely) ionized in aqueous solution. *20.4*

strong base a base that completely dissociates into metal ions and hydroxide ions in aqueous solution. *20.4*

strong electrolyte a solution in which a large portion of the solute exists as ions. *17.3*

structural formula a chemical formula that shows the arrangement of atoms in a molecule or a polyatomic ion; each dash between two atoms indicates a pair of shared electrons. *16.1*

structural isomer a compound that has the same molecular formula as another compound but that has a different molecular structure. *25.3*

sublimation the conversion of a solid to a gas or vapor without passing through the liquid state. *10.4*

substance a sample of matter having a uniform and definite composition; it can be either an element or a compound. *2.1*

substituent an atom or group of atoms that can take the place of a hydrogen atom on a parent hydrocarbon molecule. *25.1*

substitution reaction common type of organic reaction; involves the replacement of an atom or group of atoms by another atom or group of atoms. *26.1*

substrate a molecule on which an enzyme acts. *27.3*

supersaturated solution a solution that contains more solute than it can theoretically hold at a given temperature; excess solute precipitates if a seed crystal is added. *18.1*

surface tension an inward force that tends to minimize the surface area of a liquid; it causes the surface to behave as if it were a thin skin. *17.1*

surfactant a surface active agent; any substance with molecules that interfere with the hydrogen bonding between water molecules, reducing surface tension; soaps and detergents are surfactants. *17.1*

surroundings the remainder of the universe that is outside the system. *11.1*

suspension a mixture from which some of the particles settle out slowly upon standing. *17.4*

system any part of the universe upon which attention is focused. *11.1*

T

temperature a measure of the average kinetic energy of particles in matter; temperature determines the direction of heat transfer. *3.5*

ternary compound a compound containing atoms of three different elements, usually containing at least one polyatomic ion; Na_2CO_3 and $Mg(OH)_2$ are ternary ionic compounds. *6.4*

tetrahedral angle a bond angle of 109.5° created when a central atom forms four bonds directed toward the corners of a regular tetrahedron. *16.2*

theoretical yield the amount of product that could form during a reaction calculated from a balanced chemical equation; it represents the maximum amount of product that could be formed from a given amount of reactant. *9.3*

theory a thoroughly tested model that explains why experiments give certain results. *1.3*

thermochemical equation a chemical equation that includes the amount of heat produced or absorbed during the reaction. *11.2*

thermochemistry the study of heat changes in chemical reactions. *11.1*

titration method used to determine the concentration of a solution (often an acid or base); a solution of known concentration (the standard) is added to a measured amount of the solution of unknown concentration until an indicator signals the end point. *21.1*

***trans* configuration** a term applied to geometric isomers; it denotes an arrangement in which the substituted groups are on opposite sides of the double bond. *25.3*

transition metal Group B element characterized by addition of electrons to *d* suborbitals. *5.4, 14.1*

transition state a term sometimes used to refer to the activated complex. *19.1*

transmutation natural or artificial conversion of an atom of one element into an atom of another element by the emission of radiation from an unstable nucleus. *28.2*

transuranium element an element in the periodic table with an atomic number that is greater than 92. *28.2*

triglyceride an ester in which all three hydroxyl groups on a glycogen molecule have been replaced by long-chain fatty acids; fats are triglycerides. *27.4*

triple covalent bond a covalent bond in which three pairs of electrons are shared by two atoms. *16.1*

triple point the point on a phase diagram that represents the only set of conditions at which all three phases exist in equilibrium with one another. *10.4*

triprotic acid any acid that contains three ionizable protons (hydrogen ions); phosphoric acid (H_3PO_4) is a triprotic acid. *20.3*

Tyndall effect scattering of light by particles in a colloid or suspension, which causes a beam of light to become visible. *17.4*

U

unit cell the smallest group of particles within a crystal that retains the geometric shape of the crystal. *10.3*

universe the totality of all existing things. *11.1*

unsaturated a solution that contains less solute than a saturated solution at a given temperature and pressure. *18.1*

unsaturated compound an organic compound with one or more double or triple carbon–carbon bonds. *25.2*

unshared pair a pair of valence electrons that is not involved in bonding. *16.1*

V

vacuum a space where no particles of matter exist. *10.1*

valence electron an electron in the highest occupied energy level of an atom. *15.1*

van der Waals force a term used to describe the weakest intermolecular attractions; these include dispersion forces and dipole interactions. *16.3*

vapor a substance in the gaseous state that is ordinarily a liquid or solid at room temperature. *2.1*

vaporization the conversion of a liquid to a gas or a vapor. *10.2*

vapor pressure the pressure produced when vapor particles above a liquid in a sealed container collide with the container walls; a dynamic equilibrium exists between the vapor and the liquid. *10.2*

voltaic cell an electrochemical cell used to convert chemical energy into electrical energy; the energy is produced by a spontaneous redox reaction. *23.1*

volume the space occupied by a sample of matter. *3.3*

VSEPR theory valence-shell electron-pair repulsion theory; because electron pairs repel, molecules adjust their shapes so that valence-electron pairs are as far apart as possible. *16.2*

W

water of hydration water molecules that are an integral part of a crystal structure. *17.3*

wavelength (λ) the distance between two adjacent crests of a wave. *13.3*

wax an ester of a long-chain fatty acid and a long-chain alcohol. *27.4*

weak acid an acid that is only slightly ionized in aqueous solution. *20.4*

weak base a base that does not dissociate completely in aqueous solution. *20.4*

weak electrolyte a solution in which only a fraction of the solute exists as ions. *17.3*

weight force that measures the pull of gravity on a given mass. *3.3*

The page on which a term is defined is indicated in **boldface** type.

A

Absolute zero, **74,** 271–272, 336
Accepted value, **55**
Accuracy, **54**
   of measurements, evaluating, 54–55
Acid(s), 213, **578**
   Arrhenius, 594–596
   Brønsted-Lowry, 596–598
   common, 594 (table)
   common, concentrations of, 600,
     604 (table)
   conjugate, **597**
   diprotic, **594,** 602
   dissociation constants of, **601**–602
     (table)
   formulas of, 578
   Lewis, **598**
   monoprotic, **594**
   naming, 160, 578 (table), 579
   neutralization of, 613–624
   properties of, 577
   strengths of, 600 (table)–602
   triprotic, **549,** 602
Acid deterioration of books, 596
Acid dissociation constant, **601**–602,
   604–605
Acidophiles, 638
Acidic solutions, **581,** 583
Acid rain, 607
Activated complex, **536**
Activation energy, **535**
Active site, **818**–819
Activity series of metals, 217 (table)
Actual yield, **256**–258
Addition reactions, **781**–783
Adenosine triphosphate (ATP), 306,
   832–833
Aerosol sprays, 331
Agriculture, 11–12
Air, composition of, 350 (table)
Airbag inflation system, 260
Alchemy symbols, 39
Alcohols, **778**–779
   denatured, **781**
   nomenclature for, 778–779
   oxidation of, 792–793
   properties of, 779–781
   uses of, 780–781
Aldehydes, **785**–787, 786 (table)
   boiling points of, 787 (table)
   common, 786 (table)
   detection of, 793
Aliphatic alcohols, 778, 779, 780
Aliphatic compounds, **759**
Alkali metals, **125,** 394, 705–706
   physical properties of, 705–706 (table)
Alkaline earth metals, **125,** 394, 708–710
   physical properties of, 708–709
     (table)

Alkaline solutions, **581.** *See also* Basic
   solutions
Alkaliphiles, 638
Alkanes, **743**–751, 782
   boiling points of, 775 (table)
   branched-chain, **748**–751, 766
   properties of, 751
   straight-chain, **745**–747, 766
Alkenes, **752,** 773
Alkyl group, **748,** 775 (table)
Alkyl halides, **774**
Alkynes, **753,** 773, 779
Allotropes, **282**–283
   of carbon, 282–283
Alloys, 429 (table)
   copper, 729
   steel, 728
   titanium, 726
Alpha particles, 111, 112, 842 (table),
   843, 846
Alpha radiation, 842 (table), **843**
Aluminum, 419, 712–713
Amalgams, 429
Amino acids, **815** (table)–819
Amino acid sequence, **816**
Ammonia, 444, 445, 455–456
   as Brønsted-Lowry base, 596–597
   electron dot formula for, 439
   heat of vaporization of, 480
   manufacture of, 242, 715–716, 733
   melting and boiling points of,
     480 (table)
   molecule, 139
   in the nitrogen cycle, 246
Amorphous solids, **282**–283
Amphoteric substances, **598**
Amplitude, of wave, **372**
Anabolism, **834**
Analytical balance, 67
Analytical chemist, 76
Analytical chemistry, **4**
Aneroid barometer, 269
Anhydrous compounds, 485–488
Anion(s), **136,** 417
   electron configurations for, 417–418
   formation of, 136, 143
   ionic radius of, 404
   names of, 136, 578
Anode(s), **680**
   in electrolytic vs. voltaic cells,
     692–693
Anodizing, 695
Anthracite coal, 765
Antibonding orbital, **452,** 453
Antimicrobials, 570
Antioxidants, 570
Aqueous solutions, **482**–488
   symbol for, 205, 206 (table)
Archaeologist, 870
Arenes, **759**
Argon, 394
Aromatic aldehydes, 786–787
Aromatic compounds, **759**

Arrhenius, Svante, 594
Arrhenius acids and bases, 594–596
Aryl halides, **774**
Astronomy, 14
Asymmetric carbon, **755**
Atmosphere, destruction of ozone layer
   of, 13
Atmospheric pressure, **268**–269, 350
   and boiling point, 277–278, 284–285
   measurement of, 268–269
   and melting point, 284–285
   at sea level, 268
Atom(s), **108.** *See also* Subatomic
   particles
   calculating number of, in mass, 185
   Dalton's atomic theory, **107**
   determining composition of,
     from atomic number and mass
     number, 115
   estimation of size of, 398
   and ions, 135–136
   mass number of, **115**
Atomic emission spectra, **374**
   explanation of, 379–380
   light and, 372–375
Atomic mass(es), 118–121, **120**
   calculating, 120–121
   Newlands's arrangement of elements
     in order of, 405
   weighted average, 120
Atomic mass unit (amu), **118,** 176
Atomic model(s)
   Bohr's, 361, 362, 379, 380
   development of, 361–363
   quantum mechanical, 362, **363**–364
Atomic number(s), **113**–116
   and atomic size, 400
   of first ten elements, 113 (table)
   and ionization energy, **403**
Atomic orbitals, 364, **365**–366
   energy levels of, 367–369
   filling of, 367–368
   vs. molecular orbitals, 452
Atomic radii, **398**–399 (table), 400–401
   compared to ionic radii, 404
Atomic size, periodic trends in, 400
Atomic structure, 109–121 *See also*
   Atomic model(s)
   Dalton's theory of, 107–117
   electrons in, 361–382
   quantum mechanical model, 362,
     363–364
   Rutherford's theory of, 111–112, 362
   Thomson model of, 361
Atomic theory, development of, 361–364
"Atomists," 107
Aufbau principle, **367**–368, 370
Autobody repair, 538
Autoclaves, 278
Automotive design engineer, 879
Avogadro, Amedeo, 173
Avogadro's hypothesis, **347**–349
Avogadro's number, **173,** 175, 239

E

Ecologist, 871
Effloresce, **487**
Effusion, **352**
  Graham's law of, 352–353
Einstein, Albert, 377
Electrical conductivity
  electrolytes and, 483–485
  of ionic compounds, 425
Electrical energy, conversion of chemical
    energy into, 677–681
Electrical potential, **685**
Electric vehicle, 699
Electrochemical cells, 679
  shorthand representation of, 681
  zinc–copper, oxidation–reduction
    reactions in, 680–681
Electrochemical processes, 677–697, **678**
Electrochemist, 879
Electrodes, **680**
Electroforming, 696
Electrolysis, **692**
  of sodium chloride, 694–695, 706
  of water, 248, 692–694
Electrolyte(s), **483**–485, 577
  strong, **485** (table)
  weak, **485** (table)
Electrolytic cells, **692**–697
  compared to voltaic cells, 693
Electromachining, 697
Electromagnetic radiation, **372**–375, 844
Electromagnetic spectrum, **373**–375
Electron(s), **109**–110
  in atomic structure, 361–382
  charge, **109**–110
  energy levels of, **362**, 364–366
  mass, 110
  planetary model, 362
  properties, 111 (table)
  spin of, 368
  transfer of, in oxidation–reduction
    reactions, 647–650
  valence, **413**–414
Electron configuration(s), **367**–370
  for anions, 417–418
  for cations, 414–416
  and number of valence electrons
    from, 413–414
  and periodicity, 391, 394–396
  for selected elements, 368 (table)
  writing, 368–369
Electron densities, plotting, 455
Electron dot formulas, for covalent com-
    pounds, 439–440
Electron dot structures, **414** (table), 441
Electronegativity(ies), **405** (table)
  and bond types, 462 (table)
  periodic trends in, 405 406
Electroplating, 696
Electropolishing, 697
Electrorefining, 697
Element(s), **36**–38
  diatomic, 443 (table)
  electron dot structures of, **414** (table)
  ionic charges of, 143–145
  Latin names and symbols, 40 (table)
  periodic table of. See Periodic table
Elementary reactions, **568**

Emission spectra, 374–375
  of hydrogen, 380
Empirical formula(s), **192**
  calculating, 193
  molecular formulas vs., 194 (table)
Emulsifying agents, 493
Emulsion, **493**
Endothermic processes, **294**–295,
    303–304
End point, **617**
Energy, 8–10, 42, **293**–294. See also
    Kinetic energy
  free, **549**–551, 554
  heat, **293**. See also Heat
  potential, chemical, 293
  quantum concept of, 376
  solar, 320
  units of measurement, 63
Energy and carbon cycle, **810**–811
Energy levels of electrons, **362**–366,
    400–401
  designations of, 364–366
  ground state, **379**
  of various atomic orbitals, **365**,
    367–368
  within period, 400
Energy pathways, 833
Energy transformation, 293, 549
  chemical to electrical, 677–684
  in nuclear reactions, 853–855, 856
Engine knock, 766
ENIAC, 407
Enthalpy, **301**, 314–315, 551
  diagrams, 303
  measurement of, 301–302
  and phase change, 307–313
  sign convention, 301 (table)
  and spontaneous reactions, 554
Entropy, 551–555, **552**
  reaction spontaneity and, 554
    (table)–555
  standard, 558 (table)
Environmental pollutants, 12–13
Environmental Protection Agency, 196
Enzyme(s), 538, 638, **818**–819
Enzyme-substrate complex, **819**
Equations. See Chemical equation(s)
Equilibrium, chemical, **540**
  factors affecting, 541–544
Equilibrium, dynamic, 276
Equilibrium constant(s), **545**–548
Equilibrium-constant expressions,
    545–548, 603
Equilibrium position, **540**
  shift in, 541–542
Equivalence point, **622**
Equivalents, **619**–620, 622
Errors, in measurement, **55**
Esterification reactions, 790
Esters, **789**–791
Ethane, 744
Ethanol, physical properties of, 29 (table)
Ethene, bonding in, 458
Ethers, **783**–784
Ethnobiology, 816
Ethyne, bonding in, 458–459
Eukaryotic cell, 809–810
Evaporation, **275**–277
  of water, 479–480

Excess reagent, **253**–254
Exothermic processes, **294**–295, 303,
    551, 671
Experiment(s), 15–16
Experimental value, **55**
Extremophiles, 638
  acidophiles, 638
  alkaliphiles, 638
Extremozymes, 638

F

Face-centered cubic arrangement of
    atoms, 428
Face-centered cubic unit cells, 282
Fat(s), 821–822
  dietary, 821
  substitute, 835
Fat cells, brown, 306
Fatty acids, **788**
  salts of, 821–822
Fehling's test, **793**
Fermentation, **781**
Ferromagnetism, 450
Fertilizer runoff, 502
Film badge, **858**–859
Firefighter, 871
Firefighting technology, 230
First-order reactions, **566**–568
Fission, 10, **853**–855
Flameless Ration Heater (FRH), 671
Flavor developer, 790, 802
Fleming, Alexander, 15
Fluorine, 113 (table), 438, 721, 722, 850
Foams, 45
Food science, 6, 418, 570
Formula(s). See Chemical formula(s)
Formula unit, **140**, 419
Frasch, Herman, 718
Frasch process, 718
Free energy, **549**–551, 554
Freeze-drying, 285, 286
Freezing, 280
Freezing point(s), 280
Freezing point depression, 517, **519**,
    522–524
Frequency, of waves, **372**–373
Fuel
  alternative, 784
  gasoline, 766
Fuel cells, **683**–684
Fuel rods, spent, 855
Functional groups, **773**–774 (table)
Fusion, 10, **856**
  molar heat of, **307**, 308 (table)

G

Gallium, 407, 713
Gamma radiation, 372, 842 (table), **844**
  in teletherapy, 861
Gas(es), **31**
  behavior of, 326–353
  calculating gram molecular mass of,
    185
  calculating volume of mole of, at
    STP, 184–185
  composition of, 267

S

CP-Color-Pic, Inc., **FP**-Fundamental Photographs, **OPC**-Omni-Photo Communications, **PA**-Peter Arnold, Inc., **PR**-Photo Researchers, Inc., **SM**-The Stock Market

Photographs

Table of Contents iiiL Richard Megna/FP; iiiC Telegraph Colour Library/FPG International; iiiR Stephen Frisch*; ivLC Robert E. Daemmrich/Tony Stone Images; ivTR Coco McCoy/Rainbow; ivBR, Elisa Leonelli/TonyStone Images; vT Richard Megna/FP; vB Phil Degginger/CP; viL Wayne Estep/Tony Stone Images; viBL Richard Megna/FP; viBR Richard Megna/FP; viiT The Granger Collection; viiC Scott Smith/Earth Scene; viiB Hermann Lustbader/PR; viiiTR Richard Megna/FP; viiiCL, Molkenthin Studio/SM; viiiB Chris Cole/Tony Stone Images; ixT Richard Megna/FP; ixC Metcalfe/Thatcher/Tony Stone Images; ixB Ray Massey/Tony Stone Images; xTL Alvis Upitis/The Image Bank; xTR Carolyn Iverson; xBL Norbert Schafer/SM; xCR Reuters/Ho/Archive Photos; xBR E.R. Degginger/FPSA; xiT Paul Silverman/FP; xiB Richard Hutchings*; xiii R. Ian Lloyd/Westlight

Chapter 1 2, Courtesy NASA; 3T Courtesy NASA; 3B Mark A. Johnson/SM; 4TL Erik A. Svensson/SM; 4TC John Lamb/Tony Stone Images; 4TR Don Mason/SM; 4B Gregory Ochocki/PR; 5TL Telegraph Colour Library/FPG International; 5TC Courtesy NASA/PR; 5TR Thomas Braise/Tony Stone Images; 5CL Scott Camazine/PR; 5C Joe Bator/SM; 5BL Robert E. Daemmrich/Tony Stone Images; 5BC FOTOPIC/OPC; 6 Peter Johansky/FPG International; 7T Richard Laird/FPG International; 7BL BPL; 7BC James L. Amos/PA; 7BR Briolle Rapho/PR; 8L Kunio Owaki/SM; 8C Lowell Georgia/Science Source/PR; 8R Mark Lewis/Tony Stone Images; 9TL Bohdan Hrynewych/Stock, Boston; 9CR Fran Heyl Associates; 9BL Chromosohm/Sohm/PR; 9BC Ken Karp*; 9BR Ken Karp*; 10L Phil Degginger/CP; 10R Norbert Schafer/SM; 11T Gary Farber/The Image Bank; 11C Prof. K. Seddon & Dr. T. Evans, Queens Univ. Belfast Science Photo Library/PR; 11B Roslin Institute/Phototake NYC; 12TL G. David Lewis/CP; 12TC E.R. Degginger/CP; 12TR Nigel Cattlin/PR; 12B Ed Pritchard/Tony Stone Images; 13L NYC Parks Photo Archive/FP; 13R Kristen Brochmann/FP; 14TL Corbis-Bettmann; 14TR Coursesy NASA; 14CL Agence France Presse/Corbis-Bettmann; 15 Runk/Schoenberger/Grant Heilman Photography; 16TC Richard Megna/FP; 16TR Ken Karp*; 16BC Ken Karp*; 20TL Amanda Kavanaugh; 20BL Rosemary Weller/Tony Stone Images; 20BC Dr. Dennis Kunkel/Phototake; 20BR Richard Megna/FP; 21 Ken Karp*; 22 J. Nourok/PhotoEdit; 23 Ted Horowitz/SM; 25TL Telegraph Colour Library/FPG International; 25BL Telegraph Colour Library/FPG International; 25TR William Johnson/Stock, Boston; 25CRT Corbis; 25CRB Bruce Iverson; 25BR Phil Degginger/CP

Chapter 2 28 Dick Durrance II/SM; 29 Dick Durrance II/SM; 30 Geoffrey Nilsen Photography*; 31 Richard Megna/FP; 32T Neal & Mary Mishler/Tony Stone Images; 32B Ken Karp*; 33 David Lawrence*; 36T Lynn St. John/International Stock; 36B David Lawrence*; 37CL Yoav Levy/Phototake; 37C Art Stein/PR; 37CR David Lawrence*; 37BL Mike Hewitt/Tony Stone Images; 37BC Rich Treptow/PR; 37BR David Lawrence*; 38BL E. R. Degginger/CP; 38BCL Coco McCoy/Rainbow; 38BCR E.R. Degginger/CP; 38BR Monkmeyer/Conklin/Monkmeyer Press Photo; 41T Cameron Davidson/Tony Stone Images; 41BL Laurence Dutton/Tony Stone Images; 41BC Ed Pritchard/Tony Stone Images; 41BR Kim Heacox/Tony Stone Images; 42 Richard Megna/FP; 43 Richard Megna/FP; 45 James Stoots Lawrence/Livermore National Laboratory

Chapter 3 50 Dick Hanley/PR; 51T Jerry Cooke/PR; 51BL Leonard Lessin/FBPA; 51BC Comstock; 51BR Leonard Lessin/PA; 52T PA; 52B Fran Heyl Associates; 54 SYGMA; 55 Richard Hutchings*; 57 David Lawrence*; 58 Ken Karp*; 61 David Lawrence*; 63 Erich Lessing/Art Resource, NY; 64 David Lawrence*; 65TL Ken Karp*; 65TC David Lawrence*; 65CR David Lawrence*; 65CR David Lawrence*; 66TL Richard Hutchings*; 66TR Ken Karp*; 66BL Courtesy NASA; 67 Richard Hutchings*; 68 Dick Hanley/PR; 69 Richard Megna/FP; 71 Ken Karp*; 72L Phil Degginger/CP; 72R Phil Degginger/CP; 74TR Runk Schoenberger/Grant Heilman Photography; 74T PA; 74CL Gordon Wiltsie/PA; 74BL Alan Schein/SM; 76 Bureau International des Poids & Measures; 80 Geoffrey Nilsen Photography*

Chapter 4 82 Pat Kepic*; 83T Pat Kepic*; 83B Ken Karp*; 86 Richard Hutchings*; 89 Ken Reid/FPG International; 91 Richard Hutchings*; 92 P. Young-Wolff/PhotoEdit; 93 Ken Karp*; 97 Ana Nance; 98 SuperStock; 99 Gary M. Prior/Allsport; 101 Grant Heilman Photography; 104 Roy Schneider/SM

Chapter 5 106 Physics Department, Imperial College/Science Photo Library/PR; 107 Physics Department, Imperial College/Science Photo Library/PR; 108 Fran Heyl Associates; 109T Science Photo Library/PR; 109B Stephen G. St. John/National Geographic Society; 110 Richard Megna/FP; 112 Steve Bronstein/The Image Bank; 113 Richard Shiell/Earth Scenes; 116 PA; 117 Elisa Leonelli/Tony Stone Images; 118 Steven Sutton/Duomo; 123T Chuck Keeler/Tony Stone Images; 123B The Granger Collection; 125TL Ken Karp*; 125TC Ken Karp*; 125TR Ralph Reinhold/Earth Scenes; 125BL Richard Megna/FP; 125BR Kip Peticolas/FP; 126BL George Whiteley/PR; 126T Stephen Marks/The Image Bank; 126BR Dawn Goss/Phototake; 127 PR

Chapter 6 132 Dr. Pepper Museum; 133T Rob Matheson/SM; 133BL Ken Karp*; 133BR Ginger Chih/PA; 134L Alese/Mortpechter/SM; 134R Kent Wood/PR; 138 Dick Luria/PG International; 139 David Young-Wolff/PhotoEdit; 140 Bruce Iverson; 141 Ken Karp*; 143 John Michael/International Stock; 144 E.R.Degginger/CP; 145L Ken Karp*; 145R Alan Oddie/PhotoEdit; 148L Paul Silverman/FP; 148C E.R. Degginger/CP; 148R Charles D. Winters/PR; 149 Dr. Pepper Museum; 150 David Barber/PhotoEdit; 153L Ken Karp*; 153R Haroldo De Faria Castro/FPG International; 154L SuperStock; 154C Paul Silverman/FP; 154R Randy Duchaine; 158T T. Kevin Smyth/SM; 158BL Tim Davis/PR; 158BR Spencer Grant/PhotoEdit; 160 Ken Karp*; 161 Fran Heyl Associates; 162 Jerry L. Ferrara/PR; 164 Ken Karp*

Chapter 7 170 Jim Zuckerman/Westlight; 171T Jim Zuckerman/Westlight; 171BL Richard Hutchings*; 171BR David Lawrence*; 172 Ken Karp*; 173 The Granger Collection; 174TL Richard Hutchings*; 174CL David Lawrence*; 174BL David Lawrence*; 175 Ken Karp*; 176 ZEFA-Lange/SM; 177 Geoffrey Nilsen Photography*; 179 Geoffrey Nilsen Photography*; 180 David Lawrence*; 182 Corbis; 184 David Lawrence*; 185 Ken Karp*; 188TR Alice Gurlich-Jones/OPC; 188CL David Lawrence*; 189BL Ewing Galloway/American Stock Photography; 189BR Rod Planck/Tony Stone Images; 193T Phil Degginger/CP; 193B Felicia Martinez/PhotoEdit; 196 Roy Morsch/SM

Chapter 8 202 Will and Deni McIntyre/PR; 203T Archive Photos; 203BL David Lawrence*; 203BC David Lawrence*; 203BR SuperStock; 204L Jacques M. Chenet/Woodfin Camp & Associates; 204C Oliver Meckes/PR; 204R SM; 205L Ken Karp*; 205R Ken Karp*; 210 David Lawrence*; 212 Will and Deni McIntyre/PR; 213L David Lawrence*; 213C David Lawrence*; 213R Richard Megna/FP; 215TL Ken Karp*; 215TC Ken Karp*; 215TR Ken Karp*; 215B Ron Watts/Westlight; 216 David Lawrence*; 217L E.R. Degginger/CP; 217R Charles D. Winters/PR; 219 Richard Megna/FP; Richard Megna/FP; 222TL David Lawrence*; 222TR David Lawrence*; 222BL Ken Karp*; 222BC Ken Karp*; 222BR Ken Karp*; 223T David Lawrence*; 223CL Richard Megna/FP; 223C Richard Megna/FP; 223CR Richard Megna/FP; 223B Richard Megna/FP; 225 Phil Schermeister/Tony Stone Images; 227 David Lawrence*; 230 Superstock; 235TL HMS Images; 235TR HMS Images; 235BL Jody Dole; 235BC Ken Karp*; 235BR Richard Megna/FP

Chapter 9 236 David Woods/SM; 237T Ken Straiton/SM; 237B Gianni Cigolini/The Image Bank; 239 SuperStock; 240 E.R. Degginger/CP; 242T David Woods/SM; 242L&R Grant Heilman Photography; 244 Richard Hutchings*; 246TR Courtesy NASA; 246L Runk/Schoenberger/Grant Heilman Photography; 248 Runk/Schoenberger/Grant Heilman Photography; 249 Gerard Fritz/Tony Stone Images; 252T Tom Stewart/SM; 252B Ken Karp*; 254 E.R. Degginger/CP; 255 Ken Karp*; 256 Uniphoto; 257T Ken Karp*; 257B Richard Hutchings*; 260 David Young-Wolff/PhotoEdit; 265 SuperStock

Chapter 10 266 Ed Reschke/PA; 267 G.C. Kelley/PR; 268 Ken Karp*; 269 Runk/Schoenberger/Grant Heilman Photography; 274T OPC; 274B Phil Degginger/CP; 275 Richard Megna/FP; 276 Ken Karp*; 280 Ken Eward/PR; 281T Bruce Iverson; 281CL Charles D. Winters/PR; 281C BioPhoto Associates/PR; 281CR BioPhoto Associates/PR; 281BL E.R. Degginger/PR; 281BCL Gary Rutherford/PR; 281BCR Arthur Singer/Phototake NYC; 281B George Roos/PA; 283 James L. Amos/PA; 284T Ed Reschke; 284B Ken Karp*; 287 Sydney Thomson/Earth Science; 290 Richard Megna/FP

Chapter 11 292 Lee Snyder/PR.; 293T Richard A. Cooke III/Tony Stone Images; 293BL D.R. Stoecklein/SM; 293BR Brian Czobat/International Stock; 295L Richard Hutchings*; 295R William Sallaz/Duomo; 296 David Lawrence*; 297T Accuweather; 297B Wayne Eastep/Tony Stone Images; 300 Lee Snyder/PR.; 303 Richard Megna/FP; 306L Kennan Ward/SM; 306R N.R. Rowan/PR; 307 Craig Hammell/SM; 309 Bob Abraham/SM; 312L Geoffrey Nilsen Photography*; 312R Richard Hutchings*; 314 Andy Caulfield/The Image Bank; 320 John Roberts/SM

Chapter 12 326 Alese/Mort Pechter/SM; 327T W. Geiersperger/SM; 327B Romilly Lockyer/The Image Bank; 328 Ken Karp*; 330T S.L. Craig Jr./Bruce Coleman Inc.; 330C Phil Degginger/CP; 331 Ken Karp*; 333 Alese/Mort Pechter/SM; 337 Ken Karp*; 341 Roger Tully/Tony Stone Images; 342 Erik Leigh Simmons/The Image Bank; 344 Barry L. Runk/Grant Heilman Photography; 345 Diane Hirsch/FP; 347 Butch Adams/The Image Bank; 351L Joe Towers/SM; 351R Keren Su/Stock, Boston; 352 Ken Karp*; 354 David & Doris Krumholz/FP; 357 Diane Hirsch/FP

Chapter 13 360 Richard Pasley/Stock, Boston; 361T Embry Riddle Aeronautical Univ.; 361BL Science Photo Library/PR; 361BCL Science Photo Library/PR; 361BCR Corbis-Bettman; 361BR Science Photo Library/PR; 367 Allan Morgan/PA; 370TL Doug Martin/PR; 370TR Guy Gillette/PR; 372 Richard Pasley/Stock, Boston; 374BL Kunio Owaki/SM; 374BC Richard Megna/FP; 374BR Richard Megna/FP; 374 Wabash Instrument Corp./FP; 375L Ray Pfortner/PA; 375R Blair Seitz/PR; 376T European Space Agency/PR; 376B Phil Degginger/CP; 377 Chromosohm/Sohm/SM; 381 Martin Dohrn/PR; 384 David Parker/PR; 387 Richard Megna/FP

Chapter 14 390 The Granger Collection; 391 The Granger Collection; 394L John Michael/International Stock; 394R E.R. Degginger/CP; 395TL David Sailors/SM; 395TR Charles O'Rear/Westlight; 395L Stephen Frisch/Stock, Boston; 395BR E.R. Degginger/CP; 398 SuperStock; 402 Phil Degginger/CP; 407 Dr. Jeremy Burgess/Science Photo Library/PR

Chapter 15 412 Pat Lynch/PR; 413T Pat Lynch/PR; 413BL Amos Zezmer/OPC; 413BR Pawel Kumelowski/OPC; 414T Yoav Levy/Phototake; 414B Joel Greenstein/OPC; 416L Erich Lessing/Art Resource; 416R Nathan Beck/OPC; 419T Gary Retherford/PR; 419R Ken Karp*; 422TL Breck P. Kent; 422TR J&L Weber/PA; 422CL J&L Weber/PA; 422CC Breck P. Kent/Earth Scenes; 422CR Grace Davies/OPC; 422BL George Whiteley/PR; 422BC Tomisch/PR; 422BR Paul Silverman/FP; 423T Omikron/Science Source/PR; 423B Tomisch/PR; 424 Phil Degginger/Earth Scenes; 427 Bruce Frisch/PR; 428T Steve Elmore/SM; 428B Fran Heyl Associates; 429L Scott Smith/Earth Scenes; 429R Kourosh Behbahani/Tony Stone Images; 430 Barry L. Runk/Grant Heilman Photography

Chapter 16 436 Gerben Oppermans/Tony Stone Images; 437 Courtesy NASA; 438L Robert Frerck/Woodfin Camp and Assoc.; 438R Garry Hunter/Tony Stone Images; 442 Hugh Sitton/Tony Stone Images; 443 Susan M. Klemens/Stock, Boston; 444 Richard Hutchings*; 449 A. Ramey/Woodfin Camp and Assoc.; 452 James Schnepf/Liaison International; 453 United States Dept. of Interior Geological Survey; 460T Gerben Oppermans/Tony Stone Images; 460B George Disario/SM; 464 Dr. Arthur Lesk, Laboratory for Molecular Biology/SPL/PR; 465 Craig Tuttle/SM; 468 Allen Penn*

Chapter 17 474 Frank Rossotto/SM; 475T Frank Rossotto/SM; 475R William and Marcia Levy/PR; 476 Hermann Eisenbeiss/PR; 477L Michael Lustbader/PR; 477R Ken Karp*; 478L Richard Hutchings*; 478R Four by Five; 479T Critical Position of H.M.S. Investigator on the North Coast of Baring Island, August 20th 1851, drawn by Lieu. S. Gurney Cresswell, pub. 1854 by Day & Son and Ackermann & Co.; Royal Geographical Society, London, UK/Bridgeman Art Library, London/New York; 479BL Thomas R. Fletcher/Stock, Boston; 479BC E.R. Degginger/CP; 479BR SuperStock; 481T Nuridsany et Perennou/Science Source PR; 481B Richard Hutchings*; 482 Russ Lappa*; 483 Cary Wolinsky/Stock, Boston; 484 FP; 486T Ken Karp*; 486L Kristen Brochman/FP*; 487 Ken Karp*; 490 Russ Lappa*; 491 Ken Karp*; 491(2nd from bottom) Johnathan T. Wright/Bruce Coleman, Inc.; 492 Robert Essel/SM; 493 Ken Karp*; 494 SuperStock

Chapter 18 500 St. Petersburg Times/Liason International; 501T St. Petersburg Times/Liason International; 501BR Richard Megna/FP; 501B Ken Karp*; 503BL Phil Degginger/Tony Stone Images; 503BR Jim Olive/PA; 505 Runk/Schoenberger/Grant Heilman Photography; 506T 1990 Richard Megna/FP; 506B John Lamb/Tony Stone Images; 507 Jim Brandenburg; 508 Richard Megna/FP*; 509T Tony Stone Images; 509B Ken Karp*; 510L Tom McCarthy/Rainbow; 510R Richard Hutchings*; 512T Ken Karp*; 512B Richard Hutchings; 514 Ken Karp*; 517 John M Burnley/PR; 518 Ken Karp*; 519 Ken Karp*; 520 Ken Karp*; 522 Phil Degginger/CP; 526 Dan McCoy/Rainbow

Chapter 19 532 Associated Press; 533T J. Langevin/Sygma; 533B Gray Mortimore/Tony Stone Images; 534TL Thomas Brase/Tony Stone Images; 534TR Nathan Beck/OPC; 534BL Erika Stone/PA; 534BR Werner H. Muller/PA; 536 Ken Karp*; 537 The Bettman Archives; 538 Richard Hutchings*; 539 Chuck Kuhn/The Image Bank; 540 Martin Rogers/Stock, Boston; 542 Chris Cole/Tony Stone Images; 545 Geoffrey Nilsen Photography*; 549T Associated Press; 549B Chris Hamilton/SM; 550 Ken Karp*; 551 John Kaprielian/PR; 552 Richard Hutchings*; 558 Frank Siteman/OPC; 561 AP/Wide World Photos; 562 Fotopic/OPC; 566 Reuters/Corbis-Bettman; 570 Ken Karp*

Chapter 20 576 Ken Karp*; 577T J. H. Robinson/PR; 577TR Richard Megna/FP; 577C Bill Bachman/PR; 577L Don Mason/SM; 577BR Russ Lappa*; 578T Molkenthin Studio/SM; 578B Tom Hollyman/PR; 580 Martyn F. Chillmaid/Science Photo Library/PR; 581L Michael Dalton/FP; 581C E.R. Degginger/CP; 581R Ken Karp*; 589 Richard Megna/FP*; 591 Richard Megna/FP*; 592T E.R. Degginger/CP; 592BL Richard Hutchings*; 592BR Matt Meadows/PA; 594T Stephen Kraseman/Nature Conservancy/PR; 594BL Mike Neumann/PR; 594, John Maher/Stock Boston/Picture Quest; 594BR Bob Daemmrich/ Stock, Boston; 600 Ken Karp*; 607 Simon Fraser/Science Photo Library/PR

Chapter 21 612 Paul Silverman/FP*; 613T Paul Silverman/FP*; 613BL E.R. Degginger/CP; 613BR Roy Morsch/SM; 616 Ken Karp*; 617 Richard Megna/FP*; 617B Ken Karp*; 626 Bill Longcore/PR; 627T Richard Megna/FP; 627B Ken Karp*; 628 Ken Karp*; 629 No credit; 631 Ken Karp*; 632 CNRI/Science Photo Library/PR; 635 Ken Karp*; 638 Pete Saloutos/SM; 642 Ken Karp*

Chapter 22 644 Bill Stormont/SM; 645T Bill Stormont/SM; 645B Ken Karp*; 646T Richard Megna/FP*; 646B E.R. Degginger/CP*; 647L The Granger Collection; 647R Crown Copyright/Health & Safety Laboratory/Science Photo Library/PR; 648L Paul Silverman/FP*; 648C Ken Karp*; 648R Ken Karp*; 650 Jens J. Jensen/World Images, Inc./SM; 651 Jan Halaska/PR; 652L Michael Newman/Photo Edit; 652R Julie Houck/Stock, Boston; 653T No credit; 653B Jonathan Blair/Corbis; 654T Werner H. Muller/PA; 654B Ken Karp*; 655 Ken Karp*; 657 Ken Karp*; 660T The Granger Collection-New York; 660B Richard Megna/FP; 661T E.R. Degginger/CP; 661B Ken Karp*; 664 Ken Karp*; 667 Ivan Polunin/Bruce Coleman Inc.; 669 Leonard Lessin/FBPA; 671 Photri-Microstock/OPC; 674 Ken Karp*

Chapter 23 676 Clay Wiseman/Animals Animals; 677T Clay Wiseman/Animals Animals; 677B Richard Megna/FP*; 679L Science Photo/PR; 679C The Granger Collection; 679R Paul Silverman/FP; 682 Leonard Lessin/FBPA; 684 Frank Rosotto/SM; 685 D. Young-Wolff/Photo Edit; 692T Robert Rathe/Stock, Boston; 692TL John Clark/SM; 692BL Stephen Frisch/Stock, Boston; 692BR Occidental Chemical Corp.; 694 Charles D. Winters/PR; 695 E.R. Degginger/CP; 696 Felicia Martinez/Photo Edit; 699 Will and Deni McIntyre/PR

Chapter 24 704 Erich Lessing/Art Resource; 705T Corbis/Bettman; 705B Jim Wark/PA; 706 Richard Megna/FP; 708TL Charles D. Winters/PR; 708TC E.R. Degginger/CP; 708BL E.R. Degginger/CP; 708BC Paul Silverman/FP; 708R Agra Uttar Pradesh/SuperStock; 709T E.R. Degginger/CP*; 709C E.R. Degginger/PR; 709B Ken Karp*;710L Paul Silverman/FP; 710R Jim Olive/Uni Photo Picture Agency; 712T Erich Lessing/Art Resource; 712BL S.J. Krasemann/PA; 712BR American Stock; 713T Paul Silverman/FP; 713B Matthew McVay/All Stock; 714L C. Falco/PR; 714R Kristen Brochmann/PR; 715 Richard Megna/FP; 716T Grant Heilman Photography; 716BL Metcalfe/Thatcher/Tony Stone Images; 716BR Geoffrey Nilsen Photography*; 717L Barrie Fanton/OPC; 717R Richard Megna/FP; 718 Phil Degginger/CP; 719L Richard Megna/FP; 719R Charles D. Winters/PR; 720 Dr. Ken McDonald/Science Photo Library; 721 Ken Karp*; 722TL Stephen Frisch*; 722TR Richard Megna/FP; 722B Geoffrey Nilsen Photography*; 724T Mauritius-Wesche/The Stock Shop Inc.; 724B E.R. Degginger/CP; 725T Geoffrey Nilsen Photography*; 725BL Stephen Frisch; 726L Thomas Brase/Tony Stone Images; 726C Ray Massey/Tony Stone Images; 726R Ken Karp*; 728 Runk/Scheonberger/Grant Heilman Photography; 729TL Paul Silverman/FP; 729TC John Cancalosi/PA; 729TR E.R. Degginger/CP; 729B Paul Silverman/FP; 730T Ken Karp*; 730BL Egyptian Museum, Cairo, Egypt/Giraudon/SuperStock; 730BR Sepp Seitz/Woodfin Camp & Associates; 731L Alberto Incrocci/The Image Bank; 731C Derek Berwin/The Image Bank; 731R Maximilian Stock Ltd/Science Photo Library/PR; 732T Courtesy NASA; 732B Ken Karp*; 733 Mary Evans/PR; 734T E.R. Degginger; 734B Cralle/The Image Bank; 734R E.R. Degginger; 736 Peter Lamberti/Tony Stone Images

Chapter 25 742 Jet Propulsion Lab; 743TL Richard A. Cooke III/Tony Stone Images; 743BL Michael P. Gadomski/PR; 743CR James H. Robinson/PR; 743BR David R. Frazier/PR; 746L Jacques Cochin/Agence Vandystadt; 746R Leonard Lessin/FBPA; 747 Andrew McClenaghan/Science Photo Library/PR; 751 Edward Parker/PA; 752TR Nigel Cattlin/PR; 752CL Alan & Linda Detrick/PR; 752BL Ross M. Horowitz/The Image Bank; 754 Martin Dohrn/Science Photo Library/PR; 759 Miwako Ikeda/International Stock; 760L Barry L. Runk/Grant Heilman Photography; 760R Malcolm Fielding, Johnson Matthey/Science Photo Library/PR; 762T Jet Propulsion Lab; 762B Joseph Sohm/Chromosohm/PR; 764C Earth History Hall, American Museum of Natural History; 764CL Bob O'Shaughnessy/SM; 764BC E.R. Degginger/CP; 764BR Carolina Biological Supply Company/Phototake; 764CR E.R. Degginger/CP; 765 William Felger/Grant Heilman Photography; 766 Jeffrey Mark Dunn/Stock, Boston

Chapter 26 772 Ken Karp*; 773T Robert Fried/Stock, Boston; 773B Michael Groen*; 776 Alan Levenson/Tony Stone Images; 778 Brown Brothers; 779 Michael Groen*; 780L Michael Groen*; 780C Michael A. Keller/SM; 780R Phil Degginger/CP; 781T Ken Karp*; 781B Ken Karp*; 782 Richard Megna/FP; 785 Ken Karp*; 787 Jane Grushow/Grant Heilman Photography; 788 Michael Groen*; 790L Steve Solum/Bruce Coleman Inc.; 790C Danny Eilers/Grant Heilman Photography; 790R Barry L. Runk/Grant Heilman Photography; 792L Tony Freeman/PhotoEdit; 792R Berenholtz/SM; 793 Richard Megna/FP; 795 Andrea Pistolesi/The Image Bank; 796L Bob Masini/Phototake; 796C Alan Schein/SM; 796R Grant Heilman Photography; 797TR Leonard Lessin/FBPA; 797CL Bill Stanton/International Stock; 797CR Rosemary Weller/Tony Stone Images; 797BL Chris Sorensen/SM; 797BR Garry Gay/The Image Bank; 798L Michael English/Custom Medical Stock Photo; 798R Michelle Del Guercio/Custom Medical Stock Photo; 799L Zephyr/Camerique; 799R Alvis Upitis/The Image Bank; 800 Bob Daemmrich/Stock, Boston; 802 Michael Busselle/Tony Stone Images; 802Inset Michael Groen*

Chapter 27 808 George W. Disario/SM; 809T Randy Wells/Tony Stone Images; 809B Carlyn Iverson; 811 Kunio Owaki/SM; 812T Paul Skelcher/Rainbow; 812B Ken Karp*; 815 J. Barry O'Rourke/SM; 816 John Mitchell/PR; 817T A.J. Wasserman/Visuals Unlimited; 817B E.R. Degginger/CP; 819 NIBSC/Science Photo Library/PR; 821T Dennis Blachut/SM; 821B Richard Hutchings*; 822 Richard Hutchings*; 823T Dr. Dennis Kunkel; 823B Hans Pfletschinger/PA; 824T George W. Disario/SM; 824B Phil A. Harrington/PA; 825 Richard Megna/FP; 828T Jackie Lewin, Royal Free Hospital-Science Photo Library/PR; 828B Ken Eward/Science Source; 829 Dan McCoy/Rainbow; 831T Caloene/PA; 831B Reuters/Ho/Archive Photos; 832 John Paulkay/PA; 835 Michael Pohuski/Envision; 839 Leonard Lessin/PA

Chapter 28 840 Lawrence Radiation/PR; 841T Novosti/Science Photo Library/PR; 841BL The Granger Collection; 841BR Science Photo Library/PR; 845 Richard Megna/FP*; 847 Archive Photos; 851 Robert Isaacs/Science Source PR; 853T Courtesy NASA; 853B Ken Karp*; 854R Dr. Jeremy Burgess/PR; 855 Daniel MacDonald/Stock Boston/Pictue Quest; 857 Lawrence Radiation Lab/PR; 857B Hank Morgan/PR; 859T Yoav Levy/Phototake NYC; 859B Runk/Schoen Erger/Grant Heilman Photography; 860 CNRI/Phototake NYC; 861 Larry Mulvehill/PR; 862 Alan Rostro/Waste Isolation Pilot Plant (WIPP)

Chemistry In Careers 868T Bill Varie/Westlight; 868B Iowa State University/Science Photo Library/PR; 869T Steve Chenn Photography/Westlight; 869B Mac Donald Photography/The Stockhouse, Inc.; 870T Wesley Bocxe/PR; 870B Super-Stock; 871T Peter French/Bruce Coleman, Inc.; 871B Alvis Upitis/The Image Bank; 872T Jeff Greenberg/Unicorn Photos; 872B Michael Sewell/PA; 873T US Department of Energy/Mark Marten/PR; 873B Lawrence Migdale/Stock, Boston; 874T Firefly Productions/Firefly; 874B George Haling/PR; 875T Tom Hollyman/PR; 875B Michael A. Keller Studios LTD./SM; 876T Brian Smith/Stock, Boston; 876B Giancarlo DeBellis/OPC; 877T C.E. Mitchell/Black Star; 877B Y. Arthus Bertrand/PA; 878T Stephen Derr/The Image Bank; 878B Chris Jones/SM; 879T Randy Duchaine/SM; 879B Andy Duchaine; 880T Matt Meadows/PA; 880B Russ Lappa*; 881T Hank Morgan/Rainbow; 881B Archive Photos

Chem Serving Borders SOCIETY Nick Wheeler/Westlight; THE ENVIRONMENT, INDUSTRY C. Murray/Westlight; THE CONSUMER R. Ian Lloyd/Westlight

*Photographs taken expressly for Addison-Wesley Chemistry © 2000 and © 2002.

Special thanks to Kris Wynne-Jones

Illustrations

Academy Artworks iv, vii, ix, xi, 21, 117, 118, 129, 179, 192, 213, 215, 216, 219, 221, 239, 248, 253, 362, 382, 389, 423, 437, 438, 439, 442, 443, 444, 449, 451, 453, 454, 455, 456, 457, 458, 459, 461, 463, 464, 465, 466, 563, 694, 719, 745, 746, 747, 749, 753, 754, 755, 757, 758, 759, 760, 769, 771, 774, 776, 780, 783, 785, 789, 791, 806, 807, 839

Jim DeLapine 295, 303, 307, 310, 315, 317, 318

Guilbert Gates 4, 16, 21, 39, 43, 52, 54, 58, 62, 75, 84, 89, 99, 169, 177, 192, 239, 247, 253, 263

Network Graphics iii, viTL, 19, 27, 49, 81, 105, 169, 178, 201, 208, 209, 235, 265, 268, 274, 281, 283, 285, 291, 325, 359, 389, 411, 435, 473, 475, 476, 481, 484, 499, 518, 531, 539, 553, 575, 580, 595, 597, 598, 611, 614, 626, 631, 643, 645, 646, 648, 675, 677, 680, 703, 741, 771, 807, 822, 839, 843, 850, 853, 856, 867

J/B Woolsey Associates v, viCR, vii, 30, 34, 49, 56, 68, 107, 108, 109, 110, 111, 124, 131, 169, 186, 199, 235, 259, 268, 269, 275, 277, 278, 280, 281, 282, 286, 291, 294, 328, 330, 331, 332, 333, 336, 338, 345, 347, 350, 363, 373, 374, 377, 380, 392, 394, 395, 398, 399, 400, 401, 403, 404, 404, 406, 410, 411, 412, 419, 424, 425, 427, 433, 460, 467, 477, 492, 493, 503, 505, 512, 517, 520, 522, 533, 534, 535, 543, 545, 552, 553, 573, 593, 621, 622, 652, 672, 680, 681, 682, 683, 684, 686, 693, 695, 696, 702, 718, 727, 817, 818, 823, 825, 826, 830, 833, 842, 844, 845, 847, 849, 854, 857, 858, 859, 860, 867

Precision Graphics 811, 819, 822, 828

Molly K. Scanlon 273, 629

Michael Sloan 15, 16

Steven Stankiewicz 9, 13, 16, 26, 38, 48, 105, 188, 272, 279, 284, 291, 335, 336, 344, 372, 373, 504, 505, 523, 538, 583, 584, 584, 590, 709, 715, 739, 740, 833, 834

Nina Wallace 35, 72, 207, 238, 300, 301, 427, 762, 763

Table A.3 Symbols of Common Elements

Ag	silver	Cu	copper	O	oxygen
Al	aluminum	F	fluorine	P	phosphorus
As	arsenic	Fe	iron	Pb	lead
Au	gold	H	hydrogen	Pt	platinum
Ba	barium	Hg	mercury	S	sulfur
Bi	bismuth	I	iodine	Sb	antimony
Br	bromine	K	potassium	Sn	tin
C	carbon	Mg	magnesium	Sr	strontium
Ca	calcium	Mn	manganese	Ti	titanium
Cl	chlorine	N	nitrogen	U	uranium
Co	cobalt	Na	sodium	W	tungsten
Cr	chromium	Ni	nickel	Zn	zinc

Table A.4 Symbols of Common Polyatomic Ions

$C_2H_3O_2^-$	acetate	$Cr_2O_7^{2-}$	dichromate	NO_3^-	nitrate
ClO^-	hypochlorite	HCO_3^-	hydrogen carbonate	NO_2^-	nitrite
ClO_2^-	chlorite	H_3O^+	hydronium	O_2^{2-}	peroxide
ClO_3^-	chlorate	HPO_4^{2-}	hydrogen phosphate	OH^-	hydroxide
ClO_4^-	perchlorate	HSO_3^-	hydrogen sulfite	PO_4^{3-}	phosphate
CN^-	cyanide	HSO_4^-	hydrogen sulfate	SiO_3^{2-}	silicate
CO_3^{2-}	carbonate	MnO_4^-	permanganate	SO_3^{2-}	sulfite
CrO_4^{2-}	chromate	NH_4^+	ammonium	SO_4^{2-}	sulfate

Table A.5 Other Symbols and Abbreviations

α	alpha rays	gmm	gram molecular mass	m	mass
β	beta rays	H	enthalpy	m	molality
γ	gamma rays	H_f	heat of formation	mL	milliliter (*volume*)
Δ	change in	h	hour	mm	millimeter (*length*)
$\delta+, \delta-$	partial ionic charge	h	Planck's constant	mol	mole (*amount*)
λ	wavelength	Hz	hertz (*frequency*)	mp	melting point
π	pi bond	J	joule (*energy*)	N	normality
σ	sigma bond	K	kelvin (*temperature*)	n^0	neutron
ν	frequency	K_a	acid dissociation constant	n	number of moles
amu	atomic mass unit	K_b	base dissociation constant	n	principal quantum number
(*aq*)	aqueous solution	K_b	molal boiling point	P	pressure
atm	atmosphere (*pressure*)		elevation constant	p^+	proton
bp	boiling point	K_{eq}	equilibrium constant	Pa	pascal (*pressure*)
°C	degree Celsius (*temperature*)	K_f	molal freezing point	R	ideal gas constant
c	speed of light in a vacuum		depression constant	S	entropy
cm	centimeter (*length*)	K_w	ion product constant	s	second
D	density		for water	(*s*)	solid
E	energy	K_{sp}	solubility product constant	SI	International System
e^-	electron	kcal	kilocalorie (*energy*)		of Units
fp	freezing point	kg	kilogram (*mass*)	STP	standard temperature
G	Gibb's free energy	kPa	kilopascal (*pressure*)		and pressure
g	gram (*mass*)	L	liter (*volume*)	T	temperature
(*g*)	gas	(*l*)	liquid	$t_{\frac{1}{2}}$	half-life
gam	gram atomic mass	M	molarity	V	volume
gfm	gram formula mass	m	meter (*length*)	v	velocity, speed